386

PRENTICE HALL
LITERATURE
THE AMERICAN EXPERIENCE

PRENTICE HALL
LITERATURE

BRONZE

Annotated Teacher's Edition
Teaching Portfolio
Novel Study Guides

SILVER

Annotated Teacher's Edition
Teaching Portfolio
Novel Study Guides

GOLD

Annotated Teacher's Edition
Teaching Portfolio
Novel Study Guides

PLATINUM

Annotated Teacher's Edition
Teaching Portfolio
Novel Study Guides

THE AMERICAN EXPERIENCE

Annotated Teacher's Edition
Teaching Portfolio
Novel Study Guides

THE ENGLISH TRADITION

Annotated Teacher's Edition
Teaching Portfolio
Novel Study Guides

PROPERTY OF SCHOOL DIST. #1
LARAMIE, WY.

NO. _____ DATE _____
PUPILS ARE HELD RESPONSIBLE FOR
CARE AND RETURN OF THIS BOOK

Master Teacher Board

Roger Babusci
(Pennsylvania Teacher
of the Year, 1983)
Schenley High School
Pittsburgh, Pennsylvania

Loutish Burns
(Teacher of the Year, 1981)
Louie Welch Middle School
Houston, Texas

Guy Doud
(National Teacher of the Year, 1986)
Brainerd Senior High School
Brainerd, Minnesota

Terri Fields
(Arizona Teacher of the Year, 1986)
Sunnyslope High School
Phoenix, Arizona

Kermeen Fristrom
(1985 Distinguished Service Award)
San Diego City Schools
San Diego, California

LeRoy Hay
(National Teacher of the Year, 1983)
Manchester High School
Manchester, Connecticut

Beth Johnson
(Florida Teacher of the Year, 1982)
Kathleen Senior High School
Lakeland, Florida

Evaline Kruse
(California Teacher of the Year, 1985)
Audubon Junior High School
Los Angeles, California

Jane McKee
(West Virginia Teacher
of the Year, 1986)
Man High School
Man, West Virginia

Robert Seney
(Texas Curriculum Association's
Exemplary Showcase Award
for Literature, 1986)
Albright Middle School
Houston, Texas

Pat Weaver
(1985 National Outstanding
Dissertation for Curriculum)
Arlington Independent School District
Arlington, Texas

Consultants

Joan Baron
University of Connecticut
Storrs, Connecticut

Charles Cooper
University of California
San Diego, California

Robert D. Yanni
Pace University
Pleasantville, New York

Nancy Spivey
Carnegie-Mellon Institute
Pittsburgh, Pennsylvania

Contributing Writers

Frances Earle
former English teacher
Miralest High School
Palos Verdes, California

Marcia Muth
former English teacher
Glendora High School
Glendora, California

Cosmo Ferrara
former English teacher
Riverdell Regional
High School
Oradell, New Jersey

Howard Portnoy
former English teacher
Boston Latin School
Boston, Massachusetts

Gerald Tomlinson
former English teacher
Horseheads Jr. High School
Horseheads, New York

PRENTICE HALL
LITERATURE
THE AMERICAN EXPERIENCE

PRENTICE HALL, Englewood Cliffs, New Jersey 07632

Copyright © 1989 by Prentice-Hall, Inc., Englewood Cliffs, New Jersey 07632.
All rights reserved. No part of this book may be reproduced in any form or by any means without permission in writing from the publisher. Printed in the United States of America.

ISBN 0-13-698614-5

10 9 8 7 6 5

Art credits begin on page 1393.

COVER AND TITLE PAGE: OLD FRIENDS, 1894, Winslow Homer Worcester Art Museum

PRENTICE HALL
A Division of Simon & Schuster
Englewood Cliffs, New Jersey 07632

ACKNOWLEDGMENTS

Grateful acknowledgment is made to the following for permission to reprint copyrighted material:

Samuel Allen
"To Satch" by Samuel Allen, reprinted by permission of the author.

The American Scholar
Lines from the poem "Garden of My Childhood" by Kuang-chi C. Chang. Reprinted from *The American Scholar*, Volume 26, Number 3, Summer 1957. Copyright © 1957 by the United Chapters of Phi Beta Kappa. Reprinted by permission of the publishers.

Atheneum Publishers, an imprint of Macmillan Publishing Co.
Donald Justice, "Poem" from *Selected Poems.* Copyright © 1979 Donald Justice. Reprinted with the permission of Atheneum Publishers, an imprint of Macmillan Publishing Co.

Elizabeth Barnett, Literary Executor of the Estate of Norma Millay Ellis
Excerpts from "I Shall Go Back Again to the Bleak Shore" and "Recuerdo" by Edna St. Vincent Millay. Copyright 1922, 1923, 1950, 1951 by Edna St. Vincent Millay and Normal Millay Ellis. Reprinted by permission. "Renascence" by Edna St. Vincent Millay. From *Collected Poems*, Harper & Row. Copyright 1912, 1940 by Edna St. Vincent Millay. Reprinted by permission.

Robert Bly
One line from "Solitude Late at Night in the Woods" by Robert Bly, reprinted by permission of the author.

Gwendolyn Brooks
"The Explorer" from *The World of Gwendolyn Brooks* by Gwendolyn Brooks. Reprinted by permission of the author. Lines from "Life for my child is simple, and is good" from "Blacks" by Gwendolyn Brooks, 1987, The David Company.

Century-Hutchinson Ltd.:
"The Watch" from *Collected Poems* by Frances Cornford, published by Cresset Press Ltd., 1954, now a part of Century-Hutchinson Ltd. Copyright Frances Cornford. Reprinted by permission of Century-Hutchinson Ltd.

Diana Chang
"Most Satisfied by Snow" by Diana Chang. Reprinted by permission of the author.

Curtis Brown Ltd.
Lines from "Untitled" ("the thirty eighth year of my life") from *An Ordinary Woman* by Lucille Clifton. Copyright 1974 by Lucille Clifton. Reprinted by permission of Curtis Bown Ltd.

J. M. Dent & Sons, Ltd.
From "Letters from an American Farmer" by Michel-Guillaume Jean de Crèvecoeur in *An Everyman's Library.*

Dodd, Mead & Company, Inc.
"Douglass" and "We Wear the Mask" reprinted by permission of Dodd, Mead & Company, Inc. from *The Complete Poems of Paul Laurence Dunbar.*

Elizabeth Dos Passos
"Tin Lizzie" from *U.S.A.*, Houghton Mifflin Co. Copyright by John Dos Passos and Elizabeth Dos Passos, Co-Executor of the Estate of John Dos Passos.

Doubleday, a division of Bantam, Doubleday, Dell Publishing Group, Inc.
"Imagined Scenes" by Ann Beattie originally appeared in *The Texas Quarterly*. From the book *Distortions*, copyright © 1974,

(continued on page 1390)

CONTENTS

A GROWING NATION
1800–1840

NEW ENGLAND RENAISSANCE
1840–1855

New England Poets

DIVISION, WAR, AND RECONCILIATION
1855–1865

REALISM AND THE FRONTIER
1865–1915

Prose

CONTEMPORARY WRITERS
1946–Present

PRENTICE HALL
LITERATURE
THE AMERICAN EXPERIENCE

LANDING OF COLUMBUS
John Vanderlyn
Three Lions

THE NEW LAND
To 1750

Let England know our willingnesse,
    For that our worke is good;
Wee hope to plant a nation,
    Where none before hath stood.

Thomas Dale
Governor of the Jamestown Colony

More than a century after European explorers discovered North America, there were no permanent settlements in the New World north of St. Augustine, Florida. By 1607, however, a small group of English settlers was struggling to survive on a marshy island in the James River in the present state of Virginia. In 1611, Thomas Dale, governor of the colony, wrote a report to the king expressing the colonists' determination to succeed. Despite disease and starvation, Jamestown did survive.

The first settlers were entranced by the presence and, to them, the strangeness of the native inhabitants. They did not at first realize that these earlier Americans, like Europeans, had cultural values and literary traditions of their own. The literature was entirely oral, for the tribes of North America had not yet developed writing systems. This extensive oral literature, along with the first written works of the colonists, forms the beginning of the American literary heritage.

THE HISTORICAL SETTING

When Christopher Columbus reached North America in 1492, the continent was already populated, though sparsely, by several hundred Native American tribes. Europeans did not encounter these tribes all at once. Explorers from different nations came into contact with them at different times. As we now know, these widely dispersed tribes of Native Americans differed greatly from one another in language, government, social organization, customs, housing, and methods of survival.

The Native Americans

No one knows for certain when or how the first Americans arrived in what is now the United States. It may have been as recently as 12,000 years ago or as long ago as 70,000 years. Even if the shorter estimate is correct, Native Americans have been on the continent thirty times longer than the Europeans. Colonists from Europe did not begin arriving on the East Coast of North America until the late 1500's.

What were the earliest Americans doing for those many centuries? To a great extent, the answer is shrouded in mystery. As the historian Samuel Eliot Morison noted, "Even now we cannot write 'The History of America before 1492,' because history presupposes a more or less continuous and dated story." No such story of the Native Americans exists. Archeologists have deduced a great deal from artifacts, however, and folklorists have recorded a rich variety of songs, legends, and myths.

What we do know is that the Native Americans usually, but by no means always, greeted the earliest Europeans as friends. They instructed the newcomers in New World agriculture and woodcraft, introduced them to maize, beans, squash, maple sugar, snow-shoes, toboggans, and birch bark canoes. Indeed, many more of the European settlers would have succumbed to the bitter Northeastern winters had it not been for the help of these first Americans.

Pilgrims and Puritans

A small group of Europeans sailed from England on the *Mayflower* in 1620. The passengers were religious reformers, Puritans who were critical of the Church of England. Having given up hope of "purifying" the church from within, they chose instead to withdraw from the church. This action earned them the name Separatists. We know them as the Pilgrims. They landed in the New World and established a settlement at what is now Plymouth, Massachusetts. With help from friendly tribes of Native Americans, the Plymouth settlement managed to survive the rigors of the New World. The colony never grew very large, however. Eventually, it was engulfed by the Massachusetts Bay Colony, the much larger settlement to the north.

Like the Plymouth Colony, the Massachusetts Bay Colony was also founded by religious reformers. These reformers, however, did not withdraw from the Church of England. Unlike the Separatists

THE BEGINNING OF NEW ENGLAND
After the Painting by Clyde O. Deland
The Granger Collection

AMERICAN EVENTS

Pre–
1492   Native American tribes occupy what is now the United States.

1492   Crew of Christopher Columbus discovers America, sighting land in the Bahamas.

1565   St. Augustine, Florida, first permanent settlement in U.S., founded by Pedro Menéndez.

1570   Iroquois Confederacy established to stop warfare among the Five Nations.

1587   English colony at Roanoke Island disappears; known as the Lost Colony.

1607   First permanent English settlement at Jamestown, Virginia.

1608   **Captain John Smith** writes *A True Relation... of Virginia*.

1609   Henry Hudson in the *Half Moon* explores New York harbor and the Hudson River.

1619   House of Burgesses established in Virginia; first legislature in the New World.

1620   Pilgrims land at Plymouth, Massachusetts.

1629   Formation of Massachusetts Bay Company leads to influx of Puritans into New England.

1630   **William Bradford** begins writing *Of Plymouth Plantation*, completes it in 1651.

1636   Harvard University founded in Cambridge, Massachusetts.

1638   First printing press in English-speaking North America arrives in Massachusetts.

1640   *Bay Psalm Book* published; first book printed in the colonies.

Columbus Lands at San Salvador

Captain John Smith

Jamestown

Galileo

The *Mayflower*

The *Mona Lisa*

William Shakespeare

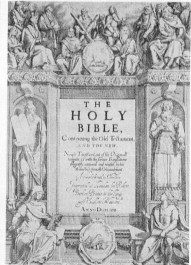

THE
HOLY
BIBLE,

The King James Bible

WORLD EVENTS

AMERICAN EVENTS

Nat Bacon's Rebellion

Woman Accused of Witchcraft in Salem

The Trial of John Peter Zenger   Baron de Montesquieu

The *Night Watch*

Johann Sebastian Bach

Illustration from *Gulliver's Travels*

Illustration from *Robinson Crusoe*

WORLD EVENTS

1642	Holland: Rembrandt paints *Night Watch*.
	England: Civil War begins.
1644	France: Descartes publishes *Principia Philosophicae*.
	China: Ming Dynasty ends.
1660	South Africa: First Dutch settlers arrive.
1667	England: Milton publishes *Paradise Lost*.
1669	France: Molière's *Tartuffe* first performed.
1678	England: John Bunyan publishes *The Pilgrim's Progress*.
1685	China: All ports opened to foreign trade.
1690	India: Calcutta founded by British.
1702	England: First daily newspaper begins publication.
1712	England: Alexander Pope publishes *The Rape of the Lock*.
1719	England: Daniel Defoe publishes *Robinson Crusoe*.
1721	Germany: Bach composes *Brandenburg Concertos*.
1726	England: Jonathan Swift publishes *Gulliver's Travels*.
1727	Brazil: First coffee planted.
1748	France: Montesquieu publishes *The Spirit of the Law*.
1749	Portugal: Sign language invented.

Introduction 7

THE FIRST THANKSGIVING
J. L. G. Ferris
Three Lions

they were Puritans who intended instead to reform the church from within. In America, the Puritans hoped to establish what John Winthrop, governor of the colony, called a "city upon a hill," a community guided in all aspects by the Bible. Their form of government would be a theocracy, a state under the immediate guidance of God.

Religion affected every aspect of Puritan life, although the Puritans were not always as stern and otherworldly as they are sometimes pictured. Their writings occasionally reveal a sense of humor, and the hardships of daily life forced them to be practical. In one sense, the Puritans were radical, since they demanded fundamental changes in the Church of England. In another sense, however, they were conservative. They preached a plain, unadorned Christianity that contrasted sharply with the cathedrals, vestments, ceremony, and hierarchy of the Church of England.

What exactly did the Puritans believe? Their beliefs were far from simple, but they agreed that human beings exist for the glory of God and that the Bible is the sole expression of God's will. They believed in predestination—John Calvin's doctrine that God has already decided who will achieve salvation and who will not. The elect, or saints, who are to be saved cannot take election for granted, however. Because of that, all devout Puritans searched their souls with great rigor and frequency for signs of grace. The Puritans believed in original sin and felt that they could accomplish good only through continual hard work and self-discipline. When people today speak of the "Puritan ethic," that is what they mean.

Puritanism was in decline throughout New England by the early 1700's, as more liberal Protestant congregations attracted followers. A reaction against this new freedom, however, set in around 1735. The Great Awakening, a series of religious revivals led by such eloquent ministers as Jonathan Edwards and George Whitefield, swept the colonies. The Great Awakening attracted thousands of converts to many Protestant groups, but it did little to revive old-fashioned Puritanism. What had been the dominant religion of New England had all but vanished by the time of the American Revolution. Nevertheless, Puritanism made a lasting impression on American attitudes. Its ideals of hard work, frugality, self-improvement, and self-reliance are still regarded as basic American virtues.

The Southern Planters

The Southern colonies differed from New England in climate, crops, social organization, and religion. Prosperous coastal cities grew up in the South, just as in the North, but beyond the Southern cities lay large plantations, not small farms. Despite its romantic image, the plantation was in fact a large-scale agricultural enterprise and a center of commerce. Up to a thousand people, many of them slaves, might live and work on a single plantation. The first black

LANDING AT JAMESTOWN, 1608–09 (ALSO CALLED HOPE OF JAMESTOWN)
John Gadsby Chapman
Mr. and Mrs. Paul Mellon, Upperville, VA

slaves were brought to Virginia in 1619, a year before the Pilgrims landed at Plymouth. The plantation system and the institution of slavery were closely connected from the very beginning, although slavery existed in every colony, including Massachusetts.

Most of the plantation owners were Church of England members who regarded themselves as aristocrats. The first generation of owners, the men who established the great plantations, were ambitious, energetic, self-disciplined, and resourceful, just as the Puritans were. But the way of life on most plantations was more sociable and elegant than that of any Puritan. By 1750, Puritanism was in decline everywhere, despite the Great Awakening, while the plantation system in the South was just reaching its peak.

THE EARLIEST AMERICAN LITERATURE

It was an oddly assorted group that established the foundations of American literature: the Native Americans with their oral traditions, the Puritans with their preoccupation with sin and salvation, and the Southern planters with their busy social lives. Indeed, much of the literature that the colonists read was not produced in the colonies. It came from England. Yet by 1750 there were the clear beginnings of a native literature that would one day be honored throughout the English-speaking world.

Their Name Is on Your Waters

For a long time, Native American literature was viewed mainly as folklore. The consequence was that song lyrics, hero tales, migration legends, and accounts of the creation were studied more for their content than for their literary qualities. In an oral tradition, the telling of the tale may change with each speaker, and the words are almost sure to change over time. Thus, no fixed versions of such literary works exist. Still, in cases where the words of Native American lyrics or narratives have been captured in writing, the language is often poetic and moving. As might be expected in an oral setting, oratory was much prized among Native Americans. The names of certain orators, such as Logan and, later, Red Jacket, were widely known.

The introductory literature in this unit suggests the depth and power of those original American voices. Interestingly, you can find familiar, one-word examples of the various tribal languages, simply by looking at a map or at road signs. A remarkable number of American place names, including the names of more than half of our fifty states, come from Native American words. In the nineteenth century, Lydia Sigourney wrote a popular poem called "Indian Names."

> Ye say they all have pass'd away
>   That noble race and brave;
> That their light canoes have vanish'd,
>   From off the crested wave;

PILGRIMS ON THE WAY TO CHURCH
Charles Yardley Turner
Three Lions

That mid the forests where they roam'd,
　There rings no hunter's shout;
But their name is on your waters,
　Ye may not wash it out. . . .

"In Adam's Fall/We Sinned All"

Just as religion dominated the lives of the Puritans, it also dominated their writings, most of which would not be considered literary works by modern standards. Typically, the Puritans wrote theological studies, hymns, histories, biographies, and autobiographies. The purpose of such writing was to provide spiritual insight and instruction. When Puritans wrote for themselves, in journals or diaries, their aim was the serious kind of self-examination they practiced in other aspects of their lives. The Puritans produced neither fiction nor drama, since they regarded both as sinful.

The Puritans did write poetry, however, as a vehicle of spiritual enlightenment. Although they were less concerned with a poem's literary form than with its message, some writers were naturally more gifted than others. A few excellent Puritan poets emerged in the 1600's, among them Anne Bradstreet and Edward Taylor. Anne Bradstreet's moving, personal voice and Edward Taylor's devotional intensity shine through the conventional Puritanism of their themes.

The Puritans were highly literate, with a strong belief in education for both men and women. In 1636, they founded Harvard University to ensure a well-educated ministry. Two years later, they set up the first printing press in the colonies. In 1647, free public schools were established in Massachusetts to combat the influence of "ye ould deluder, Satan." *The New England Primer,* first published around 1690, combined instruction in spelling and reading with moralistic teachings, such as "In Adam's fall/We sinned all."

One of the first books printed in the colonies was the *Bay Psalm Book,* the standard hymnal of the time. Richard Mather, a prominent preacher, was one of its three authors. Increase Mather, Richard's youngest son, served for many years as pastor of the North Church in Boston. He was the author of some 130 books. *Cases of Conscience Concerning Evil Spirits,* published in 1693, was a discourse on the Salem witchcraft trials of the previous year. The trials, conducted in an atmosphere of hysteria, resulted in the hanging of nineteen people as witches.

Increase's eldest son, Cotton Mather, far exceeded his father's literary output, publishing at least 450 works in his lifetime. Cotton Mather, like his father, is remembered in part because of his connection with the Salem witchcraft trials. Although he did not actually take part in the trials, his works on witchcraft had helped to stir up some of the hysteria. Still, Cotton Mather was one of the most learned men of his time, a power in the state, and a notable author.

**HARVARD HALL (COLLEGE)
CAMBRIDGE, MASSACHUSETTS,
BUILT 1672–82**
Colored Engraving
The Granger Collection

His theory of writing was simple (although his writing was not): the more information a work contains, the better its style.

In fact, the Puritans in general had a theory of literary style. They believed in a plain style of writing, one in which clear statement is the highest goal. An ornate or clever style would be a sign of vanity and, as such, would not be in accordance with God's will. Despite the restrictions built into their life and literature, the Puritans succeeded in producing a small body of excellent writing.

The Planter from Westover

Considering the number of brilliantly literate statesmen who would later emerge in the South, especially in Virginia, it seems surprising that only a few notable Southern writers appeared prior to 1750. As in Puritan New England, those who were educated produced a substantial amount of writing, but it was mostly of a practical nature. Many planters spent long hours each day writing letters. Unlike the Puritans, Southerners did not oppose fiction or drama, and the first theater in America opened in Williamsburg, Virginia, in 1716.

The important literature of the pre-Revolutionary South can be summed up in one name—William Byrd. Byrd lived at Westover, a magnificent plantation on the James River bequeathed to him by his wealthy father. Commissioned in 1738 to survey the boundary line between Virginia and North Carolina, he kept a journal of his experiences. That journal served as the basis for Byrd's book, *The History of the Dividing Line*, which was circulated in manuscript form among Byrd's friends in England. Published nearly a century after Byrd's death, the book was immediately recognized as a minor humorous masterpiece. More of Byrd's papers were published later, establishing his reputation as the finest writer in the pre-Revolutionary South.

The writers whose work appears in this unit are not the great names in American literature. They are the founders, the men and women who laid the groundwork for the towering achievements that followed. The modest awakening of American literature seen in this unit had repercussions that echo down the years.

THE TRIAL OF TWO "WITCHES" AT SALEM, MASSACHUSETTS, IN 1692
Illustration by Howard Pyle
The Granger Collection

AMERICAN VOICES
Quotations by Prominent Figures of the Period

The voice that beautifies the land,
The voice above,
The voice of the grasshopper,
Among the plants,
Again and again it sounds,—
The voice that beautifies the land.
—Navaho

The sun . . . ever shineth on one part or the other [of the Spanish dominions] we have conquered for our king.
Captain John Smith, Advertisements for the Unexperienced

They knew they were pilgrims.
William Bradford, Of Plymouth Plantation

Welcome, Englishmen.
Squanto

The public must and will be served.
William Penn, Some Fruits of Solitude

Resolved, never to do anything which I should be afraid to do if it were the last hour of my life.
Jonathan Edwards, Seventy Resolutions

Brother! Our lands were once large, and yours were very small. You have now become a great people, and we have scarcely a place left to spread our blankets. You have got our country, but are not satisfied.
Red Jacket, Seneca Council Speech

The Literature to 1750

When you read literature written during particular time periods, it is important to know the historical background.

Historical Context

Before settlers came to North America, Native Americans lived lives close to the land. Their interaction with nature shows in their literature. The early settlers came from Europe seeking freedom to live and worship as they pleased. For most, their strong religious convictions sustained them as they endured the hardships of life in the New World.

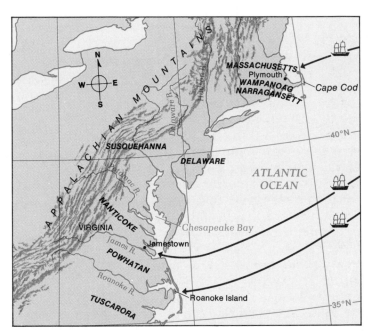

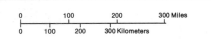

THE FIRST ENGLISH SETTLEMENTS

Literary Movements

The traditional literature of the Native Americans related to their tribal knowledge, customs, and rituals. This literature consists of myths, songs, and chants in the oral tradition.

The early settlers who came from Europe brought with them their knowledge of written communication with its particular style and content. They wrote about their new experiences in forms that were familiar to them—letters, factual records, sermons, and poems.

Writers' Techniques

During this period most writers wrote in a simple, direct, unadorned style, known as the Puritan plain style. Occasionally, writers employed strong images to emphasize their ideas.

On the following pages is a poem by Anne Bradstreet, a devout Puritan woman who lived in the Massachusetts Bay Colony.

Upon the Burning of Our House

July 10th, 1666

Anne Bradstreet

In silent night when rest I took
For sorrow near I did not look
I wakened was with thund'ring noise
And piteous shrieks of dreadful voice.
5   That fearful sound of "Fire!" and "Fire!"
Let no man know is my desire.
I, starting up, the light did spy,
And to my God my heart did cry
To strengthen me in my distress
10 And not to leave me succorless.
Then, coming out, beheld a space
The flame consume my dwelling place.
And when I could no longer look,
I blest His name that gave and took,
15 That laid my goods now in the dust.
Yea, so it was, and so 'twas just.
It was His own, it was not mine,
Far be it that I should repine;
He might of all justly bereft
20 But yet sufficient for us left.
When by the ruins oft I past
My sorrowing eyes aside did cast,
And here and there the places spy
Where oft I sat and long did lie:
25 Here stood that trunk, and there that chest,
There lay that store I counted best.
My pleasant things in ashes lie,
And them behold no more shall I.
Under thy roof no guest shall sit,
30 Nor at thy table eat a bit.
No pleasant tale shall e'er be told,
Nor things recounted done of old.

Literary Movement: Bradstreet writes in a personal voice, sharing her feelings about this incident.

Writer's Technique: Bradstreet uses vivid words to make her purpose clear.

Historical Context: A Puritan's thoughts turn to God on every occasion.

Historical Context: These lines express the Puritan attitude that God's ways are not to be understood so much as simply accepted.

Writer's Technique: Bradstreet's medium is a lyric poem; it expresses her thoughts and feelings.

THE PARSON BARNARD HOUSE
Henry Marsh
North Andover Historical Society

Writer's Technique: Bradstreet writes mostly in the Puritan plain style—clear and precise, making her points directly.

No candle e'er shall shine in thee,
Nor bridegroom's voice e'er heard shall be.
35 In silence ever shall thou lie,
Adieu, Adieu,[1] all's vanity.
Then straight I 'gin my heart to chide,
And did thy wealth on earth abide?
Didst fix thy hope on mold'ring dust?
40 The arm of flesh didst make thy trust?
Raise up thy thoughts above the sky
That dunghill mists away may fly.
Thou hast an house on high erect,

---

1. adieu (ə dyoo′): "Farewell" (French).

Framed by that mighty Architect,
45 With glory richly furnished,
Stands permanent though this be fled.
It's purchased and paid for too
By Him who hath enough to do.
A price so vast as is unknown
50 Yet by His gift is made thine own;
There's wealth enough, I need no more,
Farewell, my pelf,[2] farewell my store.
The world no longer let me love,
My hope and treasure lies above.

Writer's Technique: This image presents a Puritan lesson—one's true home is with God, not here on Earth.

Historical Context: The poet ends with her message—not to be attached to earthly things but to live by spiritual ideals.

---

2. pelf *n.*: Money or wealth regarded with contempt.

THINKING ABOUT THE SELECTION

Recalling

1. What does the speaker do when she can no longer look at her burning house?
2. What does the speaker see when she passes by her house?
3. In the end, where do the speaker's "hope and treasure" lie?

Interpreting

4. Why does the speaker bless God as her house is burning down?
5. (a) With what emotions is the speaker filled when she passes by the ruins of her house? (b) How does she react to these emotions?
6. To what is the speaker referring when she speaks of the "house on high" in line 43?
7. (a) On the basis of this poem, what generalization would you make about the Puritan attitude toward worldly goods? (b) What seems to be the theme of the poem?

Applying

8. Do you think the contemporary attitude toward worldly goods is similar to or different from that expressed in this poem? Explain your answer.

ANALYZING LITERATURE

The Puritan Plain Style

The writing style of the Puritans reflected the plain style of their lives—spare, simple, and straightforward, with a focus on the essentials of life, not on frivolities. Short words, direct statements, and references to ordinary everyday objects—these were the characteristics of the style. Anne Bradstreet writes mainly in this plain style; however, she does occasionally allow herself some strong, vivid images to present her ideas.

1. Point out three basic, plain words referring to everyday items.
2. Point out three examples of more vivid, colorful words.
3. Find a line that is an example of a direct statement reflecting her Puritan beliefs.

CRITICAL THINKING AND READING

Appreciating Connotations

The **connotation** of a word refers to the suggestions or associations evoked by it—beyond its literal meaning. For example, the word *sky* literally refers to the upper atmosphere or the appearance of this atmosphere. However, *sky* has the connotation of soaring, extreme height. Therefore, when Bradstreet writes "raise up thy thoughts above the sky," in line 41, she is reminding herself of God's province—the highest attainment.

Explain the connotation of the italicized words in each of the following lines.
1. "And did thy *wealth* on earth abide?"
2. "Didst fix thy hope on *mold'ring* dust?"

UNDERSTANDING LANGUAGE

Finding Word Origins

One characteristic of the plain style is the use of short, simple words rather than longer, more difficult words. Many simple words come from Old English, an earlier form of our language, whereas many more difficult words derive from Latin.

Determine whether the following words from the poem come from Old English or Latin. Tell the meaning of the original word.
1. bride 2. bless 3. vanity 4. earth 5. permanent

THINKING AND WRITING

Writing About Lyric Poetry

In her lyrics Anne Bradstreet conveys important Puritan beliefs and concerns. Reread "Upon the Burning of Our House" carefully, noting concerns expressed in the poem. What seems to be her major concern in this poem? Write an essay in which you show how this one concern seems to dominate the poem. Include passages from the poem to support your thesis. Once you have finished writing a draft, revise your paper where needed, and prepare a final copy.

Native American Voices

PHILIP (METACOMET), AMERICAN WAMPANOAG INDIAN CHIEF
Colored Engraving, 1772, by Paul Revere
The Granger Collection

Delaware

Long before the first Europeans arrived in North America, the people of the Delaware tribe lived in parts of what is now Delaware, Pennsylvania, New York, and New Jersey. The Delaware hunted, fished, and farmed. For the most part, the Delaware lived in peace, except when threatened by their powerful enemies, the Iroquois.

In the seventeenth century, European colonists settled in Delaware territory. In 1682 the Delaware signed a treaty with William Penn, the colonial leader, but colonists took the tribe's land. During the next hundred years, eighteen treaties between the colonists and the Delaware were made and broken as the Delaware were pushed westward—eventually, to a reservation in Oklahoma. Today, there are fewer then three thousand Delaware, living primarily in Oklahoma, Wisconsin, and southern Canada.

Living close to the land as they did, the Delaware sought explanations for natural phenomena. Some of their explanations, like *The Walam Olum,* are recorded in pictographs, symbols painted on wood or stone.

Navaho

The Navaho are believed to have settled in the American Southwest between A.D. 1000 and 1400. Fierce warriors and hunters, they intermarried with members of the peaceful Pueblo tribe, who taught them how to weave and raise fruits and vegetables. The Spanish gave the tribe the name "Navaho," which means "cultivator of fields," but the Navaho usually referred to themselves as Dine, "the people." After the Spanish introduced domestic animals to the Navaho, many became herders of sheep and goats.

In the early 1800's, as American settlers began establishing ranches on Navaho land, the Navaho fought to drive the ranchers away. In 1864 U.S. Army troops defeated the Navaho, and seven thousand captives were marched to New Mexico, a trek of more than three hundred miles through the desert. Four years later, they were allowed to return to a reservation on their old land. The Navaho reservation, covering more than 24,000 square miles in Arizona, Utah, and New Mexico, is the largest in the United States. At more than 110,000 people, the Navaho are also the nation's biggest tribe. Today thousands of tribe members choose to live in the traditional Navaho manner, inhabiting earth and log structures as their ancestors did, and practicing their tribal religion.

GUIDE FOR READING

from The Walam Olum;
from The Navaho Origin Legend

Literary Forms

Myths. Myths are traditional stories passed down from generation to generation, characteristically involving immortal beings. Myths attempt to explain natural phenomena, the origin of humans, the customs, institutions or religious rites of a people, or events beyond people's control. Indirectly, myths teach the values and ideals of a culture.

The Walam Olum and *The Navaho Origin Legend* are both myths. *The Walam Olum* is the Delaware origin myth. Originally it consisted of a long series of pictographs explaining the origin of the Delaware people as a result of the actions of a manito, or spirit. At traditional ceremonies, a person who had inherited the right to keep *The Walam Olum* would interpret its meaning for the other members of the tribe. *The Navaho Origin Legend*, an important part of the Navaho tradition, also explains the origin of life.

Look For

What is the role of the manito in *The Walam Olum*? What events do the two myths explain? As you read the excerpts from *The Walam Olum* and *The Navaho Origin Legend,* look for the answers to these questions. What cultural ideals and values are conveyed through these myths?

Writing

What events that defy explanation occur in the modern world? Are there natural phenomena, such as black holes, that you find mysterious or difficult to understand? List events that are not fully understandable and freewrite about one of them.

Vocabulary

Knowing the following words will help you as you read the excerpts from the *The Walam Olum* and *The Navaho Origin Legend.*

ablutions (ab loo' shənz) *n.*: A washing or cleansing of the body as part of a religious rite (p. 26)

protruded (prō trood id) *v.*: Jutted out (p. 27)

from The Walam Olum
Delaware

At first, in that place, at all times, above the earth,

On the earth was an extended fog, and there the great Manito was.

At first, forever, lost in space, everywhere, the great Manito was.

He made the extended land and the sky.

He made the sun, the moon, the stars.

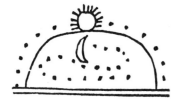

He made them all to move evenly.

Then the wind blew violently, and it cleared, and the water flowed off far and strong.

 And groups of islands grew newly, and there remained.

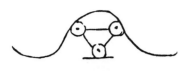 Anew spoke the great Manito, a manito to manitos,

 To beings, mortals, souls and all,

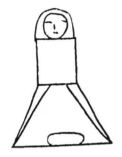 And ever after he was a manito to men, and their grandfather.

 He gave the first mother, the mother of beings.

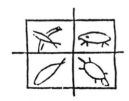 He gave the fish, he gave the turtles, he gave the beasts, he gave the birds.

 But an evil Manito made evil beings only, monsters.

He made the flies, he made the gnats.

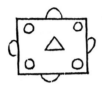

All beings were then friendly.

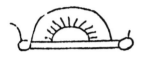

Truly the manitos were active and kindly

To those very first men, and to those first mothers; fetched them wives,

And fetched them food, when first they desired it.

All had cheerful knowledge, all had leisure, all thought in gladness.

But very secretly an evil being, a mighty magician, came on earth,

And with him brought badness, quarreling, unhappiness,

Brought bad weather, brought sickness, brought death.

All this took place of old on the earth, beyond the great tidewater, at the first.

THINKING ABOUT THE SELECTION

Recalling

1. List five of the great Manito's creations.
2. What did the evil Manito create?
3. What six troubles did a "mighty magician" bring to the earth?

Interpreting

4. According to *The Walam Olum,* what constitutes a happy life for the Delaware?
5. Examine the pictographs carefully. What evidence is there that the "evil Manito" and the "evil being, a mighty magician" might be the same spirit?

Applying

6. Identify three evils of the twentieth century. Provide an imaginative explanation for the origin of each of these evils.

ANALYZING LITERATURE

Recognizing Myths

Myths, like *The Walam Olum,* are ancient stories, generally involving immortal characters, that explain the mysteries of nature or the customs and religious rites of a people. For example, the excerpt from *The Walam Olum* explains how the universe was created.

1. What supernatural powers does the great Manito have?
2. According to *The Walam Olum,* how did human beings come to inhabit the earth?
3. How does *The Walam Olum* explain bad weather, sickness, and death?

CRITICAL THINKING AND READING

Inferring Cultural Values

Myths like *The Walam Olum* reveal the ideals and values of the people who created them. These ideals and values may not be stated directly, but by reading closely, you can infer them. For example, in *The Walam Olum,* when you read that the first inhabitants of the earth "all had cheerful knowledge, all had leisure, all thought in gladness," you can probably infer that the Delaware value knowledge and leisure, because the statement indicates that knowledge and leisure make people happy.

What can you infer that the Delaware valued from each of the following statements?

1. "He gave the fish, he gave the turtles, he gave the beasts, he gave the birds. . . . All beings were then friendly."
2. ". . . an evil being, a mighty magician, came on earth, And with him brought badness, quarreling, unhappiness. . . ."

from The Navaho Origin Legend

Navaho

On the morning of the twelfth day the people washed themselves well. The women dried themselves with yellow cornmeal; the men with white cornmeal. Soon after the ablutions were completed they heard the dis-tant call of the approaching gods.[1] It was shouted, as before, four times—nearer and

---

1. the approaching gods: The four Navaho gods: White Body, Blue Body, Yellow Body, and Black Body.

THE PLACE OF EMERGENCE AND THE FOUR WORLDS
Navaho
Wheelwright Museum of the American Indian

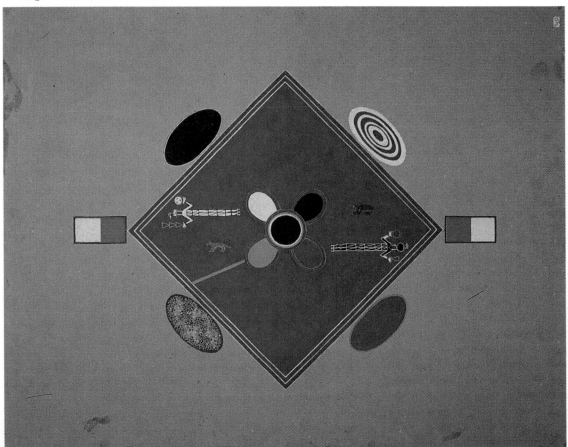

louder at each repetition—and, after the fourth call, the gods appeared. Blue Body and Black Body each carried a sacred buckskin. White Body carried two ears of corn, one yellow, one white, each covered at the end completely with grains.

The gods laid one buckskin on the ground with the head to the west; on this they placed the two ears of corn, with their tips to the east, and over the corn they spread the other buckskin with its head to the east; under the white ear they put the feather of a white eagle, under the yellow ear the feather of a yellow eagle. Then they told the people to stand at a distance and allow the wind to enter. The white wind blew from the east, and the yellow wind blew from the west, between the skins. While the wind was blowing, eight of the Mirage People[2] came and walked around the objects on the ground four times, and as they walked the

_____

2. Mirage People: Mirages personified.

eagle feathers, whose tips protruded from between the buckskins, were seen to move. When the Mirage People had finished their walk the upper buckskin was lifted; the ears of corn had disappeared, a man and a woman lay there in their stead.

The white ear of corn had been changed into a man, the yellow ear into a woman. It was the wind that gave them life. It is the wind that comes out of our mouths now that gives us life. When this ceases to blow we die. In the skin at the tips of our fingers we see the trail of the wind; it shows us where the wind blew when our ancestors were created.

The pair thus created were First Man and First Woman (Atsé *Hastín* and Atsé Estsán). The gods directed the people to build an enclosure of brushwood for the pair. When the enclosure was finished, First Man and First Woman entered it, and the gods said to them: "Live together now as husband and wife."

THINKING ABOUT THE SELECTION
Recalling

1. What items do the gods place on the ground?
2. What brings First Man and First Woman to life?
3. What do the gods direct First Man and First Woman to build?

Interpreting

4. Why do the Navaho associate the skin at the tips of the fingers with the trail of the wind?
5. Find evidence in the passage that suggests that the number four is sacred to the Navaho religion.

Applying

6. State two ways in which the wind affects the animals or plants living on the earth.

THINKING AND WRITING
Comparing and Contrasting Myths

Find a myth explaining the origin of life in another culture. Compare and contrast it with the Navaho origin myth. First, prepare a list of similarities and differences between the excerpt from *The Navaho Origin Legend* and the myth you have chosen. Organize your information into an outline, and write a thesis statement about the similarities and differences between the two myths. Then write a short essay in which you support your thesis statement with the information in your lists. When you revise, make sure that you have included corresponding points of comparison and contrast for each myth to support your thesis and that you have used appropriate transitions to show either comparison or contrast.

from The Iroquois Constitution

The **Iroquois** were a powerful tribe of Native Americans who lived in what is now the northeast United States. During the fourteenth century, an Iroquoian mystic and prophet named Dekanawidah traveled from village to village urging the Iroquoian-speaking peoples to stop fighting and to band together in peace and brotherhood. Dekanawidah's efforts led to the foundation of the Iroquois Confederation of the Five Nations, a league of five Iroquois tribes: Mohawk, Oneida, Seneca, Cayuga, and Onondaga.

Literary Forms

Constitutions. A constitution is a written or unwritten system of fundamental laws and principles governing a society. The Iroquois Constitution, which was unwritten, was first presented to confederate lords of the Five Nations in a speech by Dekanawidah. The confederate lords memorized it and recorded it in symbols on strings of shells.

In most constitutions, laws and principles are listed in a straightforward, factual manner. Because the Iroquois Constitution was spoken rather than written, it had to be presented in a way that would hold the listeners' attention. As a result, the Iroquois Constitution uses elegant phrasing and metaphors, or comparisons, to describe the foundation of the confederation and the system by which the confederation will be governed.

Look For

The Iroquois Constitution outlines a system of laws and principles. What are they? What purpose do they serve? As you read this excerpt, look for the language and metaphors that might help to hold the listeners' attention.

Writing

Try to imagine a society without laws and principles. What would it be like living there? Freewrite about the function of the laws and principles that govern a society.

Vocabulary

Knowing the following words will help you as you read the excerpt from The Iroquois Constitution.

confederate (kən fed′ ər it) *adj.*: United with others for a common purpose (p. 29)

disposition (dis′ pə zish′ ən) *n.*: An inclination or tendency (p. 29)

deliberation (di lib′ə rā′ shən) *n.*: Careful consideration (p. 30)

from The Iroquois Constitution

Iroquois

I am Dekanawidah and with the Five Nations[1] confederate lords I plant the Tree of the Great Peace. I name the tree the Tree of the Great Long Leaves. Under the shade of this Tree of the Great Peace we spread the soft white feathery down of the globe thistle as seats for you, Adodarhoh, and your cousin lords.

We place you upon those seats, spread soft with the feathery down of the globe thistle, there beneath the shade of the spreading branches of the Tree of Peace. There shall you sit and watch the council fire of the confederacy of the Five Nations, and all the affairs of the Five Nations shall be transacted at this place before you.

Roots have spread out from the Tree of the Great Peace, one to the north, one to the east, one to the south and one to the west. The name of these roots is the Great White Roots and their nature is peace and strength.

If any man or any nation outside the Five Nations shall obey the laws of the Great Peace and make known their disposition to the lords of the confederacy, they may trace the roots to the tree and if their minds are clean and they are obedient and promise to obey the wishes of the confederate council, they shall be welcomed to take shelter beneath the Tree of the Long Leaves.

We place at the top of the Tree of the Long Leaves an eagle who is able to see afar. If he sees in the distance any evil approach-

RED JACKET
George Catlin
The Thomas Gilcrease Institute of American History and Art, Tulsa, Oklahoma

---

1. Five Nations: The Mohawk, Oneida, Onondaga, Cayuga, and Seneca tribes. Together, these tribes formed the Iroquois Confederation.

ing or any danger threatening he will at once warn the people of the confederacy.

The smoke of the confederate council fire shall ever ascend and pierce the sky so that other nations who may be allies may see the council fire of the Great Peace. . .

Whenever the confederate lords shall assemble for the purpose of holding a council, the Onondaga lords shall open it by expressing their gratitude to their cousin lords and greeting them, and they shall make an address and offer thanks to the earth where men dwell, to the streams of water, the pools, the springs and the lakes, to the maize and the fruits, to the medicinal herbs and trees, to the forest trees for their usefulness, to the animals that serve as food and give their pelts for clothing, to the great winds and the lesser winds, to the thunderers, to the sun, the mighty warrior, to the moon, to the messengers of the Creator who reveal his wishes and to the Great Creator who dwells in the heavens above, who gives all the things useful to men, and who is the source and the ruler of health and life.

Then shall the Onondaga lords declare the council open. . .

All lords of the Five Nations' Confederacy must be honest in all things. . . It shall be a serious wrong for anyone to lead a lord into trivial affairs, for the people must ever hold their lords high in estimation out of respect to their honorable positions.

When a candidate lord is to be installed he shall furnish four strings of shells (or wampum)[2] one span in length bound together at one end. Such will constitute the evidence of his pledge to the confederate lords that he will live according to the constitution of the Great Peace and exercise justice in all affairs.

When the pledge is furnished the speaker of the council must hold the shell strings in his hand and address the opposite side of the council fire and he shall commence his address saying: "Now behold him. He has now become a confederate lord. See how splendid he looks." An address may then follow. At the end of it he shall send the bunch of shell strings to the opposite side and they shall be received as evidence of the pledge. Then shall the opposite side say:

"We now do crown you with the sacred emblem of the deer's antlers, the emblem of your lordship. You shall now become a mentor of the people of the Five Nations. The thickness of your skin shall be seven spans—which is to say that you shall be proof against anger, offensive actions and criticism. Your heart shall be filled with peace and good will and your mind filled with a yearning for the welfare of the people of the confederacy. With endless patience you shall carry out your duty and your firmness shall be tempered with tenderness for your people. Neither anger nor fury shall find lodgement in your mind and all your words and actions shall be marked with calm deliberation. In all of your deliberations in the confederate council, in your efforts at law making, in all your official acts, self-interest shall be cast into oblivion. Cast not over your shoulder behind you the warnings of the nephews and nieces should they chide you for any error or wrong you may do, but return to the way of the Great Law which is just and right. Look and listen for the welfare of the whole people and have always in view not only the present but also the coming generations, even those whose faces are yet beneath the surface of the ground—the unborn of the future nation."

---

2. wampum (wäm′ pəm) n.: Small beads made of shells.

THINKING ABOUT THE SELECTION

Recalling

1. Describe the roots of the Tree of Great Peace.
2. What is the role of the eagle at the top of the Tree of the Long Leaves?
3. How will the Onondaga lords open each council meeting?
4. Why will a candidate lord furnish a string of shells when he is installed?

Interpreting

5. What does the council fire of the Five Nations represent?
6. The constitution tells the lords to "offer thanks to the earth where men dwell." What does this decree suggest about the Iroquois?
7. What conclusions can you draw about Dekanawidah from the constitution he created?

Applying

8. In the constitution, Dekanawidah outlines the qualities he expects the Iroquois lords to possess. What qualities do you think that the leaders of a contemporary society should possess? Explain your answer.

ANALYZING LITERATURE

Recognizing a Constitution

A **constitution** is a written or unwritten system of fundamental principles, laws, and customs that governs a nation or union of nations. The Iroquois Constitution outlines the principles on which the union of the Five Nations is based and presents the manner in which the confederation will be governed.

1. List three principles emphasized in the Iroquois Constitution.
2. (a) What is the function of the confederate council? (b) What sort of behavior is expected of its members?

CRITICAL THINKING AND READING

Interpreting Metaphors

A **metaphor** is an implied comparison between two seemingly dissimilar things. In most constitutions the rules and principles outlined are presented in a direct manner. In contrast, many of the ideas in The Iroquois Constitution are revealed through metaphors. As a result, you must interpret the comparison being made in each metaphor. For example, Dekanawidah uses the thickness of the council lords' skin as a metaphor for their ability to resist anger, offensive actions, and criticism.

1. For what is the planting of the Tree of Great Peace a metaphor?
2. What does Dekanawidah mean when he says that any nation outside the Five Nations that obeys the laws of the Great Peace "shall be welcomed to take shelter beneath the Tree of Long Leaves"?

UNDERSTANDING LANGUAGE

Using Native American Words

The American vocabulary includes many place names and common nouns from Native American languages. For example, the word *Connecticut* was taken from the Algonquian language family, in which it means "place of long river." Using a dictionary, find the Native American language from which each of the following words came, and find the meaning of the word in that language.

1. raccoon
2. Iowa
3. Oklahoma
4. Massachusetts
5. husky
6. Missouri
7. opossum
8. Nebraska
9. totem
10. Kentucky

THINKING AND WRITING

Comparing and Contrasting

Write a short essay contrasting the Iroquois constitution and the United States constitution. Carefully study both documents. In your prewriting, list the similarities and differences between the two documents. Then write a short essay in which you support a thesis statement about the contrasts between the two constitutions. When you revise, make sure that you have organized your writing so that your ideas are clear.

Pima

The Pima have lived in the Gila and Salt River valleys in southern Arizona for hundreds of years. A peaceful people, the Pima were friendly to both the Spanish explorers and the American settlers who ventured into their region. In the nineteenth century, as American pioneers flooded through Pima land on their way to the new frontier, the Pima fought against only their traditional enemies, the Apaches. Today about 5,500 Pima live on reservations near the Gila and Salt Rivers. Many maintain their oral literature, including songs like "From the Houses of Magic."

Chippewa

When the European settlers arrived in America, the Chippewa were a nomadic people living on the shores of Lake Superior. They sustained themselves by hunting and fishing. After the French gave them guns in exchange for furs, the Chippewa drove the Sioux and Fox tribes out of the Wisconsin area, seizing control of their land. The Chippewa's territory eventually extended from Lake Huron to central North Dakota. Today there are about 30,000 Chippewa living on reservations in North Dakota, Michigan, Wisconsin, and Minnesota, in addition to about 50,000 Chippewa living in Canada. Their early nomadic life made them sensitive to nature. This sensitivity is apparent in "Spring Song."

Teton Sioux

The Teton Sioux are the largest of seven tribes in the Sioux, or Dakota, Confederation. Originally living in the northeastern and north-central part of the country, the Teton Sioux were pushed westward to the midwestern plains by the Chippewa. Like the other tribes of the plains, the Teton Sioux were nomadic hunters who lived in tepees and depended on buffalo for food. In 1874, after gold was discovered on Teton Sioux land, the Teton Sioux became involved in conflicts with the United States Army with increasing frequency. In June of 1876, an army of Sioux defeated General Custer at the Battle of the Little Bighorn. In the months following the battle, the American forces began an intensive campaign that led to the final defeat of the Sioux at Wounded Knee, South Dakota in 1890. Today 40,000 Sioux live on reservations in Minnesota, Nebraska, Montana, North Dakota, and South Dakota.

GUIDE FOR READING

From the Houses of Magic; Spring Song; Song Concerning a Dream of the Thunderbirds

Literary Forms

The Oral Tradition. The oral tradition refers to the process of passing down sayings, songs, tales, and myths from one generation to the next by word of mouth. Native Americans did not have a written language, though they occasionally recorded myths or historical events in pictographs engraved on wood or hide or in symbols painted on strings of beads. Therefore, members of a tribe memorized the tribal literature and communicated it orally to the next generations. In some tribes, the person who had the best memory became the "keeper" of the tribe's history, songs, and myths.

Native American poetry began as songs chanted to a regular beat. Sometimes complicated melodies accompanied the words. To help the singer remember the poem or song, lines were often repeated, sometimes with a slight variation in the second line. Each line usually contained the same number of accented syllables or beats. Certain images and comparisons were also used so often that the listeners expected to hear them in tribal songs.

Look For

The following three songs survived for generations in the oral tradition. As you read them, listen to the rhythm and look for repeated lines and images.

Writing

The lyrics of songs often stand out in our memories. What qualities make lyrics memorable? Freewrite about the feelings you associate with one of your favorite songs and the qualities that make the lyrics easy to remember.

Vocabulary

Knowing the following words will help you as you read "From the Houses of Magic," "Spring Song," and "Song Concerning a Dream of the Thunderbirds."

gourd (gôrd) n.: The dried, hollowed-out shell of a fruit, used as a drinking vessel (p. 35, l. 27)

behold (bi hōld') v.: Look (p. 38, l. 1)

From the Houses of Magic

Pima

1

Down from the houses of magic,
Down from the houses of magic;
Blow the winds, and from my antlers
And my ears, they stronger gather.

5 Over there I ran trembling,
Over there I ran trembling,
For bows and arrows pursued me,
Many bows were on my trail.

2

I ran into the swamp confused,
10 There I heard the tadpoles singing.
I ran into the swamp confused,
Where the bark-clothed tadpoles sang.

In the west the dragonfly wanders,
Skimming the surfaces of the pools,
15 Touching only with his tail. He skims
With flapping and rustling wings.

Thence I ran as the darkness gathers,
Wearing cactus flowers in my hair.
Thence I ran as the darkness gathers,
20 In fluttering darkness to the singing-place.

3

At the time of the white dawning,
At the time of the white dawning,
I arose and went away,
At Blue Nightfall I went away.

INDIAN VILLAGE, RIVER GILA
Seth Eastman
Rhode Island School of Design Museum of Art

4

25 The evening glow yet lingers,
The evening glow yet lingers:
And I sit with my gourd rattle
Engaged in the sacred chant.
As I wave the eagle feathers
30 We hear the magic sounding.

The strong night is shaking me,
Just as once before he did
When in spirit I was taken
To the great magician's house.

5

35 Pitiable harlot though I am,
My heart glows with the singing
While the evening yet is young.
My heart glows with the singing.

6

Now the swallow begins his singing;
40 Now the swallow begins his singing;
And the women who are with me,
The poor women commence to sing.

The swallows met in the standing cliff;
The swallows met in the standing cliff;
45 And the rainbows arched above me,
There the blue rainbow-arches met.

7

In the reddish glow of the nightfall,
In the reddish glow of the nightfall.
I return to my burrow
50 About which the flowers bloom.

With the four eagle feathers,
With the four eagle feathers,
I stir the air. When I turn
My magic power is crossed.

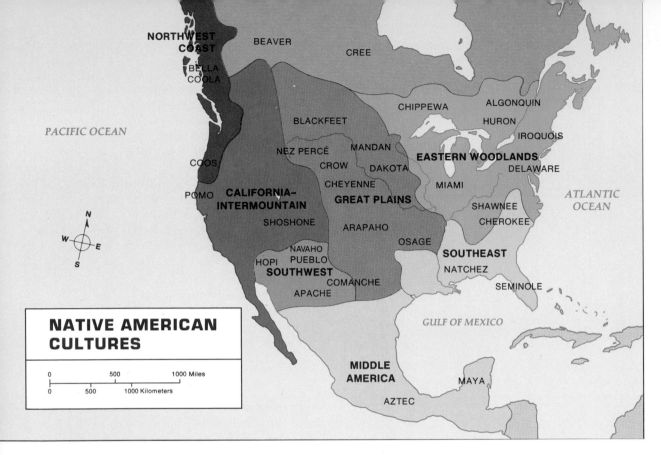

NATIVE AMERICAN CULTURES

0 — 500 — 1000 Miles
0 — 500 — 1000 Kilometers

THINKING ABOUT THE SELECTION

Recalling

1. Summarize the narrator's movements. What does the narrator do "at the time of the white dawning"?

2. (a) What does the narrator hear while waving the eagle feathers? (b) Where do the swallows meet? (c) What does the narrator do with four eagle feathers at the end of the song?

Interpreting

3. (a) What time of day is described in the poem? (b) What details indicate that it is that time?

4. List three emotions or feelings that the song conveys. How are they conveyed?

Applying

5. The Pima, as well as many other Native American tribes, considered the deer to be a sacred animal. (a) What qualities of deer make them appropriate for being considered sacred? (b) How does the way in which most people today regard deer differ from the Pima view? (c) What does this difference suggest about the contrasts between Pima society and today's society?

ANALYZING LITERATURE

Understanding the Oral Tradition

The oral tradition is the process of passing down literature from generation to generation. Poems and songs were an important part of the Native American oral tradition. Because they had to be memorized, various techniques, such as repeated lines and images and the use of lines with same number of accented syllables, or beats, were used to make them easier to remember. For example, many lines in "From the Houses of Magic" are repeated.

1. What one image, or word picture, is repeated several times in the song?

2. Aside from the use of repetition, in what way are many of the lines similar?

Spring Song

Chippewa

As my eyes
search
the prairie
I feel the summer
in the spring.

THINKING ABOUT THE SELECTION

Recalling

1. What two seasons are mentioned in the poem?

Interpreting

2. What type of weather does the speaker of the poem seem to be experiencing?

3. What is meant by the statement "I feel the summer in the spring"?

Applying

4. What seasonal change do you consider to to the most dramatic? Why?

Song Concerning a Dream of the Thunderbirds

Teton Sioux

Friends, behold!
Sacred I have been made.
Friends, behold!
In a sacred manner
5 I have been influenced
At the gathering of the clouds.
Sacred I have been made,
Friends, behold!
Sacred I have been made.

THE MYSTIC
William R. Leigh
The Thomas Gilcrease Institute of American History and Art,
Tulsa, Oklahoma

THINKING ABOUT THE SELECTION

Recalling

1. What two lines appear three times in the song?

Interpreting

2. (a) To what does the "gathering of the clouds" refer? (b) How does it relate to the title of the poem?
3. How does the pattern of the song add emphasis to lines 4–6?

Applying

4. In many ancient cultures, thunderstorms inspired fear and awe. (a) Why did the people of these cultures react this way? (b) What other natural occurrences might have inspired such emotions in these cultures?

THINKING AND WRITING

Writing a Song

Today's songwriters often use some of the same techniques when writing lyrics that the Native American tribes did. Try some of these techniques as you compose a song. First decide on a topic you might like to write a song about and an audience for the song. Brainstorm for ideas about your topic and select some that might work for your audience. Then review your notes about song lyrics and look over the Native American songs once again, taking note of the qualities that make them easy to remember. Once you have a topic and an audience, write a song using the techniques you observed in the songs of the Native American tribes and other songwriters. Then, revise your song, making sure that it is appropriate for your audience, and prepare a final draft.

Living in the New Land

THE ARRIVAL OF THE ENGLISHMEN IN VIRGINIA
Colored Line Engraving, 1590, by Theodor de Bry
The Granger Collection

JOHN SMITH

1580–1631

John Smith was a leader in the settlement of Jamestown, Virginia, the first successful English colony in America, and was one of England's most famous New World explorers. The stories of his adventures, often embellished by his own pen, fascinated European readers of his day and continue to provide a wealth of details about the early exploration and colonization of America.

The son of a farmer, Smith was born in Lincolnshire, England. He left home at the age of sixteen to become a soldier. During the next ten years, Smith traveled throughout Europe and the Near East, fought in numerous battles, and was promoted to captain. Then, in 1606, a year after his return to England, Smith led a group of colonists across the Atlantic to establish a settlement in the New World. The group landed in Virginia in 1607 and founded Jamestown.

As president of the colony from 1608 to 1609, Smith helped assure the colony's success, obtaining food, enforcing discipline, and dealing with the native tribes who inhabited the region. In 1608 Smith published *A True Relation of Virginia,* the first English book describing life in America. In 1609, after being burned in a gunpowder accident and involved in disputes with other colonists, Smith traveled back to England.

Smith made two more voyages to America in 1614 and 1615, exploring and mapping the coast of the region he named New England. Then Smith returned to England, settling in London, where he lived for the remainder of his life. During his later years, he published his two most famous works, *A Description of New England* (1616) and *The General History of Virginia, New England, and the Summer Isles* (1624).

In *The General History of Virginia,* which describes the founding of Jamestown, Smith attempts to dispel English misconceptions about America and encourages others to settle in the New World. The book also includes an account of what has become Smith's most famous adventure. According to his story, Smith was captured by the Native Americans and faced execution until the chief's daughter Pocahontas saved him from death. This episode, along with the other experiences Smith describes, provides an understanding and appreciation of what the early colonists' lives were like.

GUIDE FOR READING

Literary Forms

from The General History of Virginia

History. A history is a factual account of events in the life or development of a people, nation, institution, or culture. Histories, which usually recount events chronologically, often include analysis and explanation. Some histories are firsthand accounts by people who lived through the events. Other histories are secondhand, or secondary, accounts by people who have researched the events but did not live through them.

Firsthand accounts are likely to be subjective because of the writer's personal involvement with the events. Also, they sometimes lack accuracy because the writer often wrote to persuade or entertain the audiences of the time. For example, John Smith often exaggerates events in *The General History of Virginia*. At the same time, firsthand accounts often capture the flavor of living through those events.

Look For

The General History of Virginia is about life in Jamestown, the first colony. As you read the excerpt, look for the details that capture the essence of life there. What events does Smith tell subjectively? What events might he have exaggerated?

Writing

The early American settlers faced a great number of hardships. List the problems you think the colonists faced. Then freewrite about how you would have dealt with each of these hardships if you had been in their situation.

Vocabulary

Knowing the following words will help you as you read the excerpt from *The General History of Virginia*.

pilfer (pil′ fər) *v.*: Steal (p. 42)
palisades (pal′e sādz′) *n.*: Large pointed stakes set in the ground to form a fence used for defense (p. 42).

conceits (kən sētz′) *n.*: Strange for fanciful ideas (p. 43).
mollified (mäl′ə fīd) *v.*: Soothed; calmed (p. 45).

from The General History of Virginia

John Smith

What Happened Till the First Supply

Being thus left to our fortunes, it fortuned[1] that within ten days, scarce ten amongst us could either go[2] or well stand, such extreme weakness and sickness oppressed us. And thereat none need marvel if they consider the cause and reason, which was this: While the ships stayed, our allowance was somewhat bettered by a daily proportion of biscuit which the sailors would pilfer to sell, give, or exchange with us for money, sassafras,[3] or furs. But when they departed, there remained neither tavern, beer house, nor place of relief but the common kettle.[4] Had we been as free from all sins as gluttony and drunkenness we might have been canonized for saints, but our President[5] would never have been admitted for engrossing to his private,[6] oatmeal, sack,[7] oil, aqua vitae,[8] beef, eggs, or what not but the kettle; that indeed he allowed equally to be distributed, and that was half a pint of wheat and as much barley boiled with water for a man a day, and this, having fried some twenty-six weeks in the ship's hold, contained as many worms as grains so that we might truly call it rather so much bran than corn; our drink was water, our lodgings castles in the air.

With this lodging and diet, our extreme toil in bearing and planting palisades so strained and bruised us and our continual labor in the extremity of the heat had so weakened us, as were cause sufficient to have made us as miserable in our native country or any other place in the world.

From May to September, those that escaped lived upon sturgeon and sea crabs. Fifty in this time we buried; the rest seeing the President's projects to escape these miseries in our pinnace[9] by flight (who all this time had neither felt want nor sickness) so

---

1. **fortuned:** Happened.
2. **go:** Be active.
3. **sassafras:** A tree, the root of which was valued for its supposed medicinal qualities.
4. **common kettle:** Communal cooking pot.
5. **President:** Wingfield, the leader of the colony.
6. **engrossing to his private:** Taking for his own use.

7. **sack** *n.*: A type of white wine.
8. **aqua vitae** (ak′wə vīt′ē): Brandy.
9. **pinnace** (pin′ is) *n.*: A small sailing ship.

moved our dead spirits as we deposed him and established Ratcliffe in his place . . .

But now was all our provision spent, the sturgeon gone, all helps abandoned, each hour expecting the fury of the savages; when God, the patron of all good endeavors, in that desperate extremity so changed the hearts of the savages that they brought such plenty of their fruits and provision as no man wanted.

And now where some affirmed it was ill done of the Council[10] to send forth men so badly provided, this incontradictable reason will show them plainly they are too ill advised to nourish such ill conceits: First, the fault of our going was our own; what could be thought fitting or necessary we had, but what we should find, or want, or where we should be, we were all ignorant and supposing to make our passage in two months, with victual to live and the advantage of the spring to work; we were at sea five months where we both spent our victual and lost the opportunity of the time and season to plant, by the unskillful presumption of our ignorant transporters that understood not at all what they undertook.

Such actions have ever since the world's beginning been subject to such accidents, and everything of worth is found full of difficulties, but nothing so difficult as to establish a commonwealth so far remote from men and means and where men's minds are so untoward[11] as neither do well themselves nor suffer others. But to proceed.

The new President and Martin, being little beloved, of weak judgment in dangers, and less industry in peace, committed the managing of all things abroad[12] to Captain Smith, who, by his own example, good words, and fair promises, set some to mow, others to bind thatch, some to build houses, others to thatch them, himself always bearing the greatest task for his own share, so that in short time he provided most of them lodgings, neglecting any for himself . . .

Leading an expedition on the Chickahominy River, Captain Smith and his men are attacked by Indians, and Smith is taken prisoner.

When this news came to Jamestown, much was their sorrow for his loss, few expecting what ensued.

Six or seven weeks those barbarians kept him prisoner, many strange triumphs and conjurations they made of him, yet he so demeaned himself amongst them, as he not only diverted them from surprising the fort, but procured his own liberty, and got himself and his company such estimation amongst them, that those savages admired him.

The manner how they used and delivered him is as followeth:

The savages having drawn from George Cassen whither Captain Smith was gone, prosecuting that opportunity they followed him with three hundred bowmen, conducted by the King of Pamunkee,[13] who in divisions searching the turnings of the river found Robinson and Emry by the fireside; those they shot full of arrows and slew. Then finding the Captain, as is said, that used the savage that was his guide as his shield (three of them being slain and divers[14] others so galled),[15] all the rest would not come near him. Thinking thus to have returned to his boat, regarding them, as he marched, more than his way, slipped up to the middle in an oozy creek and his savage with him; yet dared they not come to him till being near dead with cold he threw away his

---

10. Council: The seven persons in charge of the expedition.
11. untoward: Stubborn.
12. abroad: Outside the palisades.

13. Pamunkee: The Pamunkee River.
14. divers (dī′ vərz) *adj.*: Several.
15. galled: Wounded.

arms. Then according to their composition[16] they drew him forth and led him to the fire where his men were slain. Diligently they chafed his benumbed limbs.

He demanding for their captain, they showed him Opechancanough, King of Pamunkee, to whom he gave a round ivory double compass dial. Much they marveled at the playing of the fly and needle,[17] which they could see so plainly and yet not touch it because of the glass that covered them. But when he demonstrated by that globe-like jewel the roundness of the earth and skies, the sphere of the sun, moon, and stars, and how the sun did chase the night round about the world continually, the greatness of the land and sea, the diversity of nations, variety of complexions, and how we were to them antipodes[18] and many other such like matters, they all stood as amazed with admiration.

Nothwithstanding, within an hour after, they tied him to a tree, and as many as could stand about him prepared to shoot him, but the King holding up the compass in his hand, they all laid down their bows and arrows and in a triumphant manner led him to Orapaks where he was after their manner kindly feasted and well used. . . .

At last they brought him to Werowocomoco, where was Powhatan, their Emperor. Here more than two hundred of those grim courtiers stood wondering at him, as he had been a monster, till Powhatan and his train had put themselves in their greatest braveries. Before a fire upon a seat like a bedstead, he sat covered with a great robe made of raccoon skins and all the tails hanging by. On either hand did sit a young wench of sixteen or eighteen years and along on each side the house, two rows of men and behind them as many women, with all their heads and shoulders painted red, many of their heads bedecked with the white down of birds, but every one with something, and a great chain of white beads about their necks.

At his entrance before the King, all the people gave a great shout. The Queen of Appomattoc was appointed to bring him water to wash his hands, and another brought him a bunch of feathers, instead of a towel, to dry them; having feasted him after their best barbarous manner they could, a long consultation was held, but the conclusion was, two great stones were brought before Powhatan; then as many as could, laid hands on him, dragged him to them, and thereon laid his head and being ready with their clubs to beat out his brains, Pocahontas, the King's dearest daughter, when no entreaty could prevail, got his head in her arms and laid her own upon his to save him from death; whereat the Emperor was contented he should live to make him hatchets, and her bells, beads, and copper, for they thought him as well of all occupations as themselves.[19] For the King himself will make his own robes, shoes, bows, arrows, pots; plant, hunt, or do anything so well as the rest.

Two days after, Powhatan, having disguised himself in the most fearfulest manner he could, caused Captain Smith to be brought forth to a great house in the woods and there upon a mat by the fire to be left alone. Not long after, from behind a mat that divided the house, was made the most dolefulest noise he ever heard; then Powhatan more like a devil than a man, with some two hundred more as black as himself, came unto him and told him now they were friends, and presently he should go to Jamestown to send him two great guns and a grindstone for which he would give him the country of Capahowasic and forever esteem him as his son Nantaquond.

---

16. **composition:** Ways.
17. **fly and needle:** Parts of a compass.
18. **antipodes** (an tip′ ə dēz′): On the opposite side of the globe.

19. **as well . . . themselves:** Capable of making them just as well as they could themselves.

FOUNDING OF THE FIRST PERMANENT ENGLISH SETTLEMENT
IN AMERICA
A. C. Warren
New York Public Library

So to Jamestown with twelve guides Powhatan sent him. That night they quartered in the woods, he still expecting (as he had done all this long time of his imprisonment) every hour to be put to one death or other, for all their feasting. But almighty God (by His divine providence) had mollified the hearts of those stern barbarians with compassion. The next morning betimes they came to the fort, where Smith having used the savages with what kindness he could, he showed Rawhunt, Powhatan's trusty servant, two demiculverins[20] and a millstone to carry Powhatan; they found them somewhat too heavy, but when they did see him discharge them, being loaded with stones, among the boughs of a great tree loaded with icicles, the ice and branches came so tumbling down that the poor savages ran away

---

20. demiculverins (dem′ ē kul′ vər inz): Large cannons.

half dead with fear. But at last we regained some conference with them and gave them such toys and sent to Powhatan, his women, and children such presents as gave them in general full content.

Now in Jamestown they were all in combustion,[21] the strongest preparing once more to run away with the pinnace; which, with the hazard of his life, with saker falcon[22] and musket shot, Smith forced now the third time to stay or sink.

Some, no better than they should be, had plotted with the President the next day to have him put to death by the Levitical law,[23] for the lives of Robinson and Emry; pretending the fault was his that had led

them to their ends; but he quickly took such order with such lawyers that he laid them by their heels till he sent some of them prisoners for England.

Now every once in four or five days, Pocahontas with her attendants brought him so much provision that saved many of their lives, that else for all this had starved with hunger.

His relation of the plenty he had seen, especially at Werowocomoco, and of the state and bounty of Powhatan (which till that time was unknown), so revived their dead spirits (especially the love of Pocahontas) as all men's fear was abandoned.

Thus you may see what difficulties still crossed any good endeavor; and the good success of the business being thus oft brought to the very period of destruction; yet you see by what strange means God hath still delivered it.

---

21. **combustion:** Tumult.
22. **saker falcon:** Small cannon.
23. **Levitical law:** "He that killeth man shall surely be put to death" (Leviticus 24:17).

THINKING ABOUT THE SELECTION

Recalling

1. (a) What hardships do the colonists face during their first several months in the New World? (b) What assistance do they receive?
2. (a) What criticisms does Smith make of the new president and colonist Martin? (b) What does Smith praise?
3. (a) What happens to Smith during his expedition on the Chickahominy River? (b) How is he saved from death?
4. What does Smith discover when he returns to Jamestown after his release?

Interpreting

5. What impression of Smith do you get from this account?
6. What seems to be Smith's attitude toward the Native Americans?
7. Why does Smith write in the third person, referring to himself as "he" instead of "I"?

Applying

8. What are some situations in the world today in which people are coping with great hardships?

ANALYZING LITERATURE

Understanding a History

A **history** is a nonfiction account of events that occurred to a people, nation, institution, or culture. Histories may be either firsthand accounts, written by someone who was involved with the events, or secondhand accounts, written by someone who was not involved in the events. Firsthand accounts, which sometimes lack factual accuracy, tend to be subjective, but they often capture the flavor of the time. For example, while *The General History of Virginia* conveys a sense of life in the Jamestown settlement, most historians consider Smith's account of his rescue by Pocahontas to be greatly exaggerated.

1. Find two examples in which Smith displays subjectivity in recounting events.
2. List three details that capture the flavor of life in Jamestown.

CRITICAL THINKING AND READING

Recognizing Author's Purpose

While the **purpose** of most secondhand historical accounts is to inform, many firsthand accounts are written to entertain or persuade. For example, Smith's primary purpose in writing *The General History of Virginia* was probably to encourage other English men and women to settle in the New World.

1. In what way is the primary purpose of *The General History of Virginia* made apparent?
2. What other purposes does Smith appear to have had?

THINKING AND WRITING

Writing a Historical Account

During our lifetime we all live through or are in some way a part of important events. Think of an important historical event that occurred during your lifetime or an event in your community. Brainstorm to recall details of the event, and, if necessary, research the event in your library. Then, after listing the details in chronological order, write a brief secondhand account. Try to be as objective as possible. When you revise, make sure you have included enough information to inform thoroughly a reader who has no prior knowledge of the event. Try to remove any subjective details you may have included. At this point, you might decide to include tables or maps to make your information clearer. Tables, like the one below, present facts and figures in rows and columns.

Founding of the Colonies

Colony/Date Founded	Leader	Reasons Founded
New England Colonies		
Massachusetts		
Plymouth/1620	William Bradford	Religious freedom
Massachusetts Bay/1630	John Winthrop	Religious freedom
New Hampshire/1622	Ferdinando Gorges John Mason	Profit from trade and fishing
Connecticut		
Hartford/1636	Thomas Hooker	Expand trade; religious and political freedom
New Haven/1639		
Rhode Island/1636	Roger Williams	Religious freedom
Middle Colonies		
New York/1624	Peter Minuit	Expand trade
Delaware/1638	Swedish settlers	Expand trade
New Jersey/1664	John Berkeley George Carteret	Profit from land sales; religious and political freedom
Pennsylvania/1682	William Penn	Profit from land sales; religious and political freedom
Southern Colonies		
Virginia/1607	John Smith	Trade and farming
Maryland/1632	Lord Baltimore	Profit from land sales; religious and political freedom
The Carolinas/1663	Group of eight proprietors	Trade and farming; religious freedom
North Carolina/1712		
South Carolina/1712		
Georgia/1732	James Oglethorpe	Profit, home for debtors; buffer against Spanish Florida

WILLIAM BRADFORD

1590–1657

Thirteen years after the first permanent English settlement was established in Jamestown, another group of colonists, known as the Pilgrims, landed on the shore of what is now Massachusetts. William Bradford, one of their leaders, recorded the experiences of these early settlers in a factually accurate account.

Bradford was born in Yorkshire, England. Having developed a strong devotion to religion early in life, Bradford joined a group of Puritan extremists, who felt that the Church of England was corrupt and wished to separate themselves from it entirely. In the face of stiff persecution, Bradford's group eventually fled to Leyden, Holland, where Bradford worked as a weaver. Later Bradford and many other group members left Holland to establish a settlement in the New World.

After a difficult voyage aboard the *Mayflower,* a small ship with a cracked beam, the Pilgrims reached North America in 1620, landing much farther north than they had planned. They settled in Plymouth, Massachusetts. There they encountered not only the hardships experienced by Jamestown's first settlers but also the added problem of a harsh New England winter. After the death of their first governor, John Carver, the Pilgrims elected William Bradford as their leader. Bradford was reelected governor thirty times. During his tenure as governor, he organized the repayment of debts to financial backers, encouraged new immigration, and, unlike many later settlers, established good relations with the Native Americans, without whose help the colony never would have survived.

In 1630 Bradford began writing *Of Plymouth Plantation,* an account of the Pilgrims' voyage to the New World, the founding of Plymouth Plantation, and the Pilgrims' experiences during the early years of the colony's existence. Bradford's work, which was not published until 1856, provides a firsthand view of the Pilgrims' struggle to endure and the courage and unbending religious faith that helped them survive. Written in the simple language that has come to be known as Puritan plain style, *Of Plymouth Plantation* stands as a tribute to the fortitude of Bradford and the other Pilgrim settlers.

GUIDE FOR READING

from Of Plymouth Plantation

Literary Forms

Modes of Discourse. Prose is often classified into four modes, or forms, of discourse: narration, description, exposition, and persuasion. Narration is writing that relates a story. The subject may be fictional, as in novels and short stories, or factual, as in historical accounts and biographies. Description presents the details of something, often through appeal to one or more of the five senses—sight, sound, taste, smell, and touch. Exposition uses logical patterns, such as comparison and contrast or definition, to inform or explain. Grammar textbooks and repair manuals are two examples of books containing expository writing. The fourth mode of discourse is persuasion, writing that attempts to convince readers to adopt an opinion or act in a certain way. Examples of persuasion include television advertisements and newspaper editorials.

Most often, the author's main purpose determines which of these categories a work best fits into. However, an author usually uses more than one form of discourse. For example, when writing a narrative, an author is likely to include descriptions of people and places and information about historical events.

Look For

The following selection relates events in the founding of Plymouth Plantation. As you read, look for the hardships the Pilgrims endured and the qualities and resources they were able to draw upon to survive.

Writing

The belief that we should be thankful for what we have, regardless of how difficult our circumstances may be, is often associated with the Pilgrims. What associations do you normally have when you think of the Pilgrims? Write a journal entry in which you discuss the ideas you associate with the Pilgrims.

Vocabulary

Knowing the following words will help you as you read the excerpt from *Of Plymouth Plantation*.

loath (lōth) *adj.*: Reluctant; unwilling (p. 50)

lusty (lus′ tē) *adj.*: Strong; hearty (p. 51)

sundry (sun′ drē) *adj.*: Various, different (p. 51)

from Of Plymouth Plantation

William Bradford

Of Their Voyage and How They Passed the Sea; and of Their Safe Arrival at Cape Cod

After they had enjoyed fair winds and weather for a season, they were encountered many times with cross winds and met with many fierce storms with which the ship was shroudly[1] shaken, and her upper works made very leaky; and one of the main beams in the midships was bowed and cracked, which put them in some fear that the ship could not be able to perform the voyage. So some of the chief of the company, perceiving the mariners to fear the sufficiency of the ship as appeared by their mutterings, they entered into serious consultation with the master and other officers of the ship, to consider in time of the danger, and rather to return than to cast themselves into a desperate and inevitable peril. And truly there was great distraction and difference of opinion amongst the mariners themselves; fain would they do what could be done for their wages' sake (being now near half the seas over) and on the other hand they were loath to hazard their lives too desperately. But in examining of all opinions, the master and others affirmed they knew the ship to be strong and firm under water; and for the buckling of the main beam, there was a great iron screw the passengers brought out of Holland, which would raise the beam into his place; the which being done, the carpenter and master affirmed that with a post put under it, set firm in the lower deck and otherways bound, he would make it sufficient. And as for the decks and upper works, they would caulk them as well as they could, and though with the working of the ship they would not long keep staunch, yet there

THE COMING OF THE MAYFLOWER
N. C. Wyeth
From the Collection of the Metropolitan Life Insurance Company, New York City

---

1. shroudly: Wickedly.

would otherwise be no great danger, if they did not overpress her with sails. So they committed themselves to the will of God and resolved to proceed.

In sundry of these storms the winds were so fierce and the seas so high, as they could not bear a knot of sail, but were forced to hull² for divers days together. And in one of them, as they thus lay at hull in a mighty storm, a lusty young man called John Howland, coming upon some occasion above the gratings was, with a seel³ of the ship, thrown into sea; but it pleased God that he

---

2. **hull:** Drift with the wind.
3. **seel:** Rolling.

caught hold of the topsail halyards⁴ which hung overboard and ran out at length. Yet he held his hold (though he was sundry fathoms under water) till he was hauled up by the same rope to the brim of the water, and then with a boat hook and other means got into the ship again and his life saved. And though he was something ill with it, yet he lived many years after and became a profitable member both in church and commonwealth. In all this voyage there died but one of the passengers, which was William Butten, a youth, servant to Samuel Fuller, when they drew near the coast.

But to omit other things (that I may be brief) after long beating at sea they fell with that land which is called Cape Cod; the which being made and certainly known to be it, they were not a little joyful. After some deliberation had amongst themselves and with the master of the ship, they tacked about and resolved to stand for the southward (the wind and weather being fair) to find some place about Hudson's River for their habitation. But after they had sailed that course about half the day, they fell amongst dangerous shoals and roaring breakers, and they were so far entangled therewith as they conceived themselves in great danger; and the wind shrinking upon them withal,⁵ they resolved to bear up again for the Cape and thought themselves happy to get out of those dangers before night overtook them, as by God's good providence they did. And the next day they got into the Cape Harbor⁶ where they rid in safety.

Being thus arrived in a good harbor, and brought safe to land, they fell upon their knees and blessed the God of Heaven who had brought them over the vast and furious ocean, and delivered them from all the perils and miseries thereof, again to set their feet on the firm and stable earth, their proper element.

---

4. **halyards** *n*.: Ropes for raising or lowering sails.
5. **withal:** Also.
6. **Cape Harbor:** Now Provincetown Harbor.

THE LANDING OF THE PILGRIMS AT PLYMOUTH, MASSACHUSETTS, December 22nd, 1620
Currier & Ives, 1876
Museum of the City of New York

The Starving Time

But that which was most sad and lamentable was, that in two or three months' time half of their company died, especially in January and February, being the depth of winter, and wanting houses and other comforts; being infected with the scurvy[7] and other diseases which this long voyage and their inaccommodate[8] condition had brought upon them. So as there died sometimes two or three of a day in the foresaid time, that of one hundred and odd persons, scarce fifty remained. And of these, in the time of most distress, there was but six or seven sound persons who to their great commendations, be it spoken, spared no pains night or day, but with abundance of toil and hazard of their own health, fetched them wood, made them fires, dressed them meat, made their beds, washed their loathsome clothes, clothed and unclothed them. In a word, did all the homely[9] and necessary offices for them which dainty and queasy stomachs cannot endure to hear named; and all this

---

7. scurvy *n.*: A disease caused by vitamin C deficiency.
8. inaccommodate *adj.*: Unfit.

9. homely *adj.*: Domestic.

willingly and cheerfully, without any grudging in the least, showing herein their true love unto their friends and brethren; a rare example and worthy to be remembered. Two of these seven were Mr. William Brewster, their reverend Elder, and Myles Standish, their Captain and military commander, unto whom myself and many others were much beholden in our low and sick condition. And yet the Lord so upheld these persons as in this general calamity they were not at all infected either with sickness or lameness. And what I have said of these I may say of many others who died in this general visitation,[10] and others yet living; that whilst they had health, yea, or any strength continuing, they were not wanting to any that had need of them. And I doubt not but their recompense is with the Lord.

But I may not here pass by another remarkable passage not to be forgotten. As this calamity fell among the passengers that were to be left here to plant, and were hasted ashore and made to drink water that the seamen might have the more beer, and one[11] in his sickness desiring but a small can of beer, it was answered that if he were their own father he should have none. The disease began to fall amongst them also, so as almost half of their company died before they went away, and many of their officers and lustiest men, as the boatswain, gunner, three quartermasters, the cook and others. At which the Master was something strucken and sent to the sick ashore and told the Governor he should send for beer for them that had need of it, though he drunk water homeward bound.

But now amongst his company there was far another kind of carriage[12] in this misery than amongst the passengers. For they that before had been boon[13] companions in drinking and jollity in the time of their health and welfare, began now to desert one another in this calamity, saying they would not hazard their lives for them, they should be infected by coming to help them in their cabins; and so, after they came to lie by it, would do little or nothing for them but, "if they died, let them die." But such of the passengers as were yet aboard showed them what mercy they could which made some of their hearts relent, as the boatswain (and some others) who was a proud young man and would often curse and scoff at the passengers. But when he grew weak, they had compassion on him and helped him; then he confessed he did not deserve it at their hands, he had abused them in word and deed. "Oh!" (saith he) "you, I now see, show your love like Christians indeed one to another, but we let one another lie and die like dogs." Another lay cursing his wife, saying if it had not been for her he had never come this unlucky voyage, and anon cursing his fellows, saying he had done this and that for some of them; he had spent so much and so much amongst them, and they were now weary of him and did not help him, having need. Another gave his companion all he had, if he died, to help him in his weakness; he went and got a little spice and made him a mess[14] of meat once or twice. And because he died not so soon as he expected, he went amongst his fellows and swore the rogue would cozen[15] him, he would see him choked before he made him any more meat; and yet the poor fellow died before morning.

Indian Relations

All this while the Indians came skulking about them, and would sometimes show themselves aloof off, but when any approached near them, they would run away; and once they stole away their tools where they had been at work and were gone to dinner. But about the sixteenth of March, a certain Indian came boldly amongst them and

---

10. visitation *n.*: Affliction.
11. one: William Bradford.
12. carriage *n.*: Behavior.
13. boon *adj.*: Close.

14. mess *n.*: Meal.
15. cozen (kuz′ n) *v.*: Cheat.

spoke to them in broken English, which they could well understand but marveled at it. At length they understood by discourse with him, that he was not of these parts, but belonged to the eastern parts where some English ships came to fish, with whom he was acquainted and could name sundry of them by their names, amongst whom he had got his language. He became profitable to them in acquainting them with many things concerning the state of the country in the east parts where he lived, which was afterwards profitable unto them; as also of the people here, of their names, number and strength, of their situation and distance from this place, and who was chief amongst them. His name was Samoset. He told them also of another Indian whose name was Squanto, a native of this place, who had been in England and could speak better English than himself.

Being, after some time of entertainment and gifts dismissed, a while after he came again, and five more with him, and they brought again all the tools that were stolen away before, and made way for the coming of their great Sachem,[16] called Massasoit. Who, about four or five days after, came with the chief of his friends and other attendance, with the aforesaid Squanto. With whom, after friendly entertainment and some gifts given him, they made a peace with him

---

16. **Sachem** (sā′ chəm): Chief.

(which hath now continued this twenty-four years) in these terms:

1. That neither he nor any of his should injure or do hurt to any of their people.
2. That if any of his did hurt to any of theirs, he should send the offender, that they might punish him.
3. That if anything were taken away from any of theirs, he should cause it to be restored; and they should do the like to his.
4. If any did unjustly war against him, they would aid him; if any did war against them, he should aid them.
5. He should send to his neighbors confederates to certify them of this, that they might not wrong them, but might be likewise comprised in the conditions of peace.
6. That when their men came to them, they should leave their bows and arrows behind them.

After these things he returned to his place called Sowams, some 40 miles from this place, but Squanto continued with them and was their interpreter and was a special instrument sent of God for their good beyond their expectation. He directed them how to set their corn, where to take fish, and to procure other commodities, and was also their pilot to bring them to unknown places for their profit, and never left them till he died.

THINKING ABOUT THE SELECTION

Recalling

1. What hardships do the Pilgrims endure during their trip across the Atlantic?
2. What is the Pilgrims' first act when they are "brought safe to land?"
3. Explain the situation between the sick and the healthy crew members during the first winter.
4. What are the terms of the peace agreement between the Pilgrims and Native Americans?

Interpreting

5. How would you characterize the Pilgrims' reactions to the hardships they encountered during their first winter in Plymouth?
6. Find two statements by Bradford that convey the Pilgrims' belief that they were being guided and protected by God.
7. (a) What change occurs in Bradford's attitude toward the Native Americans? (b) How does the Native Americans' attitude toward the Pilgrims change? (c) Based on Bradford's descriptions, what do you think brought about these changes in attitude?

Applying

8. Do you feel that the changing attitudes of the settlers toward the Native Americans and the Native Americans toward the settlers reflect typical experiences with newcomers? Why or why not?

ANALYZING LITERATURE

Using Modes of Discourse

Prose is often classified into four modes of discourse: narration, description, exposition, and persuasion. Most often, the author's main purpose determines into which of these modes a work is best classified. However, a writer rarely uses only one form of discourse in a work. For example, while *Of Plymouth Plantation* is primarily a narrative, because Bradford's main purpose is to tell about a series of events, the work contains many descriptive passages.

1. Find at least two examples of Bradford's use of description.
2. Find two examples of Bradford's use of a third form of discourse.

CRITICAL THINKING AND READING

Making Inferences About Attitudes

Many narratives, such as *Of Plymouth Plantation,* reveal the attitudes and values of the people being portrayed. However, in most cases cultural attitudes and values are revealed indirectly. As a result, you must make inferences, or draw conclusions, by carefully examining the characters' actions, thoughts, and comments. For example, from Bradford's statement that the Pilgrims "committed themselves to the will of God" you can conclude that Pilgrims had a strong faith in God.

What inferences can you make about the Pilgrims' attitudes and values from each of the following passages?

1. ". . . there was but six or seven sound persons who . . . did all the homely and necessary offices for them [sick Pilgrims] . . . willingly and cheerfully, without any grudging in the least. . . ."
2. "The boatswain . . . would often curse and scoff at the passengers. But when he grew weak, they had compassion on him and helped him. . . ."

THINKING AND WRITING

Comparing and Contrasting Accounts

Write an essay comparing and contrasting *The General History of Virginia* and *Of Plymouth Plantation* in such areas as style, purpose, objectivity, accuracy, and content. First prepare a list of similarities and differences, and then organize your information into an outline or map. In the essay, use specific examples and passages from both works to support your thesis. When you revise, make sure your essay is well organized and includes supporting information.

To My Dear and Loving Husband

Anne Bradstreet (1612–1672) was born in Northampton, England, and raised as a Puritan. In 1630, she and her husband, Simon Bradstreet, left England and settled in the Massachusetts Bay Colony. Bradstreet endured the hardships of life in the New World and raised eight children. In 1650 a collection of her scholarly poems, *The Tenth Muse Lately Sprung Up in America, By a Gentlewoman of Those Parts,* was published in England. Bradstreet's later poems, like "To My Dear and Loving Husband," are more personal, expressing the feeling arising from the joyful but difficult and sometimes tragic experiences of everyday Puritan life.

Literary Forms

Lyric Poetry. Lyric poems, or lyrics, are brief poems that express the writer's personal feelings and thoughts. These poems, which in ancient Greece were sung to the accompaniment of a stringed instrument called a lyre, tend to be melodic and focus on producing a single, unified effect.

Although Bradstreet's early poetry consisted of scholarly poems on such subjects as physics, history, and philosophy, most of her later poems are lyrics. As she became more deeply immersed in her life in the New World, Bradstreet expressed her personal feelings about her family and the difficulties of colonial life.

Look For

As you read "To My Dear and Loving Husband," look for the thoughts and feelings Bradstreet expresses. How does she relate her married life to eternity?

Writing

Like most other Puritans, Anne Bradstreet had a deep devotion to her family. List ways in which people may demonstrate such devotion to others.

Vocabulary

Knowing the following words will help you as you read "To My Dear and Loving Husband."
recompense (rek′ əm pens′) *n.*: Reward (p. 57, l. 8)

manifold (man′ ə fold) *adv.*: In many ways (p. 57, l. 10)

To My Dear and Loving Husband

Anne Bradstreet

If ever two were one, then surely we.
If ever man were lov'd by wife, then thee;
If ever wife was happy in a man,
Compare with me ye women if you can.
5   I prize thy love more than whole mines of gold,
Or all the riches that the East doth hold.
My love is such that rivers cannot quench,
Nor ought[1] but love from thee, give recompense.
Thy love is such I can no way repay,
10   The heavens reward thee manifold, I pray.
Then while we live, in love let's so persevere,
That when we live no more, we may live ever.

---

1. ought: Anything whatever.

READING WOMAN
Terborch
Three Lions

THINKING ABOUT THE SELECTION

Recalling

1. (a) What does the speaker prize more than "all the riches that the East doth hold"? (b) What "is such that rivers cannot quench"?

Interpreting

2. What does Bradstreet mean by the apparent paradox in the last two lines: ". . . let's so persevere / That when we live no more, we may live ever"?
3. What ideas about heaven and the afterlife does the poem convey?

Applying

4. Do you think personal devotion is as much esteemed today as it was in Anne Bradstreet's day? Support your answer.

ANALYZING LITERATURE

Understanding Lyric Poetry

A **lyric poem** expresses the personal thoughts and feelings of the poet in lively, musical language. For example, "To My Dear and Loving Husband" is a lyric poem that conveys the poet's happiness.

1. What is the main feeling Bradstreet expresses?
2. What other thoughts or feelings does Bradstreet express?
3. How do Bradstreet's repetition and images help to convey the strength of the emotion being expressed?

EDWARD TAYLOR

1642–1729

Edward Taylor is now generally regarded as the best of the colonial poets. Yet, because Taylor thought of his poetry as a form of personal religious worship, he permitted only two stanzas from one of his poems to be printed while he was alive, and he instructed his heirs not to have any more of his poetry published. As a result, few people knew about his work until his poems were first published more than two centuries after his death.

Before the English government's lack of tolerance for his Puritan beliefs prompted him to emigrate to America, Taylor worked as a teacher in England. After arriving in Boston in 1668, Taylor entered Harvard College and graduated in 1671. Taylor was then asked to serve as the minister and physician of the small farming community of Westfield, Massachusetts. After accepting the position, Taylor walked more than one hundred miles, partly through knee-deep snow, to get to his new home.

Taylor spent the rest of his life in Westfield. It was a life filled with hardships. Because of the fierce battles between the Native Americans and the colonists, Taylor and the other people of Westfield lived in a state of constant fear. Taylor also experienced many personal tragedies. Five of the eight children he had with his first wife died in infancy, and his first wife died while still a young woman.

In spite of the difficulties of his life and the demands of his position, Taylor wrote a considerable amount of poetry. Nearly all of his poems are expressions of his extremely conservative religious beliefs. Taylor believed that only a select few people were predestined to escape eternal damnation. Taylor's poetry is not characteristic of most Puritan poetry. Yet his poems convey the intensity of the conservative Puritans' devotion to God and the strength of their desire for salvation perhaps better than any of the other poetry of his day.

GUIDE FOR READING

Huswifery; Upon a Wasp Chilled with Cold

Figurative Language. Figurative language is language that is not intended to be interpreted literally. To interpret figurative language, you must examine the suggestions and associations it evokes. Writers use figurative language for strength and freshness of expression, to illustrate similarities between things that are seemingly quite different, or to express abstract ideas with concrete images, or word pictures. For example, the statement that a character's "thoughts were like scattered leaves" is figurative. In suggesting that the character's thoughts lacked focus, the phrase creates a concrete picture of an abstract idea and presents an interesting and unusual comparison.

Conceits. One kind of figurative language is a conceit, an elaborate and unusual comparison between two startlingly different subjects. Conceits are often lengthy and intricate, frequently developing through a series of shorter, less elaborate comparisons into the framework for an entire poem. Like the seventeenth-century English poets such as John Donne and George Herbert, whose work he greatly admired, Edward Taylor often used extended conceits in his writing. Yet, while Donne and Herbert used conceits primarily to surprise or shock readers, Taylor used conceits to emphasize the close relationship between God and the natural world.

As you read "Huswifery" and "Upon a Wasp Chilled with Cold," look for Taylor's figurative language. What elaborate comparisons form the basis for each poem?

When figurative language is used to express abstract ideas through concrete images, or word pictures, it often adds to our understanding and appreciation of these ideas. Taylor uses figurative language in the poems you will read. List five abstract words, such as *love* and *sorrow*. Then brainstorm about concrete images that could be applied to each of these ideas, and record each image beside the idea that it is intended to express.

Knowing the following words will help you as you read "Huswifery" and "Upon a Wasp Chilled with Cold."

chafes (chāfz) *v.*: Rubs to make warm (p. 62, l. 5)

precepts (prē′ septz) *n.*: Rules of conduct (p. 62, l. 16)

EVENING
Wanda Gág
University of New Mexico

Huswifery

Edward Taylor

Make me, O Lord, Thy spinning wheel complete.
    Thy holy word my distaff[1] make for me.
Make mine affections[2] Thy swift flyers[3] neat
    And make my soul Thy holy spoole to be.
5   My conversation make to be Thy reel
    And reel the yarn thereon spun of Thy wheel.

Make me Thy loom then, knit therein this twine:
    And make Thy holy spirit, Lord, wind quills:[4]

---

1. distaff *n.*: A staff on which flax or wool is wound
for use in spinning.
2. affections: Emotions.
3. flyers *n.*: The part of a spinning wheel which
twists fibers into yarn.
4. quills *n.*: A weaver's spindles or bobbins.

Then weave the web Thyself. The yarn is fine.
10   Thine ordinances[5] make my fulling mills.[6]
    Then dye the same in heavenly colors choice,
    All pinked[7] with varnished flowers of paradise.

    Then clothe therewith mine understanding, will,
    Affections, judgment, conscience, memory
15 My words, and actions, that their shine may fill
    My ways with glory and Thee glorify.
    Then mine apparel shall display before Ye
    That I am clothed in holy robes for glory.

---

5. ordinances: Sacraments.
6. fulling mills *n.*: Mills used for cleaning and thickening cloth.
7. pinked: Decorated.

THINKING ABOUT THE SELECTION
Recalling
1. To whom is the poem addressed?
2. (a) What type of machine does Taylor describe? (b) What process does he describe? (c) In what does the speaker ask to be clothed?

Interpreting
3. What does the poem suggest about the speaker's attitude toward God?
4. (a) What seems to be the poem's overall purpose? (b) How do the final two lines convey Taylor's belief that religious grace comes as a gift from God, rather than as a result of a person's efforts?

Applying
5. What process do you think Taylor might have described in the poem if he had written it while living in today's society?

ANALYZING LITERATURE
Noting Figurative Language and Conceits

Figurative language is language that is not meant to be interpreted literally. To grasp the meaning of figurative language, you must examine the suggestions and associations it evokes. For example, the first line of "Huswifery"—"Make me, O Lord, Thy spinning wheel complete"—suggests that the speaker is asking to be made an instrument or agent of God.

A **conceit** is an elaborate, often lengthy comparison between two startlingly different subjects. For example, in "Huswifery," Taylor creates an intricate, extended comparison between the making of cloth and the granting of God's grace.

1. What do each of the following lines from "Huswifery" suggest?
   a. "And make my soul Thy holy spoole to be."
   b. "That I am clothed in holy robes for glory."
2. Taylor believed that the granting of grace involved the transformation of a person from a flawed and imperfect state of being to a state of purity and perfection. How does Taylor's conceit express this belief?
3. What does Taylor's comparison of a common household task with the granting of grace suggest about his beliefs concerning the relationship between God and the earthly world?

Upon a Wasp Chilled with Cold

Edward Taylor

The bear[1] that breathes the northern blast
Did numb, torpedo-like,[2] a wasp
Whose stiffened limbs encramped, lay bathing
In Sol's[3] warm breath and shine as saving,
5   Which with her hands she chafes and stands
Rubbing her legs, shanks, thighs, and hands.
Her petty[4] toes, and fingers' ends
Nipped with this breath, she out extends
Unto the sun, in great desire
10   To warm her digits at that fire.
Doth hold her temples in this state
Where pulse doth beat, and head doth ache.
Doth turn, and stretch her body small,
Doth comb her velvet capital.[5]
15   As if her little brain pan were
A volume of choice precepts clear.
As if her satin jacket hot
Contained apothecary's shop[6]
Of Nature's receipts,[7] that prevails
20   To remedy all her sad ails,[8]
As if her velvet helmet high
Did turret[9] rationality.
She fans her wing up to the wind
As if her petticoat were lined,
25   With reason's fleece, and hoists sails
And humming flies in thankful gails
Unto her dun curled[10] palace hall
Her warm thanks offering for all.

---

1. The bear: The constellation of Ursa Major, commonly called the Big Dipper.
2. torpedo-like: Capable of producing a strong electrical charge.
3. Sol: Personification of the sun.
4. petty: Small.
5. capital: Head.
6. apothecary's shop: Shop where medicines are prepared and sold.
7. nature's receipts: Natural remedies.
8. ails: Ailments.
9. turret: Contain.
10. dun curled: Dark curved.

Lord clear my misted sight that I
30 May hence view thy divinity.
Some sparks whereof thou up dost hasp[11]
Within this little downy wasp
In whose small corporation[12] we
A school and a schoolmaster see
35 Where we may learn, and easily find
A nimble spirit bravely mind
Her work in every limb: and lace
It up neat with a vital grace,
Acting each part though ne'er so small
40 Here of this fustian[13] animal.
Till I enravished climb into
The godhead[14] on this lather do.
Where all my pipes inspired upraise
An heavenly music furred with praise.

---

11. **hasp:** Fasten.
12. **corporation:** Here, body.
13. **fustian:** Coarsely coated.
14. **godhead:** Paradise.

THINKING ABOUT THE SELECTION

Recalling

1. (a) What human features does Taylor use in describing the wasp? (b) How does the wasp warm itself? (c) What does the wasp do after it has warmed itself?
2. (a) To whom is the second stanza addressed? (b) For what does the speaker ask?

Interpreting

3. In the first stanza, the speaker creates a comparison between the warming of the wasp and the granting of God's grace. (a) What does the manner in which the wasp is warmed suggest about Taylor's beliefs concerning the granting of God's grace? (b) With what can the actions of the wasp at the end of the first stanza be compared?

Applying

4. In this poem, the wasp serves as an example for the speaker. List two other insects or animals you feel could serve as an example for humans, and explain what you think we could learn from them.

THINKING AND WRITING

Writing a Conceit

Think of two seemingly different processes that are in some way similar to each other. Then list the stages of each process and try to think of vivid images, or word pictures, to describe each stage. Write a poem in which you develop an extended conceit by directly comparing each of the corresponding stages of the two processes. Your poem does not need to have rhythm or a definite structure. When you revise, make sure that the comparison you are making is clear and that you have used vivid imagery in your descriptions.

from The History of the Dividing Line

William Byrd (1674–1744) helped to develop and expand the early southern colonies. Throughout the course of his life in America, Byrd, a Virginian who spent much of his early life in England, kept diaries that provide us with a firsthand view of early southern life. After his return to Virginia, when he was about thirty years old, Byrd ran his estate while attending to the mapping and expansion of the colonies. Byrd wrote numerous poems, essays, and travel books, and recorded his personal experiences in a diary, *The History of the Dividing Line* (1729), which recounts his experiences during a surveying expedition undertaken to settle a border dispute between the colonies of Virginia and North Carolina.

Literary Forms

Journals. A journal, or diary, is a personal record of events, conversations, thoughts, feelings, and observations. Because journals are written on a day-to-day basis, they allow people to record their immediate reactions to their experiences. Most often, people keep journals for their personal use, never intending to have them published. However, keeping a journal allows writers to record descriptions, ideas, and events that they may eventually use in a story, poem, or essay.

William Byrd was a dedicated journal writer, recording his experiences in a code that only he could interpret. *The History of the Dividing Line* is based on an account from Byrd's journal. Though Byrd refined and toned down the original material in preparing *The History,* the work remains in journal form and still captures Byrd's spontaneous responses to the events of the surveying expedition.

Look For

In this excerpt from *The History of the Dividing Line,* Byrd shares his experiences on a surveying expedition. Look for his personal comments about the incidents that occur.

Writing

What experiences have you had that you feel were adventures? Write a journal entry describing one of these experiences.

Vocabulary

Knowing the following words will help you as you read the excerpt from *The History of the Dividing Line.*

unconscionable (un kän′ shən ə b′l) *adj.*: Unreasonable (p. 65)
practicable (prak′ ti kə b′l) *adj.*: Capable of being put into practice; feasible (p. 65)
quagmire (kwag′ mīr) *n.*: Wet, boggy ground (p. 65)

cumbersome (kum′ bər səm) *adj.*: Hard to handle or deal with because of size or weight (p. 65)

from The History of the Dividing Line

William Byrd

Into the Dismal Swamp

March 14 Before nine of the clock this morning the provisions, bedding, and other necessaries were made up into packs for the men to carry on their shoulders into the Dismal. They were victualed for eight days at full allowance, nobody doubting but that would be abundantly sufficient to carry them through that inhospitable place; nor indeed was it possible for the poor fellows to stagger under more. As it was, their loads weighed from sixty to seventy pounds, in just proportion to the strength of those who were to bear them. 'Twould have been unconscionable to have saddled them with burdens heavier than that, when they were to lug them through a filthy bog which was hardly practicable with no burden at all. Besides this luggage at their backs, they were obliged to measure the distance, mark the trees, and clear the way for the surveyors every step they went. It was really a pleasure to see with how much cheerfulness they undertook and with how much spirit they went through all this drudgery. For their greater safety, the commissioners took care to furnish them with Peruvian bark,[1] rhubarb, and ipecacuanha,[2] in case they might happen, in that wet journey, to be taken with fevers or fluxes.

Although there was no need of example to inflame persons already so cheerful, yet to enter the people with the better grace, the author and two more of the commissioners accompanied them half a mile into the Dismal. The skirts of it were thinly planted with dwarf reeds and gall bushes, but when we got into the Dismal itself we found the reeds grew there much taller and closer and, to mend the matter, were so interlaced with bamboo briers that there was no scuffling through them without the help of pioneers. At the same time we found the ground moist and trembling under our feet like a quagmire, insomuch that it was an easy matter to run a ten-foot pole up to the head in it without exerting any uncommon strength to do it. Two of the men whose burdens were the least cumbersome had orders to march before with their tomahawks and clear the way in order to make an opening for the surveyors. By their assistance we made a shift to push the line half a mile in three hours and then reached a small piece of firm land about a hundred yards wide, standing up above the rest like an island. Here the people were glad to lay down their loads and take a little refreshment, while the happy man whose lot it was to carry the jug of rum began already, like Aesop's bread carriers,[3] to find it grow a good deal lighter.

After reposing about an hour, the com-

---

1. Peruvian bark: Quinine, used in medicine for treating malaria and other fevers.
2. ipecacuanha (ip′ ə kak′ yoo wan′ ə) *n.*: A plant with roots used for medicinal purposes.

3. Aesop's bread carriers: From a fable in which the man who wanted to carry the lightest load on a journey chose the bread because, though it was the heaviest load at the start of the journey, he knew once it had been distributed he would have only an empty basket to carry.

DISMAL SWAMP
Flavius J. Fisher
Randolph-Macon Women's College, Maier Museum of Art

missioners recommended vigor and constancy to their fellow travelers, by whom they were answered with three cheerful huzzas, in token of obedience. This ceremony was no sooner over but they took up their burdens and attended the motion of the surveyors, who, though they worked with all their might, could reach but one mile farther, the same obstacles still attending them which they had met with in the morning. However small this distance may seem to such as are used to travel at their ease, yet our poor men, who were obliged to work with an unwieldy load at their backs, had reason to think it a long way; especially in a bog where they had no firm footing but every step made a deep impression which was instantly filled with water. At the same time they were laboring with their hands to cut down the reeds, which were ten feet high, their legs were hampered with briers. Besides, the weather happened to be warm, and the tallness of the reeds kept off every friendly breeze from coming to refresh them. And indeed it was a little provoking to hear the wind whistling among the branches of the white cedars, which grew here and there amongst the reeds, and at the same time

not to have the comfort to feel the least breath of it.

In the meantime the three commissioners returned out of the Dismal the same way they went in and, having joined their brethren, proceeded that night as far as Mr. Wilson's. This worthy person lives within sight of the Dismal, in the skirts whereof his stocks range and maintain themselves all the winter, and yet he knew as little of it as he did of *Terra Australis Incognita.*[4] He told us a Canterbury tale[5] of a North Briton whose curiosity spurred him a long way into this great desert,[6] as he called it, near twenty years ago, but he, having no compass nor seeing the sun for several days together, wandered about till he was almost famished; but at last he bethought himself of[7] a secret his countrymen make use of to pilot themselves in a dark day. He took a fat louse out

---

4. *Terra Australis Incognita* (tĕr′ ə ô strâl′ əs ĭn kăg′ nə tə): An unknown southern land.
5. Canterbury tale: Here, a remarkable story. *The Canterbury Tales* is a literary work written by medieval English poet Geoffrey Chaucer.
6. desert: Here, referring to the swamp.
7. bethought himself of: Remembered.

of his collar and exposed it to the open day on a piece of white paper, which he brought along with him for his journal. The poor insect, having no eyelids, turned himself about till he found the darkest part of the heavens and so made the best of his way toward the North. By this direction he steered himself safe out and gave such a frightful account of the monsters he saw and the distresses he underwent that no mortal since has been hardy enough to go upon the like dangerous discovery.

THINKING ABOUT THE SELECTION

Recalling

1. Describe the contents of the men's packs. How much do their loads weigh?
2. Name two obstacles that the men encounter in the dismal swamp.
3. (a) What, according to Mr. Wilson, did the North Briton use to find his way out of the swamp after becoming lost in it? (b) How did it help him find his way out?

Interpreting

4. How does Byrd's detailed description of the vegetation and surface of the swamp reflect his knowledge of science?
5. Give one example of Byrd's use of humorous exaggeration in this excerpt.

Applying

6. How might this account be different if it had been written by a New England Puritan?

ANALYZING LITERATURE

Understanding Journals

A **journal** is a personal record of thoughts, feelings, insights, conversations, and events. Writers often use material they have recorded in their journals in writing short stories, novels, poems, essays, or other works. For example, *The History of the Dividing Line,* which is written in journal form, is based on an account from William Byrd's journal.

1. How might this account be different if Byrd had written it twenty years after the experience without having a journal to refer to?
2. In his original journal account, Byrd is critical of a number of the other members of the surveying party. In *The History,* however, Byrd is far less critical of these people. Why do you think Byrd toned down his original material when he prepared *The History*?
3. What other changes would you guess Byrd made when revising his original journal account? Explain your answer.

CRITICAL THINKING AND READING

Recognizing the Author's Purpose

William Byrd's decision to tone down his original material when he prepared *The History* shows that the purpose of his journal was different from the purpose of *The History*. While Byrd's journal account served as his personal record of the surveying expedition, *The History* was intended to inform members of the British aristocracy about life in America.

1. What impression of himself and the other colonists does Byrd seem to be trying to convey?
2. What impression of the American wilderness does he seem to be trying to convey?
3. Aside from informing readers, what other purpose does *The History* serve?

THINKING AND WRITING

Writing a Narrative Account

Refer to the journal entry that you wrote before reading this selection. Turn your journal entry into a narrative designed to achieve a certain effect. First determine the effect you would like to achieve. For instance, do you want to persuade someone to undertake an adventure similar to yours? Then, using the information from your journal entry, write your narrative. Revise your narrative, changing or adding details necessary to achieve your effect.

JONATHAN EDWARDS

1703–1758

Though he also wrote extensively, Jonathan Edwards is remembered mainly as one of the most powerful and persuasive Puritan preachers of colonial New England.

Born in East Windsor, Connecticut, Edwards grew up in an atmosphere of devout Puritan discipline. As a young boy, he is said to have demonstrated his religious devotion by preaching sermons to his playmates from a makeshift pulpit he built behind his home. Edwards also displayed academic brilliance at an early age. By the time he was twelve, he had learned to speak Latin, Greek, and Hebrew and had written numerous philosophical and scientific essays. Edwards entered Yale at the age of thirteen and graduated four years later as the valedictorian of his class. Edwards went on to earn his master's degree in theology.

In 1727 Edwards became the assistant to his grandfather, Solomon Stoddard, who was the pastor of the church at Northampton, Massachusetts, one of the largest and wealthiest congregations in the Puritan world. Edwards became the church pastor two years later when his grandfather died, and he also began preaching as a visiting minister throughout New England. Strongly desiring a return to the simplicity and orthodoxy of the Puritan past, Edwards became one of the leaders of the Great Awakening, a religious revival that swept the colonies in the 1730's and 1740's.

The Great Awakening did not last long, however, and in 1750 Edwards was dismissed from his position after many members of his congregation had become displeased with his conservative beliefs. Edwards then moved to Stockbridge, Massachusetts, where he preached to the Native Americans and wrote a number of theological works. In 1757 Edwards became the president of the College of New Jersey (now Princeton University), but he died shortly after taking office.

Although in most of his sermons, books, and essays Edwards appeals to reason and logic, his highly emotional "fire and brimstone" sermon *Sinners in the Hands of an Angry God* is by far his most famous work. This sermon, which was delivered to a congregation in Enfield, Connecticut, in 1741, and is said to have caused listeners to rise from their seats in a state of hysteria, demonstrates Edwards's tremendous powers of persuasion and captures the religious fervor of the Great Awakening.

from Sinners in the Hands of an Angry God

Literary Forms

Persuasive Speeches. A persuasive speech attempts to convince listeners to think or act in a certain way. The effectiveness of a persuasive speech depends to a large extent on the audience's perception of the speaker, the speaker's consideration of the audience and setting, and the choice of persuasive techniques.

The Speaker's Qualifications. A speaker must establish his or her qualifications to speak on the subject. In many cases the speaker's reputation alone convinces an audience of his or her qualifications. In other cases the speaker must gain the audience's trust by displaying his or her knowledge of the subject or presenting his or her credentials.

Audience. It is also important for the speaker to be aware of the audience he or she is addressing. The writer must take into account the backgrounds, ages, interests, and beliefs of the audience.

Occasion. The time and place at which a persuasive speech is to be presented will also affect its content. Often the speaker will include references to current events or examples that will appeal to current interests.

Technique. Finally, the speaker must decide which persuasive techniques will best serve his or her purpose. A speaker may choose to present a logical argument or may appeal to past traditions or to the audience's emotions or sense of reason, or he or she may use a variety of other techniques.

Look For

As you read the excerpt from *Sinners in the Hands of an Angry God*, look for evidence of the writer's qualifications, awareness of audience and occasion, and his use of specific techniques.

Writing

Some of the factors that determine the effectiveness of a television commercial are similar to the factors that determine the effectiveness of a persuasive speech. Brainstorm about television commercials that you consider effective. Then list them and jot down the reasons why you think each one is effective.

Vocabulary

Knowing the following words will help you as you read the excerpt from *Sinners in the Hands of an Angry God*.

omnipotent (äm nip′ ə tənt) *adj.*: All-powerful (p. 71)

ineffable (in ef′ ə bl) *adj.*: Inexpressible (p. 72)

dolorous (dō′ lər əs) *adj.*: Sad; mournful (p. 72)

from Sinners in the Hands of an Angry God

Jonathan Edwards

This is the case of every one of you that are out of Christ:[1] That world of misery, that lake of burning brimstone, is extended abroad under you. There is the dreadful pit of the glowing flames of the wrath of God; there is Hell's wide gaping mouth open; and you have nothing to stand upon, nor anything to take hold of; there is nothing between you and Hell but the air; it is only the power and mere pleasure of God that holds you up.

You probably are not sensible of this; you find you are kept out of Hell, but do not see the hand of God in it; but look at other things, as the good state of your bodily constitution, your care of your own life, and the means you use for your own preservation. But indeed these things are nothing; if God should withdraw his hand, they would avail no more to keep you from falling than the thin air to hold up a person that is suspended in it.

Your wickedness makes you as it were heavy as lead, and to tend downwards with great weight and pressure towards Hell; and if God should let you go, you would immediately sink and swiftly descend and plunge into the bottomless gulf, and your healthy constitution, and your own care and prudence, and best contrivance, and all your righteousness, would have no more influence to uphold you and keep you out of Hell, than a spider's web would have to stop a fallen rock. Were it not for the sovereign

pleasure of God, the earth would not bear you one moment . . . The world would spew you out, were it not for the sovereign hand of Him who hath subjected it in hope. There are black clouds of God's wrath now hanging directly over your heads, full of the dreadful storm, and big with thunder; and were it not for the restraining hand of God, it would immediately burst forth upon you. The sovereign pleasure of God, for the present, stays[2] his rough wind; otherwise it would come with fury, and your destruction would come like a whirlwind, and you would be like the chaff of the summer threshing floor.

The wrath of God is like great waters that are dammed for the present; they increase more and more, and rise higher and higher, till an outlet is given; and the longer the stream is stopped, the more rapid and mighty is its course, when once it is let loose. It is true, that judgment against your evil works has not been executed hitherto; the floods of God's vengeance have been withheld; but your guilt in the meantime is constantly increasing, and you are every day treasuring up more wrath; the waters are constantly rising, and waxing more and more mighty; and there is nothing but the mere pleasure of God, that holds the waters back, that are unwilling to be stopped, and press hard to go forward. If God should only withdraw his hand from the floodgate, it would immediately fly open, and the fiery floods of the fierceness and wrath of God,

---

1. out of Christ: Not in God's grace.

2. stays: Restrains.

would rush forth with inconceivable fury, and would come upon you with omnipotent power; and if your strength were ten thousand times greater than it is, yea, ten thousand times greater than the strength of the stoutest, sturdiest devil in Hell, it would be nothing to withstand or endure it.

The bow of God's wrath is bent, and the arrow made ready on the string, and justice bends the arrow at your heart, and strains the bow, and it is nothing but the mere pleasure of God, and that of an angry God, without any promise or obligation at all, that keeps the arrow one moment from being made drunk with your blood. Thus all you that never passed under a great change of heart, by the mighty power of the spirit of God upon your souls; all you that were never born again, and made new creatures, and raised from being dead in sin, to a state of new, and before altogether unexperienced light and life, are in the hands of an angry God. However you may have reformed your life in many things, and may have had religious affections, and may keep up a form of religion in your families and closets,[3] and in the house of God, it is nothing but His mere pleasure that keeps you from being this moment swallowed up in everlasting destruction. However unconvinced you may now be of the truth of what you hear, by and by you will be fully convinced of it.

Those that are gone from being in the like circumstances with you, see that it was so with them; for destruction came suddenly upon most of them; when they expected nothing of it, and while they were saying, peace and safety: now they see, that those things on which they depended for peace and safety, were nothing but thin air and empty shadows.

The God that holds you over the pit of Hell, much as one holds a spider, or some loathsome insect over the fire, abhors you, and is dreadfully provoked: his wrath towards you burns like fire; he looks upon you as worthy of nothing else, but to be cast

THE PURITAN
Frank E. Schoonover
Collection of the Brandywine River Museum

into the fire; he is of purer eyes than to bear to have you in his sight; you are ten thousand times more abominable in his eyes, than the most hateful venomous serpent is in ours. . . .

O sinner! Consider the fearful danger you are in: it is a great furnace of wrath, a wide and bottomless pit, full of the fire of wrath, that you are held over in the hand of that God, whose wrath is provoked and incensed as much against you, as against many of the damned in Hell. You hang by a slender thread, with the flames of divine wrath flashing about it, and ready every moment to singe it, and burn it asunder; and you have no interest in any mediator, and nothing to lay hold of to save yourself, noth-

---

3. closets *n.*: Small, private rooms for meditation.

ing to keep off the flames of wrath, nothing of your own, nothing that you ever have done, nothing that you can do, to induce God to spare you one moment. . . .

When God beholds the ineffable extremity of your case, and sees your torment to be so vastly disproportioned to your strength, and sees how your poor soul is crushed, and sinks down, as it were, into an infinite gloom; he will have no compassion upon you, he will not forbear the executions of his wrath, or in the least lighten his hand; there shall be no moderation or mercy, nor will God then at all stay his rough wind; he will have no regard to your welfare, nor be at all careful lest you should suffer too much in any other sense, than only that you shall *not suffer beyond what strict justice requires.* . . .

God stands ready to pity you; this is a day of mercy; you may cry now with some encouragement of obtaining mercy. But once the day of mercy is past, your most lamentable and dolorous cries and shrieks will be in vain; you will be wholly lost and thrown away of God, as to any regard to your welfare. God will have no other use to put you to, but to suffer misery; you shall be continued in being to no other end; for you will be a vessel of wrath fitted to destruction; and there will be no other use of this vessel, but to be filled full of wrath. . . .

Thus it will be with you that are in an unconverted state, if you continue in it; the infinite might, and majesty, and terribleness of the omnipotent God shall be magnified upon you, in the ineffable strength of your torments. You shall be tormented in the presence of the holy angels, and in the presence of the Lamb,[4] and when you shall be in this state of suffering, the glorious inhabitants of Heaven shall go forth and look on the awful spectacle, that they may see what the wrath and fierceness of the Almighty is; and when they have seen it, they will fall down and adore that great power and majesty. . . .

---

4. the Lamb: Jesus.

It would be dreadful to suffer this fierceness and wrath of Almighty God one moment; but you must suffer it to all eternity. There will be no end to this exquisite horrible misery. When you look forward, you shall see a long forever, a boundless duration before you, which will swallow up your thoughts and amaze your soul; and you will absolutely despair of ever having any deliverance, any end, any mitigation, any rest at all. . . .

How dreadful is the state of those that are daily and hourly in the danger of this great wrath and infinite misery! But this is the dismal case of every soul in this congregation that has not been born again, however moral and strict, sober and religious, they may otherwise be. Oh that you would consider it, whether you be young or old! . . . Those of you that finally continue in a natural condition, that shall keep you out of Hell longest will be there in a little time! Your damnation does not slumber; it will come swiftly, and, in all probability, very suddenly upon many of you. You have reason to wonder that you are not already in Hell. It is doubtless the case of some whom you have seen and known, that never deserved Hell more than you, and that heretofore appeared as likely to have been now alive as you. Their case is past all hope; they are crying in extreme misery and perfect despair; but here you are in the land of the living and in the house of God, and have an opportunity to obtain salvation. What would not those poor damned hopeless souls give for one day's opportunity such as you now enjoy!

And now you have an extraordinary opportunity, a day wherein Christ has thrown the door of mercy wide open, and stands in calling and crying with a loud voice to poor sinners; a day wherein many are flocking to him, and pressing into the kingdom of God. Many are daily coming from the east, west, north and south; many that were very lately in the same miserable condition that you are in, are now in a happy state, with their hearts filled with love to him who has loved them, and washed them from their sins in his own blood, and rejoicing in hope of the glory of God. How awful is it to be left behind at such a day! To see so many others feasting, while you are pining and perishing! To see so many rejoicing and singing for joy of heart, while you have cause to mourn for sorrow of heart, and howl for vexation of spirit! . . .

Therefore, let everyone that is out of Christ, now awake and fly from the wrath to come. The wrath of Almighty God is now un-doubtedly hanging over a great part of this congregation: let everyone fly out of Sodom.[5] "Haste and escape for your lives, look not behind you, escape to the mountain, lest you be consumed."[6]

---

5. Sodom: In the Bible, a city destroyed by fire because of the sinfulness of its people.
6. "Haste . . . consumed": From Genesis 19:17, the angels' warning to the only virtuous man in Sodom, Lot, to flee the city before they destroy it.

THINKING ABOUT THE SELECTION

Recalling

1. (a) According to the opening paragraph, what keeps sinners from falling into Hell? (b) What power would the sinners have to keep themselves out of Hell if this were withdrawn?
2. For how long will the damned suffer in Hell?
3. Toward the end of the selection, what does Edwards say the sinners can obtain?
4. According to the last paragraph, over what portion of the congregation is God's wrath hanging?

Interpreting

5. Why do you think Edwards begins his sermon with a vivid description of Hell?
6. (a) State two comparisons Edwards uses to describe God's wrath. (b) How do these comparisons add to the speech's impact?
7. (a) At what point is there a change in Edwards's tone and emphasis? (b) How is this change related to the purpose of the sermon?

Applying

8. Do you think the approach Edwards takes in this sermon would be effective in today's society? Explain your answer.

ANALYZING LITERATURE

Understanding Persuasive Speeches

A **persuasive speech** attempts to convince an audience to think or act in a certain way. For example, in this excerpt from *Sinners in the Hands of an Angry God*, Edwards tries to convince members of a church congregation who "are out of Christ" that they must dedicate their lives to God to escape eternal damnation. The effectiveness of Edwards's sermon depended to a large extent on the listeners' perception of him, his consideration of the audience and setting, and his choice of persuasive techniques.

1. Why would this sermon have been less effective if Edwards had not had a reputation as a brilliant spiritual leader?
2. In what ways does Edwards exhibit his understanding of the people he is addressing?
3. What emotion does Edwards appeal to? Considering Edwards's purpose, why is this an appropriate choice?
4. This sermon was delivered during the midst of the Great Awakening, a religious revival during which thousands of people converted to Puritanism. Toward the end of his sermon, how does Edwards draw on the occasion to support his argument?

THINKING AND WRITING

Evaluating Persuasive Techniques

Write an essay in which you explain why Edwards's choice of persuasive techniques was appropriate for his audience, setting, and purpose. Carefully reread Edwards's sermon, keeping in mind his audience, setting, and purpose and taking note of the persuasive techniques he uses. Then take some time to think about the relationship between his choice of persuasive techniques and the other factors. After developing a thesis statement, write your essay, making sure that you include passages from the sermon to support your thesis. When you revise, make sure you have touched on all important factors.

from *Sinners in the Hands of an Angry God*   73

from The Wonders of the Invisible World

Cotton Mather (1663–1728), a descendant of a prominent family of Puritan church leaders, was born in Boston. After receiving two degrees from Harvard College, Mather entered the ministry. He devoted his life to preaching and writing and produced more than four hundred books and pamphlets. His books include *Memorable Providences, Relating to Witchcraft and Possessions* (1689) and *The Wonders of the Invisible World* (1693), a report of the testimony at the Salem witchcraft trials.

Writer's Techniques

Style. Style refers to the manner in which a writer puts his or her thoughts into words. It involves the characteristics of a literary selection that concern form of expression—the choice and arrangement of words, the length and structure of sentences, the relationship between sentences and paragraphs, and the use of literary devices—rather than the ideas conveyed.

Cotton Mather's style is usually characterized by his use of ornate, elegant language and his frequent use of allusions—short references to literary works or figures, places, or events from history, religion, or mythology. In *The Wonders of the Invisible World,* however, Mather used a plain, direct, journalistic style. At the same time, Mather's choice of words in his report of the witchcraft trials clearly indicates his biased point of view. Mather's purpose in writing the report was to justify the outcome of the trials, and he was careful to choose language that served this purpose.

Look For

As you read the excerpt from *The Wonders of the Invisible World,* take note of Mather's plain, journalistic style, and look for words that reveal his biased point of view. How does his choice of words serve his purpose?

Writing

What sort of impressions do you have of the Salem witchcraft trials? Freewrite about the witchcraft trials, describing the causes of the trials and the lessons we can learn from them.

Vocabulary

Knowing the following words will help you as you read the excerpt from *The Wonders of the Invisible World.*

calamities (kə lam′ə tēs) *n.*: Disasters (p. 76)
preternatural (prēt′ ər nach′ ər əl) *adj.*: Differing from or beyond what is normally expected from nature (p. 77)
diabolical (dī′ ə bäl′ ək'l) *adj.*: Of the Devil (p. 78)
rampant (ram′ pənt) *adj.*: Spreading unchecked (p. 78)

from The Wonders of the Invisible World

Cotton Mather

The Trial of Martha Carrier at the Court of Oyer and Terminer,[1] Held by Adjournment at Salem, August 2, 1692

I. Martha Carrier was indicted for the bewitching of certain persons, according to the form usual in such cases, pleading not guilty to her indictment. There were first brought in a considerable number of the bewitched persons who not only made the court sensible[2] of an horrid witchcraft committed upon them, but also deposed that it

---

1. Court of Oyer and Terminer: A court authorized to hear (oyer) and determine (terminer) cases.

2. sensible: Aware.

A WITCH TRIAL IN SALEM, MASSACHUSETTS, in 1692
The Granger Collection

was Martha Carrier, or her shape, that grievously tormented them by biting, pricking, pinching and choking of them. It was further deposed that while this Carrier was on her examination before the magistrates, the poor people were so tortured that everyone expected their death upon the very spot, but that upon the binding of Carrier they were eased. Moreover the look of Carrier then laid the afflicted people for dead; and her touch, if her eye at the same time were off them, raised them again; which things were also now seen upon her trial. And it was testified that upon the mention of some having their necks twisted almost round, by the shape of this Carrier, she replied, "It's no matter though their necks had been twisted quite off."

II. Before the trial of this prisoner several of her own children had frankly and fully confessed not only that they were witches themselves, but that this, their mother, had made them so. This confession they made with great shows of repentance and with much demonstration of truth. They related place, time, occasion; they gave an account of journeys, meetings, and mischiefs by them performed, and were very credible in what they said. Nevertheless, this evidence was not produced against the prisoner at the bar,[3] inasmuch as there was other evidence enough to proceed upon.

III. Benjamin Abbot gave his testimony that last March was a twelvemonth this Carrier was very angry with him upon laying out some land near her husband's. Her expressions in this anger were that she would stick as close to Abbot as the bark stuck to the tree, and that he should repent of it afore seven years came to an end, so as Doctor Prescot should never cure him. These words were heard by others besides Abbot himself, who also heard her say she would hold his nose as close to the grindstone as ever it was held since his name was Abbot. Presently af-

ter this, he was taken with a swelling in his foot, and then with a pain in his side, and exceedingly tormented. It bred into a sore, which was lanced by Doctor Prescot, and several gallons of corruption ran out of it. For six weeks it continued very bad, and then another sore bred in the groin, which was also lanced by Doctor Prescot. Another sore then bred in his groin, which was likewise cut, and put him to very great misery. He was brought unto death's door and so remained until Carrier was taken and carried away by the constable, from which very day he began to mend and so grew better every day and is well ever since.

Sarah Abbot also, his wife, testified that her husband was not only all this while afflicted in his body, but also that strange, extraordinary, and unaccountable calamities befell his cattle, their death being such as they could guess at no natural reason for.

IV. Allin Toothaker testified that Richard, the son of Martha Carrier, having some difference with him, pulled him down by the hair of the head. When he rose again he was going to strike at Richard Carrier but fell down flat on his back to the ground and had not power to stir hand or foot until he told Carrier he yielded, and then he saw the shape of Martha Carrier go off his breast.

This Toothaker had received a wound in the wars, and he now testified that Martha Carrier told him he should never be cured. Just afore the apprehending of Carrier, he could thrust a knitting needle into his wound four inches deep; but presently after her being seized, he was thoroughly healed.

He further testified that when Carrier and he sometimes were at variance she would clap her hands at him and say he should get nothing by it; whereupon he several times lost his cattle by strange deaths, whereof no natural causes could be given.

V. John Rogger also testified that upon the threatening words of this malicious Carrier his cattle would be strangely bewitched, as was more particularly then described.

---

3. bar: Court.

A WITCH TRIAL IN SALEM, MASSACHUSETTS, in 1692
Tha Granger Collection

VI. Samuel Preston testified that about two years ago, having some difference with Martha Carrier, he lost a cow in a strange, preternatural, unusual manner; and about a month after this, the said Carrier, having again some difference with him, she told him he had lately lost a cow, and it should not be long before he lost another; which accordingly came to pass; for he had a thriving and well-kept cow which without any known cause quickly fell down and died.

VII. Phebe Chandler testified that about a fortnight before the apprehension of Martha Carrier, on a Lord's day while the psalm was singing in the Church, this Carrier then took her by the shoulder and, shaking her, asked her where she lived. She made her no answer, although as Carrier, who lived next door to her father's house, could not in reason but know who she was. Quickly after this, as she was at several times crossing the fields, she heard a voice that she took to be Martha Carrier's, and it seemed as if it was over her head. The voice told her she should within two or three days be poisoned. Accordingly, within such a little time, one half of her right hand became greatly swollen and very painful, as also part of her face, whereof she can give no account how it came. It continued very bad for some days, and several times since she has had a great pain in her breast and been so seized on her legs that she has hardly been able to go. She added that lately, going well to the house of God, Richard, the son of Martha Carrier, looked very earnestly upon her; and immediately her hand, which had formerly been poisoned, as is abovesaid, began to pain her greatly, and she had a strange burning at her stomach; but was then struck deaf so that she could not hear any of the prayer or singing till the two or three last words of the psalm.

VIII. One Foster, who confessed her own share in the witchcraft for which the prisoner stood indicted, affirmed that she had seen the prisoner at some of their witch meetings, and that it was this Carrier who persuaded her to be a witch. She confessed that the devil carried them on a pole to a witch meeting; but the pole broke, and she hanging about Carrier's neck, they both fell down, and she then received an hurt by the fall, whereof she was not at this very time recovered.

IX. One Lacy, who likewise confessed her share in this witchcraft, now testified that she and the prisoner were once bodily present at a witch meeting in Salem village, and that she knew the prisoner to be a witch and to have been at a diabolical sacrament, and that the prisoner was the undoing of her and her children by enticing them into the snare of the devil.

X. Another Lacy, who also confessed her share in this witchcraft, now testified that the prisoner was at the witch meeting in Salem village, where they had bread and wine administered unto them.

XI. In the time of this prisoner's trial, one Susanna Sheldon in open court had her hands unaccountably tied together with a wheel band[4] so fast that without cutting it it could not be loosed. It was done by a specter, and the sufferer affirmed it was the prisoner's.

Memorandum. This rampant hag, Martha Carrier, was the person of whom the confessions of the witches and of her own children among the rest agreed that the devil had promised her she should be queen of Hell.

---

4. wheel band: A band or strap that goes around a wooden wheel.

THINKING ABOUT THE SELECTION

Recalling

1. For what was Martha Carrier indicted?
2. Who was brought in to testify against her?
3. To what had Carrier's children confessed prior to the trial?
4. According to Benjamin Abbot's testimony, what happened to Abbot after Martha Carrier became angry with him?
5. (a) According to Phoebe Chandler's testimony, what did Martha Carrier do to Chandler "on a Lord's day"? (b) What happened "quickly after" this incident?
6. What information does Mather present in his "memorandum" at the end of the excerpt?

Interpreting

7. What detail in Abbot's description of his physical ailments is clearly exaggerated?
8. What does Chandler's testimony that she heard a voice above her head "that she took to be Martha Carrier's" imply about Carrier?

Applying

9. Do you think witnesses might have been likely to fabricate their testimony during the Salem witchcraft trials? Explain your answer.

ANALYZING LITERATURE

Recognizing a Writer's Style

Style refers to the way in which a writer expresses his or her thoughts. For example, in *The Wonders of the Invisible World,* Cotton Mather writes in a plain, direct, journalistic style.

1. How does Mather's style make his report of the trial seem like an objective, factual account?
2. Why would the report be less effective if it had been written in the elaborate, elegant style Mather used in his other works?

CRITICAL THINKING AND READING

Recognizing Author's Bias

Bias means "partiality" or an inclination toward a certain position. Although Mather's report is supposedly an objective account of the trial, his choice of words makes it clear that in reality his report is written from a biased point of view. For example, his reference to Martha Carrier as a "rampant hag" clearly indicates his negative attitude toward her.

1. How does Mather's statement that "a number of bewitched persons" were brought in to testify against Carrier reveal his bias?
2. Find two other examples of language that clearly indicates Mather's bias.
3. Do you think it possible for a person to be completely free of bias? Explain your answer.

THINKING AND WRITING

Writing a Journal Entry

Write a journal entry in which you describe the trial of Martha Carrier from Carrier's point of view. Reread the selection, thinking about how Martha Carrier might have viewed the proceedings. Then write your journal entry, using a plain, journalistic style similar to Mather's. When you revise, make sure your entry is simple and clear.

YOU THE WRITER

Assignment

1. Imagine that you are an early settler living in either Plymouth or Jamestown. Write a series of five journal entries describing some of the hardships you and the other settlers face and discussing your impressions of the new land.

Prewriting. Review the unit introduction (p. 2) and the selections by William Bradford (p. 50) and John Smith (p. 42), noting the hardships the early settlers encountered.

Writing. When you write your journal entries, use simple, direct language, and use sensory details in describing the landscape.

Revising. When you revise, make sure your descriptions are clear and coherent. After you have finished revising, proofread your entries and prepare a final copy.

Assignment

2. Because the early settlers and the Native Americans came from dramatically different cultures, it was difficult for them to understand one another when the settlers first arrived. Write a dialogue between a Native American and a settler occurring shortly after the settlers' arrival in the new land. (For the purpose of this assignment, imagine that both speak English.)

Prewriting. Review the selections by William Bradford (p. 50) and John Smith (p. 42), noting what they reveal about the relationship between the settlers and the Native Americans. Brainstorm about the types of things the early settlers and the Native Americans might have discussed with one another. Then select two characters to have this dialogue.

Writing. Write the first draft of your dialogue. Try to make your dialogue seem realistic, as if you were recording a conversation that actually occurred.

Revising. When you revise, make sure your dialogue reveals some of the differences between the two cultures.

Assignment

3. Origin myths were an important part of the Native-American oral tradition. Write a myth describing the origin of the world and the human race. Your myth should be modeled after one of the myths you have read and should include superhuman or supernatural beings.

Prewriting. Reread the origin myths in this unit. Try to put yourself in the place of the Native Americans, and think of other ways in which they might have explained the origin of the world. Then develop the plot of your origin myth, organizing the events in chronological order.

Writing. Write your myth in either prose or verse, and model your writing style after the style used in the myths you have read.

Revising. When you revise, make sure the events in your myth are described clearly. After you have finished revising, proofread your myth and prepare a final copy.

Assignment

1. Reading the literature of the new land helps provide us with an awareness of the differences between life in the early settlements in the North and those in the South. Write an essay in which you compare and contrast life in the northern and southern settlements, using evidence from the selections you have read to support your argument.

Prewriting. Review the selections in this unit, noting what they reveal about the similarities and differences between life in the northern and southern settlements.

Writing. When you write your essay, organize your argument according to corresponding points of contrast.

Revising. When you revise, make sure you have used transitions and other linking devices to connect your ideas.

Assignment

2. The literature of the new land is important because of what it reveals about the lives of the settlers. Write an essay in which you discuss the historical significance of early American literature.

Prewriting. Review the selections in this unit, noting what they reveal about life in the early American settlements. Prepare a thesis statement, then organize your information into an outline.

Writing. When you write your essay, use evidence from at least two selections to support your thesis.

Revising. When you revise, make sure your argument is clear and coherent and is organized in a logical manner. After you have finished revising, proofread your essay and prepare a final copy.

Assignment

3. Literature often reveals a great deal about the attitudes and beliefs of different cultures. Write an essay in which you discuss what the literature of the Puritans reveals about their attitudes and values.

Prewriting. Review the selections by Puritan writers that you have read, noting what they reveal about Puritan beliefs. Prepare a thesis statement and organize your notes into an outline.

Writing. When you write your essay, use evidence from at least four selections to support your thesis.

Revising. When you revise, make sure you have thoroughly supported your thesis and have not included any unnecessary information. After you have finished revising, proofread your essay and prepare a final copy.

THE SIGNING OF THE CONSTITUTION, 1787
Howard Chandler Christy
The Granger Collection

THE COLONIAL PERIOD
1750–1800

Yesterday the greatest question was decided which ever was debated in America; and a greater perhaps never was, nor will be, decided among men. A resolution was passed without one dissenting colony, that these united colonies are, and of right ought to be, free and independent states.

John Adams

John Adams, who was to become the second President of the United States, wrote these sentences in a letter to his wife Abigail on the eve of the adoption of the Declaration of Independence. The momentous event of July 4, 1776, capped more than a decade of controversy between England and the American colonies. More than a decade of struggle to establish the new nation followed. During those years—indeed, during the entire second half of the eighteenth century—American literature was largely political. So dominant was the question of our relationship to England, and so talented and literate were the statesmen of the emerging nation, that some of the most notable writers of the period were the founders of the republic.

THE HISTORICAL SETTING

It is easy to forget how long the thirteen original states had been colonies. By 1750, there were fourth- and fifth-generation Americans of European descent living in Virginia and New England. These people were English subjects, and, on the whole, they were well satisfied with that status. Royal governors irritated them from time to time, but the colonial assemblies were locally elected and exercised considerable power, particularly over money. Year by year, decade by decade, Americans acquired experience in the art of self-government. As late as the early 1760's, however, few Americans had given much thought to the prospect of independence.

Between the mid-1760's and the mid-1770's, however, attitudes changed dramatically. King George III and Parliament imposed a number of unwise regulations that threatened the liberties of the colonists. With each succeeding measure, the outrage in America grew, finally erupting into war. As one Revolutionary veteran put it, "We always had governed ourselves, and we always meant to."

The Age of Reason

Great upheavals in history occur when circumstances are ripe. The American Revolution was such an upheaval, and the groundwork for it had been laid by European writers and thinkers as well as by the English king and Parliament. The eighteenth century is often characterized as the Age of Reason, or the Enlightenment. Spurred by the work of seventeenth-century scientists such as Galileo and Sir Isaac Newton, the writers and thinkers of the Enlightenment valued reason over faith. Unlike the Puritans, they had little interest in the hereafter, believing instead in the power of reason and science to further human progress. They spoke of a social contract that forms the basis of government. Above all, they believed that people are by nature good, not evil. A perfect society seemed to them to be more than just an idle dream.

Among the most influential figures of the Enlightenment were the French writer Voltaire, the French philosopher Jean Jacques Rousseau, the English political theorist John Locke, and the Scottish historian David Hume. Educated readers in the American colonies were familiar with the writings of these men.

The American statesmen of the Revolutionary period were themselves figures of the Enlightenment. No history of the period would be complete without mention of the thought and writings of Benjamin Franklin, Thomas Paine, and Thomas Jefferson. These Americans not only expressed the ideas of the Age of Reason, but they also helped to put them spectacularly into practice.

Toward a Clash of Arms

The American Revolution was preceded by the French and Indian War, a struggle between England and France for control of North America. The conflict broke out in the colonies in 1754 and continued for nearly a decade. British forces won the decisive battle of the war at the city of Quebec, Canada, in 1759. When the French and Indian War officially ended in 1763, France gave up its claims to North American territory. There was general jubilation in the thirteen English colonies.

The good feelings were short-lived, however. The British government, wanting to raise revenue in the colonies to pay its war debt, passed the Stamp Act in 1765. This was the first tax other than customs duties ever imposed on the colonists by Great Britain. The act required buying and affixing stamps to each of fifty-four kinds of items, including newspapers, playing cards, legal documents, licenses, and almanacs. Colonial reaction to the Stamp Act was swift and bitter. Stamps were burned. Stamp distributors were

EMBOSSED TAX STAMP ISSUED BY THE BRITISH GOVERNMENT IN 1765 FOR USE IN THE AMERICAN COLONIES
The Granger Collection

AMERICAN EVENTS

Benjamin Franklin Conducts His Experiment

1752   **Benjamin Franklin** conducts his kite and key experiment with lightning.

1754   French and Indian War begins for control of North American continent.

1758   *Poor Richard's Almanack* sold to new owner after 25 years under **Benjamin Franklin.**

1763   France, after French and Indian War, gives up claims to North American territory.

1765   Stamp Act passed by British Parliament; colonists protest bitterly.

1767   Townshend Acts impose new taxes, angering colonists further.

        Thomas Godfrey's *The Prince of Parthia* produced as first American play.

1770   British troops fire on an unruly mob in Boston, resulting in Boston Massacre.

        William Billings offers new American hymns in *The New England Psalm–Singer.*

1771   **Benjamin Franklin** begins writing his famous, uncompleted *Autobiography.*

1773   Parliament's Tea Act prompts Boston Tea Party, which led to Intolerable Acts.

        Phillis Wheatley's *Poems on Various Subjects* published in England.

1774   First Continental Congress meets in Philadelphia in response to the Intolerable Acts.

1775   **Patrick Henry** gives his "liberty or death" speech at the Virginia Convention.

        Skirmishes at Lexington and Concord open the American Revolution.

1776   **Thomas Paine's** *Common Sense* helps spur the movement for independence.

        Second Continental Congress adopts Declaration of Independence.

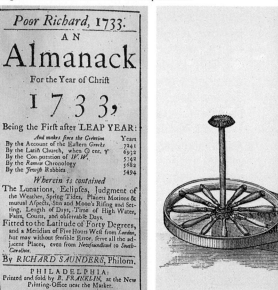

Poor Richard, 1733:
AN
Almanack
For the Year of Christ
1733,
Being the First after LEAP YEAR:

	Years
By the Account of the Eastern *Greeks*	7241
By the Latin Church, when ☉ ent. ♈	6932
By the Con. putation of *W.W.*	5742
By the *Roman* Chronology	5682
By the *Jewish* Rabbies	5494

Wherein is contained

The Lunations, Eclipses, Judgment of the Weather, Spring Tides, Planets Motions & mutual Aspects, Sun and Moon's Rising and Setting, Length of Days, Time of High Water, Fairs, Courts, and observable Days.
Fitted to the Latitude of Forty Degrees, and a Meridian of Five Hours West from *London,* but may without sensible Error, serve all the adjacent Places, even from *Newfoundland* to *South-Carolina.*

By *RICHARD SAUNDERS,* Philom.

PHILADELPHIA:
Printed and sold by B. FRANKLIN, at the New Printing-Office near the Market.

Poor Richard's Almanack

Richard Arkwright's

Phillis Wheatley

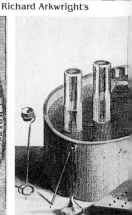

Apparatus Used in

Voltaire

NING-FRAME.

Spinning Frame

Colonists Protest Stamp Act

Priestley's Experiments

William Hershel

WORLD EVENTS

1751   England: Thomas Gray completes "Elegy Written in a Country Churchyard."

1755   England: Samuel Johnson publishes *Dictionary of the English Language.*

1757   England: Robert Clive defeats native army at Plassey, India.

1759   France: Voltaire publishes *Candide*, satirizing optimism of Rousseau.

1762   France: Jean Jacques Rousseau states his political philosophy in *The Social Contract.*

1763   Seven Years War ends (including French and Indian War in America).

1765   Scotland: James Watt invents an improved steam engine.

1769   England: Richard Arkwright invents a frame for spinning; helped bring about factory system.

1770   Germany: Goethe begins 50 years of work on the dramatic poem *Faust.*

       Germany: Ludwig von Beethoven is born.

1771   England: Tobias Smollett publishes his novel *Humphrey Clinker.*

1772   Poland: First of three major partitions of Poland gives land to Russia, Prussia, and Austria.

1774   England: Joseph Priestley discovers oxygen, named later by Lavoisier.

1778   England: Captain James Cook becomes first European to see Hawaii.

1779   South Africa: First of many Kaffir Wars between blacks and whites breaks out.

1781   Germany: Immanuel Kant publishes his *Critique of Pure Reason.*

       England: William Herschel discovers planet Uranus.

Introduction   87

AMERICAN EVENTS

1777 American forces defeat British at Battle of Saratoga, a turning point.

1778 France recognizes U.S. independence and signs treaty of alliance.

1781 General Cornwallis surrenders British army to George Washington at Yorktown.

1782 **Michel–Guillaume Jean de Crèvecoeur's** *Letters from an American Farmer* published in London.

1783 Noah Webster's *Spelling Book* first appears; 60 million copies would be sold.

Peace of Paris ends Revolutionary War and recognizes U.S. independence.

1784 *Pennsylvania Packet and General Advertiser* becomes first long-term daily paper.

1787 Constitutional Convention meets in Philadelphia to draft Constitution.

Royall Tyler's *The Contrast*, a satiric comedy, is produced in New York City.

1788 *The Federalist*, mainly the work of Alexander Hamilton, appears as a book.

1789 William Hill Brown's *The Power of Sympathy*, first American novel, published anonymously.

George Washington elected unanimously as first President of United States.

1793 Eli Whitney invents cotton gin.

1795 University of North Carolina opens as America's first state university.

1800 **Thomas Jefferson,** principal author of Declaration of Independence, elected President.

The Constitutional Convention

Eli Whitney's Cotton Gin

Independence Hall, Philadelphia

The Storming of

The British Surrender at Yorktown

The *Death of Socrates*

James Boswell

the Bastille

Napoleon Bonaparte

WORLD EVENTS

1785 France: Jean–Pierre Blanchard makes first balloon crossing of English Channel.

1786 Scotland: Robert Burns is widely acclaimed for his first book of poems.

Austria: Wolfgang Amadeus Mozart creates the comic opera *The Marriage of Figaro*.

1787 France: Jacques–Louis David paints *Death of Socrates*.

1789 France: Storming of Bastille in Paris sets off French Revolution.

1791 England: James Boswell publishes *The Life of Samuel Johnson*.

1793 France: King Louis XVI and Marie Antoinette go to death on guillotine.

1794 England: William Blake publishes *Songs of Experience*, including "Tyger! Tyger!"

1796 England: Edward Jenner develops vaccine against smallpox.

1798 England: Samuel Taylor Coleridge completes "The Rime of the Ancient Mariner."

England: William Wordsworth publishes *Lyrical Ballads*.

1799 Egypt: Rosetta Stone, key to translating hieroglyphics, found.

Spain: Goya creates powerfully satiric *Capichos* etchings.

France: Napoleon Bonaparte becomes First Consul in a coup d'état.

1800 Germany: Ludwig von Beethoven composes *First Symphony*.

beaten and their shops destroyed. No blood was shed, but the hated stamps were withdrawn within six months, and the Stamp Act was repealed.

Other acts and reactions followed. The Townshend Acts of 1767 taxed paper, paint, glass, lead, and tea. When the colonists organized a boycott, the British dissolved the Massachusetts legislature and sent two regiments of British troops to Boston. In 1770, these Redcoats fired into a taunting mob, causing five fatalities. This so-called Boston Massacre further inflamed passions. Parliament repealed the Townshend duties except for the tax on tea, but a separate Tea Act soon greeted the colonists. The Tea Act gave an English company a virtual monopoly of the American tea trade. Furious, a group of Bostonians dressed as Mohawks dumped a shipment of tea into Boston harbor. As punishment for this Boston Tea Party, the English Parliament passed the Coercive Acts. Colonists immediately dubbed them the Intolerable Acts.

The situation had in fact become intolerable to both the colonists and the British. Colonial leaders, although not speaking

**THE BOSTON MASSACRE,
5 MARCH 1770**
*Colored Engraving, 1770, by
Paul Revere After the Drawing
by Henry Pelham*
The Granger Collection

openly of independence, met in Philadelphia for the First Continental Congress. The British, their authority slipping away, appointed General Thomas Gage governor of Massachusetts. The stage was set for war.

"The World Turned Upside Down"

On the night of April 18, 1775, General Gage sent a detail of about 700 British troops from Boston to destroy colonial munitions at Concord. The next morning, these troops met a drawn-up line of some seventy colonial Minutemen on the Lexington green. A musket shot was fired (from which side, no one knows), and the firing became widespread. Before it was over, eight Americans lay dead.

The British continued marching west to Concord, where another skirmish took place. Two more Americans fell, but so did three Redcoats. The British commander ordered a retreat to Boston. American snipers fired on the British troops all the way back, causing a total of 273 casualties.

The encounters at Lexington and Concord, a landmark in American history, have been referred to as "the shot heard round the world." The American revolution had begun, and there would be

THE BATTLE OF LEXINGTON AT THE BEGINNING OF THE COMBAT
*Line Engraving, 1832,
by Amos Doolittle
and John W. Barber*
The Granger Collection

**THE BATTLE OF CONCORD, THE ENGAGEMENT AT THE NORTH
BRIDGE, APRIL 19, 1775**
Line Engraving, 1775, by Amos Doolittle
The Granger Collection

no turning back. In June, the Americans killed or wounded more than a thousand British soldiers at the Battle of Bunker Hill. Although all the fighting up to this point had taken place in Massachusetts, the revolt involved all the colonies. Two days before Bunker Hill, the Second Continental Congress, meeting in Philadelphia, had named a commander in chief of the official American army. He was George Washington of Virginia.

More than a year would pass before the colonies declared their independence. More than six years would pass before the war ended, although the Battle of Saratoga, in the fall of 1777, marked a turning point. At Saratoga, in upstate New York, the British were surrounded and forced to surrender 5,700 men. When news of this American victory reached Paris, the government of France formally recognized the independence of the United States. Soon afterward, France began to commit troops to aid the American cause.

The war finally came to an end at Yorktown, Virginia, on October 19, 1781. Aided by the French army and the French navy, General Washington bottled up the 8,000-man British force under General Cornwallis. Seeing that escape was impossible, Cornwallis surrendered. After the British regiments had stacked their arms, they marched back to camp between rows of American and French soldiers. The British bands played a number of tunes during this ceremony. One of them was an old English song that seemed appropriate to the American troops: "The World Turned Upside Down."

The New Nation

One of the most impressive aspects of the American Revolution is that its original aims were realized. The revolt did not end in a bloodbath, or a military dictatorship, or a regime worse than the one overthrown. Thomas Jefferson recognized the danger of this in 1776 when he warned that "should a bad government be instituted for us in the future, it had been as well to have accepted . . . the bad one offered to us from beyond the water. . . ."

The path to self-government was not always smooth. After the Revolution, the Articles of Confederation established a "league of friendship" among the new states. This arrangement did not work well, however. The federal Constitution that replaced the Articles required many compromises and was ratified only after a long fight. Even then, a Bill of Rights had to be added to placate those who feared the centralized power that the Constitution conferred.

The old revolutionaries, by and large, remained true to their principles and continued their public duties. George Washington became the nation's first President. John Adams, a signer of the Declaration of Independence, succeeded him in that office. Then in 1800, Americans elected as their President the brilliant statesman who had drafted the Declaration, one of the heroes of the Enlightenment, Thomas Jefferson.

GEORGE WASHINGTON ADDRESSING THE SECOND CONTINENTAL CONGRESS AT PHILADELPHIA
Contemporary Colored Line Engraving
The Granger Collection

LITERATURE IN A TIME OF CRISIS

Like the Puritans in New England, educated Americans in the Age of Reason did a great deal of writing. Unlike the private soul-searching of the Puritans, however, much of what was produced during the Revolutionary period was public writing. By the time of the War for Independence, nearly fifty newspapers had been established in the coastal cities. At the time of Washington's inauguration, there were nearly forty magazines. Almanacs were popular from Massachusetts to Georgia.

During this period, the mind of the nation was on politics. Journalists and printers provided a forum for the expression of ideas. After 1763, those ideas were increasingly focused on relations with Great Britain and, more broadly, on the nature of government. The writing of permanent importance from the Revolutionary era is mostly political writing.

PATRICK HENRY SPEAKING AGAINST
THE STAMP ACT IN THE VIRGINIA
HOUSE OF BURGESSES IN 1765
*Colored Line Engraving, 19th
Century*
The Granger Collection

Politics as Literature

The public writing and speaking of American statesmen in two tumultuous decades, the 1770's and 1780's, helped to reshape not only the nation but also the world. James Otis of Massachusetts defended colonial rights vigorously in speeches and pamphlets. Otis, an eloquent speaker, is credited with giving Americans their rallying cry: "Taxation without representation is tyranny."

Another spellbinder was Patrick Henry, whose speech against the Stamp Act in the Virginia House of Burgesses brought cries of "Treason!" Ten years later, his electrifying speech to the Virginia Convention expressed the rising sentiment for independence.

One man was more influential than any other in swaying public opinion in favor of independence. He was Thomas Paine, and his pamphlet *Common Sense,* published in January 1776, created an immediate sensation. It swept the colonies, selling 100,000 copies in three months. George Washington praised its "sound doctrine and unanswerable reasoning," as did countless other readers. "Independence rolls in on us like a torrent," said John Adams, who set forth his own ideas in *Thoughts on Government,* published in 1776.

The Declaration of Independence was first drafted by Thomas Jefferson in June 1776. The finished document is largely his work, although a committee of five, including Benjamin Franklin, was involved in its creation. The Declaration, despite some exaggerated charges against King George III, is well reasoned and superbly written. It is one of the most influential political statements ever made.

Another document written by committee that has stood the test of time is the Constitution of the United States, drafted in 1787. The framers, whose new nation contained about four million people, hoped that the Constitution would last a generation. It still survives, amended many times, as the political foundation of a superpower of fifty states and nearly 230 million people. Not everyone in 1787 was pleased with the Constitution. Alexander Hamilton called it a "weak and worthless fabric," and Benjamin Franklin supported it only because "I expect no better."

The doubts of the framers were reflected in the controversy over ratification. Delaware ratified the Constitution within three months, thus becoming the first state in the Union. But the ratification of nine states was necessary before the document could go into effect. The last few states proved difficult. The contest between supporters and opponents was especially hard-fought in New York. Alexander Hamilton, whose opinion of the Constitution was none too high, nevertheless wanted to see it pass in his home state. With James Madison and John Jay, he wrote a series of essays that were first published as letters to three New York newspapers. These essays, collected as *The Federalist,* served their immediate purpose. New York ratified the Constitution by a vote of 30 to 27. Over time, they have also come to be recognized as authoritative statements on the principles of American government.

The Cultural Scene

While politics dominated the literature of the Revolutionary period, not every writer of note was a statesman. Verse appeared in most of the newspapers, and numerous broadside ballads were published. (A broadside is a single sheet of paper, printed on one or both sides, dealing with a current topic.) One of the most popular broadside ballads was called "The Dying Redcoat," supposedly written by a British sergeant mortally wounded in the Revolution. The sergeant in the ballad realizes too late that his sympathy lies with the American cause:

> Fight on, America's noble sons,
> Fear not Britannia's thundering guns:
> Maintain your cause from year to year,
> God's on your side, you need not fear.

One poet of the time whose works were more sophisticated than the broadside ballads was Philip Freneau, a 1771 graduate of Princeton. A journalist and newspaper editor by profession, Freneau wrote poetry throughout his life. A few of his poems, such as "The Wild Honeysuckle" and "The Indian Burying Ground," earned his reputation as America's earliest important lyric poet.

Two other poets of the day were Joel Barlow and Phillis Wheatley. Barlow, a 1778 Yale graduate, is best remembered for "The Hasty Pudding," a mock-heroic tribute to cornmeal mush. Phillis Wheatley, born in Africa and brought to Boston in early childhood as a slave, showed signs of literary genius. A collection of her poems was published in England while she was still a young woman.

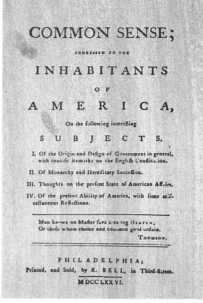

COVER OF TOM PAINE'S *COMMON SENSE,* 1776
The Granger Collection

TITLE PAGE OF VOLUME I OF THE *FEDERALIST,* NEW YORK, 1788
The Granger Collection

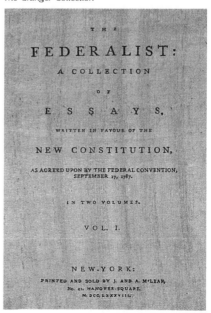

One writer of the Revolutionary period recorded his impressions of everyday American life. He was Michel-Guillaume Jean de Crèvecoeur. Born of an aristocratic French family, Crèvecoeur became a soldier of fortune, a world traveler, and a farmer. For fifteen years he owned a plantation in Orange County, New York, and his impressions of life there were published in London in 1782 as *Letters from an American Farmer*.

Perhaps the best-known writing of the period outside the field of politics was done by Benjamin Franklin. His *Poor Richard's Almanack* became familiar to most households in the colonies. A statesman, printer, author, inventor, and scientist, Franklin was a true son of the Enlightenment. His *Autobiography,* covering only his early years, is regarded as one of the finest autobiographies in any language.

During this period, America began to establish a cultural identity of its own. Theaters were built from New York to Charleston. A number of new colleges were established after the war, especially in the South. Several outstanding painters were at work in the colonies and the young republic. Among them were John Singleton Copley, Gilbert Stuart, John Trumbull, and Charles Willson Peale. Patience Wright, famous in the colonies as a sculptor of wax portraits, moved to London before the war. While there, she acted as a Revolutionary spy. In music, William Billings produced *The New England Psalm-Singer* and a number of patriotic hymns. This was a turbulent time, a time of action, and its legacy was cultural as well as political.

American Literature at Daybreak

By the early 1800's, America could boast a small body of national literature. The Native Americans had contributed haunting poetry and legends through their oral traditions. The Puritans had written a number of powerful, inward-looking works. The statesmen of the Revolutionary period had produced political documents for the ages. A few poets and essayists had made a permanent mark on the literature of the young republic. There were, however, no American novels or plays of importance. The modern short story had yet to be invented.

The raw materials for a great national literature were at hand, waiting to be used. The nation stood on the threshold of a territorial and population explosion unique in the history of the world. It would take almost exactly a century to close the frontier on the vast and varied continent beyond the Appalachians. During that century, American literature would burst forth with a vitality that might have surprised even the farsighted founders of the nation. The colonial age ended with a narrow volume of memorable literature. The nineteenth century would close with a library of works that form a major part of America's literary heritage.

AMERICAN VOICES
Quotations by Prominent Figures of the Period

Experience keeps a dear school, but fools will learn in no other.
Benjamin Franklin, *Poor Richard's Almanack*

We must all hang together, or assuredly we shall all hang separately.
Benjamin Franklin, At signing of Declaration of Independence

Caesar had his Brutus; Charles the First his Cromwell; and George the Third ["Treason!" cried the Speaker] *may profit by their example.* If *this* be treason, make the most of it.
Patrick Henry, Speech on the Stamp Act, Virginia House of Burgesses

He that would make his own liberty secure must guard even his enemy from oppression.
Thomas Paine, *Dissertation on First Principles of Government*

For bright Aurora now demands my song.
  Aurora, hail, and all the thousand dyes,
Which deck thy progress through the vaulted skies.
Phillis Wheatley, "An Hymn to the Morning"

The tree of liberty must be refreshed from time to time with the blood of patriots and tyrants.
Thomas Jefferson, Letter to William Stevens Smith

It is not in the still calm of life, or the repose of a pacific station, that great characters are formed. . . . All history will convince you of this. . . . Great necessities call out great virtues.
Abigail Adams, Letter to her son, John Quincy Adams

What then is the American, this new man?
Michel-Guillaume Jean de Crèvecoeur, *Letters from an American Farmer*

Thus briefly sketched the sacred RIGHTS OF MAN,
How inconsistent with the ROYAL PLAN!
Philip Freneau, "On Mr. Paine's *Rights of Man*"

READING CRITICALLY

The Literature of 1750–1800

During the years from 1750–1800, almost all writing in America was influenced by the revolutionary spirit or the spirit of the new nation. Recognizing this spirit and the ideas of this period will enable you to understand better the purpose and techniques of the writers of the period.

Historical Context

It was during these years that the American colonists reached the point where they were no longer able to tolerate the British rule. The colonies united and took a stand against Britain. The Revolution was successful, and a proud and practical new nation emerged.

Literary Movements

This was the Age of Reason. The ideas of reason and discipline prevailed in the writing of the time. Because the attention of the nation was on the political events surrounding the Revolution, the literature was mostly political also. There was some personal writing—poetry and letters, for example—but most writing was public—pamphlets, speeches, and other documents—advocating and supporting a break with England.

Writers' Techniques

Logical reasoning is the major technique used by the writers of this period. Public writing offered sound clear arguments in support of the causes. Personal writing too showed the reasoning process.

On the following pages is a selection by Benjamin Franklin. Franklin wrote both political and personal documents. Always interested in self-improvement, he was a thoughtful, forthright, practical representative of the period.

Dialogue Between Franklin and the Gout

Benjamin Franklin

This dialogue was written during the six-week period in 1780 when Franklin, suffering from gout, was confined to his house.

Midnight, October 22, 1780.

FRANKLIN. Eh! Oh! Eh! What have I done to merit these cruel sufferings?

GOUT. Many things; you have ate and drank too freely, and too much indulged those legs of yours in their indolence.

FRANKLIN. Who is it that accuses me?

GOUT. It is I, even I, the Gout.

FRANKLIN. What! my enemy in person?

GOUT. No, not your enemy.

FRANKLIN. I repeat it: my enemy, for you would not only torment my body to death but ruin my good name, you reproach me as a glutton and a tippler. Now all the world that knows me will allow that I am neither the one nor the other.

GOUT. The world may think as it pleases. It is always very complaisant to itself and sometimes to its friends, but I very well know that the quantity of meat and drink proper for a man who takes a reasonable degree of exercise would be too much for another who never takes any.

FRANKLIN. I take—Eh! Oh!—as much exercise—Eh!—as I can, Madam Gout. You know my sedentary state, and on that account, it would seem, Madam Gout, as if you might spare me a little, seeing it is not altogether my own fault.

GOUT. Not a jot, your rhetoric and your politeness are thrown away, your apology avails nothing. If your situation in life is a sedentary one, your amusements, your recreations, at least, should be active. You ought to walk or ride, or, if the weather prevents that, play at billiards. But let us examine

Literary Movement: Reason prevails during this period. Franklin applies reasoning to determine the cause of his pain.

Writer's Technique: Franklin presents his arguments in the form of a rational but humorous discourse.

Literary Movement: Franklin advocates "reasonable" and responsible behavior on the part of the individual.

Writer's Technique: Franklin has the Gout present reasonable arguments for her case.

BENJAMIN FRANKLIN IN 1777
Augustus de Sainte Aubin
Philadelphia Museum of Art

Historical Context: Note the reference to the great number of documents (newspapers, and so on) available.

Writer's Technique: Franklin presents a clear appeal to a man of sense.

your course of life. While the mornings are long, and you have leisure to go abroad, what do you do? Why, instead of gaining an appetite for breakfast by salutary exercise you amuse yourself with books, pamphlets, or newspapers, which commonly are not worth the reading. Yet you eat an inordinate breakfast: four dishes of tea with cream and one or two buttered toasts with slices of hung beef, which I fancy are not things the most easily digested. Immediately afterward you sit down to write at your desk or converse with persons who apply to you on business. Thus the time passes till one without any kind of bodily exercise. But all this I could pardon in regard, as you say, to your sedentary condition. But what is your practice after dinner? Walking in the beautiful gardens of those friends with whom you have dined would be the choice of men of sense; yours is to be fixed down to chess where you are found engaged for two or three hours! This is your perpetual recreation, which is the least eligible of any for a sedentary man, because, instead of accelerating the motion of the fluids, the rigid attention it requires helps to retard the circulation and obstruct internal secretions. Wrapped in the speculations of this wretched game you destroy your constitution. What can be expected from such a course of living but a body replete with stagnant humors[1] ready to fall a prey to all kinds of dangerous maladies, if I, the Gout, did not occasionally bring you relief by agitating those humors and so purifying or dissipating them? If it was in some nook or alley in Paris, deprived of walks, that you played awhile at chess after dinner, this might

---

1. humors: At the time it was believed that the body contained four fluids (humors) which were responsible for a person's health and disposition.

be excusable; but the same taste prevails with you in Passy, Auteuil, Montmartre, or Sanoy, places where there are the finest gardens and walks, a pure air, beautiful women, and most agreeable and instructive conversation, all which you might enjoy by frequenting the walks. But these are rejected for this abominable game of chess. Fie then, Mr. Franklin! But amidst my instructions I had almost forgot to administer my wholesome corrections, so take that twinge, and that.

FRANKLIN. Oh! Eh! Oh! Ohhh! As much instruction as you please, Madam Gout, and as many reproaches; but pray, Madam, a truce with your corrections!

GOUT. No, Sir, no, I will not abate a particle of what is so much for your good—therefore—

FRANKLIN. Oh! Ehhh! It is not fair to say I take no exercise when I do very often, going out to dine and returning in my carriage.

GOUT. That, of all imaginable exercises, is the most slight and insignificant, if you allude to the motion of a carriage suspended on springs. By observing the degree of heat obtained by different kinds of motion we may form an estimate of the quantity of exercise given by each. Thus, for example, if you turn out to walk in winter with cold feet, in an hour's time you will be in a glow all over; ride on horseback, the same effect will scarcely be perceived by four hours' round trotting; but if you loll in a carriage, such as you have mentioned, you may travel all day and gladly enter the last inn to warm your feet by a fire. Flatter yourself then no longer that half an hour's airing in your carriage deserves the name of exercise. Providence has appointed few to roll in carriages, while he has given to all a pair of legs, which are machines infinitely more commodious and serviceable. Be grateful, then, and make a proper use of yours. Would you know how they forward the circulation of your fluids in the very action of transporting you from place to place; observe when you walk that all your weight is alternately thrown from one leg to the other; this occasions a great pressure on the vessels of the foot and repels their contents; when relieved by the weight being thrown on the other foot, the vessels of the first are allowed to replenish, and by a return of this weight this repulsion again succeeds, thus accelerating the circulation of the blood. The heat produced in any given time depends on the degree of this acceleration; the fluids are shaken, the humors attenuated, the secretions facilitated, and all goes well, the cheeks are ruddy and health is established. Behold your fair friend at Auteuil, a lady who received from bounteous nature more really useful science than half a dozen such pretenders to philosophy as you have been able to

Historical Context: The use of battle terminology reflects the ongoing revolutionary events.

Literary Movement: The interest in scientific experiments reflects the attitude of the Age of Reason.

extract from all your books. When she honors you with a visit, it is on foot. She walks all hours of the day and leaves indolence and its concomitant maladies to be endured by her horses. In this see at once the preservative of her health and personal charms. But when you go to Auteuil, you must have your carriage, though it is no farther from Passy to Auteuil than from Auteuil to Passy.

FRANKLIN. Your reasonings grow very tiresome.

GOUT. I stand corrected. I will be silent and continue my office. Take that, and that.

FRANKLIN. Oh! Ohh! Talk on, I pray you!

GOUT. No, no, I have a good number of twinges for you tonight, and you may be sure of some more tomorrow.

FRANKLIN. What, with such a fever! I shall go distracted. Oh! Eh! Can no one bear it for me?

GOUT. Ask that of your horses, they have served you faithfully.

FRANKLIN. How can you so cruelly sport with my torments?

GOUT. Sport! I am very serious. I have here a list of offenses against your own health distinctly written and can justify every stroke inflicted on you.

FRANKLIN. Read it, then.

GOUT. It is too long a detail, but I will briefly mention some particulars.

FRANKLIN. Proceed. I am all attention.

GOUT. Do you remember how often you have promised yourself, the following morning, a walk in the grove of Boulogne, in the garden de la Muette, or in your own garden, and have violated your promise, alleging, at one time, it was too cold, at another, too warm, too windy, too moist, or what else you pleased, when in truth it was too nothing but your insuperable love of ease?

FRANKLIN. That I confess may have happened occasionally, probably ten times in a year.

GOUT. Your confession is very far short of the truth. The gross amount is one hundred and ninety-nine times.

FRANKLIN. Is it possible?

GOUT. So possible, that it is fact. You may rely on the accuracy of my statement. You know M. Brillon's gardens and what fine walks they contain, you know the handsome flight of a hundred steps which lead from the terrace above to the lawn below. You have been in the practice of visiting this amiable family twice a week, after dinner, and it is a maxim of your own that "a man may take as much exercise in walking a mile up and down stairs as in ten on level ground." What an oppor-

Historical Context: Franklin served as diplomat to France, where these gardens are located.

tunity was here for you to have had exercise in both these ways! Did you embrace it, and how often?

FRANKLIN. I cannot immediately answer that question.

GOUT. I will do it for you: not once.

FRANKLIN. Not once?

GOUT. Even so. During the summer you went there at six o'clock. You found the charming lady with her lovely children and friends eager to walk with you and entertain you with their agreeable conversation, and what has been your choice? Why to sit on the terrace, satisfying yourself with the fine prospect and passing your eye over the beauties of the garden below, without taking one step to descend and walk about in them. On the contrary, you call for tea and the chessboard, and lo! you are occupied in your seat till nine o'clock, and that besides two hours' play after dinner; and then, instead of walking home, which would have bestirred you a little, you step into your carriage. How absurd to suppose that all this carelessness can be reconcilable with health without my inter-position!

FRANKLIN. I am convinced now of the justness of poor Richard's remark that "Our debts and our sins are always greater than we think for."[2]

Literary Movement: Franklin refers to his own publication, *Poor Richard's Almanack.*

GOUT. So it is. You philosophers are sages in your maxims and fools in your conduct.

FRANKLIN. But do you charge among my crimes that I return in a carriage from Mr. Brillon's?

GOUT. Certainly, for, having been seated all the while, you cannot object the fatigue of the day and cannot want therefore the relief of a carriage.

FRANKLIN. What then would you have me do with my carriage?

GOUT. Burn it if you choose, you would at least get heat out of it once in this way; or, if you dislike that proposal, here's another for you: observe the poor peasants who work in the vineyards and grounds about the villages of Passy, Auteuil, Chaillot, etc., you may find every day among these deserving creatures four or five old men and women bent and perhaps crippled by weight of years and too long and too great labor. After a most fatiguing day these people have to trudge a mile or two to their smoky huts. Order your coachman to set them down. This is an act that will be good for your soul; and, at the same time, after your visit to the Brillons, if you return on foot, that will be good for your body.

Writer's Technique: The Gout presents a logical solution, with a double benefit, in response to Franklin's question.

---

2. **"Our debts . . . for":** From Franklin's *Poor Richard's Almanack.*

FRANKLIN. Ah! how tiresome you are!

GOUT. Well, then, to my office, it should not be forgotten that I am your physician. There.

FRANKLIN. Ohhh! what a devil of a physician!

GOUT. How ungrateful you are to say so! Is it not I who, in the character of your physician, have saved you from the palsy, dropsy, and apoplexy,[3] one or other of which would have done for you long ago but for me?

FRANKLIN. I submit and thank you for the past, but entreat the discontinuance of your visits for the future; for, in my mind, one had better die than be cured so dolefully. Permit me just to hint that I have also not been unfriendly to *you*. I never feed physician or quack of any kind to enter the list against you. If, then, you do not leave me to my repose, it may be said you are ungrateful too.

GOUT. I can scarcely acknowledge that as any objection. As to quacks, I despise them; they may kill you indeed, but cannot injure me. And, as to regular physicians, they are at last convinced that the gout in such a subject as you are is no disease but a remedy, and wherefore cure a remedy?—but to our business—there.

FRANKLIN. Oh! oh!—for Heaven's sake leave me! and I promise faithfully never more to play at chess but to take exercise daily and live temperately.

GOUT. I know you too well. You promise fair, but, after a few months of good health, you will return to your old habits; your fine promises will be forgotten like the forms of last year's clouds. Let us then finish the account, and I will go. But I leave you with an assurance of visiting you again at a proper time and place, for my object is your good, and you are sensible now that I am your *real friend.*

Historical Context: In line with tenets of the Age of Reason, Franklin promises to work on self-improvement.

---

3. apoplexy (ap′ ə plek′ sē) *n.*: Stroke.

THINKING ABOUT THE SELECTION

Recalling

1. What has Franklin done to merit his suffering?
2. (a) How does Franklin spend his mornings? (b) What is his "practice after dinner"?
3. According to the Gout, how does walking help "forward the circulation of your fluids"?
4. What maxim of Franklin's does the Gout use in her argument?
5. (a) Why does the Gout disregard Franklin's promise "to take exercise daily and live temperately"? (b) With what assurance does the Gout leave Franklin?

Interpreting

6. What do you think might have prompted Franklin to write this dialogue?
7. What does the dialogue reveal about Franklin's personal interests?

Applying

8. Do you think most people today get enough exercise? Why or why not?

ANALYZING LITERATURE

Understanding the Age of Reason

The eighteenth century is often referred to as the Age of Reason because it was characterized by an emphasis on rational thought. At the time, people believed that they could discover all the truths about the world and human existence through scientific observation and the process of reasoning. Because of their faith in reason, people possessed a great deal of optimism about the present and future. People also generally possessed a deep interest in science, a desire to preserve cultural standards and traditions, and a belief in moderation and self-restraint. These attitudes and beliefs are reflected in the literature of the period, which is also characterized by the use of elegant, ornate language.

1. How does Franklin's dialogue reflect a belief in reason?
2. How does the dialogue reflect a belief in moderation and self-restraint?
3. How does the dialogue reflect an interest in science?

CRITICAL THINKING AND READING

Understanding Reasoning

In his dialogue Franklin uses the process of reasoning to analyze his condition. First he assesses the causes of his condition. Then he provides a body of evidence to support his assessment and ends the dialogue by presenting possible solutions to his problem.

1. What are the causes of his condition?
2. Find three examples that he uses to support his assessment of the cause.

THINKING AND WRITING

Writing a Dialogue

Write a dialogue in which you present a logical argument, as Franklin does in "Franklin and the Gout." Think of an ailment or condition that occurs when people do not care for themselves properly. Then write a dialogue between this ailment and a fictional character who suffers from the ailment. Analyze the condition, following the process of reasoning that Franklin uses in his dialogue. When you revise make sure you have included enough evidence to thoroughly support the character's assessment of the causes of his or her condition.

BENJAMIN FRANKLIN

1706–1800

No other colonial American better embodied the promise of America than Benjamin Franklin. Through hard work, dedication, and ingenuity, Franklin was able to rise out of poverty to become a wealthy, famous, and influential person. Although he never received a formal education, Franklin made important contributions in a variety of fields, including literature, journalism, science, diplomacy, education, and philosophy.

Franklin was born in Boston, one of seventeen children. After leaving school at the age of ten, Franklin spent two years working for his father, before becoming an apprentice to his older brother, who was a printer. When he was seventeen, Franklin left Boston and traveled to Philadelphia, hoping to open his own print shop. Once he established himself as a printer, Franklin began producing a newspaper and an annual publication called *Poor Richard's Almanack,* which contained information, observations, and advice. The *Almanack,* which Franklin published from 1733 through 1758, was very popular and earned Franklin a reputation as a talented writer.

When Franklin was forty-two, he retired from the printing business to devote himself to science. Franklin proved to be as successful a scientist as he had been a printer. Over the course of his lifetime, he was responsible for inventing the lightning rod, bifocals, and a new type of stove; confirming the laws of electricity; and contributing to the scientific understanding of earthquakes and ocean currents.

In spite of his other contributions, Franklin probably is remembered by most as a statesman and diplomat. Franklin played an important role in drafting the Declaration of Independence, enlisting French support during the Revolutionary War, negotiating a peace treaty with Britain, and drafting the United States Constitution.

Though it was never completed, Franklin's *Autobiography,* filled with his opinions and suggestions about self-discipline and moral perfection, provides not only a record of his achievements but also an understanding of his character.

from The Autobiography

Literary Forms

Autobiography. An autobiography is a person's account of his or her life. Generally written in the first person, with the author speaking as "I," autobiographies present the life events as the writer views them. As a result, the author's portrayals are colored by his or her attitudes, thoughts, and feelings. Thus, they can provide unique insights into the beliefs and perceptions of the author.

People write autobiographies because they feel that their lives are interesting or important or can in some way serve as an example for others. The autobiography has been a popular literary form in America.

Look For

What kind of a person was Benjamin Franklin? As you read this excerpt from his *Autobiography,* look for Franklin's beliefs and opinions reflected in his portrayal of himself, other people, and events.

Writing

What experiences would you choose to write about if you were preparing your own autobiography? List the experiences that you would be most likely to include.

Vocabulary

Knowing the following words will help you as you read the excerpt from Benjamin Franklin's *Autobiography.*

approbation (ap′ rə bā′ sh-ən) *n.*: Approval (p. 108)
arduous (är jōō wəs) *adj.*: Difficult (p. 112)
avarice (av′ ər is) *n.*: Greed (p. 113)
vigilance (vij′ ə ləns) *n.*: Watchfulness (p. 114)

disposition (dis′ pə zish′ ən) *n.*: Management (p. 116)
foppery (fäp′ ər ē) *n.*: Foolishness (p. 116)
felicity (fə lis′ə tē) *n.*: Happiness; bliss (p. 116)

from The Autobiography

Benjamin Franklin

My brother had in 1720 or '21, begun to print a newspaper. It was the second that appeared in America and was called the *New England Courant.* The only one before it was *the Boston News Letter.* I remember his being dissuaded by some of his friends from the undertaking, as not likely to succeed, one newspaper being in their judgment enough for America. At this time (1771) there are not less than five-and-twenty. He went on, however, with the undertaking, and after having worked in composing the types and printing off the sheets, I was employed to carry the papers through the streets to the customers. He had some ingenious men among his friends who amused themselves by writing little pieces for this paper, which gained it credit and made it more in demand, and these gentlemen often visited us. Hearing their conversations and their accounts of the approbation their papers were received with, I was excited to try my hand among them; but, being still a boy, and suspecting that my brother would object to printing anything of mine in his paper if he knew it to be mine, I contrived to disguise my hand, and writing an anonymous paper, I put it in at night under the door of the printing house. It was found in the morning and communicated to his writing friends when they called in as usual. They read it, commented on it in my hearing, and I had the exquisite pleasure of finding it met with their approbation, and that, in their different guesses at the author, none were named but men of some character among us for learning and ingenuity. I suppose now that I was rather lucky in my judges, and that perhaps they were not really so very good ones as I then esteemed them.

Encouraged however by this, I wrote and conveyed in the same way to the press several more papers, which were equally approved; and I kept my secret till my small fund of sense for such performances was pretty well exhausted, and then I discovered[1] it, when I began to be considered a little more by my brother's acquaintance, and in a manner that did not quite please him, as he thought, probably with reason, that it tended to make me too vain. And perhaps this might be one occasion of the differences that we began to have about this time. Though a brother, he considered himself as my master, and me as his apprentice, and accordingly expected the same services from me as he would from another; while I thought he demeaned me too much in some he required of me, who from a brother expected more indulgence. Our disputes were often brought before our father, and I fancy I was either generally in the right or else a better pleader, because the judgment was generally in my favor. But my brother was passionate and had often beaten me, which I took extremely amiss; and, thinking my apprenticeship very tedious, I was continually wishing for some opportunity of shortening it, which at length offered in a manner unexpected.

One of the pieces in our newspaper, on some political point which I have now forgotten, gave offense to the assembly. He was taken up, censured and imprisoned for a

---

1. discovered: Revealed.

month, by the speaker's warrant, I suppose because he would not discover his author. I too was taken up and examined before the council; but though I did not give them any satisfaction, they contented themselves with admonishing me, and dismissed me, considering me perhaps as an apprentice who was bound to keep his master's secrets.

During my brother's confinement, which I resented a good deal, notwithstanding our private differences, I had the management of the paper; and I made bold to give our rulers some rubs in it, which my brother took very kindly, while others began to consider me in an unfavorable light, as a young genius that had a turn for libeling and satire. My brother's discharge was accompanied with an order of the House (a very odd one) "that James Franklin should no longer print the paper called the *New England Courant*."

There was a consultation held in our printing house among his friends what he should do in this case. Some proposed to evade the order by changing the name of the paper; but my brother seeing inconveniences in that, it was finally concluded on as a better way to let it be printed for the future under the name of Benjamin Franklin. And to avoid the censure of the Assembly that might fall on him as still printing it by his apprentice, the contrivance was that my old indenture should be returned to me with a full discharge on the back of it, to be shown on occasion; but to secure to him the benefit of my service, I was to sign new indentures for the remainder of the term, which were to be kept private. A very flimsy scheme it was; however, it was immediately executed, and the paper went on accordingly under my name for several months.

At length a fresh difference arising between my brother and me, I took upon me to assert my freedom, presuming that he would not venture to produce the new indentures. It was not fair in me to take this advantage, and this I therefore reckon one of the first errata[2] of my life; but the unfairness of it

BENJAMIN FRANKLIN'S BIRTHPLACE IN BOSTON, MASSACHUSETTS
J. H. Buffords
Metropolitan Museum of Art

weighed little with me when under the impressions of resentment for the blows his passion too often urged him to bestow upon me, though he was otherwise not an ill-natured man: perhaps I was too saucy and provoking.

When he found I would leave him, he took care to prevent my getting employment in any other printing house of the town by going round and speaking to every master, who accordingly refused to give me work. I then thought of going to New York as the nearest place where there was a printer; and I was the rather inclined to leave Boston when I reflected that I had already made myself a little obnoxious to the governing party, and, from the arbitrary proceedings of the Assembly in my brother's case, it was likely I might if I stayed soon bring myself into scrapes. I determined on the point, but my

---

2. errata (e rät′ ə): Errors.

from *The Autobiography* 109

father now siding with my brother, I was sensible that if I attempted to go openly, means would be used to prevent me. My friend Collins, therefore, undertook to manage a little for me. He agreed with the captain of a New York sloop for my passage. So I sold some of my books to raise a little money, was taken on board privately, and as we had a fair wind, in three days I found myself in New York near three hundred miles from home, a boy of but seventeen, without the least recommendation to, or knowledge of, any person in the place, and with very little money in my pocket.

My inclinations for the sea were by this time worn out, or I might now have gratified them. But, having a trade, and supposing myself a pretty good workman, I offered my service to the printer in the place, old Mr. William Bradford, who had been the first printer in Pennsylvania, but removed from thence upon the quarrel of George Keith. He could give me no employment, having little to do and help enough already; but, says he, "My son at Philadelphia has lately lost his principal hand, Aquila Rose, by death. If you go thither I believe he may employ you." Philadelphia was one hundred miles farther. I set out, however, in a boat for Amboy,[3] leaving my chest and things to follow me round by sea. In crossing the bay we met with a squall that tore our rotten sails to pieces, prevented our getting into the kill,[4] and drove us upon Long Island. . . .

When we drew near the island, we found it was at a place where there could be no landing, there being a great surf on the stony beach. So we dropped anchor and swung round towards the shore. Some people came down to the water edge and hallowed[5] to us, as we did to them. But the wind was so high and the surf so loud, that we could not hear so as to understand each other. There were canoes on the shore, and we made signs and hallowed that they should fetch us, but they either did not understand us, or thought it impracticable. So they went away, and night coming on, we had no remedy but to wait till the wind should abate; and in the meantime the boatman and I concluded to sleep if we could, and so crowded into the scuttle,[6] and the spray beating over the head of our boat, leaked through to us. In this manner we lay all night with very little rest. But the wind abating the next day, we made a shift to reach Amboy before night, having been thirty hours on the water without victuals or any drink but a bottle of filthy rum, the water we sailed on being salt.

In the evening I found myself very feverish, and went in to bed. But having read somewhere that cold water drank plentifully was good for a fever, I followed the prescription, sweat plentifully most of the Night; my Fever left me, and in the morning crossing the ferry, I proceeded on my journey, on foot, having fifty miles to Burlington, where I was told I should find boats that would carry me the rest of the way to Philadelphia.

It rained very hard all day, I was thoroughly soaked, and by noon a good deal tired; so I stopped at a poor inn where I stayed all night, beginning now to wish I had never left home. I cut so miserable a figure, too, that I found by the questions asked me I was suspected to be some runaway servant, and in danger of being taken up on that suspicion. However I proceeded the next day and got in the evening to an inn within eight to ten miles of Burlington, kept by one Dr. Brown.

He entered into conversation with me while I took some refreshment, and finding I had read a little, became very sociable and friendly. Our acquaintance continued as long as he lived. . . .

At his house I lay that night, and the next morning reached Burlington, but had

---

3. Amboy: A town on the New Jersey coast.
4. kill *n.*: Channel.
5. halloed: Called.

6. scuttle *n.*: A small, covered opening or hatchway in the outer hull or deck of a ship.

the mortification to find that the regular boats were gone a little before my coming and no other expected to go till Tuesday, this being Saturday. Wherefore I returned to an old woman in the town of whom I had bought gingerbread to eat on the water and asked her advice. She invited me to lodge at her house till a passage by water should offer, and, being tired with my foot traveling, I accepted the invitation. She, understanding I was a printer, would have had me stay at that town and follow my business, being ignorant of the stock necessary to begin with. She was very hospitable, gave me a dinner of oxcheek with great good will, accepting only a pot of ale in return; and I thought myself fixed till Tuesday should come. However, walking in the evening by the side of the river, a boat came by, which I found was going towards Philadelphia with several people in her. They took me in, and as there was no wind, we rowed all the way; and about midnight not having yet seen the city, some of the company were confident we must have passed it, and would row no farther; the others knew not where we were; so we put towards the shore, got into a creek, landed near an old fence, with the rails of which we made a fire, the night being cold in October, and there we remained till daylight. Then one of the company knew the place to be Cooper's Creek, a little above Philadelpia, which we saw as soon as we got out of the creek, and arrived there about eight or nine o'clock on the Sunday morning, and landed at the Market Street Wharf.

I have been the more particular in this description of my journey, and shall be so of

DELAWARE RIVER FRONT, PHILADELPHIA
Thomas Birch
Museum of Fine Arts, Boston

my first entry into that city, that you may in your mind compare such unlikely beginnings with the figure I have since made there. I was in my working dress, my best clothes being to come round by sea. I was dirty from my journey; my pockets were stuffed out with shirts and stockings; I knew no soul, nor where to look for lodging. I was fatigued with traveling, rowing, and want of rest; I was very hungry; and my whole stock of cash consisted of a Dutch dollar and about a shilling in copper. The latter I gave the people of the boat for my passage, who at first refused it, on account of my rowing; but I insisted on their taking it, a man being sometimes more generous when he has but a little money than when he has plenty, perhaps through fear of being thought to have but little.

Then I walked up the street, gazing about, till near the markethouse I met a boy with bread. I had made many a meal on bread, and inquiring where he got it, I went immediately to the baker's he directed me to in Second Street, and asked for biscuit, intending such as we had in Boston; but they, it seems, were not made in Philadelphia. Then I asked for a threepenny loaf and was told they had none such. So, not considering or knowing the difference of money and the greater cheapness nor the names of his bread, I bade him give me threepenny worth of any sort. He gave me, accordingly, three great puffy rolls. I was surprised at the quantity, but took it, and, having no room in my pockets, walked off with a roll under each arm and eating the other. Thus I went up Market Street as far as Fourth Street, passing by the door of Mr. Read, my future wife's father; when she, standing at the door, saw me and thought I made, as I certainly did, a most awkward, ridiculous appearance. Then I turned and went down Chestnut Street and part of Walnut Street, eating my roll all the way, and, coming round, found myself again at Market Street Wharf, near the boat I came in, to which I went for a draft of the river water; and, being filled with one of my rolls,

gave the other two to a woman and her child that came down the river in the boat with us and were waiting to go farther.

Thus refreshed, I walked again up the street, which by this time had many clean-dressed people in it, who were all walking the same way. I joined them, and thereby was led into the great meetinghouse of the Quakers near the market. I sat down among them, and, after looking round awhile and hearing nothing said, being very drowsy through labor and want of rest the preceding night, I fell fast asleep, and continued so till the meeting broke up, when one was kind enough to rouse me. This was therefore the first house I was in, or slept in, in Philadelphia.

The following excerpt relates events that occurred several years later.

It was about this time I conceived the bold and arduous project of arriving at moral perfection. I wished to live without committing any fault at any time; I would conquer all that either natural inclination, custom, or company might lead me into. As I knew, or thought I knew, what was right and wrong, I did not see why I might not always do the one and avoid the other. But I soon found I had undertaken a task of more difficulty than I had imagined. While my care was employed in guarding against one fault, I was often surprised by another; habit took the advantage of inattention; inclination was sometimes too strong for reason. I concluded, at length, that the mere speculative conviction that it was our interest to be completely virtuous was not sufficient to prevent our slipping; and that the contrary habits must be broken, and good ones acquired and established, before we can have any dependence on a steady, uniform rectitude of conduct. For this purpose I therefore contrived the following method.

In the various enumerations of the moral virtues I had met with in my reading, I found the catalog more or less numerous, as dif-

QUAKER MEETING
British, fourth quarter 18th century or first quarter 19th century
Museum of Fine Arts, Boston

ferent writers included more or fewer ideas under the same name. Temperance, for example, was by some confined to eating and drinking, while by others it was extended to mean the moderating every other pleasure, appetite, inclination, or passion, bodily or mental, even to our avarice and ambition. I proposed to myself, for the sake of clearness, to use rather more names, with fewer ideas annexed to each, than a few names with more ideas; and I included under thirteen names of virtues all that at that time oc-

curred to me as necessary or desirable, and annexed to each a short precept, which fully expressed the extent I gave to its meaning.

These names of virtues, with their precepts, were:

1. TEMPERANCE Eat not to dullness; drink not to elevation.

2. SILENCE Speak not but what may benefit others or yourself; avoid trifling conversation.

from *The Autobiography*   113

3. ORDER   Let all your things have their places; let each part of your business have its time.

4. RESOLUTION   Resolve to perform what you ought; perform without fail what you resolve.

5. FRUGALITY   Make no expense but to do good to others or yourself; *i.e.*, waste nothing.

6. INDUSTRY   Lose no time; be always employed in something useful; cut off all unnecessary actions.

7. SINCERITY   Use no hurtful deceit; think innocently and justly, and, if you speak, speak accordingly.

8. JUSTICE   Wrong none by doing injuries, or omitting the benefits that are your duty.

9. MODERATION   Avoid extremes; forebear resenting injuries so much as you think they deserve.

10. CLEANLINESS   Tolerate no uncleanliness in body, clothes, or habitation.

11. TRANQUILLITY   Be not disturbed at trifles, or at accidents common or unavoidable.

12. CHASTITY

13. HUMILITY   Imitate Jesus and Socrates.[7]

⁓ My intention being to acquire the *habitude* of all these virtues, I judged it would be well not to distract my attention by attempting the whole at once but to fix it on one of them at a time; and, when I should be master of that, then to proceed to another, and so on, till I should have gone through the thirteen; and, as the previous acquisition of some might facilitate the acquisition of certain others, I arranged them with that view,

as they stand above. *Temperance* first, as it tends to procure that coolness and clearness of head, which is so necessary where constant vigilance was to be kept up, and guard maintained against the unremitting attraction of ancient habits and the force of perpetual temptations. This being acquired and established, *Silence* would be more easy; and my desire being to gain knowledge at the same time that I improved in virtue, and considering that in conversation it was obtained rather by the use of the ears than of the tongue, and therefore wishing to break a habit I was getting into of prattling, punning, and joking, which only made me acceptable to trifling company, I gave *Silence* the second place. This and the next, *Order*, I expected would allow me more time for attending to my project and my studies. *Resolution*, once become habitual, would keep me firm in my endeavors to obtain all the subsequent virtues; *Frugality* and *Industry* freeing me from my remaining debt and producing affluence and independence, would make more easy the practice of *Sincerity* and *Justice*, etc., etc. Conceiving then, that, agreeably to the advice of Pythagoras[8] in his *Golden Verses*, daily examination would be necessary, I contrived the following method for conducting that examination.

I made a little book, in which I allotted a page for each of the virtues. I ruled each page with red ink, so as to have seven columns, one for each day of the week, marking each column with a letter for the day. I crossed these columns with thirteen red lines, marking the beginning of each line with the first letter of one of the virtues, on which line and in its proper column I might mark, by a little black spot, every fault I found upon examination to have been committed respecting that virtue upon that day.

I determined to give a week's strict attention to each of the virtues successively.

---

7. Socrates (säk′ rə tēz′): Ancient Greek philosopher and teacher (470?–399 B.C.).

8. Pythagoras (pi thag′ ər əs): An ancient Greek philosopher and mathematician who lived in the sixth century B.C.

Thus, in the first week, my great guard was to avoid every[9] the least offense against *Temperance*, leaving the other virtues to their ordinary chance, only marking every evening the faults of the day. Thus, if in the first week I could keep my first line, marked *T*, clear of spots, I supposed the habit of that virtue so much strengthened, and its opposite weakened, that I might venture extending my attention to include the next, and for the following week keep both lines clear of spots. Proceeding thus to the last, I could go through a course complete in thirteen weeks, and four courses in a year. And like him who, having a garden to weed, does not attempt to eradicate all the bad herbs at once, which would exceed his reach and his strength, but works on one of the beds at a time, and, having accomplished the first, proceeds to a second, so I should have, I hoped, the encouraging pleasure of seeing on my pages the progress I made in virtue, by clearing successively my lines of their spots, till in the end, by a number of courses, I should be happy in viewing a clean book, after a thirteen weeks' daily examination . . .

The precept of *Order* requiring that *every part of my business should have its allotted time*, one page in my little book contained the following scheme of employment for the twenty-four hours of a natural day.

THE MORNING. *Question.* What good shall I do this day?	5 6 7	Rise, wash, and address *Powerful Goodness!* Contrive day's business, and take the resolution of the day; prosecute the present study, and breakfast.
	8 9 10 11	Work.
NOON.	12 1	Read, or over-look my accounts, and dine.
	2 3 4 5	Work.
EVENING. *Question.* What good have I done today?	6 7 8 9	Put things in their places. Supper. Music or diversion, or conversation. Examination of the day.
	10 11 12	
NIGHT.	1 2 3 4	Sleep.

I entered upon the execution of this plan for self-examination, and continued it with occasional intermissions for some time. I was surprised to find myself so much fuller of faults than I had imagined; but I had the satisfaction of seeing them diminish. To avoid the trouble of renewing now and then my little book, which, by scraping out the marks on the paper of old faults to make room for new ones in a new course, became full of holes, I transferred my tables and precepts to the ivory leaves of a memorandum book, on which the lines were drawn with red ink that made a durable stain, and on those lines I marked my faults with a black-lead pencil, which marks I could easily wipe out with a wet sponge. After a while I went through one course only in a year, and afterward only one in several years, till at length I omitted them entirely, being employed in voyages and business abroad, with a multiplicity of affairs that interfered; but I always carried my little book with me.

My scheme of *Order* gave me the most trouble; and I found that, though it might be

---

9. every: Even.

practicable where a man's business was such as to leave him the disposition of his time, that of a journeyman printer, for instance, it was not possible to be exactly observed by a master, who must mix with the world and often receive people of business at their own hours. *Order,* too, with regard to places for things, papers, etc., I found extremely difficult to acquire. I had not been early accustomed to it, and, having an exceeding good memory, I was not so sensible of the inconvenience attending want of method. This article, therefore, cost me so much painful attention, and my faults in it vexed me so much, and I made so little progress in amendment, and had such frequent relapses, that I was almost ready to give up the attempt, and content myself with a faulty character in that respect, like the man who, in buying an ax of a smith, my neighbor, desired to have the whole of its surface as bright as the edge. The smith consented to grind it bright for him if he would turn the wheel; he turned, while the smith pressed the broad face of the ax hard and heavily on the stone, which made the turning of it very fatiguing. The man came every now and then from the wheel to see how the work went on, and at length would take his ax as it was, without farther grinding. "No," said the smith, "turn on, turn on; we shall have it bright by and by; as yet, it is only speckled." "Yes," says the man, *"but I think I like a speckled ax best."* And I believe this may have been the case with many, who, having, for want of some such means as I employed, found the difficulty of obtaining good and breaking bad habits in other points of vice and virtue, have given up the struggle, and concluded that *"a speckled ax was best"*; for something, that pretended to be reason, was every now and then suggesting to me that such extreme nicety as I exacted of myself might be a kind of foppery in morals, which, if it were known, would make me ridiculous; that a perfect character might be

attended with the inconvenience of being envied and hated; and that a benevolent man should allow a few faults in himself, to keep his friends in countenance.

In truth, I found myself incorrigible with respect to *Order;* and now I am grown old, and my memory bad, I feel very sensibly the want of it. But, on the whole, though I never arrived at the perfection I had been so ambitious of obtaining, but fell far short of it, yet I was, by the endeavor, a better and a happier man than I otherwise should have been if I had not attempted it; as those who aim at perfect writing by imitating the engraved copies, though they never reached the wished-for excellence of those copies, their hand is mended by the endeavor, and is tolerable while it continues fair and legible.

It may be well my posterity should be informed that to this little artifice, with the blessing of God, their ancestor owed the constant felicity of his life, down to his seventy-ninth year in which this is written. What reverses may attend the remainder is in the hand of Providence; but, if they arrive, the reflection on past happiness enjoyed ought to help his bearing them with more resignation. To *Temperance* he ascribes his long-continued health, and what is still left to him of a good constitution; to *Industry* and *Frugality,* the early easiness of his circumstances and acquisition of his fortune, with all that knowledge that enabled him to be a useful citizen, and obtained for him some degree of reputation among the learned; to *Sincerity* and *Justice,* the confidence of his country, and the honorable employs it conferred upon him; and to the joint influence of the whole mass of the virtues, even in the imperfect state he was able to acquire them, all that evenness of temper, and that cheerfulness in conversation, which makes his company still sought for, and agreeable even to his younger acquaintance. I hope, therefore, that some of my descendants may follow the example and reap the benefit.

THINKING ABOUT THE SELECTION

Recalling

1. Why does Franklin choose not to sign the first papers he submits for publication?
2. (a) Why is Franklin's brother sent to prison? (b) Who runs the paper while Franklin's brother is confined?
3. (a) What order is given to Franklin's brother when he is released? (b) How does he evade the order?
4. (a) Why does Franklin leave Boston? (b) How old is Franklin when he leaves?
5. What is Franklin's condition when he arrives in Philadelphia?
6. (a) What thirteen virtues does Franklin feel are necessary for moral perfection? (b) Summarize Franklin's plan for arriving at moral perfection. (c) How successful is Franklin in carrying out his plan?

Interpreting

7. (a) What characteristics does Franklin display in his dealings with his brother? (b) What qualities does he display during his trip to Philadelphia?
8. (a) What does Franklin's plan for moral perfection reveal about him? (b) Why is it surprising that the virtue of order gives him the most trouble?
9. (a) Find five examples of self-analysis in the selection. (b) How does Franklin's character change as he grows older?

Applying

10. How can analyzing behavior contribute to personal growth?

ANALYZING LITERATURE

Understanding an Autobiography

An **autobiography** is the story of a person's life written by that person. Because the author's attitudes, thoughts, and feelings color the self-portrayal as well as the portrayal of other people and events, the autobiography is subjective. However, for this same reason, autobiographies often provide insights into the beliefs and perceptions of the author. For example, Franklin's sense of morality is revealed in the excerpt from his *Autobiography.*

1. What impression does Franklin convey of himself as a young man?
2. How might the account of Franklin's early years be different if it had been written by his brother or his father?

CRITICAL THINKING AND READING

Making Inferences About the Author

Because an autobiographical account is colored by the author's viewpoint, you can make **inferences,** or draw conclusions, about the author's personality by examining the manner in which the self, other people, and events are portrayed. For example, one of the inferences that you might make from Franklin's portrayal of himself is that he was a very proud man.

1. What inference can you make about Franklin from his portrayal of his brother? Explain the evidence that supports your inferences.
2. What inference can you make about Franklin from his description of his journey to Philadelphia? Explain the evidence that supports your inference.

THINKING AND WRITING

Writing an Autobiographical Account

Examine the list of experiences you wrote before reading this selection. Decide which one you think others would find most interesting. Outline the events that led up to the experience, and think of what it taught you. Then write an autobiographical account, relating events in chronological order and including descriptive details that help bring the experience to life for your readers. When you finish writing, revise your account; and prepare a final copy.

GUIDE FOR READING

from Poor Richard's Almanack

Literary Forms

Aphorisms. An aphorism is a short, concise statement expressing a wise or clever observation or a general truth. A variety of devices make aphorisms easy to remember. Some aphorisms contain rhymes or repeated words or sounds; others contain two phrases that present contrasting ideas using the same grammatical structure. For example, the contemporary aphorism "when the going gets tough, the tough get going," contains repeated words and contrasting ideas.

Most of Benjamin Franklin's aphorisms are adapted from proverbs, anonymous traditional sayings. Franklin, who believed that clarity and brevity were two of the most important characteristics of good prose, rewrote the traditional sayings, making them short, direct, and witty.

Franklin put an aphorism at the top or bottom of most pages in his almanacs. The aphorisms allowed Franklin to include many moral messages in very little space. Because readers found them entertaining, Franklin's aphorisms contributed to the popularity of *Poor Richard's Almanack.*

Look For

Which of Franklin's aphorisms do you already know? Under what circumstances have you heard them? As you read the aphorisms from *Poor Richard's Almanack,* look for the messages they convey. What methods does Franklin use to make these messages memorable and entertaining?

Writing

People often use aphorisms or proverbs in everyday speech. What sayings do you use or hear others use? Brainstorm for such sayings, and list as many as you can.

Vocabulary

Knowing the following words will help you as you read the aphorisms from *Poor Richard's Almanack.*

fasting (fast′ iŋ) *v.:* Eating very little or nothing (p. 119)
squander (skwän dər) *v.:* Spend or use wastefully (p. 120)

from Poor Richard's Almanack

Benjamin Franklin

Hunger is the best pickle.

He that lives upon hope will die fasting.

Fish and visitors smell in three days.

Keep thy shop, and thy shop will keep thee.

If your head is wax, don't walk in the sun.

Necessity never made a good bargain.

Love your neighbor; yet don't pull down your hedge.

A slip of the foot you may soon recover, but a slip of
the tongue you may never get over.

Early to bed, early to rise, makes a man healthy,
wealthy, and wise.

God helps them that help themselves.

Three may keep a secret if two of them are dead.

Fools make feasts, and wise men eat them.

God heals and the doctor takes the fee.

The rotten apple spoils his companions.

If you would know the value of money, try to
borrow some.

A small leak will sink a great ship.

Drive thy business; let it not drive thee.

Dost thou love life? Then do not squander time; for
  that's the stuff life is made of.

Genius without education is like silver in the mine.

The cat in gloves catches no mice.

POOR RICHARD'S ALMANACK
The Granger Collection

THINKING ABOUT THE SELECTION

Recalling

1. According to Franklin, what will happen to a person who "lives upon hope"?
2. What makes a person "healthy, wealthy, and wise"?
3. To what does Franklin compare "genius without education"?

Interpreting

4. In what way are the ninth and eighteenth aphorisms related to each other?
5. How are the fourteenth and sixteenth aphorisms related?
6. Which aphorisms express Franklin's belief in the need for self-discipline and self-motivation? Explain why.

Applying

7. Which aphorisms would Franklin apply to business? Which to education? Explain your answers.

ANALYZING LITERATURE

Recognizing Aphorisms

Aphorisms are brief statements expressing wise observations or general truths. A variety of techniques, such as rhymes or repeated words or sounds, are used to make aphorisms easy to remember. For example, in his aphorism "Keep thy shop, and thy shop will keep thee," Franklin uses word repetition to make his saying memorable.

1. Identify Franklin's techniques in each of the following aphorisms, and list them. Then state the meaning of each aphorism, and explain why the aphorisms have more of an impact than the simple statements of their meaning.
   a. "A slip of the foot you may soon recover, but a slip of the tongue you may never get over."
   b. "Early to bed and early to rise, makes a man healthy, wealthy, and wise."
   c. "Fools make feasts, and wise men eat them."
2. Using Franklin's techniques, write three aphorisms for contemporary life.

THINKING AND WRITING

Responding to a Statement About Style

In his essay "On Literary Style," Franklin states that good writing must be "smooth, clear, and short." Examine the excerpt from Franklin's *Autobiography* and the aphorisms from *Poor Richard's Almanack*. Does Franklin's writing meet his own requirements? List passages that support your opinion. Organize your information into an outline. Then write a thesis statement and an essay in which you use transitions to link your ideas and support your argument with examples of Franklin's writing. When you revise, make sure that your paper meets Franklin's requirements for good writing.

PATRICK HENRY

1736–1799

Remembered most for his fiery battle cry, "Give me liberty or give me death," Patrick Henry is considered the most powerful orator of the American Revolution. Using his talents as a speaker, Henry helped to inspire colonists to unite in an effort to win their independence.

Born on his father's plantation in Hanover County, Virginia, Henry attended school only until the age of ten, though his father continued his schooling at home. After unsuccessfully attempting to run a store with his brother, Henry married at the age of eighteen and took up farming. When his farm was destroyed by a fire several years later, Henry found himself deeply in debt, with several children to support. He then began studying law, and in 1760 he received his license to practice. His talent as a speaker contributed to his reputation as an excellent lawyer.

In 1765 Henry was elected to the Virginia House of Burgesses. Shortly after his election, Henry delivered one of his most powerful speeches, declaring his opposition to the Stamp Act. At the end of his speech, Henry mentioned two kings who had been killed for political reasons and declared that King George III of Britain might "profit by their example." According to legend, this shocked the members of the audience so much that they accused Henry of treason. To this accusation Henry replied, "If this be treason, make the most of it!"

In 1775, after he had served as a member of the First Continental Congress, Henry delivered his most famous speech at the Virginia Provincial Convention. While most of the speakers that day argued that the colony should seek a compromise with the British, Henry boldly and dramatically urged armed resistance to England. Henry's speech had a powerful impact on the audience, reinforcing the revolutionary spirit that led to the signing of the Declaration of Independence. In the years that followed, Henry continued to be an important political leader, serving as the governor of Virginia and as a member of the Virginia General Assembly. It was this speech that secured him a place in American history.

GUIDE FOR READING

Speech in the Virginia Convention

Oratory. Oratory is the art of skilled, eloquent public speaking. Throughout history talented orators have used their skills to spread messages, gain support, and sway opinions. Oratory has always played an important role in American politics. In fact, to a great extent, America owes its independence to gifted speakers such as Patrick Henry who were responsible for influencing colonists to resist British rule.

An effective orator uses a variety of devices to emphasize important points. Four of these devices are rhetorical questions, restatement, repetition, and parallelism.

Rhetorical questions are questions that the speaker does not expect people to answer verbally. Because people generally will try to answer the questions in their mind, however, the questions force them to think actively about what the speaker is saying.

Restatement, repetition, and parallelism are methods used to highlight important points. A speaker uses restatement to state an idea in a variety of ways. When a speaker uses repetition, he or she restates an idea using the same words. Parallelism involves the use of a repeated grammatical structure.

What made Patrick Henry such an effective orator? As you read his "Speech in the Virginia Convention," look for the oratorical devices he used to emphasize his points and to force the audience to contemplate what he is saying.

What were the main reasons the colonies rebelled against British rule? Spend five minutes brainstorming about the causes of the American Revolution, and list them.

Knowing the following words will help you as you read the "Speech in the Virginia Convention."

arduous (är′ jōō wəs) *adj.*: Difficult (p. 124)

insidious (in sid′ē əs) *adj.*: Deceitful; treacherous (p. 124)

subjugation (sub′ jə gā′ sʰən)

n.: The act of conquering (p. 124)

vigilant (vij′ə lənt) *n.*: Alert to danger (p. 126)

Speech in the Virginia Convention

Patrick Henry

Mr. President: No man thinks more highly than I do of the patriotism, as well as abilities, of the very worthy gentlemen who have just addressed the house. But different men often see the same subject in different lights; and, therefore, I hope it will not be thought disrespectful to those gentlemen, if, entertaining, as I do, opinions of a character very opposite to theirs, I shall speak forth my sentiments freely and without reserve. This is no time for ceremony. The question before the house is one of awful moment[1] to this country. For my own part, I consider it as nothing less than a question of freedom or slavery. And in proportion to the magnitude of the subject ought to be the freedom of the debate. It is only in this way that we can hope to arrive at truth, and fulfill the great responsibility which we hold to God and our country. Should I keep back my opinions at such a time, through fear of giving offense, I should consider myself as guilty of treason toward my country, and of an act of disloyalty toward the Majesty of Heaven, which I revere above all earthly kings.

Mr. President, it is natural to man to indulge in the illusions of hope. We are apt to shut our eyes against a painful truth, and listen to the song of that siren till she transforms us into beasts.[2] Is this the part of wise men, engaged in a great and arduous struggle for liberty? Are we disposed to be of the number of those who having eyes see not, and having ears hear not,[3] the things which so nearly concern their temporal salvation? For my part, whatever anguish of spirit it may cost, I am willing to know the whole truth; to know the worst and to provide for it.

I have but one lamp by which my feet are guided, and that is the lamp of experience. I know of no way of judging of the future but by the past. And judging by the past, I wish to know what there has been in the conduct of the British ministry for the last ten years to justify those hopes with which gentlemen have been pleased to solace themselves and the house? Is it that insidious smile with which our petition has been lately received? Trust it not, sir; it will prove a snare to your feet. Suffer not yourselves to be betrayed with a kiss.[4] Ask yourselves how this gracious reception of our petition comports with those warlike preparations which cover our waters and darken our land. Are fleets and armies necessary to a work of love and reconciliation? Have we shown ourselves so unwilling to be reconciled that force must be called in to win back our love? Let us not deceive ourselves, sir. These are the implements of war and subjugation—the last arguments to which kings resort.

I ask gentlemen, sir, what means this martial array, if its purpose be not to force

---

1. moment: Importance.
2. listen . . . beasts: In Homer's *Odyssey* the enchantress Circe transforms men into swine after charming them with her singing.

3. having eyes . . . hear not: In Ezekiel 12:2 those "who have eyes to see, but see not, who have ears to hear, but hear not" are addressed.
4. betrayed with a kiss: In Luke 22:47–48 Jesus is betrayed with a kiss.

PATRICK HENRY BEFORE THE VIRGINIA HOUSE OF BURGESSES
Peter F. Rothermel
Red Hill, The Patrick Henry National Memorial

Speech in the Virginia Convention   125

us to submission? Can gentlemen assign any other possible motive for it? Has Great Britain any enemy in this quarter of the world, to call for all this accumulation of navies and armies? No, sir, she has none. They are meant for us: they can be meant for no other. They are sent over to bind and rivet upon us those chains which the British ministry have been so long forging.

And what have we to oppose to them? Shall we try argument? Sir, we have been trying that for the last ten years. Have we anything new to offer upon the subject? Nothing. We have held the subject up in every light of which it is capable; but it has been all in vain. Shall we resort to entreaty and humble supplication? What terms shall we find which have not been already exhausted? Let us not, I beseech you, sir, deceive ourselves longer.

Sir, we have done everything that could be done to avert the storm which is now coming on. We have petitioned; we have remonstrated; we have supplicated; we have prostrated ourselves before the throne, and have implored its interposition[5] to arrest the tyrannical hands of the ministry and Parliament. Our petitions have been slighted; our remonstrances have produced additional violence and insult; our supplications have been disregarded; and we have been spurned with contempt from the foot of the throne! In vain, after these things, may we indulge the fond[6] hope of peace and reconciliation. There is no longer any room for hope. If we wish to be free, if we mean to preserve inviolate those inestimable privileges for which we have been so long contending, if we mean not basely to abandon the noble struggle in which we have been so long engaged, and which we have pledged ourselves never to abandon until the glorious object of our contest shall be obtained—we must fight! I repeat it, sir, we must fight! An appeal to arms and to the God of Hosts is all that is left us!

They tell us, sir, that we are weak—un-able to cope with so formidable an adversary. But when shall we be stronger? Will it be the next week, or the next year? Will it be when we are totally disarmed, and when a British guard shall be stationed in every house? Shall we gather strength by irresolution and inaction? Shall we acquire the means of effectual resistance by lying supinely on our backs and hugging the delusive phantom of hope until our enemies shall have bound us hand and foot? Sir, we are not weak, if we make a proper use of those means which the God of nature hath placed in our power. Three millions of people, armed in the holy cause of liberty, and in such a country as that which we possess, are invincible by any force which our enemy can send against us. Besides, sir, we shall not fight our battles alone. There is a just God who presides over the destinies of nations and who will raise up friends to fight our battles for us. The battle, sir, is not to the strong alone;[7] it is to the vigilant, the active, the brave. Besides, sir, we have no election.[8] If we were base enough to desire it, it is now too late to retire from the contest. There is no retreat but in submission and slavery! Our chains are forged! Their clanging may be heard on the plains of Boston! The war is inevitable—and let it come! I repeat it, sir, let it come!

It is in vain, sir, to extenuate the matter. Gentlemen may cry, "Peace, peace"—but there is no peace. The war is actually begun! The next gale that sweeps from the north[9] will bring to our ears the clash of resounding arms! Our brethren are already in the field! Why stand we here idle? What is it that gentlemen wish? What would they have? Is life so dear, or peace so sweet, as to be purchased at the price of chains and slavery? Forbid it, Almighty God! I know not what course others may take; but as for me, give me liberty or give me death!

---

5. interposition: Intervention.
6. fond: Foolish.

7. The battle . . . alone: "The race is not to the swift, nor the battle to the strong." (Ecclesiastes 9:11).
8. election: Choice.
9. The next gale . . . north: In Massachusetts some colonists had already shown open resistance to the British.

THINKING ABOUT THE SELECTION

Recalling

1. What comment does Henry make about the delegates who have just addressed the House?
2. What does Henry say he would be guilty of if he holds back his opinion?
3. How does Henry say that he judges the future?
4. (a) What does Henry say is the reason for the British military buildup in America? (b) What course of action must the colonists take?
5. What does Henry say "the next gale that sweeps from the north" will bring?
6. To what does Henry compare the colonists' situation?

Interpreting

7. Why do you think Henry begins his speech by stating his opinions of the previous speakers?
8. Why does Henry believe that compromise with the British is not a workable solution?
9. How does Henry answer the objection that the colonists are not ready to fight?

Applying

10. What occasion or situation might prompt a statesman to deliver such a formal, dramatic speech today?

ANALYZING LITERATURE

Recognizing Oratory

Oratory is the art of formal public speaking. A skilled orator uses such devices as rhetorical questions, restatement, repetition, and parallelism to emphasize points. For example, Henry uses restatement in his speech, repeating his declaration, "We must fight!"

1. (a) Find one instance where Henry answers a possible objection to his argument with a series of rhetorical questions. (b) What purpose does this series of questions serve?
2. List two ideas that Henry repeats, using different words.
3. Find one example of parallelism.

CRITICAL THINKING AND READING

Understanding Persuasive Techniques

An effective orator may use a number of persuasive techniques to try to convince an audience to think or act in a certain way. For example, Patrick Henry uses a blend of logical arguments and emotional appeals in his speech.

1. Considering the purpose of Henry's speech, why do you feel these two techniques were appropriate?
2. Why do you think Henry chose to end his speech with an emotional appeal?
3. Rational thought is thinking based on reason. (a) What is the difference between rational thought and rationalization? (b) Which characterizes Henry's speech? Explain.

SPEAKING AND LISTENING

Delivering a Speech

Part of what made Henry's speech successful was his dramatic delivery. Recite Henry's "Speech in the Virginia Convention" to your class, emphasizing the most important points by using gestures and varying the pitch and loudness of your voice. Speak slowly and clearly so that your audience can understand what you are saying.

THINKING AND WRITING

Writing a Speech

Imagine that you are another speaker in the Virginia Provincial Convention and you do not agree with Patrick Henry. Write a speech in which you rebut Henry's points. In your prewriting, list the arguments against Henry's ideas. Then, using some of the same oratorical devices that Henry used, write your speech. As you revise it, strengthen your arguments to make them as persuasive as you can.

THOMAS PAINE

1737–1809

Though he did not become a journalist until he was in his late thirties, Thomas Paine was the most effective American political writer of the Revolution. Throughout the war, Paine's pamphlets convinced people of the justness of the American cause and helped to inspire faltering American troops.

Born in Thetford, England, Paine left school at thirteen and worked unsuccessfully as a teacher, corset maker, sailor, and grocer. After meeting Benjamin Franklin in London, Paine decided to emigrate to the colonies to start a new life. With a letter of introduction from Franklin, Paine came to America in 1774 and began a career in journalism.

In January 1776, less than two years after his arrival in America, Paine published *Common Sense,* a pamphlet in which he accused the English king of tyranny and argued that Americans had no choice but to fight for their independence. *Common Sense,* which sold more than 120,000 copies in three months, had a powerful effect on the American public. Less than six months after the pamphlet's publication, America declared its independence.

After enlisting in the American army toward the end of 1776, Paine wrote the first of a series of sixteen essays called *The American Crisis.* Paine joined Washington's troops after they had retreated from the British in New York. Suffering from the cold weather and a shortage of provisions, the soldiers were extremely disheartened. As the troops prepared to leave Valley Forge to fight the British at Trenton, General Washington had the first of Paine's inspirational essays read to the men to raise their spirits.

In 1787, several years after the end of the Revolution, Paine traveled to Europe and became involved with the French Revolution. Though Paine supported the revolutionary cause in *The Rights of Man* (1791–1792), the French revolutionaries imprisoned him for pleading against the execution of the overthrown French king. While in prison, he began writing *The Age of Reason* (1784–1785), a sharp attack on organized religion.

When he returned to America in 1802, Paine was treated harshly by the American public for supporting the French Revolution and criticizing religion. Paine died in New York in 1809, an unhappy man, not to be recognized as an American revolutionary hero until years after his death.

from The Crisis, Number I

Writer's Techniques

Aphorisms. An aphorism is a short, pointed statement expressing a wise or clever observation or a general truth. Though aphorisms may appear by themselves, they can also be used as a part of a longer work. Because aphorisms capture our attention and are easy to remember, writers may use them to express or emphasize important points.

Thomas Paine uses aphorisms throughout *The American Crisis* to make his argument strong and memorable. By defending the American cause through a series of statements expressing general truths, Paine creates the impression that the American forces are fighting not only for their own independence but also for the cause of liberty and justice for all humankind.

Look For

As you read the excerpt from *The Crisis, Number I,* look for the aphorisms Paine uses. How do the aphorisms affect Paine's argument?

Writing

What inspirational sayings or slogans from the American Revolution can you think of? Spend five minutes brainstorming about revolutionary sayings and slogans, and list them.

Vocabulary

Knowing the following words will help you as you read the excerpt from *The Crisis, Number I.*

tyranny (tir′ə nē) *n*.: Oppressive and unjust government (p. 130)
celestial (sə les′ chəl) *adj*.: Of the heavens (p. 130)
impious (im′ pē əs) *adj*.: Lacking reverence for God (p. 130)
infidel (in′ fə d'l) *n*.: A person who holds no religious belief (p. 130)
ardor (är′ dər) *n*.: Emotional warmth; passion (p. 131)

from The Crisis, Number I

Thomas Paine

These are the times that try men's souls. The summer soldier and the sunshine patriot will in this crisis, shrink from the service of his country; but he that stands it NOW, deserves the love and thanks of man and woman. Tyranny, like hell, is not easily conquered; yet we have this consolation with us, that the harder the conflict, the more glorious the triumph. What we obtain too cheap, we esteem too lightly; 'tis dearness only that gives everything its value. Heaven knows how to put a proper price upon its goods; and it would be strange indeed, if so celestial an article as FREEDOM should not be highly rated. Britain, with an army to enforce her tyranny, has declared that she has a right (*not only to* TAX) but "to BIND *us in* ALL CASES WHATSOEVER," and if being *bound in that manner*, is not slavery, then is there not such a thing as slavery upon earth. Even the expression is impious, for so unlimited a power can belong only to God . . .

I have as little superstition in me as any man living, but my secret opinion has ever been, and still is, that God Almighty will not give up a people to military destruction, or leave them unsupportedly to perish, who have so earnestly and so repeatedly sought to avoid the calamities of war, by every decent method which wisdom could invent. Neither have I so much of the infidel in me, as to suppose that he has relinquished the government of the world, and given us up to the care of devils; and as I do not, I cannot see on what grounds the king of Britain can look up to heaven for help against us: a common murderer, a highwayman, or a housebreaker, has as good a pretense as he . . .

I once felt all that kind of anger, which a man ought to feel, against the mean[1] principles that are held by the Tories:[2] a noted one, who kept a tavern at Amboy, was standing at his door, with as pretty a child in his hand, about eight or nine years old, as I ever saw, and after speaking his mind as freely as he thought was prudent, finished with this unfatherly expression, *"Well! give me peace in my day."* Not a man lives on the continent but fully believes that a separation must some time or other finally take place, and a generous parent should have said, *"If there must be trouble let it be in my day, that my child may have peace"*; and this single reflection, well applied, is sufficient to awaken every man to duty. Not a place upon earth might be so happy as America. Her situation is remote from all the wrangling world, and she has nothing to do but to trade with them. A man can distinguish himself between temper and principle, and I am as confident, as I am that God governs the world, that America will never be happy

---

1. mean *adj.*: Here, small-minded.
2. Tories: Colonists who remained loyal to Great Britain.

RECRUITING FOR THE CONTINENTAL ARMY
William T. Ranney
Munson-Williams Proctor Institute

till she gets clear of foreign dominion. Wars, without ceasing, will break out till that period arrives, and the continent must in the end be conqueror; for though the flame of liberty may sometimes cease to shine, the coal can never expire . . .

I turn with the warm ardor of a friend to those who have nobly stood, and are yet determined to stand the matter out: I call not upon a few, but upon all; not on *this* state or *that* state, but on *every* state; up and help us; lay your shoulders to the wheel; better

have too much force than too little, when so great an object is at stake. Let it be told to the future world, that in the depth of winter, when nothing but hope and virtue could survive, that the city and the country, alarmed at one common danger, came forth to meet and to repulse it. Say not that thousands are gone, turn out your tens of thousands; throw not the burden of the day upon Providence, but *"show your faith by your works,"* that God may bless you. It matters not where you live, or what rank of life you hold, the evil or the blessing will reach you all. The far and the near, the home counties and the back, the rich and the poor, will suffer or rejoice alike. The heart that feels not now, is dead: the blood of his children will curse his cowardice, who shrinks back at a time when a little might have saved the whole, and made *them* happy. (I love the man that can smile at trouble; that can gather strength from distress, and grow brave by reflection.) 'Tis the business of little minds to shrink; but he whose heart is firm, and whose conscience approves his conduct, will pursue his principles unto death. My own line of reasoning is to myself as straight and clear as a ray of light. Not all the trea-sures of the world, so far as I believe, could have induced me to support an offensive war, for I think it murder; but if a thief breaks into my house, burns and destroys my property, and kills or threatens to kill me, or those that are in it, and to *"bind me in all cases whatsoever,"* to his absolute will, am I to suffer it? What signifies it to me, whether he who does it is a king or a common man; my countryman, or not my countryman; whether it be done by an individual villain or an army of them? If we reason to the root of things we shall find no difference; neither can any just cause be assigned why we should punish in the one case and pardon in the other.

THINKING ABOUT THE SELECTION

Recalling

1. (a) According to the first paragraph, who will "shrink from the service of his country"? (b) What will the people who do not shrink from service deserve?
2. According to the first paragraph, what has Britain declared?
3. Of what is Paine confident in the third paragraph?
4. According to the final paragraph, what will a person "whose heart is firm" pursue "unto death"?
5. What opinion of offensive wars does Paine express in the final paragraph?

Interpreting

6. What does Paine mean when he refers to "the summer soldier" and "the sunshine patriot"?
7. What is the point of Paine's story about the tavernkeeper at Amboy?
8. Name two emotions to which Paine appeals in his essay.
9. (a) What is the main idea of this essay? (b) How does Paine support his main idea?

Applying

10. How might a colonist who had remained loyal to the British react to Paine's argument?

ANALYZING LITERATURE
Using Aphorisms

An **aphorism** is a brief, pointed statement expressing a wise or clever observation or a general truth. Sometimes writers use aphorisms in their works to express or emphasize important points. For example, Paine uses the aphorism, "the harder the conflict, the more glorious the triumph," to express his belief that hardships faced by the American forces during the war will make their eventual victory more meaningful.

1. Find three more aphorisms used in Paine's essay.
2. What point does each of these aphorisms emphasize or express?

CRITICAL THINKING AND READING
Understanding the Effect of Aphorisms

Aphorisms can make a work more forceful and memorable. Because aphorisms express general truths, they can create the impression that the specific argument being presented has a more general application. For example, Paine's use of aphorisms helps to convey his belief that the American Revolution is a part of a greater struggle aimed at attaining liberty and justice for all humankind.

1. Why does the universal application of Paine's argument add to the essay's value as a work of literature?
2. What other historical situations can you think of for which Paine's essay would have been appropriate?

UNDERSTANDING LANGUAGE
Noting Synonyms

Synonyms are words that have the same or almost the same meaning. However, sometimes the slight difference in meaning is very important.

Each group below contains synonyms. Explain the difference in meaning.

1. rational   reasonable   sensible
2. irrational   unreasonable   absurd
3. reason   speculate   deliberate

THINKING AND WRITING
Writing About Revolutionary Literature

Reread the "Speech in the Virginia Convention," "The Declaration of Independence," and the excerpt from *The Crisis, Number 1,* taking notes that will help you to write an essay discussing the common purpose of revolutionary speeches and documents and the various methods used to achieve this purpose. Organize your notes into an outline, and prepare a thesis statement. Then write your essay, being sure to include passages that demonstrate the different methods and arguments used by revolutionary writers to achieve their purpose. When you finish writing, revise your essay, and prepare a final copy.

PHILLIS WHEATLEY

1753[?]–1784

Although she was a black slave whose native language was not English, Phillis Wheatley achieved success as a poet at an early age and went on to become a highly regarded American poet in the Revolutionary period.

Born in West Africa, she was brought to America on a slave ship when she was about eight years old. She was purchased by the Wheatley family of Boston, who gave her their name and converted her to Christianity. Recognizing her extraordinary intelligence, the Wheatleys taught her to read and write. Wheatley learned quickly and was soon reading the Bible, the Latin and Greek classics, and the works of the contemporary English poets. Wheatley also began writing poetry, and when she was thirteen her first poem was published.

In 1770, when she published a poem about the death of George Whitehead, a celebrated English clergyman, Wheatley became famous. Two years later, she accompanied the Wheatley's son on a trip to England, where she was introduced to a number of British aristocrats who were impressed by her poetry and helped to have *Poems on Various Subjects: Religious and Moral* published in London in 1773.

After returning to Boston in the fall of 1773, Wheatley continued to write poetry. During the Revolutionary War, she wrote several poems supporting the American cause, including a poem addressed to George Washington, the commander of the American forces. Washington was so impressed with this poem, "To His Excellency, George Washington," that he invited her to visit him at his headquarters.

Though she was freed in 1778 when John Wheatley died, the last several years of Wheatley's life were filled with hardships. She married John Peters, a free black man, but Peters had trouble maintaining a job and was eventually imprisoned for failing to pay his debts. They had three children, but two of them died in infancy. In addition, Wheatley fell into obscurity as a poet. Though she assembled a second collection of her poetry, the manuscript was lost before it could be published. With her husband in jail and her fame having faded, Phillis Wheatley died alone and impoverished in 1784.

GUIDE FOR READING

To His Excellency, General Washington

Writer's Techniques

Personification. Personification is the attribution of human powers and characteristics to something that is not human, such as an object, an aspect of nature, or an abstract idea. For instance, in the sentence, "The angry wind mercilessly pounded the walls," the wind is personified with two human qualities: anger and lack of mercy.

Throughout history, personification has fulfilled people's need to understand the world in human terms. In ancient religions, gods personified elements of the universe and the natural world. For example, the Greek god Poseidon and the Roman god Neptune were personifications of the ocean. Today, personification is often used as a part of everyday speech. In fact, certain personifications, such as "the screaming of the siren" and "the sighing of the wind," are so common that we do not even think of them as personifications.

In eighteenth-century English literature, poets often drew upon the traditions of the ancient Greek and Roman religions, personifying abstract ideas and elements of the natural world as gods or goddesses. Phillis Wheatley was greatly influenced by the work of the eighteenth-century English poets. This influence is reflected in Wheatley's personification of both America and Great Britain as goddesses in "To His Excellency, General Washington."

Look For

What does Wheatley think of General Washington? As you read "To His Excellency, General Washington" look for Wheatley's use of personification. What does it add to the poem?

Writing

Brainstorm for examples of personification in everyday language, listing your examples.

Vocabulary

Knowing the following words will help you as you read "To His Excellency, General Washington."

celestial (sə les′ chəl) *adj.*: Of the heavens (p. 137, l. 1)
refulgent (ri ful′ jənt) *adj.*: Radiant; shining (p. 137, l. 4)
propitious (prə pish′ əs) *adj.*: Favorably inclined or disposed (p. 137, l. 13)

refluent (ref′ lōō wənt) *adj.*: Flowing back (p. 137, l. 18)
pensive (pen′ siv) *adj.*: Thinking deeply or seriously (p. 138, l. 35)

GEORGE WASHINGTON AT THE BATTLE OF PRINCETON
Charles Wilson Peale
Yale University Art Gallery

To His Excellency, General Washington

Phillis Wheatley

Celestial choir! enthron'd in realms of light,
    Columbia's[1] scenes of glorious toils I write.
While freedom's cause her anxious breast alarms,
She flashes dreadful in refulgent arms.
5 See mother earth her offspring's fate bemoan,
And nations gaze at scenes before unknown!
See the bright beams of heaven's revolving light
Involved in sorrows and the veil of night!
    The goddess comes, she moves divinely fair,
10 Olive and laurel binds her golden hair:
Wherever shines this native of the skies,
Unnumber'd charms and recent graces rise.
    Muse![2] bow propitious while my pen relates
How pour her armies through a thousand gates,
15 As when Eolus[3] heaven's fair face deforms,
Enwrapp'd in tempest and a night of storms;
Astonish'd ocean feels the wild uproar,
The refluent surges beat the sounding shore;
Or thick as leaves in Autumn's golden reign,
20 Such, and so many, moves the warrior's train.
In bright array they seek the work of war,
Where high unfurl'd the ensign[4] waves in air.
Shall I to Washington their praise recite?
Enough thou know'st them in the fields of fight.
25 Thee, first in peace and honors,—we demand
The grace and glory of thy martial band.
Fam'd for thy valor, for thy virtues more,
Hear every tongue thy guardian aid implore!
    One century scarce perform'd its destined round,
30 When Gallic[5] powers Columbia's fury found;

---

1. Columbia: America personified as a goddess.
2. Muse: The goddess who presides over poetry; one
of nine muses presiding over literature, the arts, and
the sciences.
3. Eolus (ē' ə ləs): The Greek god of the winds.
4. ensign (en' s'n): Flag.
5. Gallic (găl' ik): French. The colonists, led by
Washington, defeated the French in the French and
Indian War (1754–1763).

And so may you, whoever dares disgrace
The land of freedom's heaven-defended race!
Fix'd are the eyes of nations on the scales,
For in their hopes Columbia's arm prevails.
35   Anon Britannia[6] droops the pensive head,
While round increase the rising hills of dead.
Ah! cruel blindness to Columbia's state!
Lament thy thirst of boundless power too late.
    Proceed, great chief, with virtue on thy side,
40   Thy ev'ry action let the goddess guide.
A crown, a mansion, and a throne that shine,
With gold unfading, WASHINGTON! be thine.

---

6. Britannia: England.

THINKING ABOUT THE SELECTION

Recalling

1. What cause does Columbia's "anxious breast" alarm?
2. (a) What question does Wheatley ask in line 23? (b) How does she answer this question?
3. According to line 33, whose eyes are fixed "on the scales"?
4. What outcome of the war does Wheatley say that other nations hope for?
5. According to line 39, what does Washington have on his side?

Interpreting

6. (a) Find three instances in which Wheatley indicates a relationship between God and the American cause. (b) What is the nature of this relationship?
7. What does Wheatley suggest about the American forces in comparisons made in lines 13–20?
8. (a) What are the "scales" Wheatley refers to in line 33? (b) Why are eyes fixed on them?
9. What do the last two lines indicate about the influence of the British social and political systems on American thinking?

Applying

10. What does this poem suggest about Wheatley's feelings regarding her country?

ANALYZING LITERATURE

Recognizing Personification

Personification is the attribution of human powers to something that is not human, such as an inanimate object or an abstract idea. For example, in "To His Excellency, General Washington," Phillis Wheatley personifies America as the goddess Columbia.

1. How does Wheatley characterize Columbia?
2. What details does she use in describing Columbia's physical appearance?
3. What is the significance of the physical details Wheatley uses in describing Columbia?
4. What does the god Eolus (line 15) personify?
5. How does Wheatley personify Britain?

CRITICAL THINKING AND READING

Evaluating the Effect of Personification

Personification makes it possible for us to understand a subject in human terms. For example, in "To His Excellency, General Washington" we are able to view American ideals and beliefs as character traits of the goddess Columbia.

1. Explain how Wheatley's use of personification makes us sympathize more readily with the American cause.
2. Compare and contrast Wheatley's personification of America as the goddess Columbia with the common personification of the United States as Uncle Sam.

THINKING AND WRITING

Developing a Personification

What type of person would best personify America today? Prepare to write a poem or several paragraphs in which you personify America. First, develop a list of character traits that express the ideals and beliefs of today's society. Think of how you would describe the physical appearance of a man or woman who personifies America, and think about how this person would behave. Then develop your personification of America as a man or woman through your description of his or her appearance, behavior, and character traits. When you finish writing, revise your poem or paragraphs and prepare a final copy.

THOMAS JEFFERSON

1743–1826

Thomas Jefferson is one of the most widely respected and admired figures in American history. A gifted writer, diplomat, political leader, inventor, architect, philosopher, and educator, with an intense belief in equal rights and individual freedoms, Jefferson played a significant role in the creation and shaping of America.

Born into a wealthy Virginia family, Jefferson received a thorough classical education as a boy. After graduating from the College of William and Mary in 1762, Jefferson spent five years studying law. In 1769, two years after Jefferson received his license to practice law, he was elected to the Virginia House of Burgesses. While serving in the House, Jefferson became an outspoken defender of American rights. After Jefferson displayed his persuasive abilities in his pamphlet *A Summary View of the Rights of British America* (1774), he was chosen to draft the Declaration of Independence at the Second Continental Congress in 1776.

When the Revolutionary War ended, Jefferson served as the American minister to France for several years. He then became America's first Secretary of State in 1789. In 1801, after he served as Vice-President under John Adams, Jefferson became the third American President. While in office, Jefferson nearly doubled the size of the nation by authorizing the purchase of the Louisiana Territory from France.

In 1809 Jefferson retired to Monticello, the Virginia home he had designed, and devoted his time to reading, conducting scientific experiments, collecting paintings, and playing the violin. Jefferson also helped to found the University of Virginia, designing the campus and planning the curriculum.

On July 4, 1826, the fiftieth anniversary of the Declaration of Independence, Thomas Jefferson died.

GUIDE FOR READING

The Declaration of Independence

Writer's Techniques

Parallelism. Parallelism refers to the repeated use of phrases, clauses, or sentences that are similar in structure or meaning. Writers use this technique to emphasize important ideas, create rhythm, and make their writing forceful and direct. In the Declaration of Independence, Thomas Jefferson uses parallelism when listing the reasons that Americans feel compelled to declare their independence. Jefferson's use of parallelism makes his argument grow stronger with each reason he presents.

Look For

The Declaration of Independence is a well-known and internationally respected document. One of its memorable features is its style. As you read it, look for the parallel statements that add force to Jefferson's arguments.

Writing

What does freedom mean to you? Prepare a journal entry in which you discuss your ideas about the concept of freedom. Include specific examples.

Vocabulary

Knowing the following words will help you as you read the Declaration of Independence.

unalienable (un āl′ yən ə b′l) *adj.*: Not to be taken away (p. 142)

usurpations (yoo′ sər pā shənz) *n.*: Unlawful seizures of rights or privileges (p. 142)

candid (kan′ did) *adj.*: Impartial (p. 142)

perfidy (pər′ fə dē) *n.*: Betrayal of trust (p. 144)

redress (ri dres′) *v.*: Compensation for a wrong done (p. 144)

magnanimity (mag′nə nim′ə tē) *n.*: Ability to rise above pettiness or meanness (p. 144)

consanguinity (kän′ saŋ gwin′ə tē) *n.*: Kinship (p. 144)

acquiesce (ak′ wē es′) *v.*: Agree without protest (p. 144)

The Declaration of Independence

Thomas Jefferson

When in the course of human events, it becomes necessary for one people to dissolve the political bands which have connected them with another, and to assume among the powers of the earth, the separate and equal station to which the laws of nature and of nature's God entitle them, a decent respect to the opinions of mankind requires that they should declare the causes which impel them to the separation.

We hold these truths to be self-evident: that all men are created equal; that they are endowed by their Creator with certain unalienable rights; that among these are life, liberty and the pursuit of happiness; that to secure these rights, governments are instituted among men, deriving their just powers from the consent of the governed; that whenever any form of government becomes destructive of these ends, it is the right of the people to alter or to abolish it, and to institute new government, laying its foundation on such principles and organizing its powers in such form, as to them shall seem most likely to effect their safety and happiness. Prudence, indeed, will dictate that governments long established should not be changed for light and transient causes; and accordingly all experience hath shown, that mankind are more disposed to suffer while evils are sufferable than to right themselves by abolishing the forms to which they are accustomed. But when a long train of abuses and usurpations, pursuing invariably the same object, evinces a design to reduce them under absolute despotism,[1] it is their right, it is their duty, to throw off such government, and to provide new guards for their future security. Such has been the patient sufferance of these colonies; and such is now the necessity which constrains[2] them to alter their former systems of government. The history of the present king of Great Britain is a history of repeated injuries and usurpations, all having in direct object the establishment of an absolute tyranny over these states. To prove this, let facts be submitted to a candid world.

He has refused his assent to laws the most wholesome and necessary for the public good.

He has forbidden his governors to pass laws of immediate and pressing importance, unless suspended in their operation till his assent should be obtained; and when so suspended, he has utterly neglected to attend to them.

He has refused to pass other laws for the accommodation of large districts of people, unless those people would relinquish the right of representation in the legislature, a right inestimable to them and formidable to tyrants only.

He has called together legislative bodies at places unusual, uncomfortable, and distant from the depository of their public rec-

---

1. despotism (des′ pə tiz′m) *n.*: Tyranny.
2. constrains *v.*: Forces.

THE DECLARATION OF INDEPENDENCE
John Trumbull
Yale University Art Gallery

ords, for the sole purpose of fatiguing them into compliance with his measures.

He has dissolved representative houses repeatedly, for opposing with manly firmness his invasions on the rights of the people.

He has refused for a long time after such dissolutions to cause others to be elected, whereby the legislative powers, incapable of annihilation, have returned to the people at large for their exercise, the state remaining in the mean time exposed to all the dangers of invasion from without, and convulsions within.

He has endeavored to prevent the population of these states; for that purpose obstructing the laws for naturalization of foreigners, refusing to pass others to encourage their migration hither, and raising the conditions of new appropriations of lands.

He has obstructed the administration of justice, by refusing his assent to laws for establishing judiciary powers.

He has made judges dependent on his will alone, for the tenure of their offices, and the amount and payment of their salaries.

He has erected a multitude of new offices, and sent hither swarms of officers to harass our people and eat out their substance.

He has kept among us in times of peace standing armies without the consent of our legislatures.

He has affected to render the military independent of, and superior to, the civil power.

He has combined with others to subject us to a jurisdiction foreign to our constitution and unacknowledged by our laws, giving his assent to their acts of pretended legislation: for quartering large bodies of armed troops among us; for protecting them by a mock trial from punishment for any murders which they should commit on the inhabitants of these states; for cutting off our trade with all parts of the world; for imposing taxes on us without our consent; for depriving us, in many cases, of the benefits of trial by jury; for transporting us beyond seas to be tried for pretended offenses; for abolishing the free system of English laws in a neighboring province,[3] establishing therein an arbitrary government, and enlarging its boundaries, so as to render it at once an example and fit instrument for introducing the same absolute rule into these colonies; for taking away our charters, abolishing our most valuable laws, and altering fundamentally the forms of our governments; for suspending our own legislatures, and declaring themselves invested with power to legislate for us in all cases whatsoever.

He has abdicated government here, by declaring us out of his protection and waging war against us.

He has plundered our seas, ravaged our coasts, burned our towns, and destroyed the lives of our people.

He is at this time transporting large armies of foreign mercenaries to complete the works of death, desolation, and tyranny, already begun with circumstances of cruelty and perfidy scarcely paralleled in the most barbarous ages, and totally unworthy the head of a civilized nation.

He has constrained our fellow citizens taken captive on the high seas to bear arms against their country, to become the executioners of their friends and brethren, or to fall themselves by their hands.

He has excited domestic insurrections amongst us, and has endeavored to bring on the inhabitants of our frontiers, the merciless Indian savages, whose known rule of warfare is an undistinguished destruction of all ages, sexes, and conditions.

In every stage of these oppressions we have petitioned for redress in the most humble terms. Our repeated petitions have been answered only by repeated injury.

A prince whose character is thus marked by every act which may define a tyrant is unfit to be the ruler of a free people.

Nor have we been wanting in attentions to our British brethren. We have warned them from time to time of attempts by their legislature to extend an unwarrantable jurisdiction over us. We have reminded them of the circumstances of our emigration and settlement here. We have appealed to their native justice and magnanimity and we have conjured[4] them by the ties of our common kindred to disavow these usurpations which would inevitably interrupt our connections and correspondence. They too have been deaf to the voice of justice and of consanguinity. We must therefore acquiesce in the necessity which denounces[5] our separation and hold them, as we hold the rest of mankind, enemies in war, in peace friends.

We, therefore, the representatives of the United States of America in general congress assembled, appealing to the Supreme Judge of the world for the rectitude of our intentions, do in the name and by authority of the good people of these colonies, solemnly publish and declare that these united colonies are and of right ought to be free and independent states; that they are absolved from all allegiance to the British Crown, and that all political connection between them and the state of Great Britain is and ought to be totally dissolved; and that as free and independent states, they have full power to levy war, conclude peace, contract alliances, establish commerce, and to do all other acts and things which independent states may of right do.

And for the support of this declaration, with a firm reliance on the protection of divine providence, we mutually pledge to each other our lives, our fortunes and our sacred honor.

---

3. **neighboring province:** Quebec.

4. **conjured:** Solemnly appealed to.
5. **denounces:** Here, announces.

THINKING ABOUT THE SELECTION

Recalling

1. What are the three "unalienable rights" listed in the second paragraph?
2. (a) According to Jefferson, what is the purpose of a government? (b) When should a government be abolished?
3. List three of the statements Jefferson presents to support his claim that the king's objective is "the establishment of an absolute tyranny over these states"?
4. (a) What does Jefferson claim the colonists have done at "every stage of these oppressions"? (b) How has the king responded to the colonists' actions?
5. What pledge is made in the last paragraph?

Interpreting

6. What effect does Jefferson's long list of specific grievances have on his argument?
7. Why does Jefferson focus his attack on King George III rather than on the British Parliament or people?
8. How is the eighteenth-century faith in reason reflected in the Declaration?

Applying

9. Considering Jefferson's views concerning the purpose of a government, to what governments in today's world might he object?

ANALYZING LITERATURE

Recognizing Parallelism

Parallelism refers to the repeated use of phrases, clauses, or sentences that are similar in structure or meaning. For example, Jefferson lists the colonists' grievances in a series of sentences with the same structure.

1. Find another example of Jefferson's use of parallel structure.
2. In what ways does Jefferson's use of parallelism strengthen his argument?

CRITICAL THINKING AND READING

Recognizing Charged Words

In presenting an argument, a writer may appeal to emotions indirectly through the use of emotionally charged words. **Charged words** are words with strong connotations beyond their literal meanings that are likely to produce an emotional response. For example, the word *tyranny* evokes a feeling of fear. It suggests living in a state of terror, afraid of being jailed or executed for disagreeing with governmental policies.

What associations are evoked by each of the following words from the Declaration of Independence?

1. liberty   2. justice   3. honor

THINKING AND WRITING

Comparing and Contrasting Arguments

The Declaration of Independence and Patrick Henry's "Speech in the Virginia Convention" are both powerful arguments for American independence. In what ways are the two arguments similar? In what ways are they different? Reread both documents carefully and list similarities and differences in format, content, and persuasive techniques. Review your notes to help you develop your thesis statement; then prepare an outline. When you write your essay, make sure that you include passages from both selections to support your argument. After you finish writing, review your essay, making sure you have included enough information to support your thesis.

ABIGAIL SMITH ADAMS

1744–1818

Abigail Smith Adams, the wife of John Adams, the second President of the United States, and the mother of John Quincy Adams, the sixth President, was one of the most important and influential American women of her time. A dedicated supporter of women's rights and the American Revolutionary movement, Adams wrote many letters to her husband and other members of her family expressing her opinions. In these letters, Adams included vivid descriptions that capture the essence of life in early America.

Abigail Smith was born in Weymouth, Massachusetts. At the age of twenty, she married John Adams. The couple had four sons and one daughter, and Abigail made sure that her daughter received a thorough education—something few American girls received at the time.

In 1774, when John left home to serve as a member of the Continental Congress, Abigail assumed the responsibility of managing the family farm in what is now Quincy, Massachusetts. Because of John's political involvement, John and Abigail were separated from each other for most of the next ten years. During this period Abigail became an avid letter writer. In her letters, Abigail provided her husband with information about British troops and ships in the Boston area, stressed the importance of women's rights, and voiced her opposition to slavery.

When John Adams was elected President of the United States, John and Abigail Adams became the first couple to live in the White House. Among the letters Abigail wrote while living there is one to her daughter describing her temporary home. This letter and the others she wrote during this period provide an interesting view of life in the new nation.

Abigail Adams died in 1818, after spending the last seventeen years of her life at the Adams's family home in Massachusetts. In 1840 a volume of her letters was published, and since then three more volumes have been published. Today, Abigail Adams is widely recognized as a writer and a pioneer of the American women's movement.

GUIDE FOR READING

Writer's Techniques

Letter to Her Daughter from the New White House

Description. Descriptive writing creates an impression of a person, place, or thing through the use of details appealing to one or more of the five senses—sight, sound, taste, smell, and touch. In a description, a writer includes enough details to enable us to visualize the subject. Because a writer cannot use all the details of the subject in a description, he or she selects those details that create a desired impression.

Abigail Adams lived in the days before cameras were invented. Her descriptions provided the equivalent of snapshots. In passages in her letters, she described for her daughter what the White House looked like and what it was like to live there. When we read Adams's letter, the contrast between her description of the White House and our perceptions of today's White House make the impression created by Adams even more striking.

Look For

How do you envision the White House? As you read "Letter to Her Daughter from the New White House," look for Abigail Adams's impression of the White House. What details does she use to convey her impression?

Writing

What details would you include in a description of your city hall? List its most significant and striking details.

Vocabulary

Knowing the following words will help you as you read "Letter to Her Daughter from the New White House."

extricate (eks′ trə kāt) v. To set free (p. 148)

agues (ā gyōōz) n.: Fits of shivering (p. 148)

Letter to Her Daughter from the New White House

Abigail Adams

Washington, 21 November, 1800

My Dear Child:

I arrived here on Sunday last, and without meeting with any accident worth noticing, except losing ourselves when we left Baltimore and going eight or nine miles on the Frederick road, by which means we were obliged to go the other eight through woods, where we wandered two hours without finding a guide or the path. Fortunately, a straggling black came up with us, and we engaged him as a guide to extricate us out of our difficulty; but woods are all you see from Baltimore until you reach *the city*, which is only so in name. Here and there is a small cot, without a glass window, interspersed amongst the forests, through which you travel miles without seeing any human being. In the city there are buildings enough, if they were compact and finished, to accommodate Congress and those attached to it; but as they are, and scattered as they are, I see no great comfort for them. The river, which runs up to Alexandria,[1] is in full view of my window, and I see the vessels as they pass and repass. The house is upon a grand and superb scale, requiring about thirty servants to attend and keep the apartments in proper order, and perform the ordinary business of the house and stables; an establishment very well proportioned to the President's salary. The lighting of the apartments, from the kitchen to parlors and chambers, is a tax indeed; and the fires we are obliged to keep to secure us from daily agues is another very cheering comfort. To assist us in this great castle, and render less attendance necessary, bells are wholly wanting, not one single one being hung through the whole house, and promises are all you can obtain. This is so great an inconvenience, that I know not what to do, or how to do. The ladies from Georgetown[2] and in the city have many of them visited me. Yesterday I returned fifteen visits—but such a place as Georgetown appears—why, our Milton is beautiful. But no comparisons—if they will put me up some bells and let me have wood enough to keep fires, I design to be pleased. I could content myself almost anywhere three months; but, surrounded with forests, can you believe that wood is not to be had because people cannot be found to cut and cart it? Briesler entered into a contract with a man to supply him with wood. A small part, a few cords only, has he been able to get. Most of that was expended to dry the walls of the house before we came in, and yesterday the man told him it was impossible for him to procure it to be cut and carted. He has had recourse to coals; but we cannot get grates made and set. We have, indeed, come into a *new country.*

---

1. Alexandria: A city in northeastern Virginia.

2. Georgetown: A section of Washington, D.C.

BUILDING THE FIRST WHITE HOUSE
N. C. Wyeth
Copyrighted by the White House Historical Association

You must keep all this to yourself, and, when asked how I like it, say that I write you the situation is beautiful, which is true. The house is made habitable, but there is not a single apartment finished, and all within-side, except the plastering, has been done since Briesler came. We have not the least fence, yard, or other convenience, without, and the great unfinished audience room I make a drying-room of, to hang up the clothes in. The principal stairs are not up, and will not be this winter. Six chambers are made comfortable; two are occupied by the President and Mr. Shaw; two lower rooms, one for a common parlor, and one for a levee room. Upstairs there is the oval room, which is designed for the drawing room, and has the crimson furniture in it. It is a very handsome room now; but, when completed, it will be beautiful. If the twelve years, in which this place has been considered as the future seat of government, had been improved, as they would have been if in New England, very many of the present inconveniences would have been removed. It is a beautiful spot, capable of every improvement, and, the more I view it, the more I am delighted with it.

Since I sat down to write, I have been called down to a servant from Mount Vernon,[3] with a billet[4] from Major Custis, and a haunch of venison, and a kind, congratulatory letter from Mrs. Lewis, upon my arrival in the city, with Mrs. Washington's love, inviting me to Mount Vernon, where, health permitting, I will go before I leave this place.

Affectionately, your mother,
Abigail Adams

---

3. Mount Vernon: Home of George Washington, located in northern Virginia.
4. billet (bil′ it) *n*.: A brief letter.

THINKING ABOUT THE SELECTION
Recalling

1. By what is Washington, D.C., surrounded?
2. (a) Why are the Adamses "obliged to keep" a fire burning in the fireplace? (b) Why is there very little firewood?
3. Describe the state of the living quarters in the White House.
4. At the end of her letter, what invitation does Adams mention receiving?

Interpreting

5. What do you think is Adams's attitude toward living in the White House? Explain how her selection of details conveys this attitude.

6. Why do you think Adams tells her daughter to keep her complaints about the White House to herself?

Applying

7. Name two contrasts between Adams's description of the White House and Washington, D.C., and the appearance of the building and the city today.

ANALYZING LITERATURE
Recognizing Descriptive Writing

Descriptive writing creates an impression of a person, place, or thing through details appealing to one or more of the five senses. For example, one of the details Abigail Adams includes in her description of the surroundings of the White House is "the river, which runs up to Alexandria."

1. Name four details, including some that appeal to senses other than sight, that Adams includes in her description of the interior of the White House.
2. What impression of the White House does Adams's description create?
3. How does her description of the area surrounding the White House add to this impression?

CRITICAL THINKING AND READING
Inferring a Writer's Attitude

Writers often convey their attitude toward a subject through their description of it. Though in some cases the writer's attitude may be directly stated, most often you have to make inferences, or draw conclusions, about the writer's attitude by examining his or her choice of words or details. For example, from Adams's statement that "woods are all you see from Baltimore until you reach the city, which is so only in name" you can infer that Adams felt that Washington, D.C., was isolated and undeveloped.

What inference can you make from each of the following passages from the "Letter to Her Daughter"?

1. "In the city there are buildings enough, if they were compact and finished, to accommodate Congress and those attached to it; but as they are, and scattered as they are, I see no great comfort for them."
2. "The house is upon a grand and superb scale. . . ."
3. "We have not the least fence, yard, or other convenience, without. . . ."

UNDERSTANDING LANGUAGE
Tracing Word Origins

Many words in English were borrowed or derived from other languages. For example, the word *extricate* comes from the Latin *extricare* meaning "to disentangle."

Using a dictionary that provides etymologies, find the earliest language or origin of each of the following words found in the "Letter to Her Daughter from the New White House."

1. interspersed
2. superb
3. apartment
4. furniture
5. congratulatory

THINKING AND WRITING
Writing a Description

Review your list of details about your city hall. Selecting appropriate details from your list, write a description of some aspect of your city hall, such as the exterior. Write a description, presenting your details in spatial order. When you revise try to think about how someone who has never seen your city hall would respond to your description. Have you included enough details to enable a person to visualize it? Have you included too many for a brief description?

MICHEL-GUILLAUME JEAN DE CRÈVECOEUR

1735–1813

The first writer to compare America to a melting pot, Michel-Guillaume Jean de Crèvecoeur chronicled his experiences and observations as a European immigrant adjusting to life in America. His idealistic descriptions confirmed many people's vision of America as a land of great promise.

Born into a wealthy French aristocratic family, Crèvecoeur emigrated to Canada at the age of nineteen and served for several years as a member of the French army in Quebec. After his military career ended in 1759, Crèvecoeur spent ten years traveling throughout the colonies as a surveyor and Indian trader. In 1769, Crèvecoeur married and settled on a 120-acre farm in Orange County, New York. While living on his farm, which he named Pine Hill, Crèvecoeur began writing about his experiences in America.

Because his position during the Revolutionary War was ambiguous, Crèvecoeur was at one point forced by the revolutionaries to leave his farm; another time he was imprisoned for several months by the British. In 1780 Crèvecoeur sailed to London, where his *Letters from an American Farmer* was published two years later. The book, which was translated into several languages, was successful and made Crèvecoeur famous.

Crèvecoeur's good fortune did not last, however. When he returned to America in 1783 as the French consul to New York, New Jersey, and Connecticut, he discovered that his farm had been burned, his wife killed, and his children sent to live with foster parents in Boston. In 1790 he returned to France, where he spent the remainder of his life.

GUIDE FOR READING

from Letters from an American Farmer

Literary Forms

Epistles. An epistle, or literary letter, is a formal composition written in the form of a letter addressed to a distant person or group of people. Unlike common personal letters, which tend to be conversational and private compositions, epistles are carefully-crafted works of literature, intended for a general audience.

The epistle has been a popular literary form throughout history. In ancient Greece and Rome, philosophers recorded their thoughts in epistle form. Centuries later the epistle form was used in the New Testament. During the eighteenth century, European writers frequently composed their works—poems, essays, and novels—using the epistle form.

Influenced by the eighteenth-century European writers, Crèvecoeur chose the epistle form for his essays about life in America. Crèvecoeur's letters are supposedly written by an American farmer named "James" to his friend "Mr. F. B.," but in reality they are intended for a general audience. By presenting his essays in this form, Crèvecoeur is able to maintain a personal tone, while attempting to convince the general pubic to accept his ideas and opinions.

Look For

As you read the excerpt from *Letters from an American Farmer,* look for the details through which Crèvecoeur creates an intimate tone while expressing opinions intended for a general audience.

Writing

What does being an American mean to you? Freewrite about what you associate with being an American.

Vocabulary

Knowing the following words will help you as you read the excerpt from *Letters from an American Farmer.*

asylum (ə sī′ ləm) *n.*: Place of refuge (p. 154)

penury (pen′ yə rē) *n.*: Lack of money, property, or necessities (p. 154)

metamorphosis (met′ ə môr′ fə sis) *n.*: Transformation (p. 154)

despotic (de spät′ ik) *adj.*: Harsh, cruel, unjust (p. 156)

servile (ser′ v'l) *adj.*: Humbly yielding or submissive (p. 156)

subsistence (səb sis′ təns) *n.*: Means of support (p. 156)

from Letters from an American Farmer

Michel-Guillaume Jean de Crèvecoeur

In this great American asylum, the poor of Europe have by some means met together, and in consequence of various causes; to what purpose should they ask one another what countrymen they are? Alas, two thirds of them had no country. Can a wretch who wanders about, who works and starves, whose life is a continual scene of sore affliction or pinching penury, can that man call England or any other kingdom his country? A country that had no bread for him, whose fields procured him no harvest, who met with nothing but the frowns of the rich, the severity of the laws, with jails and punishments; who owned not a single foot of the extensive surface of this planet? No! Urged by a variety of motives, here they came. Everything has tended to regenerate them; new laws, a new mode of living, a new social system; here they are become men: in Europe they were as so many useless plants, wanting vegetative mold[1] and refreshing showers; they withered, and were mowed down by want, hunger, and war; but now by the power of transplantation, like all other plants they have taken root and flourished! Formerly they were not numbered in any civil lists[2] of their country, except in those of the poor; here they rank as citizens. By what invisible power has this surprising metamorphosis been performed? By that of the laws and that of their industry. The laws, the indulgent laws, protect them as they arrive, stamping on them the symbol of adoption; they receive ample rewards for their labors; these accumulated rewards procure them lands; those lands confer on them the title of freemen, and to that title every benefit is affixed which men can possibly require. This is the great operation daily performed by our laws. From whence proceed these laws? From our government. Whence the government? It is derived from the original genius and strong desire of the people ratified and confirmed by the crown. . . .

What attachment can a poor European emigrant have for a country where he had nothing? The knowledge of the language, the love of a few kindred as poor as himself, were the only cords that tied him: his country is now that which gives him land, bread, protection, and consequence: *Ubi panis ibi patria*[3] is the motto of all emigrants. What then is the American, this new man? He is either a European, or the descendant of a European, hence that strange mixture of blood, which you will find in no other country. I could point out to you a family whose grandfather was an Englishman, whose wife was Dutch, whose son married a French woman, and whose present four sons have now four wives of different nations. *He* is an American, who, leaving behind him all his ancient prejudices and manners, receives

---

1. vegetative mold: Enriched soil.
2. civil lists: Lists of distinguished persons.

3. *Ubi . . . patria*: "Where there is bread, there is one's fatherland" (Latin).

new ones from the new mode of life he has embraced, the new government he obeys, and the new rank he holds. He becomes an American by being received in the broad lap of our great *Alma Mater*.[4] Here individuals of all nations are melted into a new race of men, whose labors and posterity will one day cause great changes in the world. Americans are the western pilgrims, who are carrying along with them that great mass of arts, sciences, vigor, and industry which began long since in the east; they will finish the great circle. The Americans were once scattered all over Europe; here they are incorporated into one of the finest systems of population

---

4. *Alma Mater* (al′ mə mä′ tər): "Fostering mother." Here, referring to America; usually used in reference to a school or college.

INDEPENDENCE (SQUIRE JACK PORTER) 1858
Frank Blackwell Mayer
National Museum of American Art, Smithsonian Institution

from *Letters from an American Farmer* 155

which has ever appeared, and which will hereafter become distinct by the power of the different climates they inhabit. The American ought therefore to love this country much better than that wherein either he or his forefathers were born. Here the rewards of his industry follow with equal steps the progress of his labor; his labor is founded on the basis of nature, *self-interest;* can it want a stronger allurement? Wives and children, who before in vain demanded of him a morsel of bread, now, fat and frolicsome, gladly help their father to clear those fields whence exuberant crops are to arise to feed and to clothe them all; without any part being claimed, either by a despotic prince, a rich abbot,[5] or a mighty lord. Here religion demands but little of him; a small voluntary salary to the minister, and gratitude to God; can he refuse these? The American is a new man, who acts upon new principles; he must therefore entertain new ideas, and form new opinions. From involuntary idleness, servile dependence, penury, and useless labor, he has passed to toils of a very different nature, rewarded by ample subsistence—This is an American.

---

5. abbot *n.:* The head of a monastery.

THINKING ABOUT THE SELECTION

Recalling

1. What has "tended to regenerate" the European immigrants into America?
2. From what is the colonial system of government "derived"?
3. According to the second paragraph, "what attachment can a poor European have for a country where he had nothing"?
4. What prediction does Crèvecoeur make about the impact the "new race of men" in America will one day have on the rest of the world?

Interpreting

5. (a) What is the logic of Crèvecoeur's arguments? (b) What are his premises? (c) What is his support?
6. (a) How would you summarize Crèvecoeur's definition of an American? (b) Why does he refer to an American as a "new man"?
7. (a) Find two examples of exaggeration in Crèvecoeur's description of life in America. (b) Why does he use exaggeration?

Applying

8. Do you think Crèvecoeur would have written his epistle today? If so, what has stayed essentially the same? If not, what are the important differences?

ANALYZING LITERATURE

Understanding Epistles

An **epistle,** or literary letter, is a formal composition written in the form of a letter addressed to a distant person or group of people. Crèvecoeur's essays in *Letters from an American Farmer* are written in epistle form. The letters are addressed to a fictional character named "Mr. F. B.," though in reality they are intended for a general audience.

One way that Crèvecoeur establishes a personal tone is to use the pronoun *you* in addressing his audience. How does does the epistle form allow him to maintain a personal tone, while attempting to convince the general public to accept his ideas and opinions? Support your answer with passages from the selection.

CRITICAL THINKING AND READING

Supporting Opinions

A **fact** can be proved true or false. An **opinion** is a personal belief, altitude, or judgment that cannot be proved. However, an opinion that is supported by facts, we call well-grounded or sound.

Identify the facts de Crèvecoeur uses to back up each of the following opinions.
1. ". . . here they are become men: in Europe they were so many useless plants . . ."
2. "The American ought therefore to love this country much better than that wherein either he or his forefathers were born."

THINKING AND WRITING

Writing an Epistle

What does it mean to be an American today? Review your freewriting about being an American. Spend some time brainstorming about the people who live in America, the opportunities they have, and the difficulties they may face. Record your thoughts so that you can write an epistle discussing what it means to be an American today. Address your letter to a fictional person in a foreign country. Then write your letter, using examples to support your opinions. Try to maintain a personal tone. When you revise, make sure that your letter is well-organized and that your opinions are stated clearly.

YOU THE WRITER

Assignment

1. Imagine that you are an American colonist and it has become increasingly apparent to you that a war with the British is inevitable. Write a journal entry in which you express your thoughts and feelings about the impending Revolution.

Prewriting. Spend some time reflecting about how the colonists must have felt as the Revolutionary War approached. List some of the thoughts, hopes, and fears you imagine they must have had.

Writing. When you write your journal entry, use an informal, conversational writing style.

Revising. When you revise, make sure your entry clearly conveys your thoughts and feelings. After you finish revising, proofread your entry and prepare a final copy.

Assignment

2. When the Revolutionary War finally ended and the colonists had won their independence, many of the colonial leaders were viewed as national heroes. Imagine that you are an American who has just lived through the war, and write a letter to a Revolutionary hero, discussing his or her contributions to the American cause and expressing your gratitude.

Prewriting . Choose a Revolutionary hero. Then outline his or her contributions to the American cause.

Writing. When you write your letter, use an informal writing style but make sure the letter is organized in a logical manner.

Revising. When you revise, make sure you have used transitions and other linking devices to connect your ideas. After you finish revising, proofread your letter and prepare a final copy.

Assignment

3. Imagine that it is 1775 and you are a colonial leader who has become increasingly dissatisfied with British rule. Write an essay in which you attempt to persuade other colonists to join together in a unified revolt against British rule.

Prewriting. Start by reviewing the unit introduction (p. 84) and the selections by Patrick Henry (p. 124), Thomas Paine (p. 130), and Thomas Jefferson (p. 142), noting the reasons why the colonists felt compelled to revolt against the British.

Writing. In your essay, present a series of reasons why the colonists must revolt, and use such persuasive devices as restatement and repetition.

Revising. When you revise, make sure your essay is logically organized and that you have used examples to support your argument.

Assignment

1. During the Colonial Period there was a great deal of emphasis on discipline and restraint. Write an essay in which you discuss how this emphasis is reflected in one of the selections you have read.

Prewriting. Review the selections in this unit, and choose a selection that reflects the colonial emphasis on discipline and restraint. Then reread the selection, noting how the emphasis is reflected in its form and content and in the style in which it is written.

Writing. When you write your essay, use evidence from the selection to support your argument.

Revising. When you revise, make sure your essay is logically organized and that you have thoroughly supported your argument. After you finish revising, proofread your essay and prepare a final copy.

Assignment

2. The Colonial Period is often called the Age of Reason, because it was characterized by an emphasis on reason and logic. Write an essay in which you analyze how the process of reasoning is used in one of the selections you have read.

Prewriting. Choose a selection in which the reasoning process is used. Then review this selection, noting how the writer uses the reasoning process to develop a logical argument.

Writing. Include your thesis statement in the introduction of your essay. In the body of the essay, present evidence from the selection to support your thesis.

Revising. When you revise, make sure you have included enough evidence to thoroughly support your thesis.

Assignment

3. During the Colonial Period, a revolutionary spirit swept through the land, inspiring the colonists to fight for their independence. Write an essay in which you discuss how this spirit is expressed in the literature of the period.

Prewriting. Choose three selections that express the revolutionary spirit. Reread each of these selections, noting how the spirit is conveyed. Prepare a thesis statement and organize your notes into an outline.

Writing. When you write your essay, use passages from each of the selections to support your thesis.

Revising. When you revise, make sure you have thoroughly supported your thesis and have not included any unnecessary information. After you finish revising, proofread your essay and prepare a final copy.

NIAGARA FALLS, ABOUT 1832—1840
Thomas Chambers
Wadsworth Atheneum, Hartford

A GROWING NATION
1800–1840

America is a land of wonders, in which everything is in constant motion and every change seems an improvement. . . . No natural boundary seems to be set to the efforts of man; and in his eyes what is not yet done is only what he has not yet attempted to do.

Alexis de Tocqueville

In 1831, Alexis de Tocqueville, a young Frenchman, journeyed to the United States to report on the American penitentiary system for his government. He observed far more than prisons during his stay, however. His observations were compiled in a monumental four-volume work, *Democracy in America,* that is considered a classic of political literature. While Tocqueville was impressed by the bustle and optimism that he noted, he was not as impressed by American literature. "America has produced very few writers of distinction," he wrote, adding that the literary output of England "still darts its rays into the forests of the New World."

Tocqueville had perhaps arrived a few years too soon. At the very time he was in the United States, a number of writers of distinction were at work. Among them were Washington Irving, James Fenimore Cooper, William Cullen Bryant, and Edgar Allan Poe, all of whom would achieve fame and acceptance far beyond "the forests of the New World."

THE HISTORICAL SETTING

When Thomas Jefferson was elected President in 1800, three new states, Vermont, Kentucky, and Tennessee, had joined the original thirteen. Then in 1803, at the stroke of a pen, the Louisiana Purchase doubled the nation's territory. By 1837, when Michigan became a state, more than half the present-day fifty states were in the Union.

The rapid growth of the nation brought with it an upsurge of na-

LOUISIANA PURCHASE CEREMONY AT NEW ORLEANS, 20 DECEMBER 1803
Thor de Thulstrup
The Granger Collection

ERIE CANAL NEAR LITTLE FALLS
W. R. Miller
Three Lions

tional pride and identity. Improved transportation helped bind the old and the new states together. Canals, turnpikes, and railroads boomed during this period. Steamboats and sailing packets helped speed people and goods to their destinations. The westward expansion of the United States and its explosive growth in population had profound effects on American life and literature.

Old New York

By 1800, the country's frontier had moved far away from the East Coast. Yet there were other kinds of national frontiers. In the early 1800's, New York, the city that Washington Irving called "Gotham," was becoming a sort of American literary frontier.

New York City had a population of 60,000 in 1800, making it the second largest city in the nation after Philadelphia. A decade later, it passed Philadelphia and was never again challenged for population leadership. By 1840, the population of New York City was 312,000, or about the size of Philadelphia and Boston combined.

The earliest Dutch settlement on Manhattan Island had been at the very southern tip. In 1820, the built-up area extended north to 14th Street and was advancing rapidly up the island. The commercial buildings of the day were low, three or four stories at most.

Despite New York's prosperity, it was not looked upon as a cultural capital. Tocqueville saw it as a center of "all our greatest vices, without any of those interests which counteract their baneful influence." In many people's eyes, Philadelphia remained "the Athens of America," but that was changing. New York, cultivated or not, was attracting America's first professional writers. All four authors represented in this section—Irving, Cooper, Bryant, and Poe—spent important parts of their careers in New York City.

The Growth of Democracy

When Tocqueville looked at American cities such as New York, he foresaw problems. A firm believer in democratic ideals, Tocqueville was concerned about the possible excesses of democracy in urban areas. He thought that cities were too likely to put power "in the hands of a populace carrying out its own impulses."

In fact, the people of the United States had already moved toward giving themselves more direct power over government. The election in 1828 of Andrew Jackson, "the People's President," ushered in the era of the common man. Property requirements for voting began to be eliminated. Presidential electors were increasingly chosen by popular vote, rather than by state legislatures.

Not everyone shared in the triumph of the common man, however. Despite early stirrings of feminism, little political attention was paid to women. The majority of blacks were still slaves, and each slave counted as 3/5 of a person for purposes of congressional rep-

TRADE AND COMMERCE IN MANHATTAN
Karoly and Santo
Three Lions

AMERICAN EVENTS

The Lewis and Clark Expedition

1803   Louisiana Purchase extends nation's territory to Rocky Mountains.

1804   Lewis and Clark begin expedition exploring and mapping vast region of West.

1807   Robert Fulton's steamboat makes first trip from New York City to Albany.

1809   *A History of New York...by Diedrich Knickerbocker* brings recognition to **Washington Irving.**

1812   U.S. declares war on Great Britain; early battles in War of 1812 are at sea.

1814   Bombardment of Fort McHenry inspires Francis Scott Key to write "The Star-Spangled Banner."

1815   Battle of New Orleans occurs after war is officially over.

1817   **William Cullen Bryant** publishes early draft of "Thanatopsis" in a Boston magazine.

1819   **Washington Irving's** *Sketch Book*, including "Rip Van Winkle," begins to appear serially in U.S.

      Spain relinquishes claims to Florida for $5 million.

1820   Missouri Compromise bans slavery in some parts of new territories.

1821   **James Fenimore Cooper** gains widespread fame with *The Spy*, his second novel.

      Emma Willard founds Troy Female Seminary, first women's college in United States.

1823   *The Pioneers* by **James Fenimore Cooper** introduces Natty Bumppo and *Leatherstocking Tales.*

      Monroe Doctrine warns European powers to keep hands off Latin America.

1825   Completion and success of Erie Canal spurs canal building throughout the nation.

The Battle of New Orleans

Rip Van Winkle

The Monroe Doctrine

The Erie Canal

Napoleon in Coronation Robes

Is Established

Jane Austen

John Keats

René Laënnec

1800 England: Samuel Taylor Coleridge finishes writing "Kubla Khan."

1802 England: J. M. W. Turner, romantic landscape artist, paints *Calais Pier*.

1804 France: Napoleon Bonaparte, proclaims himself emperor.

Germany: Friedrich von Schiller gives Swiss their national festival play, *William Tell*.

England: William Wordsworth completes "Ode on Intimations of Immortality."

1805 Germany: Ludwig von Beethoven breaks formal musical conventions with *Third Symphony*.

1812 France: Napoleon Bonaparte suffers disastrous military defeat in Russia.

1813 England: Jane Austen publishes *Pride and Prejudice*, one of the world's great novels.

1815 Belgium: French army under Napoleon routed at Waterloo, Belgium, by British and Prussian forces.

Austria: Congress of Vienna redraws map of Europe following Napoleon's downfall.

1818 England: Mary Wollstonecraft Shelley creates a legend with *Frankenstein*.

1819 England: John Keats writes "Ode to a Nightingale" and "Ode on a Grecian Urn."

France: René Laënnec, a physician, invents the stethoscope.

Scotland: Sir Walter Scott completes *Ivanhoe*, a pioneering historical romance.

1820 England: Percy Bysshe Shelley publishes the four-act drama *Prometheus Unbound*.

1821 Mexico: Mexico gains independence from Spain.

England: George Gordon, Lord Byron completes final work of verse satire, *Don Juan*.

1826 *Leatherstocking* saga continues with **James Fenimore Cooper's** *The Last of the Mohicans.*

1827 Serial publication of John James Audubon's *The Birds of America* begins in England.

Edgar Allan Poe publishes *Tamerlane,* his first collection of poems.

1828 Noah Webster's *An American Dictionary of the English Language* makes its appearance.

1830 Peter Cooper builds *Tom Thumb,* America's first steam-driven locomotive.

1831 *Poems* by **Edgar A. Poe**, published in New York, includes "To Helen."

1832 **Washington Irving's** *The Alhambra* causes some critics to think he prefers Europe.

1833 "MS. Found in a Bottle" wins contest for **Edgar Allan Poe** and attracts attention to his work.

1834 Cyrus McCormick invents mechanical reaper.

1836 Battles at the Alamo and San Jacinto fought while Texas is a republic.

Ralph Waldo Emerson's essay, *Nature,* signals start of New England's literary renaissance.

1837 *Twice-Told Tales* by **Nathaniel Hawthorne** contains masterpieces that few critics noted.

Samuel F. B. Morse, painter and inventor, patents electromagnetic telegraph.

1838 U.S. army marches Cherokees of Georgia on long "Trail of Tears" to Oklahoma.

1839 "The Fall of the House of Usher," short story by **Edgar Allan Poe**, first appears in print.

1840 After many years, **James Fenimore Cooper's** *Leatherstocking Tales* resume with *The Pathfinder.*

The Last of the Mohicans

Locomotive "Tom Thumb" Races Horse Car

Samuel Morse

The "Trail of Tears"

Decembrist Uprising in Russia

Stendhal

Alfred, Lord Tennyson

Charles Dickens

1823 Germany: Jakob and Wilhelm Grimm have *Grimm's Fairy Tales* translated into English.

1824 Hawaii: King Kamehameha III, who favors U.S. interests, ascends the throne.

1825 Denmark: Hans Oersted becomes first scientist to isolate aluminum.

Russia: Decembrist uprising crushed by czarist forces.

1826 Italy: Alessandro Manzoni completes work on his classic novel *The Betrothed*.

1829 England: George Stephenson perfects a steam locomotive for Liverpool-Manchester Railway.

1830 France: Stendhal publishes *The Red and the Black*, first of his great novels.

1831 France: Victor Hugo publishes *Notre Dame de Paris*, popularly called *The Hunchback of Notre Dame*.

1832 England: Alfred, Lord Tennyson completes "The Lady of Shalott," a poem.

1834 France: Eugène Delacroix, a Romantic artist, paints *Women of Algiers*.

1835 Denmark: Hans Christian Andersen publishes his first book of fairy tales.

France: Honoré de Balzac shows his mastery of the novel in *Father Goriot*.

1837 England: Charles Dickens achieves great success with *Oliver Twist*.

England: Thomas Carlyle publishes renowned *The French Revolution, A History*.

1838 England: Elizabeth Barrett Browning adds to her fame with *The Seraphim and Other Poems*.

ANDREW JACKSON ENCOURAGING HIS
RIFLEMEN AT THE BATTLE OF NEW ORLEANS,
JANUARY 8, 1815
Colored Engraving, 19th Century
The Granger Collection

THE BOMBARDMENT
OF FORT MCHENRY,
BALTIMORE, ON 13–14
SEPTEMBER 1814
*Contemporary
American
Aquatint Engraving
by John Bower*
The Granger Collection

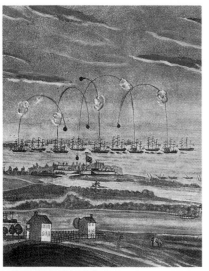

resentation. Still, this period saw the beginnings of the feminist and antislavery movements.

One of the tragic aspects of the Jackson era was "Indian removal," the forcible seizure of tribal lands. In the South, many thousands of native Americans were uprooted and moved to open lands in the West. The most publicized removal was that of the Cherokees from northwestern Georgia to the Indian Territory, now Oklahoma. This 1838 "Trail of Tears" took the lives of about 4,000 of the 15,000 Cherokees who began the long trek.

Despite all this, the first four decades of the 1800's were, on the whole, hopeful ones. The young republic seemed able to weather any storm.

America on the World Stage

One of the storms to be weathered was the War of 1812. This two-and-a-half-year conflict was fought to settle a number of grievances against Great Britain, including the impressment of American seamen by the Royal Navy. Although neither side gained or lost, the war created a number of American military heroes. The British bombardment of Fort McHenry in Baltimore Harbor inspired Francis Scott Key to write "The Star-Spangled Banner." After the war, there was a feeling of solidarity in the United States. Most important, perhaps, the war convinced Europeans that the United States was on the world stage to stay.

That fact was emphasized again in 1823 with the Monroe Doctrine. President James Monroe, fearing European intervention in the newly free nations of Latin America, stated that "the American continents . . . are henceforth not to be considered as subjects for future colonization by any European powers." Monroe's statement attracted little attention at the time. As the United States gained strength and prestige, however, European nations were not eager to challenge it.

Florida and the Southwest raised special problems for the young nation. As late as 1818, Florida was still a Spanish province. Border troubles created tension, and some Americans were killed. The resulting invasion by Andrew Jackson's Tennessee militia convinced Spain to sell Florida rather than have it seized. In 1819 the United States purchased all of Spain's land east of the Mississippi for $5 million.

The situation in Texas was more complicated. Originally a part of Mexico, Texas seceded from Mexico in 1835. The following year, the Mexican army made its famous assault on the Alamo, where every Texan defender was killed. President Jackson recognized the Republic of Texas in 1837. Although Texas wanted to be annexed by the United States, it was not admitted to the Union until 1845. The annexation brought about war between Mexico and the United States. American victory in this war added further territory in the Southwest to the United States.

AMERICAN LITERATURE COMES OF AGE

In 1783, when the Peace of Paris ended the American Revolution, an eleventh child was born into the family of a wealthy merchant in New York City. The child, Washington Irving, would become the first professional author of the new nation and the first American literary figure to win an international reputation. Other notable writers appeared on the scene in the early nineteenth century. By 1840, Americans could offer convincing answers to British writer Sydney Smith's taunt from 20 years earlier: "In the four quarters of the globe, who reads an American book, or goes to an American play, or looks at an American picture or statue?"

The Professionals

From early colonial times, there were journalists who wrote and edited for a living. Their works were meant for the moment and did not survive as literature. The important literary figures who do survive from those days were outstanding writers, but none made writing his profession. Thomas Jefferson, for example, was a statesman, and Benjamin Franklin was a printer, inventor, and statesman.

America's cultural independence did not come easily. For nearly 200 years American readers had been looking to Europe, mainly Great Britain, for most of their reading material other than the Bible, almanacs, newspapers, magazines, and broadsides. Susanna Rowson, raised in Massachusetts but living in England, wrote America's first best-selling novel, *Charlotte Temple*. It was published in London in 1791 and reprinted in Philadelphia in 1794.

In the early nineteenth century, two Scottish writers, Robert Burns and Sir Walter Scott, were popular in the United States. So, too, were three young English poets, Lord Byron, Percy Bysshe Shelley, and John Keats. In addition, classic English works dating back hundreds of years were in print. Tocqueville observed, "There is hardly a pioneer's hut that does not contain a few odd volumes of Shakespeare."

Most American writers of the time could not compete in that company. The names of dozens of writers in the early national period, familiar in their own time, are all but forgotten today. Charles Brockden Brown, James Paulding, Fitz-Greene Halleck, Caroline Kirkland, and N. P. Willis achieved substantial reputations in the early 1800's. All lived in or near New York City, except Kirkland, who was born in New York but moved to frontier Michigan, where she wrote realistic sketches of backwoods life.

A New York Biblical scholar, Clement Clarke Moore, gained more lasting fame with a poem he wrote for his family, with no thought of publication. A relative of Moore's gave a copy of the poem to a newspaper editor in Troy, New York. The poem, popularly known as " 'Twas the Night Before Christmas," thus made its first appearance in 1823.

LAST STAND AT THE ALAMO
N. C. Wyeth
Three Lions

One writer who had a national reputation was William Gilmore Simms of Charleston, South Carolina. As a young man, Simms lived briefly in New York City and published his first novel, *Martin Faber,* there in 1833. His reputation rests mainly on the romantic novels set in South Carolina that he wrote after returning to Charleston.

The major American authors of the day have already been mentioned. Washington Irving achieved his first great success in 1809 with the satiric *History of New York,* supposedly written by Diedrich Knickerbocker. James Fenimore Cooper introduced his frontier hero Natty Bumppo in *The Pioneers,* published in 1823. William Cullen Bryant, born in Massachusetts, wrote the first draft of his famous poem "Thanatopsis" when he was 17. Edgar Allan Poe, today the most widely read of the four, was a tormented genius. Poe's life, though brief and tragic, produced poems, stories, and criticism that have had a powerful influence on the course of American literature.

Knickerbocker and Leatherstocking

The North American continent offered a vast and exciting vista for American writers, whether in the settled regions or on the advancing edge of settlement. The first who took artistic advantage of this view in any sustained way were New Yorkers, members of two informal literary and artistic groups.

One was the Knickerbocker Group, led by Washington Irving. A notable member of this group was William Cullen Bryant, who moved to New York City in 1825. He remained a dominant literary figure in the city for the rest of his eighty-four years. Other members of stature were James Paulding and Fitz-Greene Halleck. Many Knickerbocker members were of lesser talent. Edgar Allan Poe ridiculed them in a critical review, *The Literati of New York City,* as writers with grand pretensions but limited abilities.

The second New York group, whose leader was James Fenimore Cooper, was called the Bread and Cheese Club. Basically a social club, its members' interests were not restricted to literature. Samuel F. B. Morse, renowned as both a painter and the inventor of the telegraph, was a member. So, too, was William Dunlap, an artist, the founder of the National Academy of Design, and the first professional American playwright and producer.

Not only were these groups located in New York, but the subject matter of their members' work was often local. Irving's *History of New York* and some of the stories in *The Sketch Book* (particularly "Rip Van Winkle" and "The Legend of Sleepy Hollow") make vivid use of local scenes and events. Irving, a world traveler, also used many European settings. The sketches in *The Alhambra,* for example, all involve Spain. Even so, Irving's use of regional materials sparked an interest in American locales, especially the Hudson River valley.

James Fenimore Cooper's fearless, straight-shooting frontier hero enthralled readers here and abroad. Natty Bumppo, a man of complete moral integrity, established the pattern for countless Western heroes to come (although Bumppo himself was not a westerner). Four of the novels about Natty Bumppo, which are collectively known as *The Leatherstocking Tales,* are set on the upstate New York frontier, which was already a dim memory in Cooper's time.

Cooper, like Irving, was a world traveler, and some of his novels have European settings. Yet Cooper, too, found much near at hand to write about, helping to focus attention on the varied literary wellsprings within the new nation.

In 1831, while Irving was in London and Cooper was in Paris, Samuel Francis Smith, a Boston Baptist clergyman, wrote new words for the British song "God Save the King." Smith's words, simple and stirring, expressed the national mood in a timeless hymn: "My country, 'tis of thee,/Sweet land of liberty,/Of thee I sing."

ILLUSTRATION FROM AN 1872 EDITION OF JAMES FENIMORE COOPER'S *THE LAST OF THE MOHICANS*
Felix Octavius Carr Darley
The Granger Collection

From Reason to Romance

The Puritans were religious fundamentalists who sought salvation. The founders of the republic were political realists who pursued reason. So, then, how can the writers of the early nineteenth century—Irving, Cooper, Bryant, and Poe—be described? Despite unmistakable differences among them, they were all Romantics.

That name can be misleading, because the Romantics do not necessarily write about love. Romanticism can be viewed as an artistic movement, or a state of mind, or both. Romantic writers favor the imagination over reason, intuition over facts. Irving's *History of New York* is not a dry account of actual events; it is a rollicking history that ignores and alters facts at will. Cooper's *The Deerslayer,* the first in the *Leatherstocking* plot sequence, is not a realistic novel of life on the New York frontier. It is a mythical tale of the "natural" man and of lost innocence, of nature versus civilization.

There are other aspects of Romanticism. One is its intense interest in and reverence for nature. The poems of William Cullen Bryant are nearly perfect examples of this characteristic of Romanticism. Most of Bryant's best-known poems exalt the virtues of nature, whatever the poems' individual themes may be. Their titles show this emphasis: "The Yellow Violet," "A Forest Hymn," "Green River," "Summer Wind," and "The Prairies."

Another aspect of Romanticism is its accent on mystery—on the strange and fantastic aspects of human experience. In this realm, Edgar Allan Poe stands supreme. Poe wrote forty-eight brilliantly original lyric poems and a number of short stories whose characters, in the words of a biographer, "are either grotesques or the inhabitants of another world than this."

Not all Romantics were writers. Romanticism pervaded all the

KINDRED SPIRITS
Asher B. Durand
New York Public Library

arts in this time of America's youth. Of special note were the landscape painters who came to be known as the Hudson River School. The most influential of this New York group was English-born Thomas Cole. His haunting and dramatic views of the Hudson River and Catskill Mountains have often been compared to Irving's word images. Perhaps the most famous Hudson River School painting is Asher B. Durand's *Kindred Spirits,* in which Thomas Cole and William Cullen Bryant stand on a jutting rock overlooking a picturesque valley.

Seedtime in New England

Although many of the significant literary accomplishments from 1800 to 1840 occurred in New York, cultural activity was by no means limited to that city. Small groups of writers could be found in most major cities on the East Coast, notably Philadelphia, Richmond, and Charleston. After 1840, as New York writing lost its preeminence, an impressive burst of literary activity took place in and around Boston. By that date, the movement that one critic has called, "the flowering of New England," had already begun. In the next fifteen years, it would produce an array of important writers and enduring literary works.

AMERICAN VOICES
Quotations by Prominent Figures of the Period

How convenient it would be to many of our great men and great families of doubtful origin, could they have the privilege of the heroes of yore, who, whenever their origin was involved in obscurity, modestly announced themselves descended from a god.

Washington Irving, *A History of New York*

To see him striding along the profile of a hill on a windy day, with his clothes bagging and fluttering about him, one might have mistaken him for the genius of famine descending upon the earth, or some scarecrow eloped from a cornfield.

Washington Irving, "The Legend of Sleepy Hollow"

I am always at a loss to know how much to believe of my own stories.

Washington Irving, *Tales of a Traveler*

All is contradiction in the settlements, while all is concord in the woods. Forts and churches almost always go together, and yet they're downright contradictions, churches being for peace and forts for war.

James Fenimore Cooper, *The Deerslayer*

Ignorance and superstition ever bear a close, and even a mathematical, relationship to each other.

James Fenimore Cooper, *Jack Tier*

Loveliest of lovely things are they,
On earth, that soonest pass away.

William Cullen Bryant, "A Scene on the Banks of the Hudson"

These are the gardens of the Desert, these
The unshorn fields, boundless and beautiful,
For which the speech of England has no name—
The Prairies.

William Cullen Bryant, "The Prairies"

True!—nervous—very, very dreadfully nervous I had been and am; but why *will* you say that I am mad?

Edgar Allan Poe, "The Tell-Tale Heart"

For the moon never beams without bringing me dreams
Of the beautiful Annabel Lee.

Edgar Allan Poe, "Annabel Lee"

The Literature of 1800–1840

During the years from 1800–1840, the new nation grew and expanded at a rapid pace. During this time, the country began developing its own distinctive literary tradition. Because the United States was now an established nation, writers were able to turn from the subject of politics and create literature equal in quality to the work of European writers.

Historical Context

In 1803 President Jefferson completed the Louisiana Purchase, extending the American boundary to the Rocky Mountains. During the years that followed, many Americans traveled westward, seeking new homes and new opportunities. At the same time, the eastern cities grew rapidly, as the United States developed into an industralized and self-sufficient nation.

Literary Movements

Following the turn of the century, an artistic movement that had originated in Europe swept through the United States. This movement, which came to be known as Romanticism, grew out of a reaction against the dominant attitudes and approaches of the eighteenth century. Unlike the eighteenth-century writers, who emphasized reason, logic, and scientific observation, the Romantics stressed the examination of inner feelings and emotions and the use of the imagination. The Romantic movement was also characterized by an interest in nature and the supernatural, a strong belief in democracy, and a deep awareness of the past.

Writers' Techniques

The attitudes, concerns, and interests of the Romantics are reflected in the themes of the majority of the literary works written between 1800 and 1840. Writers explored the mysteries of nature and the inner self and the relationship between nature and the human imagination. With the establishment of the American identity, writers also began focusing on distinctively American themes and delving into the history of the young nation.

On the following pages is a selection by William Cullen Bryant, the first American poet to win worldwide critical acclaim. The notes in the side column draw your attention to Bryant's literary techniques and to the Romantic concerns which are reflected in the selection.

To a Waterfowl
William Cullen Bryant

Literary Movement: The title indicates this poem will be about nature, which is a characteristic interest of the Romantic movement.

    Whither, midst falling dew,
While glow the heavens with the last steps of day,
Far, through their rosy depths, dost thou pursue
    Thy solitary way?

Literary Movement: Bryant creates vivid images, or word pictures, that capture the beauty of nature.

5   Vainly the fowler's[1] eye
Might mark thy distant flight to do thee wrong,

---

1. fowler's: Referring to a hunter.

Writer's Techniques: Like most Romantic works, the poem is written in the language of common people.

As, darkly seen against the crimson sky,
    Thy figure floats along.

Literary Movements: The mystery concerning the bird's destination prompts the speaker to use his imagination.

        Seek'st thou the plashy brink
10 Of weedy lake, or marge[2] of river wide,
Or where the rocking billows rise and sink
    On the chafed ocean-side?

There is a Power whose care
Teaches thy way along that pathless coast—
15 The desert and illimitable air—
    Lone wandering, but not lost.

Writer's Techniques: The poem is written in quatrains, or four-line stanzas, with an *abab* rhyme scheme.

        All day thy wings have fanned,
At that far height, the cold, thin atmosphere,
Yet stoop not, weary, to the welcome land,
20   Though the dark night is near.

And soon that toil shall end;
Soon shalt thou find a summer home, and rest,
And scream among thy fellows; reeds shall bend
    Soon, o'er thy sheltered nest.

Literary Movement: The poem reflects the Romantics' emphasis on the heart rather than the mind.

25   Thou'rt gone, the abyss of heaven
Hath swallowed up thy form; yet, on my heart
Deeply has sunk the lesson thou hast given,
    And shall not soon depart.

Literary Movement: The poem reflects the Romantics' view of nature as a source of inspiration and understanding.

        He who, from zone to zone,
30 Guides through the boundless sky thy certain flight,
In the long way that I must tread alone,
    Will lead my steps aright.

---

2. marge: Edge or border.

THINKING ABOUT THE SELECTION

Recalling

1. What questions does the speaker ask the waterfowl in the first three stanzas?
2. What does the "Power" referred to in the fourth stanza teach the waterfowl?
3. What will the waterfowl soon find?
4. What lesson does the speaker learn from the waterfowl?

Interpreting

5. How does the speaker's interest in the waterfowl contrast with the fowler's concern with the bird?
6. What does the speaker learn from his observations of the waterfowl?

Applying

7. What are some other lessons that people might learn from birds or other animals?

ANALYZING LITERATURE

Understanding Romanticism

Romanticism was an artistic movement that grew out of a reaction against the dominant attitudes and approaches of the eighteenth century. The Romantics stressed the examination of inner feelings and emotions and the use of the imagination, rather than the use of reason and logic. They were interested in nature and its mysteries and even in the supernatural. Often, the Romantics sought inspiration and understanding through the observation and contemplation of nature. Possessing a deep awareness of the past, the Romantics turned to legends and folklore as sources of inspiration.

The use of legends and folklore reflected the Romantics' interest in and concern for common people. This concern was also reflected in the Romantics' frequent use of the language of common people in their works.

1. Bryant's poem focuses on the migration of birds, a subject that scientists still cannot fully explain. Why is this an appropriate subject for a Romantic poem?
2. How does the speaker's approach to understanding the waterfowl's flight reflect the concerns of the Romantics?
3. Unlike the writers of the eighteenth century, the Romantics were generally concerned with specific experiences of individuals, rather than with general, universal experiences. How is this concern reflected in Bryant's poem?
4. In writing about the concerns of the Romantic movement, some writers capitalize *Nature.* Explain why this would be appropriate.

THINKING AND WRITING

Responding to Criticism

In discussing "To a Waterfowl," Edgar Allan Poe commented that the poem's main strength is its "completeness," adding that the poem's "rounded and didactic termination has done wonders." Write an essay in which you discuss the poem in relation to this comment. Reread the poem, keeping Poe's comment in mind. Do you think his statement is accurate? Why or why not? When writing your essay, use evidence from the poem to support your argument. When you finish writing, revise your essay, making sure it supports your opinion of the quotation. Proofread your essay and prepare a final draft.

WASHINGTON IRVING

1783–1859

Named after the first American President, Washington Irving became the first American writer to achieve an international reputation.

Born into a wealthy New York family, Irving began studying law at the age of sixteen. He had little interest in his studies, however, and spent much time traveling throughout Europe and New York's Hudson Valley and reading European literature. Irving also wrote satirical essays using the pen name Jonathan Oldstyle. When Irving was twenty-four, he and his brother began publishing an anonymous magazine, *Salmagundi* (the name of a spicy appetizer), which carried humorous sketches and essays about New York society.

In 1809 Irving published his first major work, *A History of New York from the Beginning of the World to the End of the Dutch Dynasty,* using the pseudonym Diedrich Knickerbocker. The *History,* a humorous examination of New York during colonial times, was popular and made Irving famous.

From 1815 to 1832, Irving lived in Europe, traveling extensively and learning about European customs, traditions, and folklore. Inspired by the European folk heritage, Irving created two of his most famous stories, "The Legend of Sleepy Hollow" and "Rip Van Winkle," transforming two traditional German tales into distinctly American stories set in the Hudson Valley. When Irving published these two stories in *The Sketch Book* (1820) under the pseudonym Geoffrey Crayon, writers and critics throughout Europe and the United States responded enthusiastically.

Irving produced a number of other books while living in Europe, including *Bracebridge Hall* (1822), *Tales of a Traveller* (1824), and *The Alhambra* (1832). Another of Irving's more famous stories, "The Devil and Tom Walker," an American adaptation of a German legend about a man who sells his soul to the devil, appeared in *Tales of a Traveller*.

Although Irving continued to write after returning to the United States in 1832, he is remembered mainly for a few of the stories he wrote while in Europe. Like the folk tales from which they were adapted, these stories have remained popular for generations, becoming an important part of the American literary heritage.

GUIDE FOR READING

The Devil and Tom Walker

Literary Forms

Folk Tales. Folk tales are stories handed down orally among the common people of a particular culture. These stories often relate events that are unrealistic or unlikely to happen in the real world in order to teach a lesson or express a general truth about life. The characters in folk tales tend to be stereotypes or stock characters embodying a single human trait, quality, or emotion. For example, a character in a folktale may embody hatred or greed.

Washington Irving created "The Devil and Tom Walker" by reshaping a German folk tale about a man who sells his soul to the devil. Irving makes the tale distinctly American by setting it in New England during the late 1720's—a time when Puritanism, especially the belief that a person's life should be devoted to God, was being replaced by commercialism and the desire for personal gain. Like the tale from which it was adapted, Irving's story relates a series of unlikely events, involves stereotyped characters, and teaches an important lesson about life. Because Irving's story is grounded in a specific time and place, it also reveals a great deal about life in New England in the 1720's.

Look For

Washington Irving once wrote, "He is the true enchanter, whose spell operates, not upon the senses, but upon the imagination and the heart." As you read "The Devil and Tom Walker," look for how the story makes its point by playing upon the heart.

Writing

Do you think that some people today sometimes become so concerned with acquiring money and power that they forget to be sympathetic and compassionate toward other people? Freewrite about your thoughts regarding this question.

Vocabulary

Knowing the following words will help you as you read "The Devil and Tom Walker."

termagant (tʉr′ mə gənt) *n.*: A quarrelsome woman (p. 180)
avarice (av′ ər is) *n.*: Greed (p. 183)
usurer (yo͞o′ zho͞o rər) *n.*: A moneylender who charges very high interest (p. 185)

extort (ik stôrt′) *v.*: To obtain by threat or violence (p. 186)
ostentation (äs′tən tā′ shən) *n.*: Boastful display (p. 186)
parsimony (pär′sə mō′ nē) *n.*: Stinginess (p. 186)

The Devil and Tom Walker

Washington Irving

A few miles from Boston in Massachusetts, there is a deep inlet, winding several miles into the interior of the country from Charles Bay, and terminating in a thickly wooded swamp or morass. On one side of this inlet is a beautiful dark grove; on the opposite side the land rises abruptly from the water's edge into a high ridge, on which grow a few scattered oaks of great age and immense size. Under one of these gigantic trees, according to old stories, there was a great amount of treasure buried by Kidd the pirate.[1] The inlet allowed a facility to bring the money in a boat secretly and at night to the very foot of the hill; the elevation of the place permitted a good look-out to be kept that no one was at hand; while the remarkable trees formed good landmarks by which the place might easily be found again. The old stories add, moreover, that the Devil presided at the hiding of the money, and took it under his guardianship; but this it is well known he always does with buried treasure, particularly when it has been ill-gotten. Be that as it may, Kidd never returned to recover his wealth; being shortly after seized at Boston, sent out to England, and there hanged for a pirate.

About the year 1727, just at the time that earthquakes were prevalent in New England, and shook many tall sinners down upon their knees, there lived near this place a meager, miserly fellow, of the name of Tom Walker. He had a wife as miserly as himself: they were so miserly that they even conspired to cheat each other. Whatever the woman could lay hands on, she hid away; a hen could not cackle but she was on the alert to secure the new-laid egg. Her husband was continually prying about to detect her secret hoards, and many and fierce were the conflicts that took place about what ought to have been common property. They lived in a forlorn-looking house that stood alone, and had an air of starvation. A few straggling savin trees, emblems of sterility, grew near it; no smoke ever curled from its chimney; no traveler stopped at its door. A miserable horse, whose ribs were as articulate as the bars of a gridiron, stalked about a field, where a thin carpet of moss, scarcely covering the ragged beds of puddingstone, tantalized and balked his hunger; and sometimes he would lean his head over the fence, look piteously at the passerby, and seem to petition deliverance from this land of famine.

The house and its inmates had altogether a bad name. Tom's wife was a tall termagant, fierce of temper, loud of tongue, and strong of arm. Her voice was often heard in wordy warfare with her husband; and his face sometimes showed signs that their conflicts were not confined to words. No one ventured, however, to interfere between them. The lonely wayfarer shrunk within himself at the horrid clamor and clapperclawing;[2] eyed the den of discord askance; and hurried on his way, rejoicing, if a bachelor, in his celibacy.

One day that Tom Walker had been to a

---

1. Kidd the pirate: Captain William Kidd (1645–1701).

2. clapperclawing (klap′ ər klô′ ing): Clawing or scratching.

distant part of the neighborhood, he took what he considered a shortcut homeward, through the swamp. Like most shortcuts, it was an ill-chosen route. The swamp was thickly grown with great gloomy pines and hemlocks, some of them ninety feet high, which made it dark at noonday, and a retreat for all the owls of the neighborhood. It was full of pits and quagmires, partly covered with weeds and mosses, where the green surface often betrayed the traveler into a gulf of black, smothering mud; there were also dark and stagnant pools, the abodes of the tadpole, the bullfrog, and the water-snake; where the trunks of pines and hemlocks lay half-drowned, half-rotting, looking like alligators sleeping in the mire.

Tom had long been picking his way cautiously through this treacherous forest; stepping from tuft to tuft of rushes and roots, which afforded precarious footholds among deep sloughs; or pacing carefully, like a cat, along the prostrate trunks of trees; startled now and then by the sudden screaming of the bittern, or the quacking of a wild duck, rising on the wing from some solitary pool. At length he arrived at a piece of firm ground, which ran out like a peninsula into the deep bosom of the swamp. It had been one of the strongholds of the Indians during their wars with the first colonists. Here they had thrown up a kind of fort, which they had looked upon as almost impregnable, and had used as a place of refuge for their squaws and children. Nothing remained of the old Indian fort but a few embankments, gradually sinking to the level of the surrounding earth, and already overgrown in part by oaks and other forest trees, the foliage of which formed a contrast to the dark pines and hemlocks of the swamp.

It was late in the dusk of evening when Tom Walker reached the old fort, and he paused there awhile to rest himself. Anyone but he would have felt unwilling to linger in this lonely, melancholy place, for the common people had a bad opinion of it, from the stories handed down from the time of the In-

dian wars; when it was asserted that the savages held incantations here, and made sacrifices to the evil spirit.

Tom Walker, however, was not a man to be troubled with any fears of the kind. He reposed himself for some time on the trunk of a fallen hemlock, listening to the boding cry of the tree toad, and delving with his walking staff into a mound of black mold at his feet. As he turned up the soil unconsciously, his staff struck against something hard. He raked it out of the vegetable mold, and lo! a cloven skull, with an Indian tomahawk buried deep in it, lay before him. The rust on the weapon showed the time that had elapsed since this deathblow had been given. It was a dreary memento of the fierce struggle that had taken place in this last foothold of the Indian warriors.

"Humph!" said Tom Walker, as he gave it a kick to shake the dirt from it.

"Let that skull alone!" said a gruff voice. Tom lifted up his eyes, and beheld a great black man seated directly opposite him, on the stump of a tree. He was exceedingly surprised, having neither heard nor seen anyone approach; and he was still more perplexed on observing, as well as the gathering gloom would permit, that the stranger was neither Negro nor Indian. It is true he was dressed in a rude half-Indian garb, and had a red belt or sash swathed round his body; but his face was neither black nor copper color, but swarthy and dingy, and begrimed with soot, as if he had been accustomed to toil among fires and forges. He had a shock of coarse black hair, that stood out from his head in all directions, and bore an ax on his shoulder.

He scowled for a moment at Tom with a pair of great red eyes.

"What are you doing on my grounds?" said the black man, with a hoarse growling voice.

"Your grounds!" said Tom with a sneer, "no more your grounds than mine; they belong to Deacon Peabody."

"Deacon Peabody be d——d," said the

stranger, "as I flatter myself he will be, if he does not look more to his own sins and less to those of his neighbors. Look yonder, and see how Deacon Peabody is faring."

Tom looked in the direction that the stranger pointed, and beheld one of the great trees, fair and flourishing without, but rotten at the core, and saw that it had been nearly hewn through, so that the first high wind was likely to blow it down. On the bark of the tree was scored the name of Deacon Peabody, an eminent man, who had waxed wealthy by driving shrewd bargains with the Indians. He now looked round, and found most of the tall trees marked with the name of some great man of the colony, and all more or less scored by the ax. The one on which he had been seated, and which had evidently just been hewn down, bore the

name of Crowninshield; and he recollected a mighty rich man of that name, who made a vulgar display of wealth, which it was whispered he had acquired by buccaneering.

"He's just ready for burning!" said the black man, with a growl of triumph. "You see I am likely to have a good stock of firewood for winter."

"But what right have you," said Tom, "to cut down Deacon Peabody's timber?"

"The right of a prior claim," said the other. "This woodland belonged to me long before one of your white-faced race put foot upon the soil."

"And pray, who are you, if I may be so bold?" said Tom.

"Oh, I go by various names. I am the wild huntsman in some countries; the black miner in others. In this neighborhood I am known by the name of the black woodsman. I am he to whom the red men consecrated this spot, and in honor of whom they now and then roasted a white man, by way of sweet-smelling sacrifice. Since the red men have been exterminated by you white savages, I amuse myself by presiding at the per-

secutions of Quakers and Anabaptists;[3] I am the great patron and prompter of slave dealers, and the grandmaster of the Salem witches."

"The upshot of all which is, that, if I mistake not," said Tom, sturdily, "you are he commonly called Old Scratch."

"The same, at your service!" replied the black man, with a half-civil nod.

Such was the opening of this interview, according to the old story; though it has almost too familiar an air to be credited. One would think that to meet with such a singular personage, in this wild, lonely place, would have shaken any man's nerves; but Tom was a hard-minded fellow, not easily daunted, and he had lived so long with a termagant wife, that he did not even fear the Devil.

It is said that after this commencement they had a long and earnest conversation together, as Tom returned homeward. The black man told him of great sums of money buried by Kidd the pirate, under the oak trees on the high ridge, not far from the morass. All these were under his command, and protected by his power, so that none could find them but such as propitiated his favor. These he offered to place within Tom Walker's reach, having conceived an especial kindness for him; but they were to be had only on certain conditions. What these conditions were may easily be surmised, though Tom never disclosed them publicly. They must have been very hard, for he required time to think of them, and he was not a man to stick at trifles where money was in view. When they had reached the edge of the swamp, the stranger paused—"What proof have I that all you have been telling me is true?" said Tom. "There is my signature," said the black man, pressing his finger on Tom's forehead. So saying, he turned off among the thickets of the swamp, and seemed, as Tom said, to go down, down, down, into the earth, until nothing but his head and shoulders could be seen, and so on, until he totally disappeared.

When Tom reached home, he found the black print of a finger, burnt, as it were, into his forehead, which nothing could obliterate.

The first news his wife had to tell him was the sudden death of Absalom Crowninshield, the rich buccaneer. It was announced in the papers with the usual flourish, that "A great man had fallen in Israel."[4]

Tom recollected the tree which his black friend had just hewn down, and which was ready for burning, "Let the freebooter roast," said Tom, "who cares!" He now felt convinced that all he had heard and seen was no illusion.

He was not prone to let his wife into his confidence; but as this was an uneasy secret, he willingly shared it with her. All her avarice was awakened at the mention of hidden gold, and she urged her husband to comply with the black man's terms and secure what would make them wealthy for life. However Tom might have felt disposed to sell himself to the Devil, he was determined not to do so to oblige his wife; so he flatly refused, out of the mere spirit of contradiction. Many and bitter were the quarrels they had on the subject, but the more she talked, the more resolute was Tom not to be damned to please her.

At length she determined to drive the bargain on her own account, and if she succeeded, to keep all the gain to herself. Being of the same fearless temper as her husband, she set off for the old Indian fort towards the close of a summer's day. She was many hours absent. When she came back, she was reserved and sullen in her replies. She spoke something of a black man, whom she had met about twilight, hewing at the root of a tall tree. He was sulky, however, and would not come to terms: she was to go again with a propitiatory offering, but what it was she forbore to say.

---

3. Quakers and Anabaptists: Two religious groups that were persecuted for their beliefs.

4. A . . . Israel: A reference to II Samuel 3:38 in the Bible. The Puritans often called New England "Israel."

The next evening she set off again for the swamp, with her apron heavily laden. Tom waited and waited for her, but in vain; midnight came, but she did not make her appearance: morning, noon, night returned, but still she did not come. Tom now grew uneasy for her safety, especially as he found she had carried off in her apron the silver teapot and spoons, and every portable article of value. Another night elapsed, another morning came; but no wife. In a word, she was never heard of more.

What was her real fate nobody knows, in consequence of so many pretending to know. It is one of those facts which have become confounded by a variety of historians. Some asserted that she lost her way among the tangled mazes of the swamp, and sank into some pit or slough; others, more uncharitable, hinted that she had eloped with the household booty, and made off to some other province; while others surmised that the tempter had decoyed her into a dismal quagmire, on the top of which her hat was found lying. In confirmation of this, it was said a great black man, with an ax on his shoulder, was seen late that very evening coming out of the swamp, carrying a bundle tied in a checked apron, with an air of surly triumph.

The most current and probable story, however, observes, that Tom Walker grew so anxious about the fate of his wife and his property, that he set out at length to seek them both at the Indian fort. During a long summer's afternoon he searched about the gloomy place, but no wife was to be seen. He called her name repeatedly, but she was nowhere to be heard. The bittern alone responded to his voice, as he flew screaming by; or the bullfrog croaked dolefully from a neighboring pool. At length, it is said, just in the brown hour of twilight, when the owls began to hoot, and the bats to flit about, his attention was attracted by the clamor of carrion crows hovering about a cypress tree. He looked up, and beheld a bundle tied in a checked apron, and hanging in the branches of the tree, with a great vulture perched hard

by, as if keeping watch upon it. He leaped with joy; for he recognized his wife's apron, and supposed it to contain the household valuables.

"Let us get hold of the property," said he, consolingly to himself, "and we will endeavor to do without the woman."

As he scrambled up the tree, the vulture spread its wide wings, and sailed off screaming into the deep shadows of the forest. Tom seized the checked apron, but woeful sight! found nothing but a heart and liver tied up in it!

Such, according to the most authentic old story, was all that was to be found of Tom's wife. She had probably attempted to deal with the black man as she had been accustomed to deal with her husband; but though a female scold is generally considered a match for the Devil, yet in this instance she appears to have had the worst of it. She must have died game, however; for it is said Tom noticed many prints of cloven feet deeply stamped about the tree, and found handfuls of hair, that looked as if they had been plucked from the coarse black shock of the woodsman. Tom knew his wife's prowess by experience. He shrugged his shoulders, as he looked at the signs of a fierce clapperclawing. "Egad," said he to himself, "Old Scratch must have had a tough time of it!"

Tom consoled himself for the loss of his property, with the loss of his wife, for he was a man of fortitude. He even felt something like gratitude towards the black woodsman, who, he considered, had done him a kindness. He sought, therefore, to cultivate a further acquaintance with him, but for some time without success; the old blacklegs played shy, for whatever people may think, he is not always to be had for calling for: he knows how to play his cards when pretty sure of his game.

At length, it is said, when delay had whetted Tom's eagerness to the quick, and prepared him to agree to anything rather than not gain the promised treasure, he met the black man one evening in his usual woodsman's dress, with his ax on his shoulder,

saunter-
ing along the
swamp, and
humming a tune.
He affected to re-
ceive Tom's ad-
vances with great
indifference, made
brief replies, and
went on humming
his tune.

By degrees, however,
Tom brought him to busi-
ness, and they began to haggle
about the terms on which the
former was to have the pirate's
treasure. There was one condition which need not be mentioned, being generally understood in all cases where the
Devil grants favors; but there
were others about which, though
of less importance, he was inflexi-
bly obstinate. He insisted that the
money found through his means
should be employed in his service.
He proposed, therefore, that Tom
should employ it in the black traffic;
that is to say, that he should fit out a
slave ship. This, however, Tom resolutely
refused: he was bad enough in all conscience, but the Devil himself could not
tempt him to turn slave-trader.

Finding Tom so squeamish on this
point, he did not insist upon it, but proposed, instead, that he should turn usurer;
the Devil being extremely anxious for the increase of usurers, looking upon them as his
peculiar[5] people.

To this no objections were made, for it
was just to Tom's taste.

"You shall open a broker's shop in Boston next month," said the black man.

"I'll do it tomorrow, if you wish," said
Tom Walker.

"You shall lend money at two per cent a
month."

---

5. peculiar: Particular, special.

"Egad, I'll charge four!" replied Tom Walker.

"You shall extort bonds, foreclose mortgages, drive the merchant to bankruptcy——"

"I'll drive him to the D——l," cried Tom Walker.

"You are the usurer for my money!" said the blacklegs with delight. "When will you want the rhino?"[6]

"This very night."

"Done!" said the Devil.

"Done!" said Tom Walker. So they shook hands and struck a bargain.

A few days' time saw Tom Walker seated behind his desk in a countinghouse in Boston.

His reputation for a ready-moneyed man, who would lend money out for a good consideration, soon spread abroad. Everybody remembers the time of Governor Belcher,[7] when money was particularly scarce. It was a time of paper credit. The country had been deluged with government bills; the famous Land Bank[8] had been established; there had been a rage for speculating; the people had run mad with schemes for new settlements, for building cities in the wilderness; land jobbers[9] went about with maps of grants, and townships, and El Dorados,[10] lying nobody knew where, but which everybody was ready to purchase. In a word, the great speculating fever which breaks out every now and then in the country, had raged to an alarming degree, and everybody was dreaming of making sudden fortunes from nothing. As usual the fever had subsided; the dream had gone off, and the imaginary fortunes with it; the patients were left in doleful plight, and the whole country resounded with the consequent cry of "hard times."

At this propitious time of public distress did Tom Walker set up as usurer in Boston. His door was soon thronged by customers. The needy and adventurous, the gambling speculator, the dreaming land jobber, the thriftless tradesman, the merchant with cracked credit, in short, everyone driven to raise money by desperate means and desperate sacrifices, hurried to Tom Walker.

Thus Tom was the universal friend of the needy, and acted like a "friend in need"; that is to say, he always exacted good pay and good security. In proportion to the distress of the applicant was the hardness of his terms. He accumulated bonds and mortgages; gradually squeezed his customers closer and closer, and sent them at length, dry as a sponge, from his door.

In this way he made money hand over hand, became a rich and mighty man, and exalted his cocked hat upon 'Change.[11] He built himself, as usual, a vast house, out of ostentation; but left the greater part of it unfinished and unfurnished, out of parsimony. He even set up a carriage in the fullness of his vainglory, though he nearly starved the horses which drew it; and as the ungreased wheels groaned and screeched on the axletrees, you would have thought you heard the souls of the poor debtors he was squeezing.

As Tom waxed old, however, he grew thoughtful. Having secured the good things of this world, he began to feel anxious about those of the next. He thought with regret on the bargain he had made with his black friend, and set his wits to work to cheat him out of the conditions. He became, therefore, all of a sudden, a violent churchgoer. He prayed loudly and strenuously, as if heaven were to be taken by force of lungs. Indeed, one might always tell when he had sinned most during the week, by the clamor of his Sunday devotion. The quiet Christians who

---

6. **rhino** (rī′ nō): Slang term for money.

7. **Governor Belcher:** Jonathan Belcher, the governor of Massachusetts Bay Colony from 1730 through 1741.

8. **Land Bank:** A bank that financed transactions in real estate.

9. **land jobbers:** People who bought and sold undeveloped land.

10. **El Dorados** (el′ də rä′ dōz): Places that are rich in gold or opportunity. El Dorado was a legendary country in South America sought by early Spanish explorers for its gold and precious stones.

11. **'Change:** The exchange, where bankers and merchants did business.

had been modestly and steadfastly traveling Zionward,[12] were struck with self-reproach at seeing themselves so suddenly outstripped in their career by this new-made convert. Tom was as rigid in religious as in money matters; he was a stern supervisor and censurer of his neighbors, and seemed to think every sin entered up to their account became a credit on his own side of the page. He even talked of the expediency of reviving the persecution of Quakers and Anabaptists. In a word, Tom's zeal became as notorious as his riches.

Still, in spite of all this strenuous attention to forms, Tom had a lurking dread that the Devil, after all, would have his due. That he might not be taken unawares, therefore, it is said he always carried a small Bible in his coat pocket. He had also a great folio Bible on his countinghouse desk, and would frequently be found reading it when people called on business; on such occasions he would lay his green spectacles in the book, to mark the place, while he turned round to drive some usurious bargain.

Some say that Tom grew a little crack-brained in his old days, and that fancying his end approaching, he had his horse newly shod, saddled and bridled, and buried with his feet uppermost; because he supposed that at the last day the world would be turned upside down, in which case he should find his horse standing ready for mounting, and he was determined at the worst to give his old friend a run for it. This, however, is probably a mere old wives' fable. If he really did take such a precaution, it was totally superfluous; at least so says the authentic old legend, which closes his story in the following manner.

One hot summer afternoon in the dog days, just as a terrible black thunder-gust was coming up, Tom sat in his counting-house in his white linen cap and India silk morning gown. He was on the point of foreclosing a mortgage, by which he would complete the ruin of an unlucky land speculator

for whom he had professed the greatest friendship. The poor land jobber begged him to grant a few months' indulgence. Tom had grown testy and irritated, and refused another day.

"My family will be ruined and brought upon the parish," said the land jobber. "Charity begins at home," replied Tom; "I must take care of myself in these hard times."

"You have made so much money out of me," said the speculator.

Tom lost his patience and his piety— "The Devil take me," said he, "if I have made a farthing!"

Just then there were three loud knocks at the street door. He stepped out to see who was there. A black man was holding a black horse, which neighed and stamped with impatience.

"Tom, you're come for," said the black fellow, gruffly. Tom shrunk back, but too late. He had left his little Bible at the bottom of his coat pocket, and his big Bible on the desk buried under the mortgage he was about to foreclose: never was sinner taken more unawares. The black man whisked him like a child into the saddle, gave the horse the lash, and away he galloped, with Tom on his back, in the midst of the thunderstorm. The clerks stuck their pens behind their ears, and stared after him from the windows. Away went Tom Walker, dashing down the streets, his white cap bobbing up and down, his morning gown fluttering in the wind, and his steed striking fire out of the pavement at every bound. When the clerks turned to look for the black man he had disappeared.

Tom Walker never returned to foreclose the mortgage. A countryman who lived on the border of the swamp, reported that in the height of the thunder-gust he had heard a great clattering of hoofs and a howling along the road, and running to the window caught sight of a figure, such as I have described, on a horse that galloped like mad across the fields, over the hills and down into the black hemlock swamp towards the

---

12. Zionward (zī′ ən wôrd): Toward heaven.

old Indian fort; and that shortly after a thunderbolt falling in that direction seemed to set the whole forest in a blaze.

The good people of Boston shook their heads and shrugged their shoulders, but had been so much accustomed to witches and goblins and tricks of the Devil, in all kind of shapes from the first settlement of the colony, that they were not so much horror struck as might have been expected. Trustees were appointed to take charge of Tom's effects. There was nothing, however, to administer upon. On searching his coffers all his bonds and mortgages were found reduced to cinders. In place of gold and silver his iron chest was filled with chips and shavings; two skeletons lay in his stable instead of his half-starved horses, and the very next day his great house took fire and was burned to the ground.

Such was the end of Tom Walker and his ill-gotten wealth. Let all griping money brokers lay this story to heart. The truth of it is not to be doubted. The very hole under the oak trees, whence he dug Kidd's money, is to be seen to this day; and the neighboring swamp and old Indian fort are often haunted in stormy nights by a figure on horseback, in morning gown and white cap, which is doubtless the troubled spirit of the usurer. In fact, the story has resolved itself into a proverb, and is the origin of that popular saying, so prevalent throughout New England, of "The Devil and Tom Walker."

THINKING ABOUT THE SELECTION
Recalling

1. Describe Tom Walker and his wife.
2. Describe Tom Walker's first encounter with the stranger in the forest.
3. (a) Why does Walker's wife decide to venture into the forest? (b) What does she bring with her?
4. (a) How does Tom Walker react when his wife does not return? (b) What does he discover when he sets out to find her?
5. (a) What arrangement does Walker finally make with the stranger? (b) What does Walker do when he begins to regret making this arrangement?
6. What happens to Tom Walker and his possessions in the end?

Interpreting

7. What does Irving's description of the Walkers' house and the surrounding land indicate about the kind of people they are?
8. What details indicate that while Tom Walker's condition changes during the story his nature remains the same?
9. (a) What does Irving mean when he says that Walker became "a *violent* church-goer"? (b) How is the manner in which Walker approaches religion similar to the way he approaches his financial dealings?

Applying

10. Would this story be effective if it were set in contemporary America? Why or why not?

ANALYZING LITERATURE
Recognizing Folk Tales

Folk tales are stories passed down from generation to generation in a particular culture. These stories usually relate unlikely or unrealistic events, involve stereotypes or stock characters, and teach a lesson or express a general truth about life.
1. What trait does Tom Walker embody?
2. What trait does Tom Walker's wife embody?
3. What general truth about life does the story express?

CRITICAL THINKING AND READING
Inferring Cultural Attitudes

"The Devil and Tom Walker" reveals many of the attitudes of the people living in New England in the late 1720's and early 1730's. Because these attitudes are revealed indirectly, you must make inferences, or draw conclusions, about them by examining the evidence presented in the story. For example, when describing the old Indian fort Irving states that, "the stories handed down from the time of the Indian wars . . . asserted that the savages held incantations here, and made sacrifices to the evil spirit." From this passage you can infer that the colonists had a suspicious attitude toward the Native Americans and a firm belief in the devil.

What inferences about the cultural attitudes of the New Englanders of this period can you make from each of the following passages?
1. ". . . the great speculating fever which breaks out every now and then in the country had raged to an alarming degree, and everybody was dreaming of making sudden fortunes from nothing."
2. "The quiet Christians who had been moving modestly and steadfastly traveling Zionward were struck with self-reproach at seeing themselves so suddenly outstripped of their career by this new-made convert."

THINKING AND WRITING
Adapting a Folk Tale

In your library find a folk tale that interests you, perhaps the tale of John Henry, for example. In what ways would this tale be different if it were set in twentieth-century America? Think about how you can reshape the characters and events to make them fit into a contemporary setting. List the qualities that each character in your adaptation will embody, prepare an outline of events, and decide what lesson your tale will teach. When you write your tale, include details of the setting that will ground it in time and place. After you finish writing, revise your tale and prepare a final copy.

JAMES FENIMORE COOPER

1789–1851

James Fenimore Cooper was the first successful American novelist. Although his novels were popular when they were published, their literary value was not recognized until decades after Cooper's death.

Cooper grew up on his family's large estate in Cooperstown, New York. When he was thirteen, he entered Yale, but he was expelled during his second year for repeated pranks. He worked for two years as a sailor on a merchant ship; then he joined the navy. Later, when his father died, Cooper left the navy and assumed the life of a gentleman farmer.

According to legend Cooper wrote his first novel after making a bet with his wife that he could write a better book than the British novel he had been reading to her. The novel he wrote, *Precaution* (1820), was actually no better than the one he had been reading, but Cooper developed an interest in writing that led him to write many other successful novels. In fact, his second book, *The Spy* (1821), a historical novel set during the Revolution, was extremely popular and earned critical acclaim.

In 1823 Cooper published *The Pioneers,* the first of five related novels collectively known as *The Leatherstocking Tales*. These novels—*The Deerslayer, The Last of the Mohicans, The Pathfinder, The Pioneers,* and *The Prairie*—portray the life of Natty Bumppo, an American frontiersman, who spends his life moving westward as American civilization expands and the wilderness disappears.

During the course of his literary career, Cooper wrote thirty-two novels and a number of nonfiction books. Though readers throughout Europe and the United States responded with enthusiasm to *The Leatherstocking Tales* and many of Cooper's other novels, Cooper's characters and his books were often attacked by the press of his day.

Following Cooper's death in 1851, his novels came to be thought of as appropriate reading only for schoolchildren. In the 1920's, however, scholars began to reassess Cooper's work, and came to regard Cooper as America's first social critic and one of the first writers to explore enduring themes in American literature.

GUIDE FOR READING

from The Prairie

Writer's Techniques

Setting. Setting is the time, environment, and conditions in which the events in a work of literature occur. Though it is rarely the most important element of a literary work, the setting may directly or indirectly affect the characters and events and may be related to the theme, or central idea. Just as real people are often shaped by their environment, characters are often shaped by the setting. As a result, in many literary works, your understanding of the characters' values, attitudes, and behavior depends to some extent on your awareness of the setting. By affecting the characters' behavior, the setting also influences the events in a work. In fact, in some cases, the events are a direct result of the characters' interaction with the setting. The setting may also be closely related to the theme of a work. For example, the theme of a story about a man stranded in the mountains, struggling to survive, might concern the powerlessness of man when confronted with the forces of nature.

Throughout James Fenimore Cooper's *Leatherstocking Tales,* the setting plays a vital role. The novels portray the life of Natty Bumppo, a character molded by the wilderness. During Bumppo's lifetime the American wilderness is being eroded by the westward expansion of civilization. As a result, Bumppo finds himself continually moving westward—from western New York, where he spends his youth, to the midwestern prairies, where he spends his final years—to escape the growth of society. Set on the fringes of the constantly moving frontier, the novels explore the effects of expansion on the American wilderness and people.

Look For

How has the wilderness shaped Natty Bumppo's character? As you read the selection, look for the relationship between the details of the setting and the events.

Writing

Brainstorm and list the events, characters, and descriptive details that you associate with the expanding American frontier. Before reading, share your list with your classmates.

Vocabulary

Knowing the following words will help you as you read the excerpt from *The Prairie.*

solicitous (sə lis′ ə təs) *adj.:* Showing concern (p. 192)

emaciated (i mā′shē āt′ id) *adj.:* Abnormally thin (p. 197)

from The Prairie

James Fenimore Cooper

In the following excerpt, Natty Bumppo is close to death. He is visited by Duncan Uncas Middleton, an army officer whose life Bumppo had saved a year earlier, and Middleton's scouting party. Bumppo has been living with the tribe of Hard-Heart, a young Pawnee chief, whom Bumppo had adopted as a son. As Bumppo's death approaches, both the Indians and the white men are deeply saddened.

When they entered the town, its inhabitants were seen collected in an open space, where they were arranged with the customary deference to age and rank. The whole formed a large circle, in the center of which were perhaps a dozen of the principal chiefs. Hard-Heart waved his hand as he approached, and as the mass of bodies opened he rode through, followed by his companions. Here they dismounted; and as the beasts were led apart, the strangers found themselves environed by a thousand grave, composed, but solicitous faces.

Middleton gazed about him in growing concern, for no cry, no song, no shout welcomed him among a people from whom he had so lately parted with regret. His uneasiness, not to say apprehensions, was shared by all his followers. Determination and stern resolution began to assume the place of anxiety in every eye, as each man silently felt for his arms, and assured himself that his several weapons were in a state for service. But there was no answering symptom of hostility on the part of their hosts. Hard-Heart beckoned for Middleton and Paul[1] to follow, lead-ing the way towards the cluster of forms that occupied the center of the circle. Here the visitors found a solution of all the movements which had given them so much reason for apprehension.

The trapper[2] was placed on a rude seat, which had been made, with studied care, to support his frame in an upright and easy attitude. The first glance of the eye told his former friends that the old man was at length called upon to pay the last tribute of nature. His eye was glazed and apparently as devoid of sight as of expression. His features were a little more sunken and strongly marked than formerly; but there, all change, so far as exterior was concerned, might be said to have ceased. His approaching end was not to be ascribed to any positive disease, but had been a gradual and mild decay of the physical powers. Life, it is true, still lingered in his system; but it was as if at times entirely ready to depart, and then it would appear to reanimate the sinking form, reluctant to give up the possession of a tenement[3] that had never been corrupted by vice or undermined by disease. It would have been no violent fancy to have imagined that the spirit fluttered about the placid lips of the old woodsman, reluctant to depart from a shell that had so long given it an honest and an honorable shelter.

His body was placed so as to let the light of the setting sun fall full upon the solemn features. His head was bare, the long, thin locks of gray fluttering lightly in the evening breeze. His rifle lay upon his knee, and the

---

1. Paul: Paul Hover, a young pioneer.

2. the trapper: Natty Bumppo.
3. tenement (ten′ ə mənt) *n*.: Here, body.

other accouterments of the chase were placed at his side, within reach of his hand. Between his feet lay the figure of a hound, with its head crouching to the earth, as if it slumbered; and so perfectly easy and natural was its position, that a second glance was necessary to tell Middleton he saw only the skin of Hector, stuffed, by Indian tenderness and ingenuity, in a manner to represent the living animal. His own dog was playing at a distance with the child of Tachechana and Mahtoree.[4] The mother herself stood at hand, holding in her arms a second offspring, that might boast of a parentage no less honorable than that which belonged to the son of Hard-Heart. Le Balafré[5] was seated nigh the dying trapper, with every mark about his person that the hour of his own departure was not far distant. The rest of those immediately in the center were aged men who had apparently drawn near in order to observe the manner in which a just and fearless warrior would depart on the greatest of his journeys.

The old man was reaping the rewards of a life remarkable for temperance and activity, in a tranquil and placid death. His vigor in a manner endured to the very last. Decay, when it did occur, was rapid, but free from pain. He had hunted with the tribe in the spring, and even throughout most of the summer, when his limbs suddenly refused to perform their customary offices. A sympathizing weakness took possession of all his faculties; and the Pawnees believed that they were going to lose, in this unexpected manner, a sage and counselor whom they had begun both to love and respect. But, as we have already said, the immortal occupant seemed unwilling to desert its tenement. The lamp of life flickered without becoming extinguished. On the morning of the day on which Middleton arrived, there was a general reviving of the powers of the whole man. His tongue was again heard in wholesome maxims, and his eye from time to time recognized the persons of his friends. It merely proved to be a brief and final intercourse with the world on the part of one who had already been considered, as to mental communion, to have taken his leave of it forever.

When he had placed his guests in front of the dying man, Hard-Heart, after a pause, that proceeded as much from sorrow as decorum, leaned a little forward and demanded:

"Does my father hear the words of his son?"

"Speak," returned the trapper, in tones that issued from his chest, but which were rendered awfully distinct by the stillness that reigned in the place. "I am about to depart from the village of the Loups,[6] and shortly shall be beyond the reach of your voice."

"Let the wise chief have no cares for his journey," continued Hard-Heart with an earnest solicitude that led him to forget, for the moment, that others were waiting to address his adopted parent; "a hundred Loups shall clear his path from briars."

"Pawnee, I die as I have lived, a Christian man," resumed the trapper with a force of voice that had the same startling effect upon his hearers as is produced by the trumpet when its blast rises suddenly and freely on the air after its obstructed sounds have been heard struggling in the distance; "as I came into life so will I leave it. Horses and arms are not needed to stand in the presence of the Great Spirit of my people. He knows my color, and according to my gifts will he judge my deeds."

"My father will tell my young men how many Mingoes[7] he has struck, and what acts of valor and justice he has done, that they may know how to imitate him."

---

4. **Tachechana and Mahtoree:** Two Sioux Indians. During a battle between the Pawnees and the Sioux, Hard-Heart had killed Mahtoree and taken Mahtoree's widow, Tachechana, as his wife.
5. **Le Balafré:** An aging Pawnee chief.

---

6. **Loups:** A Pawnee tribe.
7. **Mingoes:** Enemy warriors.

"A boastful tongue is not heard in the heaven of a white man!" solemnly returned the old man. "What I have done He has seen. His eyes are always open. That which has been well done will he remember; wherein I have been wrong will he not forget to chastise, though he will do the same in mercy. No, my son; a paleface may not sing his own praises and hope to have them acceptable before his God!"

A little disappointed, the young partisan stepped modestly back, making way for the recent comers to approach. Middleton took one of the meager hands of the trapper, and, struggling to command his voice, he succeeded in announcing his presence. The old

THE DEATH OF LEATHERSTOCKING
Felix O. C. Darly
New York Public Library

man listened like one whose thoughts were dwelling on a very different subject; but when the other had succeeded in making him understand that he was present, an expression of joyful recognition passed over his faded features.

"I hope you have not so soon forgotten those whom you so materially served!" Middleton concluded. "It would pain me to think my hold on your memory was so light."

"Little that I have ever seen is forgotten," returned the trapper; "I am at the close of many weary days, but there is not one among them all that I could wish to overlook. I remember you with the whole of your company; aye, and your gran'ther that went before you. I am glad that you have come back upon these plains, for I had need of one who speaks the English, since little faith can be put in the traders of these regions. Will you do a favor to an old and dying man?"

"Name it," said Middleton; "it shall be done."

"It is a far journey to send such trifles," resumed the old man, who spoke at short intervals, as strength and breath permitted; "a far and weary journey is the same; but kindnesses and friendships are things not to be forgotten. There is a settlement among the Otsego hills—"

"I know the place," interrupted Middleton, observing that he spoke with increasing difficulty; "proceed to tell me what you would have done."

"Take this rifle and pouch and horn, and send them to the person whose name is graven on the plates of the stock—a trader cut the letters with his knife—for it is long that I have intended to send him such a token of my love."

"It shall be so. Is there more that you could wish?"

"Little else have I to bestow. My traps I give to my Indian son; for honestly and kindly has he kept his faith. Let him stand before me."

Middleton explained to the chief what the trapper had said, and relinquished his own place to the other.

"Pawnee," continued the old man, always changing his language to suit the person he addressed, and not unfrequently according to the ideas he expressed, "it is a custom of my people for the father to leave his blessing with the son before he shuts his eyes forever. This blessing I give to you; take it, for the prayers of a Christian man will never make the path of a just warrior to the blessed prairies either longer or more tangled. May the God of a white man look on your deeds with friendly eyes, and may you never commit an act that shall cause him to darken his face. I know not whether we shall ever meet again. There are many traditions concerning the place of Good Spirits. It is not for one like me, old and experienced though I am, to set up my opinions against a nation's. You believe in the blessed prairies, and I have faith in the sayings of my fathers. If both are true, our parting will be final; but if it should prove that the same meaning is hid under different words, we shall yet stand together, Pawnee, before the face of your Wahcondah, who will then be no other than my God. There is much to be said in favor of both religions, for each seems suited to its own people, and no doubt it was so intended. I fear I have not altogether followed the gifts of my color, inasmuch as I find it a little painful to give up forever the use of the rifle and the comforts of the chase. But then the fault has been my own, seeing that it could not have been His. Aye, Hector," he continued, leaning forward a little, and feeling for the ears of the hound, "our parting has come at last, dog, and it will be a long hunt. You have been an honest, and a bold, and a faithful hound. Pawnee, you cannot slay the pup on my grave, for where a Christian dog falls, there he lies forever; but you can be kind to him after I am gone, for the love you bear his master."

"The words of my father are in my ears," returned the young partisan, making a grave and respectful gesture of assent.

"Do you hear, what the chief has promised, dog?" demanded the trapper, making an effort to attract the notice of the insensible effigy of his hound. Receiving no answering look, nor hearing any friendly whine, the old man felt for the mouth and endeavored to force his hand between the cold lips. The truth then flashed upon him, although he was far from perceiving the whole extent of the deception. Falling back in his seat, he hung his head, like one who felt a severe and unexpected shock. Profiting by this momentary forgetfulness, two young Indians removed the skin with the same delicacy of feeling that had induced them to attempt the pious[8] fraud.

"The dog is dead!" muttered the trapper, after a pause of many minutes; "a hound has his time as well as a man; and well has he filled his days! Captain," he added, making an effort to wave his hand for Middleton, "I am glad you have come; for though kind and well-meaning according to the gifts of their color, these Indians are not the men to lay the head of a white man in his grave. I have been thinking, too, of this dog at my feet; it will not do to set forth the opinion that a Christian can expect to meet his hound again; still there can be little harm in placing what is left of so faithful a servant nigh the bones of his master."

"It shall be as you desire."

"I'm glad you think with me in this matter. In order then to save labor, lay the pup at my feet; or for that matter, put him side by side. A hunter need never be ashamed to be found in company with his dog!"

"I charge myself with your wish."

The old man made a long and apparently a musing pause. At times he raised his eyes wistfully, as if he would again address Middleton, but some innate feeling appeared always to suppress his words. The other, who observed his hesitation, enquired in a way most likely to encourage him to proceed whether there was aught else that he could wish to have done.

"I am without kith or kin in the wide world!" the trapper answered; "when I am gone, there will be an end of my race. We have never been chiefs; but honest, and useful in our way. I hope it cannot be denied, we have always proved ourselves. My father lies buried near the sea, and the bones of his son will whiten on the prairies—"

---

8. pious (pī′ əs) *adj.*: Dutiful.

"Name the spot, and your remains shall be placed by the side of your father," interrupted Middleton.

"Not so, not so, Captain. Let me sleep, where I have lived, beyond the din of the settlements! Still I see no need why the grave of an honest man should be hid, like a redskin in his ambushment. I paid a man in the settlements to make and put a graven stone at the head of my father's resting place. It was of the value of twelve beaver skins, and cunningly and curiously was it carved! Then it told to all comers that the body of such a Christian lay beneath; and it spoke of his manner of life, of his years, and of his honesty. When we had done with the Frenchers in the old war[9] I made a journey to the spot, in order to see that all was rightly performed, and glad I am to say, the workman had not forgotten his faith."

"And such a stone you would have at your grave?"

"I! no, no, I have no son, but Hard-Heart, and it is little that an Indian knows of white fashions and usages. Besides I am his debtor, already, seeing it is so little I have done since I have lived in his tribe. The rifle might bring the value of such a thing—but then I know it will give the boy pleasure to hang the piece in his hall, for many is the deer and the bird that he has seen it destroy. No, no, the gun must be sent to him whose name is graven on the lock!"

"But there is one who would gladly prove his affection in the way you wish; he who owes you not only his own deliverance from so many dangers, but who inherits a heavy debt of gratitude from his ancestors. The stone shall be put at the head of your grave."

The old man extended his emaciated hand, and gave the other a squeeze of thanks.

"I thought you might be willing to do it, but I was backward in asking the favor," he said, "seeing that you are not of my kin. Put no boastful words on the same, but just the name, the age, and the time of the death, with something from the Holy Book; no more, no more. My name will then not be altogether lost on 'arth; I need no more."

Middleton intimated his assent, and then followed a pause that was only broken by distant and broken sentences from the dying man. He appeared now to have closed his accounts with the world, and to await merely for the final summons to quit it. Middleton and Hard-Heart placed themselves on the opposite sides of his seat, and watched with melancholy solicitude the variations of his countenance. For two hours there was no very sensible alteration. The expression of his faded and timeworn features was that of a calm and dignified repose. From time to time he spoke, uttering some brief sentence in the way of advice, or asking some simple questions concerning those in whose fortunes he still took a friendly interest. During the whole of that solemn and anxious period each individual of the tribe kept his place, in the most self-restrained patience. When the old man spoke, all bent their heads to listen; and when his words were uttered, they seemed to ponder on their wisdom and usefulness.

As the flame drew nigher to the socket, his voice was hushed, and there were moments when his attendants doubted whether he still belonged to the living. Middleton, who watched each wavering expression of his weather-beaten visage with the interest of a keen observer of human nature, softened by the tenderness of personal regard, fancied he could read the workings of the old man's soul in the strong lineaments of his countenance. Perhaps what the enlightened soldier took for the delusion of mistaken opinion did actually occur—for who has returned from that unknown world to explain by what forms, and in what manner, he was introduced into its awful precincts? Without pretending to explain what

---

9. the old war: The French and Indian War (1754–1763).

must ever be a mystery to the quick, we shall simply relate facts as they occurred.

The trapper had remained nearly motionless for an hour. His eyes alone had occasionally opened and shut. When opened, his gaze seemed fastened on the clouds, which hung around the western horizon, reflecting the bright colors, and giving form and loveliness to the glorious tints of an American sunset. The hour—the calm beauty of the season—the occasion, all conspired to fill the spectators with solemn awe. Suddenly, while musing on the remarkable position in which he was placed, Middleton felt the hand which he held, grasp his own with incredible power, and the old man, supported on either side by his friends, rose upright to his feet. For a moment he looked about him, as if to invite all in presence to listen (the lingering remnant of human frailty), and then, with a fine military elevation of the head, and with a voice that might be heard in every part of that numerous assembly, he pronounced the word:

"Here!"

A movement so entirely unexpected, and the air of grandeur and humility which were so remarkably united in the mien of the trapper, together with the clear and uncommon force of his utterance, produced a short period of confusion in the faculties of all present. When Middleton and Hard-Heart, each of whom had involuntarily extended a hand to support the form of the old man, turned to him again, they found that the subject of their interest was removed forever beyond the necessity of their care. They mournfully placed the body in its seat, and Le Balafré arose to announce the termination of the scene to the tribe. The voice of the old Indian seemed a sort of echo from that invisible world to which the meek spirit of the trapper had just departed.

"A valiant, a just, and a wise warrior has gone on the path which will lead him to the blessed grounds of his people!" he said. "When the voice of the Wahcondah called him, he was ready to answer. Go, my children; remember the just chief of the palefaces, and clear your own tracks from briars!"

The grave was made beneath the shade of some noble oaks. It has been carefully watched to the present hour by the Pawnees of the Loup, and is often shown to the traveler and the trader as a spot where a just white man sleeps. In due time the stone was placed at its head, with the simple inscription, which the trapper had himself requested. The only liberty, taken by Middleton, was to add, *"May no wanton hand ever disturb his remains!"*

THINKING ABOUT THE SELECTION
Recalling

1. Why does Middleton grow concerned when he and his troops enter the Pawnee village?
2. In what condition does Middleton find Natty Bumppo?
3. (a) How does Bumppo respond when Hard-Heart suggests that Bumppo should "tell my young men how many Mingoes he has struck"? (b) How does Hard-Heart react to Bumppo's response?
4. (a) Who is the second person to address Bumppo? (b) What favor does Bumppo ask of this person?
5. (a) According to Bumppo what will happen when he dies? (b) Where does he ask to be buried? (c) What does Middleton promise to put at the head of Bumppo's grave?
6. (a) What is Bumppo's final word? (b) What words does Middleton add to the inscription on Bumppo's gravestone?

Interpreting

7. (a) What do Bumppo's comments about the Christian and Pawnee religions suggest about his character? (b) What differences between the two religions does Bumppo state?
8. How would you describe Bumppo's attitude concerning his death?
9. What is the significance of the fact that both Middleton and Hard-Heart are supporting Bumppo when he dies?

Applying

10. What does Natty Bumppo's life illustrate about relationships between different groups of people?

ANALYZING LITERATURE
Understanding Setting

The **setting** is the time and place in which the events in a work of literature occur. In *The Prairie* the setting is the fringe of the rapidly changing frontier. Setting may directly or indirectly affect the characters and events and may be related to the theme. For example, in Cooper's *Leatherstocking Tales,* there is an obvious relationship between the setting and the theme—that the wilderness provided Americans with an opportunity to free themselves from the restraints of society and live according to the laws of nature.

1. What evidence is there in this selection to indicate that Bumppo's values, attitudes, and behavior have been shaped by the wilderness?
2. What details of the setting are given toward the end of the selection? How are these details related to the events in the selection?

CRITICAL THINKING AND READING
Predicting Later Events

The Prairie is set in the midwestern plains, where Natty Bumppo has settled to escape from the growth of society. Only several years after his death, however, settlers would begin arriving in the area.

1. Considering their relationship with Bumppo, how do you think Hard-Heart and his tribe might react to the arrival of settlers?
2. In what ways might the arrival of settlers have changed the lives of Hard-Heart and the members of his tribe?

THINKING AND WRITING
Responding to Criticism

Commenting on Natty Bumppo's movement westward throughout the *Leatherstocking Tales,* a critic has remarked that, "Natty runs from civilization yet opens up the path for civilization to follow." What evidence is there in the excerpt from *The Prairie* to support this statement? Review the excerpt, thinking about what it suggests about the ways in which Bumppo may have opened the path for civilization. Then write a short essay in which you use evidence from the excerpt to support the critic's statement. In your conclusion briefly discuss the irony of the fact that Bumppo dislikes civilization yet opens the way for its expansion. When you finish writing, revise your essay and prepare a final copy.

WILLIAM CULLEN BRYANT

1794–1878

During William Cullen Bryant's long life, America emerged from its infancy to become a large and powerful nation, and American literature blossomed, earning its place among the world's literature. As a journalist and political activist, Bryant fought to make sure that industrialization and rapid growth did not obscure the democratic values and principles upon which the country was built. As a poet Bryant helped to establish an American literary tradition by producing a number of poems that could be matched against the work of the European poets of his day.

Bryant, a descendant of idealistic Puritans, was born in a rural area in western Massachusetts. His father, a country doctor with a deep interest in nature, encouraged him to explore the surrounding wilderness. Bryant's father also taught his son Greek and Latin and urged him to become an avid reader. As a boy he read the work of eighteenth-century English poets, and during his teens he developed a strong interest in the work of the nineteenth-century English Romantic poets. Bryant began writing poetry at the age of nine, and at nineteen he wrote the first version of "Thanatopsis," his most famous poem. When "Thanatopsis" was published in the *North American Review* in 1817, it was greeted with great enthusiasm. In spite of the poem's success, however, Bryant decided to revise it several years later.

Finding that pursuing a full-time career as a poet was economically impossible, Bryant earned a law degree and practiced law for ten years, continuing to write poetry in his spare time. In 1825 Bryant moved to New York City and began a new career as a journalist. By 1829 he had become editor-in-chief and part owner of the New York *Evening Post,* one of the most highly regarded newspapers in the country. In this position Bryant became an influential and enthusiastic defender of human rights and personal freedoms. He supported such causes as women's rights, freedom of speech and religion, and the abolition of slavery.

Though Bryant did not produce a great quantity of poetry, he was the first American poet to win worldwide critical acclaim. Like the European poets of his day, Bryant explored the connection between nature and humanity in his poetry. His work played a major role in establishing the Romantic movement in American literature and influenced the next generation of American poets.

Thanatopsis

Blank Verse. Though "Thanatopsis" is not written in rhyme, its lines do have a regular rhythm, that is, a recurring pattern of stressed and unstressed syllables, known as meter. The basic unit of meter is the foot. Usually a *foot* consists of one stressed syllable and one or more unstressed syllables. The most frequently used foot in American and English verse is the *iamb,* which consists of one unstressed syllable followed by a stressed syllable. When the lines in a poem consist of five iambs, as in "Thanatopsis," the poem is written in iambic pentameter. Verse consisting of unrhymed lines of iambic pentameter is called *blank verse*. Below is an example of blank verse from "Thanatopsis." The unstressed syllables are marked with ˘; the stressed syllables with ′.

> Yet not to thine eternal resting place
> Shalt thou retire alone, nor couldst thou wish

Because it effectively re-creates the smooth natural flow of everyday speech in English, blank verse is one of the most common metrical patterns in American and English poetry. However, when poets use blank verse, they often introduce slight variations in the rhythm to avoid monotony.

"Thanatopsis" has a smooth, natural rhythm. As you read the poem, notice the way that Bryant's use of blank verse creates this rhythm. Also, look for any variations in the rhythm.

What thoughts does nature bring to your mind? Freewrite about nature, considering the relationship between humanity and nature.

Knowing the following words will help you as you read "Thanatopsis."

eloquence (el′ ə kwəns) *n.*: Persuasive power (l. 5)

sepulcher (sep′′l kər) *n.*: Grave; tomb (l. 37)

pensive (pen′ siv) *adj.*: Thinking deeply or seriously (l. 39)

venerable (ven′ ər ə b'l) *adj.*: Worthy of respect or reverence (l. 40)

melancholy (mal′ ən käl′ē) *adj.*: Gloomy (l. 43)

VERNAL FALLS, YOSEMITE VALLEY
Thomas Moran
Three Lions

Thanatopsis

William Cullen Bryant

To him who in the love of Nature holds
Communion with her visible forms, she speaks
A various language; for his gayer hours
She has a voice of gladness, and a smile
5   And eloquence of beauty, and she glides
Into his darker musings, with a mild
And healing sympathy, that steals away
Their sharpness, ere[1] he is aware. When thoughts
Of the last bitter hour come like a blight
10 Over thy spirit, and sad images
Of the stern agony, and shroud, and pall,
And breathless darkness, and the narrow house,[2]
Make thee to shudder, and grow sick at heart—
Go forth, under the open sky, and list
15 To Nature's teachings, while from all around—
Earth and her waters, and the depths of air—
Comes a still voice—Yet a few days, and thee
The all-beholding sun shall see no more
In all his course; nor yet in the cold ground,
20 Where thy pale form was laid, with many tears,
Nor in the embrace of ocean, shall exist
Thy image. Earth, that nourished thee, shall claim
Thy growth, to be resolved to earth again,
And, lost each human trace, surrendering up
25 Thine individual being, shalt thou go
To mix forever with the elements,
To be a brother to the insensible rock
And to the sluggish clod, which the rude swain[3]
Turns with his share,[4] and treads upon. The oak
30 Shall send his roots abroad, and pierce thy mold.

Yet not to thine eternal resting place
Shalt thou retire alone, nor couldst thou wish
Couch[5] more magnificent. Thou shalt lie down
With patriarchs of the infant world—with kings,
35 The powerful of the earth—the wise, the good,
Fair forms, and hoary seers of ages past,
All in one mighty sepulcher. The hills
Rock-ribbed and ancient as the sun—the vales

---

1. ere: Before.
2. narrow house: coffin.
3. swain: A country youth.
4. share: Plowshare.
5. couch: Bed.

.ching in pensive quietness between;
ie venerable woods—rivers that move
n majesty, and the complaining brooks
That make the meadows green; and, poured round all,
Old Ocean's gray and melancholy waste—
Are but the solemn decorations all
45 Of the great tomb of man. The golden sun,
The planets, all the infinite host of heaven,
Are shining on the sad abodes of death,
Through the still lapse of ages. All that tread
The globe are but a handful to the tribes
50 That slumber in its bosom. Take the wings
Of morning,[6] pierce the Barcan[7] wilderness,
Or lose thyself in the continuous woods
Where rolls the Oregon,[8] and hears no sound,
Save his own dashings—yet the dead are there:
55 And millions in those solitudes, since first
The flight of years began, have laid them down
In their last sleep—the dead reign there alone.
So shalt thou rest, and what if thou withdraw
In silence from the living, and no friend
60 Take note of thy departure? All that breathe
Will share thy destiny. The gay will laugh
When thou art gone, the solemn brood of care
Plod on, and each one as before will chase
His favorite phantom; yet all these shall leave
65 Their mirth and their employments, and shall come
And make their bed with thee. As the long train
Of ages glide away, the sons of men,
The youth in life's green spring, and he who goes
In the full strength of years, matron and maid,
70 The speechless babe, and the gray-headed man—
Shall one by one be gathered to thy side,
By those, who in their turn shall follow them.

So live, that when thy summons comes to join
The innumerable caravan, which moves
75 To that mysterious realm, where each shall take
His chamber in the silent halls of death,
Thou go not, like the quarry-slave at night,
Scourged to his dungeon, but, sustained and soothed
By an unfaltering trust, approach thy grave,
80 Like one who wraps the drapery of his couch
About him, and lies down to pleasant dreams.

---

6. Take . . . morning: An allusion to Psalm 139:9.
7. Barcan (bär′ kən): Referring to Barca, a desert region in North Africa.
8. Oregon: A river flowing between Oregon and Washington, now known as the Columbia River.

THINKING ABOUT THE SELECTION

Recalling

1. (a) According to lines 1–3, to whom does nature speak? (b) In what language does nature speak?
2. According to lines 8–15, when should a person "Go forth, under the open sky, and list/To Nature's teachings"?
3. According to lines 22–30, what will eventually happen to you?
4. According to lines 60 and 61, who shares your destiny?
5. According to lines 78 and 79, by what should you be "sustained and soothed"?

Interpreting

6. (a) According to the speaker, how is nature related to human life? (b) How is nature related to death?
7. How is the attitude toward death expressed in the first part of the poem (lines 1–30) different from the attitude expressed in the second half (lines 31–81)?

Applying

8. Bryant's conservative Puritan ancestors believed that only a select few were predestined to go to Heaven. How would the message of this poem be different if it had been written by one of Bryant's ancestors?
9. The contemporary writer Edwin Way Teale has written, "In nature, there is less death and destruction than death and transmutation." First discuss the meaning of this quotation. Then explain how Teale's view of nature compares with Bryant's.

ANALYZING LITERATURE

Recognizing Blank Verse

Blank verse is composed of unrhymed lines of iambic pentameter. In iambic pentameter there are five feet, or beats, per line, and every second syllable is stressed. Below is an example of blank verse from "Thanatopsis."

Shall one by one be gathered to thy side,

By those, who in their turn shall follow them.

1. Find four more lines of blank verse in "Thanatopsis."
2. Find two lines in which the rhythm is varied. Is there any apparent reason why the rhythm is varied besides to break the monotony?

SPEAKING AND LISTENING

Reading with Expression

Recite "Thanatopsis" to your class, being aware of the poem's basic iambic rhythm and its variations. Try to recite the poem at a slow, steady pace, and pronounce each word clearly. Rather than pausing after each line, pause only where a pause is indicated by punctuation.

THINKING AND WRITING

Writing a Poem Using Blank Verse

Think of a natural scene that you could describe in a short poem using iambic pentameter. You might consider one of the following subjects: a waterfall cascading down a mountainside, large snowflakes drifting gently down onto a bed of decaying leaves, large waves crashing on the shore, or a scorching wind screaming across the desert. Once you have decided on your topic, compose a list of details that describe it. Arrange your details in a logical order. Then, using your list of details, compose a brief poem in iambic pentameter. You may vary your rhythm slightly to avoid monotony. When you finish writing, revise your poem and prepare a final copy.

EDGAR ALLAN POE

1809–1849

Throughout the years following Edgar Allan Poe's death, there have been disagreements among writers and critics concerning the quality of his work. In spite of these disagreements, Poe has remained the most influential and widely read American writer of his time.

Poe was born in Boston in 1809, the son of impoverished traveling actors. Shortly after Poe's birth, his father deserted the family. A year later, Poe's mother died. Young Edgar was taken in, though never formally adopted, by the family of John Allan, a wealthy Virginia merchant. The Allans provided for Poe's education, and in 1826 Poe entered the University of Virginia. However, when he contracted large gambling debts which his stepfather refused to pay, Poe was forced to leave the school.

In 1827, after joining the army under an assumed name, Poe published his first volume of poetry, *Tamerlane and Other Poems,* and in 1829 he published a second volume, *Al Aaraaf.* The following year Poe's stepfather helped him to win an appointment to the United States Military Academy at West Point. Poe was expelled for academic violations within a year, however, and his dismissal resulted in an irreparable break with his stepfather.

During the second half of his life, Poe pursued a literary career in New York, Richmond, Philadelphia, and Baltimore, barely supporting himself by writing and working as an editor for a number of magazines. After his third volume of poetry, *Poems* (1831), failed to bring him either money or acclaim, he turned from poetry to fiction and literary criticism. Five of his short stories were published in newspapers in 1832, and in 1838 he published his only novel, *The Narrative of Arthur Gordon Pym.* Though Poe's short stories gained him some recognition and his poem "The Raven" (1845) was greeted with enthusiasm, he was never able to escape from poverty. In 1849, two years after the death of his beloved wife Virginia, Poe died alone and unhappy.

In the years since his death, Poe's work has received much attention. Some writers and critics have harshly criticized Poe's writing. Others have praised his use of vivid imagery and sound effects and his exploration of altered mental states and the dark side of human nature. Despite Poe's uncertain status among writers and critics, however, his work has remained extremely popular among generations of American readers.

GUIDE FOR READING

The Fall of the House of Usher

Writer's Techniques

The Single Effect. More than any other writer, Edgar Allan Poe is responsible for the emergence of the short story as a popular and respected literary form. Poe was the first writer to classify and define the short story as a distinct literary genre and argue that the short story deserved the same status as such other genres as the poem and the novel. In his definition, which first appeared in his review of Nathaniel Hawthorne's *Twice-Told Tales,* Poe asserted that a story should be constructed to achieve "a certain unique or single effect." Poe believed that every character, detail, and incident in a story should contribute to this effect, commenting that "in the whole composition there should be no word written, of which the tendency, direct or indirect, is not to the one preestablished design." Poe even stated that if a writer's "very initial sentence tend not to the outbringing of this effect, then he has failed in his first step."

Look For

With what impression does "The Fall of the House of Usher" leave you? As you read the story, look for the single effect that the story creates. How do the characters, details, and incidents contribute to this effect?

Writing

What sorts of characters, events, and details make a book or movie terrifying? Brainstorm about terrifying books you have read or movies you have seen. Then compose a list of the characters, events, and details that contributed to the effect of these books or movies.

Vocabulary

Knowing the following words will help you as you read "The Fall of the House of Usher."

importunate (im pôr′ chə nit) *adj.*: Insistent (p. 208-210)

munificent (myoo nif′ ə s'nt) *adj.*: Generous (p. 210)

equivocal (i kwiv′ ə k'l) *adj.*: Having more than one possible interpretation (p. 210)

appellation (ap′ ə lā′ s∕hən) *n.*: Name or title (p. 210)

paradoxical (par′ ə däks′i k'l) *adj.*: Expressing an apparent contradiction (p. 210)

specious (spē′ s∕həs) *adj.*: Seeming to be good or sound without actually being so (p. 211)

anomalous (ə näm′ ə ləs) *adj.*: Abnormal (p. 212)

sentience (sen′ s∕həns) *n.*: Capacity of feeling (p. 215)

The Fall of the House of Usher

Edgar Allan Poe

Son cœur est un luth suspendu;
Sitôt qu'on le touche il résonne.[1]

During the whole of a dull, dark, and soundless day in the autumn of the year, when the clouds hung oppressively low in the heavens, I had been passing alone, on horseback, through a singularly dreary tract of country, and at length found myself, as the shades of evening drew on, within view of the melancholy House of Usher. I know not how it was—but, with the first glimpse of the building, a sense of insufferable gloom pervaded my spirit. I say insufferable; for the feeling was unrelieved by any of that half-pleasurable, because poetic, sentiment, with which the mind usually receives even the sternest natural images of the desolate or terrible. I looked upon the scene before me—upon the mere house, and the simple landscape features of the domain—upon the bleak walls—upon the vacant eyelike windows—upon a few rank sedges[2]—and upon a few white trunks of decayed trees—with an utter depression of soul, which I can compare to no earthly sensation more properly than to the afterdream of the reveler upon opium—the bitter lapse into everyday life—the hideous dropping off of the veil. There was an iciness, a sinking, a sickening of the heart—an unredeemed dreariness of thought which no goading of the imagination could torture into aught[3] of the sublime. What was it—I paused to think—what was it that so unnerved me in the contemplation of the House of Usher? It was a mystery all insoluble; nor could I grapple with the shadowy fancies that crowded upon me as I pondered. I was forced to fall back upon the unsatisfactory conclusion, that while, beyond doubt, there *are* combinations of very simple natural objects which have the power of thus affecting us, still the analysis of this power lies among considerations beyond our depth. It was possible, I reflected, that a mere different arrangement of the particulars of the scene, of the details of the picture, would be sufficient to modify, or perhaps to annihilate its capacity for sorrowful impression; and, acting upon this idea, I reined my horse to the precipitous brink of a black and lurid tarn[4] that lay in unruffled luster by the dwelling, and gazed down—but with a shudder even more thrilling than before—upon the remodeled and inverted images of the gray sedge, and the ghastly tree stems, and the vacant and eyelike windows.

Nevertheless, in this mansion of gloom I now proposed to myself a sojourn of some weeks. Its proprietor, Roderick Usher, had been one of my boon companions in boyhood; but many years had elapsed since our last meeting. A letter, however, had lately reached me in a distant part of the country—a letter from him—which, in its wildly im-

---

1. Son . . . résonne: "His heart is a suspended lute; as one touches it, it resounds." From "Le Rufus" by Pierre Jean de Béranger (1780–1857).
2. sedges (sej′ ez) *n.*: Grasslike plants.

3. aught (ôt): Anything.
4. tarn (tärn) *n.*: A small lake.

"I AT LENGTH . . . ," EDGAR ALLAN POE'S TALES OF MYSTERY AND IMAGINATION
Arthur Rackham
New York Public Library, Astor, Lenox and Tilden Foundations

The Fall of the House of Usher　209

portunate nature, had admitted of no other than a personal reply. The MS.[5] gave evidence of nervous agitation. The writer spoke of acute bodily illness—of a mental disorder which oppressed him—and of an earnest desire to see me, as his best and indeed his only personal friend, with a view of attempting, by the cheerfulness of my society, some alleviation of his malady. It was the manner in which all this, and much more, was said—it was the apparent *heart* that went with his request—which allowed me no room for hesitation; and I accordingly obeyed forthwith what I still considered a very singular summons.

Although, as boys, we had been even intimate associates, yet I really knew little of my friend. His reserve had been always excessive and habitual. I was aware, however, that his very ancient family had been noted, time out of mind, for a peculiar sensibility of temperament, displaying itself, through long ages, in many works of exalted art, and manifested, of late, in repeated deeds of munificent yet unobtrusive charity, as well as in a passionate devotion to the intricacies, perhaps even more than to the orthodox and easily recognizable beauties, of musical science. I had learned, too, the very remarkable fact, that the stem of the Usher race, all time-honored as it was, had put forth, at no period, any enduring branch; in other words, that the entire family lay in the direct line of descent, and had always, with very trifling and very temporary variations, so lain. It was this deficiency, I considered, while running over in thought the perfect keeping of the character of the premises with the accredited character of the people, and while speculating upon the possible influence which the one, in the long lapse of centuries, might have exercised upon the other—it was this deficiency, perhaps of collateral[6] issue, and the consequent undeviating transmission, from sire to son, of the patrimony[7] with the name, which had, at length, so identified the two as to merge the original title of the estate in the quaint and equivocal appellation of the "House of Usher"—an appellation which seemed to include, in the minds of the peasantry who used it, both the family and the family mansion.

I have said that the sole effect of my somewhat childish experiment—that of looking down within the tarn—had been to deepen the first singular impression. There can be no doubt that the consciousness of the rapid increase of my superstition—for why should I not so term it?—served mainly to accelerate the increase itself. Such, I have long known, is the paradoxical law of all sentiments having terror as a basis. And it might have been for this reason only, that, when I again uplifted my eyes to the house itself, from its image in the pool, there grew in my mind a strange fancy—a fancy so ridiculous, indeed, that I but mention it to show the vivid force of the sensations which oppressed me. I had so worked upon my imagination as really to believe that about the whole mansion and domain there hung an atmosphere peculiar to themselves and their immediate vicinity—an atmosphere which had no affinity with the air of heaven, but which had reeked up from the decayed trees, and the gray wall, and the silent tarn—a pestilent and mystic vapor, dull, sluggish, faintly discernible and leaden-hued.

Shaking off from my spirit what *must* have been a dream, I scanned more narrowly the real aspect of the building. Its principal feature seemed to be that of an excessive antiquity. The discoloration of ages had been great. Minute fungi overspread the whole exterior, hanging in a fine tangled web-work from the eaves. Yet all this was apart from any extraordinary dilapidation. No portion of the masonry had fallen; and there appeared to be a wild inconsistency between its still perfect adaptation of parts, and the crum-

---

5. MS.: Manuscript.
6. collateral (kə lat′ ər əl) *adj.*: Descended from the same ancestors, but in a different line.

7. patrimony (pat′ rə mō′ nē) *n.*: Property inherited from one's father.

bling condition of the individual stones. In this there was much that reminded me of the specious totality of old woodwork which has rotted for long years in some neglected vault, with no disturbance from the breath of the external air. Beyond this indication of extensive decay, however, the fabric gave little token of instability. Perhaps the eye of a scrutinizing observer might have discovered a barely perceptible fissure, which, extending from the roof of the building in front, made its way down the wall in a zigzag direction, until it became lost in the sullen waters of the tarn.

Noticing these things, I rode over a short causeway to the house. A servant in waiting took my horse, and I entered the Gothic[8] archway of the hall. A valet, of stealthy step, then conducted me, in silence, through many dark and intricate passages in my progress to the *studio* of his master. Much that I encountered on the way contributed, I know not how, to heighten the vague sentiments of which I have already spoken. While the objects around me—while the carvings of the ceilings, the somber tapestries of the walls, the ebon blackness of the floors, and the phantasmagoric[9] armorial trophies which rattled as I strode, were but matters to which, or to such as which, I had been accustomed from my infancy—while I hesitated not to acknowledge how familiar was all this—I still wondered to find how unfamiliar were the fancies which ordinary images were stirring up. On one of the staircases, I met the physician of the family. His countenance, I thought, wore a mingled expression of low cunning and perplexity. He accosted me with trepidation and passed on. The valet now threw open a door and ushered me into the presence of his master.

The room in which I found myself was very large and lofty. The windows were long, narrow, and pointed, and at so vast a distance from the black oaken floor as to be al-together inaccessible from within. Feeble gleams of encrimsoned light made their way through the trellised panes, and served to render sufficiently distinct the more prominent objects around; the eye, however, struggled in vain to reach the remoter angles of the chamber, or the recesses of the vaulted and fretted[10] ceiling. Dark draperies hung upon the walls. The general furniture was profuse, comfortless, antique, and tattered. Many books and musical instruments lay scattered about, but failed to give any vitality to the scene. I felt that I breathed an atmosphere of sorrow. An air of stern, deep, and irredeemable gloom hung over and pervaded all.

Upon my entrance, Usher arose from a sofa on which he had been lying at full length, and greeted me with a vivacious warmth which had much in it, I at first thought, of an overdone cordiality—of the constrained effort of the *ennuyé*[11] man of the world. A glance, however, at his countenance convinced me of his perfect sincerity. We sat down; and for some moments, while he spoke not, I gazed upon him with a feeling half of pity, half of awe. Surely, man had never before so terribly altered, in so brief a period, as had Roderick Usher! It was with difficulty that I could bring myself to admit the identity of the wan being before me with the companion of my early boyhood. Yet the character of his face had been at all times remarkable. A cadaverousness of complexion; an eye large, liquid, and luminous beyond comparison; lips somewhat thin and very pallid, but of a surpassingly beautiful curve; a nose of a delicate Hebrew model, but with a breadth of nostril unusual in similar formations; a finely molded chin, speaking, in its want of prominence, of a want of moral energy; hair of a more than weblike softness and tenuity—these features, with an inordinate expansion above the regions of the temple, made up altogether a countenance not easily to be forgotten. And now in the mere

---

8. Gothic: High and ornate.
9. phantasmagoric (fan taz′ mə gôr′ ik) *adj.*: Fantastic or dreamlike.

10. fretted: Ornamented.
11. ennuyé (än′ nwē ā′): Bored (French).

exaggeration of the prevailing character of these features, and of the expression they were wont to convey, lay so much of change that I doubted to whom I spoke. The now ghastly pallor of the skin, and the now miraculous luster of the eye, above all things startled and even awed me. The silken hair, too, had been suffered to grow all unheeded, and as, in its wild gossamer texture, it floated rather than fell about the face, I could not, even with effort, connect its Arabesque[12] expression with any idea of simple humanity.

In the manner of my friend I was at once struck with an incoherence—an inconsistency; and I soon found this to arise from a series of feeble and futile struggles to overcome an habitual trepidancy—an excessive nervous agitation. For something of this nature I had indeed been prepared, no less by his letter than by reminiscences of certain boyish traits, and by conclusions deduced from his peculiar physical conformation and temperament. His action was alternately vivacious and sullen. His voice varied rapidly from a tremulous indecision (when the animal spirits seemed utterly in abeyance) to that species of energetic concision—that abrupt, weighty, unhurried, and hollow-sounding enunciation—that leaden, self-balanced, and perfectly modulated guttural utterance, which may be observed in the lost drunkard, or the irreclaimable eater of opium, during the periods of his most intense excitement.

It was thus that he spoke of the object of my visit, of his earnest desire to see me, and of the solace he expected me to afford him. He entered, at some length, into what he conceived to be the nature of his malady. It was, he said, a constitutional and a family evil and one for which he despaired to find a remedy—a mere nervous affection,[13] he immediately added, which would undoubtedly soon pass off. It displayed itself in a host of

unnatural sensations. Some of these, as he detailed them, interested and bewildered me; although, perhaps, the terms and the general manner of their narration had their weight. He suffered much from a morbid acuteness of the senses; the most insipid food was alone endurable; he could wear only garments of certain texture; the odors of all flowers were oppressive; his eyes were tortured by even a faint light; and there were but peculiar sounds, and these from stringed instruments, which did not inspire him with horror.

To an anomalous species of terror I found him a bounden slave. "I shall perish," said he, "I *must* perish in this deplorable folly. Thus, thus, and not otherwise, shall I be lost. I dread the events of the future, not in themselves, but in their results. I shudder at the thought of any, even the most trivial, incident, which may operate upon this intolerable agitation of soul. I have, indeed, no abhorrence of danger, except in its absolute effect—in terror. In this unnerved, in this pitiable, condition I feel that the period will sooner or later arrive when I must abandon life and reason together, in some struggle with the grim phantasm, FEAR."

I learned, moreover, at intervals, and through broken and equivocal hints, another singular feature of his mental condition. He was enchained by certain superstitious impressions in regard to the dwelling which he tenanted, and whence, for many years, he had never ventured forth—in regard to an influence whose supposititious[14] force was conveyed in terms too shadowy here to be restated—an influence which some peculiarities in the mere form and substance of his family mansion had, by dint of long sufferance, he said, obtained over his spirit—an effect which the physique of the gray walls and turrets, and of the dim tarn into which they all looked down, had at length, brought about upon the morale of his existence.

---

12. Arabesque (ar′ ə besk′) *n.*: Of complex and elaborate design.
13. affection: Affliction.

---

14. supposititious (sə päz′ ə tish′ əs) *adj.*: Supposed.

He admitted, however, although with hesitation, that much of the peculiar gloom which thus afflicted him could be traced to a more natural and far more palpable origin—to the severe and long-continued illness—indeed to the evidently approaching dissolution—of a tenderly beloved sister, his sole companion for long years, his last and only relative on earth. "Her decease," he said, with a bitterness which I can never forget, "would leave him (him, the hopeless and the frail) the last of the ancient race of the Ushers." While he spoke, the lady Madeline (for so was she called) passed through a remote portion of the apartment, and, without having noticed my presence, disappeared. I regarded her with an utter astonishment not unmingled with dread; and yet I found it impossible to account for such feelings. A sensation of stupor oppressed me as my eyes followed her retreating steps. When a door, at length, closed upon her, my glance sought instinctively and eagerly the countenance of the brother; but he had buried his face in his hands, and I could only perceive that a far more than ordinary wanness had overspread the emaciated fingers through which trickled many passionate tears.

The disease of the lady Madeline had long baffled the skill of her physicians. A settled apathy, a gradual wasting away of the person, and frequent although transient affections of a partially cataleptical[15] character were the unusual diagnosis. Hitherto she had steadily borne up against the pressure of her malady, and had not betaken herself finally to bed; but on the closing in of the evening of my arrival at the house, she succumbed (as her brother told me at night with inexpressible agitation) to the prostrating power of the destroyer; and I learned that the glimpse I had obtained of her person would thus probably be the last I should obtain—that the lady, at least while living, would be seen by me no more.

For several days ensuing, her name was unmentioned by either Usher or myself; and during this period I was busied in earnest endeavors to alleviate the melancholy of my friend. We painted and read together, or I listened, as if in a dream, to the wild improvisations of his speaking guitar. And thus, as a closer and still closer intimacy admitted me more unreservedly into the recesses of his spirit, the more bitterly did I perceive the futility of all attempt at cheering a mind from which darkness, as if an inherent positive quality, poured forth upon all objects of the moral and physical universe in one unceasing radiation of gloom.

I shall ever bear about me a memory of the many solemn hours I thus spent alone with the master of the House of Usher. Yet I should fail in any attempt to convey an idea of the exact character of the studies, or of the occupations, in which he involved me, or led me the way. An excited and highly distempered ideality[16] threw a sulfureous[17] luster over all. His long improvised dirges will ring forever in my ears. Among other things, I hold painfully in mind a certain singular perversion and amplification of the wild air of the last waltz of von Weber.[18] From the paintings over which his elaborate fancy brooded, and which grew, touch by touch, into vaguenesses at which I shuddered the more thrillingly, because I shuddered knowing not why—from these paintings (vivid as their images now are before me) I would in vain endeavor to educe more than a small portion which should lie within the compass of merely written words. By the utter simplicity, by the nakedness of his designs, he arrested and overawed attention. If ever mortal painted an idea, that mortal was Roderick Usher. For me at least, in the circumstances then surrounding me, there arose out of the pure abstractions which the hypochondriac contrived to throw upon his

---

15. **cataleptical** (kat′ 'l ep′ tik 'l) *adj.*: In a state in which consciousness and feeling are suddenly and temporarily lost and the muscles become rigid.

16. **ideality** (ī′ dē al′ ə tē) *n.*: Something that is ideal and has no reality.
17. **sulfureous** (sul fyoor′ ē əs) *adj.*: Greenish-yellow.
18. **von Weber:** Karl Maria von Weber (1786–1826), a German Romantic composer.

The Fall of the House of Usher **213**

canvas, an intensity of intolerable awe, no shadow of which felt I ever yet in the contemplation of the certainly glowing yet too concrete reveries of Fuseli.[19]

One of the phantasmagoric conceptions of my friend, partaking not so rigidly of the spirit of abstraction, may be shadowed forth, although feebly, in words. A small picture presented the interior of an immensely long and rectangular vault or tunnel, with low walls, smooth, white and without interruption or device. Certain accessory points of the design served well to convey the idea that this excavation lay at an exceeding depth below the surface of the earth. No outlet was observed in any portion of its vast extent, and no torch or other artificial source of light was discernible; yet a flood of intense rays rolled throughout, and bathed the whole in a ghastly and inappropriate splendor.

I have just spoken of that morbid condition of the auditory nerve which rendered all music intolerable to the sufferer, with the exception of certain effects of stringed instruments. It was, perhaps, the narrow limits to which he thus confined himself upon the guitar which gave birth, in great measure, to the fantastic character of his performances. But the fervid facility of his impromptus could not be so accounted for. They must have been, and were, in the notes, as well as in the words of his wild fantasias (for he not unfrequently accompanied himself with rhymed verbal improvisations), the result of that intense mental collectedness and concentration to which I have previously alluded as observable only in particular moments of the highest artificial excitement. The words of one of these rhapsodies I have easily remembered. I was, perhaps, the more forcibly impressed with it as he gave it because, in the under or mystic current of its meaning, I fancied that I perceived, and for the first time, a full consciousness on the part of Usher of the tottering of his lofty reason upon her throne. The verses, which were entitled "The Haunted Palace," ran very nearly, if not accurately, thus:

I

In the greenest of our valleys,
*   By good angels tenanted,*
Once a fair and stately palace—
*   Radiant palace—reared its head.*
In the monarch Thought's dominion—
*   It stood there!*
Never seraph[20] spread a pinion
*   Over fabric half so fair.*

II

Banners yellow, glorious, golden,
*   On its roof did float and flow*
(This—all this—was in the olden
*   Time long ago)*
And every gentle air that dallied,
*   In that sweet day,*
Along the ramparts plumed and
*   pallid,*
*   A winged odor went away.*

III

Wanderers in that happy valley
*   Through two luminous windows saw*
Spirits moving musically
*   To a lute's well-tunèd law;*
Round about a throne, where sitting
*   (Porphyrogene!)[21]*
In state his glory well befitting,
*   The ruler of the realm was seen.*

IV

And all with pearl and ruby glowing
*   Was the fair palace door,*
Through which came flowing, flowing,
*   flowing*
*   And sparkling evermore,*

---

19. Fuseli: Johann Heinrich Fuseli (1742–1825), a Swiss-born painter who lived in England and was noted for his work in the supernatural.

20. seraph (ser′ əf): Angel.
21. Porphyrogene (pôr fər ō jēn′): Born to royalty or "the purple."

A troop of Echoes whose sweet duty
  Was but to sing,
In voices of surpassing beauty,
  The wit and wisdom of their king.

V

But evil things, in robes of sorrow,
  Assailed the monarch's high estate;
(Ah, let us mourn, for never morrow
  Shall dawn upon him, desolate!)
And, round about his home, the glory
  That blushed and bloomed
Is but a dim-remembered story
  Of the old time entombed.

VI

And travelers now within that valley,
  Through the red-litten[22] windows see
Vast forms that move fantastically
  To a discordant melody;
While, like a rapid ghastly river,
  Through the pale door,
A hideous throng rush out forever,
  And laugh—but smile no more.

I well remember that suggestions arising from this ballad led us into a train of thought wherein there became manifest an opinion of Usher's which I mention not so much on account of its novelty (for other men have thought thus), as on account of the pertinacity with which he maintained it. This opinion, in its general form, was that of the sentience of all vegetable things. But, in his disordered fancy the idea had assumed a more daring character, and trespassed, under certain conditions, upon the kingdom of inorganization.[23] I lack words to express the full extent, or the earnest abandon of his persuasion. The belief, however, was connected (as I have previously hinted) with the gray stones of the home of his forefathers. The conditions of the sentience had been here, he imagined, fulfilled in the method of collocation of these stones—in the order of

their arrangement, as well as in that of the many fungi which overspread them, and of the decayed trees which stood around—above all, in the long undisturbed endurance of this arrangement, and in its reduplication in the still waters of the tarn. Its evidence—the evidence of the sentience—was to be seen, he said (and I here started as he spoke), in the gradual yet certain condensation of an atmosphere of their own about the waters and the walls. The result was discoverable, he added, in that silent yet importunate and terrible influence which for centuries had molded the destinies of his family, and which made him what I now saw him—what he was. Such opinions need no comment, and I will make none.

Our books—the books which, for years, had formed no small portion of the mental existence of the invalid—were, as might be supposed, in strict keeping with this character of phantasm. We pored together over such works as the *Ververt et Chartreuse*[24] of Gresset; the *Belphegor* of Machiavelli; the *Heaven and Hell* of Swedenborg; the *Subterranean Voyage of Nicholas Klimm* by Holberg; the *Chiromancy* of Robert Flud, of Jean D'Indaginé and of De la Chambre; the *Journey into the Blue Distance* of Tieck; and the *City of the Sun* of Campanella. One favorite volume was a small octavo edition of the *Directorium Inquisitorium*, by the Dominican Eymeric de Gironne; and there were passages in Pomponius Mela, about the old African Stayrs and Œgipans, over which Usher would sit dreaming for hours. His chief delight, however, was found in the perusal of an exceedingly rare and curious book in quarto Gothic—the manual of a forgotten church—the *Vigiliæ Mortuorum secundum Chorum Ecclesiae Maguntinae.*

I could not help thinking of the wild ritual of this work, and of its probable influence upon the hypochondriac, when, one evening, having informed me abruptly that the lady Madeline was no more, he stated his

---

22. litten: Lighted.
23. inorganization: Inanimate objects.

24. *Ververt et Chartreuse*, etc.: All of the books listed deal with magic or mysticism.

intention of preserving her corpse for a fortnight (previously to its final interment), in one of the numerous vaults within the main walls of the building. The worldly reason, however, assigned for this singular proceeding, was one which I did not feel at liberty to dispute. The brother had been led to his resolution (so he told me) by consideration of the unusual character of the malady of the deceased, of certain obstrusive and eager inquiries on the part of her medical men, and of the remote and exposed situation of the burial ground of the family. I will not deny that when I called to mind the sinister countenance of the person whom I met upon the staircase, on the day of my arrival at the house, I had no desire to oppose what I regarded as at best but a harmless, and by no means an unnatural precaution.

At the request of Usher, I personally aided him in the arrangements for the temporary entombment. The body having been encoffined, we two alone bore it to its rest. The vault in which we placed it (and which had been so long unopened that our torches, half smothered in its oppressive atmosphere, gave us little opportunity for investigation) was small, damp, and entirely without means of admission for light; lying, at great depth, immediately beneath that portion of the building in which was my own sleeping apartment. It had been used, apparently, in remote feudal times, for the worst purposes of a donjon-keep, and, in later days, as a place of deposit for powder, or some other highly combustible substance, as a portion of its floor, and the whole interior of a long archway through which we reached it, were carefully sheathed with copper. The door, of massive iron, had been, also, similarly protected. Its immense weight caused an unusually sharp, grating sound, as it moved upon its hinges.

Having deposited our mournful burden upon trestles within this region of horror, we partially turned aside the yet unscrewed lid of the coffin, and looked upon the face of the tenant. A striking similitude between the brother and sister now first arrested my attention; and Usher, divining, perhaps, my thoughts, murmured out some few words from which I learned that the deceased and himself had been twins, and that sympathies of a scarcely intelligible nature had always existed between them. Our glances, however, rested not long upon the dead—for we could not regard her unawed. The disease which had thus entombed the lady in the maturity of youth, had left, as usual in all maladies of a strictly cataleptical character, the mockery of a faint blush upon the bosom and the face, and that suspiciously lingering smile upon the lip which is so terrible in death. We replaced and screwed down the lid, and, having secured the door of iron, made our way, with toil, into the scarcely less gloomy apartments of the upper portion of the house.

And now, some days of bitter grief having elapsed, an observable change came over the features of the mental disorder of my friend. His ordinary manner had vanished. His ordinary occupations were neglected or forgotten. He roamed from chamber to chamber with hurried, unequal, and objectless step. The pallor of his countenance had assumed, if possible, a more ghastly hue—but the luminousness of his eye had utterly gone out. The once occasional huskiness of his tone was heard no more; and a tremulous quaver, as if of extreme terror, habitually characterized his utterance. There were times, indeed, when I thought his unceasingly agitated mind was laboring with some oppressive secret, to divulge which he struggled for the necessary courage. At times, again, I was obliged to resolve all into the mere inexplicable vagaries[25] of madness, for I beheld him gazing upon vacancy for long hours, in an attitude of the profoundest attention, as if listening to some imaginary sound. It was no wonder that his condition terrified—that it infected me. I felt creeping

---

25. vagaries (və ger′ ēz) *n*.: Odd, unexpected actions or notions.

upon me, by slow yet uncertain degrees, the wild influences of his own fantastic yet impressive superstitions.

It was, especially, upon retiring to bed late in the night of the seventh or eighth day after the placing of the lady Madeline within the donjon, that I experienced the full power of such feelings. Sleep came not near my couch—while the hours waned and waned away. I struggled to reason off the nervousness which had dominion over me. I endeavored to believe that much, if not all of what I felt, was due to the bewildering influence of the gloomy furniture of the room—of the dark and tattered draperies, which, tortured into motion by the breath of a rising tempest, swayed fitfully to and fro upon the walls, and rustled uneasily about the decorations of the bed. But my efforts were fruitless. An irrepressible tremor gradually pervaded my frame; and, at length, there sat upon my very heart an incubus[26] of utterly causeless alarm. Shaking this off with a gasp and a struggle, I uplifted myself upon the pillows, and, peering earnestly within the intense darkness of the chamber, hearkened—I know not why, except that an instinctive spirit prompted me—to certain low and indefinite sounds which came, through the pauses of the storm, at long intervals, I knew not whence. Overpowered by an intense sentiment of horror, unaccountable yet unendurable, I threw on my clothes with haste (for I felt that I should sleep no more during the night), and endeavored to arouse myself from the pitiable condition into which I had fallen by pacing rapidly to and fro through the apartment.

I had taken but few turns in this manner, when a light step on an adjoining staircase arrested my attention. I presently recognized it as that of Usher. In an instant afterward he rapped, with a gentle touch, at my door, and entered, bearing a lamp. His countenance was, as usual, cadaverously wan—but, moreover, there was a species of mad hilarity in his eyes—an evidently restrained hysteria in his whole demeanor. His air appalled me—but anything was preferable to the solitude which I had so long endured, and I even welcomed his presence as a relief.

"And you have not seen it?" he said abruptly, after having stared about him for some moments in silence—"you have not then seen it?—but, stay! you shall." Thus speaking, and having carefully shaded his lamp, he hurried to one of the casements, and threw it freely open to the storm.

The impetuous fury of the entering gust nearly lifted us from our feet. It was, indeed, a tempestuous yet sternly beautiful night, and one wildly singular in its terror and its beauty. A whirlwind had apparently collected its force in our vicinity; for there were frequent and violent alterations in the direction of the wind; and the exceeding density of the clouds (which hung so low as to press upon the turrets of the house) did not prevent our perceiving the lifelike velocity with which they flew careering from all points against each other, without passing away into the distance. I say that even their exceeding density did not prevent our perceiving this—yet we had no glimpse of the moon or stars, nor was there any flashing forth of the lightning. But the under surfaces of the huge masses of agitated vapor, as well as all terrestrial objects immediately around us, were glowing in the unnatural light of a faintly luminous and distinctly visible gaseous exhalation which hung about and enshrouded the mansion.

"You must not—you shall not behold this!" said I, shuddering, to Usher, as I led him, with a gentle violence, from the window to a seat. "These appearances, which bewilder you, are merely electrical phenomena not uncommon—or it may be that they have their ghastly origin in the rank miasma[27] of

---

26. incubus (iŋ′ kyə bəs) *n*.: Something nightmarishly burdensome.

27. miasma (mī az′ mə) *n*.: An unwholesome atmosphere.

the tarn. Let us close this casement:—the air is chilling and dangerous to your frame. Here is one of your favorite romances. I will read, and you shall listen:—and so we will pass away this terrible night together."

The antique volume which I had taken up was the *Mad Trist* of Sir Launcelot Canning;[28] but I had called it a favorite of Usher's more in sad jest than in earnest; for, in truth, there is little in its uncouth and unimaginative prolixity which could have had interest for the lofty and spiritual ideality of my friend. It was, however, the only book immediately at hand; and I indulged a vague hope that the excitement which now agitated the hypochondriac, might find relief (for the history of mental disorder is full of similar anomalies) even in the extremeness of the folly which I should read. Could I have judged, indeed, by the wild overstrained air of vivacity with which he hearkened, or apparently hearkened, to the words of the tale, I might well have congratulated myself upon the success of my design.

I had arrived at that well-known portion of the story where Ethelred, the hero of the Trist, having sought in vain for peaceable admission into the dwelling of the hermit, proceeds to make good an entrance by force. Here, it will be remembered, the words of the narrative run thus:

"And Ethelred, who was by nature of a doughty heart, and who was now mighty withal, on account of the powerfulness of the wine which he had drunken, waited no longer to hold parley with the hermit, who, in sooth, was of an obstinate and maliceful turn, but feeling the rain upon his shoulders, and fearing the rising of the tempest, uplifted his mace outright, and, with blows, made quickly room in the plankings of the door for his gauntleted hand; and now pulling therewith sturdily, he so cracked, and ripped, and tore all asunder, that the noise of the dry and hollow-sounding wood alar-

umed and reverberated throughout the forest."

At the termination of this sentence I started and, for a moment, paused; for it appeared to me (although I at once concluded that my excited fancy had deceived me)—it appeared to me that, from some very remote portion of the mansion, there came, indistinctly to my ears, which might have been, in its exact similarity of character, the echo (but a stifled and dull one certainly) of the very cracking and ripping sound which Sir Launcelot had so particularly described. It was, beyond doubt, the coincidence alone which had arrested my attention; for, amid the rattling of the sashes of the casements, and the ordinary commingled noises of the still increasing storm, the sound, itself, had nothing, surely, which should have interested or disturbed me. I continued the story:

"But the good champion Ethelred, now entering within the door, was sore enraged and amazed to perceive no signal of the maliceful hermit; but, in the stead thereof, a dragon of a scaly and prodigious demeanor, and of a fiery tongue, which sate in guard before a palace of gold, with a floor of silver; and upon the wall there hung a shield of shining brass with this legend enwritten—

*Who entereth herein, a conqueror
  hath bin;
Who slayeth the dragon, the
  shield he shall win.*

And Ethelred uplifted his mace, and struck upon the head of the dragon, which fell before him, and gave up his pesty breath, with a shriek so horrid and harsh, and withal so piercing, that Ethelred had fain to close his ears with his hands against the dreadful noise of it, the like whereof was never before heard."

Here again I paused abruptly, and now with a feeling of wild amazement—for there could be no doubt whatever that, in this instance, I did actually hear (although from

---

28. *Mad Trist* of Sir Launcelot Canning: A fictional book and author.

what direction it proceeded I found it impossible to say) a low and apparently distant, but harsh, protracted, and most unusual screaming or grating sound—the exact counterpart of what my fancy had already conjured up for the dragon's unnatural shriek as described by the romancer.

Oppressed, as I certainly was, upon the extraordinary coincidence, by a thousand conflicting sensations, in which wonder and extreme terror were predominant, I still retained sufficient presence of mind to avoid exciting, by an observation, the sensitive nervousness of my companion. I was by no means certain that he had noticed the sounds in question; although, assuredly, a strange alteration had, during the last few minutes, taken place in his demeanor. From a position fronting my own, he had gradually brought round his chair; so as to sit with his face to the door of the chamber; and thus I could but partially perceive his features, although I saw that his lips trembled as if he were murmuring inaudibly. His head had dropped upon his breast—yet I knew that he was not asleep, from the wide and rigid opening of the eye as I caught a glance of it in profile. The motion of his body, too, was at variance with this idea—for he rocked from side to side with a gentle yet constant and uniform sway. Having rapidly taken notice of all this, I resumed the narrative of Sir Launcelot, which thus proceeded:

"And now, the champion, having escaped from the terrible fury of the dragon, bethinking himself of the brazen shield, and of the breaking up of the enchantment which was upon it, removed the carcass from out of the way before him, and approached valorously over the silver pavement of the castle to where the shield was upon the wall; which in sooth tarried not for his full coming, but fell down at his feet upon the silver floor, with a mighty great and terrible ringing sound."

No sooner had these syllables passed my lips, than—as if a shield of brass had indeed, at the moment, fallen heavily upon a floor of silver—I became aware of a distinct, hollow, metallic, and clangorous, yet apparently muffled, reverberation. Completely unnerved, I leaped to my feet; but the measured rocking movement of Usher was undisturbed. I rushed to the chair in which he sat. His eyes were bent fixedly before him, and throughout his whole countenance there reigned a stony rigidity. But, as I placed my hand upon his shoulder, there came a strong shudder over his whole person; a sickly smile quivered about his lips; and I saw that he spoke in a low, hurried, and gibbering murmur, as if unconscious of my presence. Bending closely over him I at length drank in the hideous import of his words.

"Not hear it?—yes, I hear it, and have heard it. Long—long—long—many minutes, many hours, many days, have I heard it—yet I dared not—oh, pity me, miserable wretch that I am!—I dared not—I *dared* not speak! *We have put her living in the tomb!* Said I not that my senses were acute? I *now* tell you that I heard her first feeble movement in the hollow coffin. I heard them—many, many days ago—yet I dared not—*I dared not speak!* and now—tonight—Ethelred—ha! ha!—the breaking of the hermit's door, and the death cry of the dragon, and the clangor of the shield—say, rather, the rending of her coffin, and the grating of the iron hinges of her prison, and her struggles within the coppered archway of the vault! Oh! wither shall I fly? Will she not be here anon? Is she not hurrying to upbraid me for my haste? Have I not heard her footstep on the stair? Do I not distinguish that heavy and horrible beating of her heart? Madman!"—here he sprang furiously to his feet, and shrieked out his syllables, as if in the effort he were giving up his soul—"*Madman! I tell you that she now stands without the door!*"

As if in the superhuman energy of his utterance there had been found the potency of a spell, the huge antique panels to which the speaker pointed threw slowly back, upon the instant, their ponderous and ebony jaws. It was the work of the rushing gust—but then without those doors there *did* stand the lofty and enshrouded figure of the lady Madeline of Usher. There was blood upon her white robes, and the evidence of some bitter struggle upon every portion of her emaciated frame. For a moment she remained trembling and reeling to and fro upon the threshold—then, with a low moaning cry, fell heavily inward upon the person of her brother, and in her violent and now final death agonies, bore him to the floor a corpse, and a victim to the terrors he had anticipated.

From that chamber, and from that mansion, I fled aghast. The storm was still abroad in all its wrath as I found myself crossing the old causeway. Suddenly there shot along the path a wild light, and I turned to see whence a gleam so unusual could have issued; for the vast house and its shadows were alone behind me. The radiance was that of the full, setting, and blood-red moon, which now shone vividly through that once barely discernible fissure, of which I have before spoken as extending from the roof of the building, in a zigzag direction, to the base. While I gazed, this fissure rapidly widened—there came a fierce breath of the whirlwind—the entire orb of the satellite burst at once upon my sight—my brain reeled as I saw the mighty walls rushing asunder—there was a long tumultuous shouting sound like the voice of a thousand waters—and the deep and dank tarn at my feet closed sullenly and silently over the fragments of the *"House of Usher."*

THINKING ABOUT THE SELECTION

Recalling

1. (a) What is the narrator's first impression of the House of Usher? (b) Why has he come to the house?
2. (a) When the narrator meets Usher, what startles him most about Usher's appearance? (b) What strikes him about Usher's behavior?
3. (a) According to Usher, what is "the nature of his malady"? (b) To what is Usher a "bounden slave"?
4. (a) Why is the narrator "forcibly impressed" with Usher's performance of "The Haunted Palace"? (b) What opinion does Usher offer following his performance?
5. (a) What does the narrator assist Usher with following the death of Usher's sister, Madeline? (b) What does the narrator notice when he and Usher turn aside the cover of Madeline's coffin?

6. (a) What noises does the narrator hear in the midst of reading the *Mad Trist*? (b) How does Usher explain these noises? (c) What happens immediately after Usher finishes his explanation?
7. What happens to the House of Usher at the end of the story?

Interpreting

8. (a) How is the physical appearance of the interior of the House of Usher related to the condition of Usher's mind? (b) How is it related to his physical appearance?
9. What details early in the story foreshadow, or hint at, the ending?
10. Critics have argued that Madeline and Roderick are not only twins but are physical and mental components of the same being. What evidence is there in the story to support this claim?
11. What is the significance of the fact that, rather than helping Usher, the narrator finds

himself becoming infected by Usher's condition?

12. Explain the two meanings of the story's title.

13. (a) In what way is the ending of the story ambiguous? (b) What do you think has happened?

Applying

14. Poe's story may suggest that the human imagination is capable of producing false perceptions of reality. Do you agree with this suggestion? Why or why not?

ANALYZING LITERATURE

Understanding the Single Effect

In his definition of a short story, Edgar Allan Poe asserted that a story should be constructed to achieve a single effect and that every word, detail, character, and incident in a story should contribute to this effect. Carefully constructed to create a growing sense of terror, "The Fall of the House of Usher" is a perfect illustration of Poe's theory.

How do each of the following events or details contribute to the growing sense of terror in "The Fall of the House of Usher"?

1. The description of the House of Usher
2. The description of Usher's painting
3. The entombment of Madeline
4. Storms and other natural phenomena.
5. Madeline's appearance at the end of the story

CRITICAL THINKING AND READING

Supporting Statements of Theme

In his definition of the short story, Poe went on to state that "truth is often, and in very great degree, the aim" of the short story. In other words, in addition to being constructed to achieve a single effect, short stories are often written to make a point, or express a general truth about life. The general truth a story expresses is the story's **theme.** There have been many different interpretations of the theme of "The Fall of the House of Usher." Find evidence from the story to support each of the following statements of possible themes.

1. In the absence of contact with the real world, the human imagination can produce a distorted perception of reality.
2. When isolated from the real world, a person can be infected by another person's fears and false perceptions of reality.
3. If artists (many critics believe that Roderick Usher represents a typical creative artist) completely turn away from the external world and become drawn into the internal world of their imaginations, they ultimately destroy their capacity to create and may eventually destroy themselves.

THINKING AND WRITING

Supporting a Statement of Theme

Develop one of your answers from the Critical Thinking and Reading exercise into an essay. Review the story to see if there is additional evidence you can use to support the statement. Take note of specific passages from the story that you can use in your essay. Organize your support into an outline. Develop the statement of theme into a thesis statement. When you write your essay, use transitions to link your ideas. When you revise make sure that your argument is well organized and clearly presented.

The Raven

Sound Devices. Alliteration, consonance, and assonance are three sound devices that poets use to give their writing a musical quality. Alliteration is the repetition of similar sounds, usually consonants, at the beginnings of words or accented syllables. Notice the repetition of the *n* sound in the following line from "The Raven": "While I nodded, nearly napping, suddenly there came a tapping." Consonance is the repetition of consonant sounds at the ends of words or accented syllables. For example, Poe ends several stanzas of "The Raven" with a line containing a repeated *v* sound: "Quoth the Raven, 'Nevermore.'" Assonance is the repetition of vowel sounds. For example, the *ur* sound is repeated in line 13 of "The Raven": "And the silken, sad, uncertain rustling of each purple curtain."

The repetition of similar sounds in poetry pleases the ear and reinforces meaning by emphasizing important words. Poe's use of alliteration, consonance, and assonance throughout "The Raven" creates a hypnotic effect that draws us into the speaker's irrational world. As a result, we are persuaded temporarily to abandon our conception of reality and accept the speaker's vision as reality. At the same time, the repetition of sounds emphasizes certain words that contribute to the mood and reinforce the meaning of the poem.

Look For

Poe has effectively used sound devices in "The Raven." As you read the poem, look for Poe's use of alliteration, consonance, and assonance. How do these devices create a hypnotic effect?

Writing

Describe a creature that you find frightening or mysterious. Try to use descriptive details that convey the fear or uncertainty that you associate with this creature.

Vocabulary

Knowing the following words will help you as you read "The Raven."

obeisance (ō'bā' s'ns) *n.*: Gesture of respect (l. 39)

beguiling (bi gīl' iŋ) *v.*: Charming (l. 43)

countenance (koun' tə nəns) *n.*: Facial expression (l. 44)

craven (krā' vən) *adj.*: Very cowardly (l. 45)

ominous (äm' ə nəs) *adj.*: Threatening; sinister (l. 71)

THE RAVEN
Edouard Manet
Courtesy, Museum of Fine Arts, Boston

The Raven

Edgar Allan Poe

Once upon a midnight dreary, while I pondered, weak and weary,
Over many a quaint and curious volume of forgotten lore,
While I nodded, nearly napping, suddenly there came a tapping,
As of someone gently rapping, rapping at my chamber door.
5 " 'Tis some visitor," I muttered, "tapping at my chamber door—
                    Only this, and nothing more."

Ah, distinctly I remember it was in the bleak December,
And each separate dying ember wrought its ghost upon the floor.
Eagerly I wished the morrow—vainly I had tried to borrow
10 From my books surcease[1] of sorrow—sorrow for the lost Lenore—
For the rare and radiant maiden whom the angels name Lenore—
                    Nameless here for evermore.

And the silken, sad, uncertain rustling of each purple curtain
Thrilled me—filled me with fantastic terrors never felt before;
15 So that now, to still the beating of my heart, I stood repeating
" 'Tis some visitor entreating entrance at my chamber door—
Some late visitor entreating entrance at my chamber door—
                    This it is and nothing more."

---

1. **surcease** (sʉr sēs'): End.

Presently my soul grew stronger; hesitating then no longer,
20 "Sir," said I, "or Madam, truly your forgiveness I implore;
But the fact is I was napping, and so gently you came rapping,
And so faintly you came tapping, tapping at my chamber door,
That I scarce was sure I heard you"—here I opened wide the door—
                    Darkness there, and nothing more.

25 Deep into that darkness peering, long I stood there wondering,
    fearing,
Doubting, dreaming dreams no mortal ever dared to dream before;
But the silence was unbroken, and the darkness gave no token,
And the only word there spoken was the whispered word, "Lenore!"
This *I* whispered, and an echo murmured back the word, "Lenore!"
30   Merely this, and nothing more.

Then into the chamber turning, all my soul within me burning,
Soon I heard again a tapping somewhat louder than before.
"Surely," said I, "surely that is something at my window lattice;
Let me see, then, what thereat is, and this mystery explore—
35 Let my heart be still a moment and this mystery explore—
                 'Tis the wind, and nothing more!"

Open here I flung the shutter, when, with many a flirt and flutter,
In there stepped a stately raven of the saintly days of yore;
Not the least obeisance made he; not an instant stopped or stayed
    he;
40 But, with mien of lord or lady, perched above my chamber door—
Perched upon a bust of Pallas² just above my chamber door—
               Perched, and sat, and nothing more.

Then this ebony bird beguiling my sad fancy into smiling,
By the grave and stern decorum of the countenance it wore,
45 "Though thy crest be shorn and shaven, thou," I said, "art sure no
    craven,
Ghastly grim and ancient raven wandering from the Nightly
    shore—
Tell me what thy lordly name is on the Night's Plutonian³ shore!"
             Quoth the raven, "Nevermore."

Much I marveled this ungainly fowl to hear discourse so plainly,
50 Though its answer little meaning—little relevancy bore;
For we cannot help agreeing that no sublunary being
Ever yet was blessed with seeing bird above his chamber door—
Bird or beast upon the sculptured bust above his chamber door,
             With such name as "Nevermore."

---

2. Pallas (pal' əs): Pallas Athena, the ancient Greek goddess of
wisdom.
3. Plutonian (ploo tŏ' nē ən) *adj.*: Referring to Pluto, the Greek and
Roman god of the underworld.

55 But the raven, sitting lonely on the placid bust, spoke only
That one word, as if his soul in that one word he did outpour.
Nothing farther then he uttered—not a feather then he fluttered—
Till I scarcely more than muttered, "Other friends have flown
before—
On the morrow *he* will leave me, as my hopes have flown before."
60   Quoth the raven, "Nevermore."

Wondering at the stillness broken by reply so aptly spoken,
"Doubtless," said I, "what it utters is its only stock and store,
Caught from some unhappy master whom unmerciful Disaster
Followed fast and followed faster—so, when Hope he would adjure,
65 Stern Despair returned, instead of the sweet Hope he dared
adjure—
                    That sad answer, "Nevermore!"

But the raven still beguiling all my sad soul into smiling,
Straight I wheeled a cushioned seat in front of bird, and bust, and
door;
Then upon the velvet sinking, I betook myself to linking
70 Fancy unto fancy, thinking what this ominous bird of yore—

THE RAVEN
Edouard Manet
Courtesy, Museum of Fine Arts, Boston

What this grim, ungainly, ghastly, gaunt, and ominous bird of yore
                    Meant in croaking "Nevermore."

This I sat engaged in guessing, but no syllable expressing
To the fowl whose fiery eyes now burned into my bosom's core;
75 This and more I sat divining, with my head at ease reclining
On the cushion's velvet lining that the lamplight gloated o'er,
But whose velvet violet lining with the lamplight gloating o'er,
                   She shall press, ah, nevermore!

Then, methought, the air grew denser, perfumed from an unseen censer
80 Swung by angels whose faint foot-falls tinkled on the tufted floor.
"Wretch," I cried, "thy God hath lent thee—by these angels he hath sent thee
Respite—respite and nepenthe[4] from thy memories of Lenore!
Let me quaff this kind nepenthe and forget this lost Lenore!"
                   Quoth the raven, "Nevermore."

85 "Prophet!" said I, "thing of evil!—prophet still, if bird or devil!—
Whether Tempter sent, or whether tempest tossed thee here ashore,
Desolate, yet all undaunted, on this desert land enchanted—
On this home by Horror haunted—tell me truly, I implore—
Is there—*is* there balm in Gilead?[5]—tell me—tell me, I implore!"
90   Quoth the raven, "Nevermore."

"Prophet!" said I, "thing of evil!—prophet still, if bird or devil!
By that Heaven that bends above us—by that God we both adore—
Tell this soul with sorrow laden if, within the distant Aidenn,[6]
It shall clasp a sainted maiden whom the angels name Lenore—
95 Clasp a rare and radiant maiden whom the angels name Lenore."
                   Quoth the raven, "Nevermore."

"Be that word our sign of parting, bird or fiend!" I shrieked, upstarting—
"Get thee back into the tempest and the Night's Plutonian shore!
Leave no black plume as a token of that lie thy soul hath spoken!
100 Leave my loneliness unbroken!—quit the bust above my door!
Take thy beak from out my heart, and take thy form from off my door!"
                   Quoth the raven, "Nevermore."

---

4. nepenthe (ni pen′ thē) *n.*: A drug that the ancient Greeks
believed could relieve sorrow.
5. balm in Gilead (gil′ ē əd): In the Bible, a healing ointment was
made in Gilead, a region of ancient Palestine.
6. Aidenn (ā′den): Arabic for *Eden* or *heaven*.

And the raven, never flitting, still is sitting, still is sitting
On the pallid bust of Pallas just above my chamber door;
105 And his eyes have all the seeming of a demon that is dreaming,
And the lamplight o'er him streaming throws his shadow on the
     floor;
And my soul from out that shadow that lies floating on the floor
                              Shall be lifted—nevermore!

THINKING ABOUT THE SELECTION

Recalling

1. (a) How does the speaker respond to the noise he hears? (b) How does he try to explain this noise?
2. (a) How does the raven get into the chamber? (b) Upon what does it land?
3. According to lines 81-83, what does the speaker want to forget?
4. (a) What does the speaker implore the raven to tell him in lines 88 and 89? (b) What question does the speaker ask the raven in lines 93–95? (c) What does the speaker order in lines 97–101?

Interpreting

5. (a) What is the mood? (b) How is the mood established in the first two stanzas?
6. (a) During the course of the poem, what changes occur in the speaker's attitude toward the raven? (b) What brings about each of these changes? (c) What does the raven finally come to represent?
7. (a) How does the speaker's emotional state change during the poem? (b) How are these changes related to the changes in his attitude toward the raven?
8. How is the word spoken by the raven related to the speaker's emotional state at the end of the poem?

Applying

9. "The Raven" has been popular for well over one hundred years. What do you think accounts for its continuing appeal?

ANALYZING LITERATURE

Using Sound Devices

Alliteration, consonance, and **assonance** are three sound devices used in poetry. Alliteration is the repetition of similar sounds, usually consonants, at the beginnings of words or accented syllables (for example, "surcease of sorrow," line 10). Consonance is the repetition of consonant sounds at the ends of words or accented syllables (for example, "chamber door," line 14). Assonance is the repetition of vowel sounds (for example, "weak and weary," line 1).

Find three more examples of each of these techniques in "The Raven." Explain how each contributes to the poem's hypnotic effect.

THINKING AND WRITING

Responding to a Statement

Poe stated, "A poem, in my opinion, is opposed to a work of science by having, for its *immediate* object, pleasure, not truth. . . ." Review the poem, considering how Poe's use of sound devices and his choice of subject relate to the poem's *immediate* purpose. Try to determine the general truth, or theme, the poem expresses. Think about how the theme relates to the poem's *overall* purpose. Then, after deciding how you will respond to Poe's statement, find passages from the poem to support your response. Start your essay with Poe's statement, followed by your response. Then develop an argument supporting your response. When you finish writing, revise your essay, and prepare a final copy.

The Oval Portrait

Literary Forms

The Frame Story. A frame story is a story told within the framework of another story. For example, in "The Oval Portrait" a story about a painter's attempt to capture the beauty of his young wife on canvas is told within the framework of a story about a wounded man's retreat into an abandoned chateau.

In "The Oval Portrait," Poe uses the frame, or outer story, to provide a setting and create an atmosphere for the frame story. At the same time, the reactions and observations of the wounded man, the narrator, in the frame reinforce the symbolic, or hidden, meaning of the frame story. In a sense the two stories also parallel each other, because both relate the story of a character's temporary retreat from consciousness.

Look For

How does the frame create a setting and provide an atmosphere in "The Oval Portrait"? Look for the events in the frame that reinforce the frame story's symbolic meaning.

Writing

Think of a person, place, or animal that you find exceptionally beautiful. Write a short description of this person, place, or animal. Then write a few sentences about how you think the passage of time will affect the beauty of your subject, and reflect upon how its beauty might be captured permanently in a work of art.

Vocabulary

Knowing the following words will help you as you read "The Oval Portrait."

incipient (in sip′ ē ənt) *adj.*: Just beginning (p. 229)

delirium (di lir′ ē əm) *n.*: A temporary state of extreme mental confusion (p. 229)

countenance (koun′ tə nəns) *n.*: Facial expression (p. 230)

austere (ô stir′) *adj.*: Showing strict self-discipline (p. 230)

reveries (rev′ ər ēz) *n.*: Daydreaming (p. 230)

tremulous (trem′ yōō ləs) *adj.*: Quivering (p. 232)

pallid (pal′ id) *adj.*: Pale (p. 232)

aghast (ə gast′) *adj.*: Horrified (p. 232)

The Oval Portrait

Edgar Allan Poe

The chateau into which my valet had ventured to make forcible entrance, rather than permit me, in my desperately wounded condition, to pass a night in the open air, was one of those piles of commingled gloom and grandeur which have so long frowned among the Apennines,[1] not less in fact than in the fancy of Mrs. Radcliffe.[2] To all appearance it had been temporarily and very lately abandoned. We established ourselves in one of the smallest and least sumptuously furnished apartments. It lay in a remote turret of the building. Its decorations were rich, yet tattered and antique. Its walls were hung with tapestry and bedecked with manifold and multiform armorial trophies, together with an unusually great number of very spirited modern paintings in frames of rich golden arabesque.[3] In these paintings, which depended from the walls not only in their main surfaces, but in very many nooks which the bizarre architecture of the chateau rendered necessary—in these paintings my incipient delirium, perhaps, had caused me to take deep interest; so that I bade Pedro to close the heavy shutters of the room—since it was already night—to light the tongues[4] of a tall candelabrum which stood by the head of my bed—and to throw open far and wide the fringed curtains of black velvet which enveloped the bed itself. I wished all this done that I might resign myself, if not to sleep, at least alternately to the contemplation of these pictures, and the perusal of a small volume which had been found upon the pillow, and which purported to criticize and describe them.

Long—long I read—and devoutly, devotedly I gazed. Rapidly and gloriously the hours flew by and the deep midnight came. The position of the candelabrum displeased me, and outreaching my hand with difficulty, rather than disturb my slumbering valet, I placed it so as to throw its rays more fully upon the book.

But the action produced an effect altogether unanticipated. The rays of the numerous candles (for there were many) now fell within a niche of the room which had hitherto been thrown into deep shade by one of the bedposts. I thus saw in vivid light a picture all unnoticed before. It was the portrait of a young girl just ripening into womanhood. I glanced at the painting hurriedly, and then closed my eyes. Why I did this was not at first apparent even to my own perception. But while my lids remained thus shut, I ran over in my mind my reason for so shutting them. It was an impulsive movement to gain time for thought—to make sure that my vision had not deceived me—to calm and subdue my fancy for a more sober and more certain gaze. In a very few moments I again looked fixedly at the painting.

---

1. Apennines (ap′ ə nīnz): A mountain range located in central Italy.
2. Mrs. Radcliffe: Ann Radcliffe (1764–1823), an English novelist.
3. arabesque (ar′ ə besk′): Of complex and elaborate design.
4. tongues (tuŋz): Candles.

That I now saw aright I could not and would not doubt; for the first flashing of the candles upon that canvas had seemed to dissipate the dreamy stupor which was stealing over my senses, and to startle at once into waking life.

The portrait, I have already said, was that of a young girl. It was a mere head and shoulders, done in what is technically termed a *vignette*[5] manner; much in the style of the favorite heads of Sully.[6] The arms, the bosom, and even the ends of the radiant hair melted imperceptibly into the vague yet deep shadow which formed the background of the whole. The frame was oval, richly gilded and filigreed in *Moresque*.[7] As a thing of art nothing could be more admirable than the painting itself. But it could have been neither the execution of the work, nor the immortal beauty of the countenance, which had so suddenly and so vehemently moved me. Least of all, could it have been that my fancy, shaken from its half slumber, had mistaken the head for that of a living person. I saw at once that the peculiarities of the design, of the *vignetting*, and of the frame, must have instantly dispelled such idea—must have prevented even its momentary entertainment. Thinking earnestly upon these points, I remained, for an hour perhaps, half sitting, half reclining, with my vision riveted upon the portrait. At length, satisfied with the true secret of its effect, I fell back within the bed. I had found the spell of the picture in an absolute life-likeliness of expression, which, at first startling, finally confounded, subdued, and appalled me. With deep and reverent awe I replaced the candelabrum in its former position. The cause of my deep agitation being thus shut from view, I sought eagerly the volume which

discussed the paintings and their histories. Turning to the number which designated the oval portrait, I there read the vague and quaint words which follow:

"She was a maiden of rarest beauty, and not more lovely than full of glee. And evil was the hour when she saw, and loved, and wedded the painter. He, passionate, studious, austere, and having already a bride in his art; she a maiden of rarest beauty, and not more lovely than full of glee; all light and smiles, and frolicsome as the young fawn; loving and cherishing all things; hating only the art which was her rival; dreading only the pallet and brushes and other untoward instruments which deprived her of the countenance of her lover. It was thus a terrible thing for this lady to hear the painter speak of his desire to portray even his young bride. But she was humble and obedient, and sat meekly for many weeks in the dark, high turret chamber where the light dripped upon the pale canvas only from overhead. But he, the painter, took glory in his work, which went on from hour to hour, and from day to day. And he was a passionate, and wild, and moody man, who became lost in reveries; so that he *would* not see that the light which fell so ghastly in that lone turret withered the health and the spirits of his bride, who pined visibly to all but him. Yet she smiled on and still on, uncomplainingly, because she saw that the painter (who had high renown) took a fervid and burning pleasure in his task, and wrought day and night to depict her who so loved him, yet who grew daily more dispirited and weak. And in sooth[8] some who beheld the portrait spoke of its resemblance in low words, as of a mighty marvel, and a proof not less of the power of the painter than of his deep love for her whom he depicted so surpassingly well. But at length, as the labor drew nearer to its conclusion, there were admitted none into the

---

5. vignette (vin yet') *n.*: A picture or photograph with no definite border.
6. Sully: Thomas Sully (1783–1872), an American painter born in England.
7. Moresque (mô resk'): Decoration characterized by intricate tracery and bright colors.

---

8. sooth (sooth): Truth; fact.

"HE TURNED SUDDENLY . . . ," EDGAR ALLAN POE'S TALES OF MYSTERY AND IMAGINATION
Arthur Rackham
New York Public Library, Astor, Lenox and Tilden Foundations

turret; for the painter had grown wild with the ardor of his work, and turned his eyes from canvas rarely, even to regard the countenance of his wife. And he *would* not see that the tints which he spread upon the canvas were drawn from the cheeks of her who sat beside him. And when many weeks had passed, and but little remained to do, save one brush upon the mouth and one tint upon the eye, the spirit of the lady again flickered up as the flame within the socket of the lamp. And then the brush was given, and then the tint was placed; and, for one moment, the painter stood entranced before the work which he had wrought; but in the next, while he yet gazed, he grew tremulous and very pallid, and aghast, and crying with a loud voice, 'This is indeed *Life* itself!' turned suddenly to regard his beloved—*She was dead!*"

THINKING ABOUT THE SELECTION
Recalling

1. (a) Why does the narrator's valet break into the chateau? (b) How does the narrator describe the chateau's appearance?
2. (a) What painting does the narrator see when he moves the candelabrum? (b) What is his immediate reaction to the painting? (c) What causes this reaction?
3. (a) What is the relationship between the subject of the painting and the artist? (b) What happens to the subject when the artist finally finishes the painting?

Interpreting

4. (a) What details in the first few paragraphs suggest that the narrator experiences a temporary retreat from consciousness? (b) What details in the frame story indicate that the painter experiences a temporary retreat from consciousness while painting his wife?
5. What makes the artist's remark at the end of the story ironic, or surprising?
6. When this story was first published, it was called "Life in Death." Which title do you find the most effective? Explain your answer.
7. The critic G. R. Thompson has suggested that the entire story can be read as "the dream of a man delirious from pain and lack of sleep." What is your opinion of this interpretation? Support your opinion with details from the story.

Applying

8. In "The Oval Portrait," the narrator has a strong emotional reaction to the painting of the young woman. What do you think causes people to react in this way to certain works of art?
9. Jacques Barzun has written, "Art distills sensation and embodies it with enhanced meaning in memorable form—or else it is not art." (a) How do Barzun's words relate to painting? (b) How do they relate to writing?

ANALYZING LITERATURE
Recognizing a Frame Story

The story of the painter and his wife in "The Oval Portrait" is an example of a **frame story,** a story told within the framework of another story. In the "Oval Portrait," the **frame,** or outer story, provides a setting and creates an atmosphere for the frame story. The narrator's reactions and observations in the frame also reinforce the symbolic, or hidden, meaning of the frame story.

1. What details of the setting in the frame create an appropriate atmosphere for the frame story?
2. In the frame story, the young woman's spirit and beauty are symbolically drawn out of her and into her husband's painting. Through this process her beauty and passion are released from their mortal bonds and permanently cap-

tured in her husband's painting. How does the narrator's response to the painting reinforce this interpretation?

CRITICAL THINKING AND READING
Understanding Cause and Effect

A **cause** is the reason why something happens. An **effect** is what happens, or the result.

Answer each of the following questions by finding the result of each cause.

1. The narrator is in a desperately wounded condition. As a result, what does his servant do?
2. The narrator is feeling delirious as he looks at the paintings. What is the result?
3. The narrator wants to study the paintings. As a result, what does he ask his servant to do?
4. The narrator moves the candle. What is the unanticipated effect?
5. The picture has "an absolute life-likeliness of expression." What is its effect?

UNDERSTANDING LANGUAGE
Understanding Word Origins

Many words in English originated in other languages. For example, in the book the narrator reads this description of the painter: "And he was a passionate, and wild, and moody man, who became lost in *reveries* . . ." The word *reverie* means "dreamy thinking or imagining." It comes from a Middle French word that meant "to wander." Do you see the connection? When you engage in reverie, you let your mind wander.

Find the origin of each of the words below. Explain the connection between the original word and the word today.

1. oval
2. arabesque
3. bizarre
4. candelabrum
5. vignette
6. filigree

THINKING AND WRITING
Comparing and Contrasting Stories

Write an essay comparing and contrasting "The Oval Portrait" with "The Fall of the House of Usher." First review both stories and take note of the characters, setting, mood, and theme of each story. List the similarities and differences between the two stories in each of these areas. Organize your information into an outline and write a thesis statement. Then write an essay in which you support your thesis statement with the information from your lists. When you revise make sure that have used appropriate transitions to indicate either comparison or contrast.

To Helen

Allusions. An allusion is a reference to another literary work or a figure, place, or event from history, religion, or mythology. For example, in the first stanza of "To Helen," Poe alludes to Helen of Troy, a legendary Greek woman known for her incomparable beauty.

The theme or central idea of "To Helen"—that the purest, most enduring form of beauty is spiritual beauty rather than physical beauty—is revealed through the progression of allusions Poe uses in the poem. By interpreting the meaning of each allusion, we can see through the course of the poem the speaker's ideal conception of beauty transformed from an actual woman to a nymph, and ultimately to the mind and soul.

As you read "To Helen," identify Poe's allusions. Once you finish reading, look up the meaning of each allusion in a dictionary or encyclopedia. Then reread the poem.

What does beauty mean to you? Freewrite about the thoughts and feelings you associate with the concept of beauty.

Knowing the following word will help you as you read "To Helen."
grandeur (gran′ jər) *adj.*: Magnificence (l. 10)

To Helen

Edgar Allan Poe

Helen, thy beauty is to me
    Like those Nicéan barks[1] of yore,
That gently, o'er a perfumed sea,
    The weary, way-worn wanderer bore
5   To his own native shore.

On desperate seas long wont to roam,
    Thy hyacinth[2] hair, thy classic face,
Thy Naiad airs have brought me home
    To the glory that was Greece,
10   And the grandeur that was Rome.

Lo! in yon brilliant window-niche
    How statue-like I see thee stand,
The agate lamp within thy hand!
    Ah, Psyche, from the regions which
15   Are Holy Land!

---

1. Nicean (nī sē′ ən) **barks:** Boats from the
shipbuilding city of Nicea in Asia Minor.
2. hyacinth (hī′ ə sinth′) *adj.:* Wavy, lustrous.

PROSERPINE
Dante Gabriel Rossetti
The Tate Gallery, London

THINKING ABOUT THE SELECTION

Recalling

1. To what does the speaker compare Helen's beauty in lines 2–5?
2. To what is the speaker brought home in lines 9 and 10?
3. (a) How is Helen standing in line 12? (b) What does she have in her hand?

Interpreting

4. During the course of the poem, Helen leads the speaker on a journey. What type of journey is the speaker taking?
5. Toward the end of the poem, the speaker looks to art as a possible source of the purest form of beauty. How is this indicated in lines 11–13?

Applying

6. What do you think is the purest form of beauty? Explain your answer.

ANALYZING LITERATURE

Recognizing Allusions

An **allusion** is a reference to another literary work or a figure, place, or event from history, religion, or mythology. For example, in the first stanza, Poe alludes to Helen of Troy, a woman known for her incomparable beauty.

1. Identify the meaning of each of the following allusions. a. Naiad b. Psyche
2. How do these allusions relate to the overall meaning of the poem?

YOU THE WRITER

Assignment

1. Imagine that the year is 1840 and you have lived through the period of rapid growth that occurred in the years between 1800 and 1840. Write a journal entry describing some of the changes that have occurred during your lifetime and present your reactions to these changes.

   Prewriting.   Review the unit introduction to refresh your memory about the important events that occurred during the period. Prepare a list of these events.

   Writing.   When you write your journal entry, use an informal writing style and organize your information in chronological order.

   Revising.   When you revise, make sure your descriptions are clear and complete. After you have finished revising, proofread your entry and prepare a final copy.

Assignment

2. The Romantics had a strong interest in nature and in humanity's relationship with nature. Write a lyric poem in the Romantic tradition, focusing on an aspect of nature or exploring the relationship between humanity and nature.

   Prewriting.   After deciding on a subject, develop a list of sensory details you can use in your poem. Arrange these details in a logical order.

   Writing.   When writing your poem, focus on having the speaker express his or her thoughts about the subject. Use a regular rhythm and pattern of rhyme.

   Revising.   When you revise, make sure any abstract ideas are linked to concrete images, or word pictures. After you have finished revising, proofread your poem and share it with your classmates.

Assignment

3. The attitudes and concerns of the Romantics were dramatically different from those of the writers of the Colonial Period. Write a dialogue in which a Romantic and a writer from the Colonial Period discuss their ideas and interests.

   Prewriting.   Review the unit introductions for the Colonial Period and for a Growing Nation, noting the differences in the attitudes and concerns of the writers of the two periods.

   Writing.   Develop a dialogue between an important writer from each period. Try to make the conversation seem realistic, as if it might have actually occurred had the two writers been alive at the same time.

   Revising.   When you revise, make sure your dialogue captures the contrast between Romantic and eighteenth-century attitudes.

Assignment

1. The Romantics had a strong interest in mystery and the supernatural. Write an essay in which you discuss how this interest is reflected in one of the Romantic selections you have read.

Prewriting. Choose a selection that reflects the Romantic interest in mystery and the supernatural. Carefully reread the selection, noting the elements of mystery and/or the supernatural that it includes.

Writing. Include a thesis statement in the introduction of your essay. Develop and support your thesis in the body paragraphs.

Revising. When you revise, make sure you have thoroughly supported your thesis and have not included any unnecessary information. After you finish writing, proofread your essay and prepare a final copy.

Assignment

2. Although all the writers in this unit were Romantics, they each had slightly different concerns and approaches to writing. Write an essay in which you compare and contrast two of the writers whose works you have just read.

Prewriting. After choosing two writers, review the author biography of each writer and carefully reread the selections by each writer, noting similarities and differences in their concerns and approaches.

Writing. When you write your essay, organize your argument according to corresponding points of contrast; use evidence from their works for support.

Revising. When you revise, make sure you have used transitions and other linking devices to connect your ideas and have varied the length and structure of your sentences.

Assignment

3. Romanticism is an extremely broad concept, encompassing a wide variety of different concerns and beliefs. Write an essay in which you discuss the various Romantic attitudes, interests, and approaches reflected in the literature written between 1800 and 1840.

Prewriting. Review the selections in this unit, noting the Romantic concerns and beliefs that they reflect. Prepare a thesis statement, then organize your notes into an outline.

Writing. When you write your essay, support your thesis with evidence from at least one selection by each of the writers in this unit.

Revising. When you revise, make sure your essay is organized in a logical manner. After you have finished revising, proofread your essay and prepare a final copy.

BOSTON HARBOR
Fitz Hugh Lane
Museum of Fine Arts, Boston

NEW ENGLAND RENAISSANCE
1840–1855

One man's justice is another's injustice; one man's beauty
another's ugliness; one man's wisdom another's folly.
Ralph Waldo Emerson

By 1840 it was clear that the American experiment in democracy had succeeded. England, rebuffed in the "Second American War for Independence," was no longer a threat to the survival of the republic. Andrew Jackson, the first "People's President," had served two tempestuous terms in office. New states were entering the Union; Arkansas had come in as the 25th state in 1836, and Michigan was soon to follow. Despite the Panic of 1837, the mood in America was buoyant; the best was yet to come. Alexis de Tocqueville, a French traveler in the 1830's, observed that Americans had "a lively faith in the perfectibility of man," and they "admit that what appears to them today to be good may be superseded by something better tomorrow."

Although the great early presidents of the Virginia and Massachusetts dynasties had passed from the scene, a bright new galaxy of statesmen could be seen in Washington, D.C.: Daniel Webster from Massachusetts, Henry Clay from Kentucky, Thomas Hart Benton from Missouri, and John C. Calhoun from South Carolina. As these men struggled with political issues that would ultimately break the nation apart, American literature blossomed suddenly and brilliantly in the New England states, particularly in Massachusetts, and specifically in Boston, Concord, Salem, Pittsfield, and Amherst. Historians have called this brief, sunlit era in American cultural history a "flowering," a "renaissance," and a "golden day." Its guiding spirit was Ralph Waldo Emerson, a Unitarian minister who in 1832 had left the pulpit of the Second Church of Boston for a broader stage. Wrote one historian, "The year 1836, when Emerson published his essay on *Nature*, may be taken as the focus of a period in American thought corresponding to 1776 in American politics."

Hub of the Solar System

When the New England literary group burst into flower, Boston was a vibrant, expanding city of nearly 100,000 people. Then, as now, it was the metropolis of the region, a cosmopolitan city whose clipper ships were known from Liverpool to Singapore. Oliver Wendell Holmes, a Boston physician and man of letters, said, tongue-in-cheek, "Boston State House is the hub of the solar system."

Certainly, Boston's four-story Tremont House, with 170 guest rooms, was at mid-century one of the finest hotels in America. In 1842 Charles Dickens, twenty-nine years old and already a world-famous author, stayed at the Tremont House. As a climax to his visit, the Young Men of Boston staged a great dinner in his honor, scarcely imagining that some of their close friends would one day have international literary reputations to rival that of Dickens.

Just as the city of Boston, a center of culture and commerce, was growing, so were a great many Massachusetts factory and mill towns. Of the 1,200 cotton factories in the United States in 1840, two-thirds were located in New England. Francis C. Lowell, who developed the first American power loom, devised a plan to attract conscientious workers. He hired high-principled young women, most of them from nearby farms, to work in the textile mills of Lowell, Waltham, Lawrence, and other towns on the Merrimack River. These so-called "Lowell factory girls" lived in boarding houses under strict supervision, and worked from 5:00 AM to 7:30 PM, with two half-hour breaks for meals. While the Lowell plan was far from typical, the factory system in general was an economic success. Textile companies prospered. The town of Lowell mushroomed from 200 people in 1820 to over 30,000 by 1845.

If New England was growing and changing, so was the rest of the country. The factory system, with its mass production, would eventually change the face of America, but that change was mostly in the future. America was still an agricultural nation. More often than not, the Lowell factory girls returned to their family farms after a few years, more mature, ready to marry, and by no means part of an urban American underclass. City populations were growing throughout the United States, but so was the number of American farms. The nation as a whole experienced a period of spectacular growth during these years of New England's literary prime. Cities, farms, factories—all were booming.

CORNELL FARM
Edward Hicks
Three Lions

1840 The Transcendentalist magazine, *The Dial*, begins publication.

1841 **Ralph Waldo Emerson** publishes *Essays*.

Brook Farm, the Transcendental community, established near Boston.

Henry Wadsworth Longfellow publishes "The Skeleton in Armor."

1842 Anesthesia first used for medical purposes.

Webster-Ashburton Treaty eases boundary disputes between the United States and Canada.

1843 **John Greenleaf Whittier** publishes *Lays of My Home and Other Poems*.

1844 First telegraph message sent.

Ralph Waldo Emerson publishes *Essays: Second Series*.

1845 Texas admitted to the Union.

1846 Mexican War begins.

Oliver Wendell Holmes publishes *Poems*.

Herman Melville publishes *Typee*, his first novel.

Abraham Lincoln first elected to Congress.

1847 **Henry Wadsworth Longfellow** publishes *Evangeline*.

First adhesive postage stamps issued.

John Greenleaf Whittier   Henry Wadsworth Longfellow

Mexican War

First Postage Stamps   Abraham Lincoln

Alfred, Lord Tennyson

Irish Potato Famine

Emily Brontë

Charlotte Brontë

WORLD EVENTS

1840   Canada: Upper and Lower Canada united.

England: Thomas Hardy is born.

1841   Antarctica: First explored by Englishman James Ross.

South Pacific: New Zealand becomes a British colony.

1842   Asia: Hong Kong becomes a British colony.

England: Alfred, Lord Tennyson publishes *Poems*.

France: Honoré de Balzac publishes *The Human Comedy*.

1843   England: Charles Dickens publishes *A Christmas Carol*.

1844   Germany: Heinrich Heine publishes *Germany: A Winter's Tale*.

France: Alexandre Dumas publishes *The Three Musketeers*.

1845   Ireland: Famine results from failure of potato crop.

1846   Russia: Fyodor Dostoyevsky publishes *Poor Folk*.

1847   Italy: Verdi's opera *Macbeth* first performed.

England: Charlotte Brontë publishes *Jane Eyre*.

England: Emily Brontë publishes *Wuthering Heights*.

AMERICAN EVENTS

1848   Mexican War ends; United States expands borders.

James Russell Lowell publishes *A Fable for Critics* and *The Bigelow Papers*.

California gold rush begins.

Women's Rights Convention held in Seneca Falls, New York.

1849   **Henry David Thoreau** publishes *A Week on the Concord and Merrimack Rivers*.

Edgar Allan Poe dies.

1850   *Harper's Magazine* founded.

Nathaniel Hawthorne publishes *The Scarlet Letter*.

Ralph Waldo Emerson publishes *Representative Man*.

California admitted to the Union.

1851   **Herman Melville** publishes *Moby-Dick*.

Nathaniel Hawthorne publishes *The House of Seven Gables*.

The New York Times begins publication.

1852   Harriet Beecher Stowe publishes *Uncle Tom's Cabin*.

Nathaniel Hawthorne publishes *The Blithedale Romance*.

1853   Arizona and New Mexico purchased from Mexico.

John Greenleaf Whittier publishes *The Chapel of the Hermits*.

1854   **Henry David Thoreau** publishes *Walden*.

Republican Party organized.

1855   **Henry Wadsworth Longfellow** publishes *The Song of Hiawatha*.

Henry David Thoreau

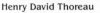

Women's Rights Convention

Japan Opens Ports to Trade

Louis Napoleon

California Gold Rush

Ralph Waldo Emerson

Taiping Rebellion

Robert Browning

1848   Belgium: Karl Marx and Friedrich Engels publish *The Communist Manifesto*.

      England: Women first admitted to University of London.

1849   England: Matthew Arnold publishes *The Strayed Reveller and Other Poems*.

1850   France: Life insurance introduced.

      England: Elizabeth Barrett Browning publishes *Sonnets from the Portuguese*.

      England: Charles Dickens publishes *David Copperfield*.

      Germany: Wagner's opera *Lohengrin* first performed.

      China: Taiping Rebellion begins.

      England: Alfred, Lord Tennyson appointed poet laureate.

1851   Australia: Gold discovered in New South Wales.

      Norway: Henrik Ibsen writes *Norma*.

1852   Russia: Leo Tolstoy publishes *Childhood*.

      Europe: Crimean War begins.

      France: Louis Napolean proclaims himself emperor.

1853   Japan: Ports opened to trade.

1854   England: Charles Dickens publishes *Hard Times*.

1855   England: Robert Browning publishes *Men and Women*.

The Way West

In one sense, the entire course of American history since 1607 can be seen as a pageant of continous westward movement. The first white settlers sailed west from Europe, establishing their homes on the East Coast of the New World. All thirteen original states were on the eastern seaboard, hemmed in by mountain barriers blocking easy access to the interior. As late as 1845 the most western state in the Union was Texas. The last of the fifty states, Hawaii, lying far away to the west of the North American continent, was at that time an independent kingdom.

During the years in which New England literature flowered, American transportation was steadily changing and improving. The Erie Canal, completed in the state of New York in 1825, set off a wave of frenzied canal building in the Northeast. Throughout the 1840's, American railroads competed not only with canals but also with plank roads. A plank road, usually constructed of hemlock boards, was strong enough to support heavy wagons and stagecoaches. Built by private turnpike companies, plank roads enjoyed a brief flurry of popularity in the 1840's. By 1855, however, it was obvious that railroads had clear-cut advantages over plank roads, and in many places railroads had already rendered canals unprofitable. As the Civil War approached, the golden age of railroading was about to begin.

Advances in agriculture followed advances in technology. John Deere, a native of Vermont, developed the steel plow out in Illinois. Cyrus McCormick, a Virginian, invented the reaper. These two inventions contributed immensely to the settlement of the prairies and later the Great Plains, for they helped make farming practical on the vast, sod-covered grasslands. Another invention of the time, the telegraph, had far-reaching effects, enabling people to communicate almost instantly across great distances. Inventor Samuel F. B. Morse's message from Washington to Baltimore in 1844 could serve as the motto for this era of innovation. "What hath God wrought!"

TELEGRAPH KEY USED BY SAMUEL F. B. MORSE TO SEND THE FIRST TELEGRAPH MESSAGE OF MAY 24, 1844
The Granger Collection

Clouds in a Summer Sky

"In this refulgent summer," wrote Emerson, "it has been a luxury to draw the breath of life. The grass grows, the buds burst, the meadow is spotted with fire and gold in the tint of flowers. The air is full of birds, and sweet with the breath of pine, the balm-of-Gilead, and the new hay. . . . One is constrained to respect the perfection of this world in which our senses converse."

Ever the optimist, Emerson, as one critic said, "counted on things to take care of themselves. He could not be angry, he could not be sad." Yet it was evident to even the most cheerful observer that the United States, in the middle of the nineteenth century, faced growing problems as well as shining promises. The factories and mills that were building prosperity did not always offer the clean boarding houses, matronly chaperons, and pleasant camaraderie of Lowell at its best. More often the factory system brought increasingly fierce competition, which sometimes led to "those dark Satanic mills" of the English poet William Blake's grim vision, in which child labor, low wages, long hours, and unsafe working conditions combined to produce a situation that cried for reform.

In the anthracite mines of Pennsylvania, boys as young as seven or eight spent long days working as slate pickers in cavernous coal breakers. These boys, blackened by coal dust, supplemented the income of their fathers, whose own twelve to fourteen hours of labor brought in too little money to support the family. Their plight was worse than most, but in time even the Lowell factory girls lost many of their benefits, saw their wages slashed, and began to think about striking.

Nor were most other women at mid-century living in idyllic circumstances. In many states women could not vote, make a will, or file a lawsuit. A woman's property was under the absolute control of her husband, making her, as one woman wrote, "a ward, an appendage." The 1840's and 1850's saw an outburst of energy directed toward increasing the rights of women. One of the pivotal events in the women's movement, the Seneca Falls Convention, organized by Lucretia Mott and Elizabeth Cady Stanton, took place in 1848. Susan B. Anthony, a superb organizer and tireless campaigner, soon joined the movement. Women were active in other reform movements as well. Dorthea Dix crusaded for better treatment of the mentally ill, while Julia Ward Howe and Harriet Beecher Stowe attacked the institution of slavery. Sarah and Angelina Grimké advocated women's rights and freedom for the slaves, as did Lucy Stone and the eloquent Sojourner Truth, who had been born a slave.

HARRIET BEECHER STOWE, 1853
Alanson Fisher
The Granger Collection

AMERICAN BOOKSELLER'S ANNOUNCEMENT FOR *UNCLE TOM'S CABIN*, **1852**
The Granger Collection

Utopias and Lyceums

"What a fertility of projects for the salvation of the world!" exclaimed Emerson. With reform in the air, it is little wonder that utopias, or "perfect communities," were on many people's minds. One of the most famous of these utopias was Brook Farm, located only nine miles from Boston. Brook Farm was established in 1841 by George Ripley, an ex-Unitarian minister like Emerson, and strongly influenced by Emerson's views. The community attracted a number of prominent writers, including Nathaniel Hawthorne. It soon fell under the influence of Fourierism, a communal system promoted by New York journalist Arthur Brisbane. Since Fourierism held scant appeal for the gentle Bostonians who had established the community, Brook Farm gradually withered away. Meanwhile, three other utopias had been founded in New England: Hopedale, Fruitlands, and Northampton. All failed.

Indeed, very few utopian communities anywhere ever prospered. Among the few that did were seven small Amana colonies, settled in 1855 near the Iowa River in east central Iowa. The woolen goods from Amana, especially blankets, became commercially popular, and today the colonies still survive, their quaint villages attracting many tourists. The 700-member Amana Church Society is virtually all that remains today of the utopian fever that swept America in the 1840's and 1850's.

Another trend of that era, also idealistic in its aims, was the movement for better public and private education. By 1850 most people in the United States seemed to agree that free public elementary and secondary schools should be provided for all children and that higher education should be available for students who were able to pay. Adult education had its advocates, too. The lyceum movement, which originated in Millbury, Massachusetts, gained great momentum during these years. A lyceum (like the chautauqua that eventually replaced it) was a popular society established for literary and scientific study. One of the most famous lyceums was Boston's Lowell Institute, founded in 1839. Lyceums offered lectures, debates, scientific demonstrations, and other entertainments. Many authors of the period, including those of the New England renaissance, appeared frequently as paid lyceum speakers.

LITERATURE IN FULL FLOWER

Elaborate theories have been devised to explain why sudden outbursts of creativity occur at certain places and times. The facts are often more fascinating than the theories—and easier to comprehend. In New England between 1840 and 1855, and mostly around Boston, an array of writers, now world-famous, produced a remarkable body of work that bulks large in the American literary tradition.

THE NOTCH OF THE WHITE MOUNTAINS (CRAWFORD NOTCH), 1839
Thomas Cole
National Gallery of Art, Washington, D. C.

Goodbye, Courtly Muses

Ralph Waldo Emerson published his first essay anonymously in 1836. The next year he delivered his famous oration, *The American Scholar,* before the Phi Beta Kappa Society of Harvard, a speech that attracted widespread attention. Oliver Wendell Holmes called the address "our intellectual Declaration of Independence," which is precisely what Emerson had in mind. Emerson believed that American writers "had listened too long to the courtly muses of Europe" and should begin to interpret their own culture in new, and not borrowed, ways. Emerson named no names, but few readers could deny that Washington Irving and James Fenimore Cooper sometimes sounded like transplanted Englishmen. Edgar Allan Poe never did, but not all American critics, then or later, took Poe seriously—"three-fifths genius," James Russell Lowell, a Bostonian, called him, "and two-fifths sheer fudge."

Critics would be much kinder to the writers who arose in New England in the 1840's and early 1850's. There was the sanguine Emerson himself, whose essays, poems, journals, and letters hold a permanent place in our literature. There was Henry David Thoreau, fourteen years younger than Emerson and something of a protégé, although a very individualistic one, who lived in the Emerson household for two years. Thoreau's classic work, *Walden,* appeared in 1854. On the darker side there was Nathaniel Hawthorne, whose powerful, sometimes enigmatic style reached its peak in *The Scarlet Letter,* published in 1850. Then there was a volatile New Yorker living in Pittsfield, the ex-sailor of the South Seas, Herman Melville, whose masterpiece, *Moby-Dick,* met with indifference at first and lavish praise later. In Amherst, living quietly and publishing almost nothing in her lifetime, was the young, brilliantly gifted poet, Emily Dickinson.

Those were the giants, or so they seem to us today. In 1850 the reading public in the United States might have pointed more quickly to four other New England writers. Henry Wadsworth Longfellow, a Harvard professor until 1854 and a tremendously popular poet, was a leading figure among New England intellectuals. So was Oliver Wendell Holmes, the unofficial poet laureate of the group. Two other celebrated writers of the day were John Greenleaf Whittier, who came from a hardworking Quaker farm family, and James Russell Lowell, born to wealth and position. Both Whittier and Lowell were antislavery crusaders as well as poets.

Transcendentalism

Most, if not all, of these writers of the period were influenced by the Transcendental movement then flourishing in New England. Emerson and Thoreau were the best-known Transcendentalists, but the ferment of Transcendental ideas affected many other writers, some of whom hovered on the fringes of the movement, some of whom opposed it.

Transcendentalism demands careful definition, yet it is very hard to define. It has many facets, many sources, and encompasses a range of beliefs whose specific principles depend on the individual writer or thinker. The term itself and some of the ideas came from the German philosopher Immanuel Kant. In his *Critique of Practical Reason,* published in 1788, Kant refers to the "transcendental," which to him meant the knowledge or understanding a person gains intuitively, although it lies beyond direct physical experience. New England Transcendentalism drew on other philosophical theories besides Kant's. These included Plato's as well as those of Pascal, the French mathematician and moralist, and Swedenborg, the Swedish scientist and mystic. In addition, it drew on Buddhist thought and German idealism.

The movement was not essentially religious, but there were religious overtones. Even though a hundred years had passed since Jonathan Edwards, a Calvinist minister in Northampton, Massachusetts, had preached that human beings can share directly in the divine light, Edwards's idea continued to exert influence in the mid-nineteenth century. More recently, William Ellery Channing, minister of the Federal Street Church, Boston, had broken with the Calvinism of his day to become the apostle of Unitarianism. Channing's sermons and essays, promoting more tolerant religious attitudes and various social causes, reflected his own optimism and idealism. The inscription on a statue of him in the Boston Public Garden reads, "He breathed into theology a humane spirit."

Beyond that, Channing helped to lay the groundwork for New England's Transcendentalism. His influence on American literature was substantial; Emerson, Longfellow, Lowell, and Holmes all acknowledged their debt to him. To a remarkable degree, his views became their views. Seven years before Emerson's *American Scholar* address, Channing's *Remarks on American Literature* had called for American writers to cease imitating British models and to find their inspiration closer to home.

Philosophy, religion, literature—all merged in New England Transcendentalism, producing a native blend that was romantic, intuitive, mystical, and considerably easier to recognize than to explain. Emerson, believing in the divinity of human nature, embodied the spirit of it. Thoreau, in *Walden,* provided it with its most sustained expression. Yet Transcendentalism was, and is, hard to pin down. To some in the luminous literary group in Boston and its environs, whose members met from time to time—a group which outsiders came to call the "Transcendental club,"—the movement meant intense individualism and self-reliance. To others it meant practically the opposite, and was considered a single-minded commitment to improving the lot of the poor and oppressed. The Transcendentalists could accept such differences, for theirs was a democracy of intellect. They recognized few absolutes beyond an all-encompassing belief in the unity of God and the world. Even self-contradictions might be necessary, as Emerson stated in a much-quoted sentence: "A foolish consistency is the hobgoblin of little minds."

For Transcendentalists the point was that the real truths, the fundamental truths, lay outside the experience of the senses, residing instead in the "Over-Soul . . . a universal and benign omnipresence . . . a God known to men only in moments of mystic enthusiasm, whose visitations leave them altered, self-reliant, and purified of petty aims."

If that seems a bit obscure, as it did to many people in the United States, and often to the press, so did the essays in *The Dial,* the quarterly magazine of New England Transcendentalism, which grew out of the informal and sporadic meetings of the Transcendentalists. Published from 1840 to 1844, *The Dial's* first editor was Margaret Fuller, a dominant personality and zealous feminist, whose book, *Woman in the Nineteenth Century,* was the first serious American exploration of feminism. Margaret Fuller, astonishingly erudite, was accepted as the intellectual equal, or even superior, of the most honored members of the circle. Under her editorship, however, *The Dial,* like Transcendentalism, seemed to lack a clear focus and may have bewildered as many people as it enlightened.

Nodding Fields and Walden Pond

If the Transcendentalists, and Emerson himself, lacked a well-defined philosophy, there were certain basic areas of agreement. The Transcendentalists revered nature. Emerson titled his first major work *Nature,* and although the essay deals with many topics—beauty, discipline, idealism, spirit, and others—Nature (with a capital N) provides its unifying theme. "The fields and woods," wrote Emerson, "nod to me, and I to them." This essay is considered the first full-scale expression of American Transcendentalism.

Both of Henry David Thoreau's important works, *Walden* and the earlier *A Week on the Concord and Merrimack Rivers,* emphasize the central importance of nature. *Walden* begins, "When I wrote the following pages, or rather the bulk of them, I lived alone, in the woods, a mile from any neighbor, in a house which I had built myself, on the shore of Walden Pond, in Concord, Massachusetts, and earned my living by the labor of my hands only." The eighteen essays that comprise the book deal with matters ranging from the pickerel in Walden Pond to a battle between red and black ants. Nature is the central subject, and from its development emerges Thoreau's philosophy of individualism, simplicity, and passive resistence to injustice.

Brook Farm, as a kind of back-to-nature venture, reflected the Transcendentalists' interest in putting theories into practice. Nathaniel Hawthorne, partly at the urging of Elizabeth Peabody, a Transcendentalist and a friend of Margaret Fuller, bought two shares of stock in Brook Farm and took up residence there in 1841. He hated it. "It is my opinion," he wrote to his fiancé, "that a man's soul may be buried and perish under a dungheap or in a furrow of the field just as well as under a pile of money." Hawthorne, who never shared the optimism of Emerson and Thoreau, found nothing at Brook Farm to alter his view that the world is more complex and less perfectible than the Transcendentalists believed.

The Possibility of Evil

Although the Transcendentalists were widely influential, their view of life seemed far too rosy to many writers. If Emerson and Thoreau can be conveniently paired as Transcendentalists, Nathaniel Hawthorne and Herman Melville can be paired as Anti-Transcendentalists. They were writers who, in Hawthorne's words, "burrowed into the depths of our common nature" and found the area not always shimmering, but often "dusky."

Just as the younger Thoreau had apprenticed, in a sense, in Emerson's household, so Melville, fifteen years younger than Hawthorne, sought the counsel and friendship of the older and more widely acclaimed Hawthorne. It happened almost by accident. Melville, in his early thirties, had moved from New York City to Pittsfield in western Massachusetts, where, on a farm he called "Arrowhead," he wrote his monumental book, *Moby-Dick*. It was published in 1851, a year after Hawthorne's *The Scarlet Letter* appeared. Although *Moby-Dick* would be recognized as a great work only after Melville's death, *The Scarlet Letter* achieved immediate fame in both the United States and England.

Meanwhile, Hawthorne had moved to Lenox, Massachusetts, in the Berkshires, a few miles south of Pittsfield. There he was working on the manuscript of *The House of the Seven Gables*. Melville, pessimistic about *Moby-Dick*—"the product is a final hash," he wrote, "and all my books are botches"—approached Hawthorne, seeking solace. According to a biographer, the young Melville was in "a state of exhaustion and hyper-excitability"; his "impetuous soul rushed out to embrace Hawthorne's . . . in headlong and abso-

THE WHALE FISHERY—THE SPERM WHALE IN A FLURRY
Undated Lithograph by Currier and Ives
The Granger Collection

lute devotion." Hawthorne may have been surprised by this adulation, but he and Melville became and remained friends.

Their visions, however, while equally dark, were very different. Hawthorne's Puritan heritage, which included an ancestor who was a judge at the Salem witchcraft trials, was never far from his consciousness. *The Scarlet Letter* is a historical romance set in Puritan Boston in the middle of the seventeenth century. In it Hawthorne deals with sin and concealed guilt, with hypocrisy and humility, in a dark tale that shows his insight into the Puritan conscience. In *The House of the Seven Gables,* he delves into seventeenth-century witchcraft, insanity, and a legendary curse. These unhappy themes do not reflect the easy optimism of the Transcendentalists, and yet Hawthorne, despite a tendency toward solitude, was stable and self-possessed, absorbed by questions of evil and moral responsibility, yet a shrewd man without illusions.

Melville, by contrast, was a maelstrom of emotions, a man at odds with the world, a tortured and cryptic personality. He was an artist raging against the fates, much like Captain Ahab was in *Moby-Dick,* when he unleashed his fury against the white whale that had torn away his leg. Melville dedicated *Moby-Dick* to Nathaniel Hawthorne "in token for my admiration for his genius." Melville was a genius, too, but an embittered one, a great writer rejected by the public. Only in his later years, with the short novel *Billy Budd,* did he affirm that the cruelties of existence might be overcome by the strength and nobility of the human spirit. Perhaps by then, after long years of obscurity as a customs inspector in New York, he had acquired in his personal life some of the serenity of Hawthorne.

When Poetry Was in Bloom

During the flowering of New England, Americans were avid readers of poetry. Newspapers and magazines published poems, and books of poetry sold briskly. Longfellow was acclaimed as the American bard; Whittier's eightieth birthday was marked by a national celebration; Holmes's comic verse made him a celebrity here and abroad. Today, when poetry is widely written but not so widely read, it may be hard to picture a time in which the names and works of poets were part of the national consciousness. "Poets," said the English poet Shelley in 1821, "are the unacknowledged legislators of the world." In the 1840's and 1850's there were Americans who still believed this.

Among the Transcendentalists, Emerson wrote poetry of an exceptionally high quality. Thoreau declared, "My life has been the poem I would have writ," but in fact he produced some fine poetry on paper as well. Hawthorne concentrated on prose, but Melville in his later years wrote a number of noteworthy poems, especially during the Civil War.

The popular poets of the day, though, were a group commonly known as the Fireside Poets: Longfellow, Whittier, Holmes, Lowell, and a few lesser-known writers. Working separately—they had no "club" as the Transcendentalists did—the Fireside Poets created verse that the average reader could understand and appreciate. Some of their poems were on inspiring or patriotic themes; others dealt with love, nature, home, family, and children. At their best, the Fireside Poets appealed to well-educated, highly literate readers as well as to the less sophisticated. Longfellow, in particular, had a towering reputation in his own time, and is the only American with a bust in the Poet's Corner of Westminster Abbey in London.

Later critics have tended to rank these poets below Emerson, Thoreau, Hawthorne, and Melville in the literary pantheon. Many of

HIAWATHA, C. 1871
Thomas Eakins
Hirshhorn Museum & Sculpture Garden, Smithsonian Institution

their works are still read, however, and the Fireside Poets appear to have earned a permanent place in the hearts of Americans. They lived in New England and were part of its literary blossoming, but they are no longer considered to have been its finest blooms. Even so, their output of memorable poetry helped to build an American myth that still survives and enriches our culture.

At Home in Amherst

At the time Charles Dickens visited Boston and met its emerging literary figures, a young girl was growing up in the valley town of Amherst, Massachusetts. She was not yet writing poetry, at least not seriously, but when she did begin to write, her achievements would catapult her (although not in her lifetime) into the company of the greatest poets in American literature.

Emily Dickinson cannot be easily assigned to any literary category. Her gem-like poetry is unique, just as her life was unique. A recluse for the last twenty-five years of her life, she did not write for publication, or even for her family. Only a few of her poems appeared in print during her lifetime, and those were released without her consent. Why, then, did she write? She may have done so partly to resolve the questions about death, immortality, and the soul that orthodox Calvinism raised but, to her inquiring mind, did not satisfactorily answer.

Since her poems were not published until 1890, and since a definitive edition of them did not appear until 1955, it is hard to pigeonhole Emily Dickinson, even historically. She was not a Transcendentalist. She wrote many of her poems during the Civil War, but she was wholly uninfluenced by the conflict. Since she was a New Englander, and since her remarkable poetry with its dazzling brevity and breath-taking images adds a special luster to the New England literary renaissance, her work appears in this unit rather than a later one.

Beyond the Flowering

The renaissance did not end abruptly in 1855, of course, but as the storm clouds of war gathered, the great sunburst of creativity in the Northeast did subside. Americans increasingly turned their attention to the coming struggle, and antislavery writers, such as Emerson, Melville, Whittier, and Lowell, strongly supported the northern war effort. Thoreau and Hawthorne died before the last shot was fired. Oliver Wendell Holmes, energetic and cheerful, lived on, outlasting all the rest of that renowned generation of writers, thus becoming "the last leaf upon the tree," to quote his own words. Holmes had written his well-known poem, "The Last Leaf," about Herman Melville's grandfather, "a venerable relic of the Revolution." The poem had been published sixty-three years earlier, in 1831, back when Holmes was a young man and before New England had even begun to bloom.

AMERICAN VOICES
Quotations by Prominent Figures of the Period

Hitch your wagon to a star.
Ralph Waldo Emerson, "Society and Solitude," from *Civilization*

Any man more right than his neighbor constitutes a majority of one.
Henry David Thoreau, *Civil Disobedience*

The mass of men lead lives of quiet desperation.
Henry David Thoreau, *Walden*

If a man does not keep pace with his companions, perhaps it is because he hears a different drummer. Let him step to the music which he hears, however measured or far away.
Henry David Thoreau, *Walden*

Life is made up of marble and mud.
Nathaniel Hawthorne, *The House of the Seven Gables*

Call me Ishmael.
Herman Melville, *Moby-Dick*

I 'spect I growed. Don't think nobody never made me.
Harriet Beecher Stowe, *Uncle Tom's Cabin*

If we could read the secret history of our enemies, we should find in each man's life sorrow and suffering enough to disarm all hostility.
Henry Wadsworth Longfellow, *Driftwood*

Put not your trust in money, but your money in trust.
Oliver Wendell Holmes, *The Autocrat of the Breakfast Table*

And what is so rare as a day in June?
  Then, if ever, come perfect days.
James Russell Lowell, *The Vision of Sir Launfal*

If I feel physically as if the top of my head were taken off, I know that is poetry.
Emily Dickinson, *Life and Letters of Emily Dickinson*

The Literature of 1840–1855

During the years from 1840–1855, the United States continued to expand rapidly. A steady flow of American pioneers traveled westward, settling in the new frontier. At the same time, a group of writers in New England brought about a literary renaissance that earned the country a place among the world's great literary traditions.

Historical Context

The rapid growth and expansion of the United States helped bring about scientific advances that established the United States as one of the most technologically advanced nations in the world. New agricultural machines were invented, new roads, canals, and railroads were built, and telegraph lines were put into place. These developments brought about an overwhelming sense of optimism about the country's future.

Literary Movements

The sense of optimism that dominated many people's thoughts during this period was reflected in the ideas of the Transcendentalists, the members of one of the main intellectual and artistic movements of the period. Possessing a deep faith in human potential, the Transcendentalists believed that all forms of being are spiritually united through a shared universal soul. In contrast, two major writers who have come to be known as Anti-Transcendentalists espoused a much darker vision of the world, believing that the truths of existence tend to be elusive and disturbing. A third group of writers known as the Fireside Poets also made important contributions during this period. By creating poetry that was inspiring and easy to read, these poets helped to establish poetry as a popular literary form among the American public.

Writers' Techniques

Focusing on popular themes such as love and nature, the Fireside Poets wrote poetry using traditional poetic forms and techniques. Although Ralph Waldo Emerson, the founder of the Transcendentalists, also wrote poetry, the Transcendentalists are remembered mainly for their essays expressing their ideas and beliefs. The Anti-Transcendentalists, on the other hand, expressed their beliefs through the themes of their novels and short stories, often using symbols to convey their themes.

On the following pages is a selection by Henry Wadsworth Longfellow. The notes in the side column should draw your attention to Longfellow's literary techniques and help you to place the selection in its historical context.

The Skeleton in Armor

Henry Wadsworth Longfellow

Literary Movements: Like much of the poetry of the Fireside Poets, this poem deals with a subject of interest to the common people.

This poem was written after a skeleton clothed in armor was unearthed near Fall River, Massachusetts.

"Speak! speak! thou fearful guest!
Who, with thy hollow breast
Still in rude armor drest,
    Comest to daunt me!
5 Wrapt not in Eastern balms,
But with thy fleshless palms
Stretched, as if asking alms,
    Why dost thou haunt me?"

Historical Context: The discovery of a skeleton in armor made it apparent that the Vikings had explored America long before the arrival of Columbus.

Then, from those cavernous eyes
10 Pale flashes seemed to rise,
As when the Northern skies
    Gleam in December;
And, like the water's flow
Under December's snow,
15 Came a dull voice of woe
    From the heart's chamber.

Writer's Technique: Notice the traditional poetic form. This poem is written in octaves, or eight-line stanzas, with an *aaabcccb* rhyme scheme.

"I was a Viking old!
My deeds, though manifold,
No Skald[1] in song has told,
20   No Saga taught thee!
Take heed, that in thy verse,
Thou dost the tale rehearse,[2]
Else dread a dead man's curse;
    For this I sought thee.

Literary Movement: The poem's subject reflects the Fireside Poets' interest in capturing the American heritage.

25 "Far in the Northern Land,
By the wild Baltic's strand,

---

1. Skald (skôld): An ancient Scandinavian poet.
2. rehearse (ri hʉrs') *v.*: Narrate.

Writer's Technique: This poem is an example of a narrative poem—a poem that tells a story. Longfellow's narrative poems played an important role in establishing poetry as a popular literary form.

I, with my childish hand,
    Tamed the gerfalcon;[3]
And, with my skates fast-bound,
30   Skimmed the half-frozen Sound,
That the poor whimpering hound
    Trembled to walk on.

"Oft to his frozen lair
Tracked I the grisly bear,
35   While from my path the hare
    Fled like a shadow;
Oft through the forest dark
Followed the werewolf's bark,
Until the soaring lark
40   Sang from the meadow.

Writer's Technique: Longfellow uses sound devices to give his poetry a musical quality.

"But when I older grew,
Joining a corsair's[4] crew,
O'er the dark sea I flew
    With the marauders.
45   Wild was the life we led;
Many the souls that sped,
Many the hearts that bled,
    By our stern orders.

"Many a wassail bout[5]
50   Wore the long Winter out;
Often our midnight shout
    Set the cocks crowing,
As we the Berserk's[6] tale
Measured in cups of ale,
55   Draining the oaken pail,
    Filled to o'erflowing.

"Once as I told in glee[7]
Tales of the stormy sea,
Soft eyes did gaze on me,
60   Burning yet tender;
And as the white stars shine

---

3. gerfalcon (jur′ fal′ k'n) *n*.: A large, fierce falcon of the Arctic.
4. corsair's (kôr′ serz): Referring to a pirate ship.
5. wassail bout (wäs′ l bout): A celebration.
6. Berserk (bər surk′): A legendary Norse warrior who worked himself into a frenzy before battle.
7. glee (glē) *n*.: An unaccompanied song.

THE FIRST CARGO, 1910
N. C. Wyeth
New York Public Library

The Skeleton in Armor 261

135 Which, to this very hour,
    Stands looking seaward.

    "There lived we many years;
    Time dried the maiden's tears;
    She had forgot her fears,
140   She was a mother;
    Death closed her mild blue eyes,
    Under that tower she lies;
    Ne'er shall the sun arise
        On such another!

145 "Still grew my bosom then,
    Still as a stagnant fen!
    Hateful to me were men,
        The sunlight hateful!
    In the vast forest here,
150 Clad in my warlike gear,
    Fell I upon my spear,
        Oh, death was grateful!

    "Thus, seamed with many scars,
    Bursting these prison bars,
155 Up to its native stars
        My soul ascended!
    There from the flowing bowl
    Deep drinks the warrior's soul,
    Skoal![12] to the Northland! *skoal!*"
160   Thus the tale ended.

---

12. *Skoal* (skōl) *interj.*: A drinking toast, meaning "to your health."

Literary Movement: Notice the heroic sentiments expressed by this poem. Such sentiments were characteristic of the Fireside Poets.

THINKING AND WRITING

Recalling

1. Why has the spirit of the Viking sought the poet?
2. Describe the Viking's activities when he was young and as he grew older?
3. How does the Viking get the woman he loves?
4. How does the Viking escape his pursuers?
5. What does the Viking do when his wife dies?

Interpreting

6. How would you characterize the Viking?
7. What does the final stanza reveal about the Viking's attitude concerning his own life?
8. Legends are traditional stories that are popularly believed to be based on fact and often serve to explain something. In what respects is Longfellow's poem similar to a legend?

Applying

9. Do you sympathize with the Viking's actions in the poem? Why or why not?

ANALYZING LITERATURE

Understanding the Fireside Poets

The Fireside Poets were a group of poets who helped to establish poetry as a popular literary form by creating poetry that the average reader could understand and appreciate. They wrote poems for a family audience, exploring such popular themes as love, nature, home and family, and patriotism. Because of their use of sound devices and regular rhythms and rhyme, their poetry is especially effective when read aloud. As a result, poetry readings developed into a popular family activity during the New England Renaissance.

1. Why might the subject of this poem be likely to appeal to a general audience?
2. Though the poems of the Fireside Poets often focus on specific subjects or situations, they usually express general, universal themes. In what sense is the theme of "The Skeleton in Armor" universal?

SPEAKING AND LISTENING

Reading with Expression

Recite Longfellow's poem to your classmates, capturing the poem's musical quality in your reading. Hesitate only where a pause is indicated by punctuation, by the meanings of words, or by the natural rhythms of the language. Vary the pitch and loudness of your voice, and be sure to speak slowly and clearly enough so that your classmates can understand you.

THINKING AND WRITING

Writing a Letter

Write a letter to Longfellow discussing the reasons why poetry is less popular today than it was during his time. Also mention the types of subjects that would appeal to a general audience today. Use informal language, but make sure that you follow the rules of grammar, usage, and punctuation. When you finish writing, revise and proofread your letter and prepare a final copy.

RALPH WALDO EMERSON

1803–1882

Ralph Waldo Emerson was an essayist, a poet, an orator, and, more than anything else, a philosopher. Throughout the course of his life, Emerson's mind was constantly in motion, bringing forth new ideas and refining and redefining his view of the world. As a result, Emerson's philosophy was reflected in all of his work—his essays, his poems, and his lectures.

Emerson was born in Boston, the son of a Unitarian minister. When Emerson was eight, his father died, leaving the family in a state of poverty. Despite his family's financial difficulties, Emerson received a thorough education. At the age of fourteen, he entered Harvard, where he began recording his ideas in a journal. After his graduation, Emerson taught for several years before deciding to become a minister. In 1825 Emerson entered Harvard Divinity School. Four years later, he became the pastor of the Second Church of Boston.

Saddened by the death of his young wife, Ellen, and dissatisfied with the spiritual restrictions of Unitarianism, Emerson resigned his ministry in 1832. Following his resignation, Emerson traveled to Europe, where he met English poets William Wordsworth and Samuel Taylor Coleridge. When Emerson returned to America, he settled in Concord, Massachusetts, remarried, and began his lifelong career of writing and lecturing.

During the 1830's and 1840's, Emerson and a small group of intellectuals gathered regularly to discuss philosophy, religion, and literature. This group, which came to be known as the Transcendental Club, developed a philosophical system that stressed intuition, individuality, and self-reliance. In 1836 Emerson—the group's most influential member—published *Nature,* a lengthy essay that became the Transcendental Club's unofficial statement of belief.

Emerson first achieved national fame in 1841 when he published *Essays,* a collection of essays based on material from his journals and lectures. Emerson went on to publish several more volumes of essays, including *Essays, Second Volume* (1844), *Representative Man* (1849), and *The Conduct of Life* (1860). Though Emerson was known mostly for his essays and lectures, he also published two successful volumes of poetry, *Poems* (1847) and *May-Day and Other Pieces* (1867).

from Nature; *from* Self-Reliance

Literary Movements

Transcendentalism. Transcendentalism was an intellectual movement that directly or indirectly affected most of the writers of the New England Renaissance. The Transcendentalists, led by Ralph Waldo Emerson, believed that the human senses can know only physical reality. The fundamental truths of being and the universe lie outside the reach of the senses and can be grasped only through intuition. As a result, in their quest for understanding, the Transcendentalists focused their attention on the human spirit. The Transcendentalists were also interested in the natural world and its relationship to humanity. They felt that if they explored nature thoroughly, they would come to know themselves and the universal truths better. Through this exploration, they discovered that the human spirit is reflected in nature. This led them to the conclusion that formed the heart of their beliefs: all forms of being—God, nature, and humanity—are spiritually united through a shared universal soul, or Over-Soul.

Emerson's lengthy essay *Nature* (1836) was the first published statement of the Transcendentalists' beliefs. As you read the following two essays, look for tenets of the Transcendentalists' beliefs.

Look For

Emerson writes about the effect of nature on him. What do *you* enjoy about nature? What effect does the natural world have on you? Freewrite about your perceptions of the natural world and its effect on you.

Writing

Knowing the following words will help you as you read the excerpts from *Nature* and *Self-Reliance*.

Vocabulary

blithe (blith) *adj.*: Carefree (p. 268)

connate (kän′ āt) *adj.*: Having the same origin or nature (p. 268)

chaos (kā′ äs) *n.*: The disorder of formless matter and infinite space, supposed to have ex- isted before the ordered universe (p. 270)

aversion (ə vʉr′ zhən) *n.*: An intense or definite dislike (p. 270)

suffrage (suf′ rij) *n.*: A vote or voting (p. 270)

divines (də vīnz′) *n.*: Clergymen (p. 270)

from Nature

Ralph Waldo Emerson

Nature is a setting that fits equally well a comic or a mourning piece. In good health, the air is a cordial of incredible virtue. Crossing a bare common,[1] in snow puddles, at twilight, under a clouded sky, without having in my thoughts any occurrence of special good fortune, I have enjoyed a perfect exhilaration. I am glad to the brink of fear. In the woods, too, a man casts off his years, as the snake his slough, and at what period soever of life is always a child. In the woods is perpetual youth. Within these plantations of God, a decorum and sanctity reign, a perennial festival is dressed, and the guest sees not how he should tire of them in a thousand years. In the woods, we return to reason and faith. There I feel that nothing can befall me in life—no disgrace, no calamity (leaving me my eyes), which nature cannot repair. Standing on the bare ground—my head bathed by the blithe air and uplifted into infinite space—all mean egotism vanishes. I become a transparent eyeball; I am nothing; I see all; the currents of the Universal Being circulate through me; I am part or parcel of God. The name of the nearest friend sounds then foreign and accidental: to be brothers, to be acquaintances, master or servant, is then a trifle and a disturbance. I am the lover of uncontained and immortal beauty. In the wilderness, I find something more dear and connate than in the streets or villages. In the tranquil landscape, and especially in the distant line of the horizon, man beholds somewhat as beautiful as his own nature.

The greatest delight which the fields and

---

1. **common:** Piece of open public land.

SUNSET
Frederick E. Church
Munson-Williams-Proctor Institute
Museum of Art, Utica, New York

woods minister is the suggestion of an occult relation between man and the vegetable. I am not alone and unacknowledged. They nod to me, and I to them. The waving of the boughs in the storm is new to me and old. It takes me by surprise, and yet is not unknown. Its effect is like that of a higher thought or a better emotion coming over me, when I deemed I was thinking justly or doing right.

Yet it is certain that the power to produce this delight does not reside in nature, but in man, or in a harmony of both. It is necessary to use these pleasures with great temperance. For nature is not always tricked[2] in holiday attire, but the same scene which yesterday breathed perfume and glittered as for the frolic of the nymphs is overspread with melancholy today. Nature always wears the colors of the spirit. To a man laboring under calamity, the heat of his own fire hath sadness in it. Then there is a kind of contempt of the landscape felt by him who has just lost by death a dear friend. The sky is less grand as it shuts down over less worth in the population.

───────────

2. tricked: Dressed.

THINKING ABOUT THE SELECTION
Recalling

1. According to Emerson, where can we "return to reason and faith"?
2. What happens to Emerson when he stands on the bare ground with his head "uplifted into infinite space"?
3. Where does man behold "somewhat as beautiful as his own nature"?
4. What is "the greatest delight which the fields and woods minister"?
5. What "colors" does nature wear?

Interpreting

6. What does Emerson mean when he comments that in the woods "a man casts off his years"?
7. What does Emerson mean when he describes himself as a "transparent eyeball"?

Applying

8. In what ways is Emerson's attitude toward nature different from a scientist's attitude?

ANALYZING LITERATURE
Understanding Transcendentalism

Transcendentalism was an intellectual movement that held that knowledge of fundamental reality was derived through intuition rather than through sensory experience. This movement focused on the human spirit and the spiritual relationship between humanity and nature. The Transcendentalists ultimately reached the conclusion that all forms of being are spiritually united through a shared universal soul, or Over-Soul.

Emerson's essay *Nature,* published in 1836, was the Transcendentalists' unofficial statement of belief.

1. What does *Nature* reveal about the Transcendentalists' attitude toward nature?
2. What does *Nature* reveal about the Transcendentalists' perceptions of human nature?
3. How does the essay convey the Transcendentalists' belief in the Over-Soul?
4. Do you find any evidence of Transcendentalist beliefs in today's poetry and song lyrics? Explain.

from Self-Reliance

Ralph Waldo Emerson

There is a time in every man's education when he arrives at the conviction that envy is ignorance; that imitation is suicide; that he must take himself for better, for worse, as his portion; that though the wide universe is full of good, no kernel of nourishing corn can come to him but through his toil bestowed on that plot of ground which is given to him to till. The power which resides in him is new in nature, and none but he knows what that is which he can do, nor does he know until he has tried. Not for nothing one face, one character, one fact makes much impression on him, and another none. This sculpture in the memory is not without preestablished harmony. The eye was placed where one ray should fall, that it might testify of that particular ray. We but half express ourselves, and are ashamed of that divine idea which each of us represents. It may be safely trusted as proportionate and of good issues, so it be faithfully imparted, but God will not have his work made manifest by cowards. A man is relieved and gay when he has put his heart into his work and done his best; but what he has said or done otherwise, shall give him no peace. It is a deliverance which does not deliver. In the attempt his genius deserts him; no muse befriends; no invention, no hope.

Trust thyself: every heart vibrates to that iron string. Accept the place the divine providence has found for you; the society of your contemporaries, the connection of events. Great men have always done so and confided themselves childlike to the genius of their age, betraying their perception that the absolutely trustworthy was stirring at their heart, working through their hands, predominating in all their being. And we are now men, and must accept in the highest mind the same transcendent destiny; and not minors and invalids in a protected corner, but guides, redeemers, and benefactors, obeying the Almighty effort and advancing on Chaos and the Dark. . . .

Society everywhere is in conspiracy against the manhood of every one of its members. Society is a joint-stock company in which the members agree for the better securing of his bread to each shareholder, to surrender the liberty and culture of the eater. The virtue in most request is conformity. Self-reliance is its aversion. It loves not realities and creators, but names and customs.

Whoso would be a man must be a nonconformist. He who would gather immortal palms must not be hindered by the name of goodness, but must explore if it be goodness. Nothing is at last sacred but the integrity of our own mind. Absolve you to yourself, and you shall have the suffrage of the world. . . .

A foolish consistency is the hobgoblin of little minds, adored by little statesmen and philosophers and divines. With consistency a great soul has simply nothing to do. He may as well concern himself with his shadow on the wall. Speak what you think now in hard words and tomorrow speak what tomorrow thinks in hard words again, though it contradict everything you said today. "Ah, so you shall be sure to be misunderstood?"—Is it so bad, then, to be misunderstood? Pythagoras was misunderstood, and Socrates, and Jesus, and Luther, and Coper-

nicus, and Galileo, and Newton,[1] and every pure and wise spirit that ever took flesh. To be great is to be misunderstood. . . .

---

1. Pythagoras . . . Newton: Individuals who made major contributions to scientific, philosophical, or religious thinking.

THINKING ABOUT THE SELECTION
Recalling

1. According to the first paragraph, at what conviction does every person arrive?
2. According to the second paragraph, what must every person accept?
3. How does Emerson describe society?
4. What is Emerson's comment about consistency?

Interpreting

5. What does he mean when he comments, "no kernel of nourishing corn can come to him but through his toil bestowed on that plot of ground which is given to him to till"?
6. Why, according to Emerson, should people trust themselves?
7. How does Emerson believe people should be affected by the way others perceive them?
8. How does Emerson support his claim that "to be great is to be misunderstood"?

Applying

9. Toward the end of the essay, Emerson writes, "Speak what you think now in hard words and tomorrow speak what tomorrow thinks in hard words again, though it contradict everything you said today." Explain your reaction to this view.

UNDERSTANDING LANGUAGE
Completing Analogies

A verbal analogy is an expression of a relationship between two words. Analogy questions on standardized tests ask you to choose two words that are related in the same way as a given pair. For example, OLD : NEW : : LONG : SHORT. In this example, the two sets of words are antonyms.

Complete each of the following analogies. Choose the pair of words whose relationship is most similar to that expressed by the capitalized pair.

1. BETTER : WORSE : :
   a. quiet : loud   c. easier : softer
   b. narrow : long   d. pompous : ambitious
2. SOCIETY : CULTURE : :
   a. resolve : ambition c. grasp : hold
   b. ambivalent : angry d. amnesty : emotion
3. SCHOOL : EDUCATION : :
   a. class : writing   c. teacher : student
   b. book : test   d. hospital : operation
4. SCULPTURE : ART : :
   a. poem : literature   c. athlete : sport
   b. flower : florist   d. water : flood

THINKING AND WRITING
Writing About Conformity

What are the advantages of conforming to society's expectations? Of not conforming? Make notes about your thoughts on the subject. Then take a stand and present your ideas in an essay. Begin by writing a draft explaining your reasons. Conclude by indicating your agreement or disagreement with Emerson's ideas on conformity. Revise your essay so that your points are clear and supported.

The Snowstorm; Concord Hymn; The Rhodora; Brahma

Writer's Techniques

Apostrophe. Apostrophe is a literary device in which a writer directly addresses an inanimate object, an abstract idea, or an absent person. A writer may address a person who is no longer living, an ocean, or a season. For example, the English poet Shelley addresses the wind in this line: "O Wind, If Winter comes, can Spring be far behind?"

The Transcendentalists believed that all living things were spiritually united through a shared universal soul, or Over-Soul. In "The Rhodora" Emerson uses apostrophe to express this spiritual unity, directly addressing a flower as if it were a person.

Look For

Emerson sees a relationship between humans and nature. As you read these poems, look for the ways in which they reflect Emerson's Transcendentalist beliefs.

Writing

Freewrite, describing a scene that suggests the majesty of nature. Explore your thoughts and reactions to this scene.

Vocabulary

Knowing the following words will help you as you read these poems.

radiant (rā′ dē ənt) *adj.*: Shining brightly (p. 273, 1.8)

tumultuous (too mult′ choo wəs) *adj.*: Greatly agitated (p. 273, 1.9)

bastions (bas′ chənz) *n.*: Fortifications (p. 273, 1.13)

rude (rood) *adj.*: Crude or rough in form or workmanship (p. 275, 1.1)

sages (sāj′ əz) *n.*: People widely respected for their wisdom (p. 277, 1.9)

pine (pīn) *v.*: To have an intense longing or desire (p. 279, 1.14)

FARM YARD, WINTER
George Henry Durrie
Courtesy of the New York Historical Society

The Snowstorm

Ralph Waldo Emerson

Announced by all the trumpets of the sky,
Arrives the snow, and, driving o'er the fields,
Seems nowhere to alight: the whited air
Hides hills and woods, the river, and the heaven,
5 And veils the farmhouse at the garden's end.
The sled and traveler stopped, the courier's feet
Delayed, all friends shut out, the housemates sit
Around the radiant fireplace, enclosed
In a tumultuous privacy of storm.

10   Come see the north wind's masonry.
Out of an unseen quarry evermore
Furnished with tile, the fierce artificer
Curves his white bastions with projected roof
Round every windward stake, or tree, or door.
15 Speeding, the myriad-handed, his wild work
So fanciful, so savage, nought cares he
For number or proportion. Mockingly,
On coop or kennel he hangs Parian[1] wreaths;
A swan-like form invests the hidden thorn;
20 Fills up the farmer's lane from wall to wall,

Maugre[2] the farmer's sighs; and at the gate
A tapering turret overtops the work.
And when his hours are numbered, and the world
Is all his own, retiring, as he were not,
25 Leaves, when the sun appears, astonished Art
To mimic in slow structures, stone by stone,
Built in an age, the mad wind's nightwork,
The frolic architecture of the snow.

---

1. Parian (per′ē ən) *adj.*: Referring to a fine, white marble of the Greek city Paros.
2. Maugre (mô′ gər) *prep.*: In spite of.

THINKING ABOUT THE SELECTION
Recalling

1. What announces the storm's arrival?
2. What does "the whited air" hide?
3. What does the speaker describe in the second stanza?
4. According to lines 25–28, what has the storm left behind "when the sun appears"?

Interpreting

5. What mood does Emerson establish in the first stanza?
6. Explain what Emerson means when he refers to the "tumultuous privacy of the storm" in line 9.

7. In this poem Emerson compares the storm and an artist at work. (a) How does he develop this comparison in the second stanza? (b) How does he extend the comparison in the final stanza? (c) How does this comparison express Emerson's belief in a spiritual unity between humanity and nature?

Applying

8. Emerson expresses a favorable attitude toward the snowstorm. Why might some people living in northern climates not share Emerson's attitude?

Concord Hymn

Sung at the Completion of the Battle Monument, April 19, 1836

Ralph Waldo Emerson

This poem was written for the unveiling of a monument commemorating the Minute Men, who fought the British in the first two battles of the Revolutionary War at Lexington and Concord, Massachusetts, in April of 1775.

By the rude bridge that arched the flood,
    Their flag to April's breeze unfurled,
Here once the embattled farmers stood,
    And fired the shot heard round the world.

5 The foe long since in silence slept;
    Alike the conqueror silent sleeps;
And Time the ruined bridge has swept
    Down the dark stream which seaward creeps.

On this green bank, by this soft stream,
10   We set today a votive[1] stone;
That memory may their deed redeem,
    When, like our sires, our sons are gone.

Spirit, that made those heroes dare
    To die, and leave their children free,
15 Bid Time and Nature gently spare
    The shaft we raise to them and thee.

---

1. votive (vōt′ iv) *adj.*: Dedicated in fulfillment of a vow or pledge.

Tell them, dear, that if eyes were made for seeing,
Then Beauty is its own excuse for being:
Why thou wert there, O rival of the rose!
I never thought to ask, I never knew:
15 But, in my simple ignorance, suppose
The self-same Power that brought me there brought you.

THINKING ABOUT THE SELECTION

Recalling

1. (a) When does the speaker find "the fresh Rhodora in the woods"? (b) Where does he find it?
2. (a) According to the speaker, what question might the sages ask the rhodora? (b) How does he suggest the rhodora should respond?
3. In the final line, how does the speaker explain the rhodora's existence?

Interpreting

4. What larger concept does the rhodora represent?
5. (a) How is the sages' attitude toward nature different from the speaker's attitude? (b) Which attitude seems to produce a more meaningful understanding of nature? Explain your answer.
6. What is unexpected about the speaker's reference to his "simple ignorance" in line 15?
7. How does the final line express Emerson's belief in a spiritual unity among all living things?

Applying

8. At another time, Ralph Waldo Emerson wrote, "Though we travel the world over to find the beautiful, we must carry it with us or we find it not." Explain the view of beauty Emerson expresses here. How is it similar to or different from the view of beauty expressed in "The Rhodora"?

ANALYZING LITERATURE
Understanding Apostrophe

Apostrophe is a literary device in which a writer directly addresses an inanimate object, an abstract idea, or an absent person. Emerson directly addresses a flower in "The Rhodora."

1. What is the effect of the use of apostrophe?
2. How does Emerson's use of apostrophe reinforce the meaning of the poem?

UNDERSTANDING LANGUAGE
Finding Antonyms

Antonyms are words that have the opposite, or nearly the opposite, meaning. For example, the words *sluggish* and *active* are antonyms.

Choose an antonym for each of the following words.

1. ARRAY:
   a. rags b. gown c. display d. splendor
2. COURT:
   a. desire b. propose c. shun d. madden
3. SAGE:
   a. wisdom b. fool c. herb d. flavor
4. RIVAL:
   a. friend b. competitor c. teacher
   d. playmate

Brahma[1]

Ralph Waldo Emerson

If the red slayer think he slays,
    Or if the slain think he is slain,
They know not well the subtle ways
    I keep, and pass, and turn again.

5 Far or forgot to me is near;
    Shadow and sunlight are the same;
The vanished gods to me appear;
    And one to me are shame and fame.

They reckon ill who leave me out;
10   When me they fly, I am the wings;
I am the doubter and the doubt,
    And I the hymn the Brahmin[2] sings.

The strong gods pine for my abode,
    And pine in vain the sacred Seven;[3]
15 But thou, meek lover of the good!
    Find me, and turn thy back on heaven.

---

1. Brahma (brä′ mə): In Hindu religion, the supreme and eternal essence or spirit of the universe.
2. Brahmin: A Hindu priest.
3. sacred Seven: The most sacred Hindu saints.

THINKING ABOUT THE SELECTION
Recalling

1. According to the first stanza, what do the red slayer and the slain "know not well"?
2. According to the final stanza, who pines for the speaker's abode?

Interpreting

3. Who is the speaker of the poem?
4. What does the speaker mean when he refers to "gods" in lines 7 and 13?
5. In the sacred Hindu writings, Brahma is the supreme essence, or spirit, of the universe. What does this poem reveal about Brahma's powers?
6. How does Emerson use the concept of Brahma to express his belief that the fundamental truths of the universe lie beyond the reach of our senses?

Applying

7. In what way is the Hindu belief in Brahma similar to the Transcendentalist belief in a universal soul, or Over-Soul?

CRITICAL THINKING AND READING
Understanding a Paradox

A **paradox** is a statement that seems contradictory but in reality contains a possible truth. In "Brahma" Emerson explores the subject of death from a Hindu perspective. In doing so he presents a series of paradoxes—apparent contradictions that are resolved in the higher reality, or the universal truth, of Brahma. For example, the paradox, "Far . . . is near," is presented in line 5. That something can be both far and near seems contradictory, but in the speaker's context, there is truth in the statement.

1. What paradox related to death is presented in the opening stanza?
2. Name three paradoxes presented in the second and third stanzas. Explain each of these paradoxes.
3. What two paradoxes are presented in the final stanza? Explain these paradoxes.

HENRY DAVID THOREAU

1817–1862

When Henry David Thoreau died of tuberculosis at the age of forty-four, his work had received little recognition. Yet he had achieved an inner success that few others have experienced. Speaking at Thoreau's funeral, Ralph Waldo Emerson commented, "The country knows not yet, or in the least part, how great a son it has lost. . . . But he, at least, is content. His soul was made for the noblest society; he had in a short life exhausted the capabilities of this world; wherever there is knowledge, wherever there is virtue, wherever there is beauty, he will find a home."

Thoreau was born and raised in Concord, Massachusetts. After graduating from Harvard, Thoreau became a teacher. When his objection to corporal punishment forced him to quit his first job, he and his older brother John opened their own school. The school was quite successful, but they had to close it when John became ill.

In 1842 Thoreau moved into Emerson's house. He lived there for two years, performing odd jobs to pay for his room and board. Thoreau became Emerson's close friend and devoted disciple. Deciding not to go back to teaching and refusing to pursue another career, Thoreau dedicated himself to testing the Transcendentalist philosophy through experience. By simplifying his needs, Thoreau was able to devote the rest of his life to exploring and writing about the spiritual relationship between humanity and nature and supporting his political and social beliefs.

For two years (1845–1847) Thoreau lived alone in a cabin he built himself at Walden Pond. Thoreau's experiences during this period provided him with the material for his masterwork, *Walden* (1854). Condensing his experiences at Walden Pond into one year, Thoreau used the four seasons as a structural framework for the book. A unique blend of natural observation, social criticism, and philosophical insight, *Walden* is now generally regarded as the supreme work of Transcendentalist literature.

Though Thoreau's work was for the most part ignored during his lifetime, his reputation has steadily grown since his death. His work has inspired and influenced writers, environmentalists, and social and political leaders. It has made generations of readers aware of the possibilities of the human spirit and the limitations of society.

GUIDE FOR READING

from Walden; *from* Civil Disobedience

Writer's Techniques

Style. Style refers to the manner in which a writer puts his or her thoughts into words. In *Walden* Thoreau's style is closely related to his purpose, which is to encourage us to examine the way we live and think. To achieve his purpose, Thoreau constructs paragraphs so that the sentences build to a climax.

Historical Context

The Mexican War. The Mexican War was a conflict between Mexico and the United States that took place from 1846 to 1848. The war was caused by a dispute over the boundary between Texas and Mexico and Mexico's refusal to discuss selling California and New Mexico to the United States. Believing that President Polk intentionally provoked the conflict before having congressional approval, Thoreau and many other Americans strongly objected to the war. To demonstrate his disapproval, Thoreau refused to pay taxes. His gesture led to his arrest, and he was forced to spend a night in jail.

Look For

In *Walden* Thoreau exhorts readers to be conscious of their acts. As you read, look for the ways in which Thoreau reveals that he is aware of his actions.

Writing

How do you think you would respond to living alone in the wilderness? Write about how you think you would manage.

Vocabulary

Knowing the following words will help you as you read the excerpts from *Walden* and *Civil Disobedience*.

dilapidated (di lap' ə dātid) *adj.*: In disrepair (p. 283)
terrestrial (tə res' trēəl) *adj.*: Of this world (p. 284-285)
sublime (sə blīm') *adj.*: Noble; majestic (p. 285)
superfluous (soo pʉr' floo wəs) *adj.*: Not needed (p. 285)
evitable (ev' ə tə b'l) *adj.*: Avoidable (p. 285)
magnanimity (mag' nə nim' ə tē) *n.*: Generosity (p. 287)
expedient (ik spē' dēənt) *n.*: Resource (p. 290)
integrity (in teg' rə tē) *n.*: Adherence to a code of values (p. 290)
posterity (päs ter' ə tē) *n.*: All succeeding generations (p. 290)
alacrity (ə lak' rə tē) *n.*: Speed (p. 290)

from **Walden**

Henry David Thoreau

from **Where I Lived, and What I Lived For**

At a certain season of our life we are accustomed to consider every spot as the possible site of a house. I have thus surveyed the country on every side within a dozen miles of where I live. In imagination I have bought all the farms in succession, for all were to be bought, and I knew their price. I walked over each farmer's premises, tasted his wild apples, discoursed on husbandry[1] with him, took his farm at his price, at any price, mortgaging it to him in my mind; even put a higher price on it—took everything but a deed of it—took his word for his deed, for I dearly love to talk—cultivated it, and him too to some extent, I trust, and withdrew when I had enjoyed it long enough, leaving him to carry it on. This experience entitled me to be regarded as a sort of real-estate broker by my friends. Wherever I sat, there I might live, and the landscape radiated from me accordingly. What is a house but a *sedes*, a seat?— better if a country seat. I discovered many a site for a house not likely to be soon improved, which some might have thought too far from the village, but to my eyes the village was too far from it. Well, there I might live, I said; and there I did live, for an hour, a summer and a winter life; saw how I could let the years run off, buffet the winter through, and see the spring come in. The future inhabitants of this region, wherever they may place their houses, may be sure that they have been anticipated. An afternoon sufficed to lay out the land into orchard woodlot and pasture, and to decide what fine oaks or pines should be left to stand before the door, and whence each blasted tree could be seen to the best advantage; and then I let it lie, fallow[2] perchance, for a man is rich in proportion to the number of things which he can afford to let alone.

My imagination carried me so far that I even had the refusal of several farms—the refusal was all I wanted—but I never got my fingers burned by actual possession. The nearest that I came to actual possession was when I bought the Hollowell Place, and had begun to sort my seeds, and collected materials with which to make a wheelbarrow to carry it on or off with; but before the owner gave me a deed of it, his wife—every man has such a wife—changed her mind and wished to keep it, and he offered me ten dollars to release him. Now, to speak the truth, I had but ten cents in the world, and it surpassed my arithmetic to tell, if I was that man who had ten cents, or who had a farm, or ten dollars, or all together. However, I let him keep the ten dollars and the farm too, for I had

---

1. husbandry (huz′ bən drē) *n*.: Farming.

2. fallow (fal′ō) *adj*.: Left uncultivated or unplanted.

From J. Lyndon Shanley, ed., *Walden: The Writings of Henry D. Thoreau*. Copyright © 1971 by Princeton University Press. Excerpts, pp. 81–98 and 320–333, reprinted with permission of Princeton University Press.

carried it far enough; or rather, to be generous, I sold him the farm for just what I gave for it, and, as he was not a rich man, made him a present of ten dollars, and still had my ten cents, and seeds, and materials for a wheelbarrow left. I found thus that I had been a rich man without any damage to my poverty. But I retained the landscape, and I have since annually carried off what it yielded without a wheelbarrow. With respect to landscapes:

> "I am monarch of all I *survey*,
> My right there is none to dispute."[3]

I have frequently seen a poet withdraw, having enjoyed the most valuable part of a farm, while the crusty farmer supposed that he had got a few wild apples only. Why, the owner does not know it for many years when a poet has put his farm in rhyme, the most admirable kind of invisible fence, has fairly impounded it, milked it, skimmed it, and got all the cream, and left the farmer only the skimmed milk.

The real attractions of the Hollowell farm, to me, were: its complete retirement, being about two miles from the village, half a mile from the nearest neighbor, and separated from the highway by a broad field; its bounding on the river, which the owner said protected it by its fogs from frosts in the spring, though that was nothing to me; the gray color and ruinous state of the house and barn, and the dilapidated fences, which put such an interval between me and the last occupant; the hollow and lichen-covered apple trees, gnawed by rabbits, showing what kind of neighbors I should have; but above all, the recollection I had of it from my earliest voyages up the river, when the house was concealed behind a dense grove of red maples, through which I heard the house-dog bark. I was in haste to buy it, before the proprietor finished getting out some rocks, cutting down the hollow apple trees, and grubbing up some young birches which had sprung up in the pasture, or, in short, had made any more of his improvements. To enjoy these advantages I was ready to carry it on; like Atlas,[4] to take the world on my shoulders—I never heard what compensation he received for that—and do all those things which had no other motive or excuse but that I might pay for it and be unmolested in my possession of it; for I knew all the while that it would yield the most abundant crop of the kind I wanted if I could only afford to let it alone. But it turned out as I have said.

All that I could say, then, with respect to farming on a large scale (I have always cultivated a garden) was that I had had my seeds ready. Many think that seeds improve with age. I have no doubt that time discriminates between the good and the bad; and when at last I shall plant, I shall be less likely to be disappointed. But I would say to my fellows, once for all, As long as possible live free and uncommitted. It makes but little difference whether you are committed to a farm or the county jail.

Old Cato,[5] whose "De Re Rustica" is my "Cultivator," says, and the only translation I have seen makes sheer nonsense of the passage, "When you think of getting a farm, turn it thus in your mind, not to buy greedily; nor spare your pains to look at it, and do not think it enough to go round it once. The oftener you go there the more it will please you, if it is good." I think I shall not buy greedily, but go round and round it as long as I live, and be buried in it first, that it may please me the more at last. . . .

I do not propose to write an ode to dejection, but to brag as lustily as chanticleer[6] in the morning, standing on his roost, if only to wake my neighbors up.

---

3. "I am . . . dispute.": From William Cowper's *Verses Supposed to Be Written by Alexander Selkirk*.

4. Atlas (at' ləs): From Greek mythology, a Titan who supported the heavens on his shoulders.

5. Old Cato: Roman statesman (234–149 B.C.). "De Re Rustica" is Latin for "Of Things Rustic."

6. chanticleer (chan' tə klir') *n.*: A rooster.

When first I took up my abode in the woods, that is, began to spend my nights as well as days there, which, by accident, was on Independence Day, or the fourth of July, 1845, my house was not finished for winter, but was merely a defense against the rain, without plastering or chimney, the walls being of rough weatherstained boards, with wide chinks, which made it cool at night. The upright white hewn studs and freshly planed door and window casings gave it a clean and airy look, especially in the morning, when its timbers were saturated with dew, so that I fancied that by noon some sweet gum would exude from them. To my imagination it retained throughout the day more or less of this auroral[7] character, reminding me of a certain house on a mountain which I had visited the year before. This was an airy and unplastered cabin, fit to entertain a traveling god, and where a goddess might trail her garments.The winds which passed over my dwelling were such as sweep over the ridges of mountains, bearing the broken strains, or celestial parts only, of ter-

---

7. auroral (ô rôr′ əl) *adj.*: Resembling the dawn.

restrial music. The morning wind forever blows, the poem of creation is uninterrupted; but few are the ears that hear it. Olympus[8] is but the outside of the earth everywhere. . . .

I went to the woods because I wished to live deliberately, to front only the essential facts of life, and see if I could not learn what it had to teach, and not, when I came to die, discover that I had not lived. I did not wish to live what was not life, living is so dear; nor did I wish to practice resignation, unless it was quite necessary. I wanted to live deep and suck out all the marrow of life, to live so sturdily and Spartanlike[9] as to put to rout all that was not life, to cut a broad swath and shave close, to drive life into a corner, and reduce it to its lowest terms, and, if it proved to be mean, why then to get the whole and genuine meanness of it, and publish its meanness to the world; or if it were sublime, to know it by experience, and be able to give a true account of it in my next excursion. For most men, it appears to me, are in a strange uncertainty about it, whether it is of the devil or of God, and have *somewhat hastily* concluded that it is the chief end of man here to "glorify God and enjoy him forever."[10]

Still we live meanly, like ants; though the fable tells us that we were long ago changed into men; like pygmies we fight with cranes;[11] it is error upon error, and clout upon clout, and our best virtue has for its occasion a superfluous and evitable wretchedness. Our life is frittered away by detail. An honest man has hardly need to count more than his ten fingers, or in extreme cases he may add his ten toes, and lump the rest. Simplicity, simplicity, simplicity! I say, let your affairs be as two or three, and not a hundred or a thousand; instead of a million count half a dozen, and keep your accounts on your thumbnail. In the midst of this chopping sea of civilized life, such are the clouds and storms and quicksands and thousand-and-one items to be allowed for, that a man has to live, if he would not founder and go to the bottom and not make his port at all, by dead reckoning,[12] and he must be a great calculator indeed who succeeds. Simplify, simplify. Instead of three meals a day, if it be necessary eat but one; instead of a hundred dishes, five; and reduce other things in proportion. Our life is like a German Confederacy,[13] made up of petty states, with its boundary forever fluctuating, so that even a German cannot tell you how it is bounded at any moment. The nation itself, with all its so-called internal improvements, which, by the way, are all external and superficial, is just such an unwieldy and overgrown establishment, cluttered with furniture and tripped up by its own traps, ruined by luxury and heedless expense, by want of calculation and a worthy aim, as the million households in the land; and the only cure for it as for them is in a rigid economy, a stern and more than Spartan simplicity of life and elevation of purpose. It lives too fast. Men think that it is essential that the *Nation* have commerce, and export ice, and talk through a telegraph, and ride thirty miles an hour, without a doubt, whether *they* do or not; but whether we should live like baboons or like men, is a little uncertain. If we do not get out sleepers,[14] and forge rails, and devote days and nights to the work, but go to tinkering upon our *lives* to improve *them*, who will build railroads? And if railroads are not

---

8. Olympus (ō lim′ pəs): In Greek mythology, the home of the gods.

9. Spartanlike: Like the people of Sparta, an ancient Greek state, whose citizens were known to be hardy, stoical, simple, and highly disciplined.

10. "glorify . . . forever.": The answer to the question "What is the chief end of man?" in the Westminster catechism.

11. like . . . cranes: In the *Iliad*, the Trojans are compared to cranes fighting against pygmies.

12. dead reckoning: Navigating without the assistance of stars.

13. German Confederacy: At the time, Germany was a loose union of thirty-eight independent states, with no common government.

14. sleepers (slē′ pərz) *n.*: Ties supporting railroad tracks.

built, how shall we get to heaven in season? But if we stay at home and mind our business, who will want railroads? We do not ride on the railroad; it rides upon us. . . .

Time is but the stream I go a-fishing in. I drink at it; but while I drink I see the sandy bottom and detect how shallow it is. Its thin current slides away, but eternity remains. I would drink deeper; fish in the sky, whose bottom is pebbly with stars. I cannot count one. I know not the first letter of the alphabet. I have always been regretting that I was not as wise as the day I was born. The intellect is a cleaver; it discerns and rifts its way into the secret of things. I do not wish to be any more busy with my hands than is necessary. My head is hands and feet. I feel all my best faculties concentrated in it. My instinct tells me that my head is an organ for burrowing, as some creatures use their snout and forepaws, and with it I would mine and burrow my way through these hills. I think that the richest vein is somewhere hereabouts; so by the divining rod[15] and thin rising vapors I judge; and here I will begin to mine. . . .

from The Conclusion

I left the woods for as good a reason as I went there. Perhaps it seemed to me that I had several more lives to live, and could not spare any more time for that one. It is remarkable how easily and insensibly we fall into a particular route, and make a beaten track for ourselves. I had not lived there a week before my feet wore a path from my door to the pondside; and though it is five or six years since I trod it, it is still quite distinct. It is true, I fear that others may have fallen into it, and so helped to keep it open. The surface of the earth is soft and impressible by the feet of men; and so with the paths which the mind travels. How worn and dusty, then, must be the highways of the world, how deep the ruts of tradition and conformity! I did not wish to take a cabin passage, but rather to go before the mast and on the deck of the world, for there I could best see the moonlight amid the mountains. I do not wish to go below now.

I learned this, at least, by my experiment; that if one advances confidently in the direction of his dreams, and endeavors to live the life which he has imagined, he will meet with a success unexpected in common hours. He will put some things behind, will pass an invisible boundary; new, universal, and more liberal laws will begin to establish themselves around and within him; or the old laws be expanded, and interpreted in his favor in a more liberal sense, and he will live with the license of a higher order of beings. In proportion as he simplifies his life, the laws of the universe will appear less complex, and solitude will not be solitude, nor poverty poverty, nor weakness weakness. If you have built castles in the air, your work need not be lost; that is where they should be. Now put the foundations under them. . . .

Why should we be in such desperate haste to succeed, and in such desperate enterprises? If a man does not keep pace with his companions, perhaps it is because he hears a different drummer. Let him step to the music which he hears, however measured or far away. It is not important that he should mature as soon as an apple tree or an oak. Shall he turn his spring into summer? If the condition of things which we were made for is not yet, what were any reality which we can substitute? We will not be shipwrecked on a vain reality. Shall we with pains erect a heaven of blue glass over ourselves, though when it is done we shall be sure to gaze still at the true ethereal heaven far above, as if the former were not?. . . .

However mean your life is, meet it and live it; do not shun it and call it hard names.

---

15. divining rod: A forked branch or stick alleged to reveal underground water or minerals.

It is not so bad as you are. It looks poorest when you are richest. The faultfinder will find faults even in paradise. Love your life, poor as it is. You may perhaps have some pleasant, thrilling, glorious hours, even in a poorhouse. The setting sun is reflected from the windows of the almshouse[16] as brightly as from the rich man's abode; the snow melts before its door as early in the spring. I do not see but a quiet mind may live as contentedly there, and have as cheering thoughts, as in a palace. The town's poor seem to me often to live the most independent lives of any. Maybe they are simply great enough to receive without misgiving. Most think that they are above being supported by the town; but it oftener happens that they are not above supporting themselves by dishonest means, which should be more disreputable. Cultivate poverty like a garden herb, like sage. Do not trouble yourself much to get new things, whether clothes or friends. Turn the old; return to them. Things do not change; we change. Sell your clothes and keep your thoughts. God will see that you do not want society. If I were confined to a corner of a garret[17] all my days, like a spider, the world would be just as large to me while I had my thoughts about me. The philosopher said: "From an army of three divisions one can take away its general, and put it in disorder; from the man the most abject and vulgar one cannot take away his thought." Do not seek so anxiously to be developed, to subject yourself to many influences to be played on; it is all dissipation. Humility like darkness reveals the heavenly lights. The shadows of poverty and meanness gather around us, "and lo! creation widens to our view."[18] We are often reminded that if there were bestowed on us the wealth of Croesus,[19] our aims must still be the same, and our means essentially the same. Moreover, if you are restricted in your range by poverty, if you cannot buy books and newspapers, for instance, you are but confined to the most significant and vital experiences; you are compelled to deal with the material which yields the most sugar and the most starch. It is life near the bone where it is sweetest. You are defended from being a trifler. No man loses ever on a lower level by magnanimity on a higher. Superfluous wealth can buy superfluities only. Money is not required to buy one necessary of the soul. . . .

The life in us is like the water in the river. It may rise this year higher than man has ever known it, and flood the parched uplands; even this may be the eventful year, which will drown out all our muskrats. It was not always dry land where we dwell. I see far inland the banks which the stream anciently washed, before science began to record its freshets. Everyone has heard the story which has gone the rounds of New England, of a strong and beautiful bug which came out of the dry leaf of an old table of apple-tree wood, which had stood in a farmer's kitchen for sixty years, first in Connecticut, and afterward in Massachusetts—from an egg deposited in the living tree many years earlier still, as appeared by counting the annual layers beyond it; which was heard gnawing out for several weeks, hatched perchance by the heat of an urn. Who does not feel his faith in a resurrection and immortality strengthened by hearing of this? Who knows what beautiful and winged life, whose egg has been buried for ages under many concentric layers of woodenness in

---

16. **almshouse** *n.*: A home for people too poor to support themselves.
17. **garret** (gar′ it) *n.*: Attic.
18. **"and . . . view":** From the sonnet "To Night" by British poet Joseph Blanco White (1775–1841).

---

19. **Croesus** (krē′ səs): The King of Lydia (d. 546 B.C.), believed to be the wealthiest person of his time.

the dead dry life of society, deposited at first in the alburnum[20] of the green and living tree, which has been gradually converted into the semblance of its well-seasoned tomb—heard perchance gnawing out now for years by the astonished family of man, as they sat round the festive board—may unexpectedly come forth from amidst society's most trivial and handselled furniture, to enjoy its perfect summer life at last!

I do not say that John or Jonathan[21] will realize all this; but such is the character of that morrow which mere lapse of time can never make to dawn. The light which puts out our eyes is darkness to us. Only that day dawns to which we are awake. There is more day to dawn. The sun is but a morning star.

---

20. alburnum (al bur' nəm) *n.*: Soft wood between the bark and the heartwood where water is conducted.

21. John or Jonathan: The average person.

THINKING ABOUT THE SELECTION

Recalling

1. What does Thoreau imagine doing?
2. (a) On what day does Thoreau begin spending nights in his "abode in the woods"? (b) What condition is the cabin in at the time?
3. For what reasons does Thoreau go to live in the woods?
4. Why does he leave the woods?
5. What does he learn from his "experiment"?
6. What advice does Thoreau offer to those who live in poverty?

Interpreting

7. What does Thoreau mean when he comments, "It makes but little difference whether you are committed to a farm or the county jail"?
8. (a) How does Thoreau's decription of the wind convey the Transcendentalist belief in the existence of a shared universal soul, or Over-Soul? (b) What does he suggest about peoples' awareness of the Over-Soul?
9. Why does Thoreau believe that living in the woods will enable him to "live deep and suck all the marrow out of life"?
10. Considering the attitude toward commitments that Thoreau expresses in his discussion of farms, why is it not surprising that he decides to leave Walden?
11. In your own words, describe Thoreau's attitude toward individuality and conformity?
12. Why, according to Thoreau, are people better off being poor than wealthy?
13. (a) What does the story of the "beautiful bug" reveal about our capacity to experience a spiritual awakening? (b) What does Thoreau believe we can do to help bring about this type of rebirth?

Applying

14. Explain why you either do or do not believe that it would be possible for Thoreau to conduct his "experiment" in today's society.

ANALYZING LITERATURE

Understanding Style

Style refers to the way in which a writer expresses his or her thoughts. For example, Thoreau writes in a powerfully excessive style, constantly reinforcing his main points.

1. How does the paragraph on simplicity (page 285) demonstrate Thoreau's tendency to make sentences build to a climax? Find one other paragraph that is structured in this manner.
2. Thoreau often starts a paragraph by discussing specific incidents or examples. He then applies them to a larger truth. Find one paragraph in which he uses this technique.

CRITICAL THINKING AND READING

Evaluating the Effect of Style

Some critics have argued that Thoreau overstates his main points in *Walden*. Thoreau, however, felt that it was impossible to overstate the truth about human potential. He deliberately repeated his main ideas to reinforce what he was saying.

Examine the paragraph on simplicity. Explain whether the structure of the paragraph contributes to its effectiveness.

THINKING AND WRITING

Comparing and Contrasting Essays

Write an essay in which you compare and contrast the excerpt from *Walden* with the excerpt from Emerson's *Nature* (page 268). Start by carefully rereading the two selections. Take notes on the ideas expressed in each selection. Organize your notes according to corresponding points of contrast. Then draft your essay, supporting your points with passages from each selection. When you revise, make sure that you have varied the length and structure of your sentences and connected your ideas with transitions. Proofread and prepare a final draft.

from Civil Disobedience

Henry David Thoreau

I heartily accept the motto, "That government is best which governs least";[1] and I should like to see it acted up to more rapidly and systematically. Carried out, it finally amounts to this, which also I believe: "That government is best which governs not at all"; and when men are prepared for it, that will be the kind of government which they will have. Government is at best but an expedient; but most governments are usually, and all governments are sometimes, inexpedient. The objections which have been brought against a standing army, and they are many and weighty, and deserve to prevail, may also at last be brought against a standing government. The standing army is only an arm of the standing government. The government itself, which is only the mode which the people have chosen to execute their will, is equally liable to be abused and perverted before the people can act through it. Witness the present Mexican war, the work of comparatively a few individuals using the standing government as their tool; for in the outset, the people would not have consented to this measure.

This American government—what is it but a tradition, though a recent one, endeavoring to transmit itself unimpaired to posterity, but each instant losing some of its integrity? It has not the vitality and force of a single living man; for a single man can bend it to his will. It is a sort of wooden gun to the people themselves; and, if ever they should use it in earnest as a real one against each other, it will surely split. But it is not the less necessary for this; for the people must have some complicated machinery or other, and hear its din, to satisfy that idea of government which they have. Governments show thus how successfully men can be imposed on, even impose on themselves, for their own advantage. It is excellent, we must all allow; yet this government never of itself furthered any enterprise, but by the alacrity with which it got out of its way. *It* does not keep the country free. *It* does not settle the West. *It* does not educate. The character inherent in the American people has done all that has been accomplished; and it would have done somewhat more, if the government had not sometimes got in its way. For government is an expedient by which men would fain succeed in letting one another alone; and, as has been said, when it is most expedient, the governed are most let alone by it. Trade and commerce, if they were not made of India rubber,[2] would never manage to bounce over the obstacles which legislators are continually putting in their way; and, if one were to judge these men wholly by the effects of their actions, and not partly by their intentions, they would deserve to be classed and punished with those mischievous persons who put obstructions on the railroads.

But, to speak practically and as a citizen, unlike those who call themselves no-government men, I ask for, not at once no government, but *at once* a better government. Let every man make known what kind of government would command his respect, and that will be one step toward obtaining it. . . .

---

1. "That . . . least": The motto of the *United States Magazine and Democratic Review*, a literary-political journal.

2. India rubber: A form of crude rubber.

THINKING ABOUT THE SELECTION

Recalling

1. What motto does Thoreau heartily accept?
2. According to Thoreau, what is the American public's attitude toward the Mexican War?
3. How does Thoreau suggest people can contribute to improving the government?

Interpreting

4. (a) How would you summarize Thoreau's attitude concerning the role of the government? (b) In what ways does he believe the American government has failed to serve this role?

Applying

5. (a) Considering the beliefs expressed in this essay, what government policies do you think Thoreau would object to? (b) What policies would he endorse?

ANALYZING LITERATURE

Understanding Historical Context

Thoreau wrote *Civil Disobedience* after spending a night in jail for refusing to pay his taxes to demonstrate his disapproval of the Mexican War and of slavery. In the essay he urged people to follow his example by resisting governmental policies with which they disagree. The essay has become one of Thoreau's most famous works, influencing a number of important historical figures such as Mahatma Gandhi and Martin Luther King, Jr.

1. In this excerpt, what does Thoreau suggest is responsible for the Mexican War?
2. What does he indicate about his reasons for disapproving of the war?
3. How does he use the war to support his argument concerning the role of the government?

THINKING AND WRITING

Writing a Report

Write a brief report about the Mexican War. Start by researching the war in encyclopedias and history books in your library. List the events leading up to the war, the important battles, and the outcome. Prepare an outline. Then write your report, making sure that you mention each of the important events related to the war. When you revise, make sure that the events in your report are presented in chronological order.

NATHANIEL HAWTHORNE

1804–1864

Despite his admiration for Ralph Waldo Emerson, Nathaniel Hawthorne found it impossible to accept the optimistic world view of the Transcendentalists. Haunted by the intolerance and cruelty of his Puritan ancestors, Hawthorne viewed evil as one of the dominant forces in the world. As a result, his works express a gloomy vision of the world, which contrasts sharply with the positive view of the Transcendentalists.

Hawthorne was born in Salem, Massachusetts, a descendant of a prominent Puritan family. His ancestors included a judge known for his persecution of the Quakers and a judge who played an important role in the Salem witchcraft trials. Though Hawthorne himself was not a Puritan, he was deeply aware of the actions of his ancestors, and his character was shaped by a sense of inherited guilt.

After graduating from Bowdoin College in Maine in 1825, Hawthorne lived in seclusion in his mother's house in Salem for twelve years, devoting his energy to developing his skills as a writer. Hawthorne's self-imposed isolation lasted until 1837, when he published his first collection of stories, *Twice-Told Tales*. The book sold poorly, but it established him as a respected writer.

After moving out of his mother's house, Hawthorne lived briefly at Brook Farm, the Transcendentalist commune. Then, in 1842, he married Sophia Peabody and moved to the Old Manse at Concord, Massachusetts, where Emerson had lived. While living in Concord, he became a friend of both Emerson and Thoreau and published a second collection of stories, *Mosses from an Old Manse* (1846).

When he received a political appointment at the Salem customhouse, he moved back to Salem. A change of administrations forced him out of office, and Hawthorne once again focused on his writing. In 1850 he published *The Scarlet Letter,* a powerful novel about sin and guilt among early Puritans. *The Scarlet Letter* was extremely successful, earning Hawthorne international fame. During the next two years, Hawthorne published two more novels, *The House of the Seven Gables* (1851) and *The Blithedale Romance* (1852).

When his college friend Franklin Pierce became President, Hawthorne was made the American consul at Liverpool, England. After spending several years in England and Italy, Hawthorne returned to Massachusetts. Hawthorne's experiences in Italy provided him with the material for his final novel, *The Marble Faun* (1860). Four years after the book's publication, Hawthorne died in his sleep while on a walking tour in New Hampshire.

GUIDE FOR READING

The Minister's Black Veil;
Dr. Heidegger's Experiment

Literary Movements

Anti-Transcendentalism. Anti-Transcendentalism was a literary movement that essentially consisted of only two writers. Yet these two writers, Nathaniel Hawthorne and Herman Melville, were easily the greatest fiction writers of their time. They focused on the limitations and potential destructiveness of the human spirit rather than on its possibilities.

Writer's Techniques

Allegory. An allegory is a work of literature in which events, characters, and details of setting have a symbolic meaning. For example, a character in an allegory may represent a single human trait, such as jealousy, greed, and compassion. Allegories are used to teach or explain moral principles and universal truths.

Look For

As you read the two stories, look for the details and incidents that convey a dark vision of the world.

Writing

Freewrite about how a person's physical appearance can isolate him or her from other people.

Vocabulary

Knowing the following words will help you as you read "The Minister's Black Veil" and "Dr. Heidegger's Experiment."

venerable (ven′ ər ə b′l) *adj.*: Commanding respect (p. 295)

iniquity (in ik′ wətē) *n.*: Sin (p. 296)

indecorous (in dek′ ər əs) *adj.*: Improper (p. 296)

ostentatious (äs′ tən tā′ shəs) *adj.*: Intended to attract notice (p. 296)

sagacious (sə gā′ shəs) *adj.*: Shrewd (p. 296)

vagary (və ger′ ē) *n.*: An unpredictable occurrence (p. 296)

tremulous (trem′ yōō ləs) *adj.*: Characterized by trembling (p. 297)

waggery (wag′ ər ē) *n.*: Mischievous humor (p. 298)

impertinent (im pur′ t′n ənt) *adj.*: Not showing proper respect (p. 298)

obstinacy (äb′ stə nə sē) *n.*: Stubbornness (p. 299)

mendicant (men′ di kənt) *n.*: A beggar (p. 304)

visage (viz′ ij) *n.*: Facial appearance (p. 305)

veracious (və rā′ shəs) *adj.*: Honest, truthful (p. 305)

imbibe (im bīb′) *v.*: Drink in (p. 305)

suffusion (sə fyōō′ zhən) *n.*: Fullness of color (p. 308)

deferential (def′ ə ren′ shəl) *adj.*: Very respectful (p. 308)

transient (tran′ shənt) *adj.*: Not permanent; passing away with time (p. 310)

The Minister's Black Veil

Nathaniel Hawthorne

A Parable

The sexton[1] stood in the porch of Milford meetinghouse, pulling busily at the bell rope. The old people of the village came stooping along the street. Children, with bright faces, tripped merrily beside their parents, or mimicked a graver gait, in the conscious dignity of their Sunday clothes. Spruce bachelors looked sidelong at the pretty maidens, and fancied that the Sabbath sunshine made them prettier than on weekdays. When the throng had mostly streamed into the porch, the sexton began to toll the bell, keeping his eye on the Reverend Mr. Hooper's door. The first glimpse of the clergyman's figure was the signal for the bell to cease its summons.

"But what has good Parson Hooper got upon his face?" cried the sexton in astonishment.

All within hearing immediately turned about, and beheld the semblance of Mr. Hooper, pacing slowly his meditative way towards the meetinghouse. With one accord they started, expressing more wonder than if some strange minister were coming to dust the cushions of Mr. Hooper's pulpit.

"Are you sure it is our parson?" inquired Goodman[2] Gray of the sexton.

"Of a certainty it is good Mr. Hooper," replied the sexton. "He was to have exchanged pulpits with Parson Shute, of Westbury; but Parson Shute sent to excuse himself yesterday, being to preach a funeral sermon."

The cause of so much amazement may appear sufficiently slight. Mr. Hooper, a gentlemanly person, of about thirty, though still a bachelor, was dressed with due clerical neatness, as if a careful wife had starched his band, and brushed the weekly dust from his Sunday's garb. There was but one thing remarkable in his appearance. Swathed about his forehead, and hanging down over his face, so low as to be shaken by his breath, Mr. Hooper had on a black veil. On a nearer view it seemed to consist of two folds of crape,[3] which entirely concealed his features, except the mouth and chin, but probably did not intercept his sight, further than to give a darkened aspect to all living and inanimate things. With this gloomy shade before him, good Mr. Hooper walked onward, at a slow and quiet pace, stooping somewhat, and looking on the ground, as is customary with abstracted men, yet nodding kindly to those of his parishioners who still waited on the meetinghouse steps. But so wonderstruck were they that his greeting hardly met with a return.

"I can't really feel as if good Mr. Hooper's face was behind that piece of crape," said the sexton.

"I don't like it," muttered an old woman, as she hobbled into the meetinghouse. "He has changed himself into something awful, only by hiding his face."

"Our parson has gone mad!" cried Goodman Gray, following him across the threshold.

---

1. sexton (seks' tən) *n*.: A person in charge of the maintenance of a church.
2. Goodman: A title of respect similar to "Mister."

3. crape (krāp) *n*.: A piece of black cloth worn as a sign of mourning.

WINTER SUNDAY IN NORWAY, MAINE
Unidentified Artist
New York State Historical Association, Cooperstown

A rumor of some unaccountable phenomenon had preceded Mr. Hooper into the meetinghouse, and set all the congregation astir. Few could refrain from twisting their heads towards the door; many stood upright, and turned directly about; while several little boys clambered upon the seats, and came down again with a terrible racket. There was a general bustle, a rustling of the women's gowns and shuffling of the men's feet, greatly at variance with that hushed repose which should attend the entrance of the minister. But Mr. Hooper appeared not to notice the perturbation of his people. He entered with an almost noiseless step, bent his head mildly to the pews on each side, and bowed as he passed his oldest parishioner, a white-haired great-grandsire, who occupied an armchair in the center of the aisle. It was strange to observe how slowly this venerable man became conscious of something singular in the apearance of his pastor. He seemed not fully to partake of the prevailing wonder, till Mr. Hooper had ascended the stairs, and showed himself in the pulpit, face to face with his congregation, except for the black veil. That mysterious emblem was never once withdrawn. It shook with his measured breath, as he gave out the psalm; it threw its obscurity between him and the holy page, as he read the Scriptures; and while he prayed, the veil lay heavily on his uplifted countenance. Did he seek to hide it from the dread Being whom he was addressing?

Such was the effect of this simple piece of crape, that more than one woman of delicate nerves was forced to leave the meetinghouse. Yet perhaps the palefaced congregation was almost as fearful a sight to the minister, as his black veil to them.

Mr. Hooper had the reputation of a good

preacher, but not an energetic one: he strove to win his people heavenward by mild, persuasive influences, rather than to drive them thither by the thunders of the Word. The sermon which he now delivered was marked by the same characteristics of style and manner as the general series of his pulpit oratory. But there was something, either in the sentiment of the discourse itself, or in the imagination of the auditors, which made it greatly the most powerful effort that they had ever heard from their pastor's lips. It was tinged, rather more darkly than usual, with the gentle gloom of Mr. Hooper's temperament. The subject had reference to secret sin, and those sad mysteries which we hide from our nearest and dearest, and would fain conceal from our own consciousness, even forgetting that the Omniscient[4] can detect them. A subtle power was breathed into his words. Each member of the congregation, the most innocent girl, and the man of hardened breast, felt as if the preacher had crept upon them, behind his awful veil, and discovered their hoarded iniquity of deed or thought. Many spread their clasped hands on their bosoms. There was nothing terrible in what Mr. Hooper said, at least, no violence; and yet, with every tremor of his melancholy voice, the hearers quaked. An unsought pathos came hand in hand with awe. So sensible were the audience of some unwonted attribute in their minister, that they longed for a breath of wind to blow aside the veil, almost believing that a stranger's visage would be discovered, though the form, gesture, and voice were those of Mr. Hooper.

At the close of the services, the people hurried out with indecorous confusion, eager to communicate their pent-up amazement, and conscious of lighter spirits the moment they lost sight of the black veil. Some gathered in little circles, huddled closely together, with their mouths all whispering in the center; some went homeward alone, wrapt in silent meditation; some talked loudly, and profaned the Sabbath day with ostentatious laughter. A few shook their sagacious heads, intimating that they could penetrate the mystery; while one or two affirmed that there was no mystery at all, but only that Mr. Hooper's eyes were so weakened by the midnight lamp, as to require a shade. After a brief interval, forth came good Mr. Hooper also, in the rear of his flock. Turning his veiled face from one group to another, he paid due reverence to the hoary heads, saluted the middle-aged with kind dignity as their friend and spiritual guide, greeted the young with mingled authority and love, and laid his hands on the little children's heads to bless them. Such was always his custom on the Sabbath day. Strange and bewildered looks repaid him for his courtesy. None, as on former occasions, aspired to the honor of walking by their pastor's side. Old Squire Saunders, doubtless by an accidental lapse of memory, neglected to invite Mr. Hooper to his table, where the good clergyman had been wont to bless the food, almost every Sunday since his settlement. He returned, therefore, to the parsonage, and, at the moment of closing the door, was observed to look back upon the people, all of whom had their eyes fixed upon the minister. A sad smile gleamed faintly from beneath the black veil, and flickered about his mouth, glimmering as he disappeared.

"How strange," said a lady, "that a simple black veil, such as any woman might wear on her bonnet, should become such a terrible thing on Mr. Hooper's face!"

"Something must surely be amiss with Mr. Hooper's intellects," observed her husband, the physician of the village. "But the strangest part of the affair is the effect of this vagary, even on a sober-minded man like myself. The black veil, though it covers only our pastor's face, throws its influence over his whole person, and makes him ghostlike from head to foot. Do you not feel it so?"

"Truly do I," replied the lady; "and I would not be alone with him for the world. I wonder he is not afraid to be alone with himself!"

---

4. Omniscient (äm nish' ent): All-knowing God.

"Men sometimes are so," said her husband.

The afternoon service was attended with similar circumstances. At its conclusion, the bell tolled for the funeral of a young lady. The relatives and friends were assembled in the house, and the more distant acquaintances stood about the door, speaking of the good qualities of the deceased, when their talk was interrupted by the appearance of Mr. Hooper, still covered with his black veil. It was now an appropriate emblem. The clergyman stepped into the room where the corpse was laid, and bent over the coffin, to take a last farewell of his deceased parishioner. As he stooped, the veil hung straight down from his forehead, so that, if her eyelids had not been closed forever, the dead maiden might have seen his face. Could Mr. Hooper be fearful of her glance, that he so hastily caught back the black veil? A person who watched the interview between the dead and living, scrupled not to affirm, that, at the instant when the clergyman's features were disclosed, the corpse had slightly shuddered, rustling the shroud and muslin cap, though the countenance retained the composure of death. A superstitious old woman was the only witness of this prodigy. From the coffin Mr. Hooper passed into the chamber of the mourners, and thence to the head of the staircase; to make the funeral prayer. It was a tender and heart-dissolving prayer, full of sorrow, yet so imbued with celestial hopes, that the music of a heavenly harp, swept by the fingers of the dead, seemed faintly to be heard among the saddest accents of the minister. The people trembled, though they but darkly understood him when he prayed that they, and himself, and all of mortal race, might be ready, as he trusted this young maiden had been, for the dreadful hour that should snatch the veil from their faces. The bearers went heavily forth, and the mourners followed, saddening all the street, with the dead before them, and Mr. Hooper in his black veil behind.

"Why do you look back?" said one in the procession to his partner.

"I had a fancy," replied she, "that the minister and the maiden's spirit were walking hand in hand."

"And so had I, at the same moment," said the other.

That night, the handsomest couple in Milford village were to be joined in wedlock. Though reckoned a melancholy man, Mr. Hooper had a placid cheerfulness for such occasions, which often excited a sympathetic smile where livelier merriment would have been thrown away. There was no quality of his disposition which made him more beloved than this. The company at the wedding awaited his arrival with impatience, trusting that the strange awe, which had gathered over him throughout the day, would now be dispelled. But such was not the result. When Mr. Hooper came, the first thing that their eyes rested on was the same horrible black veil, which had added deeper gloom to the funeral, and could portend nothing but evil to the wedding. Such was its immediate effect on the guests that a cloud seemed to have rolled duskily from beneath the black crape, and dimmed the light of the candles. The bridal pair stood up before the minister. But the bride's cold fingers quivered in the tremulous hand of the bridegroom, and her deathlike paleness caused a whisper that the maiden who had been buried a few hours before was come from her grave to be married. If ever another wedding were so dismal, it was that famous one where they tolled the wedding knell.[5] After performing the ceremony, Mr. Hooper raised a glass of wine to his lips, wishing happiness to the new-married couple in a strain of mild pleasantry that ought to have brightened the features of the guests, like a cheerful gleam from the hearth. At that instant, catching a glimpse of his figure in the looking glass, the black veil involved his own spirit in the horror with which it overwhelmed all others. His frame shuddered, his lips grew white, he

---

5. If . . . knell: A reference to Hawthorne's short story "The Wedding Knell." A *knell* is the slow ringing of a bell, as at a funeral.

CEMETERY
Peter McIntyre
Courtesy of the artist

with the multitude, good Mr. Hooper was irreparably a bugbear.[8] He could not walk the street with any peace of mind, so conscious was he that the gentle and timid would turn aside to avoid him, and that others would make it a point of hardihood to throw themselves in his way. The impertinence of the latter class compelled him to give up his customary walk at sunset to the burial ground; for when he leaned pensively over the gate, there would always be faces behind the gravestones, peeping at his black veil. A fable went the rounds that the stare of the dead people drove him thence. It grieved him, to the very depth of his kind heart, to observe how the children fled from his approach, breaking up their merriest sports, while his melancholy figure was yet afar off. Their instinctive dread caused him to feel more strongly than aught else, that a preternatu-

ral[9] horror was interwoven with the threads of the black crape. In truth, his own antipathy to the veil was known to be so great that he never willingly passed before a mirror, nor stooped to drink at a still fountain, lest, in its peaceful bosom, he should be affrighted by himself. This was what gave plausibility to the whispers, that Mr. Hooper's conscience tortured him for some great crime too horrible to be entirely concealed, or otherwise than so obscurely intimated. Thus, from beneath the black veil, there rolled a cloud into the sunshine, an ambiguity of sin or sorrow, which enveloped the poor minister, so that love or sympathy could never reach him. It was said that ghost and fiend consorted with him there. With self-shudderings and outward terrors, he walked continually in its shadow, groping

---

8. bugbear *n.*: Something causing needless fear.

9. preternatural (prēt′ ər nach′ ər əl) *adj.*: Supernatural.

darkly within his own soul or gazing through a medium that saddened the whole world. Even the lawless wind, it was believed, respected his dreadful secret, and never blew aside the veil. But still good Mr. Hooper sadly smiled at the pale visages of the worldly throng as he passed by.

Among all its bad influences, the black veil had the one desirable effect, of making its wearer a very efficient clergyman. By the aid of his mysterious emblem—for there was no other apparent cause—he became a man of awful power over souls that were in agony for sin. His converts always regarded him with a dread peculiar to themselves, affirming, though but figuratively, that, before he brought them to celestial light, they had been with him behind the black veil. Its gloom, indeed, enabled him to sympathize with all dark affections. Dying sinners cried aloud for Mr. Hooper, and would not yield their breath till he appeared; though ever, as he stooped to whisper consolation, they shuddered at the veiled face so near their own. Such were the terrors of the black veil, even when Death had bared his visage! Strangers came long distances to attend service at his church, with the mere idle purpose of gazing at his figure, because it was forbidden them to behold his face. But many were made to quake ere they departed! Once, during Governor Belcher's[10] administration, Mr. Hooper was appointed to preach the election sermon. Covered with his black veil, he stood before the chief magistrate, the council, and the representatives, and wrought so deep an impression that the legislative measures of that year were characterized by all the gloom and piety of our earliest ancestral sway.

In this manner Mr. Hooper spent a long life, irreproachable in outward act, yet shrouded in dismal suspicions; kind and loving, though unloved, and dimly feared; a man apart from men, shunned in their

health and joy, but ever summoned to their aid in mortal anguish. As years wore on, shedding their snows above his sable veil, he acquired a name throughout the New England churches, and they called him Father Hooper. Nearly all his parishioners, who were of mature age when he was settled, had been borne away by many a funeral: he had one congregation in the church, and a more crowded one in the churchyard; and having wrought so late into the evening, and done his work so well, it was now good Father Hooper's turn to rest.

Several persons were visible by the shaded candlelight, in the death chamber of the old clergyman. Natural connections[11] he had none. But there was the decorously grave, though unmoved physician, seeking only to mitigate the last pangs of the patient whom he could not save. There were the deacons, and other eminently pious members of his church. There, also, was the Reverend Mr. Clark, of Westbury, a young and zealous divine, who had ridden in haste to pray by the bedside of the expiring minister. There was the nurse, no hired handmaiden of death, but one whose calm affection had endured thus long in secrecy, in solitude, amid the chill of age, and would not perish, even at the dying hour. Who, but Elizabeth! And there lay the hoary head of good Father Hooper upon the death pillow, with the black veil still swathed about his brow, and reaching down over his face, so that each more difficult gasp of his faint breath caused it to stir. All through life that piece of crape had hung between him and the world: it had separated him from cheerful brotherhood and woman's love, and kept him in that saddest of all prisons, his own heart; and still it lay upon his face, as if to deepen the gloom of his darksome chamber, and shade him from the sunshine of eternity.

For some time previous, his mind had been confused, wavering doubtfully between the past and the present, and hovering forward, as it were, at intervals, into the indis-

10. Governor Belcher: Jonathan Belcher (1682–1757), the royal governor of the Massachusetts Bay Colony from 1730 through 1741.

11. natural connections: Relatives.

tinctness of the world to come. There had been feverish turns, which tossed him from side to side, and wore away what little strength he had. But in his most convulsive struggles, and in the wildest vagaries of his intellect, when no other thought retained its sober influence, he still showed an awful solicitude lest the black veil should slip aside. Even if his bewildered soul could have forgotten, there was a faithful woman at his pillow, who, with averted eyes, would have covered that aged face, which she had last beheld in the comeliness of manhood. At length the death-stricken old man lay quietly in the torpor of mental and bodily exhaustion, with an imperceptible pulse, and breath that grew fainter and fainter, except when a long, deep, and irregular inspiration seemed to prelude the flight of his spirit.

The minister of Westbury approached the bedside.

"Venerable Father Hooper," said he, "the moment of your release is at hand. Are you ready for the lifting of the veil that shuts in time from eternity?"

Father Hooper at first replied merely by a feeble motion of his head; then, apprehensive, perhaps, that his meaning might be doubtful, he exerted himself to speak.

"Yea," said he, in faint accents, "my soul hath a patient weariness until that veil be lifted."

"And is it fitting," resumed the Reverend Mr. Clark, "that a man so given to prayer, of such a blameless example, holy in deed and thought, so far as mortal judgment may pronounce; is it fitting that a father in the church should leave a shadow on his memory, that may seem to blacken a life so pure? I pray you, my venerable brother, let not this thing be! Suffer us to be gladdened by your triumphant aspect as you go to your reward. Before the veil of eternity be lifted, let me cast aside this black veil from your face!"

And thus speaking, the Reverend Mr. Clark bent forward to reveal the mystery of so many years. But, exerting a sudden energy, that made all the beholders stand aghast, Father Hooper snatched both his hands from beneath the bedclothes, and pressed them strongly on the black veil, resolute to struggle, if the minister of Westbury would contend with a dying man.

"Never!" cried the veiled clergyman. "On earth, never!"

"Dark old man!" exclaimed the affrighted minister, "with what horrible crime upon your soul are you now passing to the judgment?"

Father Hooper's breath heaved; it rattled in his throat; but, with a mighty effort, grasping forward with his hands, he caught hold of life, and held it back till he should speak. He even raised himself in bed; and there he sat, shivering with the arms of death around him, while the black veil hung down, awful, at that last moment, in the gathered terrors of a lifetime. And yet the faint, sad smile, so often there, now seemed to glimmer from its obscurity, and linger on Father Hooper's lips.

"Why do you tremble at me alone?" cried he, turning his veiled face round the circle of pale spectators. "Tremble also at each other! Have men avoided me, and women shown no pity, and children screamed and fled, only for my black veil? What, but the mystery which it obscurely typifies, has made this piece of crape so awful? When the friend shows his inmost heart to his friend; the lover to his best beloved; when man does not vainly shrink from the eye of his Creator, loathsomely treasuring up the secret of his sin; then deem me a monster, for the symbol beneath which I have lived, and die! I look around me, and, lo! on every visage a Black Veil!"

While his auditors shrank from one another, in mutual affright, Father Hooper fell back upon his pillow, a veiled corpse, with a faint smile lingering on the lips. Still veiled, they laid him in his coffin, and a veiled corpse they bore him to the grave. The grass of many years has sprung up and withered on that grave, the burial stone is mossgrown, and good Mr. Hooper's face is dust; but awful is still the thought that it moldered beneath the Black Veil!

THINKING ABOUT THE SELECTION
Recalling

1. How do the members of the parish react when they first see Parson Hooper wearing his black veil?
2. (a) What is different about Parson Hooper's sermon on the first day he wears the veil? (b) What is the subject of the sermon?
3. How does Elizabeth react when Parson Hooper refuses to remove the veil?
4. What is its "one desirable effect"?
5. (a) What happens when Reverend Mr. Clark tries to remove the veil while Parson Hooper is lying on his deathbed? (b) What does Parson Hooper suggest is the reason that people have been terrified by his veil?

Interpreting

6. (a) How does the black veil affect Parson Hooper's perceptions of the world? (b) In what ways does it isolate him from the rest of the world? (c) Why does it make him a more effective minister?
7. What does Parson Hooper mean when he tells Elizabeth, "There is an hour to come . . . when all of us shall cast aside our veils"?
8. (a) Why does the black veil have such a powerful effect on people? (b) What do you think it represents?
9. Why do you think Hawthorne chooses not to reveal the reason that Parson Hooper begins wearing the veil?

Applying

10. Hawthorne suggests that all people have certain secrets that they choose not to reveal to anyone. Explain why you either do or do not agree with this suggestion.

ANALYZING LITERATURE
Understanding Anti-Transcendentalism

In "The Minister's Black Veil" Hawthorne conveys a dark vision of the world that is characteristic of **Anti-Transcendentalist** writing.

1. In what way does the story reflect the Anti-Transcendentalists' belief that people possess the potential for both good and evil?
2. The Anti-Transcendentalists believed that the truths of existence tend to be elusive and disturbing. What disturbing truth does Hawthorne convey through Parson Hooper and his black veil?
3. How does the parishioners' inability to grasp the meaning of Parson Hooper's veil reflect the Anti-Transcendentalists' belief in the elusiveness of truth?

CRITICAL THINKING AND READING
Recognizing the Author's Attitudes

Hawthorne had a gloomy vision that was possibly shaped by his awareness of the intolerance and cruelty of his Puritan ancestors. Therefore, he was unable to accept the optimistic views of the Transcendentalists.

Like a number of Hawthorne's other works, "The Minister's Black Veil" is set in Puritan New England. Judging from the story, do you think Hawthorne had a negative attitude toward the Puritans? Support your answer.

THINKING AND WRITING
Comparing and Contrasting Attitudes

Write an essay in which you compare and contrast the attitude toward human nature expressed in "The Minister's Black Veil" with the attitude expressed by the Transcendentalists. Start by reviewing the discussions of Transcendentalism and Anti-Transcendentalism on pages 267 and 293. Take note of the beliefs characterizing each movement. Then review "The Minister's Black Veil," noting of the attitudes it expresses. Organize your notes by corresponding points of comparison and contrast. When you write your essay, make sure you support your argument with passages from the story. When you revise, make sure that you have clearly expressed the two attitudes being compared and contrasted.

Dr. Heidegger's Experiment

Nathaniel Hawthorne

That very singular man, old Dr. Heidegger, once invited four venerable friends to meet him in his study. There were three white-bearded gentlemen, Mr. Medbourne, Colonel Killigrew, and Mr. Gascoigne, and a withered gentlewoman, whose name was the Widow Wycherly. They were all melancholy old creatures, who had been unfortunate in life, and whose greatest misfortune it was that they were not long ago in their graves. Mr. Medbourne, in the vigor of his age, had been a prosperous merchant, but had lost his all by a frantic speculation and was now little better than a mendicant. Colonel Killigrew had wasted his best years, and his health and substance, in the pursuit of sinful pleasures, which had given birth to a brood of pains, such as the gout and divers other torments of soul and body. Mr. Gascoigne was a ruined politician, a man of evil fame, or at least had been so till time had buried him from the knowledge of the present generation and made him obscure instead of infamous. As for the Widow Wycherly, tradition tells us that she was a great beauty in her day; but, for a long while past, she had lived in deep seclusion, on account of certain scandalous stories which had prejudiced the gentry of the town against her. It is a circumstance worth mentioning that each of these three old gentlemen, Mr. Medbourne, Colonel Killigrew, and Mr. Gascoigne, were early lovers of the Widow Wycherly and had once been on the point of cutting each other's throats for her sake. And, before proceeding further, I will merely hint that Dr. Heidegger and all his four guests were sometimes thought to be a little beside themselves—as is not unfrequently the case with old people, when worried either by present troubles or woeful recollections.

"My dear old friends," said Dr. Heidegger, motioning them to be seated, "I am desirous of your assistance in one of those little experiments with which I amuse myself here in my study."

If all stories were true, Dr. Heidegger's study must have been a very curious place. It was a dim, old-fashioned chamber, festooned with cobwebs, and besprinkled with antique dust. Around the walls stood several oaken bookcases, the lower shelves of which were filled with rows of gigantic folios[1] and black-letter quartos,[2] and the upper with little parchment-covered duodecimos.[3] Over the central bookcase was a bronze bust of Hippocrates,[4] with which, according to some authorities, Dr. Heidegger was accustomed to hold consultations in all difficult cases of his practice. In the obscurest corner of the room stood a tall and narrow oaken closet, with its door ajar, within which doubtfully appeared a skeleton. Between two of the bookcases hung a looking glass, presenting its high and dusty plate within a tarnished gilt frame. Among many wonderful stories

---

1. folios (fō′lē ōz′) n.: The largest regular size of books, over eleven inches in height.
2. quartos (kwôr′tōz) n.: Books about nine by twelve inches.
3. duodecimos (do͞o′ə des′ ə mōz′) n.: Books about five by eight inches.
4. Hippocrates (hi päk′rə tēz′): A Greek physician (460?–370? B.C.).

related of this mirror, it was fabled that the spirits of all the doctor's deceased patients dwelt within its verge and would stare him in the face whenever he looked thitherward. The opposite side of the chamber was ornamented with the full-length portrait of a young lady, arrayed in the faded magnificence of silk, satin, and brocade, and with a visage as faded as her dress. Above half a century ago, Dr. Heidegger had been on the point of marriage with this young lady; but, being affected with some slight disorder, she had swallowed one of her lover's prescriptions and died on the bridal evening. The greatest curiosity of the study remains to be mentioned; it was a ponderous folio volume, bound in black leather, with massive silver clasps. There were no letters on the back, and nobody could tell the title of the book. But it was well known to be a book of magic; and once, when a chambermaid had lifted it, merely to brush away the dust, the skeleton had rattled in its closet, the picture of the young lady had stepped one foot upon the floor, and several ghastly faces had peeped forth from the mirror; while the brazen head of Hippocrates frowned, and said, "Forbear!"

Such was Dr. Heidegger's study. On the summer afternoon of our tale, a small round table, as black as ebony, stood in the center of the room, sustaining a cut-glass vase of beautiful form and elaborate workmanship. The sunshine came through the window, between the heavy festoons[5] of two faded damask curtains, and fell directly across this vase; so that a mild splendor was reflected from it on the ashen visages of the five old people who sat around. Four champagne glasses were also on the table.

"My dear old friends," repeated Dr. Heidegger, "may I reckon on your aid in performing an exceedingly curious experiment?"

Now Dr. Heidegger was a very strange old gentleman, whose eccentricity had become the nucleus for a thousand fantastic stories. Some of these fables, to my shame be it spoken, might possibly be traced back to my own veracious self; and if any passages of the present tale should startle the reader's faith, I must be content to bear the stigma of a fiction monger.

When the doctor's four guests heard him talk of his proposed experiment, they anticipated nothing more wonderful than the murder of a mouse in an air pump, or the examination of a cobweb by the microscope, or some similar nonsense, with which he was constantly in the habit of pestering his intimates. But without waiting for a reply, Dr. Heidegger hobbled across the chamber, and returned with the same ponderous folio, bound in black leather, which common report affirmed to be a book of magic. Undoing the silver clasps, he opened the volume, and took from among its black-letter pages a rose, or what was once a rose, though now the green leaves and crimson petals had assumed one brownish hue, and the ancient flower seemed ready to crumble to dust in the doctor's hands.

"This rose," said Dr. Heidegger, with a sigh, "this same withered and crumbling flower, blossomed five and fifty years ago. It was given me by Sylvia Ward, whose portrait hangs yonder; and I meant to wear it in my bosom at our wedding. Five and fifty years it has been treasured between the leaves of this old volume. Now, would you deem it possible that this rose of half a century could ever bloom again?"

"Nonsense!" said the Widow Wycherly, with a peevish toss of her head. "You might as well ask whether an old woman's wrinkled face could ever bloom again."

"See!" answered Dr. Heidegger.

He uncovered the vase, and threw the faded rose into the water which it contained. At first, it lay lightly on the surface of the fluid, appearing to imbibe none of its moisture. Soon, however, a singular change be-

---

5. festoons (fes tōōns') *n.*: Wreaths of flowers or leaves.

gan to be visible. The crushed and dried petals stirred, and assumed a deepening tinge of crimson, as if the flower were reviving from a deathlike slumber; the slender stalk and twigs of foliage became green; and there was the rose of half a century, looking as fresh as when Sylvia Ward had first given it to her lover. It was scarcely full blown; for some of its delicate red leaves curled modestly around its moist bosom, within which two or three dewdrops were sparkling.

"That is certainly a very pretty deception," said the doctor's friends; carelessly, however, for they had witnessed greater miracles at a conjurer's show; "pray how was it effected?"

"Did you never hear of the 'Fountain of Youth?'" asked Dr. Heidegger, "which Ponce De Leon,[6] the Spanish adventurer, went in search of two or three centuries ago?"

"But did Ponce De Leon ever find it?" said the Widow Wycherly.

"No," answered Dr. Heidegger, "for he never sought it in the right place. The famous Fountain of Youth, if I am rightly informed, is situated in the southern part of the Floridian peninsula, not far from Lake Macaco. Its source is overshadowed by several gigantic magnolias, which, though numberless centuries old, have been kept as fresh as violets by the virtues of this wonderful water. An acquaintance of mine, knowing my curiosity in such matters, has sent me what you see in the vase."

"Ahem!" said Colonel Killigrew, who believed not a word of the doctor's story; "and what may be the effect of this fluid on the human frame?"

"You shall judge for yourself, my dear colonel," replied Dr. Heidegger; "and all of you, my respected friends, are welcome to so much of this admirable fluid as may restore to you the bloom of youth. For my own part, having had much trouble in growing old, I

am in no hurry to grow young again. With your permission, therefore, I will merely watch the progress of the experiment."

While he spoke, Dr. Heidegger had been filling the four champagne glasses with the water of the Fountain of Youth. It was apparently impregnated with an effervescent gas, for little bubbles were continually ascending from the depths of the glasses, and bursting in silvery spray at the surface. As the liquor diffused a pleasant perfume, the old people doubted not that it possessed cordial and comfortable properties; and though utter skeptics as to its rejuvenescent power, they were inclined to swallow it at once. But Dr. Heidegger besought them to stay a moment.

"Before you drink, my respectable old friends," said he, "it would be well that, with the experience of a lifetime to direct you, you should draw up a few general rules for your guidance, in passing a second time through the perils of youth. Think what a sin and shame it would be if, with your peculiar advantages, you should not become patterns of virtue and wisdom to all the young people of the age!"

The doctor's four venerable friends made him no answer, except by a feeble and tremulous laugh; so very ridiculous was the idea that, knowing how closely repentance treads behind the steps of error, they should ever go astray again.

"Drink, then," said the doctor, bowing. "I rejoice that I have so well selected the subjects of my experiment."

With palsied hands, they raised the glasses to their lips. The liquor, if it really possessed such virtues as Dr. Heidegger imputed to it, could not have been bestowed on four human beings who needed it more woefully. They looked as if they had never known what youth or pleasure was, but had been the offspring of Nature's dotage and always the gray, decrepit, sapless, miserable creatures, who now sat stooping round the doctor's table, without life enough in their souls or bodies to be animated even by the prospect of growing young again. They drank off

---

6. Ponce De Leon (päns' də lē'ən): Spanish explorer who discovered Florida while searching for the "Fountain of Youth" (1460?–1521).

HERMAN MELVILLE

1819–1891

Herman Melville is one of America's great novelists. Unfortunately, his work was never fully appreciated during his lifetime, and he lived a life that was often filled with frustration and despair.

Melville was born in New York City, the son of a wealthy merchant. His family's financial situation changed drastically in 1830, however, when his father's import business failed. Two years later his father died, leaving the family in debt. Forced to leave school, Melville spent the rest of his childhood working as a clerk, a farmhand, and a teacher to help support his family.

After becoming a sailor at the age of nineteen, Melville spent several years exploring the South Pacific. Working on a number of different whaling ships, he visited many exotic places and even spent several weeks living among natives in the Marquesas Islands. He did not return to the United States until 1844, after a brief period of service in the navy.

Using his adventures in the South Pacific as material for his novels, Melville started a new career as a writer. He quickly established himself as a popular writer with two successful novels, *Typee* (1846) and *Omoo* (1847), both set in the Pacific islands. His readers found his third novel, *Mardi* (1849), confusing, however, and his fame rapidly faded.

Using the profits from his novels, Melville bought a farm near Pittsfield, Massachusetts. He became a close friend of Nathaniel Hawthorne, who lived in a neighboring village. Encouraged by Hawthorne's interest and influenced by his reading of Shakespeare, Melville's work became more sophisticated.

In 1851 he published his masterpiece *Moby-Dick*, under the title *The Whale. Moby-Dick* is a novel with several layers of meaning. On the surface it is the story of the fateful voyage of a whaling ship. On another level, it is the story of a bitter man's quest for vengeance and search for truth. On still another level, it is a philosophical examination of humanity's relationship to the natural world.

Unable to appreciate the novel's depth, readers responded unfavorably to *Moby-Dick*. They also reacted negatively to Melville's next two novels, *Pierre* (1852) and *The Confidence Man* (1859). As a result, Melville fell into debt and was forced to accept a job as an inspector at the New York customshouse.

Disillusioned and bitter, Melville turned away from writing fiction during the latter part of his life. He produced only a handful of short stories and a powerful novella, *Billy Budd*. He died in 1891, unnoticed and unappreciated. In the 1920's, his work was rediscovered by scholars, and he finally received the recognition he deserved.

GUIDE FOR READING

from Moby-Dick

Symbolism. A symbol is a person, place, or thing that has a meaning in itself and also represents something larger than itself. For example, a flag symbolizes the character, attitude, and values of the country it represents.

While some symbols are easy to interpret, others are complex, having a number of possible meanings. The white whale in Melville's *Moby-Dick* is an example of an extremely complex symbol. Only by examining all of the meanings suggested by its appearance and behavior do we realize that the whale ultimately represents all that is paradoxical, unexplainable, and uncontrollable in nature. Like nature, Moby-Dick is massive and threatening but beautiful and awe-inspiring. Moby-Dick is nourishing and destructive, powerful and graceful. Moby-Dick is apparently unpredictable and mindless, yet it is controlled by natural laws. Like nature, Moby-Dick seems indestructible and immortal and at the same time indifferent to human mortality.

Another quality that contributes to the whale's symbolism is its color. Like the other aspects of the whale's appearance, its whiteness conveys contradictions. It suggests purity and goodness but at the same time signifies emptiness and death. Because of the whale's blank whiteness, each crew member attaches a different meaning to the whale—just as each person attaches a different meaning to the mysteries of nature.

Look For

As you read the excerpt from *Moby-Dick,* look for Melville's symbolism. How does it contribute to the meaning of the novel?

Writing

Determination is often considered a positive characterictic. Freewrite, exploring how it can also be a negative characteristic.

Vocabulary

Knowing the following words will help you as you read the excerpt from *Moby-Dick.*

inscrutable (in skro͞ot′ ə b'l) *adj.*: Not able to be easily understood (p. 320)
maledictions (mal′ ə dik′ shən) *n.*: Curses (p. 322)

prescient (prē′ s‧hē ənt) *adj.*: Having foreknowledge (p. 324)
pertinaciously (pʉr′ tə nā′ s‧həs lē) *adv.*: Holding firmly to some purpose (p. 326)

from Moby-Dick
Herman Melville

Moby-Dick is the story of a man's obsession with the dangerous and mysterious white whale that years before had taken off one of his legs. The man, Captain Ahab, guides the Pequod, a whaling ship, and its crew in relentless pursuit of this whale, Moby-Dick. Among the more important members of the crew are Starbuck, the first mate; Stubb, the second mate; Flask, the third mate; Queequeg, Tashtego, and Daggoo, the harpooners; and Ishmael, the young sailor who narrates the book.

In the following excerpt, Ishmael and Queequeg sample some famous chowder before their voyage.

Chowder

It was quite late in the evening when the little Moss came snugly to anchor, and Queequeg and I went ashore; so we could attend to no business that day, at least none but a supper and a bed. The landlord of the Spouter Inn had recommended us to his cousin Hosea Hussey of the Try Pots, whom he asserted to be the proprietor of one of the best kept hotels in all Nantucket,[1] and moreover he had assured us that Cousin Hosea, as he called him, was famous for his chowders. In short, he plainly hinted that we could not possibly do better than try potluck at the Try Pots. But the directions he had given us about keeping a yellow warehouse on our starboard[2] hand till we opened a white church to the larboard, and then keeping that on the larboard hand till we made a corner three points to the starboard, and

that done, then ask the first man we met where the place was; these crooked directions of his very much puzzled us at first, especially as, at the outset, Queequeg insisted that the yellow warehouse—our first point of departure—must be left on the larboard hand, whereas I had understood Peter Coffin to say it was on the starboard. However, by dint of beating about a little in the dark, and now and then knocking up a peaceful inhabitant to inquire the way, we at last came to something which there was no mistaking.

Two enormous wooden pots painted black, and suspended by ass's ears, swung from the crosstrees of an old topmast, planted in front of an old doorway. The horns of the crosstrees were sawed off on the other side, so that this old topmast looked not a little like a gallows. Perhaps I was oversensitive to such impressions at the time, but I could not help staring at this gallows with a vague misgiving. A sort of crick was in my neck as I gazed up to the two remaining horns; yes, *two* of them, one for Queequeg, and one for me. It's ominous, thinks I.

---

1. Nantucket (nan tuk′ it): An island off the coast of Massachusetts.
2. Starboard *adj.*: The right-hand side of a ship. Larboard refers to the left-hand side.

A coffin my innkeeper upon landing in my first whaling port; tombstones staring at me in the whalemen's chapel; and here a gallows! and a pair of prodigious black pots too! Are these last throwing out oblique hints touching Tophet?[3]

I was called from these reflections by the sight of a freckled woman with yellow hair and a yellow gown, standing in the porch of the inn, under a dull red lamp swinging there, that looked much like an injured eye, and carrying on a brisk scolding with a man in a purple woolen shirt.

"Get along with ye," said she to the man, "or I'll be combing ye!"

"Come on, Queequeg," said I, "all right. There's Mrs. Hussey."

And so it turned out; Mr. Hosea Hussey being from home, but leaving Mrs. Hussey entirely competent to attend to all his affairs. Upon making known our desires for a supper and a bed, Mrs. Hussey, postponing further scolding for the present, ushered us into a little room, and seating us at a table spread with the relics of a recently concluded repast, turned round to us and said "clam or cod?"

"What's that about cods, ma'am?" said I, with much politeness.

---

3. Tophet (tō′ fĭt): Hell.

"Clam or cod?" she repeated.

"A clam for supper? a cold clam; is *that* what you mean, Mrs. Hussey?" says I! "but that's a rather cold and clammy reception in the winter time, ain't it, Mrs. Hussey?"

But being in a great hurry to resume scolding the man in the purple shirt who was waiting for it in the entry, and seeming to hear nothing but the word "clam," Mrs. Hussey hurried towards an open door leading to the kitchen, and bawling out "clam for two," disappeared.

"Queequeg," said I, "do you think that we can make a supper for us both on one clam?"

However, a warm savory steam from the kitchen served to belie[4] the apparently cheerless prospect before us. But when that smoking chowder came in, the mystery was delightfully explained. Oh! sweet friends, hearken to me. It was made of small juicy clams, scarcely bigger than hazel nuts, mixed with pounded ship biscuits, and salted pork cut up into little flakes! The whole enriched with butter, and plentifully seasoned with pepper and salt. Our appetites being sharpened by the frosty voyage, and in particular, Queequeg seeing his favorite fishing food before him, and the chowder being surpassingly excellent, we dispatched it with great expedition: when leaning back a moment and bethinking me of Mrs. Hussey's clam and cod announcement, I thought I would try a little experiment. Stepping to the kitchen door, I uttered the word "cod" with great emphasis, and resumed my seat. In a few moments the savory steam came forth again, but with a different flavor, and in good time a fine cod chowder was placed before us.

We resumed business; and while plying our spoons in the bowl, thinks I to myself, I wonder now if this here has any effect on the head? What's that stultifying saying about chowder-headed people? "But look, Quee-queg, ain't that a live eel in your bowl? Where's your harpoon?"

Fishiest of all fishy places was the Try Pots, which well deserved its name; for the pots there were always boiling chowders. Chowder for breakfast, and chowder for dinner, and chowder for supper, till you began to look for fish bones coming through your clothes. The area before the house was paved with clam shells. Mrs. Hussey wore a polished necklace of codfish vertebra; and Hosea Hussey had his account books bound in superior and old shark-skin. There was a fishy flavor to the milk, too, which I could not at all account for, till one morning happening to take a stroll along the beach among some fishermen's boats, I saw Hosea's brindled[5] cow feeding on fish remnants, and marching along the sand with each foot in a cod's decapitated head, looking very slipshod, I assure ye.

Supper concluded, we received a lamp, and directions from Mrs. Hussey concerning the nearest way to bed; but, as Queequeg was about to precede me up the stairs, the lady reached forth her arm, and demanded his harpoon; she allowed no harpoon in her chambers. "Why not?" said I; "every true whaleman sleeps with his harpoon—but why not?" "Because it's dangerous," says she. "Ever since young Stiggs coming from that unfort'nt v'y'ge of his, when he was gone four years and a half, with only three barrels of *ile*,[6] was found dead in my first floor back, with his harpoon in his side; ever since then I allow no boarders to take sich dangerous weepons in their rooms at night. So, Mr. Queequeg" (for she had learned his name), "I will just take this here iron, and keep it for you till morning. But the chowder; clam or cod tomorrow for breakfast, men?"

"Both," says I, "and let's have a couple of smoked herring by way of variety."

---

4. belie (bi lī') *v.*: Prove false.

5. brindled (brin' d'ld) *adj.*: Having a gray or tawny coat with streaks of darker color.
6. *ile* (īle): Oil.

When the crew signed aboard the Pequod, the voyage was to be nothing more than a business venture. However, early in the voyage, Ahab makes clear to the crew that his purpose is to seek revenge against Moby-Dick.

from The Quarter-Deck

One morning shortly after breakfast, Ahab, as was his wont, ascended the cabin gangway to the deck. There most sea captains usually walk at that hour, as country gentlemen, after the same meal, take a few turns in the garden.

Soon his steady, ivory stride was heard, as to and fro he paced his old rounds, upon planks so familiar to his tread, that they were all over dented, like geological stones, with the peculiar mark of his walk. Did you fixedly gaze, too, upon that ribbed and dented brow; there also, you would see still stranger footprints—the footprints of his one unsleeping, ever-pacing thought.

But on the occasion in question, those dents looked deeper, even as his nervous step that morning left a deeper mark. And, so full of his thought was Ahab, that at every uniform turn that he made, now at the mainmast and now at the binnacle,[7] you could almost see that thought turn in him as he turned, and pace in him as he paced; so completely possessing him, indeed, that it all but seemed the inward mold of every outer movement.

"D'ye mark him, Flask?" whispered Stubb; "the chick that's in him pecks the shell. 'Twill soon be out."

The hours wore on—Ahab now shut up within his cabin; anon, pacing the deck, with the same intense bigotry of purpose[8] in his aspect.

It drew near the close of day. Suddenly he came to a halt by the bulwarks, and inserting his bone leg into the auger hole there, and with one hand grasping a shroud, he ordered Starbuck to send everybody aft.

"Sir!" said the mate, astonished at an order seldom or never given on shipboard except in some extraordinary case.

"Send everybody aft," repeated Ahab. "Mastheads, there! come down!"

When the entire ship's company were assembled, and with curious and not wholly unapprehensive faces, were eyeing him, for he looked not unlike the weather horizon when a storm is coming up, Ahab, after rapidly glancing over the bulwarks, and then darting his eyes among the crew, started from his standpoint; and as though not a soul were nigh him resumed his heavy turns upon the deck. With bent head and half-slouched hat he continued to pace, unmindful of the wondering whispering among the men; till Stubb cautiously whispered to Flask, that Ahab must have summoned them there for the purpose of witnessing a pedestrian feat. But this did not last long. Vehemently pausing, he cried:

"What do ye do when ye see a whale, men?"

"Sing out for him!" was the impulsive rejoinder from a score of clubbed voices.

"Good!" cried Ahab, with a wild approval in his tones; observing the hearty animation into which his unexpected question had so magnetically thrown them.

"And what do ye next, men?"

"Lower away, and after him!"

"And what tune is it ye pull to, men?"

"A dead whale or a stove[9] boat!"

More and more strangely and fiercely glad and approving, grew the countenance of the old man at every shout; while the mariners began to gaze curiously at each other, as if marveling how it was that they them-

---

7. **binnacle** (bin′ ə k'l) *n.*: The case enclosing the ship's compass.
8. **bigotry of purpose:** Complete singlemindedness.

9. **stove:** Broken, smashed.

selves became so excited at such seemingly purposeless questions.

But, they were all eagerness again, as Ahab, now half-revolving in his pivot hole, with one hand reaching high up a shroud,[10] and tightly, almost convulsively grasping it, addressed them thus:

"All ye mastheaders have before now heard me give orders about a white whale. Look ye! d'ye see this Spanish ounce of gold?"—holding up a broad bright coin to the sun—"it is a sixteen-dollar piece, men. D'ye see it? Mr. Starbuck, hand me yon topmaul."

While the mate was getting the hammer, Ahab, without speaking, was slowly rubbing the gold piece against the skirts of his jacket, as if to heighten its luster, and without using any words was meanwhile lowly humming to himself, producing a sound so strangely muffled and inarticulate that it seemed the mechanical humming of the wheels of his vitality in him.

Receiving the topmaul from Starbuck, he advanced towards the mainmast with the hammer uplifted in one hand, exhibiting the gold with the other, and with a high raised voice exclaiming: "Whosoever of ye raises me a white-headed whale with a wrinkled brow and a crooked jaw; whosoever of ye raises me that white-headed whale, with three holes punctured in his starboard fluke[11]—look ye,

---

10. **shroud** n.: A set of ropes from a ship's side to the masthead.

11. **starboard fluke** (flook) n.: The right half of a whale's tail.

whosoever of ye raises me that same white whale, he shall have this gold ounce, my boys!"

"Huzza! huzza!" cried the seamen, as with swinging tarpaulins they hailed the act of nailing the gold to the mast.

"It's a white whale, I say," resumed Ahab, as he threw down the topmaul: "a white whale. Skin your eyes for him, men; look sharp for white water; if ye see but a bubble, sing out."

All this while Tashtego, Daggoo, and Queequeg had looked on with even more intense interest and surprise than the rest, and at the mention of the wrinkled brow and crooked jaw they had started as if each was separately touched by some specific recollection.

"Captain Ahab," said Tashtego, "that white whale must be the same that some call Moby-Dick."

"Moby-Dick?" shouted Ahab. "Do ye know the white whale then, Tash?"

"Does he fantail[12] a little curious, sir, before he goes down?" said the Gay-Header deliberately.

"And has he a curious spout, too," said Daggoo, "very bushy, even for a parmacetty,[13] and mighty quick, Captain Ahab?"

"And he have one, two, tree—oh! good many iron in him hide, too, Captain," cried Queequeg disjointedly, "all twiske-tee betwisk, like him—him—" faltering hard for a word, and screwing his hand round and round as though uncorking a bottle—"like him—him——"

"Corkscrew!" cried Ahab, "aye, Queequeg, the harpoons lie all twisted and wrenched in him; aye, Daggoo, his spout is a big one, like a whole shock of wheat, and white as a pile of our Nantucket wool after the great annual sheepshearing; aye, Tashtego, and he fantails like a split jib in a squall. Death and devils! men, it is Moby-Dick ye have seen—Moby-Dick—Moby-Dick!"

"Captain Ahab," said Starbuck, who, with Stubb and Flask, had thus far been eyeing his superior with increasing surprise, but at last seemed struck with a thought which somewhat explained all the wonder. "Captain Ahab, I have heard of Moby-Dick—but it was not Moby-Dick that took off thy leg?"

"Who told thee that?" cried Ahab; then pausing, "Aye, Starbuck; aye, my hearties all round; it was Moby-Dick that dismasted me; Moby-Dick that brought me to this dead stump I stand on now. Aye, aye," he shouted with a terrific, loud, animal sob, like that of a heart-stricken moose; "Aye, aye! it was that accursed white whale that razeed me; made a poor pegging lubber[14] for me forever and a day!" Then tossing both arms, with measureless imprecations he shouted out: "Aye, aye! and I'll chase him round Good Hope, and round the Horn, and round the Norway Maelstrom, and round perdition's flames before I give him up. And this is what ye have shipped for, men! to chase that white whale on both sides of land, and over all sides of earth, till he spouts black blood and rolls fin out. What say ye, men, will ye splice hands on it, now? I think ye do look brave."

"Aye, aye!" shouted the harpooneers and seamen, running closer to the excited old man: "A sharp eye for the white whale; a sharp lance for Moby-Dick!"

"God bless ye," he seemed to half sob and half shout. "God bless ye, men. Steward! go draw the great measure of grog. But what's this long face about, Mr. Starbuck; wilt thou not chase the white whale? art not game for Moby-Dick?"

"I am game for his crooked jaw, and for the jaws of Death too, Captain Ahab, if it fairly comes in the way of the business we follow; but I came here to hunt whales, not my commander's vengeance. How many bar-

---

12. fantail: To spread the tail like a fan.
13. parmacetty: Dialect for *spermaceti*, a waxy substance taken from a sperm whale's head and used to make candles.

---

14. lubber (lub′ ər) n.: A slow, clumsy person.

rels will thy vengeance yield thee even if thou gettest it, Captain Ahab? it will not fetch thee much in our Nantucket market."

"Nantucket market! Hoot! But come closer, Starbuck; thou requirest a little lower layer. If money's to be the measurer, man, and the accountants have computed their great countinghouse the globe, by girdling it with guineas, one to every three parts of an inch; then, let me tell thee, that my vengeance will fetch a great premium *here*!"

"He smites his chest," whispered Stubb, "what's that for? methinks it rings most vast, but hollow."

"Vengeance on a dumb brute!" cried Starbuck, "that simply smote thee from blindest instinct! Madness! To be enraged with a dumb thing, Captain Ahab, seems blasphemous."

"Hark ye yet again—the little lower layer. All visible objects, man, are but as pasteboard masks. But in each event—in the living act, the undoubted deed—there, some unknown but still reasoning thing puts forth the moldings of its features from behind the unreasoning mask. If man will strike, strike through the mask! How can the prisoner reach outside except by thrusting through the wall? To me, the white whale is that wall, shoved near to me. Sometimes I think there's naught beyond. But 'tis enough. He tasks me; he heaps me; I see in him outrageous strength, with an inscrutable malice sinewing it. That inscrutable thing is chiefly what I hate; and be the white whale agent, or be the white whale principal, I will wreak that hate upon him. Talk not to me of blasphemy, man; I'd strike the sun if it insulted me. For could the sun do that, then could I do the other; since there is ever a sort of fair play herein, jealousy presiding over all creations. But not my master, man, is even that fair play. Who's over me? Truth hath no confines. Take off thine eye! more intolerable than fiends' glarings is a doltish stare! So, so; thou reddenest and palest; my heat has melted thee to anger-glow. But look ye, Starbuck, what is said in heat, that thing unsays itself. There are men from whom warm words are small indignity. I meant not to incense thee. Let it go. Look! see yonder Turkish cheeks of spotted tawn—living, breathing pictures painted by the sun. The pagan leopards—the unrecking and unworshiping things, that live, and seek, and give no reasons for the torrid life they feel! The crew, man, the crew! Are they not one and all with Ahab, in this matter of the whale? See Stubb! he laughs! See yonder Chilean! he snorts to think of it. Stand up amid the general hurricane, thy one tossed sapling cannot, Starbuck! And what is it? Reckon it. 'Tis but to help strike a fin; no wondrous feat for Starbuck. What is it more? From this one poor hunt, then, the best lance out of all Nantucket, surely he will not hang back, when every foremasthand has clutched a whetstone. Ah! constrainings seize thee; I see! the billow lifts thee! Speak, but speak!— Aye, aye! thy silence, then, *that* voices thee. (*Aside*) Something shot from my dilated nostrils, he has inhaled it in his lungs. Starbuck now is mine; cannot oppose me now, without rebellion."

"God keep me!—keep us all!" murmured Starbuck, lowly.

But in his joy at the enchanted, tacit acquiescence of the mate, Ahab did not hear his foreboding invocation; nor yet the low laugh from the hold; nor yet the presaging vibrations of the winds in the cordage; nor yet the hollow flap of the sails against the masts, as for a moment their hearts sank in. For again Starbuck's downcast eyes lighted up with the stubbornness of life; the subterranean laugh died away; the winds blew on; the sails filled out; the ship heaved and rolled as before. Ah, ye admonitions and warnings! why stay ye not when ye come? But rather are ye predictions than warnings, ye shadows! Yet not so much predictions from without, as verifications of the foregoing things within. For with little external to constrain us, the innermost necessities in our being, these still drive us on.

"The measure! the measure!" cried Ahab.

Receiving the brimming pewter, and turning to the harpooneers, he ordered them to produce their weapons. Then ranging them before him near the capstan,[15] with their harpoons in their hands, while his three mates stood at his side with their lances, and the rest of the ship's company formed a circle round the group; he stood for an instant searchingly eyeing every man of his crew. But those wild eyes met his, as the bloodshot eyes of the prairie wolves meet the eye of their leader, ere he rushes on at their head in the trail of the bison; but, alas! only to fall into the hidden snare of the Indian.

"Drink and pass!" he cried, handing the heavy charged flagon to the nearest seamen. "The crew alone now drink. Round with it, round! Short drafts—long swallows, men; 'tis hot as Satan's hoof. So, so; it goes round excellently. It spiralizes in ye; forks out at the serpent-snapping eye. Well done; almost drained. That way it went, this way it comes. Hand it me—here's a hollow! Men, ye seem the years; so brimming life is gulped and gone. Steward, refill!

"Attend now, my braves. I have mustered ye all round this capstan; and ye mates, flank me with your lances; and ye harpooneers, stand there with your irons; and ye, stout mariners, ring me in, that I may in some sort revive a noble custom of my fishermen fathers before me. O men, you will yet see that— Ha! boy, come back? bad pennies come not sooner. Hand it me. Why, now, this pewter had run brimming again, wer't not thou St. Vitus' imp[16]—away, thou ague![17]

"Advance, ye mates! cross your lances full before me. Well done! Let me touch the axis." So saying, with extended arm, he grasped the three level, radiating lances at their crossed center; while so doing, suddenly and nervously twitched them; meanwhile glancing intently from Starbuck to Stubb; from Stubb to Flask. It seemed as though, by some nameless, interior volition, he would fain have shocked into them the same fiery emotion accumulated within the Leyden jar[18] of his own magnetic life. The three mates quailed before his strong, sustained, and mystic aspect. Stubb and Flask looked sideways from him; the honest eye of Starbuck fell downright.

"In vain!' cried Ahab; "but, maybe, 'tis well. For did ye three but once take the full-forced shock, then mine own electric thing, *that* had perhaps expired from out me. Perchance, too, it would have dropped ye dead. Perchance ye need it not. Down lances! And now, ye mates, I do appoint ye three cup-bearers to my three pagan kinsmen there— yon three most honorable gentlemen and noblemen, my valiant harpooneers. Disdain the task? What, when the great Pope washes the feet of beggars, using his tiara for ewer? Oh, my sweet cardinals! your own condescension, *that* shall bend ye to it. I do not order ye; ye will it. Cut your seizings and draw the poles, ye harpooneers!"

Silently obeying the order, the three harpooneers now stood with the detached iron part of their harpoons, some three feet long, held, barbs up, before him.

"Stab me not with that keen steel! Cant them; cant them over! know ye not the goblet end? Turn up the socket! So, so; now, ye cup-bearers, advance. The irons! take them; hold them while I fill!" Forthwith, slowly going from one officer to the other, he brimmed the harpoon sockets with the fiery waters from the pewter.

"Now, three to three, ye stand. Commend the murderous chalices! Bestow them, ye who are now made parties to this indissoluble league. Ha! Starbuck! but the deed is

---

15. capstan (kap′ stən) *n*.: A large cylinder, turned by hand, around which cables are wound.
16. St. Vitus' imp: Offspring of St. Vitus. Saint Vitus is the patron saint of people stricken with the nervous disorder chorea, characterized by irregular, jerking movements.
17. ague (ā′ gyōō) *n*.: A chill or fit of shivering.

18. Leyden (līd′'n) **jar** *n*.: A glass jar coated inside and out with tinfoil with a metal rod passing through the lid and connected to the inner lining; used to store condensed static electricity.

done! Yon ratifying sun now waits to sit upon it. Drink, ye harpooneers! drink and swear, ye men that man the deathful whaleboat's bow— Death to Moby-Dick! God hunt us all, if we do not hunt Moby-Dick to his death!" The long, barbed steel goblets were lifted; and to cries and maledictions against the white whale, the spirits were simultaneously quaffed down with a hiss. Starbuck paled, and turned, and shivered. Once more, and finally, the replenished pewter went the rounds among the frantic crew; when, waving his free hand to them, they all dispersed; and Ahab retired within his cabin.

After Moby-Dick has been sighted in the Pacific Ocean, the Pequod's *boats pursue the whale for two days. One of the boats has been sunk, and Ahab's ivory leg has been broken off. However, as the next day dawns, the chase continues.*

The Chase–Third Day

The morning of the third day dawned fair and fresh, and once more the solitary night man at the foremasthead was relieved by crowds of the daylight lookouts, who dotted every mast and almost every spar.

"D'ye see him?" cried Ahab; but the whale was not yet in sight.

"In his infallible wake, though; but follow that wake, that's all. Helm there; steady, as thou goest, and hast been going. What a lovely day again! were it a new-made world, and made for a summerhouse to the angels, and this morning the first of its throwing open to them, a fairer day could not dawn upon that world. Here's food for thought, had Ahab time to think; but Ahab never thinks; he only feels, feels, feels; *that's* tingling enough for mortal man! to think's audacity. God only has that right and privilege. Thinking is, or ought to be, a coolness and a calmness; and our poor hearts throb, and our poor brains beat too much for that. And yet, I've sometimes thought my brain was very calm—frozen calm, this old skull cracks so, like a glass in which the contents turned to ice, and shiver it. And still this hair is growing now; this moment growing, and heat must breed it; but no, it's like that sort of common grass that will grow anywhere, between the earthy clefts of Greenland ice or in Vesuvius lava. How the wild winds blow it; they whip it about me as the torn shreds of split sails lash the tossed ship they cling to. A vile wind that has no doubt blown ere this through prison corridors and cells, and wards of hospitals, and ventilated them, and now comes blowing hither as innocent as fleeces.[19] Out upon it!—it's tainted. Were I the wind, I'd blow no more on such a wicked, miserable world. I'd crawl somewhere to a cave, and slink there. And yet, 'tis a noble and heroic thing, the wind! who ever conquered it? In every fight it has the last and bitterest blow. Run tilting at it, and you but run through it. Ha! a coward wind that strikes stark-naked men, but will not stand to receive a single blow. Even Ahab is a braver thing—a nobler thing than *that*. Would now the wind but had a body but all the things that most exasperate and outrage mortal man, all these things are bodiless, but only bodiless as objects, not as agents. There's a most special, a most cunning, oh, a most malicious difference! And yet, I say again, and swear it now, that there's something all glorious and gracious in the wind. These warm trade winds, at least, that in the clear heavens blow straight on, in strong and steadfast, vigorous mildness; and veer not from their mark, however the baser currents of the sea may turn and tack, and mightiest Mississippis of the land swift and swerve about, uncertain where to go at last. And by the eternal poles! these same trades that so directly blow my good ship on; these trades, or something like them—something so unchangeable, and full as strong, blow my keeled soul along! To it! Aloft there! What d'ye see?"

"Nothing, sir."

---

19. fleeces (flēs′ əz) *n.:* Sheep.

"Nothing! and noon at hand! The doubloon[20] goes a-begging! See the sun! Aye, aye, it must be so. I've oversailed him. How, got the start? Aye, he's chasing *me* now; not I, *him*—that's bad; I might have known it, too. Fool! the lines—the harpoons he's towing. Aye, aye, I have run him by last night. About! about! Come down, all of ye, but the regular lookouts! Man the braces!"

Steering as she had done, the wind had been somewhat on the *Pequod*'s quarter, so that now being pointed in the reverse direction, the braced ship sailed hard upon the breeze as she rechurned the cream in her own white wake.

"Against the wind he now steers for the open jaw," murmured Starbuck to himself, as he coiled the new-hauled main brace upon the rail. "God keep us, but already my bones feel damp within me, and from the inside wet my flesh. I misdoubt me that I disobey my God in obeying him!"

"Stand by to sway me up!" cried Ahab, advancing to the hempen basket.[21] "We should meet him soon."

"Aye, aye, sir," and straightway Starbuck did Ahab's bidding, and once more Ahab swung on high.

A whole hour now passed; gold-beaten out to ages. Time itself now held long breaths with keen suspense. But at last, some three points off the weather bow, Ahab descried the spout again, and instantly from the three mastheads three shrieks went up as if the tongues of fire had voiced it.

"Forehead to forehead I meet thee, this third time, Moby-Dick! On deck there!—brace sharper up; crowd her into the wind's eye. He's too far off to lower yet, Mr. Starbuck. The sails shake! Stand over that helmsman with a topmaul! So, so; he travels fast, and I must down. But let me have one more good round look aloft here at the sea; there's

_____

20. doubloon (du bloon') *n.*: The gold coin Ahab offered as reward to the first man to spot the whale.
21. hempen basket: A rope basket constructed earlier by Ahab, in which he could be raised, by means of a pulley device, to the top of the mainmast.

time for that. An old, old sight, and yet somehow so young; aye, and not changed a wink since I first saw it, a boy, from the sand hills of Nantucket! The same!—the same!—the same to Noah as to me. There's a soft shower to leeward. Such lovely leewardings! They must lead somewhere—to something else than common land, more palmy than the palms. Leeward! the white whale goes that way; look to windward, then; the better if the bitterer quarter. But good-bye, good-bye, old masthead! What's this?—green? aye, tiny mosses in these warped cracks. No such green weather stains on Ahab's head! There's the difference now between man's old age and matter's. But aye, old mast, we both grow old together; sound in our hulls, though, are we not, my ship? Aye, minus a leg, that's all. By heaven this dead wood has the better of my live flesh every way. I can't compare with it; and I've known some ships made of dead trees outlast the lives of men made of the most vital stuff of vital fathers. What's that he said? he should still go before me, my pilot; and yet to be seen again? But where? Will I have eyes at the bottom of the sea, supposing I descend those endless stairs? and all night I've been sailing from him, wherever he did sink to. Aye, aye, like many more thou told'st direful truth as touching thyself, O Parsee; but, Ahab, there thy shot fell short. Good-bye, masthead—keep a good eye upon the whale, the while I'm gone. We'll talk tomorrow, nay, tonight, when the white whale lies down there, tied by head and tail."

He gave the word; and still gazing round him, was steadily lowered through the cloven blue air to the deck.

In due time the boats were lowered; but as standing in his shallop's stern, Ahab just hovered upon the point of the descent, he waved to the mate—who held one of the tackle ropes on deck—and bade him pause.

"Starbuck!"

"Sir?"

"For the third time my soul's ship starts upon this voyage, Starbuck."

"Aye, sir, thou wilt have it so."

"Some ships sail from their ports, and ever afterwards are missing, Starbuck!"

"Truth, sir: saddest truth."

"Some men die at ebb tide; some at low water; some at the full of the flood—and I feel now like a billow that's all one crested comb, Starbuck. I am old—shake hands with me, man."

Their hands met; their eyes fastened; Starbuck's tears the glue.

"Oh, my captain, my captain!—noble heart—go not—go not!—see, it's a brave man that weeps; how great the agony of the persuasion then!"

"Lower away!"—cried Ahab, tossing the mate's arm from him. "Stand by the crew!"

In an instant the boat was pulling round close under the stern.

"The sharks! the sharks!" cried a voice from the low cabin window there; "O master, my master, come back!"

But Ahab heard nothing; for his own voice was high-lifted then; and the boat leaped on.

Yet the voice spake true; for scarce had he pushed from the ship, when numbers of sharks, seemingly rising from out the dark waters beneath the hull, maliciously snapped at the blades of the oars, every time they dipped in the water; and in this way accompanied the boat with their bites. It is a thing not uncommonly happening to the whaleboats in those swarming seas; the sharks at times apparently following them in the same prescient way that vultures hover over the banners of marching regiments in the east. But these were the first sharks that had been observed by the *Pequod* since the White Whale had been first descried; and whether it was that Ahab's crew were all such tiger-yellow barbarians, and therefore their flesh more musky to the senses of the sharks—a matter sometimes well known to affect them—however it was, they seemed to follow that one boat without molesting the others.

"Heart of wrought steel!" murmured Starbuck gazing over the side, and following with his eyes the receding boat—"canst thou yet ring boldly to that sight?—lowering thy keel among ravening sharks, and followed by them, open-mouthed to the chase; and this the critical third day?—For when three days flow together in one continuous intense pursuit; be sure the first is the morning, the second the noon, and the third the evening and the end of that thing—be that end what it may. Oh! my God! what is this that shoots through me, and leaves me so deadly calm, yet expectant—fixed at the top of a shudder! Future things swim before me, as in empty outlines and skeletons; all the past is somehow grown dim. Mary, girl; thou fadest in pale glories behind me; boy! I seem to see but thy eyes grown wondrous blue.[22] Strangest problems of life seem clearing; but clouds sweep between—Is my journey's end coming? My legs feel faint; like his who has footed it all day. Feel thy heart—beats it yet? Stir thyself, Starbuck!—stave it off—move, move! speak aloud!—Masthead there! See ye my boy's hand on the hill?—Crazed—aloft there!—keep thy keenest eye upon the boats—mark well the whale!—Ho! again!—drive off that hawk! see! he pecks—he tears the vane"—pointing to the red flag flying at the maintruck—"Ha, he soars away with it!—Where's the old man now? see'st thou that sight, oh Ahab!—shudder, shudder!"

The boats had not gone very far, when by a signal from the mastheads—a downward pointed arm, Ahab knew that the whale had sounded; but intending to be near him at the next rising, he held on his way a little sideways from the vessel; the becharmed crew maintaining the profoundest silence, as the head-beat waves hammered and hammered against the opposing bow.

"Drive, drive in your nails, oh ye waves! to their uttermost heads drive them in! ye but strike a thing without a lid; and no coffin and no hearse can be mine:—and hemp only can kill me! Ha! ha!"

Suddenly the waters around them slowly

---

22. Mary . . . blue.: A reference to Starbuck's wife and son.

swelled in broad circles; then quickly up-heaved, as if sideways sliding from a sub-merged berg of ice, swiftly rising to the surface. A low rumbling sound was heard; a subterraneous hum; and then all held their breaths; as bedraggled with trailing ropes, and harpoons, and lances, a vast form shot lengthwise, but obliquely from the sea. Shrouded in a thin drooping veil of mist, it hovered for a moment in the rainbowed air; and then fell swamping back into the deep. Crushed thirty feet upwards, the waters flashed for an instant like heaps of foun-tains, then brokenly sank in a shower of flakes, leaving the circling surface creamed like new milk round the marble trunk of the whale.

"Give way!" cried Ahab to the oarsmen, and the boats darted forward to the attack; but maddened by yesterday's fresh irons that corroded in him, Moby-Dick seemed combinedly possessed by all the angels that fell from heaven. The wide tiers of welded tendons overspreading his broad white fore-head, beneath the transparent skin, looked knitted together; as head on, he came churning his tail among the boats; and once more flailed them apart; spilling out the irons and lances from the two mates' boats, and dashing in one side of the upper part of their bows, but leaving Ahab's almost with-out a scar.

While Daggoo and Queequeg were stop-ping the strained planks; and as the whale swimming out from them, turned, and showed one entire flank as he shot by them again; at that moment a quick cry went up. Lashed round and round to the fish's back; pinioned in the turns upon turns in which, during the past night, the whale had reeled the involutions of the lines around him, the half-torn body of the Parsee was seen; his sa-ble raiment frayed to shreds; his distended eyes turned full upon old Ahab.

The harpoon dropped from his hand.

"Befooled, befooled!"—drawing in a long lean breath—"Aye, Parsee! I see thee again— Aye, and thou goest before; and this, *this* then is the hearse that thou didst promise.

But I hold thee to the last letter of thy word. Where is the second hearse? Away, mates, to the ship! those boats are useless now; repair them if ye can in time, and return to me; if not, Ahab is enough to die—Down, men! the first thing that but offers to jump from this boat I stand in, that thing I harpoon. Ye are not other men, but my arms and my legs; and so obey me—Where's the whale? gone down again?"

But he looked too nigh the boat; for as if bent upon escaping with the corpse he bore, and as if the particular place of the last en-counter had been but a stage in his leeward voyage, Moby-Dick was now again steadily swimming forward; and had almost passed the ship—which thus far had been sailing in the contrary direction to him, though for the present her headway had been stopped. He seemed swimming with his utmost velocity, and now only intent upon pursuing his own straight path in the sea.

"Oh! Ahab," cried Starbuck, "not too late is it, even now, the third day, to desist. See! Moby-Dick seeks thee not. It is thou, thou, that madly seekest him!"

Setting sail to the rising wind, the lonely boat was swiftly impelled to leeward, by both oars and canvas. And at last when Ahab was sliding by the vessel, so near as plainly to distinguish Starbuck's face as he leaned over the rail, he hailed him to turn the vessel about, and follow him, not too swiftly, at a judicious interval. Glancing upwards he saw Tashtego, Queequeg, and Daggoo, eagerly mounting to the three mastheads; while the oarsmen were rocking in the two staved boats which had just been hoisted to the side, and were busily at work in repairing them. One after the other, through the port-holes, as he sped, he also caught flying glimpses of Stubb and Flask, busying them-selves on deck among bundles of new irons and lances. As he saw all this; as he heard the hammers in the broken boats; far other hammers seemed driving a nail into his heart. But he rallied. And now marking that the vane or flag was gone from the main masthead, he shouted to Tashtego, who had just gained that perch, to descend again for another flag, and a hammer and nails, and so nail it to the mast.

Whether fagged by the three days' running chase, and the resistance to his swimming in the knotted hamper he bore; or whether it was some latent deceitfulness and malice in him: whichever was true, the White Whale's way now began to abate, as it seemed, from the boat so rapidly nearing him once more; though indeed the whale's last start had not been so long a one as before. And still as Ahab glided over the waves the unpitying sharks accompanied him; and so pertinaciously stuck to the boat; and so continually bit at the plying oars, that the blades became jagged and crunched, and left small splinters in the sea, at almost every dip.

"Heed them not! those teeth but give new rowlocks to your oars. Pull on! 'tis the better rest, the sharks' jaw than the yielding water."

"But at every bite, sir, the thin blades grow smaller and smaller!"

"They will last long enough! pull on!—But who can tell"—he muttered—"whether these sharks swim to feast on the whale or on Ahab?—But pull on! Aye, all alive, now—we near him. The helm! take the helm! let me pass"—and so saying, two of the oarsmen helped him forward to the bows of the still flying boat.

At length as the craft was cast to one side, and ran ranging along with the White Whale's flank, he seemed strangely oblivious of its advance—as the whale sometimes will—and Ahab was fairly within the smoky mountain mist, which, thrown off from the whale's spout, curled round his great Monadnock[23] hump; he was even thus close to him; when, with body arched back, and both arms lengthwise high-lifted to the poise, he darted his fierce iron, and his far fiercer curse into the hated whale. As both steel and curse sank to the socket, as if sucked into a morass, Moby-Dick sidewise writhed; spasmodically rolled his nigh flank against the bow, and, without staving a hole in it, so suddenly canted the boat over, that had it not been for the elevated part of the gunwale to which he then clung, Ahab would once more have been tossed into the sea. As it was, three of the oarsmen—who foreknew not the precise instant of the dart, and were therefore unprepared for its effects—these were flung out; but so fell, that, in an instant two of them clutched the gunwale again, and rising to its level on a combing wave, hurled themselves bodily inboard again; the third man helplessly dropping astern, but still afloat and swimming.

Almost simultaneously, with a mighty volition of ungraduated, instantaneous swiftness, the White Whale darted through the weltering sea. But when Ahab cried out to the steersman to take new turns with the line, and hold it so; and commanded the crew to turn round on their seats, and tow the boat up to the mark; the moment the treacherous line felt that double strain and tug, it snapped in the empty air!

"What breaks in me? Some sinew cracks!—'tis whole again; oars! oars! Burst in upon him!"

Hearing the tremendous rush of the sea-crashing boat, the whale wheeled round to present his blank forehead at bay; but in that evolution, catching sight of the nearing black hull of the ship; seemingly seeing in it the source of all his persecutions; bethinking it—it may be—a larger and nobler foe; of a sudden, he bore down upon its advancing prow, smiting his jaws amid fiery showers of foam.

Ahab staggered; his hand smote his forehead. "I grow blind; hands! stretch out before me that I may yet grope my way. Is't night?"

"The whale! The ship!" cried the cringing oarsmen.

"Oars! oars! Slope downwards to thy depths, O sea that ere it be forever too late,

---

23. Monadnock (mə nad′ näk): A mountain in New Hampshire.

Ahab may slide this last, last time upon his mark! I see: the ship! the ship! Dash on, my men! will ye not save my ship?"

But as the oarsmen violently forced their boat through the sledge-hammering seas, the before whale-smitten bow-ends of two planks burst through, and in an instant almost, the temporarily disabled boat lay nearly level with the waves; its half-wading, splashing crew, trying hard to stop the gap and bale out the pouring water.

Meantime, for that one beholding instant, Tashtego's masthead hammer remained suspended in his hand; and the red flag, half wrapping him as with a plaid, then streamed itself straight out from him, as his own forward-flowing heart; while Starbuck and Stubb, standing upon the bowsprit beneath, caught sight of the down-coming monster just as soon as he.

"The whale, the whale! Up helm, up helm! Oh, all ye sweet powers of air, now hug me close! Let not Starbuck die, if die he must, in a woman's fainting fit. Up helm I say—ye fools, the jaw! the jaw! Is this the end of all my bursting prayers? all my life-long fidelities? Oh, Ahab, Ahab, lo, thy work. Steady! helmsman, steady. Nay, nay! Up helm again! He turns to meet us! Oh, his unappeasable brow drives on towards one, whose duty tells him he cannot depart. My God, stand by me now!"

from *Moby-Dick* 327

"Stand not by me, but stand under me, whoever you are that will now help Stubb; for Stubb, too, sticks here. I grin at thee, thou grinning whale! Who ever helped Stubb, or kept Stubb awake, but Stubb's own unwinking eye? And now poor Stubb goes to bed upon a mattress that is all too soft; would it were stuffed with brushwood! I grin at thee, thou grinning whale! Look ye, sun, moon, and stars! I call ye assassins of as good a fellow as ever spouted up his ghost. For all that, I would yet ring glasses with thee, would ye but hand the cup! Oh, oh! oh, oh! thou grinning whale, but there'll be plenty of gulping soon! Why fly ye not, O Ahab! For me, off shoes and jacket to it; let Stubb die in his drawers! A most moldy and oversalted death, though—cherries! cherries! cherries! Oh, Flask, for one red cherry ere we die!"

"Cherries? I only wish that we were where they grow. Oh, Stubb, I hope my poor mother's drawn my part-pay ere this; if not, few coppers will now come to her, for the voyage is up."

From the ship's bows, nearly all the seamen now hung inactive; hammers, bits of plank, lances, and harpoons, mechanically retained in their hands, just as they had darted from their various employments; all their enchanted eyes intent upon the whale, which from side to side strangely vibrating his predestinating head, sent a broad band of overspreading semicircular foam before him as he rushed. Retribution, swift vengeance, eternal malice were in his whole aspect, and spite of all that mortal man could do, the solid white buttress of his forehead smote the ship's starboard bow, till men and timbers reeled. Some fell flat upon their faces. Like dislodged trucks, the heads of the harpooneers aloft shook on their bull-like necks. Through the breach, they heard the waters pour, as mountain torrents down a flume.

"The ship! The hearse!—the second hearse!" cried Ahab from the boat; "its wood could only be American!"

Diving beneath the settling ship, the whale ran quivering along its keel; but turning under water, swiftly shot to the surface again, far off the other bow, but within a few yards of Ahab's boat, where, for a time, he lay quiescent.

"I turn my body from the sun. What ho, Tashtego! let me hear thy hammer. Oh! ye three unsurrendered spires of mine; thou uncracked keel; and only god-bullied hull; thou firm deck, and haughty helm, and Pole-pointed prow—death-glorious ship! must ye then perish, and without me? Am I cut off from the last fond pride of meanest ship-wrecked captains? Oh, lonely death on lonely life! Oh, now I feel my topmost greatness lies in my topmost grief. Ho, ho! from all your furthest bounds, pour ye now in, ye bold billows of my whole foregone life, and top this one piled comber of my death! Towards thee I roll, thou all-destroying but unconquering whale; to the last I grapple with thee; from hell's heart I stab at thee; for hate's sake I spit my last breath at thee. Sink all coffins and all hearses to one common pool! and since neither can be mine, let me then tow to pieces, while still chasing thee, though tied to thee, thou damned whale! *Thus*, I give up the spear!"

The harpoon was darted; the stricken whale flew forward; with igniting velocity the line ran through the groove;—ran foul. Ahab stooped to clear it; he did clear it; but the flying turn caught him round the neck, and voicelessly as Turkish mutes bowstring their victim, he was shot out of the boat, ere the crew knew he was gone. Next instant, the heavy eye splice in the rope's final end flew out of the stark-empty tub, knocked down an oarsman, and smiting the sea, disappeared in its depths.

For an instant, the tranced boat's crew stood still; then turned. "The ship? Great God, where is the ship?" Soon they through dim, bewildering mediums saw her sidelong fading phantom, as in the gaseous fata morgana,[24] only the uppermost masts out of

---

24. fata morgana: A mirage seen at sea.

water; while fixed by infatuation, or fidelity, or fate, to their once lofty perches, the pagan harpooneers still maintained their sinking lookouts on the sea. And now, concentric circles seized the lone boat itself, and all its crew, and each floating oar, and every lance pole, and spinning, animate and inanimate, all round and round in one vortex, carried the smallest chip of the *Pequod* out of sight.

But as the last whelmings intermixingly poured themselves over the sunken head of the Indian at the mainmast, leaving a few inches of the erect spar yet visible, together with long streaming yards of the flag, which calmly undulated, with ironical coincidings, over the destroying billows they almost touched—at that instant, a red arm and a hammer hovered backwardly uplifted in the open air, in the act of nailing the flag faster and yet faster to the subsiding spar. A sky hawk that tauntingly had followed the main-truck downwards from its natural home among the stars, pecking at the flag, and incommoding Tashtego there; this bird now chanced to intercept its broad fluttering wing between the hammer and the wood; and simultaneously feeling that ethereal thrill, the submerged savage beneath, in his deathgasp, kept his hammer frozen there; and so the bird of heaven, with archangelic shrieks, and his imperial beak thrust upwards, and his whole captive form folded in the flag of Ahab, went down with his ship, which, like Satan, would not sink to hell till she had dragged a living part of heaven along with her, and helmeted herself with it.

Now small fowls flew screaming over the yet yawning gulf; a sullen white surf beat against its steep sides; then all collapsed, and the great shroud of the sea rolled on as it rolled five thousand years ago.

THINKING ABOUT THE SELECTION

Recalling

1. What makes the narrator feel uncomfortable at the entrance to the Try Pots?
2. (a) What does Ahab offer to the man who spots Moby-Dick? (b) How do the men respond to his offer?
3. (a) Why is Ahab obsessed with killing Moby-Dick? (b) How does Starbuck interpret Ahab's obsession?
4. (a) What does Ahab tell Starbuck just before his whaleboat is lowered into the water? (b) What follows Ahab's boat as it pulls away from the ship?
5. (a) What happens to Ahab at the end of the novel? (b) What happens to Moby-Dick? (c) What happens to the *Pequod*?

Interpreting

6. How does the narrator's impression of the entrance to the Try Pots foreshadow the outcome of the novel?
7. (a) What does Ahab's obsession with Moby-Dick reveal about his character? (b) In what ways is Starbuck different from Ahab? (c) Why does Starbuck obey Ahab even though he disagrees with him? (d) Why does the rest of the crew join Ahab without hesitation in his quest?
8. On the morning of the third day of the chase, Ahab comments, "Thinking is, or ought to be, a coolness and a calmness; and our poor hearts throb, and our brains beat too much for that." (a) How does this comment apply to Ahab's behavior? (b) How does it apply to the crew?

9. (a) What do Ahab's comments about the wind (page 322) at the beginning of "The Chase—Third Day" indicate about his attitude toward nature? (b) How has his obsession with Moby-Dick shaped his attitude?

10. (a) What omens appear as Ahab's whaleboat pulls away from the ship? When Moby-Dick surfaces? (b) How does Ahab respond to these omens?

11. What is the significance of the fact that Moby-Dick seems "strangely oblivious" to the advance of Ahab's boat?

12. What does the final paragraph indicate about the relationship between humanity and nature?

Applying

13. In his speech at the beginning of "The Chase—Third Day," Ahab expresses his belief that people are guided by instinct and intuition rather than reason. React to Ahab's view.

14. (a) How can obsession with achieving a goal affect a person's ability to reach this goal? (b) What types of goals do you think many people are obsessed with reaching in today's world?

ANALYZING LITERATURE
Recognizing a Symbol

A **symbol** is a person, place, or thing that has a meaning in itself and also represents something larger than itself. For example, the crew of the *Pequod,* which includes representatives from many of the world's races and cultures, symbolizes humanity.

1. Given the fact that the crew of the *Pequod* symbolizes humanity and Moby-Dick symbolizes everything in nature that is paradoxical, unexplainable, and uncontrollable, what do you think the voyage of the *Pequod* symbolizes?

2. Considering the symbolic meaning and the outcome of the journey, what do you think is the theme, or central idea, of the novel?

CRITICAL THINKING AND READING
Analyzing the Meaning of a Symbol

Analyzing Ahab's comments is one effective way to understand the meaning of Moby-Dick as a symbol.

Explain how the following passage from one of Ahab's speeches supports the interpretation of Moby-Dick as a symbol of the mysteries of existence.

"All visible objects, man, are but pasteboard masks. But in each event—in the living act, the undoubted deed—there, some unknown but still reasoning thing puts forth the moldings of its features from behind the unreasoning mask. If man will strike, strike through the mask! How can the prisoner reach outside except by thrusting through the wall? To me, the white whale is that wall, shoved near me."

THINKING AND WRITING
Writing About Symbolism and Theme

Write an essay in which you discuss how the theme, or central idea, of *Moby-Dick* is revealed through Melville's use of symbolism. Start by rereading the excerpt, noting passages in which the meaning of any of the primary symbols in the novel is suggested. Define the meaning of each symbol in your own words. Prepare a chart showing the relationship between the symbols and the theme. Write a thesis statement. Then write your essay. Include enough passages from the novel to support your thesis. When you revise, make sure that your ideas are well-organized and stated clearly.

New England Poets

AFTER THE FIRST SNOW IN WINTER IN VERMONT
Charles Hughes
Three Lions

HENRY WADSWORTH LONGFELLOW

1807–1882

Henry Wadsworth Longfellow once wrote, "Music is the universal language of mankind—poetry their universal pastime and delight." During the latter half of the eighteenth century, Longfellow's poetry certainly was a "universal pastime and delight." His work, which was translated into two dozen foreign languages, was read and enjoyed by millions of readers throughout Europe and the United States.

Born in Portland, Maine, Longfellow attended Bowdoin College, where Nathaniel Hawthorne was one of his classmates. After graduating in 1825, Longfellow spent four years in Europe before returning to Bowdoin as a professor of modern languages. He taught at Bowdoin for five years. Then, after spending another year in Europe, he accepted a position at Harvard University in Cambridge, Massachusetts, which he held for eighteen years.

During his years as a professor at Bowdoin and Harvard, Longfellow had a long and successful career as a poet, publishing his first collection of poems, *Voices of the Night,* in 1839. Writing poems that appealed to a general audience, Longfellow established himself as the most popular American poet of his time.

Recognizing the need to maintain a connection to the past, Longfellow found subjects for his poetry in American history. His narrative poems, such as *Evangeline* (1847), *The Song of Hiawatha* (1855), *The Courtship of Miles Standish* (1858), and "Paul Revere's Ride" (1861), gave readers a romanticized view of America during its infancy and expressed the democratic ideals of the young nation.

Longfellow's poetry has been criticized for being overly optimistic and sentimental; yet it was Longfellow's optimism that made him so popular. By writing poetry that soothed and encouraged readers, Longfellow became the first American poet to reach a wide audience and create a national interest in poetry.

GUIDE FOR READING

The Tide Rises, The Tide Falls; A Psalm of Life; The Arsenal at Springfield

Writer's Techniques

Stanza Forms. A stanza is a unit of poetry consisting of two or more lines arranged in a pattern according to rhyme and meter, or rhythm. Like paragraphs in prose, stanzas organize ideas into units. Unlike paragraphs in prose, however, stanzas in a poem are generally of a fixed length and share the same pattern of rhyme and meter.

Stanza forms are described in terms of rhyme scheme and length. Rhyme scheme is indicated by assigning a different letter of the alphabet to each new rhyming sound in a stanza. For example, in a stanza in which every other line rhymes, the rhyme scheme is *abab*. Length is determined by the number of lines in a stanza. The following are common stanza lengths:

the couplet	(2 lines)
the tercet	(3 lines)
the quatrain	(4 lines)
the cinquain	(5 lines)
the sestet	(6 lines)
the octave	(8 lines)

Look For

Longfellow uses a variety of stanza forms. As you read his poems, look for the stanza forms used in each.

Writing

What do the ocean and the constant motion of the tide suggest to you? List the ideas you associate with the ocean and the rising and falling of the tide.

Vocabulary

Knowing the following words will help you as you read these poems.
bivouac (biv′ wak) *n.*: A temporary encampment (p. 336, l. 18)
sublime (sə blīm′) *adj.*: Noble; majestic (p. 336, l. 26)
beleaguered (bi lē′ gərd) *adj.*: Encircled by an army (p. 338, l. 24)
discordant (dis kôr′ d'nt) *adj.*: Not in harmony; clashing (p. 340, l. 29)

THE RETURN ALONE
Eugene Higgins
The Phillips Collection, Washington, D.C.

The Tide Rises, The Tide Falls

Henry Wadsworth Longfellow

The tide rises, the tide falls,
The twilight darkens, the curlew[1] calls;
Along the sea sands damp and brown
The traveler hastens toward the town,
5   And the tide rises, the tide falls.

Darkness settles on roofs and walls,
But the sea, the sea in the darkness calls;
The little waves, with their soft, white hands,
Efface the footprints in the sands,
10   And the tide rises, the tide falls.

The morning breaks; the steeds in their stalls
Stamp and neigh, as the hostler[2] calls;
The day returns, but nevermore
Returns the traveler to the shore,
15   And the tide rises, the tide falls.

---

1. curlew (kʉr′ lo͞o) *n.*: A large, long-legged wading bird whose call is associated with the evening.
2. hostler (häs′ lər) *n.*: A person who tends horses at an inn or stable.

THINKING ABOUT THE SELECTION

Recalling

1. What is the setting of the poem?
2. What do the "little waves" do in lines 8–9?
3. What happens in the third stanza?
4. What line is repeated three times in the poem?

Interpreting

5. (a) What details of the setting in the first stanza suggest that the traveler is nearing death? (b) What details in the second stanza suggest that the traveler has died?
6. What does the poem suggest about the relationship between humanity and nature?
7. (a) What is the effect of the refrain, or repeated line? (b) How does the rhythm of the refrain contribute to its meaning?
8. What do the details in lines 11–13 suggest about Longfellow's attitude toward death?

Applying

9. (a) What is the significance of the fact that Longfellow wrote "The Tide Rises, The Tide Falls" near the end of his life? (b) How might the poem have been different if he had written it earlier in life?

UNDERSTANDING LANGUAGE

Using Abstract Words

Concrete words are words that appeal to one or more of the five senses. In contrast, **abstract** words are words that express qualities or concepts apart from any particular or material object. The word *beauty,* for example, is an abstract word, while the word *flower* is concrete.

Define in your own words each of the following words. Check your definitions in a dictionary. Then think of a concrete image, or word picture, that conveys the qualities or concepts expressed by each abstract word.

1. death
2. birth
3. age

A Psalm of Life

Henry Wadsworth Longfellow

Tell me not, in mournful numbers,[1]
    Life is but an empty dream!—
For the soul is dead that slumbers,
    And things are not what they seem.

5 Life is real! Life is earnest!
    And the grave is not its goal;
Dust thou art, to dust returnest,
    Was not spoken of the soul.

Not enjoyment, and not sorrow,
10   Is our destined end or way;
But to act, that each tomorrow
    Find us farther than today.

Art is long, and Time is fleeting,
    And our hearts, though stout and brave,
15 Still, like muffled drums, are beating
    Funeral marches to the grave.

In the world's broad field of battle,
    In the bivouac of Life,
Be not like dumb, driven cattle!
20   Be a hero in the strife!

Trust no Future, howe'er pleasant!
    Let the dead Past bury its dead!
Act—act in the living Present!
    Heart within, and God o'erhead!

25 Lives of great men all remind us
    We can make our lives sublime,
And, departing, leave behind us
    Footprints on the sands of time;

Footprints, that perhaps another,
30   Sailing o'er life's solemn main,[2]
A forlorn and shipwrecked brother,
    Seeing, shall take heart again.

---

1. numbers: Verses.
2. main: The open sea.

Let us, then, be up and doing,
  With a heart for any fate;
35 Still achieving, still pursuing,
  Learn to labor and to wait.

THINKING ABOUT THE SELECTION

Recalling

1. (a) What opinion about appearances does the speaker express in line 4? (b) What opinion about life does the speaker express in line 5?
2. What comment concerning time does the speaker make in line 13?
3. (a) What advice does the speaker offer in the fifth stanza? (b) What advice does he offer in the sixth stanza?
4. According to the speaker, what can we learn from the "lives of great men"?
5. What advice does the speaker offer in the final stanza?

Interpreting

6. In your own words summarize the speaker's view of life.
7. How would you describe the speaker's attitude concerning individuality and self-reliance?
8. How does the speaker think our lives can influence future generations?

Applying

9. Give your opinion of the speaker's view of life. Explain your opinion

OLIVER WENDELL HOLMES

1809–1894

An extraordinarily energetic man with a variety of talents and interests, Oliver Wendell Holmes made important contributions to both literature and medicine. In addition to serving as a professor of anatomy at Harvard University for thirty-five years and writing numerous professional articles, Holmes wrote three novels and several volumes of poems and essays.

Holmes, a descendant of seventeenth-century poet Anne Bradstreet (page 17), was born in Cambridge, Massachusetts. He attended Harvard University, where he was named class poet in 1829. Following his graduation Holmes entered Harvard Law School. While there, he wrote the poem "Old Ironsides" to protest the planned demolition of the battleship *Constitution,* nicknamed "Old Ironsides" because of its ability to withstand the attacks of British warships during the War of 1812. The poem, which aroused such protest that the ship was preserved as a national monument, earned Holmes national recognition as a poet.

After abandoning the study of law, Holmes studied medicine in Paris for several years. Then, in 1836, he returned to Harvard to complete his medical degree. In that same year Holmes also published his first collection of poetry, *Poems*.

In 1847 Holmes began his lengthy teaching career at Harvard. During his years there, he established himself as a leading medical researcher. At the same time, he continued his literary pursuits with energy and enthusiasm. Along with James Russell Lowell, Holmes helped to found the *Atlantic Monthly,* a literary magazine that is still published today. Holmes published many of his best-known works in the *Atlantic Monthly,* including his poem "The Chambered Nautilus" and a series of humorous essays eventually collected in *The Autocrat of the Breakfast-Table* (1858), his most popular book. Drawing on his knowledge of medicine, Holmes also wrote three novels in which he expressed his views concerning heredity.

Retiring from medicine in 1882, Holmes devoted the final years of his life to writing and lecturing. He died in 1894, the last member of America's first generation of highly regarded writers.

GUIDE FOR READING

Old Ironsides; The Chambered Nautilus

Writer's Techniques

Meter and Scansion. Meter is a systematic arrangement of stressed and unstressed syllables in poetry. The basic unit of meter is the foot. Usually a foot consists of one stressed syllable and one or more unstressed syllables. The most common foot in American and English verse is the iamb, which is made up of one unstressed syllable followed by a stressed syllable. Other common feet include the trochee, a stressed syllable followed by an unstressed syllable; the anapest, two unstressed syllables followed by a stressed syllable; and the dactyl, a stressed syllable followed by two unstressed syllables.

Meter is determined by combining the type of foot with the number of feet per line: monometer (one foot), dimeter (two feet), trimeter (three feet), tetrameter (four feet), pentameter (five feet), hexameter (six feet). For example, the following line from "The Chambered Nautilus" is written in iambic pentameter:

> Its webs of living gauze no more unfurl;

Often, writers vary the number of feet per line in a poem. For example, a poet may alternate lines of iambic pentameter with lines of iambic trimeter. A poet may also introduce slight variations in the metrical pattern to avoid monotony or emphasize important words. For example, a poem written in iambic trimeter may contain several lines that end with two stressed syllables.

The analysis of the meter of poetry is called **scansion**. To scan a line of poetry, you divide it into feet and mark the stressed and unstressed syllables. You determine the meter by taking note of the type of foot being used and counting the number of feet in each line.

Look For

As you read "Old Ironsides" and "The Chambered Nautilus," look for the meaning of each poem. Then reread the poems aloud, listening to the rhythm of each poem.

Writing

Holmes's poem "Old Ironsides" aroused strong public opinion about a current issue. Make a list of social and political issues about which you have strong opinions.

Vocabulary

Knowing the following words will help you as you read "Old Ironsides" and "The Chambered Nautilus."

vanquished (vaŋ′ kwisht) *adj.*: Defeated (p. 344, l. 10)
venturous (ven′ chər əs) *adj.*: Daring (p. 346, l. 3)

crypt (kript) *n.*: An underground chamber or vault (p. 346, l. 14)
lustrous (lus′ trəs) *adj.*: Shining (p. 347, l. 16)

U.S. FRIGATE CONSTITUTION, 1823
Nicholas Cammilliri
The Mariner's Museum, Newport News, Virginia

Old Ironsides

Oliver Wendell Holmes

Ay, tear her tattered ensign down!
    Long has it waved on high,
And many an eye has danced to see
    That banner in the sky;
5 Beneath it rung the battle shout,
    And burst the cannons roar—
The meteor of the ocean air
    Shall sweep the clouds no more.

Her deck, once red with heroes' blood,
10   Where knelt the vanquished foe,
When winds were hurrying o'er the flood,
    And waves were white below,
No more shall feel the victor's tread,
    Or know the conquered knee—

15 The harpies[1] of the shore shall pluck
      The eagle of the sea!

   Oh, better that her shattered hulk
      Should sink beneath the wave;
   Her thunders shook the mighty deep,
20   And there should be her grave;
   Nail to the mast her holy flag,
      Set every threadbare sail,
   And give her to the god of storms,
      The lightning and the gale!

---

1. harpies (här′ pēz): In Greek mythology, hideous, filthy winged monsters with the head and trunk of a woman and the tail, legs, and talons of a bird. Here, the word refers to relentless, greedy, or grasping people.

THINKING ABOUT THE SELECTION
Recalling

1. Point out two images, or word pictures, the speaker uses in the first two stanzas to describe the battles in which "Old Ironsides" had been involved.
2. What does the speaker suggest might be a more fitting end for the ship?

Interpreting

3. What human qualities does "Old Ironsides" seem to represent for the speaker?
4. What does Holmes mean when he refers to "Old Ironsides" as "the eagle of the sea" (line 16)?
5. How does Holmes appeal in the poem to the American sense of patriotism?

Applying

6. When "Old Ironsides" was published, it aroused such protest that the ship was saved. Do you believe that a poem could have such a powerful effect on the American public today? Why or why not?

THINKING AND WRITING
Writing a Poem in Support of a Cause

Review your list of social and political issues. Decide which issue is most important to you. List the reasons why you feel so strongly about this issue. Think of some descriptive details that convey your feelings, and come up with some concrete images, or word pictures, related to the issue. Decide on the audience you would like to persuade to accept your opinion. Then use your list of details and images to write a poem expressing your opinion. Keep your audience in mind as you write. Do not worry about rhyme or rhythm. Focus on the content of your poem. When you revise make sure that you have included enough concrete images to allow your audience to visualize your subject.

Chambered Nautilus

endell Holmes

This is the ship of pearl, which, poets feign,
    Sails the unshadowed main—
    The venturous bark that flings
On the sweet summer wind its purpled wings
5 In gulfs enchanted, where the Siren[1] sings,
    And coral reefs lie bare,
Where the cold sea-maids rise to sun their streaming hair.

Its webs of living gauze no more unfurl;
    Wrecked is the ship of pearl!
10   And every chambered cell,
Where its dim dreaming life was wont to dwell,
As the frail tenant shaped his growing shell,
    Before thee lies revealed—
Its irised[2] ceiling rent, its sunless crypt unsealed!

---

1. Siren (sī′ rən): In Greek mythology, one of several sea nymphs
who lured sailors to their deaths by singing enchanting songs.
2. irised *adj.*: Rainbow colored.

15   Year after year beheld the silent toil
         That spread his lustrous coil;
         Still, as the spiral grew,
     He left the past year's dwelling for the new,
     Stole with soft step its shining archway through,
20   Built up its idle door,
     Stretched in his last-found home, and knew the old no more.

     Thanks for the heavenly message brought by thee,
         Child of the wandering sea,
         Cast from her lap, forlorn!
25   From thy dead lips a clearer note is born
     Than ever Triton[3] blew from wreathèd horn!
         While on mine ear it rings,
     Through the deep caves of thought I hear a voice that sings:

     Build thee more stately mansions, O my soul,
30   As the swift seasons roll!
         Leave thy low-vaulted past!
     Let each new temple, nobler than the last,
     Shut thee from heaven with a dome more vast,
         Till thou at length art free,
35   Leaving thine outgrown shell by life's unresting sea!

---

3. Triton (trīt′ 'n) *n.*: A Greek sea god with the body of a man and
the tail of a fish, who usually carried a conch-shell trumpet.

THINKING ABOUT THE SELECTION

Recalling

1. What has happened to the nautilus the speaker is describing?
2. What did the nautilus do "as the spiral grew" (line 17)?
3. What does the voice that rings "through the deep caves of thought" tell the speaker?

Interpreting

4. Each year throughout the course of its life, the nautilus creates a new chamber of shell to house its growing body. How does Holmes compare this process to the development of the human soul?

Applying

5. What is it about the chambered nautilus that makes it appropriate for Holmes's message?
6. What can you learn from the life of the chambered nautilus?

ANALYZING LITERATURE

Using Meter and Scansion

Meter is a systematic arrangement of stressed and unstressed syllables in poetry. **Scansion** is the process of analyzing meter.

1. Scan each line in the first stanza of "The Chambered Nautilus."
2. Identify the meter in each line.

JAMES RUSSELL LOWELL

1819–1891

James Russell Lowell may have been the most talented of the Fireside Poets. His literary career was disrupted by personal tragedies, however, and he was never able to fulfill his early promise as a poet. Still, Lowell did make many important contributions to the world of literature as a poet, editor, and critic.

Lowell was born in Cambridge, Massachusetts, the descendant of a prominent family. He graduated from Harvard Law School but quickly lost interest in practicing law. Instead, Lowell decided to pursue a career in literature, publishing his first book of poetry, *A Year's Life,* in 1841. While continuing to write poetry and essays, Lowell also supported the abolitionist movement. He frequently wrote editorials attacking slavery, thereby establishing himself as one of the country's leading abolitionist journalists.

In 1848 Lowell's literary career reached its peak. During that year he published three of his best works: *A Fable for Critics,* a satire of other American writers of his time; *The Biglow Papers,* a collection of poems and letters; and *The Vision of Sir Launfal,* an epic poem about medieval knighthood. All three works were very successful, earning him international fame.

Unfortunately, Lowell's literary success was overshadowed by tragic events in his personal life. Three of his four children died in infancy, and he lost his beloved wife, Maria, in 1853. Following Maria's death, Lowell lost his focus as a writer, and he found himself unable to produce poems or essays that matched his earlier work.

During the second half of his life, Lowell gradually turned away from writing toward other interests. In 1855 he succeeded Longfellow as professor of languages at Harvard, and he remained there until 1872. Lowell also helped to found the *Atlantic Monthly,* a respected literary magazine, and served as its first editor. Later Lowell became co-editor of the *North American Review,* another distinguished literary magazine. Then, in 1877, Lowell began a career in diplomacy, serving for a number of years as the American ambassador to Spain and, later, Great Britain.

GUIDE FOR READING

Auspex; The First Snowfall

Tone. Tone refers to the writer's attitude toward his or her subject, characters, or audience. The tone of a work of literature is revealed through the writer's choice of words and portrayal of characters and events. For example, in a work with a humorous tone a writer might use witty language and include amusing descriptions of characters and events.

Tone can dramatically affect the way you respond to the subject and characters in a literary work. For example, if a writer expresses a sympathetic attitude toward a character, we are also likely to be sympathetic toward that character. In contrast, if the writer expresses contempt for a character, we are likely to have a negative response to that character.

Your awareness of tone can be important to your understanding of a literary work, because tone is often closely related to the theme, or central idea. For example, a work written to convey the cruelty and destructiveness of war is likely to have a solemn or despairing tone.

Writer's Techniques

Look For

As you read "Auspex" and "The First Snowfall," look for the words or phrases that convey the tone. How does the tone affect your response to each poem?

Writing

These two poems by Lowell deal with emotional reactions to some aspect of a season. People often have strong emotional reactions to the first snowstorm of each winter. Describe your typical response to a change of season—either the end of one or the beginning of another.

Vocabulary

Knowing the following words will help you as you read "Auspex" and "The First Snowfall."

delusion (di lōō′ zhən) *n.*: Deception (p. 351, l. 13)

gloaming (glō′ miŋ) *n.*: Evening dusk; twilight (p. 352, l. 1)

LOW BRANCH, 1968
Scarlett
Courtesy New York Graphic Society

Auspex[1]

James Russell Lowell

My heart, I cannot still it,
Nest that had song birds in it;
And when the last shall go,
The dreary days, to fill it,
5 Instead of lark or linnet,
Shall whirl dead leaves and snow.

Had they been swallows only,
Without the passion stronger
That skyward longs and sings—
10 Woe's me, I shall be lonely
When I can feel no longer
The impatience of their wings!

A moment, sweet delusion,
Like birds the brown leaves hover;
15 But it will not be long
Before their wild confusion
Fall wavering down to cover
The poet and his song.

---

1. Auspex (ôs' peks) *n*.: In ancient Rome,
someone who watched for omens in the flight
of birds.

THINKING ABOUT THE SELECTION

Recalling

1. According to the first stanza, what will "fill" the speaker's heart when the songbirds have gone?
2. According to the second stanza, when will the speaker be lonely?
3. (a) What is the "sweet delusion" the speaker refers to in lines 13–14? (b) What will happen when the delusion ends?

Interpreting

4. In this poem Lowell compares songbirds to the happiness that provides him with poetic inspiration. To what does he compare the emptiness following the disappearance of his happiness?
5. (a) What do the swallows (line 7) represent? (b) How is this different from what the songbirds represent?
6. What does the image of the leaves falling and covering the poet represent?

Applying

7. What type of event in Lowell's life might have prompted him to write this poem?

The First Snowfall

James Russell Lowell

The snow had begun in the gloaming,
    And busily all the night
Had been heaping field and highway
    With a silence deep and white.

5 Every pine and fir and hemlock
    Wore ermine too dear for an earl,
And the poorest twig on the elm tree
    Was ridged inch deep with pearl.

From sheds new-roofed with Carrara[1]
10   Came Chanticleer's[2] muffled crow,
The stiff rails softened to swan's-down,
    And still fluttered down the snow.

I stood and watched by the window
    The noiseless work of the sky,
15 And the sudden flurries of snowbirds,
    Like brown leaves whirling by.

I thought of a mound in sweet Auburn[3]
    Where a little headstone stood;
How the flakes were folding it gently,
20   As did robins the babes in the wood.

Up spoke our own little Mabel,
    Saying, "Father, who makes it snow?"
And I told of the good All-Father
    Who cares for us here below.

25 Again I looked at the snowfall,
    And thought of the leaden sky
That arched o'er our first great sorrow,
    When that mound was heaped so high.

---

1. **Carrara** (kə rä′ rə) n.: Fine, white marble.
2. **Chanticleer's** (chan′ tə klirz′): Referring to a rooster.
3. **Auburn:** Mt. Auburn Cemetery in Cambridge, Massachusetts.

I remembered the gradual patience
30   That fell from that cloud like snow,
Flake by flake, healing and hiding
      The scar that renewed our woe.

And again to the child I whispered,
      "The snow that husheth all,
35 Darling, the merciful Father
      Alone can make it fall!"

Then, with eyes that saw not, I kissed her;
      And she, kissing back, could not know
That *my* kiss was given to her sister,
40   Folded close under deepening snow.

THINKING ABOUT THE SELECTION

Recalling

1. (a) When had the snowfall begun? (b) How much snow covered the "poorest twig on the elm tree" by morning?
2. Of what does the snowstorm make the speaker think?
3. (a) What question does the speaker's daughter ask him? (b) How does he respond at first? (c) What does he later add to his response?
4. What does the speaker's daughter not know when he kisses her?

Interpreting

5. How does the speaker imply that his sorrow resulted from the death of his daughter without directly stating it?
6. (a) To what does the speaker compare his sorrow (lines 25–28)? (b) To what does the speaker compare the process of recovering from his sorrow (lines 29–32)?

7. What does the speaker's comment to his daughter suggest about his belief in the source of emotional healing?
8. In your own words, describe the tone of "The First Snowfall."

Applying

9. This poem suggests that a natural event, such as a snowstorm, can both remind us of sorrow and help to heal it. Explain why you do or do not agree with this suggestion.

THINKING AND WRITING
Comparing and Contrasting Tones

Write an essay in which you compare and contrast the tones of "Auspex" and "The First Snowfall." Start by rereading the two poems, taking note of the similarities and differences in tone and the way in which the tone is revealed. Look over your notes and sum up the similarities and differences in a topic sentence. Then write your essay, using passages from each poem for support. When you finish writing, revise your essay and prepare a final copy.

JOHN GREENLEAF WHITTIER

1807–1892

John Greenleaf Whittier stands apart from the other Fireside Poets in several ways. Unlike Longfellow, Holmes, and Lowell, Whittier was born in poverty and received virtually no formal education. He was also more deeply involved with the social issues of his time than were the other poets. Finally, because of his devotion to the abolitionist movement, Whittier, unlike the other poets, did not gain national prominence as a poet until late in his life.

Whittier was born and raised on a farm near Haverhill, Massachusetts. His parents were Quakers, who taught him to believe in hard work, simplicity, pacifism, religious devotion, and social justice. Because he worked long hours on the debt-ridden family farm, Whittier suffered from poor health throughout much of his childhood. Though he was able to attend school for only one year, he educated himself by reading—primarily the Bible and other religious writings and the poetry of Scottish poet Robert Burns. During his teens he began writing poetry, and when he was eighteen his first poem was published in a local newspaper.

As a young man, Whittier became deeply committed to the abolitionist movement. He worked as a writer and editor for antislavery newspapers, wrote a large number of antislavery poems, spoke at abolitionist rallies, and became active in politics, serving a term in the Massachusetts legislature. Unfortunately, Whittier's dedication to abolitionism prevented him from gaining national recognition as a poet until after the Civil War.

When the war ended, Whittier turned away from politics, focused his attention on writing poetry, and established himself as one of the country's leading poets. He earned national fame in 1866, when he published his most highly regarded work, *Snowbound*. In this poem and in many later poems, Whittier vividly depicts the warmth and simplicity of life in rural New England.

As the way of life depicted in his poetry disappeared, the popularity of Whittier's poems grew. By the time of his death, Whittier had enjoyed more than twenty-five years of success as a poet. Yet he never allowed his success to affect his warmth, simplicity, and modesty, and he remained faithful at all times to his social and spiritual convictions.

GUIDE FOR READING

from Snowbound; Hampton Beach

Writer's Techniques

Imagery. Imagery refers to words or phrases that create mental pictures, or images, that appeal to one or more of the five senses—sight, hearing, touch, smell, or taste. Most often, images appeal to the reader's sense of sight. For example, when Whittier writes, "The sun . . . rose cheerless over hills of gray," he creates a visual picture. Sometimes, however, images present sensations that cannot be visualized. For example, when Whittier refers to "a hard, dull bitterness of cold," he presents an image that you can feel but cannot see. A single image may also appeal to more than one sense. Whittier creates an image that you can both see and feel when he writes, "Unwarmed by any sunset light the gray day darkened into night."

Look For

As you read the excerpt from *Snowbound* and "Hampton Beach," look for Whittier's use of imagery.

Writing

What images come to mind when you envision the morning after a snowstorm? What images do you associate with the beach? List the images that come to mind when you think of each of these scenes.

Vocabulary

Knowing the following words will help you as you read "Hampton Beach" and the excerpt from *Snowbound*.

ominous (äm′ ə nəs) *adj.*: Sinister (p. 356, l. 6)
prophecy (präf′ ə sē) *n.*: Prediction of the future (p. 356, l. 6)
querulous (kwer′ ə ləs) *adj.*: Complaining (p. 356, l. 30)
patriarch (pā′ trē ärk) *n.*: The father and ruler of a family or tribe (p. 358, l. 89)

luminous (l⁻⁻oo′ mə nəs) *adj.*: Shining (p. 362, l. 4)
tremulous (trem′ yoo ləs) *adj.*: Trembling (p. 362, l. 6)
asunder (ə sun′ dər) *adv.*: Into parts or pieces (p. 364, l. 36)

from Snowbound

John Greenleaf Whittier

A Winter Idyll

The sun that brief December day
Rose cheerless over hills of gray,
And, darkly circled, gave at noon
A sadder light than waning moon.
5   Slow tracing down the thickening sky
Its mute and ominous prophecy,
A portent seeming less than threat,
It sank from sight before it set.
A chill no coat, however stout,
10 Of homespun stuff could quite shut out,
A hard, dull bitterness of cold,
That checked, mid-vein, the circling race
Of lifeblood in the sharpened face,
The coming of the snowstorm told.
15 The wind blew east; we heard the roar
Of Ocean on his wintry shore,
And felt the strong pulse throbbing there
Beat with low rhythm our inland air.

Meanwhile we did our nightly chores—
20 Brought in the wood from out of doors,
Littered the stalls, and from the mows
Raked down the herd's-grass for the cows:
Heard the horse whinnying for his corn;
And, sharply clashing horn on horn,
25 Impatient down the stanchion[1] rows
The cattle shake their walnut bows;
While, peering from his early perch
Upon the scaffold's pole of birch,
The cock his crested helmet bent
30 And down his querulous challenge sent.

Unwarmed by any sunset light
The gray day darkened into night,
A night made hoary with the swarm
And whirl-dance of the blinding storm,

---

1. stanchion (stan' chən): A restraining device fitted
around the neck of a cow to confine it to its stall.

35   As zigzag, wavering to and fro,
       Crossed and recrossed the wingèd snow:
       And ere the early bedtime came
       The white drift piled the window frame,
       And through the glass the clothesline posts
40   Looked in like tall and sheeted ghosts.

       So all night long the storm roared on:
       The morning broke without a sun;
       In tiny spherule[2] traced with lines
       Of Nature's geometric signs,
45   In starry flake, and pellicle,[3]
       All day the hoary meteor fell;
       And, when the second morning shone,
       We looked upon a world unknown,
       On nothing we could call our own.
50   Around the glistening wonder bent
       The blue walls of the firmament,
       No cloud above, no earth below—
       A universe of sky and snow!
       The old familiar sights of ours
55   Took marvelous shapes; strange domes and towers
       Rose up where sty or corncrib stood,
       Or garden wall, or belt of wood;
       A smooth white mound the brush pile showed,
       A fenceless drift what once was road;
60   The bridle post an old man sat
       With loose-flung coat and high cocked hat;
       The wellcurb had a Chinese roof;
       And even the long sweep,[4] high aloof,
       In its slant splendor, seemed to tell
65   Of Pisa's leaning miracle.[5]

       A prompt, decisive man, no breath
       Our father wasted: "Boys, a path!"
       Well pleased (for when did farmer boy
       Count such a summons less than joy?)
70   Our buskins[6] on our feet we drew;
       With mittened hands, and caps drawn low,
       To guard our necks and ears from snow,
       We cut the solid whiteness through.
       And, where the drift was deepest, made

---

2. spherule (sfer' ōōl): A small sphere.
3. pellicle (pel' i k'l): A thin film.
4. sweep: A pole with a bucket at one end, used for raising water from a well.
5. Pisa's leaning miracle: The famous leaning tower of Pisa in Italy.
6. buskins: High-cut shoes.

75 A tunnel walled and overlaid
    With dazzling crystal: we had read
    Of rare Aladdin's[7] wondrous cave,
    And to our own his name we gave,
    With many a wish the luck were ours
80 To test his lamp's supernal powers.
    We reached the barn with merry din,
    And roused the prisoned brutes within,
    The old horse thrust his long head out,
    And grave with wonder gazed about;
85 The cock his lusty greeting said,
    And forth his speckled harem led;
    The oxen lashed their tails, and hooked,
    And mild reproach of hunger looked;
    The hornèd patriarch of the sheep,
90 Like Egypt's Amun[8] roused from sleep,
    Shook his sage head with gesture mute,
    And emphasized with stamp of foot.

    All day the gusty north wind bore
    The loosening drift its breath before;
95 Low circling round its southern zone,
    The sun through dazzling snow-mist shone.
    No church bell lent its Christian tone
    To the savage air, no social smoke
    Curled over woods of snow-hung oak.
100 A solitude made more intense
    By dreary-voicèd elements,
    The shrieking of the mindless wind,
    The moaning tree boughs swaying blind,
    And on the glass the unmeaning beat
105 Of ghostly fingertips of sleet.
    Beyond the circle of our hearth
    No welcome sound of toil or mirth
    Unbound the spell, and testified
    Of human life and thought outside.
110 We minded that the sharpest ear
    The buried brooklet could not hear,
    The music of whose liquid lip
    Had been to us companionship,
    And, in our lonely life, had grown
115 To have an almost human tone.

    As night drew on, and, from the crest
    Of wooded knolls that ridged the west,

---

7. Aladdin's: Referring to Aladdin, a boy in *The Arabian Nights* who found a magic lamp and through its powers discovered a treasure in a cave.
8. Amun: An Egyptian god with a ram's head.

OLD HOLLEY HOUSE, COS COB
John Henry Twachtman
Cincinnati Art Museum

The sun, a snow-blown traveler, sank
From sight beneath the smothering bank,
120 We piled, with care, our nightly stack
Of wood against the chimney back—
The oaken log, green, huge, and thick,
And on its top the stout backstick;
The knotty forestick laid apart,

from *Snowbound*   359

125 And filled between with curious art
The ragged brush; then, hovering near,
We watched the first red blaze appear,
Heard the sharp crackle, caught the gleam
On whitewashed wall and sagging beam,
130 Until the old, rude-furnished room
Burst, flowerlike, into rosy bloom;
While radiant with a mimic flame
Outside the sparkling drift became,
And through the bare-boughed lilac tree
135 Our own warm hearth seemed blazing free.
The crane and pendent trammels[9] showed,
The Turks' heads[10] on the andirons glowed;
While childish fancy, prompt to tell
The meaning of the miracle,
140 Whispered the old rhyme: "*Under the tree,*
When fire outdoors burns merrily,
There the witches are making tea."

The moon above the eastern wood
Shone at its full; the hill range stood
145 Transfigured in the silver flood,
Its blown snows flashing cold and keen,
Dead white, save where some sharp ravine
Took shadow, or the somber green
Of hemlocks turned to pitchy black
150 Against the whiteness at their back.
For such a world and such a night
Most fitting that unwarming light,
Which only seemed where'er it fell
To make the coldness visible.

155 Shut in from all the world without,
We sat the clean-winged hearth[11] about,
Content to let the north wind roar
In baffled rage at pane and door,
While the red logs before us beat
160 The frost line back with tropic heat;
And ever, when a louder blast
Shook beam and rafter as it passed,
The merrier up its roaring draft
The great throat of the chimney laughed;
165 The house dog on his paws outspread

---

9. trammels: Adjustable pothooks hanging from the movable arm, or crane, attached to the hearth.
10. Turks' heads: Turbanlike knots at the top of the andirons.
11. clean-winged hearth: A turkey wing was used for the hearth broom.

Laid to the fire his drowsy head,
The cat's dark silhouette on the wall
A couchant tiger's seemed to fall;
And, for the winter fireside meet,
170 Between the andirons' straddling feet,
The mug of cider simmered slow,
The apples sputtered in a row,
And, close at hand, the basket stood
With nuts from brown October's wood.

THINKING ABOUT THE SELECTION
Recalling

1. (a) What weather conditions forewarn the speaker of the approaching snowstorm? (b) How does the coming storm affect the family's nightly routine?
2. How long does the storm last?
3. (a) After the storm has ended, what does the speaker's father tell the boys to do? (b) How do the boys respond to the request?

Interpreting

4. What does the family's response to the coming of the storm suggest about their relationship with nature?
5. What descriptive details in lines 47–80 convey the speaker's sense of wonder and amazement upon viewing the snow-covered landscape?
6. What descriptive details in lines 93–115 convey a sense of solitude?
7. (a) What details in the final stanza convey a sense of warmth and security? (b) How do the details in lines 143–154 reinforce this?

Applying

8. Though for the most part snowstorms no longer isolate people as they did in Whittier's time, we sometimes experience a similar sense of isolation during power failures. In what ways do you think the response of today's families to a blackout is similar to and different from the family's response to their forced isolation in *Snowbound*?

ANALYZING LITERATURE
Understanding Imagery

Imagery appeals to one or more of the five senses. For example, when Whittier writes, "The sun . . . sank from sight beneath the smothering bank," he creates an image that appeals to your sense of sight.

Select three images in this excerpt from *Snowbound*. Explain to which sense each image appeals.

CRITICAL THINKING AND READING
Evaluating the Effect of Imagery

Because we all share the same capacity for physical sensations, imagery provides a natural link between the writer's observations, ideas, and experiences and our own imaginations. When used effectively, imagery allows us to picture each place and event the writer describes—even places and events unlike any we have actually seen. In *Snowbound,* for example, Whittier's imagery makes it possible for us to visualize his yard the morning after the snowstorm.

1. Explain what makes the imagery Whittier uses in describing the snowstorm effective.
2. Explain what makes the imagery used in describing the scene inside his house the night after the storm effective.

Hampton Beach

John Greenleaf Whittier

The sunlight glitters keen and bright,
   Where, miles away,
Lies stretching to my dazzled sight
A luminous belt, a misty light,
5 Beyond the dark pine bluffs and wastes of sandy gray.

The tremulous shadow of the sea!
   Against its ground
Of silvery light, rock, hill, and tree,
Still as a picture, clear and free,
10 With varying outline mark the coast for miles around.

On—on—we tread with loose-flung rein
   Our seaward way,
Through dark-green fields and blossoming grain,
Where the wild brier-rose skirts the lane,
15 And bends above our heads the flowering locust spray.

Ha! like a kind hand on my brow
   Comes this fresh breeze,
Cooling its dull and feverish glow,
While through my being seems to flow
20 The breath of a new life, the healing of the seas!

Now rest we, where this grassy mound
   His feet hath set
In the great waters, which have bound
His granite ankles greenly round
25 With long and tangled moss, and weeds with cool spray wet.

Good-bye to pain and care! I take
   Mine ease today:
Here where these sunny waters break,
And ripples this keen breeze, I shake
30 All burdens from the heart, all weary thoughts away.

I draw a freer breath, I seem
   Like all I see—
Waves in the sun, the white-winged gleam
Of sea birds in the slanting beam
35 And far-off sails which flit before the south wind free.

1. (a)
   he h
   he s
2. (a)
   does
   hear
   "sha
3. Wha
   etud
4. (a) V
   ing h
   him

Interpr

5. Wha
   vey
6. (a)
   spea
   ties
   How
   onen
7. (a) V
   dens
   to e
   mear
   wave
   Why
   him f
8. (a) V
   when
   asund
   spite
   event
9. Why
   stone
   his af

QUODDY HEAD
John Marin
Art Resource

EMILY DICKINSON

1830–1886

During her life, Emily Dickinson wrote at least 1,775 poems. Yet only seven of these were published—anonymously—in her lifetime. Dickinson was a private person, extremely reluctant to reveal herself and her work to the public. As a result, few people outside her family and small circle of friends were aware of her poetic genius until after her death. Today, however, she is generally regarded as one of the greatest American poets.

Dickinson was born in Amherst, Massachusetts, the daughter of a prominent lawyer. Though she traveled to Boston, Washington, and Philadelphia to visit friends when she was young, she rarely left her home town as she grew older. In fact, during the last ten years of her life, she refused to leave her house and garden. Her circle of friends grew smaller and smaller, and she communicated with her remaining friends mainly through notes and fragments of poems. She dressed only in white and would not allow her neighbors or any strangers to see her. When her health failed, she permitted her doctor to examine her only by observing her from a distance. In 1886, after fighting illness for two years, Dickinson died in the same house in which she was born.

Though she chose to live most of her life in virtual isolation, Emily Dickinson was a very intense, energetic person. Having a clear sense of purpose, she devoted most of her energy to her poetry. Yet, because she shared her work with few people, she sometimes doubted her abilities. In 1862 she sent four poems to Thomas Wentworth Higginson, an influential literary critic, and asked him to tell her if her verse was "alive." Like the editors who first published her work after her death, Higginson sought to change her unconventional style—her eccentric use of punctuation and her irregular use of meter and rhyme. He did not realize that Dickinson crafted her poetry with great precision and that her unique style was an important element of her poetry. Still, he did recognize her talent and encouraged her to keep writing.

The extent of Dickinson's talent was not widely recognized until 1955, when a complete, unedited edition of her poems was published. Viewing her work in its original form, writers and critics could see that Dickinson was unlike the other poets of her time. For the first time, Dickinson's unique style, her concrete imagery, and her simple but forceful language were appreciated. Dickinson's work was compared with that of the modern poets, and she was acknowledged as a poet who was truly ahead of her time.

"Hope" is the thing with feathers; There's a certain Slant of light; I like to see it lap the miles; A narrow Fellow in the Grass; I never saw a Moor; Tell all the Truth but tell it slant

Writer's Techniques

Style. Style refers to the manner in which a writer puts his or her ideas into words. It involves the characteristics that concern form of expression rather than the thoughts conveyed. In poetry, for example, style is determined by such factors as choice and arrangement of words, length and arrangement of lines, stanza length and format, use of punctuation and capitalization, and use of literary devices.

Emily Dickinson's unique style distinguishes her poetry from that of any other American poet. The most striking characteristics of her style are her unconventional use of punctuation and capitalization and the brevity of most of her lines and stanzas. Most of her poetry is written in quatrains, or four-line stanzas. In her quatrains she usually rhymes only the second and fourth lines, and she often uses slant rhymes, or partial rhymes—rhymes in which the final sounds of the words are similar but not identical. For the most part, she uses iambic rhythm—rhythm in which every second syllable is stressed—but she includes frequent variations in rhythm.

Another notable characteristic of Dickinson's style is her tendency to use figurative language—language that is not intended to be interpreted literally—to convey her ideas. Her use of figurative language adds depth to her poetry.

Look For

As you read Emily Dickinson's poetry, look for the characteristics of Dickinson's style.

Writing

Most people associate certain emotions with each of the four seasons. Freewrite about the emotions you associate with winter.

Vocabulary

Knowing the following words will help you as you read Emily Dickinson's poetry.

abash (ə bash′) v.: Make ashamed (p. 368, l. 7)

oppresses (ə pres′ əz) v.: Weighs heavily on the mind (p. 369, l. 3)

prodigious (prə dij′ əs) adj.: Wonderful (p. 370, l. 4)

supercilious (soo′ pər sil′ē əs) adj.: Disdainful (p. 370, l. 6)

docile (däs′ 'l) adj.: Obedient (p. 370, l. 15)

omnipotent (äm nip′ ə tənt) adj.: Having unlimited power or authority (p. 370, l. 15)

"Hope" is the thing with feathers—

Emily Dickinson

"Hope" is the thing with feathers—
That perches in the soul—
And sings the tune without the words—
And never stops—at all—

5   And sweetest—in the Gale—is heard—
And sore must be the storm—
That could abash the little Bird
That kept so many warm—

I've heard it in the chillest land—
10 And on the strangest Sea—
Yet, never, in Extremity,
It asked a crumb—of Me.

THINKING ABOUT THE SELECTION

Recalling

1. (a) According to the speaker, what "perches in the soul"? (b) What type of tune does it sing? (c) When does it stop singing?
2. (a) Name two places where the speaker has heard the "little Bird"? (b) What has the "little Bird" never done?

Interpreting

3. Throughout the poem Dickinson develops a comparison between hope and a "little Bird." What is the effect of this comparison?
4. (a) What qualities does the "little Bird" possess? (b) What does this suggest about the characteristics of hope?
5. In what way do the final two lines suggest that hope is something that we cannot consciously control?
6. What does this poem suggest about the human ability to endure hardships?

Applying

7. (a) What does hope mean to you? (b) In what situations do you think of hope?

There's a certain Slant of light,

Emily Dickinson

FEBRUARY 1890–1900
John Henry Twachtman
Museum of Fine Arts, Boston

> There's a certain Slant of light,
> Winter Afternoons—
> That oppresses, like the Heft
> Of Cathedral Tunes—
>
> 5 Heavenly Hurt, it gives us—
> We can find no scar,
> But internal difference,
> Where the Meanings, are—
>
> None may teach it—Any—
> 10 'Tis the Seal Despair—
> An imperial affliction
> Sent us of the Air—
>
> When it comes, the Landscape listens—
> Shadows—hold their breath—
> 15 When it goes, 'tis like the Distance
> On the look of Death—

THINKING ABOUT THE SELECTION

Recalling

1. (a) When does the "certain Slant of light" come? (b) What does it do? (c) What does it give us?
2. (a) What may none teach? (b) What is "the Seal Despair"?
3. (a) What does the landscape do when the "Slant of light" comes? (b) What do the shadows do?
4. What is the situation when the "Slant of light" goes?

Interpreting

5. (a) What mood does the "Slant of light" create? (b) What does it seem to represent to the speaker?

6. (a) What is paradoxical, or self-contradictory, about Dickinson's reference to "Heavenly Hurt" (line 5)? (b) How does this paradox suggest that suffering is precious as well as painful?
7. What does the third stanza suggest about the source of despair?
8. In the final stanza, Dickinson suggests that despair makes us more aware of our spiritual relationship with the natural world. What do the final two lines suggest about the connection between despair and our awareness of our own mortality?

Applying

9. Why do you think that weather conditions have such a powerful effect on our moods?

I like to see it lap the miles,

Emily Dickinson

I like to see it lap the miles,
And lick the valleys up,
And stop to feed itself at tanks;
And then, prodigious, step

5   Around a pile of mountains,
And, supercilious, peer
In shanties by the sides of roads;
And then a quarry pare

To fit its sides, and crawl between,
10 Complaining all the while
In horrid, hooting stanza;
Then chase itself down hill

And neigh like Boanerges;[1]
Then, prompter than a star,
15 Stop—docile and omnipotent—
At its own stable door.

---

1. Boanerges (bō′ ə ner′ jēz): A loud, forceful preacher.

AMERICAN RAILROAD SCENE
Currier and Ives
Three Lions

THINKING ABOUT THE SELECTION

Recalling

1. (a) What does "it" do to the valleys? (b) Where does it stop to feed itself? (c) What does it peer into? (d) What does it "chase itself down"? (e) Where does it stop?

Interpreting

2. In this poem Dickinson develops an implied comparison between a railroad train and a horse. With what words and images does Dickinson reveal this comparison?

3. What human qualities are attributed to the train in the second and third stanzas?
4. What does the description of the train as "docile and omnipotent" suggest?
5. (a) What seems to be Dickinson's attitude toward the train? (b) What does this suggest about her attitude toward industrialization?

Applying

6. Considering the attitude she expresses in this poem, how do you think Dickinson would have reacted to the numerous technological advances that have occurred since her death?

I like to see it lap the miles 371

WILDLIFE AND VEGETATION OF A HEDGEROW
Drawing by Peter Barrett
The Sunday Times, The Sunday Times
Magazine, 6 August, 1978

A narrow Fellow in the Grass

Emily Dickinson

A narrow Fellow in the Grass
Occasionally rides—
You may have met Him—did you not
His notice sudden is—

5 The Grass divides as with a Comb—
A spotted shaft is seen—
And then it closes at your feet
And opens further on—

He likes a Boggy Acre
10 A Floor too cool for Corn—
Yet when a Boy, and Barefoot—
I more than once at Noon

Have passed, I thought, a Whip lash
Unbraiding in the Sun
15 When stooping to secure it
It wrinkled, and was gone—

Several of Nature's People
I know, and they know me—
I feel for them a transport
20 Of cordiality—

But never met this Fellow
Attended, or alone
Without a tighter breathing
And Zero at the Bone—

THINKING ABOUT THE SELECTION

Recalling

1. How does the grass divide when the "narrow Fellow" moves through it?
2. What does the narrow fellow like?
3. What happens when the speaker tries to catch the narrow fellow?
4. What happens each time the speaker meets the narrow fellow?

Interpreting

5. (a) What is the narrow fellow? (b) Why do you think Dickinson does not name her subject?
6. In line 11 Dickinson indicates that the speaker of the poem is a boy. Why do you think she uses a male speaker?
7. What is the speaker's attitude toward the narrow fellow?

Applying

8. (a) What is your own attitude toward the subject of the poem? (b) Explain why you do or do not think most other people share your attitude.

ANALYZING LITERATURE

Understanding Style

Style refers to the way in which a writer expresses his or her thoughts. Though writers often write about similar subjects, each writer has his or her own distinctive style. As a result, we can often distinguish the work of different writers by examining style. For example, we can easily identify Emily Dickinson's poetry once we are familiar with some of the unique characteristics of her style.

1. What is unusual about Dickinson's use of punctuation?
2. What is unusual about her use of capitalization?
3. What are two other characteristics of her style revealed in this poem?

NEAR HARLECH, NORTH WALES
Benjamin William Leader
Bridgeman-Art Resource

I never saw a Moor—

Emily Dickinson

I never saw a Moor—
I never saw the Sea—
Yet know I how the Heather looks
And what a Billow[1] be.

5 I never spoke with God
Nor visited in Heaven—
Yet certain am I of the spot
As if the Checks[2] were given—

---

1. Billow: Large wave.
2. Checks: Colored seat checks indicating the
destinations of passengers on a train after their
tickets have been collected.

THINKING ABOUT THE SELECTION
Recalling

1. (a) What two things has the speaker never
   seen? (b) What does she know in spite of
   never having seen them?
2. (a) With whom has the speaker never
   spoken? (b) Where has she never visited? (c) Of what is she certain?

Interpreting

3. (a) How might the speaker have acquired the
   knowledge she claims to possess in the first
   stanza? (b) In what way is the knowledge
   presented in the second stanza different from
   that of the first stanza? (c) How might she
   have acquired the knowledge presented in
   the second stanza?
4. How does the information in the first stanza
   affect your reaction to the second stanza?

Applying

5. What things do you think you know through
   intuition rather than through experience?

Tell all the Truth but tell it slant—

Emily Dickinson

Tell all the Truth but tell it slant—
Success in Circuit lies
Too bright for our infirm Delight
The Truth's superb surprise
5 As Lightning to the Children eased
With explanation kind
The Truth must dazzle gradually
Or every man be blind—

THINKING ABOUT THE SELECTION

Recalling

1. According to the speaker, what is "too bright for our infirm Delight"?
2. Why must the Truth "dazzle gradually"?

Interpreting

3. What does Dickinson mean when she tells us to "tell all the Truth but tell it slant"?

4. To what type of "Truth" do you think Dickinson is referring?

Applying

5. To what types of truths do you think people have to be led gradually? Explain your answer.

Success is counted sweetest; I felt a Funeral, in my Brain; I heard a Fly buzz—when I died; Because I could not stop for Death; My life closed twice before its close; The Bustle in a House

Writer's Techniques

Theme. A theme is the central idea or insight into life that a writer conveys in a work of literature. In some literary works, the theme is directly stated. More often, however, the theme is implied, or revealed indirectly. In poetry, theme is often implied through figurative language—language that is not meant to be interpreted literally. It is important to look beyond the literal meaning of the words in a poem and try to determine their underlying, or hidden, meaning.

Look For

As you read Emily Dickinson's poetry, try to determine the theme of each poem.

Writing

One of Dickinson's poems is about success. What does success mean to you? Write your definition of success. Then suggest other views that people might hold about success.

Vocabulary

Knowing the following words will help you as you read Emily Dickinson's poetry.

gossamer (gäs′ ə mər) *n.*: A very thin, soft, filmy cloth (p. 380, l. 15)

cornice (kôr′ nis) *n.*: The projecting decorative molding along the top of a building (p. 380, l. 20)

surmised (sər mīzd′) *v.*: Guessed (p. 380, l. 23)

Success is counted sweetest

Emily Dickinson

Success is counted sweetest
By those who ne'er succeed.
To comprehend a nectar
Requires sorest need.

5   Not one of all the purple Host
Who took the Flag today
Can tell the definition
So clear of Victory

As he defeated—dying—
10 On whose forbidden ear
The distant strains of triumph
Burst agonized and clear!

THINKING ABOUT THE SELECTION

Recalling

1. (a) By whom is success "counted sweetest"? (b) What is required "to comprehend a nectar"?
2. For whom do the "distant strains of triumph burst agonized and clear"?

Interpreting

3. What does the "nectar" in line 3 represent?
4. In what way is the ear of the defeated man "forbidden" in line 10?
5. How do the descriptions of victorious and defeated soldiers in the second and third stanzas support the generalization made in the first two lines?
6. (a) What point does the poem make about failure? (b) What point does it make about our ability to comprehend success?

Applying

7. Explain why you do or do not agree with the points that the poem makes about success and failure.

I felt a Funeral, in my Brain,

Emily Dickinson

I felt a Funeral, in my Brain,
And Mourners to and fro
Kept treading—treading—till it seemed
That Sense was breaking through—

5   And when they all were seated,
A Service, like a Drum—
Kept beating—beating—till I thought
My Mind was going numb—

And then I heard them lift a Box
10 And creak across my Soul
With those same Boots of Lead, again,
Then Space—began to toll,

As all the Heavens were a Bell,
And Being, but an Ear,
15 And I, and Silence, some strange Race
Wrecked, solitary, here—

And then a Plank in Reason, broke,
And I dropped down, and down—
And hit a World, at every plunge,
20 And Finished knowing—then—

THINKING ABOUT THE SELECTION

Recalling

1. What does the speaker feel in her brain?
2. What keeps "beating" until she thinks her mind is going numb?
3. What begins "to toll" in the third stanza?
4. (a) What breaks in the final stanza? (b) What does the speaker do when it breaks?

Interpreting

5. (a) What do you think the mourners might represent? (b) How do the images in the second and third stanzas convey the speaker's growing sense of despair? (c) How do the images in the fourth stanza convey the speaker's sense of isolation?

Applying

6. Many of Emily Dickinson's poems grew out of reactions to events in her personal life. What type of event do you think might have led her to write this poem?

I heard a Fly buzz— when I died—

Emily Dickinson

I heard a Fly buzz—when I died—
The Stillness in the Room
Was like the Stillness in the Air—
Between the Heaves of Storm—

5   The Eyes around—had wrung them dry—
And Breaths were gathering firm
For that last Onset—when the King
Be witnessed—in the Room—

I willed my Keepsakes—Signed away
10 What portion of me be
Assignable—and then it was
There interposed a Fly—

With Blue—uncertain stumbling Buzz—
Between the light—and me—
15 And then the Windows failed—and then
I could not see to see—

ROOM WITH A BALCONY
Adolph von Menzel
Staatliche Museen Preubischer Kulturbesitz, Nationgalerie, Berlin (West)

THINKING ABOUT THE SELECTION

Recalling

1. (a) What does the speaker hear? (b) When does she hear it?
2. To what does the speaker compare the stillness in the room?
3. For what were breaths gathering firm in the second stanza?
4. What does the speaker sign away in the third stanza?
5. According to the final stanza, what happens when the windows fail?

Interpreting

6. Why does the buzzing of the fly heighten the speaker's awareness of the stillness and tension in the room?
7. (a) What does the speaker's attitude toward death seem to be? (b) How is this attitude reflected in her awareness of the fly?

Applying

8. Explain how Dickinson's attitude toward death is similar to and different from the attitude of another writer whose work you have read.

Because I could not stop for Death—

Emily Dickinson

Because I could not stop for Death—
He kindly stopped for me—
The Carriage held but just Ourselves—
And Immortality.

5   We slowly drove—He knew no haste
And I had put away
My labor and my leisure too,
For His Civility—

We passed the School, where Children strove
10   At Recess—in the Ring—
We passed the Fields of Gazing Grain—
We passed the Setting Sun—

Or rather—He passed Us—
The Dews drew quivering and chill—
15   For only Gossamer, my Gown—
My Tippet[1]—only Tulle[2]—

We paused before a House that seemed
A Swelling of the Ground—
The Roof was scarcely visible—
20   The Cornice—in the Ground—

Since then—'tis Centuries—and yet
Feels shorter than the Day
I first surmised the Horses Heads
Were toward Eternity—

---

1. Tippet: A scarflike garment worn over the shoulders and hanging down in front.
2. Tulle (tool) *n.*: A thin, fine netting used for scarves.

WAITING OUTSIDE NO. 12
Anonymous
Crane Kalman Gallery

THINKING ABOUT THE SELECTION

Recalling

1. (a) Explain why Death stops for the speaker. (b) What does Death's carriage hold?
2. What does the speaker "put away" in the second stanza?
3. (a) In the third stanza, what three things does the carriage pass? (b) Where does the carriage pause in the fifth stanza?
4. How long has it been since Death stopped for the speaker?

Interpreting

5. (a) How is Death portrayed in the first two stanzas? (b) What is ironic about this portrayal?
6. What stages of the speaker's life might be represented by the three things the carriage passes in the third stanza?
7. How does the speaker's attitude toward Death seem to change in the fourth stanza?
8. (a) What does the "House" in the fifth stanza represent? (b) Why do they pause there?
9. How does Death affect the speaker's conception of time?

Applying

10. What does Dickinson's interest in Death indicate about her?

My life closed twice before its close—

Emily Dickinson

My life closed twice before its close—
It yet remains to see
If Immortality unveil
A third event to me,

5   So huge, so hopeless to conceive
As these that twice befell.
Parting is all we know of heaven,
And all we need of hell.

THINKING ABOUT THE SELECTION

Recalling

1. (a) What has happened twice to the speaker? (b) What remains to be seen?
2. How does the speaker describe parting in the second stanza?

Interpreting

3. (a) What type of events caused the speaker's life to close "twice before its close"? (b) In what line is the nature of these events revealed?

4. (a) What is the "third event" to which the speaker refers? (b) How is this related to the first two events?
5. (a) What is paradoxical, or self-contradictory, about Dickinson's description of parting? (b) How do you explain this paradox?

Applying

6. (a) What is your own response to the departure of close friends? (b) In what ways is your own response similar to and different from Dickinson's response?

The Bustle in a House

Emily Dickinson

The Bustle in a House
The Morning after Death
Is solemnest of industries
Enacted upon Earth—

5   The Sweeping up the Heart
And putting Love away
We shall not want to use again
Until Eternity.

THINKING ABOUT THE SELECTION

Recalling

1. According to the speaker, what "is solemnest of industries/Enacted upon Earth"?
2. What shall we "not want to use again/Until Eternity"?

Interpreting

3. What does the first stanza indicate about people's attempts to subdue the grief that results from the death of a loved one?
4. (a) What does the speaker compare with house cleaning in the second stanza? (b) What makes this different from cleaning? (c) Is Dickinson's metaphor effective? Why or why not?
5. What do the last two lines suggest about Dickinson's belief in immortality?

Applying

6. It has been claimed that the true beginnings of modern American poetry can be traced to Emily Dickinson and Walt Whitman. Explain how Dickinson's poems are similar to and different from the modern and contemporary poems you have read.

THINKING AND WRITING

Responding to Criticism

A critic has stated that Emily Dickinson's poetry "is exploration on a variety of levels of the ultimate meaning of life itself and equally important of the depths and heights of her own inner nature." Using evidence from the poems you have just read, write an essay supporting this statement. Reread the poems, looking for evidence to support the critic's comment. Organize your notes into an outline, then write your essay. When you finish writing, revise and proofread your essay.

Much Madness is divinest Sense; As imperceptibly as grief; The Soul selects her own Society; How happy is the little Stone; There is a solitude of space; This is my letter to the World

Writer's Techniques

Simile and Metaphor. A simile is an explicit comparison between two seemingly dissimilar things. In a simile the comparison is clearly indicated by either *like* or *as*. For example, the word *like* signals the similarity in the sound of rain and a heartbeat in the following simile: The sound of the rain gently falling on the pavement echoed through the air *like* thousands of tiny heartbeats.

A metaphor is also a comparison between two apparently different things. In a metaphor, however, the comparison is implied rather than stated. A metaphor allows us not only to think that two dissimilar things are in some way alike but to pretend that one thing actually *is* something totally different. For example, the metaphor in Emily Dickinson's poem "Hope is the thing with feathers," leads us not only to see the similarities between a bird and hope but to imagine that hope *is* a bird.

Similes and metaphors enable us to visualize connections that our senses may not be able to perceive. By making it possible for us to relate our inner selves to the outer world, they allow us to visualize abstract concepts such as emotions and enable us to understand the external world in human terms.

Look For

As you read these poems, look for the similes and metaphors.

Writing

Prepare a list of descriptive details and emotions that you associate with the end of summer.

Vocabulary

Knowing the following words will help you as you read Emily Dickinson's poetry.

assent (ə sent′) *v.:* Agree (p. 385, l. 6)

demur (di mʉr′) *v.:* Object (p. 385, l. 7)

perfidy (pʉr′ fə dē) *n.:* Treachery (p. 386, l. 4)

sequestered (si kwes′ tərd) *v.:* Withdrawn; secluded (p. 386, l. 8)

harrowing (har′ ō iŋ) *v.:* Distressing (p. 386, l. 11)

exigencies (ek′ sə jən sēz) *n.:* Pressing needs; demands (p. 388, l. 4)

finite (fī′ nīt) *adj.:* Having measurable or definable limits (p. 389, l. 8)

Much Madness is divinest Sense—

Emily Dickinson

Much Madness is divinest Sense—
To a discerning Eye—
Much Sense—the starkest Madness—
'Tis the Majority
5   In this, as All, prevail—
Assent—and you are sane—
Demur—you're straightway dangerous—
And handled with a Chain—

THINKING ABOUT THE SELECTION

Recalling

1. (a) According to the speaker, what is "divinest Sense"? (b) What is "the starkest Madness"?
2. (a) According to the speaker, how are you judged if you assent? (b) What happens if you demur?

Interpreting

3. (a) What is paradoxical, or self-contradictory, about the first line? (b) How can this paradox be true?
4. (a) According to the speaker, how does society define sanity? (b) How does it define madness?
5. (a) What is the speaker's attitude toward individuality? (b) What is the speaker's attitude toward society?

Applying

6. In this poem Dickinson suggests that our own perceptions can be shaped by the perceptions of others. Explain how this may be so.
7. The contemporary poet Theodore Roethke wrote, "What's madness but Divinest sense at odds with circumstance?" Compare Roethke's words with the theme of Dickinson's poem.

As imperceptibly as grief

Emily Dickinson

As imperceptibly as grief
The summer lapsed away,—
Too imperceptible, at last,
To seem like perfidy.

5 A quietness distilled,
As twilight long begun,
Or Nature, spending with herself
Sequestered afternoon.

The dusk drew earlier in,
10 The morning foreign shone,—
A courteous, yet harrowing grace,
As guest that would be gone.

And thus, without a wing,
Or service of a keel,
15 Our summer made her light escape
Into the beautiful.

THINKING ABOUT THE SELECTION

Recalling

1. What lapses away "as imperceptibly as grief"?

Interpreting

2. How would you describe the mood?
3. What do you think is the meaning of the final two lines?

Applying

4. (a) How are you affected by the passing of summer? (b) What changes do you associate with it?

ANALYZING LITERATURE
Understanding Metaphors and Similes

Both **similes** and **metaphors** are comparisons between two seemingly dissimilar things.
1. (a) Find two similes in "As imperceptibly as grief." (b) What two qualities are being compared in each simile?
2. Each of the similes contributes to the development of a metaphor that extends throughout the entire poem. (a) What two things are being compared in this metaphor? (b) What details in the second and third stanzas develop this comparison?
3. How does this metaphor relate the inner self to the outer world?

The Soul selects her own society—

Emily Dickinson

The Soul selects her own Society—
Then—shuts the Door—
To her divine Majority—
Present no more—

5   Unmoved—she notes the Chariots—pausing—
At her low Gate—
Unmoved—an Emperor be kneeling
Upon her Mat—

I've known her—from an ample nation—
10   Choose One—
Then—close the Valves of her attention—
Like Stone—

PROGRESS
Asher B. Durand
The Warner Collection of Gulf States Paper Corp, Tuscaloosa, Alabama

---

THINKING ABOUT THE SELECTION

Recalling

1. According to the first stanza, what does the soul select?
2. What two things leave the soul unmoved in the second stanza?
3. (a) What does the soul choose in the third stanza? (b) What does the soul do after making this choice?

Interpreting

4. (a) What is the soul's "divine Majority"? (b) Of how many people does the soul's "Society" actually consist?
5. How would you describe the soul's attitude toward the rest of the world?
6. What does line 9 suggest about the speaker's relationship to the soul?

Applying

7. In real life people select a wide variety of different "societies." List as many as you can. What do you think this tendency indicates about human nature?

How happy is the little Stone

Emily Dickinson

How happy is the little Stone
That rambles in the Road alone,
And doesn't care about Careers
And Exigencies never fears—
5 Whose Coat of elemental Brown
A passing Universe put on,
And independent as the Sun
Associates or glows alone,
Fulfilling absolute Decree
10 In casual simplicity—

THINKING ABOUT THE SELECTION

Recalling

1. (a) Where does the little stone ramble? (b) What does it not care about? (c) What does it fulfill?

Interpreting

2. In this poem the speaker sees the little stone as a model for humanity's spiritual self-sufficiency. (a) What human qualities does she attribute to the stone? (b) Why do these qualities make it an appropriate model?

Applying

3. What other elements of the natural world do you think could serve as models for human behavior? Explain your choices.

There is a solitude of space

Emily Dickinson

There is a solitude of space
A solitude of sea
A solitude of death, but these
Society shall be
5 Compared with that profounder site
That polar privacy
A soul admitted to itself—
Finite Infinity.

GENESEE SCENERY
Thomas Cole
Museum of Art, Rhode Island School of Design

THINKING ABOUT THE SELECTION

Recalling

1. What three forms of solitude does the speaker mention in the first three lines?
2. What "profounder site" does the speaker describe in lines 6–7?

Interpreting

3. (a) What do you think the speaker means by "a soul admitted to itself"? (b) What makes this concept different from the three forms of solitude mentioned in the first three lines? (c) How does it relate to the paradox, or apparent contradiction, presented in the final line?

Applying

4. Explain how it is possible for a person to live in solitude while surrounded by other people.

This is my letter to the World

Emily Dickinson

This is my letter to the World
That never wrote to Me—
The simple News that Nature told—
With tender Majesty

5   Her Message is committed
To Hands I cannot see—
For love of Her—Sweet—countrymen—
Judge tenderly—of Me

TWILIGHT IN THE WILDERNESS
Frederick E. Church
The Cleveland Museum of Art

THINKING ABOUT THE SELECTION

Recalling

1. To whom does the speaker address her letter?
2. What request does the speaker make in the final line?

Interpreting

3. In this poem Dickinson addresses the potential audience of her poetry. What evidence in the poem suggests that she does not expect this audience to read her poetry until after her death?
4. How does Dickinson convey her sense of isolation from the rest of the world?
5. To what does Dickinson give credit for providing the material for her poetry?
6. How does Dickinson indicate that she believes her purpose should be taken into consideration when her poetry is judged?

Applying

7. Explain whether this poem would be an appropriate introduction to a collection of Dickinson's poetry.

THINKING AND WRITING

Responding to Dickinson's Poetry

Respond to Dickinson's letter to the world by writing a letter to her in which you express your personal reactions to her poetry. Review her poems and record your response to them. Then think about your reaction to her poetry. How does it affect you emotionally? Do you find it difficult to understand? If so, why? Do you find that it helps you to understand yourself? Start your letter by summing up your reaction. Then support your reactions with specific examples from several of her poems. When you finish writing, revise your letter and prepare a final copy.

YOU THE WRITER

Assignment

1. Imagine that you are a Transcendentalist living during the New England Renaissance. Like Thoreau, you have decided to test your beliefs by living in the wilderness. Write a series of five journal entries in which you describe the types of experiences you would expect to have in this situation.

    Prewriting. Brainstorm about the types of experiences you might have in the wilderness. How would you react to these experiences? What insights might you gain from the experiences?

    Writing. When you write your journal entries, use concrete details in describing your experiences. Make sure you convey what you have gained from the experiences.

    Revising. When you revise, make sure you have described your experiences and expressed your ideas clearly and coherently.

Assignment

2. In the tradition of the Fireside Poets, write a lyric poem that would have appealed to a family audience during the New England Renaissance. Your lyric should be inspiring and easy to read and should focus on one of the following themes: love, nature, home and family, or patriotism.

    Prewriting. Choose a subject for your poem. Then prepare a list of concrete details related to this subject.

    Writing. When writing your lyric, have your speaker express his or her thoughts and feelings about the subject. Use a regular rhythm and follow a regular rhyme scheme.

    Revising. When you revise, make sure you have used concrete imagery in expressing your ideas. After you have finished revising, share your poem with your classmates.

Assignment

3. As you have learned in this unit, there was a sharp contrast between the ideas of the Transcendentalists and those of the Anti-Transcendentalists. Write a dialogue in which one of the Transcendentalists and one of the Anti-Transcendentalists discuss their different philosophies.

    Prewriting. Review the discussion of the philosophies of Transcendentalism and Anti-Transcendentalism in the unit introduction (p. 240) and in the Guides for Reading on pages 267 and 293, paying close attention to the differences in the two philosophies.

    Writing. Try to make your dialogue seem realistic, as if you were merely recording a conversation that really occurred.

    Revising. When you revise, make sure you have clearly expressed the dominant ideas of both philosophies. After you have finished revising, proofread your dialogue and prepare a final copy.

Assignment

1. Although the Fireside Poets shared a common purpose, the poems they created were often quite different from one another. Write an essay in which you compare and contrast two poems by two different Fireside Poets.

Prewriting. Review the poetry of the Fireside Poets, and choose two poems that are in some ways similar and in some way different from each other. Then reread the poems, noting the similarities and differences.

Writing. Organize your essay according to corresponding points of contrast, using passages from each poem to support your argument.

Revising. When you revise, make sure you have used transitions and other linking devices to connect your ideas. After you have finished revising, proofread your essay and prepare a final copy.

Assignment

2. As the world changes, popular philosophies or views of life sometimes become outdated. Which philosophy do you think is more applicable to contemporary life: that of the Transcendentalists or that of the Anti-Transcendentalists?

Prewriting. Review the discussion of the philosophies of Transcendentalism and Anti-Transcendentalism in the unit introduction. Then spend some time thinking about how effectively each philosophy can be applied to contemporary life.

Writing. When writing your essay, make sure you thoroughly support your opinion with facts and examples.

Revising. When you revise, make sure you have expressed your ideas clearly and coherently.

Assignment

3. While the Transcendentalists, the Anti-Transcendentalists, and the Fireside Poets had very different philosophies and concerns, they were all part of the Romantic movement that began in the early 1800's. Write an essay in which you discuss the Romantic attitudes and interests reflected in the works of the writers involved with one of the three movements of the New England Renaissance.

Prewriting. Review the discussion of Romanticism in the introduction to the Growing Nation unit. Then reread one group of selections in this unit, noting the Romantic ideas and interests they reflect.

Writing. When you write your essay, use evidence from several works to support your argument.

Revising. When you revise, make sure you have thoroughly supported your argument. Proofread your essay and prepare a final draft.

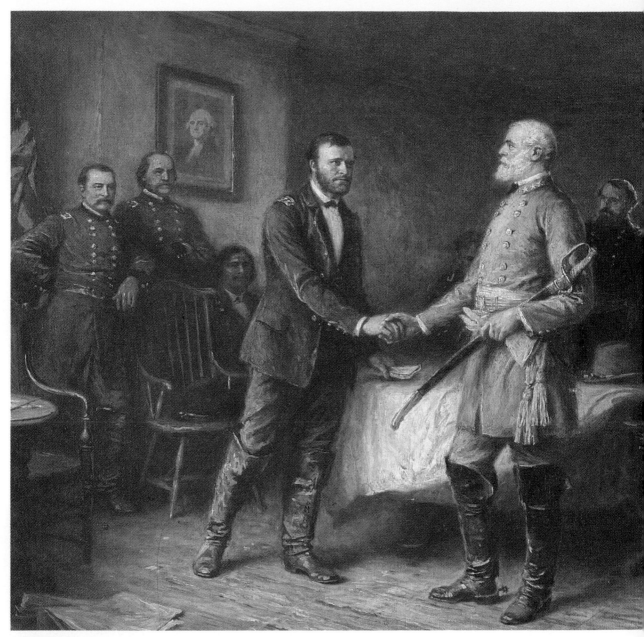

LET US HAVE PEACE (GRANT AND LEE)
J. L. G. Ferris
Three Lions

DIVISION, WAR, AND RECONCILIATION
1855–1865

Skimming lightly, wheeling still,
The swallows fly low
Over the fields in clouded days,
The forest-field of Shiloh—
Herman Melville

The Civil War moved Herman Melville to write a volume of sensitive poetry that treated incidents of the war in a quiet, mournful tone. His poem about the Battle of Shiloh is called, "A Requiem," since it was written to honor the soldiers who had died there. The battle, fought in western Tennessee in April 1862, was one of the bloodiest contests of the American Civil War. With more than 10,000 casualties on each side, Shiloh was a decisive event. It proved that the war, begun the previous spring with cheering, flag waving, and brave rhetoric, would be a long and bitter struggle.

Like the Revolution before it, the Civil War, or the War Between the States, absorbed the creative energies of the nation. Notable speeches, songs, letters, memoirs, and journals appeared, but little in the way of memorable fiction. Many writers became involved with the war, and some of the most important wartime literature was produced by the leaders from both sides. One towering literary figure did emerge during the wartime era, however—the poet Walt Whitman.

THE HISTORICAL SETTING

Opposition to slavery did not begin with the Civil War. Thomas Jefferson's first draft of the Declaration of Independence described the slave trade as a "cruel war against human nature itself, violating its most sacred rights of life and liberty." This language did not find its way into the final document, however. Slavery eventually disappeared in the North, where it had never been very profitable. In the South, however, slavery became the foundation of the plantation system.

The Missouri Compromise in 1820 and the Compromise of 1850 held off confrontations between slave states and free states for many years. But nothing short of secession from the Union (which the South often threatened) or freedom for the slaves (which many in the North demanded) could finally end the controversy. The northern and southern states entered the 1850's on a collision course. Would the new territories in the West enter the Union as free states or as slave states? Walt Whitman later saw this continuing conflict not as a "struggle between two distinct and separate peoples" but rather as one between "the passions and paradoxes" within the United States.

Passions and Paradoxes

The North and South had clearly developed along very different lines. In the North, commerce, not cotton, was king. The Industrial Revolution and cheap transportation had helped turn northern towns and cities into centers of bustling activity. Education, banking, science, and reform movements—all were topics of interest and concern. Immigration, too, was changing the face of the North. A rising tide of Irish and Germans, among others, were seeking a new life in the United States. Most of these newcomers landed at seaports between Boston and Baltimore and settled in the northern states.

The South, by contrast, was a slower-paced region of plantations and small farms. There were cities, to be sure, but the area was most truly defined by its cotton plantations, large and small. Sugar, rice, and tobacco were also important crops. The march of technological progress, with its hotly debated social issues and problems, had little impact on the prewar South.

One issue, however, made an indelible impression. That issue was slavery. The South believed its lifeblood to depend on the "peculiar institution" of slavery. Statesmen might make tactical compromises on such matters as free states or slave states being carved from the new territories, but there could be no compromise on the legality of slavery.

Firebrands on the other side of the issue, mostly northerners, were just as adamant. William Lloyd Garrison published an aboli-

A RIDE FOR LIBERTY—THE FUGITIVE SLAVES, 1862
Eastman Johnson
Brooklyn Museum

AMERICAN EVENTS

1855   **Walt Whitman** publishes first edition of *Leaves of Grass*.

My Bondage and My Freedon, **Frederick Douglass's** second autobiograpy, makes its appearance.

1858   **Oliver Wendell Holmes** publishes *The Autocrat of the Breakfast Table*.

Lincoln-Douglas debates help to make **Abraham Lincoln** a national figure.

1859   John Brown, radical abolitionist, raids federal arsenal at Harpers Ferry; he is hanged for treason.

1860   Essays by **Ralph Waldo Emerson** published as *The Conduct of Life*.

Henry Timrod's *Poems* appears; his only collection published during his lifetime.

1861   **Lincoln** inaugurated in March; Civil War begins in April with firing on Fort Sumter.

1862   **Emily Dickinson** writes many superb poems in what, for unknown reasons, is a crucial year for her.

Major battles are fought at Shiloh, Antietam, and Fredericksburg.

Julia Ward Howe writes "The Battle Hymn of the Republic."

After Antietam, **Lincoln** issues the Emancipation Proclamation.

1863   Union forces lose at Chancellorsville, but win at Gettysburg and Vicksburg.

1864   War nears an end with battles of the Wilderness, Atlanta, and Nashville.

1865   **General Robert E. Lee** surrenders to General Ulysses S. Grant at Appomattox Court House.

Within days of Lee's surrender, **President Lincoln** is assassinated.

Bombardment of Fort Sumter

Charles Darwin

Sepoy Rebellion

Battle of the Wilderness

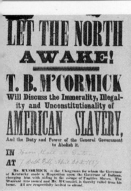

Abolitionist Poster

Frederick Douglass

John Brown

Emancipation Proclamation

The Surrender at Appomattox

1855   England: Alfred, Lord Tennyson publishes his long poem *Maud*.

1856   England: Bessemer steel process makes modern steelmaking possible.

1857   France: Gustave Flaubert completes *Madame Bovary*, classic novel of realism.

      India: Start of doomed Sepoy Rebellion; native soliders fight British rule.

1859   England: Charles Darwin introduces theory of evolution in *Origin of Species*.

      England: Charles Dickens adds to his fame with *A Tale of Two Cities*.

1860   England: Florence Nightingale founds Nightingale School for training nurses.

1861   England: George Eliot (Mary Ann Evans) publishes her popular novel *Silas Marner*.

      Italy: Unification of Italy achieved; Count Camillo Cavour led movement.

1862   France: Louis Pasteur proposes modern germ theory of disease.

      Russia: Ivan Turgenev publishes *Fathers and Sons*, his masterpiece.

1863   Mexico: French occupy Mexico City and establish Maximilian as emperor of Mexico.

      France: Jean François Millet paints *The Man with the Hoe*.

1864   England: *Dramatis Personae* by Robert Browning appears; it includes the poem "Prospice."

1865   England: Lewis Carroll completes *Alice's Adventures in Wonderland*.

tionist weekly, *The Liberator,* that demanded immediate, uncompensated freedom for all slaves. His first issue proclaimed: "I am in earnest—I will not equivocate—I will not excuse—I will not retreat a single inch—*and I will be heard*." Few people in the antislavery movement were as extreme as Garrison. Their basic goal was, nonetheless, unacceptable to most southerners.

The controversy between North and South came to a head in 1860. In that year, Abraham Lincoln was elected President of the United States in a bitter four-way race. Lincoln had once said, "If slavery is not wrong, nothing is wrong." The national paradoxes and passions that Walt Whitman observed could no longer be contained by compromise.

The Union Is Dissolved

Even before Lincoln was inaugurated, the legislature of South Carolina had declared unanimously that "the union now subsisting between South Carolina and other States . . . is hereby dissolved." Other southern states soon followed South Carolina's lead. In February 1861, delegates from seven states met in Montgomery, Alabama, to establish the Confederate States of America.

Some northerners were willing to accept secession, but President Lincoln was not. Once he had made his position clear, war seemed inevitable. The fighting began on April 12, 1861, when Confederate artillery fired on Union troops holding Fort Sumter, in Charleston Harbor. Three days later, Lincoln issued a call for 75,000 Union volunteers to put down the rebellion. Two days after that, Virginia seceded from the Union, its militia seized the United States naval yard at Norfolk. The Civil War was on.

Most people in the North expected the Union to win a quick, decisive victory over the Confederacy. It was not to be. Even with the North's formidable economic, industrial, and numerical advantages, four years of war lay ahead. The South's one main advantage over the Union was its superior military leadership. In the end, however, not even the incomparable General Robert E. Lee could prevail against the much larger Union force under General Ulysses S. Grant. Battles raged as far north as Pennsylvania, as far south as Georgia and Florida, and throughout the Mississippi Valley. The names of the major battles are carved on countless Civil War monuments across the United States: Bull Run, Fort Donelson, Shiloh, Antietam, Fredericksburg, Chancellorsville, Gettysburg, Vicksburg, Chattanooga, Atlanta, Petersburg, and, finally, Appomattox Court House.

The Civil War was the first American war in which black troops fought in large numbers. By the end of the war, there were some 180,000 black soldiers in more than a hundred Union regiments. On the Confederate side, both slaves and free blacks accompanied the army as cooks, teamsters, and laborers. A few native American

TIDINGS FROM THE FRONT
Gilbert Gaul
Three Lions

regiments served the Union cause on the frontier. Women's contributions to the war effort, North and South, were monumental. Clara Barton, organizer of the American Red Cross, became known as the "Angel of the Battlefield" for her tireless work as a nurse in army camps and hospitals.

The war finally ended in 1865, when General Lee surrendered to General Grant at Appomattox. Although the nation was reunited, deep wounds had been opened that would take decades to heal. Unfortunately, the nation's unity had to be restored without the leadership of President Lincoln. Lincoln was assassinated on the eve of the final victory.

FAITHFUL TROOPS CHEER GENERAL LEE, 1865
N. C. Wyeth
U. S. Naval Academy Museum

EPIC IN BLUE AND GRAY

Literature deals with conflict, and there was plenty of real-life conflict in the United States between 1855 and 1865. The antislavery and proslavery forces, North and South, argued vehemently in public and in private. Other notable struggles pitted the United States Army against native Americans, open-range ranchers against settlers, wage-earners against powerful new corporations, reformers against a host of real or imagined evils. All these conflicts would eventually find their way into American literature. For quite some time, however, the attention of writers was riveted on the immediate, cataclysmic event—the Civil War, its causes, clashes, and consequences.

Oh, Freedom!

When white Europeans came to America, they usually arrived with hope and the promise of a better life. Black Africans arrived as slaves, facing a life of bondage. Yet not all of them remained slaves. Some slaves, in the North and the South, were freed even before the Revolution. By the time of the Civil War, there were a great many free blacks in the United States, including a large number in the South.

Of the blacks who remained in slavery in the 1850's, more than half worked on cotton plantations. On these plantations and elsewhere, the slaves developed a unique style of music, the black spiritual. Spirituals fused traditional African music with other familiar materials—the Bible, Protestant hymns, and the popular music of the day. To the slave, spirituals were more than just deeply moving expressions of faith. They were also work songs in the fields and mills, rowing and hauling songs, war songs, laments, lullabies, and funeral dirges.

Among the best-known spirituals are "Roll, Jordan, Roll" and "Poor Rosy." Lucy McKim, a nineteenth-century collector of spirituals, quotes a slave woman who claimed that "Poor Rosy" could be sung only with "a full heart and a troubled spirit." McKim qualifies as an unsung heroine herself. Her *Slave Songs of the United States,* published in 1867, is a valuable source of music that might otherwise have been lost forever.

Not all the black voices of the period surfaced in spirituals. One of the great black abolitionist leaders was Frederick Douglass, born into slavery in Maryland. Douglass escaped as a young man and settled in the North, where he became a persuasive orator against slavery. Later he founded and published the *North Star,* a weekly antislavery newspaper. In his autobiography, *Narrative of the Life of Frederick Douglass,* Douglass agreed with the slave woman who spoke to Lucy McKim. "The songs of the slave," he wrote, "represent the sorrows of his heart; and he is relieved by them only as an aching heart is relieved by its tears."

When the Civil War broke out, the familiar spirituals went into battle. They were joined by new songs born of the conflict, such as "Many Thousand Gone" and "Oh, Freedom!" The words of these songs were still sad, but they often expressed a new-found hope:

Oh, freedom! Oh, freedom!
Oh, freedom over me;
And before I'll be a slave,
I'll be buried in my grave,
And go home to my Lord, and be free.

According to one historian, the spiritual "made it possible for human beings to accept their fate when they could do nothing else, and it summoned them to a sustained protest against that same fate whenever the hour struck."

Wartime Voices

In a symbolic sense, the hour struck in September 1862 for all the slaves who lived in the Confederate States of America. It was then, in the midst of war, that Lincoln signed the Emancipation Proclamation. This proclamation declared that as of January 1, 1863, slaves in the Confederacy would be "then, thenceforward, and forever free." In order for the promise to be kept, however, the Union had to win the war.

Abraham Lincoln is generally regarded as one of our greatest presidents. His fame rests largely on his deeds, but his words could be equally impressive. No American statesman is more often quoted. Lincoln's two inaugural addresses, his letters, and his brief, inspiring speech at Gettysburg have earned him a permanent place in American literature.

Perhaps surprisingly, Lincoln's two most able commanders—Ulysses S. Grant and William T. Sherman—produced memoirs that are still regarded as models of their kind. In fact, the quality of writing done by high-ranking officers on both sides is remarkable. Also noteworthy were the diaries of ordinary soldiers and civilians. One of the most perceptive diarists was Mary Boykin Chesnut, wife of a Confederate officer. Her vivid, close-up views of wartime life in Charleston, South Carolina, were published as *A Diary from Dixie*.

A great many patriotic songs were written and sung during the war. Among the most popular ones in the North were "The Battle Cry of Freedom" and "Tenting Tonight on the Old Campground." "Taps," composed by General Daniel Butterfield, was first played in July 1862. The most famous Union song of all is probably Julia Ward Howe's stirring "The Battle Hymn of the Republic." Among southerners, "The Bonny Blue Flag" and "The Yellow Rose of Texas" were favorites, as was the well-known "Dixie."

Countless novels have been written about the Civil War, but few of any consequence were written until many decades later. One original novel of the Confederacy, *Macaria, or Altars of Sacrifice*,

UNION SOLDIERS RALLY AROUND THE FLAG
William Winner
Art Resource

by Augusta Jane Wilson, was published in Richmond in 1864. Another novel, written from the Union viewpoint, was John W. DeForest's *Miss Ravenel's Conversion from Secession to Loyalty,* published in 1867.

Many of the northern writers who were active before the war continued to write during it. William Cullen Bryant, Ralph Waldo Emerson, Henry Wadsworth Longfellow, John Greenleaf Whittier, Oliver Wendell Holmes, James Russell Lowell, Herman Melville, and Emily Dickinson all produced wartime works. Only Melville, however, wrote memorably of the war itself. In the South, Henry Timrod composed poems that led some to call him "the laureate of the Confederacy." Born in Charleston, he developed a diamond-clear style combined with lyrical power. Illness forced Timrod's discharge from the Confederate Army. He died of tuberculosis two years after the war ended. Poets throughout the nation lamented his death, believing that his promise had been largely unfulfilled.

The Good Gray Poet

A northern poet who wrote about the war unforgettably was Walt Whitman, one of the giants of American literature. A New Yorker, Whitman worked as a journalist and editor of various newspapers, including the *Brooklyn Eagle*. In his youth, Whitman was something of a dandy, with a neatly trimmed beard, well-tailored clothes, and a spruce cane. He later acquired the better-known image of "the good gray poet"—shaggy beard, rough workman's clothes, large felt hat, and red shirt open at the collar.

Leaves of Grass, the first collection of Whitman's poems, originally appeared in 1855. Although the book achieved little public success, it was well received critically. In a letter to Whitman, Ralph Waldo Emerson hailed the work. "I greet you at the beginning of a great career," he wrote. Whitman continued to revise and expand *Leaves of Grass* throughout his life, producing several expanded editions.

After the Civil War broke out, Whitman's younger brother George enlisted in the Union army. When George was wounded at the Battle of Fredericksburg, Whitman went to Virginia to care for him. He remained in Washington, D.C., for the rest of the war, working as a volunteer in military hospitals. Out of this experience came such masterful poems as "Cavalry Crossing a Ford," "By the Bivouac's Fitful Flame," and "Beat! Beat! Drums!" Upon the assassination of Lincoln, Whitman wrote the much-quoted "O Captain! My Captain" and the classic elegy "When Lilacs Last in the Dooryard Bloom'd."

Whitman's poetry, unusual in both content and style, exalted democracy and the common man. No one had seen anything quite like it before. It was, said one critic, "impossible to transfix with a phrase or a theory." *Leaves of Grass* has been called the most influential volume of poetry in the history of American literature.

AMERICAN VOICES
Quotations by Prominent Figures of the Period

My brother sitting on the tree of life,
And he heard when Jordan roll,
  Roll, Jordan, roll, Jordan!
  Roll, Jordan, roll!
    Black Spiritual

"A house divided against itself cannot stand." I believe this government cannot endure permanently half slave and half free.
    Abraham Lincoln, Speech, Republican State Convention, 1858

With malice toward none; with charity for all; with firmness in the right, as God gives us to see the right, let us strive on to finish the work we are in. . . .
    Abraham Lincoln, Second Inaugural Address

I felt so tall within—I felt as if the power of the nation was with me.
    Frederick Douglass, *Life and Times of Frederick Douglass*

Mine eyes have seen the glory
  Of the coming of the Lord,;
He is trampling out the vintage
  Where the grapes of wrath are stored.
    Julia Ward Howe, "The Battle Hymn
    of the Republic"

I hear America singing, the varied carols I hear.
    Walt Whitman, *Leaves of Grass,* "I Hear America Singing"

I say we are no better than our judges in the North, and no worse. We are human beings of the nineteenth century, and slavery has to go, of course.
    Mary Boykin Chesnut, *A Diary from Dixie*

Christmas won't be Christmas without any presents.
    Louisa May Alcott, *Little Women*

READING CRITICALLY

The Literature of 1855–1865

Nearly all of the literary activity that occurred during the years from 1855 to 1865 was in some way related to the Civil War. By reading the literature of the period, you can gain a better understanding of the causes of the war and the ways in which it affected the American people.

Historical Context

During the early part of the nineteenth century, industrialization swept through the northern states, while the southern states clung to their traditional rural lifestyle. The division between the North and South became more and more pronounced, and a great deal of controversy developed over the issue of slavery. As a movement to abolish slavery gained force in the North, southerners, who believed that their economy depended on slavery, became increasingly concerned. This concern reached its peak when Abraham Lincoln, an opponent of slavery, was elected president in 1860. Following Lincoln's election, the southern states began seceding from the Union, and on April 12, 1861, the Civil War began. The conflict lasted four years, taking thousands of lives and causing a tremendous amount of pain and suffering among the American people.

Literary Movements

In the literary world, the decade between 1855 and 1865 was a period of transition during which no new movements developed. However, the wartime era did produce one of the most important and influential poets in the history of American literature, Walt Whitman. While the country was being torn apart by war, Whitman was reaffirming the principles upon which the country was founded by expressing American democratic ideals in his poetry.

Writers' Techniques

A number of notable speeches, songs, letters, memoirs, and journals were written by people who were directly or indirectly involved with the Civil War. At the same time, a new type of poetry was created by Walt Whitman—a type of poetry in which traditional poetic forms were abandoned in favor of free verse.

On the following pages is a selection by Walt Whitman. The notes in the side column should draw your attention to the historical context, literary movements, and writer's techniques. Understanding these features will help you to fully appreciate the selection.

When Lilacs Last in the Dooryard Bloom'd

Walt Whitman

1

When lilacs last in the dooryard bloom'd,
And the great star early droop'd in the western sky in the
    night,
I mourn'd, and yet shall mourn with ever-returning spring.

Ever-returning spring, trinity sure to me you bring,
5 Lilac blooming perennial and drooping star in the west,
And thought of him I love.

Historical Context: This poem was written in honor of President Lincoln following Lincoln's death.

2

O powerful western fallen star!
O shades of night—O moody, tearful night!
O great star disappear'd—O the black murk that hides the
    star!
10 O cruel hands that hold me powerless—O helpless soul of
    me!
O harsh surrounding cloud that will not free my soul.

Writer's Technique: The "powerful western fallen star" symbolizes President Lincoln.

3

In the dooryard fronting an old farmhouse near the white-
    wash'd palings,
Stands the lilac bush tall-growing with heart-shaped leaves
    of rich green,
With many a pointed blossom rising delicate, with the
    perfume strong I love,
15 With every leaf a miracle—and from this bush in the
    dooryard,
With delicate-color'd blossoms and heart-shaped leaves of
    rich green,
A sprig with its flower I break.

Writer's Technique: The poem is written in free verse—verse that has irregular meter and line length. Whitman was the first American writer to use free verse.

4

In the swamp in secluded recesses,
A shy and hidden bird is warbling a song.

20 Solitary the thrush,
    The hermit withdrawn to himself, avoiding the settlements,
    Sings by himself a song.

    Song of the bleeding throat,
    Death's outlet song of life, (for well dear brother I know,
25 If thou wast not granted to sing thou would'st surely die.)

5

    Over the breast of the spring, the land, amid cities,
    Amid lanes and through old woods, where lately the violets
        peep'd from the ground, spotting the gray debris,
    Amid the grass in the fields each side of the lanes, passing
        the endless grass,
    Passing the yellow-spear'd wheat, every grain from its
        shroud in the dark-brown fields uprisen,
30 Passing the apple-tree blows[1] of white and pink in the
        orchards,
    Carrying a corpse to where it shall rest in the grave,
    Night and day journeys a coffin.

---

1. blows: Blossoms.

THE FUNERAL OF PRESIDENT LINCOLN, NEW YORK, APRIL 25, 1865
Currier & Ives
Anne S. K. Brown Military Collection, Brown University Library

6

Coffin that passes through lanes and streets,
Through day and night with the great cloud darkening the
    land,
35 With the pomp of the inloop'd flags with the cities draped
    in black,
With the show of the states themselves as of crape-veil'd
    women standing,
With processions long and winding and the flambeaus[2] of
    the night,
With the countless torches lit, with the silent sea of faces
    and the unbared heads,
With the waiting depot, the arriving coffin, and the somber
    faces,
40 With dirges through the night, with the thousand voices
    rising strong and solemn,
With all the mournful voices of the dirges pour'd around
    the coffin,
The dim-lit churches and the shuddering organs—where
    amid these you journey,

Writer's Technique: Whitman uses parallelism, repeating similarly structured phrases, clauses, or sentences to establish a pattern and emphasize important ideas.

---

2. flambeaus (flam′ bōz): Torches.

With the tolling tolling bells' perpetual clang,
Here, coffin that slowly passes,
45 I give you my sprig of lilac.

7

(Nor for you, for one alone,
Blossoms and branches green to coffins all I bring,
For fresh as the morning, thus would I chant a song for
     you O sane and sacred death.

All over bouquets of roses,
50 O death, I cover you over with roses and early lilies,
But mostly and now the lilac that blooms the first,
Copious I break, I break the sprigs from the bushes,
With loaded arms I come, pouring for you,
For you and the coffins all of you O death.)

Writer's Technique: Whitman expresses his deep admiration for Lincoln, whom he viewed as a symbol of the American democratic ideal.

8

55 O western orb sailing the heaven,
Now I know what you must have meant as a month since I
     walk'd,
As I walk'd in silence the transparent shadowy night,
As I saw you had something to tell as you bent to me night
     after night,
As you droop'd from the sky low down as if to my side
     (while the other stars all look'd on,)
60 As we wander'd together the solemn night (for something I
     know not what kept me from sleep,)
As the night advanced, and I saw on the rim of the west
     how full you were of woe,
As I stood on the rising ground in the breeze in the cool
     transparent night,
As I watch'd where you pass'd and was lost in the
     netherward[3] black of the night,
As my soul in its trouble dissatisfied sank, as where you
     sad orb,
65 Concluded, dropt in the night, and was gone.

9

Sing on there in the swamp,
O singer bashful and tender, I hear your notes, I hear your
     call,

---

3. netherward *adj.:* Moving downward.

I hear, I come presently, I understand you,
But a moment I linger, for the lustrous star has detain'd
   me,
70 The star my departing comrade holds and detains me.

10

O how shall I warble myself for the dead one there I loved?
And how shall I deck my song for the large sweet soul that
   has gone?
And what shall my perfume be for the grave of him I love?

Sea winds blown from east and west,
75 Blown from the eastern sea and blown from the western
   sea, till there on the prairies meeting,
These and with these and the breath of my chant,
I'll perfume the grave of him I love.

11

O what shall I hang on the chamber walls?
And what shall the pictures be that I hang on the walls,
80 To adorn the burial house of him I love?

Pictures of growing spring and farms and homes,
With the fourth-month[4] eve at sundown, and the gray
   smoke lucid and bright,
With floods of the yellow gold of the gorgeous, indolent,
   sinking sun, burning, expanding the air,
With the fresh sweet herbage[5] under foot, and the pale
   green leaves of the trees prolific,
85 In the distance the flowing glaze, the breast of the river,
   with a wind-dapple here and there,
With ranging hills on the banks, with many a line against
   the sky, and shadows,
And the city at hand with dwellings so dense, and stacks of
   chimneys,
And all the scenes of life and the workshops, and the
   workmen homeward returning.

12

Lo, body and soul—this land,
90 My own Manhattan with spires, and the sparkling and

---

4. fourth-month: April.
5. herbage: Grass.

hurrying tides, and the ships,
The varied and ample land, the South and the North in the
    light, Ohio's shores and flashing Missouri,
And ever the far-spreading prairies cover'd with grass and
    corn.

Lo, the most excellent sun so calm and haughty,
The violet and purple morn with just-felt breezes,
95   The gentle soft-born measureless light,
The miracle spreading bathing all, the fulfill'd noon,
The coming eve delicious, the welcome night and the stars,
Over my cities shining all, enveloping man and land.

13

Sing on, sing on you gray-brown bird,
100 Sing from the swamps, the recesses, pour your chant from
    the bushes,
Limitless out of the dusk, out of the cedars and pines.

Sing on dearest brother, warble your reedy song,
Loud human song, with voice of uttermost woe.

O liquid and free and tender!
105 O wild and loose to my soul!—O wondrous singer!
You only I hear—yet the star holds me, (but will soon
    depart,)
Yet the lilac with mastering odor holds me.

14

Now while I sat in the day and look'd forth,
In the close of the day with its light and the fields of
    spring, and the farmers preparing their crops,
110 In the large unconscious scenery of my land with its lakes
    and forests,
In the heavenly aerial beauty (after the perturb'd winds and
    the storms,)
Under the arching heavens of the afternoon swift passing,
    and the voices of children and women,
The many-moving sea tides, and I saw the ships how they
    sail'd,
And the summer approaching with richness, and the fields
    all busy with labor,
115 And the infinite separate houses, how they all went on,

ABRAHAM LINCOLN
William Willard
National Portrait Gallery, Smithsonian Institution

each with its meals and minutia[6] of daily usages,
And the streets how their throbbings throbb'd, and the
 cities pent—lo, then and there,
Falling upon them all and among them all, enveloping me
 with the rest,
Appear'd the cloud, appear'd the long black trail,
And I knew death, its thought, and the sacred knowledge of
 death.

120   Then with the knowledge of death as walking one side of
 me,
And the thought of death close-walking the other side of
 me,
And I in the middle as with companions, and as holding
 the hands of companions,
I fled forth to the hiding receiving night that talks not,

---

6. minutia (mi nü′ s-hē ə) *n.*: Small and trivial detail.

Down to the shores of the water, the path by the swamp in
  the dimness,
125 To the solemn shadowy cedars and ghostly pines so still.

And the singer so shy to the rest receiv'd me,
The gray-brown bird I know receiv'd us comrades three,
And he sang the carol of death, and a verse for him I love.

From deep secluded recesses,
130 From the fragrant cedars and the ghostly pines so still,
Came the carol of the bird.

And the charm of the carol rapt me,
As I held as if by their hands my comrades in the night,
And the voice of my spirit tallied[7] the song of the bird.

135 *Come lovely and soothing death,*
Undulate[8] round the world, serenely arriving, arriving,
In the day, in the night, to all, to each,
Sooner or later delicate death.

Prais'd be the fathomless universe,
140 *For life and joy, and for objects and knowledge curious,*
And for love, sweet love—but praise! praise! praise!
For the sure-enwinding arms of cool-enfolding death.

Dark mother always gliding near with soft feet,
Have none chanted for thee a chant of fullest welcome?
145 *Then I chant it for thee, I glorify thee above all,*
I bring thee a song that when thou must indeed come,
  come unfalteringly.

Approach strong deliveress,
When it is so, when thou hast taken them I joyously sing
  the dead,
Lost in the loving floating ocean of thee,
150 *Laved[9] in the flood of thy bliss O death.*

From me to thee glad serenades,
Dances for thee I propose saluting thee, adornments and
  feastings for thee,

---

7. tallied: Corresponded with.
8. undulate *v*.: To move in waves.
9. laved *v*.: Washed.

And the sights of the open landscape and the high-spread
    sky are fitting,
And life and the fields, and the huge and thoughtful
    night.

155   *The night in silence under many a star,*
        The ocean shore and the husky whispering wave whose
            voice I know,
        And the soul turning to thee O vast and well-veil'd death,
        And the body gratefully nestling close to thee.
        Over the treetops I float thee a song,
160   *Over the rising and sinking waves, over the myriad fields*
            and the prairies wide,
        Over the dense-pack'd cities all and the teeming wharves
            and ways,
        I float this carol with joy, with joy to thee O death.

15

To the tally of my soul,
Loud and strong kept up the gray-brown bird,
165   With pure deliberate notes spreading filling the night.

Loud in the pines and cedars dim,
Clear in the freshness moist and the swamp perfume,
And I with my comrades there in the night.

While my sight that was bound in my eyes unclosed,
170   As to long panoramas of visions.

And I saw askant[10] the armies,
I saw as in noiseless dreams hundreds of battle flags,
Borne through the smoke of the battles and pierc'd with
    missiles I saw them,
And carried hither and yon through the smoke, and torn
    and bloody,
175   And at last but a few shreds left on the staffs (and all in
    silence,)
And the staffs all splinter'd and broken.

Historical Context: Whitman is referring to the armies that fought in the Civil War. The flags they carry are torn, just as the country was torn apart by the war.

I saw battle corpses, myriads of them,
And the white skeletons of young men, I saw them,

---

10. askant: Askance; with a sideways glance.

Historical Context: Whitman refers to the thousands of soldiers who lost their lives during the Civil War and to the suffering that the war caused among the American people.

I saw the debris and debris of all the slain soldiers of the war,

180 But I saw they were not as was thought,
They themselves were fully at rest, they suffer'd not,
The living remain'd and suffer'd, the mother suffer'd,
And the wife and the child and the musing comrade suffer'd,
And the armies that remain'd suffer'd.

16

185 Passing the visions, passing the night,
Passing, unloosing the hold of my comrades' hands,
Passing the song of the hermit bird and the tallying song of my soul,
Victorious song, death's outlet song, yet varying ever-altering song,
As low and wailing, yet clear the notes, rising and falling, flooding the night,
190 Sadly sinking and fainting, as warning and warning, and yet again bursting with joy,
Covering the earth and filling the spread of the heaven,
As that powerful psalm in the night I heard from recesses,
Passing, I leave thee lilac with heart-shaped leaves,
I leave thee there in the dooryard, blooming, returning with spring.

195 I cease from my song for thee,
From my gaze on thee in the west, fronting the west, communing with thee,
O comrade lustrous with silver face in the night.

Yet each to keep and all, retrievements out of the night,
The song, the wondrous chant of the gray-brown bird,
200 And the tallying chant, the echo arous'd in my soul,
With the lustrous and drooping star with the countenance full of woe,
With the holders holding my hand nearing the call of the bird,
Comrades mine and I in the midst, and their memory ever to keep, for the dead I loved so well,
For the sweetest, wisest soul of all my days and lands—and this for his dear sake,
205 Lilac and star and bird twined with the chant of my soul,
There in the fragrant pines and the cedars dusk and dim.

THINKING ABOUT THE SELECTION

Recalling

1. According to section 1, when did the speaker mourn?
2. (a) How do the people react to the funeral procession in section 6? (b) What does the speaker place on the coffin?
3. Name three of the "pictures of growing spring" presented in section 11.
4. (a) What walks on each side of the speaker in section 14? (b) To where does the speaker flee? (c) Who receives him there?
5. (a) What two things does the speaker see in section 15? (b) What does he realize about what he sees?
6. (a) Where does the speaker leave the lilac in section 16? (b) What happens to the lilac, the star, and the bird in the poem's final lines?

Interpreting

7. What is the significance of the recurring images of spring in the poem?
8. What do the images in section 6 suggest about the reaction of the American public to Lincoln's death?
9. What is the significance of the speaker's gesture at the end of section 6?
10. (a) What does the speaker learn from his observations at the beginning of section 14? (b) What does he learn from his visions in section 15?

Applying

11. What are some of the reasons why people greatly admire Abraham Lincoln?

ANALYZING LITERATURE
Understanding Elegies

Whitman's poem is an example of an elegy—a mournful poem lamenting the death of an individual or the passing of life and beauty, or meditating on the nature of death.

1. How would you describe the tone of Whitman's poem?
2. Why is this tone appropriate for an elegy?
3. What conclusion about death does the speaker ultimately reach in the poem?

UNDERSTANDING LANGUAGE
Using Synonyms

Synonyms are words that have the same or nearly the same meaning. For example, *advancement* and *development* are synonyms.

The capitalized words are from "When Lilacs Last in the Dooryard Bloom'd." Choose the word that is nearest in meaning to each of the capitalized words, as it is used in the poem.
1. HELPLESS: (a) forlorn (b) inconsiderate (c) protected (d) isolated
2. SECLUDED: (a) concealed (b) isolated (c) exclusive (d) retired
3. PERPETUAL: (a) perennial (b) constant (c) durable (d) persistent
4. LUSTROUS: (a) robust (b) colorful (c) luminous (d) luxuriant

THINKING AND WRITING
Writing an Elegy

Write an elegy mourning the death of a historical figure whom you greatly admire. Your elegy should be solemn in tone and should be written in formal language. It should capture the importance of the subject's life and should convey the sense of loss that resulted from his or her death. When you revise, make sure that you have expressed your ideas using concrete images. When you have completed your revision, share your elegy with your classmates.

SPIRITUALS

Spirituals are folk songs that originated among black slaves. They served as an important means of communication and a way of expressing the slaves' desire for freedom and religious salvation. At the same time, the songs helped to replace their lost African religious traditions and allowed them to maintain a connection to their musical heritage.

Spirituals were inspired by the religious hymns of the white revivalists of the early nineteenth century and shaped by memories of traditional African music. Because of their religious content, most slave owners openly accepted these songs. Many of the spirituals had a double meaning, however, conveying not only the slaves' religious faith but also their desire to escape from their bondage. In fact, some of the songs were used to transmit secret messages that their masters and overseers would be unable to understand. For example, the spiritual "Follow the Drinking Gourd" advised runaway slaves to follow the Big Dipper, which points to the north.

Most spirituals included references to people, places, or events in the Bible. They frequently referred to Moses, who in the Old Testament led the Jews out of slavery in Egypt. The black slaves compared their own enslavement with the plight of the ancient Jews. In spirituals such as "Swing Low, Sweet Chariot" and "Go Down, Moses" the black slaves expressed their hope that they would someday escape to their own "promised land" just as the Israelites had escaped to ancient Israel.

GUIDE FOR READING

Swing Low, Sweet Chariot;
Go Down, Moses

Writer's Techniques

Refrain. A refrain is a word, phrase, line, or group of lines repeated at regular intervals in a poem or song. For example, the line "Coming for to carry me home" is repeated throughout "Swing Low, Sweet Chariot."

Most spirituals include at least one, and sometimes more than one, refrain. The refrain emphasizes the most important ideas and establishes the rhythm. In a spiritual the refrain was usually sung by a chorus, with the other words being sung by a soloist. Because spirituals were passed orally from person to person and group to group, the words apart from the refrain often changed. In fact, soloists often improvised, creating new lyrics while singing. Since the refrains were frequently repeated, however, they were easy to remember and rarely changed. As a result, there is little variation in the refrain among different versions of a spiritual.

Look For

As you read the spirituals, look for their messages. How do the refrains emphasize the most important ideas and establish the rhythm?

Writing

Why does music often produce a strong emotional response in people? Freewrite about the emotional impact of music. Try to include examples.

Vocabulary

Knowing the following words will help you as you read "Swing Low, Sweet Chariot" and "Go Down, Moses."
oppressed (ə prest') *adj.*: Kept down by cruel or unjust power or authority (p. 423, l. 7)
smite (smīt) *v.*: To kill by a powerful blow (p. 423, l. 15)

Swing Low, Sweet Chariot

Spiritual

Swing low, sweet chariot,
Coming for to carry me home,
Swing low, sweet chariot,
Coming for to carry me home.

5   I looked over Jordan and what did I see
Coming for to carry me home,
A band of angels coming after me,
Coming for to carry me home.

If you get there before I do,
10   Coming for to carry me home,
Tell all my friends I'm coming too,
Coming for to carry me home.

Swing low, sweet chariot,
Coming for to carry me home,
15   Swing low, sweet chariot,
Coming for to carry me home.

THINKING ABOUT THE SELECTION

Recalling

1. What message does the speaker wish to convey to his friends?

Interpreting

2. (a) If you interpret this spiritual as a religious song, what does the chariot represent? (b) What does home represent? (c) What is the subject of the song?
3. (a) If you interpret this spiritual as an expression of the slaves' desire for freedom, what does the chariot represent? (b) What does home represent? (c) What does Jordan, the river that formed the boundary to the promised land of the ancient Israelites, represent? (d) What does the band of angels represent?

Applying

4. (a) For what types of events and situations do people write protest songs today? (b) Name two recent protest songs. (c) What messages do these two songs convey?

Go Down, Moses

Spiritual

Go down, Moses,
Way down in Egypt land
Tell old Pharaoh
To let my people go.

5 When Israel was in Egypt land
Let my people go
Oppressed so hard they could not stand
Let my people go.

Go down, Moses,
10 Way down in Egypt land
Tell old Pharaoh
"Let my people go."

"Thus saith the Lord," bold Moses said,
"Let my people go;
15 If not I'll smite your first-born dead
Let my people go."

Go down, Moses,
Way down in Egypt land,
Tell old Pharaoh,
20 "Let my people go!"

THINKING ABOUT THE SELECTION

Recalling

1. What does the speaker ask Moses to tell the old Pharaoh?
2. What is the condition of the people of Israel in Egypt?
3. What message does Moses deliver to the Pharaoh?

Interpreting

4. In this poem a comparison is developed between the captivity of the ancient Israelites in Egypt and the enslavement of the blacks in America. Egypt represents the South and Moses represents a leader helping blacks escape from slavery. (a) Who does the old Pharaoh represent? (b) Who do the people of Israel represent?

Applying

5. Harriet Tubman led other black slaves out of bondage to freedom in the North. Known by the code name of Moses, she once said, "We got to go free or die. And freedom's not bought with dust." What other American heroes can you think of who would agree with her words? Explain your choices.

ANALYZING LITERATURE

Recognizing a Refrain

A **refrain** is a word, phrase, line, or group of lines repeated at regular intervals in a poem or song.
1. What refrain is used in the song?
2. Explain how this refrain conveys the main idea.

THINKING AND READING

Writing About the Role of Spirituals

Write an essay in which you discuss what made spirituals such an important part of slave life. Prepare a list of reasons for the spirituals' importance. Then find passages in "Swing Low, Sweet Chariot" and "Go Down, Moses" that support your reasons. Prepare an outline and a thesis statement. Then write your essay. When you revise, eliminate any unnecessary information and make sure that your essay is coherent and well organized.

FREDERICK DOUGLASS

1817[?]–1895

Frederick Douglass rose out of slavery to become one of the most gifted writers and orators of his time. Using these talents, he dedicated his life to fighting for the abolition of slavery and for black civil rights. Douglass's life served as an inspiration and example for both blacks and whites throughout the country.

Douglass was born on a Maryland plantation. When he was eight, he was sent to live with the family of Hugh Auld in Baltimore. There, he learned to read and write, at first with the encouragement of Mrs. Auld and later despite her objections. When his desire for freedom was fueled by his reading, Douglass escaped from slavery at the age of twenty-one.

In 1841, three years after his escape, Douglass was asked to speak at a convention of the Massachusetts Anti-Slavery Society. Though he had never spoken in public before, Douglass delivered a tremendously powerful, moving speech. Impressed by his eloquence, the society immediately hired him as a lecturer.

Although he lived in constant fear of being arrested as a fugitive slave, Douglass spent the next four years lecturing throughout the Northeast. In 1845 he published his autobiography, *Narrative of the Life of Frederick Douglass*. Fearing that the book's publication would lead to his re-enslavement, Douglass fled to England, where he spent two years trying to gain British support for the abolitionist cause.

After several of his English friends raised money finally to buy his freedom, Douglass returned to the United States. Upon his return, he established the *North Star,* a newspaper for blacks, and began lecturing again. In 1855 he published *My Bondage and My Freedom,* an updated version of his autobiography.

During the Civil War, Douglass helped to recruit black soldiers for the Union army. After the war ended and slavery was abolished, he fought for black civil rights. He also held several government positions such as the marshal and recorder of deeds of the District of Columbia and the United States minister to Haiti.

from My Bondage and My Freedom

Literary Forms

Autobiography. An autobiography is a person's account of his or her own life. In an autobiography the writer presents a continuous narrative of what he or she feels are the most significant events in his or her life. Because the writer's life is presented as he or she views it, the portrayal of people and events is colored by the author's feelings and beliefs. In fact, some of the writer's attitudes and beliefs may be directly stated.

Usually, the writers of autobiographies believe that their lives are interesting or important or can in some way serve as examples for others. Frederick Douglass, for instance, wrote his autobiography because he believed that his life proved that blacks were no less perceptive, intelligent, and capable than whites. Written in a plain and direct style that was also fluent and forceful, Douglass's autobiography demonstrated not only that blacks were capable of overcoming great hardships and achieving success but also that they could express themselves eloquently.

Look For

As you read the following excerpt from *My Bondage and My Freedom,* look for what it reveals about Douglass's perceptiveness, intelligence, and capabilities.

Writing

Frederick Douglass's life served as an example for both blacks and whites throughout the country. Prepare a list of other men and women whose lives have served as an example for other people.

Vocabulary

Knowing the following words will help you as you read the excerpt from *My Bondage and My Freedom.*

congenial (kən jēn′ yəl) *adj.*: Compatible (p. 426)

benevolent (bə nev′ ə lənt) *adj.*: Kindly; charitable (p. 426)

stringency (strin′ jən ŝē) *n.*: Strictness; severity (p. 426)

depravity (di prav′ ə tē) *n.*: Corruption; wickedness (p. 426)

consternation (kän′ stər nā′ shən) *n.*: Great fear or shock that makes one feel helpless or bewildered (p. 427)

unperverted (un′ pər vʉrt′id) *adj.*: Uncorrupted (p. 428)

redolent (red′′l ənt) *adj.*: Suggestive (p. 428)

from My Bondage and My Freedom

Frederick Douglass

I lived in the family of Master Hugh, at Baltimore, seven years, during which time—as the almanac makers say of the weather—my condition was variable. The most interesting feature of my history here, was my learning to read and write, under somewhat marked disadvantages. In attaining this knowledge, I was compelled to resort to indirections by no means congenial to my nature, and which were really humiliating to me. My mistress—who had begun to teach me—was suddenly checked in her benevolent design, by the strong advice of her husband. In faithful compliance with this advice, the good lady had not only ceased to instruct me, herself, but had set her face as a flint against my learning to read by any means. It is due, however, to my mistress to say, that she did not adopt this course in all its stringency at the first. She either thought it unnecessary, or she lacked the depravity indispensable to shutting me up in mental darkness. It was, at least, necessary for her to have some training, and some hardening, in the exercise of the slaveholder's prerogative, to make her equal to forgetting my human nature and character, and to treating me as a thing destitute of a moral or an intellectual nature. Mrs. Auld—my mistress—was, as I have said, a most kind and tender-hearted woman; and, in the humanity of her heart, and the simplicity of her mind, she set out, when I first went to live with her, to treat me as she supposed one human being ought to treat another.

It is easy to see, that, in entering upon the duties of a slaveholder, some little experience is needed. Nature has done almost nothing to prepare men and women to be either slaves or slaveholders. Nothing but rigid training, long persisted in, can perfect the character of the one or the other. One cannot easily forget to love freedom; and it is as hard to cease to respect that natural love in our fellow creatures. On entering upon the career of a slaveholding mistress, Mrs. Auld was singularly deficient; nature, which fits nobody for such an office, had done less for her than any lady I had known. It was no easy matter to induce her to think and to feel that the curly-headed boy, who stood by her side, and even leaned on her lap; who was loved by little Tommy, and who loved little Tommy in turn; sustained to her only the relation of a chattel. I was *more* than that, and she felt me to be more than that. I could talk and sing; I could laugh and weep; I could reason and remember; I could love and hate. I was human, and she, dear lady, knew and felt me to be so. How could she, then, treat me as a brute, without a mighty struggle with all the noble powers of her own soul. That struggle came, and the will and power of the husband was victorious. Her noble soul was overthrown; but, he that overthrew it did not, himself, escape the consequences.

He, not less than the other parties, was injured in his domestic peace by the fall.

When I went into their family, it was the abode of happiness and contentment. The mistress of the house was a model of affection and tenderness. Her fervent piety and watchful uprightness made it impossible to see her without thinking and feeling—"that woman is a Christian." There was no sorrow nor suffering for which she had not a tear, and there was no innocent joy for which she did not a smile. She had bread for the hungry, clothes for the naked, and comfort for every mourner that came within her reach. Slavery soon proved its ability to divest her of these excellent qualities, and her home of its early happiness. Conscience cannot stand much violence. Once thoroughly broken down, *who* is he that can repair the damage? It may be broken toward the slave, on Sunday, and toward the master on Monday. It cannot endure such shocks. It must stand entire, or it does not stand at all. If my condition waxed bad, that of the family waxed not better. The first step, in the wrong direction, was the violence done to nature and to conscience, in arresting the benevolence that would have enlightened my young mind. In ceasing to instruct me, she must begin to justify herself *to* herself; and, once consenting to take sides in such a debate, she was riveted to her position. One needs very little knowledge of moral philosophy, to see *where* my mistress now landed. She finally became even more violent in her opposition to my learning to read, than was her husband himself. She was not satisfied with simply doing as *well* as her husband had commanded her, but seemed resolved to better his instruction. Nothing appeared to make my poor mistress—after her turning toward the downward path—more angry, than seeing me, seated in some nook or corner, quietly reading a book or a newspaper. I have had her rush at me, with the utmost fury, and snatch from my hand such newspaper or book, with something of the wrath and consternation which a traitor might be supposed to feel on being discovered in a plot by some dangerous spy.

Mrs. Auld was an apt woman, and the advice of her husband, and her own experience, soon demonstrated, to her entire satisfaction, that education and slavery are incompatible with each other. When this conviction was thoroughly established, I was most narrowly watched in all my movements. If I remained in a separate room from the family for any considerable length of time, I was sure to be suspected of having a book, and was at once called upon to give an account of myself. All this, however, was entirely *too late.* The first, and never to be retraced, step had been taken. In teaching me the alphabet, in the days of her simplicity and kindness, my mistress had given me the "inch," and now, no ordinary precaution could prevent me from taking the "ell."[1]

Seized with a determination to learn to read, at any cost, I hit upon many expedients to accomplish the desired end. The plea which I mainly adopted, and the one by which I was most successful, was that of using my young white playmates, with whom I met in the street, as teachers. I used to carry, almost constantly, a copy of Webster's spelling book in my pocket; and, when sent on errands, or when play time was allowed me, I would step, with my young friends, aside, and take a lesson in spelling. I generally paid my *tuition fee* to the boys, with bread, which I also carried in my pocket. For a single biscuit, any of my hungry little comrades would give me a lesson more valuable to me than bread. Not everyone, however, demanded this consideration, for there were those who took pleasure in teaching me, whenever I had a chance to be taught by them. I am strongly tempted to give the names of two or three of those little boys, as a slight testimonial of the gratitude and af-

---

1. ell *n.*: A former English measure of length, equal to forty-five inches.

fection I bear them, but prudence forbids; not that it would injure me, but it might, possibly, embarrass them; for it is almost an unpardonable offense to do anything, directly or indirectly, to promote a slave's freedom, in a slave state. It is enough to say, of my warm-hearted little play fellows, that they lived on Philpot Street, very near Durgin & Bailey's shipyard.

Although slavery was a delicate subject, and very cautiously talked about among grownup people in Maryland, I frequently talked about it—and that very freely—with the white boys. I would, sometimes, say to them, while seated on a curbstone or a cellar door, "I wish I could be free, as you will be when you get to be men." "You will be free, you know, as soon as you are twenty-one, and can go where you like, but I am a slave for life. Have I not as good a right to be free as you have?" Words like these, I observed, always troubled them; and I had no small satisfaction in wringing from the boys, occasionally, that fresh and bitter condemnation of slavery, that springs from nature, unseared and unperverted. Of all consciences let me have those to deal with which have not been bewildered by the cares of life. I do not remember ever to have met with a *boy*, while I was in slavery, who defended the slave system; but I have often had boys to console me, with the hope that something would yet occur, by which I might be made free. Over and over again, they have told me, that "they believed *I* had as good a right to be free as *they* had"; and that "they did not believe God ever made anyone to be a slave." The reader will easily see, that such little conversations with my play fellows, had no tendency to weaken my love of liberty, nor to render me contented with my condition as a slave.

When I was about thirteen years old, and had succeeded in learning to read, every increase of knowledge, especially respecting the free states, added something to the almost intolerable burden of the thought—"I am a slave for life." To my bondage I saw no end. It was a terrible reality, and I shall never be able to tell how sadly that thought chafed my young spirit. Fortunately, or unfortunately, about this time in my life, I had made enough money to buy what was then a very popular schoolbook, the *Columbian Orator.* I bought this addition to my library, of Mr. Knight, on Thames street, Fell's Point, Baltimore, and paid him fifty cents for it. I was first led to buy this book, by hearing some little boys say they were going to learn some little pieces out of it for the Exhibition. This volume was, indeed, a rich treasure, and every opportunity afforded me, for a time, was spent in diligently perusing it. . . . The dialogue and the speeches were all redolent of the principles of liberty, and poured floods of light on the nature and character of slavery. As I read, behold! the very discontent so graphically predicted by Master Hugh, had already come upon me. I was no longer the light-hearted, gleesome boy, full of mirth and play, as when I landed first at Baltimore. Knowledge had come. . . . This knowledge opened my eyes to the horrible pit, and revealed the teeth of the frightful dragon that was ready to pounce upon me, but it opened no way for my escape. I have often wished myself a beast, or a bird—anything, rather than a slave. I was wretched and gloomy, beyond my ability to describe. I was too thoughtful to be happy. It was this everlasting thinking which distressed and tormented me; and yet there was no getting rid of the subject of my thoughts. All nature was redolent of it. Once awakened by the silver trump[2] of knowledge, my spirit was roused to eternal wakefulness. Liberty! the inestimable birthright of every man, had, for me, converted every object into an asserter of this great right. It was heard in every sound, and beheld in every object. It was ever present, to torment me with a sense of my

---

2. trump: Trumpet.

A HOME ON THE MISSISSIPPI
Currier & Ives
The Museum of the City of N.Y.

GUIDE FOR READING

from Mary Chesnut's Civil War

Mary Boykin Chesnut (1823–1886) was the daughter of a United States senator from South Carolina, and she was brought up in an aristocratic family in Charleston, South Carolina. When she was seventeen, Mary Boykin married James Chesnut, Jr., a wealthy lawyer, who was later elected to the Senate. The cruelty of the war deeply disturbed her. Through her journal we can share firsthand the joy and sorrow of the people of the South in victory and defeat.

Literary Forms

Journals. A journal, or diary, is a personal record of events, conversations, thoughts, feelings, and observations. Written on a day-to-day basis, journals allow writers to record their most immediate responses to their experiences. Usually, writers keep journals for their own personal use, not intending to have them published. As a result, journals tend to be written in an informal, personal style and capture the writer's innermost thoughts and feelings.

Look For

As you read the following excerpt from *Mary Chesnut's Civil War,* look for Mary Chesnut's attitude toward the people and events she describes.

Writing

Freewrite about books you have read and movies you have seen about the Civil War. Discuss what the books and movies reveal about how the war changed people's lives. Also explain what you think the American people learned from the conflict.

Vocabulary

Knowing the following words will help you as you read the excerpt from *Mary Chesnut's Civil War.*

capitulate (kə pich' ə lāt') *v.*: Surrender conditionally (p. 434)
audaciously (ô dā' shəs lē) *adj.*: Boldly (p. 434)
foreboding (fôr bōd' iŋ) *n.*: Prediction (p. 434)

obstinate (äb' stə nit) *adj.*: Stubborn (p. 434)
imprecations (im' prə kā' shənz) *n.*: Curses (p. 434)
serenity (sə ren' ə tē) *n.*: Calmness (p. 436)

from Mary Chesnut's Civil War

Mary Chesnut

April 7, 1861. Today things seem to have settled down a little.

One can but hope still. Lincoln or Seward[1] have made such silly advances and then far sillier drawings back. There may be a chance for peace, after all.

Things are happening so fast.

My husband has been made an aide-de-camp[2] of General Beauregard.

Three hours ago we were quietly packing to go home. The convention has adjourned.

Now he tells me the attack upon Fort Sumter[3] may begin tonight. Depends upon Anderson and the fleet outside. The *Herald* says that this show of war outside of the bar is intended for Texas.

John Manning came in with his sword and red sash. Pleased as a boy to be on Beauregard's staff while the row goes on. He has gone with Wigfall to Captain Hartstene with instructions.

Mr. Chesnut is finishing a report he had to make to the convention.

Mrs. Hayne called. She had, she said, "but one feeling, pity for those who are not here."

Jack Preston, Willie Alston—"the take-life-easys," as they are called—with John Green, "the big brave," have gone down to the island—volunteered as privates.

Seven hundred men were sent over. Ammunition wagons rumbling along the streets all night. Anderson burning blue lights—signs and signals for the fleet outside, I suppose.

Today at dinner there was no allusion to things as they stand in Charleston Harbor. There was an undercurrent of intense excitement. There could not have been a more brilliant circle. In addition to our usual quartet (Judge Withers, Langdon Cheves, and Trescot) our two governors dined with us, Means and Manning.

These men all talked so delightfully. For once in my life I listened.

That over, business began. In earnest, Governor Means rummaged a sword and red sash from somewhere and brought it for Colonel Chesnut, who has gone to demand the surrender of Fort Sumter.

And now, patience—we must wait.

---

1. Seward: William Henry Seward (1801–1872), U.S. Secretary of State from 1861 through 1869.
2. aide-de-camp: An officer serving as assistant and confidential secretary to a superior.
3. Fort Sumter: A fort in Charleston Harbor, South Carolina. At the time, the fort was occupied by Union troops commanded by Major Robert Anderson.

From *Mary Chesnut's Civil War*, edited by C. Vann Woodward. Copyright © 1981 by C. Vann Woodward, Sally Bland Metts, Barbara G. Carpenter, Sally Bland Johnson, and Katherine W. Herbert. All rights reserved. Reprinted by permission of the publisher, Yale University Press.

Why did that green goose Anderson go into Fort Sumter? Then everything began to go wrong.

Now they have intercepted a letter from him, urging them to let him surrender. He paints the horrors likely to ensue if they will not.

He ought to have thought of all that before he put his head in the hole.

April 12, 1861. Anderson will not capitulate.

Yesterday was the merriest, maddest dinner we have had yet. Men were more audaciously wise and witty. We had an unspoken foreboding it was to be our last pleasant meeting. Mr. Miles dined with us today. Mrs. Henry King rushed in: "The news, I come for the latest news—all of the men of the King family are on the island"—of which fact she seemed proud.

While she was here, our peace negotiator—or envoy—came in. That is, Mr. Chesnut returned—his interview with Colonel Anderson had been deeply interesting—but was not inclined to be communicative, wanted his dinner. Felt for Anderson. Had telegraphed to President Davis[4] for instructions.

What answer to give Anderson, etc., etc. He has gone back to Fort Sumter with additional instructions.

When they were about to leave the wharf, A. H. Boykin sprang into the boat, in great excitement; thought himself ill-used. A likelihood of fighting—and he to be left behind!

I do not pretend to go to sleep. How can I? If Anderson does not accept terms—at four—the orders are—he shall be fired upon.

I count four—St. Michael chimes. I begin to hope. At half-past four, the heavy booming of a cannon.

I sprang out of bed. And on my knees—prostrate—I prayed as I never prayed before.

There was a sound of stir all over the house—pattering of feet in the corridor—all seemed hurrying one way. I put on my double gown and a shawl and went, too. It was to the housetop.

The shells were bursting. In the dark I heard a man say "waste of ammunition."

I knew my husband was rowing about in a boat somewhere in that dark bay. And that the shells were roofing it over—bursting toward the fort. If Anderson was obstinate—he was to order the forts on our side to open fire. Certainly fire had begun. The regular roar of the cannon—there it was. And who could tell what each volley accomplished of death and destruction.

The women were wild, there on the housetop. Prayers from the women and imprecations from the men, and then a shell would light up the scene. Tonight, they say, the forces are to attempt to land.

The *Harriet Lane*[5] had her wheelhouse[6] smashed and put back to sea.

We watched up there—everybody wondered. Fort Sumter did not fire a shot.

Today Miles and Manning, colonels now—aides to Beauregard—dined with us. The latter hoped I would keep the peace. I give him only good words, for he was to be under fire all day and night, in the bay carrying orders, etc.

Last night—or this morning truly—up on the housetop I was so weak and weary I sat down on something that looked like a black stool.

"Get up, you foolish woman—your dress is on fire," cried a man. And he put me out.

---

4. President Davis: Jefferson Davis (1808–1889), president of the Confederacy (1861–1865).

5. The *Harriet Lane*: A federal steamer that had brought provisions to Fort Sumter.
6. wheelhouse *n.*: An enclosed place on the upper deck of a ship, in which the helmsman stands while steering.

THE HOUSETOPS IN CHARLESTON DURING THE BOMBARDMENT OF FORT SUMTER
Harper's Weekly, May 4, 1961
Library of Congress

from *Mary Chesnut's Civil War*   435

It was a chimney, and the sparks caught my clothes. Susan Preston and Mr. Venable then came up. But my fire had been extinguished before it broke out into a regular blaze.

Do you know, after all that noise and our tears and prayers, nobody has been hurt. Sound and fury, signifying nothing.[7] A delusion and a snare. . . .

Somebody came in just now and reported Colonel Chesnut asleep on the sofa in General Beauregard's room. After two such nights he must be so tired as to be able to sleep anywhere. . . .

April 13, 1861. Nobody hurt, after all. How gay we were last night.

Reaction after the dread of all the slaughter we thought those dreadful cannons were making such a noise in doing.

Not even a battery[8] the worse for wear.

Fort Sumter has been on fire. He has not yet silenced any of our guns. So the aides—still with swords and red sashes by way of uniform—tell us.

But the sound of those guns makes regular meals impossible. None of us go to table. But tea trays pervade the corridors, going everywhere.

Some of the anxious hearts lie on their beds and moan in solitary misery. Mrs. Wig-

---

7. **Sound . . . nothing:** From Shakespeare's *Macbeth*, Act V, Scene v, lines 27–28. Macbeth is contemplating the significance of life and death, after learning of his wife's death.
8. **battery** *n.*: Artillery unit.

fall and I solace ourselves with tea in my room.

These women have all a satisfying faith.

April 15, 1861. I did not know that one could live such days of excitement.

They called, "Come out—there is a crowd coming."

A mob indeed, but it was headed by Colonels Chesnut and Manning.

The crowd was shouting and showing these two as messengers of good news. They were escorted to Beauregard's headquarters. Fort Sumter had surrendered.

Those up on the housetop shouted to us, "The fort is on fire." That had been the story once or twice before.

When we had calmed down, Colonel Chesnut, who had taken it all quietly enough—if anything, more unruffled than usual in his serenity—told us how the surrender came about.

Wigfall was with them on Morris Island when he saw the fire in the fort, jumped in a little boat and, with his handkerchief as a white flag, rowed over to Fort Sumter. Wigfall went in through a porthole.

When Colonel Chesnut arrived shortly after and was received by the regular entrance, Colonel Anderson told him he had need to pick his way warily, for it was all mined.

As far as I can make out, the fort surrendered to Wigfall.

But it is all confusion. Our flag is flying there. Fire engines have been sent to put out the fire.

Everybody tells you half of something and then rushes off to tell something else or to hear the last news. . . .

THINKING ABOUT THE SELECTION

Recalling

1. (a) When does the attack on Fort Sumter take place? (b) What happens to Mary Chesnut while she is watching the attack?
2. According to the entry for August 13, what does the sound of the guns make impossible?
3. (a) When do the Union troops at Fort Sumter surrender to the Confederate forces? (b) Who explains how the surrender came about?

Interpreting

4. What does this excerpt reveal about Mary Chesnut's attitude toward the war?
5. What does this excerpt reveal about Mary Chesnut's attitude toward the Confederacy?

Applying

6. In what ways do you think this excerpt would be different if it had been written by someone actively involved in the attack on Fort Sumter?
7. In what ways do you think this excerpt would have been different if Mary Chesnut had been from the North?

ANALYZING LITERATURE

Understanding a Journal

A **journal** is a personal record of events, conversations, thoughts, feelings, and observations. In *Mary Chesnut's Civil War,* Mary Chesnut's journal from the war years, for example, Chesnut records her personal responses to the important events and people of the Civil War.

1. Mary Chesnut's descriptions are often colored by her dislike for the war. What evidence is there in Chesnut's description of the attack on Fort Sumter and the events preceding it that she dreaded the coming of the war?
2. Name two characteristics of Mary Chesnut's personality that are revealed in her journal.

CRITICAL THINKING AND READING

Recognizing Main Ideas

When reading a journal, it is important to recognize the main ideas being expressed and the main events being described. One of the main ideas expressed in Mary Chesnut's journal entry for April 12, for example, is that her husband believes that the attack on Fort Sumter may begin that night.

List three other main ideas and events in the excerpt from *Mary Chesnut's Civil War.*

THINKING AND WRITING

Writing a Summary

Write a summary of the events described in the excerpt from *Mary Chesnut's Civil War.* Reread the selection. Then look at your list of main ideas and events from the Critical Thinking and Reading exercise, making sure that you have not omitted any. Write your summary in chronological order, using transitions to link ideas and indicate the order of events. When you revise, make sure that your summary is clear and concise.

ABRAHAM LINCOLN

1809–1865

Serving as president during one of the most tragic periods in American history, Abraham Lincoln fought to reunite a nation torn apart by war. His courage, strength, and dedication in the face of an overwhelming national crisis have made him one of the most admired and respected American presidents.

Lincoln was born in a log cabin in Kentucky. When he was seven, his family moved to Indiana. Because he had to help his family clear land, split timber, build a home, and plant crops, Lincoln was able to attend school only occasionally. Lincoln managed to educate himself, however, by reading a wide variety of books.

When Lincoln was twenty-one, his family moved to Illinois, and he took a job as a store clerk. He soon developed an interest in politics, and in 1832 he ran for the Illinois state legislature. Though he lost his first election, he won a seat in the legislature—which he held for four terms—two years later.

In 1846 Lincoln was elected to the United States Congress. He earned a reputation as a champion of emancipation by sponsoring a bill that called for the abolition of slavery. The bill was defeated, however, and Lincoln failed to win reelection. Following his defeat Lincoln left politics to practice law. Yet his interest in politics was once again aroused in 1854, when the Missouri Compromise, which protected the balance between slave states and free states, was repealed. In 1858 Lincoln ran for the United States Senate against Stephen Douglas, a strong supporter of the Missouri Compromise. Lincoln lost the election, but his heated debates with Douglas won him national recognition.

Lincoln was elected president of the United States in 1860. Soon after his election, a number of states seceded from the Union and the Civil War began. Throughout the war, Lincoln longed for the day when the states would be reunited and the country's wounds would be healed. Lincoln had little chance to celebrate the end of the war, because he was assassinated just five days after it ended.

In addition to being a strong leader, Abraham Lincoln was a gifted speaker and writer. His most famous speech, "The Gettysburg Address," was delivered at the dedication ceremonies for the national cemetery at Gettysburg. The direct, forceful speech, which captured the determination and despair of the divided nation, is one of the most significant speeches in American history.

GUIDE FOR READING

The Gettysburg Address; Letter to Mrs. Bixby

Writer's Techniques

Diction. Diction refers to a writer's choice of words. An important aspect of style, diction must be appropriate to the subject, audience, occasion, and literary form. For example, if a writer is preparing an essay describing a mountain range for people who have never been there, he or she must use vivid, concrete language that enables the reader to visualize what is being described.

Look For

Lincoln is known as an exquisite stylist. His style, though, has its roots in his early reading of Shakespeare and of the Bible. As you read "The Gettysburg Address" and "Letter to Mrs. Bixby," look for Lincoln's choice of words. What makes his word choice effective? What echoes do you hear of Shakespeare and of the Bible?

Writing

"The Gettysburg Address" is regarded as one of the most important speeches in American history because it captured the sorrow and determination of the war-torn nation. Freewrite about the Civil War and its effect on the American people.

Vocabulary

Knowing the following words will help you as you read "The Gettysburg Address" and "Letter to Mrs. Bixby."

consecrate (kän' sə krāt') *v.*: Cause to be revered or honored (p. 440)

hallow (hal' o) *v.*: Honor as sacred (p. 440)

beguile (bi gīl') *v.*: Deceive (p. 442)

assuage (ə swāj) *v.*: Lessen (p. 442)

bereavement (bi rēv' mənt) *n.*: Sadness resulting from the loss or death of a loved one (p. 442)

The Gettysburg Address

Abraham Lincoln

Four score and seven years ago our fathers brought forth on this continent, a new nation, conceived in Liberty, and dedicated to the proposition that all men are created equal.

Now we are engaged in a great civil war, testing whether that nation, or any nation so conceived and so dedicated, can long endure. We are met on a great battlefield of that war. We have come to dedicate a portion of that field, as a final resting place for those who here gave their lives that that nation might live. It is altogether fitting and proper that we should do this.

But, in a larger sense, we can not dedicate—we cannot consecrate—we cannot hallow—this ground. The brave men, living and dead, who struggled here, have consecrated it, far above our poor power to add or detract. The world will little note, nor long remember what we say here, but it can never forget what they did here. It is for us the living, rather, to be dedicated here to the unfinished work which they who fought here have thus far so nobly advanced. It is rather for us to be here dedicated to the great task remaining before us—that from these honored dead we take increased devotion to that cause for which they gave the last full measure of devotion—that we here highly resolve that these dead shall not have died in vain—that this nation, under God, shall have a new birth of freedom—and that government of the people, by the people, for the people, shall not perish from the earth.

ABRAHAM LINCOLN'S ADDRESS AT THE DEDICATION OF THE GETTYSBURG NATIONAL CEMETERY, 19 NOVEMBER 1863
The Granger Collection

THINKING ABOUT THE SELECTION

Recalling

1. To what "proposition" is the United States dedicated?
2. What is the Civil War "testing"?
3. (a) Where is the audience gathered? (b) Why have they gathered there?
4. What is the "task remaining before us"?

Interpreting

5. (a) Why does Lincoln believe that the war will have an impact on the entire world? (b) How does he convey this belief in his speech? (c) How does it add to the impact of the speech?
6. What is the purpose of Lincoln's speech?
7. Lincoln begins his speech by describing the birth of the nation and ends it by describing his vision of the nation's eventual rebirth. Considering Lincoln's purpose, why is this an effective way of structuring his speech?

Applying

8. (a) In what ways is Lincoln's speech different from the presidential addresses you have heard or seen on television? (b) How do you explain these differences?

ANALYZING LITERATURE

Understanding Diction

Diction refers to the writer's choice of words. Diction may be formal or informal, abstract or concrete. For example, "The Gettysburg Address" is written in formal, dignified language.

1. Find five words or phrases in "The Gettysburg Address" that contribute to its formal, dignified diction.
2. What words or phrases do you think Lincoln might have used in place of the five you chose in question 1 if the speech had been written using informal language?
3. The Shakespearean scholar A. L. Rowse has noted that many of Lincoln's speeches could easily be put into blank verse. In what ways do you find the language of "The Gettysburg Address" similar to the language of a poem?

CRITICAL THINKING AND READING

Analyzing Appropriateness of Diction

A writer must use language that is appropriate to the subject, audience, occasion, and literary form. For example, in writing "The Gettysburg Address," Lincoln used formal language because he felt it best suited the subject and occasion.

1. Why is Lincoln's diction appropriate?
2. Why would the speech have been less effective if it had been written using informal language?

THINKING AND WRITING

Comparing and Contrasting Speeches

Write an essay in which you compare and contrast "The Gettysburg Address" with Patrick Henry's "Speech in the Virginia Convention." Start by rereading both speeches, taking note of similarities and differences in purpose, directness, forcefulness, tone (the writer's attitude toward his or her subject), diction, structure, and methods of persuasion. Arrange your notes according to the points of contrast. Prepare a thesis statement. Then write your essay, focusing each of your body paragraphs on a single point of contrast. When you revise, make sure that you have varied the lengths and structures of your sentences and used transitions to link your ideas. Proofread your essay and prepare a final draft.

Letter to Mrs. Bixby

Abraham Lincoln

Executive Mansion, Washington,
November 21, 1864

Mrs. Bixby, Boston, Massachusetts:

Dear Madam:

I have been shown in the files of the War Department a statement of the Adjutant-General of Massachusetts that you are the mother of five sons who have died gloriously on the field of battle. I feel how weak and fruitless must be any words of mine which should attempt to beguile you from the grief of a loss so overwhelming. But I cannot refrain from tendering to you the consolation that may be found in the thanks of the Republic they died to save. I pray that our Heavenly Father may assuage the anguish of your bereavement, and leave you only the cherished memory of the loved and lost, and the solemn pride that must be yours to have laid so costly a sacrifice upon the altar of freedom.

Yours very sincerely and respectfully,

Abraham Lincoln

LINCOLN PROCLAIMING THANKSGIVING
Dean Cornwell
Louis A. Warren Lincoln Library and Museum, Fort Wayne, Indiana

THINKING ABOUT THE SELECTION

Recalling

1. What has President Lincoln been shown in the files of the War Department?
2. For what does President Lincoln pray?

Interpreting

3. What is the purpose of this letter?
4. How would you describe the tone, or the writer's attitude toward the subject?
5. (a) What does the "altar of freedom" represent? (b) What is the sacrifice which Mrs. Bixby has laid upon it?
6. What does this letter reveal about Lincoln?

Applying

7. (a) What effect do you think this letter would have on Mrs. Bixby? (b) What is it about this letter that would create this effect?
8. In the sixth century B.C., the Chinese philosopher Confucius wrote, "If language be not in accordance with the truth of things, affairs cannot be carried on to success." Explain how Lincoln's letter is in keeping with this advice. Then tell whether or not you think this is good advice for all types of writing.

UNDERSTANDING LANGUAGE

Recognizing Words with the Root *cede*

Many English words are based on the Latin root *cede,* which means "to halt or give way." For example, the word *secede* means "to withdraw or separate formally."

Keeping the definition of *cede* in mind, try to determine the meaning of each of the following words. Then check your answer in a dictionary.
1. accede   2. precede   3. recede
4. concede   5. intercede

THINKING AND WRITING

Writing a Letter

Imagine that you are Mrs. Bixby. Write a letter to Lincoln in response to his letter to you. First freewrite, exploring your reactions to Lincoln's letter. Then prepare your first draft. Choose your language carefully and remember to make the tone appropriate for the audience (the President of the United States) and the purpose. Revise your letter, making sure you have used the appropriate form for a letter.

from Preface to the 1855 Edition of *Leaves of Grass*

Walt Whitman

America does not repel the past or what it has produced under its forms or amid other politics or the idea of castes or the old religions. . . . accepts the lesson with calmness . . . is not so impatient as has been supposed that the slough still sticks to opinions and manners and literature while the life which served its requirements has passed into the new life of the new forms . . . perceives that the corpse is slowly borne from the eating and sleeping rooms of the house . . . perceives that it waits a little

WALT WHITMAN
Thomas Eakins
Courtesy of The Pennsylvania Academy of the Fine Arts

while in the door . . . that it was fittest for its days . . . that its action has descended to the stalwart and well-shaped heir who approaches . . . and that he shall be fittest for his days.

The Americans of all nations at any time upon the earth have probably the fullest poetical nature. The United States themselves are essentially the greatest poem. In the history of the earth hitherto the largest and most stirring appear tame and orderly to their ampler largeness and stir. Here at last is something in the doings of man that corresponds with the broadcast doings of the day and night. Here is not merely a nation but a teeming nation of nations. Here is action untied from strings necessarily blind to particulars and details magnificently moving in vast masses. Here is the hospitality which forever indicates heroes. . . . Here are the roughs and beards and space and ruggedness and nonchalance that the soul loves. Here the performance disdaining the trivial unapproached in the tremendous audacity of its crowds and groupings and the push of its perspective spreads with crampless and flowing breadth and showers its prolific and splendid extravagance. One sees it must indeed own the riches of the summer and winter, and need never be bankrupt while corn grows from the ground or the orchards drop apples or the bays contain fish or men beget children upon women. . . .

THINKING ABOUT THE SELECTION

Recalling

1. (a) What does America "not repel"? (b) What does it accept "with calmness"?
2. What country does Whitman say has the "fullest poetical nature"?

Interpreting

3. In the second paragraph, Whitman states that "the United States themselves are essentially the greatest poem." (a) What is the meaning of this statement? (b) How does Whitman support it?
4. What does Whitman mean when he comments that the United States "is not merely a nation but a teeming nation of nations"?
5. In your own words, describe Whitman's attitude toward America.

Applying

6. What is your definition of an American? Provide examples to clarify your definition.

from Song of Myself

Walt Whitman

1

I celebrate myself, and sing myself,
And what I assume you shall assume,
For every atom belonging to me as good belongs to you.

I loaf and invite my soul,
5   I lean and loaf at my ease observing a spear of summer
    grass.

My tongue, every atom of my blood, formed from this soil,
    this air,
Born here of parents born here from parents the same, and
    their parents the same,
I, now thirty-seven years old in perfect health begin,
Hoping to cease not till death.

10   Creeds and schools in abeyance,
Retiring back a while sufficed at what they are, but never
    forgotten,
I harbor for good or bad, I permit to speak at every hazard,
Nature without check with original energy.

6

A child said *What is the grass?* fetching it to me with full
    hands,
How could I answer the child? I do not know what it is any
    more than he.

I guess it must be the flag of my disposition, out of hopeful
    green stuff woven.

Or I guess it is the handkerchief of the Lord,
5   A scented gift and remembrancer[1] designedly dropped,
Bearing the owner's name someway in the corners, that we
    may see and remark, and say *Whose?*

        . . .

What do you think has become of the young and old men?
And what do you think has become of the women and
    children?

---

1. remembrancer: Reminder.

They are alive and well somewhere,

10   The smallest sprout shows there is really no death,
And if ever there was it led forward life, and does not wait
    at the end to arrest it,
And ceas'd the moment life appear'd.
All goes onward and outward, nothing collapses,
And to die is different from what anyone supposed, and
    luckier.

9

The big doors of the country barn stand open and ready,
The dried grass of the harvest-time loads the slow-drawn
    wagon,

Beat! Beat! Drums!

Walt Whitman

This poem was written in response to the defeat of the Union army by Confederate forces in the battle of Bull Run in 1861. The Confederate victory shocked many people who felt that the Union would easily win the war and made it clear that a long and bloody struggle lay ahead.

Beat! beat! drums!—blow! bugles! blow!
Through the windows—through doors—burst like a ruthless
    force,
Into the solemn church, and scatter the congregation,
Into the school where the scholar is studying;
5 Leave not the bridegroom quiet—no happiness must he
    have now with his bride,
Nor the peaceful farmer any peace, ploughing his field or
    gathering his grain,
So fierce you whirr and pound you drums—so shrill you
    bugles blow.

Beat! beat! drums!—blow! bugles! blow!
Over the traffic of cities—over the rumble of wheels in the
    streets;
10 Are beds prepared for sleepers at night in the houses? no
    sleepers must sleep in those beds,
No bargainers' bargains by day—no brokers or speculators—
    would they continue?
Would the talkers be talking? would the singer attempt to
    sing?
Would the lawyer rise in the court to state his case before
    the judge?
Then rattle quicker, heavier drums—you bugles wilder blow.

15 Beat! beat! drums!—blow! bugles! blow!
Make no parley—stop for no expostulation,
Mind not the timid—mind not the weeper or prayer,
Mind not the old man beseeching the young man,
Let not the child's voice be heard, nor the mother's
    entreaties,
20 Make even the trestles to shake the dead where they lie
    awaiting the hearses,
So strong you thump O terrible drums—so loud you bugles
    blow.

THE WOUNDED DRUMMER BOY
Eastman Johnson
The Union League Club, New York City

THINKING ABOUT THE SELECTION

Recalling

1. (a) What activities do the drums and bugles interrupt? (b) What do they prevent us from noticing?

Interpreting

2. What do the drums and bugles represent?
3. What does this poem suggest about the effect of war on people's everyday lives?
4. (a) How does the rhythm and repetition of lines 1, 8, and 15 add to the impact of the poem? (b) How does Whitman's use of parallelism reinforce the meaning of the poem?

Applying

5. Whitman's poem suggests that most Americans dreaded the coming of the Civil War. Why do you think the American people might have dreaded the Civil War more than other wars in which the country had participated? Explain your answer.

When I Heard the Learn'd Astronomer

Walt Whitman

When I heard the learn'd astronomer,
When the proofs, the figures, were ranged in columns
  before me,
When I was shown the charts and diagrams, to add, divide
  and measure them,
When I sitting heard the astronomer where he lectured with
  much applause in the lecture room,
5 How soon unaccountable I became tired and sick,
Till rising and gliding out I wander'd off by myself,
In the mystical moist night air, and from time to time,
Look'd up in perfect silence at the stars.

THE LAWRENCE TREE, 1929
Georgia O'Keeffe
Wadsworth Atheneum, Hartford

THINKING ABOUT THE SELECTION

Recalling

1. What visual aids does the astronomer use during his lecture?
2. How does the speaker respond to the lecture?
3. (a) Where does the speaker go when he leaves the lecture? (b) What does he look up at from time to time?

Interpreting

4. How is the speaker's attitude toward the stars different from that of the astronomer?
5. The word *mystical* means "spiritually significant." Why do you think Whitman chose this word to describe the moist night air in line 7?
6. Who do you think is more "learn'd" in regard to the stars? Explain your answer.
7. (a) What is the theme, or main point, of the poem? (b) How does Whitman's use of parallel structures in the first four lines reinforce the theme?

Applying

8. (a) How would you describe your own attitude toward the stars? (b) Is your attitude more similar to the astronomer's attitude or the speaker's attitude?

ANALYZING LITERATURE

Recognizing Free Verse

Free verse is verse that has irregular meter and line length. Walt Whitman's use of free verse reflects his belief in freedom, democracy, and individuality.

1. Considering the theme of "When I Heard a Learn'd Astronomer," why do you think free verse is an appropriate form for the poem?
2. How would this poem be different if it were written in verse with regular meter and line length?
3. Even great writers do not always receive good reviews. William Allingham wrote of Walt Whitman's poetry, "Of course, to call it poetry, in any sense, would be mere abuse of the language." Respond to Allingham's statement. Do you think Whitman's writing is poetry? Explain your answer.

THINKING AND WRITING

Writing a Poem in Free Verse

Using free verse, write a poem expressing your associations with a natural element such as grass, the ocean, the sun, or the moon. Start by reviewing the list of concrete details you prepared before you began reading. Try to think of additional details you can add to your list. Then write your poem. Structure your verse to recreate the rising and falling cadences of natural speech and vary the lengths of the lines according to intended emphasis. When you finish writing, revise your poem and share it with your classmates.

A Noiseless Patient Spider

Walt Whitman

A noiseless patient spider,
I mark'd where on a little promontory it stood isolated,
Mark'd how to explore the vacant vast surrounding,
It launch'd forth filament, filament, filament, out of itself,
5   Ever unreeling them, ever tirelessly speeding them.

And you O my soul where you stand,
Surrounded, detached, in measureless oceans of space,
Ceaselessly musing, venturing, throwing, seeking the
    spheres to connect them,
Till the bridge you will need be form'd, till the ductile
    anchor hold,
10 Till the gossamer thread you fling catch somewhere, O my
    soul.

THINKING ABOUT THE SELECTION

Recalling

1. Where is the spider standing when the speaker first sees it?
2. How does the spider explore its "vacant vast surrounding"?
3. (a) Where is the speaker's soul standing? (b) What is it doing?

Interpreting

4. What similarities does the speaker see between his soul and the spider?

5. With what do you think the speaker's soul is seeking connection (lines 8–10)?
6. Like the Transcendentalists, Whitman believed that the human spirit was mirrored in the world of nature. How does this poem reflect this belief?

Applying

7. Whitman presents a paradox, or apparent self-contradiction, in line 7 when he describes the soul as being both "surrounded" and "detached." Why do you think this paradox might be used to describe the position of the poet in society?

Assignment

1. Imagine you are one of the heroes of the American Revolution and have been transported forward in time to the time of the Civil War. Write a journal entry in which you express your thoughts and feelings concerning the war.

   Prewriting.   Choose a Revolutionary hero. Imagine how this person might have reacted to the Civil War.

   Writing.   When you write your journal entry, use an informal writing style but make sure the ideas are clearly and coherently organized.

   Revising.   When you revise, make sure you have varied the length and structure of your sentences. After you finish revising, proofread your entry and prepare a final copy.

Assignment

2. Imagine you are living in either the North or the South just before the start of the Civil War. Write a letter to the President, expressing your thoughts concerning the possible secession of the southern states.

   Prewriting.   Brainstorm about the causes of the Civil War, trying to look at the relevant issues from the points of view of the people from both the North and the South.

   Writing.   When writing your letter, express your thoughts as clearly and concisely as possible.

   Revising.   When you revise, make sure your thoughts are organized in a logical manner. After you have finished revising, proofread your letter and prepare a final copy.

Assignment

3. Many important historical figures emerged from the Civil War era. Several of these figures are represented in this book. Choose one of these people, or another figure with whom you are familiar, and write a short character sketch of that person.

   Prewriting.   Review the author biography of the figure you have chosen in addition to the selection or selections by this person, focusing on what they reveal about his or her personality.

   Writing.   When you write your sketch, focus on describing your subject's most important personality traits.

   Revising.   When you revise, make sure your sketch gives the reader a clear sense of your subject's personality. After you have finished revising, share your sketch with your classmates.

Assignment

1. Civil War literature is important because it helps us to understand how the war and the issues surrounding it affected the American people. Choose one of the selections you have read and discuss what it reveals about the effect of the Civil War and/or the issues surrounding it.

Prewriting.   Reread the selection, noting what it reveals about the effect of the war and the issues surrounding it. Then develop a thesis statement and prepare an outline.

Writing.   When you write your essay, make sure you use passages from the selection to support your thesis.

Revising.   When you revise, make sure you have thoroughly supported your thesis and have not included any unnecessary information.

Assignment

2. Although Frederick Douglass, Abraham Lincoln, Robert E. Lee, and Chief Joseph each had a different perspective of the events of the Civil War era, they all shared a number of noble ideals. Write an essay in which you compare and contrast the ideals, attitudes, and perspectives of two of these figures.

Prewriting.   After choosing the figures on which you will focus, reread the author biographies of and selections by each figure, noting similarities and differences in attitudes and points of view.

Writing.   When writing your essay, organize your ideas according to corresponding points of contrast.

Revising.   When you revise, make sure you have used transitions and other linking devices to connect your ideas.

Assignment

3. Write a critical analysis of one of the works you have read, evaluating the quality of the writing, the use of literary devices, and the selection's historical significance.

Prewriting.   Carefully reread the selection you chose. How would you evaluate the quality of the writing? How effectively does the selection achieve its purpose? What literary devices does the writer use? What is the selection's historical significance?

Writing.   When you write your essay, support your evaluation with evidence from the selection.

Revising.   When you revise, make sure you have expressed your opinions in a clear, coherent, and logically organized manner. After you finish revising, proofread your essay and prepare a final copy.

THE ADIRONDACK GUIDE
Winslow Homer
Museum of Fine Arts, Boston

REALISM AND
THE FRONTIER
1865–1915

The Palace Hotel at Fort Romper was painted a light blue, a shade that is on the legs of a kind of heron, causing the bird to declare its position against any background. The Palace Hotel, then, was always screaming and howling in a way that made the dazzling winter landscape of Nebraska seem only a gray swampish hush.

Stephen Crane

One of the characters in Stephen Crane's story "The Blue Hotel," published in 1899, is a half-mad Swede who has arrived by train in the tiny town of Fort Romper, Nebraska. Another character guesses that the Swede "has been reading dime novels, and he thinks he's right out in the middle of it—the shootin' and stabbin' and all." A visiting cowboy wonders how the man could be so mistaken, since, as he says, "this ain't Wyoming ner none of them places. This is Nebrasker."

A few years earlier, Nebraska would have been the Wild West, but no longer. America was changing dramatically in the late nineteenth and early twentieth centuries. The Civil War, although devastating to the South, was more and more becoming a hazy memory. The American frontier, which had once seemed so vast, no longer existed by 1915. (This in no way stemmed the tide of western migration, however.) A number of railroads bridged the continent. The Wright Brothers took their first aircraft aloft at Kitty Hawk, North Carolina, in 1903. Science and industry were making great leaps forward.

So was literature. After the relative quiet of the immediate postwar years, an impressive array of writers began to appear. The prewar Romantic writers were still widely read, but most of the emerging writers were not Romantics. These new writers wanted to portray life as it was lived, not sentimentally or in flights of fancy. Their goal was Realism, or Naturalism, or Regionalism.

IN SEARCH OF THE LAND OF MILK AND HONEY
Harvey Dunn
City Library, De Smet, South Dakota

THE HISTORICAL SETTING

American writers were gaining a large and increasingly diverse audience. Between 1865 and 1915, the population of the United States grew by more than 42 million people. This number was larger than the entire population of the United States at the end of the Civil War. This huge population increase stemmed in part from new immigration. Before the 1880's, most immigrants came from western Europe and the Scandanavian countries. In the 1880's immigrants began arriving from southern and eastern Europe, from Italy, Greece, Poland, and Russia. Many of the new immigrants settled in eastern cities, but some joined the relentless western march.

The populations of older cities like Boston and Baltimore tripled or quadrupled during these decades. The populations of large midwestern cities like Chicago and Detroit also skyrocketed. Major new cities sprang up almost overnight. In 1858, Denver had consisted of sixty crude log cabins. Three years later, as a result of the Pikes Peak gold rush, 3,000 people lived there. By 1890, the population of Denver exceeded 100,000.

THE MINES DURING THE GOLD RUSH, 1849, IN CALIFORNIA
Frank Tenney Johnson
Three Lions

A Nation on the Move

In many ways, the American experience has been shaped by advances in transportation. European settlers reached the shores of North America as a result of improvements in oceangoing ships. Once here, the settlers advanced westward by stagecoach, and then by railroad. Long journeys that would have been difficult for early writers of the republic were commonplace for Mark Twain. As a journeyman printer, Twain made his way from Hannibal, Missouri, to St. Louis, then New York, then Philadelphia, and back to Keokuk, Iowa. Later he went to New Orleans as a steamboat pilot, to Virginia City, Nevada, as a newspaperman, and to San Francisco as a writer and foreign correspondent. Eventually, he settled in Hartford, Connecticut. This kind of mobility helped to shape both the subject matter and the attitudes of writers in this period.

Mark Twain's *Roughing It* records his experiences in the Far West, including his days in Virginia City, Nevada. In this period, for the first time, a number of writers represented the Midwest or Far West. Some of these writers, like Bret Harte and Willa Cather, were born in the East or South, but later moved west. Harte moved as a young man from New York to California. Cather moved as a child from Virginia to Nebraska. One of the few native California writers was Jack London, born in San Francisco and raised in Oakland. Interestingly, London's first successful stories were not set in California, but farther north and west—in the Klondike, on the Alaskan-Canadian border. London had gone to this region in 1897 to prospect for gold.

1867   **Mark Twain** wins recognition with "The Notorious Jumping Frog of Calaveras County."

Lucy McKim, with others, publishes *Slave Songs of the United States*.

United States purchases Alaska from Russia for two cents an acre.

1868   Louisa May Alcott's *Little Women* becomes an immediate children's favorite.

1869   Transcontinental railroad completed with driving of golden spike in Utah.

Women in Wyoming Territory are first to win right to vote.

1870   **Bret Harte** publishes *The Luck of Roaring Camp and Other Stories*.

1876   Alexander Graham Bell patents a telephone and transmits speech over it.

Sitting Bull's Sioux wipe out General George A. Custer's cavalry at Battle of the Little Bighorn.

Mark Twain publishes *The Adventures of Tom Sawyer*.

1879   Thomas A. Edison invents electric light bulb.

1883   **Mark Twain** publishes *Life on the Mississippi*.

Brooklyn Bridge, an engineering marvel of the day, opens.

1884   **Mark Twain's** *The Adventures of Huckleberry Finn* appears.

1885   William Dean Howells publishes *The Rise of Silas Lapham*.

1886   Statue of Liberty dedicated in New York Harbor.

1887   **Sidney Lanier's** *Poems* appears six years after his death.

1888   Great mid-March blizzard in eastern United States piles 30-foot drifts in New York's Herald Square.

1889   Worst flood in American history strikes Johnstown, Pennsylvania.

Twenty Thousand Leagues Under the Sea

Proclamation of the German Empire

Thomas Edison

Blizzard of 1888

The Battle of Little Bighorn

Mark Twain

Alexander Graham Bell

Inauguration of Statue of Liberty

WORLD EVENTS

1866 Russia: Fyodor Dostoyevsky publishes *Crime and Punishment*.

Austria: Gregor Mendel reports on basic laws of biological inheritance.

1867 England: Matthew Arnold writes "Dover Beach."

1868 Japan: Emperor gains power when shogunate—Japan's feudal dictatorship—falls.

1869 France: Jules Verne publishes *Twenty Thousand Leagues Under the Sea*.

1871 Germany: End of Franco-Prussian War establishes German empire.

1872 Russia: Leo Tolstoy completes *War and Peace*.

1874 France: Claude Monet gathers Impressionist painters for first exhibition.

1875 France: People in France begin raising money to build U.S. Statue of Liberty.

1878 England: *The Return of the Native* by Thomas Hardy appears in print.

1879 Norway: Henrick Ibsen writes *The Doll's House*.

1880 Russia: Fyodor Dostoyevsky publishes *The Brothers Karamazov*.

South Africa: Cecil Rhodes founds diamond mining company.

1882 Norway: Henrik Ibsen writes *An Enemy of the People*.

1883 England: Robert Louis Stevenson publishes *Treasure Island*.

1884 Russia: Leo Tolstoy completes "The Death of Ivan Ilyich."

1885 Germany: Karl Benz builds first automobile powered by internal combustion engine.

1886 England: Thomas Hardy publishes *The Mayor of Casterbridge*.

Introduction   477

AMERICAN EVENTS

1890 First volume of **Emily Dickinson's** poems is released four years after her death.

Last major battle between U.S. troops and Native Americans fought at Wounded Knee, South Dakota.

1891 Hamlin Garland publishes *Main-Travelled Roads*.

1893 **Ambrose Bierce** publishes *Can Such Things Be?*

1894 **Kate Chopin's** *Bayou Folk* published.

1895 **Stephen Crane** publishes *The Red Badge of Courage*.

1896 **Paul Lawrence Dunbar** publishes *Lyrics of Lowly Life*.

The Country of the Pointed Firs, **Sarah Orne Jewett's** masterpiece, appears.

1897 **Edwin Arlington Robinson** publishes *The Children of the Night*.

1898 Spanish-American War begins.

1901 President William McKinley shot in Buffalo; succeeded by Theodore Roosevelt.

1903 **Jack London** publishes *The Call of the Wild*.

Boston Red Sox and Pittsburgh Pirates play in first World Series.

Wright Brothers stay aloft for 582 feet in their airplane at Kitty Hawk, North Carolina.

1905 **Willa Cather** publishes *The Troll Garden*.

Edith Wharton's *The House of Mirth* appears.

1906 Strong earthquake in San Francisco is followed by devastating fire.

1908 Ford introduces the Model T.

1909 Admiral Robert E. Peary reaches the North Pole.

National Association for the Advancement of Colored People (NAACP) founded.

Theodore Roosevelt

San Francisco Earthquake

First Flight at

Albert Einstein

Beginning of

Boxer Rebellion

Ford Model T

Kitty Hawk

Thomas Mann

Spanish-American War

Sigmund Freud

WORLD EVENTS

1891	England: Thomas Hardy publishes *Tess of the D'Urbervilles*.
1894	Sino-Japanese War breaks out; Japanese army easily defeats Chinese.
1895	Germany: Wilhelm Roentgen discovers X-rays.
1896	England: A. E. Housman publishes *A Shropshire Lad*.
1897	England: Rudyard Kipling writes *Captains Courageous*.
1898	France: Paul Cézanne begins painting *Bathers*.
	France: Pierre Curie and Marie Sklodowska Curie discovered radium.
1899	Russia: Anton Chekhov has his play *Uncle Vanya* produced at Moscow Art Theatre.
	South Africa: Boer War breaks out between British and Dutch in South Africa.
1900	Austria: Sigmund Freud publishes *The Interpretation of Dreams*.
	China: Chinese nationalists begin Boxer Rebellion to expel foreigners.
1901	Germany: Thomas Mann publishes *Buddenbrooks*.
1903	Spain: Pablo Picasso paints *The Old Guitarist*.
	Ireland: George Bernard Shaw produces *Man and Superman*.
	Ireland: William Butler Yeats publishes *In the Seven Woods*.
1904	Russo-Japanese War begins.
1905	Germany: Albert Einstein proposes his relativity theory.
1910	Mexico: Francisco Madero begins revolution that overthrows dictator Porfiorio Diaz.
1914	Europe: World War I begins.

Introduction 479

The Frontier Experience

In 1827, President John Quincy Adams's secretary of war had predicted that it would take 500 years to fill the American West. By 1890, the superintendent of the census could report that the nation's "unsettled area had been so broken into by isolated bodies of settlement that there can hardly be said to be a frontier line." To many Americans this came as quite a surprise. They had imagined that free, or at least cheap, land would always be available.

The frontier was gone, but its legacy lived on. Frontier dwellers had always been generally mobile, practical, inventive, democratic, and optimistic. Those traits colored the national character and affected American writing. Mark Twain, in his early life and writing, showed all five traits. Yet the frontier itself offered no idyllic existence. It could be lonely and cruel, as in Jack London's "To Build a Fire" or Willa Cather's "A Wagner Matinée." The great majority of Americans never lived on the frontier. American life and literature have nonetheless been enriched by those who did.

Unresolved Challenges

The Civil War and its aftermath spurred the headlong growth of industry in the North. Yet even before the Civil War, writers had observed that industrial growth created hardships as well as benefits. Along with rapid industrial expansion came urban slums, farm problems, and labor unrest. By the 1880's, some of the abuses were bringing insistent demands for reform. Back in 1873, Mark Twain and Charles Dudley Warner had published *The Gilded Age*. This novel dealt with unrestrained greed in a time of financial speculation and uncertain moral values. Around the turn of the century, a group of journalists took up this same theme. Theodore Roosevelt called them "muckrakers," because they uncovered only the muck, or dirt, of American life. Among the leading muckrakers were Ida Tarbell and Lincoln Steffens. Tarbell exposed unethical business practices, while Steffens attacked corruption in city and state governments.

A further challenge facing the nation was its great and increasing diversity. Despite the Depression of 1893, the country as a whole rejoiced in economic good times. Not everyone shared in the prosperity, however. Farmers faced falling agricultural prices, high interest rates for bank loans, and unequal railroad shipping charges. After centuries of conflict, the Native American tribes had been defeated. The slaves had been freed but had not been made full participants in American democracy. Restrictive immigration laws prohibited Chinese workers from entering the United States after 1882; European immigrants often worked long hours in sweatshops and lived in slums; and women were not allowed to vote in national elections.

The literature of the time was as diverse as the nation itself. It

THE BOWERY AT NIGHT, 1895
W. Louis Sonntag, Jr.
Museum of the City of New York

reflected both the promise and the problems of the frontier and of the dynamic expansion of industry.

REALISM IN AMERICAN LITERATURE

The Civil War and its aftermath left Americans less certain about the future than ever before, diminishing their belief in a unity of national purpose. The buoyant spirits of Emerson and the wild imaginings of Poe seemed out of date to many, especially to young writers. In the South, the Jeffersonian dream of a nation of farmers lay shattered like the land itself. The South would have to rebuild on a different foundation, and it would be a long, arduous task.

Under the circumstances, it is small wonder that writers turned away from the Romanticism that had been so popular before the war. The hopes of idealists, these new writers felt, would have to

RABBIT STEW
Gary Niblett
Photograph Courtesy of the Gerald Peters Gallery; Santa Fe, New Mexico, and Dallas, Texas

wait. Even the visions of Hawthorne and the extravagances of Melville did not fit the mood of the times. In place of Romanticism came Realism, a literary movement that sought to portray ordinary life as real people live it and attempted to show characters and events in an objective, almost factual way.

The Realistic Movement

Realistic fiction remains popular today, and it may seem strange that it was once controversial. But it was. Realistic writers saw themselves as being in revolt against Romanticism. Mark Twain wrote an amusing essay whose target was the Romantic writer James Fenimore Cooper. In *The Deerslayer,* Twain claimed, Cooper "has scored 114 offenses against literary art out of a possible 115." One of these offenses, according to Twain, is that "the personages of a tale shall confine themselves to possibilities and let miracles alone; or, if they venture a miracle, the author must plausibly set it forth to make it look possible and reasonable."

Eugene Field, a Chicago journalist, held the opposite view. Field took humorous aim at the new Realistic writers, Hamlin Garland in particular. "Mr. Garland's heroes sweat and do not wear socks," Field wrote. "His heroines eat cold huckleberry pie."

How did Realism originate? There had been Realistic writers in France for some time, notably Honore de Balzac, Stendhal, and Gustave Flaubert. Although these writers and others had great influence, American Realism had roots in this country, in the experiences of war, on the frontier, and in the cities. Science played a part as well. The objectivity of science struck many writers as a worthy goal for literature. Just as important, perhaps, was a general feeling that Romanticism was wearing thin. Students still recited Romantic poetry and read Romantic novels, but many writers believed these works to be old-fashioned.

One in particular who held that belief was William Dean Howells. Howells held prestigious editorial posts at the *Atlantic Monthly* and *Harper's* and knew virtually every important writer of the day. Although his early works were not Realistic, in the 1880's he began to champion Realism. His best Realistic novel, *The Rise of Silas Lapham,* was published in 1885. Many people considered Howells, a self-educated man, to be the leading literary figure of the time. He often advised his friend Mark Twain and encouraged many younger authors, among them Hamlin Garland and Stephen Crane. In 1891, Howells described his theories about realism in a book called *Criticism and Fiction*.

Howells and others were aware that Realistic writers ran the risk of becoming boring. A Romantic was limited only by his or her imagination, but a Realist had to find meaning in the commonplace. To do this, the Realist had to be acutely observant and to lay bare to readers the hidden meanings behind familiar words and actions. On the other hand, Realistic writers could deal honestly with characters that a Romantic writer would either avoid or gloss over: factory workers, bosses, politicians, gunfighters. This emphasis did not always please the critics, however. One journalist wrote of Willa Cather's stories: "If the writers of fiction who use western Nebraska as material would look up now and then and not keep their eyes and noses in the cattle yards, they might be more agreeable company." Despite such complaints, Realism held sway, and it remains dominant to the present day.

Naturalism

Some writers of the period went one step beyond Realism. Influenced by the French novelist Emile Zola, a literary movement known as Naturalism developed. According to Zola, a writer must

QUEENSBORO BRIDGE
Glen Odem Coleman
Hirshhorn Museum and Sculpture Garden
Smithsonian Institution

examine people and society objectively and, like a scientist, draw conclusions from what is observed. In line with this belief, Naturalistic writers viewed reality as the inescapable working out of natural forces. One's destiny, they said, is decided by heredity and environment, physical drives, and economic circumstances. Because they believed people have no control over events, Naturalistic writers tended to be pessimistic.

Only a few major American writers embraced Naturalism. One who did was Stephen Crane. His first novel, *Maggie: A Girl of the Streets,* published in 1893, is the earliest Naturalistic novel by an American writer. Jack London's "To Build a Fire" presents one of the recurring themes of Naturalism, man at the mercy of the brutal forces of nature. Another Naturalistic writer of the time was Frank Norris. *The Octopus,* his best-known novel, concerns the struggle between wheat growers and an all-powerful railroad in the San Joaquin Valley of California.

Regionalism

The third significant literary movement that developed during the latter part of the nineteenth century was Regionalism, or the "local color movement." Through the use of regional dialect and vivid descriptions of the landscape, the Regionalists sought to capture the essence of life in the various different regions of the growing nation.

At its very best, Regional writing transcends the region and becomes part of the national literature. No one today would call Mark Twain a Regionalist or a local colorist. Yet his early short story "The

Notorious Jumping Frog of Calaveras County" fits the category. Bret Harte, on the other hand, is generally regarded as the founder of the local color movement. Harte's stories, such as "The Outcasts of Poker Flat," have many of the same elements as Twain's. George Washington Cable, another leader in the local color movement, wrote sketches and novels of Creole life in Louisiana. His writings have charm and style but are seldom read today.

Various reasons have been given to explain the popularity of the local color movement. Perhaps it was the desire of people throughout the reunited nation to learn more about one another after the discord of the Civil War. Whatever its cause, the outpouring of local color was remarkable. Besides Twain, Harte, and Cable, there was Edward Eggleston. Eggleston's novel *The Hoosier Schoolmaster,* portraying the backwoods country of Indiana, became a bestseller in its day. A more critically acclaimed book was Sarah Orne Jewett's *The Country of the Pointed Firs.* Many critics regard this as the finest work of fiction about nineteenth-century rural New England. Mary Wilkins Freeman, too, wrote memorably about rural New England. Kate Chopin, a Louisiana writer, produced outstanding tales of Creole and Cajun life.

LOUISIANA INDIANS WALKING ALONG A BAYOU
Alfred Boisseau
New Orleans Museum of Art

PORTRAIT OF MARIE LAVEAU'S DAUGHTER
Attributed to Frantz Fleischbein
New Orleans Museum of Art

Poets and Popular Writers

The poets of this period cannot be easily classified, for each of them speaks in a clear, individual voice. Stephen Crane's poems are short, spare, and untitled. Sometimes they resemble fables and sometimes riddles. Sidney Lanier, whose health was shattered as a Confederate prisoner of war, fused musical and poetical principles. Among the best of his poems are "The Song of the Chattahoochee" and "The Marshes of Glynn." Paul Laurence Dunbar, the son of former slaves, used black dialect and folklore in his poetry.

In 1897, one of the finest of all volumes of American poems appeared, Edwin Arlington Robinson's *The Children of the Night*. This volume contains unforgettable psychological portraits of people, including "Luke Havergal" and "Richard Cory." Fifteen years later, the *Spoon River Anthology* by Edgar Lee Masters made that poet's name a household word.

One of the famous short story writers of the time was William Sydney Porter, better known as O. Henry. Sometimes classified as a local colorist, O. Henry portrayed New York City vividly. His stories use the surprise ending to great effect. Like many bestselling authors then and now, O. Henry wrote to formula. In other words, he worked within a customary plot structure with certain familiar character types, settings, and situations.

Rarely do formula stories survive as literature, but they can have lasting influence. One type of writing that emerged during this period, the Western, has at times dominated the popular arts. Earlier, James Fenimore Cooper had created an American frontier hero. The settlement of the American West now called for a new breed of hero more closely tied to the Great Plains. Dime-novel westerns introduced this new hero and developed the modern Western formula. Most of the elements of this formula were firmly fixed in Owen Wister's *The Virginian,* published in 1902.

In addition to the poets already named, a number of popular poets were at work during this period. James Whitcomb Riley, using a rustic Hoosier dialect, wrote "Little Orphant Annie," "Knee-Deep in June," and other favorites. Eugene Field, the Denver journalist, wrote "Little Boy Blue" and "Wynken, Blynken, and Nod." Two poets from Oregon also enjoyed a brief popularity. Edwin Markham, whose best-known poem is "The Man with the Hoe," and Joaquin Miller, who wrote "Columbus."

AMERICAN VOICES
Quotations by Prominent Figures of the Period

But I reckon I got to light out for the territory ahead of the rest, because Aunt Sally says she's going to adopt me and sivilize me, and I can't stand it. I been there before.
Mark Twain, *Adventures of Huckleberry Finn*

The reports of my death are greatly exaggerated.
Mark Twain, Cable from London to the Associated Press, 1897

Bore: a person who talks when you wish him to listen. *Prejudice:* a vagrant opinion without visible means of support.
Ambrose Bierce, *The Devil's Dictionary*

The road was new to me, as roads always are, going back.
Sarah Orne Jewett, *The Country of the Pointed Firs*

The voice of the sea speaks to the soul.
Kate Chopin, *The Awakening*

There are only two or three human stories, and they go on repeating themselves as fiercely as if they had never happened before.
Willa Cather, *O Pioneers!*

Buck did not read the newspapers, or he would have known that trouble was brewing, not alone for himself, but for every tidewater dog, strong of muscle and with warm, long hair, from Puget Sound to San Diego.
Jack London, *The Call of the Wild*

The red sun was pasted in the sky like a wafer.
Stephen Crane, *The Red Badge of Courage*

Silence may be as variously shaded as speech.
Edith Wharton, *The Reef*

We wear the mask that grins and lies,
It hides our cheeks and shades our eyes,—
Paul Laurence Dunbar, *We Wear the Mask*

I shall have more to say when I am dead.
Edwin Arlington Robinson, "John Brown"

The Literature of 1865–1915

When you read literature, it is important to place it in its historical context. Doing so will help you interpret the literary movements that were prevalent during the period and appreciate the techniques the writer used to convey the ideas of the movement.

Historical Context

During 1865–1915 the population of the United States grew dramatically, with many people moving westward and ending up on the frontier. Travel from one part of the country to another became common as a result of new advances in transportation and of the desire of people in various parts of the country to learn more about each other. During his youth, Mark Twain traveled from Hannibal, Missouri; to St. Louis; New York; Philadelphia; New Orleans; Virginia City, Nevada; and San Francisco. As a result of the westward movement and increased travel, more and more of our literature became centered on the Midwest and the Far West.

Literary Movements

During this period writers turned away from Romanticism and strove to portray life as it was actually lived. The major movements of the period were Realism, Naturalism, and Regionalism. **Realism** attempted to present "a slice of life," whereas **Naturalism** went one step further, showing life as the inexorable working out of natural forces beyond our power to control. **Regionalism,** in contrast, was in some ways a blending of Realism and Romanticism. It emphasized locale, or place, and the elements that create local color—customs, dress, speech, and other local differences.

Writer's Techniques

During this period the short story emerged as a popular literary form. In their stories writers used specific details to create a sense of realism and to capture local color. In addition, they tended to draw their characters from the mass of humanity and had them speak in dialect, capturing the flavor and rhythms of common speech.

On the following pages is a selection by Mark Twain, one of the preeminent writers of this period. The notes in the side column should draw your attention to the historical context, literary movements, and writer's techniques. Understanding these features will help you more fully appreciate the selection.

from Roughing It

Mark Twain

Tom Quartz

One of my comrades there[1]—another of those victims of eighteen years of unrequited toil and blighted hopes—was one of the gentlest spirits that ever bore its patient cross in a weary exile: grave and simple Dick Baker, pocket miner of Dead-Horse Gulch. He was forty-six, gray as a rat, earnest, thoughtful, slenderly educated, slouchily dressed, and clay-soiled, but his heart was finer metal than any gold his shovel ever brought to light—than any, indeed, that ever was mined or minted.

Whenever he was out of luck and a little downhearted, he would fall to mourning over the loss of a wonderful cat he used to own (for where women and children are not, men of kindly impulses take up with pets, for they must love something). And he always spoke of the strange sagacity of that cat with the air of a man who believed in his secret heart that there was something human about it—maybe even supernatural.

I heard him talking about this animal once. He said:

"Gentlemen, I used to have a cat here, by the name of Tom Quartz, which you'd 'a' took an interest in, I reckon—most anybody would. I had him here eight year—and he was the remarkablest cat *I* ever see. He was a large gray one of the Tom specie, an' he had more hard, natchral sense than any man in this camp—'n' a *power* of dignity—he wouldn't let the Gov'ner of Californy be familiar with him. He never ketched a rat in his life—'peared to be above it. He never cared for nothing but mining. He knowed more about mining, that cat did, than any man *I* ever, ever see. You couldn't tell *him* noth'n' 'bout placer-diggin's—'n' as for pocket mining, why he was just born for it. He would dig out after me an' Jim when we went over the hills prospect'n', and he would trot along behind us for as much as five mile, if we went so fur. An' he had the best judgment about mining-ground—why you never see anything like it.

Historical Context: Many people rushed to California in 1849 when gold was found there.

Literary Movement: This story is an example of Regionalism. It takes place in a mining camp in California. The main character is a common man, poorly educated and poorly dressed. Note how the narrator presents this character as a jewel of a man.

Writer's Technique: Twain employs a storyteller who speaks in dialect, thus adding local color to the tale.

Literary Movement: The story takes the form of a tall tale, using exaggeration to create humor. Tall tales were a major form of regional writing.

---

1. **there:** California.

Writer's Technique: Notice the use of figurative language throughout. This language is not only vivid but also contributes to character development.

Writer's Technique: Twain has Dick Baker tell this story in the first person. Notice how Twain's storyteller has a gifted imagination and is able to vividly evoke events.

Literary Movement: Twain thought the humorous story should be told in the form of a dramatic monologue. Notice that at no point in this story does Baker suggest that there is anything funny about his tale.

When we went to work, he'd scatter a glance around, 'n' if he didn't think much of the indications, he would give a look as much as to say, 'Well, I'll have to get you to excuse *me*,' 'n' without another word he'd hyste his nose into the air 'n' shove for home. But if the ground suited him, he would lay low 'n' keep dark till the first pan was washed, 'n' then he would sidle up 'n' take a look, an' if there was about six or seven grains of gold *he* was satisfied—he didn't want no better prospect 'n' that—'n' then he would lay down on our coats and snore like a steamboat till we'd struck the pocket, an' then get up 'n' superintend. He was nearly lightnin' on superintending.

"Well, by an' by, up comes this yer quartz excitement. Everybody was into it—everybody was pick 'n' 'n' blast 'n' instead of shovelin' dirt on the hillside—everybody was put 'n' down a shaft instead of scrapin' the surface. Noth 'n' would do Jim, but *we* must tackle the ledges, too, 'n' so we did. We commenced put 'n' down a shaft, 'n' Tom Quartz he begin to wonder what in the dickens it was all about. *He* hadn't ever seen any mining like that before, 'n' he was all upset, as you may say—he couldn't come to a right understanding of it no way— it was too many for *him*. He was down on it, too, you bet you— he was down on it powerful—'n' always appeared to consider it the cussedest foolishness out. But that cat, you know, was *always* agin new-fangled arrangements—somehow he never could abide 'em. *You* know how it is with old habits. But by an' by Tom Quartz begin to git sort of reconciled a little, though he never *could* altogether understand that eternal sinkin' of a shaft an' never pannin' out anything. At last he got to comin' down in the shaft, hisself, to try to cipher[2] it out. An' when he'd git the blues, 'n' feel kind o' scruffy, 'n' aggravated 'n' disgusted—knowin' as he did, that the bills was runnin' up all the time an' we warn't makin' a cent—he would curl up on a gunny-sack in the corner an' go to sleep. Well, one day when the shaft was down about eight foot, the rock got so hard that we had to put in a blast—the first blast 'n' we'd ever done since Tom Quartz was born. An' then we lit the fuse 'n' clumb out 'n' got off 'bout fifty yards—'n' forgot 'n' left Tom Quartz sound asleep on the gunny-sack. In 'bout a minute we seen a puff of smoke bust up out of the hole, 'n' then everything let go with an awful crash, 'n' about four million ton of rocks 'n' dirt 'n' smoke 'n' splinters shot up 'bout a mile an' a half into the air, an' by George, right in the dead center of it was old Tom Quartz a-goin' end over end, an' a-snortin' an' a-sneez 'n', an' a-clawin' an' a-reachin' for things like all pos-

---

2. cipher (sī' fər) *v.*: Figure.

sessed. But it warn't no use, you know, it warn't no use. An' that was the last we see of *him* for about two minutes 'n' a half, an' then all of a sudden it begin to rain rocks and rubbage, an' directly he come down ker-whop about ten foot off f'm where we stood. Well, I reckon he was p'raps the orneriest-lookin' beast you ever see. One ear was sot back on his neck, 'n' his tail was stove up, 'n' his eye-winkers was swinged off, 'n' he was all blacked up with powder an' smoke, an' all sloppy with mud 'n' slush f'm one end to the other. Well, sir, it warn't no use to try to apologize—we couldn't say a word. He took a sort of a disgusted look at hisself, 'n' then he looked at us— an' it was just exactly the same as if he had said—'Gents, maybe *you* think it's smart to take advantage of a cat that ain't had no experience of quartz minin', but *I* think *different*'—an' then he turned on his heel 'n' marched off home without ever saying another word.

"That was jest his style. An' maybe you won't believe it, but after that you never see a cat so prejudiced agin quartz mining as what he was. An' by an' by when he *did* get to goin' down in the shaft ag'in, you'd 'a' been astonished at his sagacity. The minute we'd tetch off a blast 'n' the fuse'd begin to sizzle, he'd give a look as much as to say, 'Well, I'll have to git you to excuse *me*,' an' it was surpris'n' the way he'd shin out of that hole 'n' go f'r a tree. Sagacity? It ain't no name for it. 'Twas *inspiration!*"

I said, "Well, Mr. Baker, his prejudice against quartz mining *was* remarkable, considering how he came by it. Couldn't you ever cure him of it?"

"*Cure him!* No! When Tom Quartz was sot once, he was *always* sot—and you might 'a' blowed him up as much as three million times 'n' you'd never 'a' broken him of his cussed prejudice agin quartz mining."

The affection and the pride that lit up Baker's face when he delivered this tribute to the firmness of his humble friend of other days, will always be a vivid memory with me.

Writer's Technique: Notice how Twain employs a humorless listener who takes the tale seriously. The listener acts like the "straight man" in a modern comedy routine.

THINKING ABOUT THE SELECTION

Recalling

1. What three things does Baker mention to show that Tom Quartz knew more about mining than any human did?
2. Why is Tom Quartz upset when the men turn to quartz mining?
3. Why does Tom Quartz start going down the shaft himself?
4. How is Tom Quartz's prejudice against quartz mining confirmed?

Interpreting

5. What qualities in Tom Quartz does Dick Baker admire?
6. Why does Baker consider the cat's sagacity really inspiration?
7. Are the qualities the cat displays similar to those we have come to identify as our national character? Explain your answer.

Applying

8. William Thackeray once wrote: "A good laugh is sunshine in the house." Why would the humorous story be so important to people living on the frontier?

ANALYZING LITERATURE

Understanding Point of View

Point of view is the vantage point from which a story is told. Although Twain himself serves as the narrator of this selection, the story of Tom Quartz is recounted by a storyteller, Dick Baker, one of Twain's acquaintances in the mining camp. In some ways Twain fictionalizes both himself and Dick Baker in this tale, creating a persona, or character, for each that contributes to the humor.

1. How would you describe the character Mark Twain creates for himself as the narrator?
2. How would you describe the character he creates for the storyteller, Dick Baker?
3. Compare and contrast the way this story is told with the way a modern comedy team might perform a routine.

CRITICAL THINKING AND READING

Understanding Exaggeration

Exaggeration means magnifying something beyond the limits of truth, often for humorous effect. For example, Mark Twain once joked about the length of sentences in German literature: "Whenever the literary German dives into a sentence, that is the last you are going to see of him till he emerges on the other side of the Atlantic with his verb in his mouth."

1. (a) How is the outcome of the explosion an exaggeration? (b) How is the cat's entire personality an exaggeration?
2. Baker builds his exaggerations, with each getting bigger than the previous one. Explain how this technique contributes to the humor.

UNDERSTANDING LANGUAGE

Interpreting Dialect

Dialect is the colloquial language of people living in a certain region. Writers often use dialect to give their stories local color. For example, Mark Twain has Dick Baker say, "When Tom Quartz was sot once, he was *always* sot, and you might 'a' blowed him up as much as three million times 'n' you'd never 'a' broken him of his cussed prejudice agin quartz-mining."

Find two other examples of dialect in this selection. Does the use of dialect make the tale more or less effective? Explain.

THINKING AND WRITING

Writing a Tall Tale

Write your own tall tale. Imagine someone new has just moved to your neighborhood and to entertain him you want to tell him a tall tale about the exploits of you and your friends. Brainstorm to come up with a list of incredible events. Then start writing your tale. Using a colloquial voice, begin by telling about the event that is most plausible, building to the climax with the event that is most exaggerated. Revise your tale, making sure that your tone is consistent.

Prose

TURN HIM LOOSE, BILL
Frederic Remington
Three Lions

MARK TWAIN

1835–1910

Mark Twain earned international fame early in his career by writing humorous tales that captured the local color of the West. He then went on to establish himself as one of the greatest writers in the history of American literature by transforming his childhood observations and experiences into the classic American novels *The Adventures of Tom Sawyer* (1876) and *The Adventures of Hucklebury Finn* (1884). So great was the influence of this later novel, in fact, that Ernest Hemingway wrote, "All modern American literature comes from one book by Mark Twain called *Huckleberry Finn*."

Twain, who was born Samuel Langhorne Clemens, grew up in the Mississippi River town of Hannibal, Missouri. When he was eleven, his father died, and he left school to become a printer's apprentice. Though he disliked the profession, Twain worked as a printer in a number of different cities before deciding to pursue a career as a riverboat pilot at the age of twenty-one.

When the Civil War closed the Mississippi River, Twain traveled west to Nevada. There he supported himself as a journalist and lecturer, and he developed the entertaining writing style that made him famous. In 1865, when he published "The Notorious Jumping Frog of Calaveras County," his version of a tall tale he had heard in a mining camp, he became an international celebrity.

Following the publication of *The Innocents Abroad* (1869), a successful book of humorous travel letters, Twain moved to Hartford, Connecticut, where he lived for the rest of his life. While living in his new home, Twain began using his past experiences as the raw material for his books. In *Roughing It* (1872), he drew on his experiences in the western mining regions. He turned to his childhood experiences in writing *The Adventures of Tom Sawyer, Life on the Mississippi* (1883), and *The Adventures of Hucklebury Finn*. In *Hucklebury Finn,* his masterpiece, he delved into the realities of the prewar South, portraying the adventures of a young white orphan and a runaway slave. Using his talents as a humorist and satirist, Twain confronted social injustices.

During his later years, Twain was unable to reproduce the balance between pessimism and humor that he had captured in *Hucklebury Finn*. In works such as *A Connecticut Yankee in King Arthur's Court* (1889), *Pudd'nhead Wilson* (1894), and *The Man That Corrupted Hadleyburg* (1900) he expressed an increasingly pessimistic vision of society and human nature. However, Twain displayed the same masterful command of language that had already established him as the finest American fiction writer of his time. It was this command of language that compelled the twentieth-century poet T. S. Eliot to write that in Twain he had "discovered a new way of writing . . . a literary language based on American colloquial speech."

GUIDE FOR READING

The Boys' Ambition

Literary Forms

Narration. Narration is writing that tells a story. The story being related may be fictional, as in novels and short stories, or factual, as in historical accounts, autobiographies, and biographies. However, the distinction between fictional narration and factual narration is not always clear. Fictional narratives are often inspired by or based on real-life events. For example, *The Adventures of Hucklebury Finn,* Mark Twain's finest novel, grew out of Twain's boyhood observations and experiences. Similarly, in some factual narratives certain events and details are fictionalized or exaggerated. For example, in *Life on the Mississippi,* Twain's account of his own experiences as a boy and young man living on the Mississippi River, Twain embellishes certain events and magnifies the traits of certain people.

Look For

In *Life on the Mississippi,* Twain wrote, "Your true pilot cares nothing about anything on earth but the river, and his pride in his occupation surpasses the pride of kings." As you read "The Boys' Ambition," a section from *Life on the Mississippi,* look for what it reveals about Twain's boyhood. Although Twain never achieved his ambition to be a pilot, how might his boyhood experiences have shaped his career as a writer?

Writing

In "The Boys' Ambition," Mark Twain discusses his boyhood ambition to become a steamboatman. Freewrite for five minutes about your ambitions.

Vocabulary

Knowing the following words will help you as you read "The Boys' Ambition."

transient (tran' shənt) *adj.*: Not permanent (p. 496)
prodigious (prə dij' əs) *adj.*: Powerful (p. 496)
eminence (em' ə nəns) *n.*: Greatness; celebrity (p. 498)

from Life on the Mississippi
Mark Twain

The Boys' Ambition

When I was a boy, there was but one permanent ambition among my comrades in our village[1] on the west bank of the Mississippi River. That was, to be a steamboatman. We had transient ambitions of other sorts, but they were only transient.

When a circus came and went, it left us all burning to become clowns; the first Negro minstrel show that came to our section left us all suffering to try that kind of life; now and then we had a hope that if we lived and were good, God would permit us to be pirates. These ambitions faded out, each in its turn; but the ambition to be a steamboatman always remained.

Once a day a cheap, gaudy packet[2] arrived upward from St. Louis, and another downward from Keokuk.[3] Before these events, the day was glorious with expectancy; after them, the day was a dead and empty thing. Not only the boys, but the whole village, felt this. After all these years I can picture that old time to myself now, just as it was then: the white town drowsing in the sunshine of a summer's morning; the streets empty, or pretty nearly so; one or two clerks sitting in front of the Water Street stores, with their splint-bottomed chairs tilted back against the wall, chins on breasts, hats slouched over their faces, asleep—with shingle shavings enough around to show what broke them down; a sow and a litter of pigs loafing along the sidewalk, doing a good business in watermelon rinds and seeds; two or three lonely little freight piles scattered about the levee;[4] a pile of skids[5] on the slope of the stone-paved wharf, and the fragrant town drunkard asleep in the shadow of them; two or three wood flats[6] at the head of the wharf, but nobody to listen to the peaceful lapping of the wavelets against them; the great Mississippi, the majestic, the magnificent Mississippi, rolling its mile-wide tide along, shining in the sun; the dense forest away on the other side; the point above the town, and the point below, bounding the river-glimpse and turning it into a sort of sea, and withal a very still and brilliant and lonely one. Presently a film of dark smoke appears above one of those remote points; instantly a Negro drayman,[7] famous for his quick eye and prodigious voice, lifts up the cry, "S-t-e-a-m-boat a-comin'!" and the scene changes! The town drunkard stirs, the clerks wake up, a furious clatter of drays follows, every house and store pours out a human contribution, and all in a twinkling the dead town is alive and moving. Drays, carts, men, boys, all go hurrying from many quarters to a common center, the wharf. Assembled there, the people fasten their eyes upon the coming boat as upon a wonder they are seeing for the first time.

---

1. our village: Hannibal, Missouri.
2. packet *n.*: A boat that travels a regular route, carrying passengers, freight, and mail.
3. Keokuk (kē′ ə kuk′): A town in southeastern Iowa.

4. levee (lev′ ē) *n.*: A landing place along the bank of a river.
5. skids *n.*: Low, movable wooden platforms.
6. flats *n.*: Small flat-bottomed boats.
7. drayman *n.*: The driver of a dray, a low cart with detachable sides.

And the boat *is* rather a handsome sight, too. She is long and sharp and trim and pretty; she has two tall, fancy-topped chimneys, with a gilded device of some kind swung between them; a fanciful pilothouse, all glass and gingerbread, perched on top of the texas deck[8] behind them; the paddleboxes are gorgeous with a picture or with gilded rays above the boat's name; the boiler deck, the hurricane deck, and the texas deck are fenced and ornamented with clean white railings; there is a flag gallantly flying from the jackstaff;[9] the furnace doors are open and the fires glaring bravely; the upper decks are black with passengers; the captain stands by the big bell, calm, imposing, the envy of all; great volumes of the blackest smoke are rolling and tumbling out of the chimneys—a husbanded grandeur created

with a bit of pitch pine just before arriving at a town; the crew are grouped on the forecastle;[10] the broad stage is run far out over the port bow, and an envied deckhand stands picturesquely on the end of it with a coil of rope in his hand; the pent steam is screaming through the gauge cocks; the captain lifts his hand, a bell rings, the wheels stop; then they turn back, churning the water to foam, and the steamer is at rest. Then such a scramble as there is to get aboard, and to get ashore, and to take in freight and to discharge freight, all at one and the same time; and such a yelling and cursing as the mates facilitate it all with! Ten minutes later the steamer is under way again, with no flag on the jackstaff and no black smoke issuing from the chimneys. After ten more minutes the town is dead again, and the town drunkard asleep by the skids once more.

---

8. texas deck: The deck adjoining the officers' cabins, the largest cabins on the ship.
9. jackstaff *n.*: A rope that runs up and down a ship's mast.

---

10. forecastle *n.*: The front part of the upper deck.

PADDLE STEAMBOAT MISSISSIPPI
The Shelburne Museum, Shelburne, Vermont

My father was a justice of the peace, and I supposed he possessed the power of life and death over all men and could hang anybody that offended him. This was distinction enough for me as a general thing; but the desire to be a steamboatman kept intruding, nevertheless. I first wanted to be a cabin boy, so that I could come out with a white apron on and shake a tablecloth over the side, where all my old comrades could see me; later I thought I would rather be the deckhand who stood on the end of the stage plank with the coil of rope in his hand, because he was particularly conspicuous. But these were only daydreams—they were too heavenly to be contemplated as real possibilities. By and by one of our boys went away. He was not heard of for a long time. At last he turned up as apprentice engineer or striker on a steamboat. This thing shook the bottom out of all my Sunday-school teachings. That boy had been notoriously worldly, and I just the reverse; yet he was exalted to this eminence, and I left in obscurity and misery. There was nothing generous about this fellow in his greatness. He would always manage to have a rusty bolt to scrub while his boat tarried at our town, and he would sit on the inside guard and scrub it, where we could all see him and envy him and loathe him. And whenever his boat was laid up he would come home and swell around the town in his blackest and greasiest clothes, so that nobody could help remembering that he was a steamboatman; and he used all sorts of steamboat technicalities in his talk, as if he were so used to them that he forgot common people could not understand them. He would speak of the labboard[11] side of a horse in an easy, natural way that would make one wish he was dead. And he was always talking about "St. Looey" like an old citizen; he would refer casually to occasions when he "was coming down Fourth Street," or when he was "passing by the Planter's House," or when there was a

fire and he took a turn on the brakes of "the old Big Missouri"; and then he would go on and lie about how many towns the size of ours were burned down there that day. Two or three of the boys had long been persons of consideration among us because they had been to St. Louis once and had a vague general knowledge of its wonders, but the day of their glory was over now. They lapsed into a humble silence, and learned to disappear when the ruthless cub engineer approached. This fellow had money, too, and hair oil. Also an ignorant silver watch and a showy brass watch chain. He wore a leather belt and used no suspenders. If ever a youth was cordially admired and hated by his comrades, this one was. No girl could withstand his charms. He cut out every boy in the village. When his boat blew up at last, it diffused a tranquil contentment among us such as we had not known for months. But when he came home the next week, alive, renowned, and appeared in church all battered up and bandaged, a shining hero, stared at and wondered over by everybody, it seemed to us that the partiality of Providence for an undeserving reptile had reached a point where it was open to criticism.

This creature's career could produce but one result, and it speedily followed. Boy after boy managed to get on the river. The minister's son became an engineer. The doctor's and the postmaster's sons became mud clerks; the wholesale liquor dealer's son became a barkeeper on a boat; four sons of the chief merchant, and two sons of the county judge, became pilots. Pilot was the grandest position of all. The pilot, even in those days of trivial wages, had a princely salary—from a hundred and fifty to two hundred and fifty dollars a month, and no board to pay. Two months of his wages would pay a preacher's salary for a year. Now some of us were left disconsolate. We could not get on the river—at least our parents would not let us.

So by and by I ran away. I said I never would come home again till I was a pilot and could come in glory. But somehow I could not manage it. I went meekly aboard a few of

---

11. labboard: Larboard, the left-hand side of a ship.

the boats that lay packed together like sardines at the long St. Louis wharf, and very humbly inquired for the pilots, but got only a cold shoulder and short words from mates and clerks. I had to make the best of this sort of treatment for the time being, but I had comforting daydreams of a future when I should be a great and honored pilot, with plenty of money, and could kill some of these mates and clerks and pay for them.

THINKING ABOUT THE SELECTION

Recalling

1. What is the one permanent ambition of Twain and his boyhood friends?
2. How do the people of Hannibal respond to the daily arrival of the steamboat?
3. (a) How do Twain and the other boys react when one of their friends becomes an apprentice engineer on a steamboat? (b) What does the apprentice do to make sure that the other boys do not forget that he is a steamboatman?
4. (a) What happens to the young apprentice's boat? (b) How do the other boys respond?
5. (a) Why does Twain run away from home? (b) What does he discover after he leaves?

Interpreting

6. What impression of the town of Hannibal, Missouri, is conveyed through Twain's description of the town and its response to the steamboat's arrival?
7. How does Twain's description of the steamboat reflect his boyhood desire to be a steamboatman?
8. (a) How would you describe the attitude of the boys toward the young apprentice engineer? (b) How does their attitude reflect their desire to be steamboatmen?
9. (a) What seems to be Twain's attitude toward himself as a boy? (b) What details in the selection convey his attitude?

Applying

10. Although Twain never earned fame as a steamboat pilot, he did become a famous writer. How do you think Twain's love for the Mississippi River and riverboats contributed to his success as a writer?

ANALYZING LITERATURE

Recognizing Narration

Narration is writing that tells a story. A narrative may be factual or fictional. Yet the distinction between factual narration and fictional narration is not always clear. For example, *Life on the Mississippi* is a factual narrative account of Twain's experiences while growing up on the Mississippi River, but certain details and events in the book are fictionalized or exaggerated.

1. Which details in "The Boys' Ambition" may be exaggerated? Support your answer.
2. What do you think might have been Twain's reasons for fictionalizing some of the details?

THINKING AND WRITING

Writing a Statement of Ambition

College applications often include an essay question in which applicants are asked to discuss their main ambition in life. Prepare to answer this question by reviewing your freewriting concerning your ambitions. Decide what your main ambition is. Then list the reasons for your decision. When you write your essay, make sure you include enough reasons to support your statement of ambition. When you finish writing, revise your essay and prepare a final copy.

GUIDE FOR READING

Writer's Techniques

Look For

Writing

Vocabulary

Lost in a Snowstorm

Setting. The setting is the time and place in which the events in a work of literature occur. While the setting is rarely the most important element in a literary work, it often plays a major role in shaping the characters' behavior. By affecting the characters' behavior, the setting also influences the plot in a work. In fact, in some cases, the events are a direct result of the characters' interactions with the setting. For example, the events in a story about a group of people stranded in the desert may result from the people's efforts to cope with oppressive heat and lack of water.

As you read "Lost in a Snowstorm," look for the ways that the setting shapes the characters' behavior.

As the title suggests, this story is about a group of people lost in a snowstorm. Prepare a list of details describing a snowstorm or a similar natural event, such as a hurricane or an earthquake.

Knowing the following words will help you as you read "Lost in a Snowstorm."

dubious (doo′ bē əs) *adj.*: Questionable (p. 501)

assail (ə sāl′) *v.*: To have a forceful effect on (p. 501)

lurid (loor′ id) *adj.*: Vivid in a harsh or shocking way (p. 501)

venomous (ven′ əm əs) *adj.*: Spiteful; malicious (p. 501)

placid (plas′ id) *adj.*: Tranquil; calm (p. 503)

consternation (kän′ stər nā′ shən) *n.*: Great fear or shock that makes one feel helpless or bewildered (p. 503)

eschewing (es choo′ iŋ) *v.*: Abstaining from (p. 505)

profane (prə fān′) *adj.*: Showing disrespect or contempt for sacred things (p. 506)

ruminated (roo′ mə nāt id) *v.*: Meditated (p. 506)

lamentations (lam′ ən tā′ shənz) *n.*: Outward expressions of grief (p. 506)

from Roughing It

Mark Twain

Lost in a Snowstorm

In this excerpt the narrator and two other men are traveling from Unionville, a mining town in Nevada, to Carson City, the state capital.

The next morning it was still snowing furiously when we got away with our new stock of saddles and accouterments. We mounted and started. The snow lay so deep on the ground that there was no sign of a road perceptible, and the snowfall was so thick that we could not see more than a hundred yards ahead, else we could have guided our course by the mountain ranges. The case looked dubious, but Ollendorff said his instinct was as sensitive as any compass, and that he could "strike a beeline" for Carson City and never diverge from it. He said that if he were to straggle a single point out of the true line his instinct would assail him like an outraged conscience. Consequently we dropped into his wake happy and content. For half an hour we poked along warily enough, but at the end of that time we came upon a fresh trail, and Ollendorff shouted proudly:

"I knew I was as dead certain as a compass, boys! Here we are, right in somebody's tracks that will hunt the way for us without any trouble. Let's hurry up and join company with the party."

So we put the horses into as much of a trot as the deep snow would allow, and before long it was evident that we were gaining on our predecessors, for the tracks grew more distinct. We hurried along and at the end of an hour the tracks looked still newer and fresher—but what surprised us was, that the *number* of travelers in advance of us seemed to steadily increase. We wondered how so large a party came to be traveling at such a time and in such a solitude. Somebody suggested that it must be a company of soldiers from the fort, and so we accepted that solution and jogged along a little faster still, for they could not be far off now. But the tracks still multiplied, and we began to think the platoon of soldiers was miraculously expanding into a regiment—Ballou said they had already increased to five hundred! Presently he stopped his horse and said:

"Boys, these are our own tracks, and we're actually been circussing round and round in a circle for more than two hours, out here in this blind desert! By George this is perfectly hydraulic!"

Then the old man waxed wroth and abusive. He called Ollendorff all manner of hard names—said he never saw such a lurid fool as he was, and ended with the peculiarly venomous opinion that he "did not know as much as a logarithm!"

We certainly had been following our own tracks. Ollendorff and his "mental compass" were in disgrace from that moment. After all

WHY THE MAIL WAS LATE
Oscar E. Berninghaus
Thomas Gilcrease Institute of American History and Art, Tulsa, Oklahoma

our hard travel, here we were on the bank of the stream again, with the inn beyond dimly outlined through the driving snowfall. While we were considering what to do, the young Swede landed from the canoe and took his pedestrian way Carson-ward, singing his same tiresome song about his "sister and his brother" and "the child in the grave with its mother," and in a short minute faded and disappeared in the white oblivion. He was never heard of again. He no doubt got bewildered and lost, and Fatigue delivered him over to Sleep and Sleep betrayed him to Death. Possibly he followed our treacherous tracks till he became exhausted and dropped.

Presently the Overland stage forded the now fast-receding stream and started toward Carson in its first trip since the flood came. We hesitated no longer, now, but took up our march in its wake, and trotted merrily along, for we had good confidence in the driver's bump of locality. But our horses were no match for the fresh stage team. We were soon left out of sight; but it was no matter, for we had the deep ruts the wheels made for a guide. By this time it was three in the afternoon, and consequently it was not very long before night came—and not with a lingering twilight, but with a sudden shutting down like a cellar door, as is its habit in that country. The snowfall was still as thick as ever, and of course we could not see fifteen steps before us; but all about us the white glare of the snow bed enabled us to discern the smooth sugar-loaf mounds made by the covered sage bushes, and just in front of us the two faint grooves which we knew were the steadily filling and slowly disappearing wheel tracks.

Now those sage bushes were all about the same height—three or four feet; they stood just about seven feet apart, all over the vast desert; each of them was a mere snow mound, now; in *any* direction that you proceeded (the same as in a well-laid-out orchard) you would find yourself moving down a distinctly defined avenue, with a row of these snow mounds on either side of it—an avenue the customary width of a road, nice and level in its breadth, and rising at the sides in the most natural way, by reason of the mounds. But we had not thought of this. Then imagine the chilly thrill that shot through us when it finally occurred to us, far in the night, that since the last faint trace of the wheel tracks had long ago been buried from sight, we might now be wandering down a mere sagebrush avenue, miles away from the road and diverging further and further away from it all the time. Having a cake of ice slipped down one's back is placid comfort compared to it. There was a sudden leap and stir of blood that had been asleep for an hour, and as sudden a rousing of all the drowsing activities in our minds and bodies. We were alive and awake at once—and shaking and quaking with consternation, too. There was an instant halting and dismounting, a bending low and an anxious scanning of the roadbed. Useless, of course; for if a faint depression could not be discerned from an altitude of four or five feet above it, it certainly could not with one's nose nearly against it.

We seemed to be in a road, but that was no proof. We tested this by walking off in various directions—the regular snow mounds and the regular avenues between them convinced each man that *he* had found

the true road, and that the others had found only false ones. Plainly the situation was desperate. We were cold and stiff and the horses were tired. We decided to build a sagebrush fire and camp out till morning. This was wise, because if we were wandering from the right road and the snowstorm continued another day our case would be the next thing to hopeless if we kept on.

All agreed that a campfire was what would come nearest to saving us, now, and so we set about building it. We could find no matches, and so we tried to make shift with the pistols. Not a man in the party had ever tried to do such a thing before, but not a man in the party doubted that it *could* be done, and without any trouble—because every man in the party had read about it in books many a time and had naturally come to believe it, with trusting simplicity, just as he had long ago accepted and believed *that other* common book fraud about Indians and lost hunters making a fire by rubbing two dry sticks together.

We huddled together on our knees in the deep snow, and the horses put their noses together and bowed their patient heads over us; and while the feathery flakes eddied down and turned us into a group of white statuary, we proceeded with the momentous experiment. We broke twigs from a sagebush and piled them on a little cleared place in the shelter of our bodies. In the course of ten or fifteen minutes all was ready, and then, while conversation ceased and our pulses beat low with anxious suspense, Ollendorff applied his revolver, pulled the trigger, and blew the pile clear out of the county! It was the flattest failure that ever was.

This was distressing, but it paled before a greater horror—the horses were gone! I had been appointed to hold the bridles, but in my absorbing anxiety over the pistol experiment I had unconsciously dropped them and the released animals had walked off in the storm. It was useless to try to follow them, for their footfalls could make no sound, and one could pass within two yards of the creatures and never see them. We gave them up without an effort at recovering them, and cursed the lying books that said horses would stay by their masters for protection and companionship in a distressful time like ours.

We were miserable enough, before; we felt still more forlorn, now. Patiently, but with blighted hope, we broke more sticks and piled them, and once more the Prussian shot them into annihilation. Plainly, to light a fire with a pistol was an art requiring practice and experience, and the middle of a desert at midnight in a snowstorm was not a good place or time for the acquiring of the accomplishment. We gave it up and tried the other. Each man took a couple of sticks and fell to chafing them together. At the end of half an hour we were thoroughly chilled, and so were the sticks. We bitterly execrated the Indians, the hunters, and the books that had betrayed us with the silly device, and wondered dismally what was next to be done. At this critical moment Mr. Ballou fished out four matches from the rubbish of an overlooked pocket. To have found four gold bars would have seemed poor and cheap good luck compared to this. One cannot think how good a match looks under such circumstances—or how lovable and precious, and sacredly beautiful to the eye. This time we gathered sticks with high hopes; and when Mr. Ballou prepared to light the first match, there was an amount of interest centered upon him that pages of writing could not describe. The match burned hopefully a moment, and then went out. It could not have carried more regret with it if it had been a human life. The next match simply flashed and died. The wind puffed the third one out just as it was on the imminent verge of success. We gathered together closer than ever, and developed a solicitude that was rapt and painful, as Mr. Ballou scratched our last hope on his leg. It lit, burned blue and sickly, and then budded into a robust flame. Shading it with his hands, the old gentleman bent gradually down and every

heart went with him—everybody, too, for that matter—and blood and breath stood still. The flame touched the sticks at last, took gradual hold upon them—hesitated— took a stronger hold—hesitated again—held its breath five heartbreaking seconds, then gave a sort of human gasp and went out.

Nobody said a word for several minutes. It was a solemn sort of silence; even the wind put on a stealthy, sinister quiet, and made no more noise than the falling flakes of snow. Finally a sad-voiced conversation began, and it was soon apparent that in each of our hearts lay the conviction that this was our last night with the living. I had so hoped that I was the only one who felt so. When the others calmly acknowledged their conviction, it sounded like the summons itself. Ollendorff said:

"Brothers, let us die together. And let us go without one hard feeling toward each other. Let us forget and forgive bygones. I know that you have felt hard toward me for turning over the canoe, and for knowing too much and leading you round and round in the snow—but I meant well; forgive me. I acknowledge freely that I have had hard feelings against Mr. Ballou for abusing me and calling me a logarithm, which is a thing I do not know what, but no doubt a thing considered disgraceful and unbecoming in America, and it has scarcely been out of my mind and has hurt me a great deal—but let it go; I forgive Mr. Ballou with all my heart, and—"

Poor Ollendorff broke down and the tears came. He was not alone, for I was crying too, and so was Mr. Ballou. Ollendorff got his voice again and forgave me for things I had done and said. Then he got out his bottle of whiskey and said that whether he lived or died he would never touch another drop. He said he had given up all hope of life, and although ill prepared, was ready to submit humbly to his fate; that he wished he could be spared a little longer, not for any selfish reason, but to make a thorough reform in his character, and by devoting himself to helping the poor, nursing the sick, and pleading with the people to guard themselves against the evils of intemperance, make his life a beneficent example to the young, and lay it down at last with the precious reflection that it had not been lived in vain. He ended by saying that his reform should begin at this moment, even here in the presence of death, since no longer time was to be vouchsafed wherein to prosecute it to men's help and benefit—and with that he threw away the bottle of whiskey.

Mr. Ballou made remarks of similar purport, and began the reform he could not live to continue, by throwing away the ancient pack of cards that had solaced our captivity during the flood and made it bearable. He said he never gambled, but still was satisfied that the meddling with cards in any way was immoral and injurious, and no man could be wholly pure and blemishless without eschewing them. "And therefore," continued he, "in doing this act I already feel more in sympathy with that spiritual saturnalia[1] necessary to entire and obsolete reform." These rolling syllables touched him as no intelligible eloquence could have done, and the old man sobbed with a mournfulness not unmingled with satisfaction.

My own remarks were of the same tenor as those of my comrades, and I know that the feelings that prompted them were heartfelt and sincere. We were all sincere, and all deeply moved and earnest, for we were in the presence of death and without hope. I threw away my pipe, and in doing it felt that at last I was free of a hated vice and one that had ridden me like a tyrant all my days. While I yet talked, the thought of the good I might have done in the world and the still greater good I might *now* do, with these new incentives and higher and better aims to guide me if I could only be spared a few years longer,

---

1. **saturnalia** (sat′ ər nā′ lē ə) *n.*: A period of unrestrained revelry.

A DRIFTING SNOW
William Van De Velde Bonfield
Three Lions

overcame me and the tears came again. We put our arms about each other's necks and awaited the warning drowsiness that precedes death by freezing.

It came stealing over us presently, and then we bade each other a last farewell. A delicious dreaminess wrought its web about my yielding senses, while the snowflakes wove a winding sheet about my conquered body. Oblivion came. The battle of life was done.

I do not know how long I was in a state of forgetfulness, but it seemed an age. A vague consciousness grew upon me by degrees, and then came a gathering anguish of pain in my limbs and through all my body. I shuddered. The thought flitted through my brain, "this is death—this is the hereafter."

Then came a white upheaval at my side, and a voice said, with bitterness:

"Will some gentleman be so good as to kick me behind?"

It was Ballou—at least it was a tousled snow image in a sitting posture, with Ballou's voice.

I rose up, and there in the gray dawn, not fifteen steps from us, were the frame buildings of a stage station, and under a shed stood our still saddled and bridled horses!

An arched snowdrift broke up, now, and Ollendorff emerged from it, and the three of us sat and stared at the houses without speaking a word. We really had nothing to say. We were like the profane man who could not "do the subject justice," the whole situation was so painfully ridiculous and humiliating that words were tame and we did not know where to commence anyhow.

The joy in our hearts at our deliverance was poisoned; well-nigh dissipated, indeed. We presently began to grow pettish by degrees, and sullen; and then, angry at each other, angry at ourselves, angry at everything in general, we moodily dusted the snow from our clothing and in unsociable single file plowed our way to the horses, unsaddled them, and sought shelter in the station.

I have scarcely exaggerated a detail of this curious and absurd adventure. It occurred almost exactly as I have stated it. We actually went into camp in a snowdrift in a desert, at midnight in a storm, forlorn and hopeless, within fifteen steps of a comfortable inn.

For two hours we sat apart in the station and ruminated in disgust. The mystery was gone, now, and it was plain enough why the horses had deserted us. Without a doubt they were under that shed a quarter of a minute after they had left us, and they must have overheard and enjoyed all our confessions and lamentations.

After breakfast we felt better, and the zest of life soon came back. The world looked bright again, and existence was as dear to us as ever. Presently an uneasiness came over me—grew upon me—assailed me without ceasing. Alas, my regeneration was not complete—I wanted to smoke! I resisted with all my strength, but the flesh was weak. I wandered away alone and wrestled with myself an hour. I recalled my promises of reform and preached to myself persuasively, upbraidingly, exhaustive. But it was all vain. I shortly found myself sneaking among the snowdrifts hunting for my pipe. I discovered it after a considerable search, and crept away to hide myself and enjoy it. I remained behind the barn a good while, asking myself how I would feel if my braver, stronger, truer comrades should catch me in my degradation. At last I lit the pipe, and no human being can feel meaner and baser than I did then. I was ashamed of being in my own pitiful company. Still dreading discovery, I felt that perhaps the further side of the barn would be somewhat safer, and so I turned the corner. As I turned the one corner, smoking, Ollendorff turned the other with his bottle to his lips, and between us sat unconscious Ballou deep in a game of "solitaire" with the old greasy cards!

Absurdity could go no farther. We shook hands and agreed to say no more about "reform" and "examples to the rising generation."

THINKING ABOUT THE SELECTION

Recalling

1. Why does the snowstorm make navigation difficult?
2. (a) What do the men quickly notice about the tracks they begin following? (b) How do they first explain their observations? (c) What is the true explanation?
3. Why are the men unable to follow the stage-coach tracks to Carson City?
4. (a) What happens when the men try to build a fire using a gun? (b) What happens when they try rubbing two sticks together? (c) What happens when they find four matches?
5. (a) In what ways does Ollendorff vow to reform if he survives? (b) What does Ballou vow to give up? (c) What does the narrator vow to give up?
6. What do the men discover when they awaken?

Interpreting

7. How would you describe the story's tone, or the author's attitude toward the characters and the subject?
8. What is ironic, or surprising, about the outcome of the story?
9. Considering the three men's response to the threat of death and their subsequent behavior, what do you think this story suggests about human nature?

Applying

10. How do you think you might respond if you were hopelessly lost in a snowstorm?

ANALYZING LITERATURE

Understanding the Setting of a Story

The **setting** is the time, place, and conditions in which the events in a work of literature occur. For example, "Lost in a Snowstorm" is set in a heavy snowstorm in Nevada in the mid-1800's.

1. What important details of the setting are presented in the first paragraph?
2. How does the condition of the setting change during the course of the story?

CRITICAL THINKING AND READING

Analyzing the Effect of Setting

Setting often plays an important role in shaping characters' behavior. By shaping characters' behavior, the setting also has an impact on plot.

1. In what ways does the setting affect the characters' behavior in "Lost in a Snowstorm"?
2. How does the setting affect the plot?
3. Explain why the setting is one of the most important elements of "Lost in a Snowstorm."

THINKING AND WRITING

Writing a Descriptive Essay

Write an essay describing a snowstorm or a similar natural event for someone who has never witnessed such an event. Start by reviewing the list of descriptive details you prepared. Try to think of additional details, including ones that appeal to senses other than sight. Arrange your details in a logical order, and then write your essay. When you revise, make sure that you have included enough details to enable someone who has never seen this type of event to visualize it.

The Notorious Jumping Frog of Calaveras County

Writer's Techniques

Humor. In literature, humor refers to writing that is intended to evoke laughter. To accomplish this purpose, writers must have the ability to perceive the ridiculous, comical, or ludicrous aspects of an incident, situation, or personality and to depict them in an amusing manner.

Humorists use a variety of techniques to make their work amusing. For example, the western humorists, including Mark Twain, made extensive uses of exaggeration in their writing. Certain incidents and details were exaggerated to such a great extent that they became comical. Usually, the exaggerated incidents or events were described by a narrator or storyteller in a very serious tone. This tone made the tale more humorous, because it created the impression that the storyteller was unaware of the ridiculousness of what he or she was describing.

Regional dialects—the colloquial languages of people living in certain areas—were another important element of western humor. The use of regional dialects helped to capture local color and made the characters more interesting and amusing. For example, Simon Wheeler's use of regional dialect in "The Notorious Jumping Frog of Calaveras County" helps make him a very entertaining character, and his frequent use of unexpected words adds to the humor of the story.

Look For

As you read "The Notorious Jumping Frog of Calaveras County," look for how Twain uses exaggeration and regional dialect to make the story amusing.

Writing

Think of a humorous story you have heard in which exaggeration was used. Then briefly discuss why you think the use of exaggeration in the story makes it amusing.

Vocabulary

Knowing the following words will help you as you read "The Notorious Jumping Frog of Calaveras County."

garrulous (gar′ ə ləs) *adj.*: Talking too much (p. 509)
conjectured (kən jek′ chərd) *v.*: Guessed (p. 509)
monotonous (mə nät′ nəs) *adj.*: Tiresome because unvarying (p. 509)

interminable (in tur′ mi nə b'l) *adj.*: Seeming to last forever (p. 509)
ornery (ôr′ nər ē) *adj.*: Having a mean disposition (p. 510)

The Notorious Jumping Frog of Calaveras County

Mark Twain

In compliance with the request of a friend of mine, who wrote me from the East, I called on good-natured, garrulous old Simon Wheeler, and inquired after my friend's friend, Leonidas W. Smiley, as requested to do, and I hereunto append the result. I have a lurking suspicion that *Leonidas W.* Smiley is a myth; that my friend never knew such a personage; and that he only conjectured that if I asked old Wheeler about him, it would remind him of his infamous *Jim* Smiley, and he would go to work and bore me to death with some exasperating reminiscence of him as long and as tedious as it should be useless to me. If that was the design, it succeeded.

I found Simon Wheeler dozing comfortably by the barroom stove of the dilapidated tavern in the decayed mining camp of Angel's, and I noticed that he was fat and baldheaded, and had an expression of winning gentleness and simplicity upon his tranquil countenance. He roused up, and gave me good day. I told him a friend of mine had commissioned me to make some inquiries about a cherished companion of his boyhood named *Leonidas W.* Smiley—*Rev. Leonidas W.* Smiley, a young minister of the Gospel, who he had heard was at one time a resident of Angel's Camp. I added that if Mr. Wheeler could tell me anything about this Rev. Leonidas W. Smiley, I would feel under many obligations to him.

Simon Wheeler backed me into a corner and blockaded me there with his chair, and then sat down and reeled off the monotonous narrative which follows this paragraph. He never smiled, he never frowned, he never changed his voice from the gentle-flowing key to which he tuned his initial sentence, he never betrayed the slightest suspicion of enthusiasm; but all through the interminable narrative there ran a vein of impressive earnestness and sincerity, which showed me plainly that, so far from his imagining that there was anything ridiculous or funny about his story, he regarded it as a really important matter, and admired its two heroes as men of transcendent genius in *finesse.* I let him go on in his own way, and never interrupted him once.

"Rev. Leonidas W. H'm, Reverend Le— well, there was a feller here once by the name of *Jim* Smiley, in the winter of '49—or maybe it was the spring of '50—I don't recollect exactly, somehow, though what makes me think it was one or the other is because I remember the big flume[1] warn't finished when he first come to the camp; but anyway, he was the curiousest man about always betting on anything that turned up you ever see, if he could get anybody to bet on the other side; and if he couldn't he'd change sides. Any way that suited the other man would suit *him*—any way just so's he got a bet, *he* was satisfied. But still he was lucky, uncommon lucky; he most always come out winner. He was always ready and laying for a chance; there couldn't be no solit'ry thing

---

1. flume (floom) *n.*: An artificial channel for carrying water to provide power and transport objects.

mentioned but that feller'd offer to bet on it, and take ary side you please, as I was just telling you. If there was a horse race, you'd find him flush or you'd find him busted at the end of it; if there was a dogfight, he'd bet on it; if there was a cat fight, he'd bet on it; if there was a chicken fight, he'd bet on it; why, if there was two birds setting on a fence, he would bet you which one would fly first; or if there was a camp meeting,[2] he would be there reg'lar to bet on Parson Walker, which he judged to be the best exhorter about here and so he was too, and a good man. If he even see a straddle bug[3] start to go anywheres, he would bet you how long it would take him to get to—to wherever he was going to, and if you took him up, he would foller that straddle bug to Mexico but what he would find out where he was bound for and how long he was on the road. Lots of the boys here has seen that Smiley, and can tell you about him. Why, it never made no difference to *him*—he'd bet on *any* thing—the dangdest feller. Parson Walker's wife laid very sick once, for a good while, and it seemed as if they warn't going to save her; but one morning he come in, and Smiley up and asked him how she was, and he said she was considable better—thank the Lord for his inf'nite mercy—and coming on so smart that with the blessing of Prov'dence she'd get well yet; and Smiley, before he thought, says, 'Well, I'll resk two-and-a-half she don't anyway.'

Thish-yer Smiley had a mare—the boys called her the fifteen-minute nag, but that was only in fun, you know, because of course she was faster than that—and he used to win money on that horse, for all she was so slow and always had the asthma, or the distemper, or the consumption, or something of that kind. They used to give her two or three hundred yards start, and then pass her under way; but always at the fag end[4] of the race she'd get excited and desperate like, and come cavorting and straddling up, and scattering her legs around limber, sometimes in the air, and sometimes out to one side among the fences, and kicking up m-o-r-e dust and raising m-o-r-e racket with her coughing and sneezing and blowing her nose—and *always* fetch up at the stand just about a neck ahead, as near as you could cipher it down.

And he had a little small bull-pup, that to look at him you'd think he warn't worth a cent but to set around and look ornery and lay for a chance to steal something. But as soon as money was up on him he was a different dog; his under-jaw'd begin to stick out like the fo'castle[5] of a steamboat, and his teeth would uncover and shine like the furnaces. And a dog might tackle him and bully-rag him, and bite him, and throw him over his shoulder two or three times, and Andrew Jackson—which was the name of the pup—Andrew Jackson would never let on but what *he* was satisfied, and hadn't expected nothing else—and the bets being doubled and doubled on the other side all the time, till the money was all up; and then all of a sudden he would grab that other dog jest by the j'int of his hind leg and freeze to it—not chaw, you understand, but only just grip and hang on till they throwed up the sponge, if it was a year. Smiley always come out winner on that pup, till he harnessed a dog once that didn't have no hind legs, because they'd been sawed off in a circular saw, and when the thing had gone along far enough, and the money was all up, and he come to make a snatch for his pet holt,[6] he see in a minute how he'd been imposed on, and how the other dog had him in the door, so to speak, and he 'peared surprised, and then he looked sorter discouraged-like, and didn't try no more to win the fight, and so he got shucked out bad. He give Smiley a look, as much as to say his heart was broke, and it

---

2. camp meeting: A religious gathering at the mining camp.
3. straddle bug: An insect with long legs.
4. fag end: Last part.

5. fo'castle (fōk's'l) *n.*: Forecastle; the forward part of the upper deck.
6. holt: Hold.

was *his* fault, for putting up a dog that hadn't no hind legs for him to take holt of, which was his main dependence in a fight, and then he limped off a piece and laid down and died. It was a good pup, was that Andrew Jackson, and would have made a name for hisself if he'd lived, for the stuff was in him and he had genius—I know it, because he hadn't no opportunities to speak of, and it don't stand to reason that a dog could make such a fight as he could under them circumstances if he hadn't no talent. It always makes me feel sorry when I think of that last fight of his'n, and the way it turned out.

Well, thish-yer Smiley had rat terriers,[7] and chicken cocks,[8] and tomcats and all them kind of things, till you couldn't rest, and you couldn't fetch nothing for him to bet on but he'd match you. He ketched a frog one day, and took him home, and said he cal'lated to educate him; and so he never done nothing for three months but set in his back yard and learn that frog to jump. And you bet you he *did* learn him, too. He'd give him a little punch behind, and the next minute you'd see that frog whirling in the air like a doughnut—see him turn one summerset, or maybe a couple, if he got a good start, and come down flatfooted and all right, like a cat. He got him up so in the matter of ketching flies, and kep' him in practice so constant, that he'd nail a fly every time as fur as he could see him. Smiley said all a frog wanted was education, and he could do 'most anything—and I believe him. Why, I've seen him set Dan'l Webster down here on this floor—Dan'l Webster was the name of the frog—and sing out, "Flies, Dan'l, flies!" and quicker'n you could wink he'd spring straight up and snake a fly off'n the counter there, and flop down on the floor ag'in as solid as a gob of mud, and fall to scratching the side of his head with his hind foot as indifferent as if he hadn't no idea he'd been doin' any more'n any frog might do. You never see a frog so modest and straight-for'ard as he was, for all he was so gifted. And when it come to fair and square jumping on a dead level, he could get over more ground at one straddle than any animal of his breed you ever see. Jumping on a dead level was his strong suit, you understand; and when it come to that, Smiley would ante up money on him as long as he had a red.[9] Smiley was monstrous proud of his frog, and well he might be, for fellers that had traveled and been everywheres all said he laid over any frog that ever *they* see.

Well, Smiley kep' the beast in a little lattice box, and he used to fetch him downtown sometimes and lay for a bet. One day a feller—a stranger in the camp, he was—come acrost him with his box, and says:

'What might it be that you've got in the box?'

And Smiley says, sorter indifferent-like, 'It might be a parrot, or it might be a canary, maybe, but it ain't—it's only just a frog.'

And the feller took it, and looked at it careful, and turned it round this way and that, and says, 'H'm—so 'tis. Well, what's *he* good for?'

'Well,' Smiley says, easy and careless, 'he's good enough for *one* thing, I should judge—he can outjump any frog in Calaveras county.'

The feller took the box again, and took another long, particular look, and give it back to Smiley, and says, very deliberate, 'Well,' he says, 'I don't see no p'ints about that frog that's any better'n any other frog.'

'Maybe you don't,' Smiley says. 'Maybe you understand frogs and maybe you don't understand 'em; maybe you've had experience, and maybe you ain't only a amature, as it were. Anyways, I've got *my* opinion, and I'll resk forty dollars that he can outjump any frog in Calaveras county.'

And the feller studied a minute, and then says, kinder sad like, 'Well, I'm only a

---

7. rat terriers: Dogs skilled in catching rats.
8. chicken cocks: Roosters trained to fight.

9. a red: A red cent.

**MARK TWAIN (SAMUEL L. CLEMENS) RIDING
THE CELEBRATED JUMPING FROG**
*An English Caricature
by Frederic Waddy, 1872
The Granger Collection*

stranger here, and I ain't got no frog; but if I had a frog, I'd bet you.'

And then Smiley says, 'That's all right—that's all right—if you'll hold my box a minute, I'll go and get you a frog.' And so the feller took the box, and put up his forty dollars along with Smiley's, and set down to wait.

So he set there a good while thinking and thinking to hisself, and then he got the frog out and prized his mouth open and took a teaspoon and filled him full of quail-shot[10]—filled him pretty near up to his chin—and set him on the floor. Smiley he went to the swamp and slopped around in the mud for a long time, and finally he ketched a frog, and fetched him in, and give him to this feller, and says:

'Now, if you're ready, set him alongside of Dan'l, with his forepaws just even with Dan'l's, and I'll give the word.' Then he says, 'One—two—three—*git!*' and him and the feller touched up the frogs from behind, and the new frog hopped off lively, but Dan'l give a heave, and hysted up his shoulders—so—

---

10. quailshot: Small lead pellets used for shooting quail.

like a Frenchman, but it warn't no use—he couldn't budge; he was planted as solid as a church, and he couldn't no more stir than if he was anchored out. Smiley was a good deal surprised, and he was disgusted too, but he didn't have no idea what the matter was, of course.

The feller took the money and started away; and when he was going out at the door, he sorter jerked his thumb over his shoulder—so—at Dan'l, and says again, very deliberate, 'Well,' he says, '*I* don't see no p'ints about that frog that's any better'n any other frog.'

Smiley he stood scratching his head and looking down at Dan'l a long time, and at last he says, 'I do wonder what in the nation that frog throw'd off for—I wonder if there ain't something the matter with him—he 'pears to look mighty baggy, somehow.' And he ketched Dan'l by the nap of the neck, and hefted him, and says, 'Why blame my cats if he don't weigh five pound!' and turned him upside down and he belched out a double handful of shot. And then he see how it was, and he was the maddest man—he set the frog down and took out after that feller, but he never ketched him. And——"

Here Simon Wheeler heard his name called from the front yard, and got up to see what was wanted. And turning to me as he moved away, he said: "Just set where you are, stranger, and rest easy—I ain't going to be gone a second."

But, by your leave, I did not think that a continuation of the history of the enterprising vagabond *Jim* Smiley would be likely to afford me much information concerning the Rev. *Leonidas W.* Smiley, and so I started away.

At the door I met the sociable Wheeler returning, and he buttonholed me and recommenced:

"Well, thish-yer Smiley had a yaller one-eyed cow that didn't have no tail, only just a short stump like a bannanner, and—"

However, lacking both time and inclination, I did not wait to hear about the afflicted cow, but took my leave.

THINKING ABOUT THE SELECTION
Recalling

1. Describe Simon Wheeler as the narrator encounters him.
2. What happens when the narrator asks Simon Wheeler about Leonidas W. Smiley?
3. (a) Why is Jim Smiley described as infamous? (b) What is Jim Smiley's attitude toward gambling?
4. (a) How did Smiley's mare win races? (b) How did Smiley's bull pup win fights? (c) How did the bull pup finally lose?
5. (a) Why was Smiley proud of his frog? (b) What did a stranger do to the frog? (c) What was Smiley's reaction?

Interpreting

6. The story of Jim Smiley is a frame story—a story presented within the framework of another story. How does Twain's use of this technique contribute to the story's effectiveness?
7. The narrator comments that Wheeler did not imagine "that there was anything ridiculous or funny about his story" and that he regarded it "as a really important matter." How does this add to the humor of the story?
8. (a) How would you describe Simon Wheeler's personality? (b) What makes him an interesting and unusual character?

Applying

9. Why do you think people enjoy telling and listening to tall tales such as the one told by Simon Wheeler?

ANALYZING LITERATURE
Recognizing Humor

In literature, **humor** refers to writing intended to evoke laughter. To accomplish this purpose, western humorists made extensive use of exaggeration and regional dialects in their writing. For example, in "The Notorious Jumping Frog of Calaveras County," Simon Wheeler exaggerates when describing the frog's talents. He describes the frog as if it were intelligent and thoughtful, commenting, "You never see a frog so modest and straightforward as he was, for all he was so gifted."

1. (a) Find two more examples of exaggeration in the story. (b) Explain why each of these examples is amusing.
2. (a) How does Simon Wheeler's use of dialect help make him an amusing and entertaining character? (b) Why would the story be less effective if Wheeler spoke in standard English?
3. In "How to Tell a Story" Mark Twain wrote, "The humorous story may be spun out to great length, and may wander around as much as it pleases, and arrive nowhere in particular . . ." Explain how this technique is evident in this tale.
4. Twain continued, "The humorous story is told gravely; the teller does his best to conceal the fact that he even dimly suspects there is anything funny about it." Explain how this technique is evident in this tale.

CRITICAL THINKING AND READING
Appreciating Dialect

Part of what makes Wheeler's use of **dialect** amusing is his frequently unexpected or unusual choice of words. For example, Wheeler's use of the word *monstrous* to describe the extent of Smiley's pride in his frog is unusual.

What is unexpected or unusual about the choice of words in each of the following passages from the story?

1. "And a dog might tackle him and bullyrag him . . ."
2. "Now if you're ready, set him alongside of Dan'l, with his forepaws just even with Dan'l's . . ."

THINKING AND WRITING
Writing a Story Using Dialect

Imagine that your school literary magazine has asked you to write a story in which the characters speak in a regional dialect. Think of a region in which people speak in a distinctive manner. Then develop a story in which you capture the local color of this region through the use of dialect and vivid descriptions of the setting. When you finish writing, revise your story and share it with your classmates.

BRET HARTE

1836–1902

Though relatively few of his stories were successful, Bret Harte played an important role in creating a vivid, lasting portrait of the old West. Harte's stories, filled with intriguing characters and colorful dialogue, provided much of post-Civil-War America with its first glimpse into western life and established the old West as a popular literary setting.

Harte was born and raised in Albany, New York. In 1854, when he was eighteen, he traveled across the country to California. During his first few years in California, a land in a turbulent period of rapid growth brought about by the discovery of gold in 1848, Harte worked as a schoolteacher, tutor, messenger, clerk, and prospector. While Harte's life seemed to have little direction at the time, his observations of the rugged, often violent life in the mining camps and the towns and cities of the new frontier provided him with the inspiration for his most successful short stories.

After working as a typesetter and writer for two California periodicals and publishing two books of verse, *Outcroppings* (1856) and *The Lost Galleon* (1867), Harte became the editor of the *Overland Monthly,* a new literary magazine, in 1868. When Harte published his story "The Luck of Roaring Camp" in the magazine's second issue, he immediately became famous, as the American public, eager to learn about life in the new frontier, responded to the story with enthusiasm. Over the next two years, Harte published "The Outcasts of Poker Flat" and several other similar stories in the *Overland Monthly,* and his popularity grew at a rapid pace.

Following the publication of *The Luck of Roaring Camp and Other Sketches* in 1870, Harte's popularity reached its peak. In 1871 the *Atlantic Monthly,* a distinguished literary magazine, contracted to pay Harte $10,000 for any twelve sketches or stories he contributed over the next year. Harte returned to the East to fulfill his contract, but the stories he wrote were flat and disappointing compared with his earlier work, and his celebrity waned almost as quickly as it had grown.

Harte continued to publish stories, short novels, and plays during the next twenty years, but for the most part, his later work was unsuccessful. From 1878 to 1885, he was a diplomat in Germany and Scotland. He then retired to London, where he lived for the remainder of his life.

GUIDE FOR READING

The Outcasts of Poker Flat

Literary Movements

Regionalism. The habits, speech, appearance, customs, and beliefs of people from one geographical region often differ from those of people from other areas. Regional literature captures the essence of life in a particular area, the "local color" of a region, by accurately depicting the distinctive qualities of its people and including vivid, realistic descriptions of the physical appearance of the environment.

During the nineteenth century, the United States grew at a rapid rate. New regions developed as a steady flow of immigrants settled across the land, and as a result the American population became more and more diverse. As the country grew and became more diversified, the American public became curious about the people and the style of life in different parts of the country. Regional literature, like "The Outcasts of Poker Flat" satisfied their curiosity.

Look For

The characters and events in a work of regional literature are closely tied to the geographical setting. If the setting were moved, the characters and their behavior would no longer be believable and the work would not be effective. As you read "The Outcasts of Poker Flat," look for the qualities that make the characters appropriate only for a story set in the old West. Also take note of how Harte uses descriptive details to paint a vivid portrait of the California landscape.

Writing

Brainstorm for several minutes about films, books, and other sources of your impressions of the old West. Then make a list of typical characters, clothing, speech, situations, and scenic details that you associate with the old West.

Vocabulary

Knowing the following words will help you as you read "The Outcasts of Poker Flat."

expatriated (eks pā′ trē āt′ id) *adj.*: Deported; driven from one's native land (p. 516)
anathema (ə nath′ ə mə): *n.*: Curse (p. 517)
bellicose (bel′ ə kōs) *adj.*: Quarrelsome (p. 518)
recumbent (ri kum′ bənt) *adj.*: Resting (p. 518)

equanimity (ek′ wə nim′ ə tē) *n.*: Composure (p. 518)
vociferation (vō sif′ ə rā sʰən) *n.*: Loud or vehement shouting (p. 520)
vituperative (vī too′ prə tiv) *adj.*: Spoken abusively (p. 521)
querulous (kwer′ ə ləs) *adj.*: Inclined to find fault (p. 521)

The Outcasts of Poker Flat

Bret Harte

As Mr. John Oakhurst, gambler, stepped into the main street of Poker Flat on the morning of the twenty-third of November, 1850, he was conscious of a change in its moral atmosphere since the preceding night. Two or three men, conversing earnestly together, ceased as he approached, and exchanged significant glances. There was a Sabbath lull in the air which, in a settlement unused to Sabbath influences, looked ominous.

Mr. Oakhurst's calm, handsome face betrayed small concern in these indications. Whether he was conscious of any predisposing cause was another question. "I reckon they're after somebody," he reflected; "likely it's me." He returned to his pocket the handkerchief with which he had been whipping away the red dust of Poker Flat from his neat boots, and quietly discharged his mind of any further conjecture.

In point of fact, Poker Flat was "after somebody." It had lately suffered the loss of several thousand dollars, two valuable horses, and a prominent citizen. It was experiencing a spasm of virtuous reaction, quite as lawless and ungovernable as any of the acts that had provoked it. A secret committee had determined to rid the town of all improper persons. This was done permanently in regard of two men who were then hanging from the boughs of a sycamore in the gulch, and temporarily in the banishment of certain other objectionable characters. I regret to say that some of these were ladies. It is but due to the sex, however, to state that their impropriety was professional, and it was only in such easily established standards of evil that Poker Flat ventured to sit in judgment.

Mr. Oakhurst was right in supposing that he was included in this category. A few of the committee had urged hanging him as a possible example, and a sure method of reimbursing themselves from his pockets of the sums he had won from them. "It's agin justice," said Jim Wheeler, "to let this yer young man from Roaring Camp—an entire stranger—carry away our money." But a crude sentiment of equity residing in the breasts of those who had been fortunate enough to win from Mr. Oakhurst overruled this narrower local prejudice.

Mr. Oakhurst received his sentence with philosophic calmness, none the less coolly that he was aware of the hesitation of his judges. He was too much of a gambler not to accept Fate. With him life was at best an uncertain game, and he recognized the usual percentage in favor of the dealer.

A body of armed men accompanied the deported wickedness of Poker Flat to the outskirts of the settlement. Besides Mr. Oakhurst, who was known to be a coolly desperate man, and for whose intimidation the armed escort was intended, the expatriated party consisted of a young woman familiarly known as the "Duchess"; another, who had won the title of "Mother Shipton";[1] and "Uncle Billy," a suspected sluice robber[2] and

---

1. **"Mother Shipton":** An English woman who lived in the sixteenth century and was suspected of being a witch.
2. **sluice robber:** A person who steals gold from sluices, long troughs used for sifting gold.

THE EDGE OF TOWN
Charles Burchfield
Collection of the Kelson-Atkins Museum of Art, Kansas City

confirmed drunkard. The cavalcade provoked no comments from the spectators, nor was any word uttered by the escort. Only, when the gulch which marked the uttermost limit of Poker Flat was reached, the leader spoke briefly and to the point. The exiles were forbidden to return at the peril of their lives.

As the escort disappeared, their pent-up feelings found vent in a few hysterical tears from the Duchess, some bad language from Mother Shipton, and a Parthian[3] volley of expletives from Uncle Billy. The philosophic Oakhurst alone remained silent. He listened calmly to Mother Shipton's desire to cut somebody's heart out, to the repeated state-

ments of the Duchess that she would die in the road, and to the alarming oaths that seemed to be bumped out of Uncle Billy as he rode forward. With the easy good humor characteristic of his class, he insisted upon exchanging his own riding horse, "Five Spot," for the sorry mule which the Duchess rode. But even this act did not draw the party into any closer sympathy. The young woman readjusted her somewhat draggled plumes with a feeble, faded coquetry; Mother Shipton eyed the possessor of "Five Spot" with malevolence, and Uncle Billy included the whole party in one sweeping anathema.

The road to Sandy Bar—a camp that, not having as yet experienced the regenerating influences of Poker Flat, consequently seemed to offer some invitation to the emigrants—lay over a steep mountain range. It was distant a day's severe travel. In that advanced season, the party soon passed out of

---

3. Parthian: Hostile remarks made while leaving. The Parthians were an ancient society whose cavalrymen usually shot at the enemy while retreating or pretending to retreat.

perhaps you'd better not—you can wait till Uncle Billy gets back with provisions." For some occult reason, Mr. Oakhurst could not bring himself to disclose Uncle Billy's rascality, and so offered the hypothesis that he had wandered from the camp and had accidentally stampeded the animals. He dropped a warning to the Duchess and Mother Shipton, who of course knew the facts of their associate's defection. "They'll find out the truth about us *all* when they find out anything," he added, significantly, "and there's no good frightening them now."

Tom Simson not only put all his worldly store at the disposal of Mr. Oakhurst, but seemed to enjoy the prospect of their enforced seclusion. "We'll have a good camp for a week, and then the snow'll melt, and we'll all go back together." The cheerful gaiety of the young man, and Mr. Oakhurst's calm, infected the others. The Innocent with the aid of pine boughs extemporized a thatch for the roofless cabin, and the Duchess directed Piney in the rearrangement of the interior with a taste and tact that opened the blue eyes of that provincial maiden to their fullest extent. "I reckon now you're used to fine things at Poker Flat," said Piney. The Duchess turned away sharply to conceal something that reddened her cheeks through its professional tint, and Mother Shipton requested Piney not to "chatter." But when Mr. Oakhurst returned from a weary search for the trail, he heard the sound of happy laughter echoed from the rocks. He stopped in some alarm, and his thoughts first naturally reverted to the whisky, which he had prudently cached.[7] "And yet it don't somehow sound like whisky," said the gambler. It was not until he caught sight of the blazing fire through the still-blinding storm and the group around it that he settled to the conviction that it was "square fun."

Whether Mr. Oakhurst had cached his cards with the whisky as something debarred the free access of the community, I cannot say. It was certain that, in Mother Shipton's words, he "didn't say cards once" during that evening. Haply the time was beguiled by an accordion, produced somewhat ostentatiously by Tom Simson from his pack. Notwithstanding some difficulties attending the manipulation of this instrument, Piney Woods managed to pluck several reluctant melodies from its keys, to an accompaniment by the Innocent on a pair of bone castanets. But the crowning festivity of the evening was reached in a rude camp-meeting hymn, which the lovers, joining hands, sang with great earnestness and vociferation. I fear that a certain defiant tone and Covenanter's[8] swing to its chorus, rather than any devotional quality, caused it speedily to infect the others, who at last joined in the refrain:

> "I'm proud to live in the service
>   of the Lord,
> And I'm bound to die in
>   His army."[9]

The pines rocked, the storm eddied and whirled above the miserable group, and the flames of their altar leaped heavenward as if in token of the vow.

At midnight the storm abated, the rolling clouds parted, and the stars glittered keenly above the sleeping camp. Mr. Oakhurst, whose professional habits had enabled him to live on the smallest possible amount of sleep, in dividing the watch with Tom Simson somehow managed to take upon himself the greater part of that duty. He excused himself to the Innocent by saying that he had "often been a week without sleep." "Doing what?" asked Tom. "Poker!" replied Oakhurst, sententiously; "when a man gets a streak of luck, he don't get tired. The luck gives in first. Luck," continued the gambler, reflectively, "is a mighty queer thing. All you know about it for certain is

---

7. cached (kasht) *v.*: Hidden.

8. Covenanter's (kuv' ə nan' tərz): Seventeenth-century Scottish Presbyterians who resisted the rule of the Church of England.

9. "I'm . . . army": Lines from the early American spiritual "Service of the Lord."

that it's bound to change. And it's finding out when it's going to change that makes you. We've had a streak of bad luck since we left Poker Flat—you come along, and slap you get into it, too. If you can hold your cards right along you're all right. For," added the gambler, with cheerful irrelevance,

" 'I'm proud to live in the service
    of the Lord,
And I'm bound to die in
    His army.' "

The third day came, and the sun, looking through the white-curtained valley, saw the outcasts divide their slowly decreasing store of provisions for the morning meal. It was one of the peculiarities of that mountain climate that its rays diffused a kindly warmth over the wintry landscape, as if in regretful commiseration of the past. But it revealed drift on drift of snow piled high around the hut—a hopeless, uncharted, trackless sea of white lying below the rocky shores to which the castaways still clung. Through the marvelously clear air the smoke of the pastoral village of Poker Flat rose miles away. Mother Shipton saw it, and from a remote pinnacle of her rocky fastness hurled in that direction a final malediction. It was her last vituperative attempt, and perhaps for that reason was invested with a certain degree of sublimity. It did her good, she privately informed the Duchess. "Just you go out there and cuss, and see." She then set herself to the task of amusing "the child," as she and the Duchess were pleased to call Piney. Piney was no chicken, but it was a soothing and original theory of the pair thus to account for the fact that she didn't swear and wasn't improper.

When night crept up again through the gorges, the reedy notes of the accordion rose and fell in fitful spasms and long-drawn gasps by the flickering campfire. But music failed to fill entirely the aching void left by insufficient food, and a new diversion was proposed by Piney—storytelling. Neither Mr. Oakhurst nor his female companions caring to relate their personal experiences, this plan would have failed too but for the Innocent. Some months before he had chanced upon a stray copy of Mr. Pope's[10] ingenious translation of the *Iliad*.[11] He now proposed to narrate the principal incidents of that poem—having thoroughly mastered the argument and fairly forgotten the words—in the current vernacular of Sandy Bar. And so for the rest of that night the Homeric demigods again walked the earth. Trojan bully and wily Greek wrestled in the winds, and the great pines in the canyon seemed to bow to the wrath of the son of Peleus.[12] Mr. Oakhurst listened with quiet satisfaction. Most especially was he interested in the fate of "Ash-heels," as the Innocent persisted in denominating the "swift-footed Achilles."

So with small food and much of Homer and the accordion, a week passed over the heads of the outcasts. The sun again forsook them, and again from leaden skies the snowflakes were sifted over the land. Day by day closer around them drew the snowy circle, until at last they looked from their prison over drifted walls of dazzling white that towered twenty feet above their heads. It became more and more difficult to replenish their fires, even from the fallen trees beside them, now half-hidden in the drifts. And yet no one complained. The lovers turned from the dreary prospect and looked into each other's eyes, and were happy. Mr. Oakhurst settled himself coolly to the losing game before him. The Duchess, more cheerful than she had been, assumed the care of Piney. Only Mother Shipton—once the strongest of the party—seemed to sicken and fade. At midnight on the tenth day she called Oakhurst to her side. "I'm going," she said, in a voice of querulous weakness, "but don't say anything about it. Don't waken the kids. Take the bundle from under my head and open

---

10. Mr. Pope: English poet Alexander Pope (1688–1744).
11. Iliad (il' ē əd): Greek epic poem written by Homer that tells the story of the Trojan War.
12. son of Peleus (pēl' o͞os): Achilles (ə kil' ēz), the Greek warrior hero in the *Iliad*.

it." Mr. Oakhurst did so. It contained Mother Shipton's rations for the last week, untouched. "Give 'em to the child," she said, pointing to the sleeping Piney. "You've starved yourself," said the gambler. "That's what they call it," said the woman, querulously, as she lay down again and, turning her face to the wall, passed quietly away.

The accordion and the bones were put aside that day, and Homer was forgotten. When the body of Mother Shipton had been committed to the snow, Mr. Oakhurst took the Innocent aside, and showed him a pair of snowshoes, which he had fashioned from the old pack saddle. "There's one chance in a hundred to save her yet," he said, pointing to Piney; "but it's there," he added, pointing toward Poker Flat. "If you can reach there in two days she's safe." "And you?" asked Tom Simson. "I'll stay here," was the curt reply.

The lovers parted with a long embrace. "You are not going, too?" said the Duchess as she saw Mr. Oakhurst apparently waiting to accompany him. "As far as the canyon," he replied. He turned suddenly, and kissed the Duchess, leaving her pallid face aflame and her trembling limbs rigid with amazement.

Night came, but not Mr. Oakhurst. It brought the storm again and the whirling snow. Then the Duchess, feeding the fire, found that someone had quietly piled beside the hut enough fuel to last a few days longer. The tears rose to her eyes, but she hid them from Piney.

The women slept but little. In the morning, looking into each other's faces, they read their fate. Neither spoke; but Piney, accepting the position of the stronger, drew near and placed her arm around the Duchess's waist. They kept this attitude for the rest of the day. That night the storm reached its greatest fury, and, rending asunder the protecting pines, invaded the very hut.

Toward morning they found themselves unable to feed the fire, which gradually died away. As the embers slowly blackened, the Duchess crept closer to Piney, and broke the silence of many hours: "Piney, can you pray?" "No, dear," said Piney, simply. The Duchess, without knowing exactly why, felt relieved, and, putting her head upon Piney's shoulder, spoke no more. And so reclining, the younger and purer pillowing the head of her soiled sister upon her virgin breast, they fell asleep.

The wind lulled as if it feared to waken them. Feathery drifts of snow, shaken from the long pine boughs, flew like white-winged birds, and settled about them as they slept. The moon through the rifted clouds looked down upon what had been the camp. But all human stain, all trace of earthly travail, was hidden beneath the spotless mantle mercifully flung from above.

They slept all that day and the next, nor did they waken when voices and footsteps broke the silence of the camp. And when pitying fingers brushed the snow from their wan faces, you could scarcely have told from the equal peace that dwelt upon them which was she that had sinned. Even the law of Poker Flat recognized this, and turned away, leaving them still locked in each other's arms.

But at the head of the gulch, on one of the largest pine trees, they found the deuce of clubs pinned to the bark with a bowie knife. It bore the following, written in pencil, in a firm hand:

✝

BENEATH THIS TREE

LIES THE BODY

OF

JOHN OAKHURST,

WHO STRUCK A STREAK OF BAD LUCK

ON THE 23D OF NOVEMBER, 1850,

AND

HANDED IN HIS CHECKS

ON THE 7TH DECEMBER, 1850.

✝

And pulseless and cold, with a Derringer[13] by his side and a bullet in his heart, though still calm as in life, beneath the snow lay he who was at once the strongest and yet the weakest of the outcasts of Poker Flat.

---

13. Derringer: A small pistol.

THINKING ABOUT THE SELECTION

Recalling

1. (a) At the opening of the story, what has the secret committee of Poker Flat decided? (b) Who comprises the party escorted to the outskirts of town?
2. (a) Who joins the outcasts at their camp? (b) Why are the new arrivals headed for Poker Flat?
3. What does Mr. Oakhurst discover when he awakens after his first night at the camp?
4. What does Mother Shipton do with her rations?
5. (a) In what condition are Piney and the Duchess when the rescue party arrives? (b) What else does the rescue party discover?

Interpreting

6. (a) What does Harte's statement that Poker Flat "was experiencing a spasm of virtuous reaction, quite as lawless as the acts that provoked it" suggest about his attitude toward the secret committee's decision? (b) What motivates the committee to take action against Mr. Oakhurst?
7. (a) How is Oakhurst's occupation reflected in his attitude toward life? (b) What does Harte mean when he writes that Oakhurst "was at once the strongest and yet the weakest of the outcasts of Poker Flat"?
8. How do Mother Shipton and the Duchess change over the course of the story?

Applying

9. Though the characters in this story have little in common, they band together in support of one another. What kind of situations tend to draw people together in real life?

ANALYZING LITERATURE

Understanding Regional Literature

Regional literature captures the distinctive atmosphere, or "local color," of a particular area by accurately depicting the habits, speech, appearance, customs, and beliefs of its people and vividly describing its appearance.

1. What specific details of the setting does Harte use to create a portrait of the California landscape?
2. Find three examples of a character's use of western dialect.
3. Explain why the story would not be effective if the setting were changed, for example, to New England.

CRITICAL THINKING AND READING

Making Inferences About Attitudes

Cultural attitudes and customs are important aspects of local color. In most cases, however, the distinctive attitudes and customs in regional literature are not explicitly stated by the author. As a result, you must make inferences, or draw conclusions, about the attitudes and customs being depicted by examining the characters' actions, thoughts, and comments.

What inferences about the attitudes and customs of the people of Poker Flat can you make from each of the following passages?

1. "A few of the committee had urged hanging him as a possible example, and a sure method of reimbursing themselves from his pocket of the sums he had won from them."
2. " 'It's a fine justice,' said Jim Wheeler, 'to let this yer young man—an entire stranger—carry away our money.' "

THINKING AND WRITING

Comparing and Contrasting Characters

Think of a character from a western movie, novel, or television series who is in some ways similar to John Oakhurst. In your prewriting, list the similarities and differences between Oakhurst and the character you have chosen. After preparing a thesis statement, write an essay comparing and contrasting the two characters. When you revise, make sure you have included enough information to support your thesis.

AMBROSE BIERCE

1842–1914[?]

Both Ambrose Bierce's literary career and his philosophy of life were shaped by his career as a Union officer in the Civil War. His experiences provided the material for his best short stories and helped determine the unsentimental, cynical, pessimistic view of the world he expressed in his writing.

Bierce was born in Ohio and raised on a farm in Indiana. Having educated himself by reading his father's books, Bierce left the farm during his late teens to attend a military academy in Kentucky. A year later the Civil War broke out, and he enlisted in the Union army. He fought in several important battles and rose from private to major. Toward the end of the conflict, he was seriously wounded, but he returned to battle a few months later.

When the war ended, Bierce settled in San Francisco and began a career in journalism. His column, the "Prattler," which appeared in *The Argonaut* (1877–1879), the *Wasp* (1880–1886), and the *San Francisco Sunday Examiner* (1887–1896), was a mixture of biting political and social satire, literary reviews, and gossip. Bierce also published many of his finest short stories in his column.

In the early 1890's, Bierce published two collections of his stories: *Tales of Soldiers and Civilians* (1891) and *Can Such Things Be?* (1893). The concise, carefully plotted stories in these collections, set for the most part in the Civil War, capture the cruelty and futility of war and the indifference of death and reflect Bierce's cynical view of human existence. Bierce's pessimistic outlook is also reflected in *The Devil's Dictionary* (1906), a book of humorous and cynical definitions.

Although Bierce enjoyed a successful career as a writer, his personal life was filled with tragedy and despair. His marriage ended in divorce and his two sons both died at an early age. In 1913 the lonely and disillusioned writer traveled into Mexico, a country in the midst of a bloody civil war, and never returned. The circumstances of his death are still unknown.

An Occurrence at Owl Creek Bridge

Point of View. Point of view refers to the vantage point or perspective from which a narrative is told. Most stories are told from either a first-person or third-person point of view. In a narrative with a first-person point of view, one of the characters tells the story in his or her own words, using the first-person pronoun *I*. In a narrative with a third-person point of view, the narrator does not participate in the story and refers to characters using the third-person pronouns *he* and *she*. A third-person narrator may be either limited or omniscient. A third-person limited narrator focuses on the thoughts and feelings of only one character. A third-person omniscient narrator conveys the thoughts and feelings of all the characters.

The portrayal of characters and events in a story is often shaped by the point of view. In stories with first-person or limited third-person narrators, the portrayal of characters and events may be colored by the attitudes and feelings of the character from whose point of view the story is being told.

As you read "An Occurrence at Owl Creek Bridge," look for the way the point of view affects the way you perceive characters and events.

It has often been suggested that people's lives flash before their eyes as they near death. Freewrite for five minutes about the types of thoughts and feelings that you imagine people experience during their final moments.

Knowing the following words will help you as you read "An Occurrence at Owl Creek Bridge."

acclivity (ə kliv' ə tē) *n.:* Upward slope (p. 527)

embrasure (im brā' zhər) *n.:* Opening (p. 527)

etiquette (et' i kət) *n.:* Rules for manners and ceremonies (p. 527)

imperious (im pir' ē əs) *adj.:* Overbearing (p. 528)

dictum (dik' təm) *n.:* Statement or saying (p. 528)

ramification (ram' ə fi kā' shən) *n.:* Branchlike division (p. 529)

periodicity (pir' ē ə dis' ə tē) *n.:* Recurrence at regular intervals (p. 529)

oscillation (äs' ə lā' shən) *n.:* The act of swinging regularly back and forth (p. 529)

preternaturally (prēt' ər nach ər əl ē) *adv.:* Abnormally (p. 529)

malign (mə līn') *adj.:* Evil (p. 531)

An Occurrence at Owl Creek Bridge

Ambrose Bierce

I

A man stood upon a railroad bridge in northern Alabama, looking down into the swift water twenty feet below. The man's hands were behind his back, the wrists bound with a cord. A rope closely encircled his neck. It was attached to a stout cross timber above his head and the slack fell to the level of his knees. Some loose boards laid upon the sleepers[1] supporting the metals of the railway supplied a footing for him and

his executioners—two private soldiers of the Federal army, directed by a sergeant who in civil life may have been a deputy sheriff. At a short remove upon the same temporary platform was an officer in the uniform of his rank, armed. He was a captain. A sentinel at each end of the bridge stood with his rifle in the position known as "support," that is to say, vertical in front of the left shoulder, the hammer resting on the forearm thrown straight across the chest—a formal and unnatural position, enforcing an erect carriage of the body. It did not appear to be the duty of these two men to know what was occur-

---

1. **sleepers** *n.*: Ties supporting a railroad track.

THE RED BRIDGE,
Julian Alden Weir
The Metropolitan Museum of Art

ring at the center of the bridge; they merely blockaded the two ends of the foot planking that traversed it.

Beyond one of the sentinels nobody was in sight; the railroad ran straight away into a forest for a hundred yards, then, curving, was lost to view. Doubtless there was an outpost farther along. The other bank of the stream was open ground—a gentle acclivity topped with a stockade of vertical tree trunks, loopholed for rifles, with a single embrasure through which protruded the muzzle of a brass cannon commanding the bridge. Midway of the slope between bridge and fort were the spectators—a single company of infantry in line, at "parade rest," the butts of the rifles on the ground, the barrels inclining slightly backward against the right shoulder, the hands crossed upon the stock. A lieutenant stood at the right of the line, the point of his sword upon the ground, his left hand resting upon his right. Excepting the group of four at the center of the bridge, not a man moved. The company faced the bridge, staring stonily, motionless. The sentinels, facing the banks of the stream, might have been statues to adorn the bridge. The captain stood with folded arms, silent, observing the work of his subordinates, but making no sign. Death is a dignitary who when he comes announced is to be received with formal manifestations of respect, even by those most familiar with him. In the code of military etiquette silence and fixity are forms of deference.

The man who was engaged in being hanged was apparently about thirty-five years of age. He was a civilian, if one might judge from his habit, which was that of a planter. His features were good—a straight nose, firm mouth, broad forehead, from which his long, dark hair was combed straight back, falling behind his ears to the collar of his well-fitting frock coat. He wore a mustache and pointed beard, but no whiskers; his eyes were large and dark gray, and had a kindly expression which one would hardly have expected in one whose neck was

in the hemp. Evidently this was no vulgar assassin. The liberal military code makes provision for hanging many kinds of persons, and gentlemen are not excluded.

The preparations being complete, the two private soldiers stepped aside and each drew away the plank upon which he had been standing. The sergeant turned to the captain, saluted and placed himself immediately behind that officer, who in turn moved apart one pace. These movements left the condemned man and the sergeant standing on the two ends of the same plank, which spanned three of the crossties of the bridge. The end upon which the civilian stood almost, but not quite, reached a fourth. This plank had been held in place by the weight of the captain; it was now held by that of the sergeant. At a signal from the former the latter would step aside, the plank would tilt and the condemned man go down between two ties. The arrangement commended itself to his judgment as simple and effective. His face had not been covered nor his eyes bandaged. He looked a moment at his "unsteadfast footing," then let his gaze wander to the swirling water of the stream racing madly beneath his feet. A piece of dancing driftwood caught his attention and his eyes followed it down the current. How slowly it appeared to move! What a sluggish stream!

He closed his eyes in order to fix his last thoughts upon his wife and children. The water, touched to gold by the early sun, the brooding mists under the banks at some distance down the stream, the fort, the soldiers, the piece of drift—all had distracted him. And now he became conscious of a new disturbance. Striking through the thought of his dear ones was a sound which he could neither ignore nor understand, a sharp, distinct, metallic percussion like the stroke of a blacksmith's hammer upon the anvil; it had the same ringing quality. He wondered what it was, and whether immeasurably distant or near by—it seemed both. Its recurrence was regular, but as slow as the tolling of a death knell. He awaited each stroke with impatience and—he knew not why—apprehension. The intervals of silence grew progressively longer; the delays became maddening. With their greater infrequency the sounds increased in strength and sharpness. They hurt his ear like the thrust of a knife; he feared he would shriek. What he heard was the ticking of his watch.

He unclosed his eyes and saw again the water below him. "If I could free my hands," he thought, "I might throw off the noose and spring into the stream. By diving I could evade the bullets and, swimming vigorously, reach the bank, take to the woods and get away home. My home, thank God, is as yet outside their lines; my wife and little ones are still beyond the invader's farthest advance."

As these thoughts, which have here to be set down in words, were flashed into the doomed man's brain rather than evolved from it the captain nodded to the sergeant. The sergeant stepped aside.

II

Peyton Farquhar was a well-to-do planter, of an old and highly respected Alabama family. Being a slave owner and like other slave owners a politician he was naturally an original secessionist and ardently devoted to the Southern cause. Circumstances of an imperious nature, which it is unnecessary to relate here, had prevented him from taking service with the gallant army that had fought the disastrous campaigns ending with the fall of Corinth, and he chafed under the inglorious restraint, longing for the release of his energies, the larger life of the soldier, the opportunity for distinction. That opportunity, he felt, would come, as it comes to all in war time. Meanwhile he did what he could. No service was too humble for him to perform in aid of the South, no adventure too perilous for him to undertake if consistent with the character of a civilian who was at heart a soldier, and who in good faith and without too much qualification assented to at least a part of the frankly villainous dictum that all is fair in love and war.

One evening while Farquhar and his wife were sitting on a rustic bench near the entrance to his grounds, a gray-clad soldier rode up to the gate and asked for a drink of water. Mrs. Farquhar was only too happy to serve him with her own white hands. While she was fetching the water her husband approached the dusty horseman and inquired eagerly for news from the front.

"The Yanks are repairing the railroads," said the man, "and are getting ready for another advance. They have reached the Owl Creek bridge, put it in order and built a stockade on the north bank. The commandant has issued an order, which is posted everywhere, declaring that any civilian caught interfering with the railroad, its bridges, tunnels or trains will be summarily hanged. I saw the order."

"How far is it to the Owl Creek bridge?" Farquhar asked.

"About thirty miles."

"Is there no force on this side the creek?"

"Only a picket post[2] half a mile out, on the railroad, and a single sentinel at this end of the bridge."

"Suppose a man—a civilian and student of hanging—should elude the picket post and perhaps get the better of the sentinel," said Farquhar, smiling, "what could he accomplish?"

The soldier reflected. "I was there a month ago," he replied. "I observed that the flood of last winter had lodged a great quantity of driftwood against the wooden pier at this end of the bridge. It is now dry and would burn like tow.[3]

The lady had now brought the water, which the soldier drank. He thanked her ceremoniously, bowed to her husband and rode away. An hour later, after nightfall, he re-

---

2. picket post: Troops sent ahead with news of a surprise attack.
3. tow *n.*: The coarse and broken fibers of hemp or flax before spinning.

passed the plantation, going northward in the direction from which he had come. He was a Federal scout.

III

As Peyton Farquhar fell straight downward through the bridge he lost consciousness and was as one already dead. From this state he was awakened—ages later, it seemed to him—by the pain of a sharp pressure upon his throat, followed by a sense of suffocation. Keen, poignant agonies seemed to shoot from his neck downward through every fiber of his body and limbs. These pains appeared to flash along well-defined lines of ramification and to beat with an inconceivably rapid periodicity. They seemed like streams of pulsating fire heating him to an intolerable temperature. As to his head, he was conscious of nothing but a feeling of fullness—of congestion. These sensations were unaccompanied by thought. The intellectual part of his nature was already effaced; he had power only to feel, and feeling was torment. He was conscious of motion. Encompassed in a luminous cloud, of which he was now merely the fiery heart, without material substance, he swung through unthinkable arcs of oscillation, like a vast pendulum. Then all at once, with terrible suddenness, the light about him shot upward with the noise of a loud plash; a frightful roaring was in his ears, and all was cold and dark. The power of thought was restored; he knew that the rope had broken and he had fallen into the stream. There was no additional strangulation; the noose about his neck was already suffocating him and kept the water from his lungs. To die of hanging at the bottom of a river!—the idea seemed to him ludicrous. He opened his eyes in the darkness and saw above him a gleam of light, but how distant, how inaccessible! He was still sinking, for the light became fainter and fainter until it was a mere glimmer. Then it began to grow and brighten, and he knew that he was rising toward the surface—knew it with reluctance, for he was now very comfortable. "To be hanged and drowned," he thought, "that is not so bad; but I do not wish to be shot. No; I will not be shot; that is not fair."

He was not conscious of an effort, but a sharp pain in his wrist apprised him that he was trying to free his hands. He gave the struggle his attention, as an idler might observe the feat of a juggler, without interest in the outcome. What splendid effort!—what magnificent, what superhuman strength! Ah, that was a fine endeavor! Bravo! The cord fell away; his arms parted and floated upward, the hands dimly seen on each side in the growing light. He watched them with a new interest as first one and then the other pounced upon the noose at his neck. They tore it away and thrust it fiercely aside, its undulations resembling those of a water-snake. "Put it back, put it back!" He thought he shouted these words to his hands, for the undoing of the noose had been succeeded by the direst pang that he had yet experienced. His neck ached horribly; his brain was on fire; his heart, which had been fluttering faintly, gave a great leap, trying to force itself out at his mouth. His whole body was racked and wrenched with an insupportable anguish! But his disobedient hands gave no heed to the command. They beat the water vigorously with quick, downward strokes, forcing him to the surface. He felt his head emerge; his eyes were blinded by the sunlight; his chest expanded convulsively, and with a supreme and crowning agony his lungs engulfed a great draft of air, which instantly he expelled in a shriek!

He was now in full possession of his physical senses. They were, indeed, preternaturally keen and alert. Something in the awful disturbance of his organic system had so exalted and refined them that they made record of things never before perceived. He felt the ripples upon his face and heard their separate sounds as they struck. He looked at the forest on the bank of the stream, saw the individual trees, the leaves and the veining of each leaf—saw the very insects upon them: the locusts, the brilliant-bodied flies, the gray spiders stretching their webs from twig to twig. He noted the prismatic colors in all the dewdrops upon a million blades of grass. The humming of the gnats that danced above the eddies of the stream, the beating of the dragonflies' wings, the strokes of the water spiders' legs, like oars which had lifted their boat—all these made audible music. A fish slid along beneath his eyes and he heard the rush of its body parting the water.

He had come to the surface facing down the stream; in a moment the visible world seemed to wheel slowly round, himself the pivotal point, and he saw the bridge, the fort, the soldiers upon the bridge, the captain, the sergeant, the two privates, his executioners. They were in silhouette against the blue sky. They shouted and gesticulated, pointing at him. The captain had drawn his pistol, but did not fire; the others were unarmed. Their movements were grotesque and horrible, their forms gigantic.

Suddenly he heard a sharp report and something struck the water smartly within a few inches of his head, spattering his face with spray. He heard a second report, and saw one of the sentinels with his rifle at his shoulder, a light cloud of blue smoke rising from the muzzle. The man in the water saw the eye of the man on the bridge gazing into his own through the sights of the rifle. He observed that it was a gray eye and remembered having read that gray eyes were keenest, and that all famous marksmen had them. Nevertheless, this one had missed.

A counterswirl had caught Farquhar and turned him half round; he was again looking into the forest on the bank opposite the fort. The sound of a clear, high voice in a monotonous singsong now rang out behind him and came across the water with a distinctness that pierced and subdued all other sounds, even the beating of the ripples in his ears. Although no soldier, he had frequented camps enough to know the dread signifi-

cance of that deliberate, drawling, aspirated chant; the lieutenant on shore was taking a part in the morning's work. How coldly and pitilessly—with what an even, calm intonation, presaging, and enforcing tranquillity in the men—with what accurately measured intervals fell those cruel words:

"Attention, company! . . . Shoulder arms! . . . Ready! . . . Aim! . . . Fire!"

Farquhar dived—dived as deeply as he could. The water roared in his ears like the voice of Niagara, yet he heard the dulled thunder of the volley and, rising again toward the surface, met shining bits of metal, singularly flattened, oscillating slowly downward. Some of them touched him on the face and hands, then fell away, continuing their descent. One lodged between his collar and neck; it was uncomfortably warm and he snatched it out.

As he rose to the surface, gasping for breath, he saw that he had been a long time under water; he was perceptibly farther down stream—nearer to safety. The soldiers had almost finished reloading; the metal ramrods flashed all at once in the sunshine as they were drawn from the barrels, turned in the air, and thrust into their sockets. The two sentinels fired again, independently and ineffectually.

The hunted man saw all this over his shoulder; he was now swimming vigorously with the current. His brain was as energetic as his arms and legs; he thought with the rapidity of lightning.

"The officer," he reasoned, "will not make that martinet's[4] error a second time. It is as easy to dodge a volley as a single shot. He has probably already given the command to fire at will. God help me, I cannot dodge them all!"

An appalling plash within two yards of him was followed by a loud, rushing sound, *diminuendo*,[5] which seemed to travel back

---

4. martinet *n.*: A very strict military disciplinarian.
5. diminuendo (də min' yoo wen' dō): A musical term used to describe a gradual reduction in volume.

through the air to the fort and died in an explosion which stirred the very river to its deeps! A rising sheet of water curved over him, fell down upon him, blinded him, strangled him! The cannon had taken a hand in the game. As he shook his head free from the commotion of the smitten water he heard the deflected shot humming through the air ahead, and in an instant it was cracking and smashing the branches in the forest beyond.

"They will not do that again," he thought; "the next time they will use a charge of grape.[6] I must keep my eye upon the gun; the smoke will apprise me—the report arrives too late; it lags behind the missile. That is a good gun."

Suddenly he felt himself whirled round and round—spinning like a top. The water, the banks, the forests, the now distant bridge, fort and men—all were commingled and blurred. Objects were represented by their colors only; circular horizontal streaks of color—that was all he saw. He had been caught in a vortex and was being whirled on with a velocity of advance and gyration that made him giddy and sick. In a few moments he was flung upon the gravel at the foot of the left bank of the stream—the southern bank—and behind a projecting point which concealed him from his enemies. The sudden arrest of his motion, the abrasion of one of his hands on the gravel, restored him, and he wept with delight. He dug his fingers into the sand, threw it over himself in handfuls and audibly blessed it. It looked like diamonds, rubies, emeralds; he could think of nothing beautiful which it did not resemble. The trees upon the bank were giant garden plants; he noted a definite order in their arrangement, inhaled the fragrance of their blooms. A strange, roseate light shone through the spaces among their trunks and the wind made in their branches the music of aeolian harps.[7] He had no wish to perfect his escape—was content to remain in that enchanting spot until retaken.

A whiz and rattle of grapeshot among the branches high above his head roused him from his dream. The baffled cannoneer had fired him a random farewell. He sprang to his feet, rushed up the sloping bank, and plunged into the forest.

All that day he traveled, laying his course by the rounding sun. The forest seemed interminable; nowhere did he discover a break in it, not even a woodman's road. He had not known that he lived in so wild a region. There was something uncanny in the revelation.

By night fall he was fatigued, footsore, famishing. The thought of his wife and children urged him on. At last he found a road which led him in what he knew to be the right direction. It was as wide and straight as a city street, yet it seemed untraveled. No fields bordered it, no dwelling anywhere. Not so much as the barking of a dog suggested human habitation. The black bodies of the trees formed a straight wall on both sides, terminating on the horizon in a point, like a diagram in a lesson in perspective. Overhead, as he looked up through this rift in the wood, shone great golden stars looking unfamiliar and grouped in strange constellations. He was sure they were arranged in some order which had a secret and malign significance. The wood on either side was full of singular noises, among which—once, twice, and again, he distinctly heard whispers in an unknown tongue.

His neck was in pain and lifting his hand to it he found it horribly swollen. He knew that it had a circle of black where the rope had bruised it. His eyes felt congested; he could no longer close them. His tongue was swollen with thirst; he relieved its fever by thrusting it forward from between his teeth into the cold air. How softly the turf

---

6. grape: A cluster of small iron balls that disperse once fired from a cannon.

7. aeolian (ē ō′ lē ən) **harps:** Harps with strings that produce music when air blows over them.

THE SEAT OF JOHN JULIUS PRINGLE, 1800
Charles Fraser
Carolina Art Association, Gibbes Art Gallery

had carpeted the untraveled avenue—he could no longer feel the roadway beneath his feet!

Doubtless, despite his suffering, he had fallen asleep while walking, for now he sees another scene—perhaps he has merely recovered from a delirium. He stands at the gate of his own home. All is as he left it, and all bright and beautiful in the morning sunshine. He must have traveled the entire night. As he pushes open the gate and passes up the wide white walk, he sees a flutter of female garments; his wife, looking fresh and cool and sweet, steps down from the veranda to meet him. At the bottom of the steps she stands waiting, with a smile of ineffable joy, an attitude of matchless grace and dignity. Ah, how beautiful she is! He springs forward with extended arms. As he is about to clasp her he feels a stunning blow upon the back of the neck; a blinding white light blazes all about him with a sound like the shock of a cannon—then all is darkness and silence!

Peyton Farquhar was dead; his body, with a broken neck, swung gently from side to side beneath the timbers of the Owl Creek bridge.

THINKING ABOUT THE SELECTION

Recalling

1. (a) As the condemned man is waiting to be hanged, what catches his attention? (b) What sound distracts him?
2. Describe the condemned man's background.
3. (a) What do Farquhar and his wife learn from the visitor? (b) What do you learn about the visitor after he leaves?
4. (a) What sensation does Farquhar experience "with terrible suddenness" after he has been hanged? (b) How does he interpret this sensation?
5. What is Farquhar's fate?

Interpreting

6. In Part I Bierce includes few details about the condemned man and does not reveal the reason why he is being hanged. How does this help to create suspense?
7. (a) In what ways are the condemned man's perceptions of time and motion distorted as he is waiting to be hanged? (b) Why are his distorted perceptions important?
8. (a) What seems to be the narrator's attitude toward Farquhar in Part II? (b) What is the narrator's attitude toward war?
9. (a) Considering the outcome of the story, what is ironic, or surprising, about Farquhar's longing for "the larger life of a soldier?" (b) What is ironic about the fact that Farquhar assents to the "dictum that all is fair in love and war"?
10. (a) What details in Part III suggest that Farquhar's journey occurs in his mind? (b) How is his journey connected with the plan of escape that occurs to him moments before he is hanged?

Applying

11. Explain whether you think the portrayal of Farquhar's final thoughts and sensations is realistic.

ANALYZING LITERATURE

Recognizing Point of View

Point of View refers to the vantage point from which a narrative is told.

1. Why is a limited third-person point of view appropriate for this story?
2. Why would a first-person point of view have been inappropriate?
3. How might the story be different if Bierce had used an omniscient third-person narrator?

CRITICAL THINKING AND READING

Understanding the Sequence of Events

Writers frequently do not present all of the events in a story in chronological order. For example, in "An Occurrence at Owl Creek Bridge," Bierce presents a flashback in which he describes some of the events that led up to Farquhar's hanging.

How does Bierce's use of the flashback technique contribute to the effectiveness of the story?

THINKING AND WRITING

Exploring a Different Point of View

Imagine that your school literary magazine is having a contest in which students are asked to retell "An Occurrence at Owl Creek Bridge" from the point of view of one of the Union soldiers or the Federal scout. Start by thinking about how the character you choose might have felt about the hanging of Peyton Farquhar and what he would have known about the reasons for the hanging. List the events that led up to the hanging and some details you could use in describing these events. Then, after deciding on the order in which you want to present the events, write your story. Remember to focus on the thoughts and feelings of the character you have chosen. When you finish writing, revise your story and prepare a final copy.

SARAH ORNE JEWETT

1849–1909

Like other Regionalist writers, Sarah Orne Jewett sought to capture the flavor of life in a specific region. Yet while other Regionalists wrote about the new ways of life on the developing frontier, Sarah Orne Jewett portrayed a style of life that was slowly disappearing—the simple, uncomplicated way of life of the people of rural New England.

Jewett was born in South Berwick, Maine, the daughter of a successful country doctor. During her childhood she often accompanied her father when he visited patients in rural southwestern Maine. Inspired by the people and landscapes she observed during these journeys, Jewett began writing poems and short stories during her early teens. When she was nineteen, she began submitting her work to literary journals, and one of her stories was accepted by the *Atlantic Monthly,* a prestigious magazine.

In 1877 Jewett published *Deephaven,* a collection of tales and sketches about the slow decline of a Maine seaport. Seven years later she published her first novel, *A Country Doctor,* a work that reflected her deep admiration for her father. During the next ten years, Jewett established herself as one of the country's leading Regionalist writers, publishing several more collections of stories and sketches, including *A White Heron and Other Stories* (1886), *A Native of Wimby* (1893), *The Life of Nancy* (1895), and her finest novel, *The Country of the Pointed Firs* (1896).

During Jewett's lifetime the rural lifestyle she had observed as a young girl gradually disappeared. Yet this older way of life lived on in her novels and stories, preserved in her vivid depictions of people and landscapes. In fact, Jewett portrayed life in rural New England so vividly that Willa Cather, a highly regarded American writer, would later comment that Jewett's works "melt into the land and the life of the land until they are not stories at all, but life itself."

GUIDE FOR READING

A White Heron

Imagery. Imagery refers to words or phrases that create mental pictures, or images, that appeal to one or more of the five senses—sight, hearing, touch, smell, or taste. Most often, images appeal to our sense of sight. For example, Jewett presents a visual image in the first sentence of "A White Heron": "The woods were already filled with shadows . . . though a bright sunset still glimmered through the trees." Yet many visual images also appeal to one or more of the other senses, and some images appeal only to the senses other than sight.

Sarah Orne Jewett and other Regionalist writers used imagery to present vivid, realistic descriptions of the environment. Because people's lives are often shaped by their environments, these descriptions were important in conveying the essence of life in a particular region.

As you read "A White Heron," look for the imagery through which Jewett paints a portrait of life in rural New England.

Think of something, such as an animal, a building, or a tree, that captured your interest when you were a young child. Then freewrite for five minutes about your attachment to this object or animal. Discuss the reasons why it captured your interest and what it represented to you.

Knowing the following words will help you as you read "A White Heron."

dilatory (dil′ ə tôr ē) *adj.*: Slow (p. 536)

squalor (skäl′ ər) *n.*: Filth; wretchedness (p. 538)

hermitage (hur′ mit ij) *n.*: A place where a person can live away from other people; a se-cluded retreat (p. 538)

demure (di myo͞or′) *adj.*: Modest; reserved (p. 539)

ornithologist (ôr′ nə thäl′ ə jē) *n.*: Expert on birds (p. 539)

pinions (pin′ yən) *n.*: Wings (p. 541)

A White Heron

Sarah Orne Jewett

I

The woods were already filled with shadows one June evening, just before eight o'clock, though a bright sunset still glimmered faintly among the trunks of the trees. A little girl was driving home her cow, a plodding, dilatory, provoking creature in her behavior, but a valued companion for all that. They were going away from the western light, and striking deep into the dark woods, but their feet were familiar with the path, and it was no matter whether their eyes could see it or not.

There was hardly a night the summer through when the old cow could be found waiting at the pasture bars; on the contrary, it was her greatest pleasure to hide herself away among the high huckleberry bushes, and though she wore a loud bell she had made the discovery that if one stood perfectly still it would not ring. So Sylvia had to hunt for her until she found her, and call Co'! Co'! with never an answering Moo, until her childish patience was quite spent. If the creature had not given good milk and plenty of it, the case would have seemed very different to her owners. Besides, Sylvia had all the time there was, and very little use to make of it. Sometimes in pleasant weather it was a consolation to look upon the cow's pranks as an intelligent attempt to play hide and seek, and as the child had no playmates she lent herself to this amusement with a good deal of zest. Though this chase had been so long that the wary animal herself had given an unusual signal of her whereabouts, Sylvia had only laughed when she came upon Mistress Moolly at the swampside, and urged

her affectionately homeward with a twig of birch leaves. The old cow was not inclined to wander farther, she even turned in the right direction for once as they left the pasture, and stepped along the road at a good pace. She was quite ready to be milked now, and seldom stopped to browse. Sylvia wondered what her grandmother would say because they were so late. It was a great while since she had left home at half past five o'clock, but everybody knew the difficulty of making this errand a short one. Mrs. Tilley had chased the horned torment too many summer evenings herself to blame anyone else for lingering, and was only thankful as she waited that she had Sylvia, nowadays, to give such valuable assistance. The good woman suspected that Sylvia loitered occasionally on her own account; there never was such a child for straying about out-of-doors since the world was made! Everybody said that it was a good change for a little maid who had tried to grow for eight years in a crowded manufacturing town, but, as for Sylvia herself, it seemed as if she never had been alive at all before she came to live at the farm. She thought often with wistful compassion of a wretched dry geranium that belonged to a town neighbor.

" 'Afraid of folks,' " old Mrs. Tilley said to herself, with a smile, after she had made the unlikely choice of Sylvia from her daughter's houseful of children, and was returning to the farm. " 'Afraid of folks,' they said! I guess she won't be troubled no great with 'em up to the old place!" When they reached the door of the lonely house and stopped to unlock it, and the cat came to purr loudly, and rub against them, a deserted pussy, indeed, but fat with young robins, Sylvia whispered that this was a beautiful place to live in, and she never should wish to go home.

The companions followed the shady wood-road, the cow taking slow steps, and the child very fast ones. The cow stopped long at the brook to drink, as if the pasture were not half a swamp, and Sylvia stood still and waited, letting her bare feet cool themselves in the shoal water, while the great twilight moths struck softly against her. She waded on through the brook as the cow moved away, and listened to the thrushes with a

EVENING IN THE WOODS
Worthington Whittredge
The Metropolitan Museum of Art

heart that beat fast with pleasure. There was a stirring in the great boughs overhead. They were full of little birds and beasts that seemed to be wide awake, and going about their world, or else saying good night to each other in sleepy twitters. Sylvia herself felt sleepy as she walked along. However, it was not much farther to the house, and the air was soft and sweet. She was not often in the woods so late as this, and it made her feel as if she were a part of the gray shadows and the moving leaves. She was just thinking how long it seemed since she first came to the farm a year ago, and wondering if everything went on in the noisy town just the same as when she was there; the thought of the great red-faced boy who used to chase and frighten her made her hurry along the path to escape from the shadow of the trees.

Suddenly this little woods-girl is horror-stricken to hear a clear whistle not very far away. Not a bird's whistle, which would have a sort of friendliness, but a boy's whistle, determined, and somewhat aggressive. Sylvia left the cow to whatever sad fate might await her, and stepped discreetly aside into the bushes, but she was just too late. The enemy had discovered her, and called out in a very cheerful and persuasive tone, "Halloa, little girl, how far is it to the road?" and trembling Sylvia answered almost inaudibly, "A good ways."

She did not dare to look boldly at the tall young man, who carried a gun over his shoulder, but she came out of her bush and again followed the cow, while he walked alongside.

"I have been hunting for some birds," the stranger said kindly, "and I have lost my way, and need a friend very much. Don't be afraid," he added gallantly. "Speak up and tell me what your name is, and whether you think I can spend the night at your house, and go out gunning early in the morning."

Sylvia was more alarmed than before. Would not her grandmother consider her much to blame? But who could have foreseen such an accident as this? It did not appear to be her fault, and she hung her head as if the stem of it were broken, but managed to answer "Sylvy," with much effort when her companion again asked her name.

Mrs. Tilley was standing in the doorway when the trio came into view. The cow gave a loud moo by way of explanation.

"Yes, you'd better speak up for yourself, you old trial! Where'd she tucked herself away this time, Sylvy?" Sylvia kept an awed silence; she knew by instinct that her grandmother did not comprehend the gravity of the situation. She must be mistaking the stranger for one of the farmer lads of the region.

The young man stood his gun beside the door, and dropped a heavy game bag beside it; then he bade Mrs. Tilley good evening, and repeated his wayfarer's story, and asked if he could have a night's lodging.

"Put me anywhere you like," he said. "I must be off early in the morning, before day; but I am very hungry, indeed. You can give me some milk at any rate, that's plain."

"Dear sakes, yes," responded the hostess, whose long slumbering hospitality seemed to be easily awakened. "You might fare better if you went out on the main road a mile or so, but you're welcome to what we've got. I'll milk right off, and you make yourself at home. You can sleep on husks or feathers," she proffered graciously. "I raised them all myself. There's good pasturing for geese just below here towards the ma'sh. Now step round and set a plate for the gentleman, Sylvy!" and Sylvia promptly stepped. She was glad to have something to do, and she was hungry herself.

It was a surprise to find so clean and comfortable a little dwelling in this New England wilderness. The young man had known the horrors of its most primitive housekeeping, and the dreary squalor of that level of society which does not rebel at the companionship of hens. This was the best thrift of an old-fashioned farmstead, though on such a small scale that it seemed like a hermitage. He listened eagerly to the old woman's quaint talk, he watched Sylvia's pale face and shining gray eyes with ever growing enthusiasm, and insisted that this was the best supper he had eaten for a month; then, afterward, the new-made friends sat down in the doorway together while the moon came up.

Soon it would be berry time, and Sylvia was a great help at picking. The cow was a good milker, though a plaguy[1] thing to keep track of, the hostess gossiped frankly, adding presently that she had buried four children, so that Sylvia's mother, and a son (who might be dead) in California were all the children she had left. "Dan, my boy, was a great hand to go gunning," she explained sadly. "I never wanted for pa'tridges or gray squer'ls while he was to home. He's been a great wand'rer, I expect, and he's no hand to write letters. There, I don't blame him, I'd ha' seen the world myself if it had been so I could.

"Sylvia takes after him," the grandmother continued affectionately, after a minute's pause. "There ain't a foot o' ground she don't know her way over, and the wild creatur's counts her one o' themselves. Squer'ls she'll tame to come an' feed right out o' her hands, and all sorts o' birds. Last winter she got the jay birds to bangeing[2] here, and I believe she'd 'a' scanted herself of her own meals to have plenty to throw out amongst 'em, if I hadn't kep' watch. Anything but crows, I tell her, I'm willin' to help support—though Dan he went an' tamed one o' them that did seem to have reason same as folks. It was round here a good spell after he went away. Dan an' his father they didn't hitch[3]—but he never held up his head ag'in after Dan had dared him an' gone off."

The guest did not notice this hint of family sorrows in his eager interest in something else.

"So Sylvy knows all about birds, does she?" he exclaimed, as he looked round at the little girl who sat, very demure but increasingly sleepy, in the moonlight. "I am making a collection of birds myself. I have been at it ever since I was a boy." (Mrs. Tilley smiled.) "There are two or three very rare ones I have been hunting for these five years. I mean to get them on my own ground if they can be found."

"Do you cage 'em up?" asked Mrs. Tilley doubtfully, in response to this enthusiastic announcement.

"Oh, no, they're stuffed and preserved, dozens and dozens of them," said the ornithologist, "and I have shot or snared every one myself. I caught a glimpse of a white heron three miles from here on Saturday, and I have followed it in this direction. They have never been found in this district at all. The little white heron, it is," and he turned again to look at Sylvia with the hope of discovering that the rare bird was one of her acquaintances.

But Sylvia was watching a hoptoad in the narrow footpath.

"You would know the heron if you saw it," the stranger continued eagerly. "A queer tall white bird with soft feathers and long thin legs. And it would have a nest perhaps in the top of a high tree, made of sticks, something like a hawk's nest."

Sylvia's heart gave a wild beat; she knew that strange white bird, and had once stolen softly near where it stood in some bright green swamp grass, away over at the other side of the woods. There was a open place where the sunshine always seemed strangely yellow and hot, where tall, nodding rushes grew, and her grandmother had warned her that she might sink in the soft black mud underneath and never be heard of more. Not far beyond were the salt marshes and beyond those was the sea, the sea which Sylvia wondered and dreamed about, but never had looked upon, though its great voice could often be heard above the noise of the woods on stormy nights.

"I can't think of anything I should like so much as to find that heron's nest," the handsome stranger was saying. "I would give

---

1. **plaguy** (plā´ gē) *adj.*: Disagreeable.
2. **bangeing** (ban´ jing) *v.*: Lounging around.
3. **hitch:** Relate well to each other.

ten dollars to anybody who could show it to me," he added desperately, "and I mean to spend my whole vacation hunting for it if need be. Perhaps it was only migrating, or had been chased out of its own region by some bird of prey."

Mrs. Tilley gave amazed attention to all this, but Sylvia still watched the toad, not divining, as she might have done at some calmer time, that the creature wished to get to its hole under the doorstep, and was much hindered by the unusual spectators at that hour of the evening. No amount of thought, that night, could decide how many wished-for treasures the ten dollars, so lightly spoken of, would buy.

The next day the young sportsman hovered about the woods, and Sylvia kept him company, having lost her first fear of the friendly lad, who proved to be most kind and sympathetic. He told her many things about the birds and what they knew and where they lived and what they did with themselves. And he gave her a jackknife, which she thought as great a treasure as if she were a desert islander. All day long he did not once make her troubled or afraid except when he brought down some unsuspecting singing creature from its bough. Sylvia would have liked him vastly better without his gun; she could not understand why he killed the very birds he seemed to like so much. But as the day waned, Sylvia still watched the young man with loving admiration. She had never seen anybody so charming and delightful; the woman's heart, asleep in the child, was vaguely thrilled by a dream of love. Some premonition of that great power stirred and swayed these young foresters who traversed the solemn woodlands with soft-footed silent care. They stopped to listen to a bird's song; they pressed forward again eagerly, parting the branches, speaking to each other rarely and in whispers; the young man going first and Sylvia following, fascinated, a few steps behind, with her gray eyes dark with excitement.

She grieved because the longed-for white heron was elusive, but she did not lead the guest, she only followed, and there was no such thing as speaking first. The sound of her own unquestioned voice would have terrified her—it was hard enough to answer yes or no when there was need of that. At last evening began to fall, and they drove the cow home together, and Sylvia smiled with pleasure when they came to the place where she heard the whistle and was afraid only the night before.

II

Half a mile from home, at the farther edge of the woods, where the land was highest, a great pine tree stood, the last of its generation. Whether it was left for a boundary mark, or for what reason, no one could say; the woodchoppers who had felled its mates were dead and gone long ago, and a whole forest of sturdy trees, pines and oaks and maples, had grown again. But the stately head of this old pine towered above them all and made a landmark for sea and shore miles and miles away. Sylvia knew it well. She had always believed that whoever climbed to the top of it could see the ocean; and the little girl had often laid her hand on the great rough trunk and looked up wistfully at those dark boughs that the wind always stirred, no matter how hot and still the air might be below. Now she thought of the tree with a new excitement, for why, if one climbed it at break of day, could not one see all the world, and easily discover whence the white heron flew, and mark the place, and find the hidden nest?

What a spirit of adventure, what wild ambition! What fancied triumph and delight and glory for the later morning when she could make known the secret! It was almost too real and too great for the childish heart to bear.

All night the door of the little house stood open, and the whippoorwills came and sang upon the very step. The young sportsman and his old hostess were sound asleep, but Sylvia's great design kept her broad awake and watching. She forgot to think of sleep. The short summer night seemed as long as the winter darkness, and at last when the whippoorwills ceased, and she was afraid the morning would after all come too soon, she stole out of the house and followed the pasture path through the woods, hastening toward the open ground beyond, listening with a sense of comfort and companionship to the drowsy twitter of a half-awakened bird, whose perch she had jarred in passing. Alas, if the great wave of human interest which flooded for the first time this dull little life should sweep away the satisfactions of an existence heart to heart with nature and the dumb[4] life of the forest!

There was the huge tree asleep yet in the paling moonlight, and small and hopeful Sylvia began with utmost bravery to mount to the top of it, with tingling, eager blood coursing the channels of her whole frame, with her bare feet and fingers, that pinched and held like bird's claws to the monstrous ladder reaching up, up, almost to the sky itself. First she must mount the white oak tree that grew alongside, where she was almost lost among the dark branches and the green leaves heavy and wet with dew; a bird fluttered off its nest, and a red squirrel ran to and fro and scolded pettishly at the harmless housebreaker. Sylvia felt her way easily. She had often climbed there, and knew that higher still one of the oak's upper branches chafed against the pine trunk, just where its lower boughs were set close together. There, when she made the dangerous pass from one tree to the other, the great enterprise would really begin.

She crept out along the swaying oak limb at last, and took the daring step across into the old pine tree. The way was harder than she thought; she must reach far and hold fast, the sharp dry twigs caught and held her and scratched her like angry talons, the pitch made her thin little fingers clumsy and stiff as she went round and round the tree's great stem, higher and higher upward. The

sparrows and robins in the woods below were beginning to wake and twitter to the dawn, yet it seemed much lighter there aloft in the pine tree, and the child knew that she must hurry if her project were to be of any use.

The tree seemed to lengthen itself out as she went up, and to reach farther and farther upward. It was like a great mainmast to the voyaging earth; it must truly have been amazed that morning through all its ponderous frame as it felt this determined spark of human spirit creeping and climbing from higher branch to branch. Who knows how steadily the least twigs held themselves to advantage this light, weak creature on her way! The old pine must have loved his new dependent. More than all the hawks, and bats, and moths, and even the sweet-voiced thrushes, was the brave, beating heart of the solitary gray-eyed child. And the tree stood still and held away the winds that June morning while the dawn grew bright in the east.

Sylvia's face was like a pale star, if one had seen it from the ground, when the last thorny bough was past, and she stood trembling and tired but wholly triumphant, high in the treetop. Yes, there was the sea with the dawning sun making a golden dazzle over it, and toward that glorious east flew two hawks with slow-moving pinions. How low they looked in the air from that height when before one had only seen them far up, and dark against the blue sky. Their gray feathers were as soft as moths; they seemed only a little way from the tree, and Sylvia felt as if she too could go flying away among the clouds. Westward, the woodlands and farms reached miles and miles into the distance; here and there were church steeples, and white villages; truly it was a vast and awesome world.

The birds sang louder and louder. At last the sun came up bewilderingly bright. Sylvia could see the white sails of ships out at sea, and the clouds that were purple and rose-colored and yellow at first began to fade away. Where was the white heron's nest in

---

4. dumb *adj.*: Silent.

the sea of green branches, and was this wonderful sight and pageant of the world the only reward for having climbed to such a giddy height? Now look down again, Sylvia, where the green marsh is set among the shining birches and dark hemlocks; there where you saw the white heron once you will see him again; look, look! a white spot of him like a single floating feather comes up from the dead hemlock and grows larger, and rises, and comes close at last, and goes by the landmark pine with steady sweep of wing and outstretched slender neck and crested head. And wait! wait! do not move a foot or a finger, little girl, do not send an arrow of light and consciousness from your two eager eyes, for the heron has perched on a pine bough not far beyond yours, and cries back to his mate on the nest, and plumes his feathers for the new day!

The child gives a long sigh a minute later when a company of shouting cat-birds comes also to the tree, and vexed by their fluttering and lawlessness the solemn heron goes away. She knows his secret now, the wild, light, slender bird that floats and wavers, and goes back like an arrow presently to his home in the green world beneath. Then Sylvia, well satisfied, makes her perilous way down again, not daring to look far below the branch she stands on, ready to cry sometimes because her fingers ache and her lamed feet slip. Wondering over and over again what the stranger would say to her, and what he would think when she told him how to find his way straight to the heron's nest.

"Sylvy, Sylvy!" called the busy old grandmother again and again, but nobody answered, and the small husk bed was empty, and Sylvia had disappeared.

The guest waked from a dream, and remembering his day's pleasure hurried to dress himself that it might sooner begin. He was sure from the way the shy little girl looked once or twice yesterday that she had at least seen the white heron, and now she must really be persuaded to tell. Here she comes now, paler than ever, and her worn old frock is torn and tattered, and smeared with pine pitch. The grandmother and the sportsman stand in the door together and question her, and the splendid moment has come to speak of the dead hemlock tree by the green marsh.

But Sylvia does not speak after all, though the old grandmother fretfully rebukes her, and the young man's kind appealing eyes are looking straight in her own. He can make them rich with money; he has promised it, and they are poor now. He is so well worth making happy, and he waits to hear the story she can tell.

No, she must keep silence! What is it that suddenly forbids her and makes her dumb? Has she been nine years growing, and now, when the great world for the first time puts out a hand to her, must she thrust it aside for a bird's sake? The murmur of the pine's green branches is in her ears, she remembers how the white heron came flying through the golden air and how they watched the sea and the morning together, and Sylvia cannot speak; she cannot tell the heron's secret and give its life away.

Dear loyalty, that suffered a sharp pang as the guest went away disappointed later in the day, that could have served and followed him and loved him as a dog loves! Many a night Sylvia heard the echo of his whistle haunting the pasture path as she came home with the loitering cow. She forgot even her sorrow at the sharp report of his gun and the piteous sight of thrushes and sparrows dropping silent to the ground, their songs hushed and their pretty feathers stained and wet with blood. Were the birds better friends than their hunter might have been—who can tell? Whatever treasures were lost to her, woodlands and summertime, remember! Bring your gifts and graces and tell your secrets to this lonely country child!

THINKING ABOUT THE SELECTION

Recalling

1. (a) Why is Sylvia walking through the woods at sunset? (b) Whom does she meet during her walk? (c) What is his reason for being in the woods?
2. (a) What does the young man hope Sylvia will show him? (b) How does he promise to reward her?
3. (a) What can Sylvia not understand about the young man? (b) What feelings does he awaken in her?
4. (a) How does Sylvia locate the white heron? (b) Why does Sylvia decide not to tell the young man about her discovery?

Interpreting

5. The name Sylvia is closely related to the word *sylvan,* which means "of the woods." Why is this an appropriate name for the main character?
6. (a) How would you describe Sylvia's attitude toward nature? (b) How is it different from the young man's attitude?
7. (a) What is the young man's attitude toward Sylvia and her family? (b) Find three passages in which this attitude is revealed.
8. (a) What internal conflict does Sylvia experience? (b) How is the conflict resolved?
9. (a) Considering the heron's color and gracefulness and the fact that it is rarely seen, what do you think it symbolizes, or represents? (b) What do you think the great pine tree symbolizes?
10. (a) What does this story reveal about life in the New England wilderness? (b) What details in the story suggest that this life is disappearing?

Applying

11. Explain whether you think or do not think Sylvia makes the right decision at the end of the story.

ANALYZING LITERATURE
Recognizing Imagery

Imagery refers to words or phrases that create images that appeal to one or more of the five senses. For example, in this story Jewett presents a visual image when she writes, "there was the sea with the dawning sun making a golden dazzle over it."

1. Find two other visual images in the story. Explain why these images are effective.
2. Find two images that appeal to other senses. Explain why these images are effective.

CRITICAL THINKING AND READING

Evaluating the Effect of Imagery

When used effectively, imagery allows you to visualize in your mind each place and event the writer describes—even places and events unlike any you have actually seen.

1. Explain whether Jewett's imagery makes it possible for you to visualize the setting.
2. How does Jewett's use of imagery help convey the flavor of life in the New England wilderness?

THINKING AND WRITING

Responding to Criticism

A critic has stated that Sarah Orne Jewett's stories "are always stories of character." Write an essay in which you discuss this comment in relation to "A White Heron." Reread the story keeping the critic's statement in mind. Are character and characterization the most important elements of the story? Why or why not? When you write your essay, use evidence from the story to support your argument. When you revise, make sure your argument is logically organized.

KATE CHOPIN

1851–1904

Despite her conservative, aristocratic upbringing, Kate O'Flaherty Chopin became one of the most powerful and controversial writers of her time. In her stories, sketches, and novels, she not only captured the local color of Louisiana but also boldly explored the role of women in society.

Kate O'Flaherty was born in St. Louis, Missouri, the daughter of a wealthy businessman. When she was nineteen, she married Oscar Chopin, a Louisiana cotton trader. The couple settled in New Orleans, where they lived for ten years before moving to a plantation in rural northwestern Louisiana. In 1883 Chopin's husband died, leaving her to raise her six children on her own. With her children, she returned to St. Louis and began devoting much of her energy to writing.

Influenced by American Regionalists such as Sarah Orne Jewett and fascinated by the mixture of cultures in Louisiana, Chopin focused on capturing the essence of life in Louisiana in her writing. Like most of her other works, her first novel, *At Fault* (1890), was set in a small Louisiana town inhabited by Creoles, descendants of the original French and Spanish settlers, and Cajuns, descendants of French Canadian settlers. Through her vivid descriptions and use of dialect, Chopin captured the local color of the region. In her stories, published in *Bayou Folk* (1894) and *Acadie* (1897), she exhibited her deep understanding of the different attitudes and concerns of the Louisiana natives. Yet her charming portraits of Louisiana life often obscured the fact that she explored themes considered radical at the time: the nature of marriage, racial prejudice, and women's desire for social, economic, and political equality.

Her finest novel, *The Awakening* (1899), is a psychological account of a woman's search for independence and fulfillment. Because the novel explored the issue of infidelity, it aroused a storm of protest. The book was severely attacked by critics and eventually banned, and Chopin's reputation was badly damaged. As a result, Chopin's work was virtually ignored for several decades after her death. Today, however, she is widely respected for her intense understanding of female psychology and her ability to capture local color.

GUIDE FOR READING

The Story of an Hour

Writer's Techniques

Irony. Irony is a contrast between what is stated and what is meant, or between what is expected to happen and what actually happens. A number of different types of irony are used in literature. Situational irony occurs when the actual result of an action or situation is quite different from the expected result. For example, in "An Occurrence at Owl Creek Bridge," when you are told that Peyton Farquhar assents to the "dictum that all is fair in love and war," you are led to expect that he may become involved in some type of covert or deceptive activity. As it turns out, however, Farquhar himself is the one who is deceived, when he is tricked by a Federal scout who pretends to be a Confederate soldier. Dramatic irony occurs when readers perceive something that a character in a literary work does not know. For example, in Shakespeare's *Romeo and Juliet,* Romeo poisons himself after being told that his beloved Juliet is dead. Yet the audience is aware that in reality Juliet has only been pretending to be dead as part of an elaborate plan to be united with Romeo.

Look For

In "The Story of an Hour" Mrs. Mallard receives news of her husband's death. As you read, look for the unexpected way in which she reacts to this tragedy.

Writing

Imagine an instance in which you or someone you know receives a piece of news that has a powerful effect. Then imagine that the news turns out not to be true. Describe how the news and the discovery that the news was false would affect you.

Vocabulary

Knowing the following words will help you as you read "The Story of an Hour."

forestall (fôr stôl') *v.*: Act in advance of (p. 546)

repression (ri presh' ən) *n.*: Restraint (p. 546)

elusive (i lōō' siv) *adj.*: Hard to grasp (p. 546)

tumultuously (tōō mul' chōō wəs lē) *adv.*: Agitatedly (p. 546)

importunities (im' pôr tōōn' ə tēz) *n.*: Persistent requests or demands (p. 548)

The Story of an Hour

Kate Chopin

Knowing that Mrs. Mallard was afflicted with a heart trouble, great care was taken to break to her as gently as possible the news of her husband's death.

It was her sister Josephine who told her, in broken sentences; veiled hints that revealed in half concealing. Her husband's friend Richards was there, too, near her. It was he who had been in the newspaper office when intelligence of the railroad disaster was received, with Brently Mallard's name leading the list of "killed." He had only taken the time to assure himself of its truth by a second telegram, and had hastened to forestall any less careful, less tender friend in bearing the sad message.

She did not hear the story as many women have heard the same, with a paralyzed inability to accept its significance. She wept at once, with sudden, wild abandonment, in her sister's arms. When the storm of grief had spent itself she went away to her room alone. She would have no one follow her.

There stood, facing the open window, a comfortable, roomy armchair. Into this she sank, pressed down by a physical exhaustion that haunted her body and seemed to reach into her soul.

She could see in the open square before her house the tops of trees that were all aquiver with the new spring life. The delicious breath of rain was in the air. In the street below a peddler was crying his wares. The notes of a distant song which someone was singing reached her faintly, and countless sparrows were twittering in the eaves.

There were patches of blue sky showing here and there through the clouds that had met and piled one above the other in the west facing her window.

She sat with her head thrown back upon the cushion of the chair, quite motionless, except when a sob came up into her throat and shook her, as a child who has cried itself to sleep continues to sob in its dreams.

She was young, with a fair, calm face, whose lines bespoke repression and even a certain strength. But now there was a dull stare in her eyes, whose gaze was fixed away off yonder on one of those patches of blue sky. It was not a glance of reflection, but rather indicated a suspension of intelligent thought.

There was something coming to her and she was waiting for it, fearfully. What was it? She did not know; it was too subtle and elusive to name. But she felt it, creeping out of the sky, reaching toward her through the sounds, the scents, the color that filled the air.

Now her bosom rose and fell tumultuously. She was beginning to recognize this thing that was approaching to possess her, and she was striving to beat it back with her will—as powerless as her two white slender hands would have been.

When she abandoned herself, a little whispered word escaped her slightly parted lips. She said it over and over under her breath: "free, free, free!" The vacant stare and the look of terror that had followed it went from her eyes. They stayed keen and bright. Her pulses beat fast, and the cours-

WOMAN WITH A BLACK TIE
Amedeo Modigliani
Private Collection

ing blood warmed and relaxed every inch of her body.

She did not stop to ask if it were or were not a monstrous joy that held her. A clear and exalted perception enabled her to dismiss the suggestion as trivial.

She knew that she would weep again when she saw the kind, tender hands folded in death; the face that had never looked save with love upon her, fixed and gray and dead. But she saw beyond that bitter moment a long procession of years to come that would belong to her absolutely. And she opened and spread her arms out to them in welcome.

There would be no one to live for her during those coming years; she would live for herself. There would be no powerful will bending hers in that blind persistence with which men and women believe they have a right to impose a private will upon a fellow creature. A kind intention or a cruel intention made the act seem no less a crime as she looked upon it in that brief moment of illumination.

And yet she had loved him—sometimes. Often she had not. What did it matter! What could love, the unsolved mystery, count for in face of this possession of self-assertion which she suddenly recognized as the strongest impulse of her being!

"Free! Body and soul free!" she kept whispering.

Josephine was kneeling before the closed door with her lips to the keyhole, imploring for admission. "Louise, open the door! I beg; open the door—you will make yourself ill.

What are you doing, Louise? For heaven's sake open the door."

"Go away. I am not making myself ill." No; she was drinking in a very elixir of life[1] through that open window.

Her fancy was running riot along those days ahead of her. Spring days, and summer days, and all sorts of days that would be her own. She breathed a quick prayer that life might be long. It was only yesterday she had thought with a shudder that life might be long.

She arose at length and opened the door to her sister's importunities. There was a feverish triumph in her eyes, and she carried herself unwittingly like a goddess of Victory. She clasped her sister's waist, and together they descended the stairs. Richards stood waiting for them at the bottom.

Someone was opening the front door with a latchkey. It was Brently Mallard who entered, a little travel-stained, composedly carrying his gripsack[2] and umbrella. He had been far from the scene of accident, and did not know there had been one. He stood amazed at Josephine's piercing cry; at Richards's quick motion to screen him from the view of his wife.

But Richards was too late.

When the doctors came they said she had died of heart disease—of joy that kills.

---

1. elixir of life (i lik′ sər) *n*.: An imaginary substance thought by medieval alchemists to prolong life indefinitely.
2. gripsack (grip′ sak) *n*.: A small bag for holding clothes.

THINKING ABOUT THE SELECTION

Recalling

1. Why is great care taken to break the news of Brently Mallard's death to Mrs. Mallard "as gently as possible."
2. (a) How does Mrs. Mallard first react to the news of her husband's death? (b) How does her reaction change?
3. (a) Who opens the front door toward the end of the story? (b) How does Mrs. Mallard react when she sees him?

Interpreting

4. At the beginning of the story, when Chopin states that Mrs. Mallard "was afflicted with heart trouble," she seems to be referring to a medical problem. Considering Mrs. Mallard's response to her husband's death, what other meaning do you think this statement might have?
5. How do the details of the scene outside Mrs. Mallard's room foreshadow the feelings that gradually sweep over Mrs. Mallard as she sits in her armchair?
6. What has Mrs. Mallard apparently resented about her marriage?
7. Why do you think Chopin chooses to reveal little about Mrs. Mallard's personality aside from her feelings concerning her marriage, her husband, and her independence?
8. What do you think is the actual reason for Mrs. Mallard's death?
9. What do you think is the significance of the story's title?

Applying

10. Mrs. Mallard realizes, "There would be no one to live for her during these coming years; she would live for herself." Do you think that it is important for people to live for themselves? Explain your answer.

ANALYZING LITERATURE

Recognizing Irony

Irony is a contrast between what is stated and what is meant, or between what is expected to happen and what actually happens. Situational irony and dramatic irony are two of the types of irony used in literature. An example of situational irony occurs in "The Story of an Hour," when, after you have been led to expect that Mrs. Mallard will be deeply disturbed by the news of her husband's death, she is actually overcome by a sense of joy.

1. Why is Mrs. Mallard's sudden death also an example of situational irony?
2. Why is the diagnosis of the cause of Mrs. Mallard's death an example of dramatic irony?

CRITICAL THINKING AND READING

Recognizing Details of Irony

A writer creates situational irony by including details that create certain expectations. For example, in "The Story of an Hour," Chopin leads you to expect that Mrs. Mallard will be upset by the news of her husband's death by mentioning that Josephine and Richards take great care to break the news to her as gently as possible.

Find two details that help create the situational irony of Mrs. Mallard's death.

THINKING AND WRITING

Writing About Irony

Write an essay in which you discuss the role of irony in "The Story of an Hour." Reread the story focusing on Chopin's use of irony. Develop a thesis statement. When you write your essay, use evidence from the story to support your thesis. When you revise your essay, make sure you have not included any unnecessary information.

WILLA CATHER

1873–1947

Willa Cather was born in a small town in western Virginia. When she was ten, her family moved to a farm near the frontier town of Red Cloud, Nebraska. Here, many of Cather's new neighbors were immigrants—Swedes, Germans, Slavs, and Russians—struggling to build a life for themselves in their new land and determined to preserve the culture of the land they left behind. Through her interaction with this diverse group of people, Cather developed an awareness of certain qualities shared not only by people of the frontier but by people from all over the world. She also gained a rich cultural background, studying foreign languages, history, and classical music and opera. She wrote of her childhood: "On Sundays we could drive to a Norwegian church and listen to a sermon in that language, or to a Danish or Swedish church. We could go to a French Catholic settlement or into the Bohemian township and hear one in Czech, or we could go to the church with the German Lutherans."

After graduating from the University of Nebraska in 1895, Cather worked as an editor for a Pittsburgh newspaper, while writing poems and short stories in her spare time. Her first collection of stories, *The Troll Garden,* was published in 1905. The following year she moved to New York, where she worked as the managing editor for *McClure's Magazine.* In 1912, the year after she published her first novel, *Alexander's Bridge,* she left the magazine to devote all her energy to writing. During the next several years, she produced three novels: *O Pioneers!* (1913); *The Song of the Lark* (1915); and *My Antonia* (1918), which captured the flavor of life in the midwestern prairies. In 1923 she won the Pulitzer Prize for her novel *One of Ours* (1922).

Cather shifted her attention from the Midwest to the Southwest in *Death Comes for the Archbishop* (1927) and to seventeenth-century Quebec in *Shadows on the Rock* (1931). She also published two collections of short stories: *Youth and the Bright Medusa* (1920) and *Obscure Destinies* (1932); and a collection of critical essays and recollections of earlier writers: *Not Under Forty.*

In her work Cather displayed her admiration for the courage and spirit of the immigrants and other settlers of the frontier while at the same time conveying an intense awareness of the loss felt by some of the pioneers as well as the loneliness and isolation from which they suffered. In "A Wagner Matinée" Cather captures this sense of loneliness and isolation by contrasting the stark realities of frontier life with the possibilities of life in a more cultured world.

GUIDE FOR READING

A Wagner Matinée

Writer's Techniques

Characterization. Characterization is the means by which a writer reveals a character's personality. Writers generally develop a character through one of the following methods: direct statements about the character, physical descriptions of the character, the character's actions, the character's thoughts and comments, or other characters' reactions to or comments about the character.

In the late 1800's and early 1900's, writers began turning to the first-person and third-person limited points of view. When a writer limits the point of view to one character, as Cather does in "A Wagner Matinée," most of what is revealed about the characters is shaped by the thoughts of the character from whose point of view the story is being told.

Look For

Willa Cather asked for the following words from her novel *My Antonia* to be carved on her tombstone: ". . . that is happiness, to be dissolved into something complete and great." As you read " A Wagner Matinée," look for what the young man learns about his Aunt Georgiana. How does Aunt Georgiana give flesh and blood to Cather's epitaph?

Writing

Ralph Waldo Emerson has written, "[Music] takes us out of the actual and whispers to us dim secrets that startle us to wonder as to who we are, and for what, whence, and whereth." Discuss the meaning of this quotation. Think about the powerful effect music often has on people's memories and emotions. Recall a piece of music—one that has no lyrics—that can produce a strong effect on your memories and emotions. Then freewrite about it.

Vocabulary

Knowing the following words will help you as you read "A Wagner Matinée."

callow (kal′ ō) *adj*.: Immature; inexperienced (p. 552)
reverential (rev′ ə ren′ sḥəl) *adj*.: Showing or caused by a feeling of deep respect, love, and awe (p. 554)
tremulously (trem′ yōō ləs lē) *adv*.: Fearfully; timidly (p. 554)
semi-somnambulant (sem′i

säm nam′ byōō lənt) *adj*.: Half sleepwalking (p. 554)
inert (in urt′) *adj*.: Motionless (p. 555)
trepidation (trep′ə dā′ sḥən) *n*.: Fearful anxiety; apprehension (p. 555)
jocularity (jäk′ yə lar′ə tē) *n*.: Joking good humor (p. 558)

A Wagner Matinée

Willa Cather

I received one morning a letter written in pale ink, on glassy, blue-lined notepaper, and bearing the postmark of a little Nebraska village. This communication, worn and rubbed, looking as though it had been carried for some days in a coat pocket that was none too clean, was from my Uncle Howard. It informed me that his wife had been left a small legacy by a bachelor relative who had recently died, and that it had become necessary for her to come to Boston to attend to the settling of the estate. He requested me to meet her at the station, and render her whatever services might prove necessary. On examining the date indicated as that of her arrival, I found it no later than tomorrow. He had characteristically delayed writing until, had I been away from home for a day, I must have missed the good woman altogether.

The name of my Aunt Georgiana called up not alone her own figure, at once pathetic and grotesque, but opened before my feet a gulf of recollections so wide and deep that, as the letter dropped from my hand, I felt suddenly a stranger to all the present conditions of my existence, wholly ill at ease and out of place amid the surroundings of my study. I became, in short, the gangling farmer boy my aunt had known, scourged with chilblains and bashfulness, my hands cracked and raw from the corn husking. I felt the knuckles of my thumb tentatively, as though they were raw again. I sat again before her parlor organ, thumbing the scales with my stiff, red hands, while she beside me made canvas mittens for the huskers.

The next morning, after preparing my landlady somewhat, I set out for the station. When the train arrived I had some difficulty in finding my aunt. She was the last of the passengers to alight, and when I got her into the carriage she looked not unlike one of those charred, smoked bodies that firemen lift from the *débris* of a burned building. She had come all the way in a day coach; her linen duster[1] had become black with soot and her black bonnet gray with dust during the journey. When we arrived at my boardinghouse the landlady put her to bed at once, and I did not see her again until the next morning.

Whatever shock Mrs. Springer experienced at my aunt's appearance she considerately concealed. Myself, I saw my aunt's misshapen figure with that feeling of awe and respect with which we behold explorers who have left their ears and fingers north of Franz Josef Land,[2] or their health somewhere along the upper Congo.[3] My Aunt Georgiana had been a music teacher at the Boston Conservatory, somewhere back in the latter sixties. One summer, which she had spent in the little village in the Green Mountains[4] where her ancestors had dwelt for generations, she had kindled the callow fancy of the most idle and shiftless of all the village lads, and had conceived for this Howard Carpenter one of those absurd and extravagant passions which a handsome

---

1. **duster** *n.:* A short, loose smock worn to protect clothing from dust.
2. **Franz Josef Land:** A group of islands in the Arctic Ocean that are now part of the U.S.S.R.
3. **Congo:** River in central Africa.
4. **Green Mountains:** Mountains in Vermont.

FROM ARKANSAS
George Schreiber
Sheldon Swope Art Gallery, Terre Haute, Indiana

A Wagner Matinée 553

country boy of twenty-one sometimes inspires in a plain, angular, spectacled woman of thirty. When she returned to her duties in Boston, Howard followed her; and the upshot of this inexplicable infatuation was that she eloped with him, eluding the reproaches of her family and the criticism of her friends by going with him to the Nebraska frontier. Carpenter, who of course had no money, took a homestead in Red Willow County,[5] fifty miles from the railroad. There they measured off their eighty acres by driving across the prairie in a wagon, to the wheel of which they had tied a red cotton handkerchief, and counting its revolutions. They built a dugout in the red hillside, one of those cave dwellings whose inmates usually reverted to the conditions of primitive savagery. Their water they got from the lagoons where the buffalo drank, and their slender stock of provisions was always at the mercy of bands of roving Indians. For thirty years my aunt had not been farther than fifty miles from the homestead.

But Mrs. Springer knew nothing of all this, and must have been considerably shocked at what was left of my kinswoman. Beneath the soiled linen duster, which on her arrival was the most conspicuous feature of her costume, she wore a black stuff dress whose ornamentation showed that she had surrendered herself unquestioningly into the hands of a country dressmaker. My poor aunt's figure, however, would have presented astonishing difficulties to any dressmaker. Her skin was yellow from constant exposure to a pitiless wind, and to the alkaline water which transforms the most transparent cuticle into a sort of flexible leather. She wore ill-fitting false teeth. The most striking thing about her physiognomy, however, was an incessant twitching of the mouth and eyebrows, a form of nervous disorder resulting from isolation and monotony, and from frequent physical suffering.

5. **Red Willow County:** County in southwestern Nebraska that borders on Kansas.

In my boyhood this affliction had possessed a sort of horrible fascination for me, of which I was secretly very much ashamed, for in those days I owed to this woman most of the good that ever came my way, and had a reverential affection for her. During the three winters when I was riding herd for my uncle, my aunt, after cooking three meals for half a dozen farmhands, and putting the six children to bed, would often stand until midnight at her ironing board, hearing me at the kitchen table beside her recite Latin declensions and conjugations, and gently shaking me when my drowsy head sank down over a page of irregular verbs. It was to her, at her ironing or mending, that I read my first Shakespeare; and her old textbook of mythology was the first that ever came into my empty hands. She taught me my scales and exercises, too, on the little parlor organ which her husband had bought her after fifteen years, during which she had not so much as seen any instrument except an accordion, that belonged to one of the Norwegian farmhands. She would sit beside me by the hour, darning and counting, while I struggled with the "Harmonious Blacksmith"; but she seldom talked to me about music, and I understood why. She was a pious woman; she had the consolation of religion; and to her at least her martyrdom was not wholly sordid. Once when I had been doggedly beating out some passages from an old score of "Euryanthe" I had found among her music books, she came up to me and, putting her hands over my eyes, gently drew my head back upon her shoulder, saying tremulously, "Don't love it so well, Clark, or it may be taken from you. Oh! dear boy, pray that whatever your sacrifice be it is not that."

When my aunt appeared on the morning after her arrival, she was still in a semi-somnambulent state. She seemed not to realize that she was in the city where she had spent her youth, the place longed for hungrily for half a lifetime. She had been so wretchedly trainsick throughout the journey that she had no recollection of anything but her discomfort, and, to all intents and purposes, there were but a few hours of nightmare between the farm in Red Willow County and my study on Newbury Street. I had planned a little pleasure for her that afternoon, to repay her for some of the glorious moments she had given me when we used to milk together in the straw-thatched cowshed, and she, because I was more than usually tired, or because her husband had spoken sharply to me, would tell me of the splendid performance of Meyerbeer's *Les Huguenots*[6] she had seen in Paris in her youth. At two o'clock the Boston Symphony Orchestra was to give a Wagner[7] program, and I intended to take my aunt, though as I conversed with her I grew doubtful about her enjoyment of it. Indeed, for her own sake, I could only wish her taste for such things quite dead, and the long struggle mercifully ended at last. I suggested our visiting the Conservatory and the Common[8] before lunch, but she seemed altogether too timid to wish to venture out. She questioned me absently about various changes in the city, but she was chiefly concerned that she had forgotten to leave instructions about feeding half-skimmed milk to a certain weakling calf, "Old Maggie's calf, you know, Clark," she explained, evidently having forgotten how long I had been away. She was further troubled because she had neglected to tell her daughter about the freshly opened kit of mackerel in the cellar, that would spoil if it were not used directly.

I asked her whether she had ever heard any of the Wagnerian operas, and found that she had not, though she was perfectly familiar with their respective situations and had once possessed the piano score of *The Flying Dutchman*. I began to think it would have been best to get her back to Red Willow County without waking her, and regretted having suggested the concert.

From the time we entered the concert hall, however, she was a trifle less passive and inert, and seemed to begin to perceive her surroundings. I had felt some trepidation lest one might become aware of the absurdities of her attire, or might experience some painful embarrassment at stepping suddenly into the world to which she had been dead for a quarter of a century. But again I found how superficially I had judged her. She sat looking about her with eyes as impersonal, almost as stony, as those with which the granite Ramses[9] in a museum watches the froth and fret that ebbs and flows about his pedestal, separated from it by the lonely stretch of centuries. I have seen this same aloofness in old miners who drift into the Brown Hotel at Denver, their pockets full of bullion, their linen soiled, their haggard faces unshorn, and who stand in the thronged corridors as solitary as though they were still in a frozen camp on the Yukon, or in the yellow blaze of the Arizona desert, conscious that certain experiences have isolated them from their fellows by a gulf no haberdasher could conceal.

The audience was made up chiefly of women. One lost the contour of faces and figures, indeed any effect of line whatever, and there was only the color contrast of bodices past counting, the shimmer and shading of fabrics soft and firm, silky and sheer, resisting and yielding: red, mauve, pink, blue, lilac, purple, ecru, rose, yellow, cream, and white, all the colors that an impressionist finds in a sunlit landscape, with here and there the dead black shadow of a frock coat. My Aunt Georgiana regarded them as though they had been so many daubs of tube paint on a palette.

---

6. Les Huguenots (hyo͞o′ gə nät′): Opera written in 1836 by Giacomo Meyerbeer (1791–1864).

7. Wagner (väg′ nər): Richard Wagner (1813–1883), a great German composer who is responsible for the development of the musical drama.

8. Common: Boston Common, a small park in Boston.

9. Ramses (ram′ sēz): Egyptian kings who ruled from c.1315 to c.1090 B.C.

When the musicians came out and took their places, she gave a little stir of anticipation, and looked with quickening interest down over the rail at that invariable grouping; perhaps the first wholly familiar thing that had greeted her eye since she had left old Maggie and her weakling calf. I could feel how all those details sank into her soul, for I had not forgotten how they had sunk into mine when I came fresh from plowing forever and forever between green aisles of corn, where, as in a treadmill, one might walk from daybreak to dusk without perceiving a shadow of change in one's environment. I reminded myself of the impression made on me by the clean profiles of the musicians, the gloss of their linen; the dull black of their coats, the beloved shapes of the instruments, the patches of yellow light thrown by the green-shaded stand-lamps on the smooth, varnished bellies of the cellos and the bass viols in the rear, the restless, wind-tossed forest of fiddle necks and bows; I recalled how, in the first orchestra I had ever heard, those long bow strokes seemed to draw the soul out of me, as a conjuror's stick reels out paper ribbon from a hat.

The first number was the Tannhäuser overture. When the violins drew out the first strain of the Pilgrims' chorus, my Aunt Georgiana clutched my coat sleeve. Then it was that I first realized that for her this singing of basses and stinging frenzy of lighter strings broke a silence of thirty years, the inconceivable silence of the plains. With the battle between the two motifs, with the bitter frenzy of the Venusberg[10] theme and its ripping of strings, came to me an overwhelming sense of the waste and wear we are so powerless to combat. I saw again the tall, naked house on the prairie, black and grim as a wooden fortress; the black pond where I had learned to swim, the rain-gullied clay about the naked house; the four dwarf ash seedlings on which the dishcloths were always hung to dry before the kitchen door. The world there is the flat world of the ancients; to the east, a cornfield that stretched to daybreak; to the west, a corral that stretched to sunset; between, the sordid conquests of peace, more merciless than those of war.

The overture closed. My aunt released my coat sleeve, but she said nothing. She sat staring at the orchestra through a dullness of thirty years, through the films made, little by little, by each of the three hundred and sixty-five days in every one of them. What, I wondered, did she get from it? She had been a good pianist in her day, I knew, and her musical education had been broader than that of most music teachers of a quarter of a century ago. She had often told me of Mozart's operas and Meyerbeer's, and I could remember hearing her sing, years ago, certain melodies of Verdi. When I had fallen ill with a fever she used to sit by my cot in the evening, while the cool night wind blew in through the faded mosquito netting tacked over the window, and I lay watching a bright star that burned red above the cornfield, and sing "Home to our mountains, oh, let us return!" in a way fit to break the heart of a Vermont boy near dead of homesickness already.

I watched her closely through the prelude to *Tristan and Isolde*, trying vainly to conjecture what that warfare of motifs, that seething turmoil of strings and winds, might mean to her. Had this music any message for her? Did or did not a new planet swim into her ken? Wagner had been a sealed book to Americans before the sixties. Had she anything left with which to comprehend this glory that had flashed around the world since she had gone from it? I was in a fever of curiosity, but Aunt Georgiana sat silent upon her peak in Darien.[11] She preserved

---

10. **Venusberg** (vē′ nəs bûrg′): A legendary mountain in Germany where Venus, the Roman goddess of love, held court.

11. **peak in Darien** (der′ ē ən): The mountain on the Isthmus of Panama. From "On First Looking at Chapman's Homer" by English poet John Keats (1795–1821).

AT THE OPERA
Mary Stevenson Cassatt
Museum of Fine Arts, Boston

this utter immobility throughout the numbers from the *Flying Dutchman*, though her fingers worked mechanically upon her black dress, as though of themselves they were recalling the piano score they had once played. Poor old hands! They were stretched and pulled and twisted into mere tentacles to hold, and lift, and knead with; the palms unduly swollen, the fingers bent and knotted, on one of them a thin worn band that had once been a wedding ring. As I pressed and gently quieted one of those groping hands, I remembered, with quivering eyelids, their services for me in other days.

Soon after the tenor began the "Prize Song," I heard a quick-drawn breath, and turned to my aunt. Her eyes were closed, but the tears were glistening on her cheeks, and I think in a moment more they were in my eyes as well. It never really dies, then, the

JACK LONDON

1876–1916

Jack London endured more hardships during the first twenty-one years of his life than most people experience in a lifetime. Yet he was able to learn from his experiences and use them as the inspiration for his successful career as a writer.

Born in San Francisco, London grew up in extreme poverty. At an early age, he left school to support himself through a variety of menial jobs. During his first eighteen years, he left San Francisco a number of times, sailing to Japan as part of a sealing expedition and participating in a protest march across the country with a group of unemployed men.

After being arrested for vagrancy near Buffalo, New York, London decided to educate himself and reshape his life. He quickly completed high school, then enrolled in the University of California. London remained in college for only one semester, however, before abandoning his studies and traveling to Alaska in search of gold.

Although he experienced no success as a miner, London's experiences in Alaska taught him about the human desire for wealth and power and about humankind's inability to control nature. Shortly after returning to California, London began transforming his Alaskan adventures into short stories and novels. In 1903 he earned national fame when he published the popular novel, *The Call of the Wild*. He soon became the highest paid and most industrious writer in the country. During the course of his career, he produced more than fifty books and earned more than a million dollars. Though many of his works are no longer highly regarded by critics, several of his novels, including *The Call of the Wild (1903), The Sea-Wolf* (1904), and *White Fang* (1906), have become American classics.

Many of London's best short stories and novels depict a person's struggle for survival against the powerful forces of nature. For example, "To Build a Fire" tells the story of a man's fight to survive the harsh cold of the Alaskan winter.

To Build a Fire

Conflict. Conflict, a struggle between two opposing forces or characters, plays a vital role in the plot development of a literary work. The events of a work are all related to the conflict as the plot develops. Frequently the conflict is resolved by the end of the work, though in many modern and contemporary works the conflict is left unresolved.

Conflict may be internal or external. An internal conflict is a struggle between conflicting thoughts and emotions within a character. For example, in "A White Heron" Sylvia struggles between her eagerness to please the young stranger and her desire to protect the white heron. An external conflict is a struggle between a character and an outside force, such as another character, society, nature, or fate. For example, in *Moby-Dick* Ahab struggles against a great white whale, Moby-Dick.

As you read "To Build a Fire," look for the conflict and take note of the role it plays in plot development.

Think of an incident in which you witnessed or were confronted with the tremendous power of nature. For example, you may have lived through a hurricane or tornado or experienced extremely hot or cold weather. Briefly describe your responses to this incident and how it shaped your impressions of nature.

Knowing the following words will help you as you read "To Build a Fire."

conjectural (kən jek′ chər əl) *adj.*: Based on guesswork (p. 563)
unwonted (un wun′ tid) *adj.*: Unfamiliar (p. 564)

conflagration (kän′ flə grā′ shən) *n.*: A big, destructive fire (p. 568)
peremptorily (pə remp′ tər ə lē) *adj.*: Commandingly (p. 571)

To Build a Fire

Jack London

Day had broken cold and gray, exceedingly cold and gray, when the man turned aside from the main Yukon[1] trail and climbed the high earth-bank, where a dim and little-traveled trail led eastward through the fat spruce timberland. It was a steep bank, and he paused for breath at the top, excusing the act to himself by looking at his watch. It was nine o'clock. There was no sun nor hint of sun, though there was not a cloud in the sky. It was a clear day, and yet there seemed an intangible pall over the face of things, a subtle gloom that made the day dark, and that was due to the absence of sun. This fact did not worry the man. He was used to the lack of sun. It had been days since he had seen the sun, and he knew that

1. Yukon (yōō′ kän): Territory in northwestern Canada, east of Alaska. Also a river.

a few more days must pass before that cheerful orb, due south, would just peep above the skyline and dip immediately from view.

The man flung a look back along the way he had come. The Yukon lay a mile wide and hidden under three feet of ice. On top of this ice were as many feet of snow. It was all pure white, rolling in gentle undulations where the ice jams of the freeze-up had formed. North and south, as far as his eye could see, it was unbroken white, save for a dark hairline that curved and twisted from around the spruce-covered island to the south, and that curved and twisted away into the north, where it disappeared behind another spruce-covered island. This dark hairline was the trail—the main trail—that led south five hundred miles to the Chilcoot Pass, Dyea,[2] and salt water; and that led north seventy miles to Dawson, and still on to the north a thousand miles to Nulato,[3] and finally to St. Michael on Bering Sea, a thousand miles and half a thousand more.

But all this—the mysterious, far-reaching hairline trail, the absence of sun from the sky, the tremendous cold, and the strangeness and weirdness of it all—made no impression on the man. It was not because he was long used to it. He was a newcomer in the land, a *chechaquo*,[4] and this was his first winter. The trouble with him was that he was without imagination. He was quick and alert in the things of life, but only in the things, and not in the significances. Fifty degrees below zero meant eighty-odd degrees of frost. Such fact impressed him as being cold and uncomfortable, and that was all. It did not lead him to meditate upon his frailty as a creature of temperature, and upon man's frailty in general, able only to live within certain narrow limits of heat and cold; and from there on it did not lead him to the conjectural field of

immortality and man's place in the universe. Fifty degrees below zero stood for a bite of frost that hurt and that must be guarded against by the use of mittens, earflaps, warm moccasins, and thick socks. Fifty degrees below zero was to him just precisely fifty degrees below zero. That there should be anything more to it than that was a thought that never entered his head.

As he turned to go on, he spat speculatively. There was a sharp, explosive crackle that startled him. He spat again. And again, in the air, before it could fall to the snow, the spittle crackled. He knew that at fifty below spittle crackled on the snow, but this spittle had crackled in the air. Undoubtedly it was colder than fifty below—how much colder he did not know. But the temperature did not matter. He was bound for the old claim on the left fork of Henderson Creek, where the boys were already. They had come over across the divide from the Indian Creek country, while he had come the roundabout way to take a look at the possibilities of getting out logs in the spring from the islands in the Yukon. He would be in to camp by six o'clock; a bit after dark, it was true, but the boys would be there, a fire would be going, and a hot supper would be ready. As for lunch, he pressed his hand against the protruding bundle under his jacket. It was also under his shirt, wrapped up in a handkerchief and lying against the naked skin. It was the only way to keep the biscuits from freezing. He smiled agreeably to himself as he thought of those biscuits, each cut open and sopped in bacon grease, and each enclosing a generous slice of fried bacon.

He plunged in among the big spruce trees. The trail was faint. A foot of snow had fallen since the last sled had passed over, and he was glad he was without a sled, traveling light. In fact, he carried nothing but the lunch wrapped in the handkerchief. He was surprised, however, at the cold. It certainly was cold, he concluded, as he rubbed his numb nose and cheekbones with his mittened hand. He was a warm-whiskered

2. **Dyea** (dī′ ā): A former town in Alaska at the start of the Yukon trail.
3. **Dawson** and **Nulato:** Former goldmining villages in the Yukon.
4. *chechaquo* (c̆hē c̆hä′ kwō): Slang for newcomer.

man, but the hair on his face did not protect the high cheekbones and the eager nose that thrust itself aggressively into the frosty air.

At the man's heels trotted a dog, a big native husky, the proper wolf dog, gray-coated and without any visible or temperamental difference from its brother, the wild wolf. The animal was depressed by the tremendous cold. It knew that it was no time for traveling. Its instinct told it a truer tale than was told to the man by the man's judgment. In reality, it was not merely colder than fifty below zero; it was colder than sixty below, than seventy below. It was seventy-five below zero. Since the freezing point is thirty-two above zero, it meant that one hundred and seven degrees of frost obtained. The dog did not know anything about thermometers. Possibly in its brain there was no sharp consciousness of a condition of very cold such as was in the man's brain. But the brute had its instinct. It experienced a vague but menacing apprehension that subdued it and made it slink along at the man's heels, and that made it question eagerly every unwonted movement of the man as if expecting him to go into camp or to seek shelter somewhere and build a fire. The dog had learned fire, and it wanted fire, or else to burrow under the snow and cuddle its warmth away from the air.

The frozen moisture of its breathing had settled on its fur in a fine powder of frost, and especially were its jowls, muzzle, and eyelashes whitened by its crystalled breath. The man's red beard and mustache were likewise frosted, but more solidly, the deposit taking the form of ice and increasing with every warm, moist breath he exhaled. Also, the man was chewing tobacco, and the muzzle of ice held his lips so rigidly that he was unable to clear his chin when he expelled the juice. The result was that a crystal beard of the color and solidity of amber was increasing its length on his chin. If he fell down it would shatter itself, like glass, into brittle fragments. But he did not mind the appendage. It was the penalty all tobacco-chewers paid in that country, and he had been out before in two cold snaps. They had not been so cold as this, he knew, but by the spirit thermometer[5] at Sixty Mile he knew they had been registered at fifty below and at fifty-five.

He held on through the level stretch of woods for several miles, crossed a wide flat, and dropped down a bank to the frozen bed of a small stream. This was Henderson Creek, and he knew he was ten miles from the forks. He looked at his watch. It was ten o'clock. He was making four miles an hour, and he calculated that he would arrive at the forks at half past twelve. He decided to celebrate that event by eating his lunch there.

The dog dropped in again at his heels, with a tail drooping discouragement, as the man swung along the creek bed. The furrow of the old sled trail was plainly visible, but a dozen inches of snow covered the marks of the last runners. In a month no man had come up or down that silent creek. The man held steadily on. He was not much given to thinking, and just then particularly he had nothing to think about save that he would eat lunch at the forks and that at six o'clock he would be in camp with the boys. There was nobody to talk to; and, had there been, speech would have been impossible because of the ice-muzzle on his mouth. So he continued monotonously to chew tobacco and to increase the length of his amber beard.

Once in a while the thought reiterated itself that it was very cold and that he had never experienced such cold. As he walked along he rubbed his cheekbones and nose with the back of his mittened hand. He did this automatically, now and again changing hands. But rub as he would, the instant he stopped his cheekbones went numb, and the following instant the end of his nose went numb. He was sure to frost his cheeks; he knew that, and experienced a pang of regret that he had not devised a nose strap of the

---

5. spirit thermometer: A thermometer, containing alcohol, used in extreme cold.

sort Bud wore in cold snaps. Such a strap passed across the cheeks, as well, and saved them. But it didn't matter much, after all. What were frosted cheeks? A bit painful, that was all; they were never serious.

Empty as the man's mind was of thoughts, he was keenly observant, and he noticed the changes in the creek, the curves and bends and timber jams, and always he sharply noted where he placed his feet. Once, coming around a bend, he shied abruptly, like a startled horse, curved away from the place where he had been walking, and retreated several paces back along the trail. The creek he knew was frozen clear to the bottom—no creek could contain water in that arctic winter—but he knew also that there were springs that bubbled out from the hillsides and ran along under the snow and on top the ice of the creek. He knew that the coldest snaps never froze these springs, and he knew likewise their danger. They were traps. They hid pools of water under the snow that might be three inches deep, or three feet. Sometimes a skin of ice half an inch thick covered them, and in turn was covered by the snow. Sometimes there were alternate layers of water and ice skin, so that when one broke through he kept on breaking through for a while, sometimes wetting himself to the waist.

That was why he had shied in such panic. He had felt the give under his feet and heard the crackle of a snow-hidden ice skin. And to get his feet wet in such a temperature meant trouble and danger. At the very least it meant delay, for he would be forced to stop and build a fire, and under its protection to bare his feet while he dried his socks and moccasins. He stood and studied the creek bed and its banks, and decided that the flow of water came from the right. He reflected awhile, rubbing his nose and cheeks, then skirted to the left, stepping gingerly and testing the footing for each step. Once clear of the danger, he took a fresh chew of tobacco and swung along at his four-mile gait.

In the course of the next two hours he came upon several similar traps. Usually the snow above the hidden pools had a sunken, candied apppearance that advertised the danger. Once again, however, he had a close call; and once, suspecting danger, he compelled the dog to go on in front. The dog did not want to go. It hung back until the man shoved it forward, and then it went quickly across the white, unbroken surface. Suddenly it broke through, floundered to one side, and got away to firmer footing. It had wet its forefeet and legs, and almost immediately the water that clung to it turned to ice. It made quick efforts to lick the ice off its legs, then dropped down in the snow and began to bite out the ice that had formed between the toes. This was a matter of instinct. To permit the ice to remain would mean sore feet. It did not know this. It merely obeyed the mysterious prompting that arose from the deep crypts of its being. But the man knew, having achieved a judgment on the subject, and he removed the mitten from his right hand and helped tear out the ice particles. He did not expose his fingers more than a minute, and was astonished at the swift numbness that smote them. It certainly was cold. He pulled on the mitten hastily, and beat the hand savagely across his chest.

At twelve o'clock the day was at its brightest. Yet the sun was too far south on its winter journey to clear the horizon. The bulge of the earth intervened between it and Henderson Creek, where the man walked under a clear sky at noon and cast no shadow. At half-past twelve, to the minute, he arrived at the forks of the creek. He was pleased at the speed he had made. If he kept it up, he would certainly be with the boys by six. He unbuttoned his jacket and shirt and drew forth his lunch. The action consumed no more than a quarter of a minute, yet in that brief moment the numbness laid hold of the exposed fingers. He did not put the mitten on, but, instead, struck the fingers a dozen sharp smashes against his leg. Then he sat down on a snow-covered log to eat. The sting that followed upon the striking of his fingers against his leg ceased so quickly that he was startled. He had had no chance to take a bite of biscuit. He struck the fingers repeatedly and returned them to the mitten, baring the other hand for the purpose of eating. He tried to take a mouthful, but the ice muzzle prevented. He had forgotten to build a fire and thaw out. He chuckled at his foolishness, and as he chuckled he noted the numbness creeping into the exposed fingers. Also, he noted that the stinging which had first come to his toes when he sat down was already passing away. He wondered whether the toes were warm or numb. He moved them inside the moccasins and decided that they were numb.

He pulled the mitten on hurriedly and stood up. He was a bit frightened. He stamped up and down until the stinging returned into the feet. It certainly was cold, was his thought. That man from Sulphur Creek had spoken the truth when telling how cold it sometimes got in the country. And he had laughed at him at the time! That showed one must not be too sure of things. There was no mistake about it, it *was* cold. He strode up and down, stamping his feet and threshing his arms, until reassured by the returning warmth. Then he got out matches and proceeded to make a fire. From the undergrowth, where high water of the previous spring had lodged a supply of seasoned twigs, he got his firewood. Working carefully from a small beginning, he soon had a roaring fire, over which he thawed the ice from his face and in the protection of which he ate his biscuits. For the moment the cold of space was outwitted. The dog took satisfaction in the fire, stretching out close enough for warmth and far enough away to escape being singed.

When the man had finished, he filled his pipe and took his comfortable time over a smoke. Then he pulled on his mittens, settled the earflaps of his cap firmly about his ears, and took the creek trail up the left fork. The dog was disappointed and yearned back toward the fire. This man did not know cold. Possibly all the generations of his ancestry had been ignorant of cold, of real cold, of cold one hundred and seven degrees below freezing point. But the dog knew; all its ancestry knew, and it had inherited the knowledge. And it knew that it was not good to walk abroad in such fearful cold. It was the time to lie snug in a hole in the snow and wait for a curtain of cloud to be drawn across the face of outer space whence this cold came. On the other hand, there was no keen intimacy between the dog and the man. The one was the toil slave of the other, and the only caresses it had ever received were the caresses of the whiplash and of harsh and menacing throat sounds that threatened the whiplash. So the dog made no effort to communicate its apprehension to the man. It was not concerned in the welfare of the man; it was for its own sake that it yearned back toward the fire. But the man whistled, and spoke to it with the sound of whiplashes, and the dog swung in at the man's heels and followed after.

The man took a chew of tobacco and proceeded to start a new amber beard. Also, his moist breath quickly powdered with white his mustache, eyebrows, and lashes. There did not seem to be so many springs on the left fork of the Henderson, and for half an hour the man saw no signs of any. And then it happened. At a place where there were no signs, where the soft, unbroken snow seemed to advertise solidity beneath, the man broke through. It was not deep. He wet himself halfway to the knees before he floundered out to the firm crust.

He was angry, and cursed his luck aloud. He had hoped to get into camp with the boys at six o'clock, and this would delay him an hour, for he would have to build a fire and dry out his footgear. This was imperative at that low temperature—he knew that much; and he turned aside to the bank, which he climbed. On top, tangled in the underbrush about the trunks of several small spruce trees, was a high-water deposit of dry firewood—sticks and twigs, principally, but also larger portions of seasoned branches and fine, dry, last year's grasses. He threw down several large pieces on top of the snow. This served for a foundation and prevented the young flame from drowning itself in the snow it otherwise would melt. The flame he got by touching a match to a small shred of birch bark that he took from his pocket. This burned even more readily than paper. Placing it on the foundation, he fed the young flame with wisps of dry grass and with the tiniest dry twigs.

He worked slowly and carefully, keenly aware of his danger. Gradually, as the flame grew stronger, he increased the size of the twigs with which he fed it. He squatted in the snow, pulling the twigs out from their entanglement in the brush and feeding directly to the flame. He knew there must be no failure. When it is seventy-five below zero, a man must not fail in his first attempt to build a fire—that is, if his feet are wet. If his feet are dry, and he fails, he can run along the trail for half a mile and restore his circulation. But the circulation of wet and freezing feet cannot be restored by running when it is seventy-five below. No matter how fast he runs, the wet feet will freeze the harder.

All this the man knew. The old-timer on Sulphur Creek had told him about it the previous fall, and now he was appreciating the advice. Already all sensation had gone out of his feet. To build the fire he had been forced to remove his mittens, and the fingers had quickly gone numb. His pace of four miles an hour had kept his heart pumping blood to the surface of his body and to all the extremities. But the instant he stopped, the action of the pump eased down. The cold of space smote the unprotected tip of the planet, and he, being on that unprotected tip, received the full force of the blow. The blood of his body recoiled before it. The blood was alive, like the dog, and like the dog it wanted to hide away and cover itself up from the fearful cold. So long as he walked four miles an hour, he pumped that blood, willy-nilly, to the surface; but now it ebbed away and sank down into the recesses of his body. The extremities were the first to feel its absence. His wet feet froze the faster, and his exposed fingers numbed the faster, though they had not yet begun to freeze. Nose and cheeks were already freezing, while the skin of all his body chilled as it lost its blood.

But he was safe. Toes and nose and cheeks would be only touched by the frost, for the fire was beginning to burn with strength. He was feeding it with twigs the size of his finger. In another minute he would be able to feed it with branches the size of his wrist, and then he could remove his wet foot-gear, and, while it dried, he could keep his naked feet warm by the fire, rubbing them at first, of course, with snow. The fire was a success. He was safe. He remembered the advice of the old-timer on Sulphur Creek, and smiled. The old-timer had been very serious in laying down the law that no man must travel alone in the Klondike after fifty below. Well, here he was; he had had the accident; he was alone; and he had saved himself. Those old-timers were rather womanish, some of them, he thought. All a man had to do was to keep his head, and he was all right. Any man who was a man could travel alone. But it was surprising, the rapidity with which his cheeks and nose were freezing. And he had not thought his fingers could go lifeless in so short a time. Lifeless they were, for he could scarcely make them move together to grip a twig, and they seemed remote from his body and from him. When he touched a twig, he had to look and see whether or not he had hold of it. The wires were pretty well down between him and his finger ends.

All of which counted for little. There was the fire, snapping and crackling and promising life with every dancing flame. He started to untie his moccasins. They were coated with ice; the thick German socks were like sheaths of iron halfway to the knees; and the moccasin strings were like rods of steel all twisted and knotted as by some conflagration. For a moment he tugged with his numb fingers, then, realizing the folly of it, he drew his sheath-knife.

But before he could cut the strings, it happened. It was his own fault or, rather, his mistake. He should not have built the fire under the spruce tree. He should have built it in the open. But it had been easier to pull the twigs from the brush and drop them directly on the fire. Now the tree under which he had done this carried a weight of snow on its boughs. No wind had blown for weeks, and each bough was fully freighted. Each time he had pulled a twig he had communicated a slight agitation to the tree—an imperceptible agitation, so far as he was concerned, but an agitation sufficient to bring about the disaster. High up in the tree one bough capsized its load of snow. This fell on the boughs beneath, capsizing them. This process continued, spreading out and involving the whole tree. It grew like an avalanche, and it descended without warning upon the man and the fire, and the fire was blotted out! Where it had burned was a mantle of fresh and disordered snow.

The man was shocked. It was as though he had just heard his own sentence of death. For a moment he sat and stared at the spot where the fire had been. Then he grew very calm. Perhaps the old-timer on Sulphur Creek was right. If he had only had a trail mate he would have been in no danger now. The trail mate could have built the fire. Well, it was up to him to build the fire over again, and this second time there must be no failure. Even if he succeeded, he would most likely lose some toes. His feet must be badly frozen by now, and there would be some time before the second fire was ready.

Such were his thoughts, but he did not sit and think them. He was busy all the time they were passing through his mind. He made a new foundation for a fire, this time in the open, where no treacherous tree could blot it out. Next, he gathered dry grasses and tiny twigs from the high-water flotsam. He could not bring his fingers together to pull them out, but he was able to gather them by the handful. In this way he got many rotten twigs and bits of green moss that were undesirable, but it was the best he could do. He worked methodically, even collecting an armful of the larger branches to be used later when the fire gathered strength. And all the while the dog sat and watched him, a certain yearning wistfulness in its eyes, for it looked upon him as the fire provider, and the fire was slow in coming.

When all was ready, the man reached in his pocket for a second piece of birch bark. He knew the bark was there, and, though he could not feel it with his fingers, he could hear its crisp rustling as he fumbled for it. Try as he would, he could not clutch hold of it. And all the time, in his consciousness, was the knowledge that each instant his feet were freezing. This thought tended to put him in a panic, but he fought against it and kept calm. He pulled on his mittens with his teeth, and threshed his arms back and forth, beating his hands with all his might against his sides. He did this sitting down, and he stood up to do it; and all the while the dog sat in the snow, its wolf brush of a tail curled around warmly over its forefeet, its sharp wolf ears pricked forward intently as it watched the man. And the man, as he beat and threshed with his arms and hands, felt a great surge of envy as he regarded the creature that was warm and secure in its natural covering.

After a time he was aware of the first faraway signals of sensation in his beaten fingers. The faint tingling grew stronger till it evolved into a stinging ache that was excruciating, but which the man hailed with satisfaction. He stripped the mitten from his right hand and fetched forth the birch bark. The exposed fingers were quickly going numb again. Next he brought out his bunch of sulphur matches. But the tremendous cold had already driven the life out of his fingers. In his effort to separate one match from the others, the whole bunch fell in the snow. He tried to pick it out of the snow, but failed. The dead fingers could neither touch nor clutch. He was very careful. He drove the thought of his freezing feet, and nose, and cheeks, out of his mind, devoting his whole soul to the matches. He watched, using the sense of vision in place of that of touch, and when he saw his fingers on each side the bunch, he closed them—that is, he willed to close them, for the wires were down, and the fingers did not obey. He pulled the mitten on the right hand, and beat it fiercely against his knee. Then, with both mittened hands, he scooped the bunch of matches, along with much snow, into his lap. Yet he was no better off.

After some manipulation he managed to get the bunch between the heels of his mittened hands. In this fashion he carried it to his mouth. The ice crackled and snapped when by a violent effort he opened his mouth. He drew the lower jaw in, curled the

STEPHEN CRANE

1871–1900

Stephen Crane died of tuberculosis at the age of twenty-eight. Yet during his short life he was one of the leaders of the Naturalist movement and one of the most highly regarded writers of his time.

The youngest of fourteen children, Crane was born and raised in New Jersey. After briefly attending Syracuse University, where he spent more energy playing baseball than studying, he moved to New York City and found work as a journalist. Inspired by his observations and experiences as a newspaper writer, Crane completed his first novel, *Maggie: A Girl of the Streets* (1893), which he had begun while at Syracuse. A grimly realistic depiction of life in the slums of New York City, the novel was so frank and shocking that Crane was unable to find a publisher. He eventually borrowed money and published it at his own expense, but despite praise by a number of writers and critics, the book did not sell.

Crane continued to write, however, and in 1895 he published a second novel, *The Red Badge of Courage: An Episode of the Civil War*. A psychological exploration of a young soldier's reactions under fire, the novel was a success and earned Crane international acclaim at the age of twenty-four. Readers and critics applauded the book for its realistic depiction of Civil War battles. Yet Crane had never observed military combat. Before writing the novel, however, he had interviewed Civil War veterans and studied photographs, battle plans, and the biographical accounts of military leaders.

Crane soon had the opportunity to view the realities of war first-hand, when he served as a newspaper correspondent during the Greco-Turkish War in 1897 and the Spanish-American War in 1898. His observations convinced him of the accuracy of his depiction of war in *The Red Badge of Courage* and provided material for *War Is Kind* (1899), his second collection of poetry. Crane's experiences as a correspondent also took their toll on his health. During the final months of his life, his physical condition rapidly deteriorated, and he died in Germany shortly after the turn of the century.

Like other Naturalists, Crane depicted characters who were manipulated by forces of society and nature that were beyond their control or understanding. In his best works, he explored humanity's quest to find meaning in a universe that at times seems hostile and meaningless.

GUIDE FOR READING

The Red Badge of Courage, Chapters 1–7

Literary Movements

Realism. Realism was a literary movement that emerged as a reaction against Romanticism. Unlike the Romantic writers, who often portrayed improbable situations and events, the Realist writers sought to depict real life as faithfully and accurately as possible. Generally, they attempted to present "a slice of life" by delving deeply into the realities of a small portion of the world. The Realists focused on the lives of ordinary people, often writing about lower-class and middle-class characters. In depicting the lives of people faced with poverty and other hardships, the Realists confronted many of the harsh realities of American society, often presenting pessimistic visions of the world dramatically different from the optimistic visions that dominated Romantic literature.

Naturalism. Naturalism, another major literary movement of the late nineteenth century, grew out of the Realistic movement. Like the Realists, the Naturalists attempted to depict life truthfully and accurately. Yet, while the Realists searched for the truths of existence by delving beneath the surface of everyday life, the Naturalists already possessed a well-defined view of the universe that they imposed on their works. The Naturalists believed that a person's fate is determined by heredity and environment. As a result, Naturalist writers frequently depicted characters whose lives were shaped by forces of nature or society they could not understand or control.

Look For

As you read *The Red Badge of Courage,* look for characteristics of Realism and Naturalism.

Writing

In Chapters 1–7 of *The Red Badge of Courage,* Crane examines the feelings of a young recruit who is anticipating his first battle. Freewrite for five minutes about the thoughts and feelings he might have had.

Vocabulary

Knowing the following words will help you as you read Chapters 1–7 of *The Red Badge of Courage.*

effaced (i fāsd´) *v.:* Wiped out; obliterated (p. 577)

impregnable (im preg´ nə b'l) *adj.:* Unshakable; unyielding (p. 577)

felicitating (fə lis´ ə tāt iŋ) *v.:* Congratulating (p. 585)

vociferous (vō sif´ ərəs) *adj.:* Loud, noisy, or vehement in making one's feelings known (p. 585)

facetious (fə sē´ shəs) *adj.:* Joking at an inappropriate time (p. 593)

querulous (kwer´ ə ləs) *adj.:* Complaining (p. 595)

The Red Badge of Courage

Stephen Crane

Chapter One

The cold passed reluctantly from the earth, and the retiring fogs revealed an army stretched out on the hills, resting. As the landscape changed from brown to green, the army awakened, and began to tremble with eagerness at the noise of rumors. It cast its eyes upon the roads, which were growing from long troughs of liquid mud to proper thoroughfares. A river, amber-tinted in the shadow of its banks, purled at the army's feet; and at night, when the stream had become of a sorrowful blackness, one could see across it the red, eyelike gleam of hostile campfires set in the low brows of distant hills.

Once a certain tall soldier developed virtues and went resolutely to wash a shirt. He came flying back from a brook waving his garment bannerlike. He was swelled with a tale he had heard from a reliable friend, who had heard it from a truthful cavalryman,[1] who had heard it from his trustworthy brother, one of the orderlies at division headquarters. He adopted the important air of a herald[2] in red and gold.

"We're goin' t' move t' morrah—sure," he said pompously to a group in the company street. "We're goin' 'way up the river, cut across, an' come around in behint 'em."

To his attentive audience he drew a loud and elaborate plan of a very brilliant campaign. When he had finished, the blue-clothed men scattered into small arguing groups between the rows of squat brown huts. A negro teamster who had been dancing upon a cracker box with the hilarious encouragement of two-score soldiers was deserted. He sat mournfully down. Smoke drifted lazily from a multitude of quaint chimneys.

"It's a lie! that's all it is—a thunderin' lie!" said another private loudly. His smooth face was flushed, and his hands were thrust sulkily into his trousers' pockets. He took the matter as an affront to him. "I don't believe the derned old army's ever going to move. We're set. I've got ready to move eight times in the last two weeks, and we ain't moved yet."

The tall soldier felt called upon to defend the truth of a rumor he himself had introduced. He and the loud one came near to fighting over it.

A corporal began to swear before the assemblage. He had just put a costly board floor in his house, he said. During the early spring he had refrained from adding extensively to the comfort of his environment because he had felt that the army might start on the march at any moment. Of late, however, he had been impressed that they were in a sort of eternal camp.

Many of the men engaged in a spirited debate. One outlined in a peculiarly lucid manner all the plans of the commanding general. He was opposed by men who advocated that there were other plans of campaign. They clamored at each other, numbers making futile bids for the popular attention. Meanwhile, the soldier who had

---

1. **cavalryman** *n.*: Horse soldier.
2. **herald** *n.*: An official who makes proclamations and carries messages.

fetched the rumor bustled about with much importance. He was continually assailed by questions.

"What's up, Jim?"

"Th' army's goin' t' move."

"Ah, what yeh talkin' about. How yeh know it is?"

"Well, yeh kin b'lieve me er not, jest as yeh like. I don't care a hang."

There was much food for thought in the manner in which he replied. He came near to convincing them by disdaining to produce proofs. They grew much excited over it.

There was a youthful private who listened with eager ears to the words of the tall soldier and to the varied comments of his comrades. After receiving a fill of discussions concerning marches and attacks, he went to his hut and crawled through an intricate hole that served it as a door. He wished to be alone with some new thoughts that had lately come to him.

He lay down on a wide bunk that stretched across the end of the room. In the other end, cracker boxes were made to serve as furniture. They were grouped about the fireplace. A picture from an illustrated weekly was upon the log walls, and three rifles were paralleled on pegs. Equipment hung on handy projections, and some tin dishes lay upon a small pile of firewood. A folded tent was serving as a roof. The sunlight, without, beating upon it, made it glow a light yellow shade. A small window shot an oblique square of whiter light upon the cluttered floor. The smoke from the fire at times neglected the clay chimney and wreathed into the room, and this flimsy chimney of clay and sticks made endless threats to set ablaze the whole establishment.

The youth was in a little trance of astonishment. So they were at last going to fight. On the morrow, perhaps, there would be a battle, and he would be in it. For a time he was obliged to labor to make himself believe. He could not accept with assurance an omen that he was about to mingle in one of those great affairs of the earth.

He had, of course, dreamed of battles all his life—of vague and bloody conflicts that had thrilled him with their sweep and fire. In visions he had seen himself in many struggles. He had imagined peoples secure in the shadow of his eagle-eyed prowess. But awake he had regarded battles as crimson blotches on the pages of the past. He had put them as things of the bygone with his thought-images of heavy crowns and high castles. There was a portion of the world's history which he had regarded as the time of wars, but it, he thought, had been long gone over the horizon and had disappeared forever.

From his home his youthful eyes had looked upon the war in his own country with distrust. It must be some sort of a play affair. He had long despaired of witnessing a Greeklike struggle. Such would be no more, he had said. Men were better, or more timid. Secular and religious education had effaced the throat-grappling instinct, or else firm finance held in check the passions.

He had burned several times to enlist. Tales of great movements shook the land. They might not be distinctly Homeric,[3] but there seemed to be much glory in them. He had read of marches, sieges, conflicts, and he had longed to see it all. His busy mind had drawn for him large pictures extravagant in color, lurid with breathless deeds.

But his mother had discouraged him. She had affected to look with some contempt upon the quality of his war ardor and patriotism. She could calmly seat herself and with no apparent difficulty give him many hundreds of reasons why he was of vastly more importance on the farm than on the field of battle. She had had certain ways of expression that told him that her statements on the subject came from a deep conviction. Moreover, on her side, was his belief that her ethical motive in the argument was impregnable.

---

3. Homeric: Characteristic of the heroic adventures described in the works of the ancient Greek epic poet Homer.

At last, however, he had made firm rebellion against this yellow light thrown upon the color of his ambitions. The newspapers, the gossip of the village, his own picturings, had aroused him to an uncheckable degree. They were in truth fighting finely down there. Almost every day the newspapers printed accounts of a decisive victory.

One night, as he lay in bed, the winds had carried to him the clangoring of the church bell as some enthusiast jerked the rope frantically to tell the twisted news of a great battle. This voice of the people rejoicing in the night had made him shiver in a prolonged ecstasy of excitement. Later, he had gone down to his mother's room and had spoken thus: "Ma, I'm going to enlist."

"Henry, don't you be a fool," his mother had replied. She had then covered her face with the quilt. There was an end to the matter for that night.

Nevertheless, the next morning he had gone to a town that was near his mother's farm and had enlisted in a company that was forming there. When he had returned home his mother was milking the brindle cow. Four others stood waiting. "Ma, I've enlisted," he had said to her diffidently. There was a short silence. "The Lord's will be done, Henry," she had finally replied, and had then continued to milk the brindle cow.

When he had stood in the doorway with his soldier's clothes on his back, and with the light of excitement and expectancy in his eyes almost defeating the glow of regret for the home bonds, he had seen two tears leaving their trails on his mother's scarred cheeks.

Still, she had disappointed him by saying nothing whatever about returning with his shield or on it.[4] He had privately primed himself for a beautiful scene. He had prepared certain sentences which he thought

could be used with touching effect. But her words destroyed his plans. She had doggedly peeled potatoes and addressed him as follows: "You watch out, Henry, an' take good care of yerself in this here fighting business—you watch out, an' take good care of yerself. Don't go a-thinkin' you can lick the hull rebel army at the start, because yeh can't. Yer jest one little feller amongst a hull lot of others, and yeh've got to keep quiet n' do what they tell yeh. I know how you are, Henry.

"I've knet yeh eight pair of socks, Henry, and I've put in all yer best shirts, because I want my boy to be jest as warm and comf'able as anybody in the army. Whenever

_____
4. with . . . on it: Either victorious or dead. According to legend, when the brave, stoical warriors of ancient Sparta left for battle, their wives or mothers would tell them to return with their shields or on them.

too, child, an' remember he never drunk a drop of licker in his life, and seldom swore a cross oath.

"I don't know what else to tell yeh, Henry, excepting that yeh must never do no shirking, child, on my account. If so be a time comes when yeh have to be kilt or do a mean thing, why, Henry, don't think of anything 'cept what's right, because there's many a woman has to bear up 'ginst sech things these times, and the Lord'll take keer of us all.

"Don't forgit about the socks and the shirts, child; and I've put a cup of blackberry jam with yer bundle, because I know yeh like it above all things. Good-bye, Henry. Watch out, and be a good boy."

He had, of course, been impatient under the ordeal of this speech. It had not been quite what he expected, and he had borne it with an air of irritation. He departed feeling vague relief.

Still, when he had looked back from the gate, he had seen his mother kneeling among the potato parings. Her brown face, upraised, was stained with tears, and her spare form was quivering. He bowed his head and went on, feeling suddenly ashamed of his purposes.

From his home he had gone to the seminary[5] to bid adieu[6] to many schoolmates. They had thronged about him with wonder and admiration. He had felt the gulf now between them and had swelled with calm pride. He and some of his fellows who had donned blue were quite overwhelmed with privileges for all of one afternoon, and it had been a very delicious thing. They had strutted.

A certain light-haired girl had made vivacious fun at his martial spirit, but there was another and darker girl whom he had gazed at steadfastly, and he thought she grew demure and sad at sight of his blue and brass. As he had walked down the path between the

they get holes in 'em, I want yeh to send 'em rightaway back to me, so's I kin dern 'em.

"An' allus be careful an' choose yer comp'ny. There's lots of bad men in the army, Henry. The army makes 'em wild, and they like nothing better than the job of leading off a young feller like you, as ain't never been away from home much and has allus had a mother, an' a-learning 'em to drink and swear. Keep clear of them folks, Henry. I don't want yeh to ever do anything, Henry, that yeh would be 'shamed to let me know about. Jest think as if I was a-watchin' yeh. If yeh keep that in yer mind allus, I guess yeh'll come out about right.

"Yeh must allus remember yer father,

_____
5. **seminary** *n*.: School.
6. **adieu** (ə dyoo'): "Farewell" (French).

rows of oaks, he had turned his head and detected her at a window watching his departure. As he perceived her, she had immediately begun to stare up through the high tree branches at the sky. He had seen a good deal of flurry and haste in her movement as she changed her attitude. He often thought of it.

On the way to Washington his spirit had soared. The regiment was fed and caressed at station after station until the youth had believed that he must be a hero. There was a lavish expenditure of bread and cold meats, coffee, and pickles and cheese. As he basked in the smiles of the girls and was patted and complimented by the old men, he had felt growing within him the strength to do mighty deeds of arms.

After complicated journeyings with many pauses, there had come months of monotonous life in a camp. He had had the belief that real war was a series of death struggles with small time in between for sleep and meals; but since his regiment had come to the field the army had done little but sit still and try to keep warm.

He was brought then gradually back to his old ideas. Greeklike struggles would be no more. Men were better, or more timid. Secular and religious education had effaced the throat-grappling instinct, or else firm finance held in check the passions.

He had grown to regard himself merely as a part of a vast blue demonstration. His province was to look out, as far as he could, for his personal comfort. For recreation he could twiddle his thumbs and speculate on the thoughts which must agitate the minds of the generals. Also, he was drilled and drilled and reviewed, and drilled and drilled and reviewed.

The only foes he had seen were some pickets[7] along the riverbank. They were a sun-tanned, philosophical lot, who sometimes shot reflectively at the blue pickets. When reproached for this afterward, they usually expressed sorrow, and swore by their gods that the guns had exploded without

their permission. The youth, on guard duty one night, conversed across the stream with one of them. He was a slightly ragged man, who spat skillfully between his shoes and possessed a great fund of bland and infantile assurance. The youth liked him personally.

"Yank," the other had informed him, "yer a right dum good feller." This sentiment, floating to him upon the still air, had made him temporarily regret war.

Various veterans had told him tales. Some talked of gray, bewhiskered hordes who were advancing with relentless curses and chewing tobacco with unspeakable valor; tremendous bodies of fierce soldiery who were sweeping along like the Huns.[8] Others spoke of tattered and eternally hungry men who fired despondent powders. "They'll charge through hell's fire an' brimstone t' git a holt on a haversack,[9] an' sech stomachs ain't a-lastin' long," he was told. From the stories, the youth imagined the red, live bones, sticking out through slits in the faded uniforms.

Still, he could not put a whole faith in veterans' tales, for recruits were their prey. They talked much of smoke, fire, and blood, but he could not tell how much might be lies. They persistently yelled, "Fresh fish!" at him, and were in no wise to be trusted.

However, he perceived now that it did not greatly matter what kind of soldiers he was going to fight, so long as they fought, which fact no one disputed. There was a more serious problem. He lay in his bunk pondering upon it. He tried to mathematically prove to himself that he would not run from a battle.

Previously he had never felt obliged to wrestle too seriously with this question. In his life he had taken certain things for granted, never challenging his belief in ultimate success, and bothering little about means and roads. But here he was confronted with a thing of moment. It had

7. **pickets** *n.*: Sentries; guards.

8. **Huns:** A warlike Asiatic people who invaded eastern and central Europe in the fourth and fifth centuries.

9. **haversack** *n.*: A canvas bag for carrying rations.

suddenly appeared to him that perhaps in a battle he might run. He was forced to admit that as far as war was concerned he knew nothing of himself.

A sufficient time before he would have allowed the problem to kick its heels at the outer portals of his mind, but now he felt compelled to give serious attention to it.

A little panic-fear grew in his mind. As his imagination went forward to a fight, he saw hideous possibilities. He contemplated the lurking menaces of the future, and failed in an effort to see himself standing stoutly in the midst of them. He recalled his visions of broken-bladed glory, but in the shadow of the impending tumult he suspected them to be impossible pictures.

He sprang from the bunk and began to pace nervously to and fro. "Good Lord, what's th' matter with me?" he said aloud.

He felt that in this crisis his laws of life were useless. Whatever he had learned of himself was here of no avail. He was an unknown quantity. He saw that he would again be obliged to experiment as he had in early youth. He must accumulate information of himself, and meanwhile he resolved to remain close upon his guard lest those qualities of which he knew nothing should everlastingly disgrace him. "Good Lord!" he repeated in dismay.

After a time the tall soldier slid dexterously through the hole. The loud private followed. They were wrangling.

"That's all right," said the tall soldier as he entered. He waved his hand expressively. "You can believe me or not, jest as you like. All you got to do is to sit down and wait as quiet as you can. Then pretty soon you'll find out I was right."

His comrade grunted stubbornly. For a moment he seemed to be searching for a formidable reply. Finally he said: "Well, you don't know everything in the world, do you?"

"Didn't say I knew everything in the world," retorted the other sharply. He began to stow various articles snugly into his knapsack.

The youth, pausing in his nervous walk,

looked down at the busy figure. "Going to be a battle, sure, is there, Jim?" he asked.

"Of course there is," replied the tall soldier. "Of course there is. You jest wait 'til tomorrow, and you'll see one of the biggest battles ever was. You jest wait."

"Thunder!" said the youth.

"Oh, you'll see fighting this time, my boy, what'll be regular out-and-out fighting," added the tall soldier, with the air of a man who is about to exhibit a battle for the benefit of his friends.

"Huh!" said the loud one from a corner.

"Well," remarked the youth, "like as not this story'll turn out jest like them others did."

"Not much it won't," replied the tall soldier, exasperated. "Not much it won't. Didn't the cavalry all start this morning?" He glared about him. No one denied his statement. "The cavalry started this morning," he continued. "They say there ain't hardly any cavalry left in camp. They're going to Richmond, or some place, while we fight all the Johnnies.[10] It's some dodge like that. The regiment's got orders, too. A feller what seen 'em go to headquarters told me a little while ago. And they're raising blazes all over camp—anybody can see that."

"Shucks!" said the loud one.

The youth remained silent for a time. At last he spoke to the tall soldier. "Jim!"

"What?"

"How do you think the reg'ment 'll do?"

"Oh, they'll fight all right, I guess, after they once get into it," said the other with cold judgment. He made a fine use of the third person. "There's been heaps of fun poked at 'em because they're new, of course, and all that; but they'll fight all right, I guess."

"Think any of the boys 'll run?" persisted the youth.

"Oh, there may be a few of 'em run, but there's them kind in every regiment, 'specially when they first goes under fire," said

---

10. Johnnies: Johnny Rebs, slang for Confederate soldiers.

the other in a tolerant way. "Of course it might happen that the hull kit-and-boodle might start and run, if some big fighting came first-off, and then again they might stay and fight like fun. But you can't bet on nothing. Of course they ain't never been under fire yet, and it ain't likely they'll lick the hull rebel army all-to-oncet the firs' time; but I think they'll fight better than some, if worse than others. That's the way I figger. They call the reg'ment 'Fresh fish' and everything; but the boys come of good stock, and most of 'em 'll fight like sin after they oncet git shootin'," he added, with a mighty emphasis on the last four words.

"Oh, you think you know—" began the loud soldier with scorn.

The other turned savagely upon him. They had a rapid altercation, in which they fastened upon each other various strange epithets.

The youth at last interrupted them. "Did you ever think you might run yourself, Jim?" he asked. On concluding the sentence he laughed as if he had meant to aim a joke. The loud soldier also giggled.

The tall private waved his hand. "Well," said he profoundly, "I've thought it might get too hot for Jim Conklin in some of them scrimmages, and if a whole lot of the boys started and run, why, I s'pose I'd start and run. And if I once started to run, I'd run like the devil, and no mistake. But if everybody was a-standing and a-fighting, why, I'd stand and fight. Be jiminey, I would. I'll bet on it."

"Huh!" said the loud one.

The youth of this tale felt gratitude for these words of his comrade. He had feared that all of the untried men possessed a great and correct confidence. He now was in a measure reassured.

Chapter Two

The next morning the youth discovered that his tall comrade had been the fast-flying messenger of a mistake. There was much scoffing at the latter by those who had yesterday been firm adherents of his views, and there was even a little sneering by men who had never believed the rumor. The tall one fought with a man from Chatfield Corners and beat him severely.

The youth felt, however, that his problem was in no wise lifted from him. There was, on the contrary, an irritating prolongation. The tale had created in him a great concern for himself. Now, with the newborn question in his mind, he was compelled to sink back into his old place as part of a blue demonstration.

For days he made ceaseless calculations, but they were all wondrously unsatisfactory. He found that he could establish nothing. He finally concluded that the only way to prove himself was to go into the blaze, and then figuratively to watch his legs to discover their merits and faults. He reluctantly admitted that he could not sit still and with a mental slate and pencil derive an answer. To gain it, he must have blaze, blood, and danger, even as a chemist requires this, that, and the other. So he fretted for an opportunity.

Meanwhile he continually tried to measure himself by his comrades. The tall soldier, for one, gave him some assurance. This man's serene unconcern dealt him a measure of confidence, for he had known him since childhood, and from his intimate knowledge he did not see how he could be capable of anything that was beyond him, the youth. Still, he thought that his comrade might be mistaken about himself. Or, on the other hand, he might be a man heretofore doomed to peace and obscurity, but, in reality, made to shine in war.

The youth would have liked to have discovered another who suspected himself. A sympathetic comparison of mental notes would have been a joy to him.

He occasionally tried to fathom a comrade with seductive sentences. He looked about to find men in the proper mood. All attempts failed to bring forth any statement which looked in any way like a confession to those doubts which he privately acknowledged in himself. He was afraid to make an open declaration of his concern, because he dreaded to place some unscrupulous confidant upon the high plane of the unconfessed from which elevation he could be derided.

In regard to his companions his mind wavered between two opinions, according to his mood. Sometimes he inclined to believing them all heroes. In fact, he usually admitted in secret the superior development of the higher qualities in others. He could conceive of men going very insignificantly about the world bearing a load of courage unseen, and, although he had known many of his comrades through boyhood, he began to fear that his judgment of them had been blind. Then, in other moments, he flouted these theories, and assured himself that his fellows were all privately wondering and quaking.

His emotions made him feel strange in the presence of men who talked excitedly of a prospective battle as of a drama they were about to witness, with nothing but eagerness and curiosity apparent in their faces. It was often that he suspected them to be liars.

He did not pass such thoughts without severe condemnation of himself. He dinned reproaches at times. He was convicted by himself of many shameful crimes against the gods of traditions.

In his great anxiety his heart was continually clamoring at what he considered the intolerable slowness of the generals. They seemed content to perch tranquilly on the river bank, and leave him bowed down by the weight of a great problem. He wanted it settled forthwith. He could not long bear such a load, he said. Sometimes his anger at the commanders reached an acute stage, and he grumbled about the camp like a veteran.

One morning, however, he found himself in the ranks of his prepared regiment. The men were whispering speculations and recounting the old rumors. In the gloom before the break of the day their uniforms glowed a deep purple hue. From across the river the red eyes were still peering. In the eastern sky there was a yellow patch like a rug laid for the feet of the coming sun; and against it, black and patternlike, loomed the gigantic figure of the colonel on a gigantic horse.

From off in the darkness came the trampling of feet. The youth could occasionally see dark shadows that moved like monsters. The regiment stood at rest for what seemed a long time. The youth grew impatient. It was unendurable the way these affairs were managed. He wondered how long they were to be kept waiting.

As he looked all about him and pondered upon the mystic gloom, he began to believe that at any moment the ominous distance might be aflare, and the rolling crashes of an engagement come to his ears. Staring once at the red eyes across the river, he conceived them to be growing larger, as the orbs of a row of dragons advancing. He turned toward the colonel and saw him lift his gigantic arm and calmly stroke his mustache.

At last he heard from along the road at the foot of the hill the clatter of a horse's galloping hoofs. It must be the coming of orders. He bent forward, scarce breathing. The exciting clickety-click, as it grew louder and louder seemed to be beating upon his soul. Presently a horseman with jangling equipment drew rein before the colonel of the regiment. The two held a short, sharp-worded conversation. The men in the foremost ranks craned their necks.

As the horseman wheeled his animal and galloped away he turned to shout over his shoulder, "Don't forget that box of cigars!" The colonel mumbled in reply. The youth wondered what a box of cigars had to do with war.

A moment later the regiment went swinging off into the darkness. It was now like one of those moving monsters wending with many feet. The air was heavy, and cold with dew. A mass of wet grass, marched upon, rustled like silk.

There was an occasional flash and glimmer of steel from the backs of all these huge crawling reptiles. From the road came creakings and grumblings as some surly guns were dragged away.

The men stumbled along still muttering speculations. There was a subdued debate. Once a man fell down, and as he reached for his rifle a comrade, unseeing, trod upon his hand. He of the injured fingers swore bitterly and aloud. A low tittering laugh went among his fellows.

Presently they passed into a roadway and marched forward with easy strides. A dark regiment moved before them, and from behind also came the tinkle of equipment on the bodies of marching men.

The rushing yellow of the developing day went on behind their backs. When the sun-rays at last struck full and mellowingly upon the earth, the youth saw that the landscape was streaked with two long, thin, black columns which disappeared on the brow of a hill in front and rearward vanished in a wood. They were like two serpents crawling from the cavern of the night.

The river was not in view. The tall soldier burst into praises of what he thought to be his powers of perception.

Some of the tall one's companions cried with emphasis that they, too, had evolved the same thing, and they congratulated themselves upon it. But there were others who said that the tall one's plan was not the true one at all. They persisted with other theories. There was a vigorous discussion.

The youth took no part in them. As he walked along in careless line he was engaged with his own eternal debate. He could not hinder himself from dwelling upon it. He was despondent and sullen, and threw shifting glances about him. He looked ahead, often expecting to hear from the advance the rattle of firing.

But the long serpents crawled slowly from hill to hill without bluster of smoke. A dun-colored cloud of dust floated away to the right. The sky overhead was of a fairy blue.

The youth studied the faces of his companions, ever on the watch to detect kindred emotions. He suffered disappointment. Some ardor of the air which was causing the veteran commands to move with glee—almost with song—had infected the new regiment. The men began to speak of victory as of a thing they knew. Also, the tall soldier received his vindication. They were certainly going to come around in behind the enemy. They expressed commiseration for that part of the army which had been left upon the river bank, felicitating themselves upon being a part of a blasting host.

The youth, considering himself as separated from the others, was saddened by the blithe and merry speeches that went from rank to rank. The company wags[11] all made their best endeavors. The regiment tramped to the tune of laughter.

The blatant soldier often convulsed whole files by his biting sarcasms aimed at the tall one.

And it was not long before all the men seemed to forget their mission. Whole brigades grinned in unison, and regiments laughed.

A rather fat soldier attempted to pilfer a horse from a dooryard. He planned to load his knapsack upon it. He was escaping with his prize when a young girl rushed from the house and grabbed the animal's mane. There followed a wrangle. The young girl, with pink cheeks and shining eyes, stood like a dauntless statue.

The observant regiment, standing at rest in the roadway, whooped at once, and entered whole-souled upon the side of the maiden. The men became so engrossed in this affair that they entirely ceased to remember their own large war. They jeered the piratical private, and called attention to various defects in his personal appearance; and they were wildly enthusiastic in support of the young girl.

To her, from some distance, came bold advice. "Hit him with a stick."

There were crows and catcalls showered upon him when he retreated without the horse. The regiment rejoiced at his downfall. Loud and vociferous congratulations were showered upon the maiden, who stood panting and regarding the troops with defiance.

At nightfall the column broke into regimental pieces, and the fragments went into the fields to camp. Tents sprang up like strange plants. Camp fires, like red, peculiar blossoms, dotted the night.

The youth kept from intercourse with his companions as much as circumstances would allow him. In the evening he wandered a few paces into the gloom. From this little distance the many fires, with the black forms of men passing to and fro before the crimson rays, made weird and satanic effects.

He lay down in the grass. The blades pressed tenderly against his cheek. The moon had been lighted and was hung in a treetop. The liquid stillness of the night enveloping him made him feel vast pity for himself. There was a caress in the soft

11. **wags** *n.*: Jokers.

winds; and the whole mood of the darkness, he thought, was one of sympathy for himself in his distress.

He wished, without reserve, that he was at home again making the endless rounds from the house to the barn, from the barn to the fields, from the fields to the barn, from the barn to the house. He remembered he had often cursed the brindle cow and her mates, and had sometimes flung milking stools. But, from his present point of view, there was a halo of happiness about each of their heads, and he would have sacrificed all the brass buttons on the continent to have been enabled to return to them. He told himself that he was not formed for a soldier. And he mused seriously upon the radical differences between himself and those men who were dodging implike around the fires.

As he mused thus he heard the rustle of grass, and, upon turning his head, discovered the loud soldier. He called out, "Oh, Wilson!"

The latter approached and looked down. "Why, hello, Henry; is it you? What you doing here?"

"Oh, thinking," said the youth.

The other sat down and carefully lighted his pipe. "You're getting blue, my boy. You're looking thundering peaked. What the dickens is wrong with you?"

"Oh, nothing," said the youth.

The loud soldier launched then into the subject of the anticipated fight. "Oh, we've got 'em now!" As he spoke his boyish face was wreathed in a gleeful smile, and his voice had an exultant ring. "We've got 'em now. At last, by the eternal thunders, we'll lick 'em good!"

"If the truth was known," he added, more soberly, "*they've* licked *us* about every clip up to now; but this time—this time—we'll lick 'em good!"

"I thought you was objecting to this march a little while ago," said the youth coldly.

"Oh, it wasn't that," explained the other. "I don't mind marching, if there's going to be fighting at the end of it. What I hate is this getting moved here and moved there, with no good coming of it, as far as I can see, excepting sore feet and short rations."

"Well, Jim Conklin says we'll get a-plenty of fighting this time."

"He's right for once, I guess, though I can't see how it come. This time we're in for a big battle, and we've got the best end of it, certain sure. Gee rod! how we will thump 'em!"

He arose and began to pace to and fro excitedly. The thrill of his enthusiasm made him walk with an elastic step. He was sprightly, vigorous, fiery in his belief in success. He looked into the future with clear, proud eye, and he swore with the air of an old soldier.

The youth watched him for a moment in silence. When he finally spoke his voice was as bitter as dregs. "Oh, you're going to do great things, I s'pose!"

The loud soldier blew a thoughtful cloud of smoke from his pipe. "Oh, I don't know," he remarked with dignity; "I don't know. I s'pose I'll do as well as the rest. I'm going to try like thunder." He evidently complimented himself upon the modesty of this statement.

"How do you know you won't run when the time comes?" asked the youth.

"Run?" said the loud one; "run?—of course not!" He laughed.

"Well," continued the youth, "lots of good-a-'nough men have thought they was going to do great things before the fight, but when the time come they skedaddled."

"Oh, that's all true, I s'pose," replied the other; "but I'm not going to skedaddle. The man that bets on my running will lose his money, that's all." He nodded confidently.

"Oh, shucks!" said the youth. "You ain't the bravest man in the world, are you?"

"No, I ain't," exclaimed the loud soldier indignantly; "and I didn't say I was the bravest man in the world, neither. I said I was going to do my share of fighting—that's what I said. And I am, too. Who are you, anyhow? You talk as if you thought you was Napoleon

Bonaparte."[12] He glared at the youth for a moment, and then strode away.

The youth called in a savage voice after his comrade: "Well, you needn't git mad about it!" But the other continued on his way and made no reply.

He felt alone in space when his injured comrade had disappeared. His failure to discover any mite of resemblance in their viewpoints made him more miserable than before. No one seemed to be wrestling with such a terrific personal problem. He was a mental outcast.

He went slowly to his tent and stretched himself on a blanket by the side of the snoring tall soldier. In the darkness he saw visions of a thousand-tongued fear that would babble at his back and cause him to flee, while others were going coolly about their country's business. He admitted that he would not be able to cope with this monster. He felt that every nerve in his body would be an ear to hear the voices, while other men would remain stolid and deaf.

And as he sweated with the pain of these thoughts, he could hear low, serene sentences. "I'll bid five." "Make it six." "Seven." "Seven goes."

He stared at the red, shivering reflection of a fire on the white wall of his tent until, exhausted and ill from the monotony of his suffering, he fell asleep.

Chapter Three

When another night came the columns, changed to purple streaks, filed across two pontoon bridges. A glaring fire wine-tinted the waters of the river. Its rays, shining upon the moving masses of troops, brought forth here and there sudden gleams of silver or gold. Upon the other shore a dark and mysterious range of hills was curved against the sky. The insect voices of the night sang solemnly.

After this crossing the youth assured himself that at any moment they might be suddenly and fearfully assaulted from the caves of the lowering woods. He kept his eyes watchfully upon the darkness.

But his regiment went unmolested to a camping place, and its soldiers slept the brave sleep of wearied men. In the morning they were routed out with early energy, and hustled along a narrow road that led deep into the forest.

It was during this rapid march that the regiment lost many of the marks of a new command.

The men had begun to count the miles upon their fingers, and they grew tired. "Sore feet an' short rations, that's all," said the loud soldier. There were perspiration and grumblings. After a time they began to shed their knapsacks. Some tossed them unconcernedly down; others hid them carefully, asserting their plans to return for them at some convenient time. Men extricated themselves from thick shirts. Presently few carried anything but their necessary clothing, blankets, haversacks, canteens, and arms and ammunition. "You can now eat and shoot," said the tall soldier to the youth. "That's all you want to do."

There was sudden change from the ponderous infantry[13] of theory to the light and speedy infantry of practice. The regiment, relieved of a burden, received a new impetus. But there was much loss of valuable knapsacks, and, on the whole, very good shirts.

But the regiment was not yet veteranlike in appearance. Veteran regiments in the army were likely to be very small aggregations of men. Once, when the command had first come to the field, some perambulating veterans, noting the length of their column, had accosted them thus: "Hey, fellers, what brigade is that?" And when the men had re-

---

12. Napoleon Bonaparte (nə pō′lē ən bō′ nə pärt′): (1769–1821) A French military leader and the emperor of France from 1804 to 1815.

---

13. infantry *n.*: Foot soldiers.

Directly the youth would see the skirmishers running. They were pursued by the sound of musketry fire. After a time the hot, dangerous flashes of the rifles were visible. Smoke clouds went slowly and insolently across the fields like observant phantoms. The din became crescendo,[14] like the roar of an oncoming train.

A brigade ahead of them and on the right went into action with a rending roar. It was as if it had exploded. And thereafter it lay stretched in the distance between a long gray wall, that one was obliged to look twice at to make sure that it was smoke.

The youth, forgetting his neat plan of getting killed, gazed spellbound. His eyes grew wide and busy with the action of the scene. His mouth was a little ways open.

Of a sudden he felt a heavy and sad hand laid upon his shoulder. Awakening from his trance of observation he turned and beheld the loud soldier.

"It's my first and last battle, old boy," said the latter, with intense gloom. He was quite pale and his girlish lip was trembling.

"Eh?" murmured the youth in great astonishment.

"It's my first and last battle, old boy," continued the loud soldier. "Something tells me—"

"What?"

"I'm a gone coon this first time and—and I w-want you to take these here things—to—my—folks." He ended in a quavering sob of pity for himself. He handed the youth a little packet done up in a yellow envelope.

"Why, what the devil—" began the youth again.

But the other gave him a glance as from the depths of a tomb, and raised his limp hand in a prophetic manner and turned away.

Chapter Four

The brigade was halted in the fringe of a grove. The men crouched among the trees and pointed their restless guns out at the fields. They tried to look beyond the smoke.

Out of this haze they could see running men. Some shouted information and gestured as they hurried.

The men of the new regiment watched and listened eagerly, while their tongues ran on in gossip of the battle. They mouthed rumors that had flown like birds out of the unknown.

"They say Perry has been driven in with big loss."

"Yes, Carrott went t' th' hospital. He said he was sick. That smart lieutenant is commanding 'G' Company. Th' boys say they won't be under Carrott no more if they all have t' desert. They allus knew he was a—"

"Hannises' batt'ry is took."

"It ain't either. I saw Hannises' batt'ry off on th' left not more'n fifteen minutes ago."

"Well—"

"Th' general, he ses he is goin' t 'take th' hull command of th' 304th when we go inteh action, an' then he ses we'll do sech fightin' as never another one reg'ment done."

"They say we're catchin' it over on th' left. They say th' enemy driv' our line inteh a devil of a swamp an' took Hannises' batt'ry."

"No sech thing. Hannises' batt'ry was 'long here 'bout a minute ago."

"That young Hasbrouck, he makes a good off'cer. He ain't afraid 'a nothin'."

"I met one of th' 148th Maine boys an' he ses his brigade fit th' hull rebel army fer four hours over on th' turnpike road an' killed about five thousand of 'em. He ses one more sech fight as that an' th' war 'll be over."

"Bill wasn't scared either. No, sir! It wasn't that. Bill ain't a-gettin' scared easy. He was jest mad, that's what he was. When that feller trod on his hand, he up an' sed that he was willin' t' give his hand t' his country, but he be dumbed if he was goin' t' have every dumb bushwacker in th' kentry walkin' 'round on it. So he went t' th' hospital disregardless of th' fight. Three fingers was crunched. Th' dern doctor wanted t' amputate 'm, an' Bill, he raised a heluva row, I hear. He's a funny feller."

---

14. crescendo (krə shen' dō) *adj.:* Gradually increasing in loudness or intensity.

The din in front swelled to a tremendous chorus. The youth and his fellows were frozen to silence. They could see a flag that tossed in the smoke angrily. Near it were the blurred and agitated forms of troops. There came a turbulent stream of men across the fields. A battery changing position at a frantic gallop scattered the stragglers right and left.

A shell screaming like a storm banshee[15] went over the huddled heads of the reserves. It landed in the grove, and exploding redly flung the brown earth. There was a little shower of pine needles.

Bullets began to whistle among the branches and nip at the trees. Twigs and leaves came sailing down. It was as if a thousand axes, wee and invisible, were being wielded. Many of the men were constantly dodging and ducking their heads.

The lieutenant of the youth's company was shot in the hand. He began to swear so wondrously that a nervous laugh went along the regimental line. The officer's profanity sounded conventional. It relieved the tightened senses of the new men. It was as if he had hit his fingers with a tack hammer at home.

He held the wounded member carefully away from his side so that the blood would not drip upon his trousers.

The captain of the company, tucking his sword under his arm, produced a handkerchief and began to bind with it the lieutenant's wound. And they disputed as to how the binding should be done.

The battle flag in the distance jerked about madly. It seemed to be struggling to free itself from an agony. The billowing smoke was filled with horizontal flashes.

Men running swiftly emerged from it. They grew in numbers until it was seen that the whole command was fleeing. The flag suddenly sank down as if dying. Its motion as it fell was a gesture of despair.

Wild yells came from behind the walls of smoke. A sketch in gray and red dissolved into a moblike body of men who galloped like wild horses.

The veteran regiments on the right and left of the 304th immediately began to jeer. With the passionate song of the bullets and the banshee shrieks of shells were mingled loud catcalls and bits of facetious advice concerning places of safety.

But the new regiment was breathless with horror. "Saunders's got crushed!" whispered the man at the youth's elbow. They shrank back and crouched as if compelled to await a flood.

The youth shot a swift glance along the blue ranks of the regiment. The profiles were motionless, carven; and afterward he remembered that the color sergeant was standing with his legs apart, as if he expected to be pushed to the ground.

The following throng went whirling around the flank. Here and there were officers carried along on the stream like exasperated chips. They were striking about them with their swords and with their left fists, punching every head they could reach. They cursed like highwaymen.

A mounted officer displayed the furious anger of a spoiled child. He raged with his head, his arms, and his legs.

Another, the commander of the brigade, was galloping about bawling. His hat was gone and his clothes were awry. He resembled a man who had come from bed to go to a fire. The hoofs of his horse often threatened the heads of the running men, but they scampered with singular fortune. In this rush they were apparently all deaf and blind. They heeded not the largest and longest of the oaths that were thrown at them from all directions.

Frequently over this tumult could be heard the grim jokes of the critical veterans; but the retreating men apparently were not even conscious of the presence of an audience.

---

15. banshee (ban′ shē) *n.*: In Scottish and Irish folklore, a female spirit believed to wail outside a house as a warning that a death will soon occur in the family.

The battle reflection that shone for an instant in the faces on the mad current made the youth feel that forceful hands from heaven would not have been able to have held him in place if he could have got intelligent control of his legs.

There was an appalling imprint upon these faces. The struggle in the smoke had pictured an exaggeration of itself on the bleached cheeks and in the eyes wild with one desire.

The sight of this stampede exerted a floodlike force that seemed able to drag sticks and stones and men from the ground. They of the reserves had to hold on. They grew pale and firm, and red and quaking.

The youth achieved one little thought in the midst of this chaos. The composite monster which had caused the other troops to flee had not then appeared. He resolved to get a view of it, and then, he thought he might very likely run better than the best of them.

Chapter Five

There were moments of waiting. The youth thought of the village street at home before the arrival of the circus parade on a day in the spring. He remembered how he had stood, a small, thrillful boy, prepared to follow the dingy lady upon the white horse, or the band in its faded chariot. He saw the yellow road, the lines of expectant people, and the sober houses. He particularly remembered an old fellow who used to sit upon a cracker box in front of the store and feign to despise such exhibitions. A thousand details of color and form surged in his mind. The old fellow upon the cracker box appeared in middle prominence.

Someone cried, "Here they come!"

There was rustling and muttering among the men. They displayed a feverish desire to have every possible cartridge ready to their hands. The boxes were pulled around into various positions, and adjusted with great care. It was as if seven hundred new bonnets were being tried on.

The tall soldier, having prepared his rifle, produced a red handkerchief of some kind. He was engaged in knitting it about his throat with exquisite attention to its position, when the cry was repeated up and down the line in a muffled roar of sound.

"Here they come! Here they come!" Gun locks clicked.

Across the smoke-infested fields came a brown swarm of running men who were giving shrill yells. They came on, stooping and swinging their rifles at all angles. A flag, tilted forward, sped near the front.

As he caught sight of them the youth was momentarily startled by a thought that perhaps his gun was not loaded. He stood trying to rally his faltering intellect so that he might recollect the moment when he had loaded, but he could not.

A hatless general pulled his dripping horse to a stand near the colonel of the 304th. He shook his fist in the other's face. "You've got to hold 'em back!" he shouted, savagely; "you've got to hold 'em back!"

In his agitation the colonel began to stammer. "A-all r-right, General, all right! We-we'll do our—we-we'll d-d-do—do our best, General." The general made a passionate gesture and galloped away. The colonel, perchance to relieve his feelings, began to scold like a wet parrot. The youth, turning swiftly to make sure that the rear was unmolested, saw the commander regarding his men in a highly resentful manner, as if he regretted above everything his association with them.

The man at the youth's elbow was mumbling, as if to himself: "Oh, we're in for it now! oh, we're in for it now!"

The captain of the company had been pacing excitedly to and fro in the rear. He coaxed in schoolmistress fashion, as to a congregation of boys with primers. His talk was an endless repetition. "Reserve your fire, boys—don't shoot till I tell you—save your fire—wait till they get close up—don't be fools—"

Perspiration streamed down the youth's face, which was soiled like that of a weeping urchin. He frequently, with a nervous movement, wiped his eyes with his coat sleeve. His mouth was still a little way open.

He got the one glance at the foe-swarming field in front of him, and instantly ceased to debate the question of his piece being loaded. Before he was ready to begin—before he had announced to himself that he was about to fight—he threw the obedient, well-balanced rifle into position and fired a first wild shot. Directly he was working at his weapon like an automatic affair.

He suddenly lost concern for himself, and forgot to look at a menacing fate. He became not a man but a member. He felt that something of which he was a part—a regiment, an army, a cause, or a country—was in a crisis. He was welded into a common personality which was dominated by a single desire. For some moments he could not flee, no more than a little finger can commit a revolution from a hand.

If he had thought the regiment was about to be annihilated perhaps he could have amputated himself from it. But its noise gave him assurance. The regiment was like a firework that, once ignited, proceeds superior to circumstances until its blazing vitality fades. It wheezed and banged with a mighty power. He pictured the ground before it as strewn with the discomfited.

There was a consciousness always of the presence of his comrades about him. He felt the subtle battle brotherhood more potent even than the cause for which they were fighting. It was a mysterious fraternity born of the smoke and danger of death.

He was at a task. He was like a carpenter who has made many boxes, making still another box, only there was furious haste in his movements. He, in his thought, was careering off in other places, even as the carpenter who as he works whistles and thinks of his friend or his enemy, his home or a saloon. And these jolted dreams were never perfect to him afterward, but remained a mass of blurred shapes.

Presently he began to feel the effects of the war atmosphere—a blistering sweat, a sensation that his eyeballs were about to crack like hot stones. A burning roar filled his ears.

Following this came a red rage. He developed the acute exasperation of a pestered animal, a well-meaning cow worried by dogs. He had a mad feeling against his rifle, which could only be used against one life at a time. He wished to rush forward and strangle with his fingers. He craved a power that would enable him to make a world-sweeping gesture and brush all back. His impotency appeared to him, and made his rage into that of a driven beast.

Buried in the smoke of many rifles his anger was directed not so much against the men whom he knew were rushing toward him as the swirling battle phantoms which were choking him, stuffing their smoke robes down his parched throat. He fought frantically for respite for his senses, for air, as a babe being smothered attacks the deadly blankets.

There was a blare of heated rage mingled with a certain expression of intentness on all faces. Many of the men were making low-toned noises with their mouths, and these subdued cheers, snarls, imprecations, prayers, made a wild, barbaric song that went as an undercurrent of sound, strange and chantlike with the resounding chords of the war march. The man at the youth's elbow was babbling. In it there was something soft and tender like the monologue of a babe. The tall soldier was swearing in a loud voice. From his lips came a black procession of curious oaths. Of a sudden another broke out in a querulous way like a man who has mislaid his hat. "Well, why don't they support us? Why don't they send supports? Do they think—"

The youth in his battle sleep heard this as one who dozes hears.

There was a singular absence of heroic poses. The men bending and surging in their haste and rage were in every impossible attitude. The steel ramrods clanked and clanged with incessant din as the men pounded them furiously into the hot rifle

barrels. The flaps of the cartridge boxes were all unfastened, and bobbed idiotically with each movement. The rifles, once loaded, were jerked to the shoulder and fired without apparent aim into the smoke or at one of the blurred and shifting forms which, upon the field before the regiment, had been growing larger and larger like puppets under a magician's hand.

The officers, at their intervals, rearward, neglected to stand in picturesque attitudes. They were bobbing to and fro roaring directions and encouragements. The dimensions of their howls were extraordinary. They expended their lungs with prodigal wills. And often they nearly stood upon their heads in their anxiety to observe the enemy on the other side of the tumbling smoke.

The lieutenant of the youth's company

had encountered a soldier who had fled screaming at the first volley of his comrades. Behind the lines these two were acting a little isolated scene. The man was blubbering and staring with sheeplike eyes at the lieutenant, who had seized him by the collar and was pommeling him. He drove him back into the ranks with many blows. The soldier went mechanically, dully, with his animal-like eyes upon the officer. Perhaps there was to him a divinity expressed in the voice of the other—stern, hard, with no reflection of fear in it. He tried to reload his gun, but his shaking hands prevented. The lieutenant was obliged to assist him.

The men dropped here and there like bundles. The captain of the youth's company had been killed in an early part of the action. His body lay stretched out in the position of a tired man resting, but upon his face there was an astonished and sorrowful look, as if he thought some friend had done him an ill turn. The babbling man was grazed by a shot that made the blood stream widely down his face. He clapped both hands to his head. "Oh!" he said, and ran. Another grunted suddenly as if he had been struck by a club in the stomach. He sat down and gazed ruefully. In his eyes there was mute, indefinite reproach. Farther up the line a man, standing behind a tree, had had his knee joint splintered by a ball. Immediately he had dropped his rifle and gripped the tree with both arms. And there he remained, clinging desperately and crying for assistance that he might withdraw his hold upon the tree.

At last an exultant yell went along the quivering line. The firing dwindled from an uproar to a last vindictive popping. As the smoke slowly eddied away, the youth saw that the charge had been repulsed. The enemy were scattered into reluctant groups. He saw a man climb to the top of the fence, straddle the rail, and fire a parting shot. The waves had receded, leaving bits of dark debris upon the ground.

Some in the regiment began to whoop frenziedly. Many were silent. Apparently they were trying to contemplate themselves.

After the fever had left his veins, the youth thought that at last he was going to suffocate. He became aware of the foul atmosphere in which he had been struggling. He was grimy and dripping like a laborer in a foundry. He grasped his canteen and took a long swallow of the warmed water.

A sentence with variations went up and down the line. "Well, we've helt 'em back. We've helt 'em back; derned if we haven't." The men said it blissfully, leering at each other with dirty smiles.

The youth turned to look behind him and off to the right and off to the left. He experienced the joy of a man who at last finds leisure in which to look about him.

Under foot there were a few ghastly forms motionless. They lay twisted in fantastic contortions. Arms were bent and heads were turned in incredible ways. It seemed that the dead men must have fallen from great height to get into such positions. They looked to be dumped out upon the ground from the sky.

From a position in the rear of the grove a battery was throwing shells over it. The flash of the guns startled the youth at first. He thought they were aimed directly at him. Through the trees he watched the black figures of the gunners as they worked swiftly and intently. Their labor seemed a complicated thing. He wondered how they could remember its formula in the midst of confusion.

The guns squatted in a row like savage chiefs. They argued with abrupt violence. It was a grim powwow. Their busy servants ran hither and thither.

A small procession of wounded men were going drearily toward the rear. It was a flow of blood from the torn body of the brigade.

To the right and to the left were the dark lines of other troops. Far in front he thought he could see lighter masses protruding in points from the forest. They were suggestive of unnumbered thousands.

Once he saw a tiny battery go dashing along the line of the horizon. The tiny riders were beating the tiny horses.

From a sloping hill came the sound of cheerings and clashes. Smoke welled slowly through the leaves.

Batteries were speaking with thunderous oratorical effort. Here and there were flags, the red in the stripes dominating. They splashed bits of warm color upon the dark lines of troops.

The youth felt the old thrill at the sight of the emblem. They were like beautiful birds strangely undaunted in a storm.

As he listened to the din from the hillside, to a deep pulsating thunder that came from afar to the left, and to the lesser clamors which came from many directions, it occured to him that they were fighting, too,

As he ran on he mingled with others. He dimly saw men on his right and on his left, and he heard footsteps behind him. He thought that all the regiment was fleeing, pursued by these ominous crashes.

In his flight the sound of these following footsteps gave him his one meager relief. He felt vaguely that death must make a first choice of the men who were nearest; the initial morsels for the dragons would be then those who were following him. So he displayed the zeal of an insane sprinter in his purpose to keep them in the rear. There was a race.

As he, leading, went across a little field, he found himself in a region of shells. They hurtled over his head with long wild screams. As he listened he imagined them to have rows of cruel teeth that grinned at him. Once one lit before him and the livid lightning of the explosion effectually barred the way in his chosen direction. He groveled on the ground and then springing up went careering off through some bushes.

He experienced a thrill of amazement when he came within view of a battery in action. The men there seemed to be in conventional moods, altogether unaware of the impending annihilation. The battery was disputing with a distant antagonist and the gunners were wrapped in admiration of their shooting. They were continually bending in coaxing postures over the guns. They seemed to be patting them on the back and encouraging them with words. The guns, stolid and undaunted, spoke with dogged valor.

The precise gunners were coolly enthusiastic. They lifted their eyes every chance to the smoke-wreathed hillock from whence the hostile battery addressed them. The youth pitied them as he ran. Methodical idiots! Machine like fools! The refined joy of planting shells in the midst of the other battery's formation would appear a little thing when the infantry came swooping out of the woods.

The face of a youthful rider, who was jerking his frantic horse with an abandon of temper he might display in a placid barnyard, was impressed deeply upon his mind. He knew that he looked upon a man who would presently be dead.

Too, he felt a pity for the guns, standing, six good comrades, in a bold row.

He saw a brigade going to the relief of its pestered fellows. He scrambled upon a wee hill and watched it sweeping finely, keeping formation in difficult places. The blue of the line was crusted with steel color, and the brilliant flags projected. Officers were shouting.

This sight also filled him with wonder. The brigade was hurrying briskly to be gulped into the infernal mouths of the war god. What manner of men were they, anyhow? Ah, it was some wondrous breed! Or else they didn't comprehend—the fools.

A furious order caused commotion in the artillery. An officer on a bounding horse made maniacal motions with his arms. The teams went swinging up from the rear, the guns were whirled about, and the battery scampered away. The cannon with their noses poked slantingly at the ground grunted and grumbled like stout men, brave but with objections to hurry.

The youth went on, moderating his pace since he had left the place of noises.

Later he came upon a general of division seated upon a horse that pricked its ears in an interested way at the battle. There was a great gleaming of yellow and patent leather about the saddle and bridle. The quiet man astride looked mouse-colored upon such a splendid charger.

A jingling staff was galloping hither and thither. Sometimes the general was surrounded by horsemen and at other times he was quite alone. He looked to be much harassed. He had the appearance of a business man whose market is swinging up and down.

The youth went slinking around this spot. He went as near as he dared trying to overhear words. Perhaps the general, unable to comprehend chaos, might call upon him for information. And he could tell him. He knew all concerning it. Of a surety the force was in a fix, and any fool could see that if they did not retreat while they had opportunity—why—

He felt that he would like to thrash the general, or at least approach and tell him in plain words exactly what he thought him to be. It was criminal to stay calmly in one spot and make no effort to stay destruction. He loitered in a fever of eagerness for the division commander to apply to him.

As he warily moved about, he heard the general call out irritably: "Tompkins, go over an' see Taylor, an' tell him not t' be in such an all-fired hurry; tell him t' halt his brigade in th' edge of th' woods; tell him t' detach

a reg'ment—say I think th' center 'll break if we don't help it out some; tell him t' hurry up."

A slim youth on a fine chestnut horse caught these swift words from the mouth of his superior. He made his horse bound into a gallop almost from a walk in his haste to go upon his mission. There was a cloud of dust.

A moment later the youth saw the general bounce excitedly in his saddle.

"Yes, by heavens, they have!" The officer leaned forward. His face was aflame with excitement. "Yes, by heavens, they've held 'im! They've held 'im!"

He began to blithely roar at his staff: "We'll wallop 'im now. We'll wallop 'im now. We've got 'em sure." He turned suddenly upon an aid: "Here—you—Jones—quick—ride after Tompkins—see Taylor—tell him t' go in—everlastingly—like blazes—anything."

As another officer sped his horse after the first messenger, the general beamed upon the earth like a sun. In his eyes was a desire to chant a paean.[19] He kept repeating, "They've held 'em, by heavens!"

His excitement made his horse plunge, and he merrily kicked and swore at it. He held a little carnival of joy on horseback.

Chapter Seven

The youth cringed as if discovered in a crime. By heavens, they had won after all! The imbecile line had remained and become victors. He could hear cheering.

He lifted himself upon his toes and looked in the direction of the fight. A yellow fog lay wallowing on the treetops. From beneath it came the clatter of musketry. Hoarse cries told of an advance.

He turned away amazed and angry. He felt that he had been wronged.

He had fled, he told himself, because annihilation approached. He had done a good part in saving himself, who was a little piece of the army. He had considered the time, he said, to be one in which it was the duty of every little piece to rescue itself if possible. Later the officers could fit the little pieces together again, and make a battle front. If none of the little pieces were wise enough to save themselves from the flurry of death at such a time, why, then, where would be the army? It was all plain that he had proceeded according to very correct and commendable rules. His actions had been sagacious things. They had been full of strategy. They were the work of a master's legs.

Thoughts of his comrades came to him. The brittle blue line had withstood the blows and won. He grew bitter over it. It seemed that the blind ignorance and stupidity of those little pieces had betrayed him. He had been overturned and crushed by their lack of sense in holding the position, when intelligent deliberation would have convinced them that it was impossible. He, the enlightened man who looks afar in the dark, had fled because of his superior perceptions and knowledge. He felt a great anger against his comrades. He knew it could be proved that they had been fools.

He wondered what they would remark when later he appeared in camp. His mind heard howls of derision. Their destiny would not enable them to understand his sharper point of view.

He began to pity himself acutely. He was ill used. He was trodden beneath the feet of an iron injustice. He had proceeded with wisdom and from the most righteous motives under heaven's blue only to be frustrated by hateful circumstances.

A dull, animal-like rebellion against his fellows, war in the abstract, and fate grew within him. He shambled along with bowed head, his brain in a tumult of agony and despair. When he looked loweringly up, quivering at each sound, his eyes had the expression of those of a criminal who thinks his guilt and his punishment great, and knows that he can find no words.

---

19. paean (pē′ ən) *n.*: A song of triumph.

He went from the fields into a thick wood, as if resolved to bury himself. He wished to get out of hearing of the cracking shots which were to him like voices.

The ground was cluttered with vines and bushes, and the trees grew close and spread out like bouquets. He was obliged to force his way with much noise. The creepers, catching against his legs, cried out harshly as their sprays were torn from the barks of trees. The swishing saplings tried to make known his presence to the world. He could not conciliate the forest. As he made his way, it was always calling out protestations. When he separated embraces of trees and vines the disturbed feelings waved their arms and turned their face leaves toward him. He dreaded lest these noisy motions and cries should bring men to look at him. So he went far, seeking dark and intricate places.

After a time the sound of musketry grew faint and the cannon boomed in the distance. The sun, suddenly apparent, blazed among the trees. The insects were making rhythmical noises. They seemed to be grinding their teeth in unison. A woodpecker stuck his impudent head around the side of a tree. A bird flew on lighthearted wing.

Off was the rumble of death. It seemed now that Nature had no ears.

This landscape gave him assurance. A fair field holding life. It was the religion of peace. It would die if its timid eyes were compelled to see blood. He conceived Nature to be a woman with a deep aversion to tragedy.

He threw a pine cone at a jovial squirrel, and he ran with chattering fear. High in a treetop he stopped, and, poking his head cautiously from behind a branch, looked down with an air of trepidation.

The youth felt triumphant at this exhibition. There was the law, he said. Nature had given him a sign. The squirrel, immediately upon recognizing danger, had taken to his legs without ado. He did not stand stolidly baring his furry belly to the missile, and die

with an upward glance at the sympathetic heavens. On the contrary, he had fled as fast as his legs could carry him; and he was but an ordinary squirrel, too—doubtless no philosopher of his race. The youth wended, feeling that Nature was of his mind. She reinforced his argument with proofs that lived where the sun shone.

Once he found himself almost into a swamp. He was obliged to walk upon bog tufts and watch his feet to keep from the oily mire. Pausing at one time to look about him he saw, out at some black water, a small animal pounce in and emerge directly with a gleaming fish.

The youth went again into the deep thickets. The brushed branches made a noise that drowned the sounds of cannon. He walked on, going from obscurity into promises of a greater obscurity.

At length he reached a place where the high, arching boughs made a chapel. He softly pushed the green doors aside and entered. Pine needles were a gentle brown carpet. There was a religious half light.

Near the threshold he stopped, horror-stricken at the sight of a thing.

He was being looked at by a dead man who was seated with his back against a columnlike tree. The corpse was dressed in a uniform that once had been blue, but was now faded to a melancholy shade of green. The eyes, staring at the youth, had changed to the dull hue to be seen on the side of a dead fish. The mouth was open. Its red had changed to an appalling yellow. Over the gray skin of the face ran little ants. One was trundling some sort of a bundle along the upper lip.

The youth gave a shriek as he confronted the thing. He was for moments turned to stone before it. He remained staring into the liquid-looking eyes. The dead man and the living man exchanged a long look. Then the youth cautiously put one hand behind him and brought it against a tree. Leaning upon this he retreated, step by step, with his face still toward the thing. He feared that if he turned his back the body might spring up and stealthily pursue him.

The branches, pushing against him, threatened to throw him over upon it. His unguided feet, too, caught aggravatingly in brambles; and with it all he received a subtle suggestion to touch the corpse. As he thought of his hand upon it he shuddered profoundly.

At last he burst the bonds which had fastened him to the spot and fled, unheeding the underbrush. He was pursued by a sight of the black ants swarming greedily upon the gray face and venturing horribly near to the eyes.

After a time he paused, and breathless and panting, listened. He imagined some strange voice would come from the dead throat and squawk after him in horrible menaces.

The trees about the portals of the chapel moved soughingly in a soft wind. A sad silence was upon the little guarding edifice.

THINKING ABOUT THE SELECTION

Recalling

1. (a) Why had the youth "burned" to enlist? (b) How had his mother responded to his desire? (c) How had she reacted when he left? (d) Why had her reaction disappointed him?
2. (a) What does the youth begin to fear as he lies in his bunk? (b) How does the tall soldier temporarily ease the youth's fear?
3. What does the loud soldier ask of the youth before the first battle?
4. (a) How does the youth react during his first battle? (b) What is the outcome of the battle?
5. (a) How does the youth react when the enemy mounts a second attack? (b) How does he react when he learns that the enemy's attack has failed?

Interpreting

6. Why do you think Crane chooses not to refer to the characters by their names?
7. How do the details of the setting in Chapter 3 reflect the youth's state of mind?

8. (a) What is ironic about the youth's recollection as he is marching toward his first battle that he "had never wished to come to war"? (b) What is ironic about the loud soldier's reaction when the regiment enters the first battle? (c) What do these ironies suggest about human nature?

9. (a) How does the youth's conception of himself change during his first battle? (b) How does his conception of the other members of his regiment change?

10. (a) Why does the youth respond as he does to the enemy's second attack? (b) How does he attempt to rationalize his behavior?

11. How does the youth's encounter with the dead man contradict his conclusion that nature has "a deep aversion to tragedy"?

Applying

12. Explain whether you think most people would respond as the youth does to the enemy's second attack.

ANALYZING LITERATURE
Understanding Realism and Naturalism

Realism was a literary movement that emphasized the faithful, accurate portrayal of ordinary life. The Realists attempted to present "a slice of life," focusing on the realities of a small portion of the world. For example, in *The Red Badge of Courage,* Crane focuses on one regiment's involvement in the early stages of the Civil War.

Naturalism was a literary movement in which people were generally portrayed as being manipulated by forces of society and nature beyond their understanding and control. For example, in *The Red Badge of Courage,* the characters are caught in the midst of a war and have virtually no control of their own fates.

1. Books and movies often paint unrealistic portraits of war, glamorizing combat while ignoring its grim realities. What makes Crane's portrayal of war realistic?

2. Why do you think Crane chose to portray common soldiers rather than officers?

3. How does Crane's portrayal of the soldiers in camp awaiting their first battle make it clear that the soldiers' destinies are being shaped by forces beyond their control?

4. The Naturalists believed that nature is indifferent to the troubles of humanity. How does the youth's discovery of the corpse in the woods convey this belief?

CRITICAL THINKING AND READING
Recognizing Important Passages

If you examine the novel closely, you will find that at times Crane conveys his Naturalistic beliefs directly through his descriptions and dialogue. For example, he conveys his belief in nature's indifference to the problems of humanity in his description of the setting following the first battle. He writes, "As he gazed around him the youth felt a flash of astonishment at the blue, pure sky and the sun gleaming on the trees and fields. It was surprising that Nature had gone tranquilly on with her golden process in the midst of so much bedevilment."

Find another passage, aside from the one describing the ghastly corpse, in which Crane directly conveys his Naturalistic beliefs.

THINKING AND WRITING
Writing a Letter

Write a letter from the youth to his mother describing his feelings as he awaits his first battle. Look again at Chapters 1–3, taking note of the youth's thoughts and feelings. Then write your letter, summarizing the youth's feelings in a few paragraphs. When you revise, make sure you have captured the youth's emotions as accurately as possible.

GUIDE FOR READING

The Red Badge of Courage, Chapters 8–13

Writer's Techniques

Elements of a Novel. A novel is a long work of fiction. Novels contain the same elements as short stories— including plot, characterization, setting, and point of view. Yet because novels are longer than short stories, the elements are usually more complex and well-developed.

The plot is the sequence of interrelated events or actions in a novel. Most often the events in a novel are all related to the conflict— a struggle between two opposing forces or characters—and are organized so that the conflict intensifies as the plot develops.

Characterization is the means by which the writer reveals a character's personality. The process of characterization is usually more gradual and complete in a novel than in a short story. In fact, you may continue to gain new insights into a character's personality throughout the entire course of a novel.

The setting is the time, place, and conditions under which the events in a novel occur. The general setting of *The Red Badge of Courage* is the Civil War. More specifically, the setting is the Battle of Chancellorsville, a bloody conflict that took place in Virginia in 1863. However, Crane does not name the battle in the book.

Point of view—the vantage point or perspective from which the story is told—can have a major impact on the other elements of a novel. Because Crane tells the story from the youth's point of view, you see the setting as the youth sees it, and you are presented with his impressions of the events and other characters.

Look For

As you read Chapters 8–13 of *The Red Badge of Courage,* look for the way the point of view affects the way you perceive the events of the novel.

Writing

In Chapters 8–13 of *The Red Badge of Courage,* the youth must cope with the death of a close friend. Freewrite, exploring how you think he might have responded to this situation.

Vocabulary

Knowing the following words will help you as you read Chapters 8–13 of *The Red Badge of Courage.*

perfunctory (pər fuŋk′ tər ē) *adj.*: Done without care or interest or merely as a form of routine (p. 607)

sublime (sə blīm′) *adj.*: Majestic (p. 608)

sardonic (sär dän′ ik) *adj.*: Bitterly sarcastic (p. 608)

imprecations (im′ prə kā′ shənz) *n.*: Curses (p. 615)

sinuous (sin′ yoo wəs) *adj.*: Bending or winding in and out (p. 615)

malediction (mal′ ə dik′ shən) *n.*: Curse (p. 616)

Chapter Eight

The trees began softly to sing a hymn of twilight. The sun sank until slanted bronze rays struck the forest. There was a lull in the noises of insects as if they had bowed their beaks and were making a devotional pause. There was silence save for the chanted chorus of the trees.

Then, upon this stillness, there suddenly broke a tremendous clangor of sounds. A crimson roar came from the distance.

The youth stopped. He was transfixed by this terrific medley of all noises. It was as if worlds were being rended. There was the ripping sound of musketry and the breaking crash of artillery.

His mind flew in all directions. He conceived the two armies to be at each other panther fashion. He listened for a time. Then he began to run in the direction of the battle. He saw that it was an ironical thing for him to be running thus toward that which he had been at such pains to avoid. But he said, in substance, to himself that if the earth and the moon were about to clash, many persons would doubtless plan to get upon the roofs to witness the collision.

As he ran, he became aware that the forest had stopped its music, as if at last becoming capable of hearing the foreign sounds. The trees hushed and stood motionless. Everything seemed to be listening to the crackle and clatter and ear-shaking thunder. The chorus pealed over the still earth.

It suddenly occurred to the youth that the fight in which he had been was, after all, but perfunctory popping. In the hearing of this present din he was doubtful if he had seen real battle scenes. This uproar explained a celestial battle; it was tumbling hordes a-struggle in the air.

Reflecting, he saw a sort of humor in the point of view of himself and his fellows during the late encounter. They had taken themselves and the enemy very seriously and had imagined that they were deciding the war. Individuals must have supposed that they were cutting the letters of their names deep into everlasting tablets of brass, or enshrining their reputations forever in the hearts of their countrymen, while, as to fact, the affair would appear in printed reports under a meek and immaterial title. But he saw that it was good, else, he said, in battle everyone would surely run save forlorn hopes[1] and their ilk.

He went rapidly on. He wished to come to the edge of the forest that he might peer out.

As he hastened, there passed through his mind pictures of stupendous conflicts. His accumulated thought upon such subjects was used to form scenes. The noise was as the voice of an eloquent being, describing.

Sometimes the brambles formed chains and tried to hold him back. Trees, confronting him, stretched out their arms and forbade him to pass. After its previous hostility this new resistance of the forest filled him with a fine bitterness. It seemed that Nature could not be quite ready to kill him.

But he obstinately took roundabout ways, and presently he was where he could see long gray walls of vapor where lay battle lines. The voices of cannon shook him. The musketry sounded in long irregular surges that played havoc with his ears. He stood regardant for a moment. His eyes had an awestruck expression. He gawked in the direction of the fight.

Presently he proceeded again on his forward way. The battle was like the grinding of an immense and terrible machine to him. Its complexities and powers, its grim processes, fascinated him. He must go close and see it produce corpses.

He came to a fence and clambered over it. On the far side, the ground was littered with clothes and guns. A newspaper, folded up, lay in the dirt. A dead soldier was

---

1. forlorn hopes: Groups of soldiers detached from the main group for dangerous missions.

stretched with his face hidden in his arm. Farther off there was a group of four or five corpses keeping mournful company. A hot sun had blazed upon the spot.

In this place the youth felt that he was an invader. This forgotten part of the battle-ground was owned by the dead men, and he hurried, in the vague apprehension that one of the swollen forms would rise and tell him to be gone.

He came finally to a road from which he could see in the distance dark and agitated bodies of troops, smoke-fringed. In the lane was a bloodstained crowd streaming to the rear. The wounded men were cursing, groan-ing, and wailing. In the air, always, was a mighty swell of sound that it seemed could sway the earth. With the courageous words of the artillery and the spiteful sentences of the musketry mingled red cheers. And from this region of noises came the steady current of the maimed.

One of the wounded men had a shoeful of blood. He hopped like a schoolboy in a game. He was laughing hysterically.

One was swearing that he had been shot in the arm through the commanding gen-eral's mismanagement of the army. One was marching with an air imitative of some sub-lime drum major. Upon his features was an unholy mixture of merriment and agony. As he marched he sang a bit of doggerel in a high and quavering voice:

> Sing a song 'a vic'try,
>   A pocketful 'a bullets,
> Five an' twenty dead men
>   Baked in a—pie.

Parts of the procession limped and stag-gered to this tune.

Another had the gray seal of death al-ready upon his face. His lips were curled in hard lines and his teeth were clenched. His hands were bloody from where he had passed them upon his wound. He seemed to be awaiting the moment when he should pitch headlong. He stalked like the specter of a soldier, his eyes burning with the power of a stare into the unknown.

There were some who proceeded sullenly, full of anger at their wounds, and ready to turn upon anything as an obscure cause.

An officer was carried along by two pri-vates. He was peevish. "Don't joggle so, Johnson, yeh fool," he cried. "Think m' leg is made of iron? If yeh can't carry me decent, put me down an' let someone else do it."

He bellowed at the tottering crowd who blocked the quick march of his bearers. "Say, make way there, can't yeh? Make way, dickens take it all."

They sulkily parted and went to the road-sides. As he was carried past they made pert remarks to him.

The shoulder of one of the tramping bearers knocked heavily against the spectral soldier who was staring into the unknown.

The youth joined this crowd and marched along with it. The torn bodies ex-pressed the awful machinery in which the men had been entangled.

Orderlies and couriers occasionally broke through the throng in the roadway, scatter-ing wounded men right and left, gallop-ing on, followed by howls. The melancholy march was continually disturbed by the mes-sengers, and sometimes by bustling batter-ies that came swinging and thumping down upon them, the officers shouting orders to clear the way.

There was a tattered man, fouled with dust, blood and powder stain from hair to shoes, who trudged quietly at the youth's side. He was listening with eagerness and much humility to the lurid descriptions of a bearded sergeant. His lean features wore an expression of awe and admiration. He was like a listener in a country store to wondrous tales told among the sugar barrels. He eyed the storyteller with unspeakable wonder. His mouth was agape in yokel fashion.

The sergeant, taking note of this, gave pause to his elaborate history while he ad-ministered a sardonic comment. "Be keerful, honey, you'll be a-ketchin' flies," he said.

The tattered man shrank back abashed.

After a time he began to sidle near to the youth, and in a different way try to make him a friend. His voice was gentle as a girl's voice and his eyes were pleading. The youth saw with surprise that the soldier had two wounds, one in the head, bound with a blood-soaked rag, and the other in the arm, making that member dangle like a broken bough.

After they had walked together for some time the tattered man mustered sufficient courage to speak. "Was pretty good fight, wasn't it?" he timidly said. The youth, deep in thought, glanced up at the bloody and grim figure with its lamblike eyes, "What?"

"Was pretty good fight, wa'n't it?"

"Yes," said the youth shortly. He quickened his pace.

But the other hobbled industriously after him. There was an air of apology in his manner, but he evidently thought that he needed only to talk for a time, and the youth would perceive that he was a good fellow.

"Was pretty good fight, wa'n't it?" he began in a small voice, and then he achieved the fortitude to continue. "Dern me if I ever see fellers fight so. Laws, how they did fight!

I knowed th' boys 'd like it when they onct got square at it. Th' boys ain't had no fair chanct up t' now, but this time they showed what they was. I knowed it 'd turn out this way. Yeh can't lick them boys. No, sir! They're fighters, they be."

He breathed a deep breath of humble admiration. He had looked at the youth for encouragement several times. He received none, but gradually he seemed to get absorbed in his subject.

"I was talkin' 'cross pickets with a boy from Georgie, onct, an' that boy, he ses, 'Your fellers 'll all run when they onct hearn a gun,' he ses. 'Mebbe they will,' I ses, 'but I don't b'lieve none of it,' I ses; 'an' b'jiminey,' I ses back t' 'um, 'mebbe your fellers 'll all run when they onct hearn a gun,' I ses. He larfed. Well, they didn't run t'-day, did they, hey? No, sir! They fit, an' fit, an' fit."

His homely face was suffused with a light of love for the army which was to him all things beautiful and powerful.

After a time he turned to the youth. "Where yeh hit, ol' boy?" he asked in a brotherly tone.

The youth felt instant panic at this question, although at first its full import was not borne in upon him.

"What?" he asked.

"Where yeh hit?" repeated the tattered man.

"Why," began the youth, "I–I–that is—why—I–"

He turned away suddenly and slid through the crowd. His brow was heavily flushed, and his fingers were picking nervously at one of his buttons. He bent his head and fastened his eyes studiously upon the button as if it were a little problem.

The tattered man looked after him in astonishment.

Chapter Nine

The youth fell back in the procession until the tattered soldier was not in sight. Then he started to walk on with the others.

But he was amid wounds. The mob of men was bleeding. Because of the tattered soldier's question he now felt that his shame could be viewed. He was continually casting sidelong glances to see if the men were contemplating the letters of guilt he felt burned into his brow.

At times he regarded the wounded soldiers in an envious way. He conceived persons with torn bodies to be peculiarly happy. He wished that he, too, had a wound, a red badge of courage.

The spectral soldier was at his side like a stalking reproach. The man's eyes were still fixed in a stare into the unknown. His gray, appalling face had attracted attention in the crowd, and men, slowing to his dreary pace, were walking with him. They were discussing his plight, questioning him and giving him advice. In a dogged way he repelled them, signing to them to go on and leave him alone. The shadows of his face were deepening and his tight lips seemed holding in check the moan of great despair. There could be seen a certain stiffness in the movements of his body, as if he were taking infinite care not to arouse the passion of his wounds. As he went on, he seemed always looking for a place, like one who goes to choose a grave.

Something in the gesture of the man as he waved the bloody and pitying soldiers away made the youth start as if bitten. He yelled in horror. Tottering forward he laid a quivering hand upon the man's arm. As the latter slowly turned his waxlike features toward him, the youth screamed:

"Jim Conklin!"

The tall soldier made a little commonplace smile. "Hello, Henry," he said.

The youth swayed on his legs and glared strangely. He stuttered and stammered. "Oh, Jim—oh, Jim—oh, Jim—"

The tall soldier held out his gory hand. There was a curious red and black combination of new blood and old blood upon it.

"Where yeh been, Henry?" he asked. He continued in a monotonous voice, "I thought mebbe yeh got keeled over. There's been thunder t' pay t'-day. I was worryin' about it a good deal."

The youth still lamented. "Oh, Jim—oh, Jim—oh, Jim—"

"Yeh know," said the tall soldier, "I was out there." He made a careful gesture. "An' what a circus! An', b'jiminey, I got shot—I got shot. Yes, b'jiminey, I got shot." He reiterated this fact in a bewildered way, as if he did not know how it came about.

The youth put forth anxious arms to assist him, but the tall soldier went firmly on as if propelled. Since the youth's arrival as a guardian for his friend, the other wounded men had ceased to display much interest. They occupied themselves again in dragging their own tragedies toward the rear.

Suddenly, as the two friends marched on, the tall soldier seemed to be overcome by a terror. His face turned to a semblance of gray paste. He clutched the youth's arm and looked all about him, as if dreading to be overheard. Then he began to speak in a shaking whisper:

"I tell yeh what I'm 'fraid of, Henry—I'll tell yeh what I'm 'fraid of. I'm 'fraid I'll fall down—an' then yeh know—them artillery wagons—they like as not 'll run over me. That's what I'm 'fraid of—"

The youth cried out to him hysterically: "I'll take care of yeh, Jim! I'll take care of yeh! I swear I will!"

"Sure—will yeh, Henry?" the tall soldier beseeched.

"Yes—yes—I tell yeh—I'll take care of yeh, Jim!" protested the youth. He could not speak accurately because of the gulpings in his throat.

But the tall soldier continued to beg in a lowly way. He now hung babelike to the youth's arm. His eyes rolled in the wildness of his terror. "I was allus a good friend t' yeh, wa'n't I, Henry? I've allus been a pretty good feller, ain't I? An' it ain't much t' ask, is it? Jest t' pull me along outer th' road? I'd do it fer you, wouldn't I, Henry?"

He paused in piteous anxiety to await his friend's reply.

The youth had reached an anguish where the sobs scorched him. He strove to express his loyalty, but he could only make fantastic gestures.

However, the tall soldier seemed suddenly to forget all those fears. He became again the grim, stalking specter of a soldier. He went stonily forward. The youth wished his friend to lean upon him, but the other always shook his head and strangely protested. "No—no—no—leave me be—leave me be—"

His look was fixed again upon the unknown. He moved with mysterious purpose, and all of the youth's offers he brushed aside. "No—no—leave me be—leave me be—"

The youth had to follow.

Presently the latter heard a voice talking softly near his shoulders. Turning he saw that it belonged to the tattered soldier. "Ye'd better take 'im outa th' road, pardner. There's a batt'ry comin' helitywhoop down th' road an he'll git runned over. He's a goner anyhow in about five minutes—yeh kin see that. Ye'd better take 'im outa th' road. Where th' blazes does he git his stren'th from?"

"Lord knows!" cried the youth. He was shaking his hands helplessly.

He ran forward presently and grasped the tall soldier by the arm. "Jim! Jim!" he coaxed, "come with me."

The tall soldier weakly tried to wrench himself free. "Huh," he said vacantly. He stared at the youth for a moment. At last he spoke as if dimly comprehending. "Oh! Inteh th' fields? Oh!"

He started blindly through the grass.

The youth turned once to look at the lashing riders and jouncing guns of the battery. He was startled from this view by a shrill outcry from the tattered man.

"He's runnin'!"

The tall soldier faced about as upon relentless pursuers. In his eyes there was a great appeal. "Leave me be, can't yeh? Leave me be fer a minnit."

The youth recoiled. "Why, Jim," he said, in a dazed way, "what's the matter with you?"

The tall soldier turned and, lurching dangerously, went on. The youth and the tattered soldier followed, sneaking as if whipped, feeling unable to face the stricken man if he should again confront them. They began to have thoughts of a solemn ceremony. There was something ritelike in these movements of the doomed soldier. And there was a resemblance in him to a devotee of a mad religion, blood-sucking, muscle-wrenching, bone-crushing. They were awed and afraid. They hung back lest he have at command a dreadful weapon.

At last, they saw him stop and stand motionless. Hastening up, they perceived that his face wore an expression telling that he had at last found the place for which he had struggled. His spare figure was erect; his bloody hands were quietly at his side. He was waiting with patience for something that he had come to meet. He was at the rendezvous. They paused and stood, expectant.

There was a silence.

Finally, the chest of the doomed soldier began to heave with a strained motion. It increased in violence until it was as if an animal was within and was kicking and tumbling furiously to be free.

This spectacle of gradual strangulation made the youth writhe, and once as his friend rolled his eyes, he saw something in them that made him sink wailing to the ground. He raised his voice in a last supreme call.

"Jim—Jim—Jim—"

The tall soldier opened his lips and spoke. He made a gesture. "Leave me be—don't tech me—leave me be—"

There was another silence while he waited.

Suddenly, his form stiffened and

Turning his head swiftly, the youth saw his friend running in a staggering and stumbling way toward a little clump of bushes. His heart seemed to wrench itself almost free from his body at this sight. He made a noise of pain. He and the tattered man began a pursuit. There was a singular race.

When he overtook the tall soldier he began to plead with all the words he could find. "Jim—Jim—what are you doing—what makes you do this way—you'll hurt yerself."

The same purpose was in the tall soldier's face. He protested in a dulled way, keeping his eyes fastened on the mystic place of his intentions. "No—no—don't tech me—leave me be—leave me be—"

The youth, aghast and filled with wonder at the tall soldier, began quaveringly to question him. "Where yeh goin', Jim? What you thinking about? Where you going? Tell me, won't you, Jim?"

straightened. Then it was shaken by a prolonged ague.[2] He stared into space. To the two watchers there was a curious and profound dignity in the firm lines of his awful face.

He was invaded by a creeping strangeness that slowly enveloped him. For a moment the tremor of his legs caused him to dance a sort of hideous hornpipe.[3] His arms beat wildly about his head in expression of implike enthusiasm.

His tall figure stretched itself to its full height. There was a slight rending sound. Then it began to swing forward, slow and straight, in the manner of a falling tree. A swift muscular contortion made the left shoulder strike the ground first.

The body seemed to bounce a little way from the earth.

The youth had watched, spellbound, this ceremony at the place of meeting. His face had been twisted into an expression of every agony he had imagined for his friend.

He now sprang to his feet and, going closer, gazed upon the pastelike face. The mouth was open and the teeth showed in a laugh.

As the flap of the blue jacket fell away from the body, he could see that the side looked as if it had been chewed by wolves.

The youth turned, with sudden, livid rage, toward the battlefield. He shook his fist.

The red sun was pasted in the sky like a wafer.

Chapter Ten

The tattered man stood musing.

"Well, he was a reg'lar jim-dandy fer nerve, wa'nt he," said he finally in a little awestruck voice. "A reg'lar jim-dandy." He thoughtfully poked one of the docile hands with his foot. "I wonner where he got 'is stren'th from? I never seen a man do like that before. It was a funny thing. Well, he was a reg'lar jim-dandy."

The youth desired to screech out his grief. He was stabbed, but his tongue lay dead in the tomb of his mouth. He threw himself again upon the ground and began to brood.

The tattered man stood musing.

"Look-a-here, pardner," he said, after a time. He regarded the corpse as he spoke. "He's up an' gone, ain't 'e, an' we might as well begin t' look out fer ol' number one. This here thing is all over. He's up an' gone, ain't 'e? An' he's all right here. Nobody won't bother 'im. An' I must say I ain't enjoying any great health m'self these days."

The youth, awakened by the tattered soldier's tone, looked quickly up. He saw that he was swinging uncertainly on his legs and that his face had turned to a shade of blue.

"Good Lord!" he cried, "you ain't goin' t'—not you, too."

The tattered man waved his hand. "Nary die," he said. "All I want is some pea soup an' a good bed. Some pea soup," he repeated dreamfully.

The youth arose from the ground. "I wonder where he came from. I left him over there." He pointed. "And now I find 'im here. And he was coming from over there, too." He indicated a new direction. They both turned toward the body as if to ask it a question.

"Well," at length spoke the tattered man, "there ain't no use in our stayin' here an' tryin' t' ask him anything."

The youth nodded an assent wearily. They both turned to gaze for a moment at the corpse.

The youth murmured something.

"Well, he was a jim-dandy, wa'n't 'e?" said the tattered man as if in response.

They turned their backs upon it and started away. For a time they stole softly, treading with their toes. It remained laughing there in the grass.

"I'm commencin' t' feel pretty bad," said the tattered man, suddenly breaking one of

---

2. ague (ā' gyo͞o) *n*.: Fit of shivering.
3. hornpipe *n*.: A lively dance.

his little silences. "I'm commencin' t' feel pretty bad."

The youth groaned. "O Lord!" He wondered if he was to be the tortured witness of another grim encounter.

But his companion waved his hand reassuringly. "Oh, I'm not goin' t' die yit! There's too much dependin' on me fer me t' die yit. No, sir! Nary die; I *can't*! Ye'd oughta see th' swad a' chil'ren I've got, an' all like that."

The youth glancing at his companion could see by the shadow of a smile that he was making some kind of fun.

As they plodded on the tattered soldier continued to talk. "Besides, if I died, I wouldn't die th' way that feller did. That was th' funniest thing. I'd jest flop down, I would. I never seen a feller die th' way that feller did.

"Yeh know Tom Jamison, he lives next door t' me up home. He's a nice feller, he is, an' we was allus good friends. Smart, too. Smart as a steel trap. Well, when we was a-fightin' this afternoon, all-of-a-sudden he begin t' rip up an' cuss an' beller at me. 'Yer shot, yeh blamed infernal!'—he swear horrible—he ses t' me. I put up m' hand t' m' head an' when I looked at m' fingers, I seen, sure 'nough, I was shot. I give a holler an' begin t' run, but b'fore I could git away another one hit me in th' arm an' whirl' me clean 'round. I got skeared when they was all a-shootin' b'hind me an' I run t' beat all, but I cotch it pretty bad. I've an idee I'd a' been fightin' yit, if t'wasn't fer Tom Jamison."

Then he made a calm announcement: "There's two of 'em—little ones— but they're beginnin' t' have fun with me now. I don't b'lieve I kin walk much furder."

They went slowly on in silence. "Yeh look pretty peaked yerself," said the tattered man at last. "I bet yeh 've got a worser one than yeh think. Ye'd better take keer of yer hurt. It don't do t' let sech things go. It might be inside mostly, an' them plays thunder. Where is it located?" But he continued his harangue without waiting for a reply. "I see' a feller git hit plum in th' head when my reg'ment was a-standin' at ease onct. An' ev-erybody yelled out to 'im: Hurt, John? Are yeh hurt much? 'No,' ses he. He looked kinder surprised, an' he went on tellin' 'em how he felt. He sed he didn't feel nothin'. But, by dad, th' first thing that feller knowed he was dead. Yes, he was dead—stone dead. So, yeh wanta watch out. Yeh might have some queer kind 'a hurt yerself. Yeh can't never tell. Where is your'n located?"

The youth had been wriggling since the introduction of this topic. He now gave a cry of exasperation and made a furious motion with his hand, "Oh, don't bother me!" he said. He was enraged against the tattered man, and could have strangled him. His companions seemed ever to play intolerable parts. They were ever upraising the ghost of shame on the stick of their curiosity. He turned toward the tattered man as one at bay. "Now, don't bother me," he repeated with desperate menace.

"Well, Lord knows I don't wanta bother anybody," said the other. There was a little accent of despair in his voice as he replied, "Lord knows I've gota 'nough m' own t' tend to."

The youth, who had been holding a bitter debate with himself and casting glances of hatred and contempt at the tattered man, here spoke in a hard voice. "Good-bye," he said.

The tattered man looked at him in gaping amazement. "Why—why, pardner, where yeh goin'?" he asked unsteadily. The youth looking at him, could see that he, too, like that other one, was beginning to act dumb and animal-like. His thoughts seemed to be floundering about in his head. "Now—now—look—a—here, you Tom Jamison—now—I won't have this—this here won't do. Where—where yeh goin'?"

The youth pointed vaguely. "Over there," he replied.

"Well, now look—a—here—now," said the tattered man, rambling on in idiot fashion. His head was hanging forward and his words were slurred. "This thing won't do, now, Tom Jamison. It won't do. I know yeh,

yeh pig-headed devil. Yeh wanta go trompin' off with a bad hurt. It ain't right—now—Tom Jamison—it ain't. Yeh wanta leave me take keer of yeh, Tom Jamison. It ain't—right—it ain't—fer yeh t' go—trompin' off—with a bad hurt—it ain't—ain't—ain't right—it ain't."

In reply the youth climbed a fence and started away. He could hear the tattered man bleating plaintively.

Once he faced about angrily. "What?"

"Look—a—here, now, Tom Jamison—now—it ain't—"

The youth went on. Turning at a distance he saw the tattered man wandering about helplessly in the field.

He now thought that he wished he was dead. He believed that he envied those men whose bodies lay strewn over the grass of the fields and on the fallen leaves of the forest.

The simple questions of the tattered man had been knife thrusts to him. They asserted a society that probes pitilessly at secrets until all is apparent. His late companion's chance persistency made him feel that he could not keep his crime concealed in his bosom. It was sure to be brought plain by one of those arrows which cloud the air and are constantly pricking, discovering, proclaiming those things which are willed to be forever hidden. He admitted that he could not defend himself against this agency.[4] It was not within the power of vigilance.

Chapter Eleven

He became aware that the furnace roar of the battle was growing louder. Great brown clouds had floated to the still heights of air before him. The noise, too, was approaching. The woods filtered men and the fields became dotted.

As he rounded a hillock, he perceived that the roadway was now a crying mass of wagons, teams, and men. From the heaving tangle issued exhortations, commands, imprecations. Fear was sweeping it all along.

---

4. agency *n.*: Active force.

The cracking whips bit and horses plunged and tugged. The white-topped wagons strained and stumbled in their exertions like fat sheep.

The youth felt comforted in a measure by this sight. They were all retreating. Perhaps, then, he was not so bad after all. He seated himself and watched the terror-stricken wagons. They fled like soft, ungainly animals. All the roarers and lashers served to help him to magnify the dangers and horrors of the engagement that he might try to prove to himself that the thing with which men could charge him was in truth a symmetrical act. There was an amount of pleasure to him in watching the wild march of this vindication.

Presently the calm head of a forward-going column of infantry appeared in the road. It came swiftly on. Avoiding the obstructions gave it the sinuous movement of a serpent. The men at the head butted mules with their musket stocks. They prodded teamsters indifferent to all howls. The men forced their way through parts of the dense mass by strength. The blunt head of the column pushed. The raving teamsters swore many strange oaths.

The commands to make way had the ring of a great importance in them. The men were going forward to the heart of the din. They were to confront the eager rush of the enemy. They felt the pride of their onward movement when the remainder of the army seemed trying to dribble down this road. They tumbled teams about with a fine feeling that it was no matter so long as their column got to the front in time. This importance made their faces grave and stern. And the backs of the officers were very rigid.

As the youth looked at them the black weight of his woe returned to him. He felt that he was regarding a procession of chosen beings. The separation was as great to him as if they had marched with weapons of flame and banners of sunlight. He could never be like them. He could have wept in his longings.

He searched about in his mind for an adequate malediction for the indefinite cause, the thing upon which men turn the words of final blame. It—whatever it was—was responsible for him, he said. There lay the fault.

The haste of the column to reach the battle seemed to the forlorn young man to be something much finer than stout fighting. Heroes, he thought, could find excuses in that long, seething lane. They could retire with perfect self-respect and make excuses to the stars.

He wondered what those men had eaten that they could be in such haste to force their way to grim chances of death. As he watched, his envy grew until he thought that he wished to change lives with one of them. He would have liked to have used a tremendous force, he said, throw off himself and become a better. Swift pictures of himself, apart, yet in himself, came to him—a blue desperate figure leading lurid charges with one knee forward and a broken blade high—a blue, determined figure standing before a crimson and steel assault, getting calmly killed on a high place before the eyes of all. He thought of the magnificent pathos of his dead body.

These thoughts uplifted him. He felt the quiver of war desire. In his ears, he heard the ring of victory. He knew the frenzy of a rapid successful charge. The music of the trampling feet, the sharp voices, the clanking arms of the column near him made him soar on the red wings of war. For a few moments he was sublime.

He thought that he was about to start for the front. Indeed, he saw a picture of himself, dust-stained, haggard, panting, flying to the front at the proper moment to seize and throttle the dark, leering witch of calamity.

Then the difficulties of the thing began to drag at him. He hesitated, balancing awkwardly on one foot.

He had no rifle; he could not fight with his hands, said he resentfully to his plan. Well, rifles could be had for the picking. They were extraordinarily profuse.

Also, he continued, it would be a miracle if he found his regiment. Well, he could fight with any regiment.

He started forward slowly. He stepped as if he expected to tread upon some explosive thing. Doubts and he were struggling.

He would truly be a worm if any of his comrades should see him returning thus, the marks of his flight upon him. There was a reply that the intent fighters did not care for what happened rearward saving that no hostile bayonets appeared there. In the battle-blur his face would, in a way, be hidden, like the face of a cowled man.

But then he said that his tireless fate would bring forth, when the strife lulled for a moment, a man to ask of him an explanation. In imagination he felt the scrutiny of his companions as he painfully labored through some lies.

Eventually, his courage expended itself upon these objections. The debates drained him of his fire.

He was not cast down by this defeat of his plan, for, upon studying the affair carefully, he could not but admit that the objections were very formidable.

Furthermore, various ailments had begun to cry out. In their presence he could not persist in flying high with the wings of war; they rendered it almost impossible for him to see himself in a heroic light. He tumbled headlong.

He discovered that he had a scorching thirst. His face was so dry and grimy that he thought he could feel his skin crackle. Each bone of his body had an ache in it, and seemingly threatened to break with each movement. His feet were like two sores. Also, his body was calling for food. It was more powerful than a direct hunger. There was a dull, weightlike feeling in his stomach, and, when he tried to walk, his head swayed and he tottered. He could not see with distinctness. Small patches of green mist floated before his vision.

While he had been tossed by many emotions, he had not been aware of ailments. Now they beset him and made clamor. As he was at last compelled to pay attention to them, his capacity for self-hate was multiplied. In despair, he declared that he was not like those others. He now conceded it to be impossible that he should ever become a hero. He was a craven loon. Those pictures of glory were piteous things. He groaned from his heart and went staggering off.

A certain mothlike quality within him kept him in the vicinity of the battle. He had a great desire to see, and to get news. He wished to know who was winning.

He told himself that, despite his unprecedented suffering, he had never lost his greed for a victory, yet, he said, in a half-apologetic manner to his conscience, he could not but know that a defeat for the army this time might mean many favorable things for him. The blows of the enemy would splinter regiments into fragments. Thus, many men of courage, he considered, would be obliged to desert the colors and scurry like chickens. He would appear as one of them. They would be sullen brothers in distress, and he could then easily believe he had not run any farther or faster than they. And if he himself could believe in his virtuous perfection, he conceived that there would be small trouble in convincing all others.

He said, as if in excuse for this hope, that previously the army had encountered great defeats and in a few months had shaken off all blood and tradition of them, emerging as bright and valiant as a new one; thrusting out of sight the memory of disas-

ter, and appearing with the valor and confidence of unconquered legions. The shrilling voices of the people at home would pipe dismally for a time, but various generals were usually compelled to listen to these ditties. He of course felt no compunctions for proposing a general as a sacrifice. He could not tell who the chosen for the barbs might be, so he could center no direct sympathy upon him. The people were afar and he did not conceive public opinion to be accurate at long range. It was quite probable they would hit the wrong man who, after he had recovered from his amazement would perhaps spend the rest of his days in writing replies to the songs of his alleged failure. It would be very unfortunate, no doubt, but in this case a general was of no consequence to the youth.

In a defeat there would be a roundabout vindication of himself. He thought it would prove, in a manner, that he had fled early because of his superior powers of perception. A serious prophet upon predicting a flood should be the first man to climb a tree. This would demonstrate that he was indeed a seer.

A moral vindication was regarded by the youth as a very important thing. Without salve, he could not, he thought, wear the sore badge of his dishonor through life. With his heart continually assuring him that he was despicable, he could not exist without making it, through his actions, apparent to all men.

If the army had gone gloriously on he would be lost. If the din meant that now his army's flags were tilted forward he was a condemned wretch. He would be compelled to doom himself to isolation. If the men were advancing, their indifferent feet were trampling upon his chances for a successful life.

As these thoughts went rapidly through his mind, he turned upon them and tried to thrust them away. He denounced himself as a villain. He said that he was the most unutterably selfish man in existence. His mind pictured the soldiers who would place their defiant bodies before the spear of the yelling battle fiend, and as he saw their dripping corpses on an imagined field, he said that he was their murderer.

Again he thought that he wished he was dead. He believed that he envied a corpse. Thinking of the slain, he achieved a great contempt for some of them, as if they were guilty for thus becoming lifeless. They might have been killed by lucky chances, he said, before they had had opportunities to flee or before they had been really tested. Yet they would receive laurels[5] from tradition. He cried out bitterly that their crowns were stolen and their robes of glorious memories were shams. However, he still said that it was a great pity he was not as they.

A defeat of the army had suggested itself to him as a means of escape from the consequences of his fall. He considered, now, however, that it was useless to think of such a possibility. His education had been that success for that mighty blue machine was certain; that it would make victories as a contrivance turns out buttons. He presently discarded all his speculations in the other direction. He returned to the creed of soldiers.

When he perceived again that it was not possible for the army to be defeated, he tried to bethink him of a fine tale which he could take back to his regiment, and with it turn the expected shafts of derision.

But, as he mortally feared these shafts, it became impossible for him to invent a tale he felt he could trust. He experimented with many schemes, but threw them aside one by one as flimsy. He was quick to see vulnerable places in them all.

Furthermore, he was much afraid that some arrow of scorn might lay him mentally low before he could raise his protecting tale.

He imagined the whole regiment saying: "Where's Henry Fleming? He run, didn't 'e? Oh, my!" He recalled various persons who would be quite sure to leave him no peace

_____

5. laurels *n*.: Honors.

about it. They would doubtless question him with sneers, and laugh at his stammering hesitation. In the next engagement they would try to keep watch of him to discover when he would run.

Wherever he went in camp, he would encounter insolent and lingeringly cruel stares. As he imagined himself passing near a crowd of comrades, he could hear someone say, "There he goes!"

Then, as if the heads were moved by one muscle, all the faces were turned toward him with wide, derisive grins. He seemed to hear someone make a humorous remark in a low tone. At it the others all crowed and cackled. He was a slang phrase.

Chapter Twelve

The column that had butted stoutly at the obstacles in the roadway was barely out of the youth's sight before he saw dark waves of men come sweeping out of the woods and down through the fields. He knew at once that the steel fibers had been washed from their hearts. They were bursting from their coats and their equipment as from entanglements. They charged down upon him like terrified buffaloes.

Behind them blue smoke curled and clouded above the treetops, and through the thickets he could sometimes see a distant pink glare. The voices of the cannon were clamoring in interminable chorus.

The youth was horror-stricken. He stared in agony and amazement. He forgot that he was engaged in combating the universe. He threw aside his mental pamphlets on the philosophy of the retreated and rules for the guidance of the damned.

The fight was lost. The dragons were coming with invincible strides. The army, helpless in the matted thickets and blinded by the overhanging night, was going to be swallowed. War, the red animal, war, the blood-swollen god, would have bloated fill.

Within him something bade to cry out. He had the impulse to make a rallying speech, to sing a battle hymn, but he could only get his tongue to call into the air: "Why—why—what—what's th' matter?"

Soon he was in the midst of them. They were leaping and scampering all about him. Their blanched faces shone in the dusk. They seemed, for the most part, to be very burly men. The youth turned from one to another of them as they galloped along. His incoherent questions were lost. They were heedless of his appeals. They did not seem to see him.

They sometimes gabbled insanely. One huge man was asking of the sky: "Say, where de plank road? Where de plank road!" It was as if he had lost a child. He wept in his pain and dismay.

Presently, men were running hither and thither in all ways. The artillery booming, forward, rearward, and on the flanks made jumble of ideas of direction. Landmarks had vanished into the gathered gloom. The youth began to imagine that he had got into the center of the tremendous quarrel, and he could perceive no way out of it. From the mouths of the fleeing men came a thousand wild questions, but no one made answers.

The youth, after rushing about and throwing interrogations at the heedless bands of retreating infantry, finally clutched a man by the arm. They swung around face to face.

"Why—why—" stammered the youth struggling with his balking tongue.

The man screamed: "Let go me! Let go me!" His face was livid and his eyes were rolling uncontrolled. He was heaving and panting. He still grasped his rifle, perhaps having forgotten to release his hold upon it. He tugged frantically, and the youth being compelled to lean forward was dragged several paces.

"Let go me! Let go me!"

"Why—why—" stuttered the youth.

"Well, then!" bawled the man in a lurid rage. He adroitly and fiercely swung his rifle. It crushed upon the youth's head. The man ran on.

The youth's fingers had turned to paste upon the other's arm. The energy was smitten from his muscles. He saw the flaming wings of lightning flash before his vision. There was a deafening rumble of thunder within his head.

Suddenly his legs seemed to die. He sank writhing to the ground. He tried to arise. In his efforts against the numbing pain he was like a man wrestling with a creature of the air.

There was a sinister struggle.

Sometimes he would achieve a position half erect, battle with the air for a moment, and then fall again, grabbing at the grass. His face was of a clammy pallor. Deep groans were wrenched from him.

At last, with a twisting movement, he got upon his hands and knees, and from thence, like a babe trying to walk, to his feet. Pressing his hands to his temples he went lurching over the grass.

He fought an intense battle with his body. His dulled senses wished him to swoon and he opposed them stubbornly, his mind portraying unknown dangers and mutilations if he should fall upon the field. He went tall soldier fashion. He imagined secluded spots where he could fall and be unmolested. To search for one he strove against the tide of his pain.

Once he put his hand to the top of his head and timidly touched the wound. The scratching pain of the contact made him draw a long breath through his clinched teeth. His fingers were dabbled with blood. He regarded them with a fixed stare.

Around him he could hear the grumble of jolted cannon as the scurrying horses were lashed toward the front. Once, a young officer on a besplashed charger nearly ran him down. He turned and watched the mass of guns, men, and horses sweeping in a wide curve toward a gap in a fence. The officer was making excited motions with a gauntleted hand. The guns followed the teams with an air of unwillingness, of being dragged by the heels.

Some officers of the scattered infantry were cursing and railing like fishwives. Their scolding voices could be heard above the din. Into the unspeakable jumble in the roadway rode a squadron of cavalry. The faded yellow of their facings shone bravely. There was a mighty altercation.

The artillery were assembling as if for a conference.

The blue haze of evening was upon the field. The lines of forest were long purple shadows. One cloud lay along the western sky partly smothering the red.

As the youth left the scene behind him, he heard the guns suddenly roar out. He imagined them shaking in black rage. They belched and howled like brass devils guarding a gate. The soft air was filled with the tremendous remonstrance. With it came the shattering peal of opposing infantry. Turning to look behind him, he could see sheets of orange light illumine the shadowy distance. There were subtle and sudden lightnings in the far air. At times he thought he could see heaving masses of men.

He hurried on in the dusk. The day had faded until he could barely distinguish place for his feet. The purple darkness was filled with men who lectured and jabbered. Sometimes he could see them gesticulating against the blue and somber sky. There seemed to be a great ruck of men and munitions spread about in the forest and in the fields.

The little narrow roadway now lay lifeless. There were overturned wagons like sundried boulders. The bed of the former torrent was choked with the bodies of horses and splintered parts of war machines.

It had come to pass that his wound pained him but little. He was afraid to move rapidly, however, for a dread of disturbing it. He held his head very still and took many precautions against stumbling. He was filled with anxiety, and his face was pinched and drawn in anticipation of the pain of any sudden mistake of his feet in the gloom.

His thoughts, as he walked, fixed in-

tently upon his hurt. There was a cool, liquid feeling about it and he imagined blood moving slowly down under his hair. His head seemed swollen to a size that made him think his neck to be inadequate.

The new silence of his wound made much worriment. The little blistering voices of pain that had called out from his scalp were, he thought, definite in their expression of danger. By them he believed that he could measure his plight. But when they remained ominously silent he became frightened and imagined terrible fingers that clutched into his brain.

Amid it he began to reflect upon various incidents and conditions of the past. He bethought him of certain meals his mother had cooked at home, in which those dishes of which he was particularly fond had occupied prominent positions. He saw the spread table. The pine walls of the kitchen were glowing in the warm light from the stove. Too, he remembered how he and his companions used to go from the schoolhouse to the bank of a shaded pool. He saw his clothes in disorderly array upon the grass of the bank. He felt the swash of the fragrant water upon his body. The leaves of the overhanging maple rustled with melody in the wind of youthful summer.

He was overcome presently by a dragging weariness. His head hung forward and his shoulders were stooped as if he were bearing a great bundle. His feet shuffled along the ground.

He held continuous arguments as to whether he should lie down and sleep at some near spot, or force himself on until he reached a certain haven. He often tried to dismiss the question, but his body persisted in rebellion and his senses nagged at him like pampered babies.

At last he heard a cheery voice near his shoulder: "Yeh seem t' be in a pretty bad way, boy?"

The youth did not look up, but he assented with thick tongue. "Uh!"

The owner of the cheery voice took him firmly by the arm. "Well," he said, with a round laugh, "I'm goin' your way. Th' hull gang is goin' your way. An' I guess I kin give yeh a lift."

As they went along, the man questioned the youth and assisted him with the replies like one manipulating the mind of a child. Sometimes he interjected anecdotes. "What reg'ment do yeh b'long teh? Eh? What's that? Th' 304th N' York? Why, what corps is that in? Oh, it is? Why, I thought they wasn't engaged t'-day—they're way over in th' center. Oh, they was, eh? Well, pretty nearly everybody got their share 'a fightin' t'-day. By dad, I give myself up fer dead any number 'a times. There was shootin' here an' shootin' there, an' hollerin' here an' hollerin' there, in th' darkness, until I couldn't tell t' save m' soul which side I was on. Sometimes I thought I was sure 'nough from Ohier, an' other times I could 'a swore I was from th' bitter end of Florida. It was th' most mixed up dern thing I ever see. An' these here hull woods is a reg'lar mess. It'll be a miracle if we find our reg'ments t'-night. Pretty soon, though, we'll meet a-plenty of guards an' provost-guards, an' one thing an' another. Ho! there they go with an off'cer, I guess. Look at his leg a-draggin'. He's got all th' war he wants, I bet. He won't be talkin' so big about his reputation an' all when they go t' sawin' off his leg. Poor feller! My brother's got whiskers jest like that. How did yeh git 'way over here, anyhow? Your reg'ment is a long way from here, ain't it? Well, I guess we can find it. Yeh know there was a boy killed in my comp'ny t'-day that I thought th' world an' all of. Jack was a nice feller. By ginger, it hurt like thunder t' see ol' Jack jest git knocked flat. We was a-standin' purty peaceable for a spell, 'though there was men runnin' ev'ry way all 'round us, an' while we was a-standin' like that, 'long come a big fat feller. He began t' peck at Jack's elbow, an' he ses: 'Say, where 's th' road t' th' river?' An' Jack, he never paid no attention, an' th' feller kept on a-peckin' at his elbow an' sayin': 'Say, where's th' road t' th' river?' Jack was a-lookin' ahead all th' time tryin' t' see th' Johnnies comin' through th' woods, an' he never paid no attention t' this big fat feller fer a long time, but at last he turned 'round an' he ses: 'Ah, go an' find th' road t' th' river!' An' jest then a shot slapped him bang on th' side th' head. He was a sergeant, too. Them was his last words. Thunder, I wish we was sure 'a findin' our reg'ments t'night. It's goin' t' be long huntin'. But I guess we kin do it."

In the search which followed, the man of the cheery voice seemed to the youth to possess a wand of a magic kind. He threaded the mazes of the tangled forest with a strange fortune. In encounter with guards and patrols he displayed the keenness of a detective and the valor of a gamin.[6] Obstacles fell before him and became of assistance. The youth, with his chin still on his breast, stood woodenly by while his companion beat ways and means out of sullen things.

The forest seemed a vast hive of men buzzing about in frantic circles, but the cheery man conducted the youth without mistakes, until at last he began to chuckle with glee and self-satisfaction. "Ah, there yeh are! See that fire?"

The youth nodded stupidly.

"Well, there's where your reg'ment is. An' now, good-bye, ol' boy, good luck t' yeh."

A warm and strong hand clasped the youth's languid fingers for an instant, and then he heard a cheerful and audacious whistling as the man strode away. As he who had so befriended him was thus passing out of his life, it suddenly occurred to the youth that he had not once seen his face.

---

6. gamin (gam' ən): A neglected child left to roam the streets.

Chapter Thirteen

The youth went slowly toward the fire indicated by his departed friend. As he reeled, he bethought him of the welcome his comrades would give him. He had a conviction that he would soon feel in his sore heart the barbed missiles of ridicule. He had no strength to invent a tale; he would be a soft target.

He made vague plans to go off into the deeper darkness and hide, but they were all destroyed by the voices of exhaustion and pain from his body. His ailments, clamoring, forced him to seek the place of food and rest, at whatever cost.

He swung unsteadily toward the fire. He could see the forms of men throwing black shadows in the red light, and as he went nearer it became known to him in some way that the ground was strewn with sleeping men.

Of a sudden he confronted a black and monstrous figure. A rifle barrel caught some glinting beams. "Halt! halt!" He was dismayed for a moment, but he presently thought that he recognized the nervous voice. As he stood tottering before the rifle barrel, he called out: "Why, hello, Wilson, you—you here?"

The rifle was lowered to a position of caution and the loud soldier came slowly forward. He peered into the youth's face. "That you, Henry?"

"Yes, it's—it's me."

"Well, well, ol' boy," said the other, "by ginger, I'm glad t' see yeh! I give yeh up fer a goner. I thought yeh was dead sure enough." There was husky emotion in his voice.

The youth found that now he could barely stand upon his feet. There was a sudden sinking of his forces. He thought he must hasten to produce his tale to protect him from the missiles already at the lips of his redoubtable comrades. So, staggering before the loud soldier, he began: "Yes, yes. I've—I've had an awful time. I've been all over. Way over on th' right. Ter'ble fightin' over there. I had an awful time. I got separated from th' reg'ment. Over on th' right, I got shot. In th' head. I never see sech fightin'. Awful time. I don't see how I could a' got separated from th' reg'ment. I got shot, too."

His friend had stepped forward quickly. "What? Got shot? Why didn't yeh say so first? Poor ol' boy, we must—hol' on a minnit; what am I doin'? I'll call Simpson."

Another figure at that moment loomed in the gloom. They could see that it was the corporal. "Who yeh talkin' to, Wilson?" he demanded. His voice was anger-toned. "Who yeh talkin' to? Yeh th' derndest sentinel—why—hello, Henry, you here? Why, I thought you was dead four hours ago! Great Jerusalem, they keep turnin' up every ten minutes or so! We thought we'd lost forty-two men by straight count, but if they keep on a-comin' this way, we'll git th' comp'ny all back by mornin' yit. Where was yeh?"

"Over on th' right. I got separated"—began the youth with considerable glibness.

But his friend had interrupted hastily. "Yes, an' he got shot in th' head an he's in a fix, an' we must see t' him right away." He rested his rifle in the hollow of his left arm and his right around the youth's shoulder.

"Gee, it must hurt like thunder!" he said.

The youth leaned heavily upon his friend. "Yes, it hurts—hurts a good deal," he replied. There was a faltering in his voice.

"Oh," said the corporal. He linked his arm in the youth's and drew him forward. "Come on, Henry. I'll take keer 'a yeh."

As they went on together the loud private called out after them: "Put 'im t' sleep in my blanket, Simpson. An'—hol' on a minnit—here's my canteen. It's full 'a coffee. Look at his head by th' fire an' see how it looks. Maybe it's a pretty bad un. When I git relieved in a couple 'a minnits, I'll be over an' see t' him."

The youth's senses were so deadened that his friend's voice sounded from afar and he could scarcely feel the pressure of the corporal's arm. He submitted passively to the latter's directing strength. His head was in the old manner hanging forward upon his breast. His knees wobbled.

The corporal led him into the glare of the fire. "Now, Henry," he said, "let's have a look at yer ol' head."

The youth sat down obediently and the corporal, laying aside his rifle, began to fumble in the bushy hair of his comrade. He was obliged to turn the other's head so that the full flush of the fire light would beam upon it. He puckered his mouth with a critical air. He drew back his lips and whistled through his teeth when his fingers came in contact with the splashed blood and the rare wound.

"Ah, here we are!" he said. He awkwardly made further investigations. "Jest as I thought," he added, presently. "Yeh've been grazed by a ball. It's raised a queer lump jest as if some feller had lammed yeh on th' head with a club. It stopped a-bleedin' long time ago. Th' most about it is that in th' mornin' yeh'll feel that a number ten hat wouldn't fit yeh. An' your head 'll be all het up an' feel as dry as burnt pork. An' yeh may git a lot 'a other sicknesses, too, by mornin'. Yeh can't never tell. Still, I don't much think so. It's jest a good belt on th' head, an' nothin' more. Now, you jest sit here an' don't move, while I go rout out th' relief. Then I'll send Wilson t' take keer 'a yeh."

The corporal went away. The youth remained on the ground like a parcel. He stared with a vacant look into the fire.

After a time he aroused, for some part, and the things about him began to take form. He saw that the ground in the deep shadows was cluttered with men, sprawling in every conceivable posture. Glancing narrowly into the more distant darkness, he caught occasional glimpses of visages that loomed pallid and ghostly, lit with a phosphorescent glow. These faces expressed in their lines the deep stupor of the tired soldiers.

On the other side of the fire the youth observed an officer asleep, seated bolt upright, with his back against a tree. There was something perilous in his position. Badgered by dreams, perhaps, he swayed with little bounces and starts. Dust and stains were upon his face. His lower jaw hung down as if lacking strength to assume its normal position. He was the picture of an exhausted soldier after a feast of war.

He had evidently gone to sleep with his sword in his arms. These two had slumbered in an embrace, but the weapon had been allowed in time to fall unheeded to the ground. The brass-mounted hilt lay in contact with some parts of the fire.

Within the gleam of rose and orange light from the burning sticks were other soldiers, snoring and heaving, or lying deathlike in slumber. A few pairs of legs were stuck forth, rigid and straight. The shoes displayed the mud or dust of marches and bits of rounded trousers, protruding from the blankets, showed rents and tears from hurried pitchings through the dense brambles.

The fire crackled musically. From it swelled light smoke. Overhead the foliage moved softly. The leaves, with their faces turned toward the blaze, were colored shifting hues of silver, often edged with red. Far off to the right, through a window in the forest, could be seen a handful of stars lying, like glittering pebbles, on the black level of the night.

Occasionally, in this low-arched hall, a soldier would arouse and turn his body to a new position, the experience of his sleep having taught him of uneven and objectionable places upon the ground under him. Or, perhaps, he would lift himself to a sitting position, blink at the fire for an unintelligent moment, throw a swift glance at his prostrate companion, and then cuddle down again with a grunt of sleepy content.

The youth sat in a forlorn heap until his friend, the loud young soldier, came, swinging two canteens by their light strings. "Well, now, Henry, ol' boy," said the latter, "we'll have yeh fixed up in jest about a minnit."

He had the bustling ways of an amateur nurse. He fussed around the fire and stirred the sticks to brilliant exertions. He made his patient drink largely from the canteen that contained the coffee. It was to the youth a delicious draft. He tilted his head afar back and held the canteen long to his lips. The cool mixture went caressingly down his blistered throat. Having finished, he sighed with comfortable delight.

The loud young soldier watched his comrade with an air of satisfaction. He later produced an extensive handkerchief from his pocket. He folded it into a manner of bandage and soused water from the other canteen upon the middle of it. This crude arrangement he bound over the youth's head, tying the ends in a queer knot at the back of the neck.

"There," he said, moving off and surveying his deed, "yeh look like th' devil, but I bet yeh feel better."

The youth contemplated his friend with grateful eyes. Upon his aching and swelling head the cold cloth was like a tender woman's hand.

"Yeh don't holler ner say nothin'," remarked his friend approvingly. "I know I'm a blacksmith at takin' keer 'a sick folks, an' yeh never squeaked. Yer a good un, Henry. Most 'a men would 'a been in th' hospital long ago. A shot in th' head ain't foolin' business."

The youth made no reply, but began to fumble with the buttons of his jacket.

"Well, come, now," continued his friend, "come on. I must put yeh t' bed an' see that yeh git a good night's rest."

The other got carefully erect, and the loud young soldier led him among the sleeping forms lying in groups and rows. Presently he stooped and picked up his blankets. He spread the rubber one upon the ground and placed the woolen one about the youth's shoulders.

"There now," he said, "lie down an' git some sleep."

The youth, with his manner of doglike obedience, got carefully down like a crone stooping. He stretched out with a murmur of relief and comfort. The ground felt like the softest couch.

But of a sudden he ejaculated: "Hol' on a minnit! Where you goin' t' sleep?"

His friend waved his hand impatiently. "Right down there by yeh."

"Well, but hol' on a minnit," continued the youth. "What yeh goin' t' sleep in? I've got your—"

The loud young soldier snarled: "Shet up an' go on t' sleep. Don't be makin' a fool 'a yerself," he said severely.

After the reproof the youth said no more. An exquisite drowsiness had spread through him. The warm comfort of the blanket enveloped him and made a gentle languor. His head fell forward on his crooked arm and his weighted lids went slowly down over his eyes. Hearing a splatter of musketry from the distance, he wondered indifferently if those men sometimes slept. He gave a long sigh, snuggled down into his blanket, and in a moment was like his comrades.

THINKING ABOUT THE SELECTION

Recalling

1. (a) What type of procession does the youth join on the road? (b) Why does he move toward the back of the procession?
2. Why does the youth regard the wounded soldiers with envy?
3. (a) Who is the spectral soldier? (b) What has happened to him before he meets the youth? (c) Of what is he afraid? (d) What are his final words?
4. Why does the youth abandon the tattered soldier?
5. (a) How is the youth wounded? (b) How does he find his way back to his regiment? (c) How does he explain his wound to Wilson?

Interpreting

6. (a) How is the tattered soldier's attitude toward death different from the youth's attitude? (b) What might be the reason for the difference?
7. (a) What is ironic about how the youth is wounded? (b) Why does he lie to Wilson about the cause of the wound?

8. (a) How is the youth's treatment of the tattered soldier different from the cheerful soldier's treatment of the youth? (b) What is the significance of the fact that the youth never sees the cheerful soldier's face?
9. Why do you think that throughout the novel Crane uses the color red to symbolize war?

Applying

10. When the youth returns to his regiment, it is clear that a sense of brotherhood has developed among the members of the unit. Why do such feelings develop among soldiers?

ANALYZING LITERATURE
Recognizing Elements of a Novel

Novels contain the same elements as short stories. Yet because novels are longer than short stories, the elements are usually more complex and well developed.
1. The central conflict in *The Red Badge of Courage* is internal, occurring within the youth's mind. However, there is more than one conflict in the novel. Against what external forces does the youth also struggle?
2. Characters are likely to change more dramatically during the course of a novel than during the course of a short story. What dramatic changes does the youth undergo during Chapters 1–13?
3. Considering that the story is told from the youth's point of view, why would it be inappropriate for Crane to reveal the name of the battle?

CRITICAL THINKING AND READING
Analyzing the Effect of Point of View

Point of view often affects the portrayal of characters and events in a novel. When a writer uses a first-person or limited third-person narrator, we see the characters and details through the eyes of one individual. In *The Red Badge of Courage,* for example, we are presented with the youth's impressions.
1. How do you think the novel might have been different if it had been told from the point of view of an experienced soldier?
2. How do you think the novel might have been different if it had been told from an officer's point of view?

THINKING AND WRITING
Comparing and Contrasting Writers

Using *The Red Badge of Courage* and "To Build a Fire" as characteristic works, compare and contrast the work of Stephen Crane and Jack London. Review "To Build a Fire" and the chapters you have read of *The Red Badge of Courage,* taking note of similarities and differences in style, theme, characterization, and conflict. Organize your notes into an outline and write a thesis statement. Then write your essay using passages from the works to support your argument. When you finish writing, revise your paper and prepare a final copy.

The Red Badge of Courage, Chapters 14–24

Theme. The theme is the central idea or insight about life a writer conveys in a work of literature. In some literary works, the theme is directly stated. More often, however, the theme is implied, or revealed indirectly. In fiction, the theme is usually conveyed through the portrayal of characters and events or through the use of literary devices such as irony, symbols, and allusions. While short stories often have only one theme, novels may have a number of themes. *The Red Badge of Courage,* for example, has several themes.

Look For

As you read Chapters 14–24 of *The Red Badge of Courage,* look for its major themes. How are the themes conveyed?

Writing

In Chapters 14–24 of *The Red Badge of Courage,* the youth returns to combat. Briefly discuss how you would expect him to perform during his next battle, considering his experiences in the previous chapters.

Vocabulary

Knowing the following words will help you as you read Chapters 14–24 of *The Red Badge of Courage.*

charnel (chär′ n′l) *adj.*: Like a graveyard (p. 629)

peremptory (pə remp′ tər ē) *adj.*: That cannot be denied, changed, delayed or opposed (p. 629)

petulantly (pech′ oo lənt lē) *adv.*: Impatiently or irritably (p. 629)

deprecating (dep′ rə kāt′ iŋ) *adj.*: Expressing disapproval (p. 631)

lugubrious (loo goo′ brē əs) *adj.*: Very sad or mournful (p. 632)

laggard (lag′ ərd) *adj.*: Slow or late in doing things (p. 632)

consternation (kän′ stər nā′ shən) *n.*: Great fear or shock that makes one feel helpless or bewildered (p. 634)

temerity (tə mer′ ə tē) *n.*: Foolhardiness; recklessness (p. 636)

gesticulating (jes tik′ yə lāt iŋ) *v.*: Gesturing with hands or arms (p. 641)

portentous (pôr ten′ təs) *adj.*: Ominous (p. 653)

Chapter Fourteen

When the youth awoke it seemed to him that he had been asleep for a thousand years, and he felt sure that he opened his eyes upon an unexpected world. Gray mists were slowly shifting before the first efforts of the sunrays. An impending splendor could be seen in the eastern sky. An icy dew had chilled his face, and immediately upon arousing he curled farther down into his blankets. He stared for a while at the leaves overhead, moving in a heraldic wind of the day.

The distance was splintering and blaring with the noise of fighting. There was in the sound an expression of a deadly persistency, as if it had not begun and was not to cease.

About him were the rows and groups of men that he had dimly seen the previous night. They were getting a last draft of sleep before the awakening. The gaunt, careworn features and dusty figures were made plain by this quaint light at the dawning, but it dressed the skin of the men in corpselike hues and made the tangled limbs appear pulseless and dead. The youth started up with a little cry when his eyes first swept over this motionless mass of men, thick-spread upon the ground, pallid, and in strange postures. His disordered mind interpreted the hall of the forest as a charnel place. He believed for an instant that he was in the house of the dead, and he did not dare to move lest these corpses start up, squalling and squawking. In a second, however, he achieved his proper mind. He swore a complicated oath at himself. He saw that this somber picture was not a fact of the present, but a mere prophecy.

He heard then the noise of a fire crackling briskly in the cold air, and, turning his head, he saw his friend pottering busily about a small blaze. A few other figures moved in the fog, and he heard the hard cracking of axe blows.

Suddenly there was a hollow rumble of drums. A distant bugle sang faintly. Similar sounds, varying in strength, came from near and far over the forest. The bugles called to each other like brazen gamecocks.[1] The near thunder of the regimental drums rolled.

The body of men in the woods rustled. There was a general uplifting of heads. A murmuring of voices broke upon the air. In it there was much bass of grumbling oaths. An officer's peremptory tenor rang out and quickened the stiffened movement of the men. The tangled limbs unraveled. The corpse-hued faces were hidden behind fists that twisted slowly in the eye sockets.

The youth sat up and gave vent to an enormous yawn. "Thunder!" he remarked petulantly. He rubbed his eyes, and then putting up his hand felt carefully of the bandage over his wound. His friend, perceiving him to be awake, came from the fire. "Well, Henry, ol' man, how do yeh feel this mornin'?" he demanded.

The youth yawned again. Then he puckered his mouth to a little pucker. His head, in truth, felt precisely like a melon, and there was an unpleasant sensation at his stomach.

"I feel pretty bad," he said.

"Thunder!" exlaimed the other. "I hoped ye'd feel all right this mornin'. Let's see th' bandage—I guess it's slipped." He began to tinker at the wound in rather a clumsy way until the youth exploded.

"Gosh-dern it!" he said in sharp irritation; "you're the hangdest man I ever saw! You wear muffs on your hands. Why in good thunderation can't you be more easy? I'd rather you'd stand off an' throw guns at it. Now, go slow, an' don't act as if you was nailing down carpet."

He glared with insolent command at his friend, but the latter answered soothingly. "Well, well, come now, an' git some grub," he said. "Then, maybe, yeh'll feel better."

At the fireside the loud young soldier

---

1. gamecocks _n._: Specially bred roosters trained for fighting.

watched over his comrade's wants with tenderness and care. He was very busy marshaling the little black vagabonds of tin cups and pouring into them the streaming, iron-colored mixture from a small and sooty tin pail. He had some fresh meat, which he roasted hurriedly upon a stick. He sat down then and contemplated the youth's appetite with glee.

The youth took note of a remarkable change in his comrade since those days of camp life upon the river bank. He seemed no more to be continually regarding the proportions of his personal prowess. He was not furious at small words that pricked his conceits. He was no more a loud young soldier. There was about him now a fine reliance. He showed a quiet belief in his purposes and his abilities. And this inward confidence evidently enabled him to be indifferent to little words of other men aimed at him.

The youth reflected. He had been used to regarding his comrade as a blatant child with an audacity grown from his inexperience, thoughtless, headstrong, jealous, and filled with a tinsel courage. A swaggering babe accustomed to strut in his own dooryard. The youth wondered where had been born these new eyes; when his comrade had made the great discovery that there were many men who would refuse to be subjected by him. Apparently, the other had now climbed a peak of wisdom from which he could perceive himself as a very wee thing. And the youth saw that ever after it would be easier to live in his friend's neighborhood.

His comrade balanced his ebony coffee cup on his knee. "Well, Henry," he said, "what d'yeh think th' chances are? D'yeh think we'll wallop 'em?"

The youth considered for a moment. "Day-b'fore-yesterday," he finally replied, with boldness, "you would 'a bet you'd lick the hull kit-an'-boodle all by yourself."

His friend looked a trifle amazed. "Would I?" he asked. He pondered. "Well, perhaps I would," he decided at last. He stared humbly at the fire.

The youth was quite disconcerted at this surprising reception of his remarks. "Oh, no, you wouldn't either," he said, hastily trying to retrace.

But the other made a deprecating gesture. "Oh, yeh needn't mind, Henry," he said. "I believe I was a pretty big fool in those days." He spoke as after a lapse of years.

There was a little pause.

"All th' officers say we've got th' rebs in a pretty tight box," said the friend, clearing his throat in a commonplace way. "They all seem t' think we've got 'em jest where we want 'em."

"I don't know about that," the youth replied. "What I seen over on th' right makes me think it was th' other way about. From where I was, it looked as if we was gettin' a good poundin' yestirday."

"D'yeh think so?" inquired the friend. "I thought we handled 'em pretty rough yestirday."

"Not a bit," said the youth. "Why, man, you didn't see nothing of the fight. Why!" Then a sudden thought came to him. "Oh! Jim Conklin's dead."

His friend started. "What? Is he? Jim Conklin?"

The youth spoke slowly. "Yes. He's dead. Shot in th' side."

"Yeh don't say so. Jim Conklin . . . poor cuss!"

All about them were other small fires surrounded by men with their little black utensils. From one of these near came sudden sharp voices in a row. It appeared that two light-footed soldiers had been teasing a huge, bearded man, causing him to spill coffee upon his blue knees. The man had gone into a rage and had sworn comprehensively. Stung by his language, his tormentors had immediately bristled at him with a great show of resenting unjust oaths. Possibly there was going to be a fight.

The friend arose and went over to them, making pacific motions with his arms. "Oh, here, now, boys, what's th' use?" he said. "We'll be at th' rebs in less'n an hour. What's th' good fightin' 'mong ourselves?"

One of the light-footed soldiers turned upon him red-faced and violent. "Yeh needn't come around here with yer preachin'. I s'pose yeh don't approve 'a fightin' since Charley Morgan licked yeh; but I don't see what business this here is 'a yours or anybody else."

"Well, it ain't," said the friend mildly. "Still I hate t' see—"

That was a tangled argument.

"Well, he—," said the two, indicating their opponent with accusative forefingers.

The huge soldier was quite purple with rage. He pointed at the two soldiers with his great hand, extended clawlike. "Well, they—"

But during this argumentative time the desire to deal blows seemed to pass, although they said much to each other. Finally the friend returned to his old seat. In a short while the three antagonists could be seen together in an amiable bunch.

"Jimmie Rogers ses I'll have t' fight him after th' battle t'-day," announced the friend as he again seated himself. "He ses he don't allow no interferin' in his business. I hate t' see th' boys fightin' 'mong themselves."

The youth laughed. "Yer changed a good bit. Yeh ain't at all like yeh was. I remember when you an' that Irish feller—" He stopped and laughed again.

"No, I didn't use t' be that way," said his friend thoughtfully. "That's true 'nough."

"Well, I didn't mean—" began the youth.

The friend made another deprecatory gesture. "Oh, yeh needn't mind, Henry."

There was another little pause.

"Th' reg'ment lost over half th' men yest-irday," remarked the friend eventually. "I thought 'a course they was all dead, but, laws, they kep' a-comin' back last night until it seems, after all, we didn't lose but a few. They'd been scattered all over, wanderin' around in th' woods, fightin' with other reg'ments, an' everything. Jest like you done."

"So?" said the youth.

Chapter Fifteen

The regiment was standing at order arms at the side of a lane, waiting for the command to march, when suddenly the youth remembered the little packet en-wrapped in a faded yellow envelope which the loud young soldier with lugubrious words had entrusted to him. It made him start. He uttered an exclamation and turned toward his comrade.

"Wilson!"

His friend, at his side in the ranks, was thoughtfully staring down the road. From some cause his expression was at that moment very meek. The youth, regarding him with sidelong glances, felt impelled to change his purpose. "Oh, nothing," he said.

His friend turned his head in some surprise, "Why, what was yeh goin' t' say?"

"Oh, nothing," repeated the youth.

He resolved not to deal the little blow. It was sufficient that the fact made him glad. It was not necessary to knock his friend on the head with the misguided packet.

He had been possessed of much fear of his friend, for he saw how easily question-ings could make holes in his feelings. Lately, he had assured himself that the altered com-rade would not tantalize him with a persis-tent curiosity, but he felt certain that during the first period of leisure his friend would ask him to relate his adventures of the previous day.

He now rejoiced in the possession of a small weapon with which he could prostrate his comrade at the first signs of a cross-examination. He was master. It would now be he who could laugh and shoot the shafts of derision.

The friend had, in a weak hour, spoken with sobs of his own death. He had delivered a melancholy oration previous to his funeral, and had doubtless, in the packet of letters, presented various keepsakes to relatives. But he had not died, and thus he had delivered himself into the hands of the youth.

The latter felt immensely superior to his friend, but he inclined to condescension. He adopted toward him an air of patronizing good humor.

His self-pride was now entirely restored. In the shade of its flourishing growth he stood with braced and self-confident legs, and since nothing could now be discovered he did not shrink from an encounter with the eyes of judges, and allowed no thoughts of his own to keep him from an attitude of manfulness. He had performed his mistakes in the dark, so he was still a man.

Indeed, when he remembered his for-tunes of yesterday, and looked at them from a distance he began to see something fine there. He had license to be pompous and vet-eranlike.

His panting agonies of the past he put out of his sight.

In the present, he declared to himself that it was only the doomed who roared with sincerity at circumstance. Few but they ever did it. A man with a full stomach and the re-spect of his fellows had no business to scold about anything that he might think to be wrong in the ways of the universe, or even with the ways of society. Let the unfortu-nates rail; the others may play marbles.

He did not give a great deal of thought to these battles that lay directly before him. It was not essential that he should plan his ways in regard to them. He had been taught that many obligations of a life were easily avoided. The lessons of yesterday had been that retribution was laggard and blind. With these facts before him he did not deem it

necessary that he should become feverish over the possibilities of the ensuing twenty-four hours. He could leave much to chance. Besides, a faith in himself had secretly blossomed. There was a little flower of confidence growing within him. He was now a man of experience. He had been out among the dragons, he said, and he assured himself that they were not so hideous as he had imagined them. Also, they were inaccurate; they did not sting with precision. A stout heart often defied, and, defying, escaped.

He remembered how some of the men had run from the battle. As he recalled their terror-struck faces he felt a scorn for them. They had surely been more fleet and more wild than was absolutely necessary. They were weak mortals. As for himself, he had fled with discretion and dignity.

He was aroused from this reverie by his friend, who, having hitched about nervously and blinked at the trees for a time, suddenly coughed in an introductory way, and spoke.

"Fleming!"

"What?"

The friend put his hand up to his mouth and coughed again. He fidgeted in his jacket.

"Well," he gulped, at last, "I guess yeh might as well give me back them letters." Dark, prickling blood had flushed into his cheeks and brow.

"All right, Wilson," said the youth. He

loosened two buttons of his coat, thrust in his hand, and brought forth the packet. As he extended it to his friend the latter's face was turned from him.

He had been slow in the act of producing the packet because during it he had been trying to invent a remarkable comment upon the affair. He could conjure nothing of sufficient point. He was compelled to allow his friend to escape unmolested with his packet. And for this he took unto himself considerable credit. It was a generous thing.

His friend at his side seemed suffering great shame. As he contemplated him, the youth felt his heart grow more strong and stout. He had never been compelled to blush in such manner for his acts; he was an individual of extraordinary virtues.

He reflected, with condescending pity: "Too bad! Too bad! The poor devil, it makes him feel tough!"

After this incident, and as he reviewed the battle pictures he had seen, he felt quite competent to return home and make the hearts of the people glow with stories of war. He could see himself in a room of warm tints telling tales to listeners. He could exhibit laurels. They were insignificant; still, in a district where laurels were infrequent, they might shine.

He saw his gaping audience picturing him as the central figure in blazing scenes. And he imagined the consternation and the ejaculations of his mother and the young lady at the seminary as they drank his recitals. Their vague feminine formula for beloved ones doing brave deeds on the field of battle without risk of life would be destroyed.

Chapter Sixteen

A sputtering of musketry was always to be heard. Later, the cannon had entered the dispute. In the fog-filled air their voices made a thudding sound. The reverberations were continued. This part of the world led a strange, battleful existence.

The youth's regiment was marched to relieve a command that had lain long in some damp trenches. The men took positions behind a curving line of rifle pits that had been turned up, like a large furrow, along the line of woods. Before them was a level stretch, peopled with short, deformed stumps. From the woods beyond came the dull popping of the skirmishers and pickets, firing in the fog. From the right came the noise of a terrific fracas.

The men cuddled behind the small embankment and sat in easy attitudes awaiting their turn. Many had their backs to the firing. The youth's friend lay down, buried his face in his arms, and almost instantly, it seemed, he was in a deep sleep.

The youth leaned his breast against the brown dirt and peered over at the woods and up and down the line. Curtains of trees interfered with his ways of vision. He could see the low line of trenches but for a short distance. A few idle flags were perched on the dirt hills. Behind them were rows of dark bodies with a few heads sticking curiously over the top.

Always the noise of skirmishers came from the woods on the front and left, and the din on the right had grown to frightful proportions. The guns were roaring without an instant's pause for breath. It seemed that the cannon had come from all parts and were engaged in a stupendous wrangle. It became impossible to make a sentence heard.

The youth wished to launch a joke—a quotation from newspapers. He desired to say, "All quiet on the Rappahannock,"[2] but the guns refused to permit even a comment upon their uproar. He never successfully concluded the sentence. But at last the guns stopped, and among the men in the rifle pits rumors again flew, like birds, but they were now for the most part black creatures who flapped their wings drearily near to the ground and refused to rise on any wings of

---

2. Rappahannock (rap′ ə han′ ək): A river in northeastern Virginia.

hope. The men's faces grew doleful from the interpreting of omens. Tales of hesitation and uncertainty on the part of those high in place and responsibility came to their ears. Stories of disaster were borne into their minds with many proofs. This din of musketry on the right, growing like a released genie of sound, expressed and emphasized the army's plight.

The men were disheartened and began to mutter. They made gestures expressive of the sentence: "Ah, what more can we do?" And it could always be seen that they were bewildered by the alleged news and could not fully comprehend a defeat.

Before the gray mists had been totally obliterated by the sunrays, the regiment was marching in a spread column that was retiring carefully through the woods. The disordered, hurrying lines of the enemy could sometimes be seen down through the groves and little fields. They were yelling, shrill and exultant.

At this sight the youth forgot many personal matters and became greatly enraged. He exploded in loud sentences. "B'jiminey, we're generaled by a lot 'a lunkheads."

"More than one feller has said that t'-day," observed a man.

His friend, recently aroused, was still very drowsy. He looked behind him until his mind took in the meaning of the movement. Then he sighed. "Oh, well, I s'pose we got licked," he remarked sadly.

The youth had a thought that it would not be handsome for him to freely condemn other men. He made an attempt to restrain himself, but the words upon his tongue were too bitter. He presently began a long and intricate denunciation of the commander of the forces.

"Mebbe, it wa'n't all his fault—not all together. He did th' best he knowed. It's our luck t' git licked often," said his friend in a weary tone. He was trudging along with stooped shoulders and shifting eyes like a man who has been caned and kicked.

"Well, don't we fight like the devil? Don't we do all that men can?" demanded the youth loudly.

He was secretly dumbfounded at this sentiment when it came from his lips. For a moment his face lost its valor and he looked guiltily about him. But no one questioned his right to deal in such words, and presently he recovered his air of courage. He went on to repeat a statement he had heard going from group to group at the camp that morning. "The brigadier said he never saw a new reg'ment fight the way we fought yestirday, didn' he? And we didn't do better than any another reg'ment, did we? Well, then, you can't say it's th' army's fault, can you?"

In his reply, the friend's voice was stern. "'A course not," he said. "No man dare say we don't fight like th' devil. No man will ever dare say it. But still—still, we don't have no luck."

"Well, then, if we fight like the devil an' don't ever whip, it must be the general's fault," said the youth grandly and decisively. "And I don't see any sense in fighting and fighting and fighting, yet always losing through some derned old lunkhead of a general."

A sarcastic man who was tramping at the youth's side then spoke lazily. "Mebbe yeh think yeh fit th' hull battle yestirday, Fleming," he remarked.

The speech pierced the youth. Inwardly he was reduced to an abject pulp by these chance words. His legs quaked privately. He cast a frightened glance at the sarcastic man.

"Why, no," he hastened to say in a conciliating voice, "I don't think I fought the whole battle yesterday."

But the other seemed innocent of any deeper meaning. Apparently, he had no information. It was merely his habit. "Oh!" he replied in the same tone of calm derision.

The youth, nevertheless, felt a threat. His mind shrank from going nearer to the danger, and thereafter he was silent. The significance of the sarcastic man's words took from him all loud moods that would make him appear prominent. He became suddenly a modest person.

There was low-toned talk among the troops. The officers were impatient and snappy, their countenances clouded with the tales of misfortune. The troops, sifting through the forest, were sullen. In the youth's company once a man's laugh rang out. A dozen soldiers turned their faces quickly toward him and frowned with vague displeasure.

The noise of firing dogged their footsteps. Sometimes, it seemed to be driven a little way, but it always returned again with increased insolence. The men muttered and cursed, throwing black looks in its direction.

In a clear space the troops were at last halted. Regiments and brigades, broken and detached through their encounters with thickets, grew together again and lines were faced toward the pursuing bark of the enemy's infantry.

This noise, following like the yellings of eager, metallic hounds, increased to a loud and joyous burst, and then, as the sun went serenely up the sky, throwing illuminating rays into the gloomy thickets, it broke forth into prolonged pealings. The woods began to crackle as if afire.

"Whoop-a-dadee," said a man, "here we are! Everybody fightin'. Blood an' destruction."

"I was willin' t' bet they'd attack as soon as th' sun got fairly up," savagely asserted the lieutenant who commanded the youth's company. He jerked without mercy at his little mustache. He strode to and fro with dark dignity in the rear of his men, who were lying down behind whatever protection they had collected.

A battery had trundled into position in the rear and was thoughtfully shelling the distance. The regiment, unmolested as yet, awaited the moment when the gray shadows of the woods before them should be slashed by the lines of flame. There was much growling and swearing.

The youth grumbled, "We're always being chased around like rats! It makes me sick. Nobody seems to know where we go or why we go. We just get fired around from pillar to post and get licked here and get licked there, and nobody knows what it's done for. It makes a man feel like a kitten in a bag. Now, I'd like to know what the eternal thunders we was marched into these woods for anyhow, unless it was to give the rebs a regular pot shot at us. We came in here and got our legs all tangled up in these cussed briers, and then we begin to fight and the rebs had an easy time of it. Don't tell me it's just luck! I know better. It's this derned old—"

The friend seemed jaded, but he interrupted his comrade with a voice of calm confidence. "It'll turn out all right in th' end," he said.

"Oh, the devil it will! Don't tell me! I know—"

At this time there was an interposition by the savage-minded lieutenant, who was obliged to vent some of his inward dissatisfaction upon his men. "You boys shut right up! There no need 'a your wastin' your breath in long-winded arguments about this an' that an' th' other. You've been jawin' like a lot 'a old hens. All you've got t' do is to fight, an' you'll get plenty 'a that t' do in about ten minutes. Less talkin' an' more fightin' is what's best for you boys. I never saw sech gabbling jackasses."

He paused, ready to pounce upon any man who might have the temerity to reply. No words being said, he resumed his dignified pacing.

"There's too much chin music an' too little fightin' in this war, anyhow," he said to them, turning his head for a final remark.

The day had grown more white, until the sun shed his full radiance upon the thronged forest. A sort of a gust of battle came sweeping toward that part of the line where lay the youth's regiment. The front shifted a trifle to meet it squarely. There was a wait. In this part of the field there passed slowly the intense moments that precede the tempest.

A single rifle flashed in a thicket before the regiment. In an instant it was joined by many others. There was a mighty song of clashes and crashes that went sweeping through the woods. The guns in the rear, aroused and enraged by shells that had been thrown burrlike at them, suddenly involved themselves in a hideous altercation with another band of guns. The battle roar settled to a rolling thunder, which was a single long explosion.

In the regiment there was a peculiar kind of hesitation denoted in the attitudes of the men. They were worn, exhausted, having slept but little and labored much. They rolled their eyes toward the advancing battle as they stood awaiting the shock. Some shrank and flinched. They stood as men tied to stakes.

Chapter Seventeen

This advance of the enemy had seemed to the youth like a ruthless hunting. He began to fume with rage and exasperation. He beat his foot upon the ground, and scowled with hate at the swirling smoke that was approaching like a phantom flood. There was a maddening quality in this seeming resolution of the foe to give him no rest, to give him no time to sit down and think. Yesterday he had fought and had fled rapidly. There had been many adventures. For today he felt that he had earned opportunities for contemplative repose. He could have enjoyed portraying to uninitiated listeners various scenes at which he had been a witness or ably discussing the processes of war with other proved men. Too it was important that he should have time for physical recuperation. He was sore and stiff from his experiences. He had received his fill of all exertions, and he wished to rest.

But those other men seemed never to grow weary; they were fighting with their old speed. He had a wild hate for the relentless foe. Yesterday, when he had imagined the universe to be against him, he had hated it; today he hated the army of the foe with the same great hatred. He was not going to be badgered of his life, like a kitten chased by boys, he said. It was not well to drive men into final corners; at those moments they could all develop teeth and claws.

He leaned and spoke into his friend's ear. He menaced the woods with a gesture. "If they keep on chasing us, they'd better watch out. Can't stand *too* much."

The friend twisted his head and made a calm reply. "If they keep on a-chasin' us they'll drive us all inteh th' river."

The youth cried out savagely at this statement. He crouched behind a little tree, with his eyes burning hatefully and his teeth set in a curlike snarl. The awkward bandage was still about his head, and upon it, over his wound, there was a spot of dry blood. His hair was wondrously tousled, and some straggling, moving locks hung over the cloth of the bandage down toward his forehead. His jacket and shirt were open at the throat, and exposed his young bronzed neck. There could be seen spasmodic gulpings at his throat.

His fingers twined nervously about his rifle. He wished that it was an engine of annihilating power. He felt that he and his companions were being taunted and derided from sincere convictions that they were poor and puny. His knowledge of his inability to take vengeance for it made his rage into a dark and stormy specter, that possessed him and made him dream of abominable cruelties. The tormentors were flies sucking insolently at his blood, and he thought that he would have given his life for a revenge of seeing their faces in pitiful plights.

The winds of battle had swept all about the regiment, until the one rifle, instantly followed by others, flashed in its front. A moment later the regiment roared forth its sudden and valiant retort. A dense wall of smoke settled slowly down. It was furiously slit and slashed by the knifelike fire from the rifles.

To the youth the fighters resembled animals tossed for a death struggle into a dark pit. There was a sensation that he and his fellows, at bay, were pushing back, always pushing fierce onslaughts of creatures who were slippery. Their beams of crimson seemed to get no purchase upon the bodies of their foes; the latter seemed to evade them with ease, and come through, between, around, and about with unopposed skill.

When, in a dream, it occurred to the youth that his rifle was an impotent stick, he lost sense of everything but his hate, his desire to smash into pulp the glittering smile of victory which he could feel upon the faces of his enemies.

The blue smoke-swallowed line curled and writhed like a snake stepped upon. It swung its ends to and fro in an agony of fear and rage.

The youth was not conscious that he was erect upon his feet. He did not know the direction of the ground. Indeed, once he even lost the habit of balance and fell heavily. He was up again immediately. One thought went through the chaos of his brain at the time. He wondered if he had fallen because he had been shot. But the suspicion flew away at once. He did not think more of it.

He had taken up a first position behind the little tree, with a direct determination to hold it against the world. He had not deemed it possible that his army could that day succeed, and from this he felt the ability to fight harder. But the throng had surged in all ways, until he lost directions and locations, save that he knew where lay the enemy.

The flames bit him, and the hot smoke broiled his skin. His rifle barrel grew so hot that ordinarily he could not have borne it upon his palms; but he kept on stuffing cartridges into it, and pounding them with his clanking, bending ramrod. If he aimed at some changing form through the smoke, he pulled his trigger with a fierce grunt, as if he were dealing a blow of the fist with all his strength.

When the enemy seemed falling back before him and his fellows, he went instantly forward, like a dog who, seeing his foes lagging, turns and insists upon being pursued. And when he was compelled to retire again, he did it slowly, sullenly, taking steps of wrathful despair.

Once he, in his intent hate, was almost alone, and was firing, when all those near him had ceased. He was so engrossed in his occupation that he was not aware of a lull.

He was recalled by a hoarse laugh and sentence that came to his ears in a voice of contempt and amazement. "Yeh infernal fool, don't yeh know enough t' quit when there ain't anything t' shoot at?"

He turned then and, pausing with his rifle thrown half into position, looked at the blue line of his comrades. During this moment of leisure they seemed all to be engaged in staring with astonishment at him. They had become spectators. Turning to the front again he saw, under the lifted smoke, a deserted ground.

He looked bewildered for a moment. Then there appeared upon the glazed vacancy of his eyes a diamond point of intelligence. "Oh," he said, comprehending.

He returned to his comrades and threw himself upon the ground. He sprawled like a man who had been thrashed. His flesh seemed strangely on fire, and the sounds of the battle continued in his ears. He groped blindly for his canteen.

The lieutenant was crowing. He seemed drunk with fighting. He called out to the youth: "By heavens, if I had ten thousand wildcats like you I could tear th' stomach outa this war in less'n a week!" He puffed out his chest with large dignity as he said it.

Some of the men muttered and looked at the youth in awestruck ways. It was plain that as he had gone on loading and firing and cursing without the proper intermission, they had found time to regard him. And they now looked upon him as a war devil.

The friend came staggering to him. There was some fright and dismay in his voice. "Are yeh all right, Fleming? Do yeh feel all right? There ain't nothin' th' matter with yeh, Henry, is there?"

"No," said the youth with difficulty. His throat seemed full of knobs and burrs.

These incidents made the youth ponder. It was revealed to him that he had been a barbarian, a beast. Regarding it, he saw that it was fine, wild, and, in some ways, easy. He had been a tremendous figure, no doubt. By this struggle he had overcome obstacles which he had admitted to be mountains. They had fallen like paper peaks, and he was now what he called a hero. And he had not been aware of the process. He had slept and, awakening, found himself a knight.

He lay and basked in the occasional stares of his comrades. Their faces were varied in degrees of blackness from the burned powder. Some were utterly smudged. They were reeking with perspiration, and their breaths came hard and wheezing. And from these soiled expanses they peered at him.

"Hot work! Hot work!" cried the lieutenant deliriously. He walked up and down, restless and eager. Sometimes his voice could be heard in a wild, incomprehensible laugh.

When he had a particularly profound thought upon the science of war he always unconsciously addressed himself to the youth.

There was some grim rejoicing by the men. "By thunder, I bet this army'll never see another new reg'ment like us!"

"You bet!"

"Lost a piler men, they did. If an ol' woman swep' up th' woods she'd git a dustpanful."

"Yes, an' if she'll come around ag'in in 'bout an hour she'll git a pile more."

The forest still bore its burden of clamor. From off under the trees came the rolling clatter of the musketry. Each distant thicket seemed a strange porcupine with quills of flame. A cloud of dark smoke, as from smoldering ruins, went up toward the sun now bright and gay in the blue-enameled sky.

Chapter Eighteen

The ragged line had respite for some minutes, but during its pause the struggle in the forest became magnified until the trees seemed to quiver from the firing and the ground to shake from the rushing of the men. The voices of the cannon were mingled in a long and interminable row. It seemed difficult to live in such an atmosphere. The chests of the men strained for a bit of freshness, and their throats craved water.

There was one shot through the body, who raised a cry of bitter lamentation when came this lull. Perhaps he had been calling out during the fighting also, but at that time no one had heard him. But now the men turned at the woeful complaints of him upon the ground.

"Who is it? Who is it?"

"It's Jimmie Rogers. Jimmie Rogers."

When their eyes first encountered him there was a sudden halt, as if they feared to go near. He was thrashing about in the grass, twisting his shuddering body into many strange postures. He was screaming loudly. This instant's hesitation seemed to fill him with a tremendous, fantastic contempt.

The youth's friend had a geographical illusion concerning a stream, and he obtained permission to go for some water. Immediately canteens were showered upon him. "Fill mine, will yeh?" "Bring me some, too." "And me, too." He departed, laden. The youth went with his friend, feeling a desire to throw his heated body onto the stream and, soaking there, drink quarts.

They made a hurried search for the supposed stream but did not find it. "No water here," said the youth. They turned without delay and began to retrace their steps.

From their position as they again faced toward the place of the fighting, they could of course comprehend a greater amount of the battle than when their visions had been blurred by the hurling smoke of the line. They could see dark stretches winding along the land, and on one cleared space there was

a row of guns making gray clouds, which were filled with large flashes of orange-colored flame. Over some foliage they could see the roof of a house. One window, glowing a deep murder red, shone squarely through the leaves. From the edifice a tall leaning tower of smoke went far into the sky.

Looking over their own troops, they saw mixed masses slowly getting into regular form. The sunlight made twinkling points of the bright steel. To the rear there was a glimpse of a distant roadway as it curved over a slope. It was crowded with retreating infantry. From all the interwoven forest arose the smoke and bluster of the battle. The air was always occupied by a blaring.

Near where they stood shells were flip-flapping and hooting. Occasional bullets buzzed in the air and spanged into tree trunks. Wounded men and other stragglers were slinking through the woods.

Looking down an aisle of the grove, the youth and his companion saw a jangling general and his staff almost ride upon a wounded man who was crawling on his hands and knees. The general reined strongly at his charger's opened and foamy mouth and guided it with dexterous horsemanship past the man. The latter scrambled in wild and torturing haste. His strength evidently failed him as he reached a place of safety. One of his arms suddenly weakened, and he fell, sliding over upon his back. He lay stretched out, breathing gently.

A moment later the small, creaking cavalcade was directly in front of the two soldiers. Another officer, riding with the skillful abandon of a cowboy, galloped his horse to a position directly before the general. The two unnoticed foot soldiers made a little show of going on, but they lingered near in the desire to overhear the conversation. Perhaps, they thought, some great inner historical things would be said.

The general, whom the boys knew as the commander of their division, looked at the other officer and spoke coolly, as if he were criticizing his clothes. "Th' enemy's formin' over there for another charge," he said. "It'll be directed against Whiterside, an' I fear they'll break through there unless we work like thunder t' stop them."

The other swore at his restive horse, and then cleared his throat. He made a gesture toward his cap. "It'll be hell t' pay stoppin' them," he said shortly.

"I presume so," remarked the general. Then he began to talk rapidly and in a lower tone. He frequently illustrated his words with a pointing finger. The two infantrymen could hear nothing until finally he asked: "What troops can you spare?"

The officer who rode like a cowboy reflected for an instant. "Well," he said, "I had to order in th' 12th to help th' 76th, an' I haven't really got any. But there's th' 304th. They fight like a lot 'a mule drivers. I can spare them best of any."

The youth and his friend exchanged glances of astonishment.

The general spoke sharply. "Get 'em ready, then. I'll watch developments from here, an' send you word when t' start them. It'll happen in five minutes."

As the other officer tossed his fingers toward his cap and, wheeling his horse, started away, the general called out to him in a sober voice: "I don't believe many of your mule drivers will get back."

The other shouted something in reply. He smiled.

With scared faces, the youth and his companion hurried back to the line.

These happenings had occupied an incredibly short time, yet the youth felt that in them he had been made aged. New eyes were given to him. And the most startling thing was to learn suddenly that he was very insignificant. The officer spoke of the regiment as if he referred to a broom. Some part of the woods needed sweeping, perhaps, and he merely indicated a broom in a tone properly indifferent to its fate. It was war, no doubt, but it appeared strange.

As the two boys approached the line, the lieutenant perceived them and swelled with wrath. "Fleming—Wilson—how long does it take yeh to git water, anyhow—where yeh been to?"

But his oration ceased as he saw their eyes, which were large with great tales. "We're goin' t' charge—we're goin' t' charge!" cried the youth's friend, hastening with his news.

"Charge?" said the lieutenant. "Charge? Now; this is real fightin'." Over his soiled countenance there went a boastful smile.

A little group of soldiers surrounded the two youths. "Are we, sure 'nough? Well, I'll be derned! Charge? What fer? What at? Wilson, you're lyin'."

"I hope to die," said the youth's friend, pitching his tones to the key of angry remonstrance. "Sure as shooting, I tell you."

And the youth spoke in reinforcement. "Not by a blame sight, he ain't lyin'. We heard 'em talkin'."

They caught sight of two mounted figures a short distance from them. One was the colonel of the regiment and the other was the officer who had received orders from the commander of the division. They were gesticulating at each other. The soldier, pointing at them, interpreted the scene.

One man had a final objection: "How could yeh hear 'em talkin'?" But the men, for a large part, nodded, admitting that previously the two friends had spoken truth.

They settled back into reposeful attitudes with airs of having accepted the matter. And they mused upon it, with a hundred varieties of expression. It was an engrossing thing to think about. Many tightened their belts carefully and hitched at their trousers.

A moment later the officers began to bustle among the men, pushing them into a more compact mass and into a better alignment. They chased those that straggled and fumed at a few men who seemed to show by their attitudes that they had decided to remain at that spot. They were like critical shepherds struggling with sheep.

Presently, the regiment seemed to draw itself up and heave a deep breath. None of the men's faces were mirrors of large thoughts. The soldiers were bended and stooped like sprinters before a signal. Many pairs of glinting eyes peered from the grimy faces toward the curtains of the deeper woods. They seemed to be engaged in deep calculations of time and distance.

They were surrounded by the noises of the monstrous altercation between the two armies. The world was fully interested in other matters. Apparently, the regiment had its small affair to itself.

The youth, turning, shot a quick, inquiring glance at his friend. The latter returned to him the same manner of look. They were the only ones who possessed an inner knowledge. "Mule drivers—hell t' pay—don't believe many will get back." It was an ironical secret. Still, they saw no hesitation in each other's faces, and they nodded a mute and unprotesting assent when a shaggy man near them said in a meek voice: "We'll git swallowed."

Chapter Nineteen

The youth stared at the land in front of him. Its foliage now seemed to veil powers and horrors. He was unaware of the machinery of orders that started the charge, although from the corners of his eyes he saw an officer, who looked like a boy a-horseback, come galloping, waving his hat. Suddenly he felt a straining and heaving among the men. The line fell slowly forward like a toppling wall, and, with a convulsive gasp that was intended for a cheer, the regiment began its journey. The youth was pushed and jostled for a moment before he understood the movement at all, but directly he lunged ahead and began to run.

He fixed his eye upon a distant and prominent clump of trees where he had concluded the enemy were to be met, and he ran toward it as toward a goal. He had believed throughout that it was a mere question of getting over an unpleasant matter as quickly as possible, and he ran desperately, as if pursued for a murder. His face was drawn hard and tight with the stress of his endeavor. His eyes were fixed in a lurid glare. And with his soiled and disordered dress, his red and inflamed features surmounted by the dingy rag with its spot of blood, his wildly swinging rifle and banging accouterments, he looked to be an insane soldier.

As the regiment swung from its position out into a cleared space the woods and thickets before it awakened. Yellow flames leaped toward it from many directions. The forest made a tremendous objection.

The line lurched straight for a moment. Then the right wing swung forward; it in turn was surpassed by the left. Afterward the center careered to the front until the regiment was a wedge-shaped mass, but an instant later the opposition of the bushes, trees, and uneven places on the ground split the command and scattered it into detached clusters.

The youth, light-footed, was unconsciously in advance. His eyes still kept note of the clump of trees. From all places near it the clannish yell of the enemy could be heard. The little flames of rifles leaped from it. The song of the bullets was in the air and shells snarled among the treetops. One tumbled directly into the middle of a hurrying group and exploded in crimson fury. There was an instant's spectacle of a man, almost over it, throwing up his hands to shield his eyes.

Other men, punched by bullets, fell in grotesque agonies. The regiment left a coherent trail of bodies.

They had passed into a clearer atmosphere. There was an effect like a revelation in the new appearance of the landscape.

Some men working madly at a battery were plain to them, and the opposing infantry's lines were defined by the gray walls and fringes of smoke.

It seemed to the youth that he saw everything. Each blade of the green grass was bold and clear. He thought that he was aware of every change in the thin, transparent vapor that floated idly in sheets. The brown or gray trunks of the trees showed each roughness of their surfaces. And the men of the regiment, with their starting eyes and sweating faces, running madly, or falling, as if thrown headlong, to queer, heaped-up corpses—all were comprehended. His mind took a mechanical but firm impression, so that afterward everything was pictured and explained to him, save why he himself was there.

But there was a frenzy made from this furious rush. The men, picking forward insanely, had burst into cheerings, moblike and barbaric, but tuned in strange keys that can arouse the dullard and the stoic. It made a mad enthusiasm that, it seemed, would be incapable of checking itself before granite and brass. There was the delirium that encounters despair and death, and is heedless and blind to the odds. It is a temporary but sublime absence of selfishness. And because it was of this order was the reason, perhaps, why the youth wondered, afterward, what reasons he could have had for being there.

Presently the straining pace ate up the energies of the men. As if by agreement, the leaders began to slacken their speed. The volleys directed against them had had a seeming windlike effect. The regiment snorted and blew. Among some stolid trees it began to falter and hesitate. The men, staring intently, began to wait for some of the distant walls of smoke to move and disclose to them the scene. Since much of their strength and their breath had vanished, they returned to caution. They were become men again.

The youth had a vague belief that he had run miles, and he thought, in a way, that he was now in some new and unknown land.

The moment the regiment ceased its advance the protesting splutter of musketry became a steadied roar. Long and accurate fringes of smoke spread out. From the top of a small hill came level belchings of yellow flame that caused an inhuman whistling in the air.

The men halted, had opportunity to see some of their comrades dropping with moans and shrieks. A few lay under foot, still or wailing. And now for an instant the men stood, their rifles slack in their hands, and watched the regiment dwindle. They appeared dazed and stupid. This spectacle seemed to paralyze them, overcome them with a fatal fascination. They stared woodenly at the sights, and, lowering their eyes, looked from face to face. It was a strange pause, and a strange silence.

Then, above the sounds of the outside commotion, arose the roar of the lieutenant. He strode suddenly forth, his infantile features black with rage.

"Come on, yeh fools!" he bellowed. "Come on! Yeh can't stay here. Yeh must come on." He said more, but much of it could not be understood.

He started rapidly forward, with his head turned toward the men. "Come on," he was shouting. The men stared with blank and yokel-like eyes at him. He was obliged to halt and retrace his steps. He stood then with his back to the enemy and delivered gigantic curses into the faces of the men. His body vibrated from the weight and force of his imprecations. And he could string oaths with the facility of a maiden who strings beads.

The friend of the youth aroused. Lurching suddenly forward and dropping to his knees, he fired an angry shot at the persistent woods. This action awakened the men. They huddled no more like sheep. They seemed suddenly to bethink them of their weapons, and at once commenced firing. Belabored by their officers, they began to move forward. The regiment, involved like a cart involved in mud and muddle, started unevenly with many jolts and jerks. The men stopped now every few paces to fire and load, and in this manner moved slowly on from trees to trees.

The flaming opposition in their front grew with their advance until it seemed that all forward ways were barred by the thin leaping tongues, and off to the right an ominous demonstration could sometimes be dimly discerned. The smoke lately generated was in confusing clouds that made it difficult for the regiment to proceed with intelligence. As he passed through each curling mass the youth wondered what would confront him on the farther side.

The command went painfully forward until an open space interposed between them and the lurid lines. Here, crouching and cowering behind some trees, the men clung with desperation, as if threatened by a wave. They looked wild-eyed, and as if amazed at this furious disturbance they had stirred. In the storm there was an ironical expression of their importance. The faces of the men, too, showed a lack of a certain feeling of responsibility for being there. It was as if they had been driven. It was the dominant animal failing to remember in the supreme moments the forceful causes of various superficial qualities. The whole affair seemed incomprehensible to many of them.

As they halted thus the lieutenant again began to bellow profanely. Regardless of the vindictive threats of the bullets, he went about coaxing and berating. His lips, that were habitually in a soft and childlike curve, were now writhed into contortions. He swore by all possible deities.

Once he grabbed the youth by the arm. "Come on, yeh lunkhead!" he roared. "Come on! We'll all git killed if we stay here. We've on'y got t' go across that lot. An' then"—the remainder of his idea disappeared in a blue haze of curses.

The youth stretched forth his arm.

"Cross there?" His mouth was puckered in doubt and awe.

"Certainly. Jest 'cross th' lot! We can't stay here," screamed the lieutenant. He poked his face close to the youth and waved his bandaged hand. "Come on!" Presently he grappled with him as if for a wrestling bout. It was as if he planned to drag the youth by the ear on to the assault.

The private felt a sudden unspeakable indignation against his officer. He wrenched fiercely and shook him off.

"Come on yerself, then," he yelled. There was a bitter challenge in his voice.

They galloped together down the regimental front. The friend scrambled after them. In front of the colors the three men began to bawl: "Come on! come on!" They danced and gyrated like tortured savages.

The flag, obedient to these appeals, bended its glittering form and swept toward them. The men wavered in indecision for a moment, and then with a long, wailful cry the dilapidated regiment surged forward and began its new journey.

Over the field went the scurrying mass. It was a handful of men splattered into the faces of the enemy. Toward it instantly sprang the yellow tongues. A vast quantity of blue smoke hung before them. A mighty banging made ears valueless.

The youth ran like a madman to reach the woods before a bullet could discover him. He ducked his head low, like a football player. In his haste his eyes almost closed, and the scene was a wild blur. Pulsating saliva stood at the corners of his mouth.

Within him, as he hurled himself forward, was born a love, a despairing fondness for this flag which was near him. It was a creation of beauty and invulnerability. It was a goddess, radiant, that bended its form with an imperious gesture to him. It was a woman, red and white, hating and loving, that called him with the voice of his hopes. Because no harm could come to it he endowed it with power. He kept near, as if it could be a saver of lives, and an imploring cry went from his mind.

In the mad scramble he was aware that the color sergeant[3] flinched suddenly, as if struck by a bludgeon. He faltered, and then became motionless, save for his quivering knees.

He made a spring and a clutch at the pole. At the same instant his friend grabbed it from the other side. They jerked at it, stout and furious, but the color sergeant was dead, and the corpse would not relinquish its trust. For a moment there was a grim encounter. The dead man, swinging with bended back, seemed to be obstinately tugging, in ludicrous and awful ways, for the possession of the flag.

It was past in an instant of time. They wrenched the flag furiously from the dead man, and, as they turned again, the corpse swayed forward with bowed head. One arm swung high, and the curved hand fell with heavy protest on the friend's unheeding shoulder.

Chapter Twenty

When the two youths turned with the flag they saw that much of the regiment had crumbled away, and the dejected remnant was coming back. The men, having hurled themselves in projectile fashion, had presently expended their forces. They slowly retreated, with their faces still toward the spluttering woods, and their hot rifles still replying to the din. Several officers were giving orders, their voices keyed to screams.

"Where yeh goin'?" the lieutenant was asking in a sarcastic howl. And a red-bearded officer, whose voice of triple brass[4] could plainly be heard, was commanding: "Shoot into 'em! Shoot into 'em!" There was a melee[5] of screeches, in which the men were ordered to do conflicting and impossible things.

---

3. color sergeant: Flag bearer.
4. triple brass: Strength and power.
5. melee (mā′ lā) *n*.: A noisy, confused fight.

The youth and his friend had a small scuffle over the flag. "Give it t' me!" "No, let me keep it!" Each felt satisfied with the other's possession of it, but each felt bound to declare, by an offer to carry the emblem, his willingness to further risk himself. The youth roughly pushed his friend away.

The regiment fell back to the stolid trees. There it halted for a moment to blaze at some dark forms that had begun to steal upon its track. Presently it resumed its march again, curving among the tree trunks. By the time the depleted regiment had again reached the first open space they were receiving a fast and merciless fire. There seemed to be mobs all about them.

The greater part of the men, discouraged, their spirits worn by the turmoil, acted as if stunned. They accepted the pelting of the bullets with bowed and weary heads. It was of no purpose to strive against walls. It was of no use to batter themselves against granite. And from this consciousness that they had attempted to conquer an unconquerable thing there seemed to arise a feeling that they had been betrayed. They glowered with bent brows, but dangerously, upon some of the officers, more particularly upon the red-bearded one with the voice of triple brass.

However, the rear of the regiment was fringed with men, who continued to shoot irritably at the advancing foes. They seemed resolved to make every trouble. The youthful lieutenant was perhaps the last man in the disordered mass. His forgotten back was toward the enemy. He had been shot in the arm. It hung straight and rigid. Occasionally he would cease to remember it, and be about to emphasize an oath with a sweeping gesture. The multiplied pain caused him to swear with incredible power.

The youth went along with slipping, uncertain feet. He kept watchful eyes rearward. A scowl of mortification and rage was upon his face. He had thought of a fine revenge upon the officer who had referred to him and his fellows as mule drivers. But he saw that it could not come to pass. His dreams had collapsed when the mule drivers, dwindling rapidly, had wavered and hesitated on the little clearing, and then had recoiled. And now the retreat of the mule drivers was a march of shame to him.

A dagger-pointed gaze from without his blackened face was held toward the enemy, but his greater hatred was riveted upon the man, who, not knowing him, had called him a mule driver.

When he knew that he and his comrades had failed to do anything in successful ways that might bring the little pangs of a kind of remorse upon the officer, the youth allowed the rage of the baffled to possess him. This cold officer upon a monument, who dropped epithets unconcernedly down, would be finer as a dead man, he thought. So grievous did he think it that he could never possess the secret right to taunt truly in answer.

He had pictured red letters of curious revenge. "We *are* mule drivers, are we?" And now he was compelled to throw them away.

He presently wrapped his head in the cloak of his pride and kept the flag erect. He harangued his fellows, pushing against their chests with his free hand. To those he knew well he made frantic appeals, beseeching them by name. Between him and the lieutenant, scolding and near to losing his mind with rage, there was felt a subtle fellowship and equality. They supported each other in all manner of hoarse, howling protests.

But the regiment was a machine run down. The two men babbled at a forceless thing. The soldiers who had heart to go slowly were continually shaken in their resolves by a knowledge that comrades were slipping with speed back to the lines. It was difficult to think of reputation when others were thinking of skins. Wounded men were left crying on this black journey.

The smoke fringes and flames blustered always. The youth, peering once through a sudden rift in a cloud, saw a brown mass of troops, interwoven and magnified until they appeared to be thousands. A fierce-hued flag flashed before his vision.

Immediately, as if the uplifting of the smoke had been prearranged, the discovered troops burst into a rasping yell, and a hundred flames jetted toward the retreating band. A rolling gray cloud again interposed as the regiment doggedly replied. The youth had to depend again upon his misused ears, which were trembling and buzzing from the melee of musketry and yells.

The way seemed eternal. In the clouded haze men became panic-stricken with the thought that the regiment had lost its path, and was proceeding in a perilous direction. Once the men who headed the wild procession turned and came pushing back against their comrades, screaming that they were being fired upon from points which they had considered to be toward their own lines. At this cry a hysterical fear and dismay beset the troops. A soldier, who heretofore had been ambitious to make the regiment into a wise little band that would proceed calmly amid the huge-appearing difficulties, suddenly sank down and buried his face in his arms with an air of bowing to a doom. From another a shrill lamentation rang out filled with profane illusions to a general. Men ran hither and thither, seeking with their eyes roads of escape. With serene regularity, as if controlled by a schedule, bullets buffed into men.

The youth walked stolidly into the midst of the mob, and with his flag in his hands took a stand as if he expected an attempt to push him to the ground. He unconsciously assumed the attitude of the color bearer in the fight of the preceding day. He passed over his brow a hand that trembled. His breath did not come freely. He was choking during this small wait for the crisis.

His friend came to him. "Well, Henry, I guess this is good-bye—John."

"Oh, shut up, you fool!" replied the youth, and he would not look at the other.

The officers labored like politicians to beat the mass into a proper circle to face the menaces. The ground was uneven and torn. The men curled into depressions and fitted themselves snugly behind whatever would frustrate a bullet.

The youth noted with vague surprise that the lieutenant was standing mutely with his legs far apart and his sword held in the manner of a cane. The youth wondered what had happened to his vocal organs that he no more cursed. There was something curious in this little intent pause of the lieutenant. He was like a babe which, having wept its fill, raises its eyes and fixes them upon a distant toy. He was engrossed in this contemplation, and the soft underlip quivered from self-whispered words.

Some lazy and ignorant smoke curled slowly. The men, hiding from the bullets, waited anxiously for it to lift and disclose the plight of the regiment.

The silent ranks were suddenly thrilled by the eager voice of the youthful lieutenant bawling out: "Here they come! Right on to us!" His further words were lost in a roar of wicked thunder from the men's rifles.

The youth's eyes had instantly turned in the direction indicated by the awakened and agitated lieutenant, and he had seen the haze of treachery disclosing a body of soldiers of the enemy. They were so near that he could see their features. There was a recognition as he looked at the types of faces. Also he perceived with dim amazement that their uniforms were rather gay in effect, being light gray, accented with a brilliant-hued facing. Moreover, the clothes seemed new.

These troops had apparently been going forward with caution, their rifles held in readiness, when the youthful lieutenant had discovered them and their movement had been interrupted by the volley from the blue regiment. From the moment's glimpse, it was derived that they had been unaware of the proximity of their dark-suited foes or had mistaken the direction. Almost instantly they were shut utterly from the youth's sight by the smoke from the energetic rifles of his companions. He strained his vision to learn the accomplishment of the volley, but the smoke hung before him.

The two bodies of troops exchanged blows in the manner of a pair of boxers. The fast angry firings went back and forth. The men in blue were intent with the despair of their circumstances and they seized upon the revenge to be had at close range. Their thunder swelled loud and valiant. Their curving front bristled with flashes and the place resounded with the clangor of their ramrods. The youth ducked and dodged for a time and achieved a few unsatisfactory views of the enemy. There appeared to be many of them and they were replying swiftly. They seemed moving toward the blue regiment, step by step. He seated himself gloomily on the ground with his flag between his knees.

As he noted the vicious, wolflike temper of his comrades he had a sweet thought that if the enemy was about to swallow the regimental broom as a large prisoner, it could at least have the consolation of going down with bristles forward.

But the blows of the antagonist began to grow more weak. Fewer bullets ripped the air, and finally, when the men slackened to learn of the fight, they could see only dark, floating smoke. The regiment lay still and gazed. Presently some chance whim came to the pestering blur, and it began to coil heavily away. The men saw a ground vacant of fighters. It would have been an empty stage if it were not for a few corpses that lay thrown and twisted into fantastic shapes upon the sward.

At sight of this tableau,[6] many of the men in blue sprang from behind their covers and made an ungainly dance of joy. Their

---

6. tableau (tab'lō) *n.*: A representation of a silent, motionless scene.

eyes burned and a hoarse cheer of elation broke from their dry lips.

It had begun to seem to them that events were trying to prove that they were impotent. These little battles had evidently endeavored to demonstrate that the men could not fight well. When on the verge of submission to these opinions, the small duel had showed them that the proportions were not impossible, and by it they had revenged themselves upon their misgivings and upon the foe.

The impetus of enthusiasm was theirs again. They gazed about them with looks of uplifted pride, feeling new trust in the grim, always confident weapons in their hands. And they were men.

Chapter Twenty-One

Presently they knew that no fighting threatened them. All ways seemed once more opened to them. The dusty blue lines of their friends were disclosed a short distance away. In the distance there were many colossal noises, but in all this part of the field there was a sudden stillness.

They perceived that they were free. The depleted band drew a long breath of relief and gathered itself into a bunch to complete its trip.

In this last length of journey the men began to show strange emotions. They hurried with nervous fear. Some who had been dark and unfaltering in the grimmest moments now could not conceal an anxiety that made them frantic. It was perhaps that they dreaded to be killed in insignificant ways after the times for proper military deaths had passed. Or, perhaps, they thought it would be too ironical to get killed at the portals of safety. With backward looks of perturbation, they hastened.

As they approached their own lines there was some sarcasm exhibited on the part of a gaunt and bronzed regiment that lay resting in the shade of trees. Questions were wafted to them.

"Where yeh been?"

"What yeh comin' back fer?"

"Why didn't yeh stay there?"

"Was it warm out there, sonny?"

"Goin' home now, boys?"

One shouted in taunting mimicry: "Oh, mother, come quick an' look at th' so'jers!"

There was no reply from the bruised and battered regiment, save that one man made broadcast challenges to fist fights and the red-bearded officer walked rather near and glared in great swashbuckler style at a tall captain in the other regiment. But the lieutenant suppressed the man who wished to fist fight, and the tall captain, flushing at the little fanfare of the red-bearded one, was obliged to look intently at some trees.

The youth's tender flesh was deeply stung by these remarks. From under his creased brows he glowered with hate at the mockers. He meditated upon a few revenges. Still, many in the regiment hung their heads in criminal fashion, so that it came to pass that the men trudged with sudden heaviness, as if they bore upon their bended shoulders the coffin of their honor. And the youthful lieutenant, recollecting himself, began to mutter softly in black curses.

They turned when they arrived at their old position to regard the ground over which they had charged.

The youth in this contemplation was smitten with a large astonishment. He discovered that the distances, as compared with the brilliant measurings of his mind, were trivial and ridiculous. The stolid trees, where much had taken place, seemed incredibly near. The time, too, now that he reflected, he saw to have been short. He wondered at the number of emotions and events that had been crowded into such little spaces. Elfin[7] thoughts must have exaggerated and enlarged everything, he said.

It seemed, then, that there was bitter justice in the speeches of the gaunt and

---

7. elfin *adj.*: Small.

bronzed veterans. He veiled a glance of disdain at his fellows who strewed the ground, choking with dust, red from perspiration, misty-eyed, disheveled.

They were gulping at their canteens, fierce to wring every mite of water from them, and they polished at their swollen and watery features with coat sleeves and bunches of grass.

However, to the youth there was a considerable joy in musing upon his performances during the charge. He had had very little time previously in which to appreciate himself, so that there was now much satisfaction in quietly thinking of his actions. He recalled bits of color that in the flurry had stamped themselves unawares upon his engaged senses.

As the regiment lay heaving from its hot exertions the officer who had named them as mule drivers came galloping along the line. He had lost his cap. His tousled hair streamed wildly, and his face was dark with vexation and wrath. His temper was displayed with more clearness by the way in which he managed his horse. He jerked and wrenched savagely at his bridle, stopping the hard-breathing animal with a furious pull near the colonel of the regiment. He immediately exploded in reproaches which came unbidden to the ears of the men. They were suddenly alert, being always curious about black words between officers.

"Oh, thunder, MacChesnay, what an awful bull[8] you made of this thing!" began the officer. He attempted low tones, but his indignation caused certain of the men to learn the sense of his words. "What an awful mess you made! Good Lord, man, you stopped a hundred feet this side of a very pretty success! If your men had gone a hundred feet farther you would have made a great charge, but as it is—what a lot of mud diggers you've got anyway!"

The men, listening with bated breath, now turned their curious eyes upon the colonel. They had a ragamuffin interest in this affair.

The colonel was seen to straighten his form and put one hand forth in oratorical fashion. He wore an injured air; it was as if a deacon[9] had been accused of stealing. The men were wiggling in an ecstasy of excitement.

But of a sudden the colonel's manner changed. He shrugged his shoulders. "Oh, well, general, we went as far as we could," he said calmly.

"As far as you could? Did you?" snorted the other. "Well, that wasn't very far, was it?" he added, with a glance of cold contempt into the other's eyes. "Not very far, I think. You were intended to make a diversion in favor of Whiterside. How well you succeeded your own ears can now tell you." He wheeled his horse and rode stiffly away.

The lieutenant, who had listened with an air of impotent rage to the interview, spoke suddenly in firm and undaunted tones. "I don't care what a man is—whether he is a general or what—if he says th' boys didn't put up a good fight out there he's a fool."

"Lieutenant," began the colonel, severely, "this is my own affair, and I'll trouble you—"

The lieutenant made an obedient gesture. "All right, colonel, all right," he said. He sat down with an air of being content with himself.

The news that the regiment had been reproached went along the line. For a time the men were bewildered by it. "Good thunder!" they ejaculated, staring at the vanishing form of the general. They conceived it to be a huge mistake.

Presently, however, they began to believe that in truth their efforts had been called light. The youth could see this conviction

---

8. **bull:** Slang for blunder.

9. **deacon** *n.*: A church officer who helps the priest or minister in certain Christian churches.

weigh upon the entire regiment until the men were like cuffed and cursed animals, but withal rebellious.

The friend, with a grievance in his eye, went to the youth. "I wonder what he does want," he said. "He must think we went out there an' played marbles! I never see sech a man!"

The youth developed a tranquil philosophy for these moments of irritation. "Oh, well," he rejoined, "he probably didn't see nothing of it at all and got mad as blazes, and concluded we were a lot of sheep, just because we didn't do what he wanted done. It's a pity old Grandpa Henderson got killed yesterday—he'd have known that we did our best and fought good. It's just our awful luck, that's what."

"I should say so," replied the friend. He seemed to be deeply wounded at an injustice. "I should say we did have awful luck! There's no fun in fightin' fer people when everything yeh do—no matter what—ain't done right. I have a notion t' stay behind next time an' let 'em take their ol' charge an' go t' th' devil with it."

The youth spoke soothingly to his comrade. "Well, we both did good. I'd like to see the fool what'd say we both didn't do as good as we could!"

"Of course we did," declared the friend stoutly. "An' I'd break th' feller's neck if he was as big as a church. But we're all right, anyhow, for I heard one feller say that we two fit th' best in th' reg'ment, an' they had a great argument 'bout it. Another feller, 'a course, he had t' up an' say it was a lie—he seen all what was goin' on an' he never seen us from th' beginnin' t' th' end. An' a lot more struck in an' ses it wasn't a lie—we did fight like thunder, an' they give us quite a send-off. But this is what I can't stand—these everlastin' ol' soldiers, titterin' an' laughin', an' then that general, he's crazy."

The youth exclaimed with sudden exasperation: "He's a lunkhead! He makes me mad. I wish he'd come along next time. We'd show 'im what—"

He ceased because several men had come hurrying up. Their faces expressed a bringing of great news.

"O Flem, yeh jest oughta heard!" cried one, eagerly.

"Heard what?" said the youth.

"Yeh jest oughta heard!" repeated the other, and he arranged himself to tell his tidings. The others made an excited circle. "Well, sir, th' colonel met your lieutenant right by us, an' he ses: 'Ahem! ahem!' he ses. 'Mr. Hasbrouck!' he ses, 'by th' way, who was that lad what carried th' flag?' he ses. There, Flemin', what d' yeh think 'a that? 'Who was th' lad what carried th' flag?' he ses, an' th' lieutenant, he speaks up right away: 'That's Flemin', an' he's a jimhickey,' he ses, right away. What? I say he did. 'A jimhickey,' he ses—those 'r his words. He did, too. I say he did. If you kin tell this story better than I kin, go ahead an' tell it. Well, then, keep yer mouth shet. Th' lieutenant, he ses: 'He's a jimhickey,' an' th' colonel, he ses: 'Ahem! ahem! he is, indeed, a very good man t' have, ahem! He kep' th' flag 'way t' th' front. I saw 'im. He's a good un,' ses th' colonel. 'You bet,' ses th' lieutenant, 'he an' a feller named Wilson was at th' head 'a th' charge, an' howlin' like Indians all th' time,' he ses. 'Head 'a th' charge all th' time,' he ses. 'A feller named Wilson,' he ses. There, Wilson, m'boy, put that in a letter an' send it hum t' yer mother, hay? 'A feller named Wilson,' he ses. An' th' colonel, he ses: "Were they, indeed? Ahem! ahem! My sakes!' he ses. 'At th' head 'a th' reg'ment?' he ses. 'They were,' ses th' lieutenant. 'My sakes!' ses th' colonel. He ses: 'Well, well, well,' he ses, 'those two babies?' 'They were,' ses th' lieutenant. 'Well, well,' ses th' colonel, 'they deserve t' be major generals,' he ses. 'They deserve t' be major generals.' "

The youth and his friend had said: "Huh!" "Yer lyin', Thompson." "Oh, go t' blazes!" "He never sed it." "Oh, what a lie!" "Huh!" But despite these youthful scoffings and embarrassments, they knew that their faces were deeply flushing from thrills of pleasure. They exchanged a secret glance of joy and congratulation.

They speedily forgot many things. The past held no pictures of error and disappointment. They were very happy, and their hearts swelled with grateful affection for the colonel and the youthful lieutenant.

Chapter Twenty-Two

When the woods again began to pour forth the dark-hued masses of the enemy the youth felt serene self-confidence. He smiled briefly when he saw men dodge and duck at the long screechings of shells that were thrown in giant handfuls over them. He stood, erect and tranquil, watching the attack begin against a part of the line that made a blue curve along the side of an adjacent hill. His vision being unmolested by smoke from the rifles of his companions, he had opportunities to see parts of the hard fight. It was a relief to perceive at last from whence came some of these noises which had been roared into his ears.

Off a short way he saw two regiments fighting a little separate battle with two other regiments. It was in a cleared space, wearing a set-apart look. They were blazing as if upon a wager, giving and taking tremendous blows. The firings were incredibly fierce and rapid. These intent regiments apparently were oblivious of all larger purposes of war, and were slugging each other as if at a matched game.

In another direction he saw a magnificent brigade going with the evident intention of driving the enemy from a wood. They passed in out of sight and presently there was a most awe-inspiring racket in the wood. The noise was unspeakable. Having stirred this prodigious uproar, and, apparently, finding it too prodigious, the brigade, after a little time, came marching airily out again with its fine formation in nowise disturbed. There were no traces of speed in its movements. The brigade was jaunty and seemed to point a proud thumb at the yelling wood.

On a slope to the left there was a long row of guns, gruff and maddened, denouncing the enemy, who, down through the woods, were forming for another attack in the pitiless monotony of conflicts. The round red discharges from the guns made a crimson flare and a high, thick smoke. Occasional glimpses could be caught of groups of the toiling artillerymen. In the rear of this row of guns stood a house, calm and white, amid bursting shells. A congregation of horses, tied to a long railing, were tugging frenziedly at their bridles. Men were running hither and thither.

The detached battle between the four regiments lasted for some time. There chanced to be no interference, and they settled their dispute by themselves. They struck savagely and powerfully at each other for a period of minutes, and then the lighter-hued regiments faltered and drew back, leaving the dark-blue lines shouting. The youth could see the two flags shaking with laughter amid the smoke remnants.

Presently there was a stillness, pregnant with meaning. The blue lines shifted and changed a trifle and stared expectantly at the silent woods and fields before them. The hush was solemn and churchlike, save for a distant battery that, evidently unable to remain quiet, sent a faint rolling thunder over the ground. It irritated, like the noises of unimpressed boys. The men imagined that it would prevent their perched ears from hearing the first words of the new battle.

Of a sudden the guns on the slope roared out a message of warning. A spluttering sound had begun in the woods. It swelled with amazing speed to a profound clamor that involved the earth in noises. The splitting crashes swept along the lines until an interminable roar was developed. To those in the midst of it it became a din fitted to the universe. It was the whirring and thumping of gigantic machinery, complications among the smaller stars. The youth's ears were filled up. They were incapable of hearing more.

On an incline over which a road wound he saw wild and desperate rushes of men perpetually backward and forward in riotous surges. These parts of the opposing armies were two long waves that pitched upon each other madly at dictated points. To and fro they swelled. Sometimes, one side by its yells and cheers would proclaim decisive blows, but a moment later the other side would be all yells and cheers. Once the youth saw a spray of light forms go in houndlike leaps toward the waving blue lines. There was much howling, and presently it went away with a vast mouthful of prisoners. Again, he saw a blue wave dash with such thunderous force against a gray obstruction that it seemed to clear the earth of it and leave nothing but trampled sod. And always in their swift and deadly rushes to and fro the men screamed and yelled like maniacs.

Particular pieces of fence or secure positions behind collections of trees were wrangled over, as gold thrones or pearl bedsteads. There were desperate lunges at these chosen spots seemingly every instant, and most of them were bandied like light toys between the contending forces. The youth could not tell from the battle flags flying like crimson foam in many directions which color of cloth was winning.

His emaciated[10] regiment bustled forth with undiminished fierceness when its time came. When assaulted again by bullets, the men burst out in a barbaric cry of rage and pain. They bent their heads in aims of intent hatred behind the projected hammers of their guns. Their ramrods clanged loud with fury as their eager arms pounded the cartridges into the rifle barrels. The front of the regiment was a smoke-wall penetrated by the flashing points of yellow and red.

Wallowing in the fight, they were in an astonishingly short time resmudged. They surpassed in stain and dirt all their previous appearances. Moving to and fro with strained exertion, jabbering the while, they were, with their swaying bodies, black faces, and glowing eyes, like strange and ugly friends jigging heavily in the smoke.

The lieutenant, returning from a tour after a bandage, produced from a hidden receptacle of his mind new and portentous oaths suited to the emergency. Strings of expletives he swung lashlike over the backs of his men, and it was evident that his previous efforts had in nowise impaired his resources.

The youth, still the bearer of the colors, did not feel his idleness. He was deeply absorbed as a spectator. The crash and swing of the great drama made him lean forward, intent-eyed, his face working in small contortions. Sometimes he prattled, words coming unconsciously from him in grotesque exclamations. He did not know that he breathed; that the flag hung silently over him, so absorbed was he.

A formidable line of the enemy came within dangerous range. They could be seen plainly—tall, gaunt men with excited faces running with long strides toward a wandering fence.

At sight of this danger the men suddenly ceased their cursing monotone. There was an instant of strained silence before they threw up their rifles and fired a plumping volley at the foes. There had been no order given; the men, upon recognizing the menace, had immediately let drive their flock of bullets without waiting for word of command.

But the enemy were quick to gain the protection of the wandering line of fence. They slid down behind it with remarkable celerity, and from this position they began briskly to slice up the blue men.

These latter braced their energies for a great struggle. Often, white clinched teeth shone from the dusky faces. Many heads

---

10. emaciated *adj.*: Here, thinned-out.

surged to and fro, floating upon a pale sea of smoke. Those behind the fence frequently shouted and yelped in taunts and gibelike cries, but the regiment maintained a stressed silence. Perhaps, at this new assault the men recalled the fact that they had been named mud diggers, and it made their situation thrice bitter. They were breathlessly intent upon keeping the ground and thrusting away the rejoicing body of the enemy. They fought swiftly and with a despairing savageness denoted in their expressions.

The youth had resolved not to budge whatever should happen. Some arrows of scorn that had buried themselves in his heart had generated strange and unspeakable hatred. It was clear to him that his final and absolute revenge was to be achieved by his dead body lying, torn and guttering,[11] upon the field. This was to be a poignant retaliation upon the officer who had said "mule drivers," and later "mud diggers," for in all the wild graspings of his mind for a unit responsible for his sufferings and commotions he always seized upon the man who had dubbed him wrongly. And it was his idea, vaguely formulated, that his corpse would be for those eyes a great and salt[12] reproach.

The regiment bled extravagantly. Grunting bundles of blue began to drop. The orderly sergeant of the youth's company was shot through the cheeks. Its supports being injured, his jaw hung afar down, disclosing in the wide cavern of his mouth a pulsing mass of blood and teeth. And with it all he made attempts to cry out. In his endeavor there was a dreadful earnestness, as if he conceived that one great shriek would make him well.

The youth saw him presently go rearward. His strength seemed in nowise impaired. He ran swiftly, casting wild glances for succor.

Others fell down about the feet of their companions. Some of the wounded crawled out and away, but many lay still, their bodies twisted into impossible shapes.

The youth looked once for his friend. He saw a vehement young man, powder-smeared and frowzled, whom he knew to be him. The lieutenant, also, was unscathed in his position at the rear. He had continued to curse, but it was now with the air of a man who was using his last box of oaths.

For the fire of the regiment had begun to wane and drip. The robust voice, that had come strangely from the thin ranks, was growing rapidly weak.

Chapter Twenty-Three

The colonel came running along back of the line. There were other officers following him. "We must charge'm!" they shouted. "We must charge'm!" they cried with resentful voices, as if anticipating a rebellion against this plan by the men.

The youth, upon hearing the shouts, began to study the distance between him and the enemy. He made vague calculations. He saw that to be firm soldiers they must go forward. It would be death to stay in the present place, and with all the circumstances to go backward would exalt too many others. Their hope was to push the galling foes away from the fence.

He expected that his companions, weary and stiffened, would have to be driven to this assault, but as he turned toward them he perceived with a certain surprise that they were giving quick and unqualified expressions of assent. There was an ominous, clanging overture to the charge when the shafts of the bayonets rattled upon the rifle barrels. At the yelled words of command the soldiers sprang forward in eager leaps. There was new and unexpected force in the movement of the regiment. A knowledge of its faded and jaded condition made the charge appear like a paroxysm, a display of the strength that comes before a final feebleness. The men scampered in insane fever of haste, racing as if to achieve a sudden success be-

---

11. **guttering** *adj.*: Here, bleeding.
12. **salt** *adj.*: Bitter.

fore an exhilarating fluid should leave them. It was a blind and despairing rush by the collection of men in dusty and tattered blue, over a green sward and under a sapphire sky, toward a fence, dimly outlined in smoke, from behind which spluttered the fierce rifles of enemies.

The youth kept the bright colors to the front. He was waving his free arm in furious circles, the while shrieking mad calls and appeals, urging on those that did not need to be urged, for it seemed that the mob of blue men hurling themselves on the dangerous group of rifles were again grown suddenly wild with an enthusiasm of unselfishness. From the many firings starting toward them, it looked as if they would merely succeed in making a great sprinkling of corpses on the grass between their former position and the fence. But they were in a state of frenzy, per-

haps because of forgotten vanities, and it made an exhibition of sublime recklessness. There was no obvious questioning, nor figurings, nor diagrams. There were, apparently, no considered loopholes. It appeared that the swift wings of their desires would have shattered against the iron gates of the impossible.

He himself felt the daring spirit of a savage religion-mad. He was capable of profound sacrifices, a tremendous death. He had no time for dissections, but he knew that he thought of the bullets only as things that could prevent him from reaching the place of his endeavor. There were subtle flashings of joy within him that thus should be his mind.

He strained all his strength. His eyesight was shaken and dazzled by the tension of thought and muscle. He did not see any-

thing excepting the mist of smoke gashed by the little knives of fire, but he knew that in it lay the aged fence of a vanished farmer protecting the snuggled bodies of the gray men.

As he ran a thought of the shock of contact gleamed in his mind. He expected a great concussion when the two bodies of troops crashed together. This became a part of his wild battle madness. He could feel the onward swing of the regiment about him and he conceived of a thunderous, crushing blow that would prostrate the resistance and spread consternation and amazement for miles. The flying regiment was going to have a catapulting effect. This dream made him run faster among his comrades, who were giving vent to hoarse and frantic cheers.

But presently he could see that many of the men in gray did not intend to abide the blow. The smoke, rolling, disclosed men who ran, their faces still turned. These grew to a crowd, who retired stubbornly. Individuals wheeled frequently to send a bullet at the blue wave.

But at one part of the line there was a grim and obdurate group that made no movement. They were settled firmly down behind posts and rails. A flag, ruffled and fierce, waved over them and their rifles dinned fiercely.

The blue whirl of men got very near, until it seemed that in truth there would be a close and frightful scuffle. There was an expressed disdain in the opposition of the little group, that changed the meaning of the cheers of the men in blue. They became yells of wrath, directed, personal. The cries of the two parties were now in sound an interchange of scathing insults.

They in blue showed their teeth; their eyes shone all white. They launched themselves as at the throats of those who stood resisting. The space between dwindled to an insignificant distance.

The youth had centered the gaze of his soul upon that other flag. Its possession would be high pride. It would express bloody minglings, near blows. He had a gigantic hatred for those who made great difficulties and complications. They caused it to be as a craved treasure of mythology, hung amid tasks and contrivances of danger.

He plunged like a mad horse at it. He was resolved it should not escape if wild blows and darings of blows could seize it. His own emblem, quivering and aflare, was winging toward the other. It seemed there would shortly be an encounter of strange beaks and claws, as of eagles.

The swirling body of blue men came to a sudden halt at close and disastrous range and roared a swift volley. The group in gray was split and broken by this fire, but its riddled body still fought. The men in blue yelled again and rushed in upon it.

The youth, in his leapings, saw, as through a mist, a picture of four or five men stretched upon the ground or writhing upon their knees with bowed heads as if they had been stricken by bolts from the sky. Tottering among them was the rival color bearer, whom the youth saw had been bitten vitally by the bullets of the last formidable volley. He perceived this man fighting a last struggle, the struggle of one whose legs are grasped by demons. It was a ghastly battle. Over his face was the bleach of death, but set upon it were the dark and hard lines of desperate purpose. With this terrible grin of resolution he hugged his precious flag to him and was stumbling and staggering in his design to go the way that led to safety for it.

But his wounds always made it seem that his feet were retarded, held, and he fought a grim fight, as with invisible ghouls fastened greedily upon his limbs. Those in advance of the scampering blue men, howling cheers, leaped at the fence. The despair of the lost was in his eyes as he glanced back at them.

The youth's friend went over the obstruction in a tumbling heap and sprang at the flag as a panther at prey. He pulled at it and, wrenching it free, swung up its red brilliancy with a mad cry of exultation even as the color bearer, gasping, lurched over in a final throe and, stiffening convulsively, turned his dead face to the ground. There was much blood upon the grass blades.

At the place of success there began more wild clamoring of cheers. The men gesticulated and bellowed in an ecstasy. When they spoke it was as if they considered their listener to be a mile away. What hats and caps were left to them they often slung high in the air.

At one part of the line four men had been swooped upon, and they now sat as prisoners. Some blue men were about them in an eager and curious circle. The soldiers had trapped strange birds, and there was an examination. A flurry of fast questions was in the air.

One of the prisoners was nursing a superficial wound in the foot. He cuddled it, babywise, but he looked up from it often to curse with an astonishing utter abandon straight at the noses of his captors. He consigned them to red regions; he called upon the pestilential wrath of strange gods. And with it all he was singularly free from recognition of the finer points of the conduct of prisoners of war. It was as if a clumsy clod had trod upon his toe and he conceived it to be his privilege, his duty, to use deep, resentful oaths.

Another, who was a boy in years, took his plight with great calmness and apparent good nature. He conversed with the men in blue, studying their faces with his bright and keen eyes. They spoke of battles and conditions. There was an acute interest in all their faces during this exchange of viewpoints. It seemed a great satisfaction to hear voices from where all had been darkness and speculation.

The third captive sat with a morose countenance. He preserved a stoical and cold attitude.

The last of the four was always silent and, for the most part, kept his face turned in unmolested directions. From the views the youth received he seemed to be in a state of absolute dejection. Shame was upon him, and with it profound regret that he was, perhaps, no more to be counted in the ranks of his fellows. The youth could detect no expression that would allow him to believe that the other was giving a thought to his narrowed future, the pictured dungeons, perhaps, and starvations and brutalities, liable to the imagination. All to be seen was shame for captivity and regret for the right to antagonize.

After the men had celebrated sufficiently they settled down behind the old rail fence, on the opposite side to the one from which their foes had been driven. A few shot perfunctorily at distant marks.

There was some long grass. The youth nestled in it and rested, making a convenient rail support the flag. His friend, jubilant and glorified, holding his treasure with vanity, came to him there. They sat side by side and congratulated each other.

Chapter Twenty-Four

The roarings that had stretched in a long line of sound across the face of the forest began to grow intermittent and weaker. The stentorian[13] speeches of the artillery continued in some distant encounter, but the crashes of the musketry had almost ceased. The youth and his friend of a sudden looked up, feeling a deadened form of distress at the waning of these noises, which had become a part of life. They could see changes going on among the troops. There were marchings this way and that way. A battery wheeled leisurely. On the crest of a small hill was the thick gleam of many departing muskets.

The youth arose. "Well, what now, I wonder?" he said. By his tone he seemed to be preparing to resent some new monstrosity in the way of dins and smashes. He shaded his eyes with his grimy hand and gazed over the field.

His friend also arose and stared. "I bet

_____

13. stentorian _adj._: Very loud.

we're goin' t' git along out of this an' back over th' river," said he.

"Well, I swan!" said the youth.

They waited, watching. Within a little while the regiment received orders to retrace its way. The men got up grunting from the grass, regretting the soft repose. They jerked their stiffened legs, and stretched their arms over their heads. One man swore as he rubbed his eyes. They all groaned. They had as many objections to this change as they would have had to a proposal for a new battle.

They trampled slowly back over the field across which they had run in a mad scamper.

The regiment marched until it had joined its fellows. The reformed brigade, in column, aimed through a wood at the road. Directly they were in a mass of dust-covered troops, and were trudging along in a way parallel to the enemy's lines as these had been defined by the previous turmoil.

They passed within view of a stolid white house, and saw in front of it groups of their comrades lying in wait behind a neat breast-work. A row of guns were booming at a distant enemy. Shells thrown in reply were raising clouds of dust and splinters. Horsemen dashed along the line of entrenchments.

At this point of its march the division curved away from the field and went winding off in the direction of the river. When the significance of this movement had impressed itself upon the youth he turned his head and looked over his shoulder toward the trampled and debris-strewed ground. He breathed a breath of new satisfaction. He finally nudged his friend. "Well, it's all over," he said to him.

His friend gazed backward. "It is," he assented. They mused.

For a time the youth was obliged to reflect in a puzzled and uncertain way. His mind was undergoing a subtle change. It took moments for it to cast off its battleful ways and resume its accustomed course of thought. Gradually his brain emerged from the clogged clouds, and at last he was enabled to more closely comprehend himself and circumstance.

He understood then that the existence of shot and counter-shot was in the past. He had dwelt in a land of strange, squalling upheavals and had come forth. He had been where there was red of blood and black of passion, and he was escaped. His first thoughts were given to rejoicings at this fact.

Later he began to study his deeds, his failures, and his achievements. Thus, fresh from scenes where many of his usual machines of reflection had been idle, from where he had proceeded sheeplike, he struggled to marshal all his acts.

At last they marched before him clearly. From this present viewpoint he was enabled to look upon them in spectator fashion and to criticize them with some correctness, for his new condition had already defeated certain sympathies.

Regarding his procession of memory he felt gleeful and unregretting, for in it his public deeds were paraded in great and shining prominence. Those performances which had been witnessed by his fellows marched now in wide purple and gold, having various deflections. They went gaily with music. It was pleasure to watch these things. He spent delightful minutes viewing the gilded images of memory.

He saw that he was good. He recalled with a thrill of joy the respectful comments of his fellows upon his conduct.

Nevertheless, the ghost of his flight from the first engagement appeared to him and danced. There were small shoutings in his brain about these matters. For a moment he blushed, and the light of his soul flickered with shame.

A specter of reproach came to him. There loomed the dogging memory of the tattered soldier—he who, gored by bullets and faint for blood, had fretted concerning an imagined wound in another; he who had loaned his last of strength and intellect for the tall soldier; he who, blind with weariness and pain, had been deserted in the field.

For an instant a wretched chill of sweat was upon him at the thought that he might be detected in the thing. As he stood persistently before his vision, he gave vent to a cry of sharp irritation and agony.

His friend turned. "What's the matter, Henry?" he demanded. The youth's reply was an outburst of crimson oaths.

As he marched along the little branch-hung roadway among his prattling companions this vision of cruelty brooded over him. It clung near him always and darkened his view of these deeds in purple and gold. Whichever way his thoughts turned they were followed by the somber phantom of the desertion in the fields. He looked stealthily at his companions, feeling sure that they must discern in his face evidences of this pursuit. But they were plodding in ragged array, discussing with quick tongues the accomplishments of the late battle.

"Oh, if a man should come up an' ask me, I'd say we got a dum good lickin'."

"Lickin'—in yer eye! We ain't licked, sonny. We're going down here aways, swing aroun', an' come in behint 'em."

"Oh, hush, with your comin' in behint 'em. I've seen all 'a that I wanta. Don't tell me about comin' in behint—"

"Bill Smithers, he ses he'd rather been in ten hundred battles than been in that heluva hospital. He ses they got shootin' in th' nighttime, an' shells dropped plum among 'em in th' hospital. He ses sech hollerin' he never see."

"Hasbrouck? He's th' best off'cer in this here reg'ment. He's a whale."

"Didn't I tell yeh we'd come aroun' in behint 'em? Didn't I tell yeh so? We—"

"Oh, shet yer mouth!"

For a time this pursuing recollection of the tattered man took all elation from the youth's veins. He saw his vivid error, and he was afraid that it would stand before him all his life. He took no share in the chatter of his comrades, nor did he look at them or know them, save when he felt sudden suspicion that they were seeing his thoughts and scrutinizing each detail of the scene with the tattered soldier.

Yet gradually he mustered force to put the sin at a distance. And at last his eyes seemed to open to some new ways. He found that he could look back upon the brass and bombast of his earlier gospels[14] and see them truly. He was gleeful when he discovered that he now despised them.

With the conviction came a store of assurance. He felt a quiet manhood, nonassertive but of sturdy and strong blood. He knew that he would no more quail before his guides wherever they should point. He had been to touch the great death, and found that, after all, it was but the great death. He was a man.

So it came to pass that as he trudged from the place of blood and wrath his soul changed. He came from hot plowshares[15] to prospects of clover tranquilly, and it was as if hot plowshares were not. Scars faded as flowers.

It rained. The procession of weary soldiers became a bedraggled train, despondent and muttering, marching with churning effort in a trough of liquid brown mud under a low, wretched sky. Yet the youth smiled, for he saw that the world was a world for him, though many discovered it to be made of oaths and walking sticks. He had rid himself of the red sickness of battle. The sultry nightmare was in the past. He had been an animal blistered and sweating in the heat and pain of war. He turned now with a lover's thirst to images of tranquil skies, fresh meadows, cool brooks—an existence of soft and eternal peace.

Over the river a golden ray of sun came through the hosts of leaden rain clouds.

---

14. gospels *n.*: Here, personal beliefs.
15. hot plowshares: An allusion to the end of warfare described in the Bible (Isaiah 2:4): ". . . and, they shall beat their swords into plowshares . . ."

THINKING ABOUT THE SELECTION

Recalling

1. (a) How has Wilson changed since the days of camp life? (b) Why does the youth feel superior to Wilson?
2. (a) In Chapter 17, what does the youth do when all those near him have ceased firing? (b) How does the lieutenant react to his behavior?
3. In Chapter 18, what does the officer tell the general about the 304th regiment?
4. How does the youth come into possession of the flag?
5. (a) In Chapter 21, why does the officer reproach the regiment? (b) How does the youth respond to this criticism? (c) Why is the youth praised?
6. How does Wilson capture the enemy's flag?
7. What conclusion about himself does the youth reach toward the end of the book?

Interpreting

8. (a) In Chapter 17, why is the youth overcome by hatred toward the enemy? (b) How does his hatred affect his behavior? (c) What does this suggest about the effect of war on people's attitudes and behavior?
9. (a) What is the general's attitude toward his troops? (b) What do the general's comments reveal to the youth about the realities of war? (c) What Naturalist belief does the general's attitude reflect?
10. What does the officer's criticism of the regiment indicate about the contrast between how the soldiers and the officers measure success in combat?
11. What is ironic about the fact that the soldiers are ordered back to the spot from which they started their assault?
12. (a) How do the youth's attitudes toward the war and toward himself change during the course of the novel? (b) Do the changes warrant the conclusion he reaches toward the end of the book? Support your answer.

Applying

13. In *The Red Badge of Courage,* the Civil War accelerates the youth's passage from adolescence to adulthood. Why do you think that wars often have this effect on young men?

ANALYZING LITERATURE

Understanding Theme

The **theme** is the central idea or insight into life that a writer conveys in a work of literature. A novel may have a number of themes. For example, *The Red Badge of Courage* has several themes, one of which is that war is destructive and cruel and often seems meaningless.

1. What insight does the novel express concerning the meaning of courage?
2. What point does Crane make about the passage from adolescence to adulthood?
3. What statement does Crane make about humanity's relationship to nature?

CRITICAL THINKING AND READING

Recognizing Important Details

To interpret the meaning of a novel you must be able to recognize important details that play a role in conveying the theme.

1. Find one detail in Chapters 14–24 related to the theme of maturity.
2. Find one detail in Chapters 1–7 that plays a role in conveying Crane's message concerning humanity's relationship to nature.

THINKING AND WRITING

Evaluating a Character's Behavior

Imagine that you have been hired by the military to study the behavior of young recruits during battle. Prepare a brief report in which you evaluate the youth's behavior during combat. Start by reviewing the novel, taking note of the youth's behavior during each battle. Then write your report. Start by stating your conclusion. Then support it with evidence from the novel. When you finish writing, revise your report and prepare a final copy.

Poetry

THE GRAND CANYON OF THE YELLOWSTONE, 1893–1901
Thomas Moran
Art Resource

Song of the Chattahoochee

Sidney Lanier (1842–1881) was a talented musician as well as a gifted poet. He had a strong interest in the relationship between music and poetry. As a result, he abandoned conventional poetic structures and sought to create a musical rhythm in his poetry. Born in Macon, Georgia, Lanier entered Oglethorpe University, where he studied poetry and music. In 1880 he published *The Science of English Verse*. In his book Lanier stated his belief that poetry should have the natural rhythm and fluidity of music and that the sound of a poem should reinforce its meaning.

Writer's Techniques

Sound Devices. Poets use a variety of sound devices to give their writing a musical quality. Four of the most frequently used sound devices are alliteration, consonance, assonance, and internal rhyme.

Alliteration is the repetition of similar sounds, usually consonants, at the beginnings of words or accented syllables. Notice the repetition of the *f* sound in the following line from "Song of the Chattahoochee": "And *f*lee *f*rom *f*olly on every side."

Consonance is the repetition of consonant sounds at the ends of words or accented syllables. For example, the *l* sound is repeated in the following line from "Song of the Chattahoochee": "Vei*l*ing the va*l*leys of Ha*ll*".

Assonance is the repetition of vowel sounds. For example, the long *a* sound is repeated in the following line: "Av*ai*l: I am f*ai*n for to water the pl*ai*n".

Rhyme refers to the repetition of similar or identical sounds in the accented syllables of two or more words appearing close to each other in a poem. Internal rhyme is rhyme that occurs within a line. An example of internal rhyme appears in the following line from "Song of the Chattahoochee": "With a lover's p*ain* to att*ain* the pl*ain*".

Look For

As you read "Song of the Chattahoochee," listen for sound devices that imitate the flowing of the river and reinforce the meaning of the poem.

Writing

In "Song of the Chattahoochee" Lanier personifies, or attributes human characteristics to, a river. Think of another element of nature that a writer might personify. Then prepare a list of human qualities that could be attributed to this element.

Vocabulary

Knowing the following words will help you as you read "Song of the Chattahoochee."

amain (ə mān') *adv.*: At or with great speed (p. 663, l. 3)

luminous (loo' mə nəs) *adj.*: Shining; bright (p. 664, l. 35)

Song of the Chattahoochee[1]

Sidney Lanier

Out of the hills of Habersham,
   Down the valleys of Hall,[2]
I hurry amain to reach the plain,
Run the rapid and leap the fall,
5 Split at the rock and together again,
Accept my bed, or narrow or wide,
And flee from folly on every side
With a lover's pain to attain the plain
   Far from the hills of Habersham,
10   Far from the valleys of Hall.

---

1. Chattahoochee (chat′ ə hoo′ che): A river in western Georgia.
2. Habersham . . . Hall: Two counties through which the
Chattahoochee flows.

HARPERS FERRY FROM JEFFERSON ROCK, 1857
Edward Beyer
Virginia State Library

All down the hills of Habersham,
All through the valleys of Hall,
The rushes cried *Abide, Abide,*
The willful waterweeds held me thrall,
15 The laving laurel turned my tide,
The ferns and the fondling grass said *Stay,*
The dewberry dipped for to work delay,
And the little reeds sighed *Abide, abide,*
Here in the hills of Habersham,
20 *Here in the valleys of Hall.*

High o'er the hills of Habersham,
Veiling the valleys of Hall,
The hickory told me manifold
Fair tales of shade, the poplar tall
25 Wrought me her shadowy self to hold,
The chestnut, the oak, the walnut, the pine,
Overleaning, with flickering meaning and sign,
Said, *Pass not, so cold, these manifold*
Deep shades of the hills of Habersham,
30 *These glades in the valleys of Hall.*

And oft in the hills of Habersham,
And oft in the valleys of Hall,
The white quartz shone, and the smooth brook-stone
Did bar me of passage with friendly brawl,
35 And many a luminous jewel lone
—Crystals clear or a-cloud with mist,
Ruby, garnet and amethyst—
Made lures with the lights of streaming stone
In the clefts of the hills of Habersham,
40 In the beds of the valleys of Hall.

But oh, not the hills of Habersham,
And oh, not the valleys of Hall
Avail: I am fain for to water the plain.
Downward the voices of Duty call—
45 Downward, to toil and be mixed with the main,
The dry fields burn, and the mills are to turn,
And a myriad flowers mortally yearn,
And the lordly main from beyond the plain
Calls o'er the hills of Habersham,
50 Calls through the valleys of Hall.

THINKING ABOUT THE SELECTION

Recalling

1. According to the first stanza, toward what is the river racing?
2. (a) What do the little reeds "sigh" in the second stanza? (b) What do the trees "say" in the third stanza?
3. What duties must the river perform before it mixes with the main?

Interpreting

4. Who is the speaker in this poem?
5. In this poem Lanier presents an extended personification of the Chattahoochee River. Name three other elements of nature that Lanier personifies in the poem.
6. (a) Considering Lanier's use of personification and the details he uses in describing the river's flow, what do you think the course of the river symbolizes? (b) What do the obstacles encountered by the river symbolize? (c) What does the "duty" of the plain symbolize? (d) What does the "main" symbolize?

Applying

7. Why is this poem as effective today as it was when it was written?

ANALYZING LITERATURE

Recognizing Sound Devices

Alliteration, consonance, assonance, and internal rhyme are four sound devices used in poetry. **Alliteration** is the repetition of similar sounds, usually consonants, at the beginnings of words or accented syllables (for example, "*R*un the *r*apid," line 4). **Consonance** is the repetition of consonant sounds at the ends of words or accented syllables (for example, "va*ll*eys of Ha*ll*"). **Assonance** is the repetition of vowel sounds (for example, "with fl*i*ckering," line 27). **Internal rhyme** is rhyme that occurs within a line (for example, I hurry am*ain* to reach the pl*ain*, line 3).

1. Find two more examples of each of these techniques in "Song of the Chattahoochee."
2. How do these examples convey the natural movement of the river?

CRITICAL THINKING AND READING

Analyzing the Effect of Sound Devices

Sidney Lanier believed that the sound of a poem should help to reinforce its meaning. In "Song of the Chattahoochee" he used sound devices to imitate the natural flowing of a river. For example, his use of alliteration in the line "And *f*lee *f*rom *f*olly on every side" captures the river's dancing, winding movement.

Do you agree with Lanier's contention? Support your answer.

THINKING AND WRITING

Writing an Extended Personification

What would a mountain say if it could speak? What message would the ocean give to humankind? What would a tornado say as it left behind a trail of destruction?

Write a poem or a short narrative essay in which you present an extended personification of an element of nature. Start by reviewing the list of human qualities you have already prepared. Add any other qualities you think of. Then write your personification using the element you are personifying as your speaker or narrator. When you finish writing, revise your personification and share it with your classmates.

GUIDE FOR READING

War Is Kind; Think as I Think

Stephen Crane (1871–1900), who is primarily remembered for his fiction, was also a gifted poet. He published his harshly realistic and often pessimistic poetry in two volumes, *The Black Riders* (1895) and *War is Kind* (1899). Generally composed of short, unrhymed lines with an irregular metrical pattern, his poetry was considered highly unconventional in style when it was first published. While Crane's poems were not widely accepted during his lifetime, the blatant honesty of his poems appealed to the following generation.

Writer's Techniques

Irony and **Tone.** Irony is a contrast or a difference between what is stated and what is meant, or between what is expected to happen and what actually happens. Verbal irony is one of a number of forms of irony used in literature. Verbal irony occurs when the literal meaning of a word or statement is quite different from the intended meaning. For example, a character might criticize another character's driving ability by commenting, "he is such a great driver that he's been in ten accidents in the last two years."

Verbal irony can play an important role in revealing tone—the writer's attitude toward his or her subject, characters, or audience. Most often, the use of verbal irony conveys a sarcastic attitude or a sense of anger, bitterness, or disillusionment. For example, the use of verbal irony in a number of Stephen Crane's poems conveys his pessimistic and often bitter attitude.

Look For

As you read Stephen Crane's poetry, look for his use of verbal irony and think about what it reveals about tone.

Writing

People often use verbal irony in everyday speech. Prepare a list of examples of verbal irony from conversations you have heard. Then briefly describe what made you aware that each of the statements was not meant to be interpreted literally.

Vocabulary

Knowing the following words will help you as you read Stephen Crane's poetry.

shroud (shroud) *n.*: A cloth sometimes used to wrap a corpse for burial (p. 668, l. 24)

abominably (ə bäm′ ə nə blē) *adv.*: Hatefully (p. 669, l. 2)

War Is Kind

Stephen Crane

NEWS FROM THE WAR (DETAIL)
*Winslow Homer for Harper's Weekly,
June 14, 1862*
Library of Congress

Do not weep, maiden, for war is kind.
Because your lover threw wild hands toward the sky
And the affrighted steed ran on alone,
Do not weep.
5 War is kind.

    Hoarse, booming drums of the regiment,
    Little souls who thirst for fight,
    These men were born to drill and die.
    The unexplained glory flies above them,
10   Great is the battle-god, great, and his kingdom—
    A field where a thousand corpses lie.

Do not weep, babe, for war is kind.
Because your father tumbled in the yellow trenches,
Raged at his breast, gulped and died,
15 Do not weep.
War is kind.

Swift blazing flag of the regiment,
Eagle with crest of red and gold,
These men were born to drill and die.
20   Point for them the virtue of slaughter,
Make plain to them the excellence of killing
And a field where a thousand corpses lie.

Mother whose heart hung humble as a button
On the bright splendid shroud of your son,
25 Do not weep.
War is kind.

THINKING ABOUT THE SELECTION

Recalling

1. (a) To what three people is the poem addressed? (b) What message does the speaker deliver to them?

Interpreting

2. How are the images presented in stanzas 1, 3, and 5 related to one another?

3. (a) What impressions of war do the images in stanzas 2 and 4 convey? (b) How are these images related to the speaker's message in stanzas 1, 3, and 5?

4. (a) What is the theme of the poem? (b) How does Crane's use of repetition reinforce the theme?

Applying

5. The twentieth century writer George Bernard Shaw wrote, "Peace is not only better than war, but infinitely more arduous." Discuss the meaning and implication of this statement.

ANALYZING LITERATURE

Using Irony and Tone

Verbal irony, one of a number of types of irony used in literature, occurs when the literal meaning of a word or statement is quite different from the intended meaning. For example, when the speaker states that "war is kind," he means that war is cruel.

Because writers often use it to express sarcasm, anger, bitterness, or disillusion, verbal irony is important in revealing tone.

1. Find two additional examples of verbal irony in the poem.

2. (a) How would you describe the tone of the poem? (b) How does Crane's use of verbal irony help to convey the tone?

3. Find two details from the poem that indicate the statement "war is kind" is being used ironically.

Think as I Think

Stephen Crane

"Think as I think," said a man,
"Or you are abominably wicked;
You are a toad."

And after I had thought of it,
5   I said, "I will, then, be a toad."

THINKING ABOUT THE SELECTION

Recalling

1. (a) What does the man tell the speaker?
   (b) How does the speaker respond?

Interpreting

2. (a) Explain the last line of the poem. (b) What does the speaker's response reveal about his personality?
3. What does this poem suggest about the choice between conformity and individuality?

Applying

4. In what types of situations do you think people are pressured to conform to the thoughts and desires of others?

THINKING AND WRITING

Writing About Theme

"Think as I Think" focuses on the theme of individuality versus conformity. Write a short personal essay expressing your own thoughts concerning this theme. Start by thinking about how peer pressure and societal pressure can affect people's choices and behavior. Also think about how people's lives are affected by choosing not to conform. List the types of situations in which you think people are most often pressured to conform. Organize your thoughts into an informal outline. Then write your essay expressing your ideas as clearly as possible. When you finish writing, revise your essay and share it with your classmates. Give them an opportunity to respond to it. Then revise your essay again, based on their comments.

PAUL LAURENCE DUNBAR

1872–1906

The first black American to support himself entirely by writing, Paul Laurence Dunbar displayed great versatility as a writer throughout his short career. Dunbar wrote poems, both in a formal, elegant style and in black dialect, and he wrote several novels and numerous short stories.

Dunbar was born in Dayton, Ohio, the son of former slaves. Encouraged by his mother, he began writing poetry at an early age. During high school, Dunbar, who was the only black student in his class, frequently recited his poetry before school assemblies. He also served as the president of the literary society, as class poet, and as editor of the school newspaper.

Following his graduation, he supported himself by working as an elevator operator while continuing to write. He first earned recognition among writers and critics in 1892, when he gave a poetry reading during a meeting of the Western Association of Writers. A year later he published his first collection of poetry, *Oak and Ivy*. In 1895 he published a second collection, *Majors and Minors* (1895), which was received by critics with great enthusiasm. In fact, William Dean Howells, the leading critic of the day, was so impressed with the book that he wrote an introduction for Dunbar's next collection, *Lyrics of a Lowly Life* (1896), which sold over twelve thousand copies and established Dunbar as one of the most widely read and admired American poets of the time.

Dunbar went on to write three more volumes of poetry, four novels, and four volumes of short stories, and he gave readings throughout the United States and Europe. Unfortunately, however, his life was cut short by tuberculosis in 1906.

Despite his success as a poet, Dunbar was disillusioned by the critics' tendency to focus on his poetry written in black dialect, while virtually ignoring his more formal verse. In poems such as "Douglass" and "We Wear the Mask," Dunbar demonstrates a command of the English language that was often overlooked, capturing the despair of black people in a dignified, graceful manner.

GUIDE FOR READING

We Wear the Mask; Douglass

Literary Forms

The Sonnet. A sonnet is a fourteen-line lyric poem, usually written in rhymed iambic pentameter—verse with five feet per line, each foot consisting of an unstressed syllable followed by a stressed syllable. A sonnet usually expresses a single complete idea or theme.

The two most common types of sonnets are *English sonnets,* or *Shakespearean sonnets* (named after English playwright William Shakespeare), and *Italian sonnets,* or *Petrarchan sonnets* (named after the fourteenth-century Italian poet Francesco Petrarch). English sonnets are composed of three quatrains (four-line stanzas) followed by a couplet (two rhyming lines), with the rhyme scheme *abab cdcd efef gg.* In most English sonnets, the main idea is presented and developed in the three quatrains, and the couplet offers a conclusion. Italian sonnets consist of an octave (eight lines) followed by a sestet (six lines), usually rhyming *abbaabba cdecde* or *abbaabba cdcdcd.* In some Italian sonnets, a question is raised in the octave and the answer is presented in the sestet. In other Italian sonnets, a single idea is presented in the octave and either developed or contradicted in the sestet.

Look For

As you read Paul Laurence Dunbar's poetry, look for the elegance and dignity of his poems. How does his use of formal language and traditional forms such as the sonnet contribute to the effectiveness of his poems?

Writing

In "Douglass," Paul Laurence Dunbar addresses the deceased black leader Frederick Douglass and expresses his people's feelings of despair and their need for Douglass's guidance and comfort. Review the excerpt from Douglass's autobiography (pages 426–431). Then list reasons why Dunbar might have chosen to address his poem to Douglass.

Vocabulary

Knowing the following words will help you as you read Paul Laurence Dunbar's poetry.

guile (gīl) *n.*: Craftiness (p. 672, l. 3)

myriad (mir' ē əd) *adj.*: Countless (p. 672, l. 5)

salient (sāl' yənt) *adj.*: Standing out from the rest (p. 674, l. 4)

tempest (tem' pist) *n.*: A violent storm (p. 674, l. 8)

stark (stärk) *adj.*: Stiff or rigid, as a corpse (p. 674, l. 10)

We Wear the Mask

Paul Laurence Dunbar

We wear the mask that grins and lies,
It hides our cheeks and shades our eyes—
This debt we pay to human guile;
With torn and bleeding hearts we smile,
5   And mouth with myriad subtleties.

Why should the world be overwise,
In counting all our tears and sighs?
Nay, let them only see us, while
    We wear the mask.

10   We smile, but, O great Christ, our cries
To thee from tortured souls arise.
We sing, but oh the clay is vile
Beneath our feet, and long the mile;
But let the world dream otherwise,
15   We wear the mask!

THINKING ABOUT THE SELECTION

Recalling

1. What purpose does the mask serve?

Interpreting

2. (a) Who is the poem's speaker? (b) How would you describe the speaker's emotional state?
3. What does the mask symbolize?
4. (a) Whom does the mask deceive? (b) Why do you think the speaker chooses not to reveal what is hidden beneath the mask?
5. What is the theme of the poem?

Applying

6. Like the speaker in this poem, most people at times hide their true feelings. Why do you think this is so? Explain your answer.

UNDERSTANDING LANGUAGE

Completing Sentences

Each of the following sentences is incomplete, with one or two words missing. Read each sentence carefully. Choose the lettered word or pair of words that best completes the sentence.

1. When Sue graduated from college, she was confronted with _____ possibilities.
   a. subtle   c. tortured
   b. myriad   d. passionate
2. Plagued by _____, the panel was unable to reach an _____.
   a. dissension . . . agreement
   b. defiance . . . solution
   c. dissent . . . impasse
   d. confusion . . . arrangement
3. The climber was _____ of the potential dangers that lay ahead.
   a. suspicious   c. mindful
   b. careful   d. observant
4. The boat was trapped _____ a turbulent _____.
   a. amid . . . storm
   b. within . . . tempest
   c. inside . . . squall
   d. above . . . sea

FREDERICK DOUGLASS
Historical Pictures Services, Chicago

Douglass
Paul Laurence Dunbar

Ah, Douglass,[1] we have fall'n on evil days,
    Such days as thou, not even thou didst know,
    When thee, the eyes of that harsh long ago
Saw, salient, at the cross of devious ways,
5 And all the country heard thee with amaze.
    Not ended then, the passionate ebb and flow,
    The awful tide that battled to and fro;
We ride amid a tempest of dispraise.

Now, when the waves of swift dissension swarm,
10   And Honor, the strong pilot, lieth stark,
Oh, for thy voice high-sounding o'er the storm,
    For thy strong arm to guide the shivering bark,[2]
The blast-defying power of thy form,
    To give us comfort through the lonely dark.

---

1. Douglass: Frederick Douglass, an American abolitionist (1817?–1895).
2. bark: Boat.

THINKING ABOUT THE SELECTION

Recalling

1. How does Dunbar's time compare with the days Douglass knew?
2. What does the speaker call for in the second stanza?

Interpreting

3. (a) To what does the speaker compare the struggles of the black people in lines 6–8? (b) How is this comparison developed in the second stanza?
4. What do you think prompted Dunbar to write this poem?
5. How do you think Dunbar might characterize the present times?

Applying

6. (a) What other black leaders do you think the speaker might have called on if the poem had been written today? (b) Explain how the efforts of these leaders compare with Douglass's efforts.

ANALYZING LITERATURE

Recognizing a Sonnet

A **sonnet** is a fourteen-line lyric poem. Sonnets are usually written in rhymed iambic pentameter and express a single, complete thought. The two most common types of sonnets are the English sonnet, or Shakespearean sonnet, and the Italian sonnet, or Petrarchan sonnet. "Douglass" is an example of an Italian sonnet.

1. What is the theme expressed in "Douglass"?
2. At what point in the poem does Dunbar present the main idea?
3. How is the main idea developed in the sestet?
4. How does Dunbar's use of the sonnet form contribute to the poem's effectiveness?

THINKING AND WRITING

Writing a Sonnet

Write a sonnet in which you address an important historical figure, as Dunbar does in "Douglass." Start by thinking of a historical figure who had an important impact on American society. For example, you might select Martin Luther King, Jr., Abraham Lincoln, or Abigail Adams. How would this person respond to contemporary life? Then write a sonnet focusing on issues concerning contemporary society that would be of interest to this person. When you finish writing, revise your sonnet and share it with your classmates.

EDWIN ARLINGTON ROBINSON

1869–1935

Edwin Arlington Robinson's poetry bridged the gap between two literary eras. Like most nineteenth-century poetry, his work was traditional in form. Yet like the work of modern poets, his poetry was innovative in content, probing beneath the surface of human behavior and exploring the psychological realities of the inner self.

Robinson was raised in Gardiner, Maine, a small town that served as the model for Tilbury Town, the fictional setting of many of his finest poems. When his father, a successful lumber merchant died, Robinson's family suddenly found itself living in poverty. Robinson attended Harvard for two years before his family's financial problems forced him to leave. He returned to Gardiner and began writing poetry, depending on friends and patrons for financial support.

Just before the turn of the century, Robinson published two unsuccessful collections of poetry. *The Torrent and the Night Before* (1897) and *Children of the Night* (1898), at his own expense. Hoping to improve his financial situation, he moved to New York. As it turned out, his situation did improve when President Theodore Roosevelt appointed him to a post at a New York customshouse. Robinson also discovered success as a poet when his fourth volume of poetry, *The Town Down the River* (1910), sold well and received much critical acclaim.

Robinson went on to become a highly regarded poet. His collections *The Man Against the Sky* (1916), *Avon's Harvest* (1922), and *Collected Poems* (1922) were very successful, as was his trilogy of long narrative poems based on the legends of King Arthur: *Merlin, Lancelot,* and *Tristram*. During the 1920's Robinson received more recognition than any other American poet, winning the Pulitzer Prize three times, in 1922, 1925, and 1928.

Growing out of his childhood observations in Gardiner, most of Robinson's best poems focus on people's inner struggles. His poems paint portraits of impoverished characters whose lives are filled with frustration and despair, characters who see their lives as trivial and meaningless, and characters who long to live in another time and place. Yet despite their pessimistic outlook, his poems always possess a certain dignity, resulting from his traditional style, his command of language, and his imagination and wit.

GUIDE FOR READING

Luke Havergal; Richard Cory; Miniver Cheevy

Writer's Techniques

Irony. Irony is a contrast between what is stated and what is meant, or between what is expected to happen and what actually happens. Three types of irony used in literature are verbal irony, situational irony, and dramatic irony. Verbal irony occurs when the literal meaning of a word or statement is different from the intended meaning. Situational irony occurs when the actual result of an action or situation is different from the expected result. Dramatic irony occurs when the audience perceives something that a character in a literary work does not know.

Irony is an important element in many of Edwin Arlington Robinson's poems. Robinson possessed an intense awareness of the ironies of everyday life—the contrasts between reality and people's perceptions, between results and expectations, and between the way people view themselves and how they are seen by others—and he sought to capture these ironies in his harshly realistic poetry.

Look For

As you read Edwin Arlington Robinson's poetry, look for irony. How does the use of irony suggest the complexity of life?

Writing

People are always in search of happiness, but what is happiness? William Saroyan once wrote, "The greatest happiness you can have is knowing that you do not necessarily require happiness." Freewrite, exploring the meaning of this quotation.

Vocabulary

Knowing the following words will help you as you read Edwin Arlington Robinson's poetry.

assailed (ə sāld′) v.: Attacked violently; assaulted (p. 680, l. 2)
vagrant (vā′ grənt) n.: An idle wanderer (p. 680, l. 16)
albeit (ôl bē′ it) conj.: Although (p. 680, l. 18)

incessantly (in ses′ 'nt lē) adv.: Unceasingly (p. 680, l. 19)
imperially (im pir′ ē əl ē) adv.: Majestically (p. 682, l. 4)

Luke Havergal

Edwin Arlington Robinson

Go to the western gate, Luke Havergal,
There where the vines cling crimson on the wall,
And in the twilight wait for what will come.
The leaves will whisper there of her, and some,
5   Like flying words, will strike you as they fall;
But go, and if you listen she will call.
Go to the western gate, Luke Havergal—
Luke Havergal.

No, there is not a dawn in eastern skies
10 To rift the fiery night that's in your eyes;
But there, where western glooms are gathering,
The dark will end the dark, if anything:
God slays Himself with every leaf that flies,
And hell is more than half of paradise.
15 No, there is not a dawn in eastern skies—
In eastern skies.

THE ARTIST'S GARDEN, c. 1880
Ralph Albert Blakelock
National Gallery of Art
Art Resource

Out of a grave I come to tell you this,
Out of a grave I come to quench the kiss
That flames upon your forehead with a glow
20 That blinds you to the way that you must go.
Yes, there is yet one way to where she is,
Bitter, but one that faith may never miss.
Out of a grave I come to tell you this—
To tell you this.

25 There is the western gate, Luke Havergal,
There are the crimson leaves upon the wall.
Go, for the winds are tearing them away,—
Nor think to riddle the dead words they say,
Nor any more to feel them as they fall;
30 But go, and if you trust her she will call.
There is the western gate, Luke Havergal—
Luke Havergal.

THINKING ABOUT THE SELECTION
Recalling

1. (a) Where does the speaker tell Luke Havergal to go? (b) What will happen when he gets there?
2. (a) From where has the speaker come? (b) What is his reason for coming?

Interpreting

3. What do you think was Luke's relationship to the woman referred to in the poem?
4. (a) Considering that the sun sets in the West and considering the details used in describing the western gate, what do you think the western gate symbolizes? (b) What does the "dawn in eastern skies" symbolize?

5. The speaker may actually be part of Luke Havergal's inner self. If this is so, what does the poem reveal about Luke Havergal's state of mind?
6. Considering Luke's state of mind and the action he is being urged to take, what do you think the speaker means when he comments, "The dark will end the dark"?
7. Robinson's use of repetition in the poem creates a hypnotic effect. How is this effect related to the meaning of the poem?

Applying

8. This poem suggests that a person can never replace a loved one whom he or she has lost. Discuss this view.

Miniver Cheevy

Edwin Arlington Robinson

Miniver Cheevy, child of scorn,
    Grew lean while he assailed the seasons;
He wept that he was ever born,
    And he had reasons.

5   Miniver loved the days of old
    When swords were bright and steeds were prancing;
The vision of a warrior bold
    Would set him dancing.

Miniver sighed for what was not,
10   And dreamed, and rested from his labors;
He dreamed of Thebes[1] and Camelot,[2]
    And Priam's[3] neighbors.

Miniver mourned the ripe renown
    That made so many a name so fragrant;
15   He mourned Romance, now on the town,[4]
    And Art, a vagrant.
Miniver loved the Medici,[5]
    Albeit he had never seen one;
He would have sinned incessantly
20   Could he have been one.

Miniver cursed the commonplace
    And eyed a khaki suit with loathing;
He missed the medieval grace
    Of iron clothing.

25   Miniver scorned the gold he sought,
    But sore annoyed was he without it;
Miniver thought, and thought, and thought,
    And thought about it.

---

1. Thebes (thēbz): A city-state in ancient Greece.
2. Camelot (kam′ ə lät′): The legendary English town where King Arthur's court and Round Table were located.
3. Priam (prī′ əm): King of Troy during the Trojan War.
4. on the town: On public assistance.
5. Medici (med′ ə chē): A rich, powerful family of Florence, Italy, in the fourteenth, fifteenth, and sixteenth centuries.

Miniver Cheevy, born too late,
30   Scratched his head and kept on thinking;
Miniver coughed, and called it fate,
        And kept on drinking.

THINKING ABOUT THE SELECTION

Recalling

1. (a) About what does Miniver Cheevy weep? (b) What does he love? (c) Of what does he dream? (d) What does he mourn? (e) What does he curse? (f) What does he scorn?
2. What does the final line reveal about how Miniver Cheevy copes with his unhappiness?

Interpreting

3. The word *miniver* refers to a white fur used for trimming ceremonial robes during the Middle Ages. Why is this an appropriate name for the character in the poem?
4. Considering Cheevy's condition, what do you think might be the real reason why he eyes "a khaki suit with loathing"?
5. (a) What paradox, or apparent self-contradiction, appears in lines 23–24? (b) What does this paradox reveal about Cheevy's understanding of the past?

Applying

6. Like Miniver Cheevy, people often try to escape from their problems, rather than confronting them and trying to find a solution. Why is this an ineffective way of dealing with problems?

ANALYZING LITERATURE

Understanding Irony

Irony is a contrast between what is stated and what is meant, or between what is expected to happen and what actually happens. Three types of irony used in literature are verbal irony, situational irony, and dramatic irony.

1. In line 2 the speaker comments that Cheevy "assailed the seasons." (a) How is this image related to Cheevy's visions of the past? (b) Why is this image ironic considering Cheevy's life?
2. What is ironic about Miniver's scorning the gold?
3. Explain how the use of irony affects your attitude toward Cheevy.

Richard Cory

Edwin Arlington Robinson

Whenever Richard Cory went down town,
We people on the pavement looked at him:
He was a gentleman from sole to crown,
Clean favored, and imperially slim.

5 And he was always quietly arrayed,
And he was always human when he talked;
But still he fluttered pulses when he said,
"Good-morning," and he glittered when he walked.

THE THINKER
(Portrait of Louis N. Kenton, 1900)
Thomas Eakins
The Metropolitan Museum of Art

And he was rich—yes, richer than a king—
10 And admirably schooled in every grace:
In fine, we thought that he was everything
To make us wish that we were in his place.

So on we worked, and waited for the light,
And went without the meat, and cursed the bread;
15 And Richard Cory, one calm summer night,
Went home and put a bullet through his head.

THINKING ABOUT THE SELECTION

Recalling

1. What does the speaker notice about Richard Cory each time he comes into town?
2. What does Richard Cory do "one calm summer night"?

Interpreting

3. (a) Who is the poem's speaker? (b) In what ways is the speaker different from Richard Cory?
4. What do the words "crown" (line 3) and "imperially" (line 4) suggest about the speaker's impression of Richard Cory?
5. Why would the poem be less forceful if the speaker had used the pronoun "I" instead of "we"? Explain your answer.
6. What makes the poem's final line surprising?
7. What do you think is the theme of the poem?

Applying

8. (a) Why do you think a person like Richard Cory, who seemingly has every reason to be happy, might in fact be miserable? (b) What do you think are the keys to a person's happiness?

9. The French writer Colette wrote, "What a wonderful life I've had! I only wish I'd realized it sooner." Discuss the meaning of this quotation.

CRITICAL THINKING AND READING

This poem points out that each person has a different outlook on life and that it is often difficult for people to perceive or understand the outlooks of others. In the poem we are presented with the speaker's view of Richard Cory, which leads us to expect Cory to be happy. As a result, we are shocked by the ending of the poem and forced to realize that the speaker's impressions were false. The ending also forces us to contemplate Cory's perceptions of himself and the speaker and to think about how they are different from the speaker's perceptions.

1. Considering the outcome of the poem, how do you think Cory's attitude toward himself differs from the speaker's attitude toward him?
2. What do you think might have been Richard Cory's attitude toward the townspeople?

EDGAR LEE MASTERS

1868–1950

Edgar Lee Masters is primarily remembered for one volume of his poetry. Yet this volume, *Spoon River Anthology,* is widely regarded as one of the finest collections of poetry ever produced by an American poet.

Masters was born in Kansas but grew up in rural southern Illinois—the area where Abraham Lincoln had spent his early years. After briefly attending Knox College, Masters studied law in his father's law office and eventually passed the bar exam. In 1891 he moved to Chicago, where he became a successful criminal lawyer. During his spare time, he wrote poems, plays, and essays, and he published some of his poems in the highly regarded Chicago magazine *Poetry*.

Masters's early poems, which were traditional in form, received little attention. In 1914, however, Masters's direction as a poet changed dramatically when a friend gave him a copy of *Selected Epitaphs from the Greek Anthology*. This collection included many concise, interconnected epitaphs that each captured the essence of a person's life. Using this structure and abandoning conventional rhyme and meter for free verse, Masters wrote a series of poems about the lives of people in rural southern Illinois. Published under the title *Spoon River Anthology* in 1915, the series provoked strong reactions among critics and became a best seller.

Spoon River Anthology consists of 244 epitaphs for characters buried in the mythical Spoon River cemetery. The dead themselves serve as the speakers of the poems, often revealing secrets they kept hidden throughout their lifetimes. Many types of people are represented, including storekeepers, housewives, and murderers. Some of the characters had lived happy lives, but many more had lived lives filled with frustration and despair. Presented together the epitaphs paint a vivid portrait of the loneliness and isolation with which people living in the Midwest at the time were often confronted.

Several years after *Spoon River Anthology* was published, Masters gave up his law practice to devote all of his energy to writing. Yet, while he was able to produce many other volumes of poetry in addition to novels, biographies, and his autobiography, *Across Spoon River,* he was never able to match the success of *Spoon River Anthology*.

GUIDE FOR READING

Lucinda Matlock; Fiddler Jones

Writer's Techniques

The Speaker. The speaker is the voice of a poem. Although the speaker is often the poet, the speaker may be also be a fictional character or even an inanimate object or another type of nonhuman entity. For example, the speakers in the poems in Edgar Lee Masters's *Spoon River Anthology* are fictional characters buried in the mythical Spoon River cemetery. By using the characters themselves as the speakers, Masters is able to delve deeply into the characters' minds. In each poem a different speaker discusses his or her own life intimately and honestly, candidly expressing his or her most profound thoughts, feelings, and emotions.

Many of the characters are based on people Masters observed or was acquainted with during his childhood. For example, Lucinda Matlock, one of the most forceful speakers, represents Masters's own grandmother.

Look For

As you read Edgar Lee Masters's poetry, look for the characters' inner selves as revealed by the speakers.

Writing

In *Spoon River Anthology,* Edgar Lee Masters paints portraits of a variety of characters based on people he observed during his childhood. Think of an interesting or amusing character from books, movies, or even current affairs. Then list details describing this person's appearance, personality, and behavior.

Vocabulary

Knowing the following words will help you as you read Edgar Lee Masters's poetry.

repose (ri pōz') *n.*: The state of being at rest (p. 687, l. 17)

degenerate (di jen' ər it) *adj.*: Deteriorated (p. 687, l. 20)

BARN DANCE, 1950
Grandma Moses
Copyright © 1973, Grandma Moses Properties Co., New York,

Lucinda Matlock

Edgar Lee Masters

I went to the dances at Chandlerville,
And played snap-out[1] at Winchester.
One time we changed partners,
Driving home in the moonlight of middle June,
5 And then I found Davis.
We were married and lived together for seventy years,
Enjoying, working, raising the twelve children,
Eight of whom we lost
Ere I had reached the age of sixty.

---

1. snap-out: A game often referred to as "crack-the whip," in which
a long line of players who are holding hands spin around in a circle,
causing the players on the end to be flung off by centrifugal force.
Note about art: Anna Mary Robertson Moses (1860–1961) began painting
in old age and became known as "Grandma" Moses. She painted country
landscapes and scenes remembered from her childhood.

10   I spun, I wove, I kept the house, I nursed the sick,
     I made the garden, and for holiday
     Rambled over the fields where sang the larks,
     And by Spoon River gathering many a shell,
     And many a flower and medicinal weed—
15   Shouting to the wooded hills, singing to the green valleys.
     At ninety-six I had lived enough, that is all,
     And passed to a sweet repose.
     What is this I hear of sorrow and weariness,
     Anger, discontent and drooping hopes?
20   Degenerate sons and daughters,
     Life is too strong for you—
     It takes life to love Life.

THINKING ABOUT THE SELECTION

Recalling

1. (a) How does Lucinda Matlock meet her husband? (b) How many years do they spend together? (c) How many children do they have? (d) What happens to eight of the children before Lucinda turns sixty?
2. What does Lucinda Matlock do "for holiday"?
3. When does she decide that she "had lived enough"?
4. What question does Lucinda Matlock ask?
5. What does she say it takes "to love life"?

Interpreting

6. (a) How would you characterize Lucinda Matlock's life? (b) What seems to be Lucinda Matlock's attitude concerning her life?
7. (a) Who are the "sons and daughters" Lucinda addresses in this poem? (b) What is her attitude toward them? (c) How is their attitude toward life different from her own? (d) What is the meaning of her message to them?

Applying

8. Explain whether you agree or disagree with Lucinda Matlock's message.

9. As this poem suggests, the general attitude toward life of one generation is often quite different from that of other generations. What do you think causes these differences?
10. How do you think Lucinda Matlock would respond to people who complain that life today is too complex and confusing?

THINKING AND WRITING

Writing an Epitaph

Imagine that you have entered a contest being held by your school literary magazine in which you are asked to write an epitaph in the style of Edgar Lee Masters. Start by reviewing the list of details you prepared describing an interesting or amusing person. Try to decide which details best capture the essence of the person's life. Then decide what message about life the epitaph should convey. When you write the epitaph, use free verse and try to capture the flavor of the person's life in a limited number of lines. When you finish writing, put your epitaph aside for one day. Then reread it and make any necessary revisions.

Fiddler Jones

Edgar Lee Masters

The earth keeps some vibration going
There in your heart, and that is you.
And if the people find you can fiddle,
Why, fiddle you must, for all your life.
5   What do you see, a harvest of clover?
Or a meadow to walk through to the river?
The wind's in the corn; you rub your hands
For beeves hereafter ready for market;
Or else you hear the rustle of skirts
10 Like the girls when dancing at Little Grove.
To Cooney Potter a pillar of dust
Or whirling leaves meant ruinous drouth;[1]
They looked to me like Red-Head Sammy
Stepping it off, to "Toor-a-Loor."
15 How could I till my forty acres
Not to speak of getting more,
With a medley of horns, bassoons and piccolos
Stirred in my brain by crows and robins
And the creak of a windmill—only these?
20 And I never started to plow in my life
That someone did not stop in the road
And take me away to a dance or picnic.
I ended up with forty acres;
I ended up with a broken fiddle—
25 And a broken laugh, and a thousand memories,
And not a single regret.

---

1. drouth: Drought.

THINKING ABOUT THE SELECTION

Recalling

1. According to Fiddler Jones, what must you do if "the people find you can fiddle"?
2. What are two explanations Fiddler Jones offers for his failures as a farmer?
3. What regrets does Fiddler Jones have about the way he lived his life?

Interpreting

4. What does Fiddler Jones mean when he comments, "The earth keeps some vibration going there in your heart, and that is you"?
5. What examples does Fiddler Jones use to point out that there are many different ways of viewing the world?
6. How is Fiddler Jones's view of life different from that of other farmers?
7. Explain the last three lines of the poem.

Applying

8. How might you apply the lesson taught by the story of Fiddler Jones to your own life?

ANALYZING LITERATURE

Identifying the Speaker

The **speaker** is the voice of a poem. The speaker may be the poet himself or herself, or it may be a fictional character or even an inanimate object or another type of nonhuman entity.

For example, the speaker in "Fiddler Jones" is Fiddler Jones himself.

1. How would "Fiddler Jones" be different if Masters had used a different speaker?
2. Explain whether the poem would be more or less effective if a different speaker had been used.
3. Fiddler Jones and the other speakers of the poems in *Spoon River Anthology* are dead. Why might this allow them to discuss their lives more openly and honestly than they would have if they were alive?

THINKING AND WRITING

Comparing and Contrasting Writers

Write an essay in which you compare and contrast Edwin Arlington Robinson's poetry with that of Edgar Lee Masters. Start by rereading the poems by Robinson and Masters in this book, noting similarities and differences in style, theme, and choice of subjects. Reread the biographies of Robinson and Masters, again noting similarities and differences between the two writers. Review your notes and prepare a thesis statement. Organize your notes according to corresponding points of contrast. Then begin writing your essay, using passages from the poems to support your argument. When you revise, make sure you have included enough supporting information.

YOU THE WRITER

Assignment

1. In their efforts to capture the local color of specific regions, many of the writers of the late nineteenth century used regional dialect in their works. Using regional dialect, write a dialogue between two characters living on the western frontier.

Prewriting. Review the stories in this unit in which writers use western dialect. Take note of the distinctive characteristics of the characters' speech in these stories.

Writing. Try to make your dialogue seem realistic, as if you were recording a conversation that really occurred. Also try to reveal something about the characters' personalities through their dialogue.

Revising. When you revise, make sure the speech of your characters has the same distinctive characteristics as that of the characters in the stories you read.

Assignment

2. As the nation expanded, many Americans left their homes and traveled to the western frontier, hoping to find new opportunities. In pursuing their dreams, these pioneers often had to overcome a great deal of adversity. Write a character sketch of the type of person you imagine would have chosen to make the long and treacherous journey westward.

Prewriting. Brainstorm about the character traits of a typical American pioneer. Arrange these traits in a logical order.

Writing. When writing your sketch, focus on describing the most important traits of the character's personality.

Revising. When you revise, make sure you have conveyed a clear and complete impression of the character's personality. After you finish revising, proofread your sketch and prepare a final copy.

Assignment

3. During the New England Renaissance, the Fireside Poets wrote poetry that was inspiring and optimistic. In the late nineteenth century, however, poets began creating works that expressed a less optimistic outlook, often focusing on the unpleasant realities of human existence. Imagine you are a poet living during the late nineteenth century, and write a poem that focuses on one of the difficulties or problems involved with life at the time.

Prewriting. Review the unit introduction and the poems in the unit to come up with a topic for your poem.

Writing. Write your poem, using regular rhyme and rhythm.

Revising. When you finish writing, revise your poem. Proofread it and share it with your classmates.

Assignment

1. As the nation grew and expanded, its population became more and more diverse, and people developed a desire to understand how people lived in other regions of the country. Write an essay in which you discuss how regional literature satisfied this desire.

Prewriting. Review the selections in this unit, noting what they reveal about life in the various regions of the country. Prepare a thesis statement, then arrange your notes into an outline.

Writing. When you write your essay, use evidence from several selections to support your thesis.

Revising. When you revise, make sure you have thoroughly supported your thesis and have not included any unnecessary information.

Assignment

2. The Naturalists were a group of nineteenth-century writers who possessed a well-defined view of the universe. Write an essay in which you discuss how the beliefs of the Naturalists are reflected in their works.

Prewriting. Review the discussion of Naturalism in the unit introduction. Then review the selections by Jack London and Stephen Crane, noting how they reflect the Naturalists' beliefs.

Writing. Include a thesis statement in your introduction, and develop and support your thesis in your body paragraphs.

Revising. When you revise, make sure you have used transitions and other linking devices to connect your ideas. After you have finished revising, proofread your essay and prepare a final copy.

Assignment

3. During the late nineteenth century, writers turned away from Romanticism and began to focus on depicting life as it was actually lived. Write an essay in which you compare and contrast a romantic short story with a realistic story.

Prewriting. Review the concepts of Romanticism and Realism. Choose a romantic story and a realistic story. For example, you might choose "The Fall of the House of Usher" and "A Wagner Matinée." Carefully reread the stories you choose, focusing on similarities and differences.

Writing. Organize your essay according to corresponding points of contrast, and use evidence from both stories to support your argument.

Revising. When you revise, make sure you have varied the length and structure of your sentences.

CITY ROOFS, 1932
Edward Hopper
Courtesy of Kennedy Galleries, Inc., New York

THE MODERN AGE
1915–1946

We asked the cyclone
to go around our barn
but it didn't hear us.
Carl Sandburg
from *The People, Yes*

Carl Sandburg served as a soldier in the Spanish-American War (1898) and wrote his first novel after the Second World War (1948). In the years between, he was a day laborer, a journalist, a salesman, an advertising manager, a world-renowned poet, and a Pulitzer Prize-winning biographer. The focus of Sandburg's writing, like that of Walt Whitman, was America.

The America that Sandburg observed was a nation achieving world dominance, but at the same time losing some of its youthful innocence and brash confidence. Two world wars, a dizzying decade of prosperity, and a devastating worldwide depression marked this era. With these events came a new age in American literature. The upheavals of the early twentieth century ushered in a period of artistic experimentation and lasting literary achievement.

THE HISTORICAL SETTING

The years immediately preceding World War I were characterized by an overwhelming sense of optimism. Numerous technological advances occurred, dramatically affecting people's lives, and creating a sense of promise concerning the future. While a number of serious social problems still existed, reforms aimed at solving these problems began to be instituted. When World War I broke out in 1914, however, President Woodrow Wilson was forced to turn his attention away from the troubles at home and focus on the events in Europe.

War in Europe

World War I was one of the bloodiest and most tragic conflicts ever to occur. When the initial advances of the German forces were stalled, the conflict was transformed into a trench war. The introduction of the machine gun made it virtually impossible for one side to launch a successful attack on its opponents' trenches, however, and the war dragged on for several years with little progress being made by either side. Each unsuccessful attack resulted in the deaths of thousands of soldiers, and the war ultimately claimed almost an entire generation of European men.

President Wilson wanted the United States to remain neutral in the war, but that proved impossible. In 1915, a German submarine sank the *Lusitania,* pride of the British merchant fleet. More than 1200 people on board lost their lives, including 128 Americans. After the sinking, American public opinion tended to favor the Allies—England, France, Italy, and Russia. When Germany resumed unrestricted submarine warfare two years later, the United States abandoned neutrality and joined the Allied cause.

At first the reality of war did not sink in. Americans were confident and carefree as the troops set off overseas. That cheerful mood soon passed. A number of famous American writers saw the war firsthand and learned of its horror. E. E. Cummings, Ernest Hemingway, and John Dos Passos served as ambulance drivers. Hemingway later served in the Italian infantry and was seriously wounded. Other, less famous writers fought and died in France. Among them were the poets Joyce Kilmer, who wrote "Trees," and Alan Seeger, who wrote "I Have a Rendezvous with Death."

Prosperity and Depression

The end of the Great War in November 1918 brought little peace to Woodrow Wilson. His dream of the United States joining the League of Nations to prevent future wars failed. The war's end brought little peace to the big cities of America either. In 1919, Prohibition made the sale of liquor illegal, leading to bootlegging, speakeasies, widespread lawbreaking, and sporadic warfare among competing gangs.

Throughout the 1920's, the nation seemed on a binge. After a brief recession in 1920 and 1921, the economy boomed. New buildings rose everywhere, creating new downtown sections in many cities—Omaha, Des Moines, and Minneapolis among them. Radio arrived, and so did jazz. Movies became big business, and spectacular movie palaces sprang up across the country. Fads abounded: raccoon coats, flagpole sitting, the Charleston. The great literary interpreter of the Roaring Twenties was F. Scott Fitzgerald. In *The Beautiful and Damned* and *The Great Gatsby* Fitz-

ARMISTICE DAY, 1918
Gifford Beal
Indiana University Art Museum

AMERICAN EVENTS

1916   *Chicago Poems* by **Carl Sandburg** appears.

1917   United States enters First World War.

1919   Prohibition becomes law, followed by rum-running, speakeasies; law repealed in 1933.

        Sherwood Anderson publishes *Winesburg, Ohio*.

1920   Sinclair Lewis publishes *Main Street*.

        Nineteenth Amendment to Constitution gives U.S. women the right to vote.

1921   Eugene O'Neill's play *Beyond the Horizon* wins the Pulitzer Prize.

1922   **E. E. Cummings** publishes *The Enormous Room*.

        T. S. Eliot publishes *The Waste Land*.

1923   **Wallace Stevens** publishes Harmonium.

1925   **F. Scott Fitzgerald** publishes *The Great Gatsby*.

        William Carlos Williams publishes *In the American Grain*.

1926   **Langston Hughes** publishes *The Weary Blues*.

        Ernest Hemingway publishes *The Sun Also Rises*.

James Joyce   Langston Hughes

Signing of Treaty of Versailles

Prohibition Declared

Nineteenth Amendment Adopted

F. Scott Fitzgerald

Carl Sandburg

Mural by José Orozco

D. H. Lawrence

1917 Russia: Bolsheviks seize control of Russia in October Revolution.

1918 Worldwide influenza epidemic kills as many as 20 million people.

England: Siegfried Sassoon publishes *Counter-Attack*.

1919 France: Treaty of Versailles ends First World War but sets harsh peace terms.

1921 Mexico: Diego Rivera paints murals that, along with José Orozco's, spark Mexican Renaissance.

England: D. H. Lawrence publishes *Women in Love*.

1922 Ireland: James Joyce publishes *Ulysses*.

1923 Ireland: Nobel Prize for Literature awarded to poet William Butler Yeats.

1924 Germany: Thomas Mann publishes *The Magic Mountain*.

England: E. M. Forster publishes *A Passage to India*.

1925 Czechoslovakia-Germany: *The Trial*, a novel by Franz Kafka, published posthumously.

England: Virginia Woolf publishes *Mrs. Dalloway*.

1926 Russia: Ivan Pavlov reports his experimental findings in *Conditioned Reflexes*.

1927 Charles Lindbergh flies solo and nonstop from New York to Paris.

1929 **Ernest Hemingway** publishes *A Farewell to Arms*.

Thomas Wolfe's *Look Homeward, Angel* appears.

William Faulkner publishes *The Sound and the Fury*.

Stock market crashes in October, followed by Great Depression of 1930's.

1930 **Katherine Anne Porter** publishes *Flowering Judas*.

John Dos Passos publishes *The 42nd Parallel*, first novel in *U.S.A.* trilogy.

1931 Pearl S. Buck's *The Good Earth*, wins the Pulitzer Prize.

1933 In the worst year of The Depression, President Franklin D. Roosevelt closes banks; Congress passes New Deal laws.

1938 **Thornton Wilder's** play, *Our Town,* opens.

1939 **John Steinbeck** publishes *The Grapes of Wrath*.

United States declares neutrality as World War II breaks out in Europe.

1940 Richard Wright publishes *Native Son*.

1941 *A Curtain of Green* by **Eudora Welty** appears.

Japanese bomb American naval base at Pearl Harbor, bringing U.S. into World War II.

1945 World War II ends after U.S. drops two atomic bombs on Japan.

Charles Lindbergh

Stock Market Crash   Franklin Delano Roosevelt

Woman Working During World War II

Atomic Bombs Dropped on Japan

Adolf Hitler

Nazi Troops

George Orwell

...we here highly resolve that these dead shall not have died in vain...

REMEMBER DEC. 7th!

Japanese Bomb Pearl Harbor

1927   England: Virginia Woolf publishes *To the Lighthouse*.

1928   China: Chiang Kai-shek becomes head of Nationalist government.

   Germany: Kurt Weill and Bertolt Brecht write and produce *The Threepenny Opera*.

1930   India: Mahatma Gandhi leads famous march to the sea to protest British tax on salt.

1931   Spain: Salvador Dali paints *Persistence of Memory*.

1933   Germany: Adolf Hitler becomes German chancellor and imposes Nazism.

1934   Wales: Dylan Thomas publishes *Eighteen Poems*.

1936   USSR: Stalin starts Great Purge to rid government and armed forces of opposition.

   Spain: Spanish Civil War begins.

1938   England: George Orwell publishes *Homage to Catalonia*.

1939   Poland: German blitzkrieg invasion of Poland sets off Second World War in Europe.

1940   France surrenders to Germany in same railroad car in which Germany had surrendered to France in 1918.

1941   Arthur Koestler publishes *Darkness at Noon*, a novel on totalitarianism.

1942   Albert Camus completes *The Stranger*.

1943   France: Jean-Paul Sartre writes *Being and Nothingness*.

1945   United Nations Charter signed at end of Second World War.

THE CITY FROM GREENWICH VILLAGE, 1922
John Sloan
National Gallery of Art, Washington, D.C.

gerald showed both the glamorous and the pitiful sides of the American dream.

During the 1920's, artists and writers flocked to Greenwich Village, in New York City. Older buildings in the area, including barns, stables, and houses, were converted to studios, nightclubs, theaters, and shops. In 1923, playwright Eugene O'Neill founded the Greenwich Village Theatre, where experimental dramas were performed. Thomas Wolfe taught English at New York University in the Village while writing his autobiographical novel, *Look Homeward, Angel.*

In late October 1929, the stock market crashed, marking the beginning of the Great Depression. By mid-1932, about 12 million people, or one quarter of the work force, were out of work. Even as bread lines formed and the numbers of unemployed grew, most business leaders remained optimistic. But the situation continued to worsen. In the presidential election of 1932, New York's Governor Franklin D. Roosevelt defeated incumbent President Herbert Hoover. Roosevelt embarked on a far-reaching program, the New Deal, to turn the economic tide. He won reelection in 1936 and again in 1940. While circumstances had improved by then, prosperity did not begin to equal that of the 1920's.

World War II

Only 20 years after the Treaty of Versailles had ended the First World War, the German invasion of Poland touched off the Second World War. As in the earlier war, most Americans wanted to remain neutral. Even after the fall of France in 1940, the dominant mood in the United States was one of isolationism. But when the Japanese attacked Pearl Harbor in Hawaii on December 7, 1941, America could stay neutral no longer. The United States declared war on the Axis powers—Japan, Germany, and Italy.

After years of bitter fighting on two fronts, the Allies—including the United States, Great Britain, the Soviet Union, and France—defeated Nazi Germany. Japan surrendered three months later, after the United States had dropped atomic bombs on two Japanese cities. Peace, and the atomic age, had arrived.

THE BIRTH OF MODERNISM

The devastation of World War I brought about an end to the sense of optimism that had characterized the years immediately preceding the war. Many people were left with a feeling of uncertainty, disjointedness, and disillusionment. No longer trusting the ideas and values of the world out of which the war had developed, people sought to find new ideas that were more applicable to twentieth-century life. The quest for new ideas extended into the world of literature, and a major literary movement known as Modernism was born.

The Modernists experimented with a wide variety of new approaches and techniques, producing a remarkably diverse body of literature. Yet, the Modernists shared a common purpose. They sought to capture the essence of modern life in the form and content of their work. To reflect the fragmentation of the modern world, the Modernists constructed their works out of fragments, omitting the expositions, transitions, resolutions, and explanations used in traditional literature. In poetry, they abandoned traditional forms in favor of free verse. The themes of their works were usually implied, rather than directly stated, creating a sense of uncertainty and forcing readers to draw their own conclusions. In general, Modernist

LIBRARY
Bernard Boruch Zakheim
Coit Tower Mural (WPA)
San Francisco Art Commission

ERNEST HEMINGWAY

1899–1961

In his short stories and novels, Ernest Hemingway vividly and forcefully expressed the sentiments of many members of the post-World War I generation. Using a concise, direct style, he wrote about peoples' struggles to maintain a sense of dignity while living in a seemingly hostile and confusing world.

Hemingway was born and raised in Oak Park, Illinois. After graduating from high school, he got a job as a reporter for the Kansas City *Star*. He was eager to serve in World War I, and in 1918 he joined the Red Cross ambulance corps and was sent to the Italian front. Shortly after his arrival, he was severely wounded, and he spent several months recovering in a hospital in Milan. His experiences during the war shaped his views and provided material for his writing.

After the war Hemingway had a difficult time readjusting to life in the United States. Hoping to find personal contentment and establish himself as a writer, he went to Paris where he became friends with Ezra Pound, F. Scott Fitzgerald, Gertrude Stein, and other expatriate writers and artists. His new friends provided him with valuable advice, helped to develop his style, and encouraged his interest in writing.

In 1925 Hemingway published his first major work, *In Our Time,* a series of loosely connected short stories. A year later he published *The Sun Also Rises,* a novel about a group of British and American expatriates searching for sensations that will enable them to forget the pain and disillusionment they associate with life in the modern world. The novel earned him international acclaim, and he remained famous throughout the rest of his life. Yet he was almost as well known for his lifestyle as he was for his writing. Constantly pursuing adventure, he traveled the world, hunting in Africa, deep-sea fishing in the Caribbean, and skiing in Idaho and Europe.

Despite his thirst for adventure, Hemingway remained a productive and successful writer, transforming his observations and experiences into novels and short stories. His novels *A Farewell to Arms* (1926), based on his experiences during World War I, and *For Whom the Bell Tolls* (1940), based on his observations as a war correspondent during the Spanish Civil War, have become American classics. *The Old Man and the Sea* (1952), the story of an old fisherman's struggle to maintain dignity in the face of defeat, won the Pulitzer Prize and helped earn him the Nobel Prize for Literature in 1954.

In Another Country

Modernism. Following World War I there was a growing sense of uncertainty, disjointedness, and disillusionment among certain members of American society. Many people came to distrust the ideas and values of the past and sought to find new ideas that seemed more applicable to twentieth-century life. Similarly, writers began turning away from the style, form, and content of nineteenth-century literature and began experimenting with new themes and techniques. A new literary movement, known as Modernism, was born.

The Modernists attempted to capture the essence of modern life in both the form and the content of their work. The uncertainty, bewilderment, and apparent meaninglessness of modern life were common themes in modern literature. These themes were generally implied, rather than directly stated, to reflect a sense of uncertainty and to enable readers to draw their own conclusions. For similar reasons fiction writers began abandoning the traditional plot structure, omitting the expositions and resolutions that in the past had clarified the work for the reader. Instead, stories and novels were structured to reflect the fragmentation and uncertainty of human experience. A typical modern story or novel seems to begin arbitrarily and to end without a resolution, leaving the reader with possibilities, not solutions.

As you read "In Another Country," look for the way that the form and content of the story reflect the uncertainty of modern life.

Most of Hemingway's stories and novels were based on his observations and experiences. "In Another Country," for example, grew out of his observations during his hospitalization in Milan. Prepare a list of your own observations and experiences that you could use as topics for narratives.

Knowing the following word will help you as you read "In Another Country."
invalided (in' və lid'd) *v.*: Released because of illness or disability (p. 726)

In Another Country

Ernest Hemingway

In the fall the war[1] was always there, but we did not go to it any more. It was cold in the fall in Milan[2] and the dark came very early. Then the electric lights came on, and it was pleasant along the streets looking in the windows. There was much game hanging outside the shops, and the snow powdered in the fur of the foxes and the wind blew their tails. The deer hung stiff and heavy and empty, and small birds blew in the wind and the wind turned their feathers. It was a cold fall and the wind came down from the mountains.

We were all at the hospital every afternoon, and there were different ways of walking across the town through the dusk to the hospital. Two of the ways were alongside canals, but they were long. Always, though, you crossed a bridge across a canal to enter the hospital. There was a choice of three bridges. On one of them a woman sold roasted chestnuts. It was warm, standing in front of her charcoal fire, and the chestnuts were warm afterward in your pocket. The hospital was very old and very beautiful, and you entered through a gate and walked across a courtyard and out a gate on the other side. There were usually funerals starting from the courtyard. Beyond the old hospital were the new brick pavilions, and there we met every afternoon and were all very polite and interested in what was the matter, and sat in the machines that were to make so much difference.

The doctor came up to the machine where I was sitting and said: "What did you like best to do before the war? Did you practice a sport?"

I said: "Yes, football."

"Good," he said. "You will be able to play football again better than ever."

My knee did not bend and the leg dropped straight from the knee to the ankle without a calf, and the machine was to bend the knee and make it move as in riding a tricycle. But it did not bend yet, and instead the machine lurched when it came to the bending part. The doctor said: "That will all pass. You are a fortunate young man. You will play football again like a champion."

In the next machine was a major who had a little hand like a baby's. He winked at me when the doctor examined his hand, which was between two leather straps that bounced up and down and flapped the stiff fingers, and said: "And will I too play football, captain-doctor?" He had been a very great fencer, and before the war the greatest fencer in Italy.

The doctor went to his office in a back room and brought a photograph which showed a hand that had been withered almost as small as the major's, before it had taken a machine course, and after was a little larger. The major held the photograph with his good hand and looked at it very carefully. "A wound?" he asked.

"An industrial accident," the doctor said.

"Very interesting, very interesting," the major said, and handed it back to the doctor.

---

1. **the war:** World War I (1914–1918).
2. **Milan** (mi lan′): A city in northern Italy.

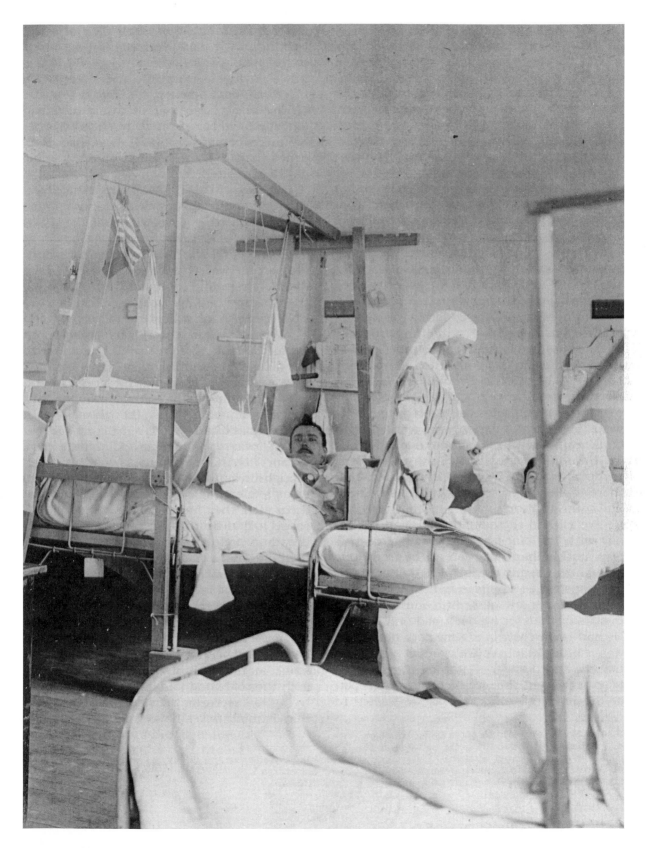

He stood there biting his lower lip. "It is very difficult," he said. "I cannot resign myself."

He looked straight past me and out through the window. Then he began to cry. "I am utterly unable to resign myself," he said and choked. And then crying, his head up looking at nothing, carrying himself straight and soldierly, with tears on both his cheeks and biting his lips, he walked past the machines and out the door.

The doctor told me that the major's wife, who was very young and whom he had not married until he was definitely invalided out of the war, had died of pneumonia. She had been sick only a few days. No one expected her to die. The major did not come to the hospital for three days. Then he came at the usual hour, wearing a black band on the sleeve of his uniform. When he came back, there were large framed photographs around the wall, of all sorts of wounds before and after they had been cured by the machines. In front of the machine the major used were three photographs of hands like his that were completely restored. I do not know where the doctor got them. I always understood we were the first to use the machines. The photographs did not make much difference to the major because he only looked out of the window.

THINKING ABOUT THE SELECTION

Recalling

1. (a) Where does the narrator go every afternoon?   (b) Why does he go there?
2. (a) What do the papers reveal about how the narrator acquired his medals?   (b) How do the boys' attitude toward the narrator change when they read the papers?
3. (a) What advice does the major give the narrator toward the end of the story?   (b) What has happened to the major's wife?
4. (a) What pictures are hanging on the wall when the major returns?   (b) Why does the narrator think the pictures are deceptive?

Interpreting

5. What mood do the details of the setting convey?
6. (a) How is the narrator's attitude toward the war different from that of the three boys?   (b) How might this difference in attitude be related to their nationalities?
7. What do you think is the significance of the major's interest in grammar?
8. In this story the machines come to symbolize the false hopes and promises of the modern age. What details convey the symbolic meaning of the machines?
9. Considering that the major waited until he was invalided out of the war to marry his wife, what is ironic about her death?

Applying

10. Gertrude Stein wrote, "You are all a lost generation." This epigraph has come to stand for the young people of Hemingway's time.   (a) In what way are the young men in this story "lost"?   (b) Are there any ways in which they are not lost? Explain your answer.
11. Explain the two meanings suggested by the title of this story.
12. World War I left many people feeling disillusioned because it caused the death of thousands of men, though it seemed to have no purpose. How does this story reflect this sense of disillusionment?

ANALYZING LITERATURE

Understanding Modernism

Modernism was a literary movement in which writers attempted to capture the essence of modern life in both the form and content of their work. One of the themes of "In Another Country," for example, is that in the modern age people are often presented with false hopes and promises.

1. Like most other Modernist stories, "In Another Country" lacks an exposition and a resolution. What Modernist perception does the use of this technique reflect?
2. In this story the narrator makes no direct statements about the war, allowing us to draw our own conclusions. How does this reflect the Modernist belief in the uncertainty of modern life?

CRITICAL THINKING AND READING

Analyzing the Effect of Style

Hemingway's style is easily distinguished from that of most other writers. He wrote in journalistic style, relating events in a straightforward manner with little elaboration and using simple and direct yet rhythmic and precise language.

1. Considering the Modernists' desire to force readers to draw their own conclusions from their works, why is Hemingway's journalistic style appropriate?
2. The nineteenth-century poet Robert Browning wrote, "Less is more." This aphorism was picked up by the twentieth-century architect Ludwig Mies van der Rohe and came to stand for a style in which design was simplified and form was made to serve function. Explain how the aphorism "less is more" can be said to characterize Hemingway's writing style.

THINKING AND WRITING

Responding to a Statement

Hemingway once commented, ". . . I always try to write on the principle of the iceberg. There is seven-eighths of it under water for every part that shows." Write an essay relating this statement to "In Another Country." Start by reviewing the story, taking note of Hemingway's concise style and how he uses such techniques as symbolism and irony to convey meaning. Organize your notes into an outline. Then write your essay, using passages from the story to support Hemingway's statement. When you finish writing, revise your essay, making sure you have backed up your thesis with details from the story. Proofread your essay and share it with your classmates.

F. SCOTT FITZGERALD

1896–1940

During the 1920's many Americans lived with reckless abandon, attending wild parties, wearing glamorous clothing, and striving for personal fulfillment through material wealth. Yet this quest for pleasure was often accompanied by a sense of inner despair. In his short stories and novels, F. Scott Fitzgerald captured both the gaiety and the emptiness of the time.

Francis Scott Key Fitzgerald was born in St. Paul, Minnesota, into a family with high social aspirations but little wealth. He entered Princeton University in 1913, but he failed to graduate. In 1917 he enlisted in the army. He was stationed in Montgomery, Alabama, where he fell in love with Zelda Sayre, a young southern belle. Shortly after being discharged from the army, Fitzgerald published his first novel, *This Side of Paradise* (1920). The novel earned him instant fame and wealth, which enabled him to persuade Zelda to marry him.

The Fitzgeralds soon became a part of the wealthy, extravagant, and hedonistic society that characterized the Roaring Twenties. Spending time in both New York and Europe, the glamorous couple mingled with rich and famous artists and aristocrats, attending countless parties and spending money recklessly. Despite his wild lifestyle, Fitzgerald remained a productive writer. During the twenties he published dozens of short stories and his most successful novel, *The Great Gatsby* (1926), the story of a self-made man whose dreams of love and social acceptance lead to scandal and corruption and ultimately end in tragedy. The novel displayed both Fitzgerald's fascination with and growing distrust of the wealthy society he had embraced.

Following the stock market crash in 1929, Fitzgerald's life changed dramatically. His wife suffered a series of nervous breakdowns, his reputation as a writer declined, and financial difficulties forced him to seek work as a Hollywood screenwriter. Despite these setbacks, however, he managed to produce many more short stories and a second fine novel, *Tender is the Night* (1934). Focusing on the decline of a young American psychiatrist following his marriage to a wealthy patient, the novel reflected Fitzgerald's awareness of the tragedy that can result from an obsession with wealth and social status.

Fitzgerald died of a heart attack in 1940. At the time he was in the midst of writing *The Last Tycoon* (1941), a novel about a Hollywood film mogul.

GUIDE FOR READING

Winter Dreams

Writer's Techniques

Characterization. Characterization is the means by which a writer reveals a character's personality. Writers generally develop a character through one or more of the following methods: direct statements about the character, physical descriptions of the character, the character's actions, the character's thoughts and comments, or another character's reactions to or comments about the character. In "Winter Dreams" F. Scott Fitzgerald develops the two main characters using a variety of these methods. For example, he reveals an important aspect of Dexter Green's personality directly, when he comments that Dexter "wanted not association with glittering things and glittering people—he wanted the glittering things themselves."

Look For

"Winter Dreams" is about a young man who becomes obsessed with a young woman and the ideals he associates with her. As you read "Winter Dreams," look for the methods Fitzgerald uses to develop the main characters. What do you learn about Dexter Green? What do you learn about Judy Jones?

Writing

In Don Marquis's poem "Unjust," Archy the cockroach writes, "beauty gets the best of it/in this world." Freewrite, exploring your reaction to Archy's comment.

Vocabulary

Knowing the following words will help you as you read "Winter Dreams."

fallowness (fal′ ō nis) *n*.: Inactivity (p. 730)

preposterous (pri päs′ tər əs) *adj*.: Ridiculous (p. 732)

ominous (äm′ə nəs) *adj*.: Threatening; sinister (p. 732)

fortuitous (fôr tōō′ə təs) *adj*.: Fortunate (p. 732)

perturbation (pʉr′ tər bā′ shən) *n*.: Agitation (p. 732)

sinuous (sin′ yoo wəs) *adj*.: Wavy (p. 735)

mundane (mun dān′) *adj*.: Commonplace; ordinary (p. 736)

poignant (poin′ yənt) *adj*.: Sharply painful to the feelings (p. 740)

pugilistic (pyōō′ jə lis′ tik) *adj*.: Like a boxer (p. 741)

somnolent (säm′ nə lənt) *adj*.: Sleepy; drowsy (p. 741)

Winter Dreams

F. Scott Fitzgerald

I

Some of the caddies were poor as sin and lived in one-room houses with a neurasthenic[1] cow in the front yard, but Dexter Green's father owned the second best grocery store in Black Bear—the best one was "The Hub," patronized by the wealthy people from Sherry Island—and Dexter caddied only for pocket money.

In the fall when the days became crisp and gray, and the long Minnesota winter shut down like the white lid of a box, Dexter's skis moved over the snow that hid the fairways of the golf course. At these times the country gave him a feeling of profound melancholy—it offended him that the links should lie in enforced fallowness, haunted by ragged sparrows for the long season. It was dreary, too, that on the tees where the gay colors fluttered in summer there were now only the desolate sandboxes knee deep in crusted ice. When he crossed the hills the wind blew cold as misery, and if the sun was out he tramped with his eyes squinted up against the hard dimensionless glare.

In April the winter ceased abruptly. The snow ran down into Black Bear Lake scarcely tarrying for the early golfers to brave the season with red and black balls. Without elation, without an interval of moist glory, the cold was gone.

Dexter knew that there was something dismal about this Northern spring, just as he knew there was something gorgeous about the fall. Fall made him clinch his hands and tremble and repeat idiotic sentences to himself, and make brisk abrupt gestures of command to imaginary audiences and armies. October filled him with hope which November raised to a sort of ecstatic triumph, and in this mood the fleeting brilliant impressions of the summer at Sherry Island were ready grist to his mill. He became a golf champion and defeated Mr. T. A. Hedrick in a marvelous match played a hundred times over the fairways of his imagination, a match each detail of which he changed about untiringly—sometimes he won with almost laughable ease, sometimes he came up magnificently from behind. Again, stepping from a Pierce-Arrow automobile, like Mr. Mortimer Jones, he strolled frigidly into the lounge of the Sherry Island Golf Club—or perhaps, surrounded by an admiring crowd, he gave an exhibition of fancy diving from the springboard of the club raft. . . . Among those who watched him in open-mouthed wonder was Mr. Mortimer Jones.

And one day it came to pass that Mr. Jones—himself and not his ghost—came up to Dexter with tears in his eyes and said that Dexter was the —— best caddy in the club, and wouldn't he decide not to quit if Mr. Jones made it worth his while, because every other —— caddy in the club lost one ball a hole for him—regularly——

"No, sir," said Dexter decisively, "I don't want to caddy any more." Then, after a pause: "I'm too old."

"You're not more than fourteen. Why the devil did you decide just this morning that

---

1. neurasthenic (noor′ əs then′ ik) *adj.*: Here, weak, tired.

FLOATING ICE, 1910
George Bellows
Collection of the Whitney Museum of American Art

you wanted to quit? You promised that next week you'd go over to the state tournament with me."

"I decided I was too old."

Dexter handed in his "A Class" badge, collected what money was due him from the caddy master, and walked home to Black Bear Village.

"The best —— caddy I ever saw," shouted Mr. Mortimer Jones over a drink that afternoon. "Never lost a ball! Willing! Intelligent! Quiet! Honest! Grateful!"

The little girl who had done this was eleven—beautifully ugly as little girls are apt to be who are destined after a few years to be inexpressibly lovely and bring no end of misery to a great number of men. The spark, however, was perceptible. There was a general ungodliness in the way her lips twisted down at the corners when she smiled, and in

the—Heaven help us!—in the almost passionate quality of her eyes. Vitality is born early in such women. It was utterly in evidence now, shining through her thin frame in a sort of glow.

She had come eagerly out on to the course at nine o'clock with a white linen nurse and five small new golf clubs in a white canvas bag which the nurse was carrying. When Dexter first saw her she was standing by the caddy house, rather ill at ease and trying to conceal the fact by engaging her nurse in an obviously unnatural conversation graced by startling and irrelevant grimaces from herself.

"Well, it's certainly a nice day, Hilda," Dexter heard her say. She drew down the corners of her mouth, smiled, and glanced furtively around, her eyes in transit falling for an instant on Dexter.

Then to the nurse:

"Well, I guess there aren't very many people out here this morning, are there?"

The smile again—radiant, blatantly artificial—convincing.

"I don't know what we're supposed to do now," said the nurse looking nowhere in particular.

"Oh, that's all right. I'll fix it up."

Dexter stood perfectly still, his mouth slightly ajar. He knew that if he moved forward a step his stare would be in her line of vision—if he moved backward he would lose his full view of her face. For a moment he had not realized how young she was. Now he remembered having seen her several times the year before—in bloomers.

Suddenly, involuntarily, he laughed, a short abrupt laugh—then, startled by himself, he turned and began to walk quickly away.

"Boy!"

Dexter stopped.

"Boy——"

Beyond question he was addressed. Not only that, but he was treated to that absurd smile, that preposterous smile—the memory of which at least a dozen men were to carry into middle age.

"Boy, do you know where the golf teacher is?"

"He's giving a lesson."

"Well, do you know where the caddy master is?"

"He isn't here yet this morning."

"Oh." For a moment this baffled her. She stood alternately on her right and left foot.

"We'd like to get a caddy," said the nurse. "Mrs. Mortimer Jones sent us out to play golf, and we don't know how without we get a caddy."

Here she was stopped by an ominous glance from Miss Jones, followed immediately by the smile.

"There aren't any caddies here except me," said Dexter to the nurse, "and I got to stay here in charge until the caddy master gets here."

"Oh."

Miss Jones and her retinue now withdrew, and at a proper distance from Dexter became involved in a heated conversation, which was concluded by Miss Jones taking one of the clubs and hitting it on the ground with violence. For further emphasis she raised it again and was about to bring it down smartly upon the nurse's bosom, when the nurse seized the club and twisted it from her hands.

"You little mean old *thing!*" cried Miss Jones wildly.

Another argument ensued. Realizing that the elements of the comedy were implied in the scene, Dexter several times began to laugh, but each time restrained the laugh before it reached audibility. He could not resist the monstrous conviction that the little girl was justified in beating the nurse.

The situation was resolved by the fortuitous appearance of the caddy master, who was appealed to immediately by the nurse.

"Miss Jones is to have a little caddy, and this one says he can't go."

"Mr. McKenna said I was to wait here till you came," said Dexter quickly.

"Well, he's here now." Miss Jones smiled cheerfully at the caddy master. Then she dropped her bag and set off at a haughty mince toward the first tee.

"Well?" The caddy master turned to Dexter. "What you standing there like a dummy for? Go pick up the young lady's clubs."

"I don't think I'll go out today," said Dexter.

"You don't——"

"I think I'll quit."

The enormity of his decision frightened him. He was a favorite caddy, and the thirty dollars a month he earned through the summer were not to be made elsewhere around the lake. But he had received a strong emotional shock, and his perturbation required a violent and immediate outlet.

It is not so simple as that, either. As so frequently would be the case in the future, Dexter was unconsciously dictated to by his winter dreams.

II

Now, of course, the quality and the seasonability of these winter dreams varied, but the stuff of them remained. They persuaded Dexter several years later to pass up a business course at the State university—his father, prospering now, would have paid his way—for the precarious advantage of attending an older and more famous university in the East, where he was bothered by his scanty funds. But do not get the impression, because his winter dreams happened to be concerned at first with musings on the rich, that there was anything merely snobbish in the boy. He wanted not association with glittering things and glittering people—he wanted the glittering things themselves. Often he reached out for the best without knowing why he wanted it—and sometimes he ran up against the mysterious denials and prohibitions in which life indulges. It is with one of those denials and not with his career as a whole that this story deals.

He made money. It was rather amazing. After college he went to the city from which Black Bear Lake draws its wealthy patrons. When he was only twenty-three and had been there not quite two years, there were already people who liked to say: "Now *there's* a boy—" All about him rich men's sons were peddling bonds precariously, or investing patrimonies precariously, or plodding through the two dozen volumes of the "George Washington Commercial Course," but Dexter borrowed a thousand dollars on his college degree and his confident mouth, and bought a partnership in a laundry.

It was a small laundry when he went into it, but Dexter made a specialty of learning how the English washed fine woolen golf stockings without shrinking them, and within a year he was catering to the trade that wore knickerbockers. Men were insisting that their Shetland hose and sweaters go to his laundry, just as they had insisted on a caddy who could find golf balls. A little later he was doing their wives' lingerie as well— and running five branches in different parts of the city. Before he was twenty-seven he owned the largest string of laundries in his section of the country. It was then that he sold out and went to New York. But the part of his story that concerns us goes back to the days when he was making his first big success.

When he was twenty-three Mr. Hart—one of the gray-haired men who like to say "Now there's a boy"—gave him a guest card to the Sherry Island Golf Club for a weekend. So he signed his name one day on the register, and that afternoon played golf in a foursome with Mr. Hart and Mr. Sandwood and Mr. T. A. Hedrick. He did not consider it necessary to remark that he had once carried Mr. Hart's bag over this same links, and that he knew every trap and gully with his eyes shut—but he found himself glancing at the four caddies who trailed them, trying to catch a gleam or gesture that would remind him of himself, that would lessen the gap which lay between his present and his past.

It was a curious day, slashed abruptly with fleeting, familiar impressions. One minute he had the sense of being a trespasser—in the next he was impressed by the tremendous superiority he felt toward Mr. T. A. Hedrick, who was a bore and not even a good golfer any more.

Then, because of a ball Mr. Hart lost near the fifteenth green, an enormous thing happened. While they were searching the stiff grasses of the rough there was a clear call of "Fore!" from behind a hill in their rear. And as they all turned abruptly from their search a bright new ball sliced abruptly over the hill and caught Mr. T. A. Hedrick in the abdomen.

"By Gad!" cried Mr. T. A. Hedrick, "they ought to put some of these crazy women off the course. It's getting to be outrageous."

A head and a voice came up together over the hill:

"Do you mind if we go through?"

"You hit me in the stomach!" declared Mr. Hedrick wildly.

"Did I?" The girl approached the group of men. "I'm sorry. I yelled 'Fore!' "

Her glance fell casually on each of the men—then scanned the fairway for her ball.

"Did I bounce into the rough?"

It was impossible to determine whether this question was ingenuous or malicious. In a moment, however, she left no doubt, for as her partner came up over the hill she called cheerfully:

"Here I am! I'd have gone on the green except that I hit something."

As she took her stance for a short mashie shot, Dexter looked at her closely. She wore a blue gingham dress, rimmed at throat and shoulders with a white edging that accentuated her tan. The quality of exaggeration, of thinness, which had made her passionate eyes and down-turning mouth absurd at eleven, was gone now. She was arrestingly beautiful. The color in her cheeks was centered like the color in a picture—it was not a "high" color, but a sort of fluctuating and feverish warmth, so shaded that it seemed at any moment it would recede and disappear. This color and the mobility of her mouth gave a continual impression of flux, of intense life, of passionate vitality—balanced only partially by the sad luxury of her eyes.

She swung her mashie impatiently and without interest, pitching the ball into a sand pit on the other side of the green. With a quick, insincere smile and a careless "Thank you!" she went on after it.

"That Judy Jones!" remarked Mr. Hedrick on the next tee, as they waited—some moments—for her to play on ahead. "All she needs is to be turned up and spanked for six months and then to be married off to an old-fashioned cavalry captain."

"My God, she's good looking!" said Mr. Sandwood, who was just over thirty.

"Good looking!" cried Mr. Hedrick contemptuously, "she always looks as if she wanted to be kissed! Turning those big cow-eyes on every calf in town!"

It was doubtful if Mr. Hedrick intended a reference to the maternal instinct.

"She'd play pretty good golf if she'd try," said Mr. Sandwood.

"She has no form," said Mr. Hedrick solemnly.

"She has a nice figure," said Mr. Sandwood.

"Better thank the Lord she doesn't drive a swifter ball," said Mr. Hart, winking at Dexter.

Later in the afternoon the sun went down with a riotous swirl of gold and varying blues and scarlets, and left the dry, rustling night of Western summer. Dexter watched from the veranda of the golf club, watched the even overlap of the waters in the little wind, silver molasses under the harvest moon. Then the moon held a finger to her lips and the lake became a clear pool, pale and quiet. Dexter put on his bathing suit and swam out to the farthest raft, where he stretched dripping on the wet canvas of the springboard.

There was a fish jumping and a star shining and the lights around the lake were gleaming. Over on a dark peninsula a piano was playing the songs of last summer and of summers before that—songs from *Chin-Chin* and *The Count of Luxemburg* and *The Chocolate Soldier*[2]—and because the sound of a piano over a stretch of water had always seemed beautiful to Dexter he lay perfectly quiet and listened.

The tune the piano was playing at that moment had been gay and new five years before when Dexter was a sophomore at college. They had played it at a prom once when he could not afford the luxury of proms, and he had stood outside the gymnasium and listened. The sound of the tune precipitated in him a sort of ecstasy and it was with that ecstasy he viewed what happened to him now. It was a mood of intense appreciation, a sense that, for once, he was magnificently attuned to life and that everything about him was radiating a brightness and a glamor he might never know again.

A low, pale oblong detached itself suddenly from the darkness of the Island, spit-

2. Chin-Chin . . . The Chocolate Soldier: Popular operettas of the time.

ting forth the reverberate sound of a racing motorboat. Two white streamers of cleft water rolled themselves out behind it and almost immediately the boat was beside him, drowning out the hot tinkle of the piano in the drone of its spray. Dexter raising himself on his arms was aware of a figure standing at the wheel, of two dark eyes regarding him over the lengthening space of water—then the boat had gone by and was sweeping in an immense and purposeless circle of spray round and round in the middle of the lake. With equal eccentricity one of the circles flattened out and headed back toward the raft.

"Who's that?" she called, shutting off her motor. She was so near now that Dexter could see her bathing suit, which consisted apparently of pink rompers.

The nose of the boat bumped the raft, and as the latter tilted rakishly he was precipitated toward her. With different degrees of interest they recognized each other.

"Aren't you one of those men we played through this afternoon?" she demanded.

He was.

"Well, do you know how to drive a motorboat? Because if you do I wish you'd drive this one so I can ride on the surfboard behind. My name is Judy Jones"—she favored him with an absurd smirk—rather, what tried to be a smirk, for, twist her mouth as she might, it was not grotesque, it was merely beautiful—"and I live in a house over there on the Island, and in that house there is a man waiting for me. When he drove up at the door I drove out of the dock because he says I'm his ideal."

There was a fish jumping and a star shining and the lights around the lake were gleaming. Dexter sat beside Judy Jones and she explained how her boat was driven. Then she was in the water, swimming to the floating surfboard with a sinuous crawl. Watching her was without effort to the eye, watching a branch waving or a sea gull flying. Her arms, burned to butternut, moved sinuously among the dull platinum ripples, elbow appearing first, casting the forearm

back with a cadence of falling water, then reaching out and down, stabbing a path ahead.

They moved out into the lake; turning, Dexter saw that she was kneeling on the low rear of the now uptilted surfboard.

"Go faster," she called, "fast as it'll go."

Obediently he jammed the lever forward and the white spray mounted at the bow. When he looked around again the girl was standing up on the rushing board, her arms spread wide, her eyes lifted toward the moon.

"It's awful cold," she shouted. "What's your name?"

He told her.

"Well, why don't you come to dinner tomorrow night?"

His heart turned over like the flywheel of the boat, and, for the second time, her casual whim gave a new direction to his life.

III

Next evening while he waited for her to come downstairs, Dexter peopled the soft deep summer room and the sun porch that opened from it with the men who had already loved Judy Jones. He knew the sort of men they were—the men who when he first went to college had entered from the great prep schools with graceful clothes and the deep tan of healthy summers. He had seen that, in one sense, he was better than these men. He was newer and stronger. Yet in acknowledging to himself that he wished his children to be like them he was admitting that he was but the rough, strong stuff from which they eternally sprang.

When the time had come for him to wear good clothes, he had known who were the best tailors in America, and the best tailors in America had made him the suit he wore this evening. He had acquired that particular reserve peculiar to his university, that set it off from other universities. He recognized the value to him of such a mannerism and he had adopted it; he knew that to be careless in dress and manner required more confidence than to be careful. But carelessness was for his children. His mother's name had been Krimelich. She was a Bohemian of the peasant class and she had talked broken English to the end of her days. Her son must keep to the set patterns.

At a little after seven Judy Jones came downstairs. She wore a blue silk afternoon dress, and he was disappointed at first that she had not put on something more elaborate. This feeling was accentuated when, after a brief greeting, she went to the door of a butler's pantry and pushing it open called: "You can serve dinner, Martha." He had rather expected that a butler would announce dinner, that there would be a cocktail. Then he put these thoughts behind him as they sat down side by side on a lounge and looked at each other.

"Father and mother won't be here," she said thoughtfully.

He remembered the last time he had seen her father, and he was glad the parents were not to be here tonight—they might wonder who he was. He had been born in Keeble, a Minnesota village fifty miles farther north, and he always gave Keeble as his home instead of Black Bear Village. Country towns were well enough to come from if they weren't inconveniently in sight and used as footstools by fashionable lakes.

They talked of his university, which she had visited frequently during the past two years, and of the nearby city which supplied Sherry Island with its patrons, and whither Dexter would return next day to his prospering laundries.

During dinner she slipped into a moody depression which gave Dexter a feeling of uneasiness. Whatever petulance she uttered in her throaty voice worried him. Whatever she smiled at—at him, at a chicken liver, at nothing—it disturbed him that her smile could have no root in mirth, or even in amusement. When the scarlet corners of her lips curved down, it was less a smile than an invitation to a kiss.

Then, after dinner, she led him out on the dark sun porch and deliberately changed the atmosphere.

"Do you mind if I weep a little?" she said.

"I'm afraid I'm boring you," he responded quickly.

"You're not. I like you. But I've just had a terrible afternoon. There was a man I cared about, and this afternoon he told me out of a clear sky that he was poor as a church mouse. He'd never even hinted it before. Does this sound horribly mundane?"

"Perhaps he was afraid to tell you."

"Suppose he was," she answered. "He didn't start right. You see, if I'd thought of him as poor—well, I've been mad about loads of poor men, and fully intended to marry them all. But in this case, I hadn't thought of him that way, and my interest in him wasn't strong enough to survive the shock. As if a girl calmly informed her fiancé that she was a widow. He might not object to widows, but——

"Let's start right," she interrupted herself suddenly. "Who are you, anyhow?"

For a moment Dexter hesitated. Then:

"I'm nobody," he announced. "My career is largely a matter of futures."

"Are you poor?"

"No," he said frankly, "I'm probably making more money than any man my age in the Northwest. I know that's an obnoxious remark, but you advised me to start right."

There was a pause. Then she smiled and the corners of her mouth drooped and an almost imperceptible sway brought her closer to him, looking up into his eyes. A lump rose in Dexter's throat, and he waited breathless for the experiment, facing the unpredictable compound that would form mysteriously from the elements of their lips. Then he saw—she communicated her excitement to him, lavishly, deeply, with kisses that were not a promise but a fulfillment. They aroused in him not hunger demanding renewal but surfeit that would demand more surfeit . . . kisses that were like charity, creating want by holding back nothing at all.

It did not take him many hours to decide

that he had wanted Judy Jones ever since he was a proud, desirous little boy.

IV

It began like that—and continued, with varying shades of intensity, on such a note right up to the dénouement. Dexter surrendered a part of himself to the most direct and unprincipled personality with which he had ever come in contact. Whatever Judy wanted, she went after with the full pressure of her charm. There was no divergence of method, no jockeying for position or premeditation of effects—there was a very little mental side to any of her affairs. She simply made men conscious to the highest degree of her physical loveliness. Dexter had no desire to change her. Her deficiencies were knit up with a passionate energy that transcended and justified them.

When, as Judy's head lay against his shoulder that first night, she whispered, "I don't know what's the matter with me. Last night I thought I was in love with a man and tonight I think I'm in love with you——" it seemed to him a beautiful and romantic thing to say. It was the exquisite excitability that for the moment he controlled and owned. But a week later he was compelled to view this same quality in a different light. She took him in her roadster to a picnic supper, and after supper she disappeared, likewise in her roadster, with another man. Dexter became enormously upset and was scarcely able to be decently civil to the other people present. When she assured him that she had not kissed the other man, he knew she was lying—yet he was glad that she had taken the trouble to lie to him.

He was, as he found before the summer ended, one of a varying dozen who circulated about her. Each of them had at one time been favored above all others—about half of them still basked in the solace of occasional sentimental revivals. Whenever one showed signs of dropping out through long neglect, she granted him a brief honeyed hour, which encouraged him to tag along for a year or so longer. Judy made these forays upon the helpless and defeated without malice, indeed half unconscious that there was anything mischievous in what she did.

When a new man came to town everyone dropped out—dates were automatically canceled.

The helpless part of trying to do anything about it was that she did it all herself. She was not a girl who could be "won" in the kinetic sense—she was proof against cleverness, she was proof against charm; if any of these assailed her too strongly she would immediately resolve the affair to a physical basis, and under the magic of her physical splendor the strong as well as the brilliant played her game and not their own. She was entertained only by the gratification of her desires and by the direct exercise of her own charm. Perhaps from so much youthful love, so many youthful lovers, she had come, in self-defense, to nourish herself wholly from within.

Succeeding Dexter's first exhilaration came restlessness and dissatisfaction. The helpless ecstasy of losing himself in her was opiate rather than tonic. It was fortunate for his work during the winter that those moments of ecstasy came infrequently. Early in their acquaintance it had seemed for a while that there was a deep and spontaneous mutual attraction—that first August, for example—three days of long evenings on her dusky veranda, of strange wan kisses through the late afternoon, in shadowy alcoves or behind the protecting trellises of the garden arbors, of mornings when she was fresh as a dream and almost shy at meeting him in the clarity of the rising day. There was all the ecstasy of an engagement about it, sharpened by his realization that there was no engagement. It was during those three days that, for the first time, he had asked her to marry him. She said "maybe some day," she said "kiss me," she said, "I'd like to marry you," she said "I love you"—she said—nothing.

The three days were interrupted by the arrival of a New York man who visited at her house for half September. To Dexter's agony, rumor engaged them. The man was the son of the president of a great trust company. But at the end of a month it was reported that Judy was yawning. At a dance one night she sat all evening in a motorboat with a local beau, while the New Yorker searched the club for her frantically. She told the local beau that she was bored with her visitor, and two days later he left. She was seen with him at the station, and it was reported that he looked very mournful indeed.

On this note the summer ended. Dexter was twenty-four, and he found himself increasingly in a position to do as he wished. He joined two clubs in the city and lived at one of them. Though he was by no means an integral part of the stag lines at these clubs, he managed to be on hand at dances where Judy Jones was likely to appear. He could have gone out socially as much as he liked—he was an eligible young man, now, and popular with downtown fathers. His confessed devotion to Judy Jones had rather solidified his position. But he had no social aspirations and rather despised the dancing men who were always on tap for the Thursday or Saturday parties and who filled in at dinners with the younger married set. Already he was playing with the idea of going East to New York. He wanted to take Judy Jones with him. No disillusion as to the world in which she had grown up could cure his illusion as to her desirability.

Remember that—for only in the light of it can what he did for her be understood.

Eighteen months after he first met Judy Jones he became engaged to another girl. Her name was Irene Scheerer, and her father was one of the men who had always believed in Dexter. Irene was light-haired and sweet and honorable, and a little stout, and she had two suitors whom she pleasantly relinquished when Dexter formally asked her to marry him.

Summer, fall, winter, spring, another summer, another fall—so much he had given of his active life to the incorrigible lips of Judy Jones. She had treated him with interest, with encouragement, with malice, with indifference, with contempt. She had inflicted on him the innumerable little slights and indignities possible in such a case—as if in revenge for having ever cared for him at all. She had beckoned him and yawned at him and beckoned him again and he had responded often with bitterness and narrowed eyes. She had brought him ecstatic happiness and intolerable agony of spirit. She had caused him untold inconvenience and not a little trouble. She had insulted him, and she had ridden over him, and she had played his interest in her against his interest in his work—for fun. She had done everything to him except to criticize him—this she had not done—it seemed to him only because it might have sullied the utter indifference she manifested and sincerely felt toward him.

When autumn had come and gone again it occurred to him that he could not have Judy Jones. He had to beat this into his mind but he convinced himself at last. He lay awake at night for a while and argued it over. He told himself the trouble and the pain she had caused him, he enumerated her glaring deficiencies as a wife. Then he said to himself that he loved her, and after a while he fell asleep. For a week, lest he imagined her husky voice over the telephone or her eyes opposite him at lunch, he worked hard and late, and at night he went to his office and plotted out his years.

At the end of a week he went to a dance and cut in on her once. For almost the first time since they had met he did not ask her to sit out with him or tell her that she was lovely. It hurt him that she did not miss these things—that was all. He was not jealous when he saw that there was a new man tonight. He had been hardened against jealousy long before.

He stayed late at the dance. He sat for an hour with Irene Scheerer and talked about books and about music. He knew very little about either. But he was beginning to be master of his own time now, and he had a

WINTER HARMONY
John Henry Twachtman
National Gallery of Art, Washington

rather priggish[3] notion that he—the young and already fabulously successful Dexter Green—should know more about such things.

That was in October, when he was twenty-five. In January, Dexter and Irene became engaged. It was to be announced in June, and they were to be married three months later.

The Minnesota winter prolonged itself interminably, and it was almost May when the winds came soft and the snow ran down into Black Bear Lake at last. For the first time in over a year Dexter was enjoying a certain tranquillity of spirit. Judy Jones had been in Florida, and afterward in Hot Springs, and somewhere she had been engaged, and somewhere she had broken it off. At first, when Dexter had definitely given her up, it had made him sad that people still linked them together and asked for news of her, but when he began to be placed at dinner next to Irene Scheerer people didn't ask him about her any more—they told him about her. He ceased to be an authority on her.

---

3. priggish (prig′ gish) *adj.*: Excessively precise.

May at last. Dexter walked the streets at night when the darkness was damp as rain, wondering that so soon, with so little done, so much of ecstasy had gone from him. May one year back had been marked by Judy's poignant, unforgivable, yet forgiven turbulence—it had been one of those rare times when he fancied she had grown to care for him. That old penny's worth of happiness he had spent for this bushel of content. He knew that Irene would be no more than a curtain spread behind him, a hand moving among gleaming teacups, a voice calling to children . . . fire and loveliness were gone, the magic of nights and the wonder of the varying hours and seasons . . . slender lips, down-turning, dropping to his lips and bearing him up into a heaven of eyes. . . . The thing was deep in him. He was too strong and alive for it to die lightly.

In the middle of May when the weather balanced for a few days on the thin bridge that led to deep summer he turned in one night at Irene's house. Their engagement was to be announced in a week now—no one would be surprised at it. And tonight they would sit together on the lounge at the University Club and look on for an hour at the dancers. It gave him a sense of solidity to go with her—she was so sturdily popular, so intensely "great."

He mounted the steps of the brownstone house and stepped inside.

"Irene," he called.

Mrs. Scheerer came out of the living room to meet him.

"Dexter," she said, "Irene's gone upstairs with a splitting headache. She wanted to go with you but I made her go to bed."

"Nothing serious, I——"

"Oh, no. She's going to play golf with you in the morning. You can spare her for just one night, can't you, Dexter?"

Her smile was kind. She and Dexter liked each other. In the living room he talked for a moment before he said good night.

Returning to the University Club, where he had rooms, he stood in the doorway for a moment and watched the dancers. He leaned against the doorpost, nodded at a man or two—yawned.

"Hello, darling."

The familiar voice at his elbow startled him. Judy Jones had left a man and crossed the room to him—Judy Jones, a slender enameled doll in cloth of gold: gold in a band at her head, gold in two slipper points at her dress's hem. The fragile glow of her face seemed to blossom as she smiled at him. A breeze of warmth and light blew through the room. His hands in the pockets of his dinner jacket tightened spasmodically. He was filled with a sudden excitement.

"When did you get back?" he asked casually.

"Come here and I'll tell you about it."

She turned and he followed her. She had been away—he could have wept at the wonder of her return. She had passed through enchanted streets, doing things that were like provocative music. All mysterious happenings, all fresh and quickening hopes, had gone away with her, come back with her now.

She turned in the doorway.

"Have you a car here? If you haven't, I have."

"I have a coupé."

In then, with a rustle of golden cloth. He slammed the door. Into so many cars she had stepped—like this—like that—her back against the leather, so—her elbow resting on the door—waiting. She would have been soiled long since had there been anything to soil her—except herself—but this was her own self outpouring.

With an effort he forced himself to start the car and back into the street. This was nothing, he must remember. She had done this before, and he had put her behind him, as he would have crossed a bad account from his books.

He drove slowly downtown and, affecting abstraction, traversed the deserted streets of the business section, peopled here and there where a movie was giving out its crowd or where consumptive or pugilistic youth lounged in front of pool halls. The clink of glasses and the slap of hands on the bars issued from saloons, cloisters of glazed glass and dirty yellow light.

She was watching him closely and the silence was embarrassing, yet in this crisis he could find no casual word with which to profane the hour. At a convenient turning he began to zigzag back toward the University Club.

"Have you missed me?" she asked suddenly.

"Everybody missed you."

He wondered if she knew of Irene Scheerer. She had been back only a day—her absence had been almost contemporaneous with his engagement.

"What a remark!" Judy laughed sadly—without sadness. She looked at him searchingly. He became absorbed in the dashboard.

"You're handsomer than you used to be," she said thoughtfully. "Dexter, you have the most rememberable eyes."

He could have laughed at this, but he did not laugh. It was the sort of thing that was said to sophomores. Yet it stabbed at him.

"I'm awfully tired of everything, darling." She called everyone darling, endowing the endearment with careless, individual camaraderie.[4] "I wish you'd marry me."

The directness of this confused him. He should have told her now that he was going to marry another girl, but he could not tell her. He could as easily have sworn that he had never loved her.

"I think we'd get along," she continued, on the same note, "unless probably you've forgotten me and fallen in love with another girl."

Her confidence was obviously enormous. She had said, in effect, that she found such a thing impossible to believe, that if it were true he had merely committed a childish indiscretion—and probably to show off. She

would forgive him, because it was not a matter of any moment but rather something to be brushed aside lightly.

"Of course you could never love anybody but me," she continued, "I like the way you love me. Oh, Dexter, have you forgotten last year?"

"No, I haven't forgotten."

"Neither have I!"

Was she sincerely moved—or was she carried along by the wave of her own acting?

"I wish we could be like that again," she said, and he forced himself to answer:

"I don't think we can."

"I suppose not. . . . I hear you're giving Irene Scheerer a violent rush."

There was not the faintest emphasis on the name, yet Dexter was suddenly ashamed.

"Oh, take me home," cried Judy suddenly; "I don't want to go back to that idiotic dance—with those children."

Then, as he turned up the street that led to the residence district, Judy began to cry quietly to herself. He had never seen her cry before.

The dark street lightened, the dwellings of the rich loomed up around them, he stopped his coupé in front of the great white bulk of the Mortimer Joneses' house, somnolent, gorgeous, drenched with the splendor of the damp moonlight. Its solidity startled him. The strong walls, the steel of the girders, the breadth and beam and pomp of it were there only to bring out the contrast with the young beauty beside him. It was sturdy to accentuate her slightness—as if to show what a breeze could be generated by a butterfly's wing.

He sat perfectly quiet, his nerves in wild clamor, afraid that if he moved he would find her irresistibly in his arms. Two tears had rolled down her wet face and trembled on her upper lip.

'I'm more beautiful than anybody else," she said brokenly, "why can't I be happy?" Her moist eyes tore at his stability—her mouth turned slowly downward with an exquisite sadness: "I'd like to marry you if

---

4. camaraderie (käm′ ə räd′ ər ē) *n*.: Warm, friendly feelings.

you'll have me, Dexter. I suppose you think I'm not worth having, but I'll be so beautfiul for you, Dexter."

A million phrases of anger, pride, passion, hatred, tenderness fought on his lips. Then a perfect wave of emotion washed over him, carrying off with it a sediment of wisdom, of convention, of doubt, of honor. This was his girl who was speaking, his own, his beautiful, his pride.

"Won't you come in?" He heard her draw in her breath sharply.

Waiting.

"All right," his voice was trembling, "I'll come in."

V

It was strange that neither when it was over nor a long time afterward did he regret that night. Looking at it from the perspective of ten years, the fact that Judy's flare for him endured just one month seemed of little importance. Nor did it matter that by his yielding he subjected himself to a deeper agony in the end and gave serious hurt to Irene Scheerer and to Irene's parents, who had befriended him. There was nothing sufficiently pictorial about Irene's grief to stamp itself on his mind.

Dexter was at bottom hard-minded. The attitude of the city on his action was of no importance to him, not because he was going to leave the city, but because any outside attitude on the situation seemed superficial. He was completely indifferent to popular opinion. Nor, when he had seen that it was no use, that he did not possess in himself the power to move fundamentally or to hold Judy Jones, did he bear any malice toward her. He loved her, and he would love her until the day he was too old for loving—but he could not have her. So he tasted the deep pain that is reserved only for the strong, just as he had tasted for a little while the deep happiness.

Even the ultimate falsity of the grounds

upon which Judy terminated the engagement that she did not want to "take him away" from Irene—Judy who had wanted nothing else—did not revolt him. He was beyond any revulsion or any amusement.

He went East in February with the intention of selling out his laundries and settling in New York—but the war came to America in March and changed his plans. He returned to the West, handed over the management of the business to his partner, and went into the first officers' training camp in late April. He was one of those young thousands who greeted the war with a certain amount of relief, welcoming the liberation from webs of tangled emotion.

VI

This story is not his biography, remember, although things creep into it which have nothing to do with those dreams he had when he was young. We are almost done with them and with him now. There is only one more incident to be related here, and it happens seven years farther on.

It took place in New York, where he had done well—so well that there were no barriers too high for him. He was thirty-two years old, and, except for one flying trip immediately after the war, he had not been West in seven years. A man named Devlin from Detroit came into his office to see him in a business way, and then and there this incident occurred, and closed out, so to speak, this particular side of his life.

"So you're from the Middle West," said the man Devlin with careless curiosity. "That's funny—I thought men like you were probably born and raised on Wall Street. You know—wife of one of my best friends in Detroit came from your city. I was an usher at the wedding."

Dexter waited with no apprehension of what was coming.

"Judy Simms," said Devlin with no particular interest; "Judy Jones she was once."

MANHATTAN TOPS
Herman Rose
Hirschorn Museum and Sculpture Garden, Smithsonian Institution

"Yes, I knew her." A dull impatience spread over him. He had heard, of course, that she was married—perhaps deliberately he had heard no more.

"Awfully nice girl," brooded Devlin meaninglessly, "I'm sort of sorry for her."

"Why?" Something in Dexter was alert, receptive, at once.

"Oh, Lud Simms has gone to pieces in a way. I don't mean he ill-uses her, but he drinks and runs around——"

"Doesn't she run around?"

"No. Stays at home with her kids."

"Oh."

"She's a little too old for him," said Devlin.

"Too old!" cried Dexter. "Why, man, she's only twenty-seven."

He was possessed with a wild notion of rushing out into the streets and taking a train to Detroit. He rose to his feet spasmodically.

"I guess you're busy," Devlin apologized quickly. "I didn't realize——"

"No, I'm not busy," said Dexter, steadying his voice. "I'm not busy at all. Not busy at all. Did you say she was—twenty-seven? No, I said she was twenty-seven."

The Jilting
of Granny Weatherall

Katherine Anne Porter

She flicked her wrist neatly out of Doctor Harry's pudgy careful fingers and pulled the sheet up to her chin. The brat ought to be in knee breeches. Doctoring around the country with spectacles on his nose! "Get along now, take your schoolbooks and go. There's nothing wrong with me."

Doctor Harry spread a warm paw like a cushion on her forehead where the forked green vein danced and made her eyelids twitch. "Now, now, be a good girl, and we'll have you up in no time."

"That's no way to speak to a woman nearly eighty years old just because she's down. I'd have you respect your elders, young man."

"Well, Missy, excuse me," Doctor Harry patted her cheek. "But I've got to warn you, haven't I? You're a marvel, but you must be careful or you're going to be good and sorry."

"Don't tell me what I'm going to be. I'm on my feet now, morally speaking. It's Cornelia. I had to go to bed to get rid of her."

Her bones felt loose, and floated around in her skin, and Doctor Harry floated like a balloon around the foot of the bed. He floated and pulled down his waistcoat and swung his glasses on a cord. "Well, stay where you are, it certainly can't hurt you."

"Get along and doctor your sick," said Granny Weatherall. "Leave a well woman alone. I'll call for you when I want you. . . .

Where were you forty years ago when I pulled through milk leg[1] and double pneumonia? You weren't even born. Don't let Cornelia lead you on," she shouted, because Doctor Harry appeared to float up to the ceiling and out. "I pay my own bills, and I don't throw my money away on nonsense!"

She meant to wave good-bye, but it was too much trouble. Her eyes closed of themselves, it was like a dark curtain drawn around the bed. The pillow rose and floated under her, pleasant as a hammock in a light wind. She listened to the leaves rustling outside the window. No, somebody was swishing newspapers: no, Cornelia and Doctor Harry were whispering together. She leaped broad awake, thinking they whispered in her ear.

"She was never like this, *never* like this!" "Well, what can we expect?" "Yes, eighty years old. . . ."

Well, and what if she was? She still had ears. It was like Cornelia to whisper around doors. She always kept things secret in such a public way. She was always being tactful and kind. Cornelia was dutiful; that was the trouble with her. Dutiful and good: "So good and dutiful," said Granny, "that I'd like to spank her." She saw herself spanking Cornelia and making a fine job of it.

---

1. **milk leg:** A painful swelling of the leg.

GARDEN OF MEMORIES, 1917
Charles Burchfield
Collection of The Museum of Modern Art,
New York

"What'd you say, Mother?"

Granny felt her face tying up in hard knots.

"Can't a body think, I'd like to know?"

"I thought you might want something."

"I do. I want a lot of things. First off, go away and don't whisper."

She lay and drowsed, hoping in her sleep that the children would keep out and let her rest a minute. It had been a long day. Not that she was tired. It was always pleasant to snatch a minute now and then. There was always so much to be done, let me see: tomorrow.

Tomorrow was far away and there was nothing to trouble about. Things were fin-ished somehow when the time came; thank God there was always a little margin over for peace: then a person could spread out the plan of life and tuck in the edges orderly. It was good to have everything clean and folded away, with the hair brushes and tonic bottles sitting straight on the white embroidered linen: the day started without fuss and the pantry shelves laid out with rows of jelly glasses and brown jugs and white stone-china jars with blue whirligigs and words painted on them: coffee, tea, sugar, ginger, cinnamon, allspice: and the bronze clock with the lion on top nicely dusted off. The dust that lion could collect in twenty-four hours! The box in the attic with all those letters tied up, well, she'd have to go through that tomorrow. All those letters—George's letters and John's letters and her letters to them both—lying around for the children to find afterwards made her uneasy. Yes, that would be tomorrow's business. No use to let them know how silly she had been once.

While she was rummaging around she found death in her mind and it felt clammy and unfamiliar. She had spent so much time preparing for death there was no need for bringing it up again. Let it take care of itself now. When she was sixty she had felt very old, finished, and went around making farewell trips to see her children and grandchildren, with a secret in her mind: This is the very last of your mother, children! Then she made her will and came down with a long fever. That was all just a notion like a lot of other things, but it was lucky too, for she had once for all got over the idea of dying for a long time. Now she couldn't be worried. She hoped she had better sense now. Her father had lived to be one hundred and two years old and had drunk a noggin of strong hot toddy on his last birthday. He told the reporters it was his daily habit, and he owed his long life to that. He had made quite a scandal and was very pleased about it. She believed she'd just plague Cornelia a little.

"Cornelia! Cornelia!" No footsteps, but a sudden hand on her cheek. "Bless you, where have you been?"

"Here, mother."

"Well, Cornelia, I want a noggin of hot toddy."

"Are you cold, darling?"

"I'm chilly, Cornelia. Lying in bed stops the circulation. I must have told you that a thousand times."

Well, she could just hear Cornelia telling her husband that Mother was getting a little childish and they'd have to humor her. The thing that most annoyed her was that Cornelia thought she was deaf, dumb, and blind. Little hasty glances and tiny gestures tossed around her and over her head saying, "Don't cross her, let her have her way, she's

eighty years old," and she sitting there as if she lived in a thin glass cage. Sometimes Granny almost made up her mind to pack up and move back to her own house where nobody could remind her every minute that she was old. Wait, wait, Cornelia, till your own children whisper behind your back!

In her day she had kept a better house and had got more work done. She wasn't too old yet for Lydia to be driving eighty miles for advice when one of the children jumped the track, and Jimmy still dropped in and talked things over: "Now, Mammy, you've a good business head, I want to know what you think of this? . . ." Old. Cornelia couldn't change the furniture around without asking. Little things, little things! They had been so sweet when they were little. Granny wished the old days were back again with the children young and everything to be done over. It had been a hard pull, but not too much for her. When she thought of all the food she had cooked, and all the clothes she had cut and sewed, and all the gardens she had made—well, the children showed it. There they were, made out of her, and they couldn't get away from that. Sometimes she wanted to see John again and point to them and say, Well, I didn't do so badly, did I? But that would have to wait. That was for tomorrow. She used to think of him as a man, but now all the children were older than their father, and he would be a child beside her if she saw him now. It seemed strange and there was something wrong in the idea. Why, he couldn't possibly recognize her. She had fenced in a hundred acres once, digging the post holes herself and clamping the wires with just a negro boy to help. That changed a woman. John would be looking for a young woman with the peaked Spanish comb in her hair and the painted fan. Digging post holes changed a woman. Riding country roads in the winter when women had their babies was another thing: sitting up nights with sick horses and sick children and hardly ever losing one. John, I hardly ever lost one of them! John would see that in a minute, that would be something he could understand, she wouldn't have to explain anything!

It made her feel like rolling up her sleeves and putting the whole place to rights again. No matter if Cornelia was determined to be everywhere at once, there were a great many things left undone on this place. She would start tomorrow and do them. It was good to be strong enough for everything, even if all you made melted and changed and slipped under your hands, so that by the time you finished you almost forgot what you were working for. What was it I set out to do? she asked herself intently, but she could not remember. A fog rose over the valley, she saw it marching across the creek swallowing the trees and moving up the hill like an army of ghosts. Soon it would be at the near edge of the orchard, and then it was time to go in and light the lamps. Come in, children, don't stay out in the night air.

Lighting the lamps had been beautiful. The children huddled up to her and breathed like little calves waiting at the bars in the twilight. Their eyes followed the match and watched the flame rise and settle in a blue curve, then they moved away from her. The lamp was lit, they didn't have to be scared and hang on to mother any more. Never, never, never more. God, for all my life I thank Thee. Without Thee, my God, I could never have done it. Hail Mary, full of grace.

I want you to pick all the fruit this year and see that nothing is wasted. There's always someone who can use it. Don't let good things rot for want of using. You waste life when you waste good food. Don't let things get lost. It's bitter to lose things. Now, don't let me get to thinking, not when I am tired and taking a little nap before supper. . . .

The pillow rose about her shoulders and pressed against her heart and the memory was being squeezed out of it: oh, push down the pillow, somebody: it would smother her if she tried to hold it. Such a fresh breeze blowing and such a green day with no threats in it. But he had not come, just the same. What does a woman do when she has put on the white veil and set out the white cake for a man and he doesn't come? She tried to remember. No, I swear he never harmed me but in that. He never harmed me but in that . . . and what if he did? There was the day, the day, but a whirl of dark smoke rose and covered it, crept up and over into the bright field where everything was planted so carefully in orderly rows. That was hell, she knew hell when she saw it. For sixty years she had prayed against remembering him and against losing her soul in the deep pit of hell, and now the two things were mingled in one and the thought of him was a smoky cloud from hell that moved and crept in her head when she had just got rid of Doctor Harry and was trying to rest a minute. Wounded vanity, Ellen, said a sharp voice in the top of her mind. Don't let your wounded vanity get the upper hand of you. Plenty of girls get jilted. You were jilted, weren't you? Then stand up to it. Her eyelids wavered and let in streamers of blue-gray light like tissue paper over her eyes. She must get up and pull the shades down or she'd never sleep. She was in bed again and the shades were not down. How could that happen? Better turn over, hide from the light, sleeping in the light gave you nightmares. "Mother, how do you feel now?" and a stinging wetness on her forehead. But I don't like having my face washed in cold water!

Hapsy? George? Lydia? Jimmy? No, Cornelia, and her features were swollen and full of little puddles. "They're coming, darling, they'll all be here soon." Go wash your face, child, you look funny.

Instead of obeying, Cornelia knelt down and put her head on the pillow. She seemed to be talking but there was no sound. "Well, are you tongue-tied? Whose birthday is it? Are you going to give a party?"

Cornelia's mouth moved urgently in strange shapes. "Don't do that, you bother me, daughter."

"Oh, no, Mother. Oh, no. . . ."

LAVENDER AND OLD LACE
Charles Burchfield, ANA
From the Collection of the New Britain Museum of American Art

Nonsense. It was strange about children. They disputed your every word. "No what, Cornelia?"

"Here's Doctor Harry."

"I won't see that boy again. He just left five minutes ago."

"That was this morning, Mother. It's night now. Here's the nurse."

"This is Doctor Harry, Mrs. Weatherall. I never saw you look so young and happy!"

"Ah, I'll never be young again—but I'd be happy if they'd let me lie in peace and get rested."

She thought she spoke up loudly, but no one answered. A warm weight on her forehead, a warm bracelet on her wrist, and a breeze went on whispering, trying to tell her something. A shuffle of leaves in the everlasting hand of God, He blew on them and they danced and rattled. "Mother, don't mind, we're going to give you a little hypodermic." "Look here, daughter, how do ants get in this bed? I saw sugar ants yesterday." Did you send for Hapsy too?

It was Hapsy she really wanted. She had to go a long way back through a great many rooms to find Hapsy standing with a baby on her arm. She seemed to herself to be Hapsy also, and the baby on Hapsy's arm was Hapsy and himself and herself, all at once, and there was no surprise in the meeting. Then Hapsy melted from within and turned flimsy as gray gauze and the baby was a gauzy shadow, and Hapsy came up close and said, "I thought you'd never come," and looked at her very searchingly and said, "You haven't changed a bit!" They leaned forward to kiss, when Cornelia began whispering from a long way off, "Oh, is there anything you want to tell me? Is there anything I can do for you?"

Yes, she had changed her mind after sixty years and she would like to see George. I want you to find George. Find him and be sure to tell him I forgot him. I want him to know I had my husband just the same and my children and my house like any other woman. A good house too and a good husband that I loved and fine children out of him. Better than I hoped for even. Tell him I was given back everything he took away and more. Oh, no, oh, God, no, there was something else besides the house and the man and the children. Oh, surely they were not all? What was it? Something not given back. . . . Her breath crowded down under her ribs and grew into a monstrous frightening shape with cutting edges; it bored up into her head, and the agony was unbelievable: Yes, John, get the Doctor now, no more talk, my time has come.

When this one was born it should be the last. The last. It should have been born first, for it was the one she had truly wanted. Everything came in good time. Nothing left out, left over. She was strong, in three days she would be as well as ever. Better. A woman needed milk in her to have her full health.

"Mother, do you hear me?"

"I've been telling you—"

"Mother, Father Connolly's here."

"I went to Holy Communion only last week. Tell him I'm not so sinful as all that."

"Father just wants to speak to you."

He could speak as much as he pleased. It was like him to drop in and inquire about her soul as if it were a teething baby, and then stay on for a cup of tea and a round of cards and gossip. He always had a funny story of some sort, usually about an Irishman who made his little mistakes and

confessed them, and the point lay in some absurd thing he would blurt out in the confessional showing his struggles between native piety and original sin. Granny felt easy about her soul. Cornelia, where are your manners? Give Father Connolly a chair. She had her secret comfortable understanding with a few favorite saints who cleared a straight road to God for her. All as surely signed and sealed as the papers for the new Forty Acres. Forever . . . heirs and assigns[2] forever. Since the day the wedding cake was not cut, but thrown out and wasted. The whole bottom dropped out of the world, and there she was blind and sweating with nothing under her feet and the walls falling away. His hand had caught her under the breast, she had not fallen, there was the freshly polished floor with the green rug on it, just as before. He had cursed like a sailor's parrot and said, "I'll kill him for you." Don't lay a hand on him, for my sake leave something to God. "Now, Ellen, you must believe what I tell you. . . ."

So there was nothing, nothing to worry about any more, except sometimes in the night one of the children screamed in a nightmare, and they both hustled out shaking and hunting for the matches and calling, "There, wait a minute, here we are!" John, get the doctor now, Hapsy's time has come. But there was Hapsy standing by the bed in a white cap. "Cornelia, tell Hapsy to take off her cap. I can't see her plain."

Her eyes opened very wide and the room stood out like a picture she had seen somewhere. Dark colors with the shadows rising towards the ceiling in long angles. The tall black dresser gleamed with nothing on it but John's picture, enlarged from a little one, with John's eyes very black when they should have been blue. You never saw him, so how do you know how he looked? But the man insisted the copy was perfect, it was very rich and handsome. For a picture, yes, but it's not my husband. The table by the

---

2. assigns: Persons to whom property is transferred.

The Far and the Near

Thomas Wolfe

On the outskirts of a little town upon a rise of land that swept back from the railway there was a tidy little cottage of white boards, trimmed vividly with green blinds. To one side of the house there was a garden neatly patterned with plots of growing vegetables, and an arbor for the grapes which ripened late in August. Before the house there were three mighty oaks which sheltered it in their clean and massive shade in summer, and to the other side there was a border of gay flowers. The whole place had an air of tidiness, thrift, and modest comfort.

Every day, a few minutes after two o'clock in the afternoon, the limited express between two cities passed this spot. At that moment the great train, having halted for a breathing space at the town nearby, was beginning to lengthen evenly into its stroke, but it had not yet reached the full drive of its terrific speed. It swung into view deliberately, swept past with a powerful swaying motion of the engine, a low smooth rumble of its heavy cars upon pressed steel, and then it vanished in the cut. For a moment the progress of the engine could be marked by heavy bellowing puffs of smoke that burst at spaced intervals above the edges of the meadow grass, and finally nothing could be heard but the solid clacking tempo of the wheels receding into the drowsy stillness of the afternoon.

Every day for more than twenty years, as the train had approached this house, the engineer had blown on the whistle, and every day, as soon as she heard this signal, a woman had appeared on the back porch of the little house and waved to him. At first she had a small child clinging to her skirts, and now this child had grown to full womanhood, and every day she, too, came with her mother to the porch and waved.

The engineer had grown old and gray in service. He had driven his great train, loaded with its weight of lives, across the land ten thousand times. His own children had grown up and married, and four times he had seen before him on the tracks the ghastly dot of tragedy converging like a cannon ball to its eclipse of horror at the boiler head[1]—a light spring wagon filled with children, with its clustered row of small stunned faces; a cheap automobile stalled upon the tracks, set with the wooden figures of people paralyzed with fear; a battered hobo walking by the rail, too deaf and old to hear the whistle's warning; and a form flung past his window with a scream—all this the man had seen and known. He had known all the grief, the joy, the peril and the labor such a man could know; he had grown seamed and weathered in his loyal service, and now, schooled by the qualities of faith and courage and humbleness that attended his labor, he had grown old, and had the grandeur and the wisdom these men have.

But no matter what peril or tragedy he had known, the vision of the little house and the women waving to him with a brave free motion of the arm had become fixed in the

---

1. boiler head: The front section of a steam locomotive.

mind of the engineer as something beautiful and enduring, something beyond all change and ruin, and something that would always be the same, no matter what mishap, grief or error might break the iron schedule of his days.

The sight of the little house and of these two women gave him the most extraordinary happiness he had ever known. He had seen them in a thousand lights, a hundred weathers. He had seen them through the harsh bare light of wintry gray across the brown and frosted stubble of the earth, and he had seen them again in the green luring sorcery of April.

He felt for them and for the little house in which they lived such tenderness as a man might feel for his own children, and at length the picture of their lives was carved so sharply in his heart that he felt that he knew their lives completely, to every hour and moment of the day, and he resolved that one day, when his years of service should be ended, he would go and find these people and speak at last with them whose lives had been so wrought into his own.

That day came. At last the engineer stepped from a train onto the station platform of the town where these two women lived. His years upon the rail had ended. He was a pensioned servant of his company, with no more work to do. The engineer

STONE CITY, IOWA
Grant Wood
Joslyn Art Museum, Omaha, Nebraska

walked slowly through the station and out into the streets of the town. Everything was as strange to him as if he had never seen this town before. As he walked on, his sense of bewilderment and confusion grew. Could this be the town he had passed ten thousand times? Were these the same houses he had seen so often from the high windows of his cab? It was all as unfamiliar, as disquieting as a city in a dream, and the perplexity of his spirit increased as he went on.

Presently the houses thinned into the straggling outposts of the town, and the street faded into a country road—the one on which the women lived. And the man plodded on slowly in the heat and dust. At length he stood before the house he sought. He knew at once that he had found the proper place. He saw the lordly oaks before the house, the flower beds, the garden and the arbor, and farther off, the glint of rails.

Yes, this was the house he sought, the place he had passed so many times, the destination he had longed for with such happiness. But now that he had found it, now that he was here, why did his hand falter on the gate; why had the town, the road, the earth, the very entrance to this place he loved turned unfamiliar as the landscape of some ugly dream? Why did he now feel this sense of confusion, doubt and hopelessness?

At length he entered by the gate, walked slowly up the path and in a moment more had mounted three short steps that led up to the porch, and was knocking at the door. Presently he heard steps in the hall, the door was opened, and a woman stood facing him.

And instantly, with a sense of bitter loss and grief, he was sorry he had come. He knew at once that the woman who stood there looking at him with a mistrustful eye was the same woman who had waved to him so many thousand times. But her face was harsh and pinched and meager; the flesh sagged wearily in sallow folds, and the small eyes peered at him with timid suspicion and uneasy doubt. All the brave freedom, the warmth and the affection that he had read into her gesture, vanished in the moment that he saw her and heard her unfriendly tongue.

And now his own voice sounded unreal and ghastly to him as he tried to explain his presence, to tell her who he was and the reason he had come. But he faltered on, fighting stubbornly against the horror of regret, confusion, disbelief that surged up in his spirit, drowning all his former joy and making his act of hope and tenderness seem shameful to him.

At length the woman invited him almost unwillingly into the house, and called her daughter in a harsh shrill voice. Then, for a brief agony of time, the man sat in an ugly little parlor, and he tried to talk while the two women stared at him with a dull, bewildered hostility, a sullen, timorous restraint.

And finally, stammering a crude farewell, he departed. He walked away down the path and then along the road toward town, and suddenly he knew that he was an old man. His heart, which had been brave and confident when it looked along the familiar vista of the rails, was now sick with doubt and horror as it saw the strange and unsuspected visage of an earth which had always been within a stone's throw of him, and which he had never seen or known. And he knew that all the magic of that bright lost way, the vista of that shining line, the imagined corner of that small good universe of hope's desire, was gone forever, could never be got back again.

THINKING ABOUT THE SELECTION

Recalling

1. Describe the engineer's daily experience for more than twenty years.
2. (a) What four tragedies has the engineer seen during his years with the railroad? (b) What vision remains fixed in his mind despite the tragedies he has known?
3. Explain what happens when the engineer carries out his resolution.
4. What realization does the engineer come to at the end of the story?

Interpreting

5. What does the house come to represent to the engineer?
6. (a) How do the engineer's observations in the final scene contrast with his expectations? (b) When does he first become aware that his experience is unlikely to match his expectations?
7. In what ways does Wolfe use distance and physical movement to symbolize the passage of time in this story?
8. What is the meaning of the story's title?
9. Explain the story's theme.

Applying

10. If you had been in the engineer's place, would you have visited the cottage? Explain your answer.

ANALYZING LITERATURE

Understanding Point of View

Point of view refers to the vantage point or perspective from which a narrative is told. "The Far and the Near" is told from a limited third-person point of view. The narrator does not participate in the story and focuses on the thoughts and feelings of one character, the engineer. The reader seems to step inside the shoes of this character and see the world through his eyes.

1. How would the story be different if Wolfe had used a first-person point of view?
2. How would it be different if Wolfe had used an omniscient third-person point of view?

CRITICAL THINKING AND READING

Recognizing Period Characteristics

Like "The Far and the Near," most modern short stories are told from a subjective point of view. The author writes in the first person or the third person but limits the perspective to one character.

1. What Modernist belief does the use of the limited third-person point of view reflect?
2. In many modern stories, the character from whose point of view the story is told is naive, lacking understanding of the nature of human existence. In what sense is the engineer naive?
3. How is the engineer's innocence shattered?
4. How does the engineer's loss of innocence reflect the Modernist belief in the uncertainty and confusion of modern life?

THINKING AND WRITING

Comparing and Contrasting Stories

Write an essay in which you compare and contrast Dexter's attachment to Judy Jones in Fitzgerald's "Winter Dreams" with the engineer's attachment to his vision of the little house in "The Far and the Near." Review both stories, noting similarities and differences between the two characters' attachments. Review your notes and prepare a thesis statement. Then write your essay. Organize it according to corresponding points of contrast. Use passages from the two stories to support your points. Then revise, eliminating any unnecessary words or details.

EUDORA WELTY

1909–

In her short stories and novels, Eudora Welty captures life in the deep South, creating vivid portraits of the landscape and conveying the shared attitudes and values of the people. She often confronts the hardships and sorrows of life in the poor rural areas. Yet despite her awareness of people's suffering, her outlook remains positive and optimistic.

Welty was born in Jackson, Mississippi, where she has spent most of her life. She attended Mississippi State College for Women, before transferring to the University of Wisconsin, from which she graduated in 1929. Hoping to pursue a career in advertising, she moved to New York and enrolled at Columbia University School of Business. However, because of the worsening Depression, she was unable to find a steady job and returned to Jackson in 1931.

After accepting a job as a publicist for a government agency, she spent several years traveling throughout Mississippi, taking photographs and interviewing people. Her experiences and observations inspired her to write fiction, and in 1936 her first short story, "Death of a Traveling Salesman," was published in a small magazine.

Welty became a leading American writer of this century. Over the years she has published numerous collections of short stories, including *A Curtain of Green* (1941), *The Wide Net and Other Stories* (1943), *The Bride of Innisfallen and Other Stories* (1955), and *Thirteen Stories* (1965). She has also written several novels, including *Delta Wedding* (1946), *The Ponder Heart* (1954), and *Losing Battles* (1970). In 1973 she was awarded the Pulitzer Prize for her novel *The Optimist's Daughter* (1972).

Throughout her work Welty displays an acute sense of detail and a deep sense of compassion toward her characters. In "A Worn Path," for example, she paints a sympathetic portrait of an old woman whose feelings of love and sense of duty motivate her to make a long, painful journey through the woods.

A Worn Path

**Writer's
Techniques**

Ambiguity. Ambiguity refers to uncertainty of intention or meaning. An ambiguous statement is one that can be interpreted in two or more ways. Similarly, when a work of literature is ambiguous or contains ambiguous elements, the work or certain elements of the work can be interpreted in more than one way. Readers may find various possible meanings and look for details that support each interpretation.

During the Modern Age, literary works became increasingly ambiguous. Writers suggested meaning and presented possibilities instead of asserting or directly stating their points. This style reflected the Modernist belief that life in the modern world is confusing and filled with uncertainties rather than definite answers.

Look For

In Egyptian and Greek mythology the phoenix is a miraculous bird that lived for 500 years, then consumed itself in fire, only to rise, renewed, from the ashes to start another long life. As you read "A Worn Path," look for ways in which Phoenix Jackson lives up to her name.

Writing

"A Worn Path" is about an old woman who repeatedly makes a long, arduous journey into town to get medicine for her grandson. Make a list of journeys that you have made repeatedly during your life. Then jot down your reasons for making each of these journeys.

Vocabulary

Knowing the following words will help you as you read "A Worn Path."

grave (grāv) *adj.*: Serious; solemn (p. 764)

limber (lim′ bər) *adj.*: Flexible (p. 764)

obstinate (äb′stə nit) *adj.*: Stubborn (p. 768)

A Worn Path

Eudora Welty

It was December—a bright frozen day in the early morning. Far out in the country there was an old Negro woman with her head tied in a red rag, coming along a path through the pinewoods. Her name was Phoenix Jackson. She was very old and small and she walked slowly in the dark pine shadows, moving a little from side to side in her steps, with the balanced heaviness and lightness of a pendulum in a grandfather clock. She carried a thin, small cane made from an umbrella, and with this she kept tapping the frozen earth in front of her. This made a grave and persistent noise in the still air, that seemed meditative like the chirping of a solitary little bird.

She wore a dark striped dress reaching down to her shoe tops, and an equally long apron of bleached sugar sacks, with a full pocket: all neat and tidy, but every time she took a step she might have fallen over her shoelaces, which dragged from her unlaced shoes. She looked straight ahead. Her eyes were blue with age. Her skin had a pattern all its own of numberless branching wrinkles and as though a whole little tree stood in the middle of her forehead, but a golden color ran underneath, and the two knobs of her cheeks were illumined by a yellow burning under the dark. Under the red rag her hair came down on her neck in the frailest of ringlets, still black, and with an odor like copper.

Now and then there was a quivering in the thicket. Old Phoenix said, "Out of my way, all you foxes, owls, beetles, jack rabbits, coons and wild animals! . . . Keep out from under these feet, little bobwhites[1]. . . . Keep the big wild hogs out of my path. Don't let none of those come running my direction. I got a long way." Under her small black-freckled hand her cane, limber as a buggy whip, would switch at the brush as if to rouse up any hiding things.

On she went. The woods were deep and still. The sun made the pine needles almost too bright to look at, up where the wind rocked. The cones dropped as light as feathers. Down in the hollow was the mourning dove—it was not too late for him.

The path ran up a hill. "Seem like there is chains about my feet, time I get this far," she said, in the voice of argument old people keep to use with themselves. "Something always take a hold of me on this hill—pleads I should stay."

After she got to the top she turned and gave a full, severe look behind her where she had come. "Up through pines," she said at length. "Now down through oaks."

Her eyes opened their widest, and she started down gently. But before she got to the bottom of the hill a bush caught her dress.

Her fingers were busy and intent, but her skirts were full and long, so that before she could pull them free in one place they were caught in another. It was not possible to allow the dress to tear. "I in the thorny bush," she said. "Thorns, you doing your appointed work. Never want to let folks pass,

---

1. **bobwhites** n.: Partridges.

no sir. Old eyes thought you was a pretty little *green* bush."

Finally, trembling all over, she stood free, and after a moment dared to stoop for her cane.

"Sun so high!" she cried, leaning back and looking, while the thick tears went over her eyes. "The time getting all gone here."

At the foot of this hill was a place where a log was laid across the creek.

"Now comes the trial," said Phoenix.

Putting her right foot out, she mounted the log and shut her eyes. Lifting her skirt, leveling her cane fiercely before her, like a festival figure in some parade, she began to march across. Then she opened her eyes and she was safe on the other side.

"I wasn't as old as I thought," she said.

But she sat down to rest. She spread her skirts on the bank around her and folded her hands over her knees. Up above her was a tree in a pearly cloud of mistletoe. She did not dare to close her eyes, and when a little boy brought her a plate with a slice of marble cake on it she spoke to him. "That would be acceptable," she said. But when she went to take it there was just her own hand in the air.

So she left that tree, and had to go through a barbed-wire fence. There she had to creep and crawl, spreading her knees and stretching her fingers like a baby trying to climb the steps. But she talked loudly to herself: she could not let her dress be torn now, so late in the day, and she could not pay for having her arm or her leg sawed off if she got caught fast where she was.

At last she was safe through the fence and risen up out in the clearing. Big dead trees, like black men with one arm, were standing in the purple stalks of the withered cotton field. There sat a buzzard.

"Who you watching?"

In the furrow she made her way along.

"Glad this not the season for bulls," she said, looking sideways, "and the good Lord made his snakes to curl up and sleep in the winter. A pleasure I don't see no two-headed snake coming around that tree, where it come once. It took a while to get by him, back in the summer."

She passed through the old cotton and went into a field of dead corn. It whispered and shook and was taller than her head. "Through the maze now," she said, for there was no path.

Then there was something tall, black, and skinny there, moving before her.

At first she took it for a man. It could have been a man dancing in the field. But she stood still and listened, and it did not make a sound. It was as silent as a ghost.

"Ghost," she said sharply, "who be you the ghost of? For I have heard of nary death close by."

But there was no answer—only the ragged dancing in the wind.

She shut her eyes, reached out her hand, and touched a sleeve. She found a coat and inside that an emptiness, cold as ice.

"You scarecrow," she said. Her face lighted. "I ought to be shut up for good," she said with laughter. "My senses is gone. I too old. I the oldest people I ever know. Dance, old scarecrow," she said, "while I dancing with you."

She kicked her foot over the furrow, and with mouth drawn down, shook her head once or twice in a little strutting way. Some husks blew down and whirled in streamers about her skirts.

Then she went on, parting her way from side to side with the cane, through the whispering field. At last she came to the end, to a wagon track where the silver grass blew between the red ruts. The quail were walking around like pullets, seeming all dainty and unseen.

"Walk pretty," she said. "This the easy place. This the easy going."

She followed the track, swaying through the quiet bare fields, through the little strings of trees silver in their dead leaves, past cabins silver from weather, with the doors and windows boarded shut, all like old women under a spell sitting there. "I walking in their sleep," she said, nodding her head vigorously.

In a ravine she went where a spring was silently flowing through a hollow log. Old Phoenix bent and drank. "Sweet gum[2] makes the water sweet," she said, and drank more. "Nobody know who made this well, for it was here when I was born."

The track crossed a swampy part where the moss hung as white as lace from every limb. "Sleep on, alligators, and blow your bubbles." Then the track went into the road.

Deep, deep the road went down between the high green-colored banks. Overhead the live-oaks met, and it was as dark as a cave.

A black dog with a lolling tongue came up out of the weeds by the ditch. She was meditating, and not ready, and when he came at her she only hit him a little with her cane. Over she went in the ditch, like a little puff of milkweed.[3]

Down there, her senses drifted away. A dream visited her, and she reached her hand up, but nothing reached down and gave her a pull. So she lay there and presently went to talking. "Old woman," she said to herself, "that black dog come up out of the weeds to stall you off, and now there he sitting on his fine tail, smiling at you."

A white man finally came along and found her—a hunter, a young man, with his dog on a chain.

"Well, Granny!" he laughed. "What are you doing there?"

"Lying on my back like a June bug waiting to be turned over, mister," she said, reaching up her hand.

He lifted her up, gave her a swing in the air, and set her down. "Anything broken, Granny?"

"No sir, them old dead weeds is springy enough," said Phoenix, when she had got her breath. "I thank you for your trouble."

2. **sweet gum:** A tree that produces a fragrant juice.
3. **milkweed:** A plant with pods which when ripe release feathery seeds.

"Where do you live, Granny?" he asked, while the two dogs were growling at each other.

"Away back yonder, sir, behind the ridge. You can't even see it from here."

"On your way home?"

"No sir, I going to town."

"Why, that's too far! That's as far as I walk when I come out myself, and I get something for my trouble." He patted the stuffed bag he carried, and there hung down a little closed claw. It was one of the bobwhites, with its beak hooked bitterly to show it was dead. "Now you go on home, Granny!"

"I bound to go to town, mister," said Phoenix. "The time come around."

He gave another laugh, filling the whole landscape. "I know you old colored people! Wouldn't miss going to town to see Santa Claus!"

But something held old Phoenix very still. The deep lines in her face went into a fierce and different radiation. Without warning, she had seen with her own eyes a flashing nickel fall out of the man's pocket onto the ground.

"How old are you, Granny?" he was saying.

"There is no telling, mister," she said, "no telling."

Then she gave a little cry and clapped her hands and said, "Git on away from here, dog! Look! Look at that dog!" She laughed as if in admiration. "He ain't scared of nobody. He a big black dog." She whispered, "Sic him!"

"Watch me get rid of that cur," said the man. "Sic him, Pete! Sic him!"

Phoenix heard the dogs fighting, and heard the man running and throwing sticks. She even heard a gunshot. But she was slowly bending forward by that time, further and further forward, the lids stretched down over her eyes, as if she were doing this in her sleep. Her chin was lowered almost to her knees. The yellow palm of her hand came out from the fold of her apron. Her fingers slid down and along the ground under the piece of money with the grace and care they would have in lifting an egg from under a setting hen. Then she slowly straightened up, she stood erect, and the nickel was in her apron pocket. A bird flew by. Her lips moved. "God watching me the whole time. I come to stealing."

The man came back, and his own dog panted about them. "Well, I scared him off that time," he said, and then he laughed and lifted his gun and pointed it at Phoenix.

She stood straight and faced him.

"Doesn't the gun scare you?" he said, still pointing it.

"No, sir, I seen plenty go off closer by, in my day, and for less than what I done," she said, holding utterly still.

He smiled, and shouldered the gun. "Well, Granny," he said, "you must be a hundred years old, and scared of nothing. I'd give you a dime if I had any money with me. But you take my advice and stay home, and nothing will happen to you."

"I bound to go on my way, mister," said Phoenix. She inclined her head in the red rag. Then they went in different directions, but she could hear the gun shooting again and again over the hill.

She walked on. The shadows hung from the oak trees to the road like curtains. Then she smelled woodsmoke, and smelled the river, and she saw a steeple and the cabins on their steep steps. Dozens of little black children whirled around her. There ahead was Natchez[4] shining. Bells were ringing. She walked on.

In the paved city it was Christmas time. There were red and green electric lights strung and criss-crossed everywhere, and all turned on in the daytime. Old Phoenix would have been lost if she had not distrusted her eyesight and depended on her feet to know where to take her.

She paused quietly on the sidewalk where people were passing by. A lady came along in the crowd, carrying an armful of red-, green- and silver-wrapped presents; she gave off perfume like the red roses in hot summer, and Phoenix stopped her.

"Please, missy, will you lace up my shoe?" She held up her foot.

"What do you want, Grandma?"

"See my shoe," said Phoenix. "Do all right for out in the country, but wouldn't look right to go in a big building."

"Stand still then, Grandma," said the lady. She put her packages down on the sidewalk beside her and laced and tied both shoes tightly.

"Can't lace 'em with a cane," said Phoenix. "Thank you, missy. I doesn't mind asking a nice lady to tie up my shoe, when I gets out on the street."

Moving slowly and from side to side, she went into the big building, and into a tower of steps, where she walked up and around and around until her feet knew to stop.

She entered a door, and there she saw nailed up on the wall the document that had been stamped with the gold seal and framed in the gold frame, which matched the dream that was hung up in her head.

"Here I be," she said. There was a fixed and ceremonial stiffness over her body.

"A charity case, I suppose," said an attendant who sat at the desk before her.

But Phoenix only looked above her head. There was sweat on her face, the wrinkles in her skin shone like a bright net.

"Speak up, Grandma," the woman said. "What's your name? We must have your history, you know. Have you been here before? What seems to be the trouble with you?"

Old Phoenix only gave a twitch to her face as if a fly were bothering her.

"Are you deaf?" cried the attendant.

But then the nurse came in.

"Oh, that's just old Aunt Phoenix," she

---

4. Natchez (nach'iz): A town in southern Mississippi.

said. "She doesn't come for herself—she has a little grandson. She makes these trips just as regular as clockwork. She lives away back off the Old Natchez Trace." She bent down. "Well, Aunt Phoenix, why don't you just take a seat? We won't keep you standing after your long trip." She pointed.

The old woman sat down, bolt upright in the chair.

"Now, how is the boy?" asked the nurse.

Old Phoenix did not speak.

"I said, how is the boy?"

But Phoenix only waited and stared straight ahead, her face very solemn and withdrawn into rigidity.

"Is his throat any better?" asked the nurse. "Aunt Phoenix, don't you hear me? Is your grandson's throat any better since the last time you came for the medicine?"

With her hands on her knees, the old woman waited, silent, erect and motionless, just as if she were in armor.

"You mustn't take up our time this way, Aunt Phoenix," the nurse said. "Tell us quickly about your grandson, and get it over. He isn't dead, is he?"

At last there came a flicker and then a flame of comprehension across her face, and she spoke.

"My grandson. It was my memory had left me. There I sat and forgot why I made my long trip."

"Forgot?" The nurse frowned. "After you came so far?"

Then Phoenix was like an old woman begging a dignified forgiveness for waking up frightened in the night. "I never did go to school, I was too old at the Surrender,[5]" she said in a soft voice. "I'm an old woman without an education. It was my memory fail me. My little grandson, he is just the same, and I forgot it in the coming."

_____

5. the Surrender: The surrender of the Confederate army, ending the Civil War.

"Throat never heals, does it?" said the nurse, speaking in a loud, sure voice to old Phoenix. By now she had a card with something written on it, a little list. "Yes. Swallowed lye. When was it?—January—two-three years ago—"

Phoenix spoke unasked now. "No, missy, he not dead, he just the same. Every little while his throat begin to close up again, and he not able to swallow. He not get his breath. He not able to help himself. So the time come around, and I go on another trip for the soothing medicine."

"All right. The doctor said as long as you came to get it, you could have it," said the nurse. "But it's an obstinate case."

"My little grandson, he sit up there in the house all wrapped up, waiting by himself," Phoenix went on. "We is the only two left in the world. He suffer and it don't seem to put him back at all. He got a sweet look. He going to last. He wear a little patch quilt and peep out holding his mouth open like a little bird. I remembers so plain now. I not going to forget him again, no, the whole enduring time. I could tell him from all the others in creation."

"All right." The nurse was trying to hush her now. She brought her a bottle of medicine. "Charity," she said, making a check mark in a book.

Old Phoenix held the bottle close to her eyes, and then carefully put it into her pocket.

"I thank you," she said.

"It's Christmas time, Grandma," said the attendant. "Could I give you a few pennies out of my purse?"

"Five pennies is a nickel," said Phoenix stiffly.

"Here's a nickel," said the attendant.

Phoenix rose carefully and held out her hand. She received the nickel and then fished the other nickel out of her pocket and laid it beside the new one. She stared at her palm closely, with her head on one side.

Then she gave a tap with her cane on the floor.

"This is what come to me to do," she said. "I going to the store and buy my child a little windmill they sells, made out of paper. He going to find it hard to believe there such a thing in the world. I'll march myself back where he is waiting, holding it straight up in this hand."

She lifted her free hand, gave a little nod, turned around, and walked out of the doctor's office. Then her slow step began on the stairs, going down.

THINKING ABOUT THE SELECTION

Recalling

1. (a) What are the first three obstacles Phoenix Jackson encounters? (b) What does she see after overcoming the third obstacle?
2. (a) What causes Phoenix to fall into a ditch? (b) Who helps her out of the ditch? (c) What does he drop from his pocket? (d) How does Phoenix divert his attention so she can pick it up?
3. (a) What does the nurse ask Phoenix? (b) How does Phoenix explain her inability to answer?

Interpreting

4. What details of the setting help to create a somber, mournful atmosphere?
5. (a) How would you characterize the hunter's attitude toward Phoenix? (b) How would you characterize the nurse's and the attendant's attitudes toward Phoenix?
6. Why do you think Phoenix does not immediately respond to the questions of the nurse and the attendant?
7. What is the significance of the story taking place at Christmas time?
8. What does Phoenix's journey symbolize?

Applying

9. Like Welty's other works, "The Worn Path" is set in the deep South. Do you think the story would be different if the setting were changed? Why or why not?

ANALYZING LITERATURE

Interpreting Ambiguity

When a work of literature is **ambiguous** or contains ambiguous elements, the work or the elements of the work can be interpreted in more than one way. For example, in "A Worn Path" Eudora Welty leaves the question of whether Phoenix Jackson's grandson is still alive open to interpretation.

1. Find two details from the story that support the interpretation that Phoenix's grandson is alive.
2. Find two details that support the interpretation that he is dead.
3. Why do you think Welty chooses not to reveal whether he is alive or dead?

THINKING AND WRITING

Writing a Continuation of the Story

Write a continuation of the story in which Phoenix returns home bearing the medicine. List details you can use to describe the setting. When you write your story, try to use these details to create an appropriate atmosphere and to foreshadow what will be waiting for her when she arrives home. When you finish writing, revise your story, making sure you have maintained a consistent point of view. Then share it with your classmates.

JOHN STEINBECK

1902–1968

Reflecting the influence of the Naturalists, John Steinbeck generally portrayed working-class characters who were manipulated by forces beyond their understanding or control. Yet although many of his characters suffered tragic fates, they almost always managed to retain a sense of dignity throughout their struggles.

Steinbeck was born in Salinas, California, the son of a county official and a schoolteacher. The people and the landscape of the area in northern California where he grew up eventually inspired many of the characters and settings of his literary works. After graduating from high school, he enrolled at Stanford University. He left before graduating, however, and spent the next five years drifting across the country, reading, writing, and working at odd jobs.

Steinbeck had little success as a writer until 1935 when he published *Tortilla Flat,* his third novel. Two years later he earned widespread recognition and critical acclaim with the publication of *Of Mice and Men*. This novel, which portrays two drifters whose dream of owning their own farm ends in tragedy, became a best-seller and was made into a Broadway play and a motion picture. Steinbeck then went on to write what is generally regarded as his finest novel, *The Grapes of Wrath* (1939), the accurate and emotional story of the "Okies," Oklahoma farmers dispossessed of their land and forced to become migrant farmers in California. The novel won the National Book Award and the Pulitzer Prize and established Steinbeck as one of the most highly regarded writers of his day.

Steinbeck produced several more successful works during his later years, including *Cannery Row* (1945), *The Pearl* (1947), *East of Eden* (1951), and *The Winter of Our Discontent* (1961). In 1963 he was awarded the Nobel Prize for Literature.

In nearly all of his works, including "Flight," Steinbeck creates vivid portraits of the landscape and demonstrates how people are shaped and manipulated by their environments. At the same time, his works reflect his belief in the need for social justice and his hope that people can learn from the suffering of others.

Flight

Setting. The setting is the time and place in which the events in a work of literature occur. Although it is not usually the most important element in a literary work, the setting can often shape and motivate the characters. In real life people are sometimes viewed as being, to some extent, products of their environments. Similarly, characters in many literary works may be viewed as products of the setting. While a character's attitudes, values, and behavior may be shaped by the long-term effect of the setting, the setting may also have a more immediate impact on a character's actions. For example, in Jack London's story "To Build a Fire," most of the character's actions result directly from his efforts to cope with the extreme cold of the Arctic wilderness.

John Steinbeck believed that people are often manipulated by forces of society and nature beyond their understanding or control. As a result, the setting usually plays an important role in his works, often having both an immediate and long-term effect on the characters. In most of his stories and novels, he describes the setting in exact detail and clearly conveys how it shapes and motivates the characters.

As you read "Flight," look for the long-term and immediate effects of the setting on the characters.

In "Flight" Steinbeck uses sensory details to paint a vivid portrait of the setting. Prepare a list of sensory details describing your environment. List them in a chart under the headings of *Sight, Smell, Taste, Touch, Hearing.*

Knowing the following words will help you as you read "Flight."
insinuating (in sin′ yo͞o wāt′iŋ) *v.*: Hinting or suggesting indirectly; implying (p. 774)
furtive (fʉr′tiv) *adj.*: Sneaky (p. 776)

monotonous (mə nät′′n əs) *adj.*: Having little or no variation or variety (p. 778)

Flight

John Steinbeck

About fifteen miles below Monterey, on the wild coast, the Torres family had their farm, a few sloping acres above a cliff that dropped to the brown reefs and to the hissing white waters of the ocean. Behind the farm the stone mountains stood up against the sky. The farm buildings huddled like little clinging aphids[1] on the mountain skirts, crouched low to the ground as though the wind might blow them into the sea. The little shack, the rattling, rotting barn were gray-bitten with sea salt, beaten by the damp wind until they had taken on the color of the granite hills. Two horses, a red cow and a red calf, half a dozen pigs and a flock of lean, multicolored chickens stocked the place. A little corn was raised on the sterile slope, and it grew short and thick under the wind, and all the cobs formed on the landward sides of the stalks.

Mama Torres, a lean, dry woman with ancient eyes, had ruled the farm for ten years, ever since her husband tripped over a stone in the field one day and fell full length on a rattlesnake. When one is bitten on the chest there is not much that can be done.

Mama Torres had three children, two undersized black ones of twelve and fourteen, Emilio and Rosy, whom Mama kept fishing on the rocks below the farm when the sea was kind and when the truant officer was in some distant part of Monterey County. And there was Pepé, the tall smiling son of nineteen, a gentle, affectionate boy, but very lazy.

Pepé had a tall head, pointed at the top, and from its peak, coarse black hair grew down like a thatch all around. Over his smiling little eyes Mama cut a straight bang so he could see. Pepé had sharp Indian cheek bones and an eagle nose, but his mouth was as sweet and shapely as a girl's mouth, and his chin was fragile and chiseled. He was loose and gangling, all legs and feet and wrists, and he was very lazy. Mama thought him fine and brave, but she never told him so. She said, "Some lazy cow must have got into thy father's family, else how could I have a son like thee." And she said, "When I carried thee, a sneaking lazy coyote came out of the brush and looked at me one day. That must have made thee so."

Pepé smiled sheepishly and stabbed at the ground with his knife to keep the blade sharp and free from rust. It was his inheritance, that knife, his father's knife. The long heavy blade folded back into the black handle. There was a button on the handle. When Pepé pressed the button, the blade leaped out ready for use. The knife was with Pepé always, for it had been his father's knife.

One sunny morning when the sea below the cliff was glinting and blue and the white surf creamed on the reef, when even the stone mountains looked kindly, Mama Torres called out the door of the shack, "Pepé, I have a labor for thee."

There was no answer. Mama listened. From behind the barn she heard a burst of laughter. She lifted her full long skirt and walked in the direction of the noise.

Pepé was sitting on the ground with his

---

1. aphids (ā′fidz) n.: Small insects that suck the juice from plants.

back against a box. His white teeth glistened. On either side of him stood the two black ones, tense and expectant. Fifteen feet away a redwood post was set in the ground. Pepé's right hand lay limply in his lap, and in the palm the big black knife rested. The blade was closed back into the handle. Pepé looked smiling at the sky.

Suddenly Emilio cried, "Ya!"

Pepé's wrist flicked like the head of a snake. The blade seemed to fly open in midair, and with a thump the point dug into the redwood post, and the black handle quivered. The three burst into excited laughter.

Rosy ran to the post and pulled out the knife and brought it back to Pepé. He closed the blade and settled the knife carefully in his listless palm again. He grinned self-consciously at the sky.

"Ya!"

The heavy knife lanced out and sunk into the post again. Mama moved forward like a ship and scattered the play.

"All day you do foolish things with the knife, like a toy baby," she stormed. "Get up on thy huge feet that eat up shoes. Get up!" She took him by one loose shoulder and hoisted at him. Pepé grinned sheepishly and came halfheartedly to his feet. "Look!" Mama cried. "Big lazy, you must catch the horse and put on him thy father's saddle. You must ride to Monterey. The medicine bottle is empty. There is no salt. Go thou now, Peanut! Catch the horse."

A revolution took place in the relaxed figure of Pepé. "To Monterey, me? Alone? *Sí*, Mama."

She scowled at him. "Do not think, big sheep, that you will buy candy. No, I will give you only enough for the medicine and the salt."

Pepé smiled. "Mama, you will put the hatband on the hat?"

She relented then. "Yes, Pepé. You may wear the hatband."

His voice grew insinuating, "And the green handkerchief, Mama?"

"Yes, if you go quickly and return with no trouble, the silk green handkerchief will go. If you make sure to take off the handkerchief when you eat so no spot may fall on it. . . ."

"*Sí*, Mama. I will be careful. I am a man."

"Thou? A man? Thou art a peanut."

He went into the rickety barn and brought out a rope, and he walked agilely enough up the hill to catch the horse.

When he was ready and mounted before the door, mounted on his father's saddle that was so old that the oaken frame showed through torn leather in many places, then Mama brought out the round black hat with the tooled leather band, and she reached up and knotted the green silk handkerchief about his neck. Pepé's blue denim coat was much darker than his jeans, for it had been washed much less often.

Mama handed up the big medicine bottle and the silver coins. "That for the medicine," she said, "and that for the salt. That for a candle to burn for the papa. That for *dulces*[2] for the little ones. Our friend Mrs. Rodriguez will give you dinner and maybe a bed for the night. When you go to the church say only

ten Paternosters[3] and only twenty-five Ave Marias.[4] Oh! I know, big coyote. You would sit there flapping your mouth over Aves all day while you looked at the candles and the holy pictures. That is not good devotion to stare at the pretty things."

The black hat, covering the high pointed head and black thatched hair of Pepé, gave him dignity and age. He sat the rangy horse well. Mama thought how handsome he was, dark and lean and tall. "I would not send thee now alone, thou little one, except for the medicine," she said softly. "It is not good to have no medicine, for who knows when the toothache will come, or the sadness of the stomach. These things are."

"Adios, Mama," Pepé cried. "I will come back soon. You may send me often alone. I am a man."

"Thou art a foolish chicken."

He straightened his shoulders, flipped the reins against the horse's shoulder and rode away. He turned once and saw that they still watched him, Emilio and Rosy and Mama. Pepé grinned with pride and gladness and lifted the tough buckskin horse to a trot.

When he had dropped out of sight over a little dip in the road, Mama turned to the black ones, but she spoke to herself. "He is nearly a man now," she said. "It will be a nice thing to have a man in the house again." Her eyes sharpened on the children. "Go to the rocks now. The tide is going out. There will be abalones[5] to be found." She put the iron hooks into their hands and saw them down the steep trail to the reefs. She brought the smooth stone *metate*[6] to the doorway and sat grinding her corn to flour and looking occasionally at the road over which Pepé had gone. The noonday came and then the afternoon, when the little ones beat the abalones on a rock to make them

---

2. dulces (do͞ol′sās) *n*.: Candy; sweets.

3. Paternosters (pät′ər nôs′tərz): Our Fathers (The Lord's Prayer).

4. Ave Marias (ä′ vä mə rē′ əz): Hail Marys.

5. abalones (ab′ə lō′nēz) *n*.: Large shellfish.

6. metate (mä tä′ tä′): A stone used in the southwestern United States for grinding meal.

tender and Mama patted the tortillas[7] to make them thin. They ate their dinner as the red sun was plunging down toward the ocean. They sat on the doorsteps and watched the big white moon come over the mountain tops.

Mama said, "He is now at the house of our friend Mrs. Rodriguez. She will give him nice things to eat and maybe a present."

Emilio said, "Some day I too will ride to Monterey for medicine. Did Pepé come to be a man today?"

Mama said wisely, "A boy gets to be a man when a man is needed. Remember this thing. I have known boys forty years old because there was no need for a man."

Soon afterwards they retired, Mama in her big oak bed on one side of the room, Emilio and Rosy in their boxes full of straw and sheepskins on the other side of the room.

The moon went over the sky and the surf roared on the rocks. The roosters crowed the first call. The surf subsided to a whispering surge against the reef. The moon dropped toward the sea. The roosters crowed again.

The moon was near down to the water when Pepé rode on a winded horse to his home flat. His dog bounced out and circled the horse yelping with pleasure. Pepé slid off the saddle to the ground. The weathered little shack was silver in the moonlight and the square shadow of it was black to the north and east. Against the east the piling mountains were misty with light; their tops melted into the sky.

Pepé walked wearily up the three steps and into the house. It was dark inside. There was a rustle in the corner.

Mama cried out from her bed. "Who comes? Pepé, is it thou?"

"Sí, Mama."

"Did you get the medicine?"

"Sí, Mama."

"Well, go to sleep, then. I thought you would be sleeping at the house of Mrs. Rodri-

---

7. tortillas (tôr tē′əz) *n.*: Thin, flat cakes of cornmeal.

guez." Pepé stood silently in the dark room. "Why do you stand there, Pepé? Did you drink wine?"

"Sí, Mama."

"Well, go to bed then and sleep out the wine."

His voice was tired and patient, but very firm. "Light the candle, Mama. I must go away into the mountains."

"What is this, Pepé? You are crazy." Mama struck a sulphur match and held the little blue burr until the flame spread up the stick. She set light to the candle on the floor beside her bed. "Now, Pepé, what is this you say?" She looked anxiously into his face.

He was changed. The fragile quality seemed to have gone from his chin. His mouth was less full than it had been, the lines of the lips were straighter, but in his eyes the greatest change had taken place. There was no laughter in them any more, nor any bashfulness. They were sharp and bright and purposeful.

He told her in a tired monotone, told her everything just as it had happened. A few people came into the kitchen of Mrs. Rodriguez. There was wine to drink. Pepé drank wine. The little quarrel—the man started toward Pepé and then the knife—it went almost by itself. It flew, it darted before Pepé knew it. As he talked, Mama's face grew stern, and it seemed to grow more lean. Pepé finished. "I am a man now, Mama. The man said names to me I could not allow."

Mama nodded. "Yes, thou art a man, my poor little Pepé. Thou art a man. I have seen it coming on thee. I have watched you throwing the knife into the post, and I have been afraid." For a moment her face had softened, but now it grew stern again. "Come! We must get you ready. Go. Awaken Emilio and Rosy. Go quickly."

Pepé stepped over to the corner where his brother and sister slept among the sheepskins. He leaned down and shook them gently. "Come, Rosy! Come, Emilio! The mama says you must arise."

The little black ones sat up and rubbed their eyes in the candlelight. Mama was out of bed now, her long black skirt over her nightgown. "Emilio," she cried. "Go up and catch the other horse for Pepé. Quickly, now! Quickly." Emilio put his legs in his overalls and stumbled sleepily out the door.

"You heard no one behind you on the road?" Mama demanded.

"No, Mama. I listened carefully. No one was on the road."

Mama darted like a bird about the room. From a nail on the wall she took a canvas water bag and threw it on the floor. She stripped a blanket from her bed and rolled it into a tight tube and tied the ends with string. From a box beside the stove she lifted a flour sack half full of black stringy jerky. "Your father's black coat, Pepé. Here, put it on."

Pepé stood in the middle of the floor watching her activity. She reached behind the door and brought out the rifle, a long 38-56, worn shiny the whole length of the barrel. Pepé took it from her and held it in the crook of his elbow. Mama brought a little leather bag and counted the cartridges into his hand. "Only ten left," she warned. "You must not waste them."

Emilio put his head in the door. " 'Qui 'st 'l caballo,[8] Mama."

"Put on the saddle from the other horse. Tie on the blanket. Here, tie the jerky to the saddle horn."

Still Pepé stood silently watching his mother's frantic activity. His chin looked hard, and his sweet mouth was drawn and thin. His little eyes followed Mama about the room almost suspiciously.

Rosy asked softly, "Where goes Pepé?"

Mama's eyes were fierce. "Pepé goes on a journey. Pepé is a man now. He has a man's thing to do."

Pepé straightened his shoulders. His mouth changed until he looked very much like Mama.

At last the preparation was finished. The loaded horse stood outside the door. The water bag dripped a line of moisture down the bay shoulder.

The moonlight was being thinned by the dawn and the big white moon was near down to the sea. The family stood by the shack. Mama confronted Pepé. "Look, my son! Do not stop until it is dark again. Do not sleep even though you are tired. Take care of the horse in order that he may not stop of weariness. Remember to be careful with the bullets—there are only ten. Do not fill thy stomach with jerky or it will make thee sick. Eat a little jerky and fill thy stomach with grass. When thou comest to the high mountains, if thou seest any of the dark watching men, go not near to them nor try to speak to them. And forget not thy prayers." She put her lean hands on Pepé's shoulders, stood on her toes and kissed him formally on both cheeks, and Pepé kissed her on both cheeks. Then he went to Emilio and Rosy and kissed both of their cheeks.

Pepé turned back to Mama. He seemed to look for a little softness, a little weakness in her. His eyes were searching, but Mama's face remained fierce. "Go now," she said. "Do not wait to be caught like a chicken."

Pepé pulled himself into the saddle. "I am a man," he said.

It was the first dawn when he rode up the hill toward the little canyon which let a trail into the mountains. Moonlight and daylight fought with each other, and the two warring qualities made it difficult to see. Before Pepé had gone a hundred yards, the outlines of his figure were misty; and long before he entered the canyon, he had become a gray, indefinite shadow.

Mama stood stiffly in front of her doorstep, and on either side of her stood Emilio and Rosy. They cast furtive glances at Mama now and then.

When the gray shape of Pepé melted into the hillside and disappeared, Mama relaxed. She began the high, whining keen[9] of the death wail. "Our beautiful—our brave," she

---

8. 'Qui 'st 'l caballo (kēst'l kä bä'yō): Here is the horse (colloquial Spanish).

9. keen: A wailing for the dead.

cried. "Our protector, our son is gone." Emilio and Rosy moaned beside her. "Our beautiful—our brave, he is gone." It was the formal wail. It rose to a high piercing whine and subsided to a moan. Mama raised it three times and then she turned and went into the house and shut the door.

Emilio and Rosy stood wondering in the dawn. They heard Mama whimpering in the house. They went out to sit on the cliff above the ocean. They touched shoulders. "When did Pepé come to be a man?" Emilio asked.

"Last night," said Rosy. "Last night in Monterey." The ocean clouds turned red with the sun that was behind the mountains.

"We will have no breakfast," said Emilio. "Mama will not want to cook." Rosy did not answer him. "Where is Pepé gone?" he asked.

Rosy looked around at him. She drew her knowledge from the quiet air. "He has gone on a journey. He will never come back."

"Is he dead? Do you think he is dead?"

Rosy looked back at the ocean again. A little steamer, drawing a line of smoke sat on the edge of the horizon. "He is not dead," Rosy explained. "Not yet."

Pepé rested the big rifle across the saddle in front of him. He let the horse walk up the hill and he didn't look back. The stony slope took on a coat of short brush so that Pepé found the entrance to a trail and entered it.

When he came to the canyon opening, he swung once in his saddle and looked back, but the houses were swallowed in the misty light. Pepé jerked forward again. The high shoulder of the canyon closed in on him. His horse stretched out its neck and sighed and settled to the trail.

It was a well-worn path, dark soft leaf-mold earth strewn with broken pieces of sandstone. The trail rounded the shoulder of the canyon and dropped steeply into the bed of the stream. In the shallows the water ran smoothly, glinting in the first morning sun. Small round stones on the bottom were as brown as rust with sun moss. In the sand along the edges of the stream the tall, rich wild mint grew, while in the water itself the cress,[10] old and tough, had gone to heavy seed.

The path went into the stream and emerged on the other side. The horse sloshed into the water and stopped. Pepé dropped his bridle and let the beast drink of the running water.

Soon the canyon sides became steep and the first giant sentinel redwoods guarded the trail, great round red trunks bearing foliage as green and lacy as ferns. Once Pepé was among the trees, the sun was lost. A perfumed and purple light lay in the pale green of the underbrush. Gooseberry bushes and blackberries and tall ferns lined the stream, and overhead the branches of the redwoods met and cut off the sky.

Pepé drank from the water bag, and he reached into the flour sack and brought out a black string of jerky. His white teeth gnawed at the string until the tough meat parted. He chewed slowly and drank occasionally from the water bag. His little eyes were slumberous and tired, but the muscles of his face were hard set. The earth of the trail was black now. It gave up a hollow sound under the walking hoofbeats.

The stream fell more sharply. Little waterfalls splashed on the stones. Five-fingered ferns hung over the water and dripped spray from their fingertips. Pepé rode half over in his saddle, dangling one leg loosely. He picked a bay leaf from a tree beside the way and put it into his mouth for a moment to flavor the dry jerky. He held the gun loosely across the pommel.

Suddenly he squared in his saddle, swung the horse from the trail and kicked it hurriedly up behind a big redwood tree. He pulled up the reins tight against the bit to keep the horse from whinnying. His face was intent and his nostrils quivered a little.

A hollow pounding came down the trail,

---

10. cress: Watercress, an edible white-flowered plant.

and a horseman rode by, a fat man with red cheeks and a white stubble beard. His horse put down its head and blubbered at the trail when it came to the place where Pepé had turned off. "Hold up!" said the man and he pulled up his horse's head.

When the last sound of the hoofs died away, Pepé came back into the trail again. He did not relax in the saddle any more. He lifted the big rifle and swung the lever to throw a shell into the chamber, and then he let down the hammer to half cock.

The trail grew very steep. Now the redwood trees were smaller and their tops were dead, bitten dead where the wind reached them. The horse plodded on; the sun went slowly overhead and started down toward the afternoon.

Where the stream came out of a side canyon, the trail left it. Pepé dismounted and watered his horse and filled up his water bag. As soon as the trail had parted from the stream, the trees were gone and only the thick brittle sage and manzanita[11] and chaparral[12] edged the trail. And the soft black earth was gone, too, leaving only the light tan broken rock for the trail bed. Lizards scampered away into the brush as the horse rattled over the little stones.

Pepé turned in his saddle and looked back. He was in the open now: he could be seen from a distance. As he ascended the trail the country grew more rough and terrible and dry. The way wound about the bases of great square rocks. Little gray rabbits skittered in the brush. A bird made a monotonous high creaking. Eastward the bare rock mountaintops were pale and powder-dry under the dropping sun. The horse plodded up and up the trail toward a little V in the ridge which was the pass.

Pepé looked suspiciously back every minute or so, and his eyes sought the tops of the ridges ahead. Once, on a white barren spur,

he saw a black figure for a moment, but he looked quickly away, for it was one of the dark watchers. No one knew who the watchers were, nor where they lived, but it was better to ignore them and never to show interest in them. They did not bother one who stayed on the trail and minded his own business.

The air was parched and full of light dust blown by the breeze from the eroding mountains. Pepé drank sparingly from his bag and corked it tightly and hung it on the horn again. The trail moved up the dry shale hillside, avoiding rocks, dropping under clefts, climbing in and out of old water scars. When he arrived at the little pass he stopped and looked back for a long time. No dark watchers were to be seen now. The trail behind was empty. Only the high tops of the redwoods indicated where the stream flowed.

Pepé rode on through the pass. His little eyes were nearly closed with weariness, but his face was stern, relentless and manly. The high mountain wind coasted sighing through the pass and whistled on the edges of the big blocks of broken granite. In the air, a red-tailed hawk sailed over close to the ridge and screamed angrily. Pepé went slowly through the broken jagged pass and looked down on the other side.

The trail dropped quickly, staggering among broken rock. At the bottom of the slope there was a dark crease, thick with brush, and on the other side of the crease a little flat, in which a grove of oak trees grew. A scar of green grass cut across the flat. And behind the flat another mountain rose, desolate with dead rocks and starving little black bushes. Pepé drank from the bag again for the air was so dry that it encrusted his nostrils and burned his lips. He put the horse down the trail. The hooves slipped and struggled on the steep way, starting little stones that rolled off into the brush. The sun was gone behind the westward mountain now, but still it glowed brilliantly on the oaks and on the grassy flat. The rocks and the hillsides still sent up waves of the heat they had gathered from the day's sun.

---

11. manzanita (man′zə nēt′ə): Shrubs or small trees.
12. chaparral (c͡hap′ə ral′) *n.*: A thicket of thorny bushes or shrubs.

Pepé looked up to the top of the next dry withered ridge. He saw a dark form against the sky, a man's figure standing on top of a rock, and he glanced away quickly not to appear curious. When a moment later he looked up again, the figure was gone.

Downward the trail was quickly covered. Sometimes the horse floundered for footing, sometimes set his feet and slid a little way. They came at last to the bottom where the dark chaparral was higher than Pepé's head. He held up his rifle on one side and his arm on the other to shield his face from the sharp brittle fingers of the brush.

Up and out of the crease he rode, and up a little cliff. The grassy flat was before him, and the round comfortable oaks. For a moment he studied the trail down which he had come, but there was no movement and no sound from it. Finally he rode out over the flat, to the green streak, and at the upper end of the damp he found a little spring welling out of the earth and dropping into a dug basin before it seeped out over the flat.

Pepé filled his bag first, and then he let the thirsty horse drink out of the pool. He led the horse to the clump of oaks, and in the middle of the grove, fairly protected from sight on all sides, he took off the saddle and the bridle and laid them on the ground. The horse stretched his jaws sideways and yawned. Pepé knotted the lead rope about the horse's neck and tied him to a sapling among the oaks, where he could graze in a fairly large circle.

When the horse was gnawing hungrily at the dry grass, Pepé went to the saddle and took a black string of jerky from the sack and strolled to an oak tree on the edge of the grove, from under which he could watch the trail. He sat down in the crisp dry oak leaves and automatically felt for his big black knife

to cut the jerky, but he had no knife. He leaned back on his elbow and gnawed at the tough strong meat. His face was blank, but it was a man's face.

The bright evening light washed the eastern ridge, but the valley was darkening. Doves flew down from the hills to the spring, and the quail came running out of the brush and joined them, calling clearly to one another.

Out of the corner of his eye Pepé saw a shadow grow out of the bushy crease. He turned his head slowly. A big spotted wildcat was creeping toward the spring, belly to the ground, moving like thought.

Pepé cocked his rifle and edged the muzzle slowly around. Then he looked apprehensively up the trail and dropped the hammer again. From the ground beside him he picked an oak twig and threw it toward the spring. The quail flew up with a roar and the doves whistled away. The big cat stood up: for a long moment he looked at Pepé with cold yellow eyes, and then fearlessly walked back into the gulch.

The dusk gathered quickly in the deep valley. Pepé muttered his prayers, put his head down on his arm and went instantly to sleep.

The moon came up and filled the valley with cold blue light, and the wind swept rustling down from the peaks. The owls worked up and down the slopes looking for rabbits. Down in the brush of the gulch a coyote gabbled. The oak trees whispered softly in the night breeze.

Pepé started up, listening. His horse had whinnied. The moon was just slipping behind the western ridge, leaving the valley in darkness behind it. Pepé sat tensely gripping his rifle. From far up the trail he heard an answering whinny and the crash of shod hooves on the broken rock. He jumped to his feet, ran to his horse and led it under the trees. He threw on the saddle and cinched it tight for the steep trail, caught the unwilling head and forced the bit into the mouth. He

felt the saddle to make sure the water bag and the sack of jerky were there. Then he mounted and turned up the hill.

It was velvet dark. The horse found the entrance to the trail where it left the flat, and started up, stumbling and slipping on the rocks. Pepé's hand rose up to his head. His hat was gone. He had left it under the oak tree.

The horse had struggled far up the trail when the first change of dawn came into the air, a steel grayness as light mixed thoroughly with dark. Gradually the sharp snaggled edge of the ridge stood out above them, rotten granite tortured and eaten by the winds of time. Pepé had dropped his reins on the horn, leaving direction to the horse. The brush grabbed at his legs in the dark until one knee of his jeans was ripped.

Gradually the light flowed down over the ridge. The starved brush and rocks stood out in the half light, strange and lonely in high perspective. Then there came warmth into the light. Pepé drew up and looked back, but he could see nothing in the darker valley below. The sky turned blue over the coming sun. In the waste of the mountainside, the poor dry brush grew only three feet high. Here and there, big outcroppings of unrotted granite stood up like moldering houses. Pepé relaxed a little. He drank from his water bag and bit off a piece of jerky. A single eagle flew over, high in the light.

Without warning Pepé's horse screamed and fell on its side. He was almost down before the rifle crash echoed up from the valley. From a hole behind the struggling shoulder, a stream of bright crimson blood pumped and stopped and pumped and stopped. The hooves threshed on the ground. Pepé lay half stunned beside the horse. He looked slowly down the hill. A piece of sage clipped off beside his head and another crash echoed up from side to side of the canyon. Pepé flung himself frantically behind a bush.

He crawled up the hill on his knees and one hand. His right hand held the rifle up off the ground and pushed it ahead of him. He moved with the instinctive care of an animal. Rapidly he wormed his way toward one of the big outcroppings of granite on the hill above him. Where the brush was high he doubled up and ran, but where the cover was slight he wriggled forward on his stomach, pushing the rifle ahead of him. In the last little distance there was no cover at all. Pepé poised and then he darted across the space and flashed around the corner of the rock.

He leaned panting against the stone. When his breath came easier he moved along behind the big rock until he came to a narrow split that offered a thin section of vision down the hill. Pepé lay on his stomach and pushed the rifle barrel through the slit and waited.

The sun reddened the western ridges now. Already the buzzards were settling down toward the place where the horse lay. A small brown bird scratched in the dead sage leaves directly in front of the rifle muzzle. The coasting eagle flew back toward the rising sun.

Pepé saw a little movement in the brush far below. His grip tightened on the gun. A little brown doe stepped daintily out on the trail and crossed it and disappeared into the brush again. For a long time Pepé waited. Far below he could see the little flat and the oak trees and the slash of green. Suddenly his eyes flashed back at the trail again. A quarter of a mile down there had been a quick movement in the chaparral. The rifle swung over. The front sight nestled in the v of the rear sight. Pepé studied for a moment and then raised the rear sight a notch. The little movement in the brush came again. The sight settled on it. Pepé squeezed the trigger. The explosion crashed down the mountain and up the other side, and came rattling back. The whole side of the slope grew still. No more movement. And then a white streak cut into the granite of the slit and a bullet whined away and a crash sounded up from below. Pepé felt a sharp pain in his right hand. A sliver of granite was sticking out from between his first and second knuckles and the point protruded from his palm. Carefully he pulled out the sliver of stone. The wound bled evenly and gently. No vein nor artery was cut.

Pepé looked into a little dusty cave in the rock and gathered a handful of spider web, and he pressed the mass into the cut, plastering the soft web into the blood. The flow stopped almost at once.

The rifle was on the ground. Pepé picked it up, levered a new shell into the chamber. And then he slid into the brush on his stomach. Far to the right he crawled, and then up the hill, moving slowly and carefully, crawling to cover and resting and then crawling again.

In the mountains the sun is high in its arc before it penetrates the gorges. The hot face looked over the hill and brought instant heat with it. The white light beat on the rocks and reflected from them and rose up quivering from the earth again, and the rocks and bushes seemed to quiver behind the air.

Pepé crawled in the general direction of the ridge peak, zig-zagging for cover. The deep cut between his knuckles began to throb. He crawled close to a rattlesnake before he saw it, and when it raised its dry head and made a soft beginning whirr, he backed up and took another way. The quick gray lizards flashed in front of him, raising a tiny line of dust. He found another mass of spider web and pressed it against his throbbing hand.

Pepé was pushing the rifle with his left hand now. Little drops of sweat ran to the ends of his coarse black hair and rolled down his cheeks. His lips and tongue were growing thick and heavy. His lips writhed to draw saliva into his mouth. His little dark eyes were uneasy and suspicious. Once when a gray lizard paused in front of him on the parched ground and turned its head sideways he crushed it flat with a stone.

When the sun slid past noon he had not gone a mile. He crawled exhaustedly a last hundred yards to a patch of high sharp manzanita, crawled desperately, and when the patch was reached he wriggled in among the tough gnarly trunks and dropped his head on his left arm. There was little shade in the meager brush, but there was cover and safety. Pepé went to sleep as he lay and the sun beat on his back. A few little birds hopped close to him and peered and hopped away. Pepé squirmed in his sleep and he raised and dropped his wounded hand again and again.

The sun went down behind the peaks and the cool evening came, and then the dark. A coyote yelled from the hillside, Pepé started awake and looked about with misty eyes. His hand was swollen and heavy; a little thread of pain ran up the inside of his arm and settled in a pocket in his armpit. He peered about and then stood up, for the mountains were black and the moon had not yet risen. Pepé stood up in the dark. The coat of his father pressed on his arm. His tongue was swollen until it nearly filled his mouth. He wriggled out of the coat and dropped it in the brush, and then he struggled up the hill, falling over rocks and tearing his way through the brush. The rifle knocked against stones as he went. Little dry avalanches of gravel and shattered stone went whispering down the hill behind him.

After a while the old moon came up and showed the jagged ridge top ahead of him. By moonlight Pepé traveled more easily. He bent forward so that his throbbing arm hung away from his body. The journey uphill was made in dashes and rests, a frantic rush up a few yards and then a rest. The wind coasted down the slope rattling the dry stems of the bushes.

The moon was at meridian when Pepé came at last to the sharp backbone of the ridge top. On the last hundred yards of the rise no soil had clung under the wearing winds. The way was on solid rock. He clambered to the top and looked down on the other side. There was a draw like the last below him, misty with moonlight, brushed with dry struggling sage and chaparral. On

the other side the hill rose up sharply and at the top the jagged rotten teeth of the mountain showed against the sky. At the bottom of the cut the brush was thick and dark.

Pepé stumbled down the hill. His throat was almost closed with thirst. At first he tried to run, but immediately he fell and rolled. After that he went more carefully. The moon was just disappearing behind the mountains when he came to the bottom. He crawled into the heavy brush feeling with his fingers for water. There was no water in the bed of the stream, only damp earth. Pepé laid his gun down and scooped up a handful of mud and put it in his mouth, and then he spluttered and scraped the earth from his tongue with his finger, for the mud drew at his mouth like a poultice. He dug a hole in

the stream bed with his fingers, dug a little basin to catch water; but before it was very deep his head fell forward on the damp ground and he slept.

The dawn came and the heat of the day fell on the earth, and still Pepé slept. Late in the afternoon his head jerked up. He looked slowly around. His eyes were slits of wariness. Twenty feet away in the the heavy brush a big tawny mountain lion stood looking at him. Its long thick tail waved gracefully, its ears were erect with interest, not laid back dangerously. The lion squatted down on its stomach and watched him.

Pepé looked at the hole he had dug in the earth. A half inch of muddy water had collected in the bottom. He tore the sleeve from his hurt arm, with his teeth ripped out a lit-tle square, soaked it in the water and put it in his mouth. Over and over he filled the cloth and sucked it.

Still the lion sat and watched him. The evening came down but there was no movement on the hills. No birds visited the dry bottom of the cut. Pepé looked occasionally at the lion. The eyes of the yellow beast drooped as though he were about to sleep. He yawned and his long thin red tongue curled out. Suddenly his head jerked around and his nostrils quivered. His big tail lashed. He stood up and slunk like a tawny shadow into the thick brush.

A moment later Pepé heard the sound, the faint far crash of horses' hooves on gravel. And he heard something else, a high whining yelp of a dog.

Pepé took his rifle in his left hand and he glided into the brush almost as quietly as the lion had. In the darkening evening he crouched up the hill toward the next ridge. Only when the dark came did he stand up. His energy was short. Once it was dark he fell over the rocks and slipped to his knees on the steep slope, but he moved on and on up the hill, climbing and scrabbling over the broken hillside.

When he was far up toward the top, he lay down and slept for a little while. The withered moon, shining on his face, awakened him. He stood up and moved up the hill. Fifty yards away he stopped and turned back, for he had forgotten his rifle. He walked heavily down, and poked about in the brush, but he could not find his gun. At last he lay down to rest. The pocket of pain in his armpit had grown more sharp. His arm seemed to swell out and fall with every heartbeat. There was no position lying down where the heavy arm did not press against his armpit.

With the effort of a hurt beast, Pepé got up and moved again toward the top of the ridge. He held his swollen arm away from his body with his left hand. Up the steep hill he dragged himself, a few steps and a rest, and a few more steps. At last he was nearing the top. The moon showed the uneven sharp back of it against the sky.

Pepé's brain spun in a big spiral up and away from him. He slumped to the ground and lay still. The rock ridge top was only a hundred feet above him.

The moon moved over the sky. Pepé half turned on his back. His tongue tried to make words, but only a thick hissing came from between his lips.

When the dawn came, Pepé pulled himself up. His eyes were sane again. He drew his great puffed arm in front of him and looked at the angry wound. The black line ran up from his wrist to his armpit. Automatically he reached in his pocket for the big black knife, but it was not there. His eyes searched the ground. He picked up a sharp blade of stone and scraped at the wound, sawed at the proud flesh and then squeezed the green juice out in big drops. Instantly he threw back his head and whined like a dog. His whole right side shuddered at the pain, but the pain cleared his head.

In the gray light he struggled up the last slope to the ridge and crawled over and lay down behind a line of rocks. Below him lay a deep canyon exactly like the last, waterless and desolate. There was no flat, no oak trees, not even heavy brush in the bottom of it. And on the other side a sharp ridge stood up, thinly brushed with starving sage, littered with broken granite. Strewn over the hill there were giant outcroppings, and on the top the granite teeth stood out against the sky.

The new day was light now. The flame of the sun came over the ridge and fell on Pepé where he lay on the ground. His coarse black hair was littered with twigs and bits of spider web. His eyes had retreated back into his head. Between his lips the tip of his black tongue showed.

He sat up and dragged his great arm into his lap and nursed it, rocking his body and moaning in his throat. He threw back his head and looked up into the pale sky. A big black bird circled nearly out of sight, and far to the left another was sailing near.

He lifted his head to listen, for a familiar sound had come to him from the valley he had climbed out of; it was the crying yelp of hounds, excited and feverish, on a trail.

Pepé bowed his head quickly. He tried to speak rapid words but only a thick hiss came from his lips. He drew a shaky cross on his breast with his left hand. It was a long struggle to get to his feet. He crawled slowly and mechanically to the top of a big rock on the ridge peak. Once there, he arose slowly, swaying to his feet, and stood erect. Far below he could see the dark brush where he had slept. He braced his feet and stood there, black against the morning sky.

There came a ripping sound at his feet. A piece of stone flew up and a bullet droned off into the next gorge. The hollow crash echoed up from below. Pepé looked down for a moment and then pulled himself straight again.

His body jarred back. His left hand fluttered helplessly toward his breast. The second crash sounded from below. Pepé swung forward and toppled from the rock. His body struck and rolled over and over, starting a little avalanche. And when at last he stopped against a bush, the avalanche slid slowly down and covered up his head.

THINKING ABOUT THE SELECTION

Recalling

1. (a) How had Pepe's father died? (b) What had Pepe inherited from him?
2. (a) Why does Mama Torres send Pepe into town? (b) Why does he return home early?
3. (a) What does Mama Torres give Pepe before he goes away into the mountains? (b) Whom does she tell him to avoid?
4. (a) How does Pepe lose his hat? (b) How does he lose his horse? (c) How is he wounded? (d) How does he lose his rifle?
5. What happens to Pepe at the end of the story?

Interpreting

6. (a) How does Pepe change during the course of the story? (b) What events bring about these changes?
7. How do the descriptions of Pepe's physical appearance during his flight reflect his state of mind?
8. What is the significance of the fact that Pepe never sees his pursuers?
9. During the course of his flight, Pepe is gradually stripped of his possessions, and his behavior becomes more and more animal-like, as he is forced to rely on his instincts. (a) Find three instances in which Steinbeck compares Pepe's actions to those of an animal? (b) What does Pepe do in the end to retain his sense of dignity as a human being?

Applying

10. Do you agree with Mama Torres's statement that "A boy gets to be a man when a man is needed"? Why or why not?

ANALYZING LITERATURE

Understanding Setting

The **setting** is the time and place in which the events in a work of literature occur. Like many of Steinbeck's other works, "Flight" is set in northern California during the later 1800's or early 1900's.

1. What do the details of the setting in the first paragraph suggest about humanity's relationship to nature?
2. How does the landscape change during the course of Pepe's flight?
3. The setting of a literary work sometimes reflects the writer's view of the world. What outlook might the setting of "Flight" reflect?
4. The American writer and social critic Ayn Rand once wrote, "Man's unique reward, however, is that while animals survive by adjusting themselves to their background, man survives by adjusting his background to himself." On the basis of "Flight," do you think John Steinbeck would agree or disagree with this statement? Explain your answer.

CRITICAL THINKING AND READING

Analyzing the Effect of Setting

The **setting** often influences the characters' personalities and behavior. For example, in "Flight" the setting directly affects Pepe's actions as he flees from his pursuers, forcing him to become more and more instinctive and animal-like in his behavior.

1. How have Pepe's and Mama Torres's personalities been shaped by the setting?
2. How do the changes in the landscape during Pepe's flight affect his chance of escape?

THINKING AND WRITING

Writing About Setting

Write an essay in which you discuss how the setting has shaped Pepe's personality and how it affects his behavior during the story. Reread the story, thinking about how the setting has shaped Pepe's character and noting the relationship between the details of the setting and Pepe's actions. When you write your essay, use evidence from the story to support your argument. When you revise make sure that your essay is logically organized.

WILLIAM FAULKNER

1897–1962

William Faulkner is generally regarded as the most innovative American novelist of his time. In his work he experimented with narrative chronology, explored multiple points of view, and delved deeply into the minds of his characters. Yet although he used a variety of forms and techniques in his novels and short stories, most of his works are linked through a common setting, the fictional world of Yoknapatawpha County, Mississippi.

Faulkner grew up in Oxford, Mississippi. Although he never finished high school, he read a great deal and developed an interest in writing at an early age. In 1918 he enlisted in the British Royal Flying Corps and was sent to Canada for training. However, World War I ended before he had a chance to see combat, and he returned to Mississippi. Several years later, longing for a change of scene, he moved to New Orleans. There he became friends with Sherwood Anderson, who offered encouragement and helped get his first novel, *A Soldier's Pay* (1926), published.

In 1926 Faulkner moved back to Oxford and concentrated on his writing. He first earned critical acclaim in 1929 when he published *The Sound and the Fury,* a complex novel exploring the downfall of an old southern family as seen through the eyes of three different characters. A year later he published *As I Lay Dying,* a novel in which the point of view constantly shifts, as Faulkner delves into the varying perceptions of death.

Faulkner went on to write several more inventive novels, including *Light in August* (1932), *Absalom, Absalom* (1936), and *The Wild Palms* (1939). His later works, such as *The Unvanquished* (1938) and *The Hamlet* (1940), were more traditional in form. Yet in these novels, Faulkner continued developing the history of Yoknapatawpha County and its people.

Despite the critical success of some of his works, Faulkner did not earn widespread public recognition until 1946, when *The Portable Faulkner*—an anthology in which many of his writings about Yoknapatawpha County were presented in chronological order—was published. Four years later he was awarded the Nobel Prize following the publication of *Intruder in the Dust* (1948), a novel in which he confronted the issue of racism.

GUIDE FOR READING

The Bear

Writer's Techniques

Symbols. A symbol is a person, place, or thing that has a meaning in itself and also represents something larger than itself. For example, gold may be used as a symbol of greed, while a rose may symbolize love.

In the aftermath of World War I, many writers came to believe that modern life was filled with uncertainty and lacked any definite meaning. To express this belief, these writers turned away from directly stating their themes and suggested rather than asserted meaning. As a result modern writers frequently used symbols as a means of expressing their themes.

Allusions. An allusion is a reference to another literary work or to a figure, place, or event from history, religion, or mythology.

Allusions serve two important purposes in literature. Like symbols they can play an important role in conveying the theme of a literary work. At the same time, they provide writers with a way of maintaining a link to the cultural roots of the past.

Look For

As you read "The Bear," look for Faulkner's descriptions of the bear. How does the bear come to represent something much larger than itself.

Writing

"The Bear" is a story about a boy whose experiences during a series of hunting expeditions gradually lead him to an understanding about life. The English novelist Charles Dickens once wrote, "There is a passion for hunting something deeply implanted in the human breast." Freewrite, exploring your reaction to this statement.

Vocabulary

Knowing the following words will help you as you read "The Bear."

malevolent (mə lev′ə lənt) *adj.*: Wishing evil or harm to others (p. 788)

anachronism (ə nak′rə niz′m) *n.*: Something that is or seems to be out of its proper time (p. 788)

apotheosis (a päth′ ē ō′sis) *n.*: Glorification (p. 788)

abjectness (ab′ jekt nəs) *n.*: Wretchedness (p. 789)

effluvium (e floo′ vē əm) *n.*: Aura (p. 789)

temerity (tə mer′ə tē) *n.*: Fool-hardy or heedless disregard of danger (p. 789)

evanescently (ev′ə nes′′nt lē) *adv.*: Fleetingly (p. 793)

immemorial (im′ə môr′ē əl) *adj.*: Extending back beyond memory or record (p. 793)

inviolable (in vī′ə lə b′l) *adj.*: Safe from danger (p. 794)

abrogated (ab′rə gāt′əd) *v.*: Canceled (p. 794)

lucidity (loo sid′ i tē) *n.*: Brightness (p. 794)

The Bear

William Faulkner

He was ten. But it had already begun, long before that day when at last he wrote his age in two figures and he saw for the first time the camp where his father and Major de Spain and old General Compson and the others spent two weeks each November and two weeks again each June. He had already inherited then, without ever having seen it, the tremendous bear with one trap-ruined foot which, in an area almost a hundred miles deep, had earned for itself a name, a definite designation like a living man.

He had listened to it for years: the long legend of corncribs rifled, of shotes[1] and grown pigs and even calves carried bodily into the woods and devoured, of traps and deadfalls[2] overthrown and dogs mangled and slain, and shotgun and even rifle charges delivered at point-blank range and with no more effect than so many peas blown through a tube by a boy—a corridor of wreckage and destruction beginning back before he was born, through which sped, not fast but rather with the ruthless and irresistible deliberation of a locomotive, the shaggy tremendous shape.

It ran in his knowledge before he ever saw it. It looked and towered in his dreams before he even saw the unaxed woods where it left its crooked print, shaggy, huge, red-eyed, not malevolent but just big—too big for the dogs which tried to bay[3] it, for the horses which tried to ride it down, for the men and the bullets they fired into it, too big for the very country which was its constricting scope. He seemed to see it entire with a child's complete divination before he ever laid eyes on either—the doomed wilderness whose edges were being constantly and punily gnawed at by men with axes and plows who feared it because it was wilderness, men myriad and nameless even to one another in the land where the old bear had earned a name, through which ran not even a mortal animal but an anachronism, indomitable and invincible, out of an old dead time, a phantom, epitome and apotheosis of the old wild life at which the puny humans swarmed and hacked in a fury of abhorrence and fear, like pygmies[4] about the ankles of a drowsing elephant; the old bear solitary, indomitable and alone, widowered, childless and absolved of mortality—old Priam[5] reft of his old wife and having outlived all his sons.

Until he was ten, each November he would watch the wagon containing the dogs and the bedding and food and guns and his father and Tennie's Jim, the Negro, and Sam Fathers, the Indian, son of a slave woman and a Chickasaw chief, depart on the road to town, to Jefferson, where Major de Spain and the others would join them. To the boy, at seven and eight and nine, they were not going into the Big Bottom to hunt bear and deer, but to keep yearly rendezvous with the bear which they did not even intend

---

1. shotes *n.*: Young hogs.
2. deadfalls *n.*: Traps arranged so that a heavy weight is dropped on prey.
3. bay *v.*: Chase and corner.

4. pygmies (pig′ mēz) *n.*: Members of African and Asiatic races known for their small stature.
5. Priam (prī′ əm): The king of Troy whose wife and children were killed when the Greeks invaded Troy during the Trojan War.

to kill. Two weeks later they would return, with no trophy, no head and skin. He had not expected it. He had not even been afraid it would be in the wagon. He believed that even after he was ten and his father would let him go too, for those two November weeks, he would merely make another one, along with his father and Major de Spain and General Compson and the others, the dogs which feared to bay it and the rifles and shotguns which failed even to bleed it, in the yearly pageant of the old bear's furious immortality.

Then he heard the dogs. It was in the second week of his first time in the camp. He stood with Sam Fathers against a big oak beside the faint crossing where they had stood each dawn for nine days now, hearing the dogs. He had heard them once before, one morning last week—a murmur, sourceless, echoing through the wet woods, swelling presently into separate voices which he could recognize and call by name. He had raised and cocked the gun as Sam told him and stood motionless again while the uproar, the invisible course, swept up and past and faded; it seemed to him that he could actually see the deer, the buck, blond, smoke-colored, elongated with speed, fleeing, vanishing, the woods, the gray solitude, still ringing even when the cries of the dogs had died away.

"Now let the hammers down," Sam said.

"You knew they were not coming here, too," he said.

"Yes," Sam said. "I want you to learn how to do when you didn't shoot. It's after the chance for the bear or the deer has done already come and gone that men and dogs get killed."

"Anyway," he said, "it was just a deer."

Then on the tenth morning he heard the dogs again. And he readied the too-long, too-heavy gun as Sam had taught him, before Sam even spoke. But this time it was no deer, no ringing chorus of dogs running strong on a free scent, but a moiling[6] yap-

ping an octave too high, with something more than indecision and even abjectness in it, not even moving very fast, taking a long time to pass completely out of hearing, leaving even then somewhere in the air that echo, thin, slightly hysterical, abject, almost grieving, with no sense of a fleeing, unseen, smoke-colored, grass-eating shape ahead of it, and Sam, who had taught him first of all to cock the gun and take position where he could see everywhere and then never move again, had himself moved up beside him; he could hear Sam breathing at his shoulder and he could see the arched curve of the old man's inhaling nostrils.

"Hah," Sam said. "Not even running. Walking."

"Old Ben!" the boy said. "But up here!" he cried. "Way up here!"

"He do it every year," Sam said. "Once. Maybe to see who in camp this time, if he can shoot or not. Whether we got the dog yet that can bay and hold him. He'll take them to the river, then he'll send them back home. We may as well go back, too; see how they look when they come back to camp."

When they reached the camp the hounds were already there, ten of them crouching back under the kitchen, the boy and Sam squatting to peer back into the obscurity where they huddled, quiet, the eyes luminous, glowing at them and vanishing, and no sound, only that effluvium of something more than dog, stronger than dog and not just animal, just beast, because still there had been nothing in front of that abject and almost painful yapping save the solitude, the wilderness, so that when the eleventh hound came in at noon and with all the others watching—even old Uncle Ash, who called himself first a cook—Sam daubed the tattered ear and the raked shoulder with turpentine and axle grease, to the boy it was still no living creature, but the wilderness which, leaning for the moment down, had patted lightly once the hound's temerity.

"Just like a man," Sam said. "Just like folks. Put off as long as she could having to be brave, knowing all the time that sooner or

6. **moiling:** Confused.

IN THE DEPTHS OF THE TIMBER
W. Herbert Dunton
Courtesy Amon Carter Museum, Fort Worth

later she would have to be brave once to keep on living with herself, and knowing all the time beforehand what was going to happen to her when she done it."

That afternoon, himself on the one-eyed wagon mule which did not mind the smell of blood nor, as they told him, of bear, and with Sam on the other one, they rode for more than three hours through the rapid, shortening winter day. They followed no path, no trail even that he could see; almost at once they were in a country which he had never seen before. Then he knew why Sam had made him ride the mule which would not spook. The sound one stopped short and tried to whirl and bolt even as Sam got down, blowing its breath, jerking and wrenching at the rein while Sam held it, coaxing it forward with his voice, since he could not risk tying it, drawing it forward while the boy got down from the marred one.

Then, standing beside Sam in the gloom of the dying afternoon, he looked down at the rotted overturned log, gutted and scored with claw marks and, in the wet earth beside it, the print of the enormous warped two-toed foot. He knew now what he had smelled when he peered under the kitchen where the dogs huddled. He realized for the first time that the bear which had run in his listening and loomed in his dreams since before he could remember to the contrary, and which, therefore, must have existed in the listening and dreams of his father and Major de Spain and even old General Compson, too, before they began to remember in their turn, was a mortal animal, and that if they had departed for the camp each November without any actual hope of bringing its trophy back, it was not because it could not be slain, but because so far they had had no actual hope to.

"Tomorrow," he said.

"We'll try tomorrow," Sam said. "We ain't got the dog yet."

"We've got eleven. They ran him this morning."

"It won't need but one," Sam said. "He ain't here. Maybe he ain't nowhere. The only other way will be for him to run by accident over somebody that has a gun."

"That wouldn't be me," the boy said. "It will be Walter or Major or—"

"It might," Sam said. "You watch close in the morning. Because he's smart. That's how come he has lived this long. If he gets hemmed up and has to pick out somebody to run over, he will pick out you."

"How?" the boy said. "How will he know—" He ceased. "You mean he already knows me, that I ain't never been here before, ain't had time to find out yet whether I—" He ceased again, looking at Sam, the old man whose face revealed nothing until it smiled. He said humbly, not even amazed, "It was me he was watching. I don't reckon he did need to come but once."

The next morning they left the camp three hours before daylight. They rode this time because it was too far to walk, even the dogs in the wagon; again the first gray light found him in a place which he had never seen before, where Sam had placed him and told him to stay and then departed. With the gun which was too big for him, which did not even belong to him, but to Major de Spain, and which he had fired only once—at a stump on the first day, to learn the recoil and how to reload it—he stood against a gum tree beside a little bayou[7] whose black still water crept without movement out of a canebrake[8] and crossed a small clearing and into cane again, where, invisible, a bird—the big woodpecker called Lord-to-God by Negroes—clattered at a dead limb.

It was a stand like any other, dissimilar only in incidentals to the one where he had stood each morning for ten days; a territory new to him, yet no less familiar than that other one which, after almost two weeks, he had come to believe he knew a little—the same solitude, the same loneliness through

---

7. bayou (bī′ o͞o) *n.*: A sluggish, marshy inlet or outlet of a lake or river.

8. canebrake *n.*: An area overgrown with cane plants.

which human beings had merely passed without altering it, leaving no mark, no scar, which looked exactly as it must have looked when the first ancestor of Sam Fathers' Chickasaw predecessors crept into it and looked about, club or stone ax or bone arrow drawn and poised; different only because, squatting at the edge of the kitchen, he smelled the hounds huddled and cringing beneath it and saw the raked ear and shoulder of the one who, Sam said, had had to be brave once in order to live with herself, and saw yesterday in the earth beside the gutted log the print of the living foot.

He heard no dogs at all. He never did hear them. He only heard the drumming of the woodpecker stop short off and knew that the bear was looking at him. He never saw it. He did not know whether it was in front of him or behind him. He did not move, holding the useless gun, which he had not even had warning to cock and which even now he did not cock, tasting in his saliva that taint as of brass which he knew now because he had smelled it when he peered under the kitchen at the huddled dogs.

Then it was gone. As abruptly as it had ceased, the woodpecker's dry, monotonous clatter set up again, and after a while he even believed he could hear the dogs—a murmur, scarce a sound even, which he had probably been hearing for some time before he even remarked it, drifting into hearing and then out again, dying away. They came nowhere near him. If it was a bear they ran, it was another bear. It was Sam himself who came out of the cane and crossed the bayou, followed by the injured bitch of yesterday. She was almost at heel, like a bird dog, making no sound. She came and crouched against his leg, trembling, staring off into the cane.

"I didn't see him," he said. "I didn't, Sam!"

"I know it," Sam said. "He done the looking. You didn't hear him neither, did you?"

"No," the boy said. "I—"

"He's smart," Sam said. "Too smart." He looked down at the hound, trembling faintly and steadily against the boy's knee. From the raked shoulder a few drops of fresh blood oozed and clung. "Too big. We ain't got the dog yet. But maybe someday. Maybe not next time. But someday."

So I must see him, he thought. *I must look at him.* Otherwise, it seemed to him that it would go on like this forever, as it had gone on with his father and Major de Spain, who was older than his father, and even with old General Compson, who had been old enough to be a brigade commander in 1865. Otherwise, it would go on so forever, next time and next time, after and after and after. It seemed to him that he could see the two of them, himself and the bear, shadowy in the limbo from which time emerged, becoming time; the old bear absolved of mortality and himself partaking, sharing a little of it, enough of it. And he knew now what he had smelled in the huddled dogs and tasted in his saliva. He recognized fear. *So I will have to see him*, he thought, without dread or even hope. *I will have to look at him.*

It was in June of the next year. He was eleven. They were in camp again, celebrating Major de Spain's and General Compson's birthdays. Although the one had been born in September and the other in the depth of winter and in another decade, they had met for two weeks to fish and shoot squirrels and turkey and run coons and wildcats with the dogs at night. That is, he and Boon Hoggenbeck and the Negroes fished and shot squirrels and ran the coons and cats, because the proved hunters, not only Major de Spain and old General Compson, who spent those two weeks sitting in a rocking chair before a tremendous iron pot of Brunswick stew, stirring and tasting, with old Ash to quarrel with about how he was making it and Tennie's Jim to pour whisky from the demijohn[9] into the tin dipper from which he drank it,

---

9. demijohn: A large bottle with a narrow neck and a wicker casing and handle.

but even the boy's father and Walter Ewell, who were still young enough, scorned such, other than shooting the wild gobblers with pistols for wagers on their marksmanship.

Or, that is, his father and the others believed he was hunting squirrels. Until the third day he thought that Sam Fathers believed that too. Each morning he would leave the camp right after breakfast. He had his own gun now, a Christmas present. He went back to the tree beside the little bayou where he had stood that morning. Using the compass which old General Compson had given him, he ranged from that point; he was teaching himself to be a better-than-fair woodsman without knowing he was doing it. On the second day he even found the gutted log where he had first seen the crooked print. It was almost completely crumbled now, healing with unbelievable speed, a passionate and almost visible relinquishment, back into the earth from which the tree had grown.

He ranged the summer woods now, green with gloom; if anything, actually dimmer than in November's gray dissolution, where, even at noon, the sun fell only in intermittent dappling upon the earth, which never completely dried out and which crawled with snakes—moccasins and water snakes and rattlers, themselves the color of the dappled gloom, so that he would not always see them until they moved, returning later and later, first day, second day, passing in the twilight of the third evening the little log pen enclosing the log stable where Sam was putting up the horses for the night.

"You ain't looked right yet," Sam said.

He stopped. For a moment he didn't answer. Then he said peacefully, in a peaceful rushing burst as when a boy's miniature dam in a little brook gives way, "All right. But how? I went to the bayou. I even found that log again. I—"

"I reckon that was all right. Likely he's been watching you. You never saw his foot?"

"I," the boy said—"I didn't—I never thought—"

"It's the gun," Sam said. He stood beside the fence, motionless—the old man, the Indian, in the battered faded overalls and the frayed five-cent straw hat which in the Negro's race had been the badge of his enslavement and was now the regalia of his freedom. The camp—the clearing, the house, the barn and its tiny lot with which Major de Spain in his turn had scratched punily and evanescently at the wilderness—faded in the dusk, back into the immemorial darkness of the woods. *The gun*, the boy thought. *The gun.*

"Be scared," Sam said. "You can't help that. But don't be afraid. Ain't nothing in the woods going to hurt you unless you corner it, or it smells that you are afraid. A bear or a deer, too, has got to be scared of a coward the same as a brave man has got to be."

The gun, the boy thought.

"You will have to choose," Sam said.

He left the camp before daylight, long before Uncle Ash would wake in his quilts on the kitchen floor and start the fire for breakfast. He had only the compass and a stick for snakes. He could go almost a mile before he would begin to need the compass. He sat on a log, the invisible compass in his invisible hand, while the secret night sounds, fallen still at his movements, scurried again and then ceased for good, and the owls ceased and gave over to the waking of day birds, and he could see the compass. Then he went fast yet still quietly; he was becoming better and better as a woodsman, still without having yet realized it.

He jumped a doe and a fawn at sunrise, walked them out of the bed, close enough to see them—the crash of undergrowth, the white scut,[10] the fawn scudding behind her faster than he had believed it could run. He was hunting right, upwind, as Sam had taught him; not that it mattered now. He had left the gun; of his own will and relinquishment he had accepted not a gambit, not a choice, but a condition in which not

---

10. scut *n.*: A short, stumpy tail.

only the bear's heretofore inviolable anonymity but all the old rules and balances of hunter and hunted had been abrogated. He would not even be afraid, not even in the moment when the fear would take him completely—blood, skin, bowels, bones, memory from the long time before it became his memory—all save that thin, clear, quenchless, immortal lucidity which alone differed him from this bear and from all the other bear and deer he would ever kill in the humility and pride of his skill and endurance, to which Sam had spoken when he leaned in the twilight on the lot fence yesterday.

By noon he was far beyond the little bayou, farther into the new and alien country than he had ever been. He was traveling now not only by the compass but by the old, heavy, biscuit-thick silver watch which had belonged to his grandfather. When he stopped at last, it was for the first time since he had risen from the log at dawn when he could see the compass. It was far enough. He had left the camp nine hours ago; nine hours from now, dark would have already been an hour old. But he didn't think that. He thought, *All right. Yes. But what?* and stood for a moment, alien and small in the green and topless solitude, answering his own question before it had formed and ceased. It was the watch, the compass, the stick—the three lifeless mechanicals with which for nine hours he had fended the wilderness off; he hung the watch and compass carefully on a bush and leaned the stick beside them and relinquished completely to it.

He had not been going very fast for the last two or three hours. He went no faster now, since distance would not matter even if he could have gone fast. And he was trying to keep a bearing on the tree where he had left the compass, trying to complete a circle which would bring him back to it or at least intersect itself, since direction would not matter now either. But the tree was not there, and he did as Sam had schooled him—made the next circle in the opposite direction, so that the two patterns would bi-

sect somewhere, but crossing no print of his own feet, finding the tree at last, but in the wrong place—no bush, no compass, no watch—and the tree not even the tree, because there was a down log beside it and he did what Sam Fathers had told him was the next thing and the last.

As he sat down on the log he saw the crooked print—the warped, tremendous, two-toed indentation which, even as he watched it, filled with water. As he looked up, the wilderness coalesced, solidified—the glade, the tree he sought, the bush, the watch and the compass glinting where a ray of sunlight touched them. Then he saw the bear. It did not emerge, appear; it was just there, immobile, solid, fixed in the hot dappling of the green and windless noon, not as big as he had dreamed it, but as big as he had expected it, bigger, dimensionless against the dappled obscurity, looking at him where he sat quietly on the log and looked back at it.

Then it moved. It made no sound. It did not hurry. It crossed the glade, walking for an instant into the full glare of the sun; when it reached the other side it stopped again and looked back at him across one shoulder while his quiet breathing inhaled and exhaled three times.

Then it was gone. It didn't walk into the woods, the undergrowth. It faded, sank back into the wilderness as he had watched a fish, a huge old bass, sink and vanish back into the dark depths of its pool without even any movement of its fins.

He thought, *It will be next fall.* But it was not next fall, nor the next nor the next. He was fourteen then. He had killed his buck, and Sam Fathers had marked his face with the hot blood, and in the next year he killed a bear. But even before that accolade he had become as competent in the woods as many grown men with the same experience; by his fourteenth year he was a better woodsman than most grown men with more. There was no territory within thirty miles of the camp that he did not know—bayou, ridge, brake, landmark tree and path. He could have led anyone to any point in it without deviation, and brought them out again. He knew game trails that even Sam Fathers did not know; in his thirteenth year he found a buck's bedding place, and unbeknown to his father he borrowed Walter Ewell's rifle and lay in wait at dawn and killed the buck when it walked back to the bed, as Sam had told him how the old Chickasaw fathers did.

But not the old bear, although by now he knew its footprint better than he did his own, and not only the crooked one. He could see any one of the three sound ones and distinguish it from any other, and not only by its size. There were other bears within those thirty miles which left tracks almost as large, but this was more than that. If Sam Fathers had been his mentor and the backyard rabbits and squirrels at home his kindergarten, then the wilderness the old bear ran was his college, the old male bear itself, so long unwifed and childless as to have become its own ungendered progenitor,[11] was his alma mater. But he never saw it.

He could find the crooked print now almost whenever he liked, fifteen or ten or five miles, or sometimes nearer the camp than that. Twice while on stand during the three years he heard the dogs strike its trail by accident; on the second time they jumped it seemingly, the voices high, abject, almost human in hysteria, as on that first morning two years ago. But not the bear itself. He would remember that noon three years ago, the glade, himself and the bear fixed during that moment in the windless and dappled blaze, and it would seem to him that it had never happened, that he had dreamed that too. But it had happened. They had looked at each other, they had emerged from the wilderness old as earth, synchronized to that instant by something more than the blood that moved the flesh and bones which bore them, and touched, pledged something, affirmed something more lasting than the frail web of bones and flesh which any accident could obliterate.

Then he saw it again. Because of the very fact that he thought of nothing else, he had forgotten to look for it. He was still-hunting with Walter Ewell's rifle. He saw it cross the end of a long blow-down, a corridor where a tornado had swept, rushing through rather than over the tangle of trunks and branches as a locomotive would have, faster than he had ever believed it could move, almost as fast as a deer even, because a deer would have spent most of that time in the air, faster than he could bring the rifle sights up to it, so that he believed the reason he never let off the shot was that he was still behind it, had never caught up with it. And now he knew what had been wrong during all the three years. He sat on a log, shaking and trembling as if he had never seen the woods before nor anything that ran them, wondering with incredulous amazement how he could have forgotten the very thing which Sam Fathers had told him and which the bear itself had proved the next day and had now returned after three years to reaffirm.

And he now knew what Sam Fathers had meant about the right dog, a dog in which size would mean less than nothing. So when he returned alone in April—school was out then, so that the sons of farmers could help with the land's planting, and at last his father had granted him permission, on his promise to be back in four days—he had the dog. It was his own, a mongrel of the sort called by Negroes a fyce, a ratter, itself not much bigger than a rat and possessing that bravery which had long since stopped being courage and had become foolhardiness.

It did not take four days. Alone again, he found the trail on the first morning. It was not a stalk; it was an ambush. He timed the meeting almost as if it were an appointment with a human being. Himself holding the fyce muffled in a feed sack and Sam Fathers

---

11. ungendered progenitor: Its own parent.

with two of the hounds on a piece of plowline rope, they lay down wind of the trail at dawn of the second morning. They were so close that the bear turned without even running, as if in surprised amazement at the shrill and frantic uproar of the released fyce, turning at bay against the trunk of a tree, on its hind feet; it seemed to the boy that it would never stop rising, taller and taller, and even the two hounds seemed to take a sort of desperate and despairing courage from the fyce, following it as it went in.

Then he realized that the fyce was actually not going to stop. He flung, threw the gun away, and ran; when he overtook and grasped the frantically pinwheeling little dog, it seemed to him that he was directly under the bear.

He could smell it, strong and hot and rank. Sprawling, he looked up to where it loomed and towered over him like a cloudburst and colored like a thunderclap, quite familiar, peacefully and even lucidly familiar, until he remembered: This was the way he had used to dream about it. Then it was gone. He didn't see it go. He knelt, holding the frantic fyce with both hands, hearing the abased wailing of the hounds drawing farther and farther away, until Sam came up. He carried the gun. He laid it down quietly beside the boy and stood looking down at him.

"You've done seed him twice now with a gun in your hands," he said. "This time you couldn't have missed him."

The boy rose. He still held the fyce. Even in his arms and clear of the ground, it yapped frantically, straining and surging after the fading uproar of the two hounds like a tangle of wire springs. He was panting a little, but he was neither shaking nor trembling now.

"Neither could you!" he said. "You had the gun! Neither did you!"

"And you didn't shoot," his father said. "How close were you?"

"I don't know, sir," he said. "There was a big wood tick inside his right hind leg. I saw that. But I didn't have the gun then."

"But you didn't shoot when you had the gun," his father said. "Why?"

But he didn't answer, and his father didn't wait for him to, rising and crossing the room, across the pelt of the bear which the boy had killed two years ago and the larger one which his father had killed before he was born, to the bookcase beneath the mounted head of the boy's first buck. It was the room which his father called the office, from which all the plantation business was transacted; in it for the fourteen years of his life he had heard the best of all talking. Major de Spain would be there and sometimes old General Compson, and Walter Ewell and Boon Hoggenbeck and Sam Fathers and Tennie's Jim, too, because they, too, were hunters, knew the woods and what ran them.

He would hear it, not talking himself but listening—the wilderness, the big woods, bigger and older than any recorded document of white man fatuous enough to believe he had bought any fragment of it or Indian ruthless enough to pretend that any fragment of it had been his to convey. It was of the men, not white nor black nor red, but men, hunters with the will and hardihood to endure and the humility and skill to survive, and the dogs and the bear and deer juxtaposed and reliefed against it, ordered and compelled by and within the wilderness in the ancient and unremitting contest by the ancient and immitigable rules which voided all regrets and brooked no quarter, the voices quiet and weighty and deliberate for retrospection and recollection and exact remembering, while he squatted in the blazing firelight as Tennie's Jim squatted, who stirred only to put more wood on the fire and to pass the bottle from one glass to another. Because the bottle was always present, so that after a while it seemed to him that those fierce instants of heart and brain and courage and wiliness and speed were concentrated and distilled into that brown liquor which not women, not boys and children, but only hunters drank, drinking not of the blood they had spilled but some condensation of the wild immortal spirit, drinking it moderately, humbly even, not with the pagan's base hope of acquiring thereby the virtues of cunning and strength and speed, but in salute to them.

His father returned with the book and sat down again and opened it. "Listen," he said. He read the five stanzas aloud, his voice quiet and deliberate in the room where there was no fire now because it was already spring. Then he looked up. The boy watched him. "All right," his father said. "Listen." He read again, but only the second stanza this time, to the end of it, the last two lines, and closed the book and put it on the table beside him. " 'She cannot fade, though thou hast not thy bliss, for ever wilt thou love, and she be fair,' "[12] he said.

"He's talking about a girl," the boy said.

"He had to talk about something," his father said. Then he said, "He was talking about truth. Truth doesn't change. Truth is one thing. It covers all things which touch the heart—honor and pride and pity and justice and courage and love. Do you see now?"

He didn't know. Somehow it was simpler than that. There was an old bear, fierce and ruthless, not merely just to stay alive, but with the fierce pride of liberty and freedom, proud enough of that liberty and freedom to see it threatened without fear or even alarm; nay, who at times even seemed deliberately to put that freedom and liberty in jeopardy in order to savor them, to remind his old strong bones and flesh to keep supple and quick to defend and preserve them. There was an old man, son of a Negro slave and an Indian king, inheritor on the one side of the long chronicle of a people who had learned humility through suffering, and pride through the endurance which survived the suffering and injustice, and on the other side, the chronicle of a people even longer in the land than the first, yet who no longer existed in the land at all save in the solitary brotherhood of an old Negro's alien blood and the wild and invincible spirit of an old bear. There was a boy who wished to learn humility and pride in order to become skillful and worthy in the woods, who suddenly found himself becoming so skillful so rapidly that he feared he would never become worthy because he had not learned humility and pride, although he had tried to, until one day and as suddenly he discovered that an old man who could not have defined either had led him, as though by the hand, to that point where an old bear and a little mongrel dog showed him that, by possessing one thing other, he would possess them both.

And a little dog, nameless and mongrel and many-fathered, grown, yet weighing less than six pounds, saying as if to itself, "I can't be dangerous, because there's nothing much smaller than I am; I can't be fierce, because they would call it just noise; I can't be humble, because I'm already too close to the ground to genuflect;[13] I can't be proud, because I wouldn't be near enough to it for anyone to know who was casting that shadow, and I don't even know that I'm not going to heaven, because they have already decided that I don't possess an immortal soul. So all I can be is brave. But it's all right. I can be that, even if they still call it just noise."

That was all. It was simple, much simpler than somebody talking in a book about a youth and a girl he would never need to grieve over, because he could never approach any nearer her and would never have to get any farther away. He had heard about a bear, and finally got big enough to trail it,

---

12. " 'She . . . fair' ": from John Keats's "Ode on a Grecian Urn."

13. genuflect (jen' yə flekt') v.: Bend the knee, as in reverence or worship.

and he trailed it four years and at last met it with a gun in his hands and he didn't shoot. Because a little dog— But he could have shot long before the little dog covered the twenty yards to where the bear waited, and Sam Fathers could have shot at any time during that interminable minute while Old Ben stood on his hind feet over them. He stopped. His father was watching him gravely across the spring-rife twilight of the room; when he spoke, his words were as quiet as the twilight, too, not loud, because they did not need to be because they would last, "Courage, and honor, and pride," his father said, "and pity, and love of justice and of liberty. They all touch the heart, and what the heart holds to becomes truth, as far as we know truth. Do you see now?"

Sam, and Old Ben, and Nip, he thought. And himself too. He had been all right too. His father had said so. "Yes, sir," he said.

THINKING ABOUT THE SELECTION
Recalling

1. (a) What had the boy "already inherited" before participating in his first hunting expedition? (b) To what had he listened?
2. According to Sam Fathers, what does the bear do every year?
3. What does the boy realize for the first time when he sees the bear's paw print?
4. (a) Why does the boy finally leave his gun behind when he is tracking the bear? (b) What other objects does he relinquish? (c) When does he first see the bear?
5. (a) What does the boy do when the fyce charges the bear? (b) What comment does Sam make after the bear has gone?
6. How does the boy's father help him to comprehend his inability to shoot the bear?

Interpreting

7. Early in the story, the narrator comments that the wilderness is "being constantly and punily gnawed at by men with axes and plows who feared it because it was wilderness." How are the men who travel to the Big Bottom twice a year different from the "men with axes"?
8. Why does the bear fear a coward more than a brave person?
9. (a) How does the boy's relationship to the wilderness change when he abandons his gun and other "lifeless mechanicals"? (b) How does this set him apart from the "men with axes"?
10. What does the narrator mean by his comment that when the bear and the boy looked at each other they were "synchronized to the instant by something more than blood that moved the flesh and bones which bore them"?
11. What understanding does the boy reach at the end of the story?

Applying

12. (a) Why do you think that people often fear the wilderness? (b) What does this fear suggest about human nature?

ANALYZING LITERATURE
Understanding Symbols

A **symbol** is a person, place, or thing that has a meaning in itself and also represents something larger than itself. The bear, for example, symbolizes the wilderness.
1. Find two descriptions of the bear that help to convey its symbolic meaning.
2. As a symbol of the wilderness, what virtues does the bear embody?
3. Considering the bear's symbolic meaning, what is the significance of its mortality?
4. Who possesses the power to destroy it?

Understanding Allusions

An **allusion** is a short reference to another literary work or to a figure, place, or event from history, religion, or mythology. For example, Faulkner alludes to the poem "Ode on a Grecian Urn" by English Romantic poet John Keats.
1. In Keats's poem the speaker comments on the permanence of a pastoral scene depicted on an urn. In "The Bear" the boy's father repeats two lines describing the urn's portrayal of a young man pursuing a beautiful maiden. How do these lines reinforce the meaning of the story?
2. Keats's poem ends with the following lines: " 'Beauty is truth, truth beauty,'—that is all/Ye know on earth, and all ye need to know." How are these lines related to the meaning of the story?

THINKING AND WRITING
Writing About Symbols and Allusions

Write an essay in which you discuss how Faulkner uses symbols and allusions in conveying the theme of "The Bear." Reread the story, focusing on Faulkner's use of symbols and allusions. Prepare a thesis statement. Then write your essay, using passages from the story to support your thesis.

ELIZABETH ENRIGHT

1909–1968

Elizabeth Enright developed an interest in writing while working as an illustrator of magazines and children's books. At first she wrote stories to accompany her illustrations, but after a time she gave up illustrating to concentrate on writing.

Born in Oak Park, Illinois, Enright spent most of her life in New York City. Inspired by her parents, who were both professional artists, she began drawing and painting at an early age. After studying art in New York and Paris, she began her career as a magazine illustrator. In 1935 she published her first book of illustrations, *Kintu: A Congo Adventure,* for which she also wrote the text.

After publishing several more children's books, Enright began writing short stories for adults, publishing them in *The New Yorker* and other respected magazines. In 1946 she published her first collection of short stories, *Borrowed Summer and Other Stories*. She went on to publish three more volumes of stories: *The Moment Before the Rain* (1955), *The Riddle of the Fly and Other Stories* (1959), and *Doublefields: Memories and Stories* (1966). Her stories also appeared in such noted anthologies as *Prize Stories: The O. Henry Awards* and *Best American Short Stories*.

GUIDE FOR READING

The Signature

Writer's Techniques

Setting. The setting is the time and place in which the events in a work of literature occur. Writers often use the setting to establish a particular atmosphere, or mood, describing it with words that convey the appropriate feeling. For example, a writer might use a secluded, decaying house as the setting of a story to create an atmosphere of loneliness and isolation, using adjectives such as *solitary, empty,* and *vacant* in describing the house.

Look For

As you read "The Signature," look for the details of the setting that establish an atmosphere, or mood.

Writing

"The Signature" tells the story of a woman who finds herself in a world that seems strange and alien. She cannot remember her name or even understand the language she hears. Freewrite, explaining how a person could go about finding out his or her identity in such a situation.

Vocabulary

Knowing the following words will help you as you read "The Signature."

unemphatic (un im′ fat′ ik) *adj.*: Not definite; not emphasized (p. 802)

laterally (lat′ər əl lē) *adv.*: In a sideways manner (p. 802).

inimical (in im′i k'l) *adj.*: Hostile; unfriendly (p. 803)

monotony (mə nät′′nē) *n.*: Tiresome sameness of uniformity (p. 803)

periphery (pə rif′ər ē) *n.*: Surrounding space or area (p. 803)

reiterated (rē it′ə rāt′d) *adj.*: Repeated (p. 804)

The Signature

Elizabeth Enright

The street was wide and sloped gently upward ahead of me. It was paved with hard-baked dust almost white in the early-afternoon light, dry as clay and decked with bits of refuse. On either side the wooden houses stood blind to the street, all their shutters closed. The one and two-story buildings—some of them set back a little; there was no sidewalk—had door yards with dusted grass and bushes, but many of them stood flush to the road itself with nothing but a powdered weed or two for grace. All of the houses had an old, foreign look, and all were unpainted, weather-scoured to the same pale color, except for the eaves of some which had been trimmed with wooden zig-zags and painted long ago, like the crude, faded shutters, in tones of blue or red.

The sky was blanched with light, fronded with cirrus,[1] unemphatic; just such a sky as one finds near the sea, and this, in addition to the scoured, dry, enduring look of the town, persuaded me that an ocean or harbor must be somewhere near at hand. But when I came up over the rise of the road, I could find no furred line of blue at any horizon. All I could see was the great town—no, it was a city—spread far and wide, low lying, sun bleached, and unknown to me. And this was only one more thing that was unknown to me, for not only was I ignorant of the name of the city, but I was ignorant of my own name, and of my own life, and nothing that I seized on could offer me a clue. I looked at my hands: they were the hands of a middle-aged woman, coarsening at the joints, faintly blotched. On the third finger of the left hand there was a golden wedding ring, but who

had put it there I could not guess. My body in the dark dress, my dust-chalked shoes were also strangers to me, and I was frightened and felt that I had been frightened for a long time, so long that the feeling had become habitual—something that I could live with in a pinch, or, more properly, something that until this moment I had felt that I could live with. But now I was in terror of my puzzle.

I had the conviction that if I could once see my own face, I would remember who and what I was, and why I was in this place. I searched for a pane of glass to give me my reflection, but every window was shuttered fast. It was a season of drought, too, and there was not so much as a puddle to look into; in my pocket there was no mirror and my purse contained only a few bills of a currency unknown to me. I took the bills out and looked at them; they were old and used and the blue numerals and characters engraved on them were also of a sort I had never seen before, or could not remember having seen. In the center of each bill, where ordinarily one finds the pictures of a statesman or a monarch, there was instead an angular, spare symbol: a laterally elongated diamond shape with a heavy vertical line drawn through it at the center, rather like an abstraction of the human eye. As I resumed my walking I was aware of an impression that I had seen this symbol recently and often, in other places, and at the very moment I was thinking this I came upon it again, drawn in chalk on the side of a house. After that, watching for it, I saw it several times: marked in the dirt of the road, marked on the shutters, carved on the railing of a fence.

---

1. cirrus (sir′əs) *n.:* High, detached wispy clouds.

It was this figure, this cross-eyed diamond, which reminded me, by its persistence, that the eye of another person can be a little mirror, and now with a feeling of excitement, of possible hope, I began walking faster, in search of a face.

From time to time I had passed other people, men and women, in the street. Their dark, anonymous clothes were like the clothes of Italian peasants, but the language they spoke was not Italian, nor did it resemble any language I had ever heard, and many of their faces had a fair Northern color. I noticed when I met these people that the answering looks they gave me, while attentive, were neither inimical nor friendly. They looked at me with that certain privilege shared by kings and children, as if they possessed the right to judge, while being ignorant of, or exempt from, accepting judgment in return. There is no answer to this look and appeal is difficult, for one is already in a defensive position. Still, I had tried to appeal to them; several times I had addressed the passers-by hoping that one of them might understand me and tell me where I was, but no one could or would. They shook their heads or lifted their empty hands, and while they did not appear hostile, neither did they smile in answer to my pleading smiles. After they had passed I thought it strange that I never heard a whisper or a laugh or any added animation in their talk. It was apparently a matter of complete indifference to them that they had been approached in the street by a stranger speaking a strange language.

Knowing these things I thought that it might be difficult to accomplish my purpose, and indeed this proved to be the case. The next people I met were three women walking together; two were young and one was middle-aged. I approached the taller of the young women, for her eyes were on a level with my own, and looking steadily into them and coming close, I spoke to her.

"Can you tell me where I am?" I said to her. "Can you understand what I am saying?"

The words were a device, I expected no answer and got none of any sort. As I drew close she looked down at the ground; she would not meet my gaze. A little smile moved the corners of her lips, and she stepped aside. When I turned to her companions they also looked away, smiling. This expression on other faces might have been called embarrassment, but not on theirs. The smile they shared seemed noncommittal, secretive, knowledgeable in a way that I could not fathom, and afterward I thought it curious that they had shown no surprise.

For a long time after that I met no one at all. I met no cat, no dog, no cabbage butterfly; not even an ant on the packed, bald dust of the road, and finally rejecting its ugliness and light I turned to the left along another street, narrower and as graceless, and walked by the same monotony of weather-beaten houses. After a few minutes I heard a sound that halted me and I stood listening. Somewhere not far away I heard children's voices. Though their words were foreign they spoke also in the common tongue of children everywhere: voices high, eruptive, excited, sparked with the universal jokes, chants, quarrels of play; and here, listening to them, my memory stirred for the first time— a memory of memory, in fact. For whatever it was that nearly illuminated consciousness was not the memory itself, but a remnant of light which glowed on the periphery of the obstacle before it: a penumbra.[2]

Where are the children, I thought; where are they! With great urgency and longing I set out in the direction of their voices, determined to find them and in doing so to find something of myself. Their voices chattered, skipped, squabbled like the voices of sparrows, never far away, but though I turned and hunted and listened and pursued I could not find them. I never found them, and after a while I could not hear them either. The ghostly light of memory faded and was

---

2. penumbra (pi num′ brə) *n.:* The partly lighted area surrounding the complete shadow of a body in full eclipse.

RED SUBURB, 1926
Paul Klee
San Francisco Museum of Modern Art

extinguished, and my despair rose up in darkness to take its place.

The next person I met was a man, young and dark-browed, and when I confronted him and asked my questions, it was without hope. I knew he would not meet my look, or let his eyes show me my longed-for, dreaded face. Yet here I was wrong; he stood before me without speaking, but the gaze with which he answered mine was so intense and undeviating that it was I who dropped my eyes and stepped aside. I could not look, and soon I heard him going on his way.

I had been walking a long time, and the light was changing; the sun was low and full in my face. West, I said to myself; at least I know west, and I know that I am a woman, and that that is the sun. When the stars come out I will know those, too, and perhaps they will tell me something else.

After a while I sat down on a wooden step

to rest. I was struck by the silence of the city around me, and I realized this was because it was a city of walkers who walked on dust instead of on pavements. I remembered that I had seen no mark of a wheel on any road, and that nothing had moved in the sky all day except for a few birds in flight.

A breath of dry wind crept along the dust at my feet, and, far away, a noise of knocking started, a sound of stakes being driven into the ground with a wooden mallet. Desolate, reiterated, it sounded as though somewhere in the city they were preparing a gallows or a barricade. Too tired and dispirited to move I sat there listening to the double knock-and-echo of each blow. A few people passed me on their way home, each of them giving me the glance of casual appraisal I had seen so often. Doors opened and doors closed, the sun went down, and soon the street was still again and the knocking stopped. Where would I sleep that night, or find a meal? I neither knew nor cared.

One by one the stars came out on the deepening sky, perfect, still, as if they were really what they seemed to be—calm ornaments for hope, promises of stillness and forever.

I looked for Venus, then Polaris,[3] then for Mars. I could not find them, and as the stars grew in number, coming imperceptibly into their light, I saw with slow-growing shock that these were not the stars I knew. The messages of this night sky were written in a language of constellations I had never seen or dreamed. I stared up at the brand-new Catherine wheels,[4] insignias, and fiery thorn crowns on the sky, and I do not think that I was really surprised when I spied at the zenith, small but bright, a constellation shaped like an elongated diamond, like the glittering abstraction of a human eye. . . .

It was just at this moment, before I could marshal or identify my thoughts in the face of such a development, that I heard a sound of trees, wind in the leaves of trees, and I realized, irrelevantly it seemed, that in all my walking in this city—how many hours, how many days?—I had not seen a single tree, and the sound of their presence was as welcome as the sound of rain is after a siege of drought. As I stood up it occurred to me that neither had I seen one child among all the strangers I had met, that though I had heard the children I had not been able to find them, and now to all the other fears was added the fear that the trees, too, would magically elude me.

The street was dark, though light was glimmering through the cracks of the closed shutters. What was left of sunset, green as water, lay on the western horizon. Yet was it really western? In a sky of new stars, was it not possible and in fact probable that what I had believed to be the sun was not really Sun at all? Then what were the compass points, what were the easts and wests of this city? And what would I find when once I found myself?

I heard the beckoning of trees again and as if they were the clue to sanity, I ran along the street in the direction of their sound. I turned a corner, and there, ah yes, there were the trees: a grove of tall, dry, paper-murmuring trees that grew in a little park or public garden where people were walking together or sitting on the dusty grass. At the center of this park or garden there was a great house of stone, the first stone building I had seen all day. It was lighted from top to bottom; the lights of its long windows twittered in gold among the small leaves of the trees, and a door stood open at the head of a flight of steps.

I passed many people on the path, but now I did not look at them or ask them questions. I knew that there was nothing they could do for me. I walked straight to the steps and up them and through the door into the lighted house. It was empty, as I had expected, a great empty ringing house, but there was a splendor about it, even in its emptiness, as if those who had left it—and left it recently—had been creatures of joy, better than people and gayer than gods. But they, who-ever they were, had gone. My footsteps sounded on the barren floor, and the talk of the loiterers outside, the foreign talk, came in the windows clearly on the night air.

The mirror was at the end of the hall. I walked toward it with my fists closed, and my heart walked, too, heavily in my chest. I watched the woman's figure in the dark dress and the knees moving forward. When I was close to it, I saw, low in the right-hand corner of the mirror, the scratched small outline of the eye-diamond, a signature, carved on the surface of the glass by whom, and in what cold spirit of raillery? Lifting my head, I looked at my own face. I leaned forward and looked closely at my face, and I remembered everything. I remembered everything. And I knew the name of the city I would never leave, and, alas, I understood the language of its citizens.

---

3. Polaris (pō lar′ is): North Star.
4. Catherine wheels: A firework like a pinwheel that whirls and throws out colored lights.

THINKING ABOUT THE SELECTION

Recalling

1. (a) What two things are unknown to the narrator? (b) What emotion does she feel? (c) What conviction does she have?
2. (a) What symbol is engraved on each bill in her purse? (b) Where else does she see this symbol?
3. (a) How do the people the narrator passes look at her? (b) How do they respond when she addresses them?
4. What happens when the narrator confronts the young, dark-browed man?
5. (a) What does the narrator realize when she hears the wind blowing through the leaves? (b) What occurs to her when she stands up?
6. (a) What happens when the narrator looks in the mirror? (b) What does she realize?

Interpreting

7. (a) How would you characterize the physical appearance of the city in which the narrator finds herself? (b) How would you characterize the people she passes?
8. (a) What evidence in the story suggests that the city has suffered a major disaster, such as a devastating war or a nuclear holocaust? (b) What is the significance of the fact that the narrator never sees any children?
9. What do you think the eye-diamond might symbolize?

Applying

10. Why do you think Enright might have chosen to write a story like this in the aftermath of World War II?

ANALYZING LITERATURE

Understanding Setting

The **setting** is the time and place in which the events in a work of literature occur. In many stories the setting establishes a particular atmosphere, or mood.

1. What atmosphere does the description of the setting in "The Signature" establish?
2. How does the description of the setting reflect the narrator's state of mind?
3. How is the atmosphere especially appropriate to the theme?

UNDERSTANDING ADJECTIVES

Appreciating Adjectives

To establish an atmosphere, a writer will describe the setting with words that convey the appropriate feeling. For example, Enright uses adjectives such as *faded* and *scoured* to help create an atmosphere in "The Signature."

1. Find five other adjectives that help to create the atmosphere in "The Signature."
2. How are these five adjectives related in meaning?

THINKING AND WRITING

Writing About Setting

Write an essay in which you discuss how Enright uses the setting to establish an atmosphere in "The Signature." Prepare a list of details that help to establish the atmosphere. Then write your essay, making sure that you support your thesis. When you finish writing, revise your essay, making sure that you have adequately supported your thesis with details from the short story.

Nonfiction

HANDBALL, 1939
Ben Shahn
The Museum of Modern Art

JOHN DOS PASSOS

1896–1970

Although he published numerous novels, essays, and biographical sketches, John Dos Passos is remembered mainly for his experimental trilogy *U.S.A.* In this work Dos Passos blends fiction and nonfiction—interweaving biographies of both fictional characters and real historical figures, newspaper excerpts, passages from popular songs, and quotations from speeches—to paint a biting portrait of early twentieth-century America.

Dos Passos was born in Chicago. He attended private schools and eventually enrolled at Harvard, from which he graduated in 1916. When the United States entered World War I, he joined the United States Army Ambulance Corps. His experiences during the war provided him with the material for his first two novels, *One Man's Initiation—1917* (1920) and *Three Soldiers* (1921).

In 1925 Dos Passos published *Manhattan Transfer,* in which he delved into the complexities of New York City life. In this novel Dos Passos developed the experimental technique which he later perfected in the *U.S.A.* trilogy. He presented scattered fragments of many characters' lives, which combine to form a complete picture of urban life.

Dos Passos published *The 42nd Parallel,* the first novel of the *U.S.A.* trilogy in 1930. The second and third novels, *1919* and *The Big Money,* appeared in 1932 and 1936. In 1937 the trilogy was published in its entirety under the title *U.S.A.*

Dos Passos went on to publish several more novels, including a second trilogy, *District of Columbia* (1952). However, critics generally agree that his later works lack the inventiveness and forcefulness of *U.S.A.*

Tin Lizzie

Literary Forms

Biographies. A biography is an account of a person's life written by another person. Most biographies focus on recounting the central events of the subject's life—the events which make that person's life worth reading about. Sometimes, however, a writer will focus on conveying his or her impressions of the subject's character, rather than merely presenting a factual account of the subject's life. The result is what is known as an impressionistic biography. In an impressionistic biography, the writer concentrates on presenting details that help to reveal the subject's personality, often intentionally omitting details that would be included in a factual biography.

In *U.S.A.* Dos Passos presents many short, impressionistic biographical sketches, including ones about Woodrow Wilson and Henry Ford. Together these sketches help to convey Dos Passos's overall impression of America during the first three decades of the twentieth century.

Look For

"Tin Lizzie" is one of the impressionistic biographical sketches included in *U.S.A.* As you read "Tin Lizzie," look for the impression of Henry Ford's character that Dos Passos is trying to convey. Notice how Dos Passos captures the fleeting quality of impressions by using his own individualistic system of capitalization, punctuation, and spelling.

Writing

Imagine that you were writing an impressionistic biography about a public figure or a person you know. Prepare a list of facts about this person's life that contribute to your impressions of his or her character.

Vocabulary

Knowing the following words will help you as you read "Tin Lizzie."
jauntily (jônt′ i lē) *adv.*: In a carefree fashion (p. 810)

practicable (prak′ ti kə b'l) *adj.*: Workable (p. 811)

Tin Lizzie

John Dos Passos

"Mr. Ford the automobileer," the feature-writer wrote in 1900,

"Mr. Ford the automobileer began by giving his steed three or four sharp jerks with the lever at the righthand side of the seat; that is, he pulled the lever up and down sharply in order, as he said, to mix air with gasoline and drive the charge into the exploding cylinder. . . . Mr. Ford slipped a small electric switch handle and there followed a puff, puff, puff. . . . The puffing of the machine assumed a higher key. She was flying along about eight miles an hour. The ruts in the road were deep, but the machine certainly went with a dreamlike smoothness. There was none of the bumping common even to a streetcar. . . . By this time the boulevard had been reached, and the automobileer, letting a lever fall a little, let her out. Whiz! She picked up speed with infinite rapidity. As she ran on there was a clattering behind, the new noise of the automobile.

For twenty years or more,

ever since he'd left his father's farm when he was sixteen to get a job in a Detroit machineshop, Henry Ford had been nuts about machinery. First it was watches, then he designed a steamtractor, then he built a horseless carriage with an engine adapted from the Otto gasengine he'd read about in *The World of Science*, then a mechanical buggy with a onecylinder fourcycle motor, that would run forward but not back;

at last, in ninetyeight, he felt he was far enough along to risk throwing up his job with the Detroit Edison Company, where

he'd worked his way up from night fireman to chief engineer, to put all his time into working on a new gasoline engine,

(in the late eighties he'd met Edison at a meeting of electriclight employees in Atlantic City. He'd gone up to Edison after Edison had delivered an address and asked him if he thought gasoline was practical as a motor fuel. Edison had said yes. If Edison said it, it was true. Edison was the great admiration of Henry Ford's life);

and in driving his mechanical buggy, sitting there at the lever jauntily dressed in a tightbuttoned jacket and a high collar and a derby hat, back and forth over the level ill-paved streets of Detroit,

scaring the big brewery horses and the skinny trotting horses and the sleekrumped pacers with the motor's loud explosions,

looking for men scatterbrained enough to invest money in a factory for building automobiles.

He was the eldest son of an Irish immigrant who during the Civil War had married the daughter of a prosperous Pennsylvania Dutch farmer and settled down to farming near Dearborn in Wayne County, Michigan;

like plenty of other Americans, young Henry grew up hating the endless sogging through the mud about the chores, the hauling and pitching manure, the kerosene lamps to clean, the irk and sweat and solitude of the farm.

He was a slender, active youngster, a good skater, clever with his hands; what he liked was to tend the machinery and let the

others do the heavy work. His mother had told him not to drink, smoke, gamble or go into debt, and he never did.

When he was in his early twenties his father tried to get him back from Detroit, where he was working as mechanic and repairman for the Drydock Engine Company that built engines for steamboats, by giving him forty acres of land.

Young Henry built himself an uptodate square white dwellinghouse with a false mansard[1] roof and married and settled down on the farm,

but he let the hired men do the farming;

he bought himself a buzzsaw and rented a stationary engine and cut the timber off the woodlots.

---

1. mansard (man′ särd): A roof with two slopes on each of the four sides.

He was a thrifty young man who never drank or smoked or gambled, but he couldn't stand living on the farm.

He moved to Detroit, and in the brick barn behind his house tinkered for years in his spare time with a mechanical buggy that would be light enough to run over the clayey wagonroads of Wayne County, Michigan.

By 1900 he had a practicable car to promote.

He was forty years old before the Ford Motor Company was started and production began to move.

Speed was the first thing the early automobile manufacturers went after. Races advertised the makes of cars.

Henry Ford himself hung up several records at the track at Grosse Pointe and on the ice on Lake St. Clair. In his 999 he did the mile in thirtynine and fourfifths seconds.

But it had always been his custom to hire others to do the heavy work. The speed he was busy with was speed in production, the records records in efficient output. He hired Barney Oldfield, a stunt bicyclerider from Salt Lake City, to do the racing for him.

Henry Ford had ideas about other things than the designing of motors, carburetors, magnetos, jigs and fixtures, punches and dies; he had ideas about sales,

that the big money was in economical quantity production, quick turnover, cheap interchangeable, easilyreplaced standardized parts;

it wasn't until 1909, after years of arguing with his partners, that Ford put out the first Model T.

Henry Ford was right.

That season he sold more than ten thousand tin lizzies, ten years later he was selling almost a million a year.

In these years the Taylor Plan was stirring up plantmanagers and manufacturers all over the country. Efficiency was the word. The same ingenuity that went into improving the performance of a machine could go into improving the performance of the workmen producing the machine.

In 1913 they established the assemblyline at Ford's. That season the profits were something like twentyfive million dollars, but they had trouble in keeping the men on the job, machinists didn't seem to like it at Ford's.

Henry Ford had ideas about other things than production.

He was the largest automobile manufacturer in the world; he paid high wages; maybe if the steady workers thought they were getting a cut (a very small cut) in the profits, it would give trained men an inducement to stick to their jobs,

wellpaid workers might save enough money to buy a tin lizzie; the first day Ford's announced that cleancut properlymarried American workers who wanted jobs had a chance to make five bucks a day (of course it turned out that there were strings to it; always there were strings to it)

such an enormous crowd waited outside the Highland Park plant

all through the zero January night

that there was a riot when the gates were opened; cops broke heads, jobhunters threw bricks; property, Henry Ford's own property, was destroyed. The company dicks[2] had to turn on the firehose to beat back the crowd.

The American Plan; automotive prosperity seeping down from above; it turned out there were strings to it.

But that five dollars a day

paid to good, clean American workmen

who didn't drink or smoke cigarettes or read or think,

and whose wives didn't take in boarders,

made America once more the Yukon of the sweated workers of the world;

made all the tin lizzies and the automotive age, and incidentally,

made Henry Ford the automobileer, the admirer of Edison, the birdlover,

the great American of his time.

_____

2. **company dicks:** Armed guards.

THINKING ABOUT THE SELECTION

Recalling

1. Why did Ford quit his job at the Detroit Edison Company?
2. Whom did Ford look for as he drove his "mechanical buggy" up and down the "illpaved streets of Detroit"?
3. (a) What had Ford grown up hating? (b) What had his mother told him?
4. How did Ford think he could make "the big money"?
5. What happened when the Ford Motor Company announced that it was looking for workers?

Interpreting

6. (a) What details in the excerpt at the beginning of the selection make it clear that the American public knew very little about automobiles in 1900? (b) How is the portrayal of Ford in this excerpt different from the way he is portrayed in the rest of the selection?
7. Find two examples of Dos Passos's use of repetition to emphasize important ideas.
8. (a) What is unconventional about the form of the final sentence? (b) How does the form help to strengthen our final impression of Ford?

Analyzing

9. Dos Passos suggests that a person's accomplishments may reveal little about his or her character. Explain why you do or do not agree with this suggestion.

ANALYZING LITERATURE

Understanding Biography

A **biography** is an account of a person's life written by another person. In an impressionistic biography, the writer focuses on conveying his or her impressions of the subject, rather than merely recounting the central events of that person's life. For example, in "Tin Lizzie" Dos Passos presents his impressions of Henry Ford.

1. What impression does Dos Passos convey of Ford as a young man?
2. How does Dos Passos suggest that Ford thought of his workers as little more than machines?
3. How is Ford's character reflected in his conception of the ideal worker?
4. Considering the impression of Ford the selection conveys, what is ironic, or surprising, about the final line?

CRITICAL THINKING AND READING

Recognizing the Writer's Attitude

Although Dos Passos mentions a number of Ford's achievements in this essay, the way in which they are presented and the way in which Ford's character is portrayed make it clear that Dos Passos actually has a very critical attitude toward Ford and his accomplishments. For example, Dos Passos conveys a negative impression of Ford when he writes that what Ford "liked to do was to tend the machinery and let the others do the heavy work."

Find three other passages that reveal Dos Passos's critical attitude toward Ford.

THINKING AND WRITING

Writing an Impressionistic Biography

Using the list of facts you prepared before reading the selection, write an impressionistic biography. As you are writing, focus on presenting details that convey your impressions of the subject's character. When you finish writing, reread your biography to make sure it conveys the proper impression. After making any necessary revisions, proofread your biography and share it with your classmates.

E. B. WHITE

1899–1985

Known for his precise, direct style, E(lwyn) B(rooks) White is generally regarded as one of the most important American essayists of the twentieth century. In fact, White's work is still the standard against which the work of many of today's essayists is judged.

After growing up in Mount Vernon, New York, White attended Cornell University. There, he studied literature and served as the editor of the Cornell *Daily Sun*. Several years after his graduation, White joined the staff of *The New Yorker* magazine. His humorous, topical essays helped to establish *The New Yorker* as one of the nation's most successful general-interest magazines.

White produced essays for *The New Yorker* on a weekly basis until 1938. In these essays, many of which are collected in his books *Every Day Is Saturday* (1935) and *Quo Vadimus?* (1939), White used his talents as a humorist to explore numerous social and political themes. Influenced by the teachings of Henry David Thoreau, he strongly believed in individualism and simplicity. In an effort to simplify his own life, he bought a farmhouse in Maine and began spending much of his time there.

While continuing to contribute essays to *The New Yorker* and other magazines, White went on to produce many more collections of essays, including *One Man's Meat* (1942), *The Second Tree From the Corner* (1954), and *The Points of My Compass* (1962). He also wrote three popular books for children, *Stuart Little* (1945), *Charlotte's Web* (1952), and *The Trumpet of the Swan* (1971); he collaborated with his wife, Katharine, in compiling the popular anthology *A Subtreasury of American Humor;* and he published a book of letters, *Letters of E. B. White,* in 1976.

"Walden (June 1939)," an essay from *One Man's Meat,* reflects White's interest in Thoreau and his concern regarding the increasing complexity of modern life. The essay also demonstrates how White's belief in simplicity is reflected in his writing style.

GUIDE FOR READING

Walden

Personal Essays. A personal essay is an informal essay that focuses on a subject that is at least to some extent autobiographical. Personal essays are prose works written in a relaxed, intimate, conversational style. They are generally brief and focus on a limited topic. Despite their narrow focus, personal essays are loosely organized, with the writer at times digressing from the topic to express opinions or discuss related matters. Because of their autobiographical nature, personal essays generally reveal something about the writer's personality. "Walden," for example, reveals White's belief in simplicity.

As you read "Walden," pay attention to the intimate, conversational style in which it is written, and think about what it reveals about White's personality.

"Walden" is written in the form of a letter addressed to Henry David Thoreau, the writer who most influenced White's work. Think of a writer whose work has had a powerful effect on you. Then jot down thoughts you would include in a letter to this writer, discussing the ways in which his or her work affected you.

Knowing the following words will help you as you read "Walden."

impetuous (im pech' ‾oo wəs) *adj.*: Moving with great force or violence (p. 816)

pertinence (pʉr't'n əns) *n.*: Appropriateness; relevance (p. 816)

stupefaction (st‾oo' pə fak' shən) *n.*: Stunned amazement or utter bewilderment (p. 816)

cryptic (krip'tik) *adj.*: Having a hidden or ambiguous meaning (p. 817)

inauspicious (in ôs pish'əs) *adj.*: Not boding well for the future (p. 818)

petulently (pəch' ‾oo lənt lē) *adv.*: Impatiently or irritably (p. 819)

Walden

E. B. White

June 1939

Miss Nims, take a letter to Henry David Thoreau. Dear Henry: I thought of you the other afternoon as I was approaching Concord doing fifty on Route 62. That is a high speed at which to hold a philosopher in one's mind, but in this century we are a nimble bunch.

On one of the lawns in the outskirts of the village a woman was cutting the grass with a motorized lawn mower. What made me think of you was that the machine had rather got away from her, although she was game enough, and in the brief glimpse I had of the scene it appeared to me that the lawn was mowing the lady. She kept a tight grip on the handles, which throbbed violently with every explosion of the one-cylinder motor, and as she sheered around bushes and lurched along at a reluctant trot behind her impetuous servant, she looked like a puppy who had grabbed something that was too much for him. Concord hasn't changed much, Henry; the farm implements and the animals still have the upper hand.

I may as well admit that I was journeying to Concord with the deliberate intention of visiting your woods; for although I have never knelt at the grave of a philosopher nor placed wreaths on moldy poets, and have often gone a mile out of my way to avoid some place of historical interest, I have always wanted to see Walden Pond. The account which you left of your sojourn there is, you will be amused to learn, a document of increasing pertinence; each year it seems to gain a little headway, as the world loses ground. We may all be transcendental yet, whether we like it or not. As our common complexities increase, any tale of individual simplicity (and yours is the best written and the cockiest) acquires a new fascination; as our goods accumulate, but not our well-being, your report of an existence without material adornment takes on a certain awkward credibility.

My purpose in going to Walden Pond, like yours, was not to live cheaply or to live dearly there, but to transact some private business with the fewest obstacles. Approaching Concord, doing forty, doing forty-five, doing fifty, the steering wheel held snug in my palms, the highway held grimly in my vision, the crown of the road now serving me (on the righthand curves), now defeating me (on the lefthand curves), I began to rouse myself from the stupefaction which a day's motor journey induces. It was a delicious evening, Henry, when the whole body is one sense, and imbibes delight through every pore, if I may coin a phrase. Fields were richly brown where the harrow, drawn by the stripped Ford, had lately sunk its teeth; pastures were green; and overhead the sky had that same everlasting great look which you will find on Page 144 of the Oxford pocket edition.[1] I could feel the road entering me, through tire, wheel, spring, and cushion; shall I not have intelligence with earth

---

1. Oxford pocket edition: An edition of Thoreau's *Walden* published by the Oxford University Press.

too? Am I not partly leaves and vegetable mold myself?—a man of infinite horsepower, yet partly leaves.

Stay with me on 62 and it will take you into Concord. As I say, it was a delicious evening. The snake had come forth to die in a bloody S on the highway, the wheel upon its head, its bowels flat now and exposed. The turtle had come up too to cross the road and die in the attempt, its hard shell smashed under the rubber blow, its intestinal yearning (for the other side of the road) forever squashed. There was a sign by the wayside which announced that the road had a "cotton surface." You wouldn't know what that is, but neither, for that matter, did I. There is a cryptic ingredient in many of our modern improvements—we are awed and pleased without knowing quite what we are enjoying. It is something to be traveling on a road with a cotton surface.

The civilization round Concord today is an odd distillation of city, village, farm, and manor. The houses, yards, fields look not quite suburban, not quite rural. Under the bronze beech and the blue spruce of the departed baron grazes the milch[2] goat of the heirs. Under the porte-cochère[3] stands the reconditioned station wagon; under the grape arbor sit the puppies for sale. (But why do

---

2. milch *adj.*: Milk-giving.
3. porte-cochère (pôrt′ kō shâr′): Carport.

ROBERT BENCHLEY

1889–1945

By producing a vast number of humorous essays that generally focused on ordinary situations, Robert Benchley established himself as one of the most popular and most prolific humorists of the modern age.

Benchley was born in Massachusetts and educated at Harvard. Following his graduation, he went into journalism and eventually became the managing editor of the respected magazine *Vanity Fair*. Later in his career, he served as the drama critic for both *Life* and *The New Yorker*.

During the course of his life, Benchley produced a large number of collections of essays, including *Pluck and Luck* (1925), *20,000 Leagues Under the Sea, or David Copperfield* (1928), *From Bed to Worse, or Comforting the Bison* (1934), *My Ten Years in the Quandry, and How They Grew* (1936), and *Benchley Beside Himself* (1943). Following his death, Benchley's work remained popular, and a number of posthumous collections were published. These books include *Chips off the Old Benchley* (1949) and *The Benchley Round-Up* (1954).

The Tooth, the Whole Tooth, and Nothing but the Tooth

Literary Forms

Informal Essays. Like other types of essays, informal essays are short prose works that generally focus on a narrow topic. However, unlike formal essays, which are dignified in style and serious in tone, informal essays are written in a relaxed, intimate, conversational style. Informal essays also tend to be more loosely organized and less serious in purpose than formal essays. While formal essays are written to inform, instruct, or persuade, informal essays are written to amuse and entertain. Often informal essays attempt to evoke laughter, either by exploring an amusing subject or by treating a serious subject in a humorous manner. For example, "The Tooth, the Whole Tooth, and Nothing but the Tooth" extracts humor from the seemingly unpleasant subject of dental problems.

Look For

The British humorist Max Beerbohm wrote, "Humor undiluted is the most depressing of all phenomena. Humor must have its background of seriousness. Without this contrast there comes none of that incongruity which is the mainspring of laughter." As you read "The Tooth, the Whole Tooth, and Nothing but the Tooth," look for the ways in which Benchley makes his essay humorous.

Writing

In "The Tooth, the Whole Tooth, and Nothing but the Tooth," Benchley suggests that most people dread visiting the dentist. Do you agree with his suggestion? Freewrite about dental visits, discussing people's responses to dental visits and exploring the reasons for these responses.

Vocabulary

Knowing the following words will help you as you read "The Tooth, the Whole Tooth, and Nothing but the Tooth."

obnoxious (əb näk′ shəs) *adj.*: Very unpleasant; objectionable (p. 824)

inscrutable (in skroōt′ ə b'l) *adj.*: Not easily understood (p. 824)

dissolutely (dis′ə loōt′ lē) *adv.*: Immorally and shamelessly (p. 828)

accost (ə kôst′) *v.*: To approach and speak to in an intrusive way (p. 828)

The Tooth, the Whole Tooth, and Nothing but the Tooth

Robert Benchley

Some well-known saying (it doesn't make much difference what) is proved by the fact that everyone likes to talk about his experiences at the dentist's. For years and years little articles like this have been written on the subject, little jokes like some that I shall presently make have been made, and people in general have been telling other people just what emotions they experience when they crawl into the old red plush guillotine.[1]

They like to explain to each other how they feel when the dentist puts "that buzzer thing" against their bicuspids,[2] and, if sufficiently pressed, they will describe their sensations on mouthing a rubber dam.

"I'll tell you what I hate," they will say with great relish, "when he takes that little nut-pick and begins to scrape. Ugh!"

"Oh, I'll tell you what's worse than that," says the friend, not to be outdone, "when he is poking around careless-like, and strikes a nerve. Wow!"

And if there are more than two people at the experience-meeting, everyone will chip in and tell what he or she considers to be the worst phase of the dentist's work, all present enjoying the narration hugely and none so much as the narrator who has suffered so.

This sort of thing has been going on ever since the first mammoth gold tooth was hung out as a bait to folks in search of a good time. (By the way, when *did* the present obnoxious system of dentistry begin? It can't be so very long ago that the electric auger[3] was invented, and where would a dentist be without an electric auger? Yet you never hear of Amalgam[4] Filling Day, or any other anniversary in the dental year. There must be a conspiracy of silence on the part of the trade to keep hidden the names of the men who are responsible for all this.)

However many years it may be that dentists have been plying their trade, in all that time people have never tired of talking about their teeth. This is probably due to the inscrutable workings of Nature who is always supplying new teeth to talk about.

As a matter of fact, the actual time and suffering in the chair is only a fraction of the gross expenditure connected with the affair. The preliminary period, about which nobody talks, is much the worse. This dates from the discovery of the wayward tooth and extends to the moment when the dentist places his foot on the automatic hoist which jacks

---

1. guillotine (gil′ ə tēn′) *n*.: An instrument for beheading by means of a heavy blade dropped between two grooved uprights.
2. bicuspids (bī kus′ pids) *n*.: Eight adult teeth with two-pointed crowns.

3. auger (ô′ gər) *n*.: A tool used for drilling teeth.
4. amalgam (ə mal′ gəm) *n*.: An alloy of mercury used with silver as a dental filling.

you up into range. Giving gas for tooth-extraction is all very humane in its way, but the time for anaesthetics is when the patient first decides that he must go to the dentist. From then on, until the first excavation is started, should be shrouded in oblivion.

There is probably no moment more appalling than that in which the tongue, running idly over the teeth in a moment of carefree play, comes suddenly upon the ragged edge of a space from which the old familiar filling has disappeared. The world stops and you look meditatively up to the corner of the ceiling. Then quickly you draw your tongue away, and try to laugh the affair off, saying to yourself:

"Stuff and nonsense, my good fellow! There is nothing the matter with your tooth. Your nerves are upset after a hard day's work, that's all."

Having decided this to your satisfaction, you slyly, and with a poor attempt at being casual, slide the tongue back along the line of adjacent teeth, hoping against hope that it will reach the end without mishap.

But there it is! There can be no doubt about it this time. The tooth simply has got to be filled by someone, and the only person who can fill it with anything permanent is a dentist. You wonder if you might not be able to patch it up yourself for the time being—a year or so—perhaps with a little spruce gum and a coating of new skin. It is fairly far back, and wouldn't have to be a very sightly job.

But this has an impracticable sound, even to you. You might want to eat some peanut brittle (you never can tell when someone might offer you peanut brittle these days), and the new skin, while serviceable enough in the case of cream soups and custards, couldn't be expected to stand up under heavy crunching.

So you admit that, since the thing has got to be filled, it might as well be a dentist who does the job.

This much decided, all that is necessary is to call him up and make an appointment.

Let us say that this resolve is made on Tuesday. That afternoon you start to look up the dentist's number in the telephone book. A great wave of relief sweeps over you when you discover that it isn't there. How can you be expected to make an appointment with a man who hasn't got a telephone? And how can you have a tooth filled without making an appointment? The whole thing is impossible, and that's all there is to it. God knows you did your best.

On Wednesday there is a slightly more insistent twinge, owing to bad management of a sip of ice-water. You decide that you simply must get in touch with that dentist when you get back from lunch. But you know how those things are. First one thing and then another came up, and a man came in from Providence who had to be shown around the office, and by the time you had a minute to yourself it was five o'clock. And,

anyway, the tooth didn't bother you again. You wouldn't be surprised if, by being careful, you could get along with it as it is until the end of the week when you will have more time. A man has to think of his business, after all, and what is a little personal discomfort in the shape of an unfilled tooth to the satisfaction of work well done in the office?

By Saturday morning you are fairly reconciled to going ahead, but it is only a half day and probably he has no appointments left, anyway. Monday is really the time. You can begin the week afresh. After all, Monday is really the logical day to start in going to the dentist.

Bright and early Monday morning you make another try at the telephone book, and find, to your horror, that some time between now and last Tuesday the dentist's name and number have been inserted into the directory. There it is. There is no getting around it: "Burgess, Jas. Kendal, DDS. . . . Courtland—2654." There is really nothing left to do but to call him up. Fortunately the line is busy, which gives you a perfectly good excuse for putting it over until Tuesday. But on Tuesday luck is against you and you get a clear connection with the doctor himself. An appointment is arranged for Thursday afternoon at 3:30.

Thursday afternoon, and here it is only Tuesday morning! Almost anything may happen between now and then. We might declare war on Mexico, and off you'd have to go, dentist appointment or no dentist appointment. Surely a man couldn't let a date to have a tooth filled stand in the way of his doing his duty to his country. Or the social revolution might start on Wednesday, and by Thursday the whole town might be in ashes. You can picture yourself standing, Thursday afternoon at 3:30, on the ruins of the city hall, fighting off marauding bands of reds, and saying to yourself, with a sigh of relief: "Only to think! At this time I was to have been climbing into the dentist's chair!" You never can tell when your luck will turn in a thing like that.

But Wednesday goes by and nothing

happens. And Thursday morning dawns without even a word from the dentist saying that he has been called suddenly out of town to lecture before the Incisor[5] Club. Apparently, everything is working against you.

By this time, your tongue has taken up a permanent resting place in the vacant tooth, and is causing you to talk indistinctly and incoherently. Somehow you feel that if the dentist opens your mouth and finds the tip of your tongue in the tooth, he will be deceived and go away without doing anything.

The only thing left is for you to call him up and say that you have just killed a man and are being arrested and can't possibly keep your appointment. But any dentist would see through that. He would laugh right into his transmitter at you. There is probably no excuse which it would be possible to invent which a dentist has not already heard eighty or ninety times. No, you might as well see the thing through now.

Luncheon is a ghastly rite. The whole left side of your jaw has suddenly developed an acute sensitiveness and the disaffection has spread to the four teeth on either side of the original one. You doubt if it will be possible for him to touch it at all. Perhaps all he intends to do this time is to look at it anyway. You might even suggest that to him. You could very easily come in again soon and have him do the actual work.

Three-thirty draws near. A horrible time of day at best. Just when a man's vitality is lowest. Before stepping in out of the sunlight into the building in which the dental parlor is, you take one look about you at the happy people scurrying by in the street. Carefree children that they are! What do they know of Life? Probably that man in the silly-looking hat never had trouble with so much as his baby teeth. There they go, pushing and jostling each other, just as if within ten feet of them there was not a man who stands on the brink of the Great Misadventure. Ah well! Life is like that!

---

5. **incisor** (in sī′zər) *n.*: A front tooth.

Into the elevator. The last hope is gone. The door clangs and you look hopelessly about you at the stupid faces of your fellow passengers. How can people be so clownish? Of course, there is always the chance that the elevator will fall and that you will all be terribly hurt. But that is too much to expect. You dismiss it from your thoughts as too impractical, too visionary. Things don't work out as happily as that in real life.

You feel a certain glow of heroic pride when you tell the operator the right floor number. You might just as easily have told him a floor too high or too low, and that would, at least, have caused delay. But after all, a man must prove himself a man and the least you can do is to meet Fate with an unflinching eye and give the right floor number.

Too often has the scene in the dentist's waiting room been described for me to try to do it again here. They are all alike. The antiseptic smell, the ominous hum from the operating rooms, the ancient *Digest*s, and the silent, sullen group of waiting patients, each trying to look unconcerned and cordially disliking everyone else in the room—all these have been sung by poets of far greater lyric powers than mine. (Not that I really think that they *are* greater than mine, but that's the customary form of excuse for not writing something you haven't got time or space to do. As a matter of fact, I think I could do it much better than it has ever been done before.)

I can only say that, as you sit looking, with unseeing eyes, through a large book entitled *The War in Pictures*, you would gladly change places with the most lowly of God's creatures. It is inconceivable that there should be anyone worse off than you, unless perhaps it is some of the poor wretches who are waiting with you.

That one over in the armchair, nervously tearing to shreds a copy of *The Dental Review and Practical Inlay Worker*. She may have something frightful the trouble with her. She couldn't possibly look more worried. Perhaps it is very, very painful. This thought cheers you up considerably. What cowards women are in times like these!

And then there comes the sound of voices from the next room.

"All right, Doctor, and if it gives me any more pain shall I call you up? . . . Do you think that it will bleed much more? . . . Saturday morning, then, at eleven. . . . Goodbye, Doctor."

And a middle-aged woman emerges (all women are middle-aged when emerging from the dentist's office) looking as if she were playing the big emotional scene in *John Ferguson*.[6] A wisp of hair waves dissolutely across her forehead between her eyes. Her face is pale, except for a slight inflammation at the corners of her mouth, and in her eyes is that far-away look of one who has been face to face with Life. But she is through. She should care how she looks.

The nurse appears, and looks inquiringly at each one in the room. Each one in the room evades the nurse's glance in one last, futile attempt to fool someone and get away without seeing the dentist. But she spots you and nods pleasantly. God, how pleasantly she nods! There ought to be a law against people being as pleasant as that.

"The doctor will see you now," she says.

The English language may hold a more disagreeable combination of words than "The doctor will see you now." I am willing to concede something to the phrase "Have you anything to say before the current is turned on." That may be worse for the moment, but it doesn't last so long. For continued, unmitigating depression, I know nothing to equal "The doctor will see you now." But I'm not narrow-minded about it. I'm willing to consider other possibilities.

Smiling feebly, you trip over the extended feet of the man next to you, and stagger into the delivery room, where amid a ghastly array of death-masks of teeth, blue flames waving eerily from Bunsen burners,

---

6. John Ferguson: A play by Irish playwright St. John Ervine.

and the drowning sound of perpetually running water which chokes and gurgles at intervals, you sink into the chair and close your eyes.

But now let us consider the spiritual exaltation that comes when you are at last let down and turned loose. It is all over, and what did it amount to? Why, nothing at all. A-ha-ha-ha-ha-ha! Nothing at all.

You suddenly develop a particular friendship for the dentist. A splendid fellow, really. You ask him questions about his instruments. What does he use this thing for, for instance? Well, well, to think of a little thing like that making all that trouble. A-ha-ha-ha-ha-ha! . . . And the dentist's family, how are they? Isn't that fine!

Gaily you shake hands with him and straighten your tie. Forgotten is the fact that you have another appointment with him for Monday. There is no such thing as Monday. You are through for today, and all's right with the world.

As you pass out through the waiting room, you leer at the others unpleasantly. The poor fishes! Why can't they take their medicine like grown people and not sit there moping as if they were going to be shot?

Heigh-ho! Here's the elevator man! A charming fellow! You wonder if he knows that you have just had a tooth filled. You feel tempted to tell him and slap him on the back. You feel tempted to tell everyone out in the bright, cheery street. And what a wonderful street it is too! All full of nice, black snow and water. After all, Life is sweet!

And then you go and find the first person whom you can accost without being arrested and explain to him just what it was that the dentist did to you, and how you felt, and what you have got to have done next time.

Which brings us right back to where we were in the beginning, and perhaps accounts for everyone's liking to divulge their dental secrets to others. It may be a sort of hysterical relief that, for the time being, it is all over with.

THINKING ABOUT THE SELECTION

Recalling

1. According to Benchley, about what does everyone like to talk?
2. (a) What is a person's immediate reaction to the discovery that a "filling has disappeared"? (b) How does the person manage to put off making an appointment to have the filling replaced? (c) How does the person imagine that he or she might be prevented from keeping the appointment?
3. What observation does Benchley make concerning dentist's waiting rooms?
4. What does Benchley view as the most disagreeable combination of words "for continued, unmitigating depression"?
5. How does a person react when his or her dental work has been completed?

Interpreting

6. (a) Why is the person so reluctant to visit the dentist? (b) Why is the person ultimately so eager to tell others about his or her visit?
7. (a) How does the person's disposition change once the dental work has been completed? (b) What is amusing about this change?

Applying

8. This essay was written before World War II. (a) How do you think people's responses to visiting the dentist have changed since then? (b) What do you think accounts for these changes?

ANALYZING LITERATURE

Understanding Informal Essays

An **informal essay** is a short prose work in which the writer uses a conversational style and a light, personal tone. Informal essays tend to be loosely organized, with the writer at times straying from the topic or interrupting the narrative flow to express related observations or opinions.

1. How does Benchley establish a light, informal tone in the first paragraph?
2. How does he maintain a personal tone throughout the remainder of the essay?
3. Find two instances in which Benchley interrupts the narrative flow to present a related opinion or observation.

CRITICAL THINKING AND READING

Evaluating an Essay

"The Tooth, the Whole Tooth, and Nothing but the Tooth" was clearly written to entertain readers and evoke laughter. For the essay to be successful, the reader must be familiar with the situation it depicts and be able to relate to the reaction it describes and to the attitude it expresses.

1. Explain whether or not you find this essay to be humorous.
2. In what ways is your own attitude toward dental visits similar to and different from the attitude expressed in the essay?
3. How do you think your attitude toward dental visits affected your appreciation of the essay?
4. Do you think this essay is less effective now than when it was written? Why or why not?

THINKING AND WRITING

Writing an Informal Essay

Imagine that your school literary magazine is having a contest to see who can write the best humorous informal essay. Think of an experience which most people dread. Then write an essay in which you describe this experience and people's responses to it in a humorous manner. When you revise, make sure that you have used a conversational style and a humorous tone.

JAMES THURBER

1894–1961

A noted humorist, James Thurber wrote essays and short stories that generally evolved from his own experiences. In his humorous autobiographical sketches, such as "The Night the Ghost Got In," Thurber embellished the facts and described events in an amusing manner. In his short stories, Thurber created characters who struggled awkwardly against the unpleasant realities of life.

Born in Columbus, Ohio, Thurber attended Ohio State University. Following his graduation, he began a career in journalism, accepting a job as a newspaper reporter in Columbus. In 1927 he joined the staff of the magazine, *The New Yorker*. Thurber remained associated with *The New Yorker* for the remainder of his life, contributing stories, essays, and cartoons. At *The New Yorker* he also worked closely with the celebrated writer E. B. White, who influenced his writing. Thurber, White, and other *New Yorker* writers such as Frank Sullivan, Robert Benchley, and S. J. Perelman helped establish a grand tradition of modern American humor. Thurber has written of humor, "Humor is emotional chaos remembered in tranquility." He has also written, "As brevity is the soul of wit, form, it seems to me, is the heart of humor and the salvation of comedy."

During the course of his career, Thurber published a great many books. Some of his books, such as *The Owl in the Attic and Other Perplexities* (1931) and *The Seal in the Bedroom and Other Predicaments* (1932), contain a mixture of short stories, parodies, and cartoons. Other books, including *My Life and Hard Times,* are composed of sketches about his childhood. He also wrote children's stories and collaborated with Elliot Nugent in writing a successful play, *The Male Animal* (1940). Thurber's best-known work is his short story, "The Secret Life of Walter Mitty," which was first published in *The New Yorker* in 1939.

During the last twenty years of his life, Thurber's vision failed, and he eventually became completely blind. He continued to write and draw as well as he could. Yet his later work is often tinged with a sense of bitterness.

The Night the Ghost Got In

Humor. In literature, humor refers to writing which attempts to evoke laughter. To accomplish this purpose, writers must have the ability to perceive the ridiculous, comical, or ludicrous aspects of an incident, situation, or personality and to depict them in an amusing manner. In "The Night the Ghost Got In," for example, Thurber captures the humorous idiosyncrasies of his family members in depicting an amusing, chaotic series of events.

Humorists often exaggerate details and embellish facts in their work. By using exaggeration, a writer can make an amusing event or character seem even more humorous, or a writer can use exaggeration to create humor in an otherwise unamusing situation. For example, in "The Night the Ghost Got In," Thurber uses exaggeration to accentuate the amusing character traits of his family members.

Another technique frequently used by humorists is malapropism—the humorous misuse of words. For example, instead of having a character say that someone "*instigated* a riot," a writer might have the character comment that someone "*insinuated* a riot".

As you read "The Night the Ghost Got In," take note of the techniques Thurber uses to create humor.

Why do we laugh when someone slips on a banana peel? Why do we find it funny when someone is hit in the face by a custard pie? Free-write, exploring your ideas on what makes someone laugh.

Knowing the following words will help you as you read "The Night the Ghost Got In."

intuitively (in tōō′ i tiv lē) *adj.*: Instinctively (p. 833)

blaspheming (blas fēm′ iŋ) *v.*: Cursing (p. 836)

The Night the Ghost Got In

James Thurber

The ghost that got into our house on the night of November 17, 1915, raised such a hullabaloo of misunderstandings that I am sorry I didn't just let it keep on walking, and go to bed. Its advent caused my mother to throw a shoe through a window of the house next door and ended up with my grandfather shooting a patrolman. I am sorry, therefore, as I have said, that I ever paid any attention to the footsteps.

They began about a quarter past one o'clock in the morning, a rhythmic, quick-cadenced walking around the dining-room table. My mother was asleep in one room upstairs, my brother Herman in another; grandfather was in the attic, in the old wal-nut bed which, as you will remember, once fell on my father. I had just stepped out of the bathtub and was busily rubbing myself with a towel when I heard the steps. They were the steps of a man walking rapidly around the dining-room table downstairs. The light from the bathroom shone down the back steps, which dropped directly into the dining-room; I could see the faint shine of plates on the plate-rail; I couldn't see the table. The steps kept going round and round the table; at regular intervals a board creaked, when it was trod upon. I supposed at first that it was my father or my brother Roy, who had gone to Indianapolis but were expected home at any time. I suspected next

THE NIGHT THE GHOST GOT IN
*Copyright © 1933, 1961, James Thurber,
From* My Life and Hard Times,
published by Harper & Row.

"The ghost got into our house on the night of November 17, 1915 and raised such a hullabaloo of misunderstandings. . . ."

that it was a burglar. It did not enter my mind until later that it was a ghost.

After the walking had gone on for perhaps three minutes, I tiptoed to Herman's room. "Psst!" I hissed, in the dark, shaking him. "Awp," he said, in the low, hopeless tone of a despondent beagle—he always half suspected that something would "get him" in the night. I told him who I was. "There's something downstairs!" I said. He got up and followed me to the head of the back staircase. We listened together. There was no sound. The steps had ceased. Herman looked at me in some alarm: I had only the bath towel around my waist. He wanted to go back to bed, but I gripped his arm. "There's something down there!" I said. Instantly the steps began again, circled the dining-room table like a man running, and started up the stairs toward us, heavily, two at a time. The light still shone palely down the stairs; we saw nothing coming; we only heard the steps. Herman rushed to his room and slammed the door. I slammed shut the door at the stairs top and held my knee against it. After a long minute, I slowly opened it again. There was nothing there. There was no sound. None of us ever heard the ghost again.

The slamming of the doors had aroused mother: she peered out of her room. "What on earth are you boys doing?" she demanded. Herman ventured out of his room. "Nothing," he said, gruffly, but he was, in color, a light green. "What was all that running around downstairs?" said mother. So she had heard the steps, too! We just looked at her. "Burglars!" she shouted intuitively. I tried to quiet her by starting lightly downstairs.

"Come on, Herman," I said.

"I'll stay with Mother," he said. "She's all excited."

I stepped back onto the landing.

"Don't either of you go a step," said mother. "We'll call the police." Since the phone was downstairs, I didn't see how we were going to call the police—nor did I want the police—but mother made one of her quick, incomparable decisions. She flung up a window of her bedroom which faced the bedroom windows of the house of a neighbor, picked up a shoe, and whammed it through a pane of glass across the narrow space that separated the two houses. Glass tinkled into the bedroom occupied by a retired engraver named Bodwell and his wife. Bodwell had been for some years in rather a bad way and was subject to mild "attacks." Most everybody we knew or lived near had *some* kind of attacks.

It was now about two o'clock of a moonless night; clouds hung black and low. Bodwell was at the window in a minute, shouting, frothing a little, shaking his fist. "We'll sell the house and go back to Peoria," we could hear Mrs. Bodwell saying. It was some time before mother "got through" to Bodwell. "Burglars!" she shouted. "Burglars in the house!" Herman and I hadn't dared to tell her that it was not burglars but ghosts, for she was even more afraid of ghosts than of burglars. Bodwell at first thought that she meant there were burglars in his house, but finally he quieted down and called the police for us over an extension phone by his bed. After he had disappeared from the window, mother suddenly made as if to throw another shoe, not because there was further need of it, but, as she later explained, because the thrill of heaving a shoe through a window glass had enormously taken her fancy. I prevented her.

The police were on hand in a commendably short time: a Ford sedan full of them, two on motorcycles, and a patrol wagon with about eight in it and a few reporters. They began banging at our front door. Flashlights shot streaks of gleam up and down the walls, across the yard, down the walk between our house and Bodwell's. "Open up!" cried a hoarse voice. "We're men from Headquarters!" I wanted to go down and let them in, since there they were, but mother wouldn't hear of it. "You haven't a stitch on," she pointed out. "You'd catch your death." I wound the towel around me again. Finally the cops put their shoulders to our big heavy

THE NIGHT THE GHOST GOT IN
Copyright © 1933, 1961, James Thurber,
From My Life and Hard Times, *published by*
Harper & Row.

front door with its thick beveled glass and broke it in: I could hear a rending of wood and a splash of glass on the floor of the hall. Their lights played all over the living-room and crisscrossed nervously in the dining-room, stabbed into hallways, shot up the front stairs and finally up the back. They caught me standing in my towel at the top. A heavy policeman bounded up the steps. "Who are you?" he demanded. "I live here," I said. "Well, whattsa matta, ya hot?" he asked. I was, as a matter of fact, cold; I went to my room and pulled on some trousers. On my way out, a cop stuck a gun into my ribs. "Whatta you doin' here?" he demanded. "I live here," I said.

The officer in charge reported to mother. "No sign of nobody, lady," he said. "Musta got away—whatt'd he look like?" "There were two or three of them," mother said, "whooping and carrying on and slamming doors." "Funny, said the cop. "All ya windows and doors was locked on the inside tight as a tick."

Downstairs, we could hear the tromping of the other police. Police were all over the place; doors were yanked open, drawers were yanked open, windows were shot up and pulled down, furniture fell with dull thumps. A half-dozen policemen emerged out of the darkness of the front hallway upstairs. They began to ransack the floor: pulled beds away from walls, tore clothes off hooks in the closets, pulled suitcases and boxes off shelves. One of them found an old zither[1] that Roy had won in a pool tournament. "Looky here, Joe," he said, strumming it with a big paw. The cop named Joe took it and turned it over. "What is it?" he asked me. "It's an old zither our guinea pig used to sleep on," I said. It was true that a pet guinea pig we once had would never sleep anywhere except on the zither, but I should never have said so. Joe and the other cop looked at me a long time. They put the zither back on a shelf.

"No sign o' nuthin'," said the cop who

1. zither (zĭth'ər) *n.*: A musical instrument with thirty to forty strings stretched across a flat soundboard and played with the fingers.

had first spoken to mother. "This guy," he explained to the others, jerking a thumb at me, "was nekked. The lady seems historical." They all nodded, but said nothing; just looked at me. In the small silence we all heard a creaking in the attic. Grandfather was turning over in bed. "What's 'at?" snapped Joe. Five or six cops sprang for the attic door before I could intervene or explain. I realized that it would be bad if they burst in on grandfather unannounced, or even announced. He was going through a phase in which he believed that General Meade's men, under steady hammering by Stonewall Jackson, were beginning to retreat and even desert.

When I got to the attic, things were pretty confused. Grandfather had evidently jumped to the conclusion that the police were deserters from Meade's army, trying to hide away in his attic. He bounded out of bed wearing a long flannel nightgown over long woolen underwear, a nightcap, and a leather jacket around his chest. The cops must have realized at once that the indignant white-haired old man belonged in the house, but they had no chance to say so. "Back, ye cowardly dogs!" roared grandfather. "Back t' the lines, ye yellow, lily-livered cattle!" With that, he fetched the officer who found the zither a flat-handed smack alongside his head that sent him sprawling. The others beat a retreat, but not fast enough; grandfather grabbed Zither's gun from its holster and let fly. The report seemed to crack the rafters; smoke filled the attic. A cop cursed and shot his hand to his shoulder. Somehow, we all finally got downstairs again and locked the door against the old gentleman. He fired once or twice more in the darkness and then went back to bed. "That was grandfather," I explained to Joe, out of breath. "He thinks you're deserters." "I'll say he does," said Joe.

THE NIGHT THE GHOST GOT IN

Copyright © 1933, 1961, James Thurber, From My Life and Hard Times, published by Harper & Row.

The cops were reluctant to leave without getting their hands on somebody besides grandfather; the night had been distinctly a defeat for them. Furthermore, they obviously didn't like the "layout"; something looked—and I can see their viewpoint—phony. They began to poke into things again. A reporter, a thin-faced, wispy man, came up to me. I had put on one of mother's blouses, not being able to find anything else. The reporter looked at me with mingled suspicion and interest. "Just what the heck is the real low-down here, Bud?" he asked. I decided to be frank with him. "We had ghosts," I said. He gazed at me a long time as if I were a slot machine into which he had, without results, dropped a nickel. Then he walked away. The cops followed him, the one grandfather shot holding his now-bandaged arm, cursing and blaspheming. "I'm gonna get my gun back from that old bird," said the zither-cop. "Yeh," said Joe. "You—and who else?" I told them I would bring it to the station house the next day.

"What was the matter with that one policeman?" mother asked, after they had gone. "Grandfather shot him," I said. "What for?" she demanded. I told her he was a deserter. "Of all things!" said mother. "He was such a nice-looking young man."

Grandfather was fresh as a daisy and full of jokes at breakfast next morning. We thought at first he had forgotten all about what had happened, but he hadn't. Over his third cup of coffee, he glared at Herman and me. "What was the idee of all them cops tarry-hootin' round the house last night?" he demanded. He had us there.

THINKING ABOUT THE SELECTION

Recalling

1. (a) What is Thurber doing when he hears the footsteps? (b) What do he and his brother do when they hear the steps coming toward them?
2. Why does Thurber's mother throw a shoe through the neighbors' window?
3. (a) Why will Thurber's mother not allow him to let the police in the house? (b) How do the police finally get in?
4. (a) How does Thurber's grandfather react when the police burst into his room? (b) What prompts this reaction?

Interpreting

5. What role does the lack of communication among the characters play in precipitating the events described?
6. (a) What does the mother's desire to throw a second shoe through the neighbors' window reveal about her character? (b) What does her response to her son's explanation of the grandfather's actions reveal about her character?
7. (a) What is surprising about the question the grandfather asks at breakfast the next morning? (b) What does it reveal about his character?
8. How is Thurber's depiction of himself different from his depiction of the other characters?

Applying

9. Thurber's stories are often filled with eccentrics—people whose idiosyncracies or peculiarities make them humorously unique. How do people react to eccentrics in real life? Explain your answer.

ANALYZING LITERATURE

Understanding Humor

In literature, **humor** refers to writing which attempts to evoke laughter. Humorists achieve this purpose by depicting comical incidents, situations, or personalities. For example, in "The Night the Ghost Got In," Thurber describes an improbable and humorous series of events involving a number of unusual characters.

1. What makes Thurber's mother an unusual and amusing character?
2. What makes Thurber's grandfather an unusual and amusing character?
3. What is comical about the behavior of the police officers?
4. What malapropism, or humorous misuse of words, does the policeman commit when he describes the mother's behavior?
5. (a) What is the usual reaction to hearing footsteps in the middle of the night? (b) How does the contrast between the usual reaction and the Thurber family's reaction add to the humor of the story?

CRITICAL THINKING AND READING

Recognizing Exaggeration

Humorists often exaggerate details and embellish facts in their work. For example, Thurber clearly exaggerates the number of police officers who showed up at his house.

1. Do you think the actions of the police officers are exaggerated? Why or why not?
2. Do you think the grandfather's personality and behavior are exaggerated? Why or why not?

THINKING AND WRITING

Writing a Humorous Essay

Write an essay describing a humorous incident that you experienced. (If you like, you may make up the incident.) Freewrite, describing an unusual predicament. Then write your essay, using exaggeration to add to the humor of your story. When you finish writing, revise your essay, making sure you have related events in chronological order. Proofread your essay and share it with your classmates.

CARL SANDBURG

1878–1967

Carl Sandburg was born in Galesburg, Illinois. The son of Swedish immigrant parents, Sandburg worked at various jobs to support himself, until volunteering for the Spanish-American War. His variety of working experiences gave an authenticity to his writing about the American worker. The dignity of the American worker is a dominant theme in his work, as is the search for meaning in American history.

Although he is remembered mostly for his poetry, Carl Sandburg was also a well-known historical biographer. In fact, he wrote what is generally regarded as the definitive biography of Abraham Lincoln, a figure who to Sandburg represented the best of the American character. Sandburg spent thirty years working on this six-volume biography, compiling and organizing information. His collection of resource material grew so large that it outgrew the Lincoln room in his home and the barn had to be set aside for additional storage. The two volumes that comprise *Abraham Lincoln: The Prairie Years* deal with Lincoln's early career. The four volumes that comprise *Abraham Lincoln: The War Years* deal with the Lincoln presidency. Sandburg was rewarded for his efforts in 1940, when his historical biography earned him the Pulitzer Prize for history.

Lincoln Speaks at Gettysburg

Literary Forms

Biography. A biography is an account of a person's life written by another person. After carefully researching his or her subject, a biographer focuses on recounting the central events of the subject's life—the events that make that person's life interesting or important. A biographer will also present his or her interpretations of the events being recounted, attempting to explain the reasons for the subject's actions and the meaning of their lives. For example, in the following chapter from *Abraham Lincoln: The War Years,* Sandburg provides insights into the events leading up to Lincoln's composing his famous Gettysburg Address.

Look For

As you read "Lincoln Speaks at Gettysburg," take note of what it reveals about how Lincoln composed his Gettysburg Address. What does it say about Lincoln—the man?

Writing

Freewrite about a person you know or a celebrity you admire, focusing on the reasons why you find this person's life interesting.

Vocabulary

Knowing the following words will help you as you read "Lincoln Speaks at Gettysburg."

eminent (em′ ə nant) *adj.*: Distinguished (p. 840)

auspices (ôs′ pə sēz′) *n.*: Approval and support (p. 842)

demeaned (di mēn′d) *v.*: Behaved; conducted (p. 843)

sallow (sal′ ō) *adj.*: Of a sickly, pale-yellow hue (p. 844)

benevolent (be nev′ ə lənt) *adj.*: Kindly; charitable (p. 845)

sovereignty (säv′ rən tē) *n.*: Supreme and independent political authority (p. 846)

sepulcher (sep′′l kər) *n.*: Tomb (p. 846)

perfunctory (pər fuŋk′ tərē) *adj.*: Done without care or interest or merely as a form or routine (p. 847)

from Abraham Lincoln: The War Years

Carl Sandburg

Lincoln Speaks at Gettysburg

A printed invitation came to Lincoln's hands notifying him that on Thursday, November 19, 1863, exercises would be held for the dedication of a National Soldiers' Cemetery at Gettysburg. The same circular invitation had been mailed to Senators, Congressmen, the governors of northern states, members of the Cabinet, by the commission of Pennsylvanians who had organized a corporation through which Maine, New Hampshire, Vermont, Massachusetts, Rhode Island, Maryland, Connecticut, New York, New Jersey, Pennsylvania, Delaware, West Virginia, Ohio, Indiana, Illinois, Michigan, Wisconsin, and Minnesota were to share the cost of a decent burying ground for the dust and bones of the Union and Confederate dead.

In the helpless onrush of the war, it was known, too many of the fallen had lain as neglected cadavers rotting in the open fields or thrust into so shallow a resting place that a common farm plow caught in their bones. Now by order of Governor Curtin of Pennsylvania seventeen acres had been purchased on Cemetery Hill, where the Union center stood its colors on the second and third of July, and plots of soil had been allotted each State for its graves.

The sacred and delicate duties of orator of the day had fallen on Edward Everett. An eminent cultural figure, perhaps foremost of all distinguished American classical orators, he was born in 1794, had been United States senator, governor of Massachusetts, member of Congress, secretary of state under Fillmore, minister to Great Britain, Phi Beta Kappa poet at Harvard, professor of Greek at Harvard, president of Harvard. . . .

The Union of States was a holy concept to Everett, and the slavery issue secondary, though when president of Harvard from 1846 to 1849 he refused to draw the color line, saying in the case of a Negro applicant, Beverly Williams, that admission to Harvard College depended on examinations. "If this boy passes the examinations, he will be admitted; and if the white students choose to withdraw, all the income of the college will be devoted to his education." Not often was he so provocative. . . .

Serene, suave, handsomely venerable in his sixty-ninth year, a prominent specimen of Northern upper-class distinction, Everett was a natural choice of the Pennsylvania commissioners, who sought an orator for a solemn national occasion. When in September they notified him that the date of the occasion would be October 23, he replied that he would need more time for preparation, and the dedication was postponed till November 19.

Lincoln meanwhile, in reply to the printed circular invitation, sent word to the commissioners that he would be present at the ceremonies. This made it necessary for the commissioners to consider whether the President should be asked to deliver an address when present. Clark E. Carr of Galesburg, Illinois, representing his state on the board of commissioners, noted that the decision of the board to invite Lincoln to speak was an afterthought. "The question was raised as to his ability to speak upon such a grave and solemn occasion . . . . Besides, it was said that, with his important duties and responsibilities, he could not possibly have the leisure to prepare an address. . . . In answer . . . it was urged that he himself, better than anyone else, could determine as to these questions, and that, if he were invited to speak, he was sure to do what, under the circumstances, would be right and proper."

And so on November 2 David Wills of Gettysburg, as the special agent of Governor Curtin and also acting for the several states, by letter informed Lincoln that the several states having soldiers in the army of the Potomac who were killed, or had since died at hospitals in the vicinity, had procured

LINCOLN
Frank E. Schoonover
Wilmington Savings Fund Society

grounds for a cemetery and proper burial of their dead. "These grounds will be consecrated and set apart to this sacred purpose by appropriate ceremonies on Thursday, the 19th instant. I am authorized by the governors of the various states to invite you to be present and participate in these ceremonies, which will doubtless be very imposing and solemnly impressive. It is the desire that after the oration, you, as chief executive of the nation, formally set apart these grounds to their sacred use by a few appropriate remarks."

Mr. Wills proceeded farther as to the solemnity of the occasion, and when Lincoln had finished reading the letter he understood definitely that the event called for no humor and that a long speech was not expected from him. "The invitation," wrote Clark E. Carr, "was not settled upon and sent to Mr. Lincoln until the second of November, more than six weeks after Mr. Everett had been invited to speak, and but little more than two weeks before the exercises were held."

On the second Sunday before the Gettysburg ceremonies were to take place Lincoln went to the studio of the photographer Gardner for a long-delayed sitting. Noah Brooks walked with him, and he carefully explained to Brooks that he could not go to the photographer on any other day without interfering with the public business and the photographer's business, to say nothing of his liability to be hindered en route by curiosity seekers "and other seekers." On the White House stairs Lincoln had paused, turned, walked back to his office, and rejoined Brooks with a long envelope in his hand, an advance copy of Edward Everett's address to be delivered at the Gettysburg dedication. It was thoughtful of Everett to take care they should not cover the same ground in their speeches, he remarked to Brooks, who exclaimed over the length of the Everett address, covering nearly two sides of a one-page supplement of a Boston newspaper. Lincoln quoted a line he said he had read

somewhere from Daniel Webster:[1] "Solid men of Boston, make no long orations." There was no danger that he should get upon the lines of Mr. Everett's oration, he told Brooks, for what he had ready to say was very short, or as Brooks recalled his emphasis, "short, short, short." He had hoped to read the Everett address between sittings, but the photographer worked fast, Lincoln got interested in talk, and did not open the advance sheets while at Gardner's. In the photograph which Lincoln later gave to Brooks an envelope lay next to Lincoln's right arm resting on a table. In one other photograph made by Gardner that Sunday the envelope was still on the table. The chief difference between the two pictures was that in one Lincoln had his knees crossed and in the other the ankles.

Lamon[2] noted that Lincoln wrote part of his intended Gettysburg address at Washington, covered a sheet of foolscap paper[3] with a memorandum of it, and before taking it out of his hat and reading it to Lamon he said that it was not at all satisfactory to him, that he was afraid he would not do himself credit nor come up to public expectation. He had been too busy to give it the time he would like to. . . .

Various definite motives besides vague intuitions may have guided Lincoln in his decision to attend and speak even though half his cabinet had sent formal declinations in response to the printed circular invitations they had all received. Though the Gettysburg dedication was to be under interstate auspices, it had tremendous national significance for Lincoln because on the platform would be the state governors whose cooperation with him was of vast importance.

---

1. Daniel Webster: An American statesman and orator (1782–1852).
2. Lamon: Ward Hill Lamon (1828–1893), an American lawyer and close associate of Abraham Lincoln.
3. foolscap paper: Paper measuring thirteen by sixteen inches in size.

Also a slander and a libel had been widely mouthed and printed that on his visit to the battlefield of Antietam nearly a year before he had laughed obscenely at his own funny stories and called on Lamon to sing a cheap comic song. Perhaps he might go to Gettysburg and let it be seen how he demeaned himself on a somber landscape of sacrifice.

His personal touch with Gettysburg, by telegraph, mail, courier, and by a throng of associations, made it a place of great realities to him. Just after the battle there, a woman had come to his office, the doorman saying she had been "crying and taking on" for several days trying to see the President. Her husband and three sons were in the army. On part of her husband's pay she had lived for a time, till money from him stopped coming. She was hard put to scrape a living and needed one of her boys to help.

The President listened to her, standing at a fireplace, hands behind him, head bowed, motionless. The woman finished her plea for one of her three sons in the army. He spoke. Slowly and almost as if talking to himself alone the words came and only those words:

"I have two, and you have none."

He crossed the room, wrote an order for the military discharge of one of her sons. On a special sheet of paper he wrote full and detailed instructions where to go and what to say in order to get her boy back.

In a few days the doorman told the President that the same woman was again on hand crying and taking on. "Let her in," was the word. She had found doors opening to her and officials ready to help on seeing the President's written words she carried. She had located her boy, camp, regiment, company. She had found him, yes, wounded at Gettysburg, dying in a hospital, and had followed him to the grave. And, she begged, would the President now give her the next one of her boys?

As before he stood at the fireplace, hands behind him, head bent low, motionless. Slowly and almost as if talking to himself alone the words came and as before only those words:

"I have two, and you have none."

He crossed the room to his desk and began writing. As though nothing else was to do she followed, stood by his chair as he wrote, put her hand on the President's head, smoothed his thick and disorderly hair with motherly fingers. He signed an order giving her the next of her boys, stood up, put the priceless paper in her hand as he choked out the one word, "There!" and with long quick steps was gone from the room with her sobs and cries of thanks in his ears.

Thus the Kentuckian, James Speed, gathered the incident and told it. By many strange ways Gettysburg was to Lincoln a fact in crimson mist. . . .

When Lincoln boarded the train for Gettysburg on November 18, his best chum in the world, Tad, lay sick abed and the doctors not sure what ailed him. The mother still remembered Willie[4] and was hysterical about Tad. But the President felt imperative duty called him to Gettysburg.

Provost Marshal General James B. Fry as a War Department escort came to the White House, but the President was late in getting into the carriage for the drive to the station. They had no time to lose, Fry remarked. Lincoln said he felt like an Illinois man who was going to be hanged and as the man passed along the road on the way to the gallows the crowds kept pushing into the way and blocking passage. The condemned man at last called out, "Boys, you needn't be in such a hurry to get ahead, there won't be any fun till I get there."

Flags and red-white-and-blue bunting decorated the four-car special train. Aboard were the three cabinet members, Nicolay and Hay,[5] army and navy representatives, newspapermen, the French and Italian ministers

---

4. Tad, Willie: Two of Lincoln's four sons. Willie had died in 1862.
5. Nicolay and Hay: John George Nicolay (1832–1901), Lincoln's private secretary, and John Milton Hay (1838–1905), the assistant private secretary.

and attachés. The rear third of the last coach had a drawing room, where from time to time the President talked with nearly everyone aboard as they came and went. Henry Clay Cochrane, lieutenant of Marines, noted:

"I happened to have a *New York Herald* and offered it to Mr. Lincoln. He took it and thanked me, saying, 'I like to see what they say about us. The news was about Burnside at Knoxville, Grant and Sherman at Chattanooga and Meade[6] on the Rapidan, all expecting trouble. He read for a little while and then began to laugh at some wild guesses of the paper about pending movements. It was pleasant to see his sad face lighted up. He was looking sallow, sunken-eyed, thin, careworn and very quiet. He returned the paper remarking among other things that when he had first passed over that road on his way to Congress in 1847 he noticed square-rigged vessels up the Patapsco River as far as the Relay House and now there seemed to be only small craft.

"At the Calvert Street Station Secretary Seward[7] began to get uneasy as we approached Baltimore. Upon reaching the Calvert Street Station in Baltimore all was quiet, less than two hundred people assembled, among them women with children in arms. They called for the President. He took two or three of the babies up and kissed them which greatly pleased the mothers. General Schenck and staff joined us and soon after the President went forward in the car and seated himself with a party of choice spirits, among whom was Mayor Frederick W. Lincoln of Boston, not a kinsman. They told stories for an hour or so, Mr. Lincoln taking his turn and enjoying it. Approaching Hanover Junction, he arose and said, 'Gentlemen, this is all very pleasant, but the people will expect me to say something to them tomorrow, and I must give the matter some thought.' He then returned to the rear room of the car. . . ."

At sundown the train pulled into Gettysburg and Lincoln was driven to the Wills residence, Seward to the Harper home fronting on the public square. A sleepy little country town of 3,500 was overflowing with human pulses again. Private homes were filled with notables and nondescripts. Hundreds slept on the floors of hotels. Military bands blared till late in the night serenading whomsoever. The weather was mild and the moon up for those who chose to go a-roaming. When serenaders called on the President for a speech, he made again one of those little addresses saying there was nothing to say. "In my position it is sometimes important that I should not say foolish things. [A voice: "If you can help it."] It very often happens that the only way to help it is to say nothing at all. Believing that is my present condition this evening, I must beg of you to excuse me from addressing you further."

The crowd didn't feel it was much of a speech. They went next door with the band and blared for Seward. He spoke so low that Hay could not hear him, but he opened the stopgaps of patriotic sentiment, saying in part, "I thank my God for the hope that this is the last fratricidal war which will fall upon the country which is vouchsafed to us by Heaven—the richest, the broadest, the most beautiful, the most magnificent, and capable of a greater destiny than has ever been given to any part of the human race." What more could a holiday crowd ask for on a fair night of moonlit November? Seward gave them more and closed: "Fellow citizens, good night." It was good night for him but not for them. They serenaded five other speakers. . . .

At dinner in the Wills home that evening Lincoln met Edward Everett, a guest under the same roof, and Governor Curtin[8] and others. About ten o'clock he was in his room, with paper and pencil ready to write, when

---

6. Burnside, Grant, Sherman, Meade: Union generals.
7. Seward: William Henry Seward (1801–1872), U.S. Secretary of State from 1861 to 1869.

8. Curtin: Andrew Gregg Curtin (1815–1894), governor of Pennsylvania from 1860 to 1867.

he sent a servant down for Judge Wills to come up. Still later, about eleven o'clock, he sent the servant down again for Judge Wills, who came up and heard Lincoln request to see Mr. Seward. Judge Wills offered to go and bring Seward from next door at the Harpers'. "No, I'll go and see him," said Lincoln, who gathered his sheets of paper and went for a half-hour with his secretary of state.

Whether Seward made slight or material alterations in the text on the sheets was known only to Lincoln and Seward. It was midnight or later that Lincoln went to sleep, probably perfectly clear in his mind as to what his speech would be the next day. The one certainty was that his "few appropriate remarks," good or bad, would go to an immense audience. Also he slept better for having a telegram from Stanton reporting there was no real war news and "On inquiry Mrs. Lincoln informs me that your son is better this evening."

Fifteen thousand, some said thirty thousand or fifty thousand people were on Cemetery Hill for the exercises the next day when the procession from Gettysburg arrived afoot and horseback representing the United States government, the army and navy, governors of states, mayors of cities, a regiment of troops, hospital corps, telegraph-company representatives, Knights Templar, Masonic Fraternity, Odd Fellows, and other benevolent associations, the press, fire departments, citizens of Pennsylvania and other States. They were scheduled to start at ten o'clock and at that hour of the clock Lincoln in a black suit, high silk hat, and white gloves came out of the Wills residence and mounted a horse. A crowd was on hand and he held a reception on horseback. At eleven the parade began to move. The President's horse seemed small for him, as some looked at it. Clark E. Carr, just behind the President, believed he noticed that the President sat erect and looked majestic to begin with and then got to thinking so that his body leaned forward, his arms hung limp, and his head bent far down.

A long telegram sent by Stanton at ten o'clock from Washington had been handed him. Burnside seemed safe though threatened at Knoxville, Grant was starting a big battle at Chattanooga, and "Mrs. Lincoln reports your son's health as a great deal better and he will be out today."

The march of the procession of military and civic bodies began. "Mr. Lincoln was mounted upon a young and beautiful chestnut horse, the largest in the Cumberland Valley," wrote Lieutenant Cochrane. This seemed the first occasion that anyone had looked at the President mounted with a feeling that just the right horse had been picked to match his physical length. "His towering figure surmounted by a high silk hat made the rest of us look small," thought Cochrane. . . . The President rode "easily, bowing occasionally to right or left," noted Cochrane, while Seward lacked dignity, his trousers working up over the shoe tops to show his homemade gray socks. Seward was "entirely unconscious" that the secretary of state looked funny—and nobody really cared. In the town of Gettysburg men with wounds still lingered in hospitals. And many flags along the main street were at half-mast for sorrow not yet over.

Minute guns spoke while the procession moved along Baltimore Street to the Emmitsburg Road, then by way of the Taneytown Road to the cemetery, where troop lines stood in salute to the President.

The march was over in fifteen minutes. But Mr. Everett, the orator of the day, had not arrived. Bands played till noon. Mr. Everett arrived. . . .

The United States House chaplain, the Reverend Thomas H. Stockton, offered a prayer while the thousands stood with uncovered heads. . . .

Benjamin B. French, officer in charge of buildings in Washington, introduced the Honorable Edward Everett, orator of the day, who rose, bowed low to Lincoln, saying, "Mr. President." Lincoln responded, "Mr. Everett." The orator of the day then stood in silence before a crowd that stretched to limits that would test his voice. Beyond and around were the wheat fields, the meadows, the peach orchards, long slopes of land, and five and seven miles farther the contemplative blue ridge of a low mountain range. His eyes could sweep them as he faced the audience. He had taken note of it in his prepared and rehearsed address. "Overlooking these broad fields now reposing from the labors of the waning year, the mighty Alleghenies dimly towering before us, the graves of our brethren beneath our feet, it is with hesitation that I raise my poor voice to break the eloquent silence of God and Nature. But the duty to which you have called me must be performed—grant me, I pray you, your indulgence and your sympathy." Everett proceeded, "It was appointed by law in Athens," and gave an extended sketch of the manner in which the Greeks cared for their dead who fell in battle. He spoke of the citizens assembled to consecrate the day. "As my eye ranges over the fields whose sods were so lately moistened by the blood of gallant and loyal men, I feel, as never before, how truly it was said of old that it is sweet and becoming to die for one's country."

Northern cities would have been trampled in conquest but for "those who sleep beneath our feet," said the orator. He gave an outline of how the war began, traversed decisive features of the three days' battles at Gettysburg, discussed the doctrine of state sovereignty and denounced it, drew parallels from European history, and came to his peroration[9] quoting Pericles[10] on dead patriots: "The whole earth is the sepulcher of illustrious men." The men of nineteen sister states had stood side by side on the perilous ridges. "Seminary Ridge, the Peach-Orchard, Cemetery, Culp, and Wolf Hill, Round Top, Little Round Top, humble names, henceforward dear and famous—no lapse of time, no distance

of space, shall cause you to be forgotten." He had spoken for an hour and fifty-seven minutes, some said a trifle over two hours, repeating almost word for word an address that occupied nearly two newspaper pages, as he had written it and as it had gone in advance sheets to many newspapers.

Everett came to his closing sentence without a faltering voice: "Down to the latest period of recorded time, in the glorious annals of our common country there will be no brighter page than that which relates THE BATTLES OF GETTYSBURG." It was the effort of his life and embodied the perfections of the school of oratory in which he had spent his career. His erect form and sturdy shoulders, his white hair and flung-back head at dramatic points, his voice, his poise, and chiefly some quality of inside goodheartedness, held most of his audience to him, though the people in the front rows had taken their seats three hours before his oration closed. . . .

Having read Everett's address, Lincoln knew when the moment drew near for him to speak. He took out his own manuscript from a coat pocket, put on his steel-bowed glasses, stirred in his chair, looked over the manuscript, and put it back in his pocket. The specially chosen Ward Hill Lamon rose and spoke the words "The President of the United States," who rose, and holding in one hand the two sheets of paper at which he occasionally glanced, delivered the address in his high-pitched and clear-carrying voice. The *Cincinnati Commercial* reporter wrote, "The President rises slowly, draws from his pocket a paper, and, when commotion subsides, in a sharp, unmusical treble voice, reads the brief and pithy remarks." Hay wrote in his diary, "The President, in a firm, free way, with more grace than is his wont, said his half dozen words of consecration." Charles Hale of the *Boston Advertiser*, also officially representing Governor Andrew of Massachusetts, had notebook and pencil in hand, took down the slow-spoken words of the President, as follows:

---

9. peroration (per′ ə rā′ shən) *n.*: The concluding part of a speech.
10. Pericles (per′ ə klēz′): Ancient Greek statesman and general (495?–429 B.C.).

Fourscore and seven years ago, our fathers brought forth upon this continent a new nation, conceived in liberty and dedicated to the proposition that all men are created equal.

Now we are engaged in a great civil war, testing whether that nation—or any nation, so conceived and so dedicated—can long endure.

We are met on a great battlefield of that war. We are met to dedicate a portion of it as the final resting place of those who have given their lives that that nation might live.

It is altogether fitting and proper that we should do this.

But, in a larger sense, we cannot dedicate, we cannot consecrate, we cannot hallow, this ground. The brave men, living and dead, who struggled here, have consecrated it, far above our power to add or to detract.

The world will very little note nor long remember what we say here; but it can never forget what they did here.

It is for us, the living, rather, to be dedicated here, to the unfinished work that they have thus far so nobly carried on. It is rather for us to be here dedicated to the great task remaining before us; that from these honored dead we take increased devotion to that cause for which they here gave the last full measure of devotion; that we here highly resolve that these dead shall not have died in vain; that the nation shall, under God, have a new birth of freedom, and that government of the people, by the people, for the people, shall not perish from the earth.

In a speech to serenaders just after the battle of Gettysburg four and a half months before, Lincoln had referred to the founding of the republic as taking place "eighty odd years since." Then he had hunted up the exact date, which was eighty-seven years since, and phrased it "Fourscore and seven years ago" instead of "Eighty-seven years since." Also in the final copy Lincoln wrote "We have come" instead of the second "We are met" that Hale reported.

In the written copy of his speech from which he read Lincoln used the phrase "our poor power." In other copies of the speech which he wrote out later he again used the phrase "our poor power." So it was evident that he meant to use the word "poor" when speaking to his audience, but he omitted it. Also in the copy held in his hands while facing the audience he had not written the words "under God," though he did include those words in later copies which he wrote. Therefore the words "under God" were decided upon after he wrote the text the night before at the Wills residence.

The *New York Tribune* and many other newspapers indicated "[Applause.]" at five places in the address and "[Long continued applause.]" at the end. The applause, however, according to most of the responsible witnesses, was formal and perfunctory, a tribute to the occasion, to the high office, to the array of important men of the nation on the platform, by persons who had sat as an audience for three hours. Ten sentences had been spoken in five minutes, and some were surprised that it should end before the orator had really begun to get his outdoor voice.

A photographer had made ready to record a great historic moment, had bustled about with his dry plates, his black box on a tripod, and before he had his head under the hood for an exposure, the President had said "by the people, for the people" and the nick of time was past for a photograph.

The New York Times reporter gave his summary of the program by writing: "The opening prayer by Reverend Mr. Stockton was touching and beautiful, and produced quite as much effect upon the audience as the classic sentences of the orator of the day. President Lincoln's address was delivered in a clear loud tone of voice, which could be distinctly heard at the extreme limits of the large assemblage. It was delivered (or rather read from a sheet of paper which the speaker held in his hand) in a very deliberate manner, with strong emphasis, and with a most businesslike air."

The *Philadelphia Press* man, John Russell Young, privately felt that Everett's speech was the performance of a great actor whose art was too evident, that it was "beautiful but cold as ice." The *New York Times* man noted: "Even while Mr. Everett was delivering his splendid oration, there were as many people wandering about the fields, made memorable by the fierce struggles of July, as stood around the stand listening to his eloquent periods. They seem to have considered, with President Lincoln, that it was not what was *said* here, but what was *done* here, that deserved their attention. . . . In wandering about these battlefields, one is astonished and indignant to find at almost every step of his progress the carcasses of dead horses which breed pestilence in the atmosphere. I am told that more than a score of deaths have resulted from this neglect in the village of Gettysburg the past summer; in the house in which I was compelled to seek lodgings, there are now two boys sick with typhoid fever attributed to this cause. Within a stone's throw of the whitewashed hut occupied as the headquarters of General Meade, I counted yesterday no less than ten carcasses of dead horses, lying on the ground where they were struck by the shells of the enemy."

The audience had expected, as the printed program stipulated, "Dedicatory Remarks, by the President of the United States." No eloquence was promised. Where eloquence is in flow the orator must have time to get tuned up, to expatiate and expand while building toward his climaxes, it was supposed. The *New York Tribune* man and other like observers merely reported the

words of the address with the one preceding sentence: "The dedicatory remarks were then delivered by the President." These reporters felt no urge to inform their readers about how Lincoln stood, what he did with his hands, how he moved, vocalized, or whether he emphasized or subdued any parts of the address. Strictly, no address as such was on the program from him. He was down for just a few perfunctory "dedicatory remarks."

According to Lamon, Lincoln himself felt that about all he had given the audience was ordinary garden-variety dedicatory remarks, for Lamon wrote that Lincoln told him just after delivering the speech that he had regret over not having prepared it with greater care. "Lamon, that speech won't *scour*. It is a flat failure and the people are disappointed." On the farms where Lincoln grew up as a boy when wet soil stuck to the mold board of a plow they said it didn't "scour."

The nearby *Patriot and Union* of Harrisburg took its fling: "The President succeeded on this occasion because he acted without sense and without constraint in a panorama that was gotten up more for the benefit of his party than for the glory of the nation and the honor of the dead. . . . We pass over the silly remarks of the President; for the credit of the nation we are willing that the veil of oblivion shall be dropped over them and that they shall no more be repeated or thought of. . . ."

Everett's opinion of the speech he heard Lincoln deliver was written in a note to Lincoln the next day and was more than mere courtesy: "I should be glad if I could flatter myself that I came as near to the central idea of the occasion in two hours as you did in two minutes." Lincoln's immediate reply was: "In our respective parts yesterday, you could not have been excused to make a short address, nor I a long one. I am pleased to know that, in your judgment, the little I did say was not entirely a failure. . . ."

The ride to Washington took until midnight. Lincoln was weary, talked little, stretched out on one of the side seats in the drawing room and had a wet towel laid across his eyes and forehead.

He had stood that day, the world's foremost spokesman of popular government, saying that democracy was yet worth fighting for. He had spoken as one in mist who might head on deeper yet into mist. He incarnated the assurances and pretenses of popular government, implied that it could and might perish from the earth. What he meant by "a new birth of freedom" for the nation could have a thousand interpretations. The taller riddles of democracy stood up out of the address. It had the dream touch of vast and furious events epitomized for any foreteller to read what was to come. He did not assume that the drafted soldiers, substitutes, and bounty-paid privates had died willingly under Lee's shot and shell, in deliberate consecration of themselves to the Union cause. His cadences sang the ancient song that where there is freedom men have fought and sacrificed for it, and that freedom is worth men's dying for. For the first time since he became President he had on a dramatic occasion declaimed, howsoever it might be read, Jefferson's proposition which had been a slogan of the Revolutionary War—"All men are created equal"—leaving no other inference than that he regarded the Negro slave as a man. His outwardly smooth sentences were inside of them gnarled and tough with the enigmas of the American experiment.

Back at Gettysburg the blue haze of the Cumberland Mountains had dimmed till it was a blur in a nocturne. The moon was up and fell with a bland golden benevolence on the new-made graves of soldiers, on the sepulchers of old settlers, on the horse carcasses of which the onrush of war had not yet permitted removal. The *New York Herald* man walked amid them and ended the story he sent his paper: "The air, the trees, the graves are silent. Even the relic hunters are gone now. And the soldiers here never wake to the sound of reveille."

In many a country cottage over the land, a tall old clock in a quiet corner told time in a ticktock deliberation. Whether the orchard branches hung with pink-spray blossoms or icicles of sleet, whether the outside news was seedtime or harvest, rain or drought, births or deaths, the swing of the pendulum was right and left and right and left in a ticktock deliberation.

The face and dial of the clock had known the eyes of a boy who listened to its ticktock and learned to read its minute and hour hands. And the boy had seen years measured off by the swinging pendulum, and grown to man size, had gone away. And the people in the cottage knew that the clock would stand there and the boy never again come into the room and look at the clock with the query, "What is the time?"

In a row of graves of the unidentified the boy would sleep long in the dedicated final resting place at Gettysburg. Why he had gone away and why he would never come back had roots in some mystery of flags and drums, of national fate in which individuals sink as in a deep sea, of men swallowed and vanished in a man-made storm of smoke and steel.

The mystery deepened and moved with ancient music and inviolable consolation because a solemn man of authority had stood at the graves of the unidentified and spoken the words "We cannot consecrate—we cannot hallow—this ground. The brave men, living and dead, who struggled here, have consecrated it far above our poor power to add or detract. . . . From these honored dead we take increased devotion to that cause for which they gave the last full measure of devotion."

To the backward and forward pendulum swing of a tall old clock in a quiet corner they might read those cadenced words while outside the windows the first flurry of snow blew across the orchard and down over the meadow, the beginnings of winter in a gunmetal gloaming to be later arched with a star-flung sky.

from *Abraham Lincoln: The War Years—Lincoln Speaks at Gettysburg*   849

THINKING ABOUT THE SELECTION

Recalling

1. (a) What was the occasion of Lincoln's speech? (b) Why did the occasion have "tremendous national significance" for Lincoln?
2. (a) How had Lincoln responded when a woman had asked him to release one of her three sons from the army? (b) Why had she returned several days later?
3. How does Lincoln respond when "serenaders call on" him for a speech just after his arrival in Gettysburg?
4. (a) How long does Edward Everett's speech last? (b) How does Lincoln know when Everett is about to finish speaking?
5. (a) What is Lincoln's assessment of his own address? (b) What is Everett's opinion of Lincoln's address?

Interpreting

6. (a) What is Sandburg's attitude toward Lincoln? (b) How is his attitude conveyed in this selection?
7. (a) How does Lincoln's speech contrast with Everett's speech? (b) What qualities of Lincoln's speech are highlighted by this contrast?

Applying

8. Considering the historical significance of the Gettysburg Address, what is surprising about the immediate responses to the address?

ANALYZING LITERATURE

Understanding Biography

A biography is an account of a person's life written by another person. Biographers recount the central facts of the subject's life and present their interpretations of these events.

1. Why is Lincoln a good subject for a biography?
2. How does Sandburg's frequent use of quotes from eyewitnesses contribute to the reliability and authenticity of his account?

3. What conclusion does Sandburg draw about the addition of the words "under God" to Lincoln's speech?
4. What does Sandburg mean when he comments that Lincoln's "outwardly smooth sentences were inside of them gnarled and tough with the enigmas of the American experience"?
5. Carl Sandburg had great admiration for the American worker—the common man. Why would he have been especially interested in Abraham Lincoln? Explain your answer.

CRITICAL THINKING AND READING

Evaluating the Subject of a Biography

Sandburg's account of the events leading up to and following the Gettysburg Address reveals a good deal about Lincoln's personality. For example, Lincoln's ability to prepare his speech in such a short amount of time reveals the fact that he was a gifted writer and a man of great energy.

1. What does Lincoln's response to the woman's request regarding her three sons reveal about his personality?
2. What does Lincoln's assessment of his own address reveal about his personality?

THINKING AND WRITING

Writing a Biographical Sketch

Imagine that you have been asked to write a biographical sketch for your school newspaper. Review the freewriting you did before reading the selection, and prepare a short list of the central events in the subject's life. When you write your biography, recount the events in chronological order. If possible, use direct quotations. When you revise, make sure that you have included your own insights into your subject's life. Proofread your sketch and prepare a final draft.

Poetry

BLACK AND WHITE, 1930
Georgia O'Keeffe
The Whitney Museum of Art

EZRA POUND

1885–1972

More than any other poet, Ezra Pound was responsible for the dramatic changes that occurred in American poetry during the Modern Age. Urging writers to "make it new," Pound influenced many poets of his day to discard the forms, techniques, and ideas of the past and to experiment with new approaches to writing poetry.

Pound was born in Hailey, Idaho, and grew up in Philadelphia. After studying at the University of Pennsylvania and at Hamilton College, he traveled in Europe where he spent most of his life. Settling in London and later moving to Paris, he became a vital part of the growing Modernist movement. He influenced the work of the noted Irish poet William Butler Yeats and that of many American writers, including T. S. Eliot, William Carlos Williams, H. D., Marianne Moore, and Ernest Hemingway. He was also responsible for the development of Imagism, a literary movement that included Williams, H. D., and Moore.

Despite Pound's preoccupation with originality and inventiveness, his poetry reflects a deep interest in the past. In his early work, he often drew upon the poetry of ancient cultures, including Chinese, Japanese, and Provençal French. His dense, complex poems tend to be filled with literary and historical allusions. Often his poems are difficult to understand, because they are void of explanations or generalizations.

After 1920 Pound focused his efforts on writing *The Cantos,* a long poetic sequence in which he expressed his beliefs, reflected upon history and politics, and alluded to a variety of foreign languages and literatures. He eventually produced 116 cantos, which are widely varied in quality.

In 1925 Pound settled in Italy. During World War II, he was an outspoken supporter of the Italian dictator Benito Mussolini, mistakenly believing that a country governed by a powerful dictator was the most conducive environment for the creation of art. In 1943 Pound was indicted by the American government for treason, and a year later he was arrested by American troops and imprisoned. After being flown back to the United States in 1945, he was judged to be psychologically unfit to stand trial and was confined to a hospital for the criminally insane. He remained there until 1958, when he was released largely because of the efforts of his friends in the literary community. After his release he returned to Italy, where he spent the remainder of his life.

GUIDE FOR READING

In a Station of the Metro; The River-Merchant's Wife: A Letter; Canto 13

Imagism. Imagism was a literary movement established in the early part of the twentieth century by Ezra Pound and other poets. As the name suggests, the Imagists concentrated on the direct presentation of images, or word pictures. An Imagist poem expressed the essence of an object, person, or incident, without explanations or generalizations. Through the spare, clean presentation of an image, the Imagists hoped to evoke an emotional response—they hoped to freeze a single moment in time and to capture the emotions of that moment. To accomplish this purpose, the Imagists used the language of everyday speech, carefully choosing each word and avoiding any unnecessary words. Avoiding traditional poetic patterns, they also attempted to create new, musical rhythms in their poetry.

Because they generally focus on a single image, Imagist poems tend to be short. In their length and focus, many Imagist poems reflect the influence of the Japanese verse forms *haiku* and *tanka*. The haiku consists of three lines of five, seven, and five syllables. The tanka is written in five lines of five, seven, five, seven, and five syllables. Like Imagist poems, haikus and tankas generally evoke an emotional response through a single image.

Look For

As you read "In a Station of the Metro," look for the qualities of Imagist poetry.

Writing

"In a Station of the Metro" captures an impression of a crowd of people waiting on a dark subway platform. Freewrite about the types of impressions you have when you glance at a large crowd of people.

Vocabulary

Knowing the following words will help you as you read Ezra Pound's poetry.

apparition (ap′ ə rish′ ən) *n.*: The act of appearing or becoming invisible (p. 854, l. 1)
dynastic (dī nas′ tik) *adj.*: Of a period during which a certain family rules (p. 859, l. 2)

savants (sə vänts′) *n.*: Learned persons; scholars (p. 860, l. 43)
deference (def′ ər əns) *n.*: Courteous regard or respect (p. 860, l. 52)

In a Station of the Metro[1]

Ezra Pound

The apparition of these faces in the crowd;
Petals on a wet, black bough.

---

1. Metro: The Paris subway.

THINKING ABOUT THE SELECTION
Recalling

1. What is the setting of this poem?

Interpreting

2. Pound compares the faces of people on a subway platform with "petals on a wet, black bough." (a) What does this comparison suggest about the effect of society on individuality? (b) What does the comparison suggest about the fraility of human beings?

Applying

3. How does the image in the poem compare with your own image of the faces of people on a subway platform or at a train station?

ANALYZING LITERATURE
Understanding Imagism

Imagism was a literary movement that focused on evoking emotions through the spare, clean presentations of images, or word pictures. The Imagists also emphasized the creation of new rhythms, the use of common language, and precision in choosing words.

1. In "In a Station of the Metro," Pound juxtaposes, or puts together, two images to capture an impression of faces quickly glimpsed at on a dark subway platform. What emotions does the combination of images evoke?
2. Considering the common meaning of apparition as a strange figure appearing suddenly and thought to be a ghost, why do you think Pound chose the word *apparition* rather than *appearance*?
3. How does this word contribute to the emotional impact of the image?

The River-Merchant's Wife: A Letter

Ezra Pound

While my hair was still cut straight across my forehead
I played about the front gate, pulling flowers.
You came by on bamboo stilts, playing horse,
You walked about my seat, playing with blue plums.
5 And we went on living in the village of Chokan:[1]
Two small people, without dislike or suspicion.

At fourteen I married My Lord you.
I never laughed, being bashful.
Lowering my head, I looked at the wall.
10 Called to, a thousand times, I never looked back.

At fifteen I stopped scowling,
I desired my dust to be mingled with yours
Forever and forever and forever.
Why should I climb the lookout?

15 At sixteen you departed,
You went into far Ku-to-yen,[2] by the river of swirling eddies,
And you have been gone five months.
The monkeys make sorrowful noise overhead.

You dragged your feet when you went out.
20 By the gate now, the moss is grown, the different mosses,
Too deep to clear them away!
The leaves fall early this autumn, in wind.
The paired butterflies are already yellow with August
Over the grass in the West garden;
25 They hurt me. I grow older.
If you are coming down through the narrows of the river
    Kiang,

---

1. **Chokan** (Chō′ kän′): A suburb of Nanking, a city in the People's Republic of China.
2. **Ku-to-yen** (kōō′ tō′ yen′): An island in the Yangtze Kiang (yäng′ tsē kyang) River.

LANDSCAPE ALBUM IN VARIOUS STYLES
Ch'a Shih-piao
The Cleveland Museum of Art

Please let me know beforehand,
And I will come out to meet you
　　As far as Cho-fu-Sa.[3]

By Rihaku

---

3. Cho-fu-Sa (chō′ fōō′ sä′): A beach along the Yangtze Kiang River,
several hundred miles from Nanking.

THINKING ABOUT THE SELECTION

Recalling

1. Summarize the events in the life of the river-merchant's wife at fourteen, at fifteen, and at sixteen?
2. How deep has the moss grown since the river-merchant left?
3. (a) What hurts the river-merchant's wife? (b) What will she do if her husband comes down "through the narrows of the river Kiang"?

Interpreting

4. This poem is adapted from a Chinese poem by Li T'ai Po. When the original poem was written, marriages were arranged by parents according to Chinese custom. (a) How did the river-merchant's wife feel at the time of her marriage? (b) How are these feelings conveyed? (c) How have her feelings for her husband changed since the time of their marriage?
5. (a) How did the river-merchant feel about leaving home? (b) How are his feelings conveyed?
6. How do the details of the setting in the fifth stanza indicate the passage of time?
7. (a) How does the river-merchant's wife feel about her husband's absence? (b) How do the descriptions of the monkeys and butterflies reflect her feelings?

8. Explain how the tone of this poem is appropriate for the society in which the river-merchant's wife lives—a society governed by custom and tradition.

Applying

9. Many societies have believed in arranged marriages. What do you think are the benefits and the drawbacks of arranged marriages both for the individuals involved and for society as a whole?

THINKING AND WRITING

Writing About Imagism

Although "The River-Merchant's Wife" is not a pure Imagist poem, it does possess a number of the characteristics of Imagist poetry. Write an essay in which you discuss these characteristics. Review the poem noting the simplicity and precision of its language, its use of imagery to evoke emotions, and its musical rhythm. Write a thesis statement, and organize your notes into an outline. Then write your essay using passages from the poem to support your argument. When you revise, add transitions to connect your ideas.

Canto 13

Ezra Pound

Kung[1] walked
    by the dynastic temple and into the cedar grove,
       and then out by the lower river,
And with him Khieu, Tchi
5   and Tian the low speaking
And "we are unknown," said Kung,
"You will take up charioteering?
    Then you will become known,
"Or perhaps I should take up charioteering, or archery?
10 "Or the practice of public speaking?"
And Tseu-lou said, "I would put the defenses in order,"
And Khieu said, "If I were lord of a province
I would put it in better order than this is."
And Tchi said, "I would prefer a small mountain temple,
15 "With order in the observances,
    with a suitable performance of the ritual,"
And Tian said, with his hand on the strings of his lute
The low sounds continuing
    after his hand left the strings,
20 And the sound went up like smoke, under the leaves,
And he looked after the sound:
    "The old swimming hole,
"And the boys flopping off the planks,
"Or sitting in the underbrush playing mandolins."
25   And Kung smiled upon all of them equally.
And Thseng-sie desired to know:
    "Which had answered correctly?"
And Kung said, "They have all answered correctly,
"That is to say, each in his nature."
30 And Kung raised his cane against Yuan Jang,
    Yuan Jang being his elder,
For Yuan Jang sat by the roadside pretending to
    be receiving wisdom.
And Kung said
35   "You old fool, come out of it,
Get up and do something useful."

---

1. **Kung:** Confucius (551?–479? B.C.), Chinese philosopher and
teacher. Confucius emphasized devotion to parents, family and
friends, ancestor worship, and the maintenance of justice and peace.
Khieu, Tchi, Tian, Tseu-lou, Thseng-sie, and Yuan Jang were his disciples.

And Kung said
"Respect a child's faculties
"From the moment it inhales the clear air,
40 "But a man of fifty who knows nothing
    Is worthy of no respect."
And "When the prince has gathered about him
"All the savants and artists, his riches will be fully
    employed."
And Kung said, and wrote on the bo leaves:
45   If a man have not order within him
He can not spread order about him;
And if a man have not order within him
His family will not act with due order;
    And if the prince have not order within him
50 He can not put order in his dominions.
And Kung gave the words "order"
and "brotherly deference"
And said nothing of the "life after death."
And he said
55   "Anyone can run to excesses,
It is easy to shoot past the mark,
It is hard to stand firm in the middle."

And they said: If a man commit murder
    Should his father protect him, and hide him?
60 And Kung said:
    He should hide him.

And Kung gave his daughter to Kong-Tch'ang
    Although Kong-Tch'ang was in prison.
And he gave his niece to Nan-Young
65   although Nan-Young was out of office.
And Kung said "Wang[2] ruled with moderation,
    In his day the State was well kept,
And even I can remember
A day when the historians left blanks in their writings,
70 I mean for things they didn't know,
But that time seems to be passing."
And Kung said, "Without character you will
    be unable to play on that instrument
Or to execute the music fit for the Odes.
The blossoms of the apricot
    blow from the east to the west,
75 And I have tried to keep them from falling."

---

2. Wang: The first emperor of the Chou Dynasty, ruling China from
1122 to 1115 B.C.

Recalling

1. (a) What would Tseu-lou do to become known? (b) What would Khieu do if he "were the lord of a province"? (c) What would Tchi "prefer"?
2. (a) What does Thseng-sie ask Kung? (b) How does Kung respond?
3. What comment does Kung make about a "man of fifty who knows nothing"?
4. What does Kung write "on the bo leaves"?
5. According to Kung, what should a man do if his son commits murder?

Interpreting

6. This poem presents a dialogue between Confucius, or Kung, and several of his disciples. Confucius first asks his disciples how they will "become known." When they have finished responding, he comments that each has answered correctly "in his nature." (a) What does this comment reveal about his attitude toward his disciples? (b) What does the fact that he "smiled upon them equally" reveal?
7. What attitude concerning youth and old age does Confucius express?
8. What does Confucius mean when he speaks of a person who has "order within him"? (b) Why is it important for a person to have "order within him"?
9. (a) If the "blossoms of the apricot" symbolize the ancient Chinese culture and its traditions, what do you think Confucius means when he says that the blossoms are blowing "from the east to the west"? (b) What does he mean when he says that he has "tried to keep them from falling"?

Applying

10. What ideas does Confucius express that are applicable to life in our society?

T. S. ELIOT

1888–1965

Thomas Stearns Eliot's poetry received more critical acclaim than that of any other American poet of his time. At the same time, his poetry, along with his literary criticism, influenced other writers of the period.

Born into a prominent family in St. Louis, Missouri, Eliot grew up in an environment that promoted his intellectual development. During his years as an undergraduate at Harvard, Eliot published a number of poems in *The Harvard Advocate,* the school's literary magazine. Then, in 1910, the same year in which he earned his master's degree in philosophy, he completed "The Love Song of J. Alfred Prufrock," his first important poem.

When World War I broke out, Eliot settled in England. There he became acquainted with Ezra Pound, another young American poet. Recognizing Eliot's talent, Pound influenced the editor of the American magazine *Poetry* to publish "The Love Song of J. Alfred Prufrock," making Eliot's work available to the public for the first time.

The publication of "Prufrock," along with the other poems in his first book, *Prufrock and Other Observations* (1917), created a stir in the literary world. Eliot had used techniques that had never before been used. Focusing on the frustration and despair of life in modern urban societies, the poems in Eliot's first book also set the tone for the other poems he would produce during the early stage of his career.

In 1922 Eliot published *The Waste Land,* his most famous poem. The poem contrasts the spiritual bankruptcy that Eliot saw as the dominant force in modern Europe with the values and unity that governed the past. The impact of *The Waste Land* on other writers, critics, and the public was enormous, and it is regarded as one of the finest literary works ever written.

In 1928 Eliot became a devout member of the Church of England, after becoming a British citizen the previous year. These changes preceded radical changes in the focus of Eliot's writing, as evidenced by his exploration of religious themes in *Ash Wednesday* (1930) and *Four Quartets* (1943). These poems suggest that Eliot felt that religious belief could be a means for healing the wounds inflicted on a person by the spiritually bankrupt society he depicted in *The Waste Land*.

During his later years, Eliot also produced a sizable body of literary criticism and wrote several plays. In 1948 he received the Nobel Prize for Literature.

The Love Song of J. Alfred Prufrock

Stream of Consciousness. Stream of consciousness is a term originated by American psychologist William James to describe the natural flow of a person's thoughts. James noted that people's thoughts do not flow together in a logical, organized manner, but rather take the form of an unorganized and seemingly unconnected series of insights, memories, and reflections. During the early 1900's, writers began incorporating the ideas of James into their work by trying to capture the random movements of a character's thoughts to re-create the natural flow of people's thoughts. In using the stream-of-consciousness technique, the writers abandoned transitions and other linking devices used in ordinary prose, instead connecting thoughts through the character's natural associations.

As you read "The Love Song of J. Alfred Prufrock," look for Eliot's stream-of-consciousness technique. Notice how it re-creates the natural flow of the narrator's thoughts. How does it capture his indecision and doubt?

William James once wrote, "There is no more miserable human being than one in whom nothing is habitual but indecision." Freewrite, exploring the meaning of this quotation.

Knowing the following words will help you as you read "The Love Song of J. Alfred Prufrock."

insidious (in sid′ ē əs) *adj.*: Secretly treacherous (p. 864, l. 9)
digress (dī gres′) *v.*: Depart temporarily from the main subject (p. 866, l. 65)
malingers (mə liŋ′ gərz) *v.*: Pretends to be ill (p. 867, l. 76)

meticulous (mə tik′ yoo ləs) *adj.*: Extremely careful about details (p. 868, l. 115)
obtuse (äb toos′) *adj.*: Slow to understand or perceive (p. 868, l. 116)

The Love Song of J. Alfred Prufrock

T. S. Eliot

*S'io credessi che mia risposta fosse
a persona che mai tornasse al mondo,
questa fiamma staria senza più scosse.
Ma per ciò che giammai di questo fondo
non tornò vivo alcun, s'i'odo il vero,
senza tema d'infamia ti rispondo.*[1]

Let us go then, you and I,
When the evening is spread out against the sky
Like a patient etherized[2] upon a table;
Let us go, through certain half-deserted streets,
5 The muttering retreats
Of restless nights in one-night cheap hotels
And sawdust restaurants with oyster-shells:
Streets that follow like a tedious argument
Of insidious intent
10 To lead you to an overwhelming question . . .
Oh, do not ask, "What is it?"
Let us go and make our visit.

In the room the women come and go
Talking of Michelangelo.[3]

The yellow fog that rubs its back upon the window-panes,
15 The yellow smoke that rubs its muzzle on the window-
panes,
Licked its tongue into the corners of the evening,

---

1. S'io credessi . . . ti rispondo: The epigraph is a passage from Dante's *Inferno* in which one of the damned, upon being requested to tell his story, says: "If I believed my answer were being given to someone who could ever return to this world, this flame (his voice) would shake no more. But since no one has ever returned alive from this depth, if what I hear is true, I will answer you without fear or disgrace."
2. etherized (ē' thə rīzd) *v*.: Anesthetized with ether.
3. Michelangelo (mī' kəl an' jə lō): A famous Italian artist (1475–1564).

Lingered upon the pools that stand in drains,
Let fall upon its back the soot that falls from chimneys,
Slipped by the terrace, made a sudden leap,
20 And seeing that it was a soft October night,
Curled once about the house, and fell asleep.

And indeed there will be time[4]
For the yellow smoke that slides along the street
Rubbing its back upon the window-panes;
25 There will be time, there will be time
To prepare a face to meet the faces that you meet;
There will be time to murder and create,
And time for all the works and days[5] of hands
That lift and drop a question on your plate;
30 Time for you and time for me,
And time yet for a hundred indecisions,
And for a hundred visions and revisions,
Before the taking of a toast and tea.

In the room the women come and go
35 Talking of Michelangelo.

And indeed there will be time
To wonder, "Do I dare?" and, "Do I dare?"
Time to turn back and descend the stair,
With a bald spot in the middle of my hair—
40 (They will say: 'How his hair is growing thin!')
My morning coat, my collar mounting firmly to the chin,
My necktie rich and modest, but asserted by a simple pin—
(They will say: "But how his arms and legs are thin!")
Do I dare
45 Disturb the universe?
In a minute there is time
For decisions and revisions which a minute will reverse.

For I have known them all already, known them all—
Have known the evenings, mornings, afternoons,
50 I have measured out my life with coffee spoons;
I know the voices dying with a dying fall
Beneath the music from a farther room.
          So how should I presume?

---

4. there will be time: Similar to the narrator's plea in English poet
Andrew Marvell's "To His Coy Mistress": "Had we but world enough
and time . . ."
5. works and days: Ancient Greek poet Hesiod wrote a poem about
farming called "Works and Days."

MOONLIGHT, DOVEHOUSE STREET, CHELSEA
Algernon Newton
Fine Art Society, London Art Resource, NY

And I have known the eyes already, known them all—
55   The eyes that fix you in a formulated phrase,
And when I am formulated, sprawling on a pin,
When I am pinned and wriggling on the wall,
Then how should I begin
To spit out all the butt-ends of my days and ways?
60   And how should I presume?
And I have known the arms already, known them all—
Arms that are braceleted and white and bare
(But in the lamplight, downed with light brown hair!)
Is it perfume from a dress
65   That makes me so digress?
Arms that lie along a table, or wrap about a shawl.

And should I then presume?
And how should I begin?

     .   .   .   .   .   .

Shall I say, I have gone at dusk through narrow streets
70 And watched the smoke that rises from the pipes
Of lonely men in shirt-sleeves, leaning out of windows?. . .

I should have been a pair of ragged claws
Scuttling across the floors of silent seas.[6]

     .   .   .   .   .   .

And the afternoon, the evening, sleeps so peacefully!
75 Smoothed by long fingers,
Asleep . . . tired . . . or it malingers,
Stretched on the floor, here beside you and me.
Should I, after tea and cakes and ices,
Have the strength to force the moment to its crisis?
80 But though I have wept and fasted, wept and prayed,
Though I have seen my head (grown slightly bald) brought
     in upon a platter,[7]
I am no prophet—and here's no great matter;
I have seen the moment of my greatness flicker,
And I have seen the eternal Footman[8] hold my coat, and
     snicker.
85 And in short, I was afraid.

And would it have been worth it, after all,
After the cups, the marmalade, the tea,
Among the porcelain, among some talk of you and me,
Would it have been worth while,
90 To have bitten off the matter with a smile,
To have squeezed the universe into a ball
To roll it towards some overwhelming question,
To say: "I am Lazarus,[9] come from the dead,
Come back to tell you all. I shall tell you all"—
95 If one, settling a pillow by her head,
     Should say: "That is not what I meant at all.
     That is not it, at all."

---

6. I should . . . seas: In Shakespeare's *Hamlet*, the hero, Hamlet,
mocks the aging Lord Chamberlain, Polonius, saying, "You yourself,
sir, should be old as I am, if like a crab you could go backward (II.ii.
205–206).
7. head . . . platter: A reference to the prophet John the Baptist,
whose head was delivered on a platter to Salome as a reward for her
dancing (Matthew 14:1–11).
8. eternal Footman: Death.
9. Lazarus (laz' ə rəs): Lazarus is resurrected from the dead by
Jesus in John 11:1–44.

And would it have been worth it, after all,
Would it have been worth while,
100   After the sunsets and the dooryards and the sprinkled
      streets,
After the novels, after the teacups, after the skirts that trail
      along the floor—
And this, and so much more?—
It is impossible to say just what I mean!
But as if a magic lantern[10] threw the nerves in patterns on
      a screen:
105   Would it have been worth while
If one, settling a pillow or throwing off a shawl,
And turning toward the window, should say:
      "That is not it at all,
      That is not what I meant, at all."

      .   .   .   .

No! I am not Prince Hamlet, nor was meant to be;
110   Am an attendant lord, one that will do
To swell a progress,[11] start a scene or two,
Advise the prince; no doubt, an easy tool,
Deferential, glad to be of use,
115   Politic, cautious, and meticulous;
Full of high sentence,[12] but a bit obtuse;
At times, indeed, almost ridiculous—
Almost, at times, the Fool.

I grow old . . . I grow old . . .
120   I shall wear the bottoms of my trousers rolled.

Shall I part my hair behind? Do I dare to eat a peach?
I shall wear white flannel trousers, and walk upon the
      beach.
I have heard the mermaids singing, each to each.

I do not think that they will sing to me.

125   I have seen them riding seaward on the waves
Combing the white hair of the waves blown back
When the wind blows the water white and black.

We have lingered in the chambers of the sea
By sea-girls wreathed with seaweed red and brown
Till human voices wake us, and we drown.

---

10. magic lantern: An early device used to project images on a
screen.
11. To swell a progress: To add to the number of people in a
parade or scene from a play.
12. Full of high sentence: Speaking in a very ornate manner, often
offering advice.

THINKING ABOUT THE SELECTION

Recalling

1. (a) To what does the speaker compare the evening? (b) To what does he compare the streets?
2. For what "will there be time"?
3. (a) In lines 73–74 what does Prufrock say he should have been? (b) In lines 110–120 how does he describe himself? (c) In lines 126–128 whom does he claim to have seen?

Interpreting

4. Prufrock sees himself as being divided into two parts, with one part being eager to take action, while the other part struggles to hold him back. (a) How does the first line suggest that Prufrock sees himself as divided? (b) What do the images in lines 1–12 suggest about his outlook on life?
5. Throughout the poem Prufrock is on his way to an afternoon tea party and is trying to build up enough courage to tell a woman of his love for her. (a) How does Prufrock convey his apprehension and uncertainty in lines 23–48? (b) In what ways does he indicate that he feels that he is growing old? (c) How does the belief that he is growing old affect his decisions?
6. (a) What feelings about the other guests he expects to find at the party does Prufrock convey in lines 49–67? (b) How does he expect to be treated by the other guests? (c) What does he mean when he remarks, "I have measured my life with coffee spoons"?
7. (a) What fears does Prufrock express in lines 80–86? (b) In lines 97–110 how does he convey the fact that he has given in to his apprehension and has decided not to express his love to the woman? (c) How does he attempt to justify his decision?
8. (a) How do the questions Prufrock asks in line 122 contrast with the questions he had found so overwhelming earlier in the poem? (b) How do the images in lines 124–130 contrast with the images in the first stanza? (c) How does the final line suggest that reality has once again intruded upon his thoughts, leaving him in the same condition as when the poem started?

Applying

9. T. S. Eliot felt that the Modern Age was a time of confusion and uncertainty. In what ways does Eliot use Prufrock as an embodiment of the general sentiments of society as a whole?
10. (a) In what ways are many of us similar to Prufrock? (b) In what instances might our behavior be similar to Prufrock's?

ANALYZING LITERATURE

Understanding Techniques

The **stream-of-consciousness technique** allows a writer to re-create the natural flow of a character's thoughts. When using this technique, a writer uses only the character's natural associations to link thoughts. For example, in lines 70–74 Prufrock's thoughts drift from a contemplation of what he will say to the woman to the philosophical observation that he "should have been a pair of ragged claws."

1. Find two other instances in which Prufrock's thoughts drift from his immediate concerns to general philosophical observations.
2. What natural associations connect Prufrock's immediate concerns with his more general concerns.

CRITICAL THINKING AND READING

Interpreting Allusions

Interpreting the meaning of an **allusion**—a reference to another literary work or a figure, place, or event from history, religion, or mythology—may involve research. For example, to interpret the meaning of Eliot's allusion to Shakespeare's *Hamlet* (lines 111–119), you would have to consult the play itself, a critical essay, or a plot summary.

1. (a) Find two other allusions used by Eliot in the poem. (b) Interpret the meaning of each.
2. Do you think the use of allusions enriches the poem? Explain your answer.

WALLACE STEVENS

1879–1955

Wallace Stevens believed that the goal of poetry is to capture the interaction of the imagination and the real world. As a result he spent his career writing poems that delved into the ways in which the physical world is perceived through the imagination.

Stevens was born and raised in Reading, Pennsylvania. After graduating from Harvard, he worked briefly as a journalist before deciding to attend law school. He practiced law for a short time, then accepted a job in the legal department of an insurance company in Hartford, Connecticut. Eventually he became the company's vice-president.

Stevens did not publish his first collection of poetry, *Harmonium* (1923), until he was over forty. Although the book received little recognition from the general public, it earned praise from critics and other poets. In the poems in this book, Stevens uses dazzling imagery to capture the beauty of the physical world, while at the same time expressing the dependence of this beauty on the perceptions of the observer.

During the second half of his life, Stevens published many more volumes of poetry, including *Ideas of Order* (1935), *Parts of a World* (1942), *Transport to Summer* (1947), *The Auroras of Autumn* (1950), and *Collected Poems* (1955), which earned him the Pulitzer Prize. Despite his success as a poet, however, Stevens continued his career in insurance. He rarely appeared in public and only began giving readings toward the end of his life.

While Stevens's early poems explore the ways in which the imagination shapes reality, his later work tended to be more abstract. He began focusing on such philosophical subjects as death and humanity's relationship with nature. Instead of exploring different ways of perceiving reality, he delved into different ways of contemplating and comprehending reality.

Throughout his career, however, Stevens's goal as a poet was "to help people live their lives." Stevens believed that life in the Modern Age was often uncertain and confusing, and that it was the duty of the poet to provide new ways of understanding the world. By writing poems that help us to see our role in shaping reality, he was able to accomplish his goal.

GUIDE FOR READING

Disillusionment of Ten O'Clock; Anecdote of the Jar

Literary Movements

Symbolism. Like many other writers of his time, Stevens was influenced by Symbolism, a literary movement that originated in France in the last half of the nineteenth century. Because people perceive the physical world in different ways, the Symbolist poets believed that the ideas and emotions that people experience are personal and difficult to communciate. As a result these poets avoided directly stating their own ideas and emotions in their poetry. Instead they tried to convey meaning through clusters of symbols—people, places, objects, or actions that have meanings in themselves and also represent something larger than themselves. Because of this reliance on symbols, Symbolist poems can often be interpreted in a number of different ways. Similarly many of Stevens's poems can be interpreted in more than one way.

Look For

As you read Wallace Stevens's poetry, look for the symbols he uses to convey meaning.

Writing

In "Disillusionment of Ten O'Clock" the subject is people's dreams. Freewrite about dreams and their meanings. How do dreams relate to a person's life? What can dreams reveal about a person? How can people be affected by their dreams?

Vocabulary

Knowing the following words will help you as you read the poetry of Wallace Stevens.

slovenly (sluv′ ən lē) *adj.*: Untidy (p. 873, l. 3)

dominion (də min′ yən) *n.*: Power to rule (p. 873, l. 9)

Disillusionment of Ten O'Clock

Wallace Stevens

> The houses are haunted
> By white night-gowns.
> None are green,
> Or purple with green rings,
> 5 Or green with yellow rings,
> Or yellow with blue rings.
> None of them are strange,
> With socks of lace
> And beaded ceintures.
> 10 People are not going
> To dream of baboons and periwinkles.
> Only, here and there, an old sailor,
> Drunk and asleep in his boots,
> Catches tigers
> 15 In red weather.

THINKING ABOUT THE SELECTION

Recalling

1. By what are the houses haunted?
2. About what are the people "not going to dream"?
3. What happens "only here and there"?

Interpreting

4. In this poem Stevens contrasts an interesting, imaginative way of life with a dull, unimaginative way of life. (a) How does Stevens develop this contrast through his description of nightgowns? (b) How does his description of dreams further develop the contrast?
5. (a) Considering the poem's title and the reference to the houses as "haunted," which way of life do you think Stevens favors? (b) What comment does he seem to be making about modern life?

Applying

6. (a) What are some other things Stevens could have used to symbolize an unimaginative way of life? (b) What are some other things he could have used to symbolize an imaginative way of life?

THINKING AND WRITING

Responding to a Statement

Stevens felt that the goal of a poet was "to help people live their lives." Write an essay in which you discuss Stevens's comment in relation to the poem you have just read. Does it help people to live their lives? If so, how? When you finish writing, revise your essay, making sure that you have included enough evidence to thoroughly support your argument.

Anecdote of the Jar

Wallace Stevens

I placed a jar in Tennessee,
And round it was, upon a hill.
It made the slovenly wilderness
Surround that hill.

5   The wilderness rose up to it,
And sprawled around, no longer wild.
The jar was round upon the ground
And tall and of a port in air.

It took dominion everywhere.
10 The jar was gray and bare.
It did not give of bird or bush,
Like nothing else in Tennessee.

THINKING ABOUT THE SELECTION

Recalling

1. Where does the speaker place the jar?

Interpreting

2. In your own words, describe the jar's effect on the wilderness.
3. How is the impression of the jar that the speaker conveys in the third stanza different from that conveyed in the first two stanzas?

Applying

4. What types of objects do people create that have a dramatic effect on nature?

ANALYZING LITERATURE

Interpreting Symbolism

Symbolism was a literary movement that originated in France in the late nineteenth century and that influenced many English and American writers of the twentieth century. The Symbolist poets avoided directly stating ideas and emotions in their poetry. Instead they suggested meaning through the use of symbols.

How does this poem reflect the influence of the Symbolist poets?

CRITICAL THINKING AND READING

Supporting an Interpretation

Because of the Symbolists' reliance on symbols, their poetry can often be interpreted in several ways. Similarly, many of Wallace Stevens's poems can be interpreted in more than one way.

Find evidence in the poem to support each of the following interpretations.

1. The jar symbolizes the human imagination, and the poem points out how the appearance of nature is shaped by our perceptions. The poem also points out that our imaginations depend on the physical world for input.
2. The jar symbolizes human interference with nature, and the poem explores the effects of human creations on nature.

AMY LOWELL

1874–1925

A descendant of New England Renaissance poet James Russell Lowell, Amy Lowell was a strong-minded poet, whose determination helped her to establish herself as the leader of the Imagist movement.

Born in Brookline, Massachusetts, she received an excellent education and traveled extensively as a young girl. In 1913 she published her first volume of poetry, *A Dome of Many Colors,* but the book was not well received. A year later, after reading a poem by the Imagist poet H. D., she traveled to London, hoping to become part of the Imagist movement. She began focusing on creating vivid, precise images in her poetry. At the same time, she energetically promoted the Imagist movement in lectures and essays, and she eventually became the movement's leader. Unfortunately, however, Ezra Pound, the founder of the Imagist movement, found her poetry overly sentimental, and her emergence as the leader of the Imagist circle prompted him to sever his connection with the group.

Lowell published eleven volumes of poetry between 1913 and 1925, and three others appeared after her death in 1925. Her collection *What's O'Clock* (1925) won her the Pulitzer Prize.

"Patterns," one of her best-known poems, appeared in *Men, Women, and Ghosts,* published in 1916. In this poem she uses colorful images to reflect the emotions of a woman whose fiancé has just been killed in a war.

GUIDE FOR READING

Patterns

Dramatic Monologue. A dramatic monologue is a poem in which one character speaks to one or more silent listeners at a critical point in the speaker's life. The speaker's comments reveal the circumstances surrounding the conversation and offer insights into his or her personality. In T. S. Eliot's poem "The Love Song of J. Alfred Prufrock," for example, the speaker expresses his feelings of uncertainty and disjointedness while debating whether or not to declare his love for a woman.

As you read "Patterns," look for the situation that provokes the speaker's comments and take note of the insights the comments offer into the speaker's personality.

"Patterns" focuses on a woman's reaction to her fiancé's death during a war. Freewrite about the types of emotions that might be evoked by the loss of a loved one during a war.

Knowing the following words will help you as you read "Patterns."
brocaded (brō kād′ id) *adj.*: Having a raised design woven into it (p. 876, l. 5)

passion (pash′ ən) *n.*: Extreme, compelling emotion (p. 876, l. 20)

Patterns

Amy Lowell

IN A SHOREHAM GARDEN
Samuel Palmer
Victoria & Albert Museum, Trustees

I walk down the garden-paths,
And all the daffodils
Are blowing, and the bright blue squills.
I walk down the patterned garden-paths
5 In my stiff, brocaded gown.
With my powdered hair and jeweled fan,
I too am a rare
Pattern. As I wander down
The garden-paths.
10 My dress is richly figured,
And the train
Makes a pink and silver stain
On the gravel, and the thrift
Of the borders.
15 Just a plate of current fashion,
Tripping by in high-heeled, ribboned shoes.
Not a softness anywhere about me,
Only whalebone and brocade.
And I sink on a seat in the shade
20 Of a lime-tree. For my passion
Wars against the stiff brocade.
The daffodils and squills

Flutter in the breeze
As they please.
25 And I weep;
For the lime-tree is in blossom
And one small flower had dropped upon my bosom.

And the plashing of waterdrops
In the marble fountain
30 Comes down the garden-paths.
The dripping never stops.
Underneath my stiffened gown
Is the softness of a woman bathing in a marble basin,
A basin in the midst of hedges grown
35 So thick, she cannot see her lover hiding,
But she guesses he is near,
And the sliding of the water
Seems the stroking of a dear
Hand upon her.
40 What is Summer in a fine brocaded gown!
I should like to see it lying in a heap upon the ground.
All the pink and silver crumpled up on the ground.

I would be the pink and silver as I ran along the paths,
And he would stumble after,
45 Bewildered by my laughter.
I should see the sun flashing from his sword hilt and the
    buckles on his shoes.
I would choose
To lead him in a maze along the patterned paths,
A bright and laughing maze for my heavy-booted lover.
50 Till he caught me in the shade,
And the buttons of his waistcoat bruised my body as he
    clasped me
Aching, melting, unafraid.
With the shadows of the leaves and the sundrops,
And the plopping of the waterdrops,
55 All about us in the open afternoon—
I am very like to swoon
With the weight of this brocade,
For the sun sifts through the shade.
Underneath the fallen blossom
60 In my bosom,
Is a letter I have hid.
It was brought to me this morning by a rider from the
    Duke.[1]

---

1. the Duke: Probably John Churchill, Duke of Marlborough (1650–
1722), English general and statesman who commanded the united
English and Dutch armies during the War of the Spanish Succession
(1701–1714).

"Madam, we regret to inform you that Lord Hartwell
Died in action Thursday se'nnight."[2]
65 As I read it in the white, morning sunlight,
The letters squirmed like snakes.
"Any answer, Madam," said my footman.
"No," I told him.
"See that the messenger takes some refreshment.
70 No, no answer."
And I walked into the garden,
Up and down the patterned paths,
In my stiff, correct brocade.
The blue and yellow flowers stood up proudly in the sun,
75 Each one.
I stood upright too,
Held rigid to the pattern
By the stiffness of my gown.
Up and down I walked,
80 Up and down.

In a month he would have been my husband.
In a month, here, underneath this lime,
We would have broke the pattern;
He for me, and I for him,
85 He as Colonel, I as Lady,
On this shady seat.
He had a whim
That sunlight carried blessing.
And I answered, "It shall be as you have said."
90 Now he is dead.

In Summer and in Winter I shall walk
Up and down
The patterned garden-paths
In my stiff, brocaded gown.
95 The squills and daffodils
Will give place to pillared roses, and to asters, and to snow.
I shall go
Up and down,
In my gown.
100 Gorgeously arrayed,
Boned and stayed.
And the softness of my body will be guarded from embrace
By each button, hook, and lace.
For the man who should loose me is dead,
105 Fighting with the Duke in Flanders,
In a pattern called a war.
Christ! What are patterns for?

---

2. Thursday se'nnight: A week ago Thursday.

THINKING ABOUT THE SELECTION

Recalling

1. (a) Where does the speaker walk? (b) What is she wearing?
2. (a) About what had a messenger informed the speaker that morning? (b) How had she replied to the message?
3. (a) What does the speaker reveal about Lord Hartwell in the fourth stanza? (b) What does she vow to do in the fifth stanza?

Interpreting

4. The poem's speaker is an upper-class woman living in the early eighteenth century, whose life follows a rigid, formal "pattern." (a) How do her walks in the garden echo the overall pattern of her life? (b) How does the apearance of her dress reflect the pattern of her life? (c) How would getting married have broken the pattern?
5. (a) In what sense is war a "pattern"? (b) What type of "war" seems to be going on in the speaker's mind?
6. How does the final line contrast with the rest of the poem?

Applying

7. Provide your own answer to the woman's final question.

ANALYZING LITERATURE

Understanding Dramatic Monologue

A **dramatic monologue** is a poem in which one character speaks to one or more silent listeners at a critical point in the speaker's life. The speaker's comments reveal the circumstances surrounding the conversation and offer insights into his or her personality. For example, in "Pat-terns" the speaker's response to her fiancé's death provides insight into her personality.

1. What does the speaker's immediate reaction to the news of her fiancé's death reveal about her personality?
2. What is the speaker's attitude concerning her life?

UNDERSTANDING LANGUAGE

Understanding Word Origins

Many words came into English through French. For example, the English word *fatigue* comes from the French word *fatiguer,* meaning "to weary."

The following words from "Patterns" are of French origin. Use your dictionary to find the meaning of each word. Then give the French word and meaning from which it comes.

1. pattern	4. embrace
2. fashion	5. gorgeously
3. figure	

THINKING AND WRITING

Comparing and Contrasting Poems

Write an essay in which you compare and contrast "Patterns" with the Imagist poems of Ezra Pound (p. 854–860). Reread the poems, noting similarities and differences between Lowell's poem and Pound's. Organize your notes according to corresponding points of comparison and contrast. Then write your essay, using evidence from the poems to support your argument. When you finish writing, revise your essay, making sure you have quoted exactly. Proofread your essay and prepare a final draft.

H. D. (HILDA DOOLITTLE)

1886–1961

In 1913 when Ezra Pound reshaped three of Hilda Doolittle's poems and submitted them to *Poetry* magazine under the name "H. D., Imagiste," the Imagist movement was born. At the same time, it marked the beginning of a successful career for the young poet, who continued to publish her work under the name H. D. throughout the course of her career.

H. D. was born in Bethlehem, Pennsylvania. When she was fifteen she met Pound, who was a student at the University of Pennsylvania. She entered Bryn Mawr College but was forced to leave because of poor health. In 1911 she moved to London where she renewed her acquaintance with Pound. She married English poet Richard Aldington, a close friend of Pound's, in 1913. Together they studied Greek and developed a deep affection for classical literature. Unfortunately, however, their marriage failed during World War I, when Aldington enlisted in the army and was sent to France.

Like the Greek lyrics which she greatly admired, H. D.'s early poems were characteristically brief, precise, and direct. Often emphasizing light, color, and physical textures, she created vivid, emotive images. She also abandoned traditional rhythmical patterns, instead creating innovative musical rhythms in her poetry.

During the later stages of her career, H. D. focused on writing longer works. She wrote several novels, including *The Walls Do Not Fall* (1944) and *The Flowering of the Rod* (1946). She also wrote an epic poem, *Helen in Egypt*. Despite these later works, however, H. D. is remembered mainly for her early Imagist poetry.

GUIDE FOR READING

Writer's Techniques

Pear Tree; Heat

Imagery. Imagery refers to words or phrases that create mental pictures, or images, that appeal to one or more of the five senses—sight, hearing, touch, smell, or taste. Most often images appeal to our sense of sight. For example, H. D. creates a visual picture in our minds in "Pear Tree," when she writes "no flower ever opened so staunch a white leaf." Sometimes, however, images do not appeal to our sense of sight, and in some cases a single image appeals to more than one sense.

Imagery was the most vital element of Imagist poems. The Imagists focused their energy on presenting powerful and vivid images, while deleting unnecessary or abstract words and avoiding explanations and generalizations. As a result the Imagists depended on the power of their images to evoke emotions and to capture the readers' attention.

Look For

As you read H. D.'s poems, take note of how her vivid images appeal to your emotions and capture your attention.

Writing

Think of an image that you find especially striking. For example, you might think of a raging fire, a cherry tree in full bloom, or snow-covered pine trees swaying in the winter wind. Then prepare a list of sensory details you might use to capture this image.

Vocabulary

Knowing the following word will help you as you read H. D.'s poetry.
blunts (blunts) *v.*: Makes dull
(p. 885, l. 7)

Pear Tree

H. D.

Silver dust
lifted from the earth,
higher than my arms reach,
you have mounted,
5   O silver,
higher than my arms reach
you front us with great mass;

no flower ever opened
so staunch a white leaf,
10   no flower ever parted silver
from such rare silver;

O white pear,
your flower-tufts
thick on the branch
15   bring summer and ripe fruits
in their purple hearts.

ORCHARD IN BLOOM, LOUVEÇIENNES, 1872
Camille Pissarro
National Gallery of Art, Washington, D.C.

THINKING ABOUT THE SELECTION

Recalling

1. How high has the "silver dust" been "lifted"?
2. What do the flower-tufts of the white pear bring "in their purple hearts"?

Interpreting

3. (a) What is the "silver dust" referred to in the first stanza? (b) In what sense is the silver dust "lifted from the earth"?
4. (a) What time of year is the speaker describing? (b) How is this information conveyed?
5. In the final stanza, H. D. uses apostrophe, directly addressing the pear tree. How does her use of this technique help convey a sense of harmony between humanity and nature?

Applying

6. H. D. uses the color silver several times in her description. What associations do you have with the color silver?

THINKING AND WRITING

Writing an Imagist Poem

Write a poem in which you focus on creating a single vivid and emotive image. Imagine that you are writing your poem for someone who has never seen what you are describing. Start by reviewing the list of sensory details you made before. Add any additional details that come to mind. Write your poem in free verse, trying to capture the natural rhythms of ordinary speech. When you finish writing, revise your poem and share it with your classmates.

OVERHANGING CLOUD IN JULY
Charles Burchfield
The Whitney Museum

Heat

H. D.

O wind, rend open the heat,
cut apart the heat,
rend it to tatters.

Fruit cannot drop
5   through this thick air—
fruit cannot fall into heat
that presses up and blunts
the points of pears
and rounds the grapes.

10   Cut the heat—
plow through it,
turning it on either side
of your path.

THINKING ABOUT THE SELECTION

Recalling

1. What does the speaker ask of the wind?
2. According to the speaker, how does the heat affect fruit?

Interpreting

3. (a) What impression of heat does the speaker express? (b) How do the descriptions of the heat's interactions with the wind and fruit convey this impression?
4. What specific type of heat is the speaker describing?

Applying

5. (a) What is your own dominant impression of heat? (b) How does this compare with your dominant impression of cold?

ANALYZING LITERATURE

Understanding Imagery

Imagery refers to language that creates mental pictures, or images, that appeal to one or more of the five senses. For example, when H. D. writes, "Fruit cannot drop through this thick air," she creates an image that appeals to both our sense of touch and our sense of sight.

1. Find another image that appeals to both the sense of touch and the sense of sight.
2. Find an image that appeals only to our sense of touch.

CRITICAL THINKING AND READING

Analyzing the Effect of Imagery

The Imagists relied on imagery to capture the reader's interest and evoke an emotional response. For example, H. D.'s images of a blooming tree in "Pear Tree" are likely to evoke a sense of harmony and beauty and a feeling of hope.

1. What types of feelings do H. D.'s images of heat evoke?
2. Why are H. D.'s images of heat likely to capture the reader's interest?

WILLIAM CARLOS WILLIAMS

1883–1963

A close friend of Ezra Pound, William Carlos Williams was an important member of the Imagist movement. Opposing Pound's belief in using allusions to maintain a link to the past, Williams focused on capturing the common, everyday images of his time in an effort to create poetry with relevance to the lives of ordinary people.

Williams was born in Rutherford, New Jersey, where he spent most of his life. After graduating from the University of Pennsylvania Medical School, he became a pediatrician—a doctor who specializes in the care of children. In 1909 he published his first volume of poetry and began pursuing a double career as a poet and a doctor. Williams felt that his experiences as a doctor helped provide him with inspiration as a poet, crediting medicine for his ability to "gain entrance to . . . the secret gardens of the self."

While Williams's first book was modeled after the work of English Romantic poets, he soon developed his own distinctive voice. This voice emerged with the publication of *Spring and All* (1913), a book of mixed prose and poetry. In this book and in *In the American Grain* (1925), Williams made it clear that his aim was to capture the essence of modern American life by depicting a variety of ordinary people, objects, and experiences using up-to-date, everyday language. He avoided presenting explanations or making generalizations, commenting that a poet should deal in "No ideas but in things." By this he meant that a poet should present concrete images that speak for themselves, evoking emotions and stimulating thoughts and ideas.

In 1948 Williams suffered a heart attack, and three years later he had the first of a series of strokes. He was forced to abandon his medical practice and writing became increasingly difficult. However, he still managed to produce *Paterson* (1946–1958), a five-part epic poem filled with observations about life in the city of Paterson, New Jersey, and two additional collections of poetry, *The Desert Music* (1954) and *Pictures from Breughel and Other Poems* (1962). In 1963 he received the Pulitzer Prize for *Pictures of Breughel*.

The Locust Tree in Flower; The Red Wheelbarrow; This is Just to Say

Writer's Techniques

Rhythm. William Carlos Williams believed that rhythm—the arrangement of stressed and unstressed syllables in a poem—is the essence of poetry. In writing his poems, he attempted to shape the language of everyday speech into rhythmic units—lines and stanzas—that reflect and reinforce the meaning of the poems. Because each line serves as a separate rhythmic unit, you should read his poetry line by line, pausing briefly at the end of each line and pausing a bit longer at the end of each stanza. These pauses reinforce meaning by adding emphasis to important words, ideas, and images.

Look For

As you read William Carlos Williams's poetry, take note of how Williams's rhythmic units reflect and reinforce the meaning of the poems.

Writing

William Carlos Williams's poems focus on ordinary people, objects, and experiences. For example, in this group of poems, he writes about a locust tree, a red wheelbarrow, and the experience of eating plums from the icebox. Prepare a list of other ordinary experiences about which he might have written.

Vocabulary

Although Williams generally uses simple, easy-to-grasp language in his poetry, each word is carefully chosen to reflect the essence of everyday life. As you read his poetry, notice the precision of his language and the care that has gone into his choice of words.

PINK LOCUSTS AND WINDY MOON, 1959
Charles Burchfield
Collection of the Chase Manhattan Bank

The Locust Tree in Flower

William Carlos Williams

Among
of
green

stiff
5 old
bright

broken
branch
come

10 white
sweet
May

again

Recalling

1. This poem describes the locust tree during what season of the year?

Interpreting

2. How does the title help you to understand the poem?
3. (a) Which lines describe the locust tree before it blossoms? (b) Which lines describe the tree after it blossoms?
4. (a) What does this poem reveal about a locust tree's appearance? (b) How does the line arrangement add emphasis to the tree's important characteristics?
5. What is the significance of the final line?

Applying

6. How well does this poem support Williams's claim that poets should deal in "No ideas but in things"?

The Red Wheelbarrow

William Carlos Williams

so much depends
upon

a red wheel
barrow

5   glazed with rain
water

beside the white
chickens.

THINKING ABOUT THE SELECTION

Recalling

1. (a) With what is the red wheelbarrow glazed? (b) What does it sit beside?

Interpreting

2. What do you think depends on the red wheelbarrow?
3. To what sense do the images in the poem appeal?

Applying

4. (a) What types of associations do you have with the images in the poem? (b) What types of feelings do the images evoke?

ANALYZING LITERATURE

Understanding Rhythm

In writing his poems, William Carlos Williams attempted to shape the language of everyday speech into rhythmic units—lines and stanzas—that reflect and reinforce the meaning of the poems. For example, in "The Red Wheelbarrow," Williams calls our attention to the image of the wheelbarrow by breaking up the word and presenting it on two separate lines. His presentation of the word also reflects its meaning, since a wheelbarrow is composed of two separate parts.

1. What rhythmic and visual pattern does Williams establish in "The Red Wheelbarrow"?
2. How does the pattern help to emphasize each separate image?
3. How does the line break in the third stanza call our attention to and reflect the meaning of the image of rainwater?
4. What characteristic of the chickens is emphasized by the line break in the fourth stanza?

This Is Just to Say

William Carlos Williams

> I have eaten
> the plums
> that were in
> the icebox
> 5   and which
> you were probably
> saving
> for breakfast
>
> Forgive me
> 10 they were delicious
> so sweet
> and so cold

THINKING ABOUT THE SELECTION

Recalling

1. (a) What has the speaker eaten? (b) For what were the things he has eaten probably being saved?

Interpreting

2. How does the title relate to the poem?
3. To what senses do the images in the poem appeal?
4. (a) Why is the incident described in the poem important to the speaker? (b) How do the last three lines help to reveal the incident's importance?

Applying

5. Why do you think Williams might have chosen to write a poem about such a seemingly insignificant incident?

THINKING AND WRITING

Writing an Apology

"This is Just to Say" is, after all, a note of apology. However, the speaker doesn't seem to be at all sorry for what he did. Create a similar situation: a character does something he or she knows is incorrect but is actually glad to have done. For example, you might write about a sister borrowing a sweater without asking or a child giving into temptation and sneaking a piece of just-baked pie. Using Williams's poem as a model, write a note of apology. When you revise, make sure you have included details that appeal to the senses.

CARL SANDBURG

1878–1967

No poet better captured the spirit of industrial America than did Carl Sandburg. In his poems he paints a vivid portrait of the American working class, capturing its energy and enthususiasm in the lively, accessible manner that made him one of the most popular poets of his day. Sandburg wrote of poetry that it "is the opening and closing of a door, leaving those who look through to guess about what is seen during a moment."

The son of Swedish immigrants, Sandburg was born and raised in Galesburg, Illinois. Forced to go to work at an early age, Sandburg attended school on an irregular basis. After spending six years working at a variety of jobs, he enlisted in the army in 1898 to fight in the Spanish-American War. When he returned from the war, he enrolled at Lombard College. He left school shortly before his graduation, however, and spent several years traveling around the country, again working at a variety of jobs.

In 1913 Sandburg settled in Chicago, where he worked as a newspaper reporter. He began publishing poetry in *Poetry* magazine, a highly-regarded literary journal based in Chicago, and in 1916 he published his first book, *Chicago Poems*. The book sold well and was praised for its passion and vigor. Sandburg earned widespread recognition and helped establish Chicago as one of the country's leading literary centers. During the next ten years, Sandburg published three more successful collections of poetry, *Cornhuskers* (1918), *Smoke and Steel* (1920), and *Slabs of the Sunburnt West* (1922).

While continuing to write poetry, Sandburg then began touring the country delivering lectures on Walt Whitman and Abraham Lincoln—two men whom he greatly admired—and started a career as a folk singer. He also spent a great deal of time collecting material for a biography of Lincoln, and he prepared an anthology of American folk songs, *The American Songbook* (1927). His multivolume Lincoln biography won the Pulitzer Prize in 1940, and in 1951 he received a second Pulitzer Prize for his *Complete Poems*. Sandburg was also awarded the United States Presidential Medal in 1964, and he was asked to address a joint session of Congress on the 150th anniversary of Lincoln's birth. During his later years, he lived on a farm in North Carolina, where he continued to write poetry and work on his autobiography.

GUIDE FOR READING

Grass; *from* The People, Yes; Chicago

Writer's Techniques

Free Verse. Heavily influenced by the poetry of Walt Whitman, Carl Sandburg composed his poems using long open lines of free verse—verse that has irregular meter and line length. Written in simple, straightforward language, Sandburg's long free-verse lines capture the activity and energy of industrial America and mirror the natural rhythms of ordinary speech. Sandburg's use of simple language and natural rhythms reflects his interest in common people—who usually served as the subjects of his poems—and his desire to reach a wide audience.

Rather than creating a pattern through regular meter and line length, Sandburg generally establishes a pattern in his poems through the use of parallelism—the repetition of phrases or clauses that are similar in structure or meaning. His use of parallelism also helps to emphasize important ideas and contributes to the natural rhythm of his poetry.

Look For

As you read Carl Sandburg's poetry, look for how he uses free verse to recreate the natural rhythms of ordinary speech and take note of the energy and intensity of his work.

Writing

In his poem "The People, Yes," Carl Sandburg uses vivid imagery to capture the essence of the American people. Prepare a list of descriptive details you could use in describing the American people.

Vocabulary

Knowing the following words will help you as you read Carl Sandburg's poetry.

cyclonic (sī klän' ik) *adj.*: Like a cyclone, a windstorm with violent, whirling movement (p. 896, l. 7)
enigmatic (en' ig mat' ik) *adj.*: Perplexing; baffling (p. 896, l. 8)

wanton (wän' t'n) *adj.*: Senseless; unjustified (p. 898, l. 8)
cunning (kun' iŋ) *adj.*: Skillful in deception; crafty; sly (p. 898, l. 10)

Grass

Carl Sandburg

Pile the bodies high at Austerlitz and Waterloo.[1]
Shovel them under and let me work—
    I am the grass; I cover all.

And pile them high at Gettysburg
5 And pile them high at Ypres and Verdun.[2]
Shovel them under and let me work.
Two years, ten years, and passengers ask the conductor:
    What place is this?
    Where are we now?

10   I am the grass.
    Let me work.

---

1. Austerlitz (ôs′ tər lĭts′) **and Waterloo:** Sites of battles of the
Napoleonic Wars.
2. Ypres (ē′ pr) **and Verdun** (vər dŭn′): Sites of battles of World
War I.

MARSHES, DUNES AND FIELDS
Jane Freilicher

THINKING ABOUT THE SELECTION

Recalling

1. (a) What "work" does the grass perform at the battle sites mentioned in the poem? (b) What do people ask when they see the sites years after the battles?

Interpreting

2. (a) What is the attitude of the grass toward the events referred to in the poem? (b) What does this attitude suggest about humanity's relationship to nature?

3. How do the questions asked by the passengers reflect the pointlessness of war?

4. (a) Is Sandburg suggesting that it is possible for the death and destruction of war to be covered over and easily forgotten? Support your answer. (b) What is the purpose of the poem?

Applying

5. (a) What types of people do you think might share the attitude of the grass toward war? (b) What types of people do you think might strongly object to this attitude?

EDNA ST. VINCENT MILLAY

1892–1950

Although she spent only a few years in the New York City community known as Greenwich Village, Edna St. Vincent Millay will always be associated with the unconventional lifestyle and artistic experimentation characteristic of Greenwich Village during the 1920's. An enormously popular poet of her day, Millay embodied the rebellious, questing spirit that emerged in the aftermath of World War I.

Millay was born in Rockford, Maine, and began writing poetry at an early age. "Renascence," the first of her poems to attract public attention, was written when she was still in high school and appeared in a literary anthology when she was only twenty.

After graduating from Vassar College in 1917, Millay moved to Greenwich Village and quickly became part of the New York City artistic scene. While supporting herself by working as an actress and a playwright, she published a number of short stories and several collections of poetry, including *Renascence and Other Poems* (1917), *A Few Figs from Thistles* (1920), and *Second April* (1921). Her collection, *The Harp-Weaver and Other Poems* (1923), was awarded the Pulitzer Prize.

In 1923 Millay married Eugen Boissevain and moved to a farm in upstate New York where she spent the rest of her life. Although she continued to write poetry, she began turning away from writing the intensely personal lyric poems that had made her famous. Instead, deeply disturbed by the rise of fascism in Europe and the resulting war, she started focusing on current events in her poetry.

In her earlier poetry, which is generally regarded as her best, Millay displayed an ability to express the primary concerns of her time in a readily accessible, lyrical style. Like the work of other modern writers, her poetry expressed a rebellious attitude and explored the uncertainty and disillusionment of modern life. Yet her work remained linked to the past through her use of traditional verse forms and poetic devices.

GUIDE FOR READING

Renascence

Writer's Techniques

Theme. The theme is the central idea or insight about life that a writer hopes to convey in a literary work. Some themes are universal, occurring again and again in the literature of many eras. For example, the idea that nature is a powerful and wondrous force is a recurring theme in the literature of the Native Americans, the Transcendentalists, and the writers of our own century. Writers also frequently express themes that reflect specific concerns of the eras in which they lived. For example, because of rapid technological changes and the shattering effects of World War I, modern writers often focused on themes related to the uncertain, fragmentary, and confusing nature of life in the modern world.

In "Renascence," Edna St. Vincent Millay explores a universal theme—the idea that a person can be reborn or reawakened to discover a new understanding of the world. However, in describing the need to be reborn, she expresses concerns and attitudes that are characteristic of the modern period.

Look For

As you read "Renascence," look for the poem's theme and take note of how it reflects both universal concerns and concerns that are characteristic of the modern period.

Writing

Freewrite, exploring the reasons why a person might feel the need to experience a rebirth.

Vocabulary

Knowing the following words will help you as you read "Renascence."

manifold (man′ ə fōld′) *adj.*: Plentiful and varied (p. 902, l. 38)

omniscience (äm nish′ əns) *n.*: A knowledge of all things (p. 903, l. 55)

gall (gôl) *n.*: Bitterness (p. 903, l. 58)

finite (fī′ nīt) *adj.*: Having measurable limits (p. 904, l. 84)

myriad (mir′ ē əd) *adj.*: Countless (p. 905, l. 139)

sepulchered (sep′′l kərd) *v.*: Entombed; buried (p. 905, l. 140)

herald (her′ əld) *n.*: Messenger (p. 905, l. 149)

Renascence

Edna St. Vincent Millay

All I could see from where I stood
Was three long mountains and a wood;
I turned and looked another way,
And saw three islands in a bay.
5 So with my eyes I traced the line
Of the horizon, thin and fine,
Straight around till I was come
Back to where I'd started from;
And all I saw from where I stood
10 Was three long mountains and a wood.

Over these things I could not see:
These were the things that bounded me.
And I could touch them with my hand,
Almost, I thought, from where I stand!
15 And all at once things seemed so small
My breath came short, and scarce at all.
But, sure, the sky is big, I said:
Miles and miles above my head.
So here upon my back I'll lie
20 And look my fill into the sky.
And so I looked, and after all,
The sky was not so very tall.
The sky, I said, must somewhere stop . . .
And—sure enough!—I see the top!
25 The sky, I thought, is not so grand;
I 'most could touch it with my hand!
And reaching up my hand to try,
I screamed, to feel it touch the sky.

I screamed, and—lo!—Infinity
30 Came down and settled over me;
Forced back my scream into my chest;
Bent back my arm upon my breast;
And, pressing of the Undefined
The definition on my mind,
35 Held up before my eyes a glass
Through which my shrinking sight did pass
Until it seemed I must behold
Immensity made manifold;
Whispered to me a word whose sound
40 Deafened the air for worlds around,

THE SUN
Edouard Munch
Fotograf: O. Vaering

And brought unmuffled to my ears
The gossiping of friendly spheres,
The creaking of the tented sky,
The ticking of Eternity.

45 I saw and heard, and knew at last
The How and Why of all things, past,
And present, and forevermore.
The Universe, cleft to the core,
Lay open to my probing sense,
50 That, sickening, I would fain pluck thence
But could not,—nay! but needs must suck
At the great wound, and could not pluck
My lips away till I had drawn
All venom out,—Ah, fearful pawn:
55 For my omniscience paid I toll
In infinite remorse of soul.

All sin was of my sinning, all
Atoning mine, and mine the gall
Of all regret. Mine was the weight
60 Of every brooded wrong, the hate
That stood behind each envious thrust,
Mine every greed, mine every lust.

And all the while, for every grief,
Each suffering, I craved relief
65   With individual desire;
Craved all in vain! And felt fierce fire
About a thousand people crawl;
Perished with each,—then mourned for all!

A man was starving in Capri;[1]
70   He moved his eyes and looked at me;
I felt his gaze, I heard his moan,
And knew his hunger as my own.
I saw at sea a great fog bank
Between two ships that struck and sank;
75   A thousand screams the heavens smote;
And every scream tore through my throat.

No hurt I did not feel, no death
That was not mine; mine each last breath
That, crying, met an answering cry
80   From the compassion that was I.
All suffering mine, and mine its rod;
Mine, pity like the pity of God.

Ah, awful weight! Infinity
Pressed down upon the finite Me!
85   My anguished spirit, like a bird,
Beating against my lips I heard;
Yet lay the weight so close about
There was no room for it without.
And so beneath the weight lay I
90   And suffered death, but could not die.
Long had I lain thus, craving death,
When quietly the earth beneath
Gave way, and inch by inch, so great
At last had grown the crushing weight,
95   Into the earth I sank till I
Full six feet under ground did lie,
And sank no more,—there is no weight
Can follow here, however great.
From off my breast I felt it roll,
100 And as it went my tortured soul
Burst forth and fled in such a gust
That all about me swirled the dust.

Deep in the earth I rested now.
Cool is its hand upon the brow
105 And soft its breast beneath the head

---

1. Capri (ka prē'): An Italian island located near the entrance to the
Bay of Naples.

Of one who is so gladly dead.
And all at once, and over all
The pitying rain began to fall;
I lay and heard each pattering hoof
110 Upon my lowly, thatchèd roof,
And seemed to love the sound far more
Than ever I had done before.
For rain it hath a friendly sound
To one who's six feet under ground;
115 And scarce the friendly voice or face,
A grave is such a quiet place.

The rain, I said, is kind to come
And speak to me in my new home.
I would I were alive again
120 To kiss the fingers of the rain,
To drink into my eyes the shine
Of every slanting silver line,
To catch the freshened, fragrant breeze
From drenched and dripping apple trees.
125 For soon the shower will be done,
And then the broad face of the sun
Will laugh above the rain-soaked earth
Until the world with answering mirth
Shakes joyously, and each round drop
130 Rolls, twinkling, from its grass-blade top.

How can I bear it, buried here,
While overhead the sky grows clear
And blue again after the storm?
O, multi-colored, multi-form,
135 Belovèd beauty over me,
That I shall never, never see
Again! Spring-silver, autumn-gold,
That I shall never more behold!—
Sleeping your myriad magics through,
140 Close-sepulchred away from you!
O God, I cried, give me new birth,
And put me back upon the earth!
Upset each cloud's gigantic gourd[2]
And let the heavy rain, down-poured
145 In one big torrent, set me free,
Washing my grave away from me!

I ceased; and through the breathless hush
That answered me, the far-off rush
Of herald wings came whispering

---

2. gourd (gôrd) *n.:* The dried, hollowed-out shell of a piece of fruit
from a gourd plant, often used as a dipper or drinking cup.

150 Like music down the vibrant string
Of my ascending prayer, and—crash!
Before the wild wind's whistling lash
The startled storm-clouds reared on high
And plunged in terror down the sky!
155 And the big rain in one black wave
Fell from the sky and struck my grave.

I know not how such things can be;
I only know there came to me
A fragrance such as never clings
160 To aught save happy living things;
A sound as of some joyous elf
Singing sweet songs to please himself,
And, through and over everything,
A sense of glad awakening.
165 The grass, a-tiptoe at my ear,
Whispering to me I could hear;
I felt the rain's cool finger-tips
Brushed tenderly across my lips,
Laid gently on my sealèd sight,
170 And all at once the heavy night
Fell from my eyes and I could see!—
A drenched and dripping apple-tree,
A last long line of silver rain,
A sky grown clear and blue again.
175 And as I looked a quickening gust
Of wind blew up to me and thrust
Into my face a miracle
Of orchard-breath, and with the smell,—
I know not how such things can be!—
180 I breathed my soul back into me.

Ah! Up then from the ground sprang I
And hailed the earth with such a cry
As is not heard save from a man
Who has been dead, and lives again.
185 About the trees my arms I wound;
Like one gone mad I hugged the ground;
I raised my quivering arms on high;
I laughed and laughed into the sky;
Till at my throat a strangling sob
190 Caught fiercely, and a great heart-throb
Sent instant tears into my eyes:
O God, I cried, no dark disguise
Can e'er hereafter hide from me
Thy radiant identity!
195 Thou canst not move across the grass
But my quick eyes will see Thee pass,

Nor speak, however silently,
But my hushed voice will answer Thee.
I know the path that tells Thy way
200   Through the cool eve of every day;
God, I can push the grass apart
And lay my finger on Thy heart!

The world stands out on either side
No wider than the heart is wide;
205   Above the world is stretched the sky,—
No higher than the soul is high.
The heart can push the sea and land
Farther away on either hand;
The soul can split the sky in two,

210   And let the face of God shine through.
But East and West will pinch the heart
That can not keep them pushed apart;
And he whose soul is flat—the sky
Will cave in on him by and by.

THINKING ABOUT THE SELECTION

Recalling

1. (a) In the opening stanza, what does the speaker see "from where she stood"? (b) What does she see when she looks another way? (c) How do the things she sees affect her?
2. In stanza 3, what happens when the speaker screams?
3. (a) In stanza 4, what does the speaker come to know "at last"? (b) What lies open to her "probing sense"? (c) What "toll" does she pay for her "omniscience"?
4. What happens to the speaker when the earth beneath her gives way?
5. (a) What happens when the rain begins to fall? (b) What happens after the sky grows "clear and blue again"?
6. (a) According to the final stanza, how wide is the world? (b) How high is the sky? (c) What will happen to "he whose soul is flat"

Interpreting

7. In what sense is the speaker "bounded" at the beginning of the poem?
8. (a) What does the action of touching the sky symbolize? (b) Of what does the speaker become aware as a result of this action? (c) How does her awareness affect her?
9. (a) What does the speaker's death symbolize? (b) What realization does she come to that makes her want to be reborn?
10. (a) Restate the ideas presented in the final stanza in your own words? (b) How does the speaker's description of her experiences further develop this theme?

Applying

11. In what ways is the poem's theme reminiscent of Native American and Transcendentalist's themes concerning humanity's spiritual relationship with nature?
12. How does the speaker's need to be reborn reflect the Modernists' sense of disillusionment with the world?

BIOGRAPHIES

John Crowe Ransom (1884–1967)

A minister's son, John Crowe Ransom was born in Pulaski, Tennessee, and was educated at Vanderbilt University and at Oxford. He served as a professor of English at Vanderbilt and at Kenyon College. A poet, critic, and editor, he was one of the founders of both *The Fugitive* and *The Kenyon Review,* two important literary magazines. In his seemingly quiet and gentle poems, Ransom subtly expressed his awareness of life's ironies and the frailty of humankind. Much of his work reflected his affection for the rural, agrarian life of the South and his longing for the vanished culture of the pre-Civil War era. Set in a rural environment, "Janet Waking" explores the subject of the death of a child's pet in an aloof, unsentimental manner.

Archibald MacLeish (1892–1982)

A lawyer, teacher, editor, dramatist, and poet, Archibald MacLeish was born in Glencoe, Illinois. He attended Yale, where he distinguished himself in both academics and athletics. He earned a law degree but soon gave up the practice of law to devote himself to literature. His early poems, such as "Ars Poetica," reflect the influence of such Modernist poets as Ezra Pound and T. S. Eliot. However, he eventually changed his style and began using traditional poetic forms in an effort to make his work more accessible. In the 1930's, as fascism rose in Europe and social unrest grew in America, MacLeish became active in politics and began exploring social and political issues in his work. During his career, MacLeish produced more than thirty books and won three Pulitzer Prizes.

Marianne Moore (1887–1972)

Marianne Moore was born in St. Louis, Missouri, and attended Bryn Mawr College. As the editor of the highly-regarded literary journal, *The Dial,* she encouraged many new writers by publishing their work. However, she was hesitant about publishing her own work, despite the fact that it had been read and admired by many noted poets. In fact, her first book, *Poems* (1921), was published without her knowledge.

As part of the Modernist movement, Moore wrote poems that were unconventional in form, precise, inventive, and often witty. However, unlike most other Modernists, she chose not to write about the state of modern civilization. Instead, she wrote poems about such subjects as animals and other elements of nature. "Poetry," one of her most well-known poems, delves into the subject of poetry itself.

GUIDE FOR READING

Janet Waking; Ars Poetica; Poetry

Writer's Techniques

Pathos. Pathos is the quality in a work of literature that evokes a feeling of pity, compassion, or sorrow in the reader. Unlike the pity aroused by a tragedy—a drama in which a character suffers as a result of his or her own mistakes—pathos usually results from situations in which innocent characters suffer through no fault of their own. For example, "Janet Waking" arouses pity for a young girl who awakens to discover that her beloved pet has died.

Similes. A simile is an explicit comparison between two seemingly dissimilar things. This comparison is clearly indicated by a connecting word such as *like* or *as*. For example, the word *like* signals the comparison in the following simile: The sound of the explosion echoed through the air *like* thunder.

Similes force us to use our imaginations to see connections that our senses may not be able to perceive, and they make it possible for us to relate our inner selves to the outer world. Through the use of similes, a poet can enable us to visualize abstract concepts such as emotions and help us to understand the external world in human terms.

Look For

As you read "Janet Waking," take note of how the description of the young girl's suffering arouses pity. As you read "Ars Poetica," look for MacLeish's use of similes. As you read "Poetry," pay attention to the form and meaning of the poem.

Writing

In "Janet Waking" a young girl is devastated by the loss of her pet. Freewrite, exploring why you think children tend to react so strongly to the death of a pet.

Vocabulary

Knowing the following words will help you as you read the following poems.

transmogrifying (trans mäg′ rə fī′ iŋ) *v.*: Transforming in a grotesque manner (p. 911, l. 13)

rigor (rig′ ər) *n.*: Stiffness; rigidity (p. 911, l. 19)

translated (trans lāt′ id) *v.*: Transported (p. 911, l. 23)

palpable (pal′ pə b'l) *adj.*: Able to be touched, felt, or handled (p. 912, l. 1)

derivative (də riv′ ə tiv) *adj.*: Arrived at through complex reasoning (p. 914, l. 8)

literalists (lit′ ər əl ists) *n.*: People who insist on the exact meanings of words (p. 914, l. 20)

THE SICK CHICKEN
Winslow Homer
The Harold T. Pulsifer Memorial Collection
Colby College, Waterville, Maine

Janet Waking

John Crowe Ransom

Beautifully Janet slept
Till it was deeply morning. She woke then
And thought about her dainty-feathered hen,
To see how it had kept.

5   One kiss she gave her mother,
Only a small one gave she to her daddy
Who would have kissed each curl of his shining baby;
No kiss at all for her brother.

"Old Chucky, old Chucky!" she cried,
10   Running across the world upon the grass
To Chucky's house, and listening. But alas,
Her Chucky had died.

It was a transmogrifying bee
Came droning down on Chucky's old bald head
15 And sat and put the poison. It scarcely bled,
But how exceedingly

And purply did the knot
Swell with the venom and communicate
Its rigor! Now the poor comb stood up straight
20 But Chucky did not.

So there was Janet
Kneeling on the wet grass, crying her brown hen
(Translated far beyond the daughters of men)
To rise and walk upon it.

25 And weeping fast as she had breath
Janet implored us, "Wake her from her sleep!"
And would not be instructed in how deep
Was the forgetful kingdom of death.

THINKING ABOUT THE SELECTION

Recalling

1. (a) What does Janet think about when she awakens? (b) What does she do after she kisses her parents?
2. (a) How has Chucky died? (b) How does Janet respond to his death?

Interpreting

3. How do the adjectives used in describing Janet and her hen in the first two stanzas convey a sense of Janet's innocence?
4. How does Janet's behavior toward her family contrast with her behavior toward Chucky?
5. (a) Considering Janet's request in line 26, what is ironic, or surprising, about the title? (b) From what is Janet "waking" as a result of Chucky's death?

Applying

6. Do you think Janet's reaction to Chucky's death is typical for a child in her situation?

ANALYZING LITERATURE

Understanding Pathos

In describing Janet's reaction to Chucky's death, Ransom creates **pathos**—the quality in literature which evokes pity, tenderness, or sorrow in the reader. At the same time, he manages to treat the subject of death without resorting to sentimentalism—an overindulgence in emotion, usually resulting from a conscious effort to induce emotion.

1. How does the fact that the speaker maintains a detached, almost indifferent attitude throughout the poem help prevent the poem from becoming overly sentimental?
2. How does the precision with which the events are described help prevent sentimentalism?
3. Why is Ransom's precise, unsentimental description of the events enough to evoke our pity and sorrow?

Ars Poetica[1]

Archibald MacLeish

A poem should be palpable and mute
As a globed fruit,

Dumb
As old medallions to the thumb,

5 Silent as the sleeve-worn stone
Of casement ledges where the moss has grown—

A poem should be wordless
As the flight of birds.

A poem should be motionless in time
10 As the moon climbs,

1. The title is an allusion to Horace's "Ars Poetica," or "The Art of Poetry," which was composed about 20 B.C.

Leaving, as the moon releases
Twig by twig the night-entangled trees,

Leaving, as the moon behind the winter leaves,
Memory by memory the mind—

15 A poem should be motionless in time
As the moon climbs.

A poem should be equal to:
Not true.

For all the history of grief
20 An empty doorway and a maple leaf.

For love
The leaning grasses and two lights above the sea—

A poem should not mean
But be.

THINKING ABOUT THE SELECTION

Recalling

1. (a) In what sense is a poem like a "globed fruit"? (b) In what sense is a poem like "old medallions of the thumb"? (c) In what sense is a poem like "a sleeve-worn stone"? (d) In what sense is a poem like "the flight of birds"?
2. According to lines 9–16, what should a poem be like?
3. (a) According to lines 17–18, what should a poem be? (b) According to lines 23–24, what should a poem do?

Interpreting

4. (a) What does the speaker mean when he says that a poem should be "wordless"? (b) What does he mean when he says that a poem should be "motionless in time"?
5. (a) How should a poem capture "the history of grief"? (b) How should a poem express love? (c) Why do you think MacLeish chose to focus on the emotions of love and grief?

6. How does the final line sum up the ideas expressed in the poem?

Applying

7. Do you agree with MacLeish's definition of poetry? Why or why not?

ANALYZING LITERATURE

Understanding Similes

A **simile** is an explicit comparison between two seemingly dissimilar things, clearly indicated by a connecting word such as *like* or *as*. For example, MacLeish presents a simile in lines 1 and 2 in which he compares a poem to a globed fruit.

1. What does "globed" suggest about a poem?
2. (a) What comparison is made in the simile in lines 9 and 10? (b) How is this simile developed in the next four lines? (c) How does the simile in lines 9 and 10 help explain the speaker's statement that a "poem should be wordless"?
3. What is the effect of the repetition of this simile in lines 15 and 16?

E. E. CUMMINGS

1894–1962

Although E. E. Cummings's poems tend to be very unconventional in form and style, they generally embody traditional thought. In his finest poems, Cummings explores such subjects as love and nature, while innovatively using capitalization, punctuation, and grammar to reinforce meaning.

Edward Estlin Cummings was born in Cambridge, Massachusetts. After graduating from Harvard, he served in the French ambulance corps during World War I. While in France he was unjustly imprisoned for three months in a detention camp. His experiences as a prisoner later provided him with the material for a vivid war novel, *The Enormous Room* (1922).

After the war Cummings remained in Paris to study painting but soon returned to the United States and settled in Greenwich Village in New York City. There he began working full-time as an artist, devoting time to both writing and painting. He went on to produce four volumes of poetry. While some critics attacked his unconventional style, all of his collections were well received by the general public. People responded favorably to his playful use of language and his concern with the appearance as well as the content of his poems. He also became known for his concern for the individual, his ability to recognize life's ironies, his interest in human relationships and human emotions, and his humorous approach to many of the confusing aspects of modern life.

Cummings received a number of awards for his work, including the Boston Fine Arts Poetry Festival Award and the Bollingen Prize in Poetry. In 1968, six years after his death, a complete volume of his poetry, *The Complete Poems, 1913–1962,* was published.

GUIDE FOR READING

since feeling is first; anyone lived in a pretty how town; old age sticks

Style. Style refers to the manner in which a writer puts his or her ideas into words. It involves the characteristics of a literary selection that concern form of expression rather than the thoughts conveyed. In poetry style is determined by such factors as choice and arrangement of words, length and arrangement of lines, stanza length and format, use of punctuation and capitalization, and use of literary devices.

Because he was as concerned with the visual arrangement of his poems as he was with sound and meaning, E. E. Cummings's style is among the most distinctive of any American poet. Cummings strove to mold his poems into unconventional shapes through variations in line length and spaces between letters and lines. Frequently, Cummings used the shape of a poem to convey or reinforce its meaning. For example, his poem about a grasshopper, "r-p-o-p-h-e-s-s-a-g-r," forms the shape of a grasshopper hopping and reforming itself. Cummings also used capitalization and punctuation to reinforce meaning. Many of his poems contain little punctuation. As a result the few marks that are used serve to highlight important ideas. Similarly Cummings rarely used capital letters, except for emphasis. In fact Cummings even used a small *i* when his speakers referred to themselves. This reflected his perception of the self as a small part of a mass society and his belief in the need for modesty.

Look For

As you read E. E. Cummings's poetry, take note of the unique characteristics of his style. How does the way each poem is written affect its meaning?

Writing

"since feeling is first" focuses on the role of emotions in our lives. Freewrite about the ways in which feelings can affect our lives and the reasons why they can have such an impact.

Vocabulary

Knowing the following word will help you as you read E. E. Cummings's poetry.
syntax (sin' taks) *n.*: Orderly or systematic arrangement (p. 918, l. 3)

since feeling is first

E. E. Cummings

since feeling is first
who pays any attention
to the syntax of things
will never wholly kiss you;

5   wholly to be a fool
while Spring is in the world
my blood approves,
and kisses are a better fate
than wisdom
10 lady i swear by all flowers. Don't cry
—the best gesture of my brain is less than
your eyelids' flutter which says

we are for each other: then
laugh, leaning back in my arms
15 for life's not a paragraph

And death i think is no parenthesis

LOVERS WITH FLOWERS
Marc Chagall
The Israel Museum, Jerusalem

THINKING ABOUT THE SELECTION

Recalling

1. Who "will never wholly kiss you"?
2. What does the speaker "swear by all the flowers"?
3. What is more than the "best gesture" of the speaker's brain?
4. For what reasons should the lady laugh?

Interpreting

5. (a) What point does the speaker make about the relationship between reason and emotion? (b) What is his attitude concerning the role of emotions?
6. (a) What does the speaker mean when he says, "life's not a paragraph"? (b) Considering the fact that a parenthesis temporarily interrupts a sentence, what do you think the speaker means when he says, "death i think is no parenthesis"? (c) How is the speaker's perception of death related to his attitude concerning the role of emotions?

Applying

7. Do you agree with the speaker's attitude concerning the role of emotions? Why or why not?

anyone lived in a pretty how town

E. E. Cummings

anyone lived in a pretty how town
(with up so floating many bells down)
spring summer autumn winter
he sang his didn't he danced his did.

5   Women and men(both little and small)
cared for anyone not at all
they sowed their isn't they reaped their same
sun moon stars rain

children guessed(but only a few
10   and down they forgot as up they grew
autumn winter spring summer)
that noone loved him more by more

when by now and tree by leaf
she laughed his joy she cried his grief
15   bird by snow and stir by still
anyone's any was all to her

someones married their everyones
laughed their cryings and did their dance
(sleep wake hope and then)they
20   said their nevers they slept their dream

stars rain sun moon
(and only the snow can begin to explain
how children are apt to forget to remember
with up so floating many bells down)

25   one day anyone died i guess
(and noone stooped to kiss his face)
busy folk buried them side by side
little by little and was by was

all by all and deep by deep
30   and more by more they dream their sleep
noone and anyone earth by april
wish by spirit and if by yes.

Women and men(both dong and ding)
summer autumn winter spring

35   reaped their sowing and went their came
sun moon stars rain

THINKING ABOUT THE SELECTION

Recalling

1. (a) What does "anyone" sing? (b) What does he dance?
2. (a) How do "women and men" feel about "anyone"? (b) Who loves him "more by more"?
3. In the eighth stanza, what happens to "anyone"?

Interpreting

4. This poem tells about the man named "anyone" and his wife named "noone". Why do you think Cummings chose to use these names?
5. (a) What type of town is suggested by the phrase "pretty how"? (b) What type of impression does the speaker convey of the people from this town? (c) How does he convey the impression that their lives are monotonous and dull?
6. (a) What does the speaker mean when he says that the townspeople "laughed their cryings"? (b) What does he mean when he says that they "slept their dream"? (c) What does he mean when he says that they dreamed "their sleep"?
7. (a) What two lines in the poem convey the passage of time? (b) Why does Cummings vary the order of the words in these lines?

Applying

8. How do you think this poem might be different if it were set in a large city rather than a town?

old age
sticks

E. E. Cummings

old age sticks
up Keep
Off
signs)&

5 youth yanks them
down(old
age
cries No

Tres)&(pas)
10 youth laughs
(sing
old age

scolds Forbid
den Stop
15 Must
n't Don't

&)youth goes
right on
gr
20 owing old

THINKING ABOUT THE SELECTION
Recalling

1. (a) What signs does old age "stick up"?
   (b) What "yanks them down"?
2. (a) What does old age cry? (b) How does youth respond?
3. What is happening to youth?

Interpreting

4. How does youth contrast with old age in this poem?
5. What is ironic about the final stanza?

Applying

6. Why do you think the young and old often have very different attitudes toward life?

ANALYZING LITERATURE
Examining Style

Style refers to the way in which a writer expresses his or her thoughts. We can easily identify E. E. Cummings's poetry once we are familiar with his style.

1. How does Cummings's use of capitalization in "old age sticks" help to emphasize the contrast between youth and old age?
2. How does his use of parentheses in the poem highlight the contrast in the attitudes of the young and the old?
3. How does the shape of the poem reflect its content?

THINKING AND WRITING
Writing About Style

Write an essay in which you discuss how Cummings's style reinforces the meaning of his poems. Review the three poems you have just read, noting how the various elements of Cummings's style, such as his unusual use of punctuation and capitalization, reinforces the meaning of each poem. When you write your essay, use at least one passage from each of the three poems to support your argument. When you revise, make sure that you have clearly defined and thoroughly supported your thesis.

ROBERT FROST

1874–1963

In becoming one of America's most loved and respected poets, Robert Frost displayed the same rugged persistence and determination exhibited by the rural New Englanders he depicted in his poems. Although he eventually received four Pulitzer Prizes and read at a presidential inauguration, Frost had a difficult time achieving success as a poet. Only after years of rejection by book and magazine publishers did he finally receive the acceptance for which he worked so hard.

Frost was born in San Francisco, but his father died when he was eleven, and his mother moved the family to Lawrence, Massachusetts. After graduating from high school, he briefly attended Dartmouth College. Disliking college life, he left school and spent time working as a farmer, a mill hand, a newspaper writer, and a schoolteacher. During his spare time, he wrote poetry and dreamed of someday being able to support himself by writing alone.

After marrying and tending a farm in New Hampshire for ten years, Frost moved to England in 1912, hoping to establish himself as a poet. While in England he became friends with a number of well-known poets, including Ezra Pound, and published two collections of poetry, *A Boy's Will* (1913) and *North of Boston* (1914). When he returned home in 1915, he discovered that his success in England had spread to the United States.

Frost went on to publish five more volumes of poetry, for which he received many awards. He also taught at Amherst, the University of Michigan, Harvard, and Dartmouth; lectured and read at dozens of other schools; and farmed in Vermont and New Hampshire. In 1960, at John F. Kennedy's invitation, Frost became the first poet to read his work at a presidential inauguration.

Frost's poetry was popular not only among critics and intellectuals, but also among the general public. In his poems he painted vivid portraits of the New England landscape and captured the flavor of New England life using traditional verse forms and conversational language. Despite their apparent simplicity, however, his poems are filled with hidden meanings, forcing us to delve beneath the surface to fully appreciate his work.

GUIDE FOR READING

Birches; Mending Wall; The Wood-Pile; After Apple-Picking

Writer's Techniques

Symbols. A symbol is a person, place, or thing that has a meaning in itself and also represents something larger than itself. Frequently, an event or activity in a literary work may have a symbolic meaning. For example, the voyage of the *Pequod* in Herman Melville's *Moby-Dick* symbolizes humanity's quest to conquer everything in nature that seems paradoxical, unexplainable, and uncontrollable.

Symbols create different layers of meaning in a literary work. Because they generally contain symbols, Robert Frost's poems can usually be interpreted in more than one way. On the surface the poems seem straightforward and easy to grasp. Yet by analyzing his use of symbols, we become aware of larger meanings that are hidden beneath the surface.

Look For

As you read Robert Frost's poetry, take note of how he uses symbols to create different layers of meaning.

Writing

In "Birches" the speaker fondly remembers swinging on the branches of birch trees during his childhood. List some of the activities you enjoyed during the early part of your childhood. Then write down some of your reasons for liking each of these activities.

Vocabulary

Knowing the following words will help you as you read Robert Frost's poetry.

poise (poiz) *n.*: Balance; stability (p. 925, l. 35)

hoary (hôr′ ē) *adj.*: Very old; ancient (p. 932, l. 12)

NEW ENGLAND BIRCHES
Ernest Lawson
The Phillips Collection, Washington, D.C.

Birches

Robert Frost

When I see birches bend to left and right
Across the lines of straighter darker trees,
I like to think some boy's been swinging them.
But swinging doesn't bend them down to stay
5 As ice storms do. Often you must have seen them
Loaded with ice a sunny winter morning
After a rain. They click upon themselves
As the breeze rises, and turn many-colored
As the stir cracks and crazes their enamel.
10 Soon the sun's warmth makes them shed crystal shells
Shattering and avalanching on the snow crust—

Such heaps of broken glass to sweep away
You'd think the inner dome of heaven had fallen.
They are dragged to the withered bracken by the load,
15 And they seem not to break; though once they are bowed
So low for long, they never right themselves:
You may see their trunks arching in the woods
Years afterwards, trailing their leaves on the ground
Like girls on hands and knees that throw their hair
20 Before them over their heads to dry in the sun.
But I was going to say when Truth broke in
With all her matter of fact about the ice storm,
I should prefer to have some boy bend them
As he went out and in to fetch the cows—
25 Some boy too far from town to learn baseball,
Whose only play was what he found himself,
Summer or winter, and could play alone.
One by one he subdued his father's trees
By riding them down over and over again
30 Until he took the stiffness out of them,
And not one but hung limp, not one was left
For him to conquer. He learned all there was
To learn about not launching out too soon
And so not carrying the tree away
35 Clear to the ground. He always kept his poise
To the top branches, climbing carefully
With the same pains you use to fill a cup
Up to the brim, and even above the brim.
Then he flung outward, feet first, with a swish,
40 Kicking his way down through the air to the ground.
So was I once myself a swinger of birches.
And so I dream of going back to be.
It's when I'm weary of considerations,
And life is too much like a pathless wood
45 Where your face burns and tickles with the cobwebs
Broken across it, and one eye is weeping
From a twig's having lashed across it open.
I'd like to get away from earth awhile
And then come back to it and begin over.
50 May no fate willfully misunderstand me
And half grant what I wish and snatch me away
Not to return. Earth's the right place for love:
I don't know where it's likely to go better.
I'd like to go by climbing a birch tree,
55 And climb black branches up a snow-white trunk
Toward heaven, till the tree could bear no more,
But dipped its top and set me down again.
That would be good both going and coming back.
One could do worse than be a swinger of birches.

THINKING ABOUT THE SELECTION

Recalling

1. What does the speaker like to think when he sees birches "bend to the left and right"?
2. What causes the birch trees to bend "down to stay"?
3. (a) What is the only play for some boy who lives "too far from town to learn baseball"? (b) How does the boy take the stiffness out of the birch trees? (c) About what does the boy "learn all there was to learn"?
4. When does the speaker dream of "going back to be" a "swinger of birches"?
5. What does the speaker think "would be good both going and coming back"?

Interpreting

6. (a) How would you characterize the boy described in the poem? (b) Who do you think the boy actually represents? (c) How would you describe the boy's relationship with nature?
7. What type of condition is the speaker describing in lines 44–48?
8. What does the speaker mean when he comments that he hopes that fate will not "half grant" what he wishes?

Applying

9. What are some of the advantages and disadvantages of growing up "too far from town to learn baseball"?

ANALYZING LITERATURE

Interpreting Symbols

A **symbol** is a person, place, object, or action that has a meaning in itself and also represents something larger than itself. For example, in "Birches" the activity of swinging on birch trees symbolizes both a unity between humanity and nature and the notion of a temporary escape from reality.

1. Explain the following line: "One could do worse than be a swinger of birches."
2. What details in the poem suggest that the swinging on birches symbolizes the unity between humanity and nature?
3. What details suggest that the activity symbolizes a temporary escape from reality?

THINKING AND WRITING

Writing About a Symbol

Write an essay in which you discuss the symbolic meaning of the swinging on birches in Frost's poem. Review your answers from the Analyzing Literature activity. Prepare a thesis statement. Then write your essay, using passages from the poem to support your thesis. When you revise, make sure your body paragraphs are arranged in a logical order. Proofread your essay and share it with your classmates.

Mending Wall

Robert Frost

Something there is that doesn't love a wall,
That sends the frozen-ground-swell under it
And spills the upper boulders in the sun,
And makes gaps even two can pass abreast.
5 The work of hunters is another thing:
I have come after them and made repair
Where they have left not one stone on a stone,
But they would have the rabbit out of hiding,
To please the yelping dogs. The gaps I mean,
10 No one has seen them made or heard them made,
But at spring mending-time we find them there.
I let my neighbor know beyond the hill;
And on a day we meet to walk the line
And set the wall between us once again.
15 We keep the wall between us as we go.
To each the boulders that have fallen to each.
And some are loaves and some so nearly balls
We have to use a spell to make them balance:
"Stay where you are until our backs are turned!"
20 We wear our fingers rough with handling them.
Oh, just another kind of outdoor game,
One on a side. It comes to little more:
There where it is we do not need the wall:
He is all pine and I am apple orchard.
25 My apple trees will never get across
And eat the cones under his pines, I tell him.
He only says, "Good fences make good neighbors."
Spring is the mischief in me, and I wonder
If I could put a notion in his head:
30 "*Why* do they make good neighbors? Isn't it
Where there are cows? But here there are no cows.
Before I built a wall I'd ask to know
What I was walling in or walling out,
And to whom I was like to give offense.
35 Something there is that doesn't love a wall,
That wants it down." I could say "Elves" to him,
But it's not elves exactly, and I'd rather
He said it for himself. I see him there,
Bringing a stone grasped firmly by the top
40 In each hand, like an old-stone savage armed.
He moves in darkness as it seems to me,

Not of woods only and the shade of trees.
He will not go behind his father's saying,
And he likes having thought of it so well
45 He says again, "Good fences make good neighbors."

THINKING ABOUT THE SELECTION

Recalling

1. What causes the gaps in the wall?
2. How do the speaker and his neighbor go about repairing the wall?
3. (a) Why does the speaker feel the wall is unnecessary? (b) How does the neighbor respond when the speaker expresses his opinion?
4. What would the speaker ask to know before building a wall?

Interpreting

5. (a) How would you characterize the speaker? (b) How would you characterize the speaker's neighbor? (c) What is the speaker's attitude toward his neighbor?
6. What is the significance of the fact that nature breaks apart the wall each winter?
7. (a) What is suggested by the fact that the neighbor learned his favorite saying from his father? (b) What is the significance of the fact that the saying is a cliché, or an overused expression?

8. How does the speaker's relationship with his neighbor disprove the neighbor's favorite saying?

Applying

9. (a) Why might a wall be unnecessary in the type of environment described in the poem? (b) In what types of environments do you think a wall would be necessary?

THINKING AND WRITING

Writing a Poem

Write a poem that conveys a theme concerning life in contemporary American society. Prepare a list of images, or word pictures, associated with contemporary life. Then use your list of images in developing your poem. When writing your poem, try to avoid using abstract words unless they are linked to concrete images. When you finish writing, revise your poem and share it with your classmates.

WOODLOT, MAINE WOODS
Marsden Hartley
The Phillips Collection, Washington, D.C.

The Wood-Pile

Robert Frost

Out walking in the frozen swamp one gray day,
I paused and said, "I will turn back from here.
No, I will go on farther—and we shall see."
The hard snow held me, save where now and then
5   One foot went through. The view was all in lines
Straight up and down of tall slim trees
Too much alike to mark or name a place by
So as to say for certain I was here
Or somewhere else: I was just far from home.

10 A small bird flew before me. He was careful
  To put a tree between us when he lighted,
  And say no word to tell me who he was
  Who was so foolish as to think what *he* thought.
  He thought that I was after him for a feather—
15 The white one in his tail; like one who takes
  Everything said as personal to himself.
  One flight out sideways would have undeceived him.
  And then there was a pile of wood for which
  I forgot him and let his little fear
20 Carry him off the way I might have gone,
  Without so much as wishing him good-night.
  He went behind it to make his last stand.
  It was a cord of maple, cut and split
  And piled—and measured, four by four by eight.
25 And not another like it could I see.
  No runner tracks in this year's snow looped near it.
  And it was older sure than this year's cutting,
  Or even last year's or the year's before.
  The wood was gray and the bark warping off it
30 And the pile somewhat sunken. Clematis[1]
  Had wound strings round and round it like a bundle.
  What held it, though, on one side was a tree
  Still growing, and on one a stake and prop,
  These latter about to fall. I thought that only
35 Someone who lived in turning to fresh tasks
  Could so forget his handiwork on which
  He spent himself, the labor of his ax,
  And leave it there far from a useful fireplace
  To warm the frozen swamp as best it could
40 With the slow smokeless burning of decay.

---

1. clematis (klem′ ə tis) *n.*: A woody vine with bright-colored flowers.

THINKING ABOUT THE SELECTION

Recalling

1. What does the speaker say to himself when he pauses?
2. Why is the speaker unable to "mark or name a place" by the trees?
3. What causes the speaker to forget the bird in which he has developed an interest?
4. How is the speaker able to tell that the woodpile has been there for some time?
5. What type of person does the speaker imagine must have abandoned the woodpile?

Interpreting

6. (a) How does the speaker personify, or attribute human behavior to, the bird? (b) What does his personification of the bird indicate about his response to being isolated in the wilderness?
7. (a) Why is the speaker reassured by his discovery of the woodpile? (b) How does the speaker's discovery fulfill his need to "mark or name a place"?

Applying

8. Why do you think a person isolated in the wilderness might be anxious to find a sign of human life?

After Apple-Picking

Robert Frost

My long two-pointed ladder's sticking through a tree
Toward heaven still,
And there's a barrel that I didn't fill
Beside it, and there may be two or three
5   Apples I didn't pick upon some bough.
But I am done with apple-picking now.
Essence of winter sleep is on the night,
The scent of apples: I am drowsing off.
I cannot rub the strangeness from my sight
10   I got from looking through a pane of glass
I skimmed this morning from the drinking trough
And held against the world of hoary grass.
It melted, and I let it fall and break.
But I was well
15   Upon my way to sleep before it fell,
And I could tell
What form my dreaming was about to take.
Magnified apples appear and disappear,
Stem end and blossom end,
20   And every fleck of russet showing clear.
My instep arch not only keeps the ache,
It keeps the pressure of a ladder-round.
I feel the ladder sway as the boughs bend.
And I keep hearing from the cellar bin
25   The rumbling sound
Of load on load of apples coming in.
For I have had too much
Of apple-picking: I am overtired
Of the great harvest I myself desired.
30   There were ten thousand thousand fruit to touch.
Cherish in hand, lift down, and not let fall.
For all
That struck the earth,
No matter if not bruised or spiked with stubble,
35   Went surely to the cider-apple heap
As of no worth.
One can see what will trouble
This sleep of mine, whatever sleep it is.
Were he not gone,
40   The woodchuck could say whether it's like his
Long sleep, as I describe its coming on,
Or just some human sleep.

THINKING ABOUT THE SELECTION

Recalling

1. What sits beside the ladder?
2. (a) What pictures flash through the speaker's mind as he drifts off to sleep? (b) What sensations does he feel? (c) What does he hear?
3. (a) How had the speaker handled the apples? (b) What happened to the apples that fell to the ground?

Interpreting

4. (a) How would you describe the speaker's condition? (b) What is the cause of his condition?
5. What does the image, or word picture, of "magnified apples" in line 18 suggest about the speaker's desire for a great harvest?
6. How might the speaker's sleep be like the "long sleep" of the woodchuck?
7. What does this poem suggest about the effects of unrestrained ambition?

Applying

8. Why do you think people often become obsessed with reaching a goal?

The Death of the Hired Man;
"Out, Out—"

Literary Forms

Narrative Poetry. A narrative poem is one that tells a story. Like a short story, a narrative poem has one or more characters, has a setting, a conflict, and describes an event or a series of events. In a narrative poem, the story is told by a single speaker, which may be the voice of the poet or that of a fictional character.

Dramatic Poetry. Unlike narrative poetry, in which events are described in the words of the speaker, dramatic poetry re-creates an event using dialogue or monologue as well as description. In a dramatic poem we see the characters interacting with and talking to one another, and as a result it seems as if we are actually witnessing the event.

Look For

As you read "The Death of the Hired Man," take note of how Frost uses dialogue and description to make it seem as if we are actually witnessing the action. As you read " 'Out, Out—' " take note of how Frost uses a single speaker to describe an event.

Writing

" 'Out, Out—' " tells the story of the death of a young boy and how his family copes with it. Freewrite about the various ways in which people deal with death.

Vocabulary

Knowing the following words will help you as you read Robert Frost's poetry.

musing (myōōz′ iŋ) *v.*: Thinking deeply and at length (p. 935, l. 1)

harbor (här′ bər) *v.*: Shelter or house (p. 935, l. 15)

beholden (bi hōld′ ən) *adj.*: Owing thanks; indebted (p. 935, l. 21)

piqued (pēkt) *v.*: Aroused resentment in (p. 937, l. 17)

rueful (rōō′ fəl) *adj.*: Feeling or showing sorrow or pity (p. 942, l. 19)

The Death of the Hired Man

Robert Frost

Mary sat musing on the lamp-flame at the table,
Waiting for Warren. When she heard his step,
She ran on tiptoe down the darkened passage
To meet him in the doorway with the news
5 And put him on his guard. "Silas is back."
She pushed him outward with her through the door
And shut it after her. "Be kind," she said.
She took the market things from Warren's arms
And set them on the porch, then drew him down
10 To sit beside her on the wooden steps.

"When was I ever anything but kind to him?
But I'll not have the fellow back," he said.
"I told him so last haying, didn't I?
If he left then, I said, that ended it.
15 What good is he? Who else will harbor him
At his age for the little he can do?
What help he is there's no depending on.
Off he goes always when I need him most.
He thinks he ought to earn a little pay,
20 Enough at least to buy tobacco with,
So he won't have to beg and be beholden.
'All right,' I say, 'I can't afford to pay
Any fixed wages, though I wish I could.'
'Someone else can.' 'Then someone else will have to.'
25 I shouldn't mind his bettering himself
If that was what it was. You can be certain,
When he begins like that, there's someone at him
Trying to coax him off with pocket money—
In haying time, when any help is scarce.
30 In winter he comes back to us. I'm done."

"Sh! not so loud: he'll hear you," Mary said.

"I want him to: he'll have to soon or late."

"He's worn out. He's asleep beside the stove.
When I came up from Rowe's I found him here,
35 Huddled against the barn door fast asleep,

A miserable sight, and frightening, too—
You needn't smile—I didn't recognize him—
I wasn't looking for him—and he's changed.
Wait till you see."

　　　　　　　　　　"Where did you say he'd been?"

40　"He didn't say. I dragged him to the house,
And gave him tea and tried to make him smoke.
I tried to make him talk about his travels.
Nothing would do: he just kept nodding off."

"What did he say? Did he say anything?"

"But little."

45　　　　　　　"Anything? Mary, confess
He said he'd come to ditch the meadow for me."

"Warren!"
　　　　　　　"But did he? I just want to know."

"Of course he did. What would you have him say?
Surely you wouldn't grudge the poor old man
50　Some humble way to save his self-respect.
He added, if you really care to know,
He meant to clear the upper pasture, too.
That sounds like something you have heard before?
Warren, I wish you could have heard the way
55　He jumbled everything. I stopped to look
Two or three times—he made me feel so queer—
To see if he was talking in his sleep.
He ran on Harold Wilson—you remember—
The boy you had in haying four years since.
60　He's finished school, and teaching in his college.
Silas declares you'll have to get him back.
He says they two will make a team for work:
Between them they will lay this farm as smooth!
The way he mixed that in with other things.
65　He thinks young Wilson a likely lad, though daft
On education—you know how they fought
All through July under the blazing sun,
Silas up on the cart to build the load,
Harold along beside to pitch it on."

70　"Yes, I took care to keep well out of earshot."

"Well, those days trouble Silas like a dream.

You wouldn't think they would. How such things linger!
Harold's young college-boy's assurance piqued him.
After so many years he still keeps finding
75 Good arguments he sees he might have used.
I sympathize. I know just how it feels
To think of the right thing to say too late.
Harold's associated in his mind with Latin.
He asked me what I thought of Harold's saying
80 He studied Latin, like the violin,
Because he liked it—that an argument!
He said he couldn't make the boy believe
He could find water with a hazel prong—
Which showed how much good school had ever done him.
85 He wanted to go over that. But most of all
He thinks if he could have another chance
To teach him how to build a load of hay—"

"I know, that's Silas' one accomplishment.
He bundles every forkful in its place,
90 And tags and numbers it for future reference,
So he can find and easily dislodge it
In the unloading. Silas does that well.
He takes it out in bunches like big birds' nests.
You never see him standing on the hay
95 He's trying to lift, straining to lift himself."

"He thinks if he could teach him that, he'd be
Some good perhaps to someone in the world.
He hates to see a boy the fool of books.
Poor Silas, so concerned for other folk,
100 And nothing to look backward to with pride,
And nothing to look forward to with hope,
So now and never any different."

Part of a moon was falling down the west,
Dragging the whole sky with it to the hills.
105 Its light poured softly in her lap. She saw it
And spread her apron to it. She put out her hand
Among the harplike morning-glory strings,
Taut with the dew from garden bed to eaves,
As if she played unheard some tenderness
110 That wrought on him beside her in the night.
"Warren," she said, "he has come home to die:
You needn't be afraid he'll leave you this time."

"Home," he mocked gently.

                                    "Yes, what else but home?

It all depends on what you mean by home.
115 Of course he's nothing to us, any more
Than was the hound that came a stranger to us
Out of the woods, worn out upon the trail."

"Home is the place where, when you have to go there,
They have to take you in."

                    "I should have called it
120 Something you somehow haven't to deserve."

Warren leaned out and took a step or two,
Picked up a little stick, and brought it back
And broke it in his hand and tossed it by.
"Silas has better claim on us you think
125 Than on his brother? Thirteen little miles
As the road winds would bring him to his door.
Silas has walked that far no doubt today.
Why doesn't he go there? His brother's rich,
A somebody—director in the bank."

"He never told us that."

130   "We know it, though."

"I think his brother ought to help, of course.
I'll see to that if there is need. He ought of right
To take him in, and might be willing to—
He may be better than appearances.
135 But have some pity on Silas. Do you think
If he had any pride in claiming kin
Or anything he looked for from his brother,
He'd keep so still about him all this time?"

"I wonder what's between them."

                        "I can tell you.
140 Silas is what he is—we wouldn't mind him—
But just the kind that kinsfolk can't abide.
He never did a thing so very bad.
He don't know why he isn't quite as good
As anybody. Worthless though he is,
145 He won't be made ashamed to please his brother."

"*I* can't think Si ever hurt anyone."

"No, but he hurt my heart the way he lay
And rolled his old head on that sharp-edged chair-back.

GUIDE FOR READING

Writer's Techniques

Fire and Ice; Nothing Gold Can Stay; Stopping by Woods on a Snowy Evening; Acquainted with the Night

Rhythm. Rhythm is the arrangement of stressed and unstressed syllables in a poem. In poems with a regular rhythm, or meter, the arrangement of stressed and unstressed syllables forms a recurring pattern. However, poets usually introduce slight variations in the metrical pattern to avoid monotony or emphasize important words. Poets will also introduce pauses within lines to interrupt the regular rhythm. These pauses, called caesuras, are usually created by punctuation, though they may also be formed by the meanings of words or the natural rhythms of language. For example, the meanings of the words in line 7 of "Fire and Ice" ("To say that for destruction ice") cause a pause to occur between the words *destruction* and *ice*.

Another way poets can vary a regular rhythm is through the use of run-on lines. Unlike end-stopped lines, which end with a pause, run-on lines flow naturally into the next line. For example, in "Fire and Ice," line 7 ("To say that for destruction ice") flows into line 8 ("Is also great").

Look For

As you read Robert Frost's poetry, look for the techniques he uses to vary rhythm.

Writing

In "Nothing Gold Can Stay," Frost writes about the impermanence of beauty. Spend some time thinking about beautiful things that do not last, listing each item that comes to mind.

Vocabulary

Knowing the following words will help you as you read Robert Frost's poetry.

suffice (sə fīs′) *v.*: To be enough (p. 945, l. 9)

luminary (lōō′ mə ner′ ē) *adj.*: Giving of light (p. 948, l. 12)

Fire and Ice

Robert Frost

Some say the world will end in fire,
Some say in ice.
From what I've tasted of desire
I hold with those who favor fire.
5 But if it had to perish twice,
I think I know enough of hate
To say that for destruction ice
Is also great
And would suffice.

THINKING ABOUT THE SELECTION

Recalling

1. In what two ways do "some say" the world will end?
2. With whom does the speaker hold?
3. What does the speaker feel would also suffice "for destruction"?

Interpreting

4. In this poem the speaker approaches a very serious subject in a seemingly casual manner. What might have been Frost's reasons for taking this type of approach?
5. (a) What emotion does each of the natural elements in the poem represent? (b) What does the speaker suggest that these emotions have in common?

Applying

6. What emotions, aside from the ones referred to in the poem, do you think bring out destructive impulses in people?

Nothing Gold Can Stay

Robert Frost

Nature's first green is gold,
Her hardest hue to hold.
Her early leaf's a flower;
But only so an hour.
5   Then leaf subsides to leaf.
So Eden sank to grief,
So dawn goes down to day.
Nothing gold can stay.

THINKING ABOUT THE SELECTION

Recalling

1. What happens to each of the elements of nature mentioned in the poem?

Interpreting

2. What is the meaning of the first line?
3. (a) What is the poem's theme, or main point? (b) How does the allusion, or reference, to Eden help to convey the theme?

Applying

4. Do you agree with the outlook expressed in this poem? Why or why not?

Stopping by Woods on a Snowy Evening

Robert Frost

> Whose woods these are I think I know.
> His house is in the village though;
> He will not see me stopping here
> To watch his woods fill up with snow.
>
> 5 My little horse must think it queer
> To stop without a farmhouse near
> Between the woods and frozen lake
> The darkest evening of the year.
>
> He gives his harness bells a shake
> 10 To ask if there is some mistake.
> The only other sound's the sweep
> Of easy wind and downy flake.
>
> The woods are lovely, dark and deep,
> But I have promises to keep,
> 15 And miles to go before I sleep,
> And miles to go before I sleep.

THINKING ABOUT THE SELECTION

Recalling

1. Why does the speaker stop in the woods?
2. (a) What does the speaker imagine that his horse "must think"? (b) Why does the horse give "his harness bells a shake"?
3. What must the speaker do before he sleeps?

Interpreting

4. (a) What do the speaker's actions in this poem reveal about his personality? (b) What internal conflict does the speaker experience? (c) How is the conflict resolved?
5. What difference between humans and animals is revealed through the horse's behavior?

6. (a) How does the repetition of the *d* sound in line 13 reinforce the meaning of the line? (b) What is the effect of Frost's use of repetition in the final two lines?
7. Explain the last three lines of this poem.

Applying

8. Just as swinging from birch trees provides the boy in "Birches" with a temporary escape from reality, pausing to observe nature provides the speaker with a temporary escape from reality in "Stopping by Woods on a Snowy Evening." Why do you think that people at times need to find this type of temporary escape?

Acquainted with the Night

Robert Frost

I have been one acquainted with the night.
I have walked out in rain—and back in rain.
I have outwalked the furthest city light.

I have looked down the saddest city lane.
5 I have passed by the watchman on his beat
And dropped my eyes, unwilling to explain.

I have stood still and stopped the sound of feet
When far away an interrupted cry
Came over houses from another street,

10 But not to call me back or say good-by;
And further still at an unearthly height
One luminary clock against the sky

Proclaimed the time was neither wrong nor right.
I have been one acquainted with the night.

THINKING ABOUT THE SELECTION

Recalling

1. (a) Where and in what conditions has the speaker walked? (b) Where has he looked? (c) Whom has he passed?
2. What does the speaker hear that causes him to stand still and stop the sound of feet?
3. What does the "luminary clock" proclaim?

Interpreting

4. What type of mood do the images in lines 1–4 create?
5. (a) The night watchman symbolizes regularity and certainty. Given this fact, what do you think the speaker's response to the watchman suggests? (b) What is the speaker "unwilling to explain"?
6. What does the speaker's comment that "the time was neither wrong nor right" reveal about his life?
7. (a) What does night symbolize in this poem? (b) How does Frost use repetition to help convey the symbolic meaning of the night?

Applying

8. What does this poem suggest about Frost's attitude toward city life?

ANALYZING LITERATURE

Understanding Rhythm

Rhythm is the arrangement of stressed and unstressed syllables in a poem. Poets vary the regular rhythm of a poem in a number of ways. Often poets interrupt the regular rhythm by introducing pauses, or caesuras, within lines. Another way poets vary rhythm is by using run-on lines—lines that flow naturally into the next line.

1. Find two caesuras in "Acquainted with the Night."
2. Find two run-on lines in the poem.

CRITICAL THINKING AND READING

Analyzing Variations in Rhythm

Without some variation, the rhythm of a poem can become monotonous. In fact, an unvaried rhythm may even create a singsong effect that undercuts the meaning of the poem.

Read "Acquainted with the Night" aloud, disregarding run-on lines and caesuras and pausing only at the end of each line. Then reread the poem as Frost meant it to be read. Explain why the run-on lines and caesuras make the poem more effective.

THINKING AND READING

Supporting a Generalization

Write an essay in which you support a generalization about Robert Frost's poetry. Review the Frost poems in this book, noting similarities in form, content, and the attitudes expressed. Look over your notes and prepare a statement making a generalization about Frost's poetry. When you write your essay, use passages from at least four poems to support your statement. When you revise, make sure your essay is well-organized.

W. H. AUDEN

1907–1973

Although he was influenced by the Modernist poets, Wystan Hugh Auden managed to remain his own person. He adopted those aspects of Modernism with which he felt comfortable, while at the same time maintaining many elements of traditional poetry. Throughout his career he wrote with insight into the plight of people struggling to preserve their individuality in an increasingly conformist society.

Auden was born in York, England, and attended Oxford University. In 1930 he published his first collection of poetry, *Poems*. At about the same time, he became very active in politics. He spoke out about the plight of the poor in England and against the emergence of Nazism in Germany, and he actively supported the Republicans who were fighting against the Fascists in the Spanish Civil War. He also used his talents as a poet to express his political beliefs. As a result, many of his early poems focused on political issues.

In 1939 Auden moved to the United States, and in 1946 he became an American citizen. At the time of his move, he rediscovered his Christian beliefs, which grew increasingly stronger during his later years. He expressed his beliefs in *Double Man* (1941) and *For the Times Being* (1944), depicting religion as an effective way of coping with the disjointedness of modern society. In *The Age of Anxiety* (1947), a long narrative poem which earned him a Pulitzer Prize, he explored the confusion and isolation associated with *post-World War II life*. He went on to publish several more volumes of poetry, including *Nones* (1951), *The Shield of Achilles* (1955), *Homage to Clio* (1960), *About the House* (1967), and *City Without Walls* (1970), and he also produced a large body of literary criticism.

Despite being comforted by his religious beliefs, Auden became increasingly disillusioned with the modern world during his later years. Hoping to find comfort in a university community, he returned to England to teach at Oxford in the late 1950's. Several years later he moved to Austria, where he spent the remainder of his life.

GUIDE FOR READING

Who's Who; The Unknown Citizen

Writer's Techniques

Satire. Satire is a kind of writing in which certain individuals, institutions, types of behavior, or humanity in general are ridiculed or criticized in a humorous manner. The purpose of satire is to promote changes in society or humanity. Satirists write about what they perceive to be the problems and flaws of the world. By poking fun at these problems and flaws or attacking them in a humorous manner, the satirists attempt to use the force of laughter to persuade us to accept their point of view and inspire us to take action to bring about change.

Look For

As you read "The Unknown Citizen," look for how Auden satirizes the increasingly impersonal and bureaucratic nature of modern society.

Writing

"Who's Who" explores some of the facts of a famous man's life. Of what types of facts concerning a famous person's life is the public usually aware? Of what types of facts is the public usually unaware? List the sources of the public's knowledge concerning a famous person's life.

Vocabulary

Knowing the following word will help you as you read W. H. Auden's poetry.

psychology (sī kŏl′ ə jē) *n.*: The science dealing with the mind and with mental and emotional processes (p. 953, l. 12)

Who's Who

W. H. Auden

A shilling life will give you all the facts:
How Father beat him, how he ran away,
What were the struggles of his youth, what acts
Made him the greatest figure of his day:
5 Of how he fought, fished, hunted, worked all night,
Though giddy, climbed new mountains; named a sea:
Some of the last researchers even write
Love made him weep his pints like you and me.

With all his honors on, he sighed for one
10 Who, say astonished critics, lived at home;
Did little jobs about the house with skill
And nothing else; could whistle; would sit still
Or potter round the garden; answered some
Of his long marvelous letters but kept none.

THINKING ABOUT THE SELECTION

Recalling

1. What facts about the subject's youth are mentioned?
2. What acts made the subject "the greatest figure of his day"?
3. What do "some of the last researchers even write"?
4. (a) How did the one he "sighed for" spend her life? (b) What did this person do with his letters?

Interpreting

5. (a) What type of person is this poem about? (b) What do the facts suggest about his personality?

6. (a) What is surprising about the description of the woman whom he loved? (b) How do details in the poem suggest that she did not return his love?
7. (a) What is ironic, or surprising, about the fact that the subject of the poem weeped "pints like you and me"? (b) What does this suggest about the nature of happiness?
8. Explain the title of the poem.

Applying

9. Do you think that famous people are as likely to be unhappy as those who are not famous? Why or why not?

The Unknown Citizen

W. H. Auden

(To JS/07/M/378
This Marble Monument
Is Erected by the State)

He was found by the Bureau of Statistics to be
One against whom there was no official complaint,
And all the reports on his conduct agree
That, in the modern sense of an old-fashioned word, he was
    a saint,
5 For in everything he did he served the Greater Community.
Except for the War till the day he retired
He worked in a factory and never got fired,
But satisfied his employers, Fudge Motors Inc.
Yet he wasn't a scab[1] or odd in his views,
10 For his Union reports that he paid his dues,
(Our report on his Union shows it was sound)
And our Social Psychology workers found
That he was popular with his mates and liked a drink.
The Press are convinced that he bought a paper every day
15 And that his reactions to advertisements were normal in
    every way.
Policies taken out in his name prove that he was fully
    insured,
And his Health-card shows he was once in hospital but left
    it cured.
Both Producers Research and High-Grade Living declare
He was fully sensible to the advantages of the Installment
    Plan
20 And had everything necessary to the Modern Man,
A phonograph, a radio, a car and a frigidaire.
Our researchers into Public Opinion are content
That he held the proper opinions for the time of year;
When there was peace, he was for peace; when there was
    war, he went.

---

1. scab *n.*: A worker who refuses to strike or takes the place of a
striking worker.

25 He was married and added five children to the population,
    Which our Eugenist[2] says was the right number for a
      parent of his generation,
    And our teachers report that he never interfered with their
      education.
    Was he free? Was he happy? The question is absurd:
    Had anything been wrong, we should certainly have heard.

---

2. Eugenist (ū jen′ ist) *n.*: A specialist in eugenics, the movement devoted to improving the human species through genetic control.

THINKING ABOUT THE SELECTION

Recalling

1. Why is the unknown citizen remembered as a "saint"?
2. (a) Where did the unknown citizen work? (b) What does his union report about him?
3. (a) What do the social psychology workers find? (b) Of what is the press convinced? (c) What does the Eugenist say? (d) What do the teachers report?
4. Why is the question of the citizen's freedom and happiness absurd?

Interpreting

5. (a) What is suggested by the numbers and letters used by the state in referring to the citizen? (b) In what sense is the citizen "unknown" to the state?
6. (a) What is the relationship of the state to the groups mentioned in the poem? (b) What are the primary interests of these groups concerning the citizen? (c) What do the concerns of the groups and their relationship to the state reveal about the society as a whole?
7. (a) Why is it unlikely that the state would have heard anything concerning the citizen's freedom and happiness? (b) What seems to be their attitude toward his freedom and happiness?

8. How does Auden use capitalization to reinforce the meaning of the poem?

Applying

9. In what respects is the society portrayed in this poem similar to and different from our society?

ANALYZING LITERATURE

Interpreting Satire

Satire is a kind of writing in which certain individuals, institutions, types of behavior, or humanity in general are ridiculed or criticized in a humorous manner. In "The Unknown Citizen," for example, Auden criticizes the increasingly impersonal and bureaucratic nature of modern society by presenting an exaggerated vision of a state in which people have been almost completely stripped of their individuality.

1. What is Auden's attitude toward the type of society he portrays in the poem?
2. How do the final two lines help to clarify Auden's attitude?
3. Considering Auden's attitude toward the society he portrays, what type of society do you think he supports?

The Harlem Renaissance

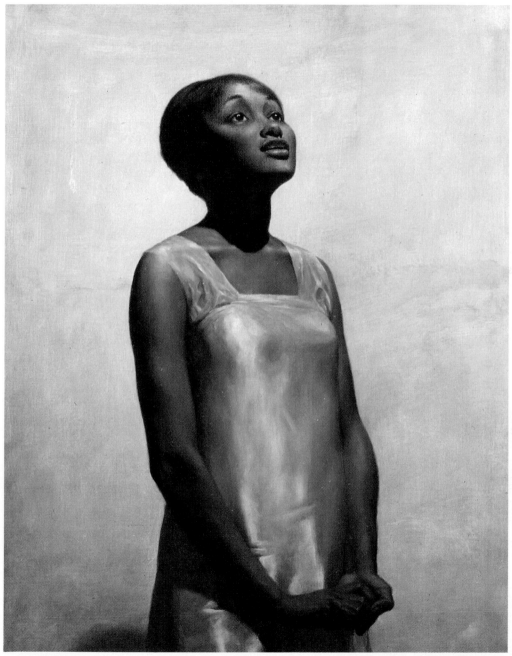

RUBY GREEN SINGING, 1928
James Chapin
Norton Gallery of Art

Countee Cullen (1903–1946)

Unlike most other poets of his time, Countee Cullen used traditional forms and methods. However, no poet expressed the general sentiments of American blacks during the early 1900's more eloquently than Cullen.

Cullen was born in New York City. He graduated from New York University and later earned a master's degree from Harvard. His first collection of poetry, *Color,* was published in 1925. This was followed by *Copper Sun* (1927), *The Ballad of the Brown Girl* (1927), and *The Black Christ* (1929). In 1932 he published *One Way to Heaven,* a satirical novel about life in Harlem. During his later years he published two children's books, *The Lost Zoo* (1940) and *My Lives and How I Lost Them* (1942).

In "Any Human to Another," one of Cullen's best-known poems, he expresses the despair of black people.

Claude McKay (1890–1948)

In much of his work, Claude McKay evokes the rich colors and the rhythms of life on his native island of Jamaica.

The son of poor farm workers, McKay moved to Kingston, the capital of the Caribbean island, when he was fourteen. While living in Kingston, he began writing poetry. When his collection, *Songs of Jamaica* (1912), won an award from the Institute of Arts and Letters, he was able to emigrate to the United States.

After studying at both the Tuskegee Institute and Kansas State College, he moved to Harlem. In 1922 while living in Harlem, he published *Harlem Shadows* (1922), a successful collection of poetry. During the remainder of his life, McKay focused mainly on writing novels protesting the injustices of black life. His novels include *Home to Harlem* (1928) and *Banana Bottom* (1933).

McKay's poem "The Tropics in New York" is marked by a nostalgia for his homeland—a feeling echoed in the title of his autobiography, *A Long Way From Home* (1937).

Any Human to Another; The Tropics in New York

Literary Movements

The Harlem Renaissance. During the late 1800's and early 1900's, many southern blacks moved north, hoping to find opportunities in the northern industrial centers. With this shift in population, the New York City community of Harlem developed into the cultural center for American blacks. There a cultural movement known as the Harlem Renaissance was established during the 1920's. The movement encompassed music, art, and literature, and included such writers as Countee Cullen, Claude McKay, Langston Hughes, Jean Toomer, and Arna Bontemps.

Although the literary forms and techniques used by the Harlem Renaissance writers varied widely, the writers all shared a common purpose: to prove that black writers could produce literature equal in quality to that of white writers. At the same time, the Harlem Renaissance writers focused on capturing the general sentiments of the American blacks of the time. In doing so they expressed their displeasure concerning their overall condition and articulated their cultural heritage.

Look For

As you read the poetry of the Harlem Renaissance poets, take note of how their work captures the general sentiments of the American blacks of the time.

Writing

In "The Tropics in New York," Claude McKay presents a series of images, or word pictures, associated with the tropics. Prepare a list of the type of images you would expect to find in this series.

Vocabulary

Knowing the following words will help you as you read "Any Human to Another" and "The Tropics in New York."

marrow (mar′ ō) *n.*: The soft tissue that fills the cavities of most bones (p. 959, l. 4)

diverse (dī vʉrs′) *adj.*: Various (p. 959, l. 11)

scorned (skôrnd) *v.*: Refused or rejected as wrong or disgraceful (p. 959, l. 22)

unsheathed (un shēthd′) *adj.*: Removed from its case (p. 959, l. 27)

BIG MEETING, 1980
Varnette P. Honeywood
Black Lifestyles, Los Angeles

Any Human to Another

Countee Cullen

The ills I sorrow at
Not me alone
Like an arrow,
Pierce to the marrow,
5 Through the fat
And past the bone.

Your grief and mine
Must intertwine
Like sea and river,
10 Be fused and mingle,
Diverse yet single,
Forever and forever.

Let no man be so proud
And confident,
15 To think he is allowed
A little tent
Pitched in a meadow
Of sun and shadow
All his little own.

20 Joy may be shy, unique,
Friendly to a few,
Sorrow never scorned to speak
To any who
Were false or true.

25 Your every grief
Like a blade
Shining and unsheathed
Must strike me down.
Of bitter aloes wreathed,
30 My sorrow must be laid
On your head like a crown.

THINKING ABOUT THE SELECTION
Recalling

1. What pierces the speaker "to the marrow"?
2. What must "intertwine like sea and river"?
3. What should no person think?
4. (a) What must strike the speaker down?
   (b) What must be done with his sorrow?

Interpreting

5. How is the image presented in the first stanza echoed in the final stanza?
6. What is the meaning of the image presented in the third stanza?
7. Why does the speaker feel that joy is more difficult to share than sorrow?

Applying

8. Why do you think sharing feelings of sorrow with others often makes a person feel better?

ANALYZING LITERATURE
Understanding the Harlem Renaissance

The **Harlem Renaissance** was a cultural movement that emerged in Harlem during the 1920's. In their work the writers of the Harlem Renaissance tried to capture the essence of black life and communicate the general sentiments of the black people.

1. What do the emotions discussed in this poem suggest about the overall sentiments of the black people at the time?
2. How does the image presented in the first stanza suggest that the suffering of the black people is deeply rooted in the past?
3. What do you think is the poem's main purpose?

The Tropics in New York

Claude McKay

Bananas ripe and green, and ginger-root,
    Cocoa in pods and alligator pears,
And tangerines and mangoes and grape fruit,
    Fit for the highest prize at parish fairs,

5 Set in the window, bringing memories
    Of fruit-trees laden by low-singing rills,
And dewy dawns, and mystical blue skies
    In benediction over nun-like hills.

My eyes grew dim, and I could no more gaze;
10   A wave of longing through my body swept,
And, hungry for the old, familiar ways
    I turned aside and bowed my head and wept.

THINKING ABOUT THE SELECTION

Recalling

1. (a) What fruits are "set in the window"? (b) Of what do they bring memories?
2. (a) What emotion sweeps through the speaker's body in the final stanza? (b) How does he respond to this emotion?

Interpreting

3. How does the title contribute to the meaning of the poem?
4. What impression does the speaker convey of his homeland?
5. Which words create especially vivid images? Explain the reason for your choices.
6. How do the speaker's observations in the first stanza lead to the emotions he experiences in the third stanza?

Applying

7. Why do you think people often idealize and long for places from their past?

THINKING AND WRITING

Writing a Poem About a Special Place

Write a poem in which the speaker describes images which lead him or her to recall a place for which he or she has very powerful feelings. Start by listing the images that lead to the speaker's recollections. Then list the speaker's emotions concerning the place he or she recalls. Present the speaker's observations in the first stanza; present his or her associations in the next stanza; and describe his or her emotions in the third stanza. When you finish writing, revise your poem and share it with your classmates.

LANGSTON HUGHES

1902–1967

Langston Hughes emerged from the Harlem Renaissance as the most prolific and successful black writer in America. Although he is best known for his poetry, he also wrote plays, fiction, autobiographical sketches, and movie screenplays.

Born in Missouri and raised in Illinois and Ohio, Hughes attended high school in Cleveland, where he contributed poetry to the school literary magazine. In 1921 he moved to New York City to attend classes at Columbia University, but a year later he left school to travel to Europe and Africa as a merchant seaman. When he returned to the United States, he met the poet Vachel Lindsay, who helped him publish his first volume of poetry, *The Weary Blues* (1926). The book attracted considerable attention and earned Hughes widespread recognition.

Hughes went on to publish several other collections of poetry, including *The Dream Keeper* (1932), *Fields of Wonder* (1947), and *Montage of a Dream Deferred* (1951). In his poetry he experimented with a variety of forms and techniques and often tried to re-create the rhythms of contemporary jazz. Using his talents as a poet, he expressed pride in his heritage and voiced his displeasure with the oppression of blacks.

During the 1950's, Hughes helped to support himself by contributing a number of prose sketches to newspapers. Among the most popular was a series of tales about a fictional character named Jesse B. Semple, whom Hughes often referred to as "Simple." In 1963 Hughes developed these sketches into a musical play, *Simply Heaven*.

Hughes's work not only helped make the general public aware of black life, but it also inspired many other black writers. By eloquently chronicling the heritage of the black people and expressing their pride and determination, Hughes provided his people with a link to their cultural roots and a promise for a better future.

The Negro Speaks of Rivers

Writer's Techniques

The Speaker. The speaker is the voice of a poem. Although the speaker is often the poet himself or herself, the speaker may also be a fictional character, a group of people, or an inanimate object or another type of nonhuman entity. For example, in Carl Sandburg's poem "Grass," the speaker is the grass itself.

Look For

As you read "The Negro Speaks of Rivers," try to identify the poem's speaker.

Writing

In "The Negro Speaks of Rivers," Hughes develops a comparison between rivers and the black people. List some of the characteristics of rivers that you feel reflect certain aspects of the experience of the black people.

Vocabulary

Knowing the following words will help you as you read "The Negro Speaks of Rivers."

lulled (luld) *v.*: Calmed or soothed by gentle sound or motion (l. 5)

dusky (dus′ kē) *adj.*: Dim; shadowy (l. 9)

The Negro Speaks of Rivers

Langston Hughes

I've known rivers:
I've known rivers ancient as the world and older than the
    flow of human blood in human veins.

My soul has grown deep like the rivers.

I bathed in the Euphrates when dawns were young.
5   I built my hut near the Congo and it lulled me to sleep.
I looked upon the Nile and raised the pyramids above it.
I heard the singing of the Mississippi when Abe Lincoln
    went down to New Orleans, and I've seen its muddy
    bosom turn all golden in the sunset.

I've known rivers:
Ancient, dusky rivers.

10   My soul has grown deep like the rivers.

THINKING ABOUT THE SELECTION

Recalling

1. (a) Who is the speaker of "The Negro Speaks of Rivers"? (b) How does the title help to reveal the speaker's identity?

2. What has happened to the speaker's soul?

3. (a) When and where did the speaker bathe? (b) Where did he build his hut? (c) What did the speaker do after looking upon the Nile? (d) What did the speaker hear when "Abe Lincoln went down to New Orleans"?

Interpreting

4. In this poem Hughes develops a comparison between rivers and the black people. What does the age of rivers imply about the black race?

5. What do the references to specific rivers in lines 4–7 convey about the black experience?

6. (a) What do lines 3 and 10 suggest about how the black race has been affected by its experiences? (b) How do these two lines reflect the poem's theme, or main point?

Applying

7. In what respects can the human race as a whole be compared with rivers?

BIOGRAPHIES

Jean Toomer (1894–1967)

Like the other Harlem Renaissance writers, Jean Toomer had a deep interest in the cultural roots of the black people. In his work Toomer expressed his belief that maintaining an awareness of and a sense of pride in the black heritage was vital to the happiness and freedom of the black people.

Born in Washington, D.C., Toomer graduated from New York University in 1918. He then taught for several years in Georgia. His observations during his years as a teacher provided him with the material for *Cane* (1923), an unconventional book which consists of prose sketches, stories, poems, and a one-act play, all focusing on the concerns, interests, and experiences of American blacks.

Toomer published few other works during the course of his life. After *Cane* fell into obscurity shortly after its publication, Toomer was virtually forgotten as a writer. In recent years, however, *Cane* has come to be recognized as one of the most important works to come out of the Harlem Renaissance and has influenced the work of a number of black writers.

Arna Bontemps (1902–1973)

A talented editor, novelist, dramatist, and poet, Arna Bontemps was one of the most scholarly figures of the Harlem Renaissance.

Bontemps was born in Louisiana and educated at the University of Chicago. He published his first novel, *God Sends Sunday,* in 1931. This book was followed by two novels about slave revolts, *Black Thunder* (1936) and *Drums at Dusk* (1939). Bontemps then went on to produce several volumes of nonfiction, including *The Story of the Negro* (1951) and *One Hundred Years of Negro Freedom* (1961). He also co-edited *The Poetry of the Negro* (1950), an anthology of black poetry, with Langston Hughes, and collaborated with Countee Cullen in writing *St. Louis Women* (1946), a musical play.

Bontemps also wrote poetry throughout his rich, varied literary career. Written in simple, direct language, using traditional forms and techniques, his poems are characterized by what Bontemps himself called "a certain simplicity of expression."

Storm Ending; A Black Man Talks of Reaping

Writer's Techniques

Metaphor. A metaphor is a comparison between two seemingly dissimilar things. This comparison is implied, rather than stated, and no connecting word is used. While metaphors are often brief, they may also be long, elaborate comparisons. This type of metaphor, in which details developing the comparison are presented throughout the poem, is known as an extended metaphor. For example, Langston Hughes uses an extended metaphor in "The Negro Speaks of Rivers," as he develops a comparison between rivers and the black people throughout the poem.

Look For

As you read "Storm Ending" and "A Black Man Talks of Reaping," look for the use of extended metaphors.

Writing

In "Storm Ending" Jean Toomer describes a thunderstorm. Freewrite about the types of images you associate with thunderstorms and discuss the reasons why people have been captivated by thunderstorms.

Vocabulary

Knowing the following words will help you as you read "Storm Ending" and "The Negro Speaks of Rivers."

stark (stärk) *adj.*: Severe (p. 970, l. 4)

reaping (rēp′ iŋ) *v.*: Cutting or harvesting grain from a field (p. 970, l. 7)

glean (glēn) *v.*: Collect the remaining grain after reaping (p. 970, l. 11)

BLACK PLACE II, 1944
Georgia O'Keeffe
The Metropolitan Museum of Art

Storm Ending

Jean Toomer

Thunder blossoms gorgeously above our heads,
Great, hollow, bell-like flowers,
Rumbling in the wind,
Stretching clappers to strike our ears . . .
5   Full-lipped flowers
Bitten by the sun
Bleeding rain
Dripping rain like golden honey—
And the sweet earth flying from the thunder.

THINKING ABOUT THE SELECTION

Recalling

1. According to line 1, what does thunder do?
2. With what is rain compared in line 8?
3. According to line 9, how does the earth respond to the thunder?

Interpreting

4. (a) What natural event does the poem describe? (b) What is the speaker's attitude toward this event? (c) How is this attitude conveyed?

Applying

5. How would you describe your own attitude toward the type of natural event described in the poem?

ANALYZING LITERATURE

Understanding Metaphors

A **metaphor** is a comparison between two seemingly dissimilar things. An extended metaphor is a comparison which is developed throughout the course of a poem.

1. What two things are compared in the extended metaphor presented in "Storm Ending"?
2. How does Toomer establish this comparison in the first four lines?
3. How does he develop the comparison in the lines that follow?

THINKING AND WRITING

Creating an Extended Metaphor

Write a poem in which you present an extended metaphor. First decide on the two things you are going to compare. Then prepare a list of details developing this comparison. When writing your poem, establish the comparison in the first several lines; then develop it throughout the rest of the poem. After you finish writing, revise your poem, making sure that you have included enough details to adequately develop the comparison. When you finish revising, proofread your poem, and share it with your classmates.

A Black Man Talks of Reaping

Arna Bontemps

I have sown beside all waters in my day.
I planted deep, within my heart the fear
that wind or fowl would take the grain away.
I planted safe against this stark, lean year.

5   I scattered seed enough to plant the land
in rows from Canada to Mexico
but for my reaping only what the hand
can hold at once is all that I can show.

Yet what I sowed and what the orchard yields
10 my brother's sons are gathering stalk and root;
small wonder then my children glean in fields
they have not sown, and feed on bitter fruit.

THINKING ABOUT THE SELECTION

Recalling

1. Why does the speaker plant "deep"?
2. (a) How much seed does the speaker scatter? (b) With how much grain does he end up?
3. Why are the speaker's brother's sons "gathering stalk and root"?

Interpreting

4. (a) What does this poem suggest about how black people are rewarded for their hard work? (b) Who is the speaker referring to when he mentions his "brother's sons" in line 10?
5. (a) What are the "fields/they have not sown" in lines 11–12? (b) What is the "bitter fruit"?

Applying

6. In what ways do all people of all races and creeds sow and reap?

Drama

THE FABULOUS INVALID, 1938
Set Design by Donald Oenslayer
The Museum of the City of New York

THORNTON WILDER

1897–1975

One of only a few American writers to achieve success as both a novelist and a playwright, Thornton Wilder gained popularity by writing polished works that the American public could easily grasp.

Wilder was born in Madison, Wisconsin, but he spent much of his childhood in China. After graduating from Yale, he studied in Rome for a year and then went on to earn a master's degree in French from Princeton. While working as a French teacher at Lawrenceville Academy in New Jersey, he published his first novel, *The Cabala* (1926). A year later, he produced another novel, *The Bridge at San Luis Rey* (1927), which became a best seller and earned him the Pulitzer Prize.

During his late thirties, Wilder began focusing much of his energy on playwriting, while continuing to write novels. In 1938 he completed *Our Town,* which earned him his second Pulitzer Prize. Five years later Wilder received another Pulitzer Prize for his play, *The Skin of Our Teeth* (1942). Wilder earned further recognition for his literary achievements when he was awarded the first National Medal for Literature in 1965.

In a number of respects, *Our Town* is a very unconventional play. The play is staged with no curtain, little scenery, and virtually no props. When the play begins, a character called the Stage Manager introduces the characters and establishes the setting. Throughout the rest of the play, the stage manager narrates and interprets the events for the audience.

Written in direct, straightforward language, *Our Town* captures the essence of life in a rural New England town in the early 1900's. Delving into the thoughts and emotions of the town's inhabitants, the play explores the underlying significance of everyday life and touches upon concerns shared by all human beings. Because of its universal quality and its accessibility, *Our Town* remains almost as popular today as it was when it first appeared on Broadway.

GUIDE FOR READING

Our Town: Act I

Writer's Techniques

Staging. Staging refers to the process of presenting a play on a stage. When a dramatist stages a play, he or she uses a number of devices, apart from dialogue, to communicate with the audience. These devices include scenery, props, costumes, lighting, special effects, and the gestures and movements of the actors and actresses. To fully appreciate the staging of a play, you must attend a live performance. However, when reading a play, you can try to envision how it would be staged by paying close attention to the stage directions.

Our Town is staged in a very unconventional manner, with no curtain, little scenery, and virtually no props. Ladders are used to indicate the second stories of houses, a wooden plank is used to represent a drugstore counter, and the actors and actresses play with invisible balls, carry invisible bags, and read invisible newspapers. As a result the audience is forced to use its imagination to envision both the setting and the invisible objects with which the characters interact. At the same time, the lack of scenery and props makes *Our Town* an easy play to stage.

Look For

As you read *Our Town,* look for the devices used in staging the play. How do these devices affect your responses to the characters and events?

Writing

Our Town focuses on the lives of the inhabitants of a rural New England town. Brainstorm about the types of activities that might be a part of the daily routines of these people.

Vocabulary

Knowing the following words will help you as you read Act I of *Our Town*.

legacy (leg′ ə sē) *n.*: Money or property left to someone by a will (p. 980)

diligent (dil′ ə jənt) *adj.*: Hardworking; industrious (p. 982)

Our Town

Thornton Wilder

CHARACTERS

Stage Manager	Emily Webb	Constable Warren
Dr. Gibbs	Professor Willard	Si Crowell
Joe Crowell	Mr. Webb	Stagehands
Howie Newsome	Woman in the Balcony	Three Baseball Players
Mrs. Gibbs	Man in the Auditorium	Sam Craig
Mrs. Webb	Lady in the Box	Joe Stoddard
George Gibbs	Simon Stimson	Men and Women
Rebecca Gibbs	Mrs. Soames	Among the Dead
Wally Webb		

The entire play takes place in Grover's Corners, New Hampshire.

Complete text of OUR TOWN by Thornton Wilder. Copyright 1938, renewed 1957 by Thornton Wilder. Reprinted by permission of Harper & Row, Publishers, Inc.

Caution! OUR TOWN is the sole property of the author and is fully protected by copyright. It may not be acted by professionals or amateurs without formal permission and the payment of a royalty. All rights, including professional, amateur, stock, radio and television, broadcasting, motion picture, recitation, lecturing, public reading, and the rights of translation into foreign languages are reserved. All professional inquiries should be addressed to the author's agent: Brandt & Brandt Literary Agents, Inc., 1501 Broadway, New York, NY 10036. All requests for amateur rights should be addressed to Samuel French, Inc., 25 West 43rd Street, New York, NY 10036.

ACT I

[*No curtain.*

No scenery.

The audience, arriving, sees an empty stage in half-light.

Presently the STAGE MANAGER, *hat on and pipe in mouth, enters and begins placing a table and three chairs downstage left, and a table and three chairs downstage right. He also places a low bench at the corner of what will be the Webb house, left.*

"Left" and "right" are from the point of view of the actor facing the audience. "Up" is toward the back wall.

As the house lights go down he has finished setting the stage and leaning against the right proscenium[1] pillar watches the late arrivals in the audience.

When the auditorium is in complete darkness he speaks.]

STAGE MANAGER. This play is called *Our Town*. It was written by Thornton Wilder; produced and directed by A ____ (*or: produced by A ____; directed by B____*). In it you will see Miss C____; Miss D____; Miss E____; and Mr. F____; Mr. G____; Mr. H ____; and many others. The name of the town is Grover's Corners, New Hampshire—just across the Massachusetts line: latitude 42 degrees 40 minutes; longitude 70 degrees 37 minutes. The first act shows a day in our town. The day is May 7, 1901. The time is just before dawn.

[*A rooster crows.*]

The sky is beginning to show some streaks of light over in the East there, behind our mount'in.

The morning star always gets wonderful bright the minute before it has to go—doesn't it? [*He stares at it for a moment, then goes upstage.*]

Well, I'd better show you how our town lies. Up here—[*That is, parallel with the* back wall] is Main Street. Way back there is the railway station; tracks go that way. Polish Town's across the tracks, and some Canuck[2] families. [*Toward the left*] Over there is the Congregational Church; across the street's the Presbyterian.

Methodist and Unitarian are over there.

Baptist is down in the holla' by the river.

Catholic Church is over beyond the tracks.

Here's the Town Hall and Post Office combined; jail's in the basement.

Bryan[3] once made a speech from these very steps here.

Along here's a row of stores. Hitching posts and horse blocks in front of them. First automobile's going to come along in about five years—belonged to Banker Cartwright, our richest citizen . . . lives in the big white house up on the hill.

Here's the grocery store and here's Mr. Morgan's drugstore. Most everybody in town manages to look into those two stores once a day.

Public school's over yonder. High school's still farther over. Quarter of nine mornings, noontimes, and three o'clock afternoons, the hull town can hear the yelling and screaming from those schoolyards. [*He approaches the table and chairs downstage right.*]

This is our doctor's house—Doc Gibbs's. This is the back door.

[*Two arched trellises, covered with vines and flowers, are pushed out, one by each proscenium pillar.*]

There's some scenery for those who think they have to have scenery.

This is Mrs. Gibbs's garden. Corn . . . peas . . . beans . . . hollyhocks . . . heliotrope . . . and a lot of burdock. [*Crosses the stage.*]

In those days our newspaper come out

---

1. proscenium [prō sē′ nē əm] *n.*: The area of the stage in front of the curtain, where action takes place when the curtain is closed.

2. Canuck [kə nuk′] *n.*: Canadian or French-Canadian.

3. Bryan: William Jennings Bryan [*1860–1925*]. Famous American lawyer, statesman, and orator.

twice a week—the Grover's Corners *Sentinel*—and this is Editor Webb's house.

And this is Mrs. Webb's garden.

Just like Mrs. Gibbs's, only it's got a lot of sunflowers, too. [*He looks upward, center stage.*]

Right here . . .'s a big butternut tree. [*He returns to his place by the right proscenium pillar and looks at the audience for a minute.*]

Nice town, y'know what I mean?

Nobody very remarkable ever come out of it, s'far as we know.

The earliest tombstones in the cemetery up there on the mountain say 1670, 1680—they're Grovers and Cartwrights and Gibbses and Herseys—same names as are here now.

Well, as I said: it's about dawn.

The only lights on in town are in a cottage over by the tracks where a Polish mother's just had twins. And in the Joe Cromwell house, where Joe Junior's getting up so as to deliver the paper. And in the depot, where Shorty Hawkins is gettin' ready to flag the 5:45 for Boston.

[*A train whistle is heard. The* STAGE MANAGER *takes out his watch and nods.*]

Naturally, out in the country—all around—there've been lights on for some time, what with milkin's and so on. But town people sleep late.

So—another day's begun.

There's Doc Gibbs comin' down Main Street now, comin' back from that baby case. And here's his wife comin' downstairs to get breakfast.

[MRS. GIBBS, *a plump, pleasant woman in the middle thirties, comes "downstairs" right. She pulls up an imaginary window shade in her kitchen and starts to make a fire in her stove.*]

Doc Gibbs died in 1930. The new hospital's named after him.

Mrs. Gibbs died first—long time ago, in fact. She went out to visit her daughter, Rebecca, who married an insurance man in Canton, Ohio, and died there—pneumonia—but her body was brought back here. She's up in the cemetery there now—in with a whole mess of Gibbses and Herseys—she was Julia Hersey 'fore she married Doc Gibbs in the Congregational Church over there.

In our town we like to know the facts about everybody.

There's Mrs. Webb, coming downstairs to get her breakfast, too.—That's Doc Gibbs. Got that call at half past one this morning. And there comes Joe Crowell, Jr., delivering Mr. Webb's *Sentinel*.

[DR. GIBBS *has been coming along Main Street from the left. At the point where he would turn to approach his house, he stops, sets down his—imaginary—black bag, takes off his hat, and rubs his face with fatigue, using an enormous handkerchief.*

MRS. WEBB, *a thin, serious, crisp woman, has entered her kitchen, left, tying on an apron. She goes through the motions of putting wood into a stove, lighting it, and preparing breakfast.*

Suddenly, JOE CROWELL, JR., *eleven, starts down Main Street from the right, hurling imaginary newspapers into doorways.*]

JOE CROWELL, JR. Morning, Doc Gibbs.

DR. GIBBS. Morning, Joe.

JOE CROWELL, JR. Somebody been sick, Doc?

DR. GIBBS. No. Just some twins born over in Polish Town.

JOE CROWELL, JR. Do you want your paper now?

DR. GIBBS. Yes, I'll take it.—Anything serious goin' on in the world since Wednesday?

JOE CROWELL, JR. Yessir. My schoolteacher, Miss Foster, 's getting married to a fella over in Concord.

DR. GIBBS. I declare.—How do you boys feel about that?

JOE CROWELL, JR. Well, of course, it's none of my business—but I think if a person starts out to be a teacher, she ought to stay one.

DR. GIBBS. How's your knee, Joe?

JOE CROWELL, JR. Fine, Doc. I never think about it at all. Only like you said, it always tells me when it's going to rain.

DR. GIBBS. What's it telling you today? Goin' to rain?

JOE CROWELL, JR. No, sir.

DR. GIBBS. Sure?

JOE CROWELL, JR. Yessir.

DR. GIBBS. Knee ever make a mistake?

JOE CROWELL, JR. No, sir.

[JOE *goes off.* DR. GIBBS *stands reading his paper.*]

STAGE MANAGER. Want to tell you something about that boy Joe Crowell there. Joe was awful bright—graduated from high school here, head of his class. So he got a scholarship to Massachusetts Tech. Graduated head of his class there, too. It was all wrote up in the Boston paper at the time. Goin' to be a great engineer, Joe was. But the war broke out and he died in France—All that education for nothing.

HOWIE NEWSOME. [*Off left*] Giddap, Bessie! What's the matter with you today?

STAGE MANAGER. Here comes Howie Newsome, deliverin' the milk.

[HOWIE NEWSOME, *about thirty, in overalls, comes along Main Street from the left, walking beside an invisible horse and wagon and carrying an imaginary rack with milk bottles. The sound of clinking milk bottles is heard. He leaves some bottles at* MRS. WEBB's *trellis, then, crossing the stage to* MRS. GIBBS's, *he stops center to talk to* DR. GIBBS.]

HOWIE NEWSOME. Morning, Doc.

DR. GIBBS. Morning, Howie.

HOWIE NEWSOME. Somebody sick?

DR. GIBBS. Pair of twins over to Mrs. Goruslawski's.

HOWIE NEWSOME. Twins, eh? This town's gettin' bigger every year.

DR. GIBBS. Goin' to rain, Howie?

HOWIE NEWSOME. No, no. Fine day—that'll burn through. Come on, Bessie.

DR. GIBBS. Hello Bessie. [*He strikes the horse, which has remained up center.*] How old is she, Howie?

HOWIE NEWSOME. Going on seventeen. Bessie's all mixed up about the route ever since the Lockharts stopped takin' their quart of milk every day. She wants to leave 'em a quart just the same—keeps scolding me the hull trip.

[*He reaches* MRS. GIBBS's *back door. She is waiting for him.*]

MRS. GIBBS. Good morning, Howie.

HOWIE NEWSOME. Morning, Mrs. Gibbs. Doc's just comin' down the street.

MRS. GIBBS. Is he? Seems like you're late today.

HOWIE NEWSOME. Yes. Somep'n went wrong with the separator.[4] Don't know what 'twas. [*He passes* DR. GIBBS *up center.*] Doc!

DR. GIBBS. Howie!

MRS. GIBBS. [*Calling upstairs.*] Children! Children! Time to get up.

HOWIE NEWSOME. Come on Bessie! [*He goes off right.*]

MRS. GIBBS. George! Rebecca!

[DR. GIBBS *arrives at his back door and passes through the trellis into his house.*]

MRS. GIBBS. Everything all right, Frank?

DR. GIBBS. Yes. I declare—easy as kittens.

MRS. GIBBS. Bacon'll be ready in a minute. Set down and drink your coffee. You can catch a couple hours' sleep this morning, can't you?

---

4. separator: A machine for separating milk from cream.

DR. GIBBS. Hm! . . . Mrs. Wentworth's coming at eleven. Guess I know what it's about, too. Her stummick ain't what it ought to be.

MRS. GIBBS. All told, you won't get more'n three hours' sleep. Frank Gibbs, I don''t know what's goin' to become of you. I do wish I could get you to go away someplace and take a rest. I think it would do you good.

MRS. WEBB. Emileeee! Time to get up! Wally! Seven o'clock!

MRS. GIBBS. I declare, you got to speak to George. Seems like something's come over him lately. He's no help to me at all. I can't even get him to cut me some wood.

DR. GIBBS. [*Washing and drying his hands at the sink.* MRS. GIBBS *is busy at the stove.*] Is he sassy to you?

MRS. GIBBS. No. He just whines! All he thinks about is that baseball—George! Rebecca! You'll be late for school.

DR. GIBBS. M-m-m . . .

MRS. GIBBS. George!

DR. GIBBS. George, look sharp!

GEORGE'S VOICE. Yes, Pa!

DR. GIBBS. [*As he goes off the stage*] Don't you hear your mother calling you? I guess I'll go upstairs and get forty winks.

MRS. WEBB. Walleee! Emileee! You'll be late for school! Walleee! You wash yourself good or I'll come up and do it myself.

REBECCA GIBBS'S VOICE. Ma! What dress shall I wear?

MRS. GIBBS. Don't make a noise. Your father's been out all night and needs his sleep. I washed and ironed the blue gingham for you special.

REBECCA. Ma, I hate that dress.

MRS. GIBBS. Oh, hush-up-with-you.

REBECCA. Every day I go to school dressed like a sick turkey.

MRS. GIBBS. Now, Rebecca, you always look *very* nice.

REBECCA. Mama, George's throwing soap at me.

MRS. GIBBS. I'll come and slap the both of you—that's what I'll do.

[*A factory whistle sounds.*

The CHILDREN *dash in and take their places at the tables. Right,* GEORGE, *about sixteen, and* REBECCA, *eleven. Left,* EMILY *and* WALLY, *same ages. They carry strapped schoolbooks.*]

STAGE MANAGER. We've got a factory in our town, too—hear it? Makes blankets. Cartwrights own it and it brung 'em a fortune.

MRS. WEBB. Children! Now I won't have it. Breakfast is just as good as any other meal and I won't have you gobbling like wolves. It'll stunt your growth—that's a fact. Put away your book, Wally.

WALLY. Aw, Ma! By ten o'clock I got to know all about Canada.

MRS. WEBB. You know the rule's well as I do—no books at table. As for me, I'd rather have my children healthy than bright.

EMILY. I'm both, Mama: you know I am. I'm the brightest girl in school for my age. I have a wonderful memory.

MRS. WEBB. Eat your breakfast.

WALLY. I'm bright, too, when I'm looking at my stamp collection.

MRS. GIBBS. I'll speak to your father about it when he's rested. Seems to me twenty-five cents a week's enough for a boy your age. I declare I don't know how you spend it all.

GEORGE. Aw, Ma—I gotta lotta things to buy.

MRS. GIBBS. Strawberry phosphates[5]—that's what you spend it on.

---

5. phosphates: Soft drinks made with soda water and syrup.

GEORGE. I don't see how Rebecca comes to have so much money. She has more'n a dollar.

REBECCA. [*Spoon in mouth, dreamily*] I've been saving it up gradual.

MRS. GIBBS. Well, dear, I think it's a good thing to spend some every now and then.

REBECCA. Mama, do you know what I love most in the world—do you?—Money.

MRS. GIBBS. Eat your breakfast.

THE CHILDREN. Mama, there's first bell.—I gotta hurry.—I don't want any more.—I gotta hurry.

[*The* CHILDREN *rise, seize their books and dash out through the trellises. They meet, down center, and chattering, walk to Main Street, then turn left.*
The STAGE MANAGER *goes off unobtrusively right.*]

MRS. WEBB. Walk fast, but you don't have to run. Wally, pull up your pants at the knee. Stand up straight, Emily.

MRS. GIBBS. Tell Miss Foster I send her my best congratulations—can you remember that?

REBECCA. Yes, Ma.

MRS. GIBBS. You look real nice, Rebecca. Pick up your feet.

ALL. Goodbye.

[MRS. GIBBS *fills her apron with food for the chickens and comes down to the footlights.*]

MRS. GIBBS. Here, chick, chick, chick.
No, go away, you. Go away.
Here, chick, chick, chick.
What's the matter with *you?* Fight, fight, fight—that's all you do.
Hm . . . *you* don't belong to me. Where'd you come from? [*She shakes her apron.*] Oh, don't be so scared. Nobody's going to hurt you.

[MRS. WEBB *is sitting on the bench by her trellis stringing beans.*]

Good morning, Myrtle. How's your cold?

MRS. WEBB. Well, I still get that tickling feeling in my throat. I told Charles I didn't know as I'd go to choir practice tonight. Wouldn't be any use.

MRS. GIBBS. Have you tried singing over your voice?

MRS. WEBB. Yes, but somehow I can't do that and stay on the key. While I'm resting myself I thought I'd string some of these beans.

MRS. GIBBS. [*Rolling up her sleeves as she crosses the stage for a chat*] Let me help you. Beans have been good this year.

MRS. WEBB. I've decided to put up forty quarts if it kills me. The children say they hate 'em, but I notice they're able to get 'em down all winter.

[*Pause. Brief sound of chickens cackling.*]

MRS. GIBBS. Now, Myrtle. I've got to tell you something, because if I don't tell somebody I'll burst.

MRS. WEBB. Why, Julia Gibbs!

MRS. GIBBS. Here, give me some more of those beans. Myrtle, did one of those second-hand-furniture men from Boston come to see you last Friday?

MRS. WEBB. No-o.

MRS. GIBBS. Well, he called on me. First I thought he was a patient wantin' to see Dr. Gibbs. 'N he wormed his way into my parlor, and, Myrtle Webb, he offered me three hundred and fifty dollars for Grandmother Wentworth's highboy, as I'm sitting here!

MRS. WEBB. Why, Julia Gibbs!

MRS. GIBBS. He did! That old thing! Why, it was so big I didn't know where to put it and I almost give it to Cousin Hester Wilcox.

MRS. WEBB. Well, you're going to take it, aren't you?

MRS. GIBBS. I don't know.

MRS. WEBB. You don't know—three hundred and fifty dollars! What's come over you?

MRS. GIBBS. Well, if I could get the Doctor to take the money and go away someplace on a real trip, I'd sell it like that.—Y'know, Myrtle, it's been the dream of my life to see Paris, France.—Oh, I don't know. It sounds crazy, I suppose, but for years I've been promising myself that if we ever had the chance—

MRS. WEBB. How does the Doctor feel about it?

MRS. GIBBS. Well, I did beat about the bush a little and said if I got a legacy—that's the way I put it—I'd make him take me somewhere.

MRS. WEBB. M-m-m . . . What did he say?

MRS. GIBBS. You know how he is. I haven't heard a serious word out of him since I've known him. No, he said, it might make him discontented with Grover's Corners to go traipsin' about Europe; better let well enough alone, he says. Every two years he makes a trip to the battlefields of the Civil War and that's enough treat for anybody, he says.

MRS. WEBB. Well, Mr. Webb just *admires* the way Dr. Gibbs knows everything about the Civil War. Mr. Webb's a good mind to give up Napoleon and move over to the Civil War, only Dr. Gibbs being one of the greatest experts in the country just makes him despair.

MRS. GIBBS. It's a fact! Dr. Gibbs is never so happy as when he's at Antietam or Gettysburg. The times I've walked over those hills, Myrtle, stopping at every bush and pacing it all out, like we were going to buy it.

MRS. WEBB. Well, if that secondhand man's really serious about buyin' it, Julia, you sell it. And then you'll get to see Paris, all right. Just keep droppin' hints from time to time—

that's how I got to see the Atlantic Ocean, y'know.

MRS. GIBBS. Oh, I'm sorry I mentioned it. Only it seems to me that once in your life before you die you ought to see a country where they don't talk in English and don't even want to.

[*The* STAGE MANAGER *enters briskly from the right. He tips his hat to the ladies, who nod their heads.*]

STAGE MANAGER. Thank you, ladies. Thank you very much.

[MRS. GIBBS *and* MRS. WEBB *gather up their things, return into their homes and disappear.*]

Now we're going to skip a few hours.

But first we want a little more information about the town, kind of a scientific account, you might say.

So I've asked Professor Willard of our State University to sketch in a few details of our past history here.

Is Professor Willard here?

[PROFESSOR WILLARD, *a rural savant,*[6] *pince-nez*[7] *on a wide satin ribbon, enters from the right with some notes in his hand.*]

May I introduce Professor Willard of our State University.

A few brief notes, thank you, Professor—unfortunately our time is limited.

PROFESSOR WILLARD. Grover's Corners . . . let me see . . . Grover's Corners lies on the old Pleistocene granite of the Appalachian range. I may say it's some of the oldest land in the world. We're very proud of that. A shelf of Devonian basalt crosses it with vestiges of Mesozoic[8] shale, and some sandstone out-

---

6. *savant* [sə vänt′]: Scholar.
7. *pince-nez* [pans′ nā′]: Eyeglasses that are clipped to the bridge of the nose.
8. Pleistocene [plīs′ tə sēn], **Devonian, Mesozoic** [mes ə zō′ ik] *adj.*: Geological eras.

croppings; but that's all more recent: two hundred, three hundred million years old.

Some highly interesting fossils have been found . . . I may say: unique fossils . . . two miles out of town, in Silas Peckham's cow pasture. They can be seen at the museum in our University at any time—that is, any reasonable time. Shall I read some of Professor Gruber's notes on the meteorological situation—mean precipitation, et cetera?

STAGE MANAGER. Afraid we won't have time for that, Professor. We might have a few words on the history of man here.

PROFESSOR WILLARD. Yes . . . anthropological data: Early Amerindian[9] stock. Cotahatchee tribes . . . no evidence before the tenth century of this era . . . hm . . . now entirely disappeared . . . possible traces in three families. Migration toward the end of the seventeenth century of English brachycephalic[10] blue-eyed stock . . . for the most part. Since then some Slav and Mediterranean—

STAGE MANAGER. And the population, Professor Willard?

PROFESSOR WILLARD. Within the town limits: 2,640.

DR. GIBBS. Just a moment, Professor. [*He whispers into the* PROFESSOR'S *ear.*]

PROFESSOR WILLARD. Oh, yes, indeed?—The population, *at the moment,* is 2,642. The postal district brings in 507 more, making a total of 3,149.—Mortality and birth rates: constant.—By MacPherson's gauge: 6,032.

STAGE MANAGER. Thank you very much, Professor. We're all very much obliged to you, I'm sure.

PROFESSOR WILLARD. Not at all, sir; not at all.

STAGE MANAGER. This way, Professor, and thank you again.

[*Exit* PROFESSOR WILLARD.]

Now the political and social report: Editor Webb—Oh, Mr. Webb?

[MRS. WEBB *appears at her back door.*]

MRS. WEBB. He'll be here in a minute. . . . He just cut his hand while he was eatin' an apple.

STAGE MANAGER. Thank you, Mrs. Webb.

MRS. WEBB. Charles! Everybody's waitin'. [*Exit* MRS. WEBB.]

STAGE MANAGER. Mr. Webb is publisher and editor of the Grover's Corners *Sentinel.* That's our local paper, y'know.

[MR. WEBB *enters from his house, pulling on his coat. His finger is bound in a handkerchief.*]

MR. WEBB. Well . . . I don't have to tell you that we're run here by a board of selectmen.[11]— All males vote at the age of twenty-one. Women vote indirect. We're a lower-middle-class: sprinkling of professional men . . . ten percent illiterate laborers. Politically, we're eighty-six percent Republicans; six percent Democrats; four percent Socialists; rest, indifferent.

Religiously, we're eighty-five percent Protestants; twelve percent Catholics; rest, indifferent.

STAGE MANAGER. Have you any comments, Mr. Webb?

MR. WEBB. Very ordinary town, if you ask me. Little better behaved than most. Probably a lot duller.

But our young people here seem to like it well enough. Ninety percent of 'em graduating from high school settle down right here

---

9. Amerindian [am′ ə rind′ ē ən] *adj.*: American Indian.
10. brachycephalic [brak′ i sə fal′ ik] *adj.*: Short-headed or broad-headed.

11. board of selectmen: A council of elected officials.

to live—even when they've been away to college.

STAGE MANAGER. Now, is there anyone in the audience who would like to ask Editor Webb anything about the town?

WOMAN IN THE BALCONY. Is there much drinking in Grover's Corners?

MR. WEBB. Well, ma'am, I wouldn't know what you'd call *much*. Satiddy nights the farmhands meet down in Ellery Greenough's stable and holler some. We've got one or two town drunks, but they're always having remorses every time an evangelist comes to town. No, ma'am, I'd say likker ain't a regular thing in the home here, except in the medicine chest. Right good for snakebite, y'know—always was.

BELLIGERENT MAN AT BACK OF AUDITORIUM. Is there no one in town aware of—

STAGE MANAGER. Come forward, will you, where we can all hear you—What were you saying?

BELLIGERENT MAN. Is there no one in town aware of social injustice and industrial inequality?

MR. WEBB. Oh, yes, everybody is—somethin' terrible. Seems like they spend most of their time talking about who's rich and who's poor.

BELLIGERENT MAN. Then why don't they do something about it? [*He withdraws without waiting for an answer.*]

MR. WEBB. Well, I dunno . . . I guess we're all hunting like everybody else for a way the diligent and sensible can rise to the top and the lazy and quarrelsome can sink to the bottom. But it ain't easy to find. Meanwhile, we do all we can to help those that can't help themselves and those that can we leave alone.—Are there any other questions?

LADY IN A BOX. Oh, Mr. Webb? Mr. Webb, is there any culture or love of beauty in Grover's Corners?

MR. WEBB. Well, ma'am, there ain't much—not in the sense you mean. Come to think of it, there's some girls that play the piano at high school commencement; but they ain't happy about it. No, ma'am, there isn't much culture; but maybe this is the place to tell you that we've got a lot of pleasures of a kind here: we like the sun comin' up over the mountain in the morning, and we all notice a good deal about the birds. We pay a lot of attention to them. And we watch the change of the seasons; yes, everybody knows about them. But those other things—you're right, ma'am—there ain't much.—*Robinson Crusoe* and the Bible; and Handel's "Largo," we all know that; and Whistler's *Mother*[12]—those are just about as far as we go.

LADY IN A BOX. So I thought. Thank you, Mr. Webb.

STAGE MANAGER. Thank you, Mr. Webb.

[MR. WEBB *retires.*]

Now, we'll go back to the town. It's early afternoon. All 2,642 have had their dinners and all the dishes have been washed.

[MR. WEBB, *having removed his coat, returns and starts pushing a lawn mower to and fro beside his house.*]

There's an early-afternoon calm in our town: a buzzin' and a hummin' from the school buildings; only a few buggies on Main Street—the horses dozing at the hitching posts; you all remember what it's like. Doc Gibbs is in his office, tapping people and making them say "ah." Mr. Webb's cuttin' his lawn over there; one man in ten thinks it's a privilege to push his own lawn mower.

---

12. *Robinson Crusoe . . . Whistler's Mother:* *Robinson Crusoe* is a novel by English writer Daniel Defoe [1660?–1731]. Handel's "Largo" is a musical piece by German-born composer George Frederick Handel [1685–1759]. Whistler's *Mother* is a reference to the painting "Arrangement in Gray and Black: Portrait of the Artist's Mother" by American artist James McNeil Whistler [1834–1903].

No, sir. It's later than I thought. There are the children coming home from school already.

[*Shrill girls' voices are heard, off left.* EMILY *comes along Main Street, carrying some books. There are some signs that she is imagining herself to be a lady of startling elegance.*]

EMILY. I *can't*, Lois, I've got to go home and help my mother. I *promised*.

MR. WEBB. Emily, walk simply. Who do you think you are today?

EMILY. Papa, you're terrible. One minute you tell me to stand up straight and the next minute you call me names. I just don't listen to you. [*She gives him an abrupt kiss.*]

MR. WEBB. Golly, I never got a kiss from such a great lady before.

[*He goes out of sight.* EMILY *leans over and picks some flowers by the gate of her house.*

GEORGE GIBBS *comes careening down Main Street. He is throwing a ball up to dizzying heights, and waiting to catch it again. This sometimes requires his taking six steps backward. He bumps into an* OLD LADY *invisible to us.*]

GEORGE. Excuse me, Mrs. Forrest.

STAGE MANAGER. [*As* MRS. FORREST] Go out and play in the fields, young man. You got no business playing baseball on Main Street.

GEORGE. Awfully sorry, Mrs. Forrest.—Hello, Emily.

EMILY. H'lo.

GEORGE. You made a fine speech in class.

EMILY. Well . . . I was really ready to make a speech about the Monroe Doctrine, but at the last minute Miss Corcoran made me talk about the Louisiana Purchase instead. I worked an awful long time on both of them.

GEORGE. Gee, it's funny, Emily. From my window up there I can just see your head

nights when you're doing your homework over in your room.

EMILY. Why, can you?

GEORGE. You certainly do stick to it, Emily. I don't see how you can sit still that long. I guess you like school.

EMILY. Well, I always feel it's something you have to go through.

GEORGE. Yeah.

EMILY. I don't mind it really. It passes the time.

GEORGE. Yeah.—Emily, what do you think? We might work out a kinda telegraph from your window to mine; and once in a while you could give me a kinda hint or two about one of those algebra problems. I don't mean the answers, Emily, of course not . . . just some little hint . . .

EMILY. Oh, I think *hints* are allowed.—So— ah—if you get stuck, George, you whistle to me; and I'll give you some hints.

GEORGE. Emily, you're just naturally bright, I guess.

EMILY. I figure that it's just the way a person's born.

GEORGE. Yeah. But, you see, I want to be a farmer, and my Uncle Luke says whenever I'm ready I can come over and work on his farm and if I'm any good I can just gradually have it.

EMILY. You mean the house and everything?

[*Enter* MRS. WEBB *with a large bowl and sits on the bench by her trellis.*]

GEORGE. Yeah. Well, thanks . . . I better be getting out to the baseball field. Thanks for the talk, Emily.—Good afternoon, Mrs. Webb.

MRS. WEBB. Good afternoon, George.

GEORGE. So long, Emily.

EMILY. So long, George.

MRS. WEBB. Emily, come and help me string these beans for the winter. George Gibbs let himself have a real conversation, didn't he? Why, he's growing up. How old would George be?

EMILY. I don't know.

MRS. WEBB. Let's see. He must be almost sixteen.

EMILY. Mama, I made a speech in class today and I was very good.

MRS. WEBB. You must recite it to your father at supper. What was it about?

EMILY. The Louisiana Purchase. It was like silk off a spool. I'm going to make speeches all my life.—Mama, are these big enough?

MRS. WEBB. Try and get them a little bigger if you can.

EMILY. Mama, will you answer me a question, serious?

MRS. WEBB. Seriously, dear—not serious.

EMILY. Seriously—will you?

MRS. WEBB. Of course, I will.

EMILY. Mama, am I good-looking?

MRS. WEBB. Yes, of course you are. All my children have got good features; I'd be ashamed if they hadn't.

EMILY. Oh, Mama, that's not what I mean. What I mean is: am I *pretty*?

MRS. WEBB. I've already told you, yes. Now that's enough of that. You have a nice young pretty face. I never heard of such foolishness.

EMILY. Oh, Mama, you never tell us the truth about anything.

MRS. WEBB. I *am* telling the truth.

EMILY. Mama, were *you* pretty?

MRS. WEBB. Yes, I was, if I do say so. I was the prettiest girl in town next to Mamie Cartwright.

EMILY. But, Mama, you've got to say *something* about me. Am I pretty enough . . . to get anybody . . . to get people interested in me?

MRS. WEBB. Emily, you make me tired. Now stop it. You're pretty enough for all normal purposes.—Come along now and bring that bowl with you.

EMILY. Oh, Mama, you're no help at all.

STAGE MANAGER. Thank you, thank you! That'll do. We'll have to interrupt again here. Thank you, Mrs. Webb; thank you, Emily.

[MRS. WEBB *and* EMILY *withdraw.*]

There are some more things we want to explore about this town.

[*He comes to the center of the stage. During the following speech the lights gradually dim to darkness, leaving only a spot on him.*]

I think this is a good time to tell you that the Cartwright interests have just begun building a new bank in Grover's Corners—had to go to Vermont for the marble, sorry to say. And they've asked a friend of mine what they should put in the cornerstone for people to dig up . . . a thousand years from now. . . . Of course, they've put in a copy of the *New York Times* and a copy of Mr. Webb's *Sentinel.* . . . We're kind of interested in this because some scientific fellas have found a way of painting all that reading matter with a glue—a silicate glue—that'll make it keep a thousand—two thousand years.

We're putting in a Bible . . . and the Constitution of the United States—and a copy of William Shakespeare's plays. What do you say, folks? What do you think?

Y'know—Babylon[13] once had two million people in it, and all we know about 'em is the names of the kings and some copies of wheat contracts . . . and contracts for the sales of

---

13. Babylon [bab′ ə lən]: Ancient city famous for wealth, luxury, and wickedness.

slaves. Yet every night all those families sat down to supper, and the father came home from his work, and the smoke went up the chimney—same as here. And even in Greece and Rome, all we know about the *real* life of the people is what we can piece together out of the joking poems and the comedies they wrote for the theater back then.

So I'm going to have a copy of this play put in the cornerstone and the people a thousand years from now'll know a few simple facts about us—more than the Treaty of Versailles[14] and the Lindbergh flight.

See what I mean?

So—people a thousand years from now—this is the way we were in the provinces north of New York at the beginning of the twentieth century.—This is the way we were: in our growing up and in our marrying and in our living and in our dying.

[*A choir partially concealed in the orchestra pit has begun singing "Blessed Be the Tie That Binds."*

SIMON STIMSON *stands directing them.*

Two ladders have been pushed onto the stage; they serve as indication of the second story in the Gibbs and Webb houses. GEORGE *and* EMILY *mount them, and apply themselves to their schoolwork.*]

DR. GIBBS *has entered and is seated in his kitchen reading.*

Well!—good deal of time's gone by. It's evening.

You can hear choir practice going on in the Congregational Church.

The children are at home doing their schoolwork.

The day's running down like a tired clock.

SIMON STIMSON. Now look here, everybody. Music come into the world to give pleasure.—Softer! Softer! Get it out of your heads that music's only good when it's loud.

You leave loudness to the Methodists. You couldn't beat 'em, even if you wanted to. Now again. Tenors!

GEORGE. Hssst! Emily!

EMILY. Hello.

GEORGE. Hello!

EMILY. I can't work at all. The moonlight's so *terrible.*

GEORGE. Emily, did you get the third problem?

EMILY. Which?

GEORGE. The *third?*

EMILY. Why, yes, George—that's the easiest of them all.

GEORGE. I don't see it. Emily, can you give me a hint?

EMILY. I'll tell you one thing: the answer's in yards.

GEORGE. !!! In yards? How do you mean?

EMILY. In *square* yards.

GEORGE. Oh . . . in square yards.

EMILY. Yes, George, don't you see?

GEORGE. Yeah.

EMILY. In square yards of *wallpaper.*

GEORGE. Wallpaper—oh, I see. Thanks a lot, Emily.

EMILY. You're welcome. My, isn't the moonlight *terrible?* And choir practice going on.— I think if you hold your breath you can hear the train all the way to Contoocook. Hear it?

GEORGE. M-m-m—What do you know!

EMILY. Well, I guess I better go back and try to work.

GEORGE. Good night, Emily. And thanks.

EMILY. Good night, George.

SIMON STIMSON. Before I forget it: how many

---

14. Treaty of Versailles [vər sī']: Treaty signed in 1919, ending World War I.

of you will be able to come in Tuesday afternoon and sing at Fred Hersey's wedding?—show your hands. That'll be fine; that'll be right nice. We'll do the same music we did for Jane Trowbridge's last month.

—Now we'll do: "Art Thou Weary, Art Thou Languid?" It's a question, ladies and gentlemen, make it talk. Ready.

DR. GIBBS. Oh, George, can you come down a minute?

GEORGE. Yes, Pa. [*He descends the ladder.*]

DR. GIBBS. Make yourself comfortable, George; I'll only keep you a minute. George, how old are you?

GEORGE. I? I'm sixteen, almost seventeen.

DR. GIBBS. What do you want to do after school's over?

GEORGE. Why, you know, Pa. I want to be a farmer on Uncle Luke's farm.

DR. GIBBS. You'll be willing, will you, to get up early and milk and feed the stock . . . and you'll be able to hoe and hay all day.

GEORGE. Sure, I will. What are you . . . what do you mean, Pa?

DR. GIBBS. Well, George, while I was in my office today I heard a funny sound . . . and what do you think it was? It was your mother chopping wood. There you see your mother—getting up early; cooking meals all day long; washing and ironing—and still she has to go out in the backyard and chop wood. I suppose she just got tired of asking you. She just gave up and decided it was easier to do it herself. And you eat her meals, and put on the clothes she keeps nice for you, and you run off and play baseball—like she's some hired girl we keep around the house but that we don't like very much. Well, I knew all I had to do was call your attention to it. Here's a handkerchief, son. George, I've decided to raise your spending money twenty-five cents a week. Not, of course, for chopping wood for your mother, because that's a present you give her, but because you're getting older—and I imagine there are lots of things you must find to do with it.

GEORGE. Thanks, Pa.

DR. GIBBS. Let's see—tomorrow's your payday. You can count on it—Hmm. Probably Rebecca'll feel she ought to have some more too. Wonder what could have happened to your mother. Choir practice never was as late as this before.

GEORGE. It's only half past eight, Pa.

DR. GIBBS. I don't know why she's in that old choir. She hasn't any more voice than an old crow. . . . Traipsin' around the streets at this hour of the night . . . Just about time you retired, don't you think?

GEORGE. Yes, Pa.

[GEORGE *mounts to his place on the ladder.*

Laughter and good-nights can be heard on stage left and presently MRS. GIBBS, MRS. SOAMES *and* MRS. WEBB *come down Main Street. When they arrive at the corner of the stage they stop.*]

MRS. SOAMES. Good night, Martha. Good night, Mr. Foster.

MRS. WEBB. I'll tell Mr. Webb; I *know* he'll want to put it in his paper.

MRS. GIBBS. My, it's late!

MRS. SOAMES. Good night, Irma.

MRS. GIBBS. Real nice choir practice, wa'n't it? Myrtle Webb! Look at that moon, will you! Tsk-tsk-tsk. Potato weather, for sure.

[*They are silent a moment, gazing up at the moon.*]

MRS. SOAMES. Naturally I didn't want to say a word about it in front of those others, but now we're alone—really, it's the worst scandal that ever was in this town!

MRS. GIBBS. What?

MRS. SOAMES. Simon Stimson!

MRS. GIBBS. Now, Louella!

MRS. SOAMES. But, Julia! To have the organist of a church *drink* and *drunk* year after year. You know he was drunk tonight.

MRS. GIBBS. Now, Louella! We all know about Mr. Stimson and we all know about the troubles he's been through, and Dr. Ferguson

knows too, and if Dr. Ferguson keeps him on there in his job the only thing the rest of us can do is just not to notice it.

MRS. SOAMES. *Not to notice it!* But it's getting worse.

MRS. WEBB. No, it isn't, Louella. It's getting better. I've been in that choir twice as long

But before they do I want you to try and remember what it was like to have been very young.

And particularly the days when you were first in love; when you were like a person sleepwalking, and you didn't quite see the street you were in, and didn't quite hear everything that was said to you.

You're just a little bit crazy. Will you remember that, please?

Now they'll be coming out of high school at three o'clock. George has just been elected president of the junior class, and as it's June, that means he'll be president of the senior class all next year. And Emily's just been elected secretary and treasurer. I don't have to tell you how important that is.

[*He places a board across the backs of two chairs, which he takes from those at the Gibbs family's table. He brings two high stools from the wings and places them behind the board. Persons sitting on the stools will be facing the audience. This is the counter of Mr. Morgan's drugstore. The sounds of young people's voices are heard off left.*]

Yepp—there they are coming down Main Street now.

[EMILY, *carrying an armful of—imaginary—schoolbooks, comes along Main Street from the left.*]

EMILY. I can't, Louise. I've got to go home. Goodbye. Oh, Ernestine! Ernestine! Can you come over tonight and do Latin? Isn't that Cicero the worst thing—! Tell your mother you *have* to. G'bye. G'bye, Helen. G'bye, Fred.

[GEORGE, *also carrying books, catches up with her.*]

GEORGE. Can I carry your books home for you, Emily?

EMILY. [*Coolly*] Why . . . uh . . . Thank you. It isn't far. [*She gives them to him.*]

GEORGE. Excuse me a minute, Emily.—Say, Bob, if I'm a little late, start practice anyway. And give Herb some long high ones.

EMILY. Goodbye, Lizzy.

GEORGE. Goodbye, Lizzy.—I'm awfully glad you were elected, too, Emily.

EMILY. Thank you.

[*They have been standing on Main Street, almost against the back wall. They take the first steps toward the audience when* GEORGE *stops and says:*]

GEORGE. Emily, why are you mad at me?

EMILY. I'm not mad at you.

GEORGE. You've been treating me so funny lately.

EMILY. Well, since you ask me, I might as well say it right out, George—[*She catches sight of a teacher passing.*] Goodbye, Miss Corcoran.

GEORGE. Goodbye, Miss Corcoran.—Wha—what is it?

EMILY. [*Not scoldingly; finding it difficult to say*] I don't like the whole change that's come over you in the last year. I'm sorry if that hurts your feelings, but I've got to—tell the truth and shame the devil.

GEORGE. A *change?*—Wha—what do you mean?

EMILY. Well, up to a year ago I used to like you a lot. And I used to watch you as you did everything . . . because we'd been friends so long . . . and then you began spending all your time at *baseball* . . . and you never stopped to speak to anybody any more. Not even to your own family you didn't . . . and, George, it's a fact, you've got awful conceited and stuck-up, and all the girls say so. They may not say so to your face, but that's what they say about you behind your back, and it hurts me to hear them say it, but I've got to agree with them a little. I'm sorry if it hurts your feelings . . . but I can't be sorry I said it.

GEORGE. I . . . I'm glad you said it, Emily. I

never thought that such a thing was happening to me. I guess it's hard for a fella not to have faults creep into his character.

[*They take a step or two in silence, then stand still in misery.*]

EMILY. I always expect a man to be perfect and I think he should be.

GEORGE. Oh . . . I don't think it's possible to be perfect, Emily.

EMILY. Well, my *father* is, and as far as I can see *your* father is. There's no reason on earth why you shouldn't be, too.

GEORGE. Well, I feel it's the other way round. That men aren't naturally good; but girls are.

EMILY. Well, you might as well know right now that I'm not perfect. It's not as easy for a girl to be perfect as a man, because we girls are more—more—nervous.—Now I'm sorry I said all that about you. I don't know what made me say it.

GEORGE. Emily—

EMILY. Now I can see it's not the truth at all. And I suddenly feel that it isn't important, anyway.

GEORGE. Emily . . . would you like an ice-cream soda, or something, before you go home?

EMILY. Well, thank you. . . . I would.

[*They advance toward the audience and*

MR. WEBB. Sh—sh—Emily. Everything's all right.

EMILY. Why can't I stay for a while just as I am? Let's go away—

MR. WEBB. No, no, Emily. Now stop and think a minute.

EMILY. Don't you remember that you used to say—all the time you used to say—all the time: that I was *your* girl! There must be lots of places we can go to. I'll work for you. I could keep house.

MR. WEBB. Sh . . . You mustn't think of such things. You're just nervous, Emily. [*He turns and calls:*] George! George! Will you come here a minute? [*He leads her toward* GEORGE.] Why, you're marrying the best young fellow in the world. George is a fine fellow.

EMILY. But Papa—

[MRS. GIBBS *returns unobtrusively to her seat.*

MR. WEBB *has one arm around his daughter. He places his hand on* GEORGE's *shoulder.*]

MR. WEBB. I'm giving away my daughter, George. Do you think you can take care of her?

GEORGE. Mr. Webb, I want to . . . I want to try. Emily, I'm going to do my best. I love you, Emily. I need you.

EMILY. Well, if you love me, help me. All I want is someone to love me.

GEORGE. I will, Emily. Emily, I'll try.

EMILY. And I mean *forever.* Do you hear me? Forever and ever.

[*They fall into each other's arms.*

The "March" from Lohengrin[3] *is heard.*

---

3. "March" from *Lohengrin* [lō′ ən grin′]: The wedding march, also known as "Here Comes the Bride," from the opera *Lohengrin,* by German composer Richard Wagner [1813–1883].

The STAGE MANAGER, *as* CLERGYMAN, *stands on the box, up center.*]

MR. WEBB. Come, they're waiting for us. Now you know it'll be all right. Come, quick.

[GEORGE *slips away and takes his place beside the* STAGE MANAGER-CLERGYMAN.

EMILY *proceeds up the aisle on her father's arm.*]

STAGE MANAGER. Do you, George, take this woman, Emily, to be your wedded wife, to have . . .

[MRS. SOAMES *has been sitting in the last row of the congregation.*

She now turns to her neighbors and speaks in a shrill voice. Her chatter drowns out the rest of the clergyman's words.]

MRS. SOAMES. Perfectly lovely wedding! Loveliest wedding I ever saw. Oh, I do love a good wedding, don't you? Doesn't she make a lovely bride?

GEORGE. I do.

STAGE MANAGER. Do you, Emily, take this man, George, to be your wedded husband—

[*Again, his further words are covered by those of* MRS. SOAMES.]

MRS. SOAMES. Don't know *when* I've seen such a lovely wedding. But I always cry. Don't know why it is, but I always cry. I just like to see young people happy, don't you? Oh, I think it's lovely.

[*The ring.*

The kiss.

The stage is suddenly arrested into silent tableau.

The STAGE MANAGER, *his eyes on the distance as though to himself:*]

STAGE MANAGER. I've married over two hundred couples in my day.

Do I believe in it?

I don't know.

M ____ marries N ____ millions of them.

The cottage, the go-cart, the Sunday-afternoon drives in the Ford, the first rheumatism, the grandchildren, the second rheumatism, the deathbed, the reading of the will—[*He now looks at the audience for the first time, with a warm smile that removes any sense of cynicism from the next line.*] Once in a thousand times it's interesting.

—Well, let's have Mendelssohn's "Wedding March"!

[*The organ picks up the "March."*

Our Town, Act III

Writer's Techniques

Theme. The theme is the central idea or insight about life that a writer hopes to convey in a work of literature. Some themes are simple and can be stated in a single sentence. Others are more complex, requiring a much longer explanation. A single literary work may also have more than one theme. In fact, a full-length play such as *Our Town* is likely to have several themes.

In drama, themes are conveyed either directly or indirectly through the comments and actions of the characters. For example, in *Our Town* the Stage Manager suggests a number of possible themes in his remarks throughout the play.

Look For

As you read *Our Town,* look for the insights about life it offers. How are these insights conveyed?

Writing

In his opening remarks in Act III, the Stage Manager comments that Grover's Corners is gradually changing in some ways but in other ways remains the same. Discuss ways in which the hometown, or city, has changed during the past several years. Then discuss some of the ways in which it has not changed.

Vocabulary

Knowing the following words will help you as you read Act III of *Our Town*.

lugubriousness (loo goo′ brē əs nəs) *n.*: Mournfulness (p. 1009)

bereaved (bi rēvd′) *n.*: The survivors of recently deceased people (p. 1011)

ACT III

[*During the intermission the audience has seen the* STAGE HANDS *arranging the stage. On the right-hand side, a little right of the center, ten or twelve ordinary chairs have been placed in three openly spaced rows facing the audience.*

These are graves in the cemetery.

Toward the end of the intermission the actors enter and take their places. The front row contains: toward the center of the stage, an empty chair; then MRS. GIBBS; SIMON STIMSON.

The second row contains, among others, MRS. SOAMES.

The third row has WALLY WEBB.

The dead do not turn their heads or their eyes to right or left, but they sit in a quiet way without stiffness. When they speak their tone is matter-of-fact, without sentimentality and, above all, without lugubriousness.

The STAGE MANAGER *takes his accustomed place and waits for the house lights to go down.*]

STAGE MANAGER. This time nine years have gone by, friends—summer, 1913.

Gradual changes in Grover's Corners. Horses are getting rarer. Farmers coming into town in Fords.

Everybody locks their house doors now at night. Ain't been any burglars in town yet, but everybody's heard about 'em.

You'd be surprised, though—on the whole, things don't change much around here.

This is certainly an important part of Grover's Corners. It's on a hilltop—a windy hilltop—lots of sky, lots of clouds—often lots of sun and moon and stars.

You come up here, on a fine afternoon and you can see range on range of hills—awful blue they are—up there by Lake Sunapee and Lake Winnipesaukee . . . and way up, if you've got a glass, you can see the White Mountains and Mt. Washington—where North Conway and Conway is. And, of course, our favorite mountain, Mt. Monadnock, 's right here—and all these towns that lie around it: Jaffrey, 'n East Jaffrey, 'n Peterborough, n' Dublin; and [*Then pointing down in the audience*] there, quite a ways down, is Grover's Corners.

Yes, beautiful spot up here. Mountain laurel and li-lacks. I often wonder why people like to be buried in Woodlawn and Brooklyn when they might pass the same time up here in New Hampshire. Over there—[*Pointing to stage left*] are the old stones—1670, 1680. Strong-minded people that come a long way to be independent. Summer people walk around there laughing at the funny words on the tombstones . . . it don't do any harm. And genealogists come up from Boston—get paid by city people for looking up their ancestors. They want to make sure they're Daughters of the American Revolution and of the *Mayflower*. . . . Well, I guess that don't do any harm, either. Wherever you come near the human race, there's layers and layers of nonsense. . . .

Over there are some Civil War veterans. Iron flags on their graves . . . New Hampshire boys . . . had a notion that the Union ought to be kept together, though they'd never seen more than fifty miles of it themselves. All they knew was the name, friends—the United States of America. The United States of America. And they went and died about it.

This here is the new part of the cemetery. Here's your friend Mrs. Gibbs. 'N let me see—Here's Mr. Stimson, organist at the Congregational Church. And Mrs. Soames, who enjoyed the wedding so—you remember? Oh, and a lot of others. And Editor Webb's boy, Wallace, whose appendix burst while he was on a Boy Scout trip to Crawford Notch.

Yes, an awful lot of sorrow has sort of quieted down up here. People just wild with grief have brought their relatives up to this hill. We all know how it is . . . and then time . . . and sunny days . . . and rainy days . . . 'n snow . . . We're all glad they're in a beautiful place and we're coming up here ourselves when our fit's over.

Now there are some things we all know, but we don't take'm out and look at'm very often. We all know that *something* is eternal. And it ain't houses and it ain't names, and it ain't earth, and it ain't even the stars . . . everybody knows in their bones that *something* is eternal, and that something has to do with human beings. All the greatest people ever lived have been telling us that for five thousand years and yet you'd be surprised how people are always losing hold of it. There's something way down deep that's eternal about every human being. [*Pause*]

You know as well as I do that the dead don't stay interested in us living people for very long. Gradually, gradually, they lose hold of the earth . . . and the ambitions they had . . . and the pleasures they had . . . and the things they suffered . . . and the people they loved.

They get weaned away from the earth— that's the way I put it—weaned away.

And they stay here while the earth part of 'em burns away, burns out; and all that time they slowly get indifferent to what's goin' on in Grover's Corners.

They're waitin'. They're waitin' for something that they feel is comin'. Something important, and great. Aren't they waitin' for the eternal part in them to come out clear?

Some of the things they're going to say maybe'll hurt your feelings—but that's the way it is: mother 'n daughter . . . husband 'n wife . . . enemy 'n enemy . . . money 'n miser . . . all those terribly important things kind of grow pale around here. And what's left when memory's gone, and your identity, Mrs. Smith? [*He looks at the audience a minute, then turns to the stage.*]

Well! There are some *living* people. There's Joe Stoddard, our undertaker, supervising a new-made grave. And here comes

a Grover's Corners boy, that left town to go out West.

[JOE STODDARD *has hovered about in the background.* SAM CRAIG *enters left, wiping his forehead from the exertion. He carries an umbrella and strolls front.*]

SAM CRAIG. Good afternoon, Joe Stoddard.

JOE STODDARD. Good afternoon, good afternoon. Let me see now: do I know you?

SAM CRAIG. I'm Sam Craig.

JOE STODDARD. Gracious sakes' alive! Of all people! I should'a knowed you'd be back for the funeral. You've been away a long time, Sam.

SAM CRAIG. Yes, I've been away over twelve years. I'm in business out in Buffalo now, Joe. But I was in the East when I got news of my cousin's death, so I thought I'd combine things a little and come and see the old home. You look well.

JOE STODDARD. Yes yes, can't complain. Very sad, our journey today, Samuel.

SAM CRAIG. Yes.

JOE STODDARD. Yes, yes. I always say I hate to supervise when a young person is taken. They'll be here in a few minutes now. I had to come here early today—my son's supervisin' at the home.

SAM CRAIG. [*Reading stones*] Old Farmer Mc-Carty, I used to do chores for him—after school. He had the lumbago.

JOE STODDARD. Yes, we brought Farmer Mc-Carty here a number of years ago now.

SAM CRAIG. [*Staring at* MRS. GIBBS's *knees*] Why, this is my Aunt Julia . . . I'd forgotten that she'd . . . of course, of course.

JOE STODDARD. Yes, Doc Gibbs lost his wife two, three years ago . . . about this time. And today's another pretty bad blow for him, too.

MRS. GIBBS. [*To* SIMON STIMSON: *in an even voice*] That's my sister Carey's boy, Sam . . . Sam Craig.

SIMON STIMSON. I'm always uncomfortable when *they're* around.

MRS. GIBBS. Simon.

SAM CRAIG. Do they choose their own verses much, Joe?

JOE STODDARD. No . . . not usual. Mostly the bereaved pick a verse.

SAM CRAIG. Doesn't sound like Aunt Julia. There aren't many of those Hersey sisters left now. Let me see: where are . . . I wanted to look at my father's and mother's . . .

JOE STODDARD. Over there with the Craigs . . . Avenue F.

SAM CRAIG. [*Reading* SIMON STIMSON's *epitaph*] He was organist at church, wasn't he?—Hm, drank a lot, we used to say.

JOE STODDARD. Nobody was supposed to know about it. He'd seen a peck of trouble. [*Behind his hands*] Took his own life, y' know?

SAM CRAIG. Oh, did he?

JOE STODDARD. Hung himself in the attic. They tried to hush it up, but of course it got around. He chose his own epy-taph. You can see it there. It ain't a verse exactly.

SAM CRAIG. Why, it's just some notes of music—what is it?

JOE STODDARD. Oh, I wouldn't know. It was wrote up in the Boston papers at the time.

SAM CRAIG. Joe, what did she die of?

JOE STODDARD. Who?

SAM CRAIG. My cousin.

JOE STODDARD. Oh, didn't you know? Had some trouble bringing a baby into the world. 'Twas her second, though. There's a little boy 'bout four years old.

SAM CRAIG. [*Opening his umbrella*] The grave's going to be over there?

JOE STODDARD. Yes, there ain't much more room over here among the Gibbses, so they're opening up a whole new Gibbs section over by Avenue B. You'll excuse me now. I see they're comin'.

[*From left to center, at the back of the stage, comes a procession.* FOUR MEN *carry a casket, invisible to us. All the rest are under umbrellas. One can vaguely see* DR. GIBBS, GEORGE, *the* WEBBS, *etc. They gather about a grave in the back center of the stage, a little to the left of center.*]

MRS. SOAMES. Who is it, Julia?

MRS. GIBBS. [*Without raising her eyes*] My daughter-in-law, Emily Webb.

MRS. SOAMES. [*A little surprised, but no emotion*] Well, I declare! The road up here must have been awfully muddy. What did she die of, Julia?

MRS. GIBBS. In childbirth.

MRS. SOAMES. Childbirth. [*Almost with a laugh*] I'd forgotten all about that. My, wasn't life awful—[*With a sigh*] and wonderful.

SIMON STIMSON. [*With a sideways glance*] Wonderful, was it?

MRS. GIBBS. Simon! Now, remember!

MRS. SOAMES. I remember Emily's wedding. Wasn't it a lovely wedding! And I remember her reading the class poem at graduation exercises. Emily was one of the brightest girls ever graduated from high school. I've heard Principal Wilkins say so time after time. I called on them at their new farm, just before I died. Perfectly beautiful farm.

A WOMAN FROM AMONG THE DEAD. It's on the same road we lived on.

A MAN AMONG THE DEAD. Yepp, right smart farm.

[*They subside. The group by the grave starts singing "Blessed Be the Tie That Binds."*]

A WOMAN AMONG THE DEAD. I always liked that hymn. I was hopin' they'd sing a hymn.

[*Pause. Suddenly* EMILY *appears from among the umbrellas. She is wearing a white dress. Her hair is down her back and tied by a white ribbon like a little girl. She comes slowly, gazing wonderingly at the dead, a little dazed. She stops halfway and smiles faintly. After looking at the mourners for a moment, she walks slowly to the vacant chair beside* MRS. GIBBS *and sits down.*]

EMILY. [*To them all, quietly, smiling*] Hello.

MRS. SOAMES. Hello, Emily.

A MAN AMONG THE DEAD. Hello, M's Gibbs.

EMILY. [*Warmly*] Hello, Mother Gibbs.

MRS. GIBBS. Emily.

EMILY. Hello. [*With surprise*] It's raining. [*Her eyes drift back to the funeral company.*]

MRS. GIBBS. Yes . . . They'll be gone soon, dear. Just rest yourself.

EMILY. It seems thousands and thousands of years since I . . . Papa remembered that that was my favorite hymn.

Oh, I wish I'd been here a long time. I don't like being new here.—How do you do, Mr. Stimson?

SIMON STIMSON. How do you do, Emily.

[EMILY *continues to look about her with a wondering smile; as though to shut out from her mind the thought of the funeral company she starts speaking to* MRS. GIBBS *with a touch of nervousness.*]

EMILY. Mother Gibbs, George and I have made that farm into just the best place you ever saw. We thought of you all the time. We wanted to show you the new barn and a great long ce-ment drinking fountain for the stock. We bought that out of the money you left us.

MRS. GIBBS. I did?

EMILY. Don't you remember, Mother Gibbs—the legacy you left us? Why, it was over three hundred and fifty dollars.

MRS. GIBBS. Yes, yes, Emily.

EMILY. Well, there's a patent device on the drinking fountain so that it never overflows, Mother Gibbs, and it never sinks below a certain mark they have there. It's fine. [*Her voice trails off and her eyes return to the funeral group.*] It won't be the same to George without me, but it's a lovely farm. [*Suddenly she looks directly at* MRS. GIBBS.] Live people don't understand, do they?

MRS. GIBBS. No, dear—not very much.

EMILY. They're sort of shut up in little boxes, aren't they? I feel as though I knew them last a thousand years ago . . . My boy is spending the day at Mrs. Carter's. [*She sees* MR. CARTER, *among the dead.*] Oh, Mr. Carter, my little boy is spending the day at your house.

MR. CARTER. Is he?

EMILY. Yes, he loves it there.—Mother Gibbs, we have a Ford, too. Never gives any trouble. I don't drive, though. Mother Gibbs, when does this feeling go away?—Of being . . . one of *them*? How long does it. . . ?

MRS. GIBBS. Sh! dear. Just wait and be patient.

EMILY. [*With a sigh*] I know.—Look, they're finished. They're going.

MRS. GIBBS. Sh—.

[*The umbrellas leave the stage.* DR. GIBBS *has come over to his wife's grave and stands before it a moment.* EMILY *looks up at his face.* MRS. GIBBS *does not raise her eyes.*]

EMILY. Look! Father Gibbs is bringing some of my flowers to you. He looks just like George, doesn't he? Oh, Mother Gibbs, I never realized before how troubled and how . . . how in the dark live persons are. Look at him. I loved him so. From morning till night, that's all they are—troubled.

[DR. GIBBS *goes off.*]

THE DEAD. Little cooler than it was.—Yes, that rain's cooled it off a little. Those northeast winds always do the same thing, don't they? If it isn't a rain, it's a three-day blow.—

[*A patient calm falls on the stage. The* STAGE MANAGER *appears at his proscenium pillar, smoking.* EMILY *sits up abruptly with an idea.*]

EMILY. But, Mother Gibbs, one can go back; one can go back there again . . . into living. I feel it, I know it. Why, then just for a moment I was thinking about . . . about the farm . . . and for a minute I *was* there, and my baby was on my lap as plain as day.

MRS. GIBBS. Yes, of course you can.

EMILY. I can go back there and live all those days over again . . . why not?

MRS. GIBBS. All I can say is, Emily, don't.

EMILY. [*She appeals urgently to the* STAGE MANAGER.] But it's true, isn't it? I can go and live . . . back there . . . again.

STAGE MANAGER. Yes, some have tried—but they soon come back here.

MRS. GIBBS. Don't do it, Emily.

MRS. SOAMES. Emily, don't. It's not what you think it'd be.

EMILY. But I won't live over a sad day. I'll choose a happy one—I'll choose the day I first knew that I loved George. Why should that be painful?

[*They are silent. Her question turns to the* STAGE MANAGER.]

STAGE MANAGER. You not only live it; but you watch yourself living it.

EMILY. Yes?

STAGE MANAGER. And as you watch it, you see the thing that they—down there—never know. You see the future. You know what's going to happen afterwards.

EMILY. But is that—painful? Why?

MRS. GIBBS. That's not the only reason why you shouldn't do it, Emily. When you've been here longer you'll see that our life here is to forget all that, and think only of what's ahead, and be ready for what's ahead. When you've been here longer, you'll understand.

EMILY. [*Softly*] But, Mother Gibbs, how can I *ever* forget that life? It's all I know. It's all I had.

MRS. SOAMES. Oh, Emily. It isn't wise. Really, it isn't.

EMILY. But it's a thing I must know for myself. I'll choose a happy day, anyway.

MRS. GIBBS. *No!*—At least, choose an unimportant day. Choose the least important day in your life. It will be important enough.

EMILY. [*To herself*] Then it can't be since I was married; or since the baby was born. [*To the* STAGE MANAGER, *eagerly*] I can choose a birthday at least, can't I?—I choose my twelfth birthday.

STAGE MANAGER. All right. February 11th, 1899. A Tuesday.—Do you want any special time of day?

EMILY. Oh, I want the whole day.

STAGE MANAGER. We'll begin at dawn. You remember it had been snowing for several days; but it had stopped the night before, and they had begun clearing the roads. The sun's coming up.

EMILY. [*With a cry; rising*] There's Main Street . . . why, that's Mr. Morgan's drugstore before he changed it! . . . And there's the livery stable.

[*The stage at no time in this act has been very dark; but now the left half of the stage gradually becomes very bright—the brightness of a crisp winter morning.* EMILY *walks toward Main Street.*]

STAGE MANAGER. Yes, it's 1899. This is fourteen years ago.

EMILY. Oh, that's the town I knew as a little girl. And, *look*, there's the old white fence that used to be around our house. Oh, I'd forgotten that! Oh, I love it so! Are they inside?

STAGE MANAGER. Yes, your mother'll be coming downstairs in a minute to make breakfast.

EMILY. [*Softly*] Will she?

STAGE MANAGER. And you remember: your father had been away for several days; he came back on the early-morning train.

EMILY. No. . . ?

STAGE MANAGER. He'd been back to his college to make a speech—in western New York, at Clinton.

EMILY. Look! There's Howie Newsome. There's our policeman. But he's *dead*; he *died.*

[*The voices of* HOWIE NEWSOME, CONSTABLE WARREN *and* JOE CROWELL, JR., *are heard at the left of the stage.* EMILY *listens in delight.*]

HOWIE NEWSOME. Whoa, Bessie!—Bessie! 'Morning, Bill.

CONSTABLE WARREN. Morning, Howie.

HOWIE NEWSOME. You're up early.

CONSTABLE WARREN. Been rescuin' a party; darn near froze to death, down by Polish Town thar. Got drunk and lay out in the snowdrifts. Thought he was in bed when I shook'm.

EMILY. Why, there's Joe Crowell. . . .

JOE CROWELL, JR. Good morning, Mr. Warren. 'Morning, Howie.

[MRS. WEBB *has appeared in her kitchen, but* EMILY *does not see her until she calls.*]

MRS. WEBB. Chil-*dren!* Wally! Emily! . . . Time to get up.

EMILY. Mama, I'm here! Oh! how young

Mama looks! I didn't know Mama was ever that young.

MRS. WEBB. You can come and dress by the kitchen fire, if you like; but hurry.

[HOWIE NEWSOME *has entered along Main Street and brings the milk to* MRS. WEBB'S *door.*]

Good morning, Mr. Newsome. Whhhh—it's cold.

HOWIE NEWSOME. Ten below by my barn, Mrs. Webb.

MRS. WEBB. Think of it! Keep yourself wrapped up. [*She takes her bottles in, shuddering.*]

EMILY. [*With an effort*] Mama, I can't find my blue hair ribbon anywhere.

MRS. WEBB. Just open your eyes, dear, that's all. I laid it out for you special—on the dresser, there. If it were a snake it would bite you.

EMILY. Yes, yes . . .

[*She puts her hand on her heart.* MR. WEBB *comes along Main Street, where he meets* CONSTABLE WARREN. *Their movements and voices are increasingly lively in the sharp air.*]

MR. WEBB. Good morning, Bill.

CONSTABLE WARREN. Good morning, Mr. Webb. You're up early.

MR. WEBB. Yes, just been back to my old college in New York State. Been any trouble here?

CONSTABLE WARREN. Well, I was called up this mornin' to rescue a Polish fella—darn near froze to death he was.

MR. WEBB. We must get it in the paper.

CONSTABLE WARREN. 'Twan't much.

EMILY. [*Whispers*] Papa.

[MR. WEBB *shakes the snow off his feet and enters his house.* CONSTABLE WARREN *goes off, right.*]

MR. WEBB. Good morning, Mother.

MRS. WEBB. How did it go, Charles?

MR. WEBB. Oh, fine, I guess. I told'm a few things.—Everything all right here?

MRS. WEBB. Yes—can't think of anything that's happened, special. Been right cold. Howie Newsome says it's ten below over to his barn.

MR. WEBB. Yes, well, it's colder than that at Hamilton College. Students' ears are falling off. It ain't Christian.—Paper have any mistakes in it?

MRS. WEBB. None that I noticed. Coffee's ready when you want it. [*He starts upstairs.*] Charles! Don't forget; it's Emily's birthday. Did you remember to get her something?

MR. WEBB. [*Patting his pocket*] Yes, I've got something here. [*Calling up the stairs*] Where's my girl? Where's my birthday girl? [*He goes off left.*]

MRS. WEBB. Don't interrupt her now, Charles. You can see her at breakfast. She's slow enough as it is. Hurry up, children! It's seven o'clock. Now, I don't want to call you again.

EMILY. [*Softly, more in wonder than in grief*] I can't bear it. They're so young and beautiful. Why did they ever have to get old? Mama, I'm here. I'm grown up. I love you all, everything.—I can't look at everything hard enough.

[*She looks questioningly at the* STAGE MANAGER, *saying or suggesting: "Can I go in?" He nods briefly. She crosses to the inner door to the kitchen, left of her mother, and as though entering the room, says, suggesting the voice of a girl of twelve:*]

Good morning, Mama.

MRS. WEBB. [*Crossing to embrace and kiss her; in her characteristic matter-of-fact manner*] Well, now, dear, a very happy birthday to my girl and many happy returns. There are some surprises waiting for you on the kitchen table.

EMILY. Oh, Mama, you *shouldn't* have. [*She throws an anguished glance at the* STAGE MANAGER] I can't—I can't.

MRS. WEBB. [*Facing the audience, over her stove*] But birthday or no birthday, I want you to eat your breakfast good and slow. I want you to grow up and be a good strong girl.

That in the blue paper is from your Aunt Carrie; and I reckon you can guess who brought the postcard album. I found it on the doorstep when I brought in the milk—George Gibbs . . . must have come over in the cold pretty early . . . right nice of him.

EMILY. [*To herself*] Oh, George! I'd forgotten that. . . .

MRS. WEBB. Chew that bacon good and slow. It'll help keep you warm on a cold day.

EMILY. [*With mounting urgency*] Oh, Mama, just look at me one minute as though you really saw me. Mama, fourteen years have gone by. I'm dead. You're a grandmother, Mama. I married George Gibbs, Mama. Wally's dead, too. Mama, his appendix burst on a camping trip to North Conway. We felt just terrible about it—don't you remember? But, just for a moment now we're all together. Mama, just for a moment we're happy. *Let's look at one another.*

MRS. WEBB. That in the yellow paper is something I found in the attic among your grandmother's things. You're old enough to wear it now, and I thought you'd like it.

EMILY. And this is from you. Why, Mama, it's just lovely and it's just what I wanted. It's beautiful!

[*She flings her arms around her mother's neck. Her* MOTHER *goes on with her cooking, but is pleased.*]

MRS. WEBB. Well, I hoped you'd like it. Hunted all over. Your Aunt Norah couldn't find one in Concord, so I had to send all the way to Boston. [*Laughing*] Wally has something for you, too. He made it at manual-training class and he's very proud of it. Be sure you make a big fuss about it.—Your father had a surprise for you, too; don't know what it is myself. Sh—here he comes.

MR. WEBB. [*Off stage*] Where's my girl? Where's my birthday girl?

EMILY. [*In a loud voice to the* STAGE MANAGER] I can't. I can't go on. It goes so fast. We don't have time to look at one another.

[*She breaks down sobbing.*

The lights dim on the left half of the stage. MRS. WEBB *disappears.*]

I didn't realize. So all that was going on and we never noticed. Take me back—up the hill—to my grave. But first: Wait! One more look.

Goodbye. Goodbye, world. Goodbye, Grover's Corners . . . Mama and Papa. Goodbye to clocks ticking . . . and Mama's sunflowers. And food and coffee. And new-ironed dresses and hot baths . . . and sleeping and waking up. Oh, earth, you're too wonderful for anybody to realize you. [*She looks toward the* STAGE MANAGER *and asks abruptly, through her tears:*] Do any human beings ever realize life while they live it?—every, every minute?

STAGE MANAGER. No. [*Pause*] The saints and poets, maybe—they do some.

EMILY. I'm ready to go back. [*She returns to her chair beside* MRS. GIBBS. *Pause.*]

MRS. GIBBS. Were you happy?

EMILY. No . . . I should have listened to you. That's all human beings are! Just blind people.

MRS. GIBBS. Look, it's clearing up. The stars are coming out.

EMILY. Oh, Mr. Stimson, I should have listened to them.

SIMON STIMSON. [*With mounting violence; bitingly*] Yes, now you know. Now you know! That's what it was to be alive. To move about in a cloud of ignorance; to go up and down trampling on the feelings of those . . . of those about you. To spend and waste time as though you had a million years. To be always at the mercy of one self-centered passion, or another. Now you know—that's the happy existence you wanted to go back to. Ignorance and blindness.

MRS. GIBBS. [*Spiritedly*] Simon Stimson, that ain't the whole truth and you know it. Emily, look at that star. I forget its name.

A MAN AMONG THE DEAD. My boy Joel was a sailor—knew 'em all. He'd set on the porch evenings and tell 'em all by name. Yes, sir, wonderful!

ANOTHER MAN AMONG THE DEAD. A star's mighty good company.

A WOMAN AMONG THE DEAD. Yes. Yes, 'tis.

SIMON STIMSON. Here's one of *them* coming.

THE DEAD. That's funny. 'Tain't no time for one of them to be here.—Goodness sakes.

EMILY. Mother Gibbs, it's George.

MRS. GIBBS. Sh, dear. Just rest yourself.

EMILY. It's George.

[GEORGE *enters from the left, and slowly comes toward them.*]

A MAN FROM AMONG THE DEAD. And my boy, Joel, who knew the stars—he used to say it took millions of years for that speck o' light to git to the earth. Don't seem like a body could believe it, but that's what he used to say—millions of years.

[GEORGE *sinks to his knees, then falls full length at* EMILY's *feet.*]

A WOMAN AMONG THE DEAD. Goodness! That ain't no way to behave!

MRS. SOAMES. He ought to be home.

EMILY. Mother Gibbs?

MRS. GIBBS. Yes, Emily?

EMILY. They don't understand, do they?

MRS. GIBBS. No, dear. They don't understand.

[*The* STAGE MANAGER *appears at the right,* one hand on a dark curtain which he slowly draws across the scene.

In the distance a clock is heard striking the hour very faintly.]

STAGE MANAGER. Most everybody's asleep in Grover's Corners. There are a few lights on: Shorty Hawkins, down at the depot, has just watched the Albany train go by. And at the livery stable somebody's setting up late and talking.—Yes, it's clearing up. There are the stars—doing their old, old crisscross journeys in the sky. Scholars haven't settled the matter yet, but they seem to think there are no living beings up there. Just chalk . . . or fire. Only this one is straining away, straining away all the time to make something of itself. The strain's so bad that every sixteen hours everybody lies down and gets a rest. [*He winds his watch.*]

Hm. . . . Eleven o'clock in Grover's Corners.—You get a good rest, too. Good night.

THINKING ABOUT THE SELECTION
Recalling

1. What changes take place in Grover's Corners between Act II and Act III?
2. According to the Stage Manager, what do "we all know"?
3. (a) How does Emily die? (b) What reason does Mrs. Gibbs give Emily for not returning to the living? (c) What day does Emily decide to relive?
4. (a) Why does Emily ask to return to the dead? (b) What does she ask the Stage Manager just before she returns? (c) How does he respond?

Interpreting

5. (a) To whom is the Stage Manager referring when he addresses "Mrs. Smith"? (b) What is the answer to his question?
6. (a) What does Emily learn about the way people live their lives when she returns to the living? (b) Why does she say, "Oh, earth, you're too wonderful for anybody to realize you"?
7. What comments do the dead people make that indicate that they still possess many of the attitudes they had during life?

Applying

8. What can you learn about life from the observations of the dead?
9. The French playwright Jean Anouilh has written, "Life is a child playing around your feet, a tool you hold firmly in your grip, a bench you sit down upon in the evening, in your garden." Discuss the meaning of this quotation.

ANALYZING LITERATURE
Understanding Theme

Although *Our Town* focuses on life in the small town of Grover's Corners, the play expresses a number of universal themes, or insights about life in general. One of these themes is that people's lives are part of an eternal and universal cycle. Controlled by nature, this cycle is moving toward the eventual perfection of the human race.

1. What insights does the play offer about the ways people typically live their lives?
2. What does the play reveal about the ways in which the world changes and the ways in which it does not change?

CRITICAL THINKING AND READING
Interpreting Theme in Drama

In drama, themes are revealed through the character's comments and actions. For example, the Stage Manager expresses the idea that people's lives are part of a natural cycle that is moving toward perfection when he remarks, "Every child born into the world is nature's attempt to make a perfect human being."

1. How do the Stage Manager's comments at the beginning of Act III reflect this theme?
2. How do his comments at the end of the play reflect this theme?
3. What comments does the Stage Manager make that express the theme of change and lack of change?

UNDERSTANDING LANGUAGE
Fitting the Context

In English words generally have more than one meaning. When you read you must choose the meaning that fits the context, or surrounding words.

Read each sentence below. Look up each italicized word in a dictionary. First tell how many meanings you find for each word. Then choose the meaning that fits the context.

1. "You come up here, on a fine afternoon and you can see *range* on range of hills . . ."
2. "Over there—[Pointing to stage left] are the old *stones*—1670, 1680."
3. "And they stay here while the earth part of 'em burns away, burns out; and all that time they slowly get *indifferent* to what's goin' on in Grover's Corners."
4. "And what's left when memory's gone, and your *identity*, Mrs. Smith?"

THINKING AND WRITING
Responding to Criticism

Another noted playwright, Arthur Miller, has commented that "Wilder sees his characters in this play not primarily as personalities, but as forces." Write an essay in which you discuss *Our Town* in relation to Miller's comment. Use passages from the play to support your argument. When you revise, make sure that your essay is organized in a logical manner and that you have used transitions and other linking devices to connect your ideas.

YOU THE WRITER

Assignment

1. During the Modern Age, writers began using the stream-of-consciousness technique, attempting to recreate the natural flow of their characters' thoughts. Use the stream-of-consciousness technique to re-create the natural flow of your own thoughts.

    Prewriting.   Start by thinking of an important or interesting experience you have had at some point in your life. Then let your thoughts flow through the natural associations created by this experience.

    Writing.   Record your thoughts as they flow through your mind. Do not add explanations or transitions. Instead, use only your natural associations to link your ideas.

    Revising.   After you have finished writing, proofread your paper and prepare a final copy.

Assignment

2. Because writers believed life in the modern world was uncertain and confusing, most modern short stories end without a resolution. Choose a modern story that ends without a resolution, and write a continuation of that story.

    Prewriting.   Carefully reread the story you chose, and try to predict the events that might occur after the ending of the story. Then develop a plot for a continuation of the story, ending your continuation with a climax and resolution.

    Writing.   When writing your continuation, model your writing style after the style of the story's author.

    Revising.   When you revise, make sure your characters' actions are consistent with their behavior in the original story.

Assignment

3. The personal essay became a popular literary form during the Modern Age. Imagine you are living during the Modern Age, and write a personal essay describing your impressions of some of the most significant events of the time.

    Prewriting.   Review the unit introduction, trying to imagine how you would have reacted to the events that occurred during the period.

    Writing.   When writing your essay, focus on presenting your impressions of one or two important events. Use an informal, conversational writing style. Relate events in chronological order.

    Revising.   When you revise, make sure you have conveyed your impressions clearly and coherently. Also make sure your essay reveals something about your personality.

YOU THE CRITIC

Assignment

1. During the Modern Age, many poets turned away from conventional poetic forms and techniques, while other poets continued to use traditional forms. Write an essay in which you compare and contrast a poem written in a conventional form with a poem written in an unconventional form.

Prewriting. Choose a conventional poem and an unconventional poem that have similar themes. Then carefully reread the two poems, noting similarities and differences in form and content.

Writing. Organize the information in your essay according to corresponding points of contrast, and use passages from both poems to support your argument.

Revising. When you revise, make sure you have thoroughly supported your argument and have not included any unnecessary information.

Assignment

2. The Modernists associated life in the modern world with a sense of uncertainty, detachment, and disillusionment. Write an essay in which you discuss how this perception of modern life is reflected in the form and content of one of the modern stories you have read.

Prewriting. Review the unit introduction. Choose a story that reflects the Modernists' perception of life in form and content. Carefully reread the story, focusing on its theme and structure.

Writing. When you write your essay, use evidence from the story to support your argument.

Revising. When you revise, make sure your argument is clear and coherent and is organized in a logical manner.

Assignment

3. Literature generally reflects the dominant attitudes and ideas of the period in which it was written. Write an essay in which you discuss the ways in which modern literature reflects the dominant attitudes and ideas of the Modern Age.

Prewriting. Review the unit introduction. Then review the selections in the unit and find at least five stories or poems that reflect the dominant attitudes of the age.

Writing. When writing your essay, use evidence from at least five selections to support your argument. State your thesis in your opening paragraph. Support your thesis in the body of your essay. Conclude with a restatement of your main idea.

Revising. When you revise, make sure your essay is logically organized and that you have used transitions and other linking devices to connect your ideas.

GOLDEN GATE, 1955
Charles Sheeler
The Metropolitan Museum of Art

CONTEMPORARY WRITERS
1946–Present

Maria lay at night in the still of Beverly Hills and saw the great signs soar overhead at seventy miles an hour: *Normandie* 1/4 Vermont 3/4 Hollywood Fwy 1. Again and again she returned to an intricate stretch just south of the interchange where successful passage from the Hollywood to the Harbor required a diagonal move across four lanes of traffic.

Joan Didion

Maria Wyeth, the heroine of Joan Didion's novel *Play It As It Lays,* thinks about freeways, the central metaphor of the story. These freeways, like the Interstate Highway System begun in 1956, speed the movement of traffic. At the same time, however, they prose tricky driving problems. Survival requires skill.

Much of the new technology that has become widespread since 1945—television and computers in particular—can also have consequences beyond their obvious ones. The new technology does make life easier and pleasanter. Paradoxically, it also introduces complexities and problems that were unknown in earlier days.

The years from the end of the Second World War to the present day have been a time of change. Great strides have been made in civil rights and women's rights. Americans have fought in two Asian wars. Popular entertainment has changed dramatically, not just in presentation (from radio to television) but also in style (from big bands to rock music). These changes and others have had an effect on American literature. Their effect seems somehow less dramatic than the changes themselves, however. In general, contemporary writers have absorbed and extended earlier techniques, but have introduced few startling innovations.

THE HISTORICAL SETTING

The United States emerged from the Second World War as the most powerful nation on earth. Proud of the part they had played in defeating the Axis, Americans now wanted life to return to normal. Soldiers and sailors came home, the rationing of scarce goods ended, and the nation prospered. But despite postwar jubilation, the dawn of the nuclear age and the ominous actions of the Soviet Union meant that nothing would be the same again.

In 1945, the United Nations was created amid high hopes that it would prevent future wars. Nonetheless, a Cold War between the Soviet Union and the West began as soon as the shooting war ended. In a speech in early 1946, Winston Churchill, Great Britain's wartime Prime Minister, said, "An iron curtain has descended across the continent" of Europe. It was in Asia, however, that the first armed conflict came. In 1950, President Harry S. Truman sent American troops to help anticommunist South Korean forces turn back a North Korean invasion.

From Quiet Pride to Activism

Americans of the 1950's are sometimes referred to as "the Silent Generation." Many of them had lived through both the Great Depression and the Second World War. When peace and prosperity finally arrived, they were only too glad to adopt a quiet, somewhat complacent attitude. They greatly admired President Dwight D. Eisenhower, one of America's wartime heroes.

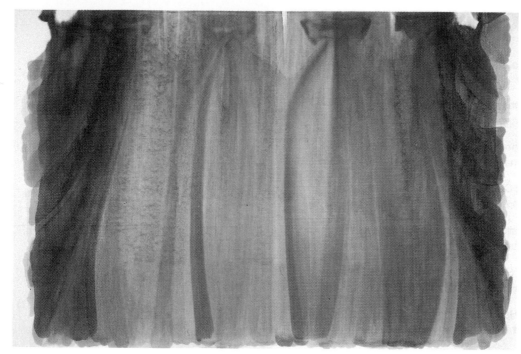

SARABAND, 1959
Morris Louis
Solomon R. Guggenheim
Museum

Near the end of the 1950's, the Soviet Union launched Sputnik, the first artificial satellite to orbit the earth. This Soviet space triumph spurred many people to call for changes in American science and education. President John F. Kennedy, elected in 1960, promised to "get the nation moving again." He had little time to do so, however, before his tragic assassination in 1963.

Kennedy's assassination was followed by an escalating and increasingly unpopular war in Vietnam. A wave of protest followed. Gone were the calm of the Eisenhower years and the high hopes of Kennedy's brief administration. In their place came idealistic but strident demands for rapid change: greater "relevance" in education, more progress on civil rights, an immediate end to the Vietnam War. It was a time of crisis and confrontations.

Real and lasting gains were made in civil rights after the Second World War. Astonishing as it may seem today, blacks could not play baseball in the major leagues until Jackie Robinson broke the color barrier in 1947. Segregation in the public schools was outlawed by the Supreme Court in 1954. Tragedy struck in 1968, when black leader Martin Luther King, Jr. was assassinated in Memphis, Tennessee. Riots broke out in many cities across the nation.

One of the bright moments in a troublesome decade occurred in 1969. In July of that year, American astronaut Neil Armstrong became the first person to set foot on the moon.

BERNARD MALAMUD

1914–1987

In his novels and short stories, Bernard Malamud depicts the struggles of ordinary people, often focusing on their desire to improve their lives. He uses the Jewish people to represent all of humanity, capturing their attempts to maintain a link to their cultural heritage while trying to cope with the realities of the modern world. While some of Malamud's characters achieve success, others experience failure. By portraying people in both victory and defeat, Malamud captures the essence of the human experience and creates a delicate balance between tragedy and comedy in his work.

Malamud was born in Brooklyn, New York, the son of Russian immigrants. His father was a grocer who worked diligently in an effort to forge a better life for his family. After attending City College of New York and Columbia University, Malamud began publishing short stories in a number of well-known magazines. In 1952 he published his first novel, *The Natural,* which depicted the life of a gifted baseball player. After that he wrote several other novels, including *The Assistant* (1957), *A New Life* (1961), *The Tenants* (1971), and *Dubin's Lives* (1979). His novel about czarist Russia, *The Fixer* (1966), earned him the Pulitzer Prize and the National Book Award. He also received the National Book Award for *The Magic Barrel* (1958), a collection of short stories.

Like most of Malamud's work, "The First Seven Years" focuses on the lives of common people. Depicting a Polish immigrant's desire to see his daughter achieve a better life, the story captures the discrepancy that often exists between parents' dreams for their children and their children's actual desires.

The First Seven Years

Epiphany. In a traditional short story, the plot moves toward a resolution, a point at which the conflict, or the struggle that the main character undergoes, is resolved and the final outcome of the action becomes clear. During the twentieth century, however, in an effort to capture the uncertainty and confusion of life in the modern world, most fiction writers have turned away from the traditional plot structure by ending their stories without a resolution. Instead, writers often construct plots that move toward an epiphany, a moment when a character has a flash of insight about himself or herself, another character, a situation, or life in general. For example, in "The First Seven Years," the main character, Feld, gains a sudden insight into his own life and his hopes for his daughter.

As you read "The First Seven Years," look for the epiphany. What revelation does Feld experience?

Like the main character in "The First Seven Years," many parents are deeply concerned with building better lives for their children. Freewrite about the reasons why parents often hope that their children's lives will be better than their own, discussing the types of actions that result from this desire.

Knowing the following words will help you as you read "The First Seven Years."

diligence (dil′ ə jəns) *n.*: Constant, careful effort; perseverance (p. 1042)

connivance (kə nī′ vəns) *n.*: Secret cooperation (p. 1042)

illiterate (i lit′ ər it) *adj.*: Unable to read or write (p. 1043)

unscrupulous (un skrōōp′ yə ləs) *adj.*: Not restrained by ideas of right and wrong (p. 1044)

repugnant (ri pug′ nənt) *adj.*: Offensive; disagreeable (p. 1045)

discern (di surn′) *v.*: To perceive or recognize; make out clearly (p. 1047)

The First Seven Years

Bernard Malamud

Feld, the shoemaker, was annoyed that his helper, Sobel, was so insensitive to his reverie that he wouldn't for a minute cease his fanatic pounding at the other bench. He gave him a look, but Sobel's bald head was bent over the last[1] as he worked and he didn't notice. The shoemaker shrugged and continued to peer through the partly frosted window at the nearsighted haze of falling February snow. Neither the shifting white blur outside, nor the sudden deep remembrance of the snowy Polish village where he had wasted his youth could turn his thoughts from Max the college boy, (a constant visitor in the mind since early that morning when Feld saw him trudging through the snowdrifts on his way to school) whom he so much respected because of the sacrifices he had made throughout the years—in winter or direst heat—to further his education. An old wish returned to haunt the shoemaker: that he had had a son instead of a daughter, but this blew away in the snow for Feld, if anything, was a practical man. Yet he could not help but contrast the diligence of the boy, who was a peddler's son, with Miriam's unconcern for an education. True, she was always with a book in her hand, yet when the opportunity arose for a college education, she had said no she would rather find a job. He had begged her to go, pointing out how many fathers could not afford to send their children to college, but she said she wanted to be independent.

As for education, what was it, she asked, but books, which Sobel, who diligently read the classics, would as usual advise her on. Her answer greatly grieved her father.

A figure emerged from the snow and the door opened. At the counter the man withdrew from a wet paper bag a pair of battered shoes for repair. Who he was the shoemaker for a moment had no idea, then his heart trembled as he realized, before he had thoroughly discerned the face, that Max himself was standing there, embarrassedly explaining what he wanted done to his old shoes. Though Feld listened eagerly, he couldn't hear a word, for the opportunity that had burst upon him was deafening.

He couldn't exactly recall when the thought had occurred to him, because it was clear he had more than once considered suggesting to the boy that he go out with Miriam. But he had not dared speak, for if Max said no, how would he face him again? Or suppose Miriam, who harped so often on independence, blew up in anger and shouted at him for his meddling? Still, the chance was too good to let by: all it meant was an introduction. They might long ago have become friends had they happened to meet somewhere, therefore was it not his duty—an obligation—to bring them together, nothing more, a harmless connivance to replace an accidental encounter in the subway, let's say, or a mutual friend's introduction in the street? Just let him once see and talk to her and he would for sure be interested. As for Miriam, what possible harm for a working girl in an office, who met only loud-mouthed

---

1. last *n.*: A block shaped like a person's foot, on which shoes are made or repaired.

salesmen and illiterate shipping clerks, to make the acquaintance of a fine scholarly boy? Maybe he would awaken in her a desire to go to college; if not—the shoemaker's mind at last came to grips with the truth— let her marry an educated man and live a better life.

When Max finished describing what he wanted done to his shoes, Feld marked them, both with enormous holes in the soles which he pretended not to notice, with large white-chalk *x*'s, and the rubber heels, thinned to the nails, he marked with *o*'s, though it troubled him he might have mixed up the letters. Max inquired the price, and

the shoemaker cleared his throat and asked the boy, above Sobel's insistent hammering, would he please step through the side door there into the hall. Though surprised, Max did as the shoemaker requested, and Feld went in after him. For a minute they were both silent, because Sobel had stopped banging, and it seemed they understood neither was to say anything until the noise began again. When it did, loudly, the shoe-maker quickly told Max why he had asked to talk to him.

"Ever since you went to high school," he said, in the dimly-lit hallway, "I watched you in the morning go to the subway to school, and I said always to myself, this is a fine boy that he wants so much an education."

"Thanks," Max said, nervously alert. He was tall and grotesquely thin, with sharply cut features, particularly a beak-like nose. He was wearing a loose, long slushy overcoat that hung down to his ankles, looking like a rug draped over his bony shoulders, and a soggy, old brown hat, as battered as the shoes he had brought in.

"I am a business man," the shoemaker abruptly said to conceal his embarrassment, "so I will explain you right away why I talk to you. I have a girl, my daughter Miriam—she is nineteen—a very nice girl and also so pretty that everybody looks on her when she passes by in the street. She is smart, always with a book, and I thought to myself that a boy like you, an educated boy—I thought maybe you will be interested sometime to meet a girl like this." He laughed a bit when he had finished and was tempted to say more but had the good sense not to.

Max stared down like a hawk. For an uncomfortable second he was silent, then he asked, "Did you say nineteen?"

"Yes."

"Would it be all right to inquire if you have a picture of her?"

"Just a minute." The shoemaker went into the store and hastily returned with a snapshot that Max held up to the light.

"She's all right," he said.

Feld waited.

"And is she sensible—not the flighty kind?"

"She is very sensible."

After another short pause, Max said it was okay with him if he met her.

"Here is my telephone," said the shoemaker, hurriedly handing him a slip of paper. "Call her up. She comes home from work six o'clock."

Max folded the paper and tucked it away into his worn leather wallet.

"About the shoes," he said. "How much did you say they will cost me?"

"Don't worry about the price."

"I just like to have an idea."

"A dollar—dollar fifty. A dollar fifty," the shoemaker said.

At once he felt bad, for he usually charged two twenty-five for this kind of job. Either he should have asked the regular price or done the work for nothing.

Later, as he entered the store, he was startled by a violent clanging and looked up to see Sobel pounding with all his might upon the naked last. It broke, the iron striking the floor and jumping with a thump against the wall, but before the enraged shoemaker could cry out, the assistant had torn his hat and coat from the hook and rushed out into the snow.

So Feld, who had looked forward to anticipating how it would go with his daughter and Max, instead had a great worry on his mind. Without his temperamental helper he was a lost man, especially since it was years now that he had carried the store alone. The shoemaker had for an age suffered from a heart condition that threatened collapse if he dared exert himself. Five years ago, after an attack, it had appeared as though he would have either to sacrifice his business upon the auction block and live on a pittance thereafter, or put himself at the mercy of some unscrupulous employee who would in the end probably ruin him. But just at the moment of his darkest despair, this Polish refugee, Sobel, appeared one night from the street and begged for work. He was a stocky man, poorly dressed, with a bald head that had once been blond, a severely plain face and soft blue eyes prone to tears over the sad books he read, a young man but old—no one would have guessed thirty. Though he confessed he knew nothing of shoemaking, he said he was apt and would work for a very little if Feld taught him the trade. Thinking that with, after all, a landsman,[2] he would have less to fear than from a complete stranger, Feld took him on and within six

---

2. **landsman** *n.*: A fellow countryman.

weeks the refugee rebuilt as good a shoe as he, and not long thereafter expertly ran the business for the thoroughly relieved shoemaker.

Feld could trust him with anything and did, frequently going home after an hour or two at the store, leaving all the money in the till, knowing Sobel would guard every cent of it. The amazing thing was that he demanded so little. His wants were few; in money he wasn't interested—in nothing but books, it seemed—which he one by one lent to Miriam, together with his profuse, queer written comments, manufactured during his lonely rooming house evenings, thick pads of commentary which the shoemaker peered at and twitched his shoulders over as his daughter, from her fourteenth year, read page by sanctified page, as if the word of God were inscribed on them. To protect Sobel, Feld himself had to see that he received more than he asked for. Yet his conscience bothered him for not insisting that the assistant accept a better wage than he was getting, though Feld had honestly told him he could earn a handsome salary if he worked elsewhere, or maybe opened a place of his own. But the assistant answered, somewhat ungraciously, that he was not interested in going elsewhere, and though Feld frequently asked himself what keeps him here? why does he stay? he finally answered it that the man, no doubt because of his terrible experiences as a refugee, was afraid of the world.

After the incident with the broken last, angered by Sobel's behavior, the shoemaker decided to let him stew for a week in the rooming house, although his own strength was taxed dangerously and the business suffered. However, after several sharp nagging warnings from both his wife and daughter, he went finally in search of Sobel, as he had once before, quite recently, when over some fancied slight—Feld had merely asked him not to give Miriam so many books to read because her eyes were strained and red—the assistant had left the place in a huff, an incident which, as usual, came to nothing for he

had returned after the shoemaker had talked to him, and taken his seat at the bench. But this time, after Feld had plodded through the snow to Sobel's house—he had thought of sending Miriam but the idea became repugnant to him—the burly landlady at the door informed him in a nasal voice that Sobel was not at home, and though Feld knew this was a nasty lie, for where had the refugee to go? still for some reason he was not completely sure of—it may have been the cold and his fatigue—he decided not to insist on seeing him. Instead he went home and hired a new helper.

Having settled the matter, though not entirely to his satisfaction, for he had much more to do than before, and so, for example, could no longer lie late in bed mornings because he had to get up to open the store for the new assistant, a speechless, dark man with an irritating rasp as he worked, whom he would not trust with the key as he had Sobel. Furthermore, this one, though able to do a fair repair job, knew nothing of grades of leather or prices, so Feld had to make his own purchases: and every night at closing time it was necessary to count the money in the till and lock up. However, he was not dissatisfied, for he lived much in his thoughts of Max and Miriam. The college boy had called her, and they had arranged a meeting for this coming Friday night. The shoemaker would personally have preferred Saturday, which he felt would make it a date of the first magnitude, but he learned Friday was Miriam's choice, so he said nothing. The day of the week did not matter. What mattered was the aftermath. Would they like each other and want to be friends? He sighed at all the time that would have to go by before he knew for sure. Often he was tempted to talk to Miriam about the boy, to ask whether she thought she would like his type—he had told her only that he considered Max a nice boy and had suggested he call her—but the one time he tried she snapped at him—justly—how should she know?

At last Friday came. Feld was not feeling

particularly well so he stayed in bed, and Mrs. Feld thought it better to remain in the bedroom with him when Max called. Miriam received the boy, and her parents could hear their voices, his throaty one, as they talked. Just before leaving, Miriam brought Max to the bedroom door and he stood there a minute, a tall, slightly hunched figure wearing a thick, droopy suit, and apparently at ease as he greeted the shoemaker and his wife, which was surely a good sign. And Miriam, although she had worked all day, looked fresh and pretty. She was a large-framed girl with a well-shaped body, and she had a fine open face and soft hair. They made, Feld thought, a first-class couple.

Miriam returned after 11:30. Her mother was already asleep, but the shoemaker got out of bed and after locating his bathrobe went into the kitchen, where Miriam, to his surprise, sat at the table, reading.

"So where did you go?" Feld asked pleasantly.

"For a walk," she said, not looking up.

"I advised him," Feld said, clearing his throat, "he shouldn't spend so much money."

"I didn't care."

The shoemaker boiled up some water for tea and sat down at the table with a cupful and a thick slice of lemon.

"So how," he sighed after a sip, "did you enjoy?"

"It was all right."

He was silent. She must have sensed his disappointment, for she added, "You can't really tell much the first time."

"You will see him again?"

Turning a page, she said that Max had asked for another date.

"For when?"

"Saturday."

"So what did you say?"

"What did I say?" she asked, delaying for a moment—"I said yes."

Afterwards she inquired about Sobel, and Feld, without exactly knowing why, said the assistant had got another job. Miriam said nothing more and began to read. The shoemaker's conscience did not trouble him; he was satisfied with the Saturday date.

During the week, by placing here and there a deft question, he managed to get from Miriam some information about Max. It surprised him to learn that the boy was not studying to be either a doctor or lawyer but was taking a business course leading to a degree in accountancy. Feld was a little disappointed because he thought of accountants as bookkeepers and would have preferred "a higher profession." However, it was not long before he had investigated the subject and discovered that Certified Public Accountants were highly respected people, so he was thoroughly content as Saturday approached. But because Saturday was a busy day, he was much in the store and therefore did not see Max when he came to call for Miriam. From his wife he learned there had been nothing especially revealing about their meeting. Max had rung the bell and Miriam had got her coat and left with him—nothing more. Feld did not probe, for his wife was not particularly observant. Instead, he waited up for Miriam with a newspaper on his lap, which he scarcely looked at so lost was he in thinking of the future. He awoke to find her in the room with him, tiredly removing her hat. Greeting her, he was suddenly inexplicably afraid to ask anything about the evening. But since she volunteered nothing he was at last forced to inquire how she had enjoyed herself. Miriam began something noncommittal but apparently changed her mind, for she said after a minute, "I was bored."

When Feld had sufficiently recovered from his anguished disappointment to ask why, she answered without hesitation, "Because he's nothing more than a materialist."

"What means this word?"

"He has no soul. He's only interested in things."

He considered her statement for a long time but then asked, "Will you see him again?"

"He didn't ask."

"Suppose he will ask you?"

"I won't see him."

He did not argue; however, as the days went by he hoped increasingly she would change her mind. He wished the boy would telephone, because he was sure there was more to him than Miriam, with her inexperienced eye, could discern. But Max didn't call. As a matter of fact he took a different route to school, no longer passing the shoemaker's store, and Feld was deeply hurt.

Then one afternoon Max came in and asked for his shoes. The shoemaker took them down from the shelf where he had placed them, apart from the other pairs. He had done the work himself and the soles and heels were well built and firm. The shoes had been highly polished and somehow looked better than new. Max's Adam's apple went up once when he saw them, and his eyes had little lights in them.

"How much?" he asked, without directly looking at the shoemaker.

"Like I told you before," Feld answered sadly. "One dollar fifty cents."

Max handed him two crumpled bills and received in return a newly-minted silver half dollar.

He left. Miriam had not been mentioned. That night the shoemaker discovered that his new assistant had been all the while stealing from him, and he suffered a heart attack.

Though the attack was very mild, he lay in bed for three weeks. Miriam spoke of going for Sobel, but sick as he was Feld rose in wrath against the idea. Yet in his heart he knew there was no other way, and the first weary day back in the shop thoroughly convinced him, so that night after supper he dragged himself to Sobel's rooming house.

He toiled up the stairs, though he knew it was bad for him, and at the top knocked at the door. Sobel opened it and the shoemaker entered. The room was a small, poor one, with a single window facing the street. It contained a narrow cot, a low table and several stacks of books piled haphazardly around on the floor along the wall, which made him think how queer Sobel was, to be uneducated and read so much. He had once asked him, Sobel, why you read so much? and the assistant could not answer him. Did you ever study in a college someplace? he had asked but Sobel shook his head. He read, he said, to know. But to know what, the shoemaker demanded, and to know, why? Sobel never explained, which proved he read much because he was queer.

Feld sat down to recover his breath. The assistant was resting on his bed with his heavy back to the wall. His shirt and trousers were clean, and his stubby fingers, away from the shoemaker's bench, were strangely pallid. His face was thin and pale, as if he had been shut in this room since the day he had bolted from the store.

"So when you will come back to work?" Feld asked him.

To his surprise, Sobel burst out, "Never."

Jumping up, he strode over to the window that looked out upon the miserable street. "Why should I come back?" he cried.

"I will raise your wages."

"Who cares for your wages!"

The shoemaker, knowing he didn't care, was at a loss what else to say.

"What do you want from me, Sobel?"

"Nothing."

"I always treated you like you was my son."

Sobel vehemently denied it. "So why you look for strange boys in the street they should go out with Miriam? Why you don't think of me?"

The shoemaker's hands and feet turned freezing cold. His voice became so hoarse he couldn't speak. At last he cleared his throat and croaked, "So what has my daughter got to do with a shoemaker thirty-five years old who works for me?"

"Why do you think I worked so long for you?" Sobel cried out. "For the stingy wages I sacrificed five years of my life so you could have to eat and drink and where to sleep?"

"Then for what?" shouted the shoemaker.

"For Miriam," he blurted—"for her."

The shoemaker, after a time, managed to say, "I pay wages in cash, Sobel," and lapsed into silence. Though he was seething with excitement, his mind was coldly clear, and he had to admit to himself he had sensed all along that Sobel felt this way. He had never so much as thought it consciously, but he had felt it and was afraid.

"Miriam knows?" he muttered hoarsely.

"She knows."

"You told her?"

"No."

"Then how does she know?"

"How does she know?" Sobel said, "because she knows. She knows who I am and what is in my heart."

Feld had a sudden insight. In some devious way, with his books and commentary, Sobel had given Miriam to understand that he loved her. The shoemaker felt a terrible anger at him for his deceit.

"Sobel, you are crazy," he said bitterly. "She will never marry a man so old and ugly like you."

Sobel turned black with rage. He cursed the shoemaker, but then, though he trembled to hold it in, his eyes filled with tears and he broke into deep sobs. With his back to Feld, he stood at the window, fists clenched, and his shoulders shook with his choked sobbing.

Watching him, the shoemaker's anger diminished. His teeth were on edge with pity for the man, and his eyes grew moist. How strange and sad that a refugee, a grown man, bald and old with his miseries, who had by the skin of his teeth escaped Hitler's incinerators,[3] should fall in love, when he had got to America, with a girl less than half his age. Day after day, for five years he had sat at his bench, cutting and hammering away, waiting for the girl to become a woman, unable to ease his heart with speech, knowing no protest but desperation.

"Ugly I didn't mean," he said half aloud.

Then he realized that what he had called ugly was not Sobel but Miriam's life if she married him. He felt for his daughter a strange and gripping sorrow, as if she were already Sobel's bride, the wife, after all, of a shoemaker, and had in her life no more than her mother had had. And all his dreams for her—why he had slaved and destroyed his heart with anxiety and labor—all these dreams of a better life were dead.

The room was quiet. Sobel was standing by the window reading, and it was curious that when he read he looked young.

"She is only nineteen," Feld said brokenly. "This is too young yet to get married. Don't ask her for two years more, till she is twenty-one, then you can talk to her."

Sobel didn't answer. Feld rose and left. He went slowly down the stairs but once outside, though it was an icy night and the crisp falling snow whitened the street, he walked with a stronger stride.

But the next morning, when the shoemaker arrived, heavy-hearted, to open the store, he saw he needn't have come, for his assistant was already seated at the last, pounding leather for his love.

---

3. Hitler's incinerators: During World War II, millions of Jews were murdered by the Nazis under the direction of German dictator Adolf Hitler (1889–1945).

THINKING ABOUT THE SELECTION
Recalling

1. (a) Why does Feld respect Max? (b) How does Feld arrange to have Max meet Miriam?
2. (a) Why did Feld hire Sobel? (b) Why does he hire a new helper?
3. Why is Miriam uninterested in seeing Max again after their second date?
4. What happens when Feld discovers that his new assistant has been stealing from him?
5. (a) What does Sobel reveal about his feelings for Miriam when Feld visits him? (b) How does Feld respond to this revelation? (c) What does he tell Sobel before he leaves his room?

Interpreting

6. How does Feld's belief that he "wasted his youth" relate to his desires concerning his daughter?
7. (a) What does education represent to Feld? (b) What does it represent to Sobel?
8. What does Feld's inability to accept Miriam's assessment of Max's personality indicate about his own personality?
9. In what ways are Sobel and Feld similar?
10. Explain the title of this story.

Applying

11. "There are only two lasting bequests we can hope to give our children," wrote Hodding Carter. "One of these is roots; the other, wings." First discuss the meaning of this quotation. Then explain how it relates to the theme of this story.

ANALYZING LITERATURE
Understanding Epiphany

In many modern and contemporary stories, the action moves toward an **epiphany,** a moment when a character has a flash of insight about himself or herself, another character, a situation, or life in general.

1. What understanding concerning himself and his hopes for his daughter does Feld reach at the end of the story?
2. Why does he walk "with a stronger stride" when he leaves Sobel's rooming house?

CRITICAL THINKING AND READING
Predicting Future Events

When a writer ends a story without a resolution, it is up to you to predict how the conflict will be resolved or whether it will be resolved at all. To make a valid prediction, you must consider what the story reveals about the characters' personalities and try to determine how they would be likely to act in the future.

1. How do you think Feld's relationship with Sobel will change following the incident at Sobel's rooming house? Support your answer.
2. Do you think Sobel will wait for two years? Explain your answer.
3. Do you think Feld will ever be able to completely accept Sobel as a son-in-law? Why or why not?

THINKING AND WRITING
Writing About a Character

Write an essay in which you analyze Feld's personality. Start by rereading the story, focusing on Feld's feelings, actions, and desires. Then try to determine what his behavior reveals about his character. At some point in your essay, discuss Feld's revelation at the end of the story. Does he change? Do you sympathize with him? When you revise, make sure that you have used passages from the story to support your argument. When you finish revising, proofread your paper and share it with your classmates.

FLANNERY O'CONNOR

1925–1964

Flannery O'Connor's work reflects her intense commitment to her personal beliefs. In her exaggerated, tragic, and at times shockingly violent tales, she forces us to confront such human faults as hypocrisy, insensitivity, self-centeredness, and prejudice.

O'Connor was born in Savannah, Georgia, and was raised in the small Georgia town of Milledgeville. She was educated at the Georgia State College for Women and studied at the University of Iowa Writers' Workshop. When she was twenty-seven, she published her first novel, *Wise Blood,* the story of a violent rivalry among the members of a fictional religious sect in the South. In 1955 she published her first collection of short stories, *A Good Man Is Hard to Find*. This was followed in 1960 by a second novel, *The Violent Bear It Away;* and in 1965 *Everything That Rises Must Converge,* another collection of her stories, was published.

Unfortunately, throughout most of her adult life, O'Connor suffered from lupus, a rare disease that eventually took her life. Because her disease set her apart from other people, O'Connor developed a deep sensitivity to misfits and outsiders. Not surprisingly, many of her most memorable characters are social outcasts or people who are in some way mentally or physically disabled. Although she portrays these characters in an unsentimental manner, there is an underlying sense of sympathy concerning their pain and suffering.

"The Life You Save May Be Your Own" is a typical O'Connor story. A grim depiction of a group of outcasts, the story conveys a powerful moral message, capturing a number of the tragic realities of life in the modern world.

GUIDE FOR READING

The Life You Save May Be Your Own

Writer's Techniques

Irony. Irony is a contrast or a difference between what is stated and what is meant, or between what is expected to happen and what actually happens. "The Life You Save May be Your Own" is filled with situational irony—one of a number of different types of irony used in literature. This type of irony occurs when the actual result of an action or situation is quite different from the expected result. Much of the situational irony in O'Connor's story results from the contrast between the main character's comments and actions. This character, Mr. Shiftlet, complains that there is a lack of morality in the world and that people have no concern for others, yet his actions in the story make it clear that he himself lacks morality and has little concern for others.

Flannery O'Connor possessed a deep awareness of the irony and hypocrisy that exist in everyday life. A devoutly religious woman, O'Connor was disturbed by the fact that many people claim to have deep religious convictions yet behave in a manner that totally contradicts this claim. This type of hypocrisy is embodied in the character of Mr. Shiftlet, whose actions clearly contradict the beliefs he professes.

Look For

As you read "The Life You Save May be Your Own," look for situational irony. In what ways do Shiftlet's actions contradict the comments he makes?

Writing

The title of the story is a slogan that commonly appeared on American highways a number of years ago. The slogan urged motorists to drive carefully to avoid killing themselves. Discuss the significance of this slogan. Freewrite about this slogan. Whom else might a motorist's reckless driving affect? To what type of motives does the slogan appeal? What does it imply about human nature?

Vocabulary

Knowing the following words will help you as you read "The Life You Save May Be Your Own."

desolate (dəs′ ə lit) *adj.*: Forlorn; wretched (p. 1052)
listed (list′ id) *v.*: Swayed (p. 1052)
ominous (äm′ ə nəs) *adj.*: Threatening; sinister (p. 1053)
ravenous (rav′ ə nəs) *adj.*: Extremely eager (p. 1056)
morose (mə rōs′) *adj.*: Gloomy, sullen (p. 1058)
guffawing (gə fô′d′) *adj.*: Laughing in a loud, coarse manner (p. 1060)

The Life You Save May Be Your Own

Flannery O'Connor

The old woman and her daughter were sitting on their porch when Mr. Shiftlet came up their road for the first time. The old woman slid to the edge of her chair and leaned forward, shading her eyes from the piercing sunset with her hand. The daughter could not see far in front of her and continued to play with her fingers. Although the old woman lived in this desolate spot with only her daughter and she had never seen Mr. Shiftlet before, she could tell, even from a distance, that he was a tramp and no one to be afraid of. His left coat sleeve was folded up to show there was only half an arm in it and his gaunt figure listed slightly to the side as if the breeze were pushing him. He had on a black town suit and a brown felt hat that was turned up in the front and down in the back and he carried a tin tool box by a handle. He came on, at an amble, up her road, his face turned toward the sun which appeared to be balancing itself on the peak of a small mountain.

The old woman didn't change her position until he was almost into her yard; then she rose with one hand fisted on her hip. The daughter, a large girl in a short blue organdy dress, saw him all at once and jumped up and began to stamp and point and make excited speechless sounds.

Mr. Shiftlet stopped just inside the yard and set his box on the ground and tipped his hat at her as if she were not in the least afflicted; then he turned toward the old woman and swung the hat all the way off. He had long black slick hair that hung flat from a part in the middle to beyond the tips of his ears on either side. His face descended in forehead for more than half its length and ended suddenly with his features just balanced over a jutting steel-trap jaw. He seemed to be a young man but he had a look of composed dissatisfaction as if he understood life thoroughly.

"Good evening," the old woman said. She was about the size of a cedar fence post and she had a man's gray hat pulled down low over her head.

The tramp stood looking at her and didn't answer. He turned his back and faced the sunset. He swung both his whole and his short arm up slowly so that they indicated an expanse of sky and his figure formed a crooked cross. The old woman watched him with her arms folded across her chest as if she were the owner of the sun, and the daughter watched, her head thrust forward and her fat helpless hands hanging at the wrists. She had long pink-gold hair and eyes as blue as a peacock's neck.

He held the pose for almost fifty seconds and then he picked up his box and came on to the porch and dropped down on the bottom step. "Lady," he said in a firm nasal voice, "I'd give a fortune to live where I could see me a sun do that every evening."

"Does it every evening," the old woman said and sat back down. The daughter sat down too and watched him with a cautious sly look as if he were a bird that had come up very close. He leaned to one side, rooting in his pants pocket, and in a second he brought out a package of chewing gum and offered her a piece. She took it and unpeeled it and began to chew without taking her eyes off him. He offered the old woman a piece but she only raised her upper lip to indicate she had no teeth.

Mr. Shiftlet's pale sharp glance had already passed over everything in the yard—the pump near the corner of the house and the big fig tree that three or four chickens were preparing to roost in—and had moved to a shed where he saw the square rusted back of an automobile. "You ladies drive?" he asked.

"That car ain't run in fifteen year," the old woman said. "The day my husband died, it quit running."

"Nothing is like it used to be, lady," he said. "The world is almost rotten."

"That's right," the old woman said. "You from around here?"

"Name Tom T. Shiftlet," he murmured, looking at the tires.

"I'm pleased to meet you," the old woman said. "Name Lucynell Crater and daughter Lucynell Crater. What you doing around here, Mr. Shiftlet?"

He judged the car to be about a 1928 or '29 Ford. "Lady," he said, and turned and gave her his full attention, "lemme tell you something. There's one of these doctors in Atlanta that's taken a knife and cut the human heart—the human heart," he repeated, leaning forward, "out of a man's chest and held it in his hand," and he held his hand out, palm up, as if it were slightly weighted with the human heart, "and studied it like it was a day-old chicken, and lady," he said, allowing a long significant pause in which his head slid forward and his clay-colored eyes brightened, "he don't know no more about it than you or me."

"That's right," the old woman said.

"Why, if he was to take that knife and cut into every corner of it, he still wouldn't know no more than you or me. What you want to bet?"

"Nothing," the old woman said wisely. "Where you come from, Mr. Shiftlet?"

He didn't answer. He reached into his pocket and brought out a sack of tobacco and a package of cigarette papers and rolled himself a cigarette, expertly with one hand, and attached it in a hanging position to his upper lip. Then he took a box of wooden matches from his pocket and struck one on his shoe. He held the burning match as if he were studying the mystery of flame while it traveled dangerously toward his skin. The daughter began to make loud noises and to point to his hand and shake her finger at him, but when the flame was just before touching him, he leaned down with his hand cupped over it as if were going to set fire to his nose and lit the cigarette.

He flipped away the dead match and blew a stream of gray into the evening. A sly look came over his face. "Lady," he said, "nowadays, people'll do anything anyways. I can tell you my name is Tom T. Shiftlet and I come from Tarwater, Tennessee, but you never have seen me before: how you know I ain't lying? How you know my name ain't Aaron Sparks, lady, and I come from Singleberry, Georgia, or how you know it's not George Speeds and I come from Lucy, Alabama, or how you know I ain't Thompson Bright from Toolafalls, Mississippi?"

"I don't know nothing about you," the old woman muttered, irked.

"Lady," he said, "people don't care how they lie. Maybe the best I can tell you is, I'm a man; but listen lady," he said and paused and made his tone more ominous still, "what is a man?"

The old woman began to gum a seed.

"What you carry in that tin box, Mr. Shiftlet?" she asked.

"Tools," he said, put back. "I'm a carpenter."

"Well, if you come out here to work, I'll be able to feed you and give you a place to sleep but I can't pay. I'll tell you that before you begin," she said.

There was no answer at once and no particular expression on his face. He leaned back against the two-by-four that helped support the porch roof. "Lady," he said slowly, "there's some men that some things mean more to them than money." The old woman rocked without comment and the daughter watched the trigger that moved up and down in his neck. He told the old woman then that all most people were interested in was money, but he asked what a man was made for. He asked her if a man was made for money, or what. He asked her what she thought she was made for but she didn't answer, she only sat rocking and wondered if a one-armed man could put a new roof on her garden house. He asked a lot of questions that she didn't answer. He told her that he was twenty-eight years old and had lived a varied life. He had been a gospel singer, a foreman on the railroad, an assistant in an undertaking parlor, and he come over the radio for three months with Uncle Roy and his Red Creek Wranglers. He said he had fought and bled in the Arm Service of his country and visited every foreign land and that everywhere he had seen people that didn't care if they did a thing one way or another. He said he hadn't been raised thataway.

A fat yellow moon appeared in the branches of the fig tree as if it were going to roost there with the chickens. He said that a man had to escape to the country to see the world whole and that he wished he lived in a desolate place like this where he could see the sun go down every evening like God made it to do.

"Are you married or are you single?" the old woman asked.

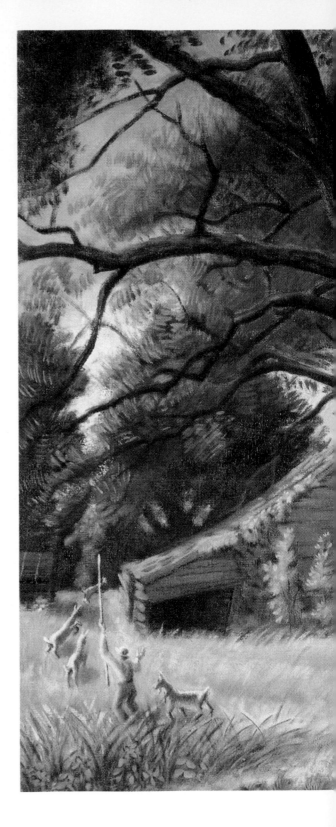

BLACK WALNUTS, 1945
Joseph Pollet
Collection of the Whitney Museum of American Art

There was a long silence. "Lady," he asked finally, "where would you find you an innocent woman today? I wouldn't have any of this trash I could just pick up."

The daughter was leaning very far down, hanging her head almost between her knees watching him through a triangular door she had made in her overturned hair; and she suddenly fell in a heap on the floor and began to whimper. Mr. Shiftlet straightened her out and helped her get back in the chair.

"Is she your baby girl?" he asked.

"My only," the old woman said "and she's the sweetest girl in the world. I would give her up for nothing on earth. She's smart too. She can sweep the floor, cook, wash, feed the chickens, and hoe. I wouldn't give her up for a casket of jewels."

"No," he said kindly, "don't ever let any man take her away from you."

"Any man come after her," the old woman said, " 'll have to stay around the place."

Mr. Shiftlet's eye in the darkness was focused on a part of the automobile bumper that glittered in the distance. "Lady," he said, jerking his short arm up as if he could point with it to her house and yard and pump, "there ain't a broken thing on this plantation that I couldn't fix for you, one-arm jackleg or not. I'm a man," he said with a sullen dignity, "even if I ain't a whole one. I got," he said, tapping his knuckles on the floor to emphasize the immensity of what he was going to say, "a moral intelligence!" and his face pierced out of the darkness into a shaft of doorlight and he stared at her as if he were astonished himself at this impossible truth.

The old woman was not impressed with the phrase. "I told you you could hang around and work for food," she said, "if you don't mind sleeping in that car yonder."

"Why listen, lady," he said with a grin of delight, "the monks of old slept in their coffins!"

"They wasn't as advanced as we are," the old woman said.

The next morning he began on the roof of the garden house while Lucynell, the daughter, sat on a rock and watched him work. He had not been around a week before the change he had made in the place was apparent. He had patched the front and back steps, built a new hog pen, restored a fence, and taught Lucynell, who was completely deaf and had never said a word in her life, to say the word "bird." The big rosy-faced girl followed him everywhere, saying "Burrttddt ddbirrrttdt," and clapping her hands. The old woman watched from a distance, secretly pleased. She was ravenous for a son-in-law.

Mr. Shiftlet slept on the hard narrow back seat of the car with his feet out the side window. He had his razor and a can of water on a crate that served him as a bedside table and he put up a piece of mirror against the back glass and kept his coat neatly on a hanger that he hung over one of the windows.

In the evenings he sat on the steps and talked while the old woman and Lucynell rocked violently in their chairs on either side of him. The old woman's three mountains were black against the dark blue sky and were visited off and on by various planets and by the moon after it had left the chickens. Mr. Shiftlet pointed out that the reason he had improved this plantation was because he had taken a personal interest in it. He said he was even going to make the automobile run.

He had raised the hood and studied the mechanism and he said he could tell that the car had been built in the days when cars were really built. You take now, he said, one man puts in one bolt and another man puts in another bolt and another man puts in another bolt so that it's a man for a bolt. That's why you have to pay so much for a car: you're paying all those men. Now if you didn't have to pay but one man, you could get you a cheaper car and one that had had a personal interest taken in it, and it would be a better car. The old woman agreed with him that this was so.

Mr. Shiftlet said that the trouble with the world was that nobody cared, or stopped and took any trouble. He said he never would have been able to teach Lucynell to say a word if he hadn't cared and stopped long enough.

"Teach her to say something else," the old woman said.

"What you want her to say next?" Mr. Shiftlet asked.

The old woman's smile was broad and toothless and suggestive. "Teach her to say 'sugarpie,' " she said.

Mr. Shiftlet already knew what was on her mind.

The next day he began to tinker with the automobile and that evening he told her that if she would buy a fan belt, he would be able to make the car run.

The old woman said she would give him the money. "You see that girl yonder?" she asked, pointing to Lucynell who was sitting on the floor a foot away, watching him, her eyes blue even in the dark. "If it was ever a man wanted to take her away, I would say, 'No man on earth is going to take that sweet girl of mine away from me!' but if he was to say, 'Lady, I don't want to take her away, I want her right here,' I would say, 'Mister, I don't blame you none. I wouldn't pass up a chance to live in a permanent place and get the sweetest girl in the world myself. You ain't no fool,' I would say."

"How old is she?" Mr. Shiftlet asked casually.

"Fifteen, sixteen," the old woman said. The girl was nearly thirty but because of her innocence it was impossible to guess.

"It would be a good idea to paint it too," Mr. Shiftlet remarked. "You don't want it to rust out."

"We'll see about that later," the old woman said.

The next day he walked into town and returned with the parts he needed and a can of gasoline. Late in the afternoon, terrible noises issued from the shed and the old woman rushed out of the house, thinking Lucynell was somewhere having a fit. Lucynell was sitting on a chicken crate, stamping her feet and screaming, "Burrddtt! bddurrd-dttt!" but her fuss was drowned out by the car. With a volley of blasts it emerged from the shed, moving in a fierce and stately way. Mr. Shiftlet was in the driver's seat, sitting very erect. He had an expression of serious modesty on his face as if he had just raised the dead.

That night, rocking on the porch, the old woman began her business, at once. "You want you an innocent woman, don't you?" she asked sympathetically. "You don't want none of this trash."

"No'm, I don't," Mr. Shiftlet said.

"One that can't talk," she continued, "can't sass you back or use foul language. That's the kind for you to have. Right there," and she pointed to Lucynell sitting cross-legged in her chair, holding both feet in her hands.

"That's right," he admitted. "She wouldn't give me any trouble."

"Saturday," the old woman said, "you and her and me can drive into town and get married."

Mr. Shiftlet eased his position on the steps.

"I can't get married right now," he said. "Everything you want to do takes money and I ain't got any."

"What you need with money?" she asked.

"It takes money," he said. "Some people'll do anything anyhow these days, but the way I think, I wouldn't marry no woman that I couldn't take on a trip like she was somebody. I mean take her to a hotel and treat her. I wouldn't marry the Duchesser Windsor," he said firmly, "unless I could take her to a hotel and giver something good to eat.

"I was raised thataway and there ain't a thing I can do about it. My old mother taught me how to do."

"Lucynell don't even know what a hotel is," the old woman muttered. "Listen here,

Mr. Shiftlet," she said, sliding forward in her chair, "you'd be getting a permanent house and a deep well and the most innocent girl in the world. You don't need no money. Lemme tell you something: there ain't any place in the world for a poor disabled friendless drifting man."

The ugly words settled in Mr. Shiftlet's head like a group of buzzards in the top of a tree. He didn't answer at once. He rolled himself a cigarette and lit it and then he said in an even voice, "Lady, a man is divided into two parts, body and spirit."

The old woman clamped her gums together.

"A body and a spirit," he repeated. "The body, lady, is like a house: it don't go anywhere; but the spirit, lady, is like a automobile: always on the move, always . . ."

"Listen, Mr. Shiftlet," she said, "my well never goes dry and my house is always warm in the winter and there's no mortgage on a thing about this place. You can go to the courthouse and see for yourself. And yonder under that shed is a fine automobile." She laid the bait carefully. "You can have it painted by Saturday. I'll pay for the paint."

In the darkness, Mr. Shiftlet's smile stretched like a weary snake waking up by a fire. After a second he recalled himself and said, "I'm only saying a man's spirit means more to him than anything else. I would have to take my wife off for the weekend without no regards at all for cost. I got to follow where my spirit says to go."

"I'll give you fifteen dollars for a weekend trip," the old woman said in a crabbed voice. "That's the best I can do."

"That wouldn't hardly pay for more than the gas and the hotel," he said. "It wouldn't feed her."

"Seventeen-fifty," the old woman said. "That's all I got so it isn't any use you trying to milk me. You can take a lunch."

Mr. Shiftlet was deeply hurt by the word "milk." He didn't doubt that she had more money sewed up in her mattress but he had already told her he was not interested in her money. "I'll make that do," he said and rose and walked off without treating with her further.

On Saturday the three of them drove into town in the car that the paint had barely dried on and Mr. Shiftlet and Lucynell were married in the Ordinary's office while the old woman witnessed. As they came out of the courthouse, Mr. Shiftlet began twisting his neck in his collar. He looked morose and bitter as if he had been insulted while someone held him. "That didn't satisfy me none," he said. "That was just something a woman in an office did, nothing but paper work and blood tests. What do they know about my blood? If they was to take my heart and cut it out," he said, "they wouldn't know a thing about me. It didn't satisfy me at all."

"It satisfied the law," the old woman said sharply.

"The law," Mr. Shiftlet said and spit. "It's the law that don't satisfy me."

He had painted the car dark green with a yellow band around it just under the windows. The three of them climbed in the front seat and the old woman said, "Don't Lucynell look pretty? Looks like a baby doll." Lucynell was dressed up in a white dress that her mother had uprooted from a trunk and there was a Panama hat on her head with a bunch of red wooden cherries on the brim. Every now and then her placid expression was changed by a sly isolated little thought like a shoot of green in the desert. "You got a prize!" the old woman said.

Mr. Shiftlet didn't even look at her.

They drove back to the house to let the old woman off and pick up the lunch. When they were ready to leave, she stood staring in the window of the car, with her fingers clenched around the glass. Tears began to seep sideways out of her eyes and run along the dirty creases in her face. "I ain't ever been parted with her for two days before," she said.

Mr. Shiftlet started the motor.

"And I wouldn't let no man have her but

you because I seen you would do right. Good-bye, Sugarbaby," she said, clutching at the sleeve of the white dress. Lucynell looked straight at her and didn't seem to see her there at all. Mr. Shiftlet eased the car forward so that she had to move her hands.

The early afternoon was clear and open and surrounded by pale blue sky. Although the car would go only thirty miles an hour, Mr. Shiftlet imagined a terrific climb and dip and swerve that went entirely to his head so that he forgot his morning bitterness. He had always wanted an automobile but he had never been able to afford one before. He drove very fast because he wanted to make Mobile by nightfall.

Occasionally he stopped his thoughts long enough to look at Lucynell in the seat beside him. She had eaten the lunch as soon as they were out of the yard and now she was pulling the cherries off the hat one by one and throwing them out the window. He became depressed in spite of the car. He had driven about a hundred miles when he decided that she must be hungry again and at the next small town they came to, he stopped in front of an aluminum-painted eating place called The Hot Spot and took her in and ordered her a plate of ham and grits. The ride had made her sleepy and as soon as she got up on the stool, she rested her head on the counter and shut her eyes. There was no one in The Hot Spot but Mr. Shiftlet and the boy behind the counter, a pale youth with a greasy rag hung over his shoulder. Before he could dish up the food, she was snoring gently.

"Give it to her when she wakes up," Mr. Shiftlet said. "I'll pay for it now."

The boy bent over her and stared at the long pink-gold hair and the half-shut sleeping eyes. Then he looked up and stared at Mr. Shiftlet. "She looks like an angel of Gawd," he murmured.

"Hitchhiker," Mr. Shiftlet explained. "I can't wait. I got to make Tuscaloosa."

The boy bent over again and very care-fully touched his finger to a strand of the golden hair and Mr. Shiftlet left.

He was more depressed than ever as he drove on by himself. The late afternoon had grown hot and sultry and the country had flattened out. Deep in the sky a storm was preparing very slowly and without thunder as if it meant to drain every drop of air from the earth before it broke. There were times when Mr. Shiftlet preferred not to be alone. He felt too that a man with a car had a responsibility to others and he kept his eye out for a hitchhiker. Occasionally he saw a sign that warned: "Drive carefully. The life you save may be your own."

The narrow road dropped off on either side into dry fields and here and there a shack or a filling station stood in a clearing. The sun began to set directly in front of the automobile. It was a reddening ball that through his windshield was slightly flat on the bottom and top. He saw a boy in overalls and a gray hat standing on the edge of the road and he slowed the car down and stopped in front of him. The boy didn't have his hand raised to thumb the ride, he was only standing there, but he had a small cardboard suitcase and his hat was set on his head in a way to indicate that he had left somewhere for good. "Son," Mr. Shiftlet said, "I see you want a ride."

The boy didn't say he did or he didn't but he opened the door of the car and got in, and Mr. Shiftlet started driving again. The child held the suitcase on his lap and folded his arms on top of it. He turned his head and looked out the window away from Shiftlet. Mr. Shiftlet felt oppressed. "Son," he said after a minute, "I got the best old mother in the world so I reckon you only got the second best."

The boy gave him a quick dark glance and then turned his face back out the window.

"It's nothing so sweet," Mr. Shiftlet continued, "as a boy's mother. She taught him his first prayers at her knee, she give him love when no other would, she told him what was right and what wasn't, and she seen that he done the right thing. Son," he said, "I never rued a day in my life like the one I rued when I left that old mother of mine."

The boy shifted in his seat but he didn't look at Mr. Shiftlet. He unfolded his arms and put one hand on the door handle.

"My mother was a angel of Gawd," Mr. Shiftlet said in a very strained voice. "He took her from heaven and giver to me and I left her." His eyes were instantly clouded over with a mist of tears. The car was barely moving.

The boy turned angrily in the seat. "You go to the devil!" he cried. "My old woman is a flea bag and yours is a stinking pole cat!" and with that he flung the door open and jumped out with his suitcase into the ditch.

Mr. Shiftlet was so shocked that for about a hundred feet he drove along slowly with the door still open. A cloud, the exact color of the boy's hat and shaped like a turnip, had descended over the sun, and another, worse looking, crouched behind the car. Mr. Shiftlet felt that the rottenness of the world was about to engulf him. He raised his arm and let it fall again to his breast. "Oh Lord!" he prayed. "Break forth and wash the slime from this earth!"

The turnip continued slowly to descend. After a few minutes there was a guffawing peal of thunder from behind and fantastic raindrops, like tin-can tops, crashed over the rear of Mr. Shiftlet's car. Very quickly he stepped on the gas and with his stump sticking out the window he raced the galloping shower into Mobile.

THINKING ABOUT THE SELECTION

Recalling

1. What does the old woman conclude about Mr. Shiftlet as she first sees him?
2. What agreement do Mr. Shiftlet and the old woman reach at the end of the first scene?
3. (a) In what way is Lucynell handicapped? (b) What arguments does the old woman use to persuade Mr. Shiftlet to marry Lucynell? (c) Why does Shiftlet say that he cannot marry her? (d) What causes him to change his mind?
4. Where does Shiftlet abandon Lucynell?
5. What happens when Shiftlet picks up a hitchhiker?

Interpreting

6. (a) What is the significance of Shiftlet's name? (b) What is the significance of the narrator's observation that Shiftlet's figure "formed a crooked cross"?
7. (a) What details in the first scene suggest that the old woman is not really listening to Shiftlet's comments? (b) With what is she preoccupied?
8. What does the narrator mean when she calls Shiftlet's claim that he has a "moral intelligence" an "impossible truth"?
9. How does Shiftlet's comment that the spirit is "always on the move" foreshadow, or hint at, the outcome of the story?
10. (a) What is the cause of Lucynell's innocence? (b) Considering the cause of her innocence, what does the story imply about a person's ability to remain innocent in the modern world?
11. How does the incident with the hitchhiker relate to the rest of the story?
12. (a) In what ways are the characters in this story realistic? (b) In what ways are they exaggerated?
13. Explain the title of this short story.

Applying

14. Do you think this story could have been written during another period of American history? Explain your answer.

ANALYZING LITERATURE
Understanding Irony

This story is filled with situational irony—irony that occurs when the actual result of an action or situation is quite different from the expected result. Much of this irony results from the contrast between Mr. Shiftlet's comments and actions.

Explain how situational irony results from each of the following comments.

1. "... people don't care how they lie."
2. "... there's some men that some things mean more to them than money."
3. Mr. Shiftlet said that the trouble with the world was that nobody cared ...
4. "Some people'll do anything anyhow these days, but the way I think, I wouldn't marry no woman that I couldn't take on a trip like she was somebody."

CRITICAL THINKING AND READING
Seeing Irony as a Key to Theme

The irony in this story plays a vital role in conveying its theme. For example, an important aspect of the theme—that people's actions often do not correspond to the beliefs they profess—is expressed through the contradictions between Mr. Shiftlet's comments and behavior.

1. What is ironic about the statement at the end of the story that "Mr. Shiftlet felt that the rottenness of the world was about to engulf him"?
2. This statement, along with Mr. Shiftlet's comment that "The world is almost rotten," suggests that the world is in a state of deterioration. What do the events in the story suggest about the cause of this deterioration?
3. What is ironic about the way in which Shiftlet's prayer at the end of the story is answered?
4. What does this incident suggest will happen to people whose behavior contradicts the beliefs they profess?

THINKING AND WRITING
Writing a Story

Develop a popular slogan into a short story, as Flannery O'Connor did in "The Life You Save May Be Your Own." Start by thinking of a slogan with deeper implications that might not occur to most people. Then develop a plot which expresses these implications. Work the slogan into the story at some point, and use it as the story's title. When you finish writing your story, revise it to make sure that the situational irony is apparent. Proofread your story and share it with your classmates.

ANNE TYLER

1941–

Inspired by the work of Eudora Welty, Anne Tyler devotes much of her fiction to exposing the latent, unusual characteristics of outwardly ordinary people.

Tyler was born in Minneapolis, Minnesota, spent most of her childhood in Raleigh, North Carolina, and now lives with her family in Baltimore, Maryland. She studied Russian at Duke and at Columbia, while at the same time developing into an enthusiastic and dedicated fiction writer. In 1964, when she was twenty-four, she published her first novel, *If Morning Ever Comes*. Since then, she has published several more novels, including *The Tin Can Tree* (1966), *The Clock Winder* (1973), *Earthly Possessions* (1977), *Dinner at the Homesick Restaurant* (1982), and *The Accidental Tourist* (1985). She has also written a vast number of short stories, many of which she has contributed to *The New Yorker*.

"Average Waves in Unprotected Waters" exhibits Tyler's ability to create well-developed, realistic characters and evoke an emotional response through an unsentimental portrayal of the characters' tragic lives.

GUIDE FOR READING

Average Waves in Unprotected Waters

Foreshadowing. Foreshadowing is a technique that writers frequently use in short stories and novels to build **suspense,** or create tension concerning the outcome of the events. When a writer uses foreshadowing, he or she presents details that hint at actions that will occur later in the story or suggest the story's outcome. For example, in her story *The Life You Save May Be Your Own,* Flannery O'Connor hints at the tragic impact that Mr. Shiftlet will have on the lives of the Crater women when she writes that Mr. Shiftlet "paused and made his tone more *ominous* still."

Flashback. A flashback is an interruption in the action of a narrative in which an earlier event is shown or described. Often a flashback takes the form of a reminiscence of one of the characters. For example, in her story "The Jilting of Granny Weatherall," Katherine Anne Porter presents numerous flashbacks as the main character's thoughts drift back to events that occurred in her younger days.

As you read "Average Waves in Unprotected Waters," look for Tyler's use of foreshadowing and flashbacks. How does her use of foreshadowing help to build suspense? How does her use of flashbacks contribute to your overall understanding of the story?

In "Average Waves in Unprotected Waters," Anne Tyler explores a mother's attempts to cope with a severely handicapped child. Freewrite about some of the difficulties that parents might have in dealing with a handicapped child. What types of emotions might parents experience in this situation? In what ways might a child's handicap affect the parents' lives? What actions might the parents take to make their child's life better?

Knowing the following words will help you as you read "Average Waves in Unprotected Waters."

staunch (stônch) *adj.*: Strong; unyielding (p. 1068)

tantrums (tan′ trəmz) *n.*: Childish fits of temper (p. 1068)

Average Waves
in Unprotected Waters

Anne Tyler

As soon as it got light, Bet woke him and dressed him, and then she walked him over to the table and tried to make him eat a little cereal. He wouldn't, though. He could tell something was up. She pressed the edge of the spoon against his lips till she heard it click on his teeth, but he just looked off at a corner of the ceiling—a knobby child with great glassy eyes and her own fair hair. Like any other nine-year-old, he wore a striped shirt and jeans, but the shirt was too neat and the jeans too blue, unpatched and un-faded, and would stay that way till he out-grew them. And his face was elderly—pinched, strained, tired—though it should have looked as unused as his jeans. He hardly ever changed his expression.

She left him in his chair and went to make the beds. Then she raised the yellowed shade, rinsed a few spoons in the bathroom sink, picked up some bits of magazines he'd torn the night before. This was a rented room in an ancient, crumbling house, and nothing you could do to it would lighten its cluttered look. There was always that feeling of too many lives layered over other lives, like the layers of brownish wallpaper her child had peeled away in the corner by his bed.

She slipped her feet into flat-heeled loaf-ers and absently patted the front of her dress, a worn beige knit she usually saved for Sundays. Maybe she should take it in a little; it hung from her shoulders like a sack.

She felt too slight and frail, too wispy for all she had to do today. But she reached for her coat anyhow, and put it on and tied a blue kerchief under her chin. Then she went over to the table and slowly spun, modeling the coat. "See, Arnold?" she said. "We're going out."

Arnold went on looking at the ceiling, but his gaze turned wild and she knew he'd heard.

She fetched his jacket from the closet—brown corduroy, with a hood. It had set her back half a week's salary. But Arnold didn't like it; he always wanted his old one, a little red duffel coat he'd long ago outgrown. When she came toward him, he started moaning and rocking and shaking his head. She had to struggle to stuff his arms in the sleeves. Small though he was, he was strong, wiry; he was getting to be too much for her. He shook free of her hands and ran over to his bed. The jacket was on, though. It wasn't buttoned, the collar was askew, but never mind; that just made him look more real. She always felt bad at how he stood inside his clothes, separate from them, passive, un-aware of all the buttons and snaps she'd fastened as carefully as she would a doll's.

She gave a last look around the room, checked to make sure the hot plate was off, and then picked up her purse and Arnold's suitcase. "Come along, Arnold," she said.

He came, dragging out every step. He

looked at the suitcase suspiciously, but only because it was new. It didn't have any meaning for him. "See?" she said. "It's yours. It's Arnold's. It's going on the train with us."

But her voice was all wrong. He would pick it up, for sure. She paused in the middle of locking the door and glanced over at him fearfully. Anything could set him off nowadays. He hadn't noticed, though. He was too busy staring around the hallway, goggling at a freckled, walnut-framed mirror as if he'd never seen it before. She touched his shoulder. "Come, Arnold," she said.

They went down the stairs slowly, both of them clinging to the sticky mahogany railing. The suitcase banged against her shins. In the entrance hall, old Mrs. Puckett stood waiting outside her door—a huge, soft lady in a black crêpe dress and orthopedic shoes. She was holding a plastic bag of peanut-butter cookies, Arnold's favorites. There were tears in her eyes. "Here, Arnold," she said, quavering. Maybe she felt to blame that he was going. But she'd done the best she could: babysat him all these years and only given up when he'd grown too strong and wild to manage. Bet wished Arnold would give the old lady some sign—hug her, make his little crowing noise, just take the cookies, even. But he was too excited. He raced on out the front door, and it was Bet who had to take them. "Well, thank you, Mrs. Puckett," she said. "I know he'll enjoy them later."

"Oh, no . . ." said Mrs. Puckett, and she flapped her large hands and gave up, sobbing.

They were lucky and caught a bus first thing. Arnold sat by the window. He must have thought he was going to work with her; when they passed the red-and-gold Kresge's sign, he jabbered and tried to stand up. "No, honey," she said, and took hold of his arm. He settled down then and let his hand stay curled in hers awhile. He had very small, cool fingers, and nails as smooth as thumbtack heads.

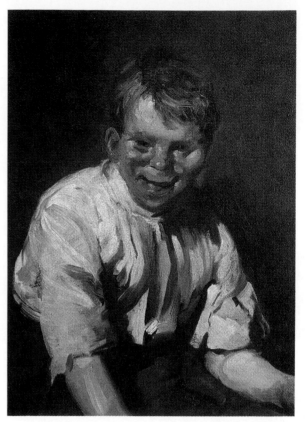

THE LAUGHING BOY
George Bellows
Hirschl & Adler Galleries, Inc.

At the train station, she bought the tickets and then a pack of Wrigley's spearmint gum. Arnold stood gaping at the vaulted ceiling, with his head flopped back and his arms hanging limp at his sides. People stared at him. She would have liked to push their faces in. "Over here, honey," she said, and she nudged him toward the gate, straightening his collar as they walked.

He hadn't been on a train before and acted a little nervous, bouncing up and down in his seat and flipping the lid of his ashtray and craning forward to see the man ahead of them. When the train started moving, he crowed and pulled at her sleeve. "That's right, Arnold. Train. We're taking a trip," Bet said. She unwrapped a stick of chewing gum and gave it to him. He loved gum. If she didn't watch him closely, he sometimes swallowed it—which worried her a little because she'd heard it clogged your kidneys; but at least it would keep him busy. She looked down at the top of his head. Through the blond prickles of his hair, cut short for practical reasons, she could see his skull bones moving as he chewed. He was so thin-skinned, almost transparent; sometimes she imagined she could see the blood traveling in his veins.

When the train reached a steady speed, he grew calmer, and after a while he nodded over against her and let his hands sag on his knees. She watched his eyelashes slowly drooping—two colorless, fringed crescents, heavier and heavier, every now and then flying up as he tried to fight off sleep. He had never slept well, not ever, not even as a baby. Even before they'd noticed anything wrong, they'd wondered at his jittery, jerky catnaps, his tiny hands clutching tight and springing open, his strange single wail sailing out while he went right on sleeping. Avery said it gave him the chills. And after the doctor talked to them Avery wouldn't have anything to do with Arnold anymore—just walked in wide circles around the crib, looking stunned and sick. A few weeks later, he left. She wasn't surprised. She even knew how he felt, more or less. Halfway, he blamed her; halfway, he blamed himself. You can't believe a thing like this will just fall on you out of nowhere.

She'd had moments herself of picturing some kind of evil gene in her husband's ordinary, stocky body—a dark little egg like a black jelly bean, she imagined it. All his fault. But other times she was sure the gene was hers. It seemed so natural; she never could do anything as well as most people. And then other times she blamed their marriage. They'd married too young, against her parents' wishes. All she'd wanted was to get away from home. Now she couldn't remember why. What was wrong with home? She

WAITING ROOM
Raphael Soyer
The Corcoran Gallery of Art

JOHN UPDIKE

1932–

In his short stories and novels, John Updike vividly captures the essence of life in contemporary America. Through his depictions of ordinary situations and events, he explores many of the more important issues of our time and offers insights into the underlying significance of everyday life.

Updike was born in Reading, Pennsylvania, and was raised in the nearby town of Shillington. After graduating from Harvard, he spent a year at the Ruskin School of Drawing and Fine Art in England. When he returned to the United States, he joined the staff of *The New Yorker,* a magazine which has published many of his short stories.

Following the publication of his first collection of poetry, *The Carpentered Hen and Other Tame Animals* (1958), Updike published several other collections of poetry, many novels and short stories, numerous essays and book reviews, and a play. His novels include *The Poorhouse Fair* (1959), *Rabbit, Run* (1960), *Of the Farm* (1965), *Couples* (1968), *Rabbit Redux* (1971), *The Coup* (1978), *Rabbit is Rich* (1981), and *Roger's Version* (1987). He earned the National Book Award for his novel *The Centaur* (1963), and his novel *The Witches of Eastwick* (1984) was made into a major motion picture. His collection of essays and criticism, *Hugging the Shore* (1983), was the winner of the 1983 National Book Critics Circle Award for criticism.

"The Slump" reflects Updike's awareness of the universal feelings and concerns that develop out of specific situations. By delving into the thoughts of a baseball player in the midst of an extended slump, he captures a sense of uncertainty and insecurity that all people have experienced at some point during their lives.

GUIDE FOR READING

The Slump

Diction. Diction refers to a writer's choice of words. When writing a short story or novel, a writer must carefully choose language that is appropriate for the characters and subject. For example, it would not be appropriate for a writer to use ornate, elevated language in a story about uneducated factory workers. However, this type of language would be suitable for a story about a group of scholars

    Style. Until the contemporary period, stories were almost always told in the past tense. "He came, she said, they did," authors would write. John Updike was one of the first of the contemporary writers to employ the present tense. In his novel *Rabbit, Run,* Updike used the present tense, a technique he called "a piece of technical daring in 1959," to "emphasize how thoroughly the zigzagging hero lived in the present. . ."

As you read "The Slump," pay close attention to Updike's choice of words. Why is the language appropriate for the story's subject and main character? What effect is created by the use of the present tense?

Updike is one of many writers who have explored the world of sports and the experiences of athletes at work. Freewrite about the reasons why sports are a common subject for literary works. Why do people enjoy reading about sports? What aspects of everyday life are embodied in the world of professional sports? What feelings and experiences do all people share with famous athletes? In what way does the field of sports serve as a metaphor for life?

Knowing the following words will help you as you read "The Slump."
vagueness (vāg′ nis) *n.:* Lack of definition in shape or form (p. 1074)
tabloid (tab′ loid) *n.:* A newspaper with many pictures and short, often sensational, stories (p. 1074)

The Slump

John Updike

They say reflexes, the coach says reflexes, even the papers now are saying reflexes, but I don't think it's the reflexes so much—last night, as a gag to cheer me up, the wife walks into the bedroom wearing one of the kids' rubber gorilla masks and I was under the bed in six-tenths of a second, she had the stopwatch on me. It's that I can't see the ball the way I used to. It used to come floating up with all seven continents showing, and the pitcher's thumbprint, and a grass smooch or two, and the Spalding guarantee in ten-point sans-serif,[1] and *whop*! I could feel the sweet wood with the bat still cocked. Now, I don't know, there's like a cloud around it, a sort of spiral vagueness, maybe the Van Allen belt,[2] or maybe I lift my eye in the last second, planning how I'll round second base, or worrying which I do first, tip my cap or slap the third-base coach's hand. You can't see a blind spot, Kierkegaard[3] says, but in there now, between when the ball leaves the bleacher background and I can hear it plop all fat and satisfied in the catcher's mitt, there's somehow just nothing, where there used to be a lot, everything in fact, because they're not keeping me around for my fielding, and already I see the afternoon tabloid has me down as trade bait.

The flutters don't come when they used to. It used to be, I'd back the convertible out of the garage and watch the electric eye put the door down again and drive in to the stadium, and at about the bridge turnoff I'd ease off grooving with the radio rock, and then on the lot there'd be the kids waiting to get a look and that would start the big butterflies, and when the attendant would take my car I'd want to shout *Stop, thief*, and walking down that long cement corridor I'd fantasize like I was going to the electric chair and the locker room was some dream after death, and I'd wonder why the suit fit, and how these really immortal guys, that I recognized from the bubble-gum cards I used to collect, knew my name. *They* knew *me*. And I'd go out and the stadium mumble would scoop at me and the grass seemed too precious to walk on, like emeralds, and by the time I got into the cage I couldn't remember if I batted left or right.

Now, heck, I move over the bridge singing along with the radio, and brush through the kids at just the right speed, not so fast I knock any of them down, and the attendant knows his Labor Day tip is coming, and we wink, and in the batting cage I own the place, and take my cuts, and pop five or six into the bullpen as easy as dropping dimes down a sewer. But when the scoreboard lights up, and I take those two steps up from the dugout, the biggest two steps in a ball-

---

1. ten-point sans-serif (san ser′ if): The size and style of the lettering.
2. Van Allen belt: A belt of radiation that encircles the earth.
3. Kierkegaard (kir′ kə gärd′): Søren (sö′rən) Kierkegaard (1813–1855), Danish philosopher and theologian.

player's life, and kneel in the circle, giving the crowd the old hawk profile, where once the flutters would ease off, now they dig down and begin.

They say I'm not hungry, but I still feel hungry, only now it's a kind of panic hungry, and that's not the right kind. Ever watch one of your little kids try to catch a ball? He gets so excited with the idea he's going to catch it he shuts his eyes. That's me now. I walk up to the plate, having come all

this way—a lot of hotels, a lot of shagging—and my eyes feel shut. And I stand up there trying to push my eyeballs through my eyelids, and my retinas register maybe a little green, and the black patch of some nuns in far left field. That's panic hungry.

Kierkegaard called it dread.[4] It queers the works. My wife comes at me without the

---

4. dread: Kierkegaard believed that fear, or dread, is a natural part of the human condition.

gorilla mask and when in the old days, *whop!*, now she slides by with a hurt expression and a flicker of gray above her temple. I go out and ride the power mower and I've already done it so often the lawn is brown. The kids get me out of bed for a little fungo and it scares me to see them trying, busting their lungs, all that shagging ahead of them. In Florida—we used to love it in Florida, the smell of citrus and marlin, the flat pink sections where the old people drift around smiling with transistor plugs in their ears—we lie on the beach after a workout and the sun seems a high fly I'm going to lose and the waves keep coming like they've been doing for a billion years, up to the plate, up to the plate. Kierkegaard probably has the clue, somewhere in there, but I picked up *Concluding Unscientific Postscript*[5] the other day and I couldn't see the print, that is, I could see the lines, but there wasn't anything on them, like the rows of deep seats in the shade of the second deck on a Thursday afternoon, just a single ice-cream vendor sitting there, nobody around to sell to, a speck

of white in all that shade, old Søren Sock himself, keeping his goods cool.

I think maybe if I got beaned. That's probably what the wife is hinting at with the gorilla mask. A change of pace, like the time DiMaggio[6] broke his slump by Topping's[7] telling him to go to a night club and get plastered. I've stopped ducking, but the trouble is, if you're not hitting, they don't brush you back. On me, they've stopped trying for even the corners; they put it right down the pike. I can see it in his evil eye as he takes the sign and rears back, I can hear the catcher snicker, and for a second of reflex there I can see it like it used to be, continents and cities and every green tree distinct as a stitch, and the hickory sweetens in my hands, and I feel the good old sure hunger. Then something happens. It blurs, skips, fades, I don't know. It's not caring enough, is what it probably is, it's knowing that none of it—the stadium, the averages—is really there, just *you* are there, and it's not enough.

---

5. ***Concluding Unscientific Postscript:*** One of Kierkegaard's major works.

6. **DiMaggio:** Joe DiMaggio (1914–   ), New York Yankee center fielder from 1936 to 1951; now a member of the baseball Hall of Fame.

7. **Topping's:** Refers to Dan Topping, one of the Yankee owners from 1945 to 1964.

THINKING ABOUT THE SELECTION

Recalling

1. (a) How do the coaches and newspapers explain the narrator's slump? (b) How does the narrator himself explain it?

2. (a) How did the narrator feel when he saw "the kids" waiting outside the stadium? (b) How does he now react when he sees them?

3. What now happens when the narrator takes "those two steps up from the dugout" and kneels "in the circle"?

4. (a) What solution does the narrator come up with in the final paragraph? (b) How does he explain his slump in the final sentence?

Interpreting

5. Explain the significance of Kierkegaard's statement, "You can't see a blind spot."

6. (a) How has the narrator's attitude toward baseball changed during the course of his career? (b) How is this change in attitude conveyed?
7. (a) What is the significance of the narrator's observations while lying on the beach in Florida? (b) How do these observations relate to his own situation?
8. Explain the meaning of the conclusion the narrator reaches in the final sentence.
9. (a) What does the story suggest about fame? (b) What does it suggest about aging? (c) What does it suggest about life in general?

Applying

10. The narrator complains, "They say I'm not hungry, but I still feel hungry, only now it's a kind of panic hunger, and that's not the right kind." (a) What does he mean by the word *hungry*? (b) What is the right kind of hunger? (c) Do you think it is necessary to be hungry to succeed? Explain.
11. What other types of situations might produce concerns and feelings similar to the ones experienced by the narrator?

ANALYZING LITERATURE
Appreciating Diction and Style

Diction refers to a writer's choice of words. In fiction a writer must use language that is appropriate for his or her subject and characters.
1. Why is the language in "The Slump" appropriate for the narrator and subject? Support your answer.
2. Would the story still be effective if Updike had used ornate, elevated language? Why or why not?

3. The narrator tells his story in the present tense. (a) How would the effect of this story be different if it were told in the past tense? (b) How effective is this technique? Explain your answer.

UNDERSTANDING LANGUAGE
Understanding Jargon

Jargon refers to the specialized vocabulary of a specific profession. In "The Slump" Updike frequently uses baseball jargon—language which can be understood only by a person with some familiarity with the game. For example, when the narrator comments that he kneels "in the *circle*," he is referring to the on-deck circle, a circle in which the next batter awaits his or her turn at bat.

Use your dictionary to find the meaning of the following baseball terms.
1. batting cage   4. fungo
2. dugout   5. beaned
3. shagging

THINKING AND WRITING
Responding to Criticism

A critic has made the following comment concerning Updike's work: "Knowledgeable about the sports because he played them, Updike understands the difficulties of success and the poignancy of diminished prowess." Write an essay in which you discuss "The Slump" in relation to this comment. Before you start, make sure you understand the critic's comment in its entirety. What does he mean when he refers to "the poignancy of diminished prowess"? Include an explanation of the critic's comment in your essay. When you revise, make sure you have thoroughly supported your argument with passages from the story.

JOYCE CAROL OATES

1938–

Joyce Carol Oates is one of the most prolific writers of our time. She has published many novels and collections of stories and has written numerous poems, plays, and critical essays, yet she has never sacrificed quality for productivity. As a result, nearly all of her work possesses a great amount of energy and intensity.

Born in Lockport, New York, Oates began writing at an early age. Her first book, *With Shuddering Fall,* was published in 1964. Since then she has produced novels, collections of short stories, and volumes of poetry at an incredibly rapid pace. Her works of fiction include *Wheel of Love and Other Stories* (1970), *The Assassins* (1975), *Do with Me What You Will* (1978), *The Seduction and Other Stories* (1980), *Bellefleur* (1980), *A Bloodsmore Romance* (1982), and *Mysteries of Winterthurn* (1984). Oates's poetry collections include *Angel Fire* (1973), *The Fabulous Beasts* (1975), and *Love and Its Derangements and Other Poems* (1977). She has received numerous awards for her work, including the 1970 National Book Award for her novel *Them* (1968).

In her fiction Oates delves into the varying states of the human mind. Her work often focuses on disturbed characters or characters who are anxiously searching for or struggling to come to terms with their identities. Oates has written, "We are stimulated to emotional response not by works that confirm our sense of the world, but by works that challenge it." "Journey" is the story of a symbolic quest for direction.

Journey

Point of View. Point of view refers to the vantage point from which a narrative is told. Most stories are told from either a first-person or a third-person point of view. In contemporary fiction, however, there are rare instances in which a writer uses a second-person point of view. In this type of narrative, the narrator does not participate in the story and refers to the story's protagonist, or main character, as *you*. Generally a second-person narrator is limited, focusing on the thoughts and feelings of only one character.

By using a second-person point of view, a writer can give his or her story a universal quality. Because the narrator refers to the main character as *you,* the reader actually assumes the role of the main character and is forced to view himself or herself performing the actions of the main character in the story. As a result, a second-person narrative may be viewed not as a story about a specific character, but about human behavior in general.

As you read "Journey," look for the effect of Oates's use of a second-person point of view. How does it contribute to the story's universal quality?

How might a person's life be described as a journey? Freewrite about the ways in which life can be viewed as a journey.

Knowing the following words will help you as you read "Journey."
monotony (mə nät′ 'n ē) *n.*: Lack of variation (p. 1080)
hypnotic (hip nät′ ik) *adj.*: Inducing a sleeplike condition (p. 1080)
convoluted (kän′ və l$\overline{oo}$t′ id) *adj.*: Intricate; complicated (p. 1080)

Journey

Joyce Carol Oates

You begin your journey on so high an elevation that your destination is already in sight—a city that you have visited many times and that, moreover, is indicated on a traveler's map you have carefully folded up to take along with you. You are a lover of maps, and you have already committed this map to memory, but you bring it with you just the same.

The highway down from the mountains is broad and handsome, constructed after many years of ingenious blasting and leveling and paving. Engineers from all over the country aided in the construction of this famous highway. Its cost is so excessive that many rumors have circulated about it—you take no interest in such things, sensing that you will never learn the true cost anyway, and that this will make no difference to your journey.

After several hours on this excellent highway, where the sun shines ceaselessly and where there is a moderate amount of traffic, cars like your own at a safe distance from you, as if to assure you that there are other people in the world, you become sleepy from the monotony and wonder if perhaps there is another, less perfect road parallel to this. You discover on the map a smaller road, not exactly parallel to the highway and not as direct, but one that leads to the same city.

You turn onto this road, which winds among foothills and forests and goes through several small villages. You sense by the attitude of the villagers that traffic on this road is infrequent but nothing to draw special attention. At some curves the road shrinks, but you are fortunate enough to meet no oncoming traffic.

The road leads deep into a forest, always descending in small cramped turns. Your turning from left to right and from right to left, in a slow hypnotic passage, makes it impossible for you to look out at the forest. You discover that for some time you have not been able to see the city you are headed for, though you know it is still somewhere ahead of you.

By mid-afternoon you are tired of this road, though it has served you well, and you come upon a smaller, unpaved road that evidently leads to your city, though in a convoluted way. After only a moment's pause you turn onto this road, and immediately your automobile registers the change—the chassis bounces, something begins to vibrate, something begins to rattle. This noise is disturbing, but after a while you forget about it in your interest in the beautiful countryside. Here the trees are enormous. There are no villages or houses. For a while the dirt road runs alongside a small river, dangerously close to the river's steep bank, and you begin to feel apprehension. It is necessary for you to drive very slowly. At times your speedometer registers less than five miles an hour. You will not get to the city before dark.

The road narrows until it is hardly more than a lane. Grass has begun to grow in its center. As the river twists and turns, so does the road twist and turn, curving around hills that consist of enormous boulders, bare of all trees and plants, covered only in patches

MARTHA'S VINEYARD, 1925
Thomas Hart Benton
Collection of Whitney Museum of American Art

by a dull, brown lichen that is unfamiliar to you. Along one stretch rocks of varying sizes have fallen down onto the road, so that you are forced to drive around them with great caution.

Navigating these blind turns, you tap your horn to give warning in case someone should be approaching. But it is all unnecessary, since you come upon no other travelers.

Late in the afternoon, your foot numb from its constant pressure on the accelerator, your body jolted by the constant bumps and vibrations of the car, you decide to make

the rest of your journey on foot, since you must be close to your destination by now.

A faint path leads through a tumble of rocks and bushes and trees, and you follow it enthusiastically. You descend a hill, slipping a little, so that a small rockslide is released; but you are able to keep your balance. At the back of your head is the precise location of your parked car, and behind that the curving dirt road, and behind that the other road, and then the magnificent highway itself: you understand that it would be no difficult feat to make your way back to any of these roads, should you decide that going by foot is unwise. But the path, though overgrown, is through a lovely forest, and then through a meadow in which yellow flowers are blooming, and you feel no inclination to turn back.

By evening you are still in the wilderness and you wonder if perhaps you have made a mistake. You are exhausted, your body aches, your eyes are seared by the need to stare so intently at everything around you. Now that the sun has nearly set, it is getting cold; evenings here in the mountains are always chilly.

You find yourself standing at the edge of a forest, staring ahead into the dark. Is that a field ahead, or a forest of small trees? Your path has long since given way to wild grass. Clouds obscure the moon, which should give you some light by which to make your way, and you wonder if you dare continue without this light.

Suddenly you remember the map you left back in the car, but you remember it as a blank sheet of paper.

You resist telling yourself you are lost. In fact, though you are exhausted and it is almost night, you are not lost. You have begun to shiver, but it is only with cold, not with fear. You are really satisfied with yourself. You are not lost. Though you can remember your map only as a blank sheet of paper, which can tell you nothing, you are not really lost.

If you had the day to begin again, on that highway which was so wide and clear, you would not have varied your journey in any way: in this is your triumph.

THINKING ABOUT THE SELECTION

Recalling

1. (a) Where does "your" journey begin? (b) What is "your" destination?
2. (a) Why do "you" turn off the highway? (b) Why do "you" turn onto an unpaved road? (c) Why do "you" decide "to make the rest of the journey on foot"?
3. (a) Where do "you" end up by evening? (b) What do "you" suddenly remember?
4. What conclusion do "you" make at the end of the story?

Interpreting

5. (a) Into what four stages can "your" journey be divided? (b) How does the appearance of the road or path that "you" follow change from stage to stage? (c) How does the appearance of the surrounding landscape change from stage to stage? (d) What other changes occur as "you" pass from stage to stage?
6. What is the significance of the fact that none of the places in the story are named?
7. In the beginning of the story, the narrator comments that "you are a lover of maps." (a) How does this attitude change during the course of the story? (b) What is the signifance of the fact that in the end "you" remember the map "as a blank sheet of paper"?
8. What is the triumph felt at the end of the story?

Applying

9. Explain how this story relates to the following lines from Robert Frost's poem "The Road Not Taken": "Two roads diverged in the wood, and I— / I took the one less traveled by, / and that has made all the difference."

ANALYZING LITERATURE
Understanding Point of View

Point of view refers to the vantage point from which a narrative is told. Unlike most other stories, "Journey" is told from a second-person point of view.

1. How does Oates's use of a second-person point of view help make it clear that the story is meant to be interpreted symbolically?
2. Why would the story be less effective if Oates had used a first-person or third-person point of view?

CRITICAL THINKING AND READING
Supporting an Interpretation

When a story is meant to be interpreted symbolically, you must examine all the details in the story and determine how they fit together and what they represent.

The following is one possible interpretation of the symbolic meaning of "Journey". Support or repute this interpretation using details from the story.

The journey symbolizes a person's life, during which he or she passes from conformity to individuality. At first this person has his or her life carefully mapped out to follow a path that many others have taken. As the person's life pro-gresses, however, he or she begins exploring new directions that fewer and fewer people have followed.

UNDERSTANDING LANGUAGE
Using Latin Roots

The Latin word *navis* means "ship." The root of this word, *nav*, has given us many English words. For example, Oates writes, "Navigating these blind turns, you tap your horn to give warning in case someone should be approaching." Originally the word *navigating* meant "directing a ship on its course on a body of water." Now the word also means "finding one's way."

Define each of the words below based on the root *nav*.

1. navy
2. navvy
3. navigator
4. navicular

THINKING AND WRITING
Writing About Symbolic Meaning

Develop your answer from the Critical Thinking and Writing activity into an essay. Review your answer and try to think of additional details that support the interpretation. Organize your essay according to the stages of the journey. When you revise, make sure you have included enough details to thoroughly support your interpretation. After revising, proofread your essay.

DONALD BARTHELME

1931–

Donald Barthelme is one of the most innovative fiction writers of our time. Experimenting with a variety of radically different approaches to writing fiction, he has frequently abandoned not only traditional forms but also the forms that characterize Modernist fiction.

Barthelme was born in Philadelphia and raised in Houston, Texas. In 1964 he published his first book, *Dr. Caligari,* a collection of satirical and surrealistic stories. Three years later, he produced his first novel, *Snow White,* an elaborately structured work that explores the underlying emptiness of many contemporary ideologies and fads. Since then, he has published several novels and numerous collections of short stories and has won a number of awards. He also produced a children's book, *The Slightly Irregular Fire Engine or the Hithering Thithering Djinn* (1971), which earned him the National Book Award for children's literature.

As is the case in most Barthelme stories, both the form and content of "Engineer-Private Paul Klee Misplaces an Aircraft Between Milbertshofen and Cambrai, March 1916" are unconventional. Barthelme uses a historical figure, Swiss abstract painter Paul Klee (1879–1940), as the story's main character. Loosely based on an incident that occurred during Klee's period of service with the German air corps during World War I, the story humorously examines the impersonal nature of military life.

GUIDE FOR READING

Engineer-Private Paul Klee Misplaces an Aircraft Between Milbertshofen and Cambrai, March 1916

Literary Movements

Experimental Fiction. During the 1960's a number of writers began searching for ways to set their work apart from the literature of the past. This quest led to the development of new and radically different types of fiction in which conventional forms and structures were often completely abandoned. Some writers discarded the use of a narrator in their stories and began composing stories from dialogue alone. Others began experimenting with the physical appearance of their work, at times even using blank pages as a part of a literary work. While basically adhering to conventional structures, other writers began exploring new and unconventional subjects in their works. A number of writers turned their focus inward, writing stories about the process of writing and the forms and techniques of the story itself. Donald Barthelme's story "Sentence," for example, is, as the title suggests, one extremely long sentence about the peculiarities of sentences. Finally, some experimental writers turned to parodying ancient literary works, while others explored the use of historical figures as characters in their works.

Look For

As you read Barthelme's story, look for its unconventional structure. How does the structure reflect the meaning of the story?

Writing

Barthelme's story focuses on the experiences of Swiss abstract painter Paul Klee during his period of service with the German air corps during World War I. List the reasons why you think it might be difficult for an artist to adjust to life in the military.

Vocabulary

Knowing the following words will help you as you read Barthelme's story.

interminable (in tʉr′ mi nə b′l) *adj.*: Without, or apparently without, end (p. 1086)
omnipresence (äm′ ni prez′ 'ns) *n.*: Presence in all places at the same time (p. 1086)

attest (ə test′) *v.*: To bear witness (p. 1087)
simulacrum (sim′ yoo lā′ krəm) *n.*: A vague representation (p. 1088)

Engineer-Private Paul Klee Misplaces an Aircraft Between Milbertshofen and Cambrai[1], March 1916

Donald Barthelme

Paul Klee said:

"Now I have been transferred to the Air Corps. A kindly sergeant effected the transfer. He thought I would have a better future here, more chances for promotion. First I was assigned to aircraft repair, together with several other workers. We presented ourselves as not just painters but artist-painters. This caused some shaking of heads. We varnished wooden fuselages, correcting old numbers and adding new ones with the help of templates. Then I was pulled off the painting detail and assigned to transport. I escort aircraft that are being sent to various bases in Germany and also (I understand) in occupied territory. It is not a bad life. I spend my nights racketing across Bavaria[2] (or some such) and my days in switching yards. There is always bread and wurst and beer in the station restaurants. When I reach a notable town I try to see the notable paintings there, if time allows. There are always unexpected delays, reroutings, backtrackings. Then the return to the base. I see Lily fairly often. We

meet in hotel rooms and that is exciting. I have never yet lost an aircraft or failed to deliver one to its proper destination. The war seems interminable. Walden has sold six of my drawings."

The Secret Police said:

"We have secrets. We have many secrets. We desire all secrets. We do not have your secrets and that is what we are after, your secrets. Our first secret is where we are. No one knows. Our second secret is how many of us there are. No one knows. Omnipresence is our goal. We do not even need real omnipresence. The theory of omnipresence is enough. With omnipresence, hand-in-hand as it were, goes omniscience. And with omniscience and omnipresence, hand-in-hand-in-hand as it were, goes omnipotence. We are a three-sided waltz. However our mood is melancholy. There is a secret sigh that we sigh, secretly. We yearn to be known, acknowledged, admired even. What is the good of omnipotence if nobody knows? However that is a secret, that sorrow. Now we are everywhere. One place we are is here watching Engineer-Private Klee, who is escorting three valuable aircraft, B.F.W. 3054/16–17–18, with spare parts, by rail from Milbertshofen to Cambrai. Do you wish to know what Engi-

---

1. Milbertshofen (mil′ berts hof′ ən) **and Cambrai** (käm brä′): Milbertshofen is a town in Bavaria. Cambrai is a town in northern France.
2. Bavaria (bə ver′ ē ə): A state in southwest Germany.

neer-Private Klee is doing at this very moment, in the baggage car? He is reading a book of Chinese short stories. He has removed his boots. His feet rest twenty-six centimeters from the baggage-car stove."

Paul Klee said:

"These Chinese short stories are slight and lovely. I have no way of knowing if the translation is adequate or otherwise. Lily will meet me in our rented room on Sunday, if I return in time. Our destination is Fighter Squadron Five. I have not had anything to eat since morning. The fine chunk of bacon given me along with my expense money when we left the base has been eaten. This morning a Red Cross lady with a squint gave me some very good coffee, however. Now we are entering Hohenbudberg."[3]

The Secret Police said:

"Engineer-Private Klee has taken himself into the station restaurant. He is enjoying a hearty lunch. We shall join him there."

Paul Klee said:

"Now I emerge from the station restaurant and walk along the line of cars to the flatcar on which my aircraft (I think of them as *my* aircraft) are carried. To my surprise and dismay, I notice that one of them is missing. There had been three, tied down on the flatcar and covered with canvas. Now I see with my trained painter's eye that instead of three canvas-covered shapes on the flatcar there are only two. Where the third aircraft had been there is only a puddle of canvas and loose rope. I look around quickly to see if anyone else has marked the disappearance of the third aircraft."

The Secret Police said:

"We had marked it. Our trained policemen's eyes had marked the fact that where three aircraft had been before, tied down on the flatcar and covered with canvas, now there were only two. Unfortunately we had been in the station restaurant, lunching, at the moment of removal, therefore we could not attest as to where it had gone or who

had removed it. There is something we do not know. This is irritating in the extreme. We closely observe Engineer-Private Klee to determine what action he will take in the emergency. We observe that he is withdrawing from his tunic a notebook and pencil. We observe that he begins, very properly in our opinion, to note down in his notebook all the particulars of the affair."

Paul Klee said:

"The shape of the collapsed canvas, under which the aircraft had rested, together with the loose ropes—the canvas forming hills and valleys, seductive folds, the ropes the very essence of looseness, lapsing—it is irresistible. I sketch for ten or fifteen minutes, wondering the while if I might not be in trouble, because of the missing aircraft. When I arrive at Fighter Squadron Five with less than the number of aircraft listed on the manifest,[4] might not some officious person become angry? Shout at me? I have finished sketching. Now I will ask various trainmen and station personnel if they have seen anyone carrying away the aircraft. If they answer in the negative, I will become extremely frustrated. I will begin to kick the flatcar."

The Secret Police said:

"Frustrated, he begins to kick the flatcar."

Paul Klee said:

"I am looking up in the sky, to see if my aircraft is there. There are in the sky aircraft of several types, but none of the type I am searching for."

The Secret Police said:

"Engineer-Private Klee is searching the sky—an eminently sound procedure, in our opinion. We, the Secret Police, also sweep the Hohenbudberg sky, with our eyes. But find nothing. We are debating with ourselves as to whether we ought to enter the station restaurant and begin drafting our preliminary report for forwarding to higher headquarters. The knotty point, in terms of the preliminary report, is that we do not have

---

3. Hohenbudberg (hō ən bud' berg): A village in northwestern Germany.

4. manifest (man' ə fest') *n*.: A cargo list.

the answer to the question 'Where is the aircraft?' The damage potential to the theory of omniscience as well as potential to our careers, dictates that this point be omitted from the preliminary report. But if this point is omitted, might not some officious person at the Central Bureau for Secrecy note the omission? Become angry? Shout at us? Omissiveness is not rewarded at the Central Bureau. We decide to observe further the actions of Engineer-Private Klee, for the time being."

Paul Klee said:

"I who have never lost an aircraft have lost an aircraft. The aircraft is signed out to me. The cost of the aircraft, if it is not found, will be deducted from my pay, meager enough already. Even if Walden sells a hundred, a thousand drawings, I will not have enough money to pay for this cursed aircraft. Can I, in the time the train remains in the Hohenbudberg yards, construct a new aircraft or even the simulacrum of an aircraft, with no materials to work with or indeed any special knowledge of aircraft construction? The situation is ludicrous. I will therefore apply Reason. Reason dictates the solution. I will diddle the manifest. With my painter's skill which is after all not so different from a forger's, I will change the manifest to reflect conveyance of *two* aircraft, B.F.W. 3054/16 and 17, to Fighter Squadron Five. The extra canvas and ropes I will conceal in an empty boxcar—this one, which according to its stickers is headed for Essigny-le-Petit.[5] Now I will walk around

<hr />

5. Essigny-le-Petit (es sē nyē′ lə pə tē′): A street or district of St. Quentin in northern France.

town and see if I can find a chocolate shop. I crave chocolate."

The Secret Police said:

"Now we observe Engineer-Private Klee concealing the canvas and ropes which covered the former aircraft into an empty boxcar bound for Essigny-le-Petit. We have previously observed him diddling the manifest with his painter's skill which resembles not a little that of the forger. We applaud these actions of Engineer-Private Klee. The contradiction confronting us in the matter of the preliminary report is thus resolved in highly satisfactory fashion. We are proud of Engineer-Private Klee and of the resolute and manly fashion in which he has dealt with the crisis. We predict he will go far. We would like to embrace him as a comrade and brother but unfortunately we are not embraceable. We are secret, we exist in the shadows, the pleasure of the comradely/brotherly embrace is one of the pleasures we are denied, in our dismal service."

Paul Klee said:

"We arrive at Cambrai. The planes are unloaded, six men for each plane. The work goes quickly. No one questions my altered manifest. The weather is clearing. After lunch I will leave to begin the return journey. My release slip and travel orders are ready, but the lieutenant must come and sign them. I wait contentedly in the warm orderly room. The drawing I did of the collapsed canvas and ropes is really very good. I eat a piece of chocolate. I am sorry about the lost aircraft but not overmuch. The war is temporary. But drawings and chocolate go on forever."

THINKING ABOUT THE SELECTION

Recalling

1. What is Klee's primary duty as a member of the air corps?
2. (a) What is the Secret Police's "first secret"? (b) What is their "second secret"? (c) What is their goal?
3. What does Klee notice when he returns to the flatcar on which his aircraft are carried?
4. (a) How does Klee solve his problem? (b) How do the Secret Police react to Klee's solution?

Interpreting

5. (a) How do the duties of the Secret Police contrast with their desires? (b) What is their attitude toward their service? (c) How is this attitude revealed?
6. (a) What concern do Klee and the Secret Police share? (b) What is the significance of the fact that they share this concern?
7. What is the significance of the mechanical fashion in which both Klee and the Secret Police speak in this story?
8. What is the meaning of Klee's comments about war, drawings, and chocolate?
9. (a) Who, or what, is Barthelme satirizing, or poking fun at, in this story? (b) What is the story's theme, or main point?

Applying

10. Explain why you do or do not think satire is an effective means of protesting war.

ANALYZING LITERATURE

Understanding Experimental Fiction

Barthelme's story is an excellent example of experimental fiction—a radically different type of fiction that developed during the 1960's, as a result of the desire of writers to create work that stood apart from the literature of the past.
1. What is unconventional about the structure of Barthelme's story?
2. How does the structure reflect its meaning?

CRITICAL THINKING AND READING

Appreciating Shades of Meaning

Frequently, words that appear to be identical in meaning actually have slightly different meanings. For example, though the words *monitor* and *observe* are quite similar, they have slightly different meanings. The word *monitor* means "to watch or check on," while *observe* means "to pay special attention to." Use your dictionary to find the slight difference in meaning between the words in each of the following pairs.
1. escort : conduct   3. opinion : belief
2. melancholy : sullen 4. ludicrous : foolish

UNDERSTANDING LANGUAGE

Using Words from Latin

The Latin word *omnis* means "all." It has given us the combining form *omni,* which we use to build new words. For example, in this story the secret police claim to be omnipresent, omnipotent, and omniscient.
1. Define the words *omnipresent, omnipotent,* and *omniscient.*
2. How are these qualities similar to the qualities usually attributed to God?
3. How does this similarity affect the meaning of the story?

THINKING AND WRITING

Responding to Criticism

A critic has commented that despair is one of Barthelme's "favorite subjects for jest." Write an essay in which you discuss this comment in relation to the story you have just read. Reread the story, noting Barthelme's use of satire. Write your essay, using passages from the story to support your argument. When you revise, make sure your essay is logically organized and that you have not included unnecessary information.

ANN BEATTIE

1947–

Generally considered to be one of today's most accomplished young fiction writers, Ann Beattie has restlessly pursued innovations in narrative structure. Like many other contemporary writers, Beattie often composes works in the form of a broken, fragmented sequence of events, thoughts, emotions, and memories. This approach reflects Beattie's perceptions of the sense of aimlessness and disorder associated with contemporary life.

Born in Washington, D.C., Beattie achieved success as a writer at an early age. She has had numerous short stories published in *The New Yorker* and has produced several collections of stories. Her collections include *Distortions* (1976), *Secrets and Surprises* (1978), *The Burning House* (1982), and *Where You'll Find Me* (1986). Although she is known more for her short stories, she has also written a number of novels, including *Chilly Scenes of Winter* (1976), *Falling into Place* (1980), and *Love Always* (1985).

A typical Beattie story, "Imagined Scenes" captures a young woman's overwhelming sense of purposelessness. Using a detached narrator to present a series of seemingly distorted scenes, Beattie makes it seem as if we are actually witnessing events from the young woman's life, rather than being told a story.

Imagined Scenes

Literary Movements

Postmodernism. Postmodernism refers to the collection of literary movements that have developed in the decades following World War II. Like their predecessors, many of the Postmodernists have attempted to capture the essence of contemporary life in the form and content of their work. Others, however, have focused on creating works that stand apart from the literature of the past. To accomplish these purposes, writers have experimented with a variety of different approaches and used a wide range of literary forms and techniques. Many writers have continued to develop the fragmentary approach of the Modernists, omitting expositions, resolutions, and transitions, and composing stories in the form of broken or distorted sequence of scenes, rather than in the form of a continuous narrative. Possessing the belief that reality is to some extent shaped by our imaginations, some writers have turned away from writing realistic fiction and begun writing fantasy or "magical realism"—fiction that blends realism and fantasy. Other writers have radically departed from traditional fictional forms and techniques, composing works from dialogue alone, creating works that blend fiction and nonfiction, and experimenting with the physical appearance of a work. Finally, a number of Postmodernist writers have confronted the problems they perceive in contemporary society through the use of satire and black humor.

Look For

As you read "Imagined Scenes," look for the form and approach Beattie uses. Also look for the story's theme. How does the theme relate to contemporary life?

Writing

"Imagined Scenes" focuses on the life of a young woman who has been forced to pattern her life to accommodate her husband's career aspirations. Freewrite about the types of problems that you think might arise from this type of situation.

Vocabulary

Knowing the following words will help you as you read "Imagined Scenes."

engrossed (in grōs′t′) v.: Absorbed (p. 1093)

impetuous (im pech′ oo wəs) adj.: Acting or done suddenly

with little thought; rash; impulsive (p. 1093)

adhere (əd hir′) v.: To stick fast; stay attached (p. 1094)

Imagined Scenes

Ann Beattie

"I've unlaced my boots and I'm standing barefoot on a beach with very brown sand, ocean in front of me and mountains in the distance, and trees making a pretty green haze around them."

"Pretty," David says.

"Where would that be?"

"Greece?"

When she wakes from a dream, David is already awake. Or perhaps he only wakes when she stirs, whispers to him. He doesn't sound sleepy; he's alert, serious, as though he'd been waiting for a question. She remembers last year, the week before Christmas, when she and David had gone out separately to shop. She got back to the house first, her keys lost—or locked in the car. Before she could look for them, headlights lit up the snowy path. David jumped out of his car, excited about his purchases, reaching around her to put the key in the door. Now she expects him to wake up when she does, that they will arrive home simultaneously. But David still surprises her—at the end of summer he told her he wouldn't be working in the fall. He was going back to college to finish the work for his Ph.D.

He sits in a gray chair by the fireplace and reads; she brings coffee to the table by his chair, and he turns off the light and goes up-

PLEASURES OF WINTER IN NEW YORK
Francis Peterson
Three Lions

stairs to bed when she is tired. By unspoken agreement, he has learned to like Roquefort dressing. He pokes the logs in the fireplace because the hot red coals frighten her.

"After I take orals in the spring we'll go to Greece to celebrate."

She wants to go to Spain. Couldn't the beach have been in Spain? No more questions—she should let him sleep. She shakes the thought out of her head.

"No?" he says. "We will. We'll go to Greece when I finish the orals."

The leaves of the plant look like worn velvet. The tops are purple, a shiny, fuzzy purple, and the underside is dark green. Suddenly the plant has begun to grow, sending up a narrow shoot not strong enough to support itself, so that it falls forward precariously, has to be staked. They agree it's strange that a plant should have such a spurt of growth in midwinter. David admires the plant, puts it in a window that gets the morning light and moves it into a side room late in the afternoon. Now when he waters the plant a little plant food is mixed in with the water. David is enthusiastic; he's started to feed the others to see if they'll grow. She comes home and finds him stretched by the fireplace, looking through a book about plants. Their plant isn't pictured, he tells her, but it may be mentioned in the text. She goes into the other room to look at the plant. The shoot appears to be taller. They bought the plant in a food store last winter— not very pretty then. It was in a small cracked pot, wrapped in plastic. They replanted it. In fact, David must have replanted it again.

She puts away the groceries and goes back to the living room. David is still on the rug reading the book. He's engrossed. The coffee would probably get cold if she brought it. She has to work that night. She goes upstairs to take a nap and sets the alarm. She rests, but can't fall asleep, listening to the quiet music downstairs. She pushes in the alarm button and goes back to the living

room. David is in his chair, reading the book, drinking coffee.

"I spent the most terrible winter in my life in Berlin. I don't know why, but birds don't leave Berlin in the winter. They're big, strong birds. They nest in the public buildings. I think the winter just comes too suddenly in Berlin, no plans can be made. The birds turn gray, like snowbirds. I think snowbirds are gray."

The old man is looking out the window. He is her patient. His daughter and son-in-law are away for a week, and his sister stays with him in the day. She has been hired to stay with him at night. He is not very ill, but old and unsteady.

She drinks tea with him, tired because she didn't nap.

"I don't sleep well," he tells her. "I want to talk all the time. My daughter doesn't sleep either. In the day we fight, or I worry her, but at night I think she's glad to have someone to talk to."

The snowplow is passing the house, slowly, the lights blinking against the newly plowed snowpiles. The lights illuminate a snowman on the next lawn—crudely made, or perhaps it's just not lit up from the right angle. She remembers her first snowman; her mother broke off the broom handle to give her and helped push the handle through the snowman. Her mother was impetuous, always letting her stay home from school to enjoy the snow, and her father had been surprised when he returned from work to see the broom head on the kitchen table. "Well, we couldn't get out. How could we go out in the snow to get anything?" her mother had asked her father. The snowplow has passed. Except for the wind, it is very quiet outside. In the room, the man is talking to her. He wants to show her his postcards. She's surprised; she hadn't realized she was being spoken to.

"Oh, not that kind of postcard. I'm an old man. Just pretty postcards."

He has opened a night-table drawer. Inside there is a box of tissues, a comb and brush, an alarm clock. He sits on the side of the bed, his feet not quite touching the floor, reaching into the drawer without looking. He finds what he wants: an envelope. He removes it and carefully pulls out the flap. He lets her look through the postcards. There is a bird's nest full of cherubs,[1] a picture of a lady elegantly dressed in a high, ruffled collar, curtseying beneath a flowering tree, and one that she looks at longer than the rest: a man in boots and a green jacket, carrying a rifle, is pictured walking down a path through the woods in the moonlight. Stars shine in the sky and illuminate a path in front of him. Tiny silver sparkles still adhere to the postcard. She holds it under the lamp on the night table: the lining of his jacket is silver, the edges of the rocks, a small area of the path. There is a caption: "Joseph Jefferson as Rip Van Winkle."[2] Beneath the caption is a message, ornately written: "Not yet but soon, Pa."

"Did your father write the postcard?"

"That's just one I found in a store long ago. I could make up a romantic story to tell you. I love to talk."

She waits, expecting the man's story. He leans back in bed, putting the envelope back in the drawer. His bedroom slippers fall to the floor, and he puts his legs under the covers.

"People get old and they can't improve things," he says, "so they lie all the time."

He waves his hand, dismissing something.

"I trust young people," he says. "I'd even tell you where my money is: in the dresser drawer, in the back of a poetry book."

The snowplow has returned, driving up the other side of the street. The lights cast patterns on the wall. He watches the shadows darken the wallpaper.

---

1. cherubs (cher' əbz) *n.*: Representations of heavenly beings as winged children with chubby, rosy faces.
2. Rip Van Winkle: A character who sleeps for twenty years without awakening in a story by Washington Irving.

"I have real stories," he says, pointing to a photograph album on a table by the chair. "Look through and I can tell you some real stories if you want to know."

He is ready to sleep. She arranges the quilt at the bottom of the bed and starts to leave.

"The light doesn't bother me," he says, waving her toward the chair. "Look through my album. I'm old and cranky. I'm afraid for my pictures to leave the room."

It's early afternoon and no one is in the house. There are dishes on the dining-room table, records and record-album covers. There's a plate, a spoon, two bowls, three coffee cups. How many people have been here? There's no one to ask. There's some food on the counter top—things she doesn't remember buying. An apple pie. She goes into the living room and sits in a chair, looking out the window. More snow is predicted, but now the day is clear and bright, the fields shining in the sun. She goes into the kitchen again to look for the note he hasn't left. On her way to the bedroom to sleep, she looks out the window and sees David coming up the road, only a sweater and scarf on, holding a stick at his side that the dog is jumping for. On the floor by the chair the plant book is open, and several others, books he's studying for his exams. The front door is open. The dog runs into the living room, jumps on her.

"You should be asleep. You can't work at night if you're not going to sleep in the day."

"I thought I'd wait for you to come back."

"You shouldn't have waited. I could have been anywhere."

"Where would you go?"

He's chilled. His knuckles are bright pink, untying the scarf at his throat. He's putting another log on the fire, pushing the screen back into place.

"How's the old man?"

"He's no trouble. Last night I fixed his photograph album for him. Some of the pictures had come loose and I glued them in."

"You look like you need sleep."

"Looks like you've been working," she says, pointing to the books by the chair.

"I've had trouble concentrating. The snow was so beautiful last night. I took the dog out for long walks in the woods."

David is stroking the dog, who lies curled by the fire, panting in his sleep.

"Get some rest," he says, looking at his watch. "I met the people who moved in down the hill and told them I'd help put a sink in. He's very nice. Katherine and Larry Duane."

David kisses her on his way out. The dog wakes and wants to go with him, but at the front door he's told to stay. The dog whines when the door closes, then waits a minute longer before going back to the living room to sleep by the fireplace.

"It's awful. When you get old you expect things to be the same. Sometimes I think the cold air could clear my head. My neighbor is ten years younger than me and he jogs every day, even through snow."

"I'm leaving now," his sister says. She puts on a blue coat and a blue velvet cap that ties under the chin. Her hair is white and copper. She has small, dainty hands. She repeats that she's leaving and pats him on the shoulder, more to make sure he's listening than out of affection. "There are oranges in the bag on your bureau. Linus Pauling says that a sufficient intake of vitamin C will prevent colds."

"How would I get a cold? Every day is the same. I don't go out."

Her coat is buttoned, her hat tied securely. "That's like asking where dust comes from," she says, and disappears down the stairs.

"She's very good to come every day. I forget to thank her. I take it for granted. Fifteen years makes so much difference. She's able to do so much more, but her hands hurt her. She does embroidery so they don't go stiff."

He is looking through a book of Currier and Ives prints.[3] "I suppose I'll have to eat her oranges. There'll be more from Florida when they get back."

She looks at a picture he holds up for her to see, offers to read him science-fiction stories.

"I don't think so. My sister read them this morning. I've had enough make-believe. No spaceships are coming to Earth today, only snow."

She looks at her watch to see if it's time for his medicine. Her watch isn't there. Did she forget to wear it? He asks for tea, and while the water is boiling in the kitchen she dials David, to see if the watch is on the night table. She hangs up and dials again, but there's still no answer. She looks out the window and sees that it has already begun to snow. Perhaps she lost the watch on the way in. The clasp was loose—she should have asked David to fix it. She turns off the burner and goes outside, looking quickly up and down the front walk before the snow begins to accumulate. She doesn't see it. The car? She looks, but it isn't there. She looks on the front steps and in the entranceway. No. It must be at home. She reheats the water, making tea, and carries the cup and saucer upstairs.

She puts it down quietly on the bureau. He's fallen asleep. She sits in a chair and watches the snow fall, and in a while she closes her eyes and begins imagining things: mountains, and blue, blue water, all the snow melted into water. This time the name of the country comes to her: Greece. She's been sent to Greece to find something on the beach, but she just stands there staring at the mountains in the distance, the water washing over her feet. Her feet are cold; she takes them out of the water, backing up onto the sandy beach. She's lifted her feet from the floor, waking up. She goes to the bureau and gets the tea, even though it's cold. The snow is falling heavily now. Everything is blanketed in whiteness; it clings to the trees, her car is covered with snow. She must have slept through the night. She hears his sister downstairs, closing the door behind her.

"I take her for granted," the old man

---

3. Currier and Ives prints: Nineteenth-century lithographs depicting the manners, people, and events of the times.

says. "Like snow. Every day I expect more snow."

The plant is gone. She looks in all the rooms and can't find it. Her watch is on the bathroom sink, where she put it when she showered. She showers again and washes her hair, blows it dry. The bathroom is steamy; she can't see her face in the glass.

"David?"

She thought she heard something, but it was only a branch brushing against the bathroom window. She walks naked up to the bedroom and puts on jeans and one of David's sweaters. She notices that some of the books he's been studying have been replaced in the bookcase. Now she's sure she hears him. The dog runs into the house. The front door bangs shut.

"Hi," she calls.

"Hi." David is climbing the steps. "I'm not used to you working for a whole week. I never see you." His cheeks are so cold they sting when he kisses her. "I was down at the Duanes'. They had puppies born this morning."

"What kind?"

"Collies."

"Take me to see them," she says.

"They were going out when I left."

"We could go later in the afternoon."

"They'll think I live there," he laughs.

"It's good for you to be out. You've been working so hard."

"I haven't done any work for a couple of days."

"Yes you have. I saw pages of notes on the dining-room table."

"Larry left his notes behind. He brought them down to read me an article he's working on. He teaches at the university, Botany."

"Botany?" she says. "Is that what happened to the plant?"

"They liked it so much I gave it to them. It was such a freak thing, to grow that way in the winter."

She calls early in the morning: 4 A.M.

The telephone rings, and there is no answer. The old man can tell that she's worried when he awakens.

"I tried to get my husband last night but there was no answer."

"Men are heavy sleepers."

"No," she says. "He'd wake up."

"All men are heavy sleepers. I can sleep when people are talking—I don't even hear the children talking on their way to school any more. I can sleep with the light on."

"I think school was canceled," she says, looking out the window.

It has snowed all night. It's still snowing.

"Call my sister and tell her not to come," he says. "If anything happens I can call."

She picks up the phone in the upstairs hallway and gives his sister the message, but the old lady is coming anyway. She has boots and an umbrella, and she's coming. He shakes his head.

"It's terrible to be old. You have no power."

He gets out of bed and opens a bureau drawer.

"Can I help you?"

"I'm putting on my things to go for a walk in the snow."

"You should stay inside. It's too cold today."

"I don't feel the cold any more. I can go out."

"Have breakfast first," she says.

"No. I want to go out before she comes."

She leaves the room while he dresses. He takes a long time. Maybe his sister will come early, before they go out. No. He opens the door and walks out without his cane, wearing a sweater and a silk scarf tucked into the neck.

"My jacket is in the hall closet," he says. "I need the air."

She helps him down the stairs. He doesn't weigh much. She asks if he'll take his cane, but he wants her arm instead. She gets his jacket and holds it for him to put on. She takes her own jacket out of the closet and zips it.

It's bright outside. They both stop, momentarily blinded by the glare. The snow is wet and deep.

"Just down the walk," she says.

"Yes. All right."

Children, off from school, are playing in the yards. Someone has already built a snowman. He likes it, wants a closer look. They go down the walk to the sidewalk. The children next door call hello. A little boy comes over to tell the old man about the snowman he's built. On another lawn some children are building a fort. Two little girls in snowsuits are carrying snow to the fort in buckets. She sees a big boy push a small boy into a snowbank. It's just fun. It's not just fun—he's kicking snow on him, kicking the little boy.

"Wait!" she says.

The big boy kicks snow in her face and runs. She pulls the younger boy out of the snow, brushing it out of his hair.

"What happened?" she asks him. He's crying, brushing himself and pointing to the boy who ran away at the same time. Now another boy is screaming. She turns and sees that the old man has slipped in the snow. She runs back. He's red in the face, but he's all right. He bent over to make a snowball and one of the children accidentally ran into him. She reaches down to help him up. He's light, but it's hard to get a good grip. The pavement is slippery, she's afraid she might slip. She sends one of the children home to get his mother. But a man walking down the sidewalk has already bent to help the old man up.

"What are you doing here?"

"I came to pick you up," David says. "Your car never would have made it up the hill. I had chains put on."

They help the old man into the house. In the hallway he brushes snow off his shoulders, embarrassed and angry. He thinks the child knocked him over on purpose. She hangs up his coat and David helps him upstairs. He goes up the stairs more quickly than he came down, talking about the boy who knocked into him. But he's forgotten about it by the time his sister arrives. He's

telling David about Berlin in the winter, about the birds. He complains about his memory—Berlin must have been beautiful in the spring. When his sister arrives she's brought fruit for her, too, saying that she's a nurse, she must know about Dr. Pauling. It's her last day. The daughter and the husband will be coming home from Florida. But the sister comes every day, even when they're home—she has an umbrella and high boots. Wait. The old man has something for her: a postcard. He's giving her the postcard. The stars twinkle brightly in her hand.

The children are still playing when she goes outside with David. The big boy she spoke to earlier hides behind a car and tries to hit them with a snowball, but he misses. David's mad at her, mad that she took the old man out. He won't speak.

"We'll have to go back for my car," she says.

No answer.

"I called you last night and there was no answer."

He looks up. "You called?"

"Yes. You weren't there."

"I didn't know it was you. I was asleep. Why were you calling?"

The snow is very deep. He's driving slowly, concentrating so the car doesn't skid. On the radio, the weather forecast calls for more snow.

"I guess you were walking the dog in the woods," she says.

"I just told you," he says. "I was asleep."

She closes her eyes, imagines him sleeping, then imagines him with the dog, pulling a broken branch out of the snow, holding it high for the dog to jump up. The dog yelps, runs in circles, but the snow is too deep to jump out of. David is asleep, under the covers. He's walking up the hill, the dog barking, jumping for the stick. She tries to imagine more, but she's afraid that if she doesn't open her eyes she'll fall asleep in the car.

Back in the house, she closes her eyes again. He's drawn the curtains, and the room is a little less bright. She's very tired. The dog whines outside the door, wanting

David. David takes his trumpet off the night table and puts it in the case. He must be practicing again.

David leaves, saying that he's going downstairs to clean up. She hears some noise: cups and saucers? and much later, ringing. She's calling David, but there's no answer. David is calling her at the foot of the stairs.

"What?"

"Someone on the phone for you."

She goes downstairs to answer the phone. She sits at a chair by the table. The table is clear. Everything has been cleared away.

"Hello?"

The voice is soft. She can hardly hear. It's the old man's sister. She's tired of the old man and his sister, tired of work. She had already dismissed the old man from her mind, like last week's dreams, but now the old man's sister has called. His sister is upset. She's talking about the snow. Apparently she's snowed in, the snow is deeper than her boots, she's been trying to reach her husband to tell him. The planes from Florida won't land. No planes are landing. The old lady is thanking her for taking care of her brother. Why is she whispering?

"I come every day. I have my umbrella and my high boots so I can do my duty. I always try to bring him things that will please him so he won't think I only do it because I have to. My niece has to get away. He's so demanding. He wants her attention all day and night."

She's still half asleep, squinting against the glare, straining to hear. His sister is at the phone outside his bedroom in the hallway. The plane is still in Florida; it hasn't left because it can't land. His sister is asking if there's any way she can come back.

As she talks, the runway is buried deeper in snow. They're trying to clear it, but the snow is heavy, the planes can't land. The planes from Greece won't land. Now no one is on the beach in Greece, or at home in the United States; they're up in the air, up above the snow. She's sitting in a chair by the table. The table is clear. What was on the table when she came in? David has cleaned the room.

"You're so lucky," the woman whispers. "You can come and go. You don't know what it's like to be caught."

THINKING ABOUT THE SELECTION

Recalling

1. (a) What is the young woman's occupation? (b) What is David's occupation? (c) How do their occupations prevent them from spending a great deal of time together?

2. Why does the old man think that "every day is the same"?

3. (a) What causes the old man to fall down while he is outside? (b) What is his reaction to the incident?

4. Why does the old man's sister call the young woman at the end of the story?

Interpreting

5. How would you describe the story's mood?

6. (a) What hints does Beattie provide that the relationship between the young woman and David is somewhat strained? (b) What might be the main cause of this tension?

7. (a) How is the old man's attitude toward his sister similar to David's attitude toward the young woman? (b) In what sense is the young woman's situation similar to the sister's situation? (c) What is ironic, or surprising, about the sister's final comment?

8. What do you think the snow symbolizes, or represents, in the story?

Applying

9. Do you think it would be possible for the young woman to change her situation? Why or why not?

ANALYZING LITERATURE
Understanding Postmodernism

"Imagined Scenes" is an excellent example of a common type of Postmodernist fiction. Written in the form of a broken sequence of scenes, the story's structure reflects the disjointed, fragmentary quality of contemporary life. Using a detached narrator, Beattie pieces together a series of events without transitions or explanations, making the reader feel as if he or she is actually witnessing the events, rather than having them described.

1. How are the beginning and ending of the story unlike those used in traditional short stories?
2. Why is the overall structure of the story appropriate for its subject?
3. What does this story suggest about the ability of people in contemporary society to communicate with one another?

CRITICAL THINKING AND READING
Thinking Metaphorically

In her story Beattie captures the human tendency to think metaphorically, or to seek to understand and explain the world through the use of implicit comparisons. For example, the old man associates the onset of winter with the birds he remembers seeing during his winter in Berlin.

1. What do the postcards represent to the old man?
2. What do the scenes the young woman imagines represent to her?

UNDERSTANDING LANGUAGE
Completing Word Analogies

One of the characteristics of Beattie's style is her use of specific words. Rarely does she simply say, "There are dishes on the dining-room table." Instead, she follows up this statement by telling you exactly what kind of dishes: "There's a plate, a spoon, two bowls, three coffee cups. . ."

Complete each word analogy below with a specific word that fits in the category.

1. TRANSPORTATION : CAR : : GROOMING AIDS:
   a. clothing   c. medicine
   b. hairbrush   d. watch
2. RAIN GEAR: UMBRELLA : : FAMILY MEMBERS:
   a. nurse   c. friend
   b. housekeeper   d. sister
3. GROCERIES: CEREAL : : BIRDS:
   a. sparrow   c. snow
   b. cats   d. Berlin
4. PUBLIC BUILDING: COURT HOUSE : : INSTRUMENTS
   a. appliances   c. musician
   b. trumpet   d. music

THINKING AND WRITING
Writing About Structure

Write an essay in which you analyze the structure of "Imagined Scenes" and discuss its relationship to the subject of the story and its theme. Reread the story, focusing on its structure. Prepare a thesis statement. Then write your essay, using evidence from the story to support your thesis. When you finish writing, revise your essay, making sure you have supported your analysis with details from the story. Proofread your essay and share it with your classmates.

GRACE PALEY

1922–

Written in a powerful, energetic style, Grace Paley's short stories capture many of the tragedies and ironies that arise in everyday life. Though few in number, Paley's stories have been praised by critics and have earned her a loyal following.

Paley was born and raised in New York City. While attending Hunter College, she developed a serious interest in writing. After her short stories had appeared in a number of major magazines, she published her first collection, *The Little Disturbances of Man: Stories of Women and Men at Love* (1959). Because she has devoted much of her time to supporting her personal beliefs, Paley has gone on to produce only two additional collections, *Enormous Changes at the Last Minute* (1974) and *Later the Same Day* (1985).

Paley has been quoted as saying about literature, "There isn't a story written that isn't about blood and money. People and their relationships to each other is the blood, the family. And how they live, the money of it."

Like many of Paley's other stories, "Anxiety" is a lively, energetic story that contains little action. Composed mainly from dialogue, the story creates a striking impression of an old woman who is haunted by her fears.

GUIDE FOR READING

Anxiety

Writer's Techniques

Point of View. Point of view refers to the vantage point from which a narrative is told. Most stories are told from either a first-person or third-person point of view. In a narrative with a first-person point of view, one of the characters tells the story in his or her own words, using the first-person pronoun *I*. In a narrative with a third-person point of view, the narrator does not participate in the story and refers to characters using the third-person pronouns *he* or *she*. A third-person narrator may be either limited or omniscient. A third-person limited narrator focuses on the thoughts and feelings of only one character. A third-person omniscient narrator conveys the thoughts and feelings of all the characters.

A story's point of view often affects the way in which the characters are developed and portrayed. By using a third-person limited or first-person point of view, a writer allows you to see directly into the mind of one of the characters. As a result, much of what you learn about the character's personality is revealed through his or her thoughts and feelings. At the same time, this character's impressions are likely to shape the way in which the other characters are depicted.

Look For

As you read "Anxiety," look for the point of view from which the story is told. How does it affect the way in which the characters are developed and portrayed?

Writing

In "Anxiety" an old woman expresses her fears about the present condition of the world. Brainstorm about the reasons why an elderly person might have a hard time coping with the state of the world today and the types of things that he or she might be likely to fear.

Vocabulary

Knowing the following words will help you as you read "Anxiety."
anxiety (aŋ zī′ ə tē) *n.* Uneasiness about the future (p. 1102)

tenements (ten′ ə mənts) *n.*: Buildings divided into apartments (p. 1102)

Anxiety

Grace Paley

The young fathers are waiting outside the school. What curly heads! Such graceful brown mustaches. They're sitting on their haunches eating pizza and exchanging information. They're waiting for the 3 P.M. bell. It's springtime, the season of first looking out the window. I have a window box of greenhouse marigolds. The young fathers can be seen through the ferny leaves.

The bell rings. The children fall out of school, tumbling through the open door. One of the fathers sees his child. A small girl. Is she Chinese? A little. Up u-u-p, he says and hoists her to his shoulders. U-u-p, says the second father, and hoists his little boy. The little boy sits on top of his father's head for a couple of seconds before sliding to his shoulders. Very funny, says the father.

They start off down the street, right under and past my window. The two children are still laughing. They try to whisper a secret. The fathers haven't finished their conversation. The frailer father is uncomfortable; his little girl wiggles too much.

Stop it this minute, he says.

Oink oink, says the little girl.

What'd you say?

Oink oink, she says.

The young father says What! three times. Then he seizes the child, raises her high above his head, and sets her hard on her feet.

What'd I do so bad, she says, rubbing her ankle. Just hold my hand, screams the frail and angry father.

I lean far out the window. Stop! Stop! I cry.

The young father turns, shading his eyes, but sees. What? he says. His friend says, Hey? Who's that? He probably thinks I'm a family friend, a teacher maybe.

Who're you? he says.

I move the pots of marigold aside. Then I'm able to lean on my elbow way out into unshadowed visibility. Once, not too long ago, the tenements were speckled with women like me in every third window up to the fifth story, calling the children from play to receive orders and instruction. This memory enables me to say strictly, Young man, I am an older person who feels free because of that to ask questions and give advice.

Oh? he says, laughs with a little embarrassment, says to his friend, Shoot if you will that old gray head. But he's joking, I know, because he has established himself, legs apart, hands behind his back, his neck arched to see and hear me out.

How old are you? I call. About thirty or so?

Thirty-three.

First I want to say you're about a generation ahead of your father in your attitude and behavior toward your child.

Really? Well? Anything else, ma'am.

Son, I said, leaning another two, three dangerous inches toward him. Son, I must tell you that madmen intend to destroy this beautifully made planet. That the murder of our children by these men has got to become

ROOM IN BROOKLYN
Edward Hopper
Museum of Fine Arts, Boston

a terror and a sorrow to you, and starting now, it had better interfere with any daily pleasure.

Speech speech, he called.

I waited a minute, but he continued to look up. So, I said, I can tell by your general appearance and loping walk that you agree with me.

I do, he said, winking at his friend; but turning a serious face to mine, he said again, Yes, yes, I do.

Well then, why did you become so angry at that little girl whose future is like a film which suddenly cuts to white. Why did you nearly slam this little doomed person to the ground in your uncontrollable anger.

Let's not go too far, said the young fa-

ther. She *was* jumping around on my poor back and hollering oink oink.

When were you angriest—when she wiggled and jumped or when she said oink?

He scratched his wonderful head of dark well-cut hair. I guess when she said oink.

Have you ever said oink oink? Think carefully. Years ago, perhaps?

No. Well maybe. Maybe.

Whom did you refer to in this way?

He laughed. He called to his friend, Hey Ken, this old person's got something. The cops. In a demonstration. Oink oink, he said, remembering, laughing.

The little girl smiled and said, Oink oink.

Shut up, he said.

What do you deduce from this?

That I was angry at Rosie because she was dealing with me as though I was a figure of authority, and it's not my thing, never has been, never will be.

I could see his happiness, his nice grin, as he remembered this.

So, I continued, since those children are such lovely examples of what may well be the last generation of humankind, why don't you start all over again, right from the school door, as though none of this had ever happened.

Thank you, said the young father. Thank you. It would be nice to be a horse, he said, grabbing little Rosie's hand. Come on Rosie, let's go. I don't have all day.

U-up, says the first father. U-up, says the second.

Giddap, shout the children, and the fathers yell neigh neigh, as horses do. The children kick their fathers' horsechests, screaming giddap giddap, and they gallop wildly westward.

I lean way out to cry once more, Be careful! Stop! But they've gone too far. Oh, anyone would love to be a fierce fast horse carrying a beloved beautiful rider, but they are galloping toward one of the most dangerous street corners in the world. And they may live beyond that trisection across other dangerous avenues.

So I must shut the window after patting the April-cooled marigolds with their rusty smell of summer. Then I sit in the nice light and wonder how to make sure that they gallop safely home through the airy scary dreams of scientists and the bulky dreams of automakers. I wish I could see just how they sit down at their kitchen tables for a healthy snack (orange juice or milk and cookies) before going out into the new spring afternoon to play.

THINKING ABOUT THE SELECTION

Recalling

1. What do the young fathers do while they are waiting outside the school?
2. (a) Why does the "frailer father" become angry with his daughter? (b) How does he respond to his anger?
3. (a) When does the father remember having said "oink oink"? (b) How does this memory help him to understand his behavior toward his daughter?

Interpreting

4. (a) Why might the narrator be so interested in the children and their "young fathers"? (b) What do the concerns she expresses reveal about her personality?
5. How does the story's title relate to the narrator's behavior?
6. What is Paley's attitude toward the narrator?
7. What does the father's response to the narrator's remarks reveal about his character?

Applying

8. How do you think most people would react to the narrator's remarks? Support your answer.

ANALYZING LITERATURE

Understanding Point of View

Point of view refers to the vantage point from which a narrative is told. "Anxiety" is told from a first-person point of view, with the old woman relating the story in her own words.

1. How would the story be different if it were told from the "frailer" father's point of view?
2. Why would a third-person omniscient point of view be less effective for this story?

CRITICAL THINKING AND READING

Generalizing About an Age

A common generalization about the period following World War II is that it is an age of anxiety. Prepare a chart with three columns. Label the first column *World,* the second, *Nation,* and the third, *Personal.* Under each heading list conditions or factors that would lead to the development of a sense of anxiety in a person living in today's world. For example, under *World* you might list nuclear war, under *Nation,* unemployment, and under *Personal,* a sense of rootlessness. Share your chart with your classmates.

UNDERSTANDING LANGUAGE

Finding Synonyms

Synonyms are words that have the same or nearly the same meaning. For example, *attitude* and *belief* are synonyms.

The words in capital letters are from "Anxiety." Choose the lettered word that is closest in meaning to each of the capitalized words, as the word is used in the selection.

1. FRAIL: (a) fragile (b) irresolute (c) resistant (d) unintelligent
2. ENABLES; (a) empowers (b) prepares (c) dictates (d) influences
3. ESTABLISHED: (a) organized (b) confirmed (c) entrenched (d) accustomed
4. DEMONSTRATION: (a) display (b) protest (c) representation (d) manifestation
5. ANXIETY: (a) calmness (b) apprehension (c) madness (d) disruption

THINKING AND WRITING

Writing a Short Story

Imagine that your school literary magazine has asked you to write a short story in which you create a striking impression of a character. Start by thinking of interesting or unusual people you know and noting the personality traits that make them interesting or unusual. Then create a fictional character who possesses some of the traits you have listed. When you write your short story, focus on conveying this character's personality through dialogue and action as well as through his or her thoughts. When you finish writing, revise your story, making sure that the character is well developed.

MARK HELPRIN

1947–

One of the most promising young writers in America today, Mark Helprin has been praised for his ability to blend realism and fantasy. Using his imagination, he transforms realistic settings into strange, mystical worlds, creating a type of fiction often referred to as "magical realism."

Helprin was born in New York City. He graduated from Harvard, where he studied Middle Eastern culture. Possessing a thirst for adventure, he is an enthusiastic mountain climber and parachutist and has served in the British merchant navy, the Israeli infantry, and the Israeli air force. Not surprisingly, Helprin has drawn upon his travel experiences in developing the settings for both his novels and short stories.

Helprin has published two novels, *Refiner's Fire* and *Winter's Tale,* and two collections of short stories, *A Dove of the East* and *Ellis Island*. His stories have also been published in many major magazines, including *The New Yorker*.

"Katherine Comes to Yellow Sky," which appears in *A Dove of the East,* exhibits Helprin's sophisticated and elegant style. Set in the late 1800's, the story depicts the westward journey of a young woman, focusing on her thoughts as she travels toward her new home.

GUIDE FOR READING

Katherine Comes to Yellow Sky

Character. A variety of types of characters are used in literary works. When a character is well developed and possesses a variety of traits, he or she is referred to as a round character. For example, Bet, the main character of Anne Tyler's "Average Waves in Unprotected Waters," is a round character who exhibits conflicting emotions and desires, possessing a deep love for her handicapped son, but also wanting to be relieved of the burden of caring for him. A character who embodies a single trait or quality is referred to as a flat character. For example, Tom Walker, the main character in Washington Irving's "The Devil and Tom Walker," is a flat character who embodies the vice of greed. Tom Walker is also an example of a stock or stereotyped character—a character type used so often that his or her nature is already familiar to readers. Characters may also be classified as static or dynamic. A static character is a character who does not change during the course of a literary work. In contrast, a dynamic character is a one whose personality undergoes some sort of permanent change. Regardless of the type of character being portrayed, the writer must provide a motivation, or a stated or implied reason for the character's behavior, to make a character's actions believable.

Look For

As you read "Katherine Comes to Yellow Sky," look for the personality traits of Katherine, the story's main character. Is she a flat character or a round character? Does she change during the course of the story? What motivates her actions?

Writing

"Katherine Comes to Yellow Sky" is about a woman who travels westward in the late 1800's to the frontier town of Yellow Sky. Why do you think so many Americans made similar journeys during the nineteenth century? Freewrite about types of motivations people may have had for leaving their homes and moving to the new frontier.

Vocabulary

Knowing the following words will help you as you read "Katherine Comes to Yellow Sky."

contemptible (kən temp′ tə b'l) *adj.*: Worthless; despicable (p. 1109)

inevitable (in ev′ ə tə b'l) *adj.*: Certain to happen; unavoidable (p. 1111)

Katherine Comes to Yellow Sky[1]

Mark Helprin

Like a French balloonist who rides above in the clear silence slowly turning in his wicker basket, Katherine rode rapidly forward on a steady-moving train. It glided down depressions and crested hills, white smoke issuing lariat-like from the funnel, but mostly it was committed to the straightness of the path, the single track, the good open way. And as an engine well loved, the locomotive ran down the rails like a horse with a rider.

Passengers sat mainly in silence, not taking one another for granted but rather deeply respectful, for they were unacquainted and there was not the familiarity of one type crossing another. From each could come the unseen, perhaps a strange resolve or stranger ability. Like athletes before a match, they had high mutual regard so that as the day passed from morning to noon each man or woman kept to windows.

Katherine too stared out the imperfect glass ahead at softly glowing grasslands, yellow seas of wheat, seas of wildflowers, and June lilies, and at the dark mountains which were always visible in one direction or another. Having neglected to get a book out of her luggage she could only look, and attempt thoughts and variations. At first it was taking off her thin gold glasses and closing the good left eye so that she could blur the deep permanent colors. This she did, but

saw an old man staring at her and at the way she tilted her head and set her mouth as if waiting for an answer she would never believe. She looked daft when she did that or as if she had some kind of rare nerve dance. Back went the glasses and for a while she stared straight and dignified directly into the distance, this soon giving her the appearance of a gorgeous lunatic. She wore a white dress with high white shoes, and an enormous wide-brimmed hat, which although it glowed as fiercely as the face of a glacier was modified in its absoluteness by the buttercup haze of a yellow saffron band. Her hair was a long bright auburn tied back, and her eyes a striking green, as hazy as the saffron glow and as cool as a spring in the mountains, and if it were not that way the burn of freckles on her face might have consumed her, for they gave this girl a hot and suncolored redness even in the stillest of white winters and a youth that carried her well into age. The daughter of an Irish quarry worker and a Dublin Jewess, she was taken when small enough to be nicknamed "Carroty" from the west of England to Boston and then to Quincy,[2] where her father became a foreman on a new opening in the granite quarry and her mother took up work in a textile mill. Katherine herself went to normal school,[3] escaping lovers because she was wedded to a dream landscape, and al-

---

1. Katherine . . . Yellow Sky: The title recalls the Stephen Crane short story "The Bride Comes to Yellow Sky."

2. Quincy: A city in eastern Massachusetts.
3. normal school: A school where teachers were trained.

though many sought her she was faithful to a vision of clouds and yellow sky far off to the West in unsettled territories. And she passed quickly from the society of the normal school to the company of a solitary idea. Convinced of new worlds her existence was animated in such a way that she had no answers, not a one, but believed incessantly in what she imagined.

She had read all her life of the openness of the West, of its red rivers and plains leafed in neutral in-breathing gold, of the miraculous Indians and the Rockies, which were mountains of mist that formed and unformed dreams so fast as to confuse even the youngest of dreamers. And strangely enough these substanceless dreams, these short electric pictures, these confused but royally intense sketches, gradually gave to her a strength, practicality, and understanding which many a substantial man would never have. Her vindication, almost God-promised, was as clear as the excellent sea air, or the deep blue pools which in summer formed at the bottom of the quarries, to her father's chagrin. Her father, whose strength had equaled the beauty of her mother, had seen in her very early what he himself had lost, and unlike many fathers he had no envy. He was too good for that. He loved her too much. He saw himself as a stone arch, unbending, sheltering around his wife and daughter, to keep them safe and await the day when his daughter could soar on her visions and be settled.

Katherine, a dreamer, was not hard but tender, and when her parents died one following the other in a general epidemic she was wild. Just to be in Quincy, as gray as a man's suit, afflicted with ice and dark winds, a shabby collection of boards amidst scrub trees like the coat of a dying mare, made her sad in a way which does no good and leads to dead ends and contemptible unbelieving. One day in winter she thought she saw her father standing by her mother, who was gentle and strong and had been the first to die. Her father held a sledgehammer, of the finest wood and with a shining gold head. He said, "I shall free you all," and went to the base of the quarry where he smashed the cast-iron braces and beams which held the rock. The iron rang like a thousand bells and black pieces shattered over the quarry, ringing the pools and echoing off the high walls. And her father continued until every chain was severed and every brace broken, until all metal and all the past were smashed, buried in the clear pools. Free air circulated away from its bounds and the muscular father said to her, a little out of breath but with as good a red color as he had had on the finest days of summer, he said, "Katherine, Katherine, my Carroty, we too have had it with this place. We are not permanently rooted here, and you must go away. I have smashed these bonds, and this I did for you. Pile your hair, tie it firmly, and find a new place."

This she did, about a year later, and headed West, for there she sensed something which would give her the moments she wanted before her death, moments of full cognizance and dream vision, the red roses of her life and its humor. It was good to abandon Quincy and its quarry.

She set her hat at an angle, trying to frame the light blue mountain ranges. The tracks threw up dust and she eyed steam from the locomotive. These billowing clouds became captions for her thoughts, and they centered on Yellow Sky, on a dream quest which had spread to all the people. Yellow Sky. It was still far off.

That night they stopped in Gibson, a town spread across a large rise in the prairie where cattle roads, a flat unnavigable river, and the railroad crossed at angles. Huge yards of seemingly spider-work boards held cattle for boxcar loading, and during the whole of the late spring night, cattle filed past her window in the darkness. Without awakening her assigned roommate, an elderly woman who looked like a tomb, Katherine stepped out of bed and went to the open

ACROSS THE CONTINENT, WESTWARD THE COURSE OF EMPIRE TAKES ITS WAY
Currier & Ives
Museum of the City of New York

window. A high wind carried occasional raindrops past the town and out into the vastly promising darkness from which an endless procession of moody steers was filing—giant animals intent upon moving to their slaughter—to feed the distant cities. She had seen the land-seas of wheat and flowers and from them came these steers, an abundance which kept her awake the rest of the night wide-eyed, waiting for the hoofbeats and dust and drovers' calls to stop, but when morning found her tears were in her eyes as she stared at the clouds of sparkling dust. From where did they come, constantly, without even the slightest break? The land

beyond was empty except for storm and mountains, and yet from there the night had been filled with a power so great it drew a shaking tense silence, a joyous fright. The endless power was born somewhere out near Yellow Sky, and Katherine couldn't sleep because she was headed there, as surely and certainly as the warm steel track, or the confident horsemen who often appeared alongside to race the train.

Leaving Gibson, they skirted the wide river and crossed a road on which thousands of cattle were backed up for miles; in the distance they were as even a brown as the drovers' felt hats. For scores of miles the landscape was the same, a rolling plain which looked like masses of brown whales, dotted flowers, banks of lilies, and grasses. The train's exact and faithful forward motion led her to expect something ahead at all moments, and although there was nothing save the glittering May landscape, the convincing direction became in itself more than enough to hold her, and hold her it did, as had her realization of the night power in and around Gibson. She was held fast, but no more than anyone on the train, no more than farmers, fencemen, or drovers outside who were passed by and left to work amid their own silence and claimed lands, no more than boys in Gibson who prodded cattle with dry white cottonwillow sticks, or distant horsemen on a ridge, galloping only to disappear, although leaving the surety of their gallop impressed upon the passengers. A detachment of pony soldiers, '75 blue,[4] rode two by two on a wagon track, swords and buckles shining. They did not always know what they did, but by God they did it, as it was inevitable. Had she not lived her life in grayness and seen the bright only by fantasy? Did she not as the daughter of a man deserve these rich lands which had been declared ready and were being gathered in the arms of those who had come from such long ways away? Yellow Sky was in the mountains, up high, beyond the timberline which was like a skirt. The air was as thin as shell and pearl bright as the lakes and plummeting black-rock streams. She would stop in Yellow Sky but others would pass right on, and yet others right down to the broken beaches of the Pacific. This young impressionable girl alone on the cool wicker-weave seat of a shady railroad car moving out West could not be stopped. The colors in her were bound for Yellow Sky.

At about six in the morning the tired train halted in a cool saddle of the mountains just above the treeline. Men began to carry wood from enormous stockpiles along the track and load it on the coaler. A wooden trough was lowered from a cable-bound barrel tank and mountain water fell into the blackened holds of the locomotive, dribbling, spraying, and steaming from valves of nickel and steel, hissing like a swarm of locusts in the convoluted boilers. The steam from the locomotive's gaskets mingled with the early morning mist, low clouds which hid white gold-flecked mountains of sunrise. The peaks had begun to shine many hours before, and after sunset they would shine even though the night was black, the price for this advanced and delayed burnishing of the mountains being shade and darkness at the extreme hours. Those who lived in that place stared each day in special communication at the shining crowns all about them. The man who had charge of the railroad depot was tall and wore hobnailed boots[5] which awakened passengers as he walked on top of the cars. His boots also awakened his children, a little bear-faced boy and two fat little girls happy to have only their own thousands of private jokes.

The one hundred or so people in the town were miners, bridge workers, and railroad men who rode small mounted donkey engines up and down the passes securing faulted track and removing obstructions. There were always bridges to build, sometimes of several yards, sometimes of a quarter of a mile, because it was ravine country, rocky, high, indifferent to smooth-trafficking men and natural only to birds such as eagles, hawks, crows, and falcons—mountain birds with eyes of wondrous and staggering capabilities. Sharp as a ten-foot glass, they still could not see veins of silver spread variously throughout the ravines and deep into rock where only men could go, and by great effort. The trackers held the land down by use of iron bands, the bridgemen smoothed

---

4. pony . . . blue: United States cavalry.

5. hobnailed boots: Heavy boots with short nails protruding slightly from the soles.

it, and the miners pierced it—as if they were hunters and it a mammoth, succumbing to their studied attack.

The attack was not studied but passionate, and not of greed alone. At each day's end the bridgemen, the railroadmen, the miners looked at the land in the quiet time when the mountains shone softly like lanterns into the dark valley, and they saw that it was not damaged. Work as they did, the peaks were high, the streams excellently fresh, the pastures rich, their iron and wood, their fences and track all but invisible due to the greatness of the land. This, as much as anything else, made them love it. It was invincible and so beckoned, challenging them to make their mark. Impossible, they said when they looked up, for the sky was as blue as a pure packet of indigo,[6] and it reached into deep unconquerable heaven.

The conductor (who had warned Katherine to be careful of sparks—prompting her to say that it was impossible to be careful of sparks) roused her from a fitful, watery-eyed, straight-backed, sitting-up, night never ends sleep and she with the rest of the passengers stepped into a mountain village where they were served tea and rolls. Katherine stood quietly at yet another window, this in the depot, and she saw in the distance the lantern mountains glowing gold in all directions, catching the future sun. There, and just then did she realize, was the source of the

---

6. indigo (in'di go') *n.*: A blue dye.

power she had sensed days before. This time it was realization which struck her, not revelation, and there were no tears or risings within. She simply realized in the deadest and most sober of moments that in those mountains was the source, glancing off high lighted rock faces where no man could ever go, split into rivers eastward and westward running in little fingers to every part of the land, to the oceans where it blended with the newly turned sea foam and sun.

As the sun became stronger, but still not visible, they re-embarked onto the train. When Katherine approached the three-stepped iron stand, the conductor offered her his hand. She wondered why, thinking that perhaps he was going to help her up, something he did not do. But he shook her hand, and barred her way. Why? she said, and then he pointed to her luggage—leather cases and white canvas duffels—and when she still did not understand, to the mountains with golden light like the warm light from a candle. She was struck dumb. The train began to pull away, conductor and all, with a vast exhalation of white steam, and he said to the stunned girl what she already knew, "This is Yellow Sky." As the train vanished she could think only of her father, her mother, and the gray oceans in between. Oceans in between, their lights had lasted, and she had found her way. It came in a flood, and she shuddered. Oceans in between. It was an end. It was a beginning. Katherine had come to Yellow Sky.

THINKING ABOUT THE SELECTION

Recalling

1. What vision dominated Katherine's thoughts while she was in normal school?
2. What did Katherine imagine seeing "one day in winter" after her mother and father had died?
3. Why does the train halt "in a cool saddle of the mountains just above the treeline"?
4. What realization strikes Katherine while she is gazing out the window of the train depot in the small mountain village?

5. Why does the conductor prevent Katherine from reboarding the train?

Interpreting

6. What type of impression does Helprin convey in his description of Quincy?
7. What overall impression of the American landscape does Helprin convey through his depiction of Katherine's observations?
8. (a) Why is the end of the story surprising? (b) What does the ending reveal about Katherine's state of mind?
9. Explain the paradox in the last three sentences: "It was an end. It was a beginning. Katherine had come to Yellow Sky."

Applying

10. Do you think that life in Yellow Sky will live up to Katherine's expectations? Why or why not?

ANALYZING LITERATURE

Understanding Characters

A variety of different types of characters are used in literature. **Round characters** are characters who possess a variety of traits. **Flat characters** are characters who embody a single trait. **Static characters** are characters whose personality does not change during the course of a literary work. **Dynamic characters** are characters whose personalities do change.

1. Is Katherine a flat character or a round character?
2. What personality traits does she possess?
3. Is she a static character or a dynamic character? Support your answer.

CRITICAL THINKING AND READING

Understanding a Character's Motivation

In portraying any type of character, the writer must provide a **motivation,** or a stated or im-plied reason for the character's behavior, to make a character's actions believable. In "Katherine Comes to Yellow Sky," for example, Katherine's decision to travel westward is motivated to a great extent by her childhood visions of the West.

1. How does Helprin's description of Quincy help explain Katherine's motivation for leaving?
2. How does the vision that Katherine has of her mother and father after they have died help explain her decision to leave?

UNDERSTANDING LANGUAGE

Understanding Differences in Meaning

The author writes of Katherine, "There, and just then did she realize, was the source of the power she had sensed before. This time it was realization which struck her, not revelation, and there were no tears or risings within."

1. Explain the difference between the words *realization* and *revelation*.
2. Why might one bring tears and the other none?

THINKING AND WRITING

Responding to Criticism

A critic has commented that "some of Mark Helprin's stories, long on mood and short on plot, seem like watercolor sketches for more finished works." Write an essay in which you discuss this statement in relation to "Katherine Comes to Yellow Sky." Reread the story. Does it seem "long on mood and short on plot"? Does it in some way seem unfinished? When writing your essay, use passages from the story to support your responses to these questions. When you revise, make sure your essay is organized in a logical manner.

LARRY McMURTRY

1936–

In his work Larry McMurtry captures the changing flavor of life in the American West. His realistic and revealing depictions of the West have established him as one of the prominent western writers of our time.

A descendant of two generations of cattle ranchers, McMurtry was born in Wichita Falls, Texas, and raised in the nearby community of Archer City. After graduating from high school, he enrolled at Rice University but soon transferred to North Texas State University. He developed an interest in writing while in college, and while pursuing a master's degree at Rice University, he started work on his first novel, *Horsemen, Pass By*. The novel, better known by its film title, *Hud,* was published in 1961.

Labeled by some critics as the creator of the "urban western," McMurtry first attracted attention as a new kind of writer of western novels who mixed the traditional elements of the genre with sharp social observation and a strong dose of dark humor. His earlier novels, such as *The Last Picture Show* (1966), *Moving On* (1970), and *Terms of Endearment* (1975), capture the changing, rootless character of the American West. These novels created resentment among some citizens of McMurtry's home town who objected to his implicit condemnation of small-town life.

Since his reputation was at first built on his portrayals of the disintegration of cowboy and western folklore, his novel *Lonesome Dove* (1985) represented a startling departure. In this novel, which won a 1986 Pulitzer Prize, he turned to the frontier heritage of the West. The novel, set in the late 1870's, tells about the fortunes of a variety of colorful characters involved in a 2,000-mile cattle drive from the Rio Grande River to northern Montana.

Although he is primarily known as a novelist, McMurtry has also received critical acclaim as an essayist and critic, writing mainly for newspapers and magazines. In a *Narrow Grave: Essays about Texas,* a collection of his nonfiction was published in 1968. He has also written film criticism and screenplays, and he is now a contributing editor to the periodical *American Film*.

GUIDE FOR READING

Writer's Techniques

from Lonesome Dove

Setting. The setting is the time and place in which the events in a work of literature occur. While short stories frequently have only one setting, novels often have one or more general settings and numerous specific settings in which the various episodes take place. An effective description of a specific setting enables us to envision the setting and imagine the characters interacting with it. To accomplish this, a writer includes details of such elements of setting as the climate and the physical composition of the land. In describing these elements, writers use sensory language, or language that appeals to one or more of the five senses. In *Lonesome Dove* McMurtry frequently uses language that appeals to our sense of sight. For example, McMurty creates a visual image, or word picture, when he writes, "The late sun shone through the dust cloud, making the white dust rosy."

Look For

As you read the excerpt from *Lonesome Dove,* look for how McMurtry uses sensory language to create a vivid portrait of the setting.

Writing

In this selection the characters are forced to cope with extremely unpleasant conditions caused by the climate. Freewrite about a time when you had to deal with unpleasant conditions related to the climate. In your freewriting explore the ways in which you coped with the conditions, the effect of the conditions on your state of mind, and what you learned from the experience.

Vocabulary

Knowing the following words will help you as you read the excerpt from *Lonesome Dove.*

deign (dān) *v.* Take or accept gracefully (p. 1116)
aggrieved (ə grēv'd') *v.*: Offended (p. 1116)
dismay (dis mā') *n.*: A loss of confidence at the prospect of trouble (p. 1118)
imperative (im per' ə tiv) *adj.*: Absolutely necessary; urgent (p. 1119)

from Lonesome Dove

Larry McMurtry

*Captain Woodrow Call and Augustus McCrae are two for-
mer Texas Rangers who helped bring peace to the Texas
frontier. Call now feels a yearning for adventure. With his
friend Augustus, he gathers together a ragtag bunch of cowboys and embarks on a cattle drive from Lonesome Dove,
Texas, on the Rio Grande, to the wilderness of Montana.*

In the late afternoon they strung a rope corral around the remuda,[1] so each hand could pick himself a set of mounts, each being allowed four picks. It was slow work, for Jasper Fant and Needle Nelson could not make up their minds. The Irishmen and the boys had to take what was left after the more experienced hands had chosen.

Augustus did not deign to make a choice at all. "I intend to ride old Malaria all the way," he said, "or if not I'll ride Greasy."

Once the horses were assigned, the positions had to be assigned as well.

"Dish, you take the right point," Call said. "Soupy can take the left and Bert and Needle will back you up."

Dish had assumed that, as a top hand, he would have a point, and no one disputed his right, but both Bert and Needle were unhappy that Soupy had the other point. They had been with the outfit longer, and felt aggrieved.

The Spettle boys were told to help Lippy with the horse herd, and Newt, the Raineys and the Irishmen were left with the drags. Call saw that each of them had bandanas, for the dust at the rear of the herd would be bad.

They spent an hour patching on the wagon, a vehicle Augustus regarded with scorn. "That dern wagon won't get us to the Brazos,"[2] he said.

"Well, it's the only wagon we got," Call said.

"You didn't assign me no duties, nor yourself either," Augustus pointed out.

"That simple," Call said. "I'll scare off bandits and you can talk to Indian chiefs."

"You boys let these cattle string out," he said to the men. "We ain't in no big hurry."

Augustus had ridden through the cattle and had come back with a count of slightly over twenty-six hundred.

"Make it twenty-six hundred cattle and two pigs," he said. "I guess we've seen the last of the dern Rio Grande. One of us ought to make a speech, Call. Think of how long we've rode this river."

Call was not willing to indulge him in any dramatics. He mounted the mare and went over to help the boys get the cattle started. It was not a hard task. Most of the

---

1. remuda (rə mōō′ də) *n*.: A group of extra saddle horses kept as a supply of remounts.

2. the Brazos (brä′ zəs): A river in central and southeastern Texas.

cattle were still wild as antelope and instinctively moved away from the horsemen. In a few minutes they were on the trail, strung out for more than a mile. The point riders soon disappeared in the low brush.

Lippy and the Spettle boys were with the wagon. With the dust so bad, they intended to keep the horses a fair distance behind.

Bolivar sat on the wagon seat, his ten-gauge across his lap. In his experience trouble usually came quick, when it came, and he meant to keep the ten-gauge handy to discourage it.

Newt had heard much talk of dust, but had paid little attention to it until they actually started the cattle. Then he couldn't help noticing it, for there was nothing else to notice. The grass was sparse, and every hoof sent up its little spurt of dust. Before they had gone a mile he himself was white with it, and for moments actually felt lost, it was so thick. He had to tie the bandana around his nose to get a good breath. He understood why Dish and the other boys were so anxious to draw assignments near the front of the herd. If the dust was going to be that bad all the way, he might as well be riding to Montana with his eyes shut. He would see

nothing but his own horse and the few cattle that happened to be within ten yards of him. A grizzly bear could walk in and eat him and his horse both, and they wouldn't be missed until breakfast the next day.

But he had no intention of complaining. They were on their way, and he was part of the outfit. After waiting for the moment so long, what was a little dust?

Once in a while, though, he dropped back a little. His bandana got sweaty, and the dust caked on it so that he felt he was inhaling mud. He had to take it off and beat it against his leg once in a while. He was riding Mouse, who looked like he could use a bandana of his own. The dust seemed to make the heat worse, or else the heat made the dust worse.

The second time he stopped to beat his bandana, he happened to notice Sean leaning off his horse as if he were trying to vomit. The horse and Sean were both white, as if they had been rolled in powder, though the horse Sean rode was a dark bay.

"Are you hurt?" he asked anxiously.

"No, I was trying to spit," Sean said. "I've got some mud in my mouth. I didn't know it would be like this."

AGAINST THE SUNSET
Frederic Remington
Peterson Galleries

DRIVING THE HERD
Frank Reaugh
The University of Texas at Austin

"I didn't either," Newt said.

"Well, we better keep up," he added nervously—he didn't want to neglect his responsibilities. Then, to his dismay, he looked back and saw twenty or thirty cattle standing behind them. He had ridden right past them in the dust. He immediately loped back to get them, hoping the Captain hadn't noticed. When he turned back, two of the wild heifers spooked. Mouse, a good cow horse, twisted and jumped a medium-sized chaparral[3] bush in an effort to gain a step on the cows. Newt had not expected the jump and lost both stirrups, but fortunately diverted the heifers so that they turned back into the main herd. He found his heart was beating fast, partly because he had almost been thrown and partly because he had nearly left thirty cattle behind. With such a start, it

seemed to him he would be lucky to get to Montana without disgracing himself.

Call and Augustus rode along together, some distance from the herd. They were moving through fairly open country, flats of chaparral with only here and there a strand of mesquite.[4] That would soon change: the first challenge would be the brush country, an almost impenetrable band of thick mesquite between them and San Antonio. Only a few of the hands were experienced in the brush, and a bad run of some kind might cost them hundreds of cattle.

"What do you think, Gus?" Call asked. "Think we can get through the brush, or had we better go around?"

Augustus looked amused. "Why, these cattle are like deer, only faster," he said. "They'll get through the brush fine. The

---

3. chaparral (chap′ ə ral′) *n.:* A thicket of shrubs or thorny bushes.

4. mesquite (mes kēt′) *n.:* A type of small, thorny tree.

problem will be the hands. Half of them will probably get their eyes poked out."

"I still don't know what you think," Call said.

"The problem is, I ain't used to being consulted," Augustus said. "I'm usually sitting on the porch drinking whiskey at this hour. As for the brush, my choice would be to go through. It's that or go down to the coast and get et by the mosquitoes."

"Where do you reckon Jake will end up?" Call asked.

"In a hole in the ground, like you and me," Augustus said.

"I don't know why I ever ask you a question," Call said.

"Well, last time I seen Jake he had a thorn in his hand," Augustus said. "He was wishing he'd stayed in Arkansas and taken his hanging."

They rode up on a little knobby hill and stopped for a moment to watch the cattle. The late sun shone through the dust cloud, making the white dust rosy. The riders to each side of the herd were spread wide, giving the cattle lots of room. Most of them were horned stock, thin and light, their hides a mixture of colors. The riders at the rear were all but hidden in the rosy dust.

"Them boys on the drags won't even be able to get down from their horses unless we take a spade and spade 'em off a little," Augustus said.

"It won't hurt 'em," Call said. "They're young."

In the clear late afternoon light they could see all the way back to Lonesome Dove and the river and Mexico. Augustus regretted not tying a jug to his saddle—he would have liked to sit on the little hill and drink for an hour. Although Lonesome Dove had not been much of a town, he felt sure that a little whiskey would have made him feel sentimental about it. Call merely sat on the hill, studying the cattle. It was clear to Augustus that he was not troubled in any way by leaving the border or the town.

"It's odd I partnered with a man like you,

Call," Augustus said. "If we was to meet now instead of when we did, I doubt we'd have two words to say to one another."

"I wish it could happen, then, if it would hold you to two words," Call said. Though everything seemed peaceful, he had an odd, confused feeling at the thought of what they had undertaken. He had quickly convinced himself it was necessary, this drive. Fighting the Indians had been necessary, if Texas was to be settled. Protecting the border was necessary, else the Mexicans would have taken south Texas back.

A cattle drive, for all its difficulty, wasn't so imperative. He didn't feel the old sense of adventure, though perhaps it would come once they got beyond the settled country.

Augustus, who could almost read his mind, almost read it as they were stopped on the little knob of a hill.

"I hope this is hard enough for you, Call," he said. "I hope it makes you happy. If it don't, I give up. Driving all these skinny cattle all that way is a funny way to maintain an interest in life, if you ask me."

"Well, I didn't," Call said.

"No, but then you seldom ask," Augustus said. "You should have died in the line of duty, Woodrow. You'd know how to do that fine. The problem is you don't know how to live."

"Whereas you do?" Call asked.

"Most certainly," Augustus said. "I've lived about a hundred to your one. I'll be a little riled if I end up being the one to die in the line of duty, because this ain't my duty and it ain't yours, either. This is just fortune hunting."

"Well, we wasn't finding one in Lonesome Dove," Call said. He saw Deets returning from the northwest, ready to lead them to the bed-ground. Call was glad to see him—he was tired of Gus and his talk. He spurred the mare on off the hill. It was only when he met Deets that he realized Augustus hadn't followed. He was still sitting on old Malaria, back on the little hill, watching the sunset and the cattle herd.

from *Lonesome Dove*   1119

THINKING ABOUT THE SELECTION

Recalling

1. Why are Bert and Needle unhappy that Soupy is given the left point?
2. (a) How does the dust affect Newt's field of vision? (b) What does he do when the dust becomes caked onto his bandana?
3. What two events cause Newt to conclude that he will be "lucky to get to Montana without disgracing himself"?
4. For what reasons is Call concerned about taking the cattle through the brush?
5. (a) Why does Augustus think it is odd that he and Call are partners? (b) According to Augustus, what does Call know?

Interpreting

6. (a) What evidence in this selection indicates that this is Newt's first cattle drive? (b) What is his attitude concerning his involvement in the cattle drive?
7. What does the conversation between Call and Augustus reveal about their personalities?

Applying

8. Do you think it is necessary for life to be filled with adventure to be interesting? Explain your answer.

ANALYZING LITERATURE

Appreciating Setting

The **setting** is the time and place in which the events in a literary work take place. To describe a setting, writers try to use specific details that create an appropriate image in the reader's mind.

1. What details does McMurtry use to enable you to visualize the setting of this selection?
2. The setting often directly or indirectly affects the characters' actions in a literary work. How does the setting affect Newt's actions in this selection?
3. Usually we think of dust as a nuisance, not as a life-threatening condition. What aspect of the dust storm did you find the most frightening.

CRITICAL THINKING AND READING

Recognizing Sensory Language

When writing a description, writers use **sensory language,** or language that appeals to one or more of the five senses. For example, McMurtry appeals to our sense of sight when he writes, "The grass was sparse, and every hoof sent up its little spurt of dust." He appeals to our sense of touch and taste when he writes, "His bandana got sweaty, and the dust caked on it so that he felt he was inhaling mud."

1. Find two more examples of language that appeals to the sense of sight.
2. Find an example of language that appeals to one of the other senses.
3. Which of these examples do you find most effective? Explain.

UNDERSTANDING LANGUAGE

Understanding Word Origins

Many words came to the English language through Spanish. For example, the English word *corral* comes from the Spanish word *corro,* meaning "a circle or ring."

The following words are of Spanish origin. Use your dictionary to find the meaning of each word. Then give the Spanish word and meaning from which it comes.

1. alcove
2. guerrilla
3. alligator
4. mosquito
5. junta

THINKING AND WRITING

Writing a Description

Describe the conditions you discussed in your freewriting for someone who has never experienced these conditions. Review your freewriting. Then prepare a list of details that you can use in your description. When you write your description, use sensory language to evoke the same types of feelings that you had when you experienced these conditions. When you revise, make sure you have included details that appeal to more than just the sense of sight.

Nonfiction

PAINTED WATER GLASSES, 1974
Janet Fish
Whitney Museum of Art

WILLIAM FAULKNER

1897–1962

William Faulkner is now generally regarded as one of the finest writers of his time, yet he received little public recognition until 1946, when *The Portable Faulkner,* an anthology of his writings, was published. Four years later he earned further recognition, when he was awarded the Nobel Prize following the publication of his novel *Intruder in the Dust* (1949). When he received the award, Faulkner delivered a powerful and moving speech concerning the duty of writers in contemporary society.

Faulkner grew up on stories of the past glories of the South. For him southern reality mingled with southern myth and memory. In *Intruder in the Dust* he wrote, "For every Southern boy fourteen years old, not once but whenever he wants it, there is the instance when it's still not two o'clock on that July afternoon in 1863, the brigades are in position behind the rail fence, the guns are laid and ready in the woods, and the furled flags are already loosened to break out. . . ."

The bulk of Faulkner's writing centers on Yoknapatawpha County—a fictional area in northern Mississippi. Here, between the 1890's and the late 1930's, the Compsons, the McCaslins, the Sartorises, and the Snopes work out their fates.

In an interview Faulkner said, "The writer's only responsibility is to his art. He will be completely ruthless if he is a good one. He has a dream. It anguishes him so much he must get rid of it. He has no peace until then."

GUIDE FOR READING

Nobel Prize Acceptance Speech

Literary Forms

Oratory. Oratory is the art of skilled, eloquent public speaking. When planning a speech, a skilled orator carefully considers his or her audience and the purpose and occasion of the speech. The speaker focuses on choosing a topic that is appropriate for the occasion and purpose, then writes the speech using language that he or she feels is suited to the audience.

When writing a speech, an orator must also be sure to emphasize his or her main points. To accomplish this, a speaker will use a variety of oratorical devices. Three of these devices are restatement, repetition, and parallelism. When a speaker uses restatement, he or she restates the same idea a number of times in a variety of different ways. When a speaker uses repetition, he or she restates the same idea using the same words. Parallelism refers to the repeated use of phrases, clauses, or sentences that are similar in structure.

Look For

As you read William Faulkner's speech, look for what makes it appropriate for the audience and occasion, and try to determine the purpose of the speech. Also look for the ways in which Faulkner emphasizes his main point. What oratorical devices does he use?

Writing

Like William Faulkner, many Nobel Prize winners have used the occasion to deliver an important message to the world. Describe the type of message that you would want to deliver if you were awarded the Nobel Prize for your special field of interest.

Vocabulary

Knowing the following words will help you as you read William Faulkner's speech.

commensurate (kə men′ shər it) *adj.*: Corresponding in amount, magnitude, or degree (p. 1124)

pinnacle (pin′ ə k'l) *n.*: A lofty peak (p. 1124)

travail (trə vāl′) *n.*: Painfully difficult or burdensome work (p. 1124)

verities (ver′ ə tēz) *n.*: Truths (p. 1124)

ephemeral (i fem′ ər əl) *adj.*: Short-lived (p. 1124)

Nobel Prize Acceptance Speech

William Faulkner

Stockholm, Sweden
December 10, 1950

I feel that this award was not made to me as a man, but to my work—a life's work in the agony and sweat of the human spirit, not for glory and least of all for profit, but to create out of the materials of the human spirit something which did not exist before. So this award is only mine in trust. It will not be difficult to find a dedication for the money part of it commensurate with the purpose and significance of its origin. But I would like to do the same with the acclaim too, by using this moment as a pinnacle from which I might be listened to by the young men and women already dedicated to the same anguish and travail, among whom is already that one who will some day stand here where I am standing.

Our tragedy today is a general and universal physical fear so long sustained by now that we can even bear it. There are no longer problems of the spirit. There is only the question: When will I be blown up? Because of this, the young man or woman writing today has forgotten the problems of the human heart in conflict with itself which alone can make good writing because only that is worth writing about, worth the agony and the sweat.

He must learn them again. He must teach himself that the basest of all things is to be afraid; and, teaching himself that, forget it forever, leaving no room in his workshop for anything but the old verities and truths of the heart, the old universal truths lacking which any story is ephemeral and doomed—love and honor and pity and pride and compassion and sacrifice. Until he does so, he labors under a curse. He writes not of love but of lust, of defeats in which nobody loses anything of value, of victories without hope and, worst of all, without pity or compassion. His griefs grieve on no universal bones, leaving no scars. He writes not of the heart but of the glands.

Until he relearns these things, he will write as though he stood among and watched the end of man. I decline to accept the end of man. It is easy enough to say that man is immortal simply because he will endure: that when the last ding-dong of doom has clanged and faded from the last worthless rock hanging tideless in the last red and dying evening, that even then there will still be one more sound: that of his puny inexhaustible voice, still talking. I refuse to accept this. I believe that man will not merely endure: he will prevail. He is immortal, not because he alone among creatures has an inexhaustible voice, but because he has a soul, a spirit capable of compassion and sacrifice and endurance. The poet's, the writer's, duty is to write about these things. It is his privilege to help man endure by lifting his heart, by reminding him of the courage and honor and hope and pride and compassion and pity and sacrifice which have been the glory of his past. The poet's voice need not merely be the record of man, it can be one of the props, the pillars to help him endure and prevail.

THINKING ABOUT THE SELECTION

Recalling

1. What does Faulkner try "to create out of the materials of the human spirit"?
2. (a) According to Faulkner, what is "our tragedy today"? (b) What have today's young writers forgotten? (c) Why have they forgotten it?
3. What must young writers teach themselves?
4. (a) What does Faulkner "decline to accept"? (b) Why does he believe that humanity "will prevail"? (c) How can young writers help humanity to prevail?

Interpreting

5. Why is fear "the basest of all things"?
6. Faulkner writes, "I believe that man will not only endure, but will prevail." What do you think Faulkner sees as the difference between prevailing and enduring?
7. (a) In your own words, restate Faulkner's message concerning a writer's duty. (b) Why does Faulkner believe that writers will help humanity to endure and prevail by fulfilling their duty?

Applying

8. Explain why you do or do not agree with Faulkner's opinion concerning a writer's duty.

ANALYZING LITERATURE

Understanding Oratory

Oratory is the art of skilled, eloquent public speaking. When preparing a speech, an effective orator considers his audience and the occasion and purpose of the speech. To emphasize his or her main points, the orator will use such oratorical devices as restatement, repetition, and parallelism.

1. What is the purpose of Faulkner's speech?
2. Why is it approrpriate for the occasion?
3. Why is the language appropriate for an intelligent, educated audience?
4. Find one example of Faulkner's use of restatement in the speech.
5. Find one example of his use of repetition.
6. Find one example of his use of parallelism.

THINKING AND WRITING

Writing About Related Themes

Write an essay in which you discuss how Faulkner's speech echoes the theme, of his short story, "The Bear." Reread "The Bear," focusing on details that reveal its theme. Then reread Faulkner's speech, noting how it echoes the theme of the story. When writing your essay, use passages from both the speech and the short story to support your argument. When you revise, make sure you have not included any unnecessary information.

CARSON McCULLERS

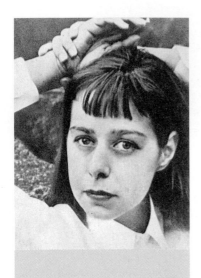

1917–1967

In her writing Carson McCullers captures the feelings of isolation and loneliness sometimes experienced by individuals living in a large, complex, and seemingly indifferent world. Although her works often express a bleak outlook, they also reflect her deep sense of compassion.

Born in Columbus, Georgia, McCullers displayed a great amount of musical talent as a young girl. When she was seventeen, she traveled to New York City to attend the Juilliard School of music, but she lost her tuition money on the subway. Unable to pursue her interest in music, she began taking writing courses at Columbia. She published her first story, "Wunderkind," when she was only nineteen, and her first novel, *The Heart is a Lonely Hunter* (1940), was published when she was twenty-three.

McCullers went on to publish several more novels, including *The Member of the Wedding* (1945), *The Ballad of the Sad Cafe* (1951), and *Clock With No Hands* (1961). Unfortunately, however, during her late twenties, she suffered a series of strokes that left her partially paralyzed and severely limited her ability to write.

Four years after McCullers's death, *The Mortgaged Heart* (1971), an edition of her previously uncollected works, was published. In the following selection from this book, McCullers explores the causes of and possible solutions to the problem of loneliness.

GUIDE FOR READING

from The Mortgaged Heart

Writer's Techniques

Argumentation. Argumentation is writing that attempts to convince the reader to accept a specific opinion or point of view. An argumentative essay, or an essay which focuses on presenting a convincing argument, can usually be divided into four parts: the introduction of the subject; the analysis of the subject; the presentation of the writer's opinion or point of view; and a brief summary of the writer's main points or ideas. In addition to following this type of logical organization, a writer must use facts and examples to support his or her opinion. The writer must also carefully consider his audience when writing the essay, making sure that his or her choice of facts and examples and use of language are appropriate.

Look For

The following excerpt from *The Mortgaged Heart* is an argumentative essay focusing on the subject of loneliness. As you read the essay, look for the opinions McCullers expresses and the way in which she organizes her argument. Do you find her essay effective? Why or why not?

Writing

What do you think are the main causes of loneliness in contemporary society? Prepare a list of reasons for people's loneliness; then list some possible solutions.

Vocabulary

Knowing the following words will help you as you read the excerpt from *The Mortgaged Heart.*

pristine (pris′ tēn) *adj.*: Pure, uncorrupted (p. 1128)

corollary (kôr′ ə ler′ ē) *n.*: An easily drawn conclusion (p. 1128)

xenophobic (zen′ə fō′bik) *adj.*: Afraid of strangers or foreigners (p. 1129)

aesthetic (es thet′ ik) *adj.*: Of beauty (p. 1129)

maverick (mav′ ər ik) *n.*: A nonconformist (p. 1129)

The Mortgaged Heart

Carson McCullers

This city, New York—consider the people in it, the eight million of us. An English friend of mine, when asked why he lived in New York City, said that he liked it here because he could be so alone. While it was my friend's desire to be alone, the aloneness of many Americans who live in cities is an involuntary and fearful thing. It has been said that loneliness is the great American malady. What is the nature of this loneliness? It would seem essentially to be a quest for identity.

To the spectator, the amateur philosopher, no motive among the complex ricochets of our desires and rejections seems stronger or more enduring than the will of the individual to claim his identity and belong. From infancy to death, the human being is obsessed by these dual motives. During our first weeks of life, the question of identity shares urgency with the need for milk. The baby reaches for his toes, then explores the bars of his crib; again and again he compares the difference between his own body and the objects around him, and in the wavering, infant eyes there comes a pristine wonder.

Consciousness of self is the first abstract problem that the human being solves. Indeed, it is this self-consciousness that removes us from lower animals. This primitive grasp of identity develops with constantly shifting emphasis through all our years. Perhaps maturity is simply the history of those mutations that reveal to the individual the relation between himself and the world in which he finds himself.

After the first establishment of identity there comes the imperative need to lose this new-found sense of separateness and to belong to something larger and more powerful than the weak, lonely self. The sense of moral isolation is intolerable to us.

In *The Member of the Wedding*[1] the lovely twelve-year-old girl, Frankie Addams, articulates this universal need: "The trouble with me is that for a long time I have just been an *I* person. All people belong to a *We* except me. Not to belong to a *We* makes you too lonesome."

Love is the bridge that leads from the *I* sense to the *We*, and there is a paradox about personal love. Love of another individual opens a new relation between the personality and the world. The lover responds in a new way to nature and may even write poetry. Love is affirmation; it motivates the *yes* responses and the sense of wider communication. Love casts out fear, and in the security of this togetherness we find contentment, courage. We no longer fear the age-old haunting questions: "Who am I?" "Why am I?" "Where am I going?"—and having cast out fear, we can be honest and charitable.

For fear is a primary source of evil. And when the question "Who am I?" recurs and is unanswered, then fear and frustration project a negative attitude. The bewildered soul can answer only: "Since I do not understand 'Who I am,' I only know what I am *not*." The corollary of this emotional incerti-

---

1. *The Member of the Wedding:* A novel and play by Carson McCullers.

NIGHT CITY
Richard Florsheim
Collection of Jane Golanty

tude is snobbism, intolerance and racial hate. The xenophobic individual can only reject and destroy, as the xenophobic nation inevitably makes war.

The loneliness of Americans does not have its source in xenophobia; as a nation we are an outgoing people, reaching always for immediate contacts, further experience. But we tend to seek out things as individuals, alone. The European, secure in his family ties and rigid class loyalties, knows little of the moral loneliness that is native to us Americans. While the European artists tend to form groups or aesthetic schools, the American artist is the eternal maverick—not only from society in the way of all creative minds, but within the orbit of his own art.

Thoreau took to the woods to seek the ultimate meaning of his life. His creed was simplicity and his *modus vivendi*[2] the deliberate stripping of external life to the Spartan[3] necessities in order that his inward life could freely flourish. His objective, as he put it, was to back the world into a corner. And in that way did he discover "What a man thinks of himself, that it is which determines, or rather indicates, his fate."

On the other hand, Thomas Wolfe turned to the city, and in his wanderings around New York he continued his frenetic and life-long search for the lost brother, the magic door. He too backed the world into a corner, and as he passed among the city's millions, returning their stares, he experienced "That silent meeting [that] is the summary of all the meetings of men's lives."

Whether in the pastoral joys of country life or in the labyrinthine city, we Americans are always seeking. We wander, question. But the answer waits in each separate heart—the answer of our own identity and the way by which we can master loneliness and feel that at last we belong.

---

2. modus vivendi (mō′ dəs vi ven′ dī): Latin for "manner of living."
3. Spartan (spär′ t'n) *adj.*: Characteristic of the people of ancient Sparta: hardy, stoical, severe, frugal.

THINKING ABOUT THE SELECTION

Recalling

1. According to the first paragraph, what is the nature of loneliness?
2. How does McCullers define maturity in the third paragraph?
3. What need develops after a person establishes his or her identity?

4. What difference between Europeans and Americans does McCullers point out in the eighth paragraph?
5. According to the final paragraph, what "waits in each separate heart"?

Interpreting

6. In the second paragraph, how does McCullers emphasize the urgency of the infant's search for identity?

7. How is Frankie Adams's age related to the statement she makes?
8. How is McCullers's method of seeking the meaning of life different from Thoreau's?
9. (a) What does McCullers mean by the terms "moral isolation" and "moral loneliness"? (b) What does she mean when she comments that love "motivates the *yes* response"?

Applying

10. Do you think that today's Americans are more likely to be lonely than the early settlers? Why or why not?

ANALYZING LITERATURE
Understanding Argumentation

Argumentation is writing that attempts to convince the reader to accept a specific opinion or point of view. In her essay Carson McCullers attempts to convince readers to accept her conclusions concerning the causes of and possible solutions to the problem of loneliness.
1. Is McCullers's essay organized like a typical argumentative essay? Support your answer.
2. What is McCullers's opinion concerning the cause of loneliness in America?
3. What conclusion does she reach about the solution to the problem?
4. What examples does she use to support her conclusion?

CRITICAL THINKING AND READING
Understanding Paradoxes

A **paradox** is a statement that seems self-contradictory but in reality contains a possible truth. For example, McCullers presents a paradox in the first paragraph of her essay, stating that a friend of hers appreciated living in New York City because it enabled him to be alone.

1. Why does the paradox concerning life in New York City serve as an effective introduction to the essay?
2. What is paradoxical about the "dual motives" of a person to both claim his or her "identity and belong"?

UNDERSTANDING LANGUAGE
Finding Word Histories

McCullers writes, "While the European artists tend to form groups or aesthetic schools, the American artist is the eternal maverick—not only from society in the way of all creative minds, but within the orbit of his own art." The word *maverick* is based on Samuel A. Maverick, a Texas pioneer who did not brand his cattle. Eventually, all unbranded cattle, especially calves separated from their mothers, came to be called mavericks. Finally, the word began to be applied to people who took independent stands. McCullers also writes, "Whether in the pastoral joys of country life or in the labyrinthine city, we Americans are always seeking." Use a dictionary to explain the history of the word *labyrinth*.

THINKING AND WRITING
Writing an Argumentative Essay

What opinions do you have that you would like to convince other people to accept? Think of a subject about which you have a strong opinion. Then write an argumentative essay focusing on this subject. Before you begin writing, decide on the type of audience you wish to address. When you write your essay, keep your intended audience in mind. Present your argument in the logical manner in which typical argumentative essays are organized. When you revise, make sure you have presented your opinions clearly and effectively.

TRUMAN CAPOTE

1924–1984

A versatile and talented writer, Truman Capote wrote novels, short stories, plays, movie scripts, and a variety of different types of nonfiction works. Achieving success early in his career, he went on to earn widespread recognition and win numerous awards.

Capote was born and raised in New Orleans. When he was eighteen he moved to New York City, where he spent a number of years working for *The New Yorker* magazine. He published his first novel, *Other Voices, Other Rooms,* in 1948. This book, along with two of his other early works, *A Tree of Night* (1949) and *The Grass Harp* (1951), explores the dark, sinister aspects of human existence. Similarly, his "nonfiction novel," *In Cold Blood* (1966), delves into the underlying motives of a violent crime. Capote also wrote several humorous works, including *The Muses are Heard* (1956) and *Breakfast at Tiffany's* (1958).

"A Ride Through Spain" is a personal account of one of Capote's more memorable experiences. The account exhibits Capote's command of language and attention to detail and his ability to bring a scene to life.

GUIDE FOR READING

A Ride Through Spain

Writer's Techniques

Narration. Narration is writing that tells a story. In nonfiction, writers often use narration to recount events and situations from their own lives. When a work focuses on describing a personal experience, it is sometimes referred to as a personal or first-person narrative. Personal narratives are quite similar to anecdotes—brief personal accounts told to make a point or reach a lesson—and autobiographies—full-length accounts of a person's entire life. Like anecdotes and autobiographies, personal narratives generally reveal something about the writer's personality. However, while autobiographies are generally written to inform, personal narratives are often written to amuse or entertain.

Look For

As you read "A Ride Through Spain," look for what the narrative reveals about Capote's personality. Also, try to determine Capote's purpose in writing the narrative. What makes the narrative interesting and entertaining?

Writing

What incident from your own life do you think might make an interesting subject for a personal narrative? Think of an appropriate incident. Then prepare a list of details that you could use in describing it.

Vocabulary

Knowing the following words will help you as you read "A Ride Through Spain."

dour (door) *adj.*: Stern; severe (p. 1134)

meandered (mē an′ dər'd) *v.*: Moved lazily (p. 1135)

somber (säm′ bər) *adj.*: Dark and gloomy or dull (p. 1136)

vigor (vig′ ər) *n.*: Active physical or mental force or strength (p. 1136)

A Ride Through Spain

Truman Capote

Certainly the train was old. The seats sagged like the jowls of a bulldog, windows were out and strips of adhesive held together those that were left; in the corridor a prowling cat appeared to be hunting mice, and it was not unreasonable to assume his search would be rewarded.

Slowly, as though the engine were harnessed to elderly coolies,[1] we crept out of Granada.[2] The southern sky was as white and burning as a desert; there was one cloud, and it drifted like a traveling oasis.

We were going to Algeciras, a Spanish seaport facing the coast of Africa. In our compartment there was a middle-aged Australian wearing a soiled linen suit; he had tobacco-colored teeth and his fingernails were unsanitary. Presently he informed us that he was a ship's doctor. It seemed curious, there on the dry, dour plains of Spain, to meet someone connected with the sea. Seated next to him there were two women, a mother and daughter. The mother was an overstuffed, dusty woman with sluggish, disapproving eyes and a faint mustache. The focus for her disapproval fluctuated; first, she eyed me rather strongly because as the sunlight fanned brighter, waves of heat blew through the broken windows and I had removed my jacket—which she considered, perhaps rightly, discourteous. Later on, she took a dislike to the young soldier who also occupied our compartment. The soldier, and the woman's not very discreet daughter, a buxom girl with the scrappy features of a prizefighter, seemed to have agreed to flirt. Whenever the wandering cat appeared at our door, the daughter pretended to be frightened, and the soldier would gallantly shoo the cat into the corridor: this byplay gave them frequent opportunity to touch each other.

The young soldier was one of many on the train. With their tasseled caps set at snappy angles, they hung about in the corridors smoking sweet black cigarettes and laughing confidentially. They seemed to be enjoying themselves, which apparently was wrong of them, for whenever an officer appeared the soldiers would stare fixedly out the windows, as though enraptured by the landslides of red rock, the olive fields and stern stone mountains. Their officers were dressed for a parade, many ribbons, much brass; and some wore gleaming, improbable swords strapped to their sides. They did not mix with the soldiers, but sat together in a first-class compartment, looking bored and rather like unemployed actors. It was a blessing, I suppose, that something finally happened to give them a chance at rattling their swords.

The compartment directly ahead was taken over by one family: a delicate, attenuated, exceptionally elegant man with a mourning ribbon sewn around his sleeve, and traveling with him, six thin, summery girls, presumably his daughters. They were beautiful, the father and his children, all of them, and in the same way: hair that had a dark shine, lips the color of pimientos,[3] eyes

---

1. **coolies:** Unskilled laborers.
2. **Granada** (grə nä′ də): A province in southern Spain.

3. **pimientos** (pi men′ tōz) *n.*: The red, bell-shaped fruit, used for stuffing green olives.

like sherry. The soldiers would glance into their compartment, then look away. It was as if they had seen straight into the sun.

Whenever the train stopped, the man's two youngest daughters would descend from the carriage and stroll under the shade of parasols. They enjoyed many lengthy promenades, for the train spent the greatest part of our journey standing still. No one appeared to be exasperated by this except myself. Several passengers seemed to have friends at every station with whom they could sit around a fountain and gossip long and lazily. One old woman was met by different little groups in a dozen-odd towns—between these encounters she wept with such abandon that the Australian doctor became alarmed: why no, she said, there was nothing he could do, it was just that seeing all her relatives made her so happy.

At each stop cyclones of barefooted women and somewhat naked children ran beside the train sloshing earthern jars of water and furrily squalling *Agua! Agua!*[4] For two pesetas[5] you could buy a whole basket of dark runny figs, and there were trays of curious white-coated candy doughnuts that looked as though they should be eaten by young girls wearing Communion dresses. Toward noon, having collected a bottle of wine, a loaf of bread, a sausage and a cheese, we were prepared for lunch. Our companions in the compartment were hungry, too. Packages were produced, wine uncorked, and for a while there was a pleasant, almost graceful festiveness. The soldier shared a pomegranate with the girl, the Australian told an amusing story, the witch-eyed mother pulled a paper-wrapped fish from between her bosoms and ate it with a glum relish.

Afterward everyone was sleepy; the doctor went so solidly to sleep that a fly meandered undisturbed over his open-mouthed face. Stillness etherized[6] the whole train; in the next compartment the lovely girls leaned loosely, like six exhausted geraniums; even the cat had ceased to prowl, and lay dreaming in the corridor. We had climbed higher, the train moseyed across a plateau of rough yellow wheat, then between the granite walls of deep ravines where wind, moving down from the mountains, quivered in strange, thorny trees. Once, at a parting in the trees, there was something I'd wanted to see, a castle on a hill, and it sat there like a crown.

It was a landscape for bandits. Earlier in the summer, a young Englishman I know (rather, know of) had been motoring through this part of Spain when, on the lonely side of a mountain, his car was surrounded by swarthy scoundrels. They robbed him, then tied him to a tree and tickled his throat with the blade of a knife. I was thinking of this when without preface a spatter of bullet fire strafed the dozy silence.

It was a machine gun. Bullets rained in the trees like the rattle of castanets,[7] and the train, with a wounded creak, slowed to a halt. For a moment there was no sound except the machine gun's cough. Then, "Bandits!" I said in a loud, dreadful voice.

"*Bandidos!*" screamed the daughter.

"*Bandidos!*" echoed her mother, and the terrible word swept through the train like something drummed on a tom-tom. The result was slapstick in a grim key. We collapsed on the floor, one cringing heap of arms and legs. Only the mother seemed to keep her head; standing up, she began systematically to stash away her treasures. She stuck a ring into the buns of her hair and without shame hiked up her skirts and dropped a pearl-studded comb into her bloomers. Like the cryings of birds at twilight, airy twitterings of distress came from the charming girls in the next compartment. In the corridor the officers bumped about yapping orders and knocking into each other.

---

4. *agua* (ag' wə): Water (Spanish).
5. *pesetas* (pə sāt' əz): The monetary unit of Spain.
6. *etherized* (ē' thə rīzd) *v.*: Anesthetized, as with ether.

---

7. *castanets* (kas' tə nets') *n.*: Small, hollowed out pieces of wood, held in the hand by a connecting cord and clicked together with the fingers.

Suddenly, silence. Outside, there was the murmur of wind in leaves, of voices. Just as the weight of the doctor's body was becoming too much for me, the outer door of our compartment swung open, and a young man stood there. He did not look clever enough to be a bandit.

"*Hay un médico en el tren?*"[8] he said, smiling.

The Australian, removing the pressure of his elbow from my stomach, climbed to his feet. "I'm a doctor," he admitted, dusting himself. "Has someone been wounded?"

"*Si, Señor.* An old man. He is hurt in the head," said the Spaniard, who was not a bandit: alas, merely another passenger. Settling back in our seats, we listened, expressionless with embarrassment, to what had happened. It seemed that for the last several hours an old man had been stealing a ride by clinging to the rear of the train. Just now he'd lost his hold, and a soldier, seeing him fall, had started firing a machine gun as a signal for the engineer to stop the train.

My only hope was that no one remembered who had first mentioned bandits. They did not seem to. After acquiring a clean shirt of mine which he intended to use as a bandage, the doctor went off to his patient, and the mother, turning her back with sour prudery, reclaimed her pearl comb. Her daughter and the soldier followed after us as we got out of the carriage and strolled under the trees, where many passengers had gathered to discuss the incident.

Two soldiers appeared carrying the old man. My shirt was wrapped around his head. They propped him under a tree and all the women clustered about vying with each other to lend him their rosary; someone brought a bottle of wine, which pleased him more. He seemed quite happy, and moaned a great deal. The children who had been on the train circled around him, giggling.

We were in a small wood that smelled of oranges. There was a path, and it led to a shaded promontory; from here, one looked across a valley where sweeping stretches of scorched golden grass shivered as though the earth were trembling. Admiring the valley, and the shadowy changes of light on the hills beyond, the six sisters, escorted by their elegant father, sat with their parasols raised above them like guests at a *fête champêtre.*[9] The soldiers moved around them in a vague, ambitious manner; they did not quite dare to approach, though one brash, sassy fellow went to the edge of the promontory and called, "*Yo te quiero mucho.*"[10] The words returned with the hollow sub-music of a perfect echo, and the sisters, blushing, looked more deeply into the valley.

A cloud, somber as the rocky hills, had massed in the sky, and the grass below stirred like the sea before a storm. Someone said he thought it would rain. But no one wanted to go: not the injured man, who was well on his way through a second bottle of wine, nor the children who, having discovered the echo, stood happily caroling into the valley. It was like a party, and we all drifted back to the train as though each of us wished to be the last to leave. The old man, with my shirt like a grand turban on his head, was put into a first-class carriage and several eager ladies were left to attend him.

In our compartment, the dark, dusty mother sat just as we had left her. She had not seen fit to join the party. She gave me a long, glittering look. "*Bandidos,*" she said with a surly, unnecessary vigor.

The train moved away so slowly butterflies blew in and out the windows.

---

8. "*Hay . . . el tren?*": "Is there a physician on the train?" (Spanish).

9. *fête champêtre* (fet shän pe' tr'): An outdoor feast or entertainment.
10. "*Yo . . . mucho*": I like you a lot (Spanish).

THINKING ABOUT THE SELECTION

Recalling

1. (a) With whom does Capote share his compartment on the train? (b) Who occupies the compartment directly ahead of him?
2. What happens each time the train stops?
3. (a) What noise does Capote hear while the other passengers are sleeping? (b) What does he immediately conclude to be the cause of this noise? (c) What turns out to be the true cause?

Interpreting

4. On what do you think Capote bases his conclusions about the attitudes of the "dusty woman" in his compartment?
5. Considering Capote's observations of this woman, why is it not surprising that she alone remembers who precipitated the passengers' reaction to the noise?
6. What seems to be Capote's attitude toward the incident he describes?

Applying

7. Do you think that most people would have reacted as Capote did, considering the circumstances? Why or why not?

ANALYZING LITERATURE

Understanding Narration

Narration is writing that tells a story. A first-person or personal narrative is an account of an event from the writer's life. Personal narratives generally focus on amusing or entertaining readers and usually offer insights into the writer's personality.

1. Why does Capote's experience make a suitable subject for a personal narrative?
2. What does Capote's reaction to the noise reveal about his personality?
3. What do his observations of the passengers reveal about his sense of humor?

CRITICAL THINKING AND READING

Appreciating the Effect of Similes

The vividness of Capote's descriptions in this account results in part from his frequent use of **similes**—comparisons indicated by a connecting word such as *like* or *as*. For example, in his description of the train, he writes that "the seats sagged like the jowls of a bulldog."

1. Find five more similes used by Capote in this selection.
2. Explain how each of these similes helps to create a vivid image, or word picture.

UNDERSTANDING LANGUAGE

Appreciating Vivid Modifiers

The clarity of Capote's descriptions also results partly from his careful choice of modifiers. For example, he uses vivid modifiers to create a clear picture of the woman in his compartment, referring to her as "an *over-stuffed, dusty* woman".

Think of a word that Capote could have used in place of the italicized word in each of the following descriptions from "A Ride Through Spain." Then explain why this word would make the description less effective.

1. *soiled* linen suit (p. 1134)
2. *sluggish,* disapproving eyes (p. 1134)
3. *stern* stone mountains (p. 1134)
4. *gleaming,* improbable swords (p. 1134)

THINKING AND WRITING

Writing a Personal Narrative

Using the list of details you prepared before reading the selection, write your own personal narrative. Focus on making your narrative entertaining. When you finish writing, revise your narrative, making sure you have included all the important details related to the incident. Then share your narrative with your classmates.

RALPH ELLISON

1914–

In both his fiction and nonfiction, Ralph Ellison has confronted many of the problems faced by black Americans during the twentieth century. He has portrayed the quests of black men and women to discover and come to terms with their identities and has depicted their struggles against the obstacles of discrimination in American society.

Born in Oklahoma City, Ellison was educated at the Tuskegee Institute in Alabama, where he pursued his strong interest in music. Hoping to become a successful jazz musician, he moved to New York City. There, he met Langston Hughes and Richard Wright, who helped inspire him to become a writer.

In 1952 Ellison published his first novel, *The Invisible Man*. The book, which recounts the often harrowing experiences of a nameless black man, earned Ellison the National Book Award. Ellison's next book, a collection of essays and interviews called *Shadow and Act,* was published in 1964. This book includes "Hidden Name and Complex Fate," an essay in which he explores the relationship between his name and his identity.

GUIDE FOR READING

from Hidden Name and Complex Fate

Literary Forms

The Essay. An essay is a short prose work that generally focuses on a narrow topic. Essays can generally be divided into two categories: formal essays and informal essays. Formal essays are written using serious, dignified language and are carefully structured to inform, instruct, or persuade. At the beginning of the essay, the topic is clearly defined and an argument is presented. The writer then develops and supports the argument in the body of the essay and concludes with a brief summary or the presentation of an additional insight into the subject. In contrast, informal essays tend to be loosely organized and are generally written in a relaxed, intimate, conversational style. Less serious in purpose than formal essays, informal essays are usually written to amuse or entertain. Often informal essays attempt to evoke laughter, either by exploring an amusing subject or by treating a serious subject in an amusing manner.

Look For

As you read Ellison's essay, look for its purpose. Also take note of Ellison's use of language and manner of organization. How would you classify his essay?

Writing

Freewrite about the relationship between people's names and their identities. How do you think most parents go about choosing names for their children? Why do you think parents often name their children after historical figures? Do you think that a person's name can in some way shape his or her development?

Vocabulary

Knowing the following words will help you as you read Ellison's essay.

furtive (fur′ tiv) *adj.*: Secretive (p. 1140)

aggregate (ag′ rə gət) *n.*: Sum total (p. 1140)

facile (fas′ 'l) *adj.*: Fluent (p. 1141)

incongruous (in käŋ′ groo wəs) *adj.*: Incompatible (p. 1141)

juxtaposition (juk′ stə pə zish′ ən) *n.*: Placing side by side (p. 1141)

arduous (är′ joo wəs) *adj.*: Very difficult (p. 1144)

from Hidden Name and Complex Fate

Ralph Ellison

Once while listening to the play of a two-year-old girl who did not know she was under observation, I heard her saying over and over again, at first with questioning and then with sounds of growing satisfaction, "I am Mimi Livisay? . . . *I* am Mimi Livisay. I *am* Mimi Livisay . . . I am *Mimi* Li-vi-say! I am Mimi . . ."

And in deed and in fact she was—or became so soon thereafter, by working playfully to establish the unity between herself and her name.

For many of us this is far from easy. We must learn to wear our names within all the noise and confusion of the environment in which we find ourselves; make them the center of all of our associations with the world, with man and with nature. We must charge them with all our emotions, our hopes, hates, loves, aspirations. They must become our masks and our shields and the containers of all those values and traditions which we learn and/or imagine as being the meaning of our familial past.

And when we are reminded so constantly that we bear, as Negroes, names originally possessed by those who owned our enslaved grandparents, we are apt, especially if we are potential writers, to be more than ordinarily concerned with the veiled and mysterious events, the fusions of blood, the furtive couplings, the business transactions, the violations of faith and loyalty, the assaults; yes, and the unrecognized and unrecognizable loves through which our names were handed down unto us. . . .

Perhaps, taken in aggregate, these European names which (sometimes with irony, sometimes with pride, but always with personal investment) represent a certain triumph of the spirit, speaking to us of those who rallied, reassembled and transformed themselves and who under dismembering pressures refused to die. "Brothers and sisters," I once heard a Negro preacher exhort, "let us make up our faces before the world, and our names shall sound throughout the land with honor! For we ourselves are our *true* names, not their epithets! So let us, I say, Make Up Our Faces and Our Minds!"

Perhaps my preacher had read T. S. Eliot, although I doubt it. And in actuality, it was unnecessary that he do so, for a concern with names and naming was very much a part of that special area of American culture from which I come, and it is precisely for this reason that this example should come to mind in a discussion of my own experience as a writer.

Undoubtedly, writers begin their *conditioning* as manipulators of words long before they become aware of literature—certain Freudians[1] would say at the breast.[2] Per-

---

1. Freudians: People who believe in the theories and methods of Sigmund Freud (1856–1939), the founder of psychoanalysis.
2. at the breast: In infancy.

haps. But if so, that is far too early to be of use at this moment. Of this, though, I am certain: that despite the misconceptions of those educators who trace the reading difficulties experienced by large numbers of Negro children in Northern schools to their Southern background, these children are, in *their* familiar South, facile manipulators of words. I know, too, that the Negro community is deadly in its ability to create nicknames and to spot all that is ludicrous in an unlikely name or that which is incongruous in conduct. Names are not qualities; nor are words, in this particular sense, actions. To assume that they are could cost one his life many times a day. Language skills depend to a large extent upon a knowledge of the details, the manners, the objects, the folkways, the psychological patterns, of a given environment. Humor and wit depend upon much the same awareness, and so does the suggestive power of names.

"A small brown bowlegged Negro with the name 'Franklin D. Roosevelt Jones' might sound like a clown to someone who looks at him from the outside," said my friend Albert Murray, "but on the other hand he just might turn out to be a fireside operator. He might just lie back in all of that comic juxtaposition of names and manipulate you deaf, dumb and blind—and you not even suspecting it, because you're thrown out of stance by his name! There you are, so dazzled by the F.D.R. image—which you *know* you can't see—and so delighted with your own superior position that you don't realize that it's *Jones* who must be confronted."

Well, as you must suspect, all of this speculation on the matter of names has a purpose, and now, because it is tied up so ironically with my own experience as a writer, I must turn to my own name.

For in the dim beginnings, before I ever thought consciously of writing, there was my own name, and there was, doubtless, a certain magic in it. From the start I was uncomfortable with it, and in my earliest years it caused me much puzzlement. Neither could I understand what a poet was, nor why, exactly, my father had chosen to name me after one. Perhaps I could have understood it perfectly well had he named me after his own father, but that name had been given to an older brother who died and thus was out of the question. But why hadn't he named me after a hero, such as Jack Johnson,[3] or a soldier like Colonel Charles Young, or a great seaman like Admiral Dewey, or an educator like Booker T. Washington, or a great orator and abolitionist like Frederick Douglass? Or again, why hadn't he named me (as so many Negro parents had done) after President Teddy Roosevelt?

Instead, he named me after someone called Ralph Waldo Emerson, and then, when I was three, he died. It was too early for me to have understood his choice, although I'm sure he must have explained it many times, and it was also too soon for me to have made the connection between my name and my father's love for reading. Much later, after I began to write and work with words, I came to suspect that he was aware of the suggestive powers of names and of the magic involved in naming.

I recall an odd conversation with my mother during my early teens in which she mentioned their interest in, of all things, prenatal culture! But for a long time I actually knew only that my father read a lot, and that he admired this remote Mr. Emerson, who was something called a "poet and philosopher"—so much so that he named his second son after him.

I knew, also, that whatever his motives, the combination of names he'd given me caused me no end of trouble from the moment when I could talk well enough to respond to the ritualized question which grownups put to very young children. Emerson's name was quite familiar to Negroes in Oklahoma during those days when World

---

3. Jack Johnson (1878–1946): The world heavyweight boxing champion from 1908 through 1915.

MAN IN A VEST, 1939–1949
William H. Johnson
National Museum of American Art, Smithsonian Institution

War I was brewing, and adults, eager to show off their knowledge of literary figures, and obviously amused by the joke implicit in such a small brown nubbin[4] of a boy carrying around such a heavy moniker,[5] would invariably repeat my first two names and then to my great annoyance, they'd add "Emerson."

And I, in my confusion, would reply, "No, no, I'm not Emerson; he's the little boy who lives next door." Which only made them laugh all the louder. "Oh no," they'd say, "you're Ralph Waldo Emerson," while I had fantasies of blue murder.

For a while the presence next door of my little friend, Emerson, made it unnecessary for me to puzzle too often over this peculiar adult confusion. And since there were other Negro boys named Ralph in the city, I came to suspect that there was something about the combination of names which produced their laughter. Even today I know of only one other Ralph who had as much comedy made out of his name, a campus politician and deep-voiced orator whom I knew at Tuskegee,[6] who was called in friendly ribbing, *Ralph Waldo Emerson Edgar Allan Poe*, spelled Powe. This must have been quite a trial for him, but I had been initiated much earlier.

During my early school years the name continued to puzzle me, for it constantly evoked in the faces of others some secret. It was as though I possessed some treasure or some defect, which was invisible to my own eyes and ears; something which I had but did not *possess*, like a piece of property in South Carolina, which was mine but which I could not have until some future time. I recall finding, about this time, while seeking adventure in back alleys—which possess for boys a superiority over playgrounds like that which kitchen utensils possess over toys designed for infants—a large photographic lens. I remember nothing of its optical qualities, of its speed or color correction, but it gleamed with crystal mystery and it was beautiful.

Mounted handsomely in a tube of shiny brass, it spoke to me of distant worlds of possibility. I played with it, looking through it with squinted eyes, holding it in shafts of sunlight, and tried to use it for a magic lantern. But most of this was as unrewarding as my attempts to make the music come from a phonograph record by holding the needle in my fingers.

I could burn holes through newspapers with it, or I could pretend that it was a telescope, the barrel of a cannon, or the third eye of a monster—*I* being the monster—but I could do nothing at all about its proper function of making images; nothing to make it yield its secret. But I could not discard it.

Older boys sought to get it away from me by offering knives or tops, agate marbles or whole zoos of grass snakes and horned toads in trade, but I held on to it. No one, not even the white boys I knew, had such a lens, and it was my own good luck to have found it. Thus I would hold on to it until such time as I could acquire the parts needed to make it function. Finally I put it aside and it remained buried in my box of treasures, dusty and dull, to be lost and forgotten as I grew older and became interested in music.

I had reached by now the grades where it was necessary to learn something about Mr. Emerson and what he had written, such as the "Concord Hymn" and the essay "Self-Reliance," and in following his advice, I reduced the "Waldo" to a simple and, I hoped, mysterious "W," and in my own reading I avoided his works like the plague. I could no more deal with my name—I shall never really master it—than I could find a creative use for my lens. . . .

If all this sounds a bit heady, remember that I did not destroy that troublesome mid-

---

4. nubbin *n.*: Anything small and undeveloped.
5. moniker *n.*: Slang for a person's name or nickname.
6. Tuskegee (tus kē′ gē): Tuskegee Institute, the Alabama college which Ellison attended.

JOAN DIDION

1934–

An innovative writer of both fiction and nonfiction, Joan Didion is known for her precise use of language and her ability to capture the essence of contemporary life using images from her own life.

Born and raised in California, Didion began writing at an early age. She earned a degree from the University of California at Berkeley and worked for a number of years as an editor for *Vogue* magazine. In 1963 she published her first novel, *Run River*. Five years later, she produced a volume of essays, *Slouching Towards Bethlehem,* which captured the flavor of life in San Francisco during the late 1960's. This book, along with a later collection of essays, *The White Album* (1979), earned Didion a reputation as one of the country's premier essayists. Since the publication of *The White Album,* she has published another work of nonfiction, *Salvador* (1983), and *Democracy* (1984), a novel that combines fiction with nonfiction.

Didion has written, "We tell ourselves stories in order to live. . . . We live entirely, especially if we are writers, by the imposition of a narrative line upon disparate images, by the 'ideas' with which we have learned to freeze the shifting phantasmagoria which is our actual experience."

In her essay "On the Mall," Didion displays her direct, precise style and her ability to transform a very ordinary subject into an interesting and entertaining work of literature.

On the Mall

Writer's Techniques

Exposition. Exposition is writing in which factual information is presented. It informs or educates the reader by presenting a series of facts, discussing their significance, and explaining how they relate to one another. In "On the Mall," for example, Didion uses exposition to inform the reader about the theories used in planning shopping malls.

Because it is vital to the reader's understanding of a literary work, exposition plays an important role in both fiction and nonfiction. In fact, many works of nonfiction are classified as expository essays because their primary purpose is to inform or educate the reader.

Look For

As you read "On the Mall," look for Didion's use of exposition. What is the main purpose of the essay? Would you classify it as an expository essay?

Writing

What sorts of impressions do you have of shopping malls? Freewrite about shopping malls, discussing the reasons for their popularity and your own thoughts concerning them.

Vocabulary

Knowing the following words will help you as you read "On the Mall."

egalitarian (i gal' ə ter' ē ən) *adj.*: Asserting, resulting from, or characterized by the belief in the equality of all people (p. 1148)

enigmatic (en' ig mat' ik) *adj.*: Perplexing; mysterious (p. 1148)

indigenous (in dij' ə nəs) *adj.*: Originating in and characterizing a particular region or country (p. 1148)

eccentric (ik sen' trik) *adj.*: Peculiar (p. 1148)

seminal (sem' ə n'l) *adj.*: Highly original and influencing the development of future events (p. 1150)

recondite (rek' ən dīt') *adj.*: Dealing with very profound, difficult, or abstruse subject matter (p. 1150)

On the Mall

Joan Didion

They float on the landscape like pyramids to the boom years, all those Plazas and Malls and Esplanades. All those Squares and Fairs. All those Towns and Dales, all those Villages, all those Forests and Parks and Lands. Stonestown. Hillsdale. Valley Fair, Mayfair, Northgate, Southgate, Eastgate, Westgate. Gulfgate. They are toy garden cities in which no one lives but everyone consumes, profound equalizers, the perfect fusion of the profit motive and the egalitarian ideal, and to hear their names is to recall words and phrases no longer quite current. Baby Boom. Consumer Explosion. Leisure Revolution. Do-It-Yourself Revolution. Backyard Revolution. Suburbia. "The Shopping Center," the Urban Land Institute could pronounce in 1957, "is today's extraordinary retail business evolvement. . . . The automobile accounts for suburbia, and suburbia accounts for the shopping center."

It was a peculiar and visionary time, those years after World War II to which all the Malls and Towns and Dales stand as climate-controlled monuments. Even the word "automobile," as in "the automobile accounts for suburbia and suburbia accounts for the shopping center," no longer carries the particular freight it once did: as a child in the late Forties in California I recall reading and believing that the "freedom of movement" afforded by the automobile was "America's fifth freedom." The trend was up. The solution was in sight. The frontier had been reinvented, and its shape was the subdivision, that new free land on which all settlers could recast their lives *tabula rasa.*[1] For one perishable moment there the American idea seemed about to achieve itself, via F.H.A.[2] housing and the acquisition of major appliances, and a certain enigmatic glamour attached to the architects of this newfound land. They made something of nothing. They gambled and sometimes lost. They staked the past to seize the future. I have difficulty now imagining a childhood in which a man named Jere Strizek, the developer of Town and Country Village outside Sacramento (143,000 square feet gross floor area, 68 stores, 1000 parking spaces, the Urban Land Institute's "prototype for centers using heavy timber and tile construction for informality"), could materialize as a role model, but I had such a childhood, just after World War II, in Sacramento. I never met or even saw Jere Strizek, but at the age of 12 I imagined him a kind of frontiersman, a romantic and revolutionary spirit, and in the indigenous grain he was.

I suppose James B. Douglas and David D. Bohannon were too.

I first heard of James B. Douglas and David D. Bohannon not when I was 12 but a dozen years later, when I was living in New York, working for *Vogue,* and taking, by correspondence, a University of California Extension course in shopping-center theory. This did not seem to me eccentric at the

1. *tabula rasa* (tab′yə lə rä′ sə): Clean slate.
2. **F.H.A.:** Federal Housing Administration.

time. I remember sitting on the cool floor in Irving Penn's studio and reading, in *The Community Builders Handbook*, advice from James B. Douglas on shopping-center financing. I recall staying late in my pale-blue office on the twentieth floor of the Graybar Building to memorize David D. Bohannon's parking ratios. My "real" life was to sit in this office and describe life as it was lived in Djakarta and Caneel Bay and in the great châteaux of the Loire Valley, but my dream life was to put together a Class-A regional shopping center with three full-line department stores as major tenants.

That I was perhaps the only person I knew in New York, let alone on the Condé Nast[3] floors of the Graybar Building, to have

memorized the distinctions among "A," "B," and "C" shopping centers did not occur to me (the defining distinction, as long as I have your attention, is that an "A," or "regional," center has as its major tenant a full-line department store which carries major appliances; a "B," or "community," center has as its major tenant a junior department store which does not carry major appliances; and a "C," or "neighborhood," center has as its major tenant only a supermarket): my interest in shopping centers was in no way casual. I did want to build them. I wanted to build them because I had fallen into the habit of writing fiction, and I had it in my head that a couple of good centers might support this habit less taxingly than a pale-blue office at *Vogue*. I had even devised an original scheme by which I planned to gain enough capital and credibility to enter the

3. Condé Nast: Company that publishes a variety of periodicals, including *Vogue* magazine.

shopping-center game: I would lease warehouses in, say, Queens, and offer Manhattan delicatessens the opportunity to sell competitively by buying cooperatively, from my trucks. I see a few wrinkles in this scheme now (the words "concrete overcoat" come to mind), but I did not then. In fact I planned to run it out of the pale-blue office.

James B. Douglas and David D. Bohannon. In 1950 James B. Douglas had opened Northgate, in Seattle, the first regional center to combine a pedestrian mall with an underground truck tunnel. In 1954 David D. Bohannon had opened Hillsdale, a forty-acre regional center on the peninsula south of San Francisco. That is the only solid bio I have on James B. Douglas and David D. Bohannon to this day, but many of their opinions are engraved on my memory. David D. Bohannon believed in preserving the integrity of the shopping center by not cutting up the site with any dedicated roads. David D. Bohannon believed that architectural setbacks in a center looked "pretty on paper" but caused "customer resistance." James B. Douglas advised that a small-loan office could prosper in a center only if it were placed away from foot traffic, since people who want small loans do not want to be observed getting them. I do not now recall whether it was James B. Douglas or David D. Bohannon or someone else altogether who passed along this hint on how to paint the lines around the parking spaces (actually this is called "striping the lot," and the spaces are "stalls"): make each space a foot wider than it need be—ten feet, say, instead of nine—when the center first opens and business is slow. By this single stroke the developer achieves a couple of important objectives, the appearance of a popular center and the illusion of easy parking, and no one will really notice when business picks up and the spaces shrink.

Nor do I recall who first solved what was once a crucial center dilemma: the placement of the major tenant vis-à-vis the parking lot. The dilemma was that the major tenant—the draw, the raison d'être[4] for the financing, the Sears, the Macy's, the May Company—wanted its customer to walk directly from car to store. The smaller tenants, on the other hand, wanted that same customer to *pass their stores* on the way from the car to, say, Macy's. The solution to this conflict of interests was actually very simple: *two major tenants*, one at each end of a mall. This is called "anchoring the mall," and represents seminal work in shopping-center theory. One thing you will note about shopping-center theory is that you could have thought of it yourself, and a course in it will go a long way toward dispelling the notion that business proceeds from mysteries too recondite for you and me.

A few aspects of shopping-center theory do in fact remain impenetrable to me. I have no idea why the Community Builders' Council ranks "Restaurant" as deserving a Number One (or "Hot Spot") location but exiles "Chinese Restaurant" to a Number Three, out there with "Power and Light Office" and "Christian Science Reading Room." Nor do I know why the Council approves of enlivening a mall with "small animals" but specifically, vehemently, and with no further explanation, excludes "monkeys." If I had a center I would have monkeys, and Chinese restaurants, and Mylar[5] kites and bands of small girls playing tambourine.

A few years ago at a party I met a woman from Detroit who told me that the Joyce Carol Oates novel with which she identified most closely was *Wonderland*.

I asked her why.

"Because," she said, "my husband has a branch there."

I did not understand.

---

4. raison d'être (rā′zōn det′rə): Justification for existence.
5. Mylar (mī′ lär): Polyester made in extremely thin sheets of great strength.

"In Wonderland the center," the woman said patiently. "My husband has a branch in Wonderland."

I have never visited Wonderland but imagine it to have bands of small girls playing tambourine.

A few facts about shopping centers.

The "biggest" center in the United States is generally agreed to be Woodfield, outside Chicago, a "super" regional or "leviathan" two-million-square-foot center with four major tenants.

The "first" shopping center in the United States is generally agreed to be Country Club Plaza in Kansas City, built in the twenties. There were some other early centers, notably Edward H. Bouton's 1907 Roland Park in Baltimore, Hugh Prather's 1931 Highland Park Shopping Village in Dallas, and Hugh Potter's 1937 River Oaks in Houston, but the developer of Country Club Plaza, the late J. C. Nichols, is referred to with ritual frequency in the literature of shopping centers, usually as "pioneering J. C. Nichols," "trailblazing J. C. Nichols," or "J. C. Nichols, father of the center as we know it."

Those are some facts I know about shopping centers because I still want to be Jere Strizek or James B. Douglas or David D. Bohannon. Here are some facts I know about shopping centers because I never will be Jere Strizek or James B. Douglas or David D. Bohannon: a good center in which to spend the day if you wake feeling low in Honolulu, Hawaii, is Ala Moana, major tenants Liberty House and Sears. A good center in which to spend the day if you wake feeling low in Ox-

nard, California, is The Esplanade, major tenants the May Company and Sears. A good center in which to spend the day if you wake feeling low in Biloxi, Mississippi, is Edgewater Plaza, major tenant Godchaux's. Ala Moana in Honolulu is larger than The Esplanade in Oxnard, and The Esplanade in Oxnard is larger than Edgewater Plaza in Biloxi. Ala Moana has carp pools. The Esplanade and Edgewater Plaza do not.

These marginal distinctions to one side, Ala Moana, The Esplanade, and Edgewater Plaza are the same place, which is precisely their role not only as equalizers but in the sedation of anxiety. In each of them one moves for a while in an aqueous suspension not only of light but of judgment, not only of judgment but of "personality." One meets no acquaintances at The Esplanade. One gets no telephone calls at Edgewater Plaza. "It's a hard place to run in to for a pair of stockings," a friend complained to me recently of Ala Moana, and I knew that she was not yet ready to surrender her ego to the idea of the center. The last time I went to Ala Moana it was to buy *The New York Times*. Because *The New York Times* was not in, I sat on the mall for a while and ate caramel corn. In the end I bought not *The New York Times* at all but two straw hats at Liberty House, four bottles of nail enamel at Woolworth's, and a toaster, on sale at Sears. In the literature of shopping centers these would be described as impulse purchases, but the impulse here was obscure. I do not wear hats, nor do I like caramel corn. I do not use nail enamel. Yet flying back across the Pacific I regretted only the toaster.

THINKING ABOUT THE SELECTION

Recalling

1. (a) When she was a young girl, what did Didion believe to be "America's fifth freedom"? (b) What impression did she have of Jere Stizek, the developer of Town and Country Village?
2. (a) Why did Didion dream of building shopping centers while she was working at *Vogue*? (b) What scheme did she devise by which she would "gain enough capital and credibility to enter the shopping-center game"?
3. (a) What theory does Didion present concerning the width of parking spaces? (b) What theory does she present concerning the placement of major tenants? (c) What is this theory called?
4. What aspects of shopping-center theory "remain impenetrable" to Didion?
5. What encounter with a woman from Detroit does Didion describe?
6. (a) What did Didion purchase the last time she visited the Ala Moana in Hawaii? (b) What did she find unusual about these purchases?

Interpreting

7. (a) What does Didion mean when she describes shopping malls as "pyramids to the boom years"? (b) In what sense are the malls "profound equalizers"?
8. What does Didion's description of her encounter with the woman from Detroit imply about the priorities of the American public?
9. (a) What seems to be Didion's current attitude concerning her earlier dreams of building shopping centers? (b) What seems to be her current attitude toward shopping malls and shopping-center theory? (c) How are these attitudes conveyed?
10. What point does Didion's essay make concerning the role of shopping centers in American society?

Applying

11. Compare your own attitude toward shopping malls with Didion's current attitude.

ANALYZING LITERATURE

Understanding Exposition

Exposition is writing in which factual information is presented. For example, in the fifth paragraph of "On the Mall," Didion presents a series of facts concerning the "distinctions among 'A,' 'B,' and 'C' shopping centers."

1. What are the distinctions among "A," "B," and "C" shopping centers?
2. Find three more examples of factual information in Didion's essay.
3. Should this essay be classified as an expository essay? Why or why not?

CRITICAL THINKING AND READING

Separating Facts from Opinions

Didion's essay contains both facts and opinions. A **fact** is an objective statement that can be verified, or proved to be true. For example, Didion presents a fact when she writes, "Woodfield Mall, outside Chicago, is a two-million-square-foot center." In contrast, an **opinion** is a subjective statement that cannot be verified. For example, Didion states an opinion when she refers to the years immediately following World War II as a "peculiar and visionary time."

1. Find three more statements of fact presented in Didion's essay.
2. Find three more opinions presented in the essay.

THINKING AND WRITING

Writing About a Writer's Attitudes

Write an essay in which you discuss the attitudes that Didion conveys about shopping malls, shopping-center theory, and the role of shopping malls in American society. Reread the essay, focusing on Didion's attitudes and noting how these attitudes are conveyed. Prepare a thesis statement. Then write your essay, using passages from the Didion's essay to support your thesis. When you revise, make sure you have varied the length and structure of your sentences.

N. SCOTT MOMADAY

1934–

Proud of his Native American heritage, N. Scott Momaday has devoted his life to teaching and writing about Native American history, folklore, and mythology.

A Kiowa Indian, Momaday was born in Lawton, Oklahoma. After graduating from the University of New Mexico, he received a doctorate in literature from Stanford University. His first novel, *House Made of Dawn* (1969), an account of a young Indian torn between his ancestral roots and contemporary mainstream society, earned him a Pulitzer Prize. He then published what has become his best-known work, *The Way to Rainy Mountain* (1969), a collection of personal anecdotes and retellings of Kiowa myths and legends. Since then, he has produced several more books, including two volumes of poetry, *Angle of Geese and Other Poems* (1973) and *The Gourd Dancer* (1976), and a collection of anecdotes entitled *The Names* (1976).

Like Momaday's other works, "A Vision Beyond Time and Place" helps provide the reader with a better understanding of traditional Native American culture. In the essay Momaday recalls and discusses the significance of an old tribe member's daily prayers to the rising sun.

GUIDE FOR READING

A Vision Beyond Time and Place

**Writer's
Techniques**

Classification. Classification refers to the process of dividing a subject into categories, or classes. In nonfiction, writers sometimes use classification to clarify the meaning of an idea or concept that may otherwise be difficult to grasp. For example, in "A Vision Beyond Time and Place," N. Scott Momaday uses classification to help define a specific type of "vision" with which most Americans are likely to be unfamiliar.

Look For

As you read "A Vision Beyond Time and Place," look for Momaday's use of classification. How does his use of the technique help clarify the significance of a traditional Native American vision quest?

Writing

Discuss the different ways in which people view the world. Why do you think people from different cultures sometimes view the same thing in completely different ways? Why is it important for different cultures to share their views? How can this contribute to their abilities to understand one another?

Vocabulary

Knowing the following words will help you as you read "A Vision Beyond Time and Place."

luminous (loo' mə nəs) *adj.*: Shining (p. 1156)

impalpable (im pal' pə b'l) *adj.*: Imperceptible to the sense of touch (p. 1156)

reverence (rev' ər əns) *n.*: A feeling or attitude of deep respect, love, or awe (p. 1156)

evanescence (ev'ə nes' 'ns) *n.*: A fading from sight (p. 1158)

quintessentially (kwin' tə sen' shə lē) *adv.*: Purely (p. 1158)

A Vision Beyond Time and Place

N. Scott Momaday

When my father was a boy, an old man used to come to [my grandfather] Mammedaty's house and pay his respects. He was a lean old man in braids and was impressive in his age and bearing. His name was Cheney, and he was an arrowmaker. Every morning, my father tells me, Cheney would paint his wrinkled face, go out, and pray aloud to the rising sun. In my mind I can see that man as if he were there now. I like to watch him as he makes his prayer. I know where he stands and where his voice goes on the rolling grasses and where the sun comes up on the land. There, at dawn, you can feel the silence. It is cold and clear and deep like water. It takes hold of you and will not let you go.[1]

I often think of old man Cheney, and of his daily devotion to the sun. He died before I was born, and I never knew where he came from or what of good and bad entered into his life. But I think I know who he was, essentially, and what his view of the world meant to him and to me. He was a man who saw very deeply into the distance, I believe, one whose vision extended far beyond the physical boundaries of his time and place. He perceived the wonder and meaning of Creation itself. In his mind's eye he could integrate all the realities and illusions of the earth and sky; they became for him profoundly intelligible and whole.

Once, in the first light, I stood where Cheney had stood, next to the house which my grandfather Mammedaty had built on a rise of land near Rainy Mountain Creek, and watched the sun come out of the black horizon of the world. It was an irresistible and awesome emergence, as waters gather to the flood, of weather and of light. I could not have been more sensitive to the cold, nor than to the heat which came upon it. And I could not have *foreseen* the break of day. The shadows on the rolling plains became large and luminous in a moment, impalpable, then faceted, dark and distinct again as they were run through with splinters of light. And the sun itself, when it appeared, was pale and immense, original in the deepest sense of the word. It is no wonder, I thought, that an old man should pray to it. It is no wonder . . . and yet, of course, wonder is the principal part of such a vision. Cheney's prayer was an affirmation of his wonder and regard, a testament to the realization of a quest for vision.

This native vision, this gift of seeing truly, with wonder and delight, into the natural world, is informed by a certain attitude of reverence and self-respect. It is a matter of extrasensory as well as sensory perception, I believe. In addition to the eye, it involves the intelligence, the instinct, and the imagination. It is the perception not only of objects

---

1. When my father . . . let you go: From N. Scott Momaday's *The Way to Rainy Mountain.*

THE MEDICINE ROBE
Maynard Dixon
Courtesy of The Buffalo Historical Center, Cody, Wyoming

PAUL THEROUX

1941–

An enthusiastic traveler, Paul Theroux has spent much of his life abroad. Possessing a keen eye for detail, he has used many of the exotic places he has visited as settings for his fiction and nonfiction.

Born in Massachusetts, Theroux has worked as a teacher in Singapore, Uganda, Italy, and the African nation of Malawi. He has written numerous essays, several volumes of short stories, and a number of novels. Included among his novels are *Girls at Play* (1969), a satirical account of schoolteachers in Kenya, and *The Mosquito Coast* (1982), the story of an American family that moves to the jungles of Honduras.

Through his travels Theroux has developed a deep awareness of the sharp cultural differences between Third World and industrialized cultures. This awareness is evident in "The Edge of a Great Rift," an essay based on an experience he had while living in the African nation of Nyasaland.

The Edge of the Great Rift

Writer's Techniques

Description. Description is writing that creates an image of a person, place, or thing in the reader's mind. To create a mental image, a writer uses sensory details—details that appeal to one or more of the five senses. For example, Theroux uses details that appeal to the sense of sight and the sense of touch in the following description of Nyasaland at noon: "there are no clouds and the heat is like a blazing rug thrown over everything."

Look For

As you read "The Edge of the Great Rift," look for Theroux's descriptions of Nyasaland. To what senses do the sensory details in the essay appeal? How does Theroux create a vivid picture of the edge of the great rift?

Writing

What types of images come to mind when you think of Africa? Freewrite about your impressions of Africa and discuss the sources of your impressions.

Vocabulary

Knowing the following words will help you as you read "The Edge of the Great Rift."

escarpments (e skärp′ mənts) *n.*: Steep slopes (p. 1162)
vulcanism (vul′ kə niz′m) *n.*: The series of phenomena connected with the origin and movement of molten rock (p. 1162)

stratosphere (strat′ ə sfir′) *n.*: A portion of the upper atmosphere (p. 1162)
luminescent (loo′ mə nes′′nt) *adj.*: Shining (p. 1162)

The Edge of the Great Rift

Paul Theroux

September 1, 1964. There is a crack in the earth which extends from the Sea of Galilee[1] to the coast of Mozambique,[2] and I am living on the edge of it, in Nyasaland.[3] This crack is the Great Rift Valley.[4] It seems to be swallowing most of East Africa. In Nyasaland it is replacing the fishing villages, the flowers, and the anthills with a nearly bottomless lake, and it shows itself in rough escarpments and troughs up and down this huge continent. It is thought that this valley was torn amid great volcanic activity. The period of vulcanism has not ended in Africa. It shows itself not only in the Great Rift Valley itself, but in the people, burning, the lava of masses, the turbulence of the humans themselves who live in the Great Rift.

My schoolroom is on the Great Rift, and in this schoolroom there is a line of children, heads shaved like prisoners, muscles showing through their rags. They are waiting to peer through the tiny lens of a cheap microscope so they can see the cells in a flower petal.

Later they will ask, "Is fire alive? Is water?"

The children appear in the morning out of the slowly drifting hoops of fog-wisp. It is chilly, almost cold. There is no visibility at six in the morning; only a fierce white-out where earth is the patch of dirt under their bare feet, a platform, and the sky is everything else. It becomes Africa at noon when there are no clouds and the heat is like a blazing rug thrown over everything to suffocate and scorch.

In the afternoon there are clouds, big ones, like war declared in the stratosphere. It starts to get gray as the children leave the school and begin padding down the dirt road.

There is a hill near the school. The sun approaches it by sneaking behind the clouds until it emerges to crash into the hill and explode yellow and pink, to paint everything in its violent fire.

At night, if there is a moon, the school, the Great Rift, become a seascape of luminescent trees and grass, whispering, silver. If there is no moon you walk from a lighted house to an infinity of space, packed with darkness.

Yesterday I ducked out of a heavy downpour and waited in a small shed for the rain to let up. The rain was far too heavy for my spidery umbrella. I waited in the shed; thunder and close bursts of lightning charged all around me; the rain spat through the palm-leaf walls of the shed.

Down the road I spotted a small African child. I could not tell whether it was a boy or a girl, since it was wearing a long shirt, a yellow one, which drooped sodden to the

---

1. Sea of Galilee (gal′ə lē′): Lake in northeastern Israel, bordering on Syria.
2. Mozambique (mō′ zəm bēk′): Country in southeastern Africa.
3. Nyasaland (nyä′ sä land′): Former name of Malawi, a country in southeastern Africa, next to Mozambique.
4. Great Rift Valley: A series of valleys extending through eastern Africa and part of southwestern Asia.

ground. The child was carrying nothing, so I assumed it was a boy.

He dashed in and out of the puddles, hopping from side to side of the forest path, his yellow shirt bulging as he twisted under it. When he came closer I could see the look of absolute fear on his face. His only defense against the thunder and the smacking of rain were his fingers stuck firmly into his ears. He held them there as he ran.

He ran into my shed, but when he saw me he shivered into a corner where he stood shuddering under his soaked shirt. We eyed each other. There were raindrops beaded on his face. I leaned on my umbrella and fumbled a Bantu[5] greeting. He moved against a

_____

5. Bantu (ban' tōō): A group of African tribes and the languages spoken by those tribes.

palm leaf. After a few moments he reinserted a finger in each ear, carefully, one at a time. Then he darted out into the rain and thunder. And his dancing yellow shirt disappeared.

I stand on the grassy edge of the Great Rift. I feel it under me and I expect soon a mighty heave to send us all sprawling. The Great Rift. And whom does this rift concern? Is it perhaps a rift with the stars? Is it between earth and man, or man and man? Is there something under this African ground seething still?

We like to believe that we are riding it and that it is nothing more than an imperfection in the crust of the earth. We do not want to be captive to this rift, as if we barely belong, as if we were scrawled on the landscape by a piece of chalk.

THINKING ABOUT THE SELECTION
Recalling

1. According to Theroux, what does the Great Rift Valley seem to be doing?
2. (a) Why does Theroux assume that the child he spots during the rainstorm is a boy? (b) How does the child react when he sees Theroux?

Interpreting

3. What overall impression does Theroux's essay convey of the physical appearance of Nyasaland?
4. (a) What do the student's questions suggest about their cultural beliefs? (b) How do their studies contrast with these beliefs?
5. In this essay Theroux uses the Great Rift to symbolize, or represent, the wide cultural gap between people from industrialized and Third World societies. In what sense are Third World cultures being swallowed up?

Applying

6. People from industrialized nations have often tried to change the beliefs of people from Third World countries. Considering the evidence in this essay, do you imagine that Theroux tried to change his students' beliefs when he worked as a teacher in Nyasaland? Why or why not?

THINKING AND WRITING
Writing a Description

Write a description of a place you have been to that you found especially interesting. Prepare a list of sensory details describing this place. Arrange these details in a logical order. Then write your description, trying to convey your overall impression of the place to readers. When you finish writing, revise your description and share it with your classmates.

BARRY LOPEZ

1945–

Although he also writes fiction, Barry Lopez is known mainly for his nonfiction works about nature and the environment. Written in a vivid, poetic style, his works explore certain aspects of nature from a variety of perspectives, creating a well-rounded view that both informs and entertains readers.

Born in Port Chester, New York, Lopez was educated at the University of Notre Dame and the University of Oregon. In 1976 he published his first book, *Desert Notes: Reflections in the Eye of a Raven,* a collection of fictional narratives. Since then he has produced several additional books and has contributed articles, essays, and short fiction to many major magazines. His most successful work, *Of Wolves and Men* (1978), a nonfiction work examining the relationships between wolves and men and between wolves and other animals, was praised by critics and earned Lopez a number of awards.

Filled with clear, descriptive language, the following excerpt from *Arctic Dreams* paints a vivid portrait of the Arctic wilderness, while examining the reasons why so many people have been drawn to this dangerous, threatening region.

GUIDE FOR READING

from Arctic Dreams

Imagery. Lopez's writing has been described as poetic, because it is filled with vivid imagery—words or phrases that create mental pictures, or images, that appeal to one or more of the five senses. While most of Lopez's images appeal to the sense of sight, he also uses some images that cannot be visualized, and some that appeal to more than one sense. For example, he creates an image that appeals to both the sense of sight and the sense of touch when he writes, "the late-night sun, small as a kite in the northern sky, poured forth an energy that burned against my cheekbones".

In *Arctic Dreams* Lopez uses imagery to create a clear, lasting impression of the Arctic wilderness—an impression that helps enlighten readers about the reasons why people are drawn to the Arctic wilderness.

As you read "Arctic Dreams," look for Lopez's use of imagery. What overall impression do the images convey?

What are your impressions of the Arctic wilderness? Freewrite about the physical appearance of the Arctic wilderness, the types of animals that inhabit it, and the dangers it poses to people who venture into it.

Knowing the following words will help you as you read the excerpt from *Arctic Dreams*.

feigning (fān′ iŋ) *v.*: Making a false show of (p. 1166)

fecundity (fi kun′ də tē) *n.*: Productivity (p. 1166)

congenial (kən jēn′ yəl) *adj.*: Friendly; sympathetic (p. 1168)

implacable (im plak′ ə b'l) *adj.*: Relentless (p. 1168)

gracile (gras′′l) *adj.*: Slender; slim (p. 1169)

magnanimous (mag nan′ ə

məs) *adj.*: Noble in mind; rising above pettiness and meanness (p. 1172)

anomalous (ə näm′ ə ləs) *adj.*: Deviating from the regular arrangement, general rule, or usual method (p. 1172)

adumbration (ad′ um brā′ shən) *n.*: Shadowy outline (p. 1172)

from Arctic Dreams

Barry Lopez

One summer evening I was camped in the western Brooks Range of Alaska with a friend. From the ridge where we had pitched our tent we looked out over tens of square miles of rolling tundra along the southern edge of the calving grounds of the Western Arctic caribou herd. During those days we observed not only caribou and wolves, which we'd come to study, but wolverine and red fox, ground squirrels, delicate-legged whimbrels and aggressive jaegers, all in the unfoldings of their obscure lives. One night we watched in awe as a young grizzly bear tried repeatedly to force its way past a yearling wolf standing guard alone before a den of young pups. The bear eventually gave up and went on its way. We watched snowy owls and rough-legged hawks hunt and caribou drift like smoke through the valley.

On the evening I am thinking about—it was breezy there on Ilingnorak Ridge, and cold; but the late-night sun, small as a kite in the northern sky, poured forth an energy that burned against my cheekbones—it was on that evening that I went on a walk for the first time among the tundra birds. They all build their nests on the ground, so their vulnerability is extreme. I gazed down at a single horned lark no bigger than my fist. She stared back resolute as iron. As I approached, golden plovers abandoned their nests in hysterical ploys, artfully feigning a broken wing to distract me from the woven grass cups that couched their pale, darkly speckled eggs. Their eggs glowed with a soft, pure light, like the window light in a Vermeer[1] painting. I marveled at this intense and concentrated beauty on the vast table of the plain. I walked on to find Lapland longspurs as still on their nests as stones, their dark eyes gleaming. At the nest of two snowy owls I stopped. These are more formidable animals than plovers. I stood motionless. The wild glare in their eyes receded. One owl settled back slowly over its three eggs, with an aura of primitive alertness. The other watched me, and immediately sought a bond with my eyes if I started to move.

I took to bowing on these evening walks. I would bow slightly with my hands in my pockets, toward the birds and the evidence of life in their nests—because of their fecundity, unexpected in this remote region, and because of the serene arctic light that came down over the land like breath, like breathing.

I remember the wild, dedicated lives of the birds that night and also the abandon with which a small herd of caribou crossed the Kokolik River to the northwest, the incident of only a few moments. They pranced through like wild mares, kicking up sheets of water across the evening sun and shaking it off on the far side like huge dogs, a bloom of spray that glittered in the air around them like grains of mica.

I remember the press of light against my face. The explosive skitter of calves among grazing caribou. And the warm intensity of

---

1. Vermeer (vər mér'): Dutch painter Jan Vermeer (1632–1675).

the eggs beneath these resolute birds. Until then, perhaps because the sun was shining in the very middle of the night, so out of tune with my own customary perception, I had never known how benign sunlight could be. How forgiving. How run through with compassion in a land that bore so eloquently the evidence of centuries of winter.

During those summer days on Iling-norak Ridge there was no dark night. Darkness never came. The birds were born. They flourished, and then flew south in the wake of the caribou.

The second incident is more fleeting. It occurred one night when I was being driven past a graveyard in Kalamazoo, Michigan. Among the gravestones was one marking the burial place of Edward Israel, a shy young man who sailed north in 1881 with Lieuten-

ant Adolphus Greely. Greely and his men established a base camp on Ellesmere Island, 450 miles from the North Pole, and explored the surrounding territory in the spring of 1882. A planned relief expedition failed to reach them that summer, and also failed again the next year. Desperate, Greely's party of twenty-five retreated south, hopeful of being met by a rescue party in 1884. They wintered at Cape Sabine, Ellesmere Island, where sixteen of them died of starvation and scurvy,[2] another committed suicide, and one man was executed for stealing food. Israel, the expedition's astronomer, died on May 27, 1884, three weeks before the others were

---

2. scurvy (skur' vē) n.: A disease caused by vitamin-C deficiency.

rescued. The survivors remembered him as the most congenial person among them.

I remember looking out the back window of the car that evening and seeing Israel's grave in the falling light. What had this man hoped to find? What sort of place did he think lay out there before him on that bright June morning in 1881 when the *Proteus* slipped its moorings at Saint John's, Newfoundland?

No one is able to say, of course. He was drawn on by the fixations of his own imagination, as were John Davis and William Baffin before him and as Robert Peary and Vilhjalmur Stefansson[3] would be after him. Perhaps he intended to make his mark as a scientist, to set his teeth in that high arctic landscape and come home like Darwin[4] to a sedate and contemplative life, in the farmlands of southern Michigan. Perhaps he merely hungered after the unusual. We can only imagine that he desired something, the fulfillment of some personal and private dream, to which he pinned his life.

Israel was buried with great public feeling and patriotic rhetoric. His gravestone reads

IN LIFE A TRUE CHILD OF GOD

IN DEATH A HERO

These two incidents came back to me often in the four or five years that I traveled in the Arctic. The one, timeless and full of light, reminded me of sublime innocence, of the innate beauty of undisturbed relationships. The other, a dream gone awry, reminded me of the long human struggle, mental and physical, to come to terms with the Far North. As I traveled, I came to believe that people's desires and aspirations were as much a part of the land as the wind, solitary animals, and the bright fields of stone and tundra. And, too, that the land itself existed quite apart from these.

The physical landscape is baffling in its ability to transcend whatever we would make of it. It is as subtle in its expression as turns of the mind, and larger than our grasp; and yet it is still knowable. The mind, full of curiosity and analysis, disassembles a landscape and then reassembles the pieces—the nod of a flower, the color of the night sky, the murmur of an animal—trying to fathom its geography. At the same time the mind is trying to find its place within the land, to discover a way to dispel its own sense of estrangement.

The particular section of the Arctic I became concerned with extends from Bering Strait in the west to Davis Strait[5] in the east. It includes great, unrelieved stretches of snow and ice that in summer become plains of open water and an ocean that is the tundra, a tawny island beneath the sky. But there are, too, surprising and riveting sights: Wilberforce Falls on the Hood River suddenly tumbles 160 feet into a wild canyon in the midst of the Canadian tundra, and its roar can be heard for miles. Humboldt Glacier, a towering, 50-mile-long sea margin of the Greenland ice sheet, calves[6] icebergs into Kane Basin with gargantuan and implacable force. The badlands of east-central Melville Island, an eroded country of desert oranges, of muted yellows and reds, reminds a traveler of canyons and arroyos in southern Utah. And there are places more exotic, like the Ruggles River, which flows out of Lake Hazen on Ellesmere Island in winter and runs 2000 feet through the Stygian[7] darkness, wreathed in frost smoke, before it disappears underneath its own ice. South of Cape Bathurst and west of the

---

3. John Davis . . . Vilhjalmur Stefansson: Arctic explorers.
4. Darwin: Charles Darwin (1809–1882), an English naturalist who formulated the theory of evolution.

5. Bering Strait . . . Davis Strait: The Bering Strait separates Siberia and Alaska. The Davis Strait separates Greenland and Baffin Island, Canada.
6. calves *v*.: Releases.
7. Stygian (stij′ ē ən) *adj*.: Characteristic of the river Styx, the river encircling Hades, the land of the dead, in Greek mythology.

Horton River in the Northwest Territories, bituminous shale fires that have been burning underground for hundreds of years make those coastal hills seem like a vast, smoldering heap of industrial slag. South of the central Kobuk River, one hundred foot dunes rise above hundreds of square miles of shifting sand. In East Greenland lies an arctic oasis called Queen Louisa Land, a valley of wild grasses and summer wildflowers surrounded by the walls of the Greenland ice cap.

The Arctic, overall, has the classic lines of a desert landscape: spare, balanced, extended, and quiet. In the Queen Elizabeth Islands the well-drained tundra plains and low-lying bogs more familiar in the south give way to expanses of weathered rock and gravel, and the illusion of a desert is even more complete. On Baffin and Ellesmere islands and in northern Alaska, sharply pitched arctic mountain ranges, which retain their remoteness even as you stand within them, complete a pervasive suggestion of austerity. The apparent monotony of the land is relieved, however, by weather systems moving through, and by the activities of animals, particularly of birds and caribou. And because so much of the country stands revealed, and because sunlight passing through the dustless air renders its edges with such unusual sharpness, animals linger before the eye. And their presence is vivid.

Like other landscapes that initially appear barren, arctic tundra can open suddenly, like the corolla of a flower, when any intimacy with it is sought. One begins to notice spots of brilliant red, orange, and green, for example, among the monotonic browns of a tundra tussock. A wolf spider lunges at a glistening beetle. A shred of muskox wool lies inert in the lavender blooms of a saxifrage. When Alwin Pederson, a Danish naturalist, first arrived on the northeast coast of Greenland, he wrote, "I must admit to strange feelings at the sight of this godforsaken desert of stone." Before he left, however, he was writing of muskoxen grazing in

lush grass that grew higher than the animals' heads in Jameson Land, and of the stark beauty of nunataks, the ice-free spires of rock that pierce the Pleistocene[8] stillness of the Greenland ice cap. I, like Pederson, when stooping to pick up the gracile rib bone of an arctic hare, would catch sudden and unexpected sight of the silken cocoon of an arctic caterpillar.

The wealth of biological detail on the tundra dispels any feeling that the land is empty; and its likeness to a stage suggests impending events. On a summer walk, the wind-washed air proves depthlessly clear. Time and again you come upon the isolated and succinct evidence of life—animal tracks, the undigested remains of a ptarmigan in an owl's casting, a patch of barren-ground willow nibbled nearly leafless by arctic hares. You are afforded the companionship of birds, which follow after you. (They know you are an animal; sooner or later you will turn up something to eat.) Sandpipers scatter before you, screaming *tuituek*, an Eskimo name for them. Coming awkwardly down a scree[9] slope of frost-riven limestone you make a glass-tinkling clatter—and at a distance a tundra grizzly rises on its hind legs to study you; the dish-shaped paws of its front legs deathly still, the stance so human it is unnerving.

Along creek washouts, in the western Arctic especially, you might stumble upon a mammoth tusk. Or in the eastern Arctic find undisturbed the ring of stones used by a hunter 1500 years ago to hold down the edge of his skin tent. These old Dorset camps, located along the coasts where arctic people have been traveling for four millennia, are poignant with their suggestion of the timeless determination of mankind. On rare occasions a traveler might come upon the more

---

8. Pleistocene (plīst′ tə sēn): A geological era characterized by the spreading and recession of continental ice sheets and the appearance of modern man.

9. scree (skrē) *adj*.: A covering of rock fragments on a slope below a rock face.

imposing stone foundations of a large house abandoned by Thule-culture[10] people in the twelfth century. (The cold, dry arctic air might have preserved, even down to its odor, the remains of a ringed seal killed and eaten by them 800 years ago.) More often, one comes upon the remains of a twentieth-century camp, artifacts far less engaging than a scrap of worked caribou bone, or carved wood, or skewered hide at a Dorset or Thule site. But these artifacts disintegrate just as slowly—red tins of Prince Albert brand crimp-cut tobacco, cans of Pet evaporated milk and Log Cabin maple syrup. In the most recent camps one finds used flashlight batteries in clusters like animal droppings, and a bewildering variety of spent rifle and shotgun ammunition.

You raise your eyes from these remains, from whatever century, to look away. The land as far as you can see is rung with a harmonious authority, the enduring force of its natural history, of which these camps are so much a part. But the most recent evidence is vaguely disturbing. It does not derive in any clear way from the land. Its claim to being part of the natural history of the region seems, somehow, false.

It is hard to travel in the Arctic today and not be struck by the evidence of recent change. What is found at modern campsites along the coast points to the sudden arrival of a foreign technology—new tools and a new way of life for the local people. The initial adjustments to this were fairly simple; the rate of change, however, has continued to accelerate. Now the adjustments required are bewildering. And the new tools bring with them ever more complicated sets of beliefs. The native culture, from Saint Lawrence Island to Greenland, is today in a state of rapid economic reorganization and of internally disruptive social readjustment. In a recent article about the residents of Nunivak

Island, for example, a scientist wrote that the dietary shift from wild to store-bought foods (with the many nutritional and social complications involved) is proceeding so quickly it is impossible to pin down. "By the time this paper appears in print," he wrote, "much of the information in it will be of historical value only."

Industrial changes have also come to the Arctic, following the discovery of oil at Prudhoe Bay, Alaska, in 1968; the 800-mile-long trans-Alaska pipeline itself, with its recent Kuparuk extension; base camps for oil exploration on Canada's Melville Island and Tuktoyaktuk Peninsula; huge lead-zinc mining operations on northern Baffin and Little Cornwallis islands; hundreds of miles of new roads; and increased ship, air, and truck traffic. The region's normally violent and unpredictable weather, its extreme cold and long periods of darkness, the great distance to supply depots, and the problem of stabilizing permanent structures over permafrost (which melts and shifts in erratic ways) have made the cost of these operations astronomical—indeed, in Canada they could not even be contemplated without massive assistance from the federal government.

Seen as widely separated dots and lines on a map, these recent, radical changes do not appear to amount to very much. But their rippling effect in the settlements and villages of the North—their economic, psychological, and social impact—is acute. And their success, though marginal and in some instances artificial, encourages additional schemes for development. Of special concern to local residents is a growing concentration of power in the hands of people with enormous economic resources but a poorly developed geographic sense of the region. A man from Tuktoyaktuk, a village near the mouth of the Mackenzie River, told me a pointed story. In the 1950's he traveled regularly up and down the coast by dogsled. When a distant early warning (DEW) line radar station went up along his accustomed route, he decided to stop to see what it was. The military

---

10. Thule (thoo′ lē) **culture:** An ancient culture that inhabited the northernmost regions of the world.

men welcomed him not as a resident of the region but as a figure of arctic fable. They enthusiastically fed his dogs a stack of raw steaks. Each time the man came, they pounded him on the back and fed his dogs piles of steak. Their largess seemed so odd and his rapport with them so unrealistic he stopped coming. For months afterward, however, he had tremendous difficulty controlling the dogs anytime they passed near the place.

Passing through the villages, even traveling across the uninhabited land, one cannot miss the evidence of upheaval, nor avoid being wrenched by it. The depression it engenders, because so much of it seems a heedless imposition on the land and on the people, a rude invasion, can lead one to despair. I brooded, like any traveler, over these things; but the presence of the land, the sheer weight of it before the senses, more often drew me away from the contemporary is-

sues. What, I wondered, had compelled me to bow to a horned lark? How do people imagine the landscapes they find themselves in? How does the land shape the imaginations of the people who dwell in it? How does desire itself, the desire to comprehend, shape knowledge? These questions seemed to me to go deeper than the topical issues, to underlie any consideration of them.

In pursuit of answers I traveled with people of differing dispositions. With Eskimos hunting narwhals off northern Baffin Island and walruses in the Bering Sea. With marine ecologists on hundreds of miles of coastal and near-shore surveys. With landscape painters in the Canadian Archipelago. In the company of roughnecks, drilling for oil on the winter ice in high winds at −30°F; and with the cosmopolitan crew of a freighter, sailing up the west coast of Greenland and into the Northwest Passage. They each assessed the land differently—the apparent emptiness of the tundra, which ran out like a shimmering mirage in the Northern Ocean; the blue-black vault of the winter sky, a cold beauty alive with scintillating stars; a herd of muskoxen, pivoting together on a hilltop to make a defensive stand, their long guard hairs swirling around them like a single, huge wave of dark water; a vein of lead-zinc ore glinting like tiny mirrors in a damp, Mesozoic[11] wall beneath the surface of Little Cornwallis Island; the moaning and wailing in the winter sea ice as the ocean's crust warped and shattered in the crystalline air. All of it, all that the land is and evokes, its actual meaning as well as its metaphorical reverberation, was and is understood differently.

These different views make a human future in that northern landscape a matter of conjecture, and it is here that one encounters dreams, projections of hope. The individual's dream, whether it be so private a wish as that the joyful determination of nesting arctic birds might infuse a distant friend weary of life, or a magnanimous wish, that a piece of scientific information wrested from the landscape might serve one's community—in individual dreams is the hope that one's own life will not have been lived for nothing. The very much larger dream, that of a people, is a story we have been carrying with us for millennia. It is a narrative of determination and hope that follows a

question: What will we do as the wisdom of our past bears down on our future? It is a story of ageless conversation, not only conversation among ourselves about what we mean and wish to do, but a conversation held with the land—our contemplation and wonder at a prairie thunderstorm, or before the jagged line of a young mountain, or at the sudden rise of ducks from an isolated lake. We have been telling ourselves the story of what *we* represent in the land for 40,000 years. At the heart of this story, I think, is a simple, abiding belief: it is possible to live wisely on the land, and to live well. And in behaving respectfully toward all that the land contains, it is possible to imagine a stifling ignorance falling away from us.

Crossing the tree line to the Far North, one leaves behind the boreal owl clutching its frozen prey to its chest feathers to thaw it. Ahead lies an open, wild landscape, pointed off on the maps with arresting and anomalous names: Brother John Glacier and Cape White Handkerchief. Navy Board Inlet, Teddy Bear Island, and the Zebra Cliffs. Dexterity Fiord, Saint Patrick Canyon, Starvation Cove. Eskimos hunt the ringed seal, still, in the broad bays of the Sons of the Clergy and Royal Astronomical Society islands.

This is a land where airplanes track icebergs the size of Cleveland and polar bears fly down out of the stars. It is a region, like the desert, rich with metaphor, with adumbration. In a simple bow from the waist before the nest of the horned lark, you are able to stake your life, again, in what you dream.

---

11. Mesozoic (mes′ ə zō′ik) *adj.*: A geological era characterized by the development and extinction of dinosaurs.

THINKING ABOUT THE SELECTION

Recalling

1. (a) What two incidents does Lopez recount in the first several paragraphs? (b) Of what do these two incidents remind Lopez?
2. What is the particular section of the Arctic with which Lopez became concerned?
3. (a) By what is the monotony of the Arctic land "relieved"? (b) What "dispels any feeling that" the Arctic land is "empty"?
4. (a) What "industrial changes" have come to the Arctic since the discovery of oil in 1968? (b) What has become a "special concern" for local residents?
5. What makes "a human future" in the Arctic "a matter of conjecture"?

Interpreting

6. What do the two incidents Lopez recounts in the first several paragraphs reveal about the relationship between man and nature in the Arctic?
7. Although the people who come to the Arctic perceive the landscape in a variety of ways, Lopez argues that they all share a common vision. What is this vision?
8. (a) What is the main point of this essay? (b) How is the title related to the main point?

Applying

9. What other types of dangerous, threatening environments have explorers ventured into during the course of history?

ANALYZING LITERATURE

Using Imagery

Imagery refers to words or phrases that create mental pictures, or images, that appeal to one or more of the five senses. Although most of the imagery in *Arctic Dreams* appeals to the sense of sight, Lopez also uses some images that cannot be visualized and others that appeal to more than one sense.

1. Find five images that appeal to the sense of sight.
2. Find two images that appeal to one of the other senses.
3. Find two images that appeal to more than one sense.

CRITICAL THINKING AND READING

Appreciating the Effect of Imagery

Through the use of imagery, Lopez creates a vivid impression of the Arctic wilderness in his essay. This impression helps provide readers with an understanding of peoples' desires to venture into this dangerous and unforgiving region.

1. What is the dominant impression of the Arctic wilderness that Lopez conveys?
2. How does this impression relate to the main point of the essay?

THINKING AND WRITING

Responding to Criticism

A critic has commented that "A poet slips quietly out of Mr. Lopez's matter-of-fact prose, like an eye on a long nerve-string, to dance and feel." Write a brief essay in which you discuss this comment in relation to the excerpt from *Arctic Dreams*. Reread the essay, focusing on Lopez's use of language. Prepare a thesis statement. Then write your essay, using passages from *Arctic Dreams* to support your thesis. When you revise, make sure you have not included any unnecessary information.

JOHN McPHEE

1931–

John McPhee is known for his detailed journalistic essays on a wide variety of subjects. In these essays he displays an ability to present a vast amount of information in an organized, unhurried, and interesting manner.

Born and raised in New Jersey, McPhee graduated from Princeton University and studied for a year at Cambridge University in England. After working for *Time* magazine for several years, McPhee became a staff writer for *The New Yorker* in 1964. Given the freedom to explore subjects of his own choice, without the pressure of deadlines, McPhee has remained with the magazine for more than two decades. In addition to publishing his essays in *The New Yorker,* McPhee has written many books, including *Oranges* (1967), *The Pine Barrens* (1968), *Confrontations with the Archdruid* (1971), *The Deltoid Pumpkin Seed* (1973), *Coming into the Country* (1977), *Basin in Range* (1981), *In Suspect Terrain* (1983), and *Rising from the Plains* (1985).

In the following excerpt from *Rising from the Plains,* McPhee recounts the experiences of geologist David Love, who grew up on his family's ranch in Wyoming, using the polished, engaging writing style that has helped to earn him a reputation as one of the finest essayists in America today.

GUIDE FOR READING

from Rising from the Plains

Writer's Techniques

Setting. The setting is the time and place in which the events in a literary work occur. In nonfiction, writers sometimes focus on capturing the flavor of life in a specific setting and exploring the effects of the setting on people's personalities and behavior. In the following excerpt from *Rising from the Plains,* for example, McPhee gives the reader a clear impression of what life was like on the Love Ranch in Wyoming during David Love's childhood. At the same time, he reveals a number of ways in which the members of the Love family were shaped by their environment.

Look For

As you read the following excerpt from *Rising from the Plains,* look for the events and details that help create a clear impression of life on Love Ranch. How is life on Love Ranch different from life in most other parts of the country? In what ways were the members of the Love family shaped by their environment?

Writing

How do you envision life on a ranch? Freewrite about your impressions of ranch life, discussing the sources of your impressions and the reasons why you think that you would or would not enjoy this type of life.

Vocabulary

Knowing the following words will help you as you read McPhee's essay.

vernacular (vər nak′ yə lər) *n.*: The native speech, language, or dialect of a country or place (p. 1176)

pragmatic (prag mat′ ik) *adj.*: Practical (p. 1176)

indigenous (in dij′ə nəs) *adj.*: Existing, growing, or produced naturally in a region or country (p. 1176)

voracity (vô ras′ə tē) *n.*: Eagerness (p. 1179)

moribund (môr′ə bund′) *adj.*: Dying; coming to an end (p. 1179)

adroit (ə droit′) *adj.*: Skillful in a physical or mental way (p. 1181)

taciturn (tas′ ə turn′) *adj.*: Almost always silent (p. 1182)

rudimentary (roo də men′ tər ē) *adj.*: Elementary (p. 1182)

truncated (truŋ′ kāt id) *v.*: Cut short (p. 1182)

magisterial (maj′ is tir′ ē əl) *adj.*: Authoritative (p. 1182)

capacious (kə pā′ shəs) *adj.*: Roomy; spacious (p. 1183)

from Rising from the Plains

John McPhee

In the United States Geological Survey's seven-and-a-half-minute series of topographic maps is a quadrangle named Love Ranch. The landscape it depicts lies just under the forty-third parallel and west of the hundred-and-seventh meridian—coordinates that place it twelve miles from the geographic center of Wyoming. The names of its natural features are names that more or less materialized around the kitchen table when David Love was young: Corral Draw, Castle Gardens, Buffalo Wallows, Jumping-Off Draw. To the fact that he grew up there his vernacular, his outlook, his pragmatic skills, and his professional absorptions about equally attest. The term "store-bought" once brightened his eyes. When one or another of the cowpunchers used a revolver, the man did not so much fire a shot as "slam a bullet." If a ranch hand was tough enough, he would "ride anything with hair on it." Coffee had been brewed properly if it would "float a horseshoe." Blankets were "sougans." A tarpaulin was a "henskin." To be off in the distant ranges was to be "gouging around the mountains." In Love's stories of the ranch, horses come and go by the "cavvy." If they are unowned and untamed, they are a "wild bunch"—led to capture by a rider "riding point." In the flavor of his speech the word "ornery" endures.

He describes his father as a "rough, kindly, strong-willed man" who would put a small son on each knee and—reciting "Ride a cockhorse to Banbury Cross to see a fine lady upon a white horse"—give the children bronco rides after dinner, explaining that his purpose was "to settle their stomachs." Their mother's complaints went straight up the stovepipe and away with the wind. When their father was not reciting such Sassenach[1] doggerel, he could draw Scottish poems out of the air like bolts of silk. He had the right voice, the Midlothian[2] timbre. He knew every syllable of *The Lady of the Lake*.[3] Putting his arms around the shoulders of his wee lads, he would roll it to them by the canto, and when they tired of Scott there were in his memory more than enough ballads to sketch the whole of Scotland, from the Caithness headlands to the Lammermuir Hills.

David was fifteen months younger than his brother, Allan. Their sister, Phoebe, was born so many years later that she does not figure in most of these scenes. They were the only children in a thousand square miles, where children outnumbered the indigenous trees. From the ranch buildings, by Muskrat Creek, the Wind River Basin reached out in buffalo grass, grama grass, and edible salt sage across the cambered erosional swells of

---

1. Sassenach (sas′ ə nak′): Saxon; English; a term used, often disparagingly, by Irish and Scots.
2. Midlothian (mid lō′ thē ən); Referring to a former county in southeastern Scotland.
3. *The Lady of the Lake*: A long poem by Scottish writer Sir Walter Scott (1771–1832).

the vast dry range. When the wind dropped, this whole wide world was silent, and they could hear from a great distance the squeak of a horned lark. The nearest neighbor was thirteen miles away. On the clearest night, they saw no light but their own.

Old buffalo trails followed the creek and branched from the creek: old but not ancient—there were buffalo skulls beside them, and some were attached to hide. The boys used the buffalo trails when they rode off on ranch chores for their father. They rode young and rode long, and often went without water. Even now, six decades later, David will pass up a cool spring, saying, "If I drink now, I'll be thirsty all day." To cut cedar fence posts, they went with a wagon to Green Mountain, near Crooks Gap—a round trip of two weeks. In early fall, each year,

they spent ten days going back and forth to the Rattlesnake Hills for stove wood. They took two wagons—four horses pulling each wagon—and they filled them with limber pine. They used axes, a two-handled saw. Near home, they mined coal with their father—from the erosional wonderland they called Castle Gardens, where a horse-drawn scraper stripped the overburden and exposed the seams of coal. Their father was adept at corralling wild horses, a skill that called for a horse and rider who could outrun these closest rivals to the wind. He caught more than he kept, put his Flatiron brand on the best ones and sold the others. Some of them escaped. David remembers seeing one clear a seven-foot bar in the wild-horse corral and not so much as touch it. When he and Allan were in their early teens,

On the walls were polished buffalo horns mounted on shields. The central piece of furniture was a gambling table from Joe Lacey's Muskrat Saloon. It was a poker-and-roulette table—round, covered with felt. Still intact were the subtle flanges that had caused the roulette wheel to stop just where the operator wished it to. And if you reached in under the table in the right place you could feel the brass slots where the dealer kept wild cards that he could call upon when the fiscal integrity of the house was threatened. If you put your nose down on the felt, you could almost smell the gunsmoke. At this table David Love received his basic education—his schoolroom a restaurant, his desk a gaming table from a saloon. His mother may have been trying to academize the table when she covered it with a red-and-white India print.

From time to time, other schoolmarms were provided by the district. They came for three months in summer. One came for the better part of a year. By and large, though, the boys were taught by their mother. She had a rolltop desk, and Peggy Doherty's glassed-in bookcases. She had the 1911 Encyclopædia Britannica, the Redpath Library, a hundred volumes of Greek and Roman literature, Shakespeare, Dickens, Emerson, Thoreau, Longfellow, Kipling, Twain. She taught her sons French, Latin, and a bit of Greek. She read to them from books in German, translating as she went along. They read the *Iliad* and the *Odyssey*.[8] The room was at the west end of the ranch house and was brightly illuminated by the setting sun. When David as a child saw sunbeams leaping off the books, he thought the contents were escaping.

In some ways, there was more chaos in this remote academic setting than there could ever be in a grade school in the heart of a city.

_____

8. ***Iliad . . . Odyssey:*** Famous epics by the ancient Greek poet Homer.

The house might be full of men, waiting out a storm, or riding on a round-up. I was baking, canning, washing clothes, making soap. Allan and David stood by the gasoline washing machine reading history or geography while I put sheets through the wringer. I ironed. They did spelling beside the ironing board, or while I kneaded bread; they gave the tables up to fifteen times fifteen to the treadle of the sewing machine. Mental problems, printed in figures on large cards, they solved while they raced across the . . . room to write the answers . . . and learned to think on their feet. Nine written problems done correctly, without help, meant no tenth problem. . . . It was surprising in how little time they finished their work—to watch the butchering, to help drive the bawling calves into the weaning pen, or to get to the corral, when they heard the hoofbeats of running horses and the cries of cowboys crossing the creek.

No amount of intellectual curiosity or academic discipline was ever going to hold a boy's attention if someone came in saying that the milk cow was mired in a bog hole or that old George was out by the wild-horse corral with the biggest coyote ever killed in the region, or if the door opened and, as David recalls an all too typical event, "they were carrying in a cowboy with guts ripped out by a saddle horn." The lessons stopped, the treadle stopped, and she sewed up the cowboy.

Across a short span of time, she had come a long way with these bunkhouse buckaroos. In her early years on the ranch, she had a lesser sense of fitting in than she would have had had she been a mare, a cow, or a ewe. She did not see another woman for as much as six months at a stretch, and if she happened to approach a group of working ranch hands they would loudly call out, "Church time!" She found "the sudden silence . . . appalling." Women were so rare in the country that when she lost a glove on the open range, at least twenty miles from home, a stranger who found it learned easily whose it must be and rode to the ranch to return it. Men did the housekeeping and the cooking, and went off to buy provisions at distant markets. Meals prepared in the bunkhouse were carried to a sheep wagon, where she and John lived while the big house was being built and otherwise assembled. The Wyoming sheep wagon was the ancestral Winnebago. It had a spring bed and a kitchenette.

After her two sons were born and became old enough to coin phrases, they called her Dainty Dish and sometimes Hooty the Owl. They renamed their food, calling it, for example, dog. They called other entrées caterpillar and coyote. The kitchen stool was Sam. They named a Christmas-tree ornament Hopping John. It had a talent for remaining unbroken. They assured each other that the cotton on the branches would not melt. David decided that he was a camel, but later changed his mind and insisted that he was "Mr. and Mrs. Booth." His mother described him as "a light-footed little elf." She noted his developing sense of scale when he said to her, "A coyote is the whole world to a flea."

One day, he asked her, "How long does a germ live?"

She answered, "A germ may become a grandfather in twenty minutes."

He said, "That's a long time to a germ, isn't it?"

She also made note that while David was the youngest person on the ranch he was nonetheless the most adroit at spotting arrowheads and chippings.

When David was five or six we began hunting arrowheads and chippings. While the rest of us labored along scanning gulches and anthills,

David rushed by chattering and picking up arrowheads right and left. He told me once, "There's a god of chippings that sends us anthills. He lives in the sky and tinkers with the clouds."

The cowboys competed with Homer in the entertainment of Allan and David. There was one who—as David remembers him—"could do magic tricks with a lariat rope,[9] making it come alive all around his horse, over our heads, under our feet, zipping it back and forth around us as we jumped up and down and squealed with delight." Sombre tableaux,[10] such as butcherings, were played out before them as well. Years later, David would write in a letter:

> We always watched the killing with horror and curiosity, although we were never permitted to participate at that age. It seemed so sad and so irrevocable to see the gushing blood when throats were cut, the desperate gasps for breath through severed windpipes, the struggle for and the rapid ebbing of life, the dimming and glazing of wide terrified eyes. We realized and accepted the fact that this was one of the procedures that were a part of our life on the range and that other lives had to be sacrificed to feed us. Throat-cutting, however, became a symbol of immediate death in our young minds, the ultimate horror, so dreadful that we tried not to use the word "throat."

He has written a recollection of the cowboys, no less frank in its bequeathed fact, and quite evidently the work of the son of his mother.

---

9. lariat (lar'ē it) **rope:** A rope used for tethering grazing horses or cattle.
10. sombre tableaux (säm' bər tab' lōz): Gloomy dramatic scenes.

The cowboys and horse runners who drifted in to the ranch in ever-increasing numbers as the spring advanced were lean, very strong, hard-muscled, taciturn bachelors, nearly all in their twenties and early thirties. They had been born poor, had only rudimentary education, and accepted their lot without resentment. They worked days that knew no hour limitations but only daylight and dark, and weeks that had no holidays. . . . Most were homely, with prematurely lined faces but with lively eyes that missed little. None wore glasses; people with glasses went into other kinds of work. Many were already stooped from chronic saddle-weariness, bowlegged, hip-sprung, with unrepaired hernias[11] that required trusses,[12] and spinal injuries that required a "hanging pole" in the bunkhouse. This was a horizontal bar from which the cowboys would hang by their hands for five to ten minutes to relieve pressure on ruptured spinal disks that came from too much bronc-fighting. Some wore eight-inch-wide heavy leather belts to keep their kidneys in place during prolonged hard rides.

When in a sense it was truly church time—when cowboys were badly injured and in need of help—they had long since learned where to go. David vividly remembers a moment in his education which was truncated when a cowboy rode up holding a bleeding hand. He had been roping a wild horse, and one of his fingers had become caught between the lariat and the saddle horn. The finger was still a part of his hand but was

hanging by two tendons. His mother boiled water, sterilized a pair of surgical scissors, and scrubbed her hands and arms. With magisterial nonchalance, she "snipped the tendons, dropped the finger into the hot coals of the fire box, sewed a flap of skin over the stump, smiled sweetly, and said: 'Joe, in a month you'll never know the difference.' "

There was a pack of ferocious wolfhounds in the country, kept by another flockmaster for the purpose of killing coyotes. The dogs seemed to relish killing rattlesnakes as well, shaking the life out of them until the festive serpents hung from the hounds' jaws like fettuccine.[13] The ranch hand in charge of them said, "They ain't happy in the spring till they've been bit. They're used to it now, and their heads don't swell up no more." Human beings (on foot) who happened to encounter these dogs might have preferred to encounter the rattlesnakes instead. One summer afternoon, John Love was working on a woodpile when he saw two of the wolfhounds streaking down to the creek in the direction of his sons, whose ages were maybe three and four. "Laddies! Run! Run to the house!" he shouted. "Here come the hounds!" The boys ran, reached the door just ahead of the dogs, and slammed it in their faces. Their mother was in the kitchen:

> The hounds, not to be thwarted so easily, leaped together furiously at the kitchen windows, high above the ground. They shattered the glass of the small panes, and tried to struggle through, their front feet catching over the inside ledge of the window frame, and their heads, with slavering mouths, reaching through the broken glass. I had only time to snatch a heavy iron frying pan from

---

11. hernias (hᵤr′ nē əz) *n.*: The protrusion of part of the intestine through the abdominal muscles.
12. trusses *n.*: Appliances for giving support in hernia cases.

13. fettuccine (fet′ o͞o chē′ nē) *n.*: Broad, flat noodles.

the stove and face them, beating at those clutching feet and snarling heads. The terrified boys cowered behind me. The window sashes held against the onslaught of the hounds, and my blows must have daunted them. They dropped back to the ground and raced away.

In the boys' vocabulary, the word "hound" joined the word "throat" in the deep shadows, and to this day when David sees a wolfhound there is a drop in the temperature of the center of his spine.

The milieu[14] of Love Ranch was not all wind, snow, freezing cattle, and killer dogs. There were quiet, lyrical days on end under blue, unthreatening skies. There were the redwing blackbirds on the corral fence, and the scent of moss flowers in spring. In a light breeze, the windmill turned slowly beside the wide log house, which was edged with flowers in bloom. Sometimes there were teal on the creek—and goldeneyes, pintails, mallards.[15] When the wild hay was ready for cutting, the harvest lasted a week.

John liked to have me ride with them for the last load. Sometimes I held the reins and called "Whoa, Dan!" while the men pitched up the hay. Then while the wagon swayed slowly back over the uneven road, I lay nestled deeply beside Allan and David in the fragrant hay. The billowy white clouds moving across the wide blue sky were close, so close, it seemed there was nothing else in the universe but clouds and hay.

When the hay house was not absolutely full, the boys cleared off the dance floor of Joe's Lacey's Muskrat Saloon and strapped on their roller skates. Bizarre as it may seem, there was also a Love Ranch croquet ground. And in winter the boys clamped ice skates to their shoes and flew with the wind up the creek. Alternatively, they lay down on their sleds and propelled themselves swiftly over wind-cleared, wind-polished black ice, with an anchor pin from a coyote trap in each hand. Almost every evening, with their parents, they played mah-jongg.[16]

One fall, their mother went to Riverton, sixty-five miles away, to await the birth of Phoebe. For her sons, eleven and twelve, she left behind a carefully prepared program of study. In the weeks that followed, they were in effect enrolled in a correspondence school run by their mother. They did their French, their spelling, their arithmetic lessons, put them in envelopes, rode fifteen miles to the post office and mailed them to her. She graded the lessons and sent them back—before and after the birth of the baby.

Her hair was the color of my wedding ring. On her cheek the fingers of one hand were outspread like a small, pink starfish.

From time to time, dust would appear on the horizon, behind a figure coming toward the ranch. The boys, in their curiosity, would climb a rooftop to watch and wait as the rider covered the intervening miles. Almost everyone who went through the region stopped at Love Ranch. It had not only the sizable bunkhouse and the most capacious horse corrals in a thousand square miles but also a spring of good water. Moreover, it had Scottish hospitality—not to mention the forbidding distance to the nearest alternative cup of coffee. Soon after Mr. Love and Miss Waxham were married, Nathaniel Thomas, the Episcopal Bishop of Wyoming, came through in his Gospel Wagon, accompanied

---

14. milieu (mēl yōō′) *n.*: Environment.
15. teal . . . goldeneyes, pintails, mallards: Types of ducks.

16. mah-jongg (mä′ jôŋ′) *n.*: A game of Chinese origin, played with pieces resembling dominoes.

by his colleague the Reverend Theodore Sedgwick. Sedgwick later reported (in a publication called *The Spirit of Missions*):

> We saw a distant building. It meant water. At this lonely ranch, in the midst of a sandy desert, we found a young woman. Her husband had gone for the day over the range. Around her neck hung a gold chain with a Phi Beta Kappa[17] key. She was a graduate of Wellesley College, and was now a Wyoming bride. She knew her Greek and Latin, and loved her house on the care-free prairie.

The bishop said he was searching for "heathen," and he did not linger.

---

17. Phi Beta Kappa (fī bāt′ə kap′ə): An honorary society of U.S. college students of high scholastic rank.

Fugitive criminals stopped at the ranch fairly often. They had to—in much the way that fugitive criminals in lonely country today will sooner or later have to stop at a filling station. A lone rider arrived at the ranch one day with a big cloud of dust on the horizon behind him. The dust might as well have formed in the air the letters of the word "posse." John Love knew the rider, knew that he was wanted for murder, and knew that throughout the country the consensus was that the victim had "needed killing." The murderer asked John Love to give him five dollars, and said he would leave his pocket watch as collateral. If his offer was refused, the man said, he would find a way to take the money. The watch was as honest as the day is long. When David does his field geology, he has it in his pocket.

People like that came along with such frequency that David's mother eventually assembled a chronicle called "Murderers I Have Known." She did not publish the manuscript, or even give it much private circulation, in her regard for the sensitivities of some of the first families of Wyoming. As David would one day comment, "they were nice men, family friends, who had put away people who needed killing, and she did not wish to offend them—so many of them were such decent people."

One of these was Bill Grace. Homesteader and cowboy, he was one of the most celebrated murderers in central Wyoming, and he had served time, but people generally disagreed with the judiciary and felt that Bill, in the acts for which he was convicted, had only been "doing his civic duty." At the height of his fame, he stopped at the ranch one afternoon and stayed for dinner. Although David and Allan were young boys, they knew exactly who he was, and in his presence were struck dumb with awe. As it happened, they had come upon and dispatched a rattlesnake that day—a big one,

over five feet long. Their mother decided to serve it creamed on toast for dinner. She and their father sternly instructed David and Allan not to use the word "rattlesnake" at the table. They were to refer to it as chicken, since a possibility existed that Bill Grace might not be an eater of adequate sophistication to enjoy the truth. The excitement was too much for the boys. Despite the parental injunction, gradually their conversation at the table fished its way toward the snake. Casually—while the meal was going down—the boys raised the subject of poisonous vipers, gave their estimates of the contents of local dens, told stories of snake encounters, and so forth. Finally, one of them remarked on how very good rattlers were to eat.

Bill Grace said, "By God, if anybody ever gave me rattlesnake meat I'd kill them."

The boys went into a state of catatonic paralysis. In the pure silence, their mother said, "More chicken, Bill?"

"Don't mind if I do," said Bill Grace.

THINKING ABOUT THE SELECTION

Recalling

1. How does David Love describe his father?
2. What was the Love Ranch policy regarding the use of tents?
3. What did John Love do when the stage route that ran through the ranch was abandoned?
4. How does David Love describe the cowboys and horse runners "who drifted in to the ranch . . . as the spring advanced"?
5. What incident involving the "celebrated" murderer, Bill Grace, does McPhee describe at the end of the selection?

Interpreting

6. How does the way in which the people in the area around Love Ranch treated newspapers reflect their sense of isolation?
7. How do the passages written by David Love and his mother contribute to the authenticity of McPhee's account?
8. What seems to be McPhee's attitude toward David Love and his family?

Applying

9. In what ways do you imagine that life on today's American ranches differs from the type of life described in this essay?

ANALYZING LITERATURE

Understanding Setting

The **setting** is the time and place in which the events in a literary work occur. In *Rising from the Plains,* McPhee focuses on capturing the flavor of life in a specific setting—the Love Ranch in Wyoming.

1. What does this selection reveal about the climate of the area in which Love Ranch is located?
2. What overall impression of life on Love Ranch does the selection convey?

CRITICAL THINKING AND READING

Understanding the Effect of Setting

McPhee's essay also reveals many of the ways in which the members of the Love family were shaped by the setting. For example, in the first paragraph McPhee points out that David Love's experiences growing up on Love Ranch shaped his use of language, his outlook on life, and "his pragmatic skills."

1. What does the way in which David Love's mother deals with the cowboy's injured finger suggest about the effect of the setting on her character?
2. In what ways has David Love's father clearly been shaped by the setting?

THINKING AND WRITING

Comparing and Contrasting Settings

Write an essay in which you compare and contrast the setting of McPhee's essay with the setting Larry McMurtry describes in the excerpt from *Lonesome Dove.* Reread each selection, noting the details of the setting. Organize your notes according to corresponding points of comparison and contrast. Then write your essay, using details from both selections to support your argument. When you revise, make sure you have used transitions to link your ideas and varied the length and structure of your sentences.

Poetry

NUMBER 3, 1949
Jackson Pollack
Joseph Hirshhorn Museum

THEODORE ROETHKE

1908–1963

Throughout the course of his career, Theodore Roethke focused his poetry on the various aspects of his own life. Although his style changed during the period between the publication of his first book, *Open House* (1941), and the appearance of his posthumous collection, *The Far Field* (1964), Roethke continued to seek a sense of self by exploring his personal experiences in his poetry.

Roethke grew up in Saginaw, Michigan, where his family owned several large commercial greenhouses. In his family's greenhouses, he observed nature putting forth roots and blossoms, as well as falling into dormancy and death. These observations later provided him with ideas and inspiration for many of his poems.

After receiving his education at the University of Michigan and Harvard, Roethke taught writing at Bennington College, the Pennsylvania State University, and the University of Washington. A slow, diligent writer, Roethke spent many years assembling poems for his first book. He went on to publish several more volumes, including *The Lost Son* (1948), *The Waking* (1953), and *Words for the Wind* (1958). In 1954 he received a Pulitzer Prize for *The Waking,* and two years after his death he was awarded the National Book Award for *The Far Field.*

The Waking; Once More, the Round

Rhyme. Rhyme refers to the repetition of sounds in the accented syllables of two or more words that appear close to each other. Rhyme that occurs at the ends of lines is called end rhyme, while rhyme that occurs within a line is called internal rhyme. When rhyme involves the repetition of identical sounds, it is called exact rhyme. For example, *snow-crow* is an exact rhyme. When the rhyme is not exact, it is called approximate rhyme or slant rhyme. For example, *dream-home* is an approximate rhyme.

As you read Roethke's poetry, look for his use of rhyme. How does his use of rhyme affect your response to his poetry?

In Roethke's poem "The Waking," the speaker comments, "I learn by going where I have to go." Do you think this is the way most people learn? Freewrite about the ways in which people acquire knowledge during the courses of their lives.

Knowing the following words will help you as you read Roethke's poetry.

abiding (ə bīd′ iŋ) *adj.*: Enduring; lasting (p. 1192, l. 6)

questing (kwest′ iŋ) *adj.*: Searching (p. 1192, l. 7)

The Waking

Theodore Roethke

I wake to sleep, and take my waking slow.
I feel my fate in what I cannot fear.
I learn by going where I have to go.

We think by feeling. What is there to know?
5   I hear my being dance from ear to ear.
I wake to sleep, and take my waking slow.

Of those so close beside me, which are you?
God bless the Ground! I shall walk softly there,
And learn by going where I have to go.

10   Light takes the Tree; but who can tell us how?
The lowly worm climbs up a winding stair;
I wake to sleep, and take my waking slow.

Great Nature has another thing to do
To you and me; so take the lively air,
15   And, lovely, learn by going where to go.

This shaking keeps me steady. I should know.
What falls away is always. And is near.
I wake to sleep, and take my waking slow.
I learn by going where I have to go.

THINKING ABOUT THE SELECTION

Recalling

1. (a) In what does the speaker feel his fate? (b) How does he learn? (c) What does he hear? (d) What keeps him steady?

Interpreting

2. (a) What is paradoxical, or seemingly self-contradictory, about the statement, "I wake to sleep"? (b) What is the meaning of this paradox? (c) Find two other paradoxes in the poem. (d) Explain the meaning of each of these paradoxes.
3. What does the speaker mean when he says that he takes his "waking slow"?
4. What is the meaning of lines 3, 9, and 19?
5. (a) What is the other "thing" that Nature has "to do/To you and me"? (b) How does the speaker's reference to this "thing" help clarify the meaning of the poem?
6. Why is the form of this poem appropriate to its subject?
7. Read this poem aloud. (a) What effect is created by the rhythm? (b) How is this effect appropriate for the subject matter?
8. What does this poem suggest about Roethke's attitude toward life?
9. Why is "The Waking" an appropriate title for this poem?

Applying

10. The American novelist Richard Wright has written, "Men can starve from lack of self-realization as much as they can from a lack of bread." Discuss the meaning of this quotation and its relation to "The Waking."

ANALYZING LITERATURE

Understanding Rhyme

Rhyme refers to the repetition of sounds in the accented syllables of two or more words that appear close to each other. Exact rhyme refers to the repetition of identical sounds. The use of the words *fear* and *ear* at the ends of lines 2 and 5 is an example of exact rhyme. When the rhyme is not exact, it is called approximate rhyme or slant rhyme. For example, Roethke uses slant rhyme in lines 5 and 8, when he rhymes the words *ear* and *there*.

1. Find two more examples of exact rhyme.
2. Find another example of slant rhyme.
3. What is the rhyme scheme, or the pattern of end rhymes in the poem?

THINKING AND WRITING

Responding to Criticism

Critic Robert Boyers has commented that Roethke's "best poems permit us to embrace the principle of change as the root of stability." Write an essay in which you discuss this comment in relation to "The Waking." Reread the poem, noting what it suggests about the concepts of change and stability. Develop a thesis statement. Then write your essay, using passages from the poem to support your argument. When you finish writing, revise your essay, making sure that you have included enough supporting information.

Once More, the Round

Theodore Roethke

What's greater, Pebble or Pond?
What can be known? The Unknown.
My true self runs toward a Hill
More! O More! visible.

5   Now I adore my life
With the Bird, the abiding Leaf,
With the Fish, the questing Snail,
And the Eye altering all;
And I dance with William Blake[1]
10 For love, for Love's sake;

And everything comes to One,
As we dance on, dance on, dance on.

---

1. William Blake: English poet (1757–1827).

WILD FLOWERS, 1978
Samuel Reindorf
Collection: George Williams

THINKING ABOUT THE SELECTION

Recalling

1. What questions does the speaker ask in the first stanza?
2. What elements of nature does the speaker mention in the second stanza?

Interpreting

3. What do the "pebble" and "pond" referred to in the first stanza represent?

4. Why does the speaker's "true self" run "toward a Hill"?
5. What does the speaker mean when he says that "the Eye" alters "all"?

Applying

6. In this poem Roethke compares life to a round dance, a type of dance in which groups of dancers move in a circle. To what other types of dances do you think life might be compared?

James Dickey (1923–)

A lover of nature and a devoted outdoorsman, James Dickey is a man of great size (he is six foot three) and energy. Dickey's energy and affection for the outdoors are exhibited in his poetry. In his work he often shows people testing their survival instincts against the primitive elements of the natural world. This reflects his belief that maintaining contact with the world of nature can help people escape from the monotony of everyday existence.

Dickey was born in Atlanta, Georgia. He was a star football player in high school and served as a bomber pilot in World War II. After returning from the war, Dickey began writing poetry while studying at Vanderbilt University. During his senior year, one of his poems was published in *Sewanee Review*.

Dickey went on to publish several volumes of poetry, including *Into the Stone* (1960), *Buckdancer's Choice* (1965), *Poems 1957–1967* (1967) and *Puella* (1982). In 1966 he received the National Book Award for *Buckdancer's Choice*. In addition to poetry, he has written literary criticism and a best-selling novel, *Deliverance* (1970).

Denise Levertov (1923–)

Denise Levertov has commented that she believes that the poem is the poet's means for discovering the divine in the real world. Acting upon this belief, Levertov writes original, inventive poetry that often explores the hidden meaning in ordinary events.

Levertov was born in Essex, England. She began writing poetry at an early age, and in 1946 she published her first collection, *The Double Image*. A year later she married American writer Mitchell Goodman and moved to the United States. She became an American citizen in 1955, and her second book of poetry was published in 1957. Since then, she has written over a dozen more books of poetry, including *With Eyes at the Back of Our Heads* (1960) and *Relearning the Alphabet* (1970). She has also published two books of translations and a book of essays about writing poetry.

GUIDE FOR READING

The Rain Guitar; Merritt Parkway

Literary Forms

Visual Poetry. Visual poetry refers to poems in which the letters, words, lines, and spaces are arranged to form a shape or create a visual effect. Often the shape of a visual poem in some way reflects or reinforces the poem's meaning. For example, seventeenth-century English George Herbert shaped his poem "The Altar" to look like a church altar and shaped his poem "Easter Wings" to resemble a pair of wings.

Look For

As you read "The Rain Guitar" and "Merritt Parkway," look for a relationship between the shape and the meaning of each poem.

Writing

In "Merritt Parkway," Levertov writes about the experience of traveling along a crowded highway. Freewrite about the thoughts and feelings that you associate with highway travel.

Vocabulary

Knowing the following words will help you as you read "The Rain Guitar" and "Merritt Parkway."

wan (wän) *adj.:* Sickly pale (p. 1198, l. 4)

continuum (ken tin′ yōō wəm) *n.:* A continuous whole with parts that cannot be separated (p. 1198, l. 10)

The Rain Guitar

James Dickey

England, 1962

The water-grass under had never waved
But one way. It showed me that flow is forever
Sealed from rain in a weir. For some reason having
To do with Winchester, I was sitting on my guitar case
5 Watching nothing but eelgrass trying to go downstream with all the right motions
But one. I had on a sweater, and my threads were opening
Like mouths with rain. It mattered to me not at all
That a bridge was stumping
With a man, or that he came near and cast a fish
10 thread into the weir. I had no line and no feeling.
I had nothing to do with fish
But my eyes on the grass they hid in, waving with the one move of trying
To be somewhere else. With what I had, what could I do?
I got out my guitar, that somebody told me was supposed to improve
15 With moisture—or was it when it dried out?—and hit the lowest
And loudest chord. The drops that were falling just then
Hammered like Georgia railroad track
With E. The man went into a kind of fishing
Turn. Play it, he said through his pipe. There
20 I went, fast as I could with cold fingers. The strings shook
With drops. A buck dance settled on the weir. Where was the city
Cathedral in all this? Out of sight, but somewhere around.
Play a little more
Of that, he said, and cast. Music-wood shone,
25 Getting worse or better faster than it liked:
Improvement or disintegration
Supposed to take years, fell on it
By the gallon. It darkened and rang
Like chimes. My sweater collapsed, and the rain reached
30 My underwear. I picked, the guitar showered, and he cast to the mountain
Music. His wood leg tapped
On the cobbles. Memories of many men
Hung, rain-faced, improving, sealed-off
In the weir. I found myself playing Australian
35 Versions of British marching songs. Mouths opened all over me; I sang,
His legs beat and marched
Like companions. I was Air Force,
I said. So was I; I picked
This up in Burma, he said, tapping his gone leg

40

> With his fly rod, as Burma and the South
> west Pacific and North Georgia reeled,
> Rapped, cast, chimed, darkened and drew down
> Cathedral water, and improved.

THINKING ABOUT THE SELECTION
Recalling

1. (a) Whom does the poet meet in the stream? (b) How does this person respond when the speaker begins playing the guitar? (c) What do the two people find they have in common?
2. (a) What are the weather conditions in the poem? (b) How does the speaker think the weather conditions will affect his guitar?

Interpreting

3. To what two senses do most of the images, or word pictures, in the poem appeal? Find examples to support your answer.
4. (a) What do the speaker's actions in the poem suggest about his state of mind? (b) What details in the poem indicate that his war experiences have had a powerful effect on him?
5. This poem is set in Winchester, England, the location of a famous cathedral, which the speaker refers to in the poem. (a) What is the relationship between the cathedral and the speaker's experiences in the poem? (b) What is the significance of the other places mentioned in the poem?

Applying

6. Why do you think music often reminds us of past experiences?

ANALYZING LITERATURE
Understanding Visual Poetry

Visual poetry refers to poems in which the letters, words, lines, and spaces are arranged to form a shape or create a visual effect. Often the shape of a visual poem reflects or reinforces the poem's meaning.

1. What is the visual effect of "The Rain Guitar"?
2. How is the visual effect related to the poem's meaning?

THINKING AND WRITING
Writing a Visual Poem

Imagine that you have been asked to write a visual poem for your school literary magazine. Start by choosing a subject for your poem. Then think about how you can shape the poem to reflect its meaning. Prepare a list of images, or word pictures, related to your subject. Then begin writing your poem, arranging the letters, words, and lines to form the appropriate shape. When you finish writing, revise and proofread your poem.

Merritt Parkway

Denise Levertov

As if it were
forever that they move, that we
keep moving—

Under a wan sky where
as the lights went on a star
pierced the haze & now
follows steadily
a constant
above our six lanes
the dreamlike continuum . . .

And the people—ourselves!
the humans from inside the
cars apparent
only at gasoline stops
unsure,
eyeing each other

drink coffee hastily at the
slot machines & hurry
back to the cars
vanish
into them forever, to
keep moving—

Houses now & then beyond the
sealed road, the trees / trees, bushes
passing by, passing
the cars that
keep moving ahead of
us, past us, pressing behind us
and
over left, those that come
toward us shining too brightly
moving relentlessly

in six lanes, gliding
north & south, speeding with
a slurred sound—

THINKING ABOUT THE SELECTION

Recalling

1. What experience does this poem describe?

Interpreting

2. Why might moving traffic seem like a "dream-like continuum"?
3. How do the details in lines 11–22 suggest that the people feel more comfortable in their cars than with other people?
4. In what sense is the road "sealed"?

5. In this poem Levertov uses highway travel as a metaphor for how people travel through life. Considering this fact, what does the poem suggest about the nature of people's lives in modern society?
6. How does the shape of "Merritt Parkway" reinforce its meaning?

Applying

7. How do the impressions of highway travel presented in the poem compare with your own impressions?

BIOGRAPHIES

Gwendolyn Brooks (1917–   )

In 1950 Gwendolyn Brooks became the first black writer to win a Pulitzer Prize, receiving the award for her second collection of poetry, *Annie Allen* (1949). Since that time, Brooks's reputation as a writer has steadily grown, and she has become one of the most highly regarded poets of our time.

Brooks was born in Topeka, Kansas, and was raised in a section of Chicago known as "Bronzeville." This area provided her with the setting for her first book of poems, *A Street in Bronzeville* (1945). In this collection and in her other early works, Brooks focused on the suffering of city blacks, whom she saw as uprooted, often abused, untrained, and unable to compete for a living. In her later works, after having, as she put it, "rediscovered her blackness," she became more outspoken, openly expressing her support for the black movement.

Elizabeth Bishop (1911–1980)

Elizabeth Bishop's poetry reflects the influence of the work of Marianne Moore. Like Moore, Bishop is known mainly for her meticulously detailed descriptions of nature and her interest in discovering meaning in ordinary observations.

Bishop was born in Worcester, Massachusetts, and was educated at Vassar College. Following her graduation, she traveled extensively outside the United States, residing in Brazil for a number of years. Bishop's travels provided her with inspiration for many of her poems.

Although she published relatively few collections of poetry during her lifetime, Bishop received many honors and awards. Her awards include the 1956 Pulitzer Prize for *Poems: North and South—A Cold Spring* and the 1969 National Book Award for *Complete Poems*.

The Explorer;
Little Exercise; House Guest

Rhythm. Rhythm is the arrangement of stressed and unstressed syllables in a poem. In poems with a regular rhythm, or meter, the arrangement of stressed and unstressed syllables forms a recurring pattern. However, poets usually introduce slight variations in the metrical pattern to avoid monotony or emphasize important words. Poets will also introduce pauses within lines to interrupt the regular rhythm. These pauses, called caesuras, are usually created by punctuation, though they may also be created by the meanings of words or the natural rhythms of language.

Another way poets can vary a regular rhythm is through the use of run-on lines. Unlike end-stopped lines, which end with a pause, run-on lines flow naturally into the next line. For example, in House Guest," line 1 ("The sad seamstress") flows into line 2 ("who stays with us this month").

As you read the following poems, look for a regular rhythm. Does the arrangement of stressed and unstressed syllables form a recurring pattern? If so, what techniques does the poet use to vary the rhythm?

In "Little Exercise" Elizabeth Bishop describes the arrival and passage of a thunderstorm as a sequence of scenes. Think of a similar natural event, such as a snowstorm or a landslide. Then describe the stages of this event in a sequence of scenes.

Knowing the following words will help you as you read the following poems.

din (din) *n.*: Loud, continuous noise or clamor (p. 1202, l. 3)

wily (wī′ lē) *adj.*: Sly; cunning (p. 1202, l. 5)

The Explorer
Gwendolyn Brooks

Somehow to find a still spot in the noise
Was the frayed inner want, the winding, the frayed hope
Whose tatters he kept hunting through the din.
A satin peace somewhere.
5 A room of wily hush somewhere within.

So tipping down the scrambled halls he set
Vague hands on throbbing knobs. There were behind
Only spiraling, high human voices,
The scream of nervous affairs,
10 Wee griefs,
Grand griefs. And choices.

He feared most of all the choices, that cried to be taken.

There were no bourns.
There were no quiet rooms.

THINKING ABOUT THE SELECTION
Recalling

1. What does "he" keep "hunting through the din"?
2. In the second stanza, what does "he" find behind the "throbbing knobs"?

Interpreting

3. To which sense do most of the images in this poem appeal? Find three examples to support your answer.
4. (a) What do the details indicate about the place in which the poem's subject lives? (b) What does this person's home symbolize, or represent? (c) What do his experiences in the poem symbolize?
5. (a) Why does the subject fear choices "most of all"? (b) What conclusions does he reach in the final two lines?

Applying

6. Why do you think people often fear having to make choices?

UNDERSTANDING LANGUAGE
Understanding Word Origins

Many words came into the English Language through Latin. For example, in "The Explorer" Brooks uses the word *vague,* which comes from the Latin word *vagus,* meaning "wandering."

The following words are of Latin origin. Use your dictionary to find the meaning of each word. Then give the Latin word and meaning from which it comes.

1. salute   4. communion
2. incubate   5. transmit
3. opinion

THE UNEXPECTED ANSWER
René Magritte
Patrimoine des Musees Royaux des Beaux-Arts

GREAT FLORIDA SUNSET, 1887
Martin Johnson Heade
Private Collection USA

Little Exercise

Elizabeth Bishop

Think of the storm roaming the sky uneasily
like a dog looking for a place to sleep in,
listen to it growling.

Think how they must look now, the mangrove[1] keys
5   lying out there unresponsive to the lightning
in dark, coarse-fibred families,

where occasionally a heron[2] may undo his head,
shake up his feathers, make an uncertain comment
when the surrounding water shines.

---

1. mangrove: A tropical tree with branches that spread and send
down roots, forming new trunks and causing a thick growth over a
large area.
2. heron (her′ ən) *n.*: A wading bird with a long neck, long legs,
and a long, tapered bill.

10   Think of the boulevard and the little palm trees
all stuck in rows, suddenly revealed
as fistfuls of limp fish-skeletons.

It is raining there. The boulevard
and its broken sidewalks with weeds in every crack
15   are relieved to be wet, the sea to be freshened.

Now the storm goes away again in a series
of small, badly lit battle-scenes,
each in "Another part of the field."[3]

Think of someone sleeping in the bottom of a rowboat
20   tied to a mangrove root or the pile of a bridge;
think of him as uninjured, barely disturbed.

---

3. "Another . . . field": A stage direction used to designate different parts of a battlefield in several of William Shakespeare's plays.

THINKING ABOUT THE SELECTION

Recalling

1. To what does the speaker compare the storm in the first stanza?
2. What happens occasionally in the mangrove keys?
3. How does the "boulevard and its broken sidewalks" respond to the rain?
4. What does the speaker describe in the final stanza?

Interpreting

5. What details indicate that the poem is set in a tropical environment?

6. In what way is the speaker's description of the storm similar to a play?
7. Considering the way in which the storm is described in the first six stanzas, what is ironic, or surprising, about the scene described in the final stanza?
8. How does the title relate to the poem?

Applying

9. How does the speaker's vision of a thunderstorm compare with your own image of a thunderstorm?

House Guest

Elizabeth Bishop

The sad seamstress
who stays with us this month
is small and thin and bitter.
No one can cheer her up.
5   Give her a dress, a drink,
roast chicken, or fried fish—
it's all the same to her.

She sits and watches TV.
No, she watches zigzags.
10   "Can you adjust the TV?"
"No," she says. No hope.
She watches on and on,
without hope, without air.

Her own clothes give us pause,
15   but she's not a poor orphan.
She has a father, a mother,
and all that, and she's earning
quite well, and we're stuffing
her with fattening foods.

20   We invite her to use the binoculars.
We say, "Come see the jets!"
We say, "Come see the baby!"
Or the knife grinder who cleverly
plays the National Anthem
25   on his wheel so shrilly.
Nothing helps.

She speaks: "I need a little
money to buy buttons."
She seems to think it's useless
30   to ask. Heavens, buy buttons,

if they'll do any good,
the biggest in the world—
by the dozen, by the gross!
Buy yourself an ice cream,
35   a comic book, a car!

Her face is closed as a nut;
closed as a careful snail
or a thousand-year-old seed.
Does she dream of marriage?
40   Of getting rich? Her sewing
is decidedly mediocre.

Please! Take our money! Smile!
What on earth have we done?
What has everyone done
45   and when did it all begin?
Then one day she confides
that she wanted to be a nun
and her family opposed her.

Perhaps we should let her go,
50   or deliver her straight off
to the nearest convent—and wasn't
her month up last week, anyway?

Can it be that we nourish
one of the Fates in our bosoms?
55   Clotho, sewing our lives
w'th a bony little foot
on a borrowed sewing machine,
and our fates will be like hers,
and our hems crooked forever?

THINKING ABOUT THE SELECTION

Recalling

1. (a) How does the speaker describe the seamstress's appearance? (b) How do the speaker and her family respond to the seamstress's clothes?
2. (a) For what does the seamstress ask? (b) How does the family respond?
3. (a) What does the seamstress reveal to the family in the seventh stanza? (b) What responses does the speaker contemplate in the eighth stanza?

Interpreting

4. (a) What do the seamstress's actions reveal about her personality? (b) What do the descriptions of her appearance reveal about her personality?
5. (a) What is the speaker's attitude toward the seamstress? (b) How is this attitude conveyed? (c) How does the speaker's attitude change after the seamstress confides in her and her family?

Applying

6. In this poem the seamstress has a strong negative reaction to her inability to fulfill her goal in life. Do you think that most people would respond as negatively as the seamstress does if they were unable to achieve their goals in life? Why or why not?

ANALYZING LITERATURE

Understanding Rhythm

Rhythm is the arrangement of stressed and unstressed syllables in a poem. Poets vary the regular rhythm of a poem in a number of ways. Often poets interrupt the regular rhythm by introducing pauses, or caesuras, within the lines. Another way poets vary rhythm is by using run-on lines—lines that flow naturally into the next line.

1. Find two caesuras in "House Guest."
2. Find two run-on lines in the poem.

THINKING AND WRITING

Responding to Criticism

Critic Candace Stalter has commented that Elizabeth Bishop's "poetry reveals more diffuse sympathy for the oppressed than definite anger at the oppressor." Write an essay in which you discuss this comment in relation to "House Guest." Reread the poem, focusing on the attitude it expresses concerning the seamstress and her unhappiness. When you write your essay, use passages from the poem to support your argument. When you finish writing, revise and proofread your essay.

BIOGRAPHIES

Robert Lowell (1917–1977)

Robert Lowell was a member of one of the country's oldest and most prominent families. His ancestors included two noted American poets, James Russell Lowell and Amy Lowell. Considering his background, it is not surprising that he was one of the most history-conscious and influential poets of his time.

Born in Boston, Lowell attended Harvard University for two years, then transferred to Kenyon College in Ohio, where he studied poetry under John Crowe Ransom. Lowell earned widespread recognition early in his career as a poet, winning a Pulitzer Prize for his collection *Lord Weary's Castle*. In the poems in this book and in those in his other early collections, Lowell relied on traditional poetic forms and techniques. During the late 1950's, however, Lowell abandoned his early style and began writing freer, more direct poems. This change first became evident when he published *Life Studies* (1959), a collection of confessional poems—poems in which Lowell openly and frankly explored his own personal life. The book had a tremendous impact on the literary world, giving rise to a school of confessional poets that included Sylvia Plath, John Berryman, and Anne Sexton.

Randall Jarrell (1914–1965)

Randall Jarrell was a talented poet, literary critic, and teacher. His poetry was praised by both writers and critics, including Robert Lowell, who called Jarrell "the most heartbreaking English poet of his day"; and his literary essays, many of which appear in his book *Poetry and the Age* (1953), have been credited with altering the dominant critical trends and tastes of his time.

Jarrell was born and raised in New Orleans, Louisiana. After graduating from Vanderbilt University, he became a teacher, a profession to which he remained dedicated for the rest of his life. During World War II, he served in the United States Air Force. His war experiences provided him with the material for the poems in his book, *Losses* (1948). Many of his other poems, including those in *The Seven League Crutches* (1951) and *The Lost World* (1965), focus on childhood and the sense of innocence with which it is associated. In contrast, the poems in *The Woman at the Washington Zoo* (1960) reflect Jarrell's concern with aging and loneliness.

Hawthorne; The Death
of the Ball Turret Gunner; Losses

Writer's Techniques

Theme. The theme is the central idea or insight about life that a writer hopes to convey in a work of literature. In some literary works, the theme is stated directly. More often, however, the theme is implied, or revealed indirectly. When interpreting an implied theme, it is important to pay close attention to the writer's choice of details, portrayal of characters and events, and use of literary devices.

Look For

As you read each of the following poems, look for the theme. How is the theme conveyed in each poem?

Writing

"The Death of the Ball Turret Gunner" and "Losses" were inspired by Randall Jarrell's experiences in the United States Air Force. Why do you think writers often use war as a subject for their writing? Freewrite about the reasons why war is such a common literary subject.

Vocabulary

Knowing these words will help you as you read the following poems.
brooding (broo͞od′ iŋ) v.: Pondering in a troubled or mournful way (p. 1212, l. 34)
furtive (fur′ tiv) adj.: Sneaky; shifty (p. 1212, l. 40)

meditation (med′ ə tā′ shən) n.: Deep reflection (p. 1212, l. 41)

Hawthorne

Robert Lowell

Follow its lazy main street lounging
from the alms house to Gallows Hill[1]
along a flat, unvaried surface
covered with wooden houses
5 aged by yellow drain
like the unhealthy hair of an old dog.
You'll walk to no purpose
in Hawthorne's Salem.

I cannot resilver the smudged plate.[2]

---

1. Gallows Hill: A hill in Salem, Massachusetts, where nineteen
people who were accused of practicing witchcraft were hanged.
2. resilver . . . plate: Early photographs were taken on a metal
plate coated with silver.

CROWNINSHIELD'S WHARF. AROUND THE
WHARF ARE THE VESSELS AMERICA, FAME,
PRUDENT, AND BELISAURIUS
George Ropes
Peabody Museum of Salem

10   I drop to Hawthorne, the customs officer,[3]
      measuring coal and mostly trying to keep warm—
      to the stunted black schooner,
      the dismal South-end dock,
      the wharf-piles with their fungus of ice.
15   On State Street[4]
      a steeple with a glowing dial-clock
      measures the weary hours,
      the merciless march of professional feet.

      Even this shy distrustful ego
20   sometimes walked on top of the blazing roof,
      and felt those flashes
      that char the discharged cells of the brain.

      Look at the faces—
      Longfellow, Lowell, Holmes and Whittier!

---

3. customs officer: Hawthorne worked as a customs officer in
Salem.
4. State Street: A street in the business district of Boston.

25 Study the grizzled silver of their beards.
    Hawthorne's picture,
    however, has a blond mustache
    and golden General Custer[5] scalp.
    He looks like a Civil War officer.
30 He shines in the firelight. His hard
    survivor's smile is touched with fire.

    Leave him alone for a moment or two,
    and you'll see him with his head
    bent down, brooding, brooding,
35 eyes fixed on some chip,
    some stone, some common plant,
    the commonest thing,
    as if it were the clue.
    The disturbed eyes rise,
40 furtive, foiled, dissatisfied
    from meditation on the true
    and insignificant.

---

5. General Custer: George Armstrong Custer (1839–1876), a
general who served in the Civil War and was killed along with his
troops by the Sioux at the Battle of Little Big Horn, had long blond
hair.

THINKING ABOUT THE SELECTION

Recalling

1. With what is the "unvaried surface" of the "lazy main street" in Salem covered?
2. (a) What is Hawthorne doing in lines 10–11? (b) According to lines 19–22, what does the "shy distrustful ego" sometimes do?
3. (a) What does the speaker reveal about the physical appearance of Longfellow, Lowell, Holmes, and Whittier? (b) How does he describe Hawthorne's appearance?
4. According to the final stanza, what will you see if you leave Hawthorne "alone for a moment or two"?

Interpreting

5. (a) What type of impression is conveyed by the description of Salem in the first stanza? (b) How does line 9 relate to the description of Salem?
6. What is the significance of the allusion, or reference, to Gallows Hill?
7. (a) What impression of time is conveyed by the image, or word picture, in lines 15–17? (b) What impression of professional people does the image in line 18 convey?
8. (a) What do lines 19–22 reveal about Hawthorne? (b) What do the descriptions in lines 23–31 imply about the contrasts between Hawthorne's personality and the personalities of some of his literary contemporaries?

9. In the final stanza, what is Hawthorne seeking through his observations of common things?

Applying

10. (a) Why do you think Lowell might have chosen to write this poem? (b) What does the poem reveal about Lowell?
11. Proverb 22:28 reads, "Remove not the ancient landmark, which the fathers have set." (a) In what way has Hawthorne served as a literary landmark for Lowell? (b) Think of your own field of interest. Who would serve as a "landmark" for you? Explain the reasons for your choice.

UNDERSTANDING LANGUAGE

Appreciating Precise Words

The effectiveness of Lowell's poetry results in part from his precise choice of words. Find a synonym for each of the italicized words below. Then explain why the synonyms are less effective than are the words Lowell chose.

1. ". . . along the flat, *unvaried* surface . . ."
2. ". . . the *merciless* march of professional feet."
3. "The *disturbed* eyes rise, furtive, foiled, dissatisfied . . ."
4. ". . . from the meditation on the true and *insignificant*."

The Death of the Ball Turret Gunner

Randall Jarrell

A ball turret was a small space, enclosed in plexiglass, on the underside of the fuselage of certain World War II bombers, which held a small man and two machine guns. When the bomber was attacked by a plane below, the gunner would fire his guns from an upside-down, hunched-up position.

From my mother's sleep I fell into the State,
And I hunched in its belly till my wet fur froze.
Six miles from earth, loosed from its dream of life,
I woke to black flak[1] and the nightmare fighters.
5   When I died they washed me out of the turret with a hose.

---

1. flak *n.*: Anti-aircraft fire.

THINKING ABOUT THE SELECTION

Recalling

1. (a) From what does the ball turret gunner fall?   (b) To what does he wake?
2. What happens when he dies?

Interpreting

3. (a) To what does the word *State* (line 1) refer?   (b) What does Jarrell mean when he writes that the gunner "fell into the State"?
4. (a) To what does Jarrell compare the ball turret gunner in the first two lines?   (b) How does this comparison add to the impact of the poem?
5. Why might the gunner view life on earth as a "dream" (line 3)?
6. What does the final line reveal about the realities of war?
7. How does the brevity of this poem add to its impact?

Applying

8. Why do you think Jarrell chose to write about a ball turret gunner rather than a pilot or another type of soldier?

Losses

Randall Jarrell

It was not dying: everybody died.
It was not dying: we had died before
In the routine crashes—and our fields
Called up the papers, wrote home to our folks,
5   And the rates rose, all because of us.
We died on the wrong page of the almanac,
Scattered on mountains fifty miles away;
Diving on haystacks, fighting with a friend,
We blazed up on the lines we never saw.
10   We died like aunts or pets or foreigners.
(When we left high school nothing else had died
For us to figure we had died like.)

In our new planes, with our new crews, we bombed
The ranges by the desert or the shore,
15   Fired at towed targets, waited for our scores—
And turned into replacements and woke up
One morning, over England, operational.
It wasn't different: but if we died
It was not an accident but a mistake
20   (But an easy one for anyone to make).
We read our mail and counted up our missions—
In bombers named for girls, we burned
The cities we had learned about in school—
Till our lives wore out; our bodies lay among
25   The people we had killed and never seen.
When we lasted long enough they gave us medals;
When we died they said, "Our casualties were low."

THINKING ABOUT THE SELECTION

Recalling

1. According to lines 6–9, where do the pilots die?
2. (a) What do the pilots bomb (line 14)? (b) At what do they fire (line 15)? (c) What do they burn (line 23)?
3. (a) What happens when the pilots last "long enough" (line 26)? (b) What happens when they die (line 27)?

Interpreting

4. (a) Do the pilots really think that their missions are not difficult? Support your answer. (b) Do they really think that if they died "it was not an accident but a mistake"? Support your answer. (c) Who might be more likely to express these opinions?
5. What is ironic, or surprising, about the fact that the bombers are named for girls?
6. What is the significance of the fact the pilots never see the people they kill?
7. (a) Who is the *they* referred to in the final line? (b) What does their comment reveal about their attitude toward the pilots?

Applying

8. How is this poem similar to and different from some of the other literary works about war you have read?

ANALYZING LITERATURE

Understanding Theme

The **theme** is the central idea or insight about life that a writer hopes to convey in a work of literature. Most often, a theme is revealed indirectly through the writer's choice of details, portrayal of characters and events, and use of literary devices.

1. What is the theme of "Losses"?
2. What details play an important role in conveying the theme?
3. How does the use of irony also help convey the theme?

THINKING AND WRITING

Writing About a Writer's Attitude

Write an essay in which you discuss what "The Death of the Ball Turret Gunner" and "Losses" reveal about Jarrell's attitude toward war. Reread both poems, focusing on their themes. Create a chart, listing details from both poems that help convey the poet's attitude. Prepare a thesis statement. Then write your essay, using passages from the two poems to support your thesis. When you revise, make sure you have included enough supporting information. Check that you have quoted precisely and have punctuated your quotations accurately. Proofread your essay and share it with your classmates.

BIOGRAPHIES

José Garcia Villa (1914–   )

José Garcia Villa's poetry reflects his concern for the individual. In fact, Villa himself has commented that his purpose as a poet is to find "man's selfhood and identity in the mystery of Creation."

Born in the Philippines, Villa came to the United States at the age of sixteen. While an undergraduate at the University of New Mexico, he established a reputation as a short-story writer. He began studying poetry while in college but did not have a collection published in the United States until 1942. This book, *Have Come, Am Here,* was followed by a second collection, *Volume Two,* in 1949. Since then Villa has published several more volumes of poetry and a collection of short stories.

Alice Walker (1944–   )

Although she is known mainly for her fiction, Alice Walker has also written a good deal of poetry. Like her other works, her poems reflect her interest in and respect for the black women of America.

Walker was born into a family of sharecroppers in Georgia. Her first book of poetry, *Once* (1968), was inspired by a trip to Africa in the summer of 1964. After publishing another book of poetry, *Revolutionary Petunias and Other Poems,* Walker focused on writing fiction. Her first novel, *Meridian* (1976), has been praised as one of the finest novels to come out of the civil rights movement; and her third novel, *The Color Purple* (1982), earned her a Pulitzer Prize.

Reed Whittemore (1919–   )

Although Reed Whittemore's poetry is often witty and fanciful, his best poems contain profound observations about contemporary American life.

Born in New Haven, Connecticut, Whittemore attended Yale University. After serving in the United States Army Air Force during World War II, he did graduate work in history at Princeton. While at Princeton, Whittemore published his first book of poetry, *Heroes and Heroines* (1946). Since then he has published many additional poetry collections, several books of essays, and a biography of the poet William Carlos Williams. He has also won numerous awards, including a grant from the National Institute of Arts and a Guggenheim Fellowship.

Be Beautiful, Noble, Like the Antique Ant; Expect Nothing; Still Life

Literary Forms

Lyric Poetry. A lyric poem expresses the personal thoughts and feelings of the speaker. One of the oldest and most popular forms of poetry, lyrics were originally sung to the accompaniment of a stringed instrument called a lyre. Although lyrics are no longer meant to be sung, they retain a musical quality. Lyrics also tend to be brief and generally focus on producing a single, unified effect.

Look For

As you read the following poems, look for the thoughts and feelings that they express.

Writing

In "Be Beautiful, Noble, like the Antique Ant," José Garcia Villa illustrates the importance of modesty. Freewrite about the value of modesty, exploring the reasons why it is an important virtue.

Vocabulary

Knowing these words will help you as you read the following poems.

frugally (froo′ g′ lē) *adv.*: Thriftily (p. 1222, l. 1)

inanimate (in an′ ə mit) *adj.*: Not endowed with life (p. 1224, l. 8)

eloquence (el′ ə kwəns) *n.*: Expressiveness; persuasive power (p. 1224, l. 19)

turbulence (tʉr′ byə ləns) *n.*: Commotion or wild disorder (p. 1224, l. 21)

Be Beautiful, Noble, Like the Antique Ant

José García Villa

Be beautiful, noble, like the antique ant,
Who bore the storms as he bore the sun,
Wearing neither gown nor helmet,
Though he was archbishop and soldier:
5   Wore only his own flesh.

Salute characters with gracious dignity:
Though what these are is left to
Your own terms. Exact: the universe is
Not so small but these will be found
10 Somewhere. Exact: they will be found.

Speak with great moderation: but think
With great fierceness, burning passion:
Though what the ant thought
No annals reveal, nor his descendants
15 Break the seal.

Trace the tracelessness of the ant,
Every ant has reached this perfection.
As he comes, so he goes,
Flowing as water flows,
20 Essential but secret like a rose.

THINKING ABOUT THE SELECTION

Recalling

1. What advice does the speaker give at the beginning of each stanza?
2. According to the final stanza, what "perfection" has the ant reached?

Interpreting

3. (a) In what sense can an ant be thought of as "antique"? (b) In what sense is an ant like an "archbishop"? (c) In what sense is an ant like a "soldier"?

4. What does the speaker mean when he refers to the "tracelessness of the ant"?
5. In what sense is a rose "essential but secret"?
6. (a) What human virtue does the speaker attribute to the ant? (b) What does he feel that people can learn from ants?

Applying

7. What other human virtues might be attributed to ants?
8. From what other insects or animals do you think people might learn? Explain your answer.

Expect Nothing

Alice Walker

Expect nothing. Live frugally
On surprise.
Become a stranger
To need of pity
5 Or, if compassion be freely
Given out
Take only enough
Stop short of urge to plead
Then purge away the need.

10 Wish for nothing larger
Than your own small heart

Or greater than a star;
Tame wild disappointment
With caress unmoved and cold
15 Make of it a parka
For your soul.

Discover the reason why
So tiny human midget
Exists at all
20 So scared unwise
But expect nothing. Live frugally
On surprise.

SOMEWHERE IN AMERICA
Robert Brackman
National Museum of American Art
Smithsonian Institution

THINKING ABOUT THE SELECTION

Recalling

1. (a) According to the speaker, to what should we "become a stranger"? (b) For what should we wish? (c) How should we deal with "wild disappointment"? (d) What should we "discover"?

Interpreting

2. (a) What is the meaning of lines 3–4? (b) What is the meaning of lines 10–12?
3. How can disappointment be made into "a parka for your soul"?
4. What do lines 18–20 reveal about the speaker's attitude concerning humanity's place in the universe?
5. Explain the title of this poem.

Applying

6. Do you agree with the advice given by the speaker of the poem? Why or why not?

ANALYZING LITERATURE

Understanding Lyric Poetry

"Expect Nothing" is an example of a lyric—a brief poem that expresses the thoughts and feelings of the speaker in lively, musical language.
1. What are the main thoughts and feelings that the speaker expresses in the poem?

2. What does the poem reveal about the speaker's attitude toward life?

UNDERSTANDING LANGUAGE

Recognizing Abstract Words

Concrete words are those which appeal to one or more of the five senses. In contrast, abstract words are ones that express qualities or concepts that exist apart from any material object. For example, the word *love* is abstract, while the word *rose* is concrete.

Define in your own words each of the following words from "Expect Nothing." Check your definitions in the dictionary. Then think of a concrete image, or word picture, that conveys the qualities or concepts expressed by the abstract word.
1. surprise   3. compassion
2. pity   4. disappointment

THINKING AND WRITING

Comparing and Contrasting Poems

Imagine you work for a literary magazine and have been asked to write an article comparing and contrasting "Expect Nothing" with "Be Beautiful, Noble, like the Antique Ant." Reread both poems, noting similarities and differences in purpose and theme. Organize your notes according to corresponding points of contrast. Then write your essay, using passages from the two poems to support your argument. When you revise, make sure you have connected your ideas using transitions and other linking devices.

Still Life

Reed Whittemore

I must explain why it is that at night, in my own house,
Even when no one's asleep, I feel I must whisper.
Thoreau and Wordsworth[1] would call it an act of devotion,
I think; others would call it fright; it is probably
5 Something of both. In my living-room there are matters I'd
    rather not meddle with
Late at night.

I prefer to sit very still on the couch, watching
All the inanimate things of my daytime life—
The furniture and the curtains, the pictures and books—
10 Come alive,
Not as in some childish fantasy, the chairs dancing
And Disney[2] prancing backstage, but with dignity,
The big old rocker presiding over a silent
And solemn assembly of all my craftsmen,
15 From Picasso[3] and other dignities gracing my walls
To the local carpenter benched at my slippered feet.

I find these proceedings
Remarkable for their clarity and intelligence, and I wish I
    might somehow
Bring into daylight the eloquence, say, of a doorknob.
20 But always the gathering breaks up; everyone there
Shrinks from the tossing turbulence
Of living,
A cough, a creaking stair.

---

1. Thoreau and Wordsworth: American author Henry David
Thoreau (1817–1862) and British poet William Wordsworth (1770–
1850).
2. Disney: Famous American film producer, Walt Disney (1901–
1966).
3. Picasso: Painter Pablo Picasso (1881–1973).

INTERIOR
Preston Dickinson
The Metropolitan Museum of Art

THINKING ABOUT THE SELECTION
Recalling
1. (a) What does the speaker watch while sitting on his couch late at night? (b) What is his attitude toward what he sees?

Interpreting
2. (a) What effect does nighttime have on the speaker? (b) How does the speaker's nighttime life contrast with his daytime life? (c) How is this contrast conveyed?
3. What does the speaker mean when he comments that he wishes he could "Bring into daylight the eloquence . . . of a doorknob"?
4. What is the significance of the poem's title?

Applying
5. Do you agree with the suggestion the poem makes concerning the effect of nighttime on the imagination? Why or why not?

CRITICAL THINKING AND READING
Analyzing the Meaning of Allusions

An allusion is a short reference to another literary work or a figure, place, or event from history, religion, or mythology. To understand the meaning of an allusion, you must have some knowledge of the work or figure to which the writer is alluding.

In "Still Life" Whittemore alludes to four men known for imagination and creativity. Look up each of these men in an encyclopedia. Then explain the meaning of each allusion and how each contributes to the poem's overall meaning.

Richard Wilbur (1921–   )

Like many other contemporary poets, Richard Wilbur is known for his elegant and imaginative use of language. Yet, unlike most of the other poets of our time, Wilbur uses traditional poetic forms and techniques in expressing an optimistic outlook toward life and an awareness of the world's beauty.

Wilbur was born in New York City but spent most of his childhood on a farm in rural northern New Jersey. After graduating from Amherst College, he served in the army infantry in Europe during World War II. He began writing poetry during the war and published his first book, *The Beautiful Changes and Other Poems* (1947), while he was a graduate student at Harvard.

Wilbur has gone on to publish many other volumes of poetry. His third book, *Things of This World* (1956), won both the Pulitzer Prize and the National Book Award. He has also published translations of a number of French dramas, a collection of essays, lyrics for an operetta based on Voltaire's novel *Candide,* and two books for children.

Robert Penn Warren (1905–   )

Robert Penn Warren is one of the most versatile, prolific, and distinguished writers of our time. He has written poetry, stories, novels, plays, criticism, essays, textbooks, and a biography, and has received three Pulitzer Prizes.

Warren was born in Guthrie, Kentucky. When he was sixteen, he entered Vanderbilt University, where he began to write poetry. After graduating from Vanderbilt in 1925, he studied at the University of California, Yale, and Oxford. In 1935 he became one of the founding editors of the literary magazine, *The Southern Review*. Just over a decade later, he was awarded his first Pulitzer Prize for his novel, *All the King's Men* (1947), which explores the subject of southern politics. He received his second Pulitzer Prize in 1959 for *Promises,* a volume of poetry; and in 1980 he won a third Pulitzer Prize for *Now and Then* (1979), another collection of poetry.

Warren has consistently used southern settings and characters in both his poetry and fiction, but at the same time he focuses on universal themes. In his work, he emphasizes love of the land, continuity between generations, and the need for self-knowledge and fulfillment in an often violent world.

GUIDE FOR READING

The Beautiful Changes; Gold Glade; Evening Hawk

Writer's Techniques

Imagery. Imagery refers to words or phrases that create mental pictures, or images, that appeal to one or more of the five senses—sight, hearing, touch, smell, or taste. Most often, images appeal to our sense of sight. For example, Warren creates a visual image in "Evening Hawk," when he writes, "From plane of light to plane, wings dipping through/Geometries and orchids that the sunset builds." Although visual imagery is the most common type of imagery, many images present sensations that we cannot visualize, and some images appeal to more than one sense. For example, in "Gold Glade" when Warren writes that there was "No breathing of air," he creates an image that appeals to both our senses of hearing and touch but not to our sense of sight.

Look For

As you read the following poems, look for the use of imagery. To what sense do most of the images appeal? Which images are especially vivid or striking?

Writing

To what do you think the title of Richard Wilbur's poem, "The Beautiful Changes," might refer? Explore the possible subjects of the poem by preparing a list of "beautiful changes" that occur in nature, in people's lives, and in people's behavior.

Vocabulary

Knowing the following words will help you as you read the following poems.

declivity (di kliv′ ə tē) *n.*: A downward slope (p. 1230, l. 12)
tumultuous (too mul′ choo wəs) *adj.*: Wild and noisy (p. 1232, l. 4)

guttural (gut′ ər əl) *adj.*: Of the throat (p. 1232, l. 5)

QUEEN ANNE'S LACE, 1957
Charles Burchfield
The Detroit Institute of Arts

The Beautiful Changes

Richard Wilbur

One wading a Fall meadow finds on all sides
The Queen Anne's Lace[1] lying like lilies
On water; it glides
So from the walker, it turns
5   Dry grass to a lake, as the slightest shade of you
Valleys my mind in fabulous blue Lucernes.[2]

---

1. Queen Anne's Lace: A weed with finely divided foliage and white flowers.
2. Lucernes (loo surnz′): The Lake of Lucerne, located in central Switzerland.

The beautiful changes as a forest is changed
By a chameleon's tuning his skin to it;
As a mantis, arranged
10   On a green leaf, grows
Into it, makes the leaf leafier, and proves
Any greenness is deeper than anyone knows.

Your hands hold roses always in a way that says
They are not only yours; the beautiful changes
15   In such kind ways,
Wishing ever to sunder
Things and things' selves for a second finding, to lose
For a moment all that it touches back to wonder.

THINKING ABOUT THE SELECTION

Recalling

1. What scene does the speaker describe in the first stanza?
2. (a) How does the chameleon change? (b) How does the mantis change?

Interpreting

3. (a) What comparison does the speaker develop in the first stanza? (b) What type of "change" does this comparison represent?
4. (a) In what sense does the change of the mantis make the "leaf leafier"? (b) Why does the change prove that "any greenness is deeper than anyone knows"?
5. What is unusual about the speaker's use of the word *beautiful*?
6. (a) What does the speaker mean when he comments that change offers a "second finding"? (b) Why does he believe that change can produce a sense of "wonder"?

Applying

7. Do you think that most people perceive changes in nature in the same way as the speaker does? Why or why not?

Gold Glade

Robert Penn Warren

Wandering, in autumn, the woods of boyhood,
Where cedar, black, thick, rode the ridge,
Heart aimless as rifle, boy-blankness of mood,
I came where ridge broke, and the great ledge,
5 Limestone, set the toe high as treetop by dark edge

Of a gorge, and water hid, grudging and grumbling,
And I saw, in mind's eye, foam white on
Wet stone, stone wet-black, white water tumbling,
And so went down, and with some fright on
10 Slick boulders, crossed over. The gorge-depth drew
      night on,

But high over high rock and leaf-lacing, sky
Showed yet bright, and declivity wooed
My foot by the quietening stream, and so I
Went on, in quiet, through the beech wood:
15 There, in gold light, where the glade gave, it stood.

The glade was geometric, circular, gold,
No brush or weed breaking that bright gold of leaf-fall.
In the center it stood, absolute and bold
Beyond any heart-hurt, or eye's grief-fall.
20 Gold-massy in air, it stood in gold light-fall,

No breathing of air, no leaf now gold-falling,
No tooth-stitch of squirrel, or any far fox bark,
No woodpecker coding, or late jay calling.
Silence: gray-shagged, the great shagbark[1]
25 Gave forth gold light. There could be no dark.

But of course dark came, and I can't recall
What county it was, for the life of me.
Montgomery, Todd, Christian—I know them all.
Was it even Kentucky or Tennessee?
30 Perhaps just an image that keeps haunting me.

---

1. **shagbark:** A hickory tree.

No, no! in no mansion under earth,
Nor imagination's domain of bright air,
But solid in soil that gave it its birth,
It stands, wherever it is, but somewhere.
35   I shall set my foot, and go there.

THINKING ABOUT THE SELECTION
Recalling

1. (a) What does the speaker hear while standing at "the great ledge"?   (b) What does he
   see in his "mind's eye"?
2. How does the speaker describe the glade?
3. What is the speaker now unable to recall
   about the glade?
4. What does the speaker vow to do at the end
   of the poem?

Interpreting

5. At what point does the action of the poem
   shift from the past to the present?
6. (a) What does the speaker mean when he
   comments that the glade is "beyond any
   heart-hurt, or eye's grief-fall"?   (b) What
   does he mean when he comments, "There
   could be no dark"?
7. (a) How many times is the word *gold* used in
   this poem?   (b) What is the significance of
   this word?

Applying

8. (a) What does the gold glade represent to
   the speaker?   (b) Why is he so anxious to
   return to the glade?

ANALYZING LITERATURE
Understanding Imagery

Imagery refers to words or phrases that create mental pictures, or images, that appeal to
one or more of the five senses—sight, hearing,
touch, smell, or taste. Although most of the imagery in "Gold Glade" appeals to our sense of
sight, Warren also uses images that appeal to
both our sense of hearing and our sense of
touch.

1. Find one image that appeals to the sense of
   hearing and one image that appeals to the
   sense of touch.
2. How do the visual images used in describing
   the woods on the ridge (lines 1–5) contrast
   with the images used in describing the glade
   (lines 15–25)?

THINKING AND WRITING
Writing a Poem Using Imagery

Write a poem in which you use vivid imagery
to re-create an important childhood experience.
Start by thinking of an important experience you
had as a child. Then prepare a list of concrete
details describing the incident. When you write
your poem, focus on creating vivid imagery and
do not worry about rhythm or rhyme. After you
finish writing, revise and proofread your poem,
and share it with your classmates.

SUMMER LANDSCAPE WITH HAWK,
1901–06
Louis M. Eilshemius
The Phillips Collection,
Washington, D.C.

Evening Hawk

Robert Penn Warren

From plane of light to plane, wings dipping through
Geometries and orchids that the sunset builds,
Out of the peak's black angularity of shadow, riding
The last tumultuous avalanche of
5 Light above pines and the guttural gorge,
The hawk comes.

His wing
Scythes[1] down another day, his motion

---

1. Scythes (sīthz) *v.*: Cuts as with a tool with a long single-edged
blade set at an angle on a long, curved handle.

Is that of the honed steel-edge, we hear
10 The crashless fall of stalks of Time.

The head of each stalk is heavy with the gold of our error.

Look! look! he is climbing the last light
Who knows neither Time nor error, and under
Whose eye, unforgiving, the world, unforgiven, swings
15 Into shadow.

       Long now,
The last thrush is still, the last bat
Now cruises in his sharp hieroglyphics.[2] His wisdom
Is ancient, too, and immense. The star
20 Is steady, like Plato,[3] over the mountain.

If there were no wind we might, we think, hear
The earth grind on its axis, or history
Drip in darkness like a leaking pipe in the cellar.

---

2. hieroglyphics (hī' ər ə glif' ikz) *n.*: Pictures or symbols,
representing words, syllables, or sounds.
3. Plato (427?–347? B.C.): A Greek philosopher.

THINKING ABOUT THE SELECTION

Recalling

1. How is the sunset described in lines 4–5?
2. What comment does the speaker make about the "last light" in lines 13–15?
3. According to the final stanza, what might we hear "If there were no wind"?

Interpreting

4. (a) What contrasting images, or word pictures, does Warren present in the first stanza? (b) How is this contrast developed throughout the rest of the poem?
5. (a) How does the speaker relate the hawk to darkness? (b) How does he relate its movement to time? (c) What does he mean when he comments that the "stalks of Time" are "heavy with the gold of our error"?
6. (a) Why might the speaker consider a bat to be wise? (b) Why might he compare a star to Plato?
7. What does the speaker mean when he describes history as dripping "in darkness like a leaking pipe in the cellar"?

Applying

8. What animals and other elements of nature, aside from the ones mentioned in the poem, do you associate with darkness?

BIOGRAPHIES

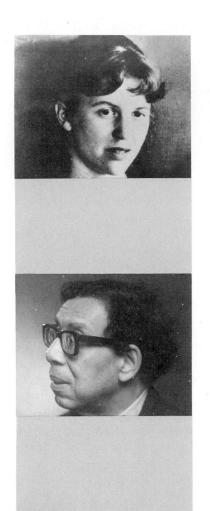

Sylvia Plath (1932–1963)

Despite her success as a poet, Sylvia Plath lived a very short, unhappy life. In many of her poems, she expresses her intense feelings of despair and her deep inner pain.

Born in Boston, Plath wrote poetry and received scholastic and literary awards as a child. Although she suffered a nervous breakdown during her junior year, she graduated with highest honors from Smith College. She went on to attend Cambridge University in England. In 1956 she married English poet Ted Hughes, and, after a year in the United States, the couple settled in England. Plath's first volume of poetry, *The Colossus* (1960), was the only collection of her work to appear during her lifetime. Two more books of her poetry and her novel, *The Bell Jar* (1963), were published posthumously.

Robert Hayden (1913–1980)

An extremely versatile poet, Robert Hayden used a variety of poetic forms and techniques and focused on a wide range of subjects. In addition to writing about his personal experiences, Hayden wrote about current and historical events, mythology, and folklore.

Born in Detroit, Hayden attended Wayne State University. He received a master's degree from the University of Michigan and taught there and at Fisk University in Tennessee. He published several collections of poetry, including *Heart-Shape in the Dust* (1940), *The Lion and the Archer* (1948), and *The Night-Blooming Dereus* (1972). His collection *A Ballad of Remembrance* received the Grand Prize for Poetry at the First World Festival for Negro Arts in 1966.

William Stafford (1914–   )

The poetry of William Stafford reflects his love for the natural world and his fear that modern technology will someday destroy the wilderness. Focusing on such subjects as the threat of nuclear war and the beauty of untamed nature, Stafford writes simply and directly about the causes in which he believes.

Born in Hutchinson, Kansas, Stafford attended the University of Kansas. Although he began submitting poems to poetry journals during the 1940's, he did not publish his first book, *West of Your City,* until he was forty-six. Since then he has published several more collections of poetry, including *Traveling Through the Dark,* which earned him the National Book Award in 1962.

GUIDE FOR READING

Mirror; Those Winter Sundays; Traveling Through the Dark

Literary Forms

Confessional Poetry. Confessional poetry is a type of poetry in which the poet speaks frankly and openly about his or her own life. This type of poetry was introduced by Robert Lowell, when he published his collection *Life Studies* in 1959. Lowell felt that the writing of poetry had become too intellectual and impersonal and needed a "breakthrough back into life." Traditionally, when writers used the first-person pronoun "I" in a poem, readers were taught to think of the "I" as the speaker of the poem, not the poet himself or herself. Even when the "I" clearly did refer to the poet, the poet tended to reveal little about his or her doubts, frustrations, and painful experiences. In *Life Studies,* however, Lowell openly expressed his thoughts and feelings concerning his family, his experiences, and his personal problems. Many other poets followed Lowell's example and confessional poetry became a popular literary form. Other poets known for their confessional poetry include John Berryman, Sylvia Plath, and Anne Sexton.

Look For

As you read "Those Winter Sundays" look for the frankness and openness with which the poet discusses his personal experiences. What does the poem reveal about the poet's personality?

Writing

In "Those Winter Sundays," Hayden writes about the sacrifices his father made for his family. Freewrite about a person who has in some way tried to make your life easier and more pleasant.

Vocabulary

Knowing these words will help you as you read the following poems.
preconceptions (prē′ kən sep′ shənz) *n.*: Ideas formed beforehand (p. 1236, l. 1)
meditate (med′ ə tāt′) *v.*: Think deeply (p. 1236, l. 6)

chronic (krän′ ik) *adj.*: Continuing indefinitely (p. 1239, l. 9)
austere (ô stir′) *adj.*: Showing strict self-discipline and self-denial (p. 1239, l. 14)

Mirror

Sylvia Plath

I am silver and exact. I have no preconceptions.
Whatever I see I swallow immediately
Just as it is, unmisted by love or dislike.
I am not cruel, only truthful—
5   The eye of a little god, four-cornered.
Most of the time I meditate on the opposite wall.
It is pink, with speckles. I have looked at it so long
I think it is a part of my heart. But it flickers.
Faces and darkness separate us over and over.
10   Now I am a lake. A woman bends over me,
Searching my reaches for what she really is.
Then she turns to those liars, the candles or the moon.
I see her back, and reflect it faithfully.
She rewards me with tears and an agitation of hands.
15   I am important to her. She comes and goes.
Each morning it is her face that replaces the darkness.
In me she has drowned a young girl, and in me an old
   woman
Rises toward her day after day, like a terrible fish.

THINKING ABOUT THE SELECTION

Recalling

1. (a) How does the mirror describe its appearance? (b) What does it do with whatever it sees?
2. (a) For what is the woman searching when she "bends over" the mirror? (b) With what does the woman reward the mirror? (c) What "rises toward" the woman in the mirror "day after day"?

Interpreting

3. In what way are the candle and the moon "liars"?

4. (a) Who is the "young girl" who has drowned? (b) Who is the "old woman"? (c) Why is the old woman "like a terrible fish"?
5. (a) How does the woman feel about aging? (b) How is her attitude revealed?

Applying

6. Do you think that most people share the woman's attitude toward aging? Why or why not?

GIRL IN WHITE DRESS
Sir William Orpen
Private Collection
Bridgeman Art Resource

Those Winter Sundays

Robert Hayden

Sundays too my father got up early
and put his clothes on in the blueblack cold,
then with cracked hands that ached
from labor in the weekday weather made
5 banked fires blaze. No one ever thanked him.

I'd wake and hear the cold splintering, breaking.
When the rooms were warm, he'd call,
and slowly I would rise and dress,
fearing the chronic angers of that house,

10 Speaking indifferently to him,
who had driven out the cold
and polished my good shoes as well.
What did I know, what did I know
of love's austere and lonely offices?

THINKING ABOUT THE SELECTION

Recalling

1. (a) Why did Hayden's father get up early on Sunday mornings? (b) Why did his father's hands ache?

Interpreting

2. What does the first stanza reveal about Hayden's father's dedication to his family?
3. What does Hayden mean when he says that he could "hear the cold splintering, breaking"?
4. What does Hayden mean when he refers to the chronic angers of his house?
5. How do you think Hayden eventually learned about "love's austere and lonely offices"?

Applying

6. Why do you think that some young people are unable to appreciate the sacrifices their parents make for them? (b) Why do you think young people sometimes have a difficult time communicating with their parents?

ANALYZING LITERATURE

Understanding Confessional Poetry

Confessional poetry is poetry that deals openly and frankly with a poet's personal life. Although confessional poems are autobiographical, the situations and problems on which they focus are often universal. For example, in "Those Winter Sundays," Hayden writes about his indifference toward the sacrifices his father made for his family—an attitude shared by many young people in contemporary society.

1. How has Hayden's attitude toward his father changed since his childhood?
2. How does he make it clear that he now regrets the way he reacted to his father?
3. What is his message to readers?

Traveling Through the Dark

William Stafford

Traveling through the dark I found a deer
dead on the edge of the Wilson River road.
It is usually best to roll them into the canyon:
that road is narrow; to swerve might make more dead.

5   By glow of the tail-light I stumbled back of the car
and stood by the heap, a doe, a recent killing;
she had stiffened already, almost cold.
I dragged her off; she was large in the belly.

My fingers touching her side brought me the reason—
10 her side was warm; her fawn lay there waiting,
alive, still, never to be born.
Beside that mountain road I hesitated.

The car aimed ahead its lowered parking lights;
under the hood purred the steady engine.
15 I stood in the glare of the warm exhaust turning red;
around our group I could hear the wilderness listen.

I thought hard for us all—my only swerving—,
then pushed her over the edge into the river.

THINKING ABOUT THE SELECTION

Recalling

1. (a) Where does the speaker find the deer? (b) What does he observe about the deer "by glow of the tail-light"? (c) What does he discover when he touches the deer? (d) What does the speaker do with the deer at the end of the poem?

Interpreting

2. (a) How does the speaker personify, or attribute human qualities to, his car in the fourth stanza? (b) How does this image of the car relate to the speaker's discovery of the deer?
3. What does this poem reveal about the relationship between humanity and nature in the modern world?
4. In literature, a journey is often used to symbolize, or represent, life. Assuming that this is the case in Stafford's poem, how might you interpret the poem's title?

Applying

5. Do you think the speaker makes the proper decision about what to do with the deer? Why or why not?

UNDERSTANDING LANGUAGE

Completing Word Analogies

Word analogies often appear on standardized tests. To complete them, you must first identify the relationship in the first pair of words and then add a word to the second pair that has the same relationship. For example,

DOE: FAWN : : COW:

The relationship between the first pair of words is mother to child. Therefore, to complete the second pair, you must find the word that names the child of a cow. This word is *calf*.

Read each word analogy below: First identify whether the relationship is mother to child or child to mother. Then complete the second pair with the appropriate word.

1. CAT : KITTEN : : BEAR:
2. SOW : PIGLET : : DOG:
3. LAMB : EWE : : DUCK:
4. CHICK : HEN : : GOSLING:

THINKING AND WRITING

Writing a Confessional Poem

Write a poem expressing your feelings of affection and appreciation for a person who has in some way tried to make your life easier or more pleasant. Start by reviewing the freewriting you did before you began reading this group of poems. When you write your poems, use concrete images, or word pictures, in describing your feelings. After revising your poem, share it with the person about whom it is written.

BIOGRAPHIES

Donald Justice (1925–   )

Thoroughout the course of his career, Donald Justice has experimented with different poetic forms and techniques. In all of his poetry, however, he displays a firm command of language and rhythm.

Born in Miami, Florida, Justice studied at the University of Miami, the University of North Carolina, Stanford University, and the University of Iowa. He began writing poetry in 1952, and in 1960 he published his first book of poems, *The Summer Anniversaries*. Since then he has published four more collections, including *The Local Storm* (1963) and *Selected Poems* (1979), which earned him a Pulitzer Prize.

Howard Nemerov (1920–   )

In his poetry Howard Nemerov has explored various themes. While some of his poems are light and witty, others focus on serious philosophical subjects such as the relationship between humanity and nature.

Born in New York City, Nemerov began writing poetry while attending Harvard. During World War II, he served as a pilot in the Royal Canadian Air Force and the United States Army Air Force. After returning from the war, he published his first collection of poetry, *The Image of the Law* (1947). Since then he has published eleven more volumes of poetry, three novels, two collections of short stories, and six books of literary criticism. In 1978 he won the National Book Award and the Pulitzer Prize for his *Collected Poems*.

James Wright (1927–1980)

In the introduction to his second book, *The Green Wall* (1957), James Wright wrote that his purpose as a poet was to say something that was "humanly important, instead of just showing off language." Throughout his career, Wright achieved this goal, while at the same time writing poetry that is filled with elegant language and rich, vivid imagery.

Wright was born in Martins Ferry, Ohio, and educated at Kenyon College and the University of Washington. During his brief life, he published five books of poetry, including *Saint Judas* (1959), *The Branch Will Not Break* (1963), and *Shall We Gather at the River* (1968). In 1972 he received the Pulitzer Prize for his *Collected Poems* (1971).

GUIDE FOR READING

Poem; Storm Windows; Lying in a Hammock at William Duffy's Farm in Pine Island, Minnesota

Writer's Techniques

Sound Devices. Poets use a variety of sound devices to give their writing a musical quality and to emphasize certain words and reinforce meaning. Alliteration, assonance, consonance, and onomatopoeia are four of the most common sound devices.

Alliteration is the repetition of similar sounds, usually consonants, at the beginnings of words or accented syllables. Notice the repetition of the *d* sound in the following line from "Traveling Through the Dark": "Traveling through the *d*ark I found a *d*eer".

Assonance is the repetition of vowel sounds. For example, the *o* sound is repeated in line 3 of "Storm Windows": "Dr*o*ve them indoors. S*o*, coming h*o*me at noon."

Consonance is the repetition of consonant sounds at the ends of words or accented syllables. For example, the *k* sound is repeated in line 2 of "Lying in a Hammock at William Duffy's Farm in Pine Island, Minnesota": "Asleep on the bla*ck* trun*k*."

Onomatopoeia refers to the use of words whose sounds in some way mimic or suggest their meanings. *Meow, bang,* and *crash* are examples of onomatopoetic words; and in the following line from Robert Penn Warren's "Gold Glade," the word *grumbling* is onomatopoetic: "Of a gorge, and water hid, grudging and *grumbling*."

Look For

As you read the following poems, look for the use of sound devices. How do the sound devices contribute to the overall effect of each poem?

Writing

In "Lying in a Hammock at William Duffy's Farm in Pine Island, Minnesota," the speaker presents his observations of a farm at sunset. What types of details do you think the speaker is likely to have observed? Prepare a list of images, or word pictures, that you associate with farms.

Vocabulary

Knowing these words will help you as you read the following poems.
spurious (spyoor′ ē əs) *adj.*: False; artificial (p. 1245, l. 8)
nostalgias (näs tal′ jəs) *n.*: Longings (p. 1245, l. 12)
illumination (i loo′ mə nā′ shən) *n.*: Supplying of light (p. 1245, l. 16)

Poem

Donald Justice

This poem is not addressed to you.
You may come into it briefly,
But no one will find you here, no one.
You will have changed before the poem will.

PORTRAIT OF DIEGO
Giacometti
Galerie Maeght, Paris

5 Even while you sit there, unmovable,
   You have begun to vanish. And it does not matter.
   The poem will go on without you.
   It has the spurious glamor of certain voids.

   It is not sad, really, only empty.
10 Once perhaps it was sad, no one knows why.
   It prefers to remember nothing.
   Nostalgias were peeled from it long ago.

   Your type of beauty has no place here.
   Night is the sky over this poem.
15 It is too black for stars.
   And do not look for any illumination.

   You neither can nor should understand what it means.
   Listen, it comes without guitar,
   Neither in rags nor any purple fashion.
20 And there is nothing in it to comfort you.

   Close your eyes, yawn. It will be over soon.
   You will forget the poem, but not before
   It has forgotten you. And it does not matter.
   It has been most beautiful in its erasures.

25 O bleached mirrors! Oceans of the drowned!
   Nor is one silence equal to another.
   And it does not matter what you think.
   This poem is not addressed to you.

THINKING ABOUT THE SELECTION

Recalling

1. (a) According to the speaker, what will happen to you before the poem changes? (b) What is happening to you "even while you sit there"?

2. According to the sixth stanza, what will happen before you forget the poem?

Interpreting

3. (a) What does the speaker mean when he comments that "Night is the sky over this poem./It is too black for stars"? (b) Why does he believe that "You neither can nor should understand what" the poem means?

4. (a) What does this poem imply about the permanence of art? (b) What does it imply about the relationship between art and humanity?

Applying

5. Do you agree with the speaker's attitude toward poetry? Why or why not?

Storm Windows

Howard Nemerov

People are putting up storm windows now,
Or were, this morning, until the heavy rain
Drove them indoors. So, coming home at noon,
I saw storm windows lying on the ground,
5 Frame-full of rain; through the water and glass
I saw the crushed grass, how it seemed to stream
Away in lines like seaweed on the tide
Or blades of wheat leaning under the wind.
The ripple and splash of rain on the blurred glass
10 Seemed that it briefly said, as I walked by,
Something I should have liked to say to you,
Something . . . the dry grass bent under the pane
Brimful of bouncing water . . . something of
A swaying clarity which blindly echoes
15 This lonely afternoon of memories
And missed desires, while the wintry rain
(Unspeakable, the distance in the mind!)
Runs on the standing windows and away.

THINKING ABOUT THE SELECTION

Recalling

1. (a) What were people doing this morning? (b) Why did they stop?
2. What does the speaker see when he comes home at noon?
3. (a) To what does the poet compare the crushed grass? (b) What does the "swaying clarity" of the grass blindly echo?

Interpreting

4. How would you describe the mood of this poem?
5. (a) Why does the speaker associate the "dry grass bent under the pane Brimful of bouncing water" with "missed desires"? (b) How does the "wintry rain" that "runs on the standing windows and away" relate to the speaker's "missed desires"?
6. What do you think is the "Something I should have liked to say to you"?
7. Why is this poem called "Storm Windows"?

Applying

8. What other types of images do you think people might associate with missed chances and desires?
9. According to a Portuguese proverb, "What was hard to bear is sweet to remember." (a) Explain the meaning of this proverb? (b) How does it relate to "Storm Windows"?

ANALYZING LITERATURE

Understanding Sound Devices

Alliteration, assonance, consonance, and onomatopoeia are four sound devices used in literature. Alliteration is the repetition of similar sounds, usually consonants, at the beginnings of words or accented syllables. Assonance is the repetition of vowel sounds. Consonance is the repetition of consonant sounds at the ends of words or accented syllables. Onomatopoeia refers to the use of words whose sounds in some way mimic or suggest their meanings.

1. Find two examples of alliteration in "Storm Windows."
2. Find two examples of assonance.
3. Find one example of consonance.
4. Find one example of onomatopoeia.

CRITICAL THINKING AND READING

Analyzing the Effect of Sound Devices

Poets use sound devices to give their writing a musical quality. Sound devices can also reinforce meaning and contribute to the mood of a poem.

1. Read "Storm Windows" aloud, paying close attention to the use of sound devices. Then explain how the sound devices contribute to the poem's musical quality.
2. (a) How do the sound devices contribute to the mood of the poem? (b) How would you describe the mood of this poem?

Lying in a Hammock at William Duffy's Farm in Pine Island, Minnesota

James Wright

Over my head, I see the bronze butterfly,
Asleep on the black trunk,
Blowing like a leaf in green shadow.
Down the ravine behind the empty house,
5   The cowbells follow one another
Into the distances of the afternoon.

THE POET RECLINING 1915
Marc Chagall
The Tate Gallery, London

To my right,
In a field of sunlight between two pines,
The droppings of last year's horses
10 Blaze into golden stones.
I lean back, as the evening darkens and comes on.
A chicken-hawk floats over, looking for home.
I have wasted my life.

THINKING ABOUT THE SELECTION

Recalling

1. (a) What does the speaker see over his head? (b) What does he observe "down the ravine behind the empty house"? (c) What does he observe to his right? (d) What observation does he make about his own life?

Interpreting

2. Metonymy is a literary device in which something very closely associated with a thing is used to suggest or represent the thing itself. Wright uses this technique in line 5, using cowbells to represent cows. How does his use of this technique help him to create an image, or word picture, that appeals to both the sense of hearing and the sense of sight?
3. What overall impression do the images, or word pictures, in the poem convey?
4. (a) Why might the speaker's observations of the farm lead him to the conclusion he reaches at the end of the poem? (b) Do you think the poet means his words to be taken at face value? Explain your answer.

Applying

5. How would you define a well-spent life?

THINKING AND WRITING

Responding to Criticism

A critic has commented that in his poetry Wright focuses "not only on his experience but also on his response to that experience." Write an essay in which you discuss this statement in relation to "Lying in a Hammock at William Duffy's Farm in Pine Island, Minnesota." Use passages from the poem to support your argument. When you revise, make sure that you have adequately supported your opinion with details from the poem.

BIOGRAPHIES

Adrienne Rich (1929–   )

Adrienne Rich's career as a poet can be divided into two distinct stages. During the early part of her career, she wrote neatly crafted traditional verse. In contrast, her later poems are written in free verse and often explore her deepest personal feelings.

Born and raised in Baltimore, Rich began writing poetry at an early age. Her first volume of poetry, *A Change of World* (1951), was published just after she graduated from Radcliffe College. Since abandoning traditional poetic forms for free verse in the early 1960's, she has produced several collections of poetry. Her later books include *Snapshots of a Daughter-in-Law* (1963), *The Will to Change* (1971), and *Diving into the Wreck* (1973).

Simon Ortiz (1941–   )

An Acoma Pueblo Indian, Simon Ortiz carries on the Native-American tradition of storytelling in his poetry. Not surprisingly, much of his poetry reflects his deep awareness of his cultural heritage.

Ortiz was born in New Mexico. After graduating from the University of New Mexico, he attended the University of Iowa Writers' Workshop. He has worked as a teacher, journalist, and public relations director, and is currently a professor at the University of New Mexico. Possessing a strong belief in the importance of education, Ortiz devotes much of his free time to educating fellow Native Americans.

Diana Chang (1934–   )

Diana Chang, who spent most of her childhood in China, is another contemporary poet whose work reflects her cultural heritage. In fact, many of her poems, including "Most Satisfied by Snow" clearly exhibit the influence of ancient Oriental verse forms.

Born in New York City and raised in China, Chang settled in the United States following World War II. She attended Barnard College, graduating in 1955. In addition to writing poetry, she has written several novels, including *The Frontiers of Love* (1956), *The Only Game in Town,* and *Eye to Eye.* She has also served as the editor of *The American Pen,* a journal published by the international writers' association, P.E.N.

The Observer; Hunger in New York City; Most Satisfied by Snow

Writer's Techniques

Parallelism. Parallelism refers to the repeated use of phrases, clauses, or sentences that are similar in structure. Poets often use parallelism to create a sense of unity and establish a pattern in their poems, especially in poems written in free verse—verse that has irregular meter and line length. The use of parallelism also adds emphasis to certain words and phrases and helps to create a rhythm.

Look For

As you read "Hunger in New York City," look for Ortiz's use of parallelism. How does he use the technique to establish a pattern in the poem?

Writing

In Adrienne Rich's poem "The Observer," the speaker contrasts her own life with the life of Dian Fossey, a scientist who studied gorillas by living among them in the African jungle. Freewrite about the type of life that you imagine Fossey might have led while living among the gorillas. Why do you think she chose to lead this sort of life? What dangers do you think she might have faced? Why might she have found the experience rewarding?

Vocabulary

Knowing these words will help you as you read the following poems.

subscribe (səb skrīb') v.: To give support, sanction, or approval (p. 1252, l. 17)

automation (ôt' ə mā' shən) n.: In manufacturing, a system or process in which many or all of the processes of production, movement, and inspection of parts and materials are automatically performed or controlled by self-operated machinery (p. 1254, l. 20)

humble (hum' b'l) adj.: Not proud; modest (p. 1254, l. 27)

pervade (pər vād') v.: To pass through; to spread throughout (p. 1256, l. 4)

The Observer

Adrienne Rich

Completely protected on all sides
by volcanoes
a woman, darkhaired, in stained jeans
sleeps in central Africa.
5 In her dreams, her notebooks, still
private as maiden diaries,
the mountain gorillas move through their life term:
their gentleness survives
observation. Six bands of them
10 inhabit, with her, the wooded highland.
When I lay me down to sleep
unsheltered by any natural guardians
from the panicky life-cycle of my tribe
I wake in the old cellblock
15 observing the daily executions,
rehearsing the laws
I cannot subscribe to,
envying the pale gorilla-scented dawn
she wakes into, the stream where she washes her hair,
20 the camera-flash of her quiet
eye.

THINKING ABOUT THE SELECTION

Recalling

1. What inhabits the wooded highland with the darkhaired woman?
2. (a) Where is the speaker when she wakes? (b) What does she observe? (c) What does she rehearse?

Interpreting

3. (a) What do the details in the poem suggest about the world in which the speaker lives? (b) How does her world contrast with the world in which the scientist lives? (c) What is the speaker's attitude toward her world? (d) How is this attitude revealed?
4. Why does the speaker envy the scientist?

Applying

5. Do you think that most people in contemporary American society would envy the scientist? Why or why not?

Hunger in New York City

Simon Ortiz

Hunger crawls into you
from somewhere out of your muscles
or the concrete or the land
or the wind pushing you.

5   It comes to you, asking
for food, words, wisdom, young memories
of places you ate at, drank cold spring water,
or held somebody's hand,
or home of the gentle, slow dances,
10 the songs, the strong gods, the world
you know.

That is, hunger searches you out.
It always asks you,
How are you, son? Where are you?
15 Have you eaten well?
Have you done what you as a person
of our people is supposed to do?

And the concrete of this city,
the oily wind, the blazing windows,
20 the shrieks of automation cannot,
truly cannot, answer for that hunger
although I have hungered,
truthfully and honestly, for them
to feed myself with.

25 So I sang to myself quietly:
I am feeding myself
with the humble presence
of all around me;
I am feeding myself
30 with your soul, my mother earth;
make me cool and humble.
Bless me.

THE LONE TENEMENT
George W. Bellows
Three Lions

THINKING ABOUT THE SELECTION

Recalling

1. (a) From where does hunger crawl into you? (b) For what does it ask? (c) What cannot "answer for" the hunger?
2. What does the speaker sing to himself?

Interpreting

3. How does Ortiz personify hunger?
4. (a) What details indicate that the speaker has moved to the city from another place? (b) How is this place different from the city? (c) What details indicate that the speaker hungers for his original home?

Applying

5. This poem clearly reflects Ortiz's Native-American heritage. What does it reveal about the traditional attitudes of his tribe?

THINKING AND WRITING

Writing a Poem Using Parallelism

Write a free-verse poem in which you use parallelism to establish a pattern. Start by thinking of a subject for your poem. You might want to write about a personal experience, an important event, or an element of nature. Prepare a list of details describing your subject. Arrange your details in logical order. Then write your poem. When you finish writing, revise and proofread your poem.

Most Satisfied by Snow

Diana Chang

Against my windows,
fog knows
what to do, too

Spaces pervade
5   us, as well

But occupied by snow,
I see

Matter
matters

10   I, too,
flowering

CHRISTMAS MORNING, ADIRONDACKS, 1946
Rockwell Kent
Sunne Savage Gallery, Boston

THINKING ABOUT THE SELECTION

Recalling

1. What does the fog against the speaker's windows know?
2. What does the speaker see when she is "occupied by snow"?

Interpreting

3. What does the speaker mean when she comments that "spaces pervade us"?

4. (a) What difference between fog and snow does this poem highlight? (b) How is this contrast embodied in human beings?
5. (a) What is the meaning of the final two lines? (b) What is the poem's overall message?

Applying

6. This poem suggests that we can learn about ourselves by observing nature. Do you agree with this suggestion? Why or why not?

BIOGRAPHIES

Lawson Fusao Inada (1938–)

The first Asian-American poet to have a book published by a major American publishing company, Lawson Fusao Inada has established himself as a widely respected member of the American literary community.

Born in Fresno, California, Inada graduated from Fresno State College and later received a master's degree from the University of Oregon. He has taught at several universities, served as a consultant for many literary organizations, and published a number of books, including *Before the War: Poems As They Happen* (1971). He was also responsible for editing *Aiiieeeee!: An Anthology of Asian-American Writers* (1974).

Rita Dove (1952–)

Rita Dove has commented that "the events of the poem should never be more important than how that event is recreated." Considering this belief, it is not surprising that her poetry can be characterized by her vivid imagery and skillful use of language.

Dove was born in Akron, Ohio. She graduated with highest honors from Miami University in Oxford, Ohio, and later earned a master's degree from the University of Iowa. She has published several collections of poetry, including *The Yellow House on the Corner* (1980) and *Museum* (1983). In 1987 she received the Pulitzer Prize for her book, *Thomas and Beulah*.

GUIDE FOR READING

Plucking Out a Rhythm; This Life

Writer's Techniques

Free Verse. The majority of contemporary poetry is written in free verse—verse that has irregular meter and line length. Though free verse lacks regular meter, it does not lack rhythm. Yet it does allow poets to experiment with new types of rhythms in their work. For example, Lawson Fusao Inada's use of free verse enables him to capture the natural rhythms of jazz in "Plucking Out a Rhythm."

Look For

As you read each of the following poems, take note of the way in which the free verse is structured. What makes the poets' use of free verse effective?

Writing

In "Plucking Out a Rhythm," Lawson Fusao Inada explores how reality affects our imaginations. Freewrite about your own thoughts concerning the effect of reality on people's imaginations.

Vocabulary

Knowing these words will help you as you read the following poems.
posturing (päs′ chər iŋ) *v.*: Posing (p. 1260, l. 15)

exuding (ig zo͞od′ iŋ) *v.*: Oozing, discharging (p. 1260, l. 25)

Plucking Out a Rhythm

Lawson Fusao Inada

Start with a simple room—
a dullish color—
and draw the one shade down.
Hot plate. Bed.
5   Little phonograph in a corner.

Put in a single figure—
medium weight and height—
but oversize, as a child might.

The features must be Japanese.

10   Then stack a black pompadour[1] on,
and let the eyes
slide behind a night of glass.

The figure is in disguise:

slim green suit
15   for posturing on a bandstand,
the turned-up shoes of Harlem[2] . . .

Then start the music playing—
thick jazz, strong jazz—

and notice that the figure
20   comes to life:
sweating, growling
over an imaginary bass—
plucking out a rhythm—
as the music rises and the room is full,
25   exuding with that rhythm . . .

---

1. pompadour (päm′pə dôr′) *n.*: A hairdo in which the hair is swept up high from the forehead.
2. Harlem: A section of New York City, located in northern Manhattan.

VAUDEVILLE, 1951
Jacob Lawrence
Hirshhorn Museum and Sculpture Garden, Smithsonian Institution

Then have the shade flap up
and daylight catch him
frozen in that pose

as it starts to snow—
30 thick snow, strong snow—

blowing in the window
while the music quiets,
the room is slowly covered,

and the figure is completely
35 out of sight.

THINKING ABOUT THE SELECTION

Recalling

1. (a) What details does the speaker use in describing the "simple room"? (b) How does he describe the appearance of the "single figure"? (c) What is this person wearing? (d) What type of music does he play?
2. What causes the figure to disappear from sight?

Interpreting

3. To what two senses do most of the images, or word pictures, in the poem appeal?
4. How does the image in line 30 echo the image in line 17?
5. What does the impact of the snow on the imaginary musician suggest about the effect of reality on the imagination?

Applying

6. In what way do people's imaginations set them apart from one another?

ANALYZING LITERATURE

Understanding Free Verse

Free verse is verse that has irregular meter and line length. Through the use of free verse, poets are able to experiment with new types of rhythms in their poetry.

1. Why is free verse an appropriate form for "Plucking Out a Rhythm"?
2. How would the poem be different if it were written in verse with regular meter and line length?

THINKING AND WRITING

Responding to a Poem

Imagine that Lawson Fusao Inada has asked you to respond to "Plucking Out a Rhythm." Reread the poem. What do you like about the poem? What do you dislike about it? Organize your thoughts. Then write your response, using passages from the poem to support your opinions. When you finish writing, revise and proofread your response.

This Life

Rita Dove

The green lamp flares on the table.
You tell me the same thing
as that one,
asleep, upstairs.
5   Now I see: the possibilities
are like golden dresses in a nutshell.

As a child, I fell in love
with a Japanese woodcut
of a girl gazing at the moon.
10   I waited with her for her lover.
He came in white breeches[1] and sandals.
He had a goatee[2]—he had

your face, though I didn't know it.
Our lives will be the same—
15   your lips, swollen from whistling
at danger,
and I a stranger
in this desert,
nursing the tough skin of figs.

---

1. breeches *n.*: Pants reaching to or just below the knees.
2. goatee (gō tē′) *n.*: A small, pointed beard.

THINKING ABOUT THE SELECTION

Recalling

1. What does the speaker "see" in the first stanza?
2. What childhood memory does the speaker describe in the second stanza?
3. How does the speaker describe her life in the final three lines?

Interpreting

4. Who might the "one" mentioned in line 3 be?

5. What is the meaning of the simile, or comparison, in lines 5 and 6?
6. (a) What is the significance of the speaker's childhood memory? (b) How does it seem to relate to her present life?
7. What attitude does "whistling at danger" suggest?
8. What impression does the image of the "tough skin of figs" convey?

Applying

9. Why do childhood memories seem so vivid?

WOMAN WITH DARK HAIR, 1959
Jacob Kainen
National Museum of American Art,
Smithsonian Institution

Assignment

1. Many contemporary poets convey a deep awareness of the American landscape in their poetry. In doing so, they use vivid, striking imagery that brings the landscape to life for the reader. Write a poem in which you use vivid imagery to describe the appearance of the landscape in the region in which you live.

    Prewriting. Prepare a list of concrete details you can use in describing the landscape. Arrange the details in spatial order.

    Writing. When you write your poem, do not worry about rhythm or rhyme. Instead, focus on using concrete imagery to create a vivid picture of the landscape you are describing.

    Revising. When you finish writing, revise and proofread your poem and share it with your classmates.

Assignment

2. Writers often focus on the dominant issues of their time. What do you feel are the most important issues of the contemporary age? Write a brief informal essay in which you discuss your perceptions of the dominant issues of our time.

    Prewriting. Brainstorm about the dominant issues of our time, and list them in order of importance. Then eliminate some of the less important issues.

    Writing. When you write your essay, use an informal writing style, but make sure the essay is organized in a logical manner.

    Revising. When you revise, make sure you have explained why you think each issue you have discussed is important.

Assignment

3. The contemporary period has been a time of rapid change. Write a short story, narrative poem, personal essay, or journal entry in which you depict some of these changes and explore the ways in which they have affected people's lives. For example, you might write a story in which a middle-aged man reflects upon some of the important events and developments that have occurred during his lifetime.

    Prewriting. Prepare a list of changes and brainstorm about how they have affected people's lives. Then decide on the type of literary form that you wish to use.

    Writing. When writing your work, make sure your writing style and choice of words are appropriate for the literary form you have chosen.

    Revising. When you revise, check for errors in grammar, usage, and mechanics.

YOU THE CRITIC

Assignment

1. Many contemporary stories reflect the writers' perception that today's world is complex and impersonal, making it difficult for people to communicate with one another. Write an essay in which you discuss how this perception is reflected in one of the contemporary stories you have read.

Prewriting. After choosing a story, carefully reread it, focusing on theme, characterization, and the characters' interactions with one another. Prepare a thesis statement and organize your notes into an outline.

Writing. When you write your essay, use passages from the story to support your thesis.

Revising. When you revise, make sure you have included enough information to thoroughly support your thesis.

Assignment

2. During the contemporary period, many writers have chosen to build on the developments of the Modernists, applying the Modernist ideas and approaches to contemporary life. Write an essay in which you compare and contrast a modern story with a contemporary story.

Prewriting. Choose a modern story and a contemporary story that are in some ways similar in form and content. For example, you might choose "In Another Country" and "Imagined Scenes." Then carefully reread the stories, noting similarities and differences in structure and theme.

Writing. When you write your essay, organize your argument according to corresponding points of contrast.

Revising. When you revise, make sure you have thoroughly supported your argument with examples from the two stories.

Assignment

3. Contemporary literature is extremely varied and diverse, with writers exploring a wide variety of subjects and approaches. Write an essay in which you discuss the diversity of contemporary poetry or contemporary fiction.

Prewriting. Reread the discussion of contemporary literature in the unit introduction. Then review the selections in the unit, noting similarities and differences in form and content.

Writing. When writing your essay, use evidence from at least five selections to support your argument.

Revising. When you revise, make sure your argument is clear and coherent and is organized in a logical manner.

Roethke
teaches

WASHINGTON

Chief Joseph's "I Will Fight No More"

NORTH DAKOTA

OREGON

Chief Joseph born

MONTANA

Sioux Territory

IDAHO

SOUTH DAKOTA

WYOMING

Ezra Pound born

CALIFORNIA

NEVADA

NEBRASKA

Twain's *Roughing It*

UTAH

Cooper's *The Prairie*
(Natty Bumpo dies)

Willa Cather's stories

Twain meets Artemus Ward

COLORADO

KANSAS

Twain's Calaveras County

Katherine Ann Porter lives

G. Brooks born

Frost born

W. Stafford born

Steinbeck's
"Flight"

ARIZONA

NEW MEXICO

OKLAHOMA

Ralph Ellison born

N. Scott Momaday
born

Navaho Legends

Simon Ortiz lives, writes

Katherine Anne Porter born

TEXAS

McMurty's
Lonesome Dove

Lopez's
Arctic Dreams

London, Melville, Twain write

ALASKA

HAWAII

Literary Map of the United States

MINNESOTA

Chippewa

WISCONSIN

MICHIGAN

Hemingway stories

Roethke born

Fitzgerald's "Winter Dreams"

Wilder born

Hemingway born

Sandberg's "Chicago"

Sandberg born

IOWA

Master's "Spoon River"

ILLINOIS

INDIANA

OHIO

S. Anderson's *Winesburg, Ohio*

Dunbar born

Lincoln's Gettysburg Address

Twain's *Life on the Mississippi*

M. Moore, T.S. Eliot born

MISSOURI

L. Hughes born

Lincoln's youth

KENTUCKY

Robert Penn Warren born

R. Jarrell born

TENNESSEE

ARKANSAS

Ransom born

Faulkner's Yoknapatawpha ("The Bear")

Walker born

MISSISSIPPI

ALABAMA

LOUISIANA

Welty stories

Capote's youth

Lanier's "Song of the Chattahoochee"

GEORGIA

James Dickey born

Flannery O'Conner born

Mary Chestnut

SOUTH CAROLINA

NORTH CAROLINA

Thomas Wolfe

WEST VIRGINIA

VIRGINIA

Henry's "Speech in the Virginia Convention"

Robert E. Lee

Washington, DC (A. Adam's "Letter to Her Daughter")

S. Crane's *Red Badge*

MD

F. Douglas's youth

Poe dies

Philadelphia B.Franklin, Declaration of Independence

DL NJ

PA

W.C. William's Patterson

Princeton (John McPhee, Joyce Carol Oates)

de Crevecoeur's *Letters*

NY

Iroquois

New York City (Harlem Renaissance, B. Malamud, H. Nemerov, S.Ortiz)

Walt Whitman's home

J. Edward's Sermons

Nantucket, Melville's "Chowder"

CN

Emily Dickenson

RI

MA

Anne Bradstreet

Boston/Cambridge (Holmes, Phillis Wheatley, J.R. Lowell, Amy Lowell, E.E. Cummings)

Salem (C.Mather, Hawthorne)

Emerson's Concord, Walden Pond

Robert Frost

Wilder's Grovers Corners

Jewett's "White Heron"

Whittier's "Hampton Beach"

NH

VT

Longfellow teaches

Robinson's Tilbury Town

MAINE

HANDBOOK OF WRITING ABOUT LITERATURE

SECTION 1: UNDERSTANDING THE WRITING PROCESS

Lesson 1: Prewriting

Someone once remarked that easy writing makes difficult reading. Good writing always takes both time and effort. Understanding that writing a paper requires not one step but many can help you to have more realistic expectations of yourself as a writer. A writer does not simply sit down and produce a final version off the top of his or her head. Instead, a writer completes a number of stages that together make up the process of writing.

1. *Prewriting:* planning the piece of writing
2. *Drafting:* getting ideas down on paper in rough form
3. *Revising:* changing and improving the rough draft
4. *Proofreading:* correcting any errors in spelling or mechanics
5. *Publishing:* letting others read and share the writing

In this lesson you will learn about the steps that make up the prewriting stage.

STEP 1: ANALYZE THE SITUATION

You may feel that you should begin any paper by just sitting down and writing. However, a better way to begin is first to think about the entire context in which you will be working. To do so, ask yourself the following questions about the writing situation.

1. *Topic* (the subject that you will be writing about): What, exactly, is this subject? Can you state it in a sentence? Is your subject too broad or too narrow?

2. *Purpose* (what you want your writing to accomplish): Is your purpose to tell a story? to describe? to explain? to persuade? to entertain? Will your writing serve some combination of these purposes?

3. *Audience* (the people for whom you are writing): What are the backgrounds of the members of your audience? Do these people already know a great deal about your topic? Will you have to provide basic background information?

4. *Voice* (the way the writing will sound to the reader): What impression do you want to make on your audience? What tone should the piece of writing have? Should your writing be formal or informal, objective or subjective, emotional or dispassionate?

5. *Content* (the subject and all the information provided about it): How much do you already know about your subject? What will you have to find out? Will you have to do some research? If so, what sources can you use? Can you use books, magazines, newspapers, reference works, or interviews with other people? Can you draw on your own memories and experiences?

6. *Form* (the shape the writing will take, including its length and organization): What will the final piece of writing look like? How long will it be? Will it be written in one or more paragraphs? Will it have a distinct introduction, body and conclusion? What method of organization or organizing principle will you use?

STEP 2: MAKE A PLAN

Ask yourself the questions outlined in Step 1 to clarify the writing task. Answer any questions you can. Then make a plan of action for answering the questions that remain. You may find, for example, that you are unsure about your topic and that you need to do more thinking about it, or you may discover that you need to gather information for your paper and therefore will have to do some research.

STEP 3: GATHER INFORMATION

Ideas and information for writing can come either from within you or from outside sources. If you decide to use outside sources, you can try looking at books, magazines, films, television programs, or reference works of various kinds. You also might try using a computer information service or conducting interviews with people who are knowledgeable about your subject. If you decide to gather information from your own memories and experiences, you might try one of the following techniques.

1. *Analyzing:* Divide your topic into parts, think about these parts, and think about the relationships among the parts and between each part and the whole.
2. *Charting:* Make lists of key ideas or concepts related to your topic. List the parts of the topic, make a pros-and-cons chart, draw a tree diagram, or construct a time line. Make any kind of list or chart that is relevant to your topic.
3. *Clustering:* Write your topic in the middle of a sheet of paper. Then think about the topic and jot down any related ideas that occur to you. Circle these related ideas and connect them, with lines, to the topic. Then think about the related ideas, jot down other ideas, and connect these with lines. Continue in this way until you have filled the paper.
4. *Freewriting:* Without stopping to punctuate or to think about spelling or form, write down everything that comes into your mind as you think about the topic.
5. *Questioning:* Prepare a list of questions that deal with various aspects of your topic. Begin the questions with words such as *who, what, where, when, why,* and *how.*

These techniques can also be used to narrow a topic or to come up with a topic idea in the first place.

STEP 4: ORGANIZE YOUR NOTES

Your next step is to organize the information that you have gathered. If you have used note cards, you might organize these. If not, you might make a rough outline. In either case, you need to choose an order in which to present your ideas and information. The order to use is one that grows logically from your materials. The following are some common methods of organization.

1. *Chronological order:* events arranged in order of occurrence in time
2. *Spatial order:* features or items arranged in a physical order or pattern, as from right to left
3. *Degree order:* points arranged from least to most or from most to least according to degree of presence or absence of some property such as complexity, familiarity, frequency, effectiveness, value, or importance

CASE STUDY: PREWRITING

Juanita's English class was studying mass communications. The teacher asked each student to choose one medium of mass communication and to write a paragraph on some topic related to that medium. At first Juanita couldn't think of a topic, so she made the following tree diagram in her notebook.

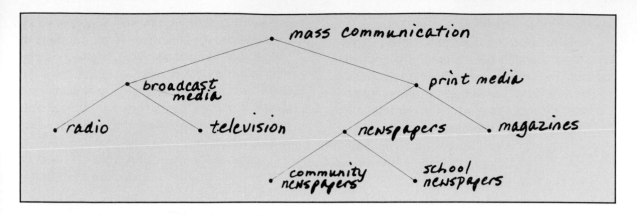

Juanita studied her diagram and decided that she wanted to write about school newspapers. However, she still needed a more narrow topic, so she did some freewriting and came up with this idea: She would write about the editorial policy of her school newspaper. This would be a good topic to write about because (1) Juanita worked on the school paper and knew something about its editorial policy and (2) because many of the students in Juanita's class probably didn't know what an editorial policy was, much less that the school paper had one.

Juanita then took the following notes.

- Topic: the editorial policy of our school newspaper

- Purpose: to explain the editorial policy to other students

- Audience: other students in my class (all readers of the school paper)

- Voice: relatively formal

- Content: information about the paper's editorial policy (but where am I going to find this information?)

- Form: one paragraph

Looking over her notes, Juanita recognized that she needed to make a plan for gathering information for her paragraph. She decided to interview the editor of the school paper, Colleen Ryan. First Juanita made a list of questions to ask Colleen, and then she arranged an interview. During the interview Juanita took notes, putting quotations around those comments that she got down word for word. Here are some of the notes that Juanita took.

- Does the school paper have an official editorial policy?
  "Yes." Policy is stated in a document called "The Editorial Policy of the Emerson High School Star Reporter"

- Who determines the editorial policy?
  "The editorial policy is determined by the editorial board, which is made up of the editor (that's me), the assistant editor, and the journalism advisor, Ms. Ortega."

- What, precisely, is the official editorial policy?
  Policy statement deals with lots of issues.
  Mostly, ensures that reporting will be fair, objective, unbiased.
  Also says that policy of paper is to print news of interest to students.
  Spells out what kinds of ads the paper can carry.
  Says who has the final word about what can go into the paper and what can't.

- Who does have the final word?

  Well, I suppose that the final word is Ms. Ortega's. She's the editor-in-chief. But the policy statement also says that the principal has the right to veto publication of any article if she considers doing so to be "in the best interest of the school."

- You mean that the principal can ask you not to print something? Doesn't that violate the freedom of the press?

  "In theory, perhaps it does. However, in practice, the principal never does stop publication of an article. Besides, every newspaper in the country has an editorial review board that turns thumbs up or thumbs down on particular articles."

- So having the materials in your paper be subject to review doesn't bother you?

  No, because the principal is only going to reject an article if it is irresponsible, and "we simply don't allow irresponsible articles to be considered in the first place."

As the interview progressed, Juanita realized that she had found a much more interesting topic to write about than the newspaper's editorial policy. She decided to change her topic to the issue of whether the student press should be completely free or subject to review by the school administration. She knew that this meant changing her statement of purpose as well. Her purpose would be to present both sides of this complicated issue.

ACTIVITIES AND ASSIGNMENTS

A. Answer the following questions about the case study:
1. What method did Juanita use to come up with a topic?
2. When Juanita analyzed the writing situation, what did she realize that she needed to do?
3. How did Juanita change her writing plan during the interview? What other parts of her writing plan will this change affect?

B. Select your own topic, or choose a reading from this book about which you want to comment. Begin work on an informal paragraph by following the prewriting steps discussed in this lesson.

Lesson 2: Drafting and Revising

DRAFTING YOUR PAPER

Once your prewriting is finished, you are ready to begin the drafting stage. *Drafting* is the process of getting ideas down on paper in rough form. When you draft, keep the following points in mind:

1. Choose a drafting style that is right for you. Some people like to write a quick and very rough draft and then go back and rework this draft considerably. Other people prefer to write a slow, careful draft, revising as they go. Choose whichever method works best for you. The quick draft has the advantage of allowing you to get all of your ideas down so they can be manipulated easily. The slow draft has the advantage of reducing the amount of revision time required later on.

2. Bear in mind that your first version is a draft and need not be perfect. If you choose to do a slow, careful draft, don't work so slowly and carefully that you interrupt your stream of thought. Make getting your ideas down the main priority. You can go back and work on the details of sentence structure, organization, spelling, and mechanics during the revision and proofreading stages.

3. Keep your audience, purpose, and voice in mind as you write. As you work, try not to stray too far from your original plan. If you find that the original plan isn't workable, go back to the prewriting stage and make a new plan.

4. As you draft, keep yourself open to new ideas. Work from your prewriting notes and your rough outline. However, remember that some of the best ideas occur while people are actually writing. If a new idea occurs to you and it is a good one, then use it. Don't forget that you can revise your prewriting plan at any time if you feel the need to do so.

5. Allow yourself enough time to write. Do not try to do all your writing at the last minute. Allow

---

CHECKLIST FOR REVISION

Topic and Purpose
- ☐ Is my main idea clear?
- ☐ Does the writing achieve its purpose?

Content and Development
- ☐ Have I developed the main idea completely?
- ☐ Have I provided examples or details that support the statements I have made?
- ☐ Are my sources of information unbiased, up-to-date, and authoritative?
- ☐ Have I avoided including unnecessary or unrelated ideas?

Form
- ☐ Have I followed a logical method of organization?
- ☐ Have I used transitions to make the connections between ideas clear?
- ☐ Does the writing have a clear introduction, body, and conclusion?

Audience
- ☐ Will my audience understand what I have said?
- ☐ Will my audience find the writing interesting?
- ☐ Will my audience respond in the way I intend?

Voice and Word Choice
- ☐ Does the writing convey the impression I intended it to convey?
- ☐ Is my language appropriate?
- ☐ Have I avoided vague, undefined terms?
- ☐ Have I used vivid, specific nouns, verbs, and adjectives?
- ☐ Have I avoided jargon?
- ☐ Have I avoided clichés, slang, euphemisms, and gobbledygook except for humorous effect?

---

yourself enough time to write a draft and then to revise and proofread it.

6. Write as many drafts as you need to write. One nice thing about writing is that you can do it over and over until you have a final product you are satisfied with.

REVISING YOUR DRAFT

Revising is the process of reworking a written draft to enhance its content and organization. After you finish your draft, use the checklist on the preceding page to identify ways to improve your paper.

CASE STUDY: DRAFTING AND REVISING

As you will recall from the preceding lesson, Juanita had decided to write a paper presenting two sides of a complicated issue: whether the student press should or should not be subject to review by academic administrators. As Juanita thought about this issue, she decided that she had firm personal opinions about it. She therefore decided to change her topic once again: She would write about why she believed that administrators should have the right to review articles before they appear in the student press.

Juanita wrote a first draft of her paper and then revised it. Here is her draft with the revisions that she made:

Recently
~~Two days ago~~ I interviewed the editor of our *Colleen Ryan,*

school newspaper, The Emerson High School
During our conversation *according to the*
Ms. Ryan told me *paper's editorial*
Star Reporter. ~~She said~~ that the Principal ~~had~~ *has*
policy,

the right to review any articles before they

could be printed in the paper. Initially I was
inscensed by
~~mad about~~ this ~~Because~~ it seemed to violate

---

the students right to *a* free press. ~~As~~ I thought *However,*

about the issue I realised that ~~their~~ were good
the review policy. First,
reasons for ~~this.~~ High school journalists are not

experienced. They need guidance regarding

such matters as what can be published in a

newspaper and what cannot. No paper can
sort of material. *for example,*
print just any ~~kind of stuff.~~ The law says that

papers can be held accountable for ~~anything~~
materials with
~~that they~~ print ~~that is libelous~~ The review policy
malice *a forethought.*
ensures that articles that violate the law will not
in the school paper. Second,
be published. *All* newspapers, including

professional ones, have review policies. The

Editor-in-Chief, and sometimes the Publisher,
ies
can veto publication of certain story. In the

case of the school paper, the journalism

sponser acts as the editor in chief, and the

Principal acts as the Publisher. They therefore

have the same right to accept or reject certain

articles as would thier counterparts in the world

of proffessional print journalism. Some

students might object to working under the

constraints of the review policy. However, these

students need to realise that they will be

working under the same constraints. When
become *ists,*
they ~~enter the world~~ of proffessional journalism.

ACTIVITIES AND ASSIGNMENTS

A. Answer the following questions about the case study:

1. Why did Juanita change the phrase "Two days ago" to the word "Recently"?
2. What transitions did Juanita add to show the logical connections between her ideas?
3. In what places did Juanita replace informal language with language that is more formal?
4. What sentence fragments did Juanita correct? How did she correct these fragments?
5. What information did Juanita add to make her statements clearer?
6. What spelling, punctuation, and capitalization errors did Juanita not correct during revision? During what stage of the writing process should such errors be corrected?

B. Use your notes and outlines from the preceding lesson to draft and revise a paragraph. Follow the procedures described in this lesson.

Lesson 3: Proofreading and Publishing

USING EDITORIAL SYMBOLS

After you have revised your draft, you are ready to begin proofreading. *Proofreading* is the process of checking for errors in spelling, grammar, mechanics, and manuscript form. As you proofread, use the editorial symbols shown on the next page to mark corrections on your draft:

USING A PROOFREADING CHECKLIST

Try to allow time between revising and proofreading. Doing so will make it easier for you to notice minor errors that you might otherwise miss. Proofread carefully, since just a few minor mistakes can distract a reader from many good ideas. Use the checklist at right to guide your proofreading.

When you have a question about some rule of spelling, grammar, mechanics, or manuscript form, check the rule in a dictionary, in a writing text, or in a grammar book. As you proofread, bear in mind the mistakes that you have made on papers in the past and try to avoid repeating these. After you proofread, make a neat final copy of your paper and check this copy as well.

PUBLISHING, OR SHARING, YOUR WORK

The neat final copy of your paper is ready for an audience. Most school papers have a teacher as the main reader, but you or your class can find other ways to share your writing. Here are some suggestions:

1. Share your writing with friends, parents, and other relatives.
2. Mail a copy of a paper you like to grandparents or to other relatives.
3. Read your paper aloud to a discussion group, to the whole class, or to a different class.

CHECKLIST FOR PROOFREADING

Grammar and Usage
- ☐ Are all my sentences complete? That is, have I avoided sentence fragments?
- ☐ Do all my sentences express just one complete thought? That is, have I avoided run-on sentences.
- ☐ Do my verbs agree with their subjects?
- ☐ Did I use all the words in my paper correctly? Am I sure the meaning and connotation of each word fits the writing?
- ☐ Does each pronoun clearly refer to something?
- ☐ Have I used adjectives and adverbs correctly?

Spelling
- ☐ Is every word correctly spelled?
- ☐ Have I double-checked the spelling of proper nouns?

Punctuation
- ☐ Does each sentence end with a punctuation mark?
- ☐ Have I used commas, semicolons, colons, hyphens, dashes, parentheses, quotation marks, and apostrophes correctly?

Capitalization
- ☐ Have I eliminated unnecessary capital letters?
- ☐ Have I correctly capitalized all words that need capital letters?

---

4. Trade papers with other students who sit nearby or who work with you on projects or in groups.
5. Create a publication containing writing by all the students in your class.
6. Make your own "book" of papers that you have written during the year. Share this book with classmates, with friends, or with relatives.

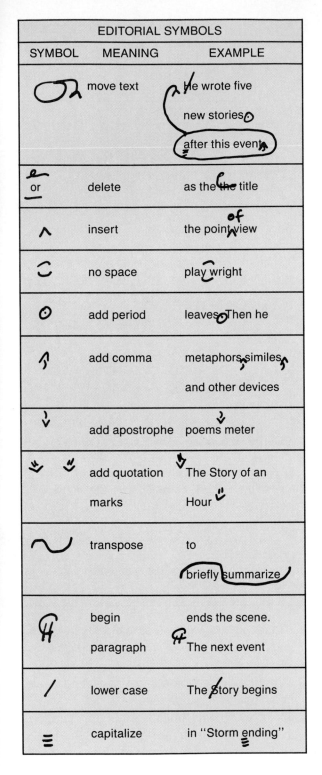

EDITORIAL SYMBOLS		
SYMBOL	MEANING	EXAMPLE
	move text	He wrote five new stories after this event
e or	delete	as the the title
∧	insert	the point view (of)
C	no space	play wright
⊙	add period	leaves Then he
⋏	add comma	metaphors similes and other devices
⋎	add apostrophe	poems meter
⋎ ⋎	add quotation marks	The Story of an Hour
∿	transpose	to briefly summarize
⌒H	begin paragraph	ends the scene. The next event
/	lower case	The Story begins
☰	capitalize	in "Storm ending"

7. Submit some of your writing to the school literary magazine.
8. Start a school literary magazine.
9. Submit your writing to your school newspaper, to the community newspaper, or to another publication that prints works by young writers.
10. Enter your work in an essay or creative writing contest.

CASE STUDY: PROOFREADING AND PUBLISHING

Juanita used the Checklist for Proofreading to find and correct the errors that remained in her rough draft. Here is Juanita's proofread paragraph:

> Recently I interviewed Colleen Ryan, the editor of our school newspaper, The Emerson High School Star Reporter. During our conversation Ms. Ryan told me that according to the paper's editorial policy, the principal has the right to review any articles before they are printed in the paper. Initially I was incensed by this policy because it seemed to violate the students' right to a free press. However, as I thought about the issue, I realized that there were good reasons for the review policy. First high-school journalists are not experienced. They need guidance regarding such matters as what can be published in a newspaper and what cannot. No paper can print just any sort of material.

The law says, for example, that papers can be held accountable for printing libelous materials with malice aforethought. The review policy ensures that articles that violate the law will not be published in the school paper. Second, all newspapers, including professional ones, have review policies. The Editor-in-Chief, and sometimes the Publisher, can veto publication of certain stories. In the case of the school paper, the journalism sponsor acts as the editor-in-chief, and the Principal acts as the Publisher. They therefore have the same right to accept or reject certain articles as would their counterparts in the world of proffessional print journalism. Some students might object to working under the constraints of the review policy. However, these students need to realise that when they become proffessional journalists, they will be working under the same constraints.

After proofreading her paper, Juanita made a clean final copy. Then she checked this copy once again for errors and shared the paper with classmates in a small-group discussion. She and her classmates had a lively debate about the issue.

ACTIVITIES AND ASSIGNMENTS

A. Answer the following questions about the case study:
1. What errors did Juanita correct in spelling, punctuation, capitalization, and manuscript form?
2. Are there any changes that Juanita should have made in her draft that she didn't make?

B. Proofread and share the paragraph that you drafted in the last lesson. Follow these steps.
1. Check your revised draft for errors, using the Checklist for Proofreading, on page 1279. Use standard editorial symbols to make any necessary corrections.
2. Make a neat final copy of your paragraph. Check this copy carefully to make sure you have added all of your final changes and have not made mistakes in copying.
3. Share your draft with your teacher and with your classmates.

3. Where did Wendy change the organization of her paragraph? Why did she make the change?
4. What other changes and corrections did Wendy make? Why did she make them?
5. What other revisions would you make in Wendy's paragraph? Why?

B. Select one of the following poems for a paragraph on images: Emily Dickinson's "There's a certain Slant of light," on page 369; Walt Whitman's "When I Heard the Learn'd Astronomer," on page 466; Edwin Arlington Robinson's "Richard Cory," on page 682; Ezra Pound's "In a Station of the Metro," on page 854; Amy Lowell's "Patterns," on page 876; or H.D.'s "Heat," on page 884. Follow these steps when planning and writing your paragraph:

1. Read the poem several times. Freewrite about the mood the poem creates.
2. Make a list in your notes of the specific images of sight, sound, touch, taste, and smell in the poem. Also note how each image contributes to the mood of the poem as a whole.
3. Use your notes to write a thesis statement that introduces the topic of your paragraph: the mood of the poem and the images that help to create it.
4. Make a rough outline for your paragraph. In the outline, show what information you will present in the introduction, body, and conclusion. Make sure that you include evidence for your thesis statement in the body of your paragraph.
5. Write a draft of your paragraph. Then revise the draft carefully, adding more specific examples from the poem and changing the organization where necessary.
6. Proofread your paper thoroughly and make a final copy of it. Share your paragraph with your classmates and with your teacher.

Lesson 5: Writing About Sound

SOUND AND MEANING

When prose or poetry is read aloud, the way the words sound contributes to the meaning that the listener attaches to the work. In the following poem, sound and meaning are closely related:

THE WORKER

Richard W. Thomas

My father lies black and hushed
Beneath white hospital sheets
He collapsed at work
His iron left him
Slow and quiet he sank
Meeting the wet concrete floor on his way
The wheels were still turning—they couldn't
  stop
And as they carried him out
The whirling and buzzing and humming
  machines
Applauded him
Lapping up his dripping iron
      They couldn't stop

Techniques of Sound

The chart at right describes some common devices of sound that writers use to enhance the meaning of their writing. The examples are from Thomas's poem.

WHY WRITERS USE DEVICES OF SOUND

Devices of sound enrich the meaning of literature in many ways. In "The Worker," for instance, Thomas contrasts the quiet hospital—emphasized by the *sh* sounds in "hu*sh*ed" and "*sh*eets"—with the noisy machinery where the father works—emphasized by the use of cacophony and onomatopoeia. Sound devices can highlight individual words, connect related words, or link words in a pattern that unites a stanza or an entire poem. Repeated sounds can also lead readers to expect and follow a musical pattern.

Alliteration: repetition of initial consonant sounds, as in "Meeting the *w*et concrete floor on his *w*ay / The *w*heels *w*ere still turning."

Assonance: repetition of vowel sounds, as in "B*e*n*ea*th . . . sh*ee*ts."

Consonance: repetition of consonant sounds at the ends of words or accented syllables, as in "whi*t*e hospi*t*al shee*t*s."

Rhyme: repetition of sounds in the final syllables of words. *Exact rhyme* means words that have identical final syllables, and *slant rhyme* refers to words whose last syllables are similar but not identical, as in "L*apping* up his dr*ipping* iron." *End rhyme* occurs when the rhyming words appear at the ends of lines of poetry, and *internal rhyme* is when they appear within the lines.

Cacophony: harsh, unpleasant sounds, as in "Gloved hands twisting knobs."

Euphony: beautiful, pleasant sounds, as in "Slow and quiet he sank."

Onomatopoeia: use of words that sound like what they mean, as in "buzzing and humming."

Parallelism: the use of phrases, clauses, or sentences that have similar grammatical structures, as in "Red and yellow lights flashing/Gloved hands twisting."

Repetition: the repeated use of a sound, word, phrase, or line. The clause "they couldn't stop" is repeated in "The Worker." Alliteration, assonance, consonance, rhyme, and parallelism are examples of repetition.

Meter: the regular rhythmical pattern of words, as in "The whirling and buzzing and humming machines."

CASE STUDY: WRITING ABOUT DEVICES OF SOUND

Clyde's English class was studying the use of sound in poetry. For a homework assignment, Clyde decided to write about the following poem:

THE WATCH
Frances Cornford

I wakened on my hot, hard bed,
Upon the pillow lay my head;
Beneath the pillow I could hear
My little watch was ticking clear
I thought the throbbing of it went
Like my continual discontent.
I thought it said in every tick:
I am so sick, so sick, so sick.
O death, come quick, come quick, come quick,
Come quick, come quick, come quick, come
   quick!

Prewriting

First Clyde read the poem aloud several times, listening carefully to its sounds. Then he made a list of the devices of sound in the poem, as follows:

- Alliteration:
  "*h*ot *h*ard bed, / . . . lay my *h*ead"
  "*th*ought the *th*robbing"

- Assonance:
  "B*enea*th . . . h*ea*r"
  "l*i*ttle . . . t*i*cking"

- Consonance:
  "har*d* . . . hea*d*"

- Rhyme:
  "bed"/"head"
  "hear"/"clear"
  "went"/"discontent"
  "tick"/"sick"/"quick"

- Cacophony:
  "I wakened on my hot, hard bed"

- Onomatopoeia:
  Last three lines sound like ticking

- Repetition:
  "so sick"
  "come quick"

- Meter:
  Iambic tetrameter—very regular, like the ticking of a watch

Clyde looked over his notes and decided to use a topic organization, discussing each sound device in turn. He then made a rough outline for his paper.

Drafting and Revising

Clyde wrote and revised the draft of his paper shown on the next page.

Proofreading and Publishing

Clyde proofread his paper for errors in grammar, usage, spelling, punctuation, and capitalization. Then he made a final copy of his writing and shared it with his family and with his teacher.

ACTIVITIES AND ASSIGNMENTS

A. Answer the following questions about the case study:
1. Why did Clyde change "show" to "suggest" in the first sentence of his paper?
2. Why did Clyde add the words "emphasizes words to introduce the rhythm of the poem" to the second sentence?
3. Why did Clyde add a reference to the mood of the poem?
4. Where did Clyde correct a run-on sentence? How did he do this?
5. How did Clyde revise his concluding sentence? Why did he revise it?
6. What other changes did Clyde make in his paper? Why did he make them?

B. Choose one of the following poems for a one- to three-paragraph composition on devices of sound: Edgar Allan Poe's "The Raven," on page 223; Ralph Waldo Emerson's "Brahma," on page 279; Henry Wadsworth Longfellow's "The Tide Rises, The Tide Falls," on page 334; Carl Sandburg's "Chicago," on page 898; E. E. Cummings's "anyone lived in a pretty now town," on page 919; or Langston Hughes's "The Negro Speaks of Rivers," on page 965.

Follow these steps when planning and writing your composition:

1. Read the poem aloud several times, listening very carefully to the sounds. Freewrite about the general effect created by these sounds.
2. Make a list in your notes of specific devices of sound used in the poem to create the general effect that you have already noted.
3. Decide in what order you will present the information in your paper. You might discuss the poem line by line, or you might explain each sound device in turn. When you have decided how you intend to organize your writing, make an outline for your composition.
4. Write a draft of your composition, referring often to your outline and to your notes. Then revise your paper, using the Checklist for Revision on page 1276.
5. Proofread your paper, using the Checklist for Proofreading on page 1279. Then make a clean final copy of your composition and share this copy with your classmates and with your teacher.

In her poem entitled "The Watch," Frances Cornford uses many devices of sound to show [*suggest*] a watch ticking. ~~A~~lliteration ~~is one of them—for~~ [*For example, the*] ~~example,~~ "on my *hot, hard* bed, / . . . lay my [*in*] [*emphasizes words to introduce the rythm of the poem*] head." ~~Then she also uses~~ assonance as in [*The*] "Beneath the pillow I could hear" and [*the*] the repetition of *t* sounds ~~as~~ in "my *little* watch was [*also shows the rythm*] *ticking* clear" and "continual discontent," End rhyme also contributes to the sound of the poem. ~~An example of~~ cacoph~~o~~ny ~~can be found~~ [*The "o"*] in the first line~~—~~ "I wakened on my hot, hard [*sets up an uncomfortable mood*] bed. Cornford uses words onomatopoetically in the last three lines, ~~which~~ sound ~~just exactly~~ [*to create the*] like a watch ticking. [*of*] Also in the last three lines, the words *so sick* and *come quick* are repeated several times for affect and the meter of the entire poem is a very regular iambic tetrameter, which ~~suggests~~ [*imitates*] the ticking of the narrator's watch as well. ~~I liked the way~~ every element in the poem contributes to a single, [*rs*] [*very*] ~~real~~ striking effect.

Lesson 6: Writing About Figures of Speech

WHAT ARE FIGURES OF SPEECH?

Figures of speech are words or phrases used imaginatively to suggest more than their literal meanings. The following chart defines and illustrates some of the common figures of speech found in literature:

Apostrophe: the direct address of an object, idea, or absent person, as in the following poem:

WHERE HAVE YOU GONE?
Mari Evans

Where have you gone

with your confident
walk with
your crooked smile

why did you leave
me
when you took your
laughter
and departed

Hyperbole: exaggeration or overstatement. The following poem uses hyperbole to describe the energetic feelings of the narrator:

TO SATCH (OR AMERICAN GOTHIC)
Samuel Allen (Paul Vesey)

Sometimes I feel like I will *never*
   stop
Just go on forever
Till one fine mornin
I'm gonna reach up and grab me a
   handfulla stars
Swing out on my long lean leg
And whip three hot strikes burnin
   down the heavens
And look over at God and say
How about that!

Irony: the use of words to suggest the opposite

---

of what they literally mean. In the following poem, the author uses the word *intelligent* ironically:

EARTH
John Hall Wheelock

"A planet doesn't explode of
   itself," said dryly
The Martian astronomer, gazing off
   into the air—
"That they were able to do it is
   proof that highly
Intelligent beings must have been
   living there."

Metaphor: writing or speaking about one thing as if it were something very different. The following poem speaks metaphorically of the task of writing poetry:

WRITING A POEM
Naomi Long Madgett

Writing a poem is trying to catch
   a fluff of cloud
With open-fingered hands.

Oxymoron: using two contradictory words to describe the same object, as in the last phrase of this poem, "Solitude Late at Night in the Woods," by Robert Bly:

Nothing but bare trunks climbing/
   like cold fire!

Paradox: a statement that seems obviously false but is somehow true. The following poem is based on a paradox:

MUCH MADNESS IS DIVINEST SENSE—
Emily Dickinson

Much Madness is divinest Sense—
To a diserning Eye—
Much Sense—the starkest Madness—
'Tis the Majority

Personification: writing or speaking about a nonhuman subject as if it had human

---

characteristics, as in these lines from "February Twilight," by Sara Teasdale:

> I stood and watched an evening star
> As long as it watched me.

Simile: a comparison between two dissimilar things using *like* or *as*. Note the examples of simile in the following poem:

UNTITLED
Lucille Clifton

> the thirty eighth year
> of my life,
> plain as bread
> round as a cake
> an ordinary woman.

Figures of speech such as metaphor, personification, and simile have two parts, called the tenor and the vehicle. The *tenor* is the subject that is being described in the figure of speech. The *vehicle* is an object that shares one or more characteristics with the tenor and that is used as a means to describe it. For instance, in the Lucille Clifton poem quoted above, the tenor of both similes is the narrator's life, and the vehicles are bread and a cake.

WHY WRITERS USE FIGURES OF SPEECH

Writers use figurative language, or figures of speech, to make their writing more vivid and concrete. Figurative language can also draw powerful emotional or imaginative responses from a reader. Through interesting comparisons and surprising combinations of words and ideas, figurative language can move the reader and enrich his or her appreciation of the human experience.

CASE STUDY: WRITING ABOUT FIGURES OF SPEECH

Leslie's English teacher asked the class to select a poem and to write a paragraph about the figures of speech used in it. Leslie decided to write about Arna Bontemps's "A Black Man Talks of Reaping," on page 970.

Prewriting

Leslie read the poem several times. She decided that the central figure of speech used in "A Black Man Talks of Reaping" is a metaphor. She made the following for her prewriting notes:

- Tenor: racism

- Vehicle: harvest/farming

- Shared characteristics:
  Planting deep
  Kept safe against lean years
  Scattered seeds
  Reap only what hand sows
  Work in fields that others have sown
  Feed on bitter fruit

Leslie decided that the metaphor would be the focus of her paragraph, and she made a rough outline organizing her information.

Drafting and Revising

Leslie used her prewriting notes and her outline to write a draft of her paragraph. Her draft, along with the revisions that she made in it, is shown on the next page.

Proofreading and Publishing

Leslie made a clean final copy of her paragraph for her teacher, who suggested that she read it aloud to the class.

ACTIVITIES AND ASSIGNMENTS

A. Answer the following questions about the draft in the case study:
1. Why did Leslie add "the persistence of" to the first sentence of her paragraph?

How did she correct her error?

¶ In the poem "A Black Man Talks of Reaping,"

Arna Bontemps employs a metaphor to illustrate *the persistence of* racial prejudice against the black man.

Bontemps*'s* metaphor ~~forces the~~ *suggests a* comparison between sowing and reaping the harvest ~~with~~ *and the* ~~the~~ sowing and reaping of racial prejudice.

Both the farmer and the black man "keep safe" against the lean years when harvests are ~~meek~~ *meager* and racial tensions are raw. Like the ~~black~~ *farmer* ~~man~~, *black man* the ~~farmer~~ reaps only what he sows. Yet,

the black man and his children continue to pay

for what others have sown, feeding on the

"bitter fruit" of prejudice.

2. Where did Leslie correct errors in word choice?
3. What spelling and punctuation corrections did Leslie make?
4. Where did Leslie originally confuse the tenor and the vehicle of the metaphor in the poem?

B. Select one of the following poems for a one- to three-paragraph composition on figures of speech: Henry Wadsworth Longfellow's "A Psalm of Life," on page 336; Emily Dickinson's "I heard a Fly buzz—when I died—," on page 379; Walt Whitman's "A Noiseless Patient Spider," on page 468; Paul Laurence Dunbar's "We Wear the Mask," on page 672; Wallace Stevens's "Anecdote of the Jar," on page 873; or Randall Jarrell's "The Death of the Ball Turret Gunner," on page 1215. Follow these steps:

1. Read the poem several times. Make a handwritten copy of the poem to familiarize yourself with the exact language used in it.
2. Find examples of figures of speech in the poem and list them in a chart in your notes.
3. Pick the one or two figures of speech that you think are most important to the poem. Write a thesis statement that tells the title and author of the poem and that introduces the central figure(s) of speech.
4. Write the rest of your composition, based on your prewriting notes. Then revise your paper, making sure that it is logically organized and clear.
5. Proofread your composition and make a clean final copy. Then share it with your classmates and with your teacher.

Lesson 7: Writing About Setting

WHAT IS SETTING?

The writer of a narrative work establishes a *setting*—a time and place in which the action occurs. The description of the setting may present details of the geographical location, the date in history, the season and the weather, the physical buildings and rooms, the social environment, and the characters' dress, manners, and customs.

Ann Petry's story "Doby's Gone" is about a young black girl beginning school. The writer opens the story in this manner:

> When Doby first came into Sue Johnson's life her family were caretakers on a farm way up in New York State. And because Sue had no one else to play with, the Johnsons reluctantly accepted Doby as a member of the family.
> The spring that Sue was six they moved to Wessex, Connecticut—a small New England town whose neat colonial houses cling to a group of hills overlooking the Connecticut River.

This description of the setting introduces the location of the story and also the characters' backgrounds.

Often the information provided about the setting includes images of sight, sound, touch, taste, and smell. Notice the imagery used in the opening of Elizabeth Sullivan's "Legend of the Trail of Tears":

> Annakee observed the beauty around her. It was a beautiful day. The fruit tree blossoms were in bloom, corn and tobacco had been planted and the cottonwood leaves were like glass. . . . The south wind sprang up. The clouds became very dark and it began to rain.

In this story the setting is especially important. It represents all that the Creek tribe lost when they had to give up their lands.

HOW WRITERS USE SETTING

The following chart describes some of the functions setting can perform in a literary work:

USES OF SETTING
To make a story seem more believable To help establish a story's mood To act as the force against which the protagonist struggles, the source of the central conflict To symbolize an idea the writer wants to reinforce in the mind of the reader To reflect or contrast with other elements of the story, such as a character's feelings or a theme

CASE STUDY: WRITING ABOUT SETTING

Alvin read Robert Frost's poem "Stopping by Woods on a Snowy Evening," on page 947. He was intrigued by the setting created by Frost, and he decided to write a paragraph about this setting for his English class.

Prewriting

Alvin reread "Stopping by Woods on a Snowy Evening" and discovered several points about the setting that he had overlooked the first time. Then he made the following notes:

- *Important details of the setting:*
  Next to woods
  Away from village
  Snowing
  "without a farmouse near"
  "frozen lake"
  "The darkest evening of the year."
  "the sweep/of easy wind and downy flake"
  "The woods are lovely, dark and deep"

- *Mood created by setting:*
  Ominous ("frozen lake," "darkest evening")
  Peaceful ("easy wind and downy flake," "lovely, dark and deep")

- *Symbolic roles of elements in setting:*
  Woods traditional symbols of confusion, of being lost
  Snow and winter traditional symbols of death

Alvin decided that although the setting does indeed provide a backdrop for the poem, there is a more important function that it serves. This function is to symbolize the main idea, or theme, of the poem. Alvin wrote a topic sentence and made a rough outline for his paragraph.

Drafting and Revising

Alvin used his notes and his outline to write the following rough draft of his paragraph:

> The Setting of Robert Frosts Stopping by Woods on a Snowey Evening creates more than just a backdrop for the poem. The setting also serves a symbolic purpose that is a key to understanding Frost's meaning. In the poem, the speaker has stopped on a country roadway to watch the "woods filling up with snow." That the speaker is in the countryside is obvious. From the fact that he refers to owner of the woods as being absent and "in the village." in the second stanza of the poem, the reader learns that the speaker beleives that his horse "must think it queer" to be stopping in the woods at this time. After all, the lake is "frozen" and this is "The darkest evening of the year." Stopping at such a time and in such a place can be dangerous, as the ominous words "frozen" and "darkest" suggest. However, the speaker is lulled by "the sweep/Of easy wind and downy flake"—by the fact that "The woods are lovely, dark and deep. In poetry, woods are traditional symbols of confusion—of being lost. Snow and winter are traditional symbols of death. On a symbolic level, therefore, the setting symbolizes the speakers attraction to and longing for the peacefullness that death would bring. In the

final stanza, the speaker reminds himself that he has "promises to keep" and should go on. However, the repetition in the final lines seems to indicate that the speaker is repeating things to himself as one does sometimes before falling off to sleep. The poem might therefor be a warning to poeple not to be attracted to the peacefulness of death or simply a warning against complacency.

Alvin revised his draft to make it more clearly organized and specific. Then he made a fresh copy of the draft for proofreading.

Proofreading and Publishing

Alvin proofread his paragraph for errors in spelling and mechanics. Then he shared the final copy of his paper with his class discussion group and with his English teacher.

ACTIVITIES AND ASSIGNMENTS

A. Revise and proofread Alvin's paragraph. Find and correct a sentence fragment, an error in a quotation, and several errors in spelling and punctuation.

B. Choose one of the following works for a composition on setting: Washington Irving's "The Devil and Tom Walker," on page 180, William Cullan Bryant's "Thanatopsis," on page 202; the selection from John Greenleaf Whittier's "Snowbound," on page 356; Jack London's "To Build a Fire," on page 562; William Faulkner's "The Bear," on page 788; or Wallace Stevens's "Disillusionment of Ten O'Clock," on page 872. Write a one- or two-paragraph analysis of the setting by following these steps:

1. Read the work once. Freewrite about the mood or atmosphere that the setting creates. Then read the story or poem again, noting specific details of the setting, used to create the mood. Also write down any other functions that the setting performs and relate these functions to details in the work.

2. Write a topic sentence for your paper that tells the title and author of the work and that introduces the most important function of the setting. Then make an outline for the rest of your paper.
3. Write a draft of your paper, based on your notes and your outline. Make sure that your writing does not stray from your purpose of showing the significance of the setting.
4. Revise your draft, making sure that it has a clear introduction, body, and conclusion. Also check to see that every statement you have made is supported by evidence from the work.
5. Proofread your revised draft for errors in grammar, usage, spelling, punctuation, capitalization, and manuscript form. Make a clean final copy of your paper, and share this copy with classmates who have read the work. Then share your writing with your English teacher.

Lesson 8: Writing About Plot

WHAT IS PLOT?

The series of events or actions in a narrative work is called the *plot.* The basis of the plot is a *conflict,* or struggle. Some plots contain more than one conflict, but most narratives focus on one central conflict involving the protagonist. Conflicts can be internal or external. An *internal conflict* takes place within the mind of a character as he or she struggles with an important decision or with a strong feeling such as fear or hatred. An *external conflict* is a struggle between a character and some outside force. This outside force may be another character or a group of characters; a natural or nonhuman force, such as a flood; or a political or social institution or custom.

THE PARTS OF A PLOT

A plot may be logically divided into six parts, as follows:

1. *Exposition:* Also called the introduction, the exposition is the opening part of a narrative in which the writer gives background information about the setting, the characters, and the basic situation.
2. *Inciting incident:* The inciting incident is the event that sets the story in motion; it introduces the central conflict.
3. *Development:* The development includes all the events that follow from the inciting incident up to the climax. In this part of a narrative, the main character normally struggles to overcome obstacles to achieve some goal.
4. *Climax:* The climax is the high point of interest or suspense in the work.
5. *Resolution:* The resolution is the point in the narrative when the central conflict is ended. In many stories the resolution and the climax are identical.
6. *Denouement:* The denouement includes all the events that take place after the central conflict has been resolved. In this part of the plot, less important conflicts may be resolved and questions still left in the mind of the reader may be answered.

Not all narratives have exactly this plot structure, of course. In some works the inciting incident takes place before the opening of the narrative. Some stories end with the resolution and thus lack a denouement. In addition, writers often employ special techniques that alter the structures of their plots.

SPECIAL TECHNIQUES OF PLOT

The following list describes some techniques writers use to make their plots more interesting and enjoyable for readers:

1. *Foreshadowing:* This technique involves hinting at an event or events that will happen later in the narrative. Foreshadowing is often very subtle, so readers must constantly be on the lookout for clues to how the plot will unfold.
2. *Flashback:* A flashback is a section of a narrative that interrupts the chronological order of events to relate something that happened in the past. Flashbacks may help to explain the motivations behind a character's actions by telling the reader about his or her past experiences.
3. *Suspense:* The tension that builds as the reader wonders how the central conflict will be resolved is known as suspense. Writers create suspense by raising questions in the reader's mind about what will happen next.
4. *Surprise ending:* An unexpected turn of events

at the resolution is called a surprise ending. An effective surprise ending is achieved by leading the reader to expect the conflict to end in a certain way and then abruptly changing the direction of the story.

CASE STUDY: WRITING ABOUT PLOT

Todd's English class learned about plot structure in narrative works. Then his teacher asked the class to select a short story and to write a paragraph analyzing its plot. Todd chose Ambrose Bierce's "An Occurrence at Owl Creek Bridge," on page 526.

Prewriting

Todd read the story several times to familiarize himself with all the techniques the author had used in constructing the plot. Then he made a list of the events in the story. He studied this list and identified the parts of the plot. Finally, he made notes about each part of the plot, as follows:

- Introduction: rich description of a military hanging of a civilian on a railroad bridge in northern Alabama during the Civil War; includes foreshadowing—"If I could free my hands"

- Inciting incident: (occurs before start of story) Peyton Farquhar was caught tampering with a Yankee-held bridge; punishment is hanging

- Development: the rope breaks; Peyton falls into the stream and escapes; detailed description of how Peyton dodges bullets and escapes

- Climax: Peyton eventually reaches the safety of his home

- False resolution: Peyton reaches out to embrace his wife; everything turns silent and dark

- Real resolution/surprise ending: Payton's body swings beneath the timbers of Owl Creek Bridge—he is dead

Drafting and Revising

Todd used his prewriting notes to write a draft of his paragraph. Then he revised his draft to make it clearer and better organized.

Proofreading and Publishing

Todd made a fresh copy of his paragraph and proofread it for errors in spelling and mechanics. Then he made a final copy and shared it with his parents, his classmates, and his teacher.

ACTIVITIES AND ASSIGNMENTS

A. Read the story "An Occurrence at Owl Creek Bridge," on page 526. Then use Todd's prewriting notes from the case study to write a paragraph about the story's plot. Follow these steps:

1. Write a topic sentence that tells the title and author of the story and introduces the main idea of your paragraph. Make an outline for your writing that shows how you will organize the information in your introduction, body, and conclusion.

2. Write a draft of your paragraph, following your outline. Make sure that you support all your main points with specific evidence from the story. Conclude with a sentence or two explaining why the story is an enjoyable one to read.

3. Revise and proofread the paragraph. Share your final copy with a small group of your classmates. Then give your paper to your teachers.

B. Select one of the following short stories for a paragraph on plot: Washington Irving's "The Devil and Tom Walker," on page 180; Edgar Allan Poe's "The Fall of the House of

Usher," on page 208; Nathaniel Hawthorne's "Dr. Heidegger's Experiment," on page 304; Bret Harte's "The Outcasts of Poker Flat," on page 516; or Willa Cather's "A Wagner Matinée," on page 552. Follow these steps:

1. Read the story once. Make a list of the events that take place in the story and group them under these headings: Introduction, Inciting incident, Deveopment, Climax, Resolution, and Denouement. Then read the story a second time and look for special techniques of plot that the author has used. Make notes about these techniques and about how they contribute to the story.

2. Write a topic sentence for your paragraph. Then make an outline for the rest of your paragraph from the information in your prewriting notes.

3. Write a draft of your paragraph. Then revise your draft, making sure that it will be clear to your readers.

4. Proofread your revised draft, checking for error in grammar, usage, spelling, punctuation, capitalization, and manuscript form. Share the final copy of your paragraph wtih your classmates and with your teacher.

Lesson 9: Writing About Character

TYPES OF CHARACTERS

The people and animals who take part in the action of a narrative work are called *characters*. The *protagonist* is the most important character in a work, the character who faces the central conflict. Other characters who play significant roles in the story are called *major characters*, and those who play less important roles are called *minor characters*. A major character who is in direct conflict with the protagonist is called the *antagonist*.

WHAT IS CHARACTERIZATION?

Characterization is the process by which a writer reveals the nature of a particular character. In this passage from "The Snow Keeps Falling," author Janet Campbell characterizes a minor character through a description of her physical appearance:

> She's sitting on the edge of her desk, casual like, one knee drawn up a little. She has greasy, thin hair, blond in places, grey-brown in places, hanging loose and stringy around her face. Little raw-looking red pimples dot her chin and forehead. She has a cold and her nose is red and runny.

By describing what the character looks like, Campbell creates certain expectations in the reader about what the character's personality is like.

James Baldwin, on the other hand, in describing the protagonist in *Go Tell It on the Mountain*, says nothing about his physical appearance:

> Everyone had always said that John would be a preacher when he grew up, just like his father. It had been said so often that John, without ever thinking about it, had come to believe it himself. Not until the morning of his fourteenth birthday did he really begin to think about it, and by then it was already too late.

This passage tells the reader something about the character's background and what people expect from him.

HOW WRITERS CREATE CHARACTER

In creating a believable character, a writer may use a number of different techniques of characterization. *Direct characterization* is the simplest method. It involves merely stating what the character is like. A statement such as "Tim had a mischievous streak" is an example of direct characterization.

A more subtle way of revealing a character is through *indirect characterization*. In this case the writer shows what a character is like by describing how the character appears, what the character says and does, and how other characters react to the character. When a writer uses indirect characterization, it is up to the reader to gather clues about the character and to draw conclusions based on those clues.

Elements of Character

A well-developed character in a literary work has many facets, just as a real person does. When you analyze a character, ask yourself the following questions about the portrayal of the character:

1. *Appearance*: How does the character look and dress? What do these aspects of appearance reveal about the character?
2. *Words and actions*: What kinds of things does the character say and do? What kind of language does the character use? What can the reader learn about the character from his or her words and actions?

3. *Background*: Where did the character grow up? What kind of educational background does the character have? What past experiences has the character had? How does the character's background affect his or her thoughts and actions in the present?
4. *Personality*: Does the character tend to be emotional or rational? principled or unscrupulous? obstinate or open-minded? caring or cold?
5. *Motivation*: What makes the character act and speak as he or she does? What does the character value? What are the character's goals? dreams? desires? needs?
6. *Relationships*: How does the character interact with other characters in the work? Who are his or her friends and enemies?
7. *Conflict*: Is the character involved in some conflict? If so, is the conflict *internal*—within the character's mind—or *external*—between the character and an outside force? How is the conflict resolved?
8. *Change*: Does the character change or grow in the course of the story? If so, how? How does the reader know that the character has changed?

CASE STUDY: WRITING ABOUT CHARACTER

Angela's English class was asked to write a paragraph about a character in a narrative work. Angela decided to write about the protagonist of Eudora Welty's short story "A Worn Path," on page 764.

Prewriting

Angela read the story several times, paying close attention to the characterization of Phoenix Jackson, the main character. In her prewriting notes, Angela answered the questions listed in the chart in this lesson. She also gathered specific details from the story to support her answers. Then she made a rough outline for her paragraph.

Drafting and Revising

Angela wrote the following draft of her paragraph:

The main character of Eudora Welty's short story: "A Worn Path" is an elderly woman named Phoenix Jackson. Phoenix lives in the country and periodically makes her way along the wooden path to reach Natchez. The author describes Phoenix as small, with her hair tied in a "red rag". Phoenix carries a cane made from an umbrella to steady her step. Phoenix appears to be an independant, courageous character, talking to the animals as she walked. Phoenix meets a hunter along the way but she shows no fear of this stranger. Upon reaching Natchez, Phoenix's motivation for her long walk is revealed—to get medicine for her grandson. With the nickle the hunter dropped and the nickle the nurse gave her she buys a paper windmill for her grandson. We maybe see how a simple windmill signifies for Phoenix the simple but more important joy of love and generosity.

Angela realized that her rough draft needed some major revisions. As she revised, Angela added details, combined sentences, eliminated sentence fragments, and clarified several of her statements.

Proofreading and Publishing

After revising her draft, Angela made a fresh copy and proofread it for errors in spelling, punctuation, and capitalization. Then Angela shared her paragraph with her class discussion group.

ACTIVITIES AND ASSIGNMENTS

A. Revise and proofread the draft in the case study. Follow these steps:
1. Read the draft, noting its overall organization. Does the draft have a topic sentence? Does it contain supporting evidence? Does it have a definite conclusion? Supply whatever parts are missing.
2. Check to see whether any sentences can be improved by combining. Notice that many of Angela's sentences begin in the same way.

Try to vary her sentence openings. Correct any sentence fragments or run-on sentences in the draft.

3. Rewrite any parts that are unclear. Check to make sure that transition words such as *however*, *although*, and *next* have been used to relate the sentences logically to one another.
4. Make sure that Angela's claims about the story are all supported by the text.
5. Make any other changes that you think are necessary. Use the Checklist for Proofreading, on page 1279, to proofread your paragraph. Then share the final copy with your classmates and with your teacher.

B. Select one of the following short stories for a paragraph about character: Edgar Allan Poe's "The Fall of the House of Usher," on page 208; Nathaniel Hawthorne's "The Minister's Black Veil," on page 294; Katherine Anne Porter's "The Jilting of Granny Weatherall," on page 748; or Flannery O'Connor's "The Life You Save May Be Your Own," on page 1052.

Follow these steps:

1. Read the story once. Choose one character from the story and freewrite about that character. Then read the story again and gather details the author has used to characterize the person.
2. Use the prewriting notes to write a draft of your paragraph. Revise your draft, making sure that it has a definite introduction, body, and conclusion.
3. Proofread your writing and make a final copy of your paragraph. Share this copy with your classmates and with your teacher.

Lesson 10: Writing About Point of View

WHAT ARE NARRATION AND POINT OF VIEW?

Narration is the act of telling a story. A literary work that tells a story is called a *narrative.* Every narrative has a speaker, or voice. This voice is called the *narrator.*

The perspective of the narrator is called the *point of view* of the story. The point of view determines who will tell the story and what details the story will include.

First-person Point of View. If the narrator is a character in the story and refers to himself or herself using "I," the story is told from the *first-person point of view.* The opening lines of Willa Cather's "A Wagner Matinée," on page 552, show that the story is told from the first-person point of view:

> I received one morning a letter written in pale ink, on glassy, blue-lined notepaper, and bearing the postmark of a little Nebraska village.

The first-person point of view is almost always *limited.* That is, the narrator does not know the thoughts and feelings of any of the other characters in the story and can offer only his or her own interpretations of their words and actions.

Third-person Point of View. When the narrator is not a character in the story but tells it from outside the action, the story is told from the third-person point of view. A third-person narrator never refers to himself or herself as "I" but uses third-person pronouns such as *she, they, his*, and *them* to talk about the characters. A writer using the third-person point of view may decide that the narrator will know what one of the characters thinks and feels but only what the others say and do. In this case, the narrator speaks from the *limited third-person point of view.* Ann Beattie's short story "Imagined Scenes," on page 1092, is told from the limited third-person point of view. Here is a passage from that story:

> When she wakes from a dream, David is already awake. Or perhaps he only wakes when she stirs, whispers to him. He doesn't sound sleepy; he's alert, serious, as though he'd been waiting for a question. She remembers last year, the week before Christmas.

If a third-person narrator is not limited but knows the thoughts and feelings of every character, that narrator is said to be *omniscient,* or "all-knowing." The following passage from Flannery O'Connor's "The Life You Save May Be Your Own," on page 1052, shows that the story is told from the *omniscient third-person point of view*:

> The old woman and her daughter were sitting on their porch when Mr. Shiftlet came up their road for the first time. The old woman slid to the edge of her chair and leaned forward, shading her eyes from the piercing sunset with her hand. The daughter could not see far in front of her and continued to play with her fingers.

Reliability and Unreliability

Besides determining what point of view a narrative is told from, a reader must also consider whether the narrator is biased or prejudiced in any way. Deciding if you can trust what a narrator says is making a judgment about the reliability or unreliability of that narrator. Another consideration is whether the narrator gives an objective or a subjective account of the story's events. An objective narrator simply presents the facts and allows the reader to draw his or her own conclusions. A subjective narrator presents his or her own opinions along with the facts, and the reader must be careful to separate the two.

CASE STUDY: WRITING ABOUT NARRATION AND POINT OF VIEW

Darrell's English class was asked to write a paragraph about the narration and point of view of a particular short story. Darrell decided to write about "The First Seven Years," by Bernard Malamud, on page 1042.

Prewriting

After reading the story once, Darrell concluded that it was told from the third-person limited point of view. Then he reread the story and made careful notes about the narration and point of view. The following are Darrell's prewriting notes:

- Point of view: third-person limited—narrator knows Feld's thoughts only

- Function of point of view: reveals the inner life of the main character; causes the reader to identify with Feld

- Narrator: reliable and objective; we see the world through Feld's eyes; narrator withholds his opinions

Darrell made an outline for his paragraph so that he would not stray from his topic when he began writing.

Drafting and Revising

Darrell used his outline and prewriting notes to write a draft of his paragraph. Then he revised his draft, using editorial symbols. Here is Darrell's revised draft:

Proofreading and Publishing

Darrell made a fresh copy of his revised draft and proofread it for errors in grammar, usage, spelling, punctuation, capitalization, and manuscript form. Finally, he shared his paragraph with his classmates by reading it aloud before the class.

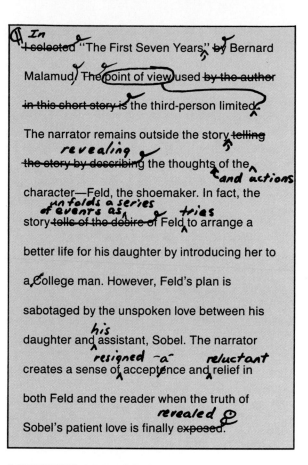

ACTIVITIES AND ASSIGNMENTS

A. Answer the following questions about the case study:

1. What error in manuscript form did Darrell correct in his draft?
2. What sentences did Darrell combine to eliminate unnecessary words?
3. What errors in spelling, punctuation, and capitalization did Darrell correct?
4. To what sentences did Darrell add clarifying details?
5. What informal words and phrases did Darrell replace with language that was more appropriate?

B. Write a two-paragraph composition analyzing the narration and point of view in one of the following short stories: Edgar Allan Poe's "The Fall of the House of Usher," on page 208;

Ambrose Bierce's "An Occurrence at Owl Creek Bridge," on page 526; Katherine Anne Porter's "The Jilting of Granny Weatherall," on page 748; or Eudora Welty's "A Worn Path," on page 764. Follow these steps:

1. Read the story once and determine whether the point of view is first-person, third-person limited, or third-person omniscient.

2. Decide whether you think the narrator is reliable or unreliable, objective or subjective. Then reread the story to gather evidence for your opinion about the narrator. Write this evidence in your prewriting notes.

3. Make an outline for your composition. Plan to introduce your topic and to discuss the narrator and point of view of the story in your first paragraph. Then use your second paragraph to discuss the effect the point of view has on a reader or on the presentation of the story.

4. Write a draft of your composition. Then revise your draft, adding details and clarifying ideas where necessary.

5. Proofread your paper and make a clean final copy of it. Share your composition with a small group of your classmates and with your teacher.

Lesson 11: Writing About Theme

WHAT IS THEME?

Although some literary works are intended merely to entertain the reader, most works contain a message that the writer wants to convey. This message is known as the *theme*. A theme usually expresses some insight into the human experience. It may deal with values, ideas, beliefs, or life in general. Complex literary works may express several perceptions about human beings and thus have several different themes.

HOW WRITERS EXPRESS THEMES

In some works the theme may be stated directly, as is the moral in a fable. More often the theme is shown by the impact of the work as a whole. Theme may be revealed through elements of a work such as the title, the characters, the setting, and the resolution of the plot. The writer expects the reader to infer the theme from clues provided by these elements.

CASE STUDY: WRITING ABOUT THEME

Hayley's English class was given an assignment to write about the theme of a poem. Hayley decided to write about the theme of Edwin Arlington Robinson's "Richard Cory," on page 682.

Prewriting

Hayley read the poem several times to make sure that she had not missed any possible clues to its theme. Then she made the following prewriting notes:

- *Title*: "Richard Cory"
- *Author*: Edwin Arlington Robinson

- *Theme*: One should not make generalizations based solely on someone's appearance.

- *Ways in which theme is revealed:*
  Poem opens with a description of Richard Cory as a gentleman whom everyone admires.
  The townspeople make assumptions about him based on the way he appears to them—handsome, well-spoken, friendly, rich, educated, well-dressed.
  The townspeople continue to work for more money and material things.
  A surprise ending—Richard Cory commits suicide. Where was the "light" in his life? The townspeople did not know him at all.

Drafting and Revising

Hayley wrote a draft of her paragraph, based on her prewriting notes. She began with a topic sentence that stated the title and author of the poem and that introduced the poem's theme. Then, in the body of her paragraph, she used evidence from the poem to show how the theme was revealed. Finally, she wrote a concluding sentence that told how the theme of the poem could be applied to real life. When she had finished her draft, Hayley revised it thoroughly, making sure that all her statements supported her topic sentence.

Proofreading and Publishing

Hayley proofread her revised draft for errors in grammar, usage, spelling, punctuation, capitalization, and manuscript form. Then she made two final copies of her paragraph—one for her English teacher and one for the class literary magazine.

ACTIVITIES AND ASSIGNMENTS

A. Using Hayley's prewriting notes from the case study, write a paragraph about the theme of "Richard Cory." Follow these steps:

1. Read the poem once and look at Hayley's prewriting notes. Then read the story a second time and add to her notes any important details that she omitted. If you think you can state the theme of the poem more accurately than Hayley did in her notes, write a sentence expressing the theme in your own words.

2. Write a topic sentence in which you state the title and author of the poem and its theme. If it will help you to organize your notes, make a rough outline for the rest of your paragraph.

3. Write the body of your paragraph. Make sure that every statement you make is supported by specific evidence from the poem.

4. Write a concluding sentence or two summarizing the theme and relating it to real life.

5. Revise and proofread the draft carefully. Then make a final copy of your paragraph and share it with a small group of your classmates and with your teacher.

B. Select one of the following works for a paragraph on theme: "Thanatopsis," on page 202; "Dr. Heidegger's Experiment," on page 304; "The Tide Rises, The Tide Falls," on page 334; "Patterns," on page 876; "since feeling is first," on page 918; "Mending Wall," on page 927; "Any Human to Another," on page 959; *Our Town*, on page 974; "Journey," on page 1080; or "Mirror," on page 1236. Follow these steps:

1. Read the work once. Try to state the theme in a sentence. Then reread the work, gathering evidence for your statement of theme in your prewriting notes. List all the elements of the work that help to reveal the theme and explain how each accomplishes this task.

2. Revise your statement of theme until it is accurate and clear.

3. Make an outline for your paragraph. In the outline, show how you will present the information in your prewriting notes in the introduction, body, and conclusion of your paragraph.

4. Use your statement of theme to write a topic sentence for your paragraph.

5. Write the body of your paragraph, explaining how each element of the work reveals the theme. Make sure that you include specific details from the work to support your ideas.

6. Write a conclusion of one or two sentences that summarize the theme of the work and show how it is relevant to real life.

7. Revise your draft, making sure that all your points are clear. Also check the overall organization of your paragraph and make sure that every statement is related to your purpose.

8. Use the Checklist for Proofreading on page 1279 to proofread your revised draft. Then make a clean final copy of your paragraph, and share this copy with a small group of your classmates before submitting it to your teacher.

Section 3: Understanding the Work as a Whole: Interpretation and Synthesis
Lesson 12: Writing About a Short Story

To interpret a short story you must analyze it. First you divide the story into its elements and consider each element separately. Then you think about how each element contributes to the meaning of the work as a whole. The following questions will help you when analyzing a short story:

1. *Author*: Who is the author of the story?
2. *Title*: What is the story's title? Does the title suggest the story's subject or theme?
3. *Setting*: Where and when does the story take place? What details does the writer use to create the setting? Does the setting create a particular mood, or feeling? Is the setting a symbol for an important idea that the writer wants to convey? Does the setting play a role in the central conflict?
4. *Point of view*: Is the story told from the first person or from the third person point of view? Is the narrator limited or omniscient? What effect does the point of view have on the way the reader experiences the story?
5. *Central conflict*: What struggle is the main character involved in? Is the central conflict *internal*—within the protagonist's mind—or *external*—between the protagonist and another character, society, or a nonhuman force? How is the conflict resolved?
6. *Plot*: What events take place in the story? Does the story have an introduction? If so, what does the reader learn in the introduction? What is the inciting incident? What happens during the development? When does the climax occur? What event marks the resolution of the central conflict? Does the story have a denouement?

Does the writer make use of special plot devices such as foreshadowing, flashbacks, or a surprise ending? Is the story suspenseful? If so, how does the writer create suspense?

7. *Characterization*: Who is the main character, or protagonist? Who are the other major and minor characters? How does the writer reveal what each of the characters is like? Which characters are in conflict with each other? Do any of the characters change in the course of the work? If so, how and why do they change?
8. *Devices of sound and figures of speech*: Does the writer make use of any devices of sound such as euphony or alliteration? Does the story contain any examples of figurative language such as hyperbole, simile, metaphor, or symbolism? What do these techniques add to the story?
9. *Theme*: What is the theme, or central idea, of the story? How is the theme revealed?

It is often convenient to use a topic organization when writing an analysis of a short story. For example, in the introductory paragraph of your paper, you might state the title, author, and theme of the story. Then you might devote each of your body paragraphs to discussing a particular element of the story and to explaining how this element is related to other elements. For example, one paragraph might explore the setting of the story and show how the setting creates a particular mood. Finally, in your concluding paragraph, you might restate the theme and summarize how each element in the story helps to reveal that theme.

CASE STUDY: WRITING ABOUT A SHORT STORY

Lynn's English teacher asked the class to write a composition presenting an interpretation of a short story. Lynn decided to write about Flannery O'Connor's "The Life You Save May Be Your Own," on page 1052.

Prewriting

Lynn read the short story carefully. She then read the chart in this lesson and wrote the answers to the questions in her notes. She decided that the main point of her composition would be the theme of the story as suggested by the title. Lynn made the following rough outline for her composition, in which each major heading represents a paragraph:

- *Introduction:*
    Author
    Title
    Theme

- *Plot:*
    Of the entire short story
    Of Mr. Shiftlet's story

- *Theme as understood by the characters:*
    What the old woman and her daughter learned from Mr. Shiftlet
    Idea of story for Mr. Shiftlet

- *Conclusion:*
    Meaning of the title of the story in light of what has been discussed in preceding paragraphs
    Significance of the theme for readers/real people

Lynn reread the story and added more details to her notes to support her ideas in each paragraph.

Drafting and Revising

Lynn wrote a draft of her four-paragraph composition and then revised it carefully. Here is the first paragraph of Lynn's draft, with her revisions marked in editorial symbols:

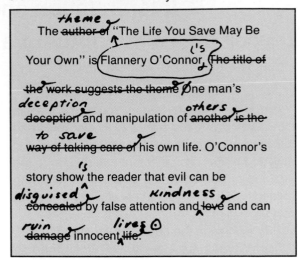

Proofreading and Publishing.

Lynn made a fresh copy of her composition and proofread it for errors in spelling and mechanics. Then she shared her composition in a class discussion.

ACTIVITIES AND ASSIGNMENTS

A. Answer the following questions about the revised paragraph in the case study:
1. What sentences did Lynn combine?
2. What words did Lynn replace with ones that were more appropriate?
3. What run-on sentence did Lynn correct?
4. What errors in spelling and punctuation did Lynn correct?

B. Select one of the following short stories for a two- to four-paragraph composition: "The Fall of the House of Usher," on page 208; "The Minister's Black Veil," on page 294; "The Story of an Hour," on page 546; "To Build a Fire," on page 562; "In Another Country," on page 722; "Flight," on page 772; "The Slump," on page 1074; or "Anxiety," on page 1102. Follow these steps:
1. Read the story carefully. Answer the questions in this lesson in your prewriting notes.

2. Decide what element of the story will be the focus of your composition. Make a rough outline showing how you will organize your writing.
3. Write a draft of your paragraph. When you revise your draft, make sure that you have provided supporting evidence for each of your statements.
4. Proofread your composition and make a clean final copy of it. Share this copy with your classmates and with your teacher.

Lesson 13:   Writing About a Poem

Before you can write an interpretation of a poem as a whole, you must make sure that you understand it thoroughly. To do this, you must analyze the poem and consider each of its parts separately. Then you can assess the meaning of the entire poem. The following steps will guide you in analyzing a poem:

1. Read the poem silently. To make sure that you understand its literal meaning, look up any words or allusions that you do not know in a dictionary or in another reference work. Then paraphrase the poem line by line, restating the literal meaning in your own words.
2. Read the poem aloud several times, listening to the sound of the words as you read them. Ask yourself what effect is created by the sound of the poem.
3. Read the poem silently again. Then make a copy of the poem and mark on the copy any examples of figures of speech and images that you can find.

   Answer the following questions in your pre-writing notes:

1. *Author:* Who is the author of the poem?
2. *Title:* What is the poem's title? Does the title suggest the poem's subject or theme?
3. *Genre:* What type of poem is it? Is it a lyric poem? a narrative poem? a dramatic poem? If it is a lyric poem, what emotion(s) does it express? Who is the speaker? What is the situation? If it is a narrative poem, what is the plot of the story that it tells? What is the setting? Who are the characters? If it is a dramatic poem, what dramatic techniques— such as monologue or dialogue—does it use? What is the plot? What is the setting? Who are the characters?

4. *Form:* Is the poem divided into stanzas? If so, how many lines are there in each stanza? Does each stanza express a complete thought, like a paragraph in prose writing?

   Is the poem written in any traditional form, such as quatrains, sonnet form, or haiku form? Is the poem written in free verse? What does the poem's form contribute to its meaning?
5. *Imagery:* What images of sight, sound, touch, taste, and smell are used in the poem? What do these images describe? What effect is created by these images?
6. *Figurative language:* Are there any examples of apostrophe in the poem? of hyperbole? of irony? of metaphor? of metonomy? of oxymoron? of paradox? of personification? of simile? of synecdoche? of understatement? What symbols, if any, does the poet use to represent other ideas or things? Does the poet make use of allusion? Is the poem an allegory?
7. *Devices of sound:* What is the ryhme scheme of the poem, if any? What examples of alliteration can you find in the poem? of assonance? of consonance? Does the poet use euphony, cacophony, parallelism, repetition, or a refrain?

   Does the poem have a regular rhythm? If so, what kind of metrical feet does the poem contain? How many feet are there in each line? What effect does the meter of the poem create?
8. *Other elements:* What is the overall mood of the poem? What literary devices create this mood?

   What is the theme of the poem? How is this theme revealed?

CASE STUDY: WRITING ABOUT A POEM

David's English teacher asked the class to select a poem and to write an interpretation of it. David chose Henry Wadsworth Longfellow's ''The Tide Rises, The Tide Falls,'' on page 334.

Prewriting

David began by reading the poem several times, both silently and aloud. Then he made the following notes about the elements of the poem:

- Title: ''The Tide Rises, The Tide Falls''

- Author: Henry Wadsworth Longfellow

- Stanza form:
    3 stanzas, 5 lines in each
    First stanza introduces the traveler at dusk.
    Second stanza tells of the traveler's disappearance.
    Third stanza suggests that the traveler is not to be seen again.

- Images of sight:
    ''The tide rises, the tide falls''
    ''Darkness settles on roofs and walls''
    ''The little waves with their soft, white hands''

- Images of sound:
    ''The tide rises, the tide falls''
    ''the steeds in their stalls stamp and neigh, as the hostler calls''

- Images of touch:
    ''sea sands damp and brown''

- Personification:
    ''waves with their soft, white hands''

- Rhyme scheme: *aabbc*

- Alliteration:
    ''*s*ea *s*ands''
    ''*st*eeds in their *st*alls *st*amp and neigh''

- Euphony/repetition:
    ''The tide rises, the tide falls''

- Mood:
    Inevitability of tides
    Acceptance of cycle of life

- Theme: The cycle of life and death is as inevitable and as predictable as the rising and falling of the tides.

Drafting and Revising

David used his prewriting notes to write a draft of his composition. In the first paragraph, he discussed the likeness between the life cycle and the ebb and flow of the tide. In the last sentence of the first paragraph, David stated his thesis, or main idea:

Henry Wadsworth Longfellow, in his poem ''The Tide Rises, The Tide Falls,'' portrays the cycle of life and death as the comforting ebb and flow of the tide.

In his second paragraph, David discussed the three stanzas of the poem. He explained how the poet suggests the cycle of life and death through the use of rhyme, repetition of phrases, and imagery.

In his third and final paragraph, David discussed the theme of the poem and explained the value of the poem to readers.

David wrote several versions of his draft. Then he revised the best of these drafts.

Proofreading and Publishing

After proofreading his draft, David made a final copy and gave it to his English teacher. His teacher suggested that he read the poem and his interpretation aloud to the class.

ACTIVITIES AND ASSIGNMENTS

A. Use David's prewriting notes to write a three-paragraph composition that offers an interpretation of ''The Tide Rises, The Tide Falls.'' Then revise and proofread your composition, and share your final copy with your classmates and with your teacher.

B. Select one of the following poems to analyze in a two- to four-paragraph composition: "A Psalm of Life," on page 336; "Hampton Beach," on page 362; "Because I could not stop for Death—," on page 380; "War Is Kind," on page 667; "Miniver Cheevy," on page 680; "The Love Song of J. Alfred Prufrock," on page 864; "Disillusionment of Ten O'Clock," on page 872; "Poetry," on page 914; "Nothing Gold Can Stay," on page 946; "The Tropics in New York," on page 960; "The Waking," on page 1190; "Expect Nothing," on page 1222; or "Most Satisfied by Snow," on page 1256. Follow these steps:

1. Read the poem several times, both silently and aloud. Follow the steps in the lesson for analyzing the poem.

2. Make an outline for your composition. Show what information from your prewriting notes you will include in each of your paragraphs. Make sure that your paper has a definite introduction, thesis statement, body, and conclusion.

3. Write a draft of your composition. Then revise your draft, adding evidence to support your claims where necessary. Also make sure that you have expressed your ideas clearly.

4. Proofread your paper and make a clean final copy of it. Share your composition with your teacher and with classmates who have analyzed the same poem.

Lesson 14: Writing About Drama

DRAMA AS LITERATURE

Dramas, like short stories, novels, and narrative poems, have plots, characters, settings, and themes. Like poetry, a drama may be written in verse and may use imagery, figures of speech, and devices of sound. In these ways, drama has many features in common with other forms of literature.

Drama as Performance

Dramas differ from other literary works in one very important respect. Dramas are written specifically for on-stage performance before an audience. The action is meant to be experienced by seeing and hearing actors move about and speak on stage. When reading a drama, therefore, it is important to try to visualize what the play would be like as a performance.

A *script*, or written form of a drama, has features that reflect the fact that the drama is meant to be performed. The title of the play is followed by a list of characters. The play itself is composed of dialogue and stage directions. *Dialogue* is the words spoken by the characters. The lines of dialogue in a drama follow the names of the characters who speak them. The *stage directions* give instructions for how the play is to be performed. They include details about how the actors should move and speak; how the set should look; what special effects of lighting and sound should be used; and what *properties*, or movable objects, should appear on stage.

When writing about drama, you may approach it as literature or as performance. The following are some suggestions for ways to write about a drama in both fashions:

The drama as literature:
1. Analyze the plot of the drama. Discuss the introduction, the inciting incident, the development, the climax, the resolution, and the denouement. Also address any special techniques of plot used by the playwright, such as suspense, foreshadowing, flashbacks, or a surprise ending.
2. Discuss how the setting of the play creates a certain mood or contributes to the action of the drama.
3. Find the central idea, or theme, of the drama and write about how other elements such as the plot, setting, and characters help to reveal this theme.
4. Select a major character in the play and discuss how the writer reveals the nature of this character. If the character changes in the course of the drama, tell why and how he or she changes.

The drama as performance:
1. Describe how you would create the set for a specific scene in the drama. Include details about the backdrop, the furniture, the properties, and the lighting you would use.
2. Imagine that you are a costume designer for the play. Describe what kinds of costumes you would have the major character wear.
3. If you have the opportunity to attend an actual performance, write a review of the play. Comment on the sets, costumes, lighting, sound, and performances by the actors.

CASE STUDY: WRITING ABOUT DRAMA

Dana's English class was asked to write a paragraph about a drama. Dana decided to write about Thornton Wilder's *Our Town*, on page 974.

Prewriting

Dana read *Our Town* carefully and thought about what aspect of the drama he would like to write about. Since he had found the Stage Manager especially intriguing, he decided to make this character the focus of his paper. Dana reread the drama and made the following notes about the Stage Manager:

- *Character:* Stage Manager

- *Characteristics:*
  Knowledgeable
  Speaks directly to audience, but also interacts with characters
  Knows what will happen in the characters' futures

- *Role he plays in the drama:*
  Establishes the setting by describing it to the audience
  Controls the action of the play
  Introduces the characters
  Explains scene transitions
  Dismisses audience after each act

Drafting and Revising

Dana wanted to make sure that the topic sentence of his paragraph clearly introduced what he intended to write about in the body of the paragraph. He drafted the following sentence:

> When I read Thornton Wilder's play *Our Town*, I thought that the Stage Manager was an important role.

Dana read his topic sentence and realized that it needed to be revised. First, he did not want to use the first-person pronoun "I" to refer to himself in the paragraph. Second, he wanted the sentence to emphasize the fact that he thought the Stage Manager was the most important character in the play. Dana rewrote his topic sentence as follows:

> The most important character in Thornton Wilder's play *Our Town* is the Stage Manager.

Next Dana wrote the body of his paragraph, in which he gave supporting evidence for his topic sentence. He concluded his paragraph with a sentence that summarized the main idea of his paper. Then Dana revised his paragraph to make sure that his ideas would be clear to his readers.

Proofreading and Publishing

Dana made a fresh copy of his paragraph and proofread it. Then he shared his paragraph with his drama teacher and with other students in the class.

ACTIVITIES AND ASSIGNMENTS

A. Use the notes in the case study to write a paragraph about the Stage Manager in *Our Town*. Follow these steps:

1. Read the play carefully. Then read Dana's notes and add to them any important details about the Stage Manager that you find are missing. Make an outline for your paragraph.
2. If you wish to do so, you may use Dana's revised sentence as the topic sentence for your paragraph, or you may write an original sentence that introduces your own main idea.
3. Write the rest of your paragraph according to your outline.
4. Revise your draft. Make sure that you have provided supporting evidence for all your statements about the Stage Manager and about *Our Town*. Also make sure that all of your ideas are clear.
5. Proofread your paragraph for errors in grammar, usage, spelling, punctuation, capitalization, and manuscript form. Make a clean final copy of your paragraph and share it with your classmates and with your teacher.

B. Select one of the following approaches for a one- to three-paragraph composition about *Our Town*, on page 974:

1. Analyze one scene and explain what elements contribute to its overall effect.
2. Describe how you would create the setting for a particular scene in the drama. Explain the mood that would be created by the setting.
3. Analyze the role of a minor character in one scene of the play.
4. Analyze the interaction of the Stage Manager with the audience in one specific scene.
5. Describe how a major character should be portrayed in a certain scene. Tell how you would instruct the actor playing the role to move, act, and speak.
6. Make up your own topic analyzing a specific element of a scene in the play.

C. Follow these steps when planning and writing your composition:

1. Carefully study the scene that you will be analyzing. Read it both silently and aloud. Think about how it would look and sound in a performance.
2. Makes notes about the details in the scene that are relevant to your topic. Then organize your notes and make an outline for your composition.
3. Write a topic sentence that introduces the main idea of your composition. Then write a draft of your paper. Make sure that your writing has a definite introduction, body, and conclusion.
4. Revise and proofread your composition. Share your final copy with your classmates and with your teacher.

SECTION 4: JUDGING A LITERARY WORK: EVALUATION

Lesson 15: Evaluating a Literary Work

WHAT IS EVALUATION?

An *evaluation* is a judgment about the quality or value of something. Every time you decide that you like or do not like something, you are making an evaluation.

To be valid, an evaluation must not be arbitrary but must be based on reasonable *criteria*, or standards. For example, if you were judging the quality of a new brand of potato chips, you might select criteria such as flavor, texture, freshness, and amount of sodium and cholesterol. You would use different criteria to evaluate an automobile, such as ease of handling and effectiveness of brakes. An evaluation must reflect facts about the object being judged. For example, if you said you did not like the flavor of Brand X potato chips because they had too much salt on them, when in fact they had no salt at all, your evaluation would be unsound.

The same principles apply when you evaluate a literary work. Your evaluation must follow a set of reasonable criteria and must reflect facts about the work you are evaluating.

CRITERIA FOR EVALUATING LITERATURE

The following list describes some of the most common criteria, or standards, that are used to evaluate literary works:

1. *Originality:* A work that deals with a subject that has not been dealt with in other literary works shows originality or creativity on the part of the writer. A work that has an unusual subject or sheds an interesting new light on a familiar subject will often be evaluated favorably on grounds of originality. Works that lack originality are trite or contain clichés.

2. *Consistency or completeness of effect:* Most works are intended to leave the reader with a certain feeling by creating an overall effect. If the reader is left feeling confused because the writer has carelessly allowed the effect of the work to be spoiled, the work will not be evaluated favorably. For example, imagine a novel that told the story of a man who had been the victim of cruel fate throughout his entire life. If the novel were to end with the words "Oh, well—that's life," the melancholy mood of the work would be ruined.

3. *Importance:* Some literary works are judged to be better than others because they deal with matters of greater importance. Works evaluated favorably according to this criterion usually have serious themes or subjects. For example, a poem that offers a profound insight into human nature might be judged to be superior to a poem that simply describes a pretty scene.

4. *Theme:* The theme of a literary work is often an idea about how one should live one's life. If a reader agrees with the theme, he or she is likely to evaluate the work favorably.

5. *Clarity:* Many great works of literature are difficult and require a great deal of study to be understood. However, if a work is incomprehensible simply because the writer has not expressed his or her ideas clearly, the work will be judged to be of poor quality.

CASE STUDY: EVALUATING A LITERARY WORK

Sara's English teacher asked the class to write an evaluation of a literary work. Sara and her classmates had saved all their writing in folders, so Sara decided to write an evaluation of a poem that she had written earlier in the year.

Prewriting

Here is Sara's poem, "Seasonal Changes":

It is springtime.
An infant crawls across
A fragrant lawn
And laughs
As she looks up at
The blossoming cherry tree.

Now it is summer
And a young girl—
Almost a woman—
Leaves a trail of footprints
On the sandy beach.
The tide washes them away.

In the fall
A mature woman
Hurries across the busy street
To her office building.
As a car horn blares
She turns up the collar of her jacket
Against a suddenly chilly wind.

It is winter.
Snow covers the ground
On the lawn outside an old woman's/
 window—
The same lawn
Across which crawled
A laughing infant.

Sara read the poem carefully and decided that it sounded trite and contained clichés. She made the following notes about why she felt the poem was ineffective:

- *Criterion for evaluation:* originality

- *How poem fails to meet criterion:*

The theme—likening cycle of life to seasonal changes—is unoriginal. Many other writers have used this analogy. The poem contains clichés such as the "young girl" who is "Almost a woman"; the "trail of footprints/On the sandy beach" that is washed away by the tide; the "suddenly chilly wind"; and the snow outside the window.

Sara made an outline for her evaluation, one that showed how she would organize her ideas in the introduction, body and conclusion of her paper.

Drafting and Revising

Sara used her notes and her outline to write a draft of her composition. Then she revised her paper, adding supporting evidence for her claims and clarifying some of her statements.

Proofreading and Publishing

Sara made a fresh copy of her paper and proofread it carefully. Then she shared the final copy of her evaluation with her class discussion group.

ACTIVITIES AND ASSIGNMENTS

A. Use Sara's prewriting notes to write an evaluation of the poem "Seasonal Changes." Follow these steps:

1. Read the poem carefully. Then look at Sara's notes. If you can think of any other criteria to evaluate the poem, add them to your notes.
2. Make an outline for your evaluation.
3. Write a topic sentence that introduces the propose of your paper. Then finish writing your draft according to your outline.
4. Revise your draft. Make sure that your purpose is clear and that your topic sentence is

supported with specific evidence from the poem.

5. Proofread your revised draft carefully. Then share your final copy with a small group of your classmates and with your teacher.

B. Select one of the following works for a one- to three-paragraph evaluation: "To a Waterfowl," on page 175; "The Raven," on page 223; "The Chambered Nautilus," on page 346; "A Noiseless Patient Spider," on page 468; "The Red Badge of Courage," on page 576; "Winter Dreams," on page 730; "Anecdote of the Jar," on page 873; "anyone lived in a pretty how town," on page 919; "The Death of the Hired Man," on page 935; "Storm Ending," on page 968; "Katherine Comes to Yellow Sky," on page 1108; "A Vision Beyond Time and Place," on page 1156; "The Explorer," on page 1202; or "Evening Hawk," on page 1232. Follow these steps:

1. Read the work carefully. Freewrite about why you like or did not like the work. Then decide which criteria you will use to evaluate the work—originality, completeness of effect, importance, moral or ethical message, or clarity. In your prewriting notes, list specific examples from the work that support your evaluation.

2. Make a rough outline for your composition. Then write a draft of your evaluation, including details to support all your statements.

3. Revise your paper to make sure that it is clear and well organized. Then proofread your revised draft for errors in spelling and mechanics.

4. Share the final copy of your evaluation with your classmates and with your teacher.

Lesson 16: Writing a Comparative Evaluation

WHAT IS A COMPARATIVE EVALUATION?

As you learned in the preceding lesson, an evaluation is a statement about the quality or value of something. A *comparative evaluation* is a statement about the relative quality or value of two or more things. Suppose, for example, that you want to buy a car and there are two models that appeal to you. To decide between these two models, you will have to do a comparative evaluation. First you will choose certain features to compare, such as safety, appearance, cost, and fuel efficiency. Then you will judge the relative value of each model with respect to these features.

COMPARING TWO LITERARY WORKS

When you choose two literary works for a comparative evaluation, the two works should have at least one feature in common—a feature that can be compared. For example, you might choose two works by the same author, two works from the same literary period, two works on the same theme or subject, or two works that make use of the same literary device. The first step in doing a comparative evaluation is to list the works and the feature to be compared in your prewriting notes. The next step is to read each work carefully and to take notes on the feature as it appears in each work. Finally, you need to decide which of the two works is better with respect to the feature you are comparing.

CASE STUDY: WRITING A COMPARATIVE EVALUATION

Marina's English teacher asked the students to choose two works for a comparative evaluation. Marina decided to write about two imagist poems—Ezra Pound's "In a Station of the Metro," on page 854, and William Carlos Williams's "The Red Wheelbarrow," on page 890.

Prewriting

Marina began by listing the works and the feature to be compared in her prewriting notes, as follows:

- Works to be compared: Ezra Pound's "In a Station of the Metro" and William Carlos Williams's "The Red Wheelbarrow"

- Feature to be compared: use of imagery

Next Marina read the two works carefully and made the following notes about the imagery in each:

- Imagery in the poem by Pound:
  faces in train station described as an "apparition," like a ghostly vision
  faces compared to "petals on a wet, black bough"
  imagery is used to report how an ordinary thing can appear to be extraordinary, like a vision or like one of those Oriental watercolors of petals against the limb of a tree, shining black after a rain
  three metaphors, all in a couple of lines (the whole scene = an apparition; the faces = petals; the people's dark clothing = a wet, black bough)

- Imagery in the poem by Williams:
  "a red wheelbarrow"
  "glazed with rain water"
  "beside the white chickens"
  contrast between the red of the wheelbarrow and the white of the chickens
  colors always more vibrant after a rain
  "So much depends" is purposefully

vague, as though Williams meant to suggest both that the overall appearance of the scene and the state of the speaker of the poem both depend on how the wheelbarrow looks

After making these notes, Marina thought about her reactions to the two poems. She decided that she liked the Pound poem better because it was more sophisticated and because it dealt with a more important subject. Therefore, she added the following comments to her notes:

- *Evaluation 1:* Ezra Pound's poem is more sophisticated than William Carlos Williams's because of its use of metaphors that bring lots of associations to mind.

- *Evaluation 2:* Ezra Pound's poem deals with an important subject—how people perceive other people. Williams's poem, on the other hand, deals with a relatively trivial subject—how the beauty of a scene can depend on a single brilliant contrast

Marina decided that she would focus her paper on the relative sophistication of the two poems. She would make the claim that Ezra Pound's poem was better because it showed more artistry in its subtle use of metaphor.

Drafting and Revising

Based on her notes, Marina wrote a four-paragraph paper. In the first paragraph she introduced the two poems, the two authors, and her subject—the imagery in the two poems. In the second paragraph she discussed how Williams used imagery in his poem to create a picture of a wheelbarrow. In the third paragraph she discussed how Pound used imagery in his poem to show that ordinary people can sometimes be strikingly beautiful. Finally, in her fourth paragraph Marina explained why she thought the Pound poem was better than the Williams poem. After finishing the rough draft of her paper, Marina made extensive revisions, using the Checklist for Revision on page 1276.

Proofreading and Publishing

Marina proofread her paper carefully and then shared it with a small group of her classmates. Several people in the group objected to Marina's paper quite strongly. They felt that Williams's poem was more powerful than Pound's precisely because the Williams poem was so simple and direct.

ACTIVITIES AND ASSIGNMENTS

A. If you haven't already done so, read Ezra Pound's "In a Station of the Metro," on page 854, and William Carlos Williams's "The Red Wheelbarrow," on page 890. Then, using the notes from the case study and notes of your own, write a comparative evaluation of the two poems.

B. Choose one of the following pairs of works for a comparative evaluation:
1. Robert Benchley's "The Tooth, the Whole Tooth, and Nothing but the Tooth," on page 824, and James Thurber's "The Night the Ghost Got In," on page 832.
2. Ralph Waldo Emerson's "Concord Hymn," on page 275, and Ralph Waldo Emerson's "Brahma," on page 279.
3. Paul Laurence Dunbar's "We Wear the Mask," on page 672, and Countee Cullen's "Any Human Being to Another," on page 959.
4. Henry Wadsworth Longfellow's "A Psalm of Life," on 336, and the excerpt from Walt Whitman's "Song of Myself," on page 456.

B. Follow these steps when writing your evaluation:
1. Choose some feature you wish to compare.
2. Read both works carefully and take notes on the feature you are comparing.
3. Write a statement of opinion that expresses the relative value of each work with respect to the feature you are comparing.
4. Write an outline for a four-paragraph paper. In the first paragraph you should state what

works and feature you are comparing. In the second paragraph you should discuss one of the works. In the third paragraph you should discuss the other work. In the fourth paragraph you should state your opinion about the relative value of the two works and support this opinion with evidence from the rest of the paper.

5. Write a rough draft based on your outline and your notes. Revise and proofread your draft. Then share it with your classmates and with your teacher.

Lesson 17: Evaluating Persuasive Writing

Persuasion, or *persuasive writing,* is a type of nonfiction in which the writer attempts to convince the audience to accept a certain idea or to act in a certain way. The purpose of persuasive writing, then, is to present the opinion of the writer in such a way as to solicit an active response from the reader. Familiar examples of persuasive writing and speech include advertisements, newspaper editorials, political speeches, and campaign brochures.

SOUND REASONING ABOUT PERSUASION

The opinions presented in persuasive writing and speech are, by definition, statements about which people may disagree. Therefore, to be effective, persuaders must present reasonable arguments to support their opinions. Readers or listeners must then decide whether these opinions are sound. The following are some criteria for evaluating the soundness of opinions:

The Consistency Principle

Is the opinion consistent with known facts? For example, the opinion that it is foolish never to check the oil level in one's car engine is consistent with the fact that to allow the oil to run low is to risk destroying the engine.

The Utility Principle

Does accepting the opinion lead to consequences that are themselves acceptable? For example, the opinion that one should engage in a program of regular exercise is sound because the result of acting on this opinion is a healthier body.

The Principle of Appeal to Authority

Is the opinion consistent with the views of knowledgeable and reliable authorities? For ex-

ample, the opinion that it will snow this evening is sound if it reflects the views of competent meteorologists. These people study the patterns of the weather and are able to make intelligent predictions about upcoming weather conditions.

Unsound Reasoning About Opinions

Not all persuasive writing and speech contains logically reasoned arguments. Instead, some persuasion makes use of propaganda and logical fallacies. *Propaganda* is language that is emotionally charged and intentionally misleading. A *logical fallacy* is an error in reasoning. The following propaganda devices and logical fallacies are often found in persuasive writing and speech:

Propaganda Devices:
1. *Bandwagon:* urging support for an opinion simply because many other people support the opinion
2. *Loaded language:* using emotionally charged words that have little meaning beyond arousing positive or negative feelings
3. *Argument ad hominem:* (literally, "argument to the person") criticizing or attacking the opponent instead of the opponent's argument
4. *Snob appeal:* urging support for an opinion solely because an admired person or group supports it.
5. *Straw man:* exaggerating or misrepresenting the opposing position so that it sounds more ridiculous than it actually is
6. *Stereotyping:* assuming, without sufficient evidence, that everyone in a particular group has certain characteristics

Logical Fallacies:
1. *Begging the question:* stating an opinion without giving evidence to support it; simply assuming the truth of the opinion to be proved

2. *Either/or fallacy:* treating a complicated issue as if there were only two sides or two alternatives when there are actually more
3. *Post hoc, ergo propter hoc:* (literally, "after this, therefore because of this") assuming that one action or event caused another simply because it came earlier in time
4. *False analogy:* falsely treating two subjects as similar in one respect simply because they are similar in some other respect
5. *Non sequitur:* (literally, "It does not follow") stating a conclusion that is not a necessary consequence of the reasons given
6. *Overgeneralization:* making a statement that is too broad in its application

When you evaluate written or spoken persuasion, you must constantly be aware of any devices of propaganda or logical fallacies that appear in the arguments. You should never accept an opinion until you are convinced that it is supported by sound reasoning.

CASE STUDY: EVALUATING PERSUASION

Jodie's English teacher asked the class to find an example of persuasive writing and to evaluate the soundness of its arguments. Jodie found a letter to the editor in a local newspaper that she decided to use for the assignment.

Prewriting

Here is the letter that Jodie found:

Dear Editor:

The outrageous behavior last Friday of five juvenile delinquents at Hampton Mall shows what trouble our country is in! These young hoodlums were playing a game by the public walkways, wildly throwing a saucer-shaped plastic disk. This unruly behavior upset all the hard-working Americans who needed to shop. I'm sure all solid citizens will agree that anyone under eighteen should be banned from malls or parents should be fined when their children run wild in public!

Sincerely,
Maudine Oxley

Jodie read the letter carefully, noting its unsupported assumptions and biased opinions. In her prewriting notes she made a list of the propaganda techniques and logical fallacies in the letter:

- Loaded language: calling the kids "juvenile delinquents" and "hoodlums"; calling shoppers "hard-working Americans"

- Bandwagon or snob appeal: calling on "all solid citizens"

- Either/or fallacy: suggesting banning or fining parents as the only choices

- Non sequitur: assuming that the kids' behavior shows trouble in the entire nation

While Jodie agreed that the behavior discussed in the letter was reprehensible, she nonetheless concluded that the letter was badly flawed because it contained unsupported claims and illogical solutions. She made an outline and drafted a topic sentence based on her prewriting notes and ideas.

Drafting and Revising

Jodie wrote a draft of her essay, including many specific examples from the letter. Then she revised her draft to clarify her points.

Proofreading and Publishing

Jodie proofread her essay and shared it with the class.

ACTIVITIES AND ASSIGNMENTS

A. Use Jodie's prewriting notes to write an essay analyzing the letter to the editor in the case study. Follow these steps:

1. Read the letter carefully. Then look at Jodie's notes and add to them any examples of propaganda devices or logical fallacies that she left out.
2. Make an outline for your essay. Make sure that it is organized logically and that it shows

how you will support each of your claims about the letter.

3. Write a draft of your essay. Then revise the draft, keeping in mind that your ideas must be presented clearly if you want to convince your readers that the letter is actually flawed.

4. Proofread your revised draft and share your final copy with a small group of your classmates before turning it in to your teacher.

B. Write an essay analyzing the propaganda devices or logical fallacies in a piece of persuasive writing. Follow these steps:

1. Find an example of persuasive writing. Look in magazines, in newspapers, and in public relations materials.

2. Analyze your example. What does the writer want the audience to do or to believe? What reasons are given for the audience to accept the opinion expressed in the writing? Look for examples of the propaganda devices and logical fallacies listed in this lesson and record them in your notes.

3. Make an outline for your essay. Then write your first draft, making sure that you include specific details to support your claims.

4. Revise your draft. Make sure that all your ideas are expressed clearly and that you have not wandered from your topic.

5. Proofread your essay, and share your final copy with your classmates.

SECTION 5: WRITING CREATIVELY
Lesson 18: Writing a Short Story

Authors have many different purposes for writing short stories. Some want to express serious themes through their narratives. Others want to entertain their audiences with intriguing or amusing tales. Still others want to sketch important or interesting characters.

An idea for a short story can come from any of a number of sources. You can work from your own experience. You can write about historical figures. You can create completely imaginary characters and events. Begin by concentrating on one element of the story—setting, characters, plot, or theme. Then build the rest of your story around this one element.

DEVELOPING YOUR IDEA

The following questions will help you to develop the various parts of your story before you begin writing:

1. *Setting:* Where does the story take place? At what date in history does the action unfold? In what season does the story occur? Are the weather conditions important to the story? What images of sight, sound, touch, taste, and smell will you use to reveal the setting?

2. *Character:* Who will be the main character, or protagonist, of the story? What other major and minor charactrers will take part in the action? What will each of the characters be like? How will you reveal the nature of each character? Will any of the characters change or grow in the course of the story? What will cause them to change? How will they be different at the end of the story? What will the reader learn from the experiences of the characters?

3. *Conflict:* What central conflict will the protagonist be involved in? Will the conflict be *internal*—within the character's mind—or *external*—between the character and some outside force? How will the conflict be resolved?

4. *Plot:* What events will take place in the story?
Introduction: What background information about the setting or the characters will you present at the beginning of the story?
Inciting incident: What event will give rise to the central conflict?
Development: What events will occur as a result of the inciting incident?
Climax: What will be the high point of interest or suspense in the story?
Resolution: How will the central conflict be resolved? Will the resolution and the climax occur at the same time?
Denouement: What events, if any, will happen after the resolution?

5. Will your story have a message for the reader? What elements in the story will serve to reveal this message, or theme?

6. *Point of view:* Who will be the narrator of the story? Will the narrator be involved in the action of the story or tell the story as an outsider? That is, will the narrator be first person or third person? How much will the narrator know about each of the characters? That is, will the narrator be limited or omniscient?

DRAFTING YOUR STORY

Perhaps the most important point to remember as you write your story is that you must keep your readers interested and involved. Do not include any pointless or unnecessary passages that will distract the reader or break the tension that you are trying to build as the plot develops. Instead, make sure that every sentence you write has a purpose and contributes to the overall effect of the story.

To make your writing especially interesting, consider where you could add vivid descriptions of people and places using images and figurative language. Also, you might want to employ special plot techniques such as foreshadowing, flashback, or surprise ending.

CASE STUDY: WRITING A SHORT STORY

Andrei's English teacher asked each student in the class to write a short story. All of the stories were to be bound together in a class booklet.

Prewriting

Andrei did not have an idea for his story, so he tried brainstorming about setting, plot, and character. Here are Andrei's brainstorming notes:

- Setting:
  a beach in California
  a stormy night in a dark, abandoned house
  the public library, where I'm studying for a math test
  the United States during the Industrial Revolution
  inside my favorite book
  ten years from now—what will I be doing?

- Plot:
  I meet the girl of my dreams on vacation, but she lives in Greece.
  A kid and his friends are snooping around where they're not supposed to be.

A poor man wants to buy his daughter an expensive doll for her birthday.
I'm reading a book and suddenly I find myself taking part in the action.

- Character:
  myself
  my best friend, Leo
  the characters in my favorite book
  a Siamese cat
  the king of an imaginary land
  a boy who can't decide whether or not to try out for the swim team

Andrei liked the idea of finding himself in the middle of his favorite book. He decided that the purpose of his short story would be to relate the humorous adventures he might have if he could participate in the action of a literary work. He made an outline of the events that would occur in the plot. He also listed the characters that would play roles in his story and described briefly what each would be like. Finally, Andrei made a list of the images he would use to describe the setting of his story.

Drafting and Revising

Andrei used his prewriting notes to write a draft of his short story. When he read the story, he realized that some passages were not essential to the plot and might seem boring to a reader. He deleted these passages.

Proofreading and Publishing

Andrei proofread his story and made a clean final copy. This copy he submitted to his teacher, who added it to the class booklet.

ACTIVITIES AND ASSIGNMENTS

A. Use Andrei's prewriting notes and ideas from the case study to write a story about a student who finds himself or herself in the setting of a literary work. Follow these steps:

1. Select a narrative work that you enjoyed reading. Then decide at what point in the story it

would be interesting for a student to enter. Make notes about what events might occur when the student suddenly appears. Think about what characters the student will meet and how he or she will interact with them.

2. Decide whether you will tell the story from the first-person or the third-person point of view. Then decide whether the narrator will be limited or omniscient.

3. Write a draft of your story. Describe the setting and characters using images and figures of speech. Tell the events of the story in order. Try to create suspense by making the reader wonder what will happen next.

4. Revise and proofread your draft. Then share your final copy with your classmates and with your teacher.

B. Write an original short story. Follow these steps:

1. If you have trouble thinking of an idea for your story, try brainstorming or freewriting. Once you have decided on a main idea, develop the other elements of the story by answering the questions in this lesson.

2. Write a draft of your story. Then revise the draft, making sure that there are no unnecessary passages that will ruin the effect of your writing. Add new passages where you need to clarify what is happening or where you want to describe something more fully.

3. Proofread your story for errors in spelling and mechanics. Then share your final copy with your classmates and with your teacher.

Lesson 19: Writing a Poem

Poetry is imaginative language that expresses ideas of truth and beauty for the enjoyment of a reader. Poems can tell stories, present dramatic moments, and express human emotions. Because American poetry during the twentieth century is especially rich and varied, you might want to try writing poems modeled on those appearing in your text. For example, you might try writing an imagist poem such as those written by Ezra Pound, H.D., and William Carlos Williams, or you might try writing a dramatic dialogue such as Robert Frost's "The Death of the Hired Man," on page 935.

WRITING AN IMAGIST POEM

An *imagist poem* presents a single vivid picture in words. See, for example, H.D.'s "Pear Tree," on page 882, and William Carlos Williams's; "The Red Wheelbarrow," on page 890. To write an imagist poem, you need first to choose a scene that you want to describe. Then you need to make a list of the elements of the scene. It might be helpful to break up this list into images of sight, sound, touch, taste, and smell. The next step is to decide what characteristic of the scene you want to emphasize. Do you want to create a particular mood? Is there some important aspect of the scene that you want to concentrate on? Decide on a focus for your description. Then make a list of descriptive words you can use in your poem. Toss out any words that are vague or abstract. You want the words in your poem to be as vivid and concrete as possible.

Use your list of words to write a rough draft of your poem. In an imagist poem, the lines do not have to be of any particular length or rhythmical pattern. As you revise, try to make your lines even more vivid and dramatic, and experiment with lines of various lengths and rhythms. Revise the poem as many times as necessary until your final product is a single, vivid picture with a single dominant effect.

WRITING A DRAMATIC POEM

A *dramatic poem* is a poem in which there are two speakers who talk to one another. Often the poem involves some conflict between the speakers and reveals the speakers' personalities. There are many ways to approach writing a dramatic poem. One way is to think, first, of a conflict involving two people. Then write a short scene, in prose, describing a confrontation between these people. In your prose version, use dialogue to reveal the characters' feelings, thoughts, opinions of one another, and the like. Begin with some incident that triggers the central conflict, show how the conflict is developed, and then show how it is resolved.

Once you are satisfied with your prose version of the dialogue, rewrite the lines in verse form. Use unrhymed verse so you will not have to make the lines fit a rhyme scheme, but make sure that each line has the same number of beats, or strong stresses—three, four, or five. Use quotation marks to show when each speaker's lines begin and end. Remember that it is acceptable to include run-on lines (ones that are not end-stopped).

As you revise your poem, check to make sure that the characters' lines sound natural by reading these lines aloud. Also check to make sure that each line has the same number of strong stresses.

CASE STUDY: WRITING A POEM

Arthur's class was studying early twentieth-century poetry. After the class finished studying the movement known as Imagism, the teacher asked each of the students to write an imagist poem.

Prewriting

At first Arthur could not think of a subject to write about. Therefore, he did the following free-writing in his journal:

> What am I going to write about? Imagism. Let's see, images are...whatever you can see or touch or taste or hear or smell or—that could be almost anything. I need a really striking, powerful image like—what about a Ferris wheel at night with its lights shining against a dark blue sky?

Arthur then made the following notes:

- Subject: a Ferris wheel at night

- Images: dark sky, Ferris wheel seen from a distance, turning, its colored lights shining

- Mood: maybe the mood could be a little bit scary, as though the Ferris wheel were some kind of creature in the darkness

Arthur also included in his notes a list of words that he could use to describe the scene.

Drafting and Revising

Arthur wrote several drafts of his poem. Here is his final draft, which he titled "The Beast at the Edge of the Wood," with some of the corrections he made:

Across the ~~farms~~ *darkened* farms and fields
Against ~~a blue~~ *an indigo* sky,

A ferris wheel turns—
A hundred eyes ~~shine~~ *burn* in the

dreamlike distance.

Proofreading and Publishing

Arthur proofread the final copy of his poem. The only error that he found to correct was the capitalization of the word *Ferris*. After correcting this error, Arthur shared his poem with his parents, with his classmates, and with his teacher.

ACTIVITIES AND ASSIGNMENTS

A. Answer the following questions about the case study:

1. Why might Arthur have added the word "darkened" to his first line?
2. Why might Arthur have changed the word "blue" to "indigo"? the word "shine" to "burn"?
3. To what sense does Arthur's poem appeal?
4. What mood does Arthur's poem create?
5. Do you think that Arthur's poem is successful? Why or why not?

B. Write your own imagist poem or dramatic poem. Follow the steps described in this lesson.

Lesson 20: Writing a Short Dramatic Sketch

A *dramatic sketch* has the same form as a full-length drama except that it has only one brief scene that makes a single point. The elements that make up a drama—dialogue and stage directions—are also found in a dramatic sketch. The *dialogue* is the words spoken by the characters. When a character speaks, his or her name appears, followed by the appropriate lines of dialogue. The *stage directions* are instructions that appear in underlined or italicized text within brackets or parentheses. They give information about how the characters should move and speak; how the stage should appear to the audience; what special effects of lighting and sound should be used; and what *properties*, or movable pieces, should be used by the actors. The setting of a dramatic sketch is often described in stage directions at the very beginning of the work.

The following excerpt from *Our Town*, on page 974, shows the form in which a dramatic sketch is written:

> MR. WEBB [*suddenly and loudly*].   Well, George, how are you?
>
> GEORGE [*startled, choking over his coffee*].   Oh, fine, I'm fine. (*Pause.*) Mr. Webb, what sense could there be in a superstition like that?

PLANNING A DRAMATIC SKETCH

Planning to write a dramatic sketch is much like planning any other narrative work. You might start by thinking of an interesting main character for the sketch, or you might begin with a creative idea for a plot. No matter how you begin your planning, before you start writing you must have a clear idea of what the setting of your sketch will be; what characters will participate in the action; how each of the characters will act and speak; and what events will take place in the sketch. If your sketch is to be a serious one with a theme, you must have a plan for revealing that theme. Finally, you must make sure that the setting and action of the sketch can be presented on a stage. For example, a scene with a car chase around mountain curves would be very difficult to reproduce on stage.

WRITING THE SKETCH

Begin your sketch with a title and a list of characters. You may include a brief description of each character, as follows:

> DR. TANAKA, a renowned surgeon
> ALISA TANAKA, Dr. Tanaka's beautiful daughter

After the list of characters, include a set of stage directions with a detailed description of the setting. The description must be explicit enough so that a director will know exactly what you had in mind when you wrote the sketch. Next write the dialogue and stage directions that describe the action of the sketch. Stop writing from time to time to read the dialogue aloud. You want to make sure that it sounds natural and not stilted or contrived. Add stage directions only where necessary to clarify a particular movement or manner of speaking of one of the characters, or where you want to indicate a special effect of lighting or sound.

When you revise your sketch, make sure that you have not included dialogue or stage directions that are unnecessary to the purpose of the sketch. Remember that the sketch should be brief and should make a single point.

CASE STUDY: WRITING A DRAMATIC SKETCH

Rosa's English class was asked to write a short dramatic sketch about a historical event in an imaginary town. Rosa decided to write about the establishment of the first trading post in a town called New Pockets, Mississippi.

Prewriting

Rosa thought about the setting, characters, and plot of her dramatic sketch. She made the following notes:

- Title: *Local Trade*

- Setting: early nineteenth century; pioneer town; wooded area near flooding stream with a cabin under construction

- Characters: Trader Wainwright, Trapper Stockton, Trapper Levar, Abigail Scully, William Scully, Jenny Scully, Nancy Scully

- Plot summary: Despite spring floods, Trader Wainwright manages to open the town's first business, thanks to the help of two trappers and the Scully family.

Drafting and Revising

Rosa used her prewriting notes to write a draft of her sketch. Then she revised the draft. Here is Rosa's revised draft:

Local Trade
[*The scene opens in a wooded area next to a flooding stream. On the left is a cabin, partly constructed. TRADER WAINWRIGHT, the Scully family, and two trappers have formed a line and are passing supplies toward the cabin, trying to safe them from the spring floods.*]

TRAPPER STOCKTON. [*Tossing a large parcel toward WAINWRIGHT*] Here you go.

TRADER WAINWRIGHT. Another bolt of fabric. [*Taking the parcel and passing it along*] Can't let the floods take your new summer outfit, can we now, Jenny, my girl?

JENNY SCULLY. No, sir, Mr. Wainwright. [*Continues passing parcel along to others and into the cabin*]

TRAPPER LEVAR. [*At the head of the line, now passing a large sack to STOCKTON*] Corn meal coming next.

TRADER WAINWRIGHT. Ready for a heavy one, Jenny?

NANCY SCULLY. Knowing what that girl eats, she'll be wanting her corn meal johnnycakes lots more than a July dress!

JENNY SCULLY. [*Turning to appeal to her mother, who is in line near the cabin*] Mother! That Nancy is makin' fun of me again! Tell her to leave me be!

ABIGAIL SCULLY. [*Eying both of them*] I do believe we have something better to do today than bicker.

TRAPPER LEVAR. [*Moving out of line*] That does it, Wainwright. Every parcel you brought here for your new trading post is safe from the flood waters now.

WILLIAM SCULLY. [*Coming down from the cabin*] Well, neighbor, we've done it. The west side of the cabin is covered and still dry. And your goods are all up on logs above ground now, too.

TRADER WAINWRIGHT. [*Shaking hands all around*] Thanks to you all. Looks like I'll still open me a trading post this spring.

WILLIAM SCULLY. [*Digging in his pocket*] When I find you a penny, you'll have your first sale, too. I'll take some of that rock candy for my two girls here.

TRADER WAINWRIGHT. Keep your penny, neighbor. The first business done at the Wainwright Trading Post is a fair exchange—neighborly help for a sweet treat. [*Brings a small bag out of the cabin and offers rock candy to the girls*] Looks like we're in business, doesn't it, girls.

Proofreading and Publishing

Rosa proofread her revised draft and made

a clean final copy. Then she and several of her friends performed the sketch for the class.

ACTIVITIES AND ASSIGNMENTS

A. Refer to the sketch in the case study to complete the following exercises:

1. Rosa's sketch lacks a list of characters. Write out a list of characters for the sketch with a brief description of each character.
2. Practice writing dialogue by adding to the sketch another brief conversation or two between characters. Be sure that the dialogue makes sense in the context of the story and that the lines sound natural when read aloud.

B. Write an original dramatic sketch. Follow these steps:

1. Select a suitable topic that can be covered in a short sketch. Decide what the purpose of your sketch will be—to make the audience laugh, to dramatize a historical event, to make a serious point, or whatever—and plan the action around that purpose. Make notes about the setting, characters, plot, and theme of your sketch.
2. Write a draft of your sketch. Then revise your draft, making sure that you have included a title, a list of characters, natural-sounding dialogue, and appropriate stage directions.
3. Proofread your sketch and share it with your classmates and with your teacher.

Lesson 21: Writing a Personal Essay

When you write a *personal essay,* you speak directly to your audience about your own experiences, knowledge, attitudes, and feelings. The way you approach your topic reflects your personal thoughts. The process of writing a personal essay is the same as the process you used to write about literature. It includes prewriting, drafting, revising, proofreading, and publishing.

PLANNING A PERSONAL ESSAY

The topic of a personal essay should be something that really matters to you. The purpose of your essay will determine how you will write about the topic. Suppose, for example, you are planning to write about your experience working at a fast-food restaurant. Depending on the purpose of your writing, you could approach the topic in a number of ways. The following list explains some of the different types of essays you might write:

1. *Narrative essay:* one that tells a story about your experience

> Just getting to work on my first day at the Burger Place turned into an unbelievable adventure.

2. *Descriptive essay:* one that describes the topic vividly so that the reader can almost experience it for himself or herself

> In the peaceful hour before dawn, the kitchen at the Burger Place is already humming with activity.

3. *Expository essay:* one that explains an idea, thing, or process

> The process of preparing a hamburger at the Burger Place involves four simple steps, each performed by a different employee in an assembly line.

4. *Persuasive essay:* one that attempts to convince the audience to accept a particular point of view or to act in a certain way

> The town loitering ordinance should be amended to allow young people to gather peacefully outside popular restaurants such as the Burger Place.

A clear and definite topic sentence, or thesis statement, like the ones in the chart, is essential to an effective essay. The topic sentence tells the audience what the writer's purpose and topic are, thus creating certain expectations in the mind of the reader. For example, the thesis statement of a persuasive essay leads the reader to expect to find solid arguments for the writer's opinion in the body of the essay. As a writer, you must make sure that these expectations are fulfilled. Regardless of what type of essay you write, you must provide supporting evidence for your topic sentence in the body of your essay.

CASE STUDY: WRITING A PERSONAL ESSAY

John's English teacher asked the class to write a personal essay of three to five paragraphs.

Prewriting

John had no idea what he would write his personal essay about. Since he knew that the prewriting stage would take him longer than usual, he started working on his essay several days before it was due.

John decided to try freewriting to gather ideas for his topic:

Maybe I could write about my future. Let's see . . . All I want is to graduate. Then I want to go to hotel school so I can get a good job working for a big chain. Maybe even manage a hotel or motel. Maybe get to pick different places to live. Plus being a trained manager. If I get tired of it I can go work for some other kind of company.

John stopped writing and read what he had written so far. He realized that his freewriting contained a good idea for his essay. He brainstormed to come up with further ideas about why he planned to attend hotel management school, and then he organized his points in an outline, as follows:

- *Topic:* Going to hotel and restaurant school

- *Reasons why I want to go:*
  - chance for good employment
    - can work for one of the major hotel chains
    - can rise to a higher-level job with one of these chains or perhaps work for an independent hotel
  - chance to have responsibility
    - eventually manage a hotel or run a big restaurant
    - take care of travelers far from home
    - be able to pick where to live, maybe in a resort area or near a beach
    - manage a big staff, which is quite a challenge
  - chance to have managerial training
    - training program combines on-the-job experience with classwork
    - managerial training is like business school
    - skills could be used in some other kind of business if I don't like the actual hotel work

John decided that his essay would have five paragraphs: an introductory paragraph, a body paragraph for each of the three major reasons listed in his outline, and a concluding paragraph.

Drafting and Revising

John wrote a thesis statement to introduce his topic and his viewpoint. Here is John's thesis statement:

> I want to go to hotel and restaurant school because it will give me a chance to get a good job, to take on important responsibilities, and to be trained as a manager.

John began his introductory paragraph with this sentence. Then he wrote the rest of his essay. When he revised his draft, he made sure that all of his points were clear.

Proofreading and Publishing

John proofread his essay and made a clean final copy of it. Then he shared it with his parents and with his English teacher.

ACTIVITIES AND ASSIGNMENTS

A. Answer the following questions about the case study:

1. What method did John use to come up with an idea for his paper? What other methods might he have used?
2. Carefully review John's outline. Do all his points support his thesis? Is the outline well organized? How might his outline be improved?
3. Look at John's thesis statement. Does it reveal his approach or viewpoint? Explain. What does the sentence make the reader expect to find in the body of John's essay? Does the reader expect to find the points covered in any particular order?

B. Write your own personal essay on any topic that is interesting or important to you. Follow these steps:

1. If you have trouble thinking of a topic, try prewriting techniques such as freewriting or clustering. Once you have settled on a topic, decide whether your essay will be narrative, descriptive, expository, or persuasive.

2. Gather all the ideas and information that you will use in your essay. Then organize your notes into a rough outline for your essay.

3. Write a thesis statement that introduces your topic and purpose. Revise this statement as necessary to make it as clear as possible.

4. Draft your essay, referring to your prewriting notes and to your outline. Make sure that your writing remains focused on your topic and purpose throughout.

5. Revise your draft. Make sure that your points are clear and that you have not made any unsupported statements.

6. Proofread your essay for errors in grammar, usage, spelling, punctuation, capitalization, and manuscript form. Make a clean final copy of your essay, and share this copy with members of your family, with your classmates, and with your teacher.

HANDBOOK OF LITERARY TERMS AND TECHNIQUES

ACT   See *Drama.*

ALLEGORY   An *allegory* is a story or tale with two or more levels of meaning—a literal level and one or more symbolic levels. The events, setting, and characters in an allegory are symbols for ideas or qualities. Many of Nathaniel Hawthorne's short stories, such as "Dr. Heidegger's Experiment," on page 304, are allegories.

ALLITERATION   *Alliteration* is the repetition of consonant sounds at the beginning of words or accented syllables. Sara Teasdale uses alliteration in the second stanza of her poem "Understanding":

> But you I never understood,
>   Your spirit's secret hides like gold
> Sunk in a Spanish galleon
>   Ages ago in waters cold.

Poets and other writers use alliteration to link and to emphasize ideas as well as to create pleasing, musical sounds.

ALLUSION   An *allusion* is a reference to a well-known person, place, event, literary work, or work of art. Writers often make allusions to stories from the Bible, to Greek and Roman myths, to plays by Shakespeare, to political and historical events, and to other materials with which they can expect their readers to be familiar. In the selection from *Hidden Name and Complex Fate,* on page 1140, Ralph Ellison alludes to Freudian psychology, to President Roosevelt's fireside chats, and to many famous Americans. By using allusions, writers can bring to mind complex ideas simply and easily.

ALMANAC   An *almanac* is a magazine or book, published monthly, seasonally, or yearly, that contains weather forecasts, tide tables, important dates, lists of upcoming events, statistics, and other information of use or interest to readers. The selection on page 119 is from *Poor Richard's Almanack* by Benjamin Franklin. Franklin's almanac is famous for its humorous and wise sayings.

ANALOGY   An *analogy* is a comparison between two unlike things. The purpose of an analogy is to describe something unfamiliar by pointing out its similarities to something that is familiar. In "A Noiseless Patient Spider," on page 468, Walt Whitman makes an analogy between a spider weaving its web and the soul seeking connections with things outside itself. See *Metaphor* and *Simile.*

ANAPEST   See *Meter.*

ANECDOTE   An *anecdote* is a brief story about an interesting, amusing, or strange event. An anecdote is told to entertain or to make a point. In the excerpt from *Life on the Mississippi,* on page 496, Mark Twain tells several anecdotes about his experiences on the Mississippi River.

ANTAGONIST   An *antagonist* is a character or force in conflict with a main character, or protagonist. In Jack London's "To Build a Fire," on page 562, the antagonist is neither a person nor an animal but is rather the extreme cold of the Yukon. Not all stories contain antagonists. However, in many stories the conflict between the antagonist and the protagonist is the basis for the plot.
See *Conflict, Plot,* and *Protagonist.*

APHORISM   An *aphorism* is a general truth or observation about life, usually stated concisely and pointedly. Often witty and wise, aphorisms appear in many kinds of works. An essay writer may have an aphoristic style, making many such statements. Ralph Waldo Emerson was famous for his aphoristic style. His essay entitled "Fate" contains the following aphorisms:

> The book of Nature is the book of Fate.
> Men are what their mothers made them.
> Nature is what you may do.
> So far as a man thinks, he is free.
> A man's fortunes are the fruit of his character.

Used in an essay, an aphorism can be a memorable way to sum up or to reinforce a point or an argument.

APOSTROPHE An *apostrophe* is a figure of speech in which a speaker directly addresses an absent person or a personified quality, object, or idea. Phillis Wheatley uses apostrophe in this line from "To the University of Cambridge, in New England":

> Students, to you 'tis given to scan the
> heights

Apostrophe is often used in poetry and in speeches to add emotional intensity.
See *Figurative Language.*

ARGUMENTATION *Argumentation* is discourse in which the writer presents and logically supports a particular view or opinion. Many critics and scholars distinguish argumentation, or reasoned discourse about opinions, from persuasion, or emotional discourse about opinions. However, some people use the two terms interchangeably.
See *Forms of Discourse* and *Persuasion.*

ASIDE In a play, an *aside* is a speech delivered by an actor in such a way that other characters on the stage are presumed not to hear it. An aside generally reveals a character's inner thoughts. In Thornton Wilder's *Our Town,* on page 974, the Stage Manager uses many asides to communicate to the audience. In the same play, when the dead speak among themselves during the funeral, they are overheard by the audience but are presumed not to be heard by the living characters.

ASSONANCE *Assonance* is the repetition of vowel sounds in conjunction with dissimilar consonant sounds. Emily Dickinson uses assonance in the line "The mountain at a g*i*ven d*i*stance." The *i* sound is repeated in the words *given* and *distance,* in the context of the dissimilar consonant sounds *g–v* and *d–s.*

ATMOSPHERE See *Mood.*

AUTOBIOGRAPHY An *autobiography* is a form of nonfiction in which a person tells his or her own life story. Notable examples of autobiographies include those by Benjamin Franklin and Frederick Douglass.
See *Biography and Journal.*

BALLAD A *ballad* is a songlike poem that tells a story, often one dealing with adventure and romance. Most ballads have the following characteristics:
1. Simple language
2. Four- or six-line stanzas
3. Rhyme
4. A regular meter

A *folk ballad* is one that originated in the oral tradition and was passed by word of mouth from generation to generation, Examples of folk ballads include "Yankee Doodle," "Casey Jones," and "John Henry." A *literary ballad* is one written by a specific person in imitation of the folk ballad. Henry Wadsworth Longfellow's "The Wreck of the Hesperus" is an example of a literary ballad. Here is its first stanza:

> 'Twas the schooner Hesperus,
>   That sailed the wintry sea;
> And the skipper had taken his little
>   daughter,
>   To bear him company.

BIOGRAPHY A *biography* is a form of nonfiction in which a writer tells the life story of another person. John Dos Passos's "Tin Lizzie," on page 810, is an example of biographical writing. See *Autobiography.*

BLANK VERSE *Blank verse* is poetry written in unrhymed iambic pentameter. An iamb is a poetic foot consisting of one weak stress followed by one strong stress. A pentameter line is a line of five poetic feet. Robert Frost's "Birches," on page 924, is written in blank verse.

CAESURA A *caesura* is a pause or break in the middle of a line of poetry. Double slanted lines (//) have been used to mark the caesuras in these lines from Jean Toomer's "November Cotton Flower":

Boll weevil's coming,//and the winter's
    cold,
Made cotton stalks look rusty,//seasons
    old

CATALOG A *catalog* is a list of people, places, or things in a literary work. In the following example from "As I Ebb'd with the Ocean of Life," Walt Whitman records what he sees along the shore:

Chaff, straw, splinters of wood,
    weeds, and the sea-gluten.
Scum, scales from shining rocks, leaves
    of salt-lettuce, left by the tide.

Whitman often used catalogs in his verse to suggest the fullness, diversity, and scope of American life or of the human experience.

CHARACTER A *character* is a person or animal who takes part in the action of a literary work. The following are some terms used to describe various types of characters:

The *main character* in a literary work is the one on whom the work focuses. *Major characters* in a literary work include the main character and any other characters who play significant roles. A *minor character* is one who does not play a significant role. A *round character* is one who is complex and multi-faceted, like a real person. A *flat character* is one who is one-dimensional. A *dynamic character* is one who changes in the course of a work. A *static character* is one who does not change in the course of a work.

See *Characterization* and *Motivation.*

CHARACTERIZATION *Characterization* is the act of creating and developing a character. There are two primary methods of characterization: direct and indirect. In *direct characterization,* a writer simply states a character's traits, as when the young girl in "A White Heron," on page 536, is called "a lonely country child." In *indirect characterization,* character is revealed by one of the following means:

1. By the words, thoughts, or actions of the character
2. By descriptions of the character's appearance or background
3. By what other characters say about the character
4. By the ways in which other characters react toward the character

See *Character.*

CINQUAIN See *Stanza.*

CLASSICISM *Classicism* is an approach to literature and the other arts that stresses reason, balance, clarity, ideal beauty, and orderly form in imitation of the arts of ancient Greece and Rome. Classicism is often contrasted with *Romanticism,* which stresses imagination, emotion, and individualism. Classicism also differs from *Realism,* which stresses the actual rather than the ideal.

See *Realism* and *Romanticism.*

CLIMAX The *climax* is the high point of inter-

est or suspense in a literary work. For example, William Faulkner's "The Bear," on page 788, reaches its climax when the boy finally meets the bear. The climax generally appears near the end of a story, play, or narrative poem.
See *Plot*.

CONCEIT   A *conceit* is an unusual or surprising comparison between two very different things. In Edward Taylor's "Huswifery," on page 60, the granting of grace is compared to spinning yarn, weaving and dyeing cloth, and making clothes. Such a far-fetched comparison is a conceit.

CONCRETE POEM   A *concrete poem* is one with a shape that suggests its subject.

CONFESSIONAL POETRY   *Confessional poetry* is verse that speaks of personal matters, often with great frankness, or candor. Famous American confessional poets include Maxine Kumin, Robert Lowell, Sylvia Plath, Anne Sexton, and John Berryman.

CONFLICT   A *conflict* is a struggle between opposing forces. Sometimes this struggle is internal, or within a character, as in Bernard Malamud's "The First Seven Years," on page 1042. At other times this struggle is external, or between a character and an outside force, as in Jack London's "To Build a Fire," on page 562. Conflict is one of the primary elements of narrative literature because most plots develop from conflicts.
See *Antagonist, Plot,* and *Protagonist*.

CONNOTATION   A *connotation* is an association that a word calls to mind in addition to the dictionary meaning of the word. Many words that are similar in their dictionary meanings, or denotations, are quite different in their connotations. Consider, for example, José Garcia Villa's line, "Be beautiful, noble, like the antique ant." This line would have a very different effect if it were "Be pretty, classy, like the old ant." Poets and other writers choose their words carefully so that the connotations of those words will be appropriate.
See *Denotation*.

CONSONANCE   *Consonance* is the repetition of consonant sounds at the ends of words or accented syllables. Emily Dickinson uses consonance in the following lines:

> But if he ask where you are hi*d*
> Until to-morrow,—happy letter!
> Gesture, coquette, an*d* shake your hea*d*!

COUPLET   See *Stanza*.

CRISIS   In the plot of a narrative, the *crisis* is the turning point for the protagonist—the point at which the protagonist's situation or understanding changes dramatically. In Bernard Malamud's "The First Seven Years," on page 1042, the crisis comes when Feld recognizes that Sobel loves Miriam.

DACTYL   See *Meter*.

DENOTATION   The *denotation* of a word is its objective meaning, independent of other associations that the word brings to mind.
See *Connotation*.

DENOUEMENT   See *Plot*.

DESCRIPTION   A *description* is a portrayal, in words, of something that can be perceived by the senses. Writers create descriptions by using images, as N. Scott Momaday does in the following lines from "A Vision Beyond Time and Place," on page 1156:

> His eyes are deep and open to the wide world.
> At sunrise, precisely, they catch fire and close, having seen. The low light descends upon him.
> And when he lifts his voice, it enters upon

the silence and carries there, like the call of a bird.

Description is one of the major forms of discourse and appears quite often in literary works of all genres.
See *Image* and *Forms of Discourse.*

DEVELOPMENT   See *Plot.*

DIALECT   A *dialect* is the form of a language spoken by people in a particular region or group. Every dialect differs from every other dialect in the details of its vocabulary, grammar, and pronunciation. Writers often use dialect to make their characters seem realistic and to create local color. See, for example, Mark Twain's "The Notorious Jumping Frog of Calaveras County," on page 509.
See *Local Color* and *Vernacular.*

DIALOGUE   A *dialogue* is a conversation between characters. Writers use dialogue to reveal character, to present events, to add variety to narratives, and to arouse their reader's interest. See *Drama.*

DICTION   *Diction* is a writer or speaker's word choice. Diction is part of a writer's style and may be described as formal or informal, plain or ornate, common or technical, abstract or concrete. In the selection from *The Mortgaged Heart,* on page 1128, Carson McCullers uses formal diction suitable to her essay's serious purpose.
See *Style.*

DIMETER   See *Meter.*

DRAMA   A *drama* is a story written to be performed by actors. The playwright supplies dialogue for the characters to speak and stage directions that give information about costumes, lighting, scenery, properties, the setting, and the characters' movements and ways of speaking. The audience accepts as believable the many dramatic conventions that are used such as soliloquies, asides, poetic language, or the passage of time between acts or scenes. An *act* is a major division in a drama. A *scene* is a minor division.
See *Genre.*

DRAMATIC CONVENTION   See *Drama.*

DRAMATIC DIALOGUE   A *dramatic dialogue* is a poem in which there are two speakers who converse with one another. An example in this text is Robert Frost's "The Death of the Hired Man," on page 935.
See *Dramatic Poem.*

DRAMATIC IRONY   See *Irony.*

DRAMATIC MONOLOGUE   A *dramatic monologue* is a poem or speech in which an imaginary character speaks to a silent listener. T.S. Eliot's "The Love Song of J. Alfred Prufrock," on page 864, is a dramatic monologue.
See *Dramatic Poem* and *Monologue.*

DRAMATIC POEM   A *dramatic poem* is one that makes use of the conventions of drama. Such poems may be monologues or dialogues or may present the speech of many characters. Examples of dramatic poems in this anthology include those from Edgar Lee Masters's *Spoon River Anthology,* on page 686, and Robert Frost's "The Death of the Hired Man," on page 935.
See *Dramatic Dialogue* and *Dramatic Monologue.*

DYNAMIC CHARACTER   See *Character.*

ELEGY   An *elegy* is a solemn and formal lyric poem about death, often one that mourns the

passing of some particular person. Walt Whitman's "When Lilacs Last in the Dooryard Bloom'd," on page 409, is an elegy lamenting the death of President Lincoln.
See *Lyric.*

END-STOPPED LINE   An *end-stopped line* is one in which the end of the line coincides with a pause or with the end of a thought. End-stopped lines are often recognizable because of their end punctuation—a period, a comma, a dash, or some other mark. These lines from "Southern Mansion," by Arna Bontemps, are end-stopped:

> The years go back with an iron clank,
> A hand is on the gate,
> A dry leaf trembles on the wall.
> Ghosts are walking.

See *Run-on Line.*

EPIGRAM   An *epigram* is a brief, pointed statement, in prose or in verse, often characterized by use of some rhetorical device or figure of speech. Benjamin Franklin was famous for his epigrams, which include "Fools make feasts, and wise men eat them," and "A plowman on his legs is higher than a gentleman on his knees."

ESSAY   An *essay* is a short, nonfiction work about a particular subject. The term *essay* comes from the Old French word *essai,* meaning "a trial or attempt." As the history of the word suggests, an essay is meant to be exploratory. It is not meant to be an exhaustive treatment of a subject. Essays can be classified as formal or informal, personal or impersonal. They can also be classified according to purpose, as expository, argumentative, descriptive, persuasive, or narrative.
See *Forms of Discourse.*

EXPOSITION   *Exposition* is writing or speech that explains, informs, or presents information. The main techniques of expository writing include analysis, classification, comparison and contrast, definition, and exemplification, or illustration. An essay may be primarily expository, as is Joan Didion's "On the Mall," on page 1148, or it may use exposition to support another purpose such as persuasion or argumentation, as in the selection from Carson McCullers's *The Mortgaged Heart,* on page 1128.

In a story or play, the exposition is that part of the plot that introduces the characters, the setting, and the basic situation.
See *Forms of Discourse* and *Plot.*

EXPRESSIONISM   *Expressionism* was an artistic movement of the early twentieth century. Expressionist painters, sculptors, and writers emphasized the inner experience of the individual rather than the time frame or physical objects of some absolute external reality. The Expressionist movement, exemplified by the works of artists like Van Gogh, influenced such writers as Eugene O'Neill and T.S. Eliot.

EXTENDED METAPHOR   See *Metaphor.*

FABLE   A *fable* is a brief story, usually with animal characters, that teaches a lesson, or moral. James Thurber was a famous American writer of fables.

FALLING ACTION   See *Plot.*

FICTION   *Fiction* is prose writing that tells about imaginary characters and events. Short stories and novels are works of fiction.
See *Genre, Narrative, Nonfiction,* and *Prose.*

FIGURATIVE LANGUAGE   *Figurative language* is writing or speech not meant to be taken literally. Writers use figurative language to express ideas in vivid and imaginative ways. For example, Emily Dickinson begins one poem with the following description of snow:

> It sifts from leaden sieves,
> It powders all the wood

By describing the snow as if it were flour,

Dickinson renders a precise and compelling picture of it.
See *Figure of Speech.*

FIGURE OF SPEECH   A *figure of speech* is an expression or a word used imaginatively rather than literally. Many types of figures of speech are used by writers in English, including apostrophe, hyperbole, irony, metaphor, metonymy, oxymoron, paradox, personification, simile, synecdoche, and understatement.
See *Figurative Language.* See also the entries for individual figures of speech.

FIRST-PERSON POINT OF VIEW   See *Point of View.*

FLASHBACK   A *flashback* is a section of a literary work that interrupts the chronological presentation of events to relate an event from an earlier time. A writer may present a flashback as a character's memory or recollection, as part of an account or story told by a character, as a dream or a daydream, or simply by having the narrator switch to a time in the past. A flashback occurs at the beginning of Ann Beattie's "Imagined Scenes," on page 1092, when the protagonist remembers a time when she arrived home from shopping, was missing her keys, and was let in by David. Writers often use flashbacks as a dramatic way of providing background information.

FLAT CHARACTER   See *Character.*

FOIL   A *foil* is a character who provides a contrast to another character. In F. Scott Fitzgerald's "Winter Dreams," on page 730, Irene Scheerer is a foil for the tantalizing Judy Jones.

FOLK BALLAD   See *Ballad.*

FOLKLORE   *Folklore* is that body of stories, legends, myths, ballads, riddles, sayings, and other works that has arisen out of the oral traditions of peoples around the globe. The folklore traditions of the United States, including those of Native Americans and of the American pioneers, are especially rich.

FOOT   See *Meter.*

FORESHADOWING   *Foreshadowing* is the use, in a literary work, of clues that suggest events that have yet to occur.

FORMS OF DISCOURSE   The *forms of discourse* are the various modes into which writing can be classified. Traditionally, writing has been divided into the following modes:
1. *Exposition,* or expository writing, which presents information
2. *Narration,* or narrative writing, which tells a story
3. *Description,* or descriptive writing, which portrays people, places, or things
4. *Persuasion,* or persuasive writing, which attempts to convince people to think or act in a certain way

Some people distinguish between *persuasion* and *argumentation,* defining the former as an attempt to move an audience by means of an emotional appeal and the latter as an attempt to move an audience by means of a reasoned or rational appeal.

Often, of course, several forms of discourse appear in a single work. A narrative, for example, may contain descriptive or expository passages.
See *Argumentation, Description, Exposition, Narration,* and *Persuasion.*

FREE VERSE   *Free verse* is poetry that lacks a regular rhythmical pattern, or meter. A writer of free verse is at liberty to use any rhythms that are appropriate to what he or she is saying. Free verse has been widely used by twentieth-century poets such as Leslie Marmon Silko, who begins "Where Mountain Lion Lay Down with Deer" with these lines:

I climb the black rock mountain
stepping from day to day
silently.

See *Meter.*

GENRE   A *genre* is a division or type of literature. Literature is commonly divided into three
major genres: poetry, prose, and drama. Each
major genre can in turn be divided into smaller
genres. Poetry can be divided into lyric, concrete, dramatic, narrative, and epic poetry.
Prose can be divided into fiction (novels and
short stories) and nonfiction (biography, autobiography, letters, essays, and reports). Drama
can be divided into series drama, tragedy, comic
drama, melodrama, and farce.
See *Drama, Poetry,* and *Prose.*

GOTHIC   *Gothic* refers to the use of primitive,
medieval, wild, or mysterious elements in literature. Gothic elements offended eighteenth-
century classical writers but appealed to the
Romantic writers who followed them. Gothic
novels feature places like mysterious and
gloomy castles, where horrifying, supernatural
events take place. Their influence on Edgar Allan Poe is evident in "The Fall of the House of
Usher," on page 208.

HARLEM RENAISSANCE   The *Harlem Renais-
sance,* which occurred during the 1920s, was a
time of black artistic creativity centered in
Harlem, in New York City. Writers of the Harlem
Renaissance include Countee Cullen, Claude
McKay, Jean Toomer, Langston Hughes, and
Arna Bontemps.

HEPTAMETER   See *Meter.*

HEPTASTICH   See *Stanza.*

HERO/HEROINE   A *hero* or *heroine* is a character whose actions are inspiring or noble. The
most obvious examples of heroes and heroines
are the larger-than-life characters of myths and
legend. More ordinary characters, however, can
also act as heroes and heroines.

HEXAMETER   See *Meter.*

HYPERBOLE   A *hyperbole* is a deliberate exaggeration or overstatement. In Mark Twain's
"The Notorious Jumping Frog of Calaveras
County," on page 509, the claim that Jim Smiley
would follow a bug as far as Mexico to win a bet
is a hyperbole. As this example shows, hyperbo-
les are often used for comic effect.

IAMB   See *Meter.*

IAMBIC PENTAMETER   *Iambic pentameter* is
a line of poetry with five iambic feet, each containing one unstressed syllable followed by one
stressed syllable ($\smile$ $\prime$). Iambic pentameter may
be rhymed or unrhymed. Unrhymed iambic pentameter is called *blank verse.* These concluding
lines from Anne Bradstreet's "The Author to Her
Book" are in iambic pentameter:

> And for thy, Mother, she alas is poor,
> Which caused her thus to send thee out
>   of door.

See *Blank Verse* and *Meter.*

IDYLL   An *idyll* is a poem or part of a poem that
describes and idealizes country life. John
Greenleaf Whittier's "Snowbound," on page
356, is an idyll.

IMAGE   An *image* is a word or phrase that
appeals to one or more of the five senses—sight,
sound, hearing, touch, taste, or smell.
See *Imagery.*

IMAGERY   *Imagery* is the descriptive or figurative language used in literature to create word

pictures for the reader. These pictures, or images, are created by details of sight, sound, taste, touch, smell, or movement. The following stanza, from Kuangchi C. Chang's "Garden of My Childhood," shows how a poet can use imagery to appeal to several senses:

> I ran past the old maple by the terraced hall
> And the singing crickets under the latticed
>   wall,
> And I kept on running down the walk
> Paved with pebbles of memory big and small
> Without turning to look until I was out of the
>   gate
> Through which there be no return at all.

IMAGISM *Imagism* was a literary movement that flourished between 1912 and 1917. Led by Ezra Pound and Amy Lowell, the Imagist poets rejected nineteenth-century poetic forms and language. Instead, they wrote short poems that used ordinary language and free verse to create sharp, exact, concentrated pictures. "Oread," by H.D., illustrates how the Imagists concentrated on describing a scene or object without making abstract comments:

> Whirl up, sea—
> whirl your pointed pines,
> splash your great pines
> on our rocks,
> hurl your green over us,
> cover us with your pools of fir.

INCITING INCIDENT See *Plot.*

INCONGRUITY *Incongruity* is the combination or juxtaposition of incompatible or opposite elements. Many examples of incongruity can be found in T.S. Eliot's "The Love Song of J. Alfred Prufrock," on page 864. The speaker constantly shifts from grand pronouncements like "Do I dare/Disturb the universe?" to pathetic ones like "Do I dare to eat a peach?"

INVERSION An *inversion* is a reversal or change in the regular word order of a sentence.

For instance, Ezra Pound begins one poem with the line, "Sing we for love and idleness." This line reverses the usual subject-verb order, "We sing."

IRONY *Irony* is a contrast between what is stated and what is meant, or between what is expected to happen and what actually happens. In *verbal irony* a word or a phrase is used to suggest the opposite of its usual meaning. In *dramatic irony,* there is a contradiction between what a character thinks and what the reader or audience knows to be true. In *irony of situation,* an event occurs that directly contradicts the expectations of the characters, of the reader, or of the audience.

IRONY OF SITUATION See *Irony.*

JOURNAL A *journal* is a daily autobiographical account of events and personal reactions. William Byrd's journal, on page 65, records events during an expedition to survey the Virginia-North Carolina boundary, while Mary Chesnut's journal, on page 433, records events during the Civil War.

LEGEND A *legend* is a traditional story. Usually a legend deals with a particular person—a hero, a saint, or a national leader. Often legends reflect a people's cultural values. American legends include those of the early Native Americans and those about folk heroes such as Davy Crockett and Daniel Boone.
See *Myth.*

LITERARY LETTER A *literary letter,* or epistle, is a work of literature created for publication and meant to be read by a large general audience but written as though it were a personal letter to an individual. Ezra Pound's "The River Merchant's Wife," on page 855, is a literary letter. See also the selection from de Crèvecoeur's *Letters from an American Farmer,* on page 154.

LOCAL COLOR *Local color* is the use in a literary work of characters and details unique to a particular geographic area. Local color can be created by the use of dialect and by descriptions of customs, clothing, manners, attitudes, scenery, and landscape. Local color stories were especially popular after the Civil War, bringing readers the West of Bret Harte, the Mississippi River of Mark Twain, and the New England of Sarah Orne Jewett.
See *Realism* and *Regionalism*.

LYRIC POEM A *lyric poem* is a melodic poem that expresses the observations and feelings of a single speaker. Unlike a narrative poem, a lyric focuses on producing a single, unified effect. Types of lyrics include the elegy, the ode, and the sonnet. Among contemporary American poets, the lyric is the most common poetic form.

MAIN CHARACTER See *Character.*

METAPHOR A *metaphor* is a figure of speech in which one thing is spoken of as though it were something else. The identification suggests a comparison between the two things that are identified as in "death *is* a long sleep" or "the sleeping dead."

A *mixed metaphor* occurs when two metaphors are jumbled together. For example, thorns and rain are illogically mixed in "the thorns of life rained down on him." A *dead metaphor* is one that has been overused and has become a common expression, such as "the arm of the chair" or "night fall." Metaphors are used to make writing, especially poetry, more vivid, imaginative, and meaningful.

METER The *meter* of a poem is its rhythmical pattern. The pattern is determined by the number and types of stresses, or beats, in each line. To describe the meter of a poem, you must *scan* its lines. *Scanning* involves marking the stressed

and unstressed syllables as follows:

> Soon as the sun forsook the eastern main
> The pealing thunder shook the heav'nly
>   plain;
> > —Phillis Wheatley, "An Hymn to the Evening"

As the example shows, each strong stress is marked with a slanted line (ˊ) and each weak stress with a horseshoe symbol (˘). The weak and strong stresses are then divided by vertical lines (|) into groups called *feet*. The following types of feet are common in poetry written in English:

1. *Iamb:* a foot with one unstressed syllable followed by one stressed syllable, as in the word "around"

2. *Trochee:* a foot with one stressed syllable followed by one unstressed syllable, as in the word "broken"

3. *Anapest:* a foot with two unstressed syllables followed by one stressed syllable, as in the phrase "in a flash"

4. *Dactyl:* a foot with one stressed syllable followed by two unstressed syllables, as in the word "argument"

5. *Spondee:* a foot with two stressed syllables, as in the word "airship"

6. *Pyrrhic:* a foot with two unstressed syllables, as in the last foot of the word "imag|ining"

7. *Amphibrach:* a foot with an unstressed syllable, one stressed syllable, and another stressed syllable, as in the word "ungainly"

8. Amphimacer: *a foot with a stressed syllable, one unstressed syllable, and another stressed syllable, as in "give and take"*

Lines of poetry are often described as *iambic, trochaic, anapestic,* or *dactylic.*

Lines are also described in terms of the number of feet that occur in them, as follows:

1. *Monometer:* verse written in one-foot lines

Évĭl

Bĕgéts

Évĭl

    —Anonymous

2. *Dimeter:* verse written in two-foot lines

Thĭs ĭs | thĕ tíme

ŏf thĕ trág|ĭc măn

      —Elizabeth Bishop, "Visits to St.
Elizabeths"

3. *Trimeter:* verse written in three-foot lines:

Óvĕr | thĕ wín|tĕr gláciĕrs

  Ĭ seé | thĕ sú|mmĕr glów,

Ănd thróugh | thĕ wíld-|pĭled snówdrĭft

  Thĕ wárm |rósebŭds | belów.

      —Ralph Waldo Emerson, "Beyond
Winter"

4. *Tetrameter:* verse written in four-foot lines:

Thĕ sún | thăt brief | Dĕcém|bĕr dáy

Rŏse chéer|lĕss óv|ĕr hílls | ŏf grây

    —John Greenleaf Whittier, '*Snowbound*'

5. *Pentameter:* verse written in five-foot lines:

Ĭ dóubt | nŏt Gód | ĭs góod, | wĕll-méan|ĭng,
  kínd,

Ănd díd | Hĕ stóop | tŏ quíb|blĕ cóuld | tĕll
  whý

Thĕ lít|tlĕ búr|ĭed móle | cŏntín|uĕs blínd

      —Countee Cullen, "Yet Do I Marvel"

A six-foot line is called a hexameter. A line with seven feet is a *heptameter.*

A complete description of the meter of a line tells both how many feet there are in the line and what kind of foot is most common. Thus the lines from Countee Cullen's poem would be described as *iambic pentameter. Blank verse* is poetry written in unrhymed iambic pentameter.

Poetry that does not have a regular meter is called *free verse.*

MINOR CHARACTER   See *Character.*

MONOLOGUE   A *monologue* is a speech delivered entirely by one person or character.
See *Dramatic Monologue* and *Soliloquy.*

MONOMETER   See *Meter.*

MOOD   *Mood,* or atmosphere, is the feeling created in the reader by a literary work or passage. Elements that can influence the mood of a work include its setting, tone, and events.
See *Setting* and *Tone.*

MOTIVATION   A *motivation* is a reason that explains a character's thoughts, feelings, actions, or speech. Characters are motivated by their values and by their wants, desires, dreams, wishes, and needs. Sometimes the reasons for a character's actions are stated directly, as in Willa Cather's "A Wagner Matinée," on page 552, when Clark explains his reception of his aunt by saying, "I owed to this woman most of the good that ever came my way in my boyhood." At other times, the writer will just suggest a character's motivation. For example, at the end of Chapter 4 of Stephen Crane's *The Red Badge of Courage,* on page 576, the loud soldier leaves a packet for his family with Henry. From the dialogue, the reader can guess that the soldier is motivated by his fear of the upcoming battle. The more effectively and persuasively a writer presents a character's motivations, the more convincing the character will be.

MYTH   A *myth* is a fictional tale that explains the actions of gods or heroes or the causes of natural phenomena. Some myths are a kind of primitive science, explaining how and why natural phenomena came about. Other myths express the central values of the people who created them. The stories of the Navaho and the Delaware peoples included in this text are examples of Native American myths.

NARRATION *Narration* is writing that tells a story. The act of telling a story is also called *narration.* The *narrative,* or story, is told by a storyteller called the *narrator.* A story is usually told chronologically, in the order that events take place in time, though it may include flashbacks and foreshadowing. Narratives may be true, as are the events recorded in Mary Chesnut's journal, on page 433, or fictional, as are the events in Flannery O'Connor's "The Life You Save May Be Your Own," on page 1052. Narration is one of the forms of discourse and is used in novels, short stories, plays, narrative poems, anecdotes, autobiographies, biographies, and reports.
See *Forms of Discourse, Narrative Poem,* and *Narrator.*

NARRATIVE A *narrative* is a story told in fiction, nonfiction, poetry, or drama.
See *Narration.*

NARRATIVE POEM A *narrative poem* tells a story in verse. Three traditional types of narrative verse are *ballads,* songlike poems that tell stories; *epics,* long poems about the deeds of gods or heroes; and *metrical romances,* poems that tell tales of love and chivalry. Examples of American narrative poems include Stephen Vincent Benét's *John Brown's Body* and the ballad "John Henry."
See *Ballad.*

NARRATOR A *narrator* is a speaker or character who tells a story. A story or novel may be narrated by a main character, by a minor character, or by someone uninvolved in the story. The narrator may speak in the first person, as in John Updike's "The Slump," on page 1074, or in the third person as in Ann Beattie's "Imagined Scenes," on page 1093. In addition, the narrator may have an omniscient or a limited point of view. The *omniscient narrator* is all-knowing, while the *limited narrator* knows only what one character does. Because the writer's choice of narrator helps determine the point of view, this decision affects what version of a story is told and how readers will react to it.
See *Point of View.*

NATURALISM *Naturalism* was a literary movement among novelists at the end of the nineteenth century and during the early decades of the twentieth century. The Naturalists tended to view people as hapless victims of immutable natural laws. Early exponents of Naturalism included Stephen Crane, Jack London, and Theodore Dreiser.
See *Realism.*

NONFICTION *Nonfiction* is prose writing that presents and explains ideas or that tells about real people, places, objects, or events. Essays, biographies, autobiographies, journals, and reports are all examples of nonfiction.
See *Fiction* and *Genre.*

NOVEL A *novel* is a long work of fiction. A novel often has a complicated plot, many major and minor characters, a significant theme, and several varied settings. Novels can be classified in many ways, based on the historical periods in which they are written, on the subjects and themes that they treat, on the techniques that are used in them, and on the literary movements that inspired them. James Fenimore Cooper, author of *The Prairie,* was the earliest well-known American novelist. Classic nineteenth-century novels include *Moby-Dick,* by Herman Melville; *The Scarlet Letter,* by Nathaniel Hawthorne; *The Adventures of Huckleberry Finn,* by Mark Twain; and *Portrait of a Lady,* by Henry James. Well-known twentieth-century novels include *The*

House of Mirth, by Edith Wharton; *O Pioneers!,* by Willa Cather; *An American Tragedy,* by Theodore Dreiser; *The Great Gatsby,* by F. Scott Fitzgerald; *The Sound and the Fury,* by William Faulkner; and *Invisible Man,* by Ralph Ellison. A *novella* is not as long as a novel but is longer than a short story. Ernest Hemingway's *The Old Man and the Sea* is a novella.

NOVELLA See *Novel.*

OCTAVE See *Stanza.*

ODE An *ode* is a long, formal lyric poem with a serious theme that may have a traditional stanza structure. An ode may be written for a private occasion or for a public ceremony. Odes often honor people, commemorate events, respond to natural scenes, or consider serious human problems.
See *Lyric.*

OMNISCIENT POINT OF VIEW See *Point of View.*

ONOMATOPOEIA *Onomatopoeia* is the use of words that imitate sounds. Examples of such words are *buzz, hiss, murmur,* and *rustle.* Isabella Stewart Gardner uses onomatopoeia in "Summer Remembered":

> Sounds sum and summon the remembering of
>   summers.
> The humming of the sun
> The mumbling in the honey-suckle vine
> The whirring in the clovered grass
> The pizzicato plinkle of ice in an auburn
>   uncle's amber glass.

ORAL TRADITION *Oral tradition* is the passing of songs, stories, and poems from generation to generation by word of mouth. The oral tradition in America has preserved Native American myths and legends, spirituals, folk ballads, and other stories or songs originally heard and memorized rather than written down.
See *Ballad, Folklore, Legend, Myth,* and *Spiritual.*

ORATORY *Oratory* is public speaking that is formal, persuasive, and emotionally appealing. Patrick Henry's "Speech in the Virginia Convention," on page 124, is an example of oratory.

ORNATE STYLE *Ornate style* is a way of writing that uses long, complicated sentences with elaborate figures of speech, parallel structures, uncommon allusions, and unfamiliar word choices. This style was used during the seventeenth and eighteenth centuries by writers such as Cotton Mather. Because of its complexity and formality, writing in the ornate style is harder to follow than that in the contrasting plain style.
See *Plain Style* and *Style.*

OVERSTATEMENT See *Hyperbole.*

OXYMORON An *oxymoron* is a figure of speech that combines two opposing or contradictory ideas. An oxymoron, such as "freezing fire" or the often used "conspicuous by his absence," suggests a paradox in just a few words.
See *Figurative Language* and *Paradox.*

PARABLE A *parable* is a brief story, usually with human characters, that teaches a moral lesson. The most famous parables are those told by Christ in the Bible. Some critics would classify Nathaniel Hawthorne's "The Minister's Black Veil," on page 294, as a parable.

PARADOX A *paradox* is a statement that seems to be contradictory but that actually presents a truth. Marianne Moore uses paradox in "Nevertheless" when she says, "Victory won't come/to me unless I go/to it." Because a paradox is surprising or even shocking, it draws

the reader's attention to what is being said.
See *Figurative Language* and *Oxymoron.*

PARALLELISM   *Parallelism* is the repetition of a grammatical structure. Robert Hayden concludes his poem "Astronauts" with these questions in parallel form:

> What do we want of these men?
> What do we want of ourselves?

Parallelism is used in poetry and in other writing to emphasize and to link related ideas.

PARODY   A *parody* is a humorous imitation of a literary work, one that exaggerates or distorts the characteristic features of the original. American author Donald Barthelme is noted for his parodic style, which he uses to point out absurd aspects of modern life.

PERSONIFICATION   *Personification* is a figure of speech in which a nonhuman subject is given human characteristics. In "April Rain Song," Langston Hughes personifies the rain:

> let the rain kiss you.
> Let the rain sing you a lullaby.

Effective personification of things or ideas makes them seem vital and alive, as if they were human.
See *Figurative Language.*

PERSUASION   *Persuasion* is writing or speech that attempts to convince a reader to think or act in a particular way. During the Revolutionary War period, leaders such as Patrick Henry, Thomas Paine, and Thomas Jefferson used persuasion in their political arguments. Persuasion is also used in advertising, in editorials, in sermons, in political speeches.
See *Argumentation* and *Forms of Discourse.*

PLAIN STYLE   *Plain style* is a way of writing that uses uncomplicated sentences and ordinary words to make simple, direct statements. This style was favored by those Puritans who rejected ornate style because they wanted to express themselves clearly and directly, in accordance with the austerity of their religious beliefs. In the twentieth century, Ernest Hemingway was a master of plain style.
See *Ornate Style* and *Style.*

PLOT   *Plot* is the sequence of events in a literary work. In most novels, dramas, short stories, and narrative poems, the plot involves both characters and a central conflict. The plot usually begins with an *exposition* that introduces the setting, the characters, and the basic situation. This is followed by the *inciting incident,* which introduces the central conflict. The conflict then increases during the *development* until it reaches a high point of interest or suspense, the *climax.* The climax is followed by the end, or *resolution,* of the central conflict. Any events that occur after the resolution make up the *denouement.* The events that lead up to the climax make up the *rising action.* The events that follow the climax make up the *falling action.*
See *Conflict.*

POETRY   *Poetry* is one of the three major types of literature. In poetry, form and content are closely connected, like the two faces of a single coin. Poems are often divided into lines and stanzas and often employ regular rhythmical patterns, or meters. Most poems make use of highly concise, musical, and emotionally charged language. Many also make use of imagery, figurative language, and special devices such as rhyme.
See *Genre.*

POINT OF VIEW   *Point of view* is the perspective, or vantage point, from which a story is told. Three commonly used points of view are first-person, omniscient third-person, and limited third-person.

In the *first-person point of view,* the narrator is a character in the story and refers to himself or herself with the first-person pronoun I. "The Fall of the House of Usher," on page 208, is told by a first-person narrator.

The two kinds of third-person point of view, limited and omniscient, are called "third person" because the narrator uses third-person pronouns such as *he* and *she* to refer to the characters. There is no *I* telling the story.

In stories told from the *omniscient third-person point of view,* the narrator knows and tells about what each character feels and thinks. "The Devil and Tom Walker," on page 180, is written from the omniscient third-person point of view.

In stories told from the *limited third-person point of view,* the narrator relates the inner thoughts and feelings of only one character, and everything is viewed from this character's perspective. "An Occurrence at Owl Creek Bridge," on page 526, is written from the limited third-person point of view.
See *Narrator.*

PROSE   *Prose* is the ordinary form of written language. Most writing that is not poetry, drama, or song is considered prose. Prose is one of the major genres of literature and occurs in two forms: fiction and nonfiction.
See *Fiction, Genre,* and *Nonfiction.*

PROTAGONIST   The *protagonist* is the main character in a literary work. In "The Jilting of Granny Weatherall," on page 748, the protagonist is the dying grandmother.
See *Antagonist.*

PUN   A *pun* is a play on words. Robert Frost's "Mending Wall," on page 927, contains a pun in the lines "Before I built a wall I'd ask to know/ What I was walling in or walling out,/And to

whom I was like to give offense." Of course, the word "offense" is meant to suggest, in addition to its normal meaning, the phrase "a fence."

PYRRHIC   See *Meter.*

QUATRAIN   See *Stanza.*

REALISM   *Realism* is the presentation in art of the details of actual life. Realism was also a literary movement that began during the nineteenth century and that stressed the actual as opposed to the imagined or the fanciful. The Realists tried to write truthfully and objectively about ordinary characters in ordinary situations. They reacted against Romanticism, rejecting heroic, adventurous, unusual, or unfamiliar subjects. The Realists, in turn, were followed by the Naturalists, who traced the effects of heredity and environment on people helpless to change their situations. American realism grew from the work of local-color writers such as Bret Harte and Sarah Orne Jewett and is evident in the writings of major figures such as Mark Twain and Henry James.
See *Local Color, Naturalism,* and *Romanticism.*

REFRAIN   A *refrain* is a repeated line or group of lines in a poem or song. Most refrains end stanzas, as does "And the tide rises, the tide falls," the refrain in Henry Wadsworth Longfellow's poem on page 334, or "Coming for to carry me home," the refrain in "Swing Low, Sweet Chariot," on page 422. Although some refrains are nonsense lines, many increase suspense or emphasize character and theme.

REGIONALISM   *Regionalism* in literature is the tendency among certain authors to write about specific geographical areas. Regional writers, like Willa Cather and William Faulkner, present the distinct culture of an area, including its speech, customs, beliefs, and history. Local-color writing may be considered a type of Re-

gionalism, but Regionalists, like the southern writers of the 1920s, usually go beyond mere presentation of cultural idiosyncracies and attempt, instead, a sophisticated sociological or anthropological treatment of the culture of a region.
See *Local Color* and *Setting*.

REPETITION   *Repetition* is the repeated use, of any element of language—a sound, a word, a phrase, a clause, a sentence, a grammatical pattern, or a rhythmical pattern. For example, in "The Mortgaged Heart," on page 1128, Carson McCullers repeats key words—*alone, lonely,* and *loneliness*—to connect and unify her arguments. Careless repetition bores a reader, but successful repetition links ideas and emphasizes main points.

RESOLUTION   See *Plot*.

RHYME   *Rhyme* is the repetition of sounds at the ends of words. Rhyming words have identical vowel sounds in their final accented syllables. The consonants before the vowels may be different, but any consonants, occurring after these vowels are the same, as in *frog* and *bog* or *willow* and *pillow*. *End rhyme* occurs when rhyming words are repeated at the ends of lines. *Internal rhyme* occurs when rhyming words fall within a line. *Approximate,* or *slant, rhyme* occurs when the rhyming sounds are similar, but not exact, as in *prove* and *glove*.
See *Rhyme Scheme*.

RHYME SCHEME   A *rhyme scheme* is a regular pattern of rhyming words in a poem. To describe a rhyme scheme, one uses a letter of the alphabet to represent each rhyming sound in a poem or stanza. Consider how letters are used to represent the rhymes in the following example:

With innocent wide penguin eyes, three	*a*
large fledgling mocking-birds below	*b*
the pussywillow tree,	*a*
stand in a row.	*b*
—Marianne Moore, "Bird-Witted"	

The rhyme scheme of this section on Moore's poem is *abab*.
See *Rhyme*.

RHYTHM   *Rhythm* is the pattern of beats, or stresses, in spoken or written language. Prose and free verse are written in the irregular rhythmical patterns of everyday speech.

Consider, for example, the rhythmical pattern in the following free verse lines by Gwendolyn Brooks:

Life for my child is simple, and is good.

He knows his wish. Yes, but that is not all.

Because I know mine too.

Traditional poetry often follows a regular rhythmical pattern, as in the following lines by America's first great female poet, Anne Bradstreet:

In critic's hands beware thou dost not come,

And take thy way where yet thou art not known

    —"The Author to Her Book"

See *Meter*.

RISING ACTION   The *rising action* is that part of the plot in a story that leads up to the climax. During the rising action, suspense increases as the complications of the conflict develop. In Mark Helprin's "Katherine Comes to Yellow Sky," on page 1108, the rising action continues until Katherine watches the sunrise and learns that she has reached Yellow Sky.
See *Plot*.

ROMANCE   A *romance* is a story that presents remote or imaginative incidents rather than ordinary, commonplace experiences. Although the events in a romance are improbable or impossible, the characters still reflect what Nathaniel

Hawthorne calls "the truth of the human heart." Hawthorne considered his writings, such as *The House of the Seven Gables,* to be "romances" rather than "novels" because they were imaginative rather than realistic.
See *Novel* and *Romanticism.*

ROMANTICISM *Romanticism* was a literary and artistic movement of the nineteenth century, one that arose in reaction against eighteenth-century Neoclassicism and that placed a premium on fancy, imagination, emotion, nature, individuality, and exotica. Romantic elements can be found in the works of American writers as diverse as Cooper, Poe, Thoreau, Emerson, Dickinson, Hawthorne, and Melville. Romanticism is particularly evident in the works of the New England Transcendentalists.
See *Classicism* and *Transcendentalism.*

ROUND CHARACTER   See *Character.*

RUN-ON LINE   A *run-on line* is one in which the thought continues, without pause, into the next line. Jean Toomer's "Song of the Son" illustrates how a line can run on to the next stanza as well as to the next line:

> O Negro slaves, dark purple ripened plums,
> Squeezed, and bursting in the pine-wood air,
> Passing, before they stripped the old tree
>   bare
> One plum was saved for me, one seed
>   becomes
>
> An everlasting song, a singing tree,

Run-on lines change a poem's rhythm, adding variety and helping avoid monotony.
See *End-Stopped Line.*

SATIRE   *Satire* is writing that ridicules or criticizes individuals, ideas, institutions, social conventions, or other works of art or literature. The writer of a satire, or satirist, may use a tolerant, sympathetic tone or an angry, bitter tone. Some satire is written in prose and some in poetry. Examples of satire in this text include Stephen Crane's "War Is Kind," on page 667, Edwin Arlington Robinson's "Miniver Cheevy," on page 680, and W.H. Auden's "The Unknown Citizen," on page 953.

SCANSION   *Scansion* is the process of analyzing a poem's metrical pattern. When a poem is scanned, its stressed and unstressed syllables are marked to show what poetic feet are used and how many feet appear in each line. The last two lines of Edna St. Vincent Millay's "I Shall Go Back Again to the Bleak Shore" may be scanned as follows:

> But I | shall find | the sul|len rocks |
>   and skies
> Unchanged | from what | they were |
>   when I | was young.

See *Meter.*

SCENE   See *Drama.*

SENSORY LANGUAGE   *Sensory language* is writing or speech that appeals to one or more of the five senses.
See *Image.*

SETTING   The *setting* of a literary work is the time and place of the action. A setting may serve any of a number of functions. It may provide a background for the action. It may be a crucial element in the plot or central conflict. It may also create a certain emotional atmosphere, or mood. The setting of Ernest Hemingway's "In Another Country," on page 722, is Milan, Italy, during World War I. The story centers on the hospital where the protagonist receives physical therapy for a war injury. The setting therefore provides a backdrop for the action and is central to the plot. Hemingway also uses his setting to suggest a mood of disillusionment and isolation. See *Mood*.

SHORT STORY A *short story* is a brief work of fiction. The short story resembles the novel but generally has a simpler plot and setting. In addition, the short story tends to reveal character at a crucial moment rather than to develop it through many incidents. For example, Thomas Wolfe's "The Far and the Near," on page 758, concentrates on what happens to the engineer when he visits the people who waved to him every day. The American writers Washington Irving, Edgar Allan Poe, and Nathaniel Hawthorne, were instrumental in creating and developing the short story genre. Other great American writers of short stories include Mark Twain, Bret Harte, Ambrose Bierce, Sarah Orne Jewett, Willa Cather, Jack London, O. Henry, Ernest Hemingway, Katherine Anne Porter, Eudora Welty, Flannery O'Connor, and John Updike.
See *Fiction* and *Genre*.

SIMILE A *simile* is a figure of speech that makes a direct comparison between two subjects using either *like* or *as*. Here are two examples of similes:

> The trees looked like pitch forks against the sullen sky.

> Her hair was as red as a robin's breast.

See *Figurative Language*.

SOLILOQUY A *soliloquy* in a play or prose work is a long speech make by a character who is alone and who reveals his or her private thoughts and feelings to the audience. By alternating the speeches of Paul Klee and of the Secret Police in his story on page 1086, Donald Barthelme adapts the soliloquy to the short story.
See *Monologue*.

SONNET A *sonnet* is a fourteen-line lyric poem focused on a single theme. Sonnets have many variations but are usually written in iambic pentameter, following one of two traditional patterns. The *Petrarchan,* or *Italian, sonnet* is divided into two parts, the eight-line octave and the six-line sestet. The octave rhymes *abba abba,* while the sestet generally rhymes *cde cde* or uses some combination of *cd* rhymes. The two parts of the Petrarchan sonnet work together: the octave raises a question, states a problem, or presents a brief narrative, and the sestet answers the question, solves the problem, or comments on the narrative.

The *Shakespearean,* or *English, sonnet* is made up of three quatrains and a concluding couplet and follows the rhyme scheme *abab cdcd efef gg.* Although the three quatrains may state and resolve a problem, as in the Petrarchan octave and sestet, each quatrain usually explores a different aspect of the main theme. The couplet then sums up the rest of the poem.
See *Lyric*.

SPEAKER The *speaker* is the voice of a poem. Although the speaker is often the poet, the speaker may also be a fictional character or even an inanimate object or another type of nonhuman entity. Interpreting a poem often depends upon recognizing who the speaker is, who the speaker is addressing, and what the speaker's attitude, or tone, is. In these lines from Sylvia Plath's "Mushrooms," the speaker is one (or perhaps all) of the mushrooms of the title:

> We shall by morning
> Inherit the earth.
> Our foot's in the door.

See *Point of View*.

SPIRITUAL A *spiritual* is a type of black American folk song dating from the period of slavery and the reconstruction. A typical spiritual deals both with religious freedom and, on an allegorical level, with political and economic freedom. For example, in some spirituals the Biblical river Jordan was used as a symbol for the Ohio River, which separated slave states from free states, and the Biblical promised land, Canaan, was used as a symbol for the free northern United States. The spirituals were developed on models derived from white American hymns and from African work songs and chants. Most spirituals contained Biblical allusions and made use of repetition, parallelism, and rhyme. Spirituals had a profound influence on the development of both poetry and song in the United States. See "Swing Low, Sweet Chariot," on page 422, and "Go Down, Moses," on page 423.

SPONDEE   See *Meter.*

STAGE DIRECTIONS   See *Drama.*

STANZA   A *stanza* is a group of lines in a poem, considered as a unit. Many poems are divided into stanzas that are separated by spaces. Stanzas often function just like paragraphs in prose. Each stanza states and develops a single main idea.

Stanzas are commonly named according to the number of lines found in them, as follows:
1. *Couplet:* a two-line stanza
2. *Tercet:* a three-line stanza
3. *Quatrain:* a four-line stanza
4. *Cinquain:* a five-line stanza
5. *Sestet:* a six-line stanza
6. *Heptastich:* a seven-line stanza
7. *Octave:* an eight-line stanza

STATIC CHARACTER   See *Character.*

STEREOTYPE   See *Character.*

STREAM OF CONSCIOUSNESS   *Stream of consciousness* is a narrative technique that presents thoughts as if they were coming directly from a character's mind. Instead of being arranged in chronological order, the events of the story are presented from the character's point of view, mixed in with the character's feelings and memories just as they might spontaneously occur in the mind of a real person. Katherine Anne Porter uses this technique in "The Jilting of Granny Weatherall," on page 748, to show Granny's dying thoughts and feelings. Ambrose Bierce also uses the stream-of-consciousness technique in his short story "An Occurrence at Owl Creek Bridge," on page 526. Stream-of-consciousness writing reveals a character's complex psychology and presents it in realistic detail.
See *Point of View.*

STYLE   A writer's *style* is his or her typical way of writing. Style includes word choice, tone, degree of formality, figurative language, rhythm, grammatical structure, sentence length, organization—in short, every feature of a writer's use of language. Ernest Hemingway, for example, is noted for a simple prose style that contrasts with Thomas Paine's aphoristic style and with N. Scott Momaday's reflective style.
See *Diction, Ornate Style,* and *Plain Style.*

SUBPLOT   A *subplot* is a second, less important plot within a story. In Stephen Crane's *The Red Badge of Courage,* on page 576, the tall soldier's story is told along with Henry's, thus adding to Crane's picture of the war. A subplot may add to, contrast with, reflect, or vary the main plot.
See *Plot.*

SURPRISE ENDING   A *surprise ending* is a conclusion that violates the expectations of the reader. Often a surprise ending is foreshadowed, or subtly hinted at, throughout the course of a work.

SUSPENSE   *Suspense* is a feeling of growing uncertainty about the outcome of events in a

literary work. Writers create suspense by raising questions in the minds of their readers. Because readers are curious or concerned, they keep reading to find out what will happen next. Suspense builds until the climax of the plot, at which point the suspense reaches its peak. Thereafter, the suspense is generally resolved.
See *Climax* and *Plot*.

SYMBOL   A *symbol* is anything that stands for or represents something else. A *conventional symbol* is one that is widely known and accepted, such as a voyage symbolizing life or a skull symbolizing death. A *personal symbol* is one developed for a particular work by a particular author. Examples in this text include Hawthorne's black veil, Melville's white whale, Jewett's white heron, and Faulkner's bear.

SYMBOLISM   *Symbolism* was a literary movement during the nineteenth century that influenced many poets, including the Imagists and T.S. Eliot. Symbolists turned away from everyday realistic details, trying instead to express emotions by using a pattern of symbols.
See *Imagism* and *Realism*.

SYNECDOCHE   *Synecdoche* is a figure of speech in which a part of something is used to stand for the whole thing. In "Recuerdo," when Edna St. Vincent Millay says, "We hailed, 'Good morrow, mother!' to a shawl-covered head," the shawl-covered head stands for the woman being greeted.
See *Figurative Language*.

TERCET   See *Stanza*.

TETRAMETER   See *Meter*.

THEME   A *theme* is a central message or insight into life revealed by a literary work. An essay's theme is often directly stated in its thesis statement. The theme of a story, poem, or play,

however, is usually not directly stated. For example, in "A Worn Path," on page 764, Eudora Welty does not directly say that Phoenix Jackson's difficult journey shows the power of love, but readers learn this indirectly by the end of the story.

THIRD-PERSON POINT OF VIEW   See *Point of View*.

TONE   The *tone* of a literary work is the writer's attitude toward his or her subject, characters, or audience. A writer's tone may be formal or informal, friendly or distant, personal or pompous. For example, William Faulkner's tone in his "Nobel Prize Acceptance Speech," on page 1124, is earnest and serious, while James Thurber's tone in "The Night the Ghost Got In," on page 832, is humorous and ironic.
See *Mood*.

TRANSCENDENTALISM   *Transcendentalism* was an American literary and philosophical movement of the nineteenth century. The Transcendentalists, who were based in New England, believed that intuition and the individual conscience "transcend" experience and thus are better guides to truth than are the senses and logical reason. Influenced by Romanticism, the Transcendentalists respected the individual spirit and the natural world, believing that divinity was present everywhere, in nature and in each person. This last notion, that of an omnipresent divinity, or Over-Soul, shows the influence on Transcendentalism of the Hindu religion and of the Swedish mystic Emanuel Swendenborg. The Transcendentalists included Ralph Waldo Emerson, Henry David Thoreau, Bronson Alcott, W.H. Channing, Margaret Fuller, and Elizabeth Peabody.
See *Romanticism*.

TRIMETER   See *Meter*.

TROCHEE   See *Meter*.

UNDERSTATEMENT   *Understatement* means saying less than is actually meant, generally in an ironic way. An example of understatement is the description of a flooded area as ''slightly soggy.''
See *Figurative Language, Hyperbole,* and *Irony*.

VERBAL IRONY   See *Irony*.

VERNACULAR   The *vernacular* is the ordinary language of people in a particular region. Instead of using a more formal literary language, writers may use the vernacular to create realistic characters or to approach readers informally. See *Dialect*.

VILLANELLE   A *villanelle* is a nineteen-line poem with only two rhymes that follows a strict pattern popular in traditional French poetry. It has two refrains formed by repeating line 1 in lines 6, 12, and 18 and by repeating line 3 in lines 9, 15, and 19. The three lines in each of the first five 3-line stanzas rhyme *aba;* the final quatrain rhymes *abaa.* An example of a villanelle in this text is Theodore Roethke's ''The Waking,'' on page 1190.

HANDBOOK OF CRITICAL THINKING AND READING TERMS

ABSTRACT *adj.* Anything that is not concrete or definite is *abstract.* The concrete is perceived by one of the senses; the abstract is conceived by the intellect. A portrait is concrete because it contains numerous concrete details—eyes, mouth, nose, hair, clothing, and so on. A stick figure drawing, on the other hand, is abstract because most of these details are left out and the mind must decide what the drawing represents. Words and the ideas that they represent can also be abstract. Some common abstract words are *truth, beauty, love, freedom,* and *courage.* Less obvious examples include *society, realism, nature, sanity,* and *history.* You can point, for instance, to concrete actions and events from history, but you cannot point to history itself.

People can make abstract ideas clear to themselves and to others by using specific examples and illustrations. Suppose, for instance, that a writer wants to convey the abstract idea that a character is wealthy. The writer might do this by showing that the character has many possessions that are normally associated with wealth, such as a sports car, a yacht, and a country estate. Another way to express abstract ideas clearly is to use figures of speech. For example, the simile "time is like a river" uses a concrete image—a river—to describe an abstraction, time.

ANALOGY *n.* An *analogy* is a comparison that explains one subject by pointing out its similarities to another subject. In his famous "Speech in the Virginia Convention," on page 124, Patrick Henry makes an analogy between the crisis facing the American colonies and the Biblical story of Christ's betrayal: "Suffer not yourselves to be betrayed with a kiss." This analogy compares the British to Judas Iscariot, who betrayed Christ by kissing his cheek. A careful writer invents or selects analogies that are likely to fall within the experience of the reader. Patrick Henry, for instance, could reasonably assume that his audience would be familiar with the Biblical story to which he referred. A careful reader evaluates a writer's analogies and rejects any that seem unfair or illogical.

An analogy may be expressed using a variety of literary techniques such as simile, metaphor, and extended metaphor. See the definition of these terms in the Handbook of Literary Terms and Techniques.

ANALYSIS *n.* *Analysis* is the process of studying the parts of a whole. The process of analysis consists of the following steps:

1. Divide the object you are studying into its parts.
2. Observe and describe the characteristics of each part.
3. Look for relationships among the parts and between each part and the whole.

An analysis might also take the form of a series of questions:

1. What are the parts that make up the whole?
2. How are they similar to one another?
3. How are they different?
4. How would the whole be affected if the parts were arranged differently?
5. What function does each part serve?

When you analyze a literary work, break it into parts, observe the characteristics of these parts, and consider how they are related. For example, you might analyze an essay by considering its subject, tone, diction, and structure. A short story or novel could be analyzed into its plot, characters, dialogue, setting, and theme.

ARGUMENT *n.* An *argument* is a set of statements consisting of one or more premises and a conclusion. *Premises* are statements assumed to be true in the context of the argument, and the *conclusion* is a statement that logically follows from the premises. If the premises are true, then the conclusion should also be true. For example, the Declaration of Independence gives a long list of premises—specific examples of King George III's treatment of the Americans—to support the conclusion that the King is a tyrant.

People also present arguments when writing about literature. They use the various parts of a literary work—plot, characters, images, and dialogue, for example—as premises, or evidence, to support their conclusions, or interpretations. For instance, a writer might argue on the basis of details mentioned in T. S. Eliot's "The Love Song of J. Alfred Prufrock", on page 864, that Prufrock is facing some crucial decision in his life.

The term *argument* is also used to describe a brief summary, or synopsis, of a literary work. Thus a paragraph summarizing the plot of Thornton Wilder's *Our Town,* on page 974, might be described as presenting "the argument of the play."
See *Conclusion, Deduction, Evidence, Induction,* and *Inference.*

BANDWAGON See *Propaganda Technique.*

BEGGING THE QUESTION See *Logical Fallacy.*

CATEGORIZATION *n.* *Categorization* is the process of placing objects or ideas into groups or classes. Objects or ideas possessing similar characteristics may be placed in the same cate-

gory. To categorize something, follow these steps:
1. Observe the characteristics of the object you are studying.
2. Think of other subjects that share these qualities.
3. Select a name or phrase that best characterizes the group.

Literary works may be placed in categories for the purpose of analysis and discussion. Prose and poetry are two very general categories into which all works of literature can be grouped. Each, however, can be further divided into more useful categories. For example, Frederick Douglass's *My Bondage and My Freedom,* on page 426, is a narrative of his own real-life experiences. Therefore, it may be placed into the category of autobiography. Usually, specific categories are more useful than general ones. A standard literary category such as the sonnet, detective story, slave narrative, or biography is called a *genre.*

CAUSE AND EFFECT *n. phrase* When one event precedes and brings about another event, the first is said to be a *cause* and the second an *effect. Cause and effect* are extremely important in the study of literature. The plot of a short story, for example, is a series of causes and effects. One event causes the next, which causes the next, and so on to the end of the story. In *Moby-Dick,* an excerpt from which appears on page 314, Captain Ahab's loss of his leg causes his obsession with the great white whale. Readers must judge whether the cause-and-effect relationships in a plot are believable or true-to-life.

In addition, writers choose their language carefully in order to cause certain effects in their readers. For example, a writer might describe a battle scene in explicit detail in order to cause the reader to feel the horror and savagery of war.

CIRCULAR REASONING See *Logical Fallacy.*

COMPARISON *n.* *Comparison* is the process of observing and pointing out similarities. For example, a comparison of the selections from Walt Whitman and Carl Sandburg might note the following similarities: Each author celebrates common people and democracy, each takes inspiration from the world of nature, and each writes in free verse.
See *Contrast.*

CONCLUSION *n.* A *conclusion* is anything that follows reasonably from something else. In an argument, the conclusion follows from supporting statements, facts, and reasons. Thus the Declaration of Independence uses a series of reasons to support the conclusion that the colonies are justified in separating from England.

CONTRAST *n.* *Contrast* is the process of observing and pointing out differences. In any kind of analysis, differences can be as significant as similarities. Contrast, therefore, is an important technique in literary study.
See *Comparison.*

DEDUCTION *n.* *Deduction* is the form of argument in which the conclusion has to be true if the premises are true. The following is a typical deductive argument:

Major premise: The Civil War was fought from 1861 to 1865.
Minor premise: Stephen Crane was born in 1871.
Conclusion: Stephen Crane did not fight in the Civil War.

If you accept the premises of the argument, then you must also accept the conclusion. Therefore, the argument is a deduction.
See *Generalization* and *Inference.*

DEFINITION *n.* *Definition* is the process of explaining the meaning of a word or phrase. Definition is essential to the process of communication because it establishes agreed-upon meanings for words. The simplest type of definition, *ostensive definition,* involves pointing to something and saying its name. If you point to an object and say, "book," you are giving an ostensive definition of the word *book.* The most common type of definition is the kind found in dictionaries, *lexical definition.* Lexical definition uses words to explain the meanings of other words and phrases. Definition by synonym, by antonym, by example, and by genus and differentia are all types of lexical definition.

In a definition by synonym, you use a word or phrase that has the same meaning: An *attorney* is a "lawyer."

In *definition by antonym,* you use a negation along with a word or a phrase that has an opposite meaning: A *coward* is one who demonstrates a "lack of courage."

In *definition by example,* you list things to which the term being defined applies: The *Trancendentalists* included Henry David Thoreau, Ralph Waldo Emerson, Margaret Fuller, and Bronson Alcott.

In a *genus and differentia definition,* you place the thing to be defined into a general category, group, or *genus.* Then you tell how it differs from other members of the group:

To be defined: *French horn*
Genus, or group: brass musical instruments
Differentia: three valves
coiled tube
flaring bell
Definition: A *French horn* is "a brass musical instrument with three valves, a coiled tube, and a flaring bell."

The purpose of definition is to make ideas as clear and exact as possible. Whenever you write about literature, make sure you define your key terms. Use the methods of lexical definition explained here.

EITHER/OR FALLACY See *Logical Fallacy.*

EVALUATION *n.* *Evaluation* is the process of making a judgment about the quality or value of something. "'Birches' is one of Robert Frost's best poems" is an evaluation. To evaluate a literary work, you must first analyze it. Only after you understand a work are you in a position to make judgments about it.

Although literary evaluation is not an exact science, there are generally accepted standards, or criteria, for judging literary works. For example, you might ask the following types of questions: Is the language fresh and imaginative? Are the characters convincing? Is the plot original and believable?

When you present an evaluation of a literary work, use elements in the work as evidence to support your evaluation. In addition, try to make your evaluation as specific as possible. Judgments such as "I hated it" are unacceptable because they are too vague.
See *Opinion* and *Judgment.*

EVIDENCE *n.* *Evidence* is factual information presented to support an argument. Trial lawyers present evidence to support their cases in court. In literary analysis or evaluation, the parts of a work—such as language, plot, characters, and tone—are the evidence that must be used to support an interpretation or judgment. For example, consider the statement, "William Carlos Williams's short poem 'The Red Wheelbarrow' asserts the primary importance of images in literature." You might support this interpretation by pointing out that the poem consists entirely of images, preceded only by the words "so much depends upon."
See *Fact, Reason,* and *Support.*

FACT *n.* A *fact* is a statement that can be proved true or false by evidence. For example, the following facts are true by definition:

Steam is vaporized water.
Plot is the series of events or actions that make up a work of fiction.

The following facts are true by observation:

Joyce Carol Oates has written many novels, short stories, and poems.
Edward Taylor's "Huswifery" contains three stanzas of six lines each.

Facts are extremely important in literary works. An author uses them to develop characters, settings, and plots. A reader uses them as the evidence or data on which to base predictions, conclusions, and evaluations.
See *Opinion.*

FALSE ANALOGY See *Logical Fallacy.*

GENERALIZATION *n.* A *generalization* is a statement that applies to more than one thing. The following are generalizations:

Emily Dickinson's poems are often about death.
Ernest Hemingway's prose style is simple and direct.

The first statement applies to more than one of Dickinson's poems, and the second applies to more than one of Hemingway's prose works.

Deductive arguments usually begin with a generalization. Consider the following deductive argument:

Premise: (a generalization) All of Mark Twain's writings are entertaining.
Conclusion: Twain's "The Notorious Jumping Frog of Calaveras County" is entertaining.

Inductive arguments, on the other hand, often end with generalizations. Consider the following:

Premise: Longfellow's "A Psalm of Life" rhymes.
Premise: Longfellow's "The Arsenal at Springfield" rhymes.
Premise: Longfellow's "The Tide Rises, The Tide Falls" rhymes.

Conclusion: (generalization) Many of Longfellow's poems rhyme.

When making generalizations, be careful not to overgeneralize. For example, the statement "All speeches are boring" is an overgeneralization because many speeches, such as Chief Joseph's "I Will Fight No More Forever," on page 450, are quite interesting. One way to avoid overgeneralization is to use qualifiers, or words that limit statements, such as *some, a few,* or *many.*
See *Conclusion* and *Stereotype.*

INDUCTION *n.* *Induction* is a form of argument in which the conclusion is probably but not necessarily true. For example, if you read several poems by E. E. Cummings and notice that each uses punctuation and syntax in unusual ways, then you might conclude that "All of E. E. Cummings's poems use punctuation and syntax in unconventional ways." This conclusion may be true, but it is not necessarily true because you have not read all of Cummings's poems. To be safe, you would have to limit your conclusion to something like, "Many of E. E. Cummings's poems use punctuation and syntax in unusual ways."
See *Generalization* and *Inference.*

INFERENCE *n.* An *inference* is any logical or reasonable conclusion based on known facts or accepted premises. The conclusions of inductive and deductive arguments are inferences. When reading or thinking about a literary work, one must constantly draw inferences from the details presented by the author. For example, the main character in Eudora Welty's "A Worn Path," on page 764, is described as wearing a dress made from bleached sugar sacks. From this detail the reader might conclude, or infer, that the main character in Welty's story is poor. Additional details in the story confirm this conclusion.
See *Conclusion, Deduction,* and *Induction.*

INTERPRETATION *n.* *Interpretation* is the process of determining the meaning or significance of speech, writing, art, music, or actions. The interpretation of a literary work involves many different processes. These include the following:
1. Reading carefully and actively and responding to each new detail, character, or incident
2. Breaking down the work into its parts, noting the characteristics of each, and looking for relationships among the parts
3. Examining your responses to the work and identifying the details in the work that help to create these responses
4. Pulling separate observations together to make generalizations about the significance of the work

Interpretation usually aims at making clear the theme of a literary work. For example, your reading of Carl Sandburg's poem "Chicago," on page 898, might lead you to this statement of theme: "Sandburg's 'Chicago' recognizes the unsavory aspects of the modern American city but nevertheless affirms and celebrates the vigor of urban life." Sound interpretations will take into account, implicitly or explicitly, all important parts of a work.
See *Analysis.*

JUDGMENT *n.* A *judgment* is a statement about the quality or value of something. Like any conclusion, a judgment must be supported by facts and reasons. A sound judgment of a literary work, therefore, must be based on evidence from the text.
See *Evaluation* and *Opinion.*

LOADED WORDS See *Propaganda Technique.*

LOGICAL FALLACY *n. phrase* A *logical fallacy* is an error in reasoning. Such errors are common in persuasive or argumentative writing and speech. The following are some of the most common types of logical fallacies:

1. *Begging the question:* This fallacy occurs when someone assumes the truth of the statement to be proved without providing any supporting evidence. For example: "Robert Frost was the greatest American poet of the twentieth century." (No evidence is provided to support the claim.)

2. *Circular reasoning:* This fallacy occurs when the evidence given to support a claim is simply a restatement of the claim. For example: "Robert Frost was the greatest American poet because his poems were better than anyone else's." (The second part of the statement simply repeats the assertion made in the first part. No evidence is supplied to support the claim.)

3. *Either/or fallacy:* This fallacy occurs when someone claims that there are only two alternatives when there are actually more. For example: "Either you love Robert Frost's poems or you hate them." (This statement ignores another alternative—that one might not feel strongly about Frost's poems one way or the other.)

4. *False analogy:* This fallacy occurs when someone falsely assumes that two subjects are similar in some respect just because they are similar in some other respect. For example: "Whitman's poems were like leaves of grass: Each was just like the others." (While there may be similarities between Whitman's poems and leaves of grass, it certainly isn't the case that Whitman's poems are all alike.)

5. *Overgeneralization:* This fallacy occurs when someone makes a statement that is too broad or too inclusive. For example: "All of Whitman's poems are about democratic ideals." (While it is true that many of Whitman's poems are about democratic ideals, it is also true that some deal with other subjects.

6. *Post hoc, ergo propter hoc:* (a Latin phrase meaning "After this, therefore because of this") This fallacy occurs when someone falsely assumes that an event is caused by another event simply because of the order of the events in time. For example: "Robert Frost became a successful poet after he moved to England. Therefore, moving to England made Frost into a great poet." (Of course, Frost's greatness depends on factors totally unrelated to his move to England.)

When you do persuasive writing or speaking, or when you present arguments, try to avoid logical fallacies. Also be on guard against logical fallacies in the speech and writing of others.

MAIN IDEA *n. phrase* The *main idea* is the central point that a speaker or writer wants to communicate. For example, the main idea of "The Gettysburg Address," on page 440, is that the living must dedicate themselves to the "unfinished work" of preserving the Union. In many literary works, especially in poetry and in fiction, the main idea is implied.
See *Purpose.*

OBJECTIVE *adj.* Something is *objective* if it has to do with a reality that is independent of any particular person's mind, or personal, internal experiences. Jurors in criminal and civil trials are expected to evaluate cases impartially and objectively. Statements of fact are objective because anyone can, at least in theory, determine whether they are true. Even apparent statements of fact, however, can mask personal or cultural biases. For example, the statement "Columbus discovered America" would seem to be a fact. However, it ignores the external reality that Native Americans and Scandinavian explorers reached this continent long before Columbus. A statement that is not objective, such as "Anne Bradstreet wrote beautiful poetry," is *subjective* because it represents only one indi-

vidual's personal, internal experience.
See *Subjective.*

OPINION *n.* An *opinion* is a statement that can be supported by facts but is not itself a fact. Opinions may be judgments, predictions, or statements of policy or obligation. The following are opinions:

Judgment: Nathaniel Hawthorne is the most profound American writer of his century.

Prediction: Hispanic writers will play an increasingly prominent role in American literature.

Obligation: We must study the past to understand the present.

Whenever you express an opinion, you should be prepared to support it with facts and with reasoned arguments. A statement that you cannot back up is merely a *prejudice,* which Ambrose Bierce once defined as "a vagrant opinion without visible means of support."
See *Fact, Judgment,* and *Prediction.*

OVERGENERALIZATION See *Logical Fallacy.*

PARAPHRASE *n.* A *paraphrase* is a restatement in other words. When you write about a literary work, paraphrasing can be a useful technique for summarizing passages that you do not wish to quote exactly, or *verbatim.* A paraphrase can be used to support an interpretive argument when the exact words of the original are not essential to the argument. When paraphrasing, be careful not to alter the meaning of the original passage. Simply put into your own words what the writer said. You can also test your understanding of a literary work by attempting to paraphrase key passages.

POST HOC, ERGO PROPTER HOC See *Logical Fallacy.*

PREDICTION *n.* *Prediction* is the act of making statements about the future. Like inference, prediction is important to active reading. An active reader continually makes and tests predictions on the basis of details presented in a literary work. For example, a reader of Jack London's "To Build a Fire," on page 562, continually predicts, based on each new detail, whether the protagonist is going to survive. Authors often provide clues to future plot developments. These clues make predictions possible. When an author presents clues to future events, he or she is using a technique known as *foreshadowing.* Sometimes an author will intentionally mislead readers into making predictions that will later prove false. This often happens, for example, in mystery stories with surprise endings.
See *Opinion.*

PROBLEM-SOLVING *n. phrase* *Problem-solving* is the process by which a person comes up with a solution to some difficulty. Advances in medicine and technology represent a common type of problem-solving. For example, polio was once a common and crippling disease among young people in the United States. The creation of a polio vaccine was the solution to that problem. The following steps can be used in any situation that requires problem-solving:

1. State the problem as precisely and as clearly as possible.
2. Identify your goal.
3. Examine the differences between the goal state (the situation that will exist when the problem is solved) and the initial state (the situation at the time when you begin working on the problem).
4. Take steps to reduce the differences between the initial state and the goal state.

The following rules of thumb, or *heuristics,* are useful in solving many problems:

1. Break the problem down into parts and solve the parts separately.

2. Think of similar problems that you have solved before. Use some or all of those solutions to solve the current problem.
3. Restate the problem in various ways or from several points of view.
4. Ask someone to help you with parts of the problem that are especially difficult.
5. Use general thinking strategies such as brainstorming, freewriting, and diagraming to come up with possible solutions.

PROPAGANDA TECHNIQUE *n. phrase* A *propaganda technique* is an improper appeal to emotion, used for the purpose of swaying the opinions of an audience. The following propaganda techniques are often found in persuasive speech and writing:

1. *Bandwagon:* This technique involves encouraging people to think or act in some way simply because other people are doing so. For example: "Everyone's buying these new fashion jeans, so rush on down to Peabody's Department Store. Supplies are limited."
2. *Loaded words:* This technique involves using words with strong positive or negative connotations, or associations. Name-calling is an example of the use of loaded words. So is any use of words that are charged with emotion. For example: "These books should be banned because they are *un-American.*"
3. *Snob appeal:* This technique involves making a claim that one should act or think in a certain way because of the high social status associated with the action or thought. For example: "Diamond jewelry from Katz Jewelers—for those who settle for nothing but the best."
4. *Transfer:* This is the technique of attempting to get readers or listeners to transfer their strong feelings about one thing onto another thing that is unrelated. For example: "To celebrate Abe Lincoln's birthday, we're slashing prices on our bedroom sets. So, come on down to the Lincoln's birthday sale at Fast Freddie's Furniture."
5. *Unreliable testimonial:* This technique involves having an unqualified person endorse a product, an action, or an opinion. For example: "Hello, I'm Anita Stratton, from television's hit series, *Crimefighters.* I'd like to talk to you about a new home security system from Ersatz Industries."
6. *Vague, undefined terms:* This technique involves promoting or challenging an opinion by using words that are so vague or so poorly defined as to be almost meaningless. For example: "This *new* cereal tastes *good* and is *good* for you."

Avoid using propaganda techniques in your own speech and writing, and be on the alert for these techniques in the speech and writing of others.

PURPOSE *n.* The *purpose* is the goal or aim of a literary work. Works are often classified, by purpose, as narrative, descriptive, expository, or persuasive. The purpose of a narrative work is to tell a story. The purpose of a descriptive work is to portray a person, place, or thing. The purpose of an expository work is to explain something or to provide information. The purpose of a persuasive work is to move an audience to take some action or to adopt some opinion. For example, Jonathan Edwards's purpose in "Sinners in the Hands of an Angry God," on page 70, is persuasive. He wants to persuade the members of his audience to change their ways. Complex literary works often involve many purposes. For example, a persuasive work may contain expository passages, or a narrative work may contain passages of description.
See *Main Idea.*

REALISTIC DETAILS/FANTASTIC DETAILS *n. phrases* A *realistic detail* is one that is drawn from actual or possible experience; a *fantastic detail* is one that is not based on actual experience and that is improbable or imaginary. Writers of fiction, poetry, and drama use realistic details to make their plots and characters seem true-to-life. Writers often use fantastic details to heighten interest or to engage the reader's imagination. In "The Raven," on page 223, Edgar Allan Poe introduces a fantastic detail—a raven who flies in and announces "Nevermore!"—into an otherwise realistic setting.

REASON *n.*   A *reason* is a statement in support of some conclusion. The term *reason* is also used as a verb to signify the human faculty for thinking logically and rationally.
See *Argument* and *Conclusion.*

SOURCE *n.*   A *source* is anything from which ideas and information are taken. Books, magazines, speeches, television programs, conversations, and personal experiences may all serve as sources. Dictionaries, encyclopedias, bibliographies, almanacs, atlases, and other reference works are specifically designed to be used as sources.

There are two basic types of sources, primary sources and secondary sources. *Primary sources* are generally preferable because they are firsthand accounts. Conversations, speeches, documents, and letters are examples of primary sources. *Secondary sources* are accounts or compilations written after the fact. The Iroquois Constitution is a primary source; a history of the Iroquois nation is a secondary source. In literary study, the work itself—the poem, play, novel, or essay—is a primary source, while a work of criticism or a biography of the author would be considered a secondary source.

STEREOTYPE *n.*   A *stereotype* is a fixed or conventional notion or characterization. It is a type of overgeneralization. Some examples include the absent-minded professor, the brainless beauty queen, the bleeding-heart liberal, and the mad scientist. Although writers occasionally use stereotypes when they do not have sufficient space in which to develop a character fully, good writers generally avoid stereotyping, preferring to create more realistic characters. See *Generalization.*

SUBJECTIVE *adj.*   Something is *subjective* if it is based on personal reactions or emotions rather than on some objective reality. A reader's reaction to a work of literature is subjective because another reader may have a different reaction. All opinions are by definition subjective. However, this does not mean that all opinions are equally valid. A credible opinion is one that is based on facts. For example, if you find Randall Jarrell's poem "Death of a Ball Turret Gunner," on page 1215, strangely disturbing, you might base this opinion on facts about the work. These facts would include all the details in the work that caused your subjective reaction.

When authors invent thoughts, dialogue, and actions for their characters, they are depicting their characters' subjective experiences. Ambrose Bierce's short story, "An Occurrence at Owl Creek Bridge," on page 526, consists almost entirely of the protagonist's subjective experiences while awaiting execution.
See *Objective.*

SUMMARIZE *v.*   To *summarize* something is to restate it briefly in other words. Generally, one summarizes long works and paraphrases short passages. A brief summary of Flannery O'Connor's "The Life You Save May Be Your Own," on page 1052, might read as follows: "A one-armed tramp named Tom Shiftlet ingratiates himself with Mrs. Crater—the owner of a broken-down farm—and with Mrs. Crater's thirty-year-old deaf-mute daughter, Lucynell. Part miracle worker and part schemer, Shiftlet fixes up the farm, rehabilitates an old, abandoned car on the property, and allows Mrs. Crater to talk him into marrying the wide-eyed Lucy. On their wedding trip, however, Shiftlet abandons Lucy at a roadside eatery and takes off for Florida. On the way he picks up a young runaway boy. The boy quickly flees the car and its one-armed driver."

SUPPORT *v.* To *support* something is to provide evidence for it.
See *Argument* and *Evidence.*

TIME ORDER *n. phrase* *Time order* is organization by order of occurrence, that is, by chronological order. Time order is one of the most common methods of organization and is used in both fiction and nonfiction works.

TRANSFER See *Propaganda Technique.*

UNRELIABLE TESTIMONIAL See *Propaganda Technique.*

GLOSSARY

This pronunciation key is from *Webster's New World Dictionary*, Second College Edition. Copyright © 1986 by Simon & Schuster. Used by permission.

READING THE GLOSSARY ENTRIES

The words in this glossary are from selections appearing in your textbook. Each entry in the glossary contains the following parts:

1. Entry Word. This word appears at the beginning of the entry, in boldface type.

2. Pronunciation. The symbols in parentheses tell how the entry word is pronounced. If a word has more than one possible pronunciation, the most common of these pronunciations is given first.

3. Part of Speech. Appearing after the pronunciation, in italics, is an abbreviation that tells the part of speech of the entry word. The following abbreviations have been used:

n. noun	**p.** pronoun	**v.** verb
adj. adjective	**adv.** adverb	**conj.** conjunction

4. Definition. This part of the entry follows the part-of-speech abbreviation and gives the meaning of the entry word as used in the selection in which it appears.

KEY TO PRONUNCIATION SYMBOLS USED IN THE GLOSSARY

The following symbols are used in the pronunciations that follow the entry words:

Symbol	Key Words	Symbol	Key Words
a	asp, fat, parrot	b	bed, fable, dub
ā	ape, date, play	d	dip, beadle, had
ä	ah, car, father	f	fall, after, off
		g	get, haggle, dog
e	elf, ten, berry	h	he, ahead, hotel
ē	even, meet, money	j	joy, agile, badge
		k	kill, tackle, bake
i	is, hit, mirror	l	let, yellow, ball
ī	ice, bite, high	m	met, camel, trim
		n	not, flannel, ton
ō	open, tone, go	p	put, apple, tap
ô	all, horn, law	r	red, port, dear
o͞o	ooze, tool, crew	s	sell, castle, pass
oo	look, pull, moor	t	top, cattle, hat
yo͞o	use, cute, few	v	vat, hovel, have
yoo	united, cure, globule	w	will, always, swear
oi	oil, point, toy	y	yet, onion, yard
ou	out, crowd, plow	z	zebra, dazzle, haze
u	up, cut, color	ch	chin, catcher, arch
ʉr	urn, fur, deter	sh	she, cushion, dash
		th	thin, nothing, truth
ə	a in ago	th	then, father, lathe
	e in agent	zh	azure, leisure
	i in sanity	ŋ	ring, anger, drink
	o in comply	'	[see explanatory note
	u in focus		below and also *Foreign sounds* below]
ər	perhaps, murder		

A

abalone (ab'ə lo'nē) *n.* A large shellfish
abash (ə bash') *v.* To make ashamed
abeyance (ə bā' əns) *n.* A temporary suspension
abiding (ə bīd' iŋ) *adj.* Enduring; lasting
abject (ab' jekt) *adj.* Wretched

ablution (ab lo͞o' shən) *n.* A washing or cleansing of the body as part of a religious rite
abominably (ə bäm' ə nə b'lē) *adv.* Hatefully
abrogated (ab'rə gāt'əd) *v.* Canceled
acclivity (ə kliv' ə tē) *n.* An upward slope
accost (ə kôst') *v.* To approach and speak to in an intrusive way
acquiesce (ak' wē es') *v.* To agree without protest
adhere (əd hir') *v.* To stick fast; stay attached
adieu (ə dyo͞o') *n.* "Farewell" (French)
adroit (ə droit') *adj.* Skillful in a physical or mental way
adumbration (ad' um brā' shən) *n.* A shadowy outline
aeolian (ē ō' lē ən) harps *n.* Harps with strings that produce music when air blows over them
aesthetic (es thet' ik) *adj.* Of beauty
aggregate (ag' rə gət) *n.* The sum total
aggrieve (ə grēv') *v.* To offend
aghast (ə gast') *adj.* Horrified
ague (ā' gyo͞o) *n.* A chill or fit of shivering
alacrity (ə lak' rə tē) *n.* Speed
albeit (ôl bē' it) *conj.* Although
alburnum (al bur' nəm) *n.* The soft wood between the bark and the heartwood where water is conducted
amain (ə mān') *adv.* At or with great speed
amalgam (əmal' gəm) *n.* An alloy of mercury used with silver as a dental filling
anachronism (ə nak'rə niz'm) *n.* Something that is or seems to be out of its proper time
anarchy (an' ər kē) *n.* The absence of government
anathema (ə nath' ə mə) *n.* Curse
anomalous (ə näm' ə ləs) *adj.* Abnormal; deviating from the regular arrangement, general rule, or usual method
antipodes (an tip' ə dēz) *n.* On the opposite side of the globe
anxiety (aŋ zī' ə tē) *n.* An uneasiness about the future
aqua vitae (ä' kwə vī' tē) *n.* Brandy
aphid (ä' fid) *n.* Small insect that suck the juice from plants
apotheosis (a päth' ē ō'sis) *n.* Glorification
apparition (ap' ə rish' ən) *n.* The act of appearing or becoming invisible
appellation (ap' ə lā shən) *n.* A name or title
approbation (ap' rə bā' shən) *n.* Approval
arabesque (ar' ə besk') *n.* A complex and elaborate design
ardor (är' dər) *n.* Emotional warmth; passion
arduous (är' jo͞o wəs) *adj.* Very difficult
assail (ə sāl') *v.* 1. To attack violently; assault; 2. to have a forceful effect on
assent (ə sent') *v.* To agree
assuage (ə swāj) *v.* To lessen
asunder (ə sun' dər) *adv.* Into parts or pieces
asylum (ə sī' ləm) *n.* A place of refuge
attest (ə test') *v.* To bear witness
audaciously (ô dā' shəs lē) *adj.* Boldly

auger (ô′ gər) *n.* A tool used for drilling teeth

auroral (ô rôr′ əl) *adj.* Resembling the dawn

Auspex (ôs′ peks) *n.* In ancient Rome, someone who watched for omens in the flight of birds

auspice (ôs′ pəs) *n.* Approval and support

austere (ô stir′) *adj.* Showing strict self-discipline and self-denial

automation (ôt′ ə mā′ shən) *n.* In manufacturing, a system or process in which many or all of the processes of production, movement, and inspection of parts and materials are automatically performed or controlled by self-operated machinery

avarice (av′ ər is) *n.* Greed

aversion (ə vʉr′ zhən) *n.* An intense or definite dislike

B

banshee (ban′ shē) *n.* In Scottish and Irish folklore, a female spirit believed to wail outside a house as a warning that a death will soon occur in the family

bastion (bas′ chən) *n.* A fortification

bayou (bī′ ōō) *n.* A sluggish, marshy inlet or outlet of a lake or river

beguile (bi gīl′) *v.* To charm; deceive

behold (bi hōld′) *v.* To look

beholden (bi hōld′ ən) *adj.* Owing thanks; indebted

beleaguered (bi lē′ gərd) *adj.* Encircled by an army

belie (bi lī′) *v.* To prove false

bellicose (bel′ ə kōs) *adj.* Quarrelsome

benevolent (bə nev′ ə lənt) *adj.* Kindly; charitable

bereaved (bi rēvd′) *n.* The survivors of recently deceased people

bereavement (bi rēv′ mənt) *n.* The sadness resulting from the loss or death of a loved one

berserk (bər sʉrk′) *adj.* In a frenzy, after a legendary Norse warrior who worked himself into a frenzy before battle

beseech (bi sēch′) *v.* To ask earnestly; implore

bicuspid (bī kus′ pid) *n.* Any of eight adult teeth with two-pointed crowns

billet (bil′ it) *n.* A brief letter

binnacle (bin′ ə k′l) *n.* The case enclosing the ship's compass

bivouac (biv′wak) *n.* A temporary encampment

blaspheme (blas fēm′) *v.* To curse

blithe (blith) *adj.* Carefree

blunt (blunt) *v.* To make dull

brachycephalic (brak′ i sə fal′ ik) *adj.* Short-headed or broad-headed

brindled (brin′ d′ld) *adj.* Having a gray or tawny coat with streaks of darker color

brocaded (brō kād id) *adj.* Having a raised design woven into it

brood (brōōd′) *v.* To pondering in a troubled or mournful way

C

cache (kash) *v.* To hide

cairn (kern) *n.* A conical heap of stones built as a monument or landmark

calamity (kə lam′ə tē) *n.* A disaster

callow (kal′ō) *adj.* Immature; inexperienced

camaraderie (käm′ əräd′ ər ē) *n.* Warm, friendly feelings

candid (kan′ did) *adj.* Impartial

capacious (kə pā′ shəs) *adj.* Roomy; spacious

capitulate (kə pich′ ə lāt′) *v.* To surrender conditionally

capstan (kap′ stən) *n.* A large cylinder, turned by hand, around which cables are wound

Carrara (kə rä′ rə) *n.* A fine, white marble

castanets (kas′ tə nets′) *n.* Small, hollowed out pieces of wood, held in the hand by a connecting cord and clicked together with the fingers

cataleptical (kat′ 'l ep′ tik 'l) *adj.* In a state in which consciousness and feeling are suddenly and temporarily lost and the muscles become rigid

celestial (sə les′ chəl) *adj.* Of the heavens

chafe (chāf) *v.* To rub to make warm

chanticleer (chan′ tə klir′) *n.* A rooster

chaos (kā′ äs) *n.* The disorder of formless matter and infinite space, supposed to have existed before the ordered universe

chaparral (chap′ə ral′) *n.* A thicket of thorny bushes or shrubs

charnel (chär′ n′l) *adj.* Like a graveyard

cherub (cher′əb) *n.* A representation of a heavenly being as a winged, child with a chubby, rosy face

chronic (krän′ ik) *adj.* Continuing indefinitely

cipher (sī′ fər) *v.* To figure

cirrus (sir′əs) *n.* High, detached wispy clouds

clematis (klem′ə tis) *n.* A woody vine with bright-colored flowers

collateral (kə lat′ ər əl) *adj.* Descended from the same ancestors, but in a different line

commensurate (kə men′ shər it) *adj.* Corresponding in amount, magnitude, or degree

conceit (kən sēt′) *n.* A strange or fanciful idea

confederate (kən fed′ ər it) *adj.* United with others for a common purpose

conflagration (kän′ flə grā shən) *n.* A big, destructive fire

congenial (kən jēn′ yəl) *adj.* Compatible; friendly; sympathetic

conjectural (kən jek′ chər əl) *adj.* Based on guesswork

conjecture (kən jek′ chər) *v.* To guessed

connate (kän′ āt) *adj.* Having the same origin or nature

connivance (kə nī′ vəns) *n.* Secret cooperation

consanguinity (kän′ saŋ gwin′ə tē) *n.* Kinship

consecrate (kän′ sə krāt′) *v.* To cause to be revered or honored

consternation (kän′ stər nā′ shən) *n.* A great fear or shock that makes one feel helpless or bewildered

contemptible (kən temp′ tə b′l) *adj.* Worthless; despicable

continuum (ken tin′ yōō wəm) *n.* A continuous whole with parts that cannot be separated

contrive (kən trīv′) *v.* To scheme

convoluted (kän′ və lōōt′ id) *adj.* Intricate; complicated

cormorant (kôr′ mə rənt) *n.* A large, diving bird with a hooked beak and webbed toes

cornice (kôr′ nis) *n.* The projecting decorative molding along the top of a building

corollary (kôr′ ə ler′ ē)   *n.* An easily drawn conclusion

countenance (koun′ tə nəns)   *n.* A facial expression

cozen (kuz′ ən)   *v.* To cheat

crape (krāp)   *n.* A piece of black cloth worn as a sign of mourning

craven (krā′ vən)   *adj.* Very cowardly

crescendo (krə shen′ dō)   *adj.* Gradually increasing in loudness or intensity

crypt (kript)   *n.* An underground chamber or vault

cryptic (krip′tik)   *adj.* Having a hidden or ambiguous meaning

cumbersome (kum′ bər səm)   *adj.* Hard to handle or deal with because of size or weight

cunning (kun′ in)   *adj.* Skillful in deception; crafty; sly

curlew (kʉr′ lo͞o)   *n.* A large, long-legged wading bird whose call is associated with the evening

cyclonic (sī klän′ ik)   *adj.* Like a cyclone, a windstorm with violent, whirling movement

cynicism (sin′ ə siz′m)   *n.* The denial of the sincerity of people's motives or actions or of the value of living

D

declivity (di kliv′ ə tē)   *n.* A downward slope

deference (def′ ər əns)   *n.* A courteous regard or respect

deferential (def′ ə ren′ shəl)   *adj.* Very respectful

degenerate (di jen′ ər it)   *adj.* Deteriorated

deign (dān)   *v.* To condescend to take or accept

deliberation (di lib′ə rā′ shən)   *n.* Careful consideration

delirium (di lir′ ē əm)   *n.* A temporary state of extreme mental confusion

delusion (di lo͞o′ zhən)   *n.* A false belief

demean (di mēn′d)   *v.* To behave; conduct

demiculverin (dem′ē kul′ vər in)   A large cannon

demur (di mʉr′)   *v.* To object

demure (di myo͞or′)   *adj.* Modest; reserved

depravity (di prav′ ə tē)   *n.* Corruption; wickedness

deprecating (dep′ rə kāt′ iŋ)   *adj.* Expressing disapproval

derivative (də riv′ə tiv)   *adj.* Arrived at through complex reasoning

desolate (dəs′ ə lit)   *adj.* Forlorn; wretched

despotic (de spät′ ik)   *adj.* Harsh, cruel, unjust

despotism (des′ pə tiz′m)   *n.* Tyranny

diabolical (dī′ ə bäl′ ə k′l)   *adj.* Of the devil

dictum (dik′ təm)   *n.* A statement or saying

digress (dī gres′)   *v.* To depart temporarily from the main subject

dilapidated (di lap′ ə dātid)   *adj.* In disrepair

dilatory (dil′ ə tôr ē)   *adj.* Slow

diligence (dil′ ə jəns)   *n.* A constant, careful effort; perseverance

diligent (dil′ ə jənt)   *adj.* Hard-working; industrious

din (din)   *n.* A loud, continuous noise or clamor

discern (di sʉrn′)   *v.* To perceive or recognize; make out clearly

discordant (dis kôr′ d′nt)   *adj.* Not in harmony; clashing

dismay (dis mā′)   *v.* To make afraid; discourage

disposition (dis′ pə zish′ ən)   *n.* An inclination or tendency

dissolutely (dis′ə lo͞ot′ lē)   *adv.* Immorally and shamelessly

diverse (dī vʉrs′)   *adj.* Various

divine (də vīn′)   *n.* A clergyman

docile (däs′ ′l)   *adj.* Obedient

dolorous (dō′ lər əs)   *adj.* Sad; mournful

dominion (də min′ yən)   *n.* The power to rule

doubloon (du blo͞on′)   *n.* The gold coin Ahab offered as reward to the first man to spot the whale

dour (do͝or)   *adj.* Stern; severe

drayman (drā′ mən)   *n.* The driver of a dray, a low cart with detachable sides

dubious (do͞o′ bē əs)   *adj.* Questionable

duodecimos (do͞o′ə des′ ə mōz′)   *n.* Books about five by eight inches

dusky (dus′ kē)   *adj.* Dim; shadowy

dynastic (dī nas′ tik)   *adj.* Of a period during which a certain family rules

dyspepsia (dis pep′ shə)   *n.* Indigestion

E

eccentric (ik sen′ trik)   *adj.* Peculiar

efface (i fās′)   *v.* To wipe out; obliterate

effluvium (e flo͞o′ vē əm)   *n.* An aura

effuse (e fyo͞oz′)   *v.* To spread out; diffuse

egalitarian (i gal′ ə ter′ ē ən)   *adj.* Asserting, resulting from, or characterized by the belief in the equality of all people

elixir of life (i lik′ sər)   *n.* An imaginary substance thought by medieval alchemists to prolong life indefinitely

eloquence (el′ə kwəns)   *n.* Expressiveness; persuasive power

elusive (i lo͞o′ siv)   *adj.* Hard to grasp

emaciated (i mā′ shē āt′ id)   *adj.* Abnormally thin

embrasure (im brā′ zhər)   *n.* An opening

eminence (em′ ə nəns)   *n.* Greatness; celebrity

eminent (em′ ə nənt)   *adj.* Distinguished

engrossed (in grōst′)   *adj.* Absorbed

enigmatic (en′ ig mat′ ik)   *adj.* Perplexing; baffling; mysterious

ephemeral (i fem′ ər əl)   *adj.* Short-lived

equanimity (ek′ wə nim′ ə tē)   *n.* Composure

equivocal (i kwiv′ ə k′l)   *adj.* Having more than one possible interpretation

escarpment (e skärp′ mənt)   *n.* A steep slope

eschew (es cho͞o′)   *v.* To abstain from

ether (ē′ thər)   *n.* A chemical compound used as an anesthetic

etherize (ē′ thə rīz)   *v.* To anesthetize as with ether

etiquette (et′ i kət)   *n.* The rules for manners and ceremonies

evanescence (ev′ə nes′ ′ns)   *n.* A fading from sight

evanescently (ev′ə nes′ ′nt lē)   *adv.* Fleetingly

evitable (ev′ ə tə b′l)   *adj.* Avoidable

exigency (ek′ sə jən sē)   *n.* A pressing need; demand

expatriated (eks pā′ trē āt′ id)   *adj.* Deported; driven from one's native land

expedient (ik spē′ dēənt)   *n.* A resource used in an emergency

expostulation (ik späs′ chə lā′ shən)   *n.* Expression of objection

extort (ik stôrt′)   *v.* To obtain by threat or violence

extricate (eks' trə kāt)   *v.* To set free
exude (ig zo͞od')   *v.* To ooze, discharge

F

facetious (fə sē' shəs)   *adj.* Joking at an inappropriate time
facile (fas' 'l)   *adj.* Fluent
fallow (fal'ō)   *adj.* Left uncultivated or unplanted
fallowness (fal' ō nis)   *n.* Inactivity
fast (fast')   *v.* To eat very little or nothing
fecundity (fi kun' də tē)   *n.* Productivity
feign (fān' in)   *v.* To make a false show of
felicitate (fə lis' ə tāt)   *v.* To congratulate
felicity (fə lis'ə tē)   *n.* Happiness; bliss
festoon (fes to͞on')   *n.* A wreath of flowers or leaves
fettuccine (fet' o͞o chē' nē)   *n.* Broad, flat noodles
finite (fī' nīt)   *adj.* Having measurable or definable limits
flume (flo͞om)   *n.* An artificial channel for carrying water to provide power and transport objects
folio (fō lē ō')   *n.* The largest regular size of books, over eleven inches in height
foppery (fäp' ər ē)   *n.* Foolishness
foreboding (fôr bōd' in)   *n.* A prediction
forestall (fôr stôl')   *v.* To act in advance of
fortuitous (fôr to͞o'ə təs)   *adj.* Fortunate
frippery (frip' ər ē)   *n.* A showy display of elegance
frugally (fro͞o' g' lē)   *adv.* Thriftily
furtive (fur' tiv)   *adj.* Sneaky; shifty; secretive

G

gall (gôl)   *n.* Bitterness
garret (gar' it)   *n.* A attic
garrulous (gar' ə ləs)   *adj.* Talking too much
genuflect (jen' yə flekt')   *v.* To bend the knee, as in reverence or worship
gerfalcon (jur' fal' k'n)   *n.* A large, fierce falcon of the Arctic
gesticulate (jes tik' yə lāt)   *v.* To gesture with hands or arms
glean (glēn)   *v.* To collect the remaining grain after reaping
gloaming (glō' min)   *n.* The evening dusk; twilight
glee (glē)   *n.* An unaccompanied song
goatee (gō tē')   *n.* A small, pointed beard
gossamer (gäs' ə mər)   *n.* A very thin, soft, filmy cloth
gourd (gôrd)   *adj.* The dried, hollowed-out shell of a piece of fruit from a gourd plant, often used as a dipper or drinking cup
gracile (gras' 'l)   *adj.* Slender; slim
grandeur (gran' jər)   *adj.* Magnificence
grave (grāv)   *adj.* Serious; solemn
gripsack (grip' sak)   *n.* A small bag for holding clothes
guile (gīl)   *n.* Craftiness
guillotine (gil' ə tēn')   *n.* An instrument for beheading by means of a heavy blade dropped between two grooved uprights
guffaw (gə fô')   *adj.* To laugh in a loud, coarse manner
guttural (gut' ər əl)   *adj.* Of the throat

H

hallow (hal'ō)   *v.* To honor as sacred
halyard (hal'yərd)   *n.* A rope for raising or lowering sail
harbor (här' bər)   *v.* A shelter or house
harrow (har' ō)   *v.* To distressing
herald (her' əld)   *n.* A messenger
hermitage (hur' mit ij)   *n.* A place where a person can live away from other people; a secluded retreat
hernia (hur' nē ə)   *n.* The protrusion of part of the intestine through the abdominal muscles
heron (her' ən)   *n.* A wading bird with a long neck, long legs, and a long, tapered bill
hieroglyphic (hī' ər ə glif' ik)   *n.* A picture or symbol representing a word, syllable, or sound
hoary (hôr' ē)   *adj.* Very old; ancient
hostler (häs' lər)   *n.* A person who tends horses at an inn or stable
humble (hum' b'l)   *adj.* Not proud; modest
husbandry (huz' bən drē)   *n.* Farming
hypnotic (hip nät' ik)   *adj.* Inducing a sleeplike condition

I

ideality (ī' dē al' ə tē)   *n.* Something that is ideal and has no reality
illiterate (i lit' ər it)   *adj.* Unable to read or write
illumination (i lo͞o' mə nā' shən)   *n.* The supplying of light
imbibe (im bīb')   *v.* To drink in
immemorial (im'ə môr'ē əl)   *adj.* Extending back beyond memory or record
impalpable (im pal' pə b'l)   *adj.* Imperceptible to the sense of touch
imperative (im per'ə tiv)   *adj.* Absolutely necessary; urgent
imperially (im pir' ē əl ē)   *adv.* Majestically
imperious (im pir' ē əs)   *adj. adj.* Urgent
impertinent (im pur' t'n ənt)   *adj.* Not showing proper respect
impetuous (im pech' oo wəs)   *adj.* Acting or done suddenly with little thought; rash; impulsive; moving with great force or violence
impious (im' pē əs)   *adj.* Lacking reverence for God
implacable (im plak'ə b'l)   *adj.* Relentless
importunate (im pôr' chə nit)   *adj.* Insistent
importunity (im' pôr to͞on' ə te)   *n.* A persistent request or demand
imprecation (im' prə kā' shən)   *n.* A curse
impregnable (im preg' nə b'l)   *adj.* Unshakable; unyielding
inanimate (in an' ə mit)   *adj.* Not endowed with life
inauspicious (in ôs pish' əs)   *adj.* Not boding well for the future
incessantly (in ses' 'nt lē)   *adv.* Unceasingly
incipient (in sip' ē ənt)   *adj.* Just beginning
incisor (in sī' zər)   *n.* A front tooth
incongruous (in kän' gro͞o wəs)   *adj.* Incompatible
incubus (in' kyə bəs)   *n.* Something nightmarishly burdensome
indecorous (in dek' ər əs)   *adj.* Improper
indigenous (in dij'ə nəs)   *adj.* Existing, growing, or produced naturally in a region or country

indigo (in′ di go′) *n.* A blue dye
ineffable (in ef′ə bl) *adj.* Inexpressible
inert (in ʉrt′) *adj.* Motionless
inevitable (in ev′ ə tə b′l) *adj.* Certain to happen; unavoidable
infidel (in′ fə d′l) *n.* A person who holds no religious belief
inimical (in im′i k′l) *adj.* Hostile; unfriendly
iniquity (in ik′ wətē) *n.* A sin
inscrutable (in skroot′ ə b′l) *adj.* Not able to be easily understood
insidious (in sid′ ē əs) *adj.* Deceitful; secretly treacherous
inscrutable (in skroot′ ə b′l) *adj.* Not easily understood
insinuate (in sin′ yoo wāt′) *v.* To hint or suggest indirectly; imply
integrity (in teg′ rə tē) *n.* The adherence to a code of values
interminable (in tʉr′ mi nə b′l) *adj.* Seeming to last forever; without, or apparently without, end
intuitively (in too′ i tiv lē) *adv.* Instinctively
invalid (in′ və lid) *v.* To release because of illness or disability
inviolable (in vī′ ə lə b′l) *adj.* Safe from danger
ipecacuanha (ip′ ə kak′ yoo wan′ ə) *n.* A plant with roots used for medicinal purposes

J

jauntily (jôn′ti lē) *adv.* In a carefree fashion
jocularity (jäk′ yə lar′ə tē) *n.* A joking good humor
juxtaposition (juk′ stə pə zish′ ən) *n.* Placing side by side

L

laggard (lag′ ərd) *adj.* Slow or late in doing things
lamentation (lam′ ən tā′ shən) *n.* The outward expression of grief
lariat (lar′ē it) rope *n.* A rope used for tethering grazing horses or cattle
laterally (lat′ ər əl lē) *adv.* In a sideways manner
legacy (leg′ə sē) *n.* The money or property left to someone by a will
levee (lev′ ē) *n.* A landing place along the bank of a river
limber (lim′ bər) *adj.* Flexible
list (list′ id) *v.* To swayed
literalist (lit′ ər əl ists) *n.* One who insists on the exact meaning of words
loath (lōth) *adj.* Reluctant; unwilling
lubber (lub′ ər) *n.* A slow, clumsy person
lucidity (loo sid′ i tē) *n.* Brightness
lugubrious (loo goo′ brē əs) *adj.* Very sad or mournful
lull (lul) *v.* To calm or soothe by gentle sound or motion
luminary (loo′ mə ner′ ē) *adj.* Giving of light
luminescent (loo′ mə nes′′nt) *adj.* Shining
luminous (loo′ mə nəs) *adj.* Shining; bright
lurid (loor′ id) *adj.* Vivid in a harsh or shocking way
lustrous (lus′ trəs) *adj.* Shining
lusty (lus′ tē) *adj.* Strong; hearty

M

magisterial (maj′ is tir′ ē əl) *adj.* Authoritative

magnanimity (mag′ nə nim′ə tē) *n.* Ability to rise above pettiness or meanness; generosity
magnanimous (mag nan′ ə məs) *adj.* Noble in mind; rising above pettiness and meanness
mah-jongg (mä′ jôŋ) *n.* A game of Chinese origin, played with pieces resembling dominoes
malediction (mal′ ə dik′ shən) *n.* A curse
malevolent (mə lev′ə lənt) *adj.* Wishing evil or harm to others
malinger (mə liŋ′ gər) *v.* To pretend to be ill
malign (mə līn′) *adj.* Evil
mammoth (mam′ əth) *n.* An extinct elephant with hairy skin
manifest (man′ ə fest′) *n.* A cargo list
manifold (man′ə fōld′) *adj.* In many ways; plentiful and varied
mansard (man′ särd) *n.* A roof with two slopes on each of the four sides
marrow (mar′ ō) *n.* The soft tissue that fills the cavities of most bones
maverick (mav′ ər ik) *n.* A nonconformist
meander (mē an′ dər) *v.* To move lazily
meditate (med′ ə tāt′) *v.* To think deeply
meditation (med′ ə tā′ shən) *n.* A deep reflection
melancholy (mal′ ən käl′ ē) *adj.* Gloomy
melee (mā′ lā) *n.* A noisy, confused fight
mendicant (men′ di kənt) *n.* A beggar
Mesozoic (mes′ ə zō′ik) *adj.* A geological era characterized by the development and extinction of dinosaurs
mesquite (mes kēt′) *n.* A type of small thorny tree
metamorphosis (met′ ə môr′ fə sis) *n.* A transformation
metate (mā tä′ tā′) *n.* A stone used in the southwestern United States for grinding meal
meticulous (mə tik′ yoo ləs) *adj.* Extremely careful about details
miasma (mī az′ mə) *n.* An unwholesome atmosphere
milieu (mēl yoo′) *n.* The environment
minutia (mi nü′ shē ə) *n.* The small and trivial details
mollifyed (mäl′ə fī) *v.* To soothe; calm
monotonous (mə nät′ ′n əs) *adj.* Having little or no variation or variety; tiresome because unvarying
monotony (mə nät′ nē) *n.* Tiresome sameness of uniformity
moribund (môr′ə bund′) *adj.* Dying; coming to an end
morose (mə rōs′) *adj.* Gloomy, sullen
mundane (mundān′) *adj.* Commonplace; ordinary
munificent (myoo nif′ ə s′nt) *adj.* Generous
musing (myooz′ iŋ) *v.* Thinking deeply and at length
myriad (mir′ ē əd) *adj.* Countless

N

nostalgia (näs tal′ jə) *n.* A longing

O

obeisance (o′bā′ s′ns) *n.* A gesture of respect
obnoxious (əb näk′ shəs) *adj.* Very unpleasant; objectionable
obstinacy (äb′stə nə sē) *n.* Stubbornness
obtuse (äb toos′) *adj.* Slow to understand or perceive
ominous (äm′ə nəs) *adj.* Threatening; sinister
omnipotent (äm nip′ə tənt) *adj.* All-powerful

omnipresence (äm′ ni prez′ 'ns) *n.* A presence in all places at the same time

omniscience (äm nish′ əns) *n.* A knowledge of all things

oppress (ə pres′) *v.* To weigh heavily on the mind

ornery (ôr′ nər ē) *adj.* Having a mean disposition

ornithologist (ôr′ nə thäl′ ə jē) *n.* An expert on birds

oscillation (äs′ ə lā′ shən) *n.* The act of swinging regularly back and forth

ostentation (äs tən tā′ shən) *n.* A boastful display

ostentatious (äs tən tā shəs) *adj.* Intended to attract notice

P

paean (pē′ ən) *n.* A song of triumph

palisade (pal′ə sād) *n.* A large pointed stake set in the ground to form a fence used for defense

pallid (pal′ id) *adj.* Pale

palpable (pal′ pə b'l) *adj.* Able to be touched, felt, or handled

paradoxical (par′ə däks′i k'l) *adj.* Expressing an apparent contradiction

Parian (per′ē ən) *adj.* Referring to a fine, white marble of the Greek city Paros

parsimony (pär′sə mō′ nē) *n.* Stinginess

passion (pash′ ən) *n.* An extreme, compelling emotion

patriarch (pā′ trē ärk) *n.* The father and ruler of a family or tribe

patrimony (pat′ rə mō′ nē) *n.* The property inherited from one's father

pelf (pelf) *n.* The money or wealth regarded with contempt

pensive (pen′ siv) *adj.* Thinking deeply or seriously

penumbra (pi num′ brə) *n.* The partly lighted area surrounding the complete shadow of a body in full eclipse

penury (pen′ yə rē) *n.* A lack of money, property, or necessities

peremptory (pə remp′ tər ē) *adj.* That cannot be denied, changed, delayed or opposed

perfidy (pur′ fə dē) *n.* A betrayal of trust; treachery

perfunctory (pər fuŋk′ tər ē) *adj.* Done without care or interest or merely as a form of routine

periodicity (pir′ ē ə dis′ ə tē) *n.* A recurrence at regular intervals

periphery (pə rif′ ər ē) *n.* A surrounding space or area

peroration (per′ ə rā′ shən) *n.* The concluding part of a speech

pertinaciously (pur′ tə nā′ səsē) *adj.* Holding firmly to some purpose

pertinence (pur′t'n əns) *n.* Appropriateness; relevance

perturbation (pur′ tər bā′ shən) *n.* Agitation

perusal (pə rōō′ z'l) *n.* The act of reading

pervade (pər vād′) *v.* To pass through; to spread throughout

petulantly (pech′ ōō lənt lē) *adv.* Impatiently or irritably

phantasmagoric (fan taz′ mə gôr′ ik) *adj.* Fantastic or dreamlike

piety (pī′ ə tē) *n.* A devotion to religious duties

pilfer (pil′ fər) *v.* To steal

pimiento (pi men′ to) *n.* A red, bell-shaped fruit, used for stuffing green olives

pine (pīn) *v.* To have an intense longing or desire

pinion (pin′ yən) *n.* Wing

pinnace (pin′ is) *n.* A small sailing ship

pinnacle (pin′ ə k'l) *n.* A lofty peak

pious (pī′ əs) *adj.* Dutiful

pique (pēk) *v.* To aroused resentment in

placid (plas′ id) *adj.* Tranquil; calm

plaguy (plā′ gē) *adj.* Disagreeable

Pleistocene (plīst′ tə sēn) *adj.* A geological era characterized by the spreading and recession of continental ice sheets and the appearance of modern man

poignant (poin′ yənt) *adj.* Sharply painful to the feelings

poise (poiz) *n.* Balance; stability

pompadour (päm′ pə dôr′) *n.* A hairdo in which the hair is swept up high from the forehead

portentous (pôr ten′ təs) *adj.* Ominous

posterity (päs ter′ ə tē) *n.* All succeeding generations

posture (päs′ chər iŋ) *v.* To pose

practicable (prak′ ti kə b'l) *adj.* Capable of being put into practice; feasible; workable

pragmatic (prag mat′ ik) *adj.* Practical

precept (prē′ sept) *n.* A rule of conduct

preconception (prē′ kən sep′ shən) *n.* An ideas formed beforehand

preposterous (pri päs′ tər əs) *adj.* Ridiculous

prescient (prē′ shē ənt) *adj.* Having foreknowledge

preternatural (prēt′ ər nach′ ər əl) *adj.* Differing from or beyond what is normally expected from nature; supernatural

priggish (prig′gish) *adj.* Excessively precise

pristine (pris′ tēn) *adj.* Pure, uncorrupted

prodigious (prə dij′ əs) *adj.* Powerful; wonderful

profane (prə fān′) *adj.* Showing disrespect or contempt for sacred things

prophecy (präf′ ə sē) *n.* Prediction of the future

propitious (prə pish′ əs) *adj.* Favorably inclined or disposed

proscenium (prō sē′ nē əm) *n.* The area of the stage in front of the curtain, where action takes place when the curtain is closed

protrude (prō trōōd′) *v.* To jut out

psychology (sī köl′ ə jē) *n.* The science dealing with the mind and with mental and emotional processes

pugilistic (pyōō′ jə lis′ tik) *adj.* Like a boxer

pygmies (pig′ mēz) *n.* Members of African and Asiatic races known for their small stature

Q

quagmire (kwag′ mīr) *n.* A wet, boggy ground

quarto (kwôr′tōz) *n.* A book about nine by twelve inches

querulous (kwer′ ə ləs) *adj.* Complaining; inclined to find fault

questing (kwest′ iŋ) *adj.* Searching

quintessentially (kwin′ tə sen′ shə lē) *adv.* Purely

R

radiant (rā dē ənt) *adj.* Shining brightly

ramification (ram′ ə fi kā′ shən)   *n.* A branchlike division

rampant (ram′ pənt)   *adj.* Spreading unchecked

ravenous (rav′ ə nəs)   *adj.* Extremely eager

reap (rēp′ iŋ)   *v.* To cut or harvest grain from a field

recompense (rek′ əm pens′)   *n.* A reward

recondite (rek′ ən dīt′)   *adj.* Dealing with very profound, difficult, or abstruse subject matter

recumbent (ri kum′ bənt)   *adj.* Resting

redolent (red″ l ənt)   *adj.* Suggestive

redress (re′ dres)   *n.* An atonement; rectification

refluent (ref′ lōō wənt)   *adj.* Flowing back

refulgent (ri ful′ jənt)   *adj.* Radiant; shinning

rehearse (ri hʉrs′)   *v.* To narrate

reiterated (rē it′ə rāt′d)   *adj.* Repeated

remuda (re mōō′ də)   *n.* A group of extra saddle horses kept as a supply of remounts

repose (ri pōz′)   *n.* The state of being at rest

repression (ri presh′ ə n)   *n.* Restraint

repugnant (ri pug′ nənt)   *adj.* Offensive; disagreeable

reverence (rev′ ər əns)   *n.* A feeling or attitude of deep respect, love or awe

reverential (rev′ ə ren′ shəl)   *adj.* Showing or caused by a feeling of deep respect, love, and awe

reverie (rev′ ər ē)   *n.* A daydream

rigor (rig′ ər)   *n.* A stiffness; rigidity

rude (rōōd)   *adj.* Crude or rough in form or workmanship

rudimentary (rōō də men′ tər ē)   *adj.* Elementary

rueful (rōō′ fəl)   *adj.* Feeling or showing sorrow or pity

ruminate (rōō′ mə nāt)   *v.* To meditate

S

sacrament (sak′ rə mənt)   *n.* Something regarded as having a sacred meaning

sagacious (sə gā′ shəs)   *adj.* Shrewd

sage (sāj′ ə)   *n.* A person widely respected for his or her wisdom

salient (sāl′ yənt)   *adj.* Standing out from the rest

sallow (sal′ ō)   *adj.* Of a sickly, pale-yellow hue

sardonic (sär dän′ ik)   *adj.* Bitterly sarcastic

saturnalia (sat′ ər nā′ lē ə)   *n.* A period of unrestrained revelry

savant (sə vänt′)   *n.* A learned person; scholar

scorn (skôrnd)   *v.* To refuse or reject as wrong or disgraceful

scree (skrē)   *adj.* A covering of rock fragments on a slope below a rock face

scurvy (skʉr′ vē)   *n.* A disease caused by vitamin-C deficiency

scythe (sīthz)   *v.* To cut as with a tool with a long single-edged blade set at an angle on a long, curved handle

sedge (sej′)   *n.* A grasslike plant

seminal (sem′ ə n'l)   *adj.* Highly original and influencing the development of future events

semi-somnambulant (sem′i säm nam′byōō lənt)   *adj.* Half sleepwalking

sentience (sen′ shəns)   *n.* A capacity of feeling

sepulcher (sep′'l kər)   *n.* A grave; tomb

sequester (si kwes′ tər)   *v.* To withdraw; seclude

serenity (sə ren′ ə tē)   *n.* Calmness

servile (ser′ v'l)   *adj.* Humbly yielding or submissive

sexton (seks′ tən)   *n.* A person in charge of the maintenance of a church

shroud (shroud)   *n.* 1. A cloth sometimes used to wrap a corpse for burial 2. A set of ropes from a ship's side to the masthead

simulacrum (sim′ yōō lā krəm)   *n.* A vague representation

sinuous (sin′ yōō wəs)   *adj.* Bending or winding in and out; wavy

Skoal (skōl)   *interj.* A drinking toast, meaning "to your health"

sleeper (slē′ pər)   *n.* A tie supporting railroad tracks

slovenly (sluv′ən lē)   *adj.* Untidy

smite (smīt)   *v.* To kill by a powerful blow

solicitous (sə lis′ ə təs)   *adj.* Showing concern

somber (säm′ bər)   *adj.* Dark and gloomy or dull

somnolent (säm nə lənt)   *adj.* Sleepy; drowsy

sovereignty (säv′ rən tē)   *n.* The supreme and independent political authority

spartan (spär′ t'n)   *adj.* Characteristic of the people of ancient Sparta: hardy, stoical, severe, frugal

specious (spē′ shəs)   *adj.* Seeming to be good or sound without actually being so

spurious (spyōōr′ ē əs)   *adj.* False; artificial

squalor (skäl′ ər)   *n.* Filth; wretchedness

squander (skwän dər)   *v.* To spend or use wastefully

starboard fluke (flōōk)   *n.* The right half of a whale's tail

stark (stärk)   *adj.* Severe

staunch (stônch)   *adj.* Strong; unyielding

stratosphere (strat′ ə sfir′)   *n.* A portion of the upper atmosphere

stringency (strin′ jən šē)   *n.* Strictness; severity

stupefaction (stōō′ pə fak′ shən)   *n.* Stunned amazement or utter bewilderment

subjugation (sub′ jə gā′ shən)   *n.* The act of conquering

sublime (sə blīm′)   *adj.* Noble; majestic

subscribe (səb skrīb′)   *v.* To give support, sanction, or approval

subsistence (səb sis′ təns)   *n.* The means of support

suffice (sə fīs′)   *v.* To be enough

suffrage (suf′ rij)   *n.* A vote or voting

suffusion (sə fyōō′ zhən)   *n.* A fullness of color

sulfureous (sul fyoor′ ē əs)   *adj.* Greenish-yellow

sullen (sul′ ən)   *adj.* Sulky; glum

sundry (sun′ drē)   *adj.* Various, different

supercilious (sōō pər sil′ē əs)   *adj.* Disdainful

superfluous (sōō pʉr′ flōō wəs)   *adj.* Not needed

supposititious (sə päz′ ə tish′ əs)   *adj.* Supposed

surmise (sər mīz′)   *v.* To guess

sylvan (sil′ vən)   *adj.* Characteristic of the forest

synod (sin′ əd)   *n.* A high governing body in certain Christian churches

syntax (sin′ taks)   *n.* An orderly or systematic arrangement

syringa (sə rin′ gə)   *n.* A plant with large clusters of tiny white flowers

T

tableau (tab′ lō)   *n.* A representation of a silent, motionless scene

tabloid (tab′ loid) *n.* A newspaper with many pictures and short, often sensational, stories

tabula rasa (tab′ yə lə rä′ sə) *n.* A clean slate

taciturn (tas′ ə tʉrn′) *adj.* Almost always silent

tantrum (tan′ trəm) *n.* A childish fit of temper

tarn (tärn) *n.* A small lake

temerity (tə mer′ə tē) *n.* Foolhardy or heedless disregard of danger; recklessness

tempest (tem′ pist) *n.* A violent storm

tenement (ten′ə mənt) *n.* A building divided into apartments

teocallis (tē′ə ka′ lis) *n.* The ancient temples erected by Aztec Indians of Mexico and Central America

termagant (tʉr′ mə gənt) *n.* A quarrelsome woman

terrestrial (tə res′ trēəl) *adj.* Of this world

timorous (tim′ ər əs) *adj.* Full of fear

tortilla (tôr tē′ə) *n.* A thin, flat cake of cornmeal

tow (tō) *n.* The coarse and broken fibers of hemp or flax before spinning

transient (tran′ shənt) *adj.* Not permanent; passing away with time

translate (trans lāt′) *v.* To transport

transmogrify (trans mäg′ rə fī′) *v.* To transform in a grotesque manner

travail (trə vāl′) *n.* Painfully difficult or burdensome work

tremulous (trem′ yōo ləs) *adj.* Characterized by trembling; quivering

trepidation (trep′ədā′ shən) *n.* A fearful anxiety; apprehension

Triton (trī′ ′n) *n.* A Greek sea god with the body of a man and the tail of a fish, who usually carried a conch-shell trumpet

truncate (trʉn′ kāt) *v.* To cut short

tulle (tool) *n.* A thin, fine netting used for scarves

tumultuous (too mul′ chŏo wəs) *adj.* Wild and noisy; greatly agitated

turbulence (tʉr′ byə ləns) *n.* A commotion or wild disorder

tyranny (tir′ə nē) *n.* An oppressive and unjust government

U

unalienable (un āl′ yən ə b′l) *adj.* Not to be taken away

unconscionable (un kän′ shən ə b′l) *adj.* Unreasonable

undulate (un dōo′ lāt) *v.* To move in waves

unempathic (un em′ pa′thik) *adj.* Unable to share in another's emotions

unobtrusively (un əb trōo′ siv lē) *adv.* Inconspicuously

unperverted (un′ pər vʉrt′id) *adj.* Uncorrupted

unscrupulous (un skrōop′ yə ləs) *adj.* Not restrained by ideas of right and wrong

unsheathed (un shēthd′) *adj.* Removed from its case

unwonted (un wun′ tid) *adj.* Unfamiliar

usurer (yōo zhōo rər) *n.* A moneylender who charges very high interest

usurpation (yōo sər pā shən) *n.* The unlawful seizure of rights or privileges

V

vagary (və ger′ ē) *n.* An unpredictable occurrence; odd, unexpected action or notion

vagrant (vā grənt) *n.* An idle wanderer

vagueness (vāg′ nis) *n.* A lack of definition in shape or form

vanquished (van′ kwisht) *adj.* Defeated

venerable (ven′ ər ə b′l) *adj.* Commanding respect

venomous (ven′ əm əs) *adj.* Spiteful; malicious

venturous (ven′ chər əs) *adj.* Daring

veracious (və rā′ shəs) *adj.* Honest, truthful

verity (ver′ ə tē) *n.* The truth

vernacular (vər nak′ yə lər) *n.* The native speech, language, or dialect of a country or place

vigilance (vij′ ə ləns) *n.* Watchfulness

vigilant (vij′ə lənt) *adj.* Alert to danger

vignette (vin yet′) *n.* A picture or photograph with no definite border

vigor (vig′ ər) *n.* An active physical or mental force or strength

visage (viz′ ij) *n.* A facial appearance

vituperative (vī tōo′ prə tiv) *adj.* Spoken abusively

vociferation (vō sif′ ə rā shən) *n.* A loud or vehement shouting

vociferous (vō sif′ər əs) *adj.* Loud, noisy, or vehement in making one's feelings known

voracity (vô ras′ ə tē) *n.* Eagerness

votive (vōt′ iv) *adj.* Dedicated in fulfillment of a vow or pledge

vulcanism (vul′ kə niz′m) *n.* The series of phenomena connected with the origin and movement of molten rock

W

waggery (wag′ ər ē) *n.* A mischievous humor

wampum (wäm′ pəm) *n.* Small beads made of shells

wan (wän) *adj.* Sickly pale

wanton (wän′ t′n) *adj.* Senseless; unjustified

wily (wī′ lē) *adj.* Sly; cunning

X

xenophobic (zen′ə fō′ bik) *adj.* Afraid of strangers or foreigners

Z

zither (zith′ ər) *n.* A musical instrument with thirty to forty strings stretched across a flat soundboard and played with the fingers

INDEX OF FINE ART

INDEX OF SKILLS

Iamb (*See* Meter)
Iambic Pentameter, *201, 205, 1341*
Idyll, *1341*
Image, *1341*
Imagery, *355, 361, 535, 543, 881, 885, 1165, 1173, 1227, 1231,*
    1341–42
Imagism, *702, 853, 854, 1342*
Inciting Incident (*See* Plot)
Incongruity, *1342*
Informal Essay, *823, 829*
Internal Conflict (*See* Conflict)
Internal Rhyme, *665*
Inversion, *1342*
Irony, *545, 549, 666, 668, 677, 681, 1051, 1061, 1342*
Irony of Situation (*See* Irony)
Journal, *64, 67, 432, 437, 1342*
Legend, *1342*
Literary Letter, *153, 157, 1342*
Local Color, *1343*
Lyric Poem, *56, 57, 1219, 1223, 1343*
Main Character (*See* Character)
Metaphor, *384, 386, 967, 969, 1343*
Meter, *343, 347, 1343–44*
Minor Character (*See* Character)
Modernism, *701–702, 721, 727*
Modes of Discourse, *49, 55*
Monologue, *1344*
Monometer (*See* Meter)
Mood, *1344*
Motivation, 1344
Myth, *21, 25, 1344–45*
Narration, *49, 495, 499, 1133, 1137, 1345*
Narrative, *1133, 1137, 1345*
Narrative Poem, *934, 943, 1345*
Narrator, *1345*
Naturalism, *575, 605, 1345*
Nonfiction, *1345*
Novel, *606, 627, 1345–46*
Novella (*See* Novel)
Octave (*See* Stanza)
Ode, *1346*
Omniscient Point of View (*See* Point of View)
Onomatopoeia, *1243, 1247, 1346*
Oral Tradition, *33, 36, 1346*
Oratory, *123, 127, 1123, 1125, 1346*
Ornate Style, *1346*
Overstatement (*See* Hyperbole)
Oxymoron, *1346*
Parable, *1346*
Paradox, *279, 1346–47*
Parallelism, *141, 145, 1251, 1347*
Parody, *1347*
Pathos, *909, 911*
Personal Essay, *815, 821*
Personification, *135, 139, 1347*
Persuasion, *49, 69, 73, 1347*

Persuasive Speech, *69, 73*
    audience, *69*
    occasion, *69*
    speaker's qualification, *69*
    technique, *69*
Plain Style, *18, 1347*
Plot, *606, 627, 1347*
Poetry, *254–56, 1033–34, 1347*
    confessional, *1235, 1239*
    dramatic, *934, 941*
    narrative, *934, 943*
    visual, *1195, 1197*
Point of View, *492, 525, 533, 757, 761, 1079, 1083, 1101, 1105,*
    1347–48
Postmodernism, *1091, 1099*
Prose, *1348*
Protagonist, *1348*
Pun, *1348*
Puritan Plain Style, *18*
Pyrrhic (*See* Meter)
Quatrain (*See* Drama)
Realism, *575, 605, 1348*
Refrain, *421, 423, 1348*
Regionalism, *515, 523, 1348–49*
Repetition, *1349*
Resolution (*See* Plot)
Rhyme, *662, 1189, 1191, 1349*
    end, *1189*
    exact, *1189*
    internal, *662, 665*
    slant, *1189*
Rhyme Scheme, *1349*
Rhythm, *887, 890, 944, 949, 1201, 1207, 1349*
Rising Action, *1349*
Romance, *1349–50*
Romanticism, *177, 1350*
Round Character (*See* Character)
Run-on Line, *1350*
Satire, *951, 954; 1350*
Scansion, *343, 347, 1350*
Scene (*See* Drama)
Sensory Language, *1350*
Setting, *191, 199, 500, 507, 771, 785, 801, 806, 1115, 1120,*
    1175, 1186, 1350–51
Short Story, *1351*
Simile, *384, 386, 909, 913, 1351*
Single Effect, *207, 221*
Soliloquy, *1351*
Sonnet, *671, 675, 1351*
Sound Device, *222, 227, 662, 665, 1243, 1247*
Speaker, *685, 689, 963, 1351*
Spiritual, *420, 1351–52*
Spondee (*See* Meter)
Stage Directions (*See* Drama)
Staging, *973, 991*
Stanza, *1352*
Stanza Form, *333, 341*
Static Character (*See* Character)

CRITICAL THINKING AND READING

Time Order, *1364*
Transfer (*See* Propaganda Technique)
Understanding a Character's Motivation, *718, 1007, 1113*
Understanding Connotation, *18*
Understanding a Paradox, *279, 1131*
Understanding the Effect of Staging, *991*
Unreliable Testimonial (*See* Propaganda Technique)

SPEAKING AND LISTENING

Delivering a Speech, *127*
Oratory, *123, 1123*
Reading with Expression, *205, 265*

STUDY AND RESEARCH

Analyzing Situation, *1272*
Catalog, *1336*
Information Gathering from Memory and Experience:
  analyzing, *1273*
  charting, *1273*
  clustering, *1273*
  freewriting, *1273*
  questioning, *1273*
Information Gathering from Outside Source:
  books, *1273*
  computer information service, *1273*
  film, *1273*
  interviews, *1273*
  magazines, *1273*
  reference works, *1273*
  television programs, *1273*
Literary Map, *1268–69*
Making a Plan, 1273
Organizing Notes:
  chronological order, *1273*
  degree order, *1273*
  spatial order, *1273*
Using Reference Works:
  almanac, *1334*

THINKING AND WRITING

Adapting a Folk tale, *189*
Comparing and Contrasting, *31*
  accounts, *55*
  arguments, *145*
  attitudes, *303*
  characters, *523*
  constitutions, *31*
  essays, *289, 821, 1159*
  origin of myths, *27*
  poems, *879, 1223*
  settings, *1186*
  speeches, *441*
  stories, *233, 761*
  tones, *353*
  writers, *627, 689*

Creating an Extended Metaphor, *969*
Developing a Personification, *139*
Drafting, *1276–77*
Editorial Symbols, *1280*
Evaluating a Character's Behavior, *660*
Evaluating a Literary Work, *1314*
Evaluating Persuasive Techniques, *73*
Evaluating Persuasive Writing, *1320*
Exploring a Different Point of View, *533*
Exposition:
  supporting a generalization, *949*
  supporting an opinion, *559*
  supporting a statement of theme, *221*
Journal, *1342*
Prewriting, *1272–75*
Proofreading, *1279–80*
Proofreading Checklist, *1279*
Responding to Criticism, *177, 199, 383, 543, 1019, 1071, 1077, 1089, 1113, 1173, 1191, 1207, 1249*
Responding to a Poem, *391, 1263*
Responding to a Statement, *121, 227, 727, 872*
Revising, *1276–77*
Revision Checklist, *1276*
Writing a Biographical Sketch, *850*
Writing About a Character, *1049*
Writing About a Poem, *1308*
Writing About a Short Story, *1305*
Writing About a Symbol, *926*
Writing About a Writer's Attitudes, *1153, 1217*
Writing About Character, *1297*
Writing About Conflict and Theme, *573*
Writing About Conformity, *271*
Writing About Critical Response, *1145*
Writing About Drama, *1311*
Writing About Figures of Speech, *1288*
Writing About Historical Context, *745*
Writing About History, *276*
Writing About Images, *1282*
Writing About Imagism, *858*
Writing About Irony, *549*
Writing About Lyric Poetry, *18*
Writing About Plot, *1294*
Writing About Point of View, *1300*
Writing About Related Themes, *1125*
Writing About Revolutionary Literature, *133*
Writing About Setting *785, 806, 1291*
Writing About Sound, *1285*
Writing About Staging, *991*
Writing About Structure, *1099*
Writing About Style, *921*
Writing About Symbolic Meaning, *1083*
Writing About Symbolism and Theme, *330*
Writing About Symbols and Allusions, *799*
Writing About Techniques, *755*
Writing About Theme, *669, 718, 1303*
Writing About the Role of Spirituals, *423*
Writing a Comparative Evaluation, *1317*
Writing a Conceit, *63*
Writing a Confessional Poem, *1241*
Writing a Continuation of the Story, *769*

UNDERSTANDING LANGUAGE

INDEX OF TITLES BY THEMES

THE INDIVIDUAL AND SOCIETY

JOURNEY TO PERSONAL FULFILLMENT

A TIME FOR COURAGE

FANTASY AND THE UNEXPLAINED

THE ENVIRONMENT AND THE TOUCHED AND UNTOUCHED EARTH

QUEST FOR UNDERSTANDING

INDEX OF AUTHORS AND TITLES

Page numbers in italics refer to biographical information.

ACKNOWLEDGMENTS (continued)

Doubleday (continued)
1975, 1976 by Ann Beattie. "An Occurrence at Owl Creek Bridge" from *The Complete Stories of Ambrose Bierce*, published by Doubleday & Company, Inc. "The Rain Guitar" by James Dickey first appeared in *The New Yorker*. From the book *The Strength of Fields*, copyright © 1972 by James Dickey. "Night Journey" and "The Waking" copyright 1940, 1948 by Theodore Roethke. "Once More, the Round" copyright © 1962 by Beatrice Roethke as administratrix of the Estate of Theodore Roethke. All poems from the book *The Collected Poems of Theodore Roethke*. Reprinted by permission of Doubleday.

Rita Dove
"This Life" from Rita Dove, *The Yellow House on the Corner*. Carnegie-Mellon University Press, Pittsburgh 1980. Reprinted by permission of the author.

Mari Evans
Lines from "Where Have You Gone" from *I Am a Black Woman* by Mari Evans, published in 1970 by William Morrow & Co., Inc. Reprinted by permission of the author.

Farrar, Straus and Giroux, Inc.
"Engineer-Private Paul Klee Misplaces an Aircraft Between Milbertshofen and Cambrai, March 1916" from *Sadness* by Donald Barthelme. Copyright © 1970, 1971, 1972 by Donald Barthelme. "House Guest" and "Little Exercise" from *The Complete Poems 1927–1979* by Elizabeth Bishop. Copyright 1946, © 1968; renewal copyright © 1980 by Alice Helen Methfessel; copyright © 1983 by Alice Helen Methfessel. Originally appeared in *The New Yorker*. Excerpt from "Visits to St. Elizabeths" from *The Complete Poems 1927–1979* by Elizabeth Bishop. Copyright 1983 by Alice Helen Methfessel. Copyright 1957 by Elizabeth Bishop. Excerpt from *Play It As It Lays* by Joan Didion. Copyright 1970 by Joan Didion. "The Death of the Ball Turret Gunner" and "Losses" from *The Complete Poems* by Randall Jarrell. Copyright 1945, 1951, © 1955 by Randall Jarrell; copyright renewed 1968, 1969 by Mrs. Randall Jarrell. "Hawthorne" from *Selected Poems* by Robert Lowell. Copyright © 1964 by Robert Lowell; copyright renewed 1972, 1974, 1975 by Robert Lowell. "The First Seven Years" from *The Magic Barrel* by Bernard Malamud. Copyright 1950, 1951, 1952, 1953, 1954, © 1955, 1956, 1958 by Bernard Malamud. Excerpt from *Rising from the Plains* by John McPhee. Copyright © 1986 by John McPhee. Reprinted by permission of Farrar, Straus and Giroux, Inc.

Harcourt Brace Jovanovich, Inc.
"anyone lived in a pretty how town" copyright 1940 by E. E. Cummings; renewed 1968 by Marion Morehouse Cummings. "old age sticks" copyright 1958 by E. E. Cummings. Both poems reprinted from his volume *Complete Poems 1913–1962* by E. E. Cummings. "The Signature" copyright © 1956 by Elizabeth Enright; renewed 1984 by Nicholas W. Gillham, Oliver Gillham, and Robert Gillham II. Reprinted from *The Riddle of the Fly and Other Stories* by Elizabeth Enright. "The Life You Save May Be Your Own" copyright 1953 by Flannery O'Connor; renewed 1981 by Mrs. Regina O'Connor. Reprinted from *A Good Man Is Hard to Find and Other Stories* by Flannery O'Connor. "The Jilting of Granny Weatherall" copyright 1930, 1958 by Katherine Anne Porter. Reprinted from her volume *Flowering Judas and Other Stories*. "Chicago" from *Chicago Poems* by Carl Sandburg, copyright 1916 by Holt,

Rinehart and Winston, Inc.; renewed 1944 by Carl Sandburg. "Grass" from *Cornhuskers* by Carl Sandburg, copyright 1918 by Holt, Rinehart and Winston, Inc.; renewed 1946 by Carl Sandburg. Excerpted from "Lincoln Speaks at Gettysburg" in *Abraham Lincoln: The War Years*, Volume Two, by Carl Sandburg, copyright 1939 by Harcourt Brace Jovanovich, Inc.; renewed 1966 by Carl Sandburg. Excerpts from *The People, Yes* by Carl Sandburg, copyright 1936 by Harcourt Brace Jovanovich, Inc.; renewed 1964 by Carl Sandburg. "Expect Nothing" from *Revolutionary Petunias & Other Poems*, copyright © 1973 by Alice Walker. "A Worn Path" copyright 1941, 1969 by Eudora Welty. Reprinted from her volume *A Curtain of Green and Other Stories*. "The Beautiful Changes" from *The Beautiful Changes and Other Poems*, copyright 1947, 1975 by Richard Wilbur. Reprinted by permission of Harcourt Brace Jovanovich, Inc.

Harcourt Brace Jovanovich, Inc. and Faber and Faber Ltd.
"The Love Song of J. Alfred Prufrock" and excerpt from "The Waste Land" from *Collected Poems 1909–1962* by T. S. Eliot, copyright 1936 by Harcourt Brace Jovanovich, Inc.; copyright © 1963, 1964 by T. S. Eliot. Reprinted by permission of the publishers.

Harper & Row, Publishers, Inc.
"The Tooth, the Whole Tooth, and Nothing but the Tooth" from *Inside Benchley* by Robert Benchley. Copyright 1922 by Harper & Row, Publishers, Inc.; renewed 1950 by Gertrude Benchley. "Any Human to Another" from *On These I Stand: An Anthology of the Best-Loved Poems by Countee Cullen*. Copyright 1935 by Harper & Row, Publishers, Inc.; renewed 1963 by Ida M. Cullen. Lines from "Yet Do I Marvel" from *On These I Stand: An Anthology of the Best-Loved Poems by Countee Cullen*. Copyright 1925 by Harper & Row, Publishers, Inc.; renewed 1953 by Ida M. Cullen. "Traveling Through the Dark" from *Stories That Could Be True: New and Collected Poems* by William Stafford. Copyright © 1960 by William Stafford. From *Roughing It* (titled "Lost in a Snowstorm") by Mark Twain. "The Boys' Ambition" from *Life on the Mississippi* by Mark Twain. "The Notorious Jumping Frog of Calaveras County" from *Sketches New and Old* by Mark Twain. "Tom Quartz" from *The Complete Short Stories of Mark Twain* edited by Charles Neider. "Walden" from *One Man's Meat* by E. B. White. Copyright 1939, renewed 1967 by E. B. White. Reprinted by permission of Harper & Row, Publishers, Inc.

Harper & Row, Publishers, Inc. and Olwyn Hughes
"Mirror" from *The Collected Poems of Sylvia Plath* edited by Ted Hughes. Copyright © 1963 by Ted Hughes. Published in London by Faber and Faber Ltd., copyright Ted Hughes 1971 and 1981. Reprinted by permission.

Harvard University Press
"Upon the Burning of Our House" from *The Complete Works of Anne Bradstreet* edited by Jeannine Hensley. Copyright © 1967 by the President and Fellows of Harvard College. From "History of the Dividing Line" in *The Prose Works of William Byrd of Westover* edited by Louis B. Wright. Copyright 1966 by the President and Fellows of Harvard College. "A narrow Fellow in the Grass," "As imperceptibly as grief," "Because I could not stop for Death—," "'Hope' is the thing with feathers—," "How happy is the little Stone," "I felt a Funeral in my Brain," "I heard a Fly buzz—when I died—," "I like to see it lap the miles—," "I never saw a Moor—," "Much Madness is divinest Sense—," "My life closed twice before

its close;" "Success is counted sweetest," "Tell all the Truth but tell it slant—," "The Bustle in a House," "The Soul selects her own Society—," "There's a certain Slant of Light," and "This is my letter to the World" reprinted by permission of the publishers and the Trustees of Amherst College from *The Poems of Emily Dickinson* edited by Thomas H. Johnson, Cambridge, Mass.: The Belknap Press of Harvard University Press, copyright 1951, © 1955, 1979, 1983 by The President and Fellows of Harvard College.

Hill and Wang, a division of Farrar, Straus and Giroux, Inc.
Adapted from "Sinners in the Hands of an Angry God" from *Jonathan Edwards: Representative Selections* by Clarence H. Faust and Thomas H. Johnson. Copyright 1935, © 1962 by Hill and Wang, Inc. Reprinted by permission of Hill and Wang, a division of Farrar, Straus and Giroux, Inc.

Henry Holt and Company, Inc.
"Stopping by Woods on a Snowy Evening" copyright 1923, © 1969 by Holt, Rinehart and Winston. Copyright 1951 by Robert Frost. Reprinted from *The Poetry of Robert Frost* edited by Edward Connery Lathem. "Acquainted with the Night," "After Apple-Picking," "Birches," "Fire and Ice," "Mending Wall," "Nothing Gold Can Stay," "Out, Out—," "The Death of the Hired Man," and "The Wood-Pile" from *The Poetry of Robert Frost* edited by Edward Connery Lathem. Copyright © 1969 by Holt, Rinehart and Winston, Inc. Copyright © 1962 by Robert Frost. Copyright © 1975 by Lesley Frost Ballantine. Reprinted by permission of Henry Holt and Company, Inc.

M. Carl Holman
Lines from "Three Brown Girls Singing" by M. Carl Holman, reprinted by permission of the author.

Houghton Mifflin Company
"A White Heron" from *A White Heron and Other Stories* by Sarah Orne Jewett. "Patterns" from *The Complete Poetical Works of Amy Lowell.* Copyright © 1955 by Houghton Mifflin Company; copyright © renewed 1983 by Houghton Mifflin Company, Brinton P. Roberts, Esquire, and G. D'Andelot Belin, Esquire. "Ars Poetica" from *New and Collected Poems 1917–1976* by Archibald MacLeish. Copyright © 1976 by Archibald MacLeish. From "The Navaho Origin Legend" in *Navaho Legends*, collected and translated by Washington Matthews. From *The Mortgaged Heart* by Carson McCullers. Copyright 1940, 1941, 1942, 1945, 1948, 1949, 1953, © 1956, 1959, 1963, 1971 by Floria V. Lasky, Executrix of the Estate of Carson McCullers; copyright © 1955, 1957, 1963 by Carson McCullers. "The Edge of the Great Rift" from *Sunrise with Seamonsters* by Paul Theroux. Copyright © 1985 by Cape Cod Scriveners Company. "A Noiseless Patient Spider,"."Beat! Beat! Drums!" and "When I Heard the Learn'd Astronomer" from *Complete Poetry and Selected Prose of Walt Whitman* edited by J. E. Miller, Jr. Reprinted by permission of Houghton Mifflin Company.

Johnson Publishing Company, Inc.
From *My Bondage and My Freedom* by Frederick Douglass.

Alfred A. Knopf, Inc.
From *Of Plymouth Plantation 1620–1647* by William Bradford, edited with Notes and Introduction by Samuel Eliot Morison. Copyright 1952 by Samuel Eliot Morison and renewed 1980 by Emily Beck. "Katherine Comes to Yellow Sky" from *A Dove of the East and Other Stories* by Mark Helprin. Copyright © 1975 by Mark Helprin. Lines from "April Rain Song" from *The Dream Keeper and Other Poems* by Langston Hughes. Copyright 1932 by Alfred A. Knopf, Inc. and renewed 1960 by Langston Hughes. "The Negro Speaks of Rivers" copyright 1926 by Alfred A. Knopf, Inc. and renewed 1954 by Langston Hughes. Reprinted from *Selected Poems of Langston Hughes* by Langston Hughes. "Janet Waking" copyright 1927 by Alfred A. Knopf, Inc. and renewed 1955 by John Crowe Ransom. Reprinted from *Selected Poems, Third Edition, Revised and Enlarged* by John Crowe Ransom. "Anecdote of the Jar" and "Disillusionment of Ten O'Clock" from *The Collected Poems of Wallace Stevens* by Wallace Stevens. Copyright 1923 and renewed 1951 by Wallace Stevens. "The Slump" copyright © 1968 by John Updike. Reprinted from *Museums and Women and Other Stories* by John Updike. Reprinted by permission of Alfred A. Knopf, Inc.

Alfred A Knopf, Inc. and Olwyn Hughes Literary Agency
Lines from "Mushrooms" copyright © 1960 by Sylvia Plath. Reprinted from *The Colossus and Other Poems* by Sylvia Plath, by permission.

Life Picture Service, a department of Time Inc.
From "A Vision Beyond Time and Place" by N. Scott Momaday, published in *Life* Magazine, 1971, © 1971 Time Inc.

Little, Brown and Company
"There is a solitude of space" from *The Complete Poems of Emily Dickinson* edited by Thomas H. Johnson. Copyright 1914, 1942 by Martha Dickinson Bianchi. By permission of Little, Brown and Company.

Liveright Publishing Corporation
"since feeling is first" reprinted from *No Thanks* by E. E. Cummings, by permission of Liveright Publishing Corporation. Copyright 1935 by E. E. Cummings, Copyright © 1968 by Marion Morehouse Cummings. Copyright © 1973, 1978 by The Trustees for the E. E. Cummings Trust. Copyright © 1973, 1978 by George James Firmage. Lines from "Astronauts" from *American Journal, Poems* by Robert Hayden, by permission of Liveright Publishing Corporation. Copyright © 1982 by Irma Hayden. Copyright © 1978 by Robert Hayden. "Those Winter Sundays" is reprinted from *Angle of Ascent, New and Selected Poems* by Robert Hayden, by permission of Liveright Publishing Corporation. Copyright © 1975, 1972, 1970, 1966 by Robert Hayden. Lines from "Song of the Son", reprinted from *Cane* by Jean Toomer, by permission of Liveright Publishing Corporation. Copyright 1923 by Boni & Liveright. Copyright © renewed 1951 by Jean Toomer. "Storm Ending" is reprinted from *Cane* by Jean Toomer, by permission of Liveright Publishing Corporation. Copyright 1923 by Boni & Liveright. Copyright renewed 1951 by Jean Toomer.

The Sterling Lord Agency, Inc.
Selections from "The Crisis, Number 1" in *The Selected Work of Tom Paine* edited by Howard Fast. Copyright 1945 by Howard Fast. Reprinted by permission of The Sterling Lord Agency, Inc.

Macmillan Publishing Company
Lines from "Bird-Witted" from *Collected Poems* by Marianne Moore. Copyright 1941, and renewed 1969, by Marianne Moore. Lines from "Nevertheless" from *Collected Poems* by

permission of Macmillan Publishing Company. ''Poetry''
reprinted with permission of Macmillan Publishing Company
from *Collected Poems* by Marianne Moore. Copyright 1935
by Marianne Moore, renewed 1963 by Marianne Moore and
T. S. Eliot. Lines from ''February Twilight'', reprinted by permission of Macmillan Publishing Company, from *Collected
Poems* by Sara Teasdale. Copyright 1926 by Macmillan Publishing Company; renewed 1954 by Mamie T. Wheless.

Naomi Long Madgett
Lines from ''Writing a Poem'' in *Pink Ladies in the Afternoon*
(Detroit: Lotus Press, 1972) by Naomi Long Madgett. Reprinted
by permission of the author.

Laureen Mar
Lines from ''Chinatown 1'' by Laureen Mar, originally published in *The Greenfield Review*. Copyright © by Laureen Mar,
and reprinted with her permission.

Ellen C. Masters
''Fiddler Jones'' and ''Lucinda Matlock'' from *Spoon River Anthology* by Edgar Lee Masters, published by Macmillan Publishing Company.

William Morrow & Company, Inc.
''Plucking Out a Rhythm'' from *Before the War: Poems As They
Happened* by Lawson Fusao Inada. Copyright © 1971 by
Lawson Fusao Inada. Reprinted by permission of William Mor-
row & Company, Inc.

Howard Nemerov
''Storm Windows'' from *The Collected Poems of Howard
Nemerov*, The University of Chicago Press, 1977. Reprinted
by permission of the author.

New Directions Publishing Corporation
''Heat'' and ''Pear Tree'' by H.D., *Collected Poems,
1912–1944*. Copyright © 1982 by The Estate of Hilda Doolittle. ''Oread'' from H.D., *Selected Poems*. Copyright 1925,
1953, © 1957 by Norman Holmes Pearson. ''Merritt Parkway''
by Denise Levertov, *Collected Earlier Poems, 1940–1960*.
Copyright © 1961 by Denise Levertov Goodman. ''Canto 13''
by Ezra Pound, *The Cantos of Ezra Pound*. Copyright 1934
by Ezra Pound. ''In a Station of the Metro'' and ''The River-
Merchant's Wife: A Letter'' by Ezra Pound, *Personae*.
Copyright 1926 by Ezra Pound. ''The Locust Tree,'' ''The Red
Wheelbarrow,'' and ''This Is Just to Say'' by William Carlos
Williams, *Collected Poems Volume I: 1909–1939*. Copyright
1938 by New Directions Publishing Corporation. Reprinted by
permission of New Directions Publishing Corporation.

New York University Press
From the ''Preface'' to *Walt Whitman: Leaves of Grass, Read-
er's Comprehensive Edition* edited by Harold W. Blodgett and
Sculley Bradley. Copyright © 1965 by New York University.
Reprinted by permission of New York University Press.

W. W. Norton & Company, Inc.
''The Observer'' is reprinted from *The Fact of A Doorframe,
Poems Selected and New, 1950–1984*, by Adrienne Rich, by
permission of W. W. Norton & Company, Inc. Copyright ©
1984 by Adrienne Rich. Copyright 1975, 1978 by W. W. Norton & Company, Inc. Copyright © 1981 by Adrienne Rich.

From ''Civil Disobedience'' reprinted from *Walden and Civil
Disobedience* by Henry David Thoreau, edited by Owen Thomas. By permission of W. W. Norton & Company, Inc. Copyright
© 1966 by W. W. Norton & Company, Inc.

Harold Ober Associates Inc.
''A Black Man Talks of Reaping'' from *Personals* by Arna Bon-
temps. Copyright © 1963 by Arna Bontemps. Lines from
''Southern Mansions'' from *Personals* by Arna Bontemps.
Copyright © 1963 by Arna Bontemps. Reprinted by permis-
sion of Harold Ober Associates Inc.

Simon J. Ortiz
''Hunger in New York City'' from *Going For the Rain: Poems*
by Simon J. Ortiz. Published by Harper & Row. Reprinted by
permission of Simon J. Ortiz.

Grace Paley
''Anxiety'' from *Later the Same Day* by Grace Paley, published
by Farrar, Straus, and Giroux. Copyright © 1985 by Grace
Paley; copyright 1985 Farrar, Straus and Giroux, Inc. Reprint-
ed by permission of Grace Paley c/o Elaine Markson Literary
Agency, Inc., New York.

Random House, Inc.
''A Ride Through Spain'' copyright 1950 by Truman Capote.
Reprinted from *The Dogs Bark: Public People and Private
Places* by Truman Capote. Excerpt from ''Hidden Name and
Complex Fate'' from *Shadow and Act* by Ralph Ellison. Copyright 1953, © 1964 by Ralph Ellison. ''The Bear'' (7,000-word
version) by William Faulkner, copyright 1942 and renewed
1970 by Estelle Faulkner and Jill Faulkner Summers. An expanded version of this story appears in *Go Down, Moses* by
William Faulkner. ''Evening Hawk'' copyright © 1975 by
Robert Penn Warren, and ''Gold Glade'' copyright © 1957
by Robert Penn Warren, reprinted from *Selected Poems,
1923–1975* by Robert Penn Warren. Reprinted by permission
of Random House, Inc.

Random House, Inc. and Faber and Faber Ltd.
''The Unknown Citizen'' copyright 1940 and renewed 1968
by W. H. Auden, and ''Who's Who'' copyright 1937 and
renewed 1965 by W. H. Auden, reprinted from *W. H. Auden:
Collected Poems* by W. H. Auden, edited by Edward Mendel-
son. Reprinted by permission of the publishers.

Russell and Volkening, Inc., as agents for the author
''Average Waves in Unprotected Waters'' by Anne Tyler, published in *The New Yorker*, February 28, 1977. Copyright ©
1977 by Anne Tyler. Reprinted by permission of Russell and
Volkening, Inc., as agents for the author.

**Charles Scribner's Sons, an imprint of Macmillan Publish-
ing Co.**
F. Scott Fitzgerald, ''Winter Dreams'' from *All The Sad Young
Men*. Copyright 1922 Frances Scott Fitzgerald Lanahan;
copyright renewed. Ernest Hemingway, ''In Another Country''
from *Men Without Women*. Copyright 1927 Charles Scribner's
Sons; copyright renewed © 1955 Ernest Hemingway. ''Song
of the Chattahoochee'' from *The Poems of Sidney Lanier*. Barry
Lopez, excerpted from *Arctic Dreams*. Copyright © 1986 Barry
Holstun Lopez. ''Luke Havergal'' and ''Miniver Cheevy'' from
Collected Poems by Edwin Arlington Robinson, published by
Charles Scribner's Sons. ''Richard Cory'' from *The Children*

of the Night by Edwin Arlington Robinson, published by Charles Scribner's Sons. John Hall Wheelock, "Earth" from *The Gardener And Other Poems.* Copyright © 1961 John Hall Wheelock. Thomas Wolfe, "The Far And the Near" from *From Death to Morning.* Copyright 1935 International Magazine Company, Inc.; copyright renewed © 1963 Paul Gitlin. Reprinted with the permission of Charles Scribner's Sons, an imprint of Macmilllan Publishing Co.

Leslie Marmon Silko
Lines from "Where Mountain Lion Lay Down With Deer" by Leslie Marmon Silko from *Voices of the Rainbow* edited by Kenneth Rosen. Reprinted by permission of Leslie Marmon Silko.

Simon & Schuster, Inc.
"On the Mall" from *The White Album* by Joan Didion. Copyright © 1979 by Joan Didion. From *Lonesome Dove* by Larry McMurtry. Copyright © 1985 by Larry McMurtry. Reprinted by permission of Simon & Schuster, Inc. Pronunciation key from *Webster's New World Dictionary*—Second College Edition. Copyright © 1984 by Simon & Schuster, Inc. Reprinted by permission.

Smithsonian Institution Press
"Song Concerning a Dream of the Thunderbirds" from *Teton Sioux Music* by Frances Densmore. Bureau of American Ethnology Bulletin 61. Smithsonian Institution, Washington, D.C., 1918. "Spring Song" from *Chippewa Music II* by Frances Densmore. Bureau of American Ethnology Bulletin 53. Smithsonian Institution, Washington, D.C., 1913. Reprinted by permission of Smithsonian Institution Press.

Donald E. Stanford
"Huswifery" and "Upon a Wasp Chilled with Cold" reprinted by permission from *The Poems of Edward Taylor* edited by Donald E. Stanford, © 1960 Donald E. Stanford.

Syracuse University Press
From "The Iroquois Constitution" from Arthur C. Parker, "The Constitution of the Five Nations" in *Parker on the Iroquois,* edited with an introduction by William N. Fenton. Syracuse, N.Y.: Syracuse University Press, 1968. By permission of the publisher.

Rosemary A. Thurber
"The Night the Ghost Got In" copyright 1933, © 1961 by James Thurber. From *My Life and Hard Times,* published by Harper & Row. Cartoon caption: "Well, if I called the wrong number, why did you answer the phone?" Copyright 1943 James Thurber; copyright © 1971 Helen Thurber and Rosemary A. Thurber. From *Men, Women and Dogs,* published by Harcourt Brace Jovanovich, Inc. Reprinted by permission.

Twayne Publishers, a division of G. K. Hall & Company, Boston
"The Tropics of New York" from *The Poems of Claude McKay* by Claude McKay, copyright © 1981. Reprinted with the permission of Twayne Publishers, a division of G. K. Hall & Co., Boston.

University of Minnesota Press
"Still Life" from *An American Takes a Walk and Other Poems* by Reed Whittemore. Reprinted with the permission of the University of Minnesota Press, Minneapolis. Copyright © 1956 by Reed Whittemore.

The University of North Carolina Press
"To His Excellency General Washington" and lines from "An Hymn to the Morning" from *The Poems of Phillis Wheatley* edited by Julian D. Mason, Jr. Copyright © 1966 by The University of North Carolina Press. Reprinted by permission of the publisher.

Vanguard Press, Inc.
"Journey" reprinted from *The Poisoned Kiss and Other Stories From the Portuguese* by Fernandes/Joyce Carol Oates, by permission of the publisher, Vanguard Press, Inc. Copyright © 1975, 1974, 1972, 1971 by Joyce Carol Oates.

Viking Penguin Inc.
"Sophistication" from *Winesburg, Ohio* by Sherwood Anderson. Copyright 1919 by B. W. Huebsch; copyright renewed 1947 by Eleanor Copenhaver Anderson. "Flight" from *The Long Valley* by John Steinbeck. Copyright 1938, renewed © 1966 by John Steinbeck. "Be beautiful, noble, like the antique ant" (Poem #39) from *Have Come, Am Here* by José Garcia Villa. Copyright 1942, renewed © 1969 by José Garcia Villa. Reprinted by permission of Viking Penguin Inc.

Wesleyan University Press
"Lying in a Hammock at William Duffy's Farm in Pine Island, Minnesota" copyright © 1961 by James Wright. Reprinted from *Collected Poems* by James Wright, by permission of Wesleyan University Press.

Note: Every effort has been made to locate the copyright owner of material reprinted in this book. Omissions brought to our attention will be corrected in subsequent editions.

ART CREDITS

Cover and Title Page: Winslow Homer, *Old Friends,* Worcester Art Museum, Worcester, Massachusetts; **p. 1:** *Landing of Columbus,* John Vanderlyn, Three Lions; **p. 3:** *The Beginning of New England,* after the painting by Clyde O. Deland, The Granger Collection; **pp. 4, 5:** *Columbus Lands at San Salvador,* The Granger Collection; *Captain John Smith,* The Granger Collection; *Galileo,* The Granger Collection; *Jamestown,* The Granger Collection; *The Mayflower,* The Granger Collection; The *Mona Lisa,* Leonardo da Vinci, Three Lions; *William Shakespeare* (1546–1616), The "Chandos" portrait, oil on canvas by an unknown artist, The Granger Collection; The King James Bible, Three Lions; **p. 6, 7:** Nat Bacon's Rebellion, The Granger Collection; *Accused of Witchcraft,* Douglas Volk, Three Lions; *The Trial of John Peter Zenger,* The Granger Collection; Rembrandt, *The Night-Watch* (Company of Franz Banningh Cocq), 1642, The Granger Collection; *Johann Sebastian Bach* (1685–1750), lithograph after the painting by Elias Gottlob Haussmann, The Granger Collection; illustration from *Gulliver's Travels,* The Granger Collection; illustration from *Robinson Crusoe,* Currier & Ives, Three Lions; **p. 8:** *The First Thanksgiving,* J. L. G. Ferris, Three Lions; **p. 9:** *Landing at Jamestown,* 1608–09 (also called *Hope of Jamestown,* John Gadsby Chapman, Mr. and Mrs. Paul Mellon, Upperville, VA; **p. 10:** *Pilgrims on the Way to Church,* Charles Yardley Turner, Three Lions; **p. 11:** Harvard Hall (College), Cambridge, Massachusetts, built 1672–82, colored engraving, The Granger Collection; **p. 12:** The Trial of Two "Witches" at Salem, Massachusetts, in 1692, illustration by Howard Pyle, The Granger Collection; **pp. 16–17:** The Parson Barnard House,

North Andover Historical Society; **p. 19:** Philip (Metacomet), American Wampanoag Indian Chief, colored engraving, 1772, by Paul Revere, The Granger Collection; **p. 20:** (top) *Song of the Aspen* (detail), Bert G. Phillips, Harrison Eiteljorg Collection; (bottom) detail from credit for p. 26; **p. 26:** The Place of Emergence and the Four Worlds, Navajo, Wheelwright Museum of the American Indian; **pp. 28** (detail), **29:** *Red Jacket,* George Catlin, The Thomas Gilcrease Institute of American History and Art, Tulsa, Oklahoma; **p. 32:** (top) detail of credit for p. 34; (middle) B. C. Seltzer, *Chief Joseph's Surrender* (detail), The Thomas Gilcrease Institute of American History and Art, Tulsa, Oklahoma; (bottom) detail from credit for p. 38; **pp. 34–35:** Eastman, Seth, *Indian Village, River Gila,* Museum of Art, Rhode Island School of Design, Gift of RISD Library; **p. 38:** *The Mystic* (detail), William R. Leight, The Thomas Gilcrease Institute of American History and Art, Tulsa, Oklahoma; **p. 39:** *The Arrival of the Englishmen in Virginia,* colored line engraving, 1590, by Theodor de Bry, The Granger Collection; **p. 40:** *John Smith,* colored lithograph, 19th century, The Granger Collection; **p. 45:** A. C. Warren, *Founding the First Permanent English Settlement in America,* Print collection, Miriam and Ira D. Wallach Division of Art, Prints & Photographs, The New York Public Library, Astor, Lenox and Tilden Foundations; **p. 48:** *William Bradford,* aquatint, French, 18th century, The Granger Collection; **pp. 50–51:** *The Coming of the Mayflower,* N. C. Wyeth, from the Collection of the Metropolitan Life Insurance Company, New York City, Photograph by Malcolm Varon; **p. 52:** *The Landing of the Pilgrims at Plymouth, Mass. Dec. 22nd 1620,* lithograph by Currier & Ives, 1876, The Harry T. Peters Collection, Museum of the City of New York; **p. 57:** *Reading Woman,* Terborch, Three Lions; **p. 60:** Wanda Gág, *Evening,* 1929, Collection of the Tamarind Institute, University of New Mexico; **p. 64:** *William Byrd* (detail), line engraving by Vander Gucht, The Granger Collection; **p. 66:** *Dismal Swamp,* Flavius J. Fisher, Randolph-Macon Women's College, Maier Museum of Art; **p. 68:** *Jonathan Edwards* (detail), 1794, Amos Doolittle, National Portrait Gallery, Smithsonian Institution; **p. 71:** Frank E. Schoonover, *The Puritan,* oil on canvas, ca. 1898, Collection of the Brandywine River Museum, Gift of Mr. and Mrs. Jacob J. Foster; **p. 74:** *Cotton Mather* (detail), 1727, mezzotint, Peter Pelham, The Granger Collection; **p. 75:** *A Witch Trial in Salem, Massachusetts, in 1692,* The Granger Collection; **p. 77:** *A Witch Trial in Salem, Massachusetts, in 1692,* The Granger Collection; **pp. 82–83:** *The Signing of the Constitution,* 1787, Howard Chandler Christy, The Granger Collection; **p. 85:** Embossed tax stamp issued by the British Government in 1765 for use in the American Colonies, The Granger Collection; **pp. 86–87:** Benjamin Franklin's experiment proving the identity of lightning and electricity, June 1752, lithograph, 1876, by Currier & Ives; *Poor Richard's Almanack,* The Granger Collection; *Phillis Wheatley,* The Granger Collection; Richard Arkwright's Spinning Frame, The Granger Collection; Apparatus Used in Priestley's Experiments, The Granger Collection; Voltaire, marble bust, 1778, by Jean Antoine Houdon, The Granger Collection; *Colonists Protest Stamp Act,* Tory stamp agents tarred and feathered and carried in a cart during an anti-Stamp Act demonstration in 1765, colored engraving from John Trumbull's M'Fingal, 1795, The Granger Collection; William Hershel, The Granger Collection; **pp. 88, 89:** *George Washington Presiding at the Constitutional Convention at Philadelphia in 1787,* after the painting by Junius Brutus Stearns, The Granger Collection; *Eli Whitney's Cotton Gin,* The Granger Collection; *Independence Hall,* Philadelphia, The Granger Collection;

Major General Benjamin Lincoln Accepting the British Surrender at Yorktown on 19 October 1781, lithograph by Nathaniel Currier after John Trumbull, The Granger Collection; *Storming of the Bastille,* 18th century, François DuPont, French, 1820–1878; Three Lions, *The Death of Socrates,* oil on canvas, 1787, by Jacques Louis David, the Granger Collection; A boastful James Boswell hawking his publications, which include his forthcoming life of Samuel Johnson, caricature etching, 1896, Thomas Rowlandson, The Granger Collection; *Napoleon Bonaparte, as First Consul,* J. A. Dominque Ingres, Three Lions, **p. 90:** *The Boston Massacre, 5 March 1770,* colored engraving, 1770, by Paul Revere after the drawing by Henry Pelham, The Granger Collection; **p. 91:** *The Battle of Lexington at the Beginning of the Combat,* line engraving, 1832, by Amos Doolittle and John W. Barber, The Granger Collection; **p. 92:** *The Battle of Concord, The Engagement at the North Bridge, April 19, 1775,* line engraving, 1775, by Amos Doolittle, The Granger Collection; **p. 93:** *George Washington Addressing the Second Continental Congress at Philadelphia,* contemporary colored line engraving, The Granger Collection; **p. 94:** *Patrick Henry Speaking Against the Stamp Act in the Virginia House of Burgesses in 1765,* colored line engraving, 19th century, The Granger Collection; **p. 95:** Cover of Tom Paine's *Common Sense,* 1776, The Granger Collection; Title page of Volume I of *The Federalist,* New York, 1788, The Granger Collection; **p. 100:** *Benjamin Franklin in 1777,* Augustus de Sainte Aubin after Cochin, Philadelphia Museum of Art, given by Mrs. John D. Rockefeller; **p. 106:** *Benjamin Franklin,* c. 1790, Pierre Michel Alix, National Portrait Gallery, Smithsonian Institution; **p. 109:** Benjamin Franklin's Birthplace in Boston, Massachusetts, J. H. Bufford, Metropolitan Museum of Art, gift of William H. Huntington, 1882; **p. 111:** *Delaware River Front, Philadelphia,* Thomas Birch, American, 1779–1851, watercolor, 10-1/8 × 13-7/8″, M. and M. Karolik Collection, Courtesy, Museum of Fine Arts, Boston; **p. 113:** *Quaker Meeting,* British, fourth quarter 18th century or first quarter 19th century, oil on canvas, 25¼ × 30″ (64 × 76.2 cm.), bequest of Maxim Karolik, Courtesy, Museum of Fine Arts, Boston; **p. 120:** *Poor Richard's Almanack,* The Granger Collection; **p. 122:** *Patrick Henry* (detail), c. 1835, James Barton Longacre after Lawrence Sully, National Portrait Gallery, Smithsonian Institution; **p. 125:** *Patrick Henry Before the Virginia House of Burgesses,* 1851, Peter F. Rothermel, Red Hill, The Patrick Henry National Memorial; **p. 128:** *Thomas Paine,* John Wesley Jarvis, The Granger Collection; **p. 131:** *Recruiting for the Continental Army,* William T. Ranney, Munson-Williams-Proctor Institute; **p. 134:** *Phillis Wheatley* (detail), 1773, unidentified artist after Scipio Moorhead, National Portrait Gallery, Smithsonian Institution; **p. 136:** *George Washington at the Battle of Princeton,* Charles Wilson Peale, Copyright Yale University Art Gallery; **p. 140:** The Granger Collection; **p. 143:** *The Declaration of Independence,* 1786, John Trumbull, Copyright Yale University Art Gallery; **p. 146:** *Abigail Adams,* 1766, Benjamin Blythe, The Granger Collection; **p. 149:** *Building the First White House,* N. C. Wyeth, Copyrighted by the White House Historical Association, Photograph by the National Geographic Society; **p. 152:** The Bettmann Archive; **p. 155:** *Independence (Squire Jack Porter),* 1858, Frank Blackwell Mayer, National Museum of American Art, Smithsonian Institution, Bequest of Harriet Lane Johnston; **pp. 160–61:** *Niagara Falls,* about 1832–1840, Thomas Chambers, Wadsworth Atheneum, Hartford, © Wadsworth Atheneum, Ella Gallup Sumner and Mary Catlin Sumner Collection; **p. 162:** *Louisiana Purchase Ceremony at New Orleans,* 20 December 1803, Thor de Thulstrup, The

Granger Collection; *Erie Canal Near Little Falls*, W. R. Miller, Three Lions; **p. 163:** *Trade and Commerce in Manhattan,* Karoly and Santo, Three Lions; **pp. 164–65:** *Lewis & Clark Expedition,* O. E. Berninghaus, Three Lions; *The Battle of New Orleans,* The Granger Collection; Washington Irving's Rip Van Winkle, drawing by James Montgomery Flagg, 1929, The Granger Collection; *The Erie Canal,* The Granger Collection; *The Birth of the Monroe Doctrine* (left to right: John Quincy Adams, W. H. Crawford, William Wirt, President James Monroe, John C. Calhoun, Daniel D. Tompkins, and ?) after the painting by Clyde O. Deland, The Granger Collection; *Napoleon in Coronation Robes, 21 March 1804,* oil by Girodet Trioson, The Granger Collection; *Jane Austen* (1775–1817), pencil and watercolor, c. 1810, by her sister Cassandra Austen, The Granger Collection; *John Keats* (1795–1821), miniature, oil on ivory, by Joseph Severn, 1819, The Granger Collection; *René Laënnec, Inventory of the Stethoscope,* at the Necker Hospital, Paris, c. 1819, after the painting by Theobald Chartran, the Granger Collection; **pp. 166–67:** Half-title of an 1872 edition of James Fenimore Cooper's *The Last of the Mohicans,* with illustrations by Felix Octavius Carr Darley, The Granger Collection; *Race Between Locomotive "Tom Thumb" and Horse Car,* Herbert D. Stitt, Three Lions; *Samuel F. B. Morse Demonstrating His Telegraph,* colored engraving, 19th century, The Granger Collection; *The Trail of Tears* (the removal of the Cherokees to the West in 1838), oil on canvas, 1942, by Robert Lindneux, The Granger Collection; *Decembrist Rising at the Senate Square, St. Petersburg, Russia,* 1825, watercolor by Kolman, The Granger Collection; *Stendhal,* 1783–1842, pseudonym of the French writer Marie Henry Beyle, oil on canvas by Loedemark, The Granger Collection; *Alfred, Lord Tennyson,* The Granger Collection; *Charles Dickens,* The Granger Collection; **p. 168:** *Andrew Jackson Encouraging His Riflemen at the Battle of New Orleans, January 8, 1815,* colored engraving, 19th century, The Granger Collection; *The Bombardment of Fort McHenry, Baltimore, on 13–14 September 1814,* contemporary American aquatint engraving by John Bower, The Granger Collection; **p. 169:** *Last Stand at the Alamo,* N. C. Wyeth, Three Lions; **p. 171:** Illustration from an 1872 edition of James Fenimore Cooper's *The Last of the Mohicans,* Felix Octavius Carr Darley, The Granger Collection; **p. 172:** *Kindred Spirits,* Asher B. Durand, New York Public Library, Astor, Lenox and Tilden Foundations; **p. 178:** *Washington Irving* (detail), Daniel Huntington, National Portrait Gallery, Smithsonian Institution; **p. 190:** *James Fenimore Cooper* (detail), Charles Loring Elliott, National Portrait Gallery, Smithsonian Institution, Gift of Alexis I. duPont de Bie; **pp. 194–95:** *The Death of Leathersotcking,* Felix O. C. Darley, New York Public Library, Astor, Lenox and Tilden Foundations; **p. 200:** William Cullen Bryant (detail), unidentified photographer, National Portrait Gallery, Smithsonian Institution; **p. 202:** *Vernal Falls, Yosemite Valley,* Thomas Moran, Three Lions; **p. 209:** ''I at Length. . .,'' Edgar Allan Poe's *Tales of Mystery and Imagination,* (London: George G. Harrap [1935]), Arthur Rackham, Print Collection, Miriam and Ira D. Wallach Division of Art, Prints and Photographs, The New York Public Library, Astor, Lenox and Tilden Foundations; **pp. 223, 225:** *The Raven,* Edouard Manet, Gift of W. G. Russell Allen, Courtesy, Museum of Fine Arts, Boston; **p. 231:** ''He Turned Suddenly . . .,'' Edgar Allan Poe's *Tales of Mystery and Imagination,* (London: George G. Harrap [1935]), Arthur Rackham, Print Collection, Miriam and Ira D. Wallach Division of Art, Prints and Photographs, New York Public Library, Astor, Lenox and Tilden Foundations; **p. 235:** *Proserpine,* Dante Gabriel Rossetti, The Tate Gallery, London; **p. 238:** *Boston Harbor,* Fitz Hugh Lane, Courtesy, Museum of Fine Arts, Boston, M. and M. Karolik Collection of American Paintings, 1815–1865 by exchange; **p. 241:** *Cornell Farm,* Edward Hicks, Three Lions: **pp. 242–43:** John Greenleaf Whittier, The Granger Collection; Mexican War, The Granger Collection; First Postage Stamps, The Granger Collection; Henry Wadsworth Longfellow, The Granger Collection; Abraham Lincoln, the earliest known photograph, a daguerrotype of 1846, The Granger Collection; Alfred, Lord Tennyson, The Granger Collection; Irish Potato Famine, The Granger Collection; Emily Brontë (1818–1848) after a drawing by her sister, Charlotte, The Granger Collection; Charlotte Brontë, The Granger Collection; **p. 244–245:** Henry David Thoreau, The Granger Collection; Commodore Matthew C. Perry meeting the Japanese Imperial Commissioners at Yokohama in 1854, colored lithograph from Perry's official report to Congress published in 1856, The Granger Collection; Louis Napoleon, The Granger Collection; Women's Rights Convention, The Granger Collection; California Gold Rush, Gold Mining in California, lithograph, 1871, by Currier & Ives, The Granger Collection; Contemporary Chinese painting of Taiping rebels storming a town during Taiping Rebellion, 1851–64, The Granger Collection; Robert Browning, The Granger Collection; **p. 247:** (left) *Harriet Beecher Stowe,* 1853, Alansori Fisher, The Granger Collection; (right) American Bookseller's Announcement for *Uncle Tom's Cabin,* 1852, The Granger Collection; **p. 249:** *The Notch of the White Mountains (Crawford Notch), 1839,* Thomas Cole, National Gallery of Art, Washington, D.C., Andrew W. Mellon Fund; **p. 253:** The Whale Fishery—The Sperm Whale in a Flurry, undated lithograph by Currier & Ives, The Granger Collection; **p. 255:** *Hiawatha,* Thomas Eakins, Hirshhorn Museum & Sculpture Garden, Smithsonian Institution, Joseph Martin/SCALA/Art Resource; **p. 261:** *The First Cargo,* N. C. Wyeth, The Central Children's Room, Donnell Library Center, The New York Public Library; **p. 268:** *Sunset,* Frederick E. Church, Collection of Munson-Williams-Proctor Institute Museum of Art, Utica, New York; **p. 273:** *Farm Yard, Winter, 1862,* George Henry Durrie, Courtesy of the New York Historical Society, New York City; **p. 280:** Henry David Thoreau, The Granger Collection; **p. 292:** *Nathaniel Hawthorne (Detail) 1862,* Emanuel Gottlieb Leutze, National Portrait Gallery, Smithsonian Institution; **p. 295:** *Winter Sunday in Norway, Maine c. 1860,* unidentified artist, New York State Historical Association, Cooperstown; **p. 300:** *Cemetery,* Peter McIntyre, Courtesy of the artist; **p. 312:** *Herman Melville,* Wyatt Eaton, The Granger Collection; **p. 331:** *After The First Snow in Winter in Vermont,* Charles Hughes, Three Lions; **p. 332:** *Henry Wadsworth Longfellow,* Thomas B. Read, National Portrait Gallery, Smithsonian Institution; **p. 334:** *The Return Alone,* Eugene Higgins, The Phillips Collection, Washington, D.C.; **p. 342:** *Oliver Wendell Holmes,* James Notman, National Portrait Gallery, Smithsonian Institution; **p. 344:** *U.S. Frigate Constitution, 1823,* Nicholas Cammilliri, Courtesy of The Mariner's Museum, Newport News, Virginia; **p. 350:** Low Branch, 1968, Scarlett, Courtesy New York Graphic Society, all rights reserved; **p. 354:** John Greenleaf Whittier, William Notman, National Portrait Gallery, Smithsonian Institution; **p. 359:** *Old Holley House, Cos Cob,* John Henry Twachtman, Cincinnati Art Museum, John J. Emery Fund; **p. 363:** *Quoddy Head,* John Martin, Art Resource; **p. 366:** Emily Dickinson, The Granger Collection; **pp. 368–69:** *February 1890–1900,* John Henry Twachtman, The Hayden Collection, Courtesy, Museum of Fine Arts, Boston; **p. 371:** American Railroad Scene, Currier & Ives,

Three Lions; **p. 372:** Wildlife and Vegetation of a Hedgerow, Drawing by Peter Barrett, The Sunday Times; **p. 374:** *Near Harlech, North Wales,* Benjamin William Leader, Bridgeman/Art Resource; **p. 379:** *Room with a Balcony,* Adolph von Menzel, Staatliche Museen Preubischer Kulturbesitz, Nationgalerie, Berlin (West); **p. 381:** *Waiting Outside No. 12,* Anonymous, Crane Kalman Gallery; **p. 386–87:** *Progress,* Asher B. Durand, The Warner Collection of Gulf States Paper Corp., Tuscaloosa, Alabama; **p. 389:** *Genesee Scenery,* Thomas Cole, Museum of Art, Rhode Island School of Design, Jesse Metcalf Fund; **p. 390:** *Twilight in the Wilderness,* Frederick E. Church, The Cleveland Museum of Art, Mr. and Mrs. William H. Marlatt Fund; **pp. 394–95:** *Let Us Have Peace (Grant and Lee),* J. L. G. Ferris, Three Lions; **p. 397:** *A Ride For Liberty— The Fugitive Slaves, c. 1862,* Eastman Johnson, The Brooklyn Museum, Gift of Miss Gwendolyn O.L. Conkling; **pp. 398–99:** Bombardment of Fort Sumter, Charleston Harbor, 1861, lithograph, 1861, by Currier & Ives, The Granger Collection; *Charles Robert Darwin (1890–82),* oil on canvas by John Collier, The Granger Collection; The Battle of the Wilderness, 6 May 1864, lithograph 1887 by Kurz & Allison, The Granger Collection; Sepoy Rebellion, The Granger Collection; Abolitionist Poster, Ohio State Historical Society; *John Brown (1800–59),* oil on canvas c. 1859 by Ole P. H. Balling, The Granger Collection; The Surrender at Appomattox, The Granger Collection; *Frederick Douglass (1817?–95),* oil on canvas c. 1844, attributed to E. Hammond, The Granger Collection; Emancipation Proclamation, The Granger Collection; **p. 401:** *Tidings From the Front,* Gilbert Gaul, Three Lions; **p. 402:** *Faithful Troops Cheer General Lee, 1865,* N. C. Wyeth, U.S. Naval Academy Museum; **p. 405:** *Union Soldiers Rally Around the Flag,* William Winner, Art Resource; **pp. 410–11:** The Funeral of President Lincoln, New York, April 25, 1865, Currier & Ives, Anne S. K. Brown Military Collection, Brown University Library; **p. 415:** *Abraham Lincoln,* William Willard, National Portrait Gallery, Smithsonian Institution, Gift of Mr. and Mrs. Daniel A. Morse; **p. 424:** *Frederick Douglass c. 1844,* attributed to Elisha Hammond, National Portrait Gallery, Smithsonian Institution; **p. 429:** A Home on the Mississippi, 1871, Currier & Ives, The Museum of the City of New York, Harry T. Peters Collection; **p. 435:** The Housetops in Charleston During the Bombardment of Fort Sumter, Harper's Weekly, May 4, 1861, Library of Congress; **p. 438:** *Abraham Lincoln (Detail) 1887,* George Peter Alexander Healy, National Portrait Gallery, Smithsonian Institution; **p. 440:** Abraham Lincoln's Address at the Dedication of the Gettysburg National Cemetery, 19 November 1863, The Granger Collection; **p. 442:** *Lincoln Proclaiming Thanksgiving,* Dean Cornwell, Louis A. Warren Lincoln Library and Museum, Fort Wayne, Indiana; **p. 444:** *Robert E. Lee, 1864–1865,* Edward Caledon Bruce, National Portrait Gallery, Smithsonian Institution; **p. 446:** *The Battle Abbey Murals: The Four Seasons of the Confederacy, The Summer Mural,* Charles Hoffbauer, The Virginia State Historical Society; **p. 448:** *Hinmaton Yalakit, Chief Joseph,* 1878, Cyrenius Hall National Portrait Gallery, Smithsonian Institution; **p. 450:** *Chief Joseph's Surrender to Colonel Nelson A. Miles,* Olaf C. Seltzer, Thomas Gilcrease Institute of American History and Art, Tulsa, Oklahoma; **p. 454:** *Walt Whitman 1887,* Thomas Eakins, Courtesy of The Pennsylvania Academy of the Fine Arts; **p. 465:** *The Wounded Drummer Boy,* Eastman Johnson, The Union League Club, New York City, Joseph Martin/SCALA/Art Resource; **p. 466:** *The Lawrence Tree, 1929,* Georgia O'Keeffe, Wadsworth Atheneum, Hartford, The Ella Gallup Sumner and Mary Catlin Sumner Collection; **pp.**

472–73: *The Adirondack Guide, 1894,* Winslow Homer, Courtesy, Museum of Fine Arts, Boston, Bequest of Mrs. Alma H. Wadleigh; **p. 474:** *In Search of the Land of Milk and Honey,* Harvey Dunn, City Library, De Smet, South Dakota; **p. 475:** *The Mines During the Gold Rush, 1849 in California.* Frank Tenney Johnson, Three Lions; **pp. 476–77:** A giant octopus attacking the submarine vessel *Nautilus,* colored engraving from Jules Verne's *Twenty Thousand Leagues Under the Sea,* 1873, The Granger Collection; *Proclamation of the German Empire at Versailles, 18 January 1871,* A. A. von Werner, The Granger Collection; Thomas A. Edison testing the first successful incandescent lamp in his laboratory at Menlo Park, New Jersey, 21 October 1879, The Granger Collection; Blizzard of 1888, The Granger Collection; Indian pictograph of Battle of Little Bighorn, 1876, The Granger Collection; Samuel L. Clemens, Huckleberry Finn, and Tom Sawyer on an early 20th century American cigar-box label, The Granger Collection; Alexander Graham Bell, The Granger Collection; Inauguration of Statue of Liberty, The Granger Collection; **pp. 478–79:** *Theodore Roosevelt,* John Singer Sargent, Three Lions; San Francisco Earthquake, The Granger Collection; Albert Einstein, Three Lions; First Flight at Kitty Hawk, The Granger Collection; Destruction of the U.S. Battleship *Maine* in Havana harbor, 15 February 1898, contemporary lithograph by Kurz & Allison, The Granger Collection; Boxers bringing captured foreigners to trial, Chinese print, 1900, The Granger Collection; Ford Model T, The Granger Collection; **p. 481:** *The Bowery at Night, 1895,* W. Lous Sonntag, Jr., Museum of the City of New York; **p. 482:** *Rabbit Stew,* Gary Niblett, photograph courtesy of the Gerald Peters Gallery, Santa Fe, New Mexico, and Dallas, Texas; **p. 484:** *Queensboro Bridge, East River* (c. 1910), Glen Oden Coleman, Hirshhorn Museum and Sculpture Garden, Smithsonian Institution, Gift of Joseph H. Hirshhorn, 1966; **p. 485:** *Louisiana Indians Walking Along a Bayou,* Alfred Boisseau, New Orleans Museum of Art, Gift of William E. Groves; **p. 486:** *Portrait of Marie Laveau's Daughter,* attributed to Frantz Fleischbein, New Orleans Museum of Art, Gift of Mr. and Mrs. William E. Groves; **p. 493:** *Turn Him Loose, Bill,* Frederic Remington, Three Lions; **p. 494:** *Samuel Langhorne Clemens (Details) 1935,* Frank Edwin Larson, National Portrait Gallery, Smithsonian Institution; **p. 497:** Paddle Steamboat Mississippi, The Shelburne Museum, Shelburne, Vermont; **p. 502:** *Why the Mail Was Late,* Oscar E. Berninghaus, Thomas Gilcrease Institute of American History and Art, Tulsa, Oklahoma; **p. 505:** *A Drifting Snow,* William Van De Velde Bonfils, Three Lions; **p. 512:** Mark Twain (Samuel L. Clemens) Riding the Celebrated Jumping Frog, An English Caricature by Frederic Waddy, 1872, The Granger Collection; **p. 514:** *Bret Harte (Detail), 1884,* John Pettie, The Granger Collection; **p. 517:** *Edge of Town,* Charles Burchfield, Collection of the Kelson-Atkins Museum of Art, Kansas City, Missouri (Gift of Friends of Art); **p. 524:** Ambrose Bierce, The Bettmann Achives; **p. 526:** *The Red Bridge,* Julian Alden Weir, The Metropolitan Museum of Art, Gift of Mrs. John A. Rutherford, 1914, © copyright 1982 by the Metropolitan Museum of Art; **p. 532:** *Seat of John Julius Pringle,* Charles Fraser, Carolina Art Association, Gibbes Art Gallery; **p. 537:** *Evening in the Woods,* Worthington Whittredge, The Metropolitan Museum of Art, Bequest of Henry H. Cook, 1905, © copyright 1984 by The Metropolitan Museum of Art; **p. 547:** *Woman With Black Tie,* Amedeo Modighani, Private Collection; **p. 553:** *From Arkansas,* George Schreiber, Sheldon Swope Art Gallery, Terre Haute, Indiana; **p. 557:** *At The Opera,* Mary Stevenson Cassatt, The Hayden Collection, Courtesy, Museum of Fine Arts,

Boston; **p. 661:** *The Grand Canyon of the Yellowstone, 1893–1901;* Thomas Moran, Art Resource; **p. 663:** *Harpers Ferry from Jefferson Rock, 1857,* Edward Beyer, Virginia State Library; **p. 667:** Detail of "News from the War", Winslow Homer for Harper's Weekly, June 14, 1862, Library of Congress; **p. 670:** Paul Lawrence Dunbar, The Granger Collection; **p. 676:** Edwin Arlington Robinson (Detail) 1933, Thomas Richard Hood, National Portrait Gallery, Smithsonian Institution; **p. 678:** *The Artist's Garden c. 1880,* Blakelock, National Gallery of Art. Art Resource; **p. 682:** *The Thinker (Portrait of Louis N. Kenton, 1900),* Thomas Eakins, The Metropolitan Museum of Art, Kennedy Fund, 1917, © copyright 1967/1984 by The Metropolitan Museum of Art; **p. 684:** *Edgar Lee Masters,* Francis J. Quirk, National Portrait Gallery, Smithsonian Institution; **p. 686:** *Barn Dance, 1950,* Grandma Moses, Copyright © 1973, Grandma Moses Properties, Co., New York; **pp. 692–93:** *City Roofs, 1932,* Edward Hopper, Courtesy of Kennedy Galleries, Inc., New York; **p. 695:** *Armistice Day, 1918,* Gifford Beal, William Lowe Bryan Memorial Collection, Indiana University Art Museum, Photograph by Michael Cavanagh, Kevin Montague; **pp. 696–97:** *James Joyce,* J. E. Blanche, Three Lions; Sir William Orpen, *The Signing of Peace in the Hall of Mirrors,* Versailles, 28th June, 1919, Imperial War Museum; The Spirit of Prohibition, cartoon by Rollin Kirby published the day after National Prohibition became law in the United States in 1920, The Granger Collection; Langston Hughes, c. 1925, Winold Reiss, The Granger Collection; *F. Scott Fitzgerald (Detail),* David Silvette, National Portrait Gallery, Smithsonian Institution, The Granger Collection; The Trench, 1921, José Clemente Orozco, National Preparatory School, Mexico City, The Granger Collection; The End of the Climb, cartoon by Rollin Kirby, 1920, upon the proclamation of the adoption of the 19th (Woman Suffrage) Amendment to the United States Constitution, The Granger Collection; *Carl Sandburg,* John Bianchi, Three Lions; **pp. 698–99:** American cartoon by Otto Soglow showing a capitalist hanging from a rope in the shape of 1929, the year of the Stock Market crash, The Granger Collection; Adolf Hitler, The Pentagon (U.S. Army Archives), Japanese bomb Pearl Harbor, The Granger Collection; **p. 700:** *The City From Greenwich Village, 1922,* John Sloan, National Gallery of Art, Washington, D.C., Gift of Helen Farr Sloan; **p. 701:** *Library,* Bernard Boruch Zakheim, Coit Tower Mural (WPA), San Francisco Art Commission; **p. 702:** *Conception Synchromy, 1914,* Stanton MacDonald-Wright, Hirshhorn Museum and Sculpture Garden, Smithsonian Institution, Scala/Art Resource; **p. 705:** *Juke Box,* Jacob Lawrence, © 1987 The Detroit Institute of Arts, Gift of Dr. D. T. Burton, Dr. M. E. Fowler, Dr. J. B. Greene and Mr. J. J. White; **p. 710:** *West Tisbury Fair,* Thomas Hart Benton, Collection of Mr. Arthur Levitt, Jr., New York, John Lei/OMNI Photo; **p. 715:** *After the Show,* Waldo Peirce, Collection of Whitney Museum of American Art, Purchase; **p. 719:** *8 December 1941,* Rockwell Kent, The Rockwell Kent Legacies; **p. 728:** *F. Scott Fitzgerald (Detail),* David Silvette, National Portrait Gallery, Smithsonian Institution; **p. 731:** *Floating Ice, 1910,* George Bellows, Collection of Whitney Museum of American Art, Gift of Gertrude Vanderbilt Whitney; **p. 739:** *Winter Harmony, 1890/1910,* John H. Twachtman, National Gallery of Art, Washington, Gift of the Avalon Foundation; **p. 743:** *Manhattan Tops,* Herman Rose, Hirshhorn Museum and Sculpture Garden, Smithsonian Institution, Gift of Joseph H. Hirshhorn, 1966; **p. 749:** *Garden of Memories, 1917,* Charles Burchfield, Collection, The Museum of Modern Art, New York, Gift of Abby Aldrich Rockefeller (by exchange); **p. 752:** *Lavender and Old Lace,* Charles Burchfield, ANA, From the Collection of the New Britain Museum of American Art, Charles F. Smith Fund, Photo credit: E. Irving Blomstrann; **p. 756:** Thomas Wolfe, Soss Melik, National Portrait Gallery, Smithsonian Institution; **p. 759:** *Stone City, Iowa,* Grant Wood, Joslyn Art Museum, Omaha, Nebraska, Gift of the Art Institute of Omaha; **p. 786:** William Faulkner, 1962, Soss Melik, National Portrait Gallery, Smithsonian Institution; **p. 790:** *In the Depths of the Timber,* W. Herbert Dunton, Courtesy Amon Carter Museum, Fort Worth; **p. 804:** *The Signature, 1920,* Red Suburb, San Francisco Museum of Modern Art, Purchase; **p. 807:** *Handball, 1939,* Ben Shahn, Collection, The Museum of Modern Art, New York, Abby Aldrich Rockefeller Fund; **pp. 832, 834, 835:** The Night the Ghost Got In, Copyright © 1933, 1961, James Thurber, From My Life and Hard Times, published by Harper & Row, **p. 838:** Carl Sandburg (Detail), Miriam Svet, National Portrait Gallery, Smithsonian Institution; **p. 841:** *Lincoln,* Frank E. Schoonover, Wilmington Savings Fund Society, Photo: Jon McDowell; **p. 851:** *Black and White,* Georgia O'Keeffe, Collection of Whitney Museum of American Art, Gift of Mr. and Mrs. R. Crosby Kemper; **p. 852:** *Ezra Pound (Detail), 1938–39,* Wyndham Lewis, The Granger Collection; **pp. 856–57:** *Landscape Album in Various Styles,* Ch'a Shih-piao, The Cleveland Museum of Art, Gift of Mr. and Mrs. Severance A. Millikin; **p. 862:** *T. S. Eliot (Detail),* Sir Gerald Kelly, National Portrait Gallery, Smithsonian Institution; **p. 866:** *Moonlight, Dovehouse Street, Chelsea,* Algernon Newton, Fine Art Society, London, Bridgeman/Art Resource; **p. 876:** *In a Shoreham Garden,* Samuel Palmer, Victoria & Albert Museum Trustees; **pp. 881, 882:** *Orchard in Bloom, Louveçiennes, 1872,* Camille Pissarro, National Gallery of Art, Washington, Ailsa Mellon Bruce Collection; **p. 884:** *Overhanging Cloud in July,* Charles Burchfield, Collection of Whitney Museum of American Art, Purchase, with funds from the Friends of the Whitney Museum of American Art; **p. 888:** *Pink Locusts and Windy Moon, 1959,* Charles Burchfield, Collection of the Chase Manhattan Bank; **p. 892:** *Carl Sandburg (Detail),* Miriam Svet, National Portrait Gallery, Smithsonian Institution; **p. 895:** *Marshes, Dunes and Fields, 1977,* Jane Freilicher, The Herbert W. Plimpton Foundation, on extended loan to the Rose Art Museum, Brandeis University, Waltham, Massachusetts, Photo credit, Herb Gallagher; **p. 900:** *Edna St. Vincent Millay (Detail),* Charles Ellis, National Portrait Gallery, Smithsonian Institution; **p. 903:** *The Sun,* Edouard Munch, Fotograf, O. Vaering; **p. 910:** *The Sick Chicken,* Winslow Homer, The Harold T. Pulsifer Memorial Collection, Colby College, Waterville, Maine; **p. 915:** *Untitled,* Alexander Calder, Solomon R. Guggenheim Museum, New York, Photo, David Heald; **p. 916:** *E. E. Cummings, 1958,* Self Portrait, National Portrait Gallery, Smithsonian Institution **p. 918:** *Lovers with Flowers, 1927,* March Chagall, The Israel Museum, Jerusalem, Gift of Baron Edmond de Rothschild, Paris; **p. 924:** *New England Birches,* Ernest Lawson, The Phillips Collection, Washington, D.C.; **p. 929:** *Woodlot, Maine Woods, 1938,* Marsden Harlety, The Phillips Collection, Washington, D.C.; **p. 955:** *Ruby Green Singing, 1928,* James Chapin, Norton Gallery and School of Art, West Palm Beach, Florida; **p. 956:** Countee Cullen (Detail) c. 1925, Winold Reiss, National Portrait Gallery, Smithsonian Institution; **p. 958:** *Big Meeting, 1980,* Varnette P. Honeywood; **p. 962:** *Langston Hughes (Detail) c. 1925,* Winold Reiss, National Portrait Gallery, Smithsonian Institution; **p. 966:** *Jean Toomer (Detail) c. 1925,* Winold Reiss, Gift of Laurence A. Fleischman and Howard Garfinkle with a matching grant from the National Endowment of the Arts, National Portrait Gallery, Smithsonian Institution; **p. 968:** *Black Place II, 1944,* Georgia O'Keeffe, The Metropolitan Museum of Art, The Alfred Stieglitz Collection, 1959, © copyright 1984/85 by the Metropolitan Museum of Art; **p. 971:** *The Fabulous Invalid, 1938,* Set design by Donald Oenslager, Theatre Collection, The Museum of the City of New York; **pp. 1022–23:** *Golden Gate, 1955,* Charles Sheeler, The Metropolitan Museum of Art, George A. Hearn Fund, 1955, © copyright 1984 by the Metropolitan Museum of Art; **p. 1025:** *Saraband, 1959,* Morris Louis, Collection Solomon R. Guggenheim Museum, New York; **p. 1030:** *Gotham News, 1955,* Willem de Kooning, Albright-Knox Gallery, Buffalo, New York, Gift of Seymour H. Knox, 1955; **p. 1031:** *Untitled, 1960–61,* Mark Rothko, Art Resource; **p. 1033:** *Ansonia 1977* (Detail) Richard Estes, Collection of the Whitney Museum of American Art, Gift of Frances and Sidney Lewis; **p. 1034:** Richard Diebenkorn, *Untitled,* 1970, color lithograph on paper, 25-5/16 × 18-7/8, 1974.12.2, National Museum of American Art, Smithsonian Institution Museum Purchase; **p. 1037:** *Railroad Train,* Edward Hopper, Addison Gallery of American Art, Phillips Academy, Andover, Massachusetts, Gift of Fred G. Murphy; **p. 1039:** *Morning Call, 1946,* Milton Avery, Hirshhorn Museum, Scala/Art Resource; **pp. 1054–55:** *Black Walnuts, 1945,* Joseph Pollet, Collection of Whitney Museum of American Art, Purchase and gift of Gertrude Vanderbilt Whitney, by exchange; **p. 1065:** *The Laughing Boy,* George Bellows, Hirschl & Adler Galleries, Inc.; **pp. 1066–67:** *Waiting Room,* Raphael Soyer, In the Collection of The Corcoran Gallery of Art, Museum Purchase, William A. Clark Fund, 1943; **p. 1081:** *Martha's Vineyard, 1925,* Thomas Hart Benton, Collection of Whitney Museum of American Art, Gift of Gertrude Vanderbilt Whitney; **p. 1092:** *Pleasures of Winter in New York,* Francis Peterson, Three Lions; **p. 1103:** *Room in Brooklyn,* Edward Hopper, The Hayden Collection, Courtesy, Museum of Fine Arts, Boston; **p. 1110:** Across the Continent, Westward the Course of Empire Takes Its Way, Currier & Ives, Museum of the City of New York; **p. 1117:** *Against the Sunset,* Frederic Remington, Courtesy of Petersen Galleries, Beverly Hills; **p. 1118:** *Driving the Herd,* Frank Reaugh, Iconography collection, Harry Ransom Humanities Research Center, The University of Texas at Austin; **p. 1121:** *Painted Water Glasses, 1974,* Janet Fish, Collection of Whitney Museum of American Art, Purchase, with funds from Susan and David Workman; **p. 1122:** William Cuthbert Faulkner, Soss Melik, National Portrait Gallery, Smithsonian Institution; **p. 1129:** *Night City,* Richard Florsheim, Collection of Jane Golanty; **p. 1132:** Truman Capote, 1974, Barnaby Conrad, National Portrait Gallery, Smithsonian Institution; **p. 1142:** *Man in a Vest, 1939–49,* William H. Johnson, National Museum of Art, Smithsonian Institution, Gift of the Harmon Foundation; **p. 1157:** *The Medicine Robe,* Maynard Dixon, Courtesy of The Buffalo Historical Center, Cody, Wyoming; **p. 1187:** *Number 3, 1949,* Jackson Pollock, Joseph Hirshhorn Museum, Joseph Martin/Scala/Art Resource; **p. 1193:** *Wild Flowers, 1978,* S. Reindorf, Collection: George Williams; **p. 1203:** *The Unexpected Answer,* René Magritte, Patrimoine des Musées Royaux des Beaux-Arts de Belgique, Bruxelles; **p. 1204:** *Great Florida Sunset, 1987,* Martin Johnson Heade, Private Collection USA, Photo Courtesy Aquavella Galleries; **pp. 1210–11:** *Crowninshield's Wharf, Around the Wharf Are the Vessels America, Fame, Prudent, and Belisaurius,* George Ropes, Peabody Museum of Salem; **p. 1222:** *Somehwere in America,* Robert Brackman, National Museum of American Art, Smithsonian Institution, Transfer from the U.S. Department of Labor; **pp. 1224–25:** *Interior,* Preston Dickinson, The Metropolitan Museum of Art, Gift of Edith Denniston 1971, © copyright 1987 by The Metropolitan Museum of Art; **p. 1226:** Robert Penn Warren, Conrad A. Albrizid, National Portrait Gallery, Smithsonian Institution; **p. 1228:** *Queen Anne's Lace, 1957,* Charles Burchfield, © 1987 The Detroit Institute of Arts, Gift of John S. Newberry; **p. 1232:** *Summer Landscape With Hawk, 1901–06,* Louis M. Eilshemius, The Phillips Collection, Washington, D.C.; **p. 1237:** *Girl in a White Dress,* Sir William Orpen, Private Collection, Bridgeman/Art Resource; **p. 1244:** *Portrait of Diego, 1954,* Giacometti, Galerie Maeght, Paris, Art Resource; **p. 1248:** *The Poet Reclining 1915,* Marc Chagall, The Tate Gallery, London; **p. 1255:** *The Lone Tenement,* George W. Bellows, Three Lions; **p. 1257:** *Christmas Morning, Adirondacks, 1946,* Rockwell Kent, Sunne Savage Gallery, Boston; **p. 1261:** *Vaudeville, 1951,* Jacob Lawrence, Hirshhorn Museum and Sculpture Garden, Smithsonian Institution, Gift of Joseph H. Hirshhorn, 1966; **p. 1265:** *Woman with Dark Hair, 1959,* Jacob Kainen, oil on canvas, 44 × 36, National Museum of American Art, Smithsonian Institution, Gift of Mrs. Mary Jane Fisher.

PHOTOGRAPH CREDITS

pp. 22–23, 24–25: John Lei/Omni; **p. 37:** Jim Brandenburg/Woodfin Camp; **p. 63:** D. Cavagnaro/DRK; **p. 175:** Rank Whitney/The Image Bank; **p. 206:** UPI/Bettmann NewsPhoto; **p. 245:** Ralph Waldo Emerson, The Granger Collection; **p. 246:** Telegraph Key Used by Samuel F. B. Morse to Send the First Telegraph Message of May 24, 1844, The Granger Collection; **p. 266:** Ralph Waldo Emerson, The Granger Collection; **p. 275:** Steve Dunwell/The Image Bank; **p. 277:** Pat O'Hara/DRK; **p. 279:** Paolo Koch/Photo Researchers; **p. 284:** Brad Parker/Thoreau Lyceum; **p. 288:** Robert Frerck/Odyssey; **p. 315:** Nantucket Historical Association; **pp. 318–27:** Culver Pictures; **pp. 336–37:** Stephanie Maze/Woodfin Camp; **p. 339:** Historical Pictures Service, Chicago; **p. 346:** James Carmichael/The Image Bank; **p. 348:** The Bettmann Archives; **p. 352:** ULRIKE Welsh; **p. 452:** Walt Whitman, UPI/Bettmann Newsphoto; **p. 457:** Don Klumpp/The Image Bank; **p. 463:** C. C. Lockwood; **p. 468:** Wolfgang Kaehler; **p. 479:** Thomas Mann, The Granger Collection; Sigmund Freud, The Granger Collection; **p. 534:** Sarah Orne Jewett, The Bettmann Archives; **p. 550:** Willa Cather, The Bettmann Archives; **p. 560:** Jack London, The Bettmann Archives; **p. 561:** Wayne Lynch/DRK; **p. 569:** Annie Griffiths/DRK; **p. 574:** Stephen Crane, UPI/Bettmann Newsphoto; **p. 578:** Library of Congress; **p. 579:** Cook Collection Valentine Museum; **pp. 584–91:** Library of Congress; **p. 596:** Cook Collection Valentine Museum; **pp. 601–09:** Library of Congress; **p. 612:** Cook Collection Valentine Museum; **p. 617:** Library of Congress; **p. 621:** Georgia Department of Archives and History; **p. 630:** Minnesota Historical Society; **pp. 633–55:** Library of Congress; **p. 662:** Sidney Lanier, The Granger Collection; **p. 666:** Stephen Crane, UPI/Bettmann Newsphoto; **p. 674:** Frederick Douglass, Historical Pictures Services, Chicago; **p. 697:** The Granger Collection; **pp. 698–99:** Charles Lindbergh, The Granger Collection; Women Working During World War II, Library of Congress; Atomic Bombs Dropped of Japan, Library of Congress; Nazi Troops, Photo Source/Three Lions; George Orwell, The Granger Collection; **p. 717:** UPI/Bettmann Newsphoto; **p. 720:** Larry Burrows/Time/Life Picture Agency; **p. 723:** American Red Cross; **p. 746:** Thomas Victor; **p. 762:** Thomas Victor; **p. 770:** UPI/Bettmann Newsphoto; **p. 773:** Art Wolfe/The Image Bank; **p. 779:** Timothy Eagan/Woodfin Camp; **pp. 782–83:** Dan

McCoy/Rainbow; **p. 808:** National Portrait Gallery, Smithsonian Institution; **p. 811:** Historical Pictures Service, Chicago; **p. 814:** AP/Wide World Photo; **p. 817:** Brad Parker/Thoreau Lyceum; **p. 822:** UPI/Bettmann Newsphoto; **p. 825:** Syd Greenberg/DPI; **p. 830:** UPI/Bettmann Newsphoto; **p. 870:** The Granger Collection; **p. 874:** The Bettmann Archives; **p. 880:** The Bettmann Archives; **p. 886:** The Granger Collection; **pp. 898–99:** Historical Pictures Service, Chicago; **p. 908:** Rollie McKenna; The Bettmann Archives; AP/Wide World Photo; **p. 912:** Janeart Ltd./The Image Bank; **p. 922:** Dmitri Kessel/Life Magazine © Time Inc.; **p. 927:** DeWitt Jones/Woodfin Camp; **p. 938:** Bill Bridge/DPI; **p. 950:** The Bettmann Archives/BBC Hulton; **p. 956:** G. K. Hall & Company; **p. 961:** Michael Skott/The Image Bank; **p. 964:** C. C. Lockwood; **p. 966:** UPI/Bettmann Newsphoto; **p. 972:** The Granger Collection; **p. 974:** Laura Inness as Emily Webb, Sally Chamberlin as Mrs. Webb—Photo Nick Gunderson, Seattle Repertory Theater; **p. 987:** Campbell Scott as George Gibbs, Mary Doyle as Mrs. Gibbs, Priscilla Hake Lauris as Mrs. Soames, Sally Chamberlin as Mrs. Webb, Laura Inness as Emily Webb, Photo by Nick Gunderson, Seattle Repertory Theater; **p. 999:** Campbell Scott as George Gibbs, Laura Inness as Emily Webb, Our Town, Seattle Repertory Theater, Photo by Chris Bennion; **pp. 1005, 1010:** Our Town—Seattle Repertory Theater, Photo by Nick Gunderson; **p. 1015:** Our Town—Seattle Repertory Theater, Laura Inness as Emily Webb, Photo by Chris Bennion; **pp. 1026–27:** School Segregation Declared Unconstitutional, Bern Keating/Black Star; Ralph Ellison, Bob Adelman/Magnum; Robert Lowell, Henri Dauman/Magnum; Flannery O'Connor, Leviton-Atlanta/Black Star; State of Israel Established, Robert Capa/Magnum; Jorge Luis Borges, S. Bassouls/Sygma; Gunter Grass, Ken Hawkins/Sygma; Fidel Castro, St. George/Magnum Photos; **pp. 1028–29:** Mrs. Martin Luther King/Flip Schulke/Black Star; First Men on the Moon, The Granger Collection; Toni Morrison, Inge Morath/Magnum;

Rachel Carson, Erich Hartman/Magnum; Violence Breaks out in Northern Ireland, M. Philppot/Sygma; The Berlin Wall, Flip Schulke/Black Star; John F. Kennedy Assassinated, Wayne Miller/Magnum; U.S. Soldier in Vietnam, Peter Garfield/Folio; President Nixon Resigns, Alex Webb/Magnum; Octavio Paz, Susan Meiselas/Magnum; **p. 1040:** Nancy Crampton; **p. 1043:** Dan McCoy/Rainbow; **p. 1062:** Thomas Victor; **p. 1072:** Thomas Victor; **p. 1075:** Ken Karp; **p. 1078:** Thomas Victor; **p. 1084:** Thomas Victor; **p. 1090:** Thomas Victor; **p. 1100:** Thomas Victor; **p. 1106:** Thomas Victor; **p. 1114:** AP/Wide World Photos; **p. 1126:** The Granger Collection; **p. 1138:** Nancy Crampton; **p. 1146:** Thomas Victor; **p. 1149:** William Rivelli/The Image Bank; **p. 1151:** David W. Hamilton/The Image Bank; **p. 1154:** Thomas Victor; **p. 1160:** Thomas Victor; **p. 1164:** Thomas Victor; **p. 1167:** Johnny Johnson/DRK/Photo; **p. 1171:** Chuck O'Rear/Woodfin Camp; **p. 1174:** Thomas Victor; **p. 1177:** J. D. Love; **p. 1184:** J. D. Love; **p. 1188:** AP/Wide World Photos; **p. 1194:** (top) Thomas Victor; (bottom) Thomas Victor; **p. 1199:** Harold Sund/The Image Bank; **p. 1200:** (top) UPI/Bettmann News Photo; (bottom) Thomas Victor; **p. 1208:** (top) Rollie McKenna; (bottom) Rollie McKenna; **p. 1214:** Historical Pictures Service, Chicago; **p. 1218:** (top) The New York Public Library; (middle) Thomas Victor; (bottom) Helen Lundeen; **p. 1221:** Jeff Foott/DRK Photo; **p. 1226:** Thomas Victor; **p. 1234:** (top) AP/Wide World Photos; (middle) PACH/Bettmann Archives; (bottom) Kit Stafford; **p. 1238:** Peter Miller/The Image Bank; **p. 1242:** (top) Thomas Victor; (middle) Thomas Victor; (bottom) Thomas Victor; **p. 1250:** (top) Thomas Victor; (middle) Marlene Foster; (bottom) Rollie McKenna; **p. 1252:** Peter Veit/DRK Photo; **p. 1258:** (top) Helga Matley; (bottom) Thomas Victor.

ILLUSTRATION CREDITS

pp. 14, 36, 182, 185, 188, 306, 1268–69: The Art Source

PRONUNCIATION GUIDE TO SELECTED TERMS

Balafré, Le: Le Balafré   (lə bä′ lä frā), 193
Barthelme   (bär′thəl mē), 1084
Barzun   (bär′ zun), 232
Bowdoin   (bō′ din), 332
Camus, Albert: Albert Camus   (al ber′ ka moo′), 699
Chambre   (sḣàm′b'r), 215
Chartreuse   (sḣär trooz′), 215
Chiromancy   (kī′ rə man′ sē), 215
Christiaan   (kris′ tyän), 1029
de Crèvecoeur, Michel-Guillaume Jean: Michel-Guillaume
   Jean de Crèvecoeur (mē shel′ gē yōm′ zhän də
   krev koor′), 152
de Gironne, Eymeric: Eymeric de Gironne   (ā mer′ēk
   də zhir ôn′), 215
Denisovich, Ivan: Ivan Denisovich   (ē′ vən den ə sō′ vich),
   1029
De Re Rustica   (də rə rus′ tik ə), 283
de Tocqueville, Alexis: Alexis de Tocqueville   (ä lek sē′ də
   tôk vēl′), 161
D'Indagine, Jean: Jean D'Indagine   (zhän din′ dä zhēn), 215
Directorium Inquisitorium   (di rek tōr′ ē əm
   in kwiz ē tōr′ē əm), 215
Fuseli   (fyoo′ zə lē), 214
Gascoigne   (gas′ koin), 304
Heidegger   (hī′ di gər), 304
Inada, Fusao: Fusao Inada   (fyoo sä′ ō i näd′ ə), 1258
Levertov   (lev′ ər tôv), 1194
Mahtoree   (mä′ tôr ē), 193
Malamud   (mal′ ə mud), 1028
Momaday   (mäm′ ə dä), 1154
Nemerov   (nem′ ər ôv), 1242
Octavio   (äk tä′ vē ō), 1029
Oegipans   (ej′ ə panz), 215
Roethke   (ret′ kē), 1188
Sartre, Jean-Paul: Jean-Paul Sartre,   (zhän pôl sàr′ tr'), 699
Solzhenitsyn, Aleksandr: Aleksandr Slozhenitsyn
   (al ik sän′ d'r sōl′ zhə nēt′ sin), 1029
Satyrs   (sat′ ərz), 215
Tachechana   (tak ə kän′ ə), 193
Theroux   (tḣər oo′), 1160
Tieck   (tēk), 215
Ververt   (vər′ vərt), 215
Vigiliae Mortuorum secundum Chorum Ecclesiae
   Maguntinae   (wē gēl′ ē ī môr too ôr′ əm si kun′ dəm
   kôr′ əm ək lā′ zē ī ma gun′ tē nī), 215
Weill, Kurt: Kurt Weill   (kʉrt vīl), 699
Yevtushenko, Yevgeny: Yevgeny Yevtushenko   (yev ge′ nē
   yev′ tooshen′ kō), 1029